Frommer's®

Eastern Europe

2nd Edition

by Mark Baker, Dr. Keith Bain, Angela Charlton, Heather Coombs, Dr. Ryan James, Hana Mastrini, Karen Tormé Olson & Sanja Bažulič Olson

Here's what the critics say about Frommer's:

"Amazingly easy to use. Very portable, very complete."
—BOOKLIST

"Detailed, accurate, and easy-to-read information for all price ranges."
—GLAMOUR MAGAZINE

"Hotel information is close to encyclopedic."
—DES MOINES SUNDAY REGISTER

"Frommer's Guides have a way of giving you a real feel for a place."
—KNIGHT RIDDER NEWSPAPERS

Wiley Publishing, Inc.

Published by:

WILEY PUBLISHING, INC.

111 River St.
Hoboken, NJ 07030-5774

ISBN 978-0-470-39908-8
Editor: Linda Barth
Production Editor: Jana M. Stefanciosa
Cartographer: Andrew Murphy
Photo Editor: Richard Fox
Production by Wiley Indianapolis Composition Services

Front cover photo: Art Noveau Cooperative Bank Building, Ljubljana, Slovenia
Back cover photo: Visitor at Plitvice Lakes National Park, Croatia

For information on our other products and services or to obtain technical support, please contact our Customer Care Department within the U.S. at 800/762-2974, outside the U.S. at 317/572-3993 or fax 317/572-4002.

Wiley also publishes its books in a variety of electronic formats. Some content that appears in print may not be available in electronic formats.

Manufactured in the United States of America

5 4 3 2 1

CONTENTS

4 BULGARIA 45

5 CROATIA 118

6 THE CZECH REPUBLIC 204

10 MOSCOW & ST. PETERSBURG 566

11 SLOVAKIA 607

12 SLOVENIA 647

INDEX 692

LIST OF MAPS

ABOUT THE AUTHORS

Mark Baker is a long-time American expat, living in Prague, and a frequent traveler to both Slovakia and Poland. He's one of the original editors of *The Prague Post* and was for years a foreign correspondent and editor for Radio Free Europe/Radio Liberty, based in Prague. He's now a freelance writer and reporter.

Dr. Keith Bain originally hails from the South African coastal city of Durban, where he developed a penchant for the beach, extra-hot curry, and all-night nightlife. He holds a doctoral degree in contemporary cinema studies and is the co-author of *Frommer's India* and a contributor to *Frommer's Dream Vacations.*

Angela Charlton first went to Russia a few weeks after the collapse of the Soviet Union in 1991, and spent the better part of the ensuing decade living and working there as a journalist. She was a Moscow-based correspondent for the Associated Press for six years and is the author of *Frommer's Moscow & St. Petersburg.*

Heather Coombs is a freelance travel writer and translator of Russian and French. She studied languages at Cambridge University while moonlighting as a correspondent for a Russian newspaper before moving to Paris where her credits include work for *Today in English* and *Living in France* magazines, and ForbesTraveler.com.

Dr. Ryan James earned a doctorate in International and Multicultural Education from the University of San Francisco. He has been living in Budapest, Hungary since 2001, and has been a full time instructor in the American Studies department at Eötvös Loránd University since 2002. He has traveled to forty-six countries, so far. He welcomes e-mail from readers. Write to him at drryanjames@gmail.com.

Hana Mastrini is a native of the western Czech spa town of Karlovy Vary who became a veteran of the "Velvet Revolution" as a student in Prague in 1989. She is the author of *Frommer's Prague & the Best of the Czech Republic.*

Karen Tormé Olson is the author of *Frommer's Croatia*. Karen is a photographer, freelance travel writer, and former *Chicago Tribune* editor. She recently earned her doctorate in administration and currently holds a day job as a high school counselor and fencing coach. She lives in a Chicago suburb with her husband, son, and three large dogs.

Sanja Bažulič Olson is the coauthor of *Frommer's Croatia* and a Croatian national who was born in Denmark, but has lived in Croatia all her life. She graduated from Zagreb University with a degree in agricultural engineering. She currently is working as a project manager for the U.S. Agency for International Development in Kabul, Afghanistan.

AN INVITATION TO THE READER

In researching this book, we discovered many wonderful places—hotels, restaurants, shops, and more. We're sure you'll find others. Please tell us about them, so we can share the information with your fellow travelers in upcoming editions. If you were disappointed with a recommendation, we'd love to know that, too. Please write to:

Frommer's Eastern Europe, 2nd Edition
Wiley Publishing, Inc. • 111 River St. • Hoboken, NJ 07030-5774

AN ADDITIONAL NOTE

Please be advised that travel information is subject to change at any time—and this is especially true of prices. We therefore suggest that you write or call ahead for confirmation when making your travel plans. The authors, editors, and publisher cannot be held responsible for the experiences of readers while traveling. Your safety is important to us, however, so we encourage you to stay alert and be aware of your surroundings. Keep a close eye on cameras, purses, and wallets, all favorite targets of thieves and pickpockets.

FROMMER'S STAR RATINGS, ICONS & ABBREVIATIONS

Every hotel, restaurant, and attraction listing in this guide has been ranked for quality, value, service, amenities, and special features using a **star-rating system.** In country, state, and regional guides, we also rate towns and regions to help you narrow down your choices and budget your time accordingly. Hotels and restaurants are rated on a scale of zero (recommended) to three stars (exceptional). Attractions, shopping, nightlife, towns, and regions are rated according to the following scale: zero stars (recommended), one star (highly recommended), two stars (very highly recommended), and three stars (must-see).

In addition to the star-rating system, we also use **seven feature icons** that point you to the great deals, in-the-know advice, and unique experiences that separate travelers from tourists. Throughout the book, look for:

Finds	Special finds—those places only insiders know about
Fun Facts	Fun facts—details that make travelers more informed and their trips more fun
Kids	Best bets for kids and advice for the whole family
Moments	Special moments—those experiences that memories are made of
Overrated	Places or experiences not worth your time or money
Tips	Insider tips—great ways to save time and money
Value	Great values—where to get the best deals

The following **abbreviations** are used for credit cards:

AE	American Express	DISC	Discover	V	Visa
DC	Diners Club	MC	MasterCard		

FROMMERS.COM

Now that you have this guidebook to help you plan a great trip, visit our website at **www.frommers.com** for additional travel information on more than 4,000 destinations. We update features regularly to give you instant access to the most current trip-planning information available. At Frommers.com, you'll find scoops on the best airfares, lodging rates, and car rental bargains. You can even book your travel online through our reliable travel booking partners. Other popular features include:

- Online updates of our most popular guidebooks
- Vacation sweepstakes and contest giveaways
- Newsletters highlighting the hottest travel trends
- Podcasts, interactive maps, and up-to-the-minute events listings
- Opinionated blog entries by Arthur Frommer himself
- Online travel message boards with featured travel discussions

1

The Best of Eastern Europe

1 THE MOST UNFORGETTABLE TRAVEL EXPERIENCES

- **Breathing the Air Inside a Thracian Tomb (Sveshtary, Bulgaria):** Entering this UNESCO-protected burial site 95km (60 miles) southeast of Ruse near the village of Sveshtary will send chills down your spine when you mull the thought that you are standing in a chamber where people who walked the earth 300 years before the birth of Christ, their servants, and their animals lay undisturbed for more than 2 millennia. You will marvel that you are viewing the same frescoes and sculptures that ushered these ancient residents to the next life. Be sure you call for reservations because the number of people allowed inside the climate-controlled space each day is limited. See p. 96.
- **Sunset on the City Wall (Dubrovnik, Croatia):** When evening approaches Dubrovnik, views from the top of Old Town's protective wall become a kaleidoscope of color and pattern as shifting light and visual perspective change position in tandem, almost to the tempo of the Adriatic Sea lapping at the wall's base. See p. 142.
- **Strolling Across Charles Bridge at Dawn or Dusk (Prague, Czech Republic):** The silhouettes of statues lining the 6-century-old crown jewel of Czech heritage hover like ghosts in the sunrise skyline. Early in the morning you can stroll across the bridge without encountering the crowds that appear by midday. With the changing light of dusk, the statues, the bridge, and the city panorama take on a whole different character. See "Crossing the Vltava: Charles Bridge," in chapter 6.
- **Stepping into History at Karlštejn Castle (Czech Republic):** A 30-minute train ride south of Prague puts you in the most visited Czech landmark in the environs, built by Charles IV (Karel IV in Czech—the namesake of Charles Bridge) in the 14th century to protect the Holy Roman Empire's crown jewels. This Romanesque hilltop bastion fits the image of the castles of medieval lore. See p. 248.
- **Discovering the Courtyards of Budapest (Hungary):** Budapest's residential streets are enchanting, but it is the buildings' courtyards that hold the city's greatest secret: Budapesters are villagers at heart. Nearly every apartment building in this city has an open-air courtyard in its center, where fruit trees and flower gardens flourish, cats lounge in the sun, and pensioners congregate on common balconies smoking cigarettes, gossiping, and watching children playing among flowerpots and laundry racks.
- **Sipping Coffee in the Heart of the City (Kraków, Poland):** Superlatives don't do Kraków's Rynek Główny justice. It's said to be central Europe's largest town square and it's also supposed to have the most bars and cafes per square

meter than any place in the world. Yet it's also one of the most beautiful spaces anywhere and the perfect spot to enjoy a beverage and watch the world go by. See p. 427.

- **Auschwitz-Birkenau (Oświęcim, Poland):** Words cannot convey what a deeply shocking and moving experience it is to visit what was the largest of the Nazi extermination camps. Plan to visit both camps (just a couple of miles apart). Auschwitz is undeniably horrible, but it's at Birkenau where you really grasp the scale of the tragedy. See p. 436.
- **Staying in a Village Home in Maramureş (Romania):** The farming villages of Maramureş occupy an idyllic mountainous landscape near Romania's northern border with the Ukraine. Here you'll discover some of the most bucolic communities in Europe, where horse-drawn carts outnumber motor vehicles and many households have a cow in the backyard. You'll be surrounded by warm, friendly people, many of whom dress exclusively in traditional costume. See p. 548.
- **Traveling by Train Through Transylvania (Romania):** You may not have Count Dracula as your guide, but the terrain encompassed by the land "beyond the forest" will set any heart racing. As you wind through vast tracts of forest and pass soaring mountains, the only signs of human habitation might be a church steeple peeking through a forest canopy, or farmers cutting grass with hand-held scythes. See p. 520.
- **Viewing Red Square at Night (Moscow, Russia):** The crimson-and-ivy-colored domes of St. Basil's Cathedral rise in a dizzying welcome to this most majestic of Russian plazas. Stand on the rise in the center of the square and feel a part of Russia's expanse. See p. 588.
- **Steam Stress Away at the Sandunovsky Baths (Sandunovskiye Banyi), (Moscow, Russia):** Thaw your eyelashes in January or escape snow flurries in May in the traditional Russian bathhouse, something between a sauna and a Turkish hammam. The pristine Sandunovsky Baths are a special treat, with Greek sculptures and marble baths. See "Banya Bliss," p. 585.
- **Watch the Neva River Drawbridges Go Up (St. Petersburg, Russia):** An unforgettable outing during White Nights, or anytime, involves perching on the quay at 2am to watch the city's bridges unfold in careful rhythm to allow ships to navigate the Neva.
- **Walking in the High Tatras (Slovakia):** During summer, trails across the peaks are open, meaning you can start in Slovakia in the morning and enjoy a well-earned dinner in Poland the same day. The High Tatras have trails suitable for walkers of all abilities; just choose a route and give it a shot. See section 5 in chapter 11.
- **Discovering Magnificence in the Bowels of the Earth (Slovenia):** Slovenia has thousands of Karstic caves, but those protected by UNESCO in the Škocjan park are unforgettable. Subterranean architecture comprises stalactites, stalagmites, and limestone pools, not to mention the world's largest underground canyon, stupendous bridges, and drop-away galleries that will reconfigure your understanding of life on earth. See p. 684.

2 THE BEST HOTEL SPLURGES

- **Cosmopolitan Hotel (Ruse, Bulgaria):** The level of sophistication, service, and value in this chic hotel that opened in March 2008 is in another stratosphere compared to properties in the rest of Bulgaria. Guest rooms are done with an eye to convenience and luxury, with flatscreen plasmas, in-room Wi-Fi, and the liberal use of original artwork. Add a world-class spa, a rooftop pool and terrace, a restaurant serving international cuisine, and lots of complementary services, and you have a runaway winner. See p. 114.

- **Hotel San Rocco (Brtonigla, Croatia):** San Rocco's location deep in Istria in northwestern Croatia adds to the romance you'll find in its impeccably restored stone buildings and grounds. Flowers, olive groves, and an assortment of ruins comprise the hotel's sensual "curb appeal." But it's the beautifully put-together guest rooms with their mélange of antique and modern touches, the inviting pool, and the gourmet restaurant that seal the deal. See p. 172.
- **Hilton Imperial (Dubrovnik, Croatia):** Rather than build a hotel from scratch, Hilton had the wisdom to restore what was salvageable from Dubrovnik's historic 19th-century Imperial and graft a modern hotel onto its base. Every detail has been addressed, and whether you hail from America or Azerbaijan, you'll feel like an honored guest. See p. 136.
- **Hotel Vestibul Palace (Split, Croatia):** The Roman Empire meets the 21st century at the Palace, where most rooms share at least part of a wall built by the Emperor Diocletian. Light, history, and gourmet delights align to make this one of the best hotel experiences in Croatia. Each room has a personality of its own, complete with cleverly designed windows carved into the stone walls to reveal views of various aspects of Old Town. See p. 157.
- **Hotel Aria (Prague, Czech Republic):** A new luxurious hotel opened in the heart of Malá Strana just around the corner from the St. Nicholas Cathedral. Its melodious theme will especially please music lovers. See p. 226.
- **Hotel Paříž (Prague, Czech Republic):** This restored Art Nouveau hotel recalls 1920s Prague, one of the wealthiest cities on earth at that time. It's across from another remodeled gem, the Municipal House (Obecní dům). See p. 227.
- **Four Seasons Gresham Palace (Budapest, Hungary):** The magnificent Gresham Palace has gained the reputation as Hungary's foremost hotel. The workmanship that recreated the Art Nouveau architecture is breathtaking. Guests get the royal treatment. See p. 295.
- **Hilton Budapest (Hungary):** The only chain hotel in the Castle Hill district, the hotel's award-winning design is incorporated into the ruins of a 13th-century Dominican church and the baroque facade of a 17th-century Jesuit college. See p. 300.
- **Królewski (Gdańsk, Poland):** Rooms to die for just across the canal from Gdańsk's Old Town. Room no. 310 is a corner room, with views over the city in two directions. The breakfast room overlooks the river at the town. See p. 453.
- **Delta Nature Resort, Danube (Delta, Romania):** This is the first luxury resort in what is widely regarded as the last wilderness in Europe. Guests are ensconced in plush cottages for the night (after enjoying local caviar), while during the day they are given endless options for wildlife encounters (including spying the 300 species of birds that find their way here each year) and cultural exploration (including rubbing shoulders with nuns and members of the small Lipovan communities that have settled in the delta). See p. 563.
- **Staying in Count Kalnoky's Guesthouses (Micloşoara, Romania):** Tudor Kalnoky was born abroad but returned to his Transylvanian homeland after the fall of Communism to reclaim his royal birthright. Having fallen in love with the Hungarian village once ruled by his

forebears, he set about restoring its old houses and ended up creating one of the best accommodations in the country. See p. 522.

- **Baltschug Kempinski (Moscow, Russia):** The hotel's views of St. Basil's Cathedral and the Kremlin are so breathtaking that TV networks set up there for their stand-ups. The brunch is fit for a tsar, and the understated elegance of the rooms complements the facade's pastel ornamentation. See p. 582.
- **Grand Hotel Europe (St. Petersburg, Russia):** This baroque confection in central St. Petersburg charmed Tchaikovsky and Bill Clinton, among other dignitaries. The harpist and the plush furniture in the mezzanine cafe provide respite from a day of touring. See p. 595.
- **Arcadia (Bratislava, Slovakia):** Bratislava now has two gorgeous boutique hotels: this one and the similarly priced Marrol's. Of the two, the Arcadia gets the nod because of its setting in a beautifully restored 13th-century town house just off the main square. Take a tour of the hotel and choose one that suits your mood: Some are done up in 19th-century Biedermeier, while others hark back to the Middle Ages, with stone walls and wood-beamed ceilings. See p. 619.
- **Grand Hotel Starý Smokovec (High Tatras, Slovakia):** You are in the Tatras, so why not spend a little extra to stay at this beautifully restored 19th-century Alpine manor that manages to match mountains for style and grace? The elegant lobby, billiard room, breakfast room, and "Rondo" dance room will have you thinking you stepped into *The Great Gatsby* or an Agatha Christie novel. See p. 633.
- **Kendov Dvorec (Slovenia):** Arguably the finest restored manor in the country, this is an idyllic retreat filled with antiques and plush furniture. Each meal is a triumph, and while you're in the country, you're never too far from everywhere else in tiny Slovenia. See p. 683.
- **Nebesa (Kobarid Slovenia):** Anywhere else in the world, this four-cottage "resort" would be considered a bargain. The real splurge is time-related: You'll need to drive several miles to get to Nebesa's mountainside location, from where you not only can see Italy, but also feel the breeze off the ocean, while at the same time you're almost eye level with soaring mountain peaks, often capped with snow. You'll feel like a private guest of the debonair owners while lounging on your private terrace and conjuring dreams of owning the world as you look down over the beautiful Soča Valley and watch the deer in the adjacent field frolicking at dusk. See p. 679.
- **Otočec Castle (Otočec Slovenia):** Dating back to the 13th century, Slovenia's only island castle is now fabulously restored and boasts some of the plushest, most beautiful (and modern) accommodations in the country. But while your luxurious bedroom will seduce you, the real thrill here is getting caught up in the fairy-tale setting, idling alongside the Krka River, then sitting down to an aristocratic feast, accompanied by the region's unique red wine. See p. 690.

3 THE BEST HOTEL BARGAINS

- **Niky (Sofia, Bulgaria):** One of the best-kept lodging secrets in Sofia, Niky's rooms often are monopolized by a cadre of repeat visitors who make reservations months in advance, and no wonder. The hotel, which billed itself as "Sofia's first all-suite hotel" when it opened in 2003, has a great location 2$^1/_2$ blocks west of Vitosha Street, friendly service, and fairly priced oversize rooms that inspire loyalty. See p. 67.

- **Hotel Gurko (Veliko Tarnovo, Bulgaria):** This timbered three-story is as traditional and charming as they come: Almost all rooms open onto balconies with geranium-filled window boxes and great views of the hillside and the Yantra River below. Every guest room in this National Revival–era home is spotless and comfortable. Gurko is one of the best options in town: an authentic family-run inn with a lively tavern on the ground floor. See p. 100.
- **Hotel Kaštel (Istria, Croatia):** The Kaštel's perch at the highest point of the walled medieval town of Motovun provides panoramic views of the Mirna valley. Each room has a different view of the terrain and the hotel has an excellent restaurant that serves homemade Istrian specialties you can't get anywhere else. The sizeable guest rooms were refurbished in 2003 but are in character with the hotel's 17th-century origin as a palace. See p. 180.
- **Valsabbion (Pula, Croatia):** The hotel's seven rooms and three suites are decorated with flair in a breezy, romantic style that carries over to its exquisite restaurant, one of the best in Croatia. There is also a spa with a long menu of beauty treatments. See p. 165.
- **Pension Unitas/Art Prison Hostel (Prague, Czech Republic):** This pension is an ideal place for budget travelers who want to take advantage of staying in the very center of Prague. See p. 228.
- **Pension Větrník (Prague, Czech Republic):** This family-run romantic hideaway is reachable in about 20 minutes by tram from the city center. Its atmosphere and prices are unbeatable. See p. 230.
- **BudaBaB Bed and Breakfast (Budapest, Hungary):** Comfortable, modern, and in the city center, it is run by two expat Americans and the author of the Hungary chapter in this book. See p. 299.
- **Hotel Fönix (Pécs, Hungary):** When in Pécs, you'll want to check out this bargain hotel that is beautifully located downtown, making it the ideal location to experience the city. See p. 373.
- **Hotel Karmel (Kraków, Poland):** This lovely family-run inn, tucked away on a quiet street in the former Jewish quarter of Kazimierz, is a total surprise. From the warm and smiling woman at the reception desk to the parquet flooring and the crisp linens on beds, everything about this place says quality. See p. 424.
- **Premiere Classe (Warsaw, Poland):** Warsaw is overpriced when it comes to decent accommodations. But here, a French-run chain came up with the novel idea of offering clean, modern rooms the size of a cubicle for a fraction of the price of other hotels. Sure the rooms are tiny, but the beds are big and comfortable, the bathrooms are clean, and the location is just a couple of tram stops from the main sights. See p. 398.
- **Casa Rozelor (Braşov, Romania):** With three of the most idiosyncratic guest suites in the country, this guesthouse is a project of love that has taken years of painstaking restoration (now continuing in a similar building nearby), followed by careful detailing with eclectic antiques bought from Gypsies, complemented by outrageous contemporary art and furniture. And it's right in the heart of Braşov's medieval center. Seldom does the blend of old and new fit so well, and feel so good. See p. 522.
- **Casa cu Cerbi (Voievodeasa, Moldavia, Romania):** One of the most beautiful guesthouses in Romania is a wooden house painted in bright, difficult-to-miss idiosyncratic green. Interiors are artfully decorated with traditional artifacts—handmade rugs, brightly painted furniture, and evidence of a life spent at work in the fields. While there are few

luxuries (aside from a lavish dinner and a pristine private bathroom), you'll spend your time getting to know a gentler way of life and exploring some of the most stunningly decorated monasteries on earth. See p. 558.

- **G&R Hostels (Moscow, Russia):** Several floors of a drab Soviet hotel have been transformed into clean, comfortable accommodations. Services include cars with drivers and visa support. While the location is not central, it's right next to a metro station. See p. 583.
- **Pulford Apartments (St. Petersburg, Russia):** Furnished, renovated flats with views of St. Petersburg's greatest monuments. A range of room sizes and services is available, including cleaning and airport transfers. Moscow apartments are also available. See p. 598.
- **Penzión pod Hradom (Trenčín, Slovakia):** Every town should have a pension as clean, quiet, delightful, and cheap as this one. And the location is ideal, perched on a small lane beside the main square and just below the castle. If the pension is empty, the owners will give you the nicest room in the house for the price of a standard. See p. 627.
- **Hiša Franko Casa (Kobarid, Slovenia):** A treasure in Soča Valley, near the Italian border. Each beautiful guest room is done in a unique combination of lively colors and all feature such treats as his-and-hers slippers and a choice of in-room amenities. It's more pension than hotel, and it is something of an afterthought to one of the country's finest restaurants, just downstairs. See p. 678.
- **Antiq Hotel (Ljubljana, Slovenia):** In the heart of Ljubljana's Old Town, right near one of the paths that leads to the Castle, this small hotel is brand new and stuffed full of lovely antique pieces in a wonderful, tasteful jumble that will remind you of the city's excellent Sunday morning market. See p. 662.

4 THE BEST FESTIVALS & CELEBRATIONS

- **Festival of the Kukeri (Bulgaria):** The days between New Year's and Lent are known as Mrasni Dni ("Dirty Days"), a time when it is said that the gates to heaven and hell are left open and demons walk the earth. To scare away evil, villagers all over Bulgaria don terrifying masks and belts sagging with huge bells while brandishing wooden weapons as they patrol the streets, making noise. You can see the best examples and photos of *kukeri* costumes in Sofia's Ethnographic Museum. For the ultimate *kukeri* show, plan to visit in an even-numbered year during the last weekend in January, when some 3,500 revelers participate in Bulgaria's largest Festival of the Kukeri in Pernik. See p. 78.
- The **Karlovy Vary International Film Festival (Czech Republic):** This is the place to see and be seen. Each summer (in early July), the country's film stars, celebrities, and wealthy folks, supported by a cast of international luminaries, can be spotted taking part in one of Europe's biggest film festivals. Nine venues screen more than 300 films during the 10-day festival. See p. 211.
- **Easter (Hollókő, Hungary):** The entire town dresses in traditional Easter garb to reenact the religious event, and it's a magical experience. These rural Palóc people speak an unusual Hungarian dialect, and they have some of the more colorful folk customs and costumes. See p. 365.
- **September Wine Festival (Budapest, Hungary):** The first weekend of September celebrates the first wheat harvest of the season and the crushing of the

grapes. A parade of traditionally costumed dancers and musicians starts the celebration with a march up to Castle Hill, signaling the opening of the weekend-long wine festival. Each year a different country is invited to share its wine heritage. Entertainment, wine tasting, food, and crafts fill the weekend with fun for the entire family. Check with TourInform, as events change from year to year due to bridge construction.

- **Winter Customs Festival (Maramureş, Romania):** Countless festivals occur throughout the year, but a favorite is over the Christmas holidays when the small town of Sighet, near the Ukraine border, comes to life on December 27 for the Winter Customs Festival, good old-fashioned fun filled with folkloric symbolism. Participants dress up in traditional costumes and young men run around with grotesque masks, cowbells dangling from their waists. See p. 551.
- **New Year's Day (Russia):** This is the major holiday of the Russian year. It's a family event centered on a fir tree, a huge feast, and gift-giving traditions transferred by Soviet leaders from Christmas to the more secular New Year's Day. See p. 574.
- **White Nights in St. Petersburg (Russia):** Two weeks of festivities in late June celebrate the longest day of the year, when the northern sun never dips below the horizon. The White Nights are more than a party; they're a buoyant, carefree attitude of summer-ness. Ride a boat through the canals as the sunset melts into a languorous sunrise, and you'll never want to go south again. See p. 574.
- **Pohoda Music Festival (Trenčín, Slovakia):** Every year in mid-July, the normally industrious town of Trenčín lets its hair down for 3 days of independent folk, rock, and pop. The festival has grown in recent years and now lures some of the best bands around. But don't just think traffic jams, mud, and long lines for beer: The word *pohoda* means "relax," and that's the whole idea. See p. 614.
- **The Kurentovanje Festival (Slovenia):** Each winter in Ptuj, revelers don crazy masks and take to the streets in a positively pagan celebration that once had some bearing on trying to control the climate. Now it's a spirited reminder that Slovenes love to party. See p. 689.

5 THE BEST OUTDOOR ACTIVITIES

- **Hiking Rila's Seven Lakes (Rila, Bulgaria):** This moderate 2-day (or more) hike from Rila Monastery into Bulgaria's Alps to view the eerily beautiful Seven Lakes is the most rewarding hike in the country. After the first day (a fairly strenuous 6-hr. hike), you reach the Ivan Vazov hut, which you can use as a base to visit the Seven Lakes. Better still, push on to one of the *Sedemte ezera* huts on the shores of the lowest lakes. If you can, book the newest, which has the best facilities. See "Outdoors in the Rila, Pirin & Rhodope Mountains" in chapter 4.
- **Plitvice Lakes National Park (Croatia):** Plitvice is Croatia's best-known natural wonder. You can choose the difficulty of your exploration, from challenging 8-hour hikes to shorter treks eased by ferry and tram rides. The park's 16 crystal-clear turquoise lakes and their countless waterfalls are the marquee attraction, and you'll be fascinated by these pristine ponds, which flow into one another and tumble over deposits of

travertine, creating waterfalls that drop a few feet or plunge as much as 64m (210 ft.). All this beauty is set in a dense forest accessed via footpaths, ferries, and fuel-friendly people-movers. See section 9 in chapter 5.

- **Taking a Slow Boat Down the Vltava (Czech Republic):** You can see many striking architectural landmarks from the low-angle and low-stress vantage point of a rowboat you pilot yourself. At night, you can rent a dinghy with lanterns for a very romantic ride.
- **Riding a Faster Boat Down the Vltava (Czech Republic):** For those not willing to test their navigational skills or rowing strength, tour boats offer floating views, many with meals. Be sure to check the float path to be certain your boat travels past the castles and palaces.
- **Hiking in the Hills Outside Szigliget (Hungary):** You can hike up to the fantastic ruins of a 13th-century castle above this scenic village in the Lake Balaton region, or go farther north and hike into hills covered with vineyards. See "Top Attraction & Special Moments" in chapter 7.
- **Swimming in the Thermal Lake at Hévíz (Hungary):** Even in the depths of winter, the temperature in Europe's largest thermal lake seldom dips below 85° to 90°F (30°–32°C). Hungarians swim here year-round, and you can, too! If you visit in winter, it'll be a memorable experience. See "An Excursion to the Thermal Lake in Hévíz" in chapter 7.
- **Hiking in the Tatras (Poland):** Zakopane is the jumping-off point to hundreds of kilometers of gorgeous hiking trails. You can choose one of the 2,000m-plus (6,560-ft.) assaults on the peaks, or a more leisurely stroll along breathtaking valleys, carved out by tiny mountain streams. See "Outside of Zakopane" in chapter 8.
- **Idling Through the Backwaters of the Danube Delta (Romania):** Considered by some to be Europe's most important wildlife sanctuary, the Danube Delta once was threatened by Communism's unchecked industrial program. Now the Delta once again is a haven for bird life, including its famous pelican population, which you can observe while on a boat safari through this unique ecosystem of waterways, lakes, reed beds, sand dunes, and subtropical forests. See "The Danube Delta" in chapter 9.
- **Picnic at Kolomenskoye (Moscow, Russia):** This architectural reserve boasts the breathtaking 16th-century Church of the Assumption and the wooden house where Peter the Great sought refuge before assuming Russia's throne. The surrounding lawns beckon visitors to stretch out with caviar or cucumber sandwiches and a thermos of strong Russian tea. See p. 586.
- **Rafting the Dunajec (Slovakia):** This is fun for the whole family. It's not intense white-water rafting, but a gentle group-float down a winding, twisting river that marks the boundary between Poland and Slovakia. The guides are good-natured and bedecked in the traditional folk costumes of the region. See "Rafting on the Dunajec" in chapter 11.
- **Having the Ride of Your Life (Slovenia):** Compact and oozing spectacular scenery, Slovenia may be the ultimate cycling destination. Verdant valleys, dark forests, and rural countryside and hills beckon, but the challenge that your muscles will remember forever is the steep ascent up and over the Vršič Pass in the Julian Alps; the 50 hairpin bends will exhaust you, but the views along the way will leave you breathless. Of course, it's less tiring by car! See "Outdoor Activities in the Soča Valley" in chapter 12.

6 THE BEST LOCAL DINING EXPERIENCES

- **Manastinska Magernitza (Sofia, Bulgaria):** Its name translates to "Monastery Kitchen," and the traditional recipes from 161 Bulgarian monasteries executed here translate to culinary bliss. There is plenty on the menu you won't find elsewhere in Bulgaria, like *plakovsjka hayverna,* peeled garlic mashed with salt, oil, lemon, bread, and walnuts. This is a place to linger over your meal and make plans to return. See p. 70.
- **Kopitoto (St. Konstantin, Bulgaria):** "Folk restaurant" might be the best way to describe Kopitoto, located about 10 minutes north of Varna on the road to Sunny Beach. Bulgarian bells and other folk objects are used in the decor and there is a fire pit in the center of the outdoor dining area that provides ashes for the nightly "ember dance" during which dancers stomp around on warm ashes to music. Entertainment aside, you should go to Kopitoto (translation: horse hoof) for traditional Bulgarian food. See p. 109.
- **Bitoraj (Fužine, Croatia):** Bitoraj is a 75-year-old restaurant in a new building, which only enhances the dining experience. The menu offers game dishes available nowhere else in Croatia, plus a huge selection of traditional delicacies. From bear ham to Bitoraj's signature dish of wild boar baked under a lid *(peka)* on an open fire, all dishes utilize the best ingredients the surrounding woods can offer. See p. 183.
- **Paprika Vendéglő (Budapest, Hungary):** Escape the city without leaving Budapest when entering this restaurant. Whether you want to sample wild boar or a more domestic dish, the overflowing portions and excellent service will fill all your needs. See p. 307.
- **Karczma Jana (Olsztyn, Poland):** You'd expect to find excellent food in Warsaw, Kraków, and Gdańsk (and you do), but in Olsztyn, it's a surprise. Karczma Jana is one of the distinctly Polish restaurants with traditional decor and local specialties done very well. See p. 414.
- **Piwnicka Świdnicka (Wrocław, Poland):** It looks like a classic tourist trap with big wooden tables set right on the main square, but Piwnicka Świdnicka is actually an excellent traditional Polish restaurant. Come for big plates of classic dishes like pork knuckle or beef roulade served with puréed beets. See p. 446.
- **Casa cu Cerbi (Voievodeasa, Moldavia, Romania):** As a guest at the House of the Stags in this tiny village near the painted monastery at Suceviţ, you'll be treated like family. You'll be served huge portions of soup, bread, meat, and vegetables in the kitchen-cum–dining room of this new-but-traditional wooden house. See p. 558.
- **The Aristocratic Atmosphere at Cafe Pushkin (Moscow, Russia):** Plunge into the refined opulence of 19th-century Russia as you spear a bite of suckling pig or sip fine tea from a silver samovar. See p. 584.
- **Fresh Fish at Staraya Tamozhnya (St. Petersburg, Russia):** The spare stone arches of this restaurant evoke the building's history as an 18th-century Customs house. See p. 599.
- **Le Colonial (Košice, Slovakia):** Too many Slovak chefs still follow the old recipes by rote, but here they mix it up a bit, to good effect: Fried chicken breast is a staple on every Slovak menu, but here it comes stuffed with tart sheep's cheese and served with freshly cooked string beans. The interior is perfect for a romantic meal. See p. 644.
- **Hiša Franko (near Kobarid, Slovenia):** Fans of this renowned family restaurant (where you can bed down for the night

in the sumptuous rooms upstairs) come from all over Europe to join chef Ana Roš's latest culinary adventure. Leave the choice of wine to her husband, Valter Kramer, Slovenia's most accomplished sommelier. See p. 678.

7 THE BEST MUSEUMS

- **Varna Archaeological Museum (Bulgaria):** The fine detail in a gold figure of Victory carved on an earring taken from the tomb of a Thracian noble woman will reveal the skill of the goldsmith who made this exquisite piece 2,400 years ago. With 15,000 tombs and 400 ancient settlements scattered throughout the country, Bulgaria is so rich in Thracian burial mounds that archaeologists think some of Europe's oldest artifacts are waiting to be unearthed there. See p. 111.
- **Roman Amphitheater (Pula, Croatia):** Smaller than Rome's coliseum but in much better shape, the amphitheater is more accessible than its Rome counterpart. Don't miss the restored underground chambers, which house museum exhibits featuring Istrian history. And if you happen to be in town when a concert is scheduled, buy a ticket no matter who is headlining. See p. 166.
- **Ivan Meštrović Gallery and Kaštelet (Split, Croatia):** The Meštrović Gallery occupies the mansion Croatian sculptor Ivan Meštrović built from 1937 to 1939 as a home/atelier for his family. Meštrović lived there for just 2 years before emigrating from Croatia, but he left behind a house and garden on a hill overlooking the Adriatic that showcase some of his best work. Up the road is the 16th-century **Kaštelet,** a Renaissance-style summer house Meštrović purchased and remodeled in 1939 as a showcase for his "Life of Christ" reliefs. See p. 159.
- **Alfons Mucha Museum (Prague, Czech Republic):** Posters, decorative panels, objects, excerpts from sketchbooks, and oil paintings from this well-known Art Nouveau master are displayed at the Baroque Kaunický Palace near Václavské náměstí. See p. 244.
- **Holocaust Memorial Center (Budapest, Hungary):** Opened on the 60th anniversary of the Holocaust, the center is the first of its kind in central Europe to be government funded. A refurbished eclectic synagogue is located in the center of the building. See p. 312.
- **Museum of Fine Arts (Budapest, Hungary):** Critics agree that this museum has one of the most important collections in Europe. The collection of Spanish masters is second only to Madrid. See p. 313.
- **Museum of the Warsaw Uprising (Poland):** The audiovisual displays and sound effects are an assault on the eyes and ears, but when you're done walking through the exhibitions and watching the startling documentaries filmed during the fighting in 1944, you'll understand a lot more about Poles' resolve to preserve their nation. The photos of Warsaw's destruction alone will leave you in awe that a modern city actually still exists. See p. 403.
- **Museum of Zakopane Style (Zakopane, Poland):** This low-key museum is dedicated to the fine woodworking craft of the early Zakopane architects of the late 19th and early 20th centuries. No stunning high-tech visuals, just beautifully carved furnishings and a wonderful aesthetic feel. It's a log cabin made into a palace. See p. 441.
- **Peleş (Sinaia, Romania):** Built as a summer residence for Romania's first king in what is now a popular ski resort, Peleş Castle looks like it was built for the next *Harry Potter* blockbuster: It's

an architectural triumph of German neo-Renaissance architecture that is at once stylish and fantastical. It remains one of the finest castles in Europe, with 170 opulent rooms, only some of which are open during the country's best guided museum tour. See p. 516.

- **Memorial Museum of the Victims of Communism and the Resistance (Sighet, Romania):** This evocative memorial to people who died because of Communism in Romania occupies a chilling former prison in Maramureş, not far from the Ukraine border. Each of the cells, including the one where former Prime Minister Iuliu Maniu died, is an exhibition space. See p. 554.
- **Armory Museum (Moscow, Russia):** Fabergé eggs, coronation robes, royal carriages, and jewels fill what was once the tsarist weapons storehouse. See p. 587.
- **State Hermitage Museum (St. Petersburg, Russia):** The museum holds one of the world's biggest art collections, from Egyptian carvings to Impressionist masterpieces. It is in the Winter Palace, stormed in 1917 by revolutionaries. See p. 601.
- **Kobarid Museum (Slovenia):** The Kobarid is Slovenia's best antiwar museum, dedicated to the memory of those who lost their lives in the fierce battle of Caporetto (Kobarid), which took place near this peaceful town, now a center for adventure activities. See p. 681.

8 THE BEST TOWNS & VILLAGES

- **The Heritage Villages of Pirin, Rhodope, Balkan, and Sredna Gora Mountains (Bulgaria):** Besides the charm of the 18th- and 19th-century stone-and-timber architecture, village life here appears untainted by the 21st century, with toothless old-timers in headscarves sunning themselves on benches while young lovers holding hands head off to the fields, hoes casually slung over their shoulders. The most photogenic and evocative villages are hidden deep in the mountains: Kovachevitsa and Dolen are surrounded by the forested Rhodope ranges, Zheravna by the lush Balkan foothills, and pretty Koprivishtitsa in the undulating Sredna Gora. See "Outdoors in the Rila, Pirin & Rhodope Mountains" in chapter 4.
- **Hum (Croatia):** It calls itself the smallest town in the world, and population-wise, it might be. But so many people visit this village high in the Istrian interior that it almost always seems crowded. The village elders have done a wonderful job of restoring buildings to make Hum tourist-friendly. See "Motovun, Roč & Hum" in chapter 5.
- **Český Krumlov (Czech Republic):** If you have time for only one excursion from Prague, make it Český Krumlov. This living gallery of Renaissance-era buildings housing many galleries, shops, and restaurants is 167km (104 miles) south of Prague. Above it towers the second-largest castle complex in the country, with the Vltava River running below. No wonder UNESCO named this town a World Heritage Site. See "Český Krumlov" in chapter 6.
- **Karlovy Vary (Czech Republic):** A slow pace and pedestrian promenades lined with turn-of-the-20th-century Art Nouveau buildings turn strolling into an art form here. Nighttime walks take on a mystical feel as the sewers, the river, and multiple major cracks in the roads emit steam from the mineral waters running underneath. Sample the

town's 12 hot spring waters; each is full of healing power. See "Karlovy Vary (Carlsbad)" in chapter 6.

- **Pécs (Hungary):** This delightful city in southern Hungary is home to one of the country's most pleasing central squares and some great examples of Turkish architecture. See "Pécs: The 2,000-Year-Old City" in chapter 7.
- **Szentendre (Hungary):** Right along the Danube bend and only 45 minutes from Budapest, this small Serbian village has a different cultural flavor than the rest of the country. It is worth a trip outside the capital for a half-day to see the architecture. See "Szentendre" in chapter 7.
- **Gdańsk (Poland):** If you were expecting a dirty port city on the Baltic, you're in for the surprise of your life. Gdańsk is a beautifully restored Hanseatic town that's brimming with life. The hotels and restaurants are superb and the city couldn't be more inviting. And when you tire of Gdańsk, there's Sopot and the beaches and nightclubs just up the road. See "Gdańsk" in chapter 8.
- **Wrocław (Poland):** This city feels (at least in terms of the architecture) very much like a provincial German capital. The Old Town is gorgeous. The Baroque and Renaissance facades sing with color, and elevate your mood in any season. Wrocław is also filled with students, ensuring lots of great little clubs tucked away in places you'd least expect. See "Wrocław" in chapter 8.
- **Sibiu (Romania):** A joint European City of Culture in 2007, Sibiu has received a remarkable makeover, transforming it into a whitewashed version of its former self: a walled city with bastion towers, large open squares, impossible alleyways, and countless marvelous Gothic, Baroque, and Renaissance buildings. See "Sibiu" in chap-ter 9.
- **Sighişoara (Romania):** This medieval citadel was the birthplace of the man who inspired Bram Stoker's Count Dracula. Today, it remains inhabited, and despite its compact size, it is one of the best preserved hilltop fortress cities in Europe, a jumble of ancient crannies, cobbled streets, medieval homes, and towers protruding from battlements. See "Sighişoara" in chap-ter 9.
- **Old Town (Bratislava, Slovakia):** Yes, it's technically part of a city, but Old Town feels more like a village. Indeed, it's hard to imagine a more active, fun, and user-friendly town center than Bratislava's Old Town. The past decade has witnessed a major effort to bring new life into what once was a quiet part of town. The result is a nightly street party. See "Exploring Bratislava" in chapter 11.
- **Piran (Slovenia):** Piran is Slovenia's Venice, occupying a sharp promontory on the Istrian Coast. Piran doesn't have canals, but it will make your head spin as you get lost in a jumble of narrow cobblestone streets lined with lovely architecture, some beautifully preserved, some crumbling perfectly. See "Piran & the Istrian Coast" in chapter 12.

9 THE BEST LOCAL BEER & WINE

- **Mitko Manolev (Melnik, Bulgaria):** Mitko, aka "Six Fingers," may not make the best wine, but he sure offers a great tasting experience. Seated in the cool sandstone cave burrowed into the side of a cliff in Melnik, Mitko lets you taste his wines directly from the barrel, then bottles your choice (two types of red, not dissimilar to grape juice); it's worth it if only to watch him fill, cork, and label right in front of you. See "Drinking Wine with 'Six Fingers' Manolev" in chapter 4.

- **Grgić Vina (Trstenik, Croatia):** About 32km (20 miles) north of Dubrovnik lies a turnoff for Trstenik, an out-of-the-way town with a couple of small, uncrowded beaches, a few restaurants, and a concrete pier for diving. Along the way, you'll find the Croatian branch of Grgich Hills, one of the world's great wineries. Grgić Vina is modest compared to its California counterpart—it's basically a concrete bunker—but it produces some of Croatia's most sought-after wines. Buy a bottle of the latest vintage at about half the cost elsewhere. See "Pelješac Peninsula" in chapter 5.
- **Plzeňské Pivovary/Pilsner Brewery (Prague, Czech Republic):** At U Prazdroje 7, Plzeň will interest anyone who wants to learn more about the brewing process. The brewery actually comprises several breweries, pumping out brands like Pilsner Urquell and Gambrinus, the most widely consumed beer in the Czech Republic. See "Touring the Beer Shrines" in chapter 6.
- **House of Hungarian Wines (Budapest, Hungary):** Located on castle hill, here you can savor the flavors of more than 60 of the most important Hungarian wines in one spot while being educated about them at the same time. Hungary is famous for its Tokai, the king of wines and the wine of kings, and it is the only country where Tokai is legally produced. See p. 338.
- **Okocim Beer (Poland):** Of the big national beers, Poles seem to favor Żywiec (maybe it's folk dancing on the label that wins them over?). For our money, Okocim is the brew of choice. The slightly sweetish taste is reminiscent of Czech Budvar (Budweiser), and all the other beers more or less taste blandly the same. Drink it straight or add a shot of fruit syrup to the mix (but don't try this if you're male). See "Polish Cuisine" in chapter 8.
- **Ţuică (Romania):** Ţuică (also referred to as Pălinca) is a homemade brandy distilled from plums, pears, apples, or other fruit, and it is a popular after-dinner or welcome drink, particularly in Romania's village communities. You can purchase some of the country's best-known Ţuică from Teo Coroian, who runs a small distilling business from his home in the medieval fortress town of Sighişoara. See "Getting Fortified in the Citadel" in chapter 9.
- **The Jeruzalem Wine Road (Slovenia):** This route in Slovenia's "far" east is perfect for purveyors of fine wine and gentle drives through rambling vineyards. You can stop at many farms, with private tastings conducted by one of the owners, and should things get out of hand, you simply can stay the night and pick up where you left off after a scrumptious farm breakfast. See "Touring the Jeruzalem Wine Road" in chapter 12.

2

Introducing Eastern Europe

If you talk with anyone living in one of the countries included in this guide and refer to his or her homeland's location as Eastern European, you'll quickly be corrected. It's in *central* Europe, you'll be told, whether you are referring to Croatia, Romania, or sometimes even Russia. So why the semantic dispute about geography? Perhaps it's an attempt to shake off persistent suspicions that Eastern Europe is still in the thrall of Soviet socialism. Or perhaps it's just the desire to be accepted without having to deal with the past's unpleasant baggage. Whatever the reason, there is no doubt that this diverse, politically complicated region is coming into its own and revamping its image.

1 THE REGION TODAY

Eastern Europe's diverse delights translate to a long list of options for vacationers. With so many choices, how can you see everything in a single trip or even decide which is the most worthwhile itinerary? In this chapter, we provide an overall view of the region and explain each country's unique attractions to help you decide what you want to see most. In subsequent chapters, we'll help you plan your trip.

Geographically, the countries of Eastern Europe are blessed with breathtaking scenery, deep-seated history, and a menu of natural wonders that offers something for everyone. Croatia's crystal-blue Adriatic seacoast, Romania's snowcapped Carpathian peaks, and Poland's lush forests and golden farmland are just three examples of the countless treasures found there. Add Roman ruins, sophisticated metropolitan areas, medieval castles, and Kremlin-era architecture and you have a recipe for a singular adventure.

Culturally Eastern Europe is a cross section of influences from Turkey, Italy, Germany, and other European nations. Many Westerners routinely lump Eastern European nations under a single umbrella and assume they are interchangeable variations on one depressing theme. Nothing could be further from the truth. If anything, the countries that lie roughly between the Baltic, Adriatic, and Black seas are a remarkably diverse bunch with intersecting but distinct cultures, complicated histories, lusty political traditions, and a list of attractions that run the gamut from religious shrines to opulent palaces to Soviet-era monuments.

But there are similarities among these countries, too. Each has rejected Soviet-style ideology, each is in a different stage of recovery from years of oppression, and each is on a trajectory to become a full and participating member of the global community.

The dilemma lies in the realization that the fate of the Balkan nations depends on the ability of the divergent people who live there to coexist peacefully. The burden is on each group in the region being strong enough in its own identity and tolerant enough of differences to not feel threatened by any of the other groups.

0 200 mi
0 200 km
N
NORWAY
SWEDEN
FINLAND
Gulf of Bothnia
L. Onega
Lake Ladoga
Oslo
Helsinki
Gulf of Finland
St. Petersburg
Stockholm
Vänern
Skagerrak
Tallinn
Rybinsk Res.
Gothenburg
Saaremaa
ESTONIA
L. Peipus
Yaroslavl
Ivanovo
Gotland
LATVIA
DEN.
Riga
Tver
Copenhagen
BALTIC SEA
RUSSIA
Moscow
Daugava
Bornholm
LITHUANIA
Vitsyebsk
Ryazan
RUSSIA
Kaliningrad
Hamburg
Gdańsk
Vilnius
Smolensk
Tula
Szczecin
Don R.
Minsk
GERMANY
Berlin
POLAND
BELARUS
Orel
Poznań
Gomel
Leipzig
Warsaw
Voronezh
Łódź
Kursk
Dresden
Wrocław
Bug R.
Dnieper R.
Oder R.
Kiev Res.
Prague
Kiev
Kharkiv
CZECH REP.
Kraków
Zhytomyr
L'viv
Poltava
Brno
Kremenchuk Res.
Munich
Danube R.
CARPATHIAN MTS.
Dniester R.
UKRAINE
SLOVAKIA
Vienna
Bratislava
Dnipropetrovs'k
Donets'k
ALPS
Chernivtsi
Zaporiyhzhya
AUSTRIA
Budapest
MOLD.
Kakhovka Res.
HUNGARY
Cluj-Napoca
Chişinău
SLOVENIA
Ljubljana
Sea of Azov
Venice
Drava R.
Odessa
Zagreb
Sava R.
Timişoara
Crimea
DINARIC ALPS
ROMANIA
Sevastopol'
CROATIA
Belgrade
B.H.
Bucharest
ADRIATIC SEA
Sarajevo
Constanţa
SERBIA
Danube R.
BLACK SEA
Dubrovnik
MONT.
Varna
Podgorica
Sofia
BULGARIA
Skopje
RHODOPE MTS.
ITALY
Naples
Bari
Tirana
MACE.
ALBANIA
Istanbul
Thessaloniki
Bursa
Ankara
Corfu
GREECE
TURKEY
AEGEAN SEA
Izmir
Athens
Konya
Sicily
Ceyhan
Antalya
MEDITERRANEAN SEA
Rhodes
SYRIA
Crete
Nicosia
CYPRUS
LEBANON

Serbs and Croats, Hungarians and Russians; Catholics, Eastern Orthodox, and Muslims—each of these groups has a claim on the culture, and each is in competition with the other for the same piece of real estate. Will they be able to recognize the need for peaceful coexistence and prosper together in peace, or will they find they are unable to give up a little to gain a lot?

Even in the face of warring traditions, economic and political developments related to the European Union have transformed Eastern Europe. The road to European Union membership has been difficult for some of the region's countries, but their efforts to join the larger European community also reflect a new stability. That, in turn, has attracted foreign development and a new tourism demographic.

Bulgaria and Romania in particular are working hard to overcome the off-putting perception that they are countries still operating with an iron-curtain mentality. Bulgaria's tourism industry is in its infancy and hopes that E.U. membership will help dispel inaccuracies about its image. Bulgarian officials are working hard at a makeover that will more accurately reflect the country as it is today.

The vetting process for E.U. membership also has reduced the shroud of uncertainty surrounding Eastern Europeans' ability to live together peacefully and it has given their citizens—and the world—the hope that the region's future might turn out to be prosperous.

BULGARIA

The fall of the Berlin Wall did little to boost this nation on the Black Sea from its plight as one of the poorest in the old Soviet bloc. In 1999, 10% of the population still lived in impoverished conditions, but that is slowly changing.

The old Communist regime ruled the country until 1997 under the guise of "Socialists," but the state still controlled the economy. The result was hunger, disarray, and eventually an economic collapse.

After the Socialist government fell, there seemed to be little chance that this nation with a heritage dating from Byzantine times would turn around quickly, but governmental and currency reform have been moving rapidly.

Situated on the southeastern tip of the Balkans, Bulgaria has pushed hard to become an accepted member of the world cultural and economic community by seeking full membership in the E.U.

Publicity surrounding that effort has put a spotlight on both the good and the bad of Bulgaria's emergence from Communist control.

Tourists are uncovering the complex history of cities like Sofia, which can trace its lineage back 4,000 years. They can savor the mélange of cultures from the Romans to the Ottomans to remnants of the iron-curtain years.

The Byzantine Church of St. George, the Sofia Synagogue, and the Ottoman Banya Bashi Mosque all are within easy walking distance of each other.

Skiers are finding banner skiing at bargain prices in resorts such as Borovets and Bansko, while sun worshippers are basking at Black Sea havens like Sunny Beach and Golden Sands.

Right now, Bulgaria is a travel bargain thanks to a relatively low-cost but well-educated workforce. The country's tourism infrastructure still needs a lot of work, but there are signs that the means to improve it are building because investment, construction, and tourism all showed strong growth in 2008.

Bulgaria joined the E.U. on January 1, 2007, and accepted the World Bank's first infusion of cash ($300 million). Some of the results of that deposit (improved highways, restored monuments) were visible in the summer of 2008, but how the future plays out remains to be seen. The challenge is in putting aside the totalitarian mindset and sustaining reforms that will control widespread corruption and increase the standard of living for Bulgaria's citizens.

CROATIA

Contemporary Croatia is a land of contrasts and contradictions, a land with diverse geography and cultures that include primitive Stone Age settlements, glittering seaside resorts, vestiges of Greek and Roman antiquity, pristine natural wonders, and newly cosmopolitan cities. It is famous as a sun-drenched tourist destination and infamous as the site of one of the most vicious European wars in modern times.

Croatia has successfully protected its heritage despite invasions by neighboring nations. Those invaders played keep-away with the land itself while pushing aside Croatian culture in favor of their own.

Modern Croats are survivors, fiercely independent people who through the ages again and again emerged from ethnic conflicts and foreign occupations to reassert their national identity. Fortunately, Croatia's wars are in the past and the newly vibrant nation is now solidly in the 21st century, poised to embrace progress, global commerce, tourism, and independence as it pushes forward to claim a place in the European Union.

Signs of economic recovery are everywhere, from packed luxury hotels on the Adriatic coast to thriving upscale boutiques and gourmet restaurants in Zagreb. There is no doubt that Croatia is beginning to shake off its down-in-the-mouth persona and present a more sophisticated, savvy face to the world. Tourism is booming; international hoteliers such as Hilton (Dubrovnik), Le Meridien (Split), and Sheraton (Zagreb) have established a presence in the country; and local hoteliers especially have been courting an upscale international crowd by upgrading properties on the Dalmatian Coast at a dizzying pace.

Meanwhile, the Croatian government is working to reduce foreign debt, boost the economy, and promote the country's natural treasures while it waits for admittance to the European Union, an event that was stalled until mid-2006 but is now moving ahead following the arrest of one of Croatia's alleged war criminals. If the process proceeds without any more glitches, E.U. membership could become a reality for Croatia as early as 2010.

Croatian travel professionals are anticipating a healthy increase in tourism when that happens. In the meantime, they are getting the word out about their country's considerable appeal: Croatia's stunning Adriatic seacoast, idyllic islands, vibrant cities, historic sites, and warmhearted people are the things tour operators' dreams are made of. If Croatia achieves its economic and social goals, there will be no limits to its future.

CZECH REPUBLIC

The landlocked Czech Republic is a crossroads for Eastern Europe, thanks to its location in the heart of the region. In some ways the Czech Republic has been the "heart" of the region's emergence from Communist domination, too.

Leaders like Alexander Dubček, who instituted the freedoms that led to the Prague Spring of 1968, and Václav Havel, who engineered the split from Moscow, embody the spirit of the Czech people.

Havel stayed on to lead the new Czech Republic when the former Czechoslovakia split into two nations during the "Velvet Divorce" of 1993.

The two regions that now make up the Czech Republic—Bohemia and Moravia—have fostered a booming tourism industry, especially in Prague, where a multitude of spires punctuate the skyline in the heart of Bohemia.

Visiting Prague provides a typical glimpse of the contrasts that exist throughout the country, with designer boutiques and chain restaurants around the corner from ancient cobbled streets and crumbling facades. Prague's timeline is visible in its architecture, from the 9th-century Prague Castle to the houses and palaces of Old Town, the synagogues of the Jewish Quarter, and the Charles Bridge, where street performers entertain passersby. Visitors to Prague have a lot to take in because the city has a lot to offer. So if you're weary of entertainment delivered by sidewalk violinists and jugglers, take a walk to the Estates Theater, formerly Count Nostitz's Theater. If you listen carefully you might pick up the sounds of *Don Giovanni* floating past and the sense that Mozart is smiling.

Prague may be the destination du jour in the Czech Republic, but the country has much more to offer outside the capital. In Bohemia, you can visit the center of the Czech beer-brewing industry and the birthplace of lager. Stop at a tavern in Bohemia, and a beer appears in front of you almost automatically.

In contrast, Moravia's beverage of choice is wine. Moravia's soil is conducive to growing grapes. That fortunate topographical feature supports a robust wine industry that in turn has spawned numerous wine bars serving local vintages.

Both regions are home to numerous castles and châteaux, which provide visitors with a view into the country's cultural heritage. The state of these architectural treasures varies from pristinely preserved to near ruins. Those still in good shape offer glimpses into a vanished way of life.

Outdoor enthusiasts have numerous options. Miles of flat, quiet roads await bicyclists outside the large cities, and mountainous regions of both Bohemia and Moravia maintain an extensive network of marked trails that connect the smaller towns.

Winter sports enthusiasts in Bohemia can choose between the Alpine resorts of the Giant Mountains of the north and Nordic areas of the Sumava in the south. And no matter which sport you fancy, at the end of the day you can soothe your muscles at one of the many thermal spas that dot every corner of the country.

Since January 2007, Mirek Topolánek (ODS) has been prime minister of Czech Republic, whose government comprises the right-wing Civic Democrats (ODS), the Christian Democrats (KDU-ČSL), and the Greens (SZ). The prime minister is the head of the government. President Vaclav Klaus is was re-elected for a second 5-year term as the head of state in the spring of 2008. Even with changes in its diverse leadership, the Czech Republic is flourishing and keeping in step with its European Union compatriots on the road to prosperity.

HUNGARY

Like many of its neighbors, Hungary has had to battle a series of would-be foreign conquerors on the way to its current state of independence. Hungarians have had to rout occupiers repeatedly over the last 1,000 years or so: They took on the Turks in the 17th century, the Habsburgs in the 19th century, and the Soviets in the 20th century in a 1956 rebellion that is the most infamous of all the country's uprisings.

What began on October 23, 1956, as a student protest to demand the withdrawal of Soviet troops from Hungarian soil ended on November 11, 1956, when the Soviets flexed their military muscle and sent tanks into Budapest to quash the dissidents. When the guns finally fell silent nearly 3 weeks later, more than 25,000 people had died. Shortly afterward, the Soviets arrested or executed thousands of others, and a quarter of a million Hungarians fled to Austria. The last Soviet troops left Hungary in 1991, and the beleaguered nation then began its transformation into an independent citizen of the world community in earnest.

Since then, Hungary has joined NATO (1999), become a member of the European Union (2004), and experienced a powerful economic growth spurt thanks to investments by foreign companies that amount to billions of dollars.

Hungary has been a free country for more than a decade, and visitors will find a new order softened by courtly old-world customs such as gentlemen kissing their ladies' hands.

Hungary also has undergone an image change in the nearly 20 years since the fall of Communism, and with it tourism has brought hordes of visitors to the country's restored castles, palaces, and museums and to its festivals, fairs, and harvest celebrations.

Today Hungary's travel specialists can arrange general or special-interest tours for English speakers, among them a tour with an itinerary that helps visitors research their roots or just walk around the same land where their ancestors once lived.

There is a new national pride evident in big cities and rural villages in Hungary as fear of foreign invasion fades. Many restaurants have revived traditional recipes, museums display artifacts that trace Hungary's turbulent 1,000-year past, and lively Hungarian folk music fills the air everywhere.

Above all, visitors feel welcome thanks to the contagious goodwill and optimism of the Hungarian people, who have endured and prospered no matter how high the odds.

POLAND

Since Poland joined the European Union in May 2004, many of its tourist sites have acquired an international reputation as "must-sees" for foreign visitors. **Kraków, Warsaw, Gdańsk, Czestochowa, Auschwitz,** and the **Tatra Mountains** are just some of the stops that are attracting large crowds these days, and with good reason.

With a population of more than three-quarters of a million people, **Kraków** is Poland's third-largest city and its former capital. Kraków was left virtually untouched by World War II hostilities, so much of its original architecture and most of its monuments are still intact, and today it is Poland's unofficial cultural center. Kraków always has been one of Poland's most popular tourist centers, but is also the birthplace of the late Pope John Paul II and as such its popularity with tourists has surged since his death in 2005.

Warsaw is Poland's capital. Unlike Kraków, Warsaw was devastated during World War II and had to be almost totally rebuilt. Today Warsaw is a sophisticated, modern city with a vibrant business district that exudes an Eastern European aura. If you visit, be sure to see **Old Town,** the **Royal Route,** the **Chopin museum,** and the former **Jewish ghetto.**

Gdańsk is a seaport city where in 1978 shipyard electrician **Lech Wałęsa** started the **Solidarity** movement on behalf of workers' rights. Wałęsa's efforts eventually resulted in the defeat of Communism in Poland and made him a national hero. Gdańsk also is a tourist town thanks to a mild climate, beautiful beaches, and architectural treasures that include the largest brick Gothic church in Europe.

The town of **Czestochowa** is usually associated with **Jasna Gora Monastery,** which is the biggest Marian sanctuary in Poland. For Catholic Poland it is a sacred pilgrimage destination that is home to an icon known as the **Black Madonna of Czestochowa.** There are several legends associated with the Black Madonna, but the most common is that the painting saved its church from being destroyed in a fire, but not before the flames darkened the Virgin Mary's flesh tones. Catholics honor the Madonna as Poland's protector and she is credited with many miracles.

The provincial town of **Oświęcim,** aka **Auschwitz,** was the site of the largest Nazi extermination camp during World War II. An estimated 1.5 million people were tortured, starved, and murdered there. Today Auschwitz has been preserved as a monument to man's inhumanity to his fellow man.

The **Tatras** are the highest mountains between the Alps and the Caucasus and the range's rocky peaks are covered with snow year-round. About 250km (155 miles) of trails and ski slopes delight hikers and skiers.

In spite of a turbulent history and dramatic changes in its world standing, Poland has maintained its culture, its faith, and its sense of humor. Coupled with the country's considerable natural wonders, historical sites, and hospitality, these elements are a potent combination for tourists.

ROMANIA

Romania's history is marked by a legacy of bloodthirsty leaders, one of whom inspired the Count Dracula legend (Vlad the Impaler) because of his cruel method of killing his enemies, and another (Nicolae Ceauşescu) who parlayed personal excesses, repressive policies, and economic miscues to suck a different sort of life force from the people he governed. But the cold-blooded nature of Romania's political leaders has never been able to dull the beauty of the country and the warmth of its people.

Breathtaking scenery and traditional values mark the rural heartland, while Bucharest boasts broad boulevards and a sophistication that demonstrate why it once was called the "Paris of the East."

The contrasts between the lavish architecture of the past and the ugly, utilitarian facades of the Ceauşescu era are pervasive throughout Bucharest. Orthodox churches and 18th-century monasteries are neighbors to concrete high-rises, a dichotomy that also symbolizes Romania's current state of mind, an attitude that still straddles the chasm between the country's iron-curtain past and its 21st-century future.

Hotels in Bucharest are upgrading to accommodate an expected influx of international guests, tour operators are planning ski trips and other excursions to Romania's mountains (Poiana Brasov), and budget carrier Wizz Air has been running daily round-trip flights between Bucharest and London's Luton Airport since 2007. At the same time, the country's economy is struggling, some of its leaders are under suspicion for war crimes, and Romania's European Union brethren are nervous about the politics of its Balkan member.

Romania's tourism board says the country realized a 23% increase in visitor traffic in 2007 over the previous year. But despite that positive sign, the country has a long way to go to catch up with industry accommodations and service standards appropriate for an international destination.

Romania's modern capital represents just a small portion of this country, which covers about the same acreage as the state of Oregon. Actually, most of Romania is a "wild" country, terrain that has pockets of primitive roads that can be difficult to navigate, especially in winter.

Attractions include Transylvania, a name that's recognizable to any horror-movie fan because it is the birthplace of the infamous Vlad, and by association the home of filmdom's most famous vampire. The "Dracula Castle" there is a popular stop.

Romania also is home to the rugged Carpathian Mountains, the Danube Delta wetland ecosystem, the amazing painted monasteries of Bucovina, countless rural villages untouched by time for centuries, and a string of Black Sea resorts that always have attracted a crowd.

RUSSIAN FEDERATION (MOSCOW & ST. PETERSBURG)

The Russian landscape depicted in the film *Doctor Zhivago* was characterized by vast expanses of snow-covered land dotted with opulent palaces inhabited by aristocrats and humble homes where ordinary people lived. The discrepancy between the haves and the have-nots in Russia may not be as visual today, but an economic chasm definitely exists in the newly flush country.

Oil money has created a superwealthy class of nouveau riche, and at the same time relegated the elderly and longtime patriots to poverty. Perhaps this gap was inevitable: The sheer size of the Russian Federation almost guarantees an adventure in diversity, spreading across 11 time zones and numerous ethnic cultures. But cultural and socioeconomic strata are obvious even in the western portion of the country known as "European Russia."

Visits to Russia's two largest cities amplify the differences: the hectic, modern bustle of Moscow, contrasted with the historical, sophisticated aura of imperial St. Petersburg.

Moscow flaunts its links to Western culture, with chain restaurants, dance clubs, and a cutthroat club scene. Its residents have discarded the dour, gray mood that characterized the city during the Soviet years in favor of a pursuit of hedonism and wealth.

The city has more billionaires than any other city in the world, but it also is home to vast numbers of beggars, as if to accentuate the city's stark differences.

Moscow's economy has been booming since the dissolution of the Soviet Union, opening the door to increased tourism from the West. The city's more than 12 million citizens crowd the subways and clubs. Visitors will find that hotel prices rival or exceed those charged in Paris, and restaurant tabs can run as high or higher than a three-star dining room in New York. Add to that a rising crime rate and police corruption (tourist shakedowns are common) and you have "big city" problems.

But Moscow still is a fascinating city to explore. Cupolas and cathedrals compete with Soviet-era skyscrapers for visitors' attention, while the brooding specter of the Kremlin reminds them of the events from recent history. Red Square, St. Basil's Cathedral, and Lenin's Mausoleum all beckon to the tourists, while the Bolshoi and Chekhov theaters offer a glimpse into the classical Russian soul.

St. Petersburg is Moscow's cultural counterpoint, a city filled with architectural and artistic wonders. Built by Peter the Great in 1703 on the site of a swamp, St. Petersburg has evolved into the fourth-largest city in Europe. Its role in the arts world is solidified by author Fyodor Dostoevski and composer Dmitri Shostakovich.

The Heritage Museum in the Winter Palace contains one of the world's great collections of art, but intellectual and artistic excellence has not translated into economic progress for St. Petersburg, as it has for Moscow.

SLOVAKIA

Slovakia's tourism industry has burgeoned since that country declared independence in 1993. By the late 1990s Slovakia was receiving more than half a million visitors annually; in 2007, the number of visitors was just over 1.6 million.

Slovakia is situated between Austria, Hungary, and Russia, a position that had a strong influence on its history and architecture. Of the three influential styles, the sensibilities of Austria and Hungary won out. However, in the eastern part of the country the architectural landscape is more Eastern Orthodox than Austro-Hungarian.

Almost every town in Slovakia has a historic church, and each house of worship has something to commend it. However, the most interesting churches in the country are the centuries-old **wooden churches** in the northeastern part of the country. Unfortunately, these are difficult to reach.

Throughout history Slovakia never was a dominant nation, and it never became a wealthy nation, either. Consequently the historic sections of Slovak cities are less ornate than those in wealthier countries like Austria.

Slovakian **town squares** deserve special note for their architectural interest. Some (like Stiavnica) even have been designated UNESCO Cultural Heritage Sites.

Slovak castles and ruins are another source of interest for architecture buffs. Many have been restored, but even those that have fallen into ruin are notable and every region of the country offers a few examples of each.

If poking around rock piles isn't your passion, check out Slovakia's historic towns and its mountain ski resorts, which seem to ban westernization and the commercialism that go hand in hand with capitalism. Here you can comfortably go back in time and experience life as it was lived in Slovakia for centuries.

Finally, Slovakia's capital city, **Bratislava,** is homey and friendly, but with a surprisingly rich cultural life. Bratislava is a capital city without the usual congestion of most seats of government. Quaint, gentle, and old world are apt terms to describe this charming city, and they extend to food and lodging options, too. Slovakia joined the European Union in 2004, but the country has not yet caught up with its neighbors when it comes to developing a thriving tourism infrastructure. If you visit, don't expect things to be up to western standards, but that could be a good thing. Instead, luxuriate in an atmosphere that lets you truly experience a bygone era.

SLOVENIA

Slovenia is a country of firsts. As the westernmost country in the region defined as Eastern Europe in this guide, Slovenia was the first to declare its independence (1990). It also was one of the first of this group to join the European Union, and on January 1, 2007, it was the first to adopt the euro as its official currency. Slovenia is definitely the first of this group to boast the lowest crime rate in all of Europe. In fact, this efficient country has moved into the ranks of successful European Union nations with laserlike precision, and the result is a nation that works. Slovenia has a well-oiled tourism industry with facilities and sites that consistently attract an international crowd. It even has exported its expertise in spa design and management to Croatia, where Slovenian firms are taking over and rehabbing that country's aging spa facilities.

Business acumen isn't the only Slovenian virtue. Legend has it that after God created the world he had a fistful of leftover beauty, which he sprinkled over Slovenia. A glimpse of **St. Martin's Pilgrimage Church** rising through the mist from its island perch in the middle of **Lake Bled,** a walk through the subterranean majesty of **Škocjan Caves,** the panoramic view of **Ljubljana** from its namesake castle, or an Adriatic sunset over coastal **Portorož** are enough hard evidence to convince even atheists that the legend is fact.

Slovenia certainly is one of the most easily accessible Eastern European nations from Europe's capitals: It is just 230km (143 miles) from Vienna, 240km (149 miles) from Budapest, and 460km (285 miles) from Milan. It is linked to the world by modern highways, numerous air routes, efficient train service, and even by ferry.

Slovenia's position on land surrounded by the mountains of Austria and Italy, Hungary's plains, and the Adriatic makes for a surprisingly diverse landscape. What's even more of a pleasant surprise is that nothing in Slovenia is more than a 2-hour drive from anything else in the country. You can ski an Olympic training run on the slopes above picturesque **Kranjska Gora** in the morning, and take a dip in the warm sea at languid Portorož before the sun goes down. You can hike through gorgeous **Triglav National Park** and marvel at its glacial valleys, gorges, and waterfalls. You even can launch your kayak in rushing water that moves fast enough to challenge the most expert white-water fan and finish your run in time for dinner in enchanting Ljubljana the same day.

Of all the countries profiled in this guide, Slovenia has proven to be the most "together" in its plan to become a full member of the global community. Not only has Slovenia's government gone out of its way to attract, and keep, foreign investment since its accession to the E.U. in 2004, but it also has shared the resulting wealth with its citizens by taking steps to improve public services and to enhance everyone's everyday life.

3

Planning Your Trip to Eastern Europe

When the Berlin Wall fell in 1989, the iron curtain slowly lifted to give the world its first unobstructed view of Eastern Europe since World War II. What materialized was a region numbed by economic disaster, iron-fisted suppression of the individual, and the neglect of the aesthetic. Almost 2 decades later, Eastern Europe's fortunes have changed dramatically, but most North Americans still picture the region east of Berlin and the Adriatic in grim, forbidding Cold War terms and consequently eliminate it from their lists of desirable vacation destinations. Western Europeans, however, always viewed Eastern European countries as places to explore and relax, and as soon as they were free to travel there without much restriction, they returned in droves to Croatia's Adriatic resorts, the Czech Republic's majestic churches, Hungary's intriguing spa towns, Slovenia's picturesque Alpine villages, Romania's Carpathian mountains, Russia's historic cities, and Poland's bustling markets. North Americans' long-held preconceptions of Eastern Europe are dissipating, and more and more English-speaking folks are riding the tourism wave that is sweeping the region. Eastern Europe finally is emerging as a trendy travel frontier where friendly people, stunning natural beauty, compelling history, and relatively low prices are drawing a crowd of savvy travelers. Even though North American travelers must tolerate one-stop flights and must obtain a visa if Russia is their destination, gaining entry to Eastern Europe is no more difficult than accessing Western Europe. Furthermore, you'll find an OPEN sign on these formerly restricted destinations and you'll wonder why it took you so long to get there.

1 VISITOR INFORMATION

The country chapters in this guide provide specific information on traveling to and getting around individual Eastern European countries. In this chapter we offer region-wide tips and general information that will help you plan your trip.

2 ENTRY REQUIREMENTS

PASSPORTS

For information on how to get a passport, go to "Getting Your Passport in Order" later in this chapter—the websites listed provide downloadable passport applications as well as the current fees for processing passport applications. For an up-to-date, country-by-country listing of passport requirements around the world, go to the "Foreign Entry Requirement" Web page of the U.S. State Department at **http://travel.state.gov**. For children under 14, **both** parents/legal guardians must consent to the passport application, either in writing or in person. Parents with sole custody must present documentation of

Getting Your Passport in Order

Allow plenty of time before your trip to apply for a passport; processing normally takes 3 weeks but can take longer during busy periods (especially spring). And keep in mind that if you need a passport in a hurry, you'll pay a much higher processing fee.

For Residents of Australia: You can pick up an application from your local post office or any branch of Passports Australia, but you must schedule an interview at the passport office to present your application materials. Call the **Australian Passport Information Service** at ✆ **131-232,** or visit the government website at www.passports.gov.au.

For Residents of Canada: Passport applications are available at travel agencies throughout Canada or from the central **Passport Office,** Department of Foreign Affairs and International Trade, Ottawa, ON K1A 0G3 (✆ **800/567-6868;** www.ppt.gc.ca).

For Residents of Ireland: You can apply for a 10-year passport at the **Passport Office,** Setanta Centre, Molesworth Street, Dublin 2 (✆ **01/671-1633;** www.irlgov.ie/iveagh). Those under age 18 and over 65 must apply for a 3-year passport. You also can apply at 1A South Mall, Cork (✆ **021/272-525**) or at most main post offices.

For Residents of New Zealand: You can pick up a passport application at any New Zealand Passports Office or download it from the website. Contact the **Passports Office** at ✆ **0800/225-050** in New Zealand or 04/474-8100, or log on to www.passports.govt.nz.

For Residents of the United Kingdom: To pick up an application for a standard 10-year passport (5-year passport for children under 16), visit your nearest passport office, major post office, or travel agency; or contact the **United Kingdom Passport Service** at ✆ **0870/521-0410** or search its website at www.ukpa.gov.uk.

For Residents of the United States: Whether you're applying in person or by mail, you can download passport applications from the U.S. State Department website at **http://travel.state.gov**. To find your regional passport office, either check the U.S. State Department website or call the **National Passport Information Center** toll-free number (✆ **877/487-2778**) for automated information.

their status when applying for a child's passport. Acceptable documentation includes: a court order listing the parent as sole custodian and a court document granting the parent permission to travel with the child, a death certificate for the absent parent, and a certified copy of the child's birth certificate that lists **only** the parent applying for the child's passport. Ask your airline what's required when you book the ticket. Also check the State Department's **Single Parent Travel Forum,** which also has a helpful FAQ section at www.singleparenttravel.net.

Note: See the "**Planning Your Trip to . . .**" sections of the individual country chapters for detailed information on entry/visa requirements for each country covered in this book.

VISAS

Visitors from the U.S., Canada, Australia, and E.U. countries do not need visas to visit Bulgaria, Croatia, the Czech Republic, Hungary, Poland, Romania, Slovakia, or Slovenia. Visas *are* required for all visitors entering Russia. Visas for entry to Russia are issued by the Russian embassy or consulate in your home country. For specifics on how to get a visa, go to the "**Planning Your Trip to . . .**" sections of the individual country chapters.

MEDICAL REQUIREMENTS

For information on medical requirements and recommendations, see "Health," p. 33.

CUSTOMS

What You Can Take Home

U.S. Citizens

Returning **U.S. citizens** who have been away for at least 48 hours are allowed to bring back, once every 30 days, $800 worth of merchandise duty-free. You'll pay a flat rate of duty on the next $1,000 worth of purchases. Any dollar amount beyond that is subject to duties at whatever rates apply. On mailed gifts, the duty-free limit is $200. Be sure to keep your receipts or purchases accessible to expedite the declaration process. ***Note:*** If you owe duty, you are required to pay on your arrival in the United States—by cash, personal check, government or traveler's check, or money order (and, in some locations, a Visa or MasterCard).

To avoid paying duty on foreign-made personal items you owned before your trip, bring along a bill of sale, insurance policy, jeweler's appraisal, or receipts of purchase. Or you can register items that can be readily identified by a permanently affixed serial number or marking—think laptop computers, cameras, and CD players—with Customs before you leave. Take the items to the nearest Customs office or register them with Customs at the airport from which you're departing. You'll receive, at no cost, a Certificate of Registration, which allows duty-free entry for the life of the item.

With few exceptions, you cannot bring fresh fruits and vegetables into the United States. For specifics on what you can bring back and the corresponding fees, download the invaluable free pamphlet *Know Before You Go!* online at **www.cbp.gov**. (Click on "Travel," and then click on "Know Before You Go.") Or contact the **U.S. Customs & Border Protection (CBP),** 1300 Pennsylvania Ave. NW, Washington, DC 20229 (✆ **877/287-8667**) and request the pamphlet.

Canadian Citizens

Canada allows its citizens a C$750 exemption. Canadians are allowed to bring back duty-free one carton of cigarettes, one can of tobacco, 40 imperial ounces of liquor, and 50 cigars. In addition, they can mail gifts to Canada valued at less than C$60 a day, provided they're unsolicited and don't contain alcohol or tobacco (write on the package "Unsolicited gift, under $60 value"). All valuables should be declared on the Y-38 form before departure from Canada, including serial numbers of valuables you already own, such as expensive foreign cameras. ***Note:*** The C$750 exemption can be used only once a year and only after an absence of 7 days.

For a clear summary of Canadian rules, write for the booklet *I Declare,* issued by the **Canada Border Services Agency** (✆ **800/461-9999** in Canada, or 204/983-3500; **www.cbsa-asfc.gc.ca**).

U.K. Citizens

U.K. citizens returning from a **non-E.U. country** have a Customs allowance of 200 cigarettes; 50 cigars; 250 grams of smoking tobacco; 2 liters of still table wine;

1 liter of spirits or strong liqueurs (over 22% volume); 2 liters of fortified wine, sparkling wine or other liqueurs; 60cc (ml) perfume; 250cc (ml) of toilet water; and £145 worth of all other goods, including gifts and souvenirs. People under 17 cannot have the tobacco or alcohol allowance.

For information, contact **HM Customs & Excise** at ✆ **0845/010-9000** in the U.K., or 020/8929-0152, or consult the website at **www.hmce.gov.uk**.

Australian Citizens

The duty-free allowance in **Australia** is A$400 or, for those under 18, A$200. Citizens can bring in 250 cigarettes or 250 grams of loose tobacco, and 1,125 milliliters of alcohol. If you're returning with valuables you already own, such as foreign-made cameras, you should file form B263. A helpful brochure available from Australian consulates or Customs offices is *Know Before You Go.* For more information, call the **Australian Customs Service** at ✆ **1300/363-263,** or log on to **www.customs.gov.au.**

New Zealand Citizens

The duty-free allowance for **New Zealand** is NZ$700. Citizens over 17 can bring in 200 cigarettes, 50 cigars, or 250 grams of tobacco (or a mixture of all three if their combined weight doesn't exceed 250 grams); plus 4.5 liters of wine and beer, or 1.125 liters of liquor. New Zealand currency does not carry import or export restrictions. Fill out a certificate of export, listing the valuables you are taking out of the country; that way, you can bring them back without paying duty. Most questions are answered in a free pamphlet available at New Zealand consulates and Customs offices: *New Zealand Customs Guide for Travellers, Notice no. 4.* For more information, contact **New Zealand Customs,** the Customhouse, 17–21 Whitmore St., Box 2218, Wellington (✆ **04/473-6099** or 0800/428-786; **www.customs.govt.nz**).

3 WHEN TO GO

Eastern Europe sprawls over a huge geographic area with multiple climates that range from Mediterranean to alpine to something that approaches arctic. In general, the tourist season runs from May through September, with the greatest influx of visitors occurring in July and August, especially in coastal areas, where the weather is sunny and dry almost every day. (See the chapter specific to your destination for detailed weather information). During these 2 months all sites, attractions, and special events operate at full throttle and charge top dollar. July and August are also when rooms are in shortest supply and when crowds can be overwhelming.

Travelers to Eastern Europe have more elbow room in May and June and from September until mid-October. The weather is more temperate and prices are lower than in the summer months, but some attractions, restaurants, and hotels may operate on reduced schedules during this time. Check ahead if something that is a must-see is open or closed.

During the winter months, tourism shifts to Eastern Europe's mountain ranges and metropolitan areas, leaving coastal areas deserted. In fact, many island and seaside attractions are closed altogether from November to April, and even if they aren't, visitors are few.

Eastern Europe's ski season lasts from December to mid-March (longer in Romania) and except for other snow sports enthusiasts, you won't run into many people outside ski resort areas if you're traveling in the mountains.

Eastern Europe's city dwellers tend to hunker down in winter, when the days can be short, cold, and gray and the nights long, colder, and silent. Concerts and theater productions are in full swing in big cities during the winter but they attract mostly locals, unlike the flamboyant outdoor music festivals that seem to go nonstop in the summer months and attract an international crowd.

Each Eastern European country covered in this guide has its own optimal "season."

HOLIDAYS, CELEBRATIONS & EVENTS

Many of Eastern Europe's holidays and festivals correspond to religious holy days (Catholic and Orthodox) and to national commemorations.

JANUARY

New Year's Day. January 1 is the first day of the Gregorian calendar, which is used by most countries in Eastern Europe. This day is both a secular and a religious holiday commemorating the circumcision of Christ. In countries where Eastern Orthodoxy is the predominant religion, many celebrate January 1 as a civic holiday and January 14 as a religious holiday. The Eastern Church in Bulgaria, Romania, and Poland has adopted a modified Julian calendar, which incorporates both religious and civic holidays on January 1. In Russia, January 1 is a civil holiday and the biggest of the year, a holdover from the atheist Soviet government, which banned religious celebrations.

FEBRUARY

Feast of St. Blaise. The patron saint of Dubrovnik (Croatia) is honored each February 3 by Catholics worldwide as a healer of throat ailments. But in Dubrovnik, the saint is revered as the city's savior, a man who thwarted an attack of invading Turks. He is feted with parades, food, wine, and a workers' day off.

Carnival. This pre-Lenten celebration begins in mid-February and ends at midnight on Shrove Tuesday in cities and villages all over the globe. It is celebrated to various degrees throughout Eastern Europe, but lavishly so in Rijeka, Croatia.

MARCH

National Days. March is a good month for national days in Eastern Europe. **Bulgaria National Day** is March 3 while Hungary's is March 15. Bulgaria also hosts **March Music Days,** a festival of classical music and composers, in March.

APRIL

Easter Sunday and Easter Monday. These movable feasts can fall in March or April, but they are both religious and civic holidays for Catholics and Eastern Rite Christians throughout Eastern Europe whenever they occur. Eastern Rite Easter is usually 1 or 2 weeks after Catholic/Protestant Easter. The day has taken on greater significance in Russia since the collapse of Soviet atheism. The **International Festival of Ghosts and Phantoms** materializes in Bojnice, Slovakia, at the end of April. On **National Resistance Day** Slovenia stops to remember the movement that stood up to occupying forces during World War II.

MAY

Labor Day. May 1 is a workers' holiday throughout Eastern Europe.

National Days. Poland's Constitution Day is May 3; Bulgaria has Bulgarian Army Day on May 6; the Czech Republic and Slovakia celebrate Liberation Day on May 8; Hungary commemorates Emancipation Day on May 24; and Croatia celebrates Statehood Day on May 30.

June

Pentecost Sunday. Another movable church feast, Pentecost is celebrated 40 days after Easter throughout Eastern Europe. Pentecost, aka Whit Monday, is also a civic holiday.

Corpus Christi Day. This Catholic holy day also merits some civic closures in Croatia, Poland, Slovakia, and Slovenia. It usually falls in June but can be in late May when Easter falls early in the season.

Summer Festivals. June is the traditional start of the summer festival season in Eastern Europe, which kicks off with dance festivals in Zagreb, Croatia (June 1), and Prague, Czech Republic (June 2).

National Days. Croatia stops everything for **Antifascist Struggle Day** on June 22, and closes down again 3 days later on June 25 for **Statehood Day,** a date it shares with Slovenia's **National Day** holiday. In late June or early July St. Petersburg hosts **White Nights,** a series of concerts, film festivals, all-night boat tours, and other events.

July & August

These 2 months equate with Eastern Europe's high tourism season and the summer festival season all over the region. Choose from **Dubrovnik's Summer Festival** in Croatia, a more-than-50-year-old theater and music marathon that goes from the second week of July through the third week of August, to **Formula I racing** in Budapest (Hungary) at the beginning of August. The **Maiden Festival** in Romania is a vestige of Targu de Fete, a day when guys picked out their brides. Today it is more of a folk festival. Look for single-day or weekend celebrations in specific towns in every country and you can eat, drink, sing, and dance your way across Eastern Europe for 2 months. **Split's Summer Festival** showcases open-air opera, theater, and dance performances and Poreč is the venue for a series of **jazz concerts.** August 15 is the **Feast of the Assumption,** which is a holy day for the world's Catholics, including Eastern Europe's Catholic countries (Croatia, Poland, Slovakia, and Slovenia). See specific country chapters for detailed festival information.

September

The festival season winds down and kids in Eastern Europe go back to school in September. You still can take in a concert or two at the **Prague Autumn Music Festival** from mid-September to October or watch a **Marco Polo naval battle reenactment** off Korčula (Croatia) in early September. The **Apollonia Festival of the Arts** takes place in Bulgaria in September and it is followed by the **Golden Rose International Film Festival** at the end of the month.

October

Lots of civic commemorations across Eastern Europe mean plenty of days off work and store closures in October. Croatia, Hungary, the Czech Republic, and Slovenia each close down for a day (Oct 8, 23, 28, and 31, respectively) to celebrate political milestones. The harvest season goes into full swing, too, with village celebrations in progress across the region. Warsaw hosts a **Jazz Jamboree** this month. It is purported to be the oldest jazz festival in Europe.

November

All Saints' Day (Nov 1) is another holy day for Catholics and a day to close up shop in Eastern Europe's Catholic countries (Croatia, Poland, Slovakia, Slovenia). Polish people place lighted candles on the graves of the dear departed on this day. November 11 is **St. Martin's Day** and the first day of the wine season in grape-growing regions (Croatia, Slovenia) and a day to eat, drink, and be merry.

December

Christmas fairs abound in the Czech Republic in the days leading up to that holiday. Polish children delight on **St. Nicholas Day** (Dec 6) because they receive gifts. Except for Russia, **Christmas Day and St. Stephen's Day** (Dec 25–26) are celebrated throughout Eastern Europe as both religious and civic holidays, as is **New Year's Eve,** aka **St. Sylvester's Day,** on December 31.

For an exhaustive list of events beyond those listed here, check http://events.frommers.com, where you'll find a searchable, up-to-the-minute roster of what's happening in cities all over the world.

4 GETTING THERE & GETTING AROUND EASTERN EUROPE

GETTING TO EASTERN EUROPE

Prague, Warsaw, Zagreb, Budapest, and Moscow receive the greatest number of international flights to Eastern Europe. If you're planning to explore the entire region, you might consider starting at one of these gateways and catching connecting flights to less-serviced destinations. See the **"Getting There"** sections of the individual country chapters for detailed information.

By Plane

While most airports in the Eastern European countries covered in this book accommodate flights from a variety of international airlines, each welcomes most of its tourists on connecting flights run by its national carriers from major western European hubs. These are:

Bulgaria: Sofia Airport (SOF); Bulgaria Air, ✆ +359 2 402 0400, www.air.bg/en.

Croatia: Zagreb Airport (ZAG); Croatia Air, ✆ **+385 (0) 91 77 312,** www.croatiaairlines.com.

Czech Republic: Prague Airport (PRG); Czech Airlines, ✆ **+420 239 007 007,** www.csa.cz/en/portal/homepage/cz_homepage.htm.

Hungary: Budapest Airport (BUD); Malév Hungarian Airlines, ✆ +36 1 235 3888, www.malev.com/bp/eng/index.asp.

Poland: Warsaw Frederic Chopin Airport (WAW); LOT Polish Airline, ✆ +48 801 703 703, www.lot.com/default.aspx?_lang=en&_cid=1013.

Romania: Bucharest Henri Coanda/Otopeni Airport (OTP); TAROM Romania Air Transport, ✆ +40 **021 317 4444,** www.tarom.ro/en.

Moscow: Sheremetevo-2 Airport (SVO); Aeroflot, ✆ +7 495 223-55-55, www.aeroflot.ru.

Slovakia: Bratislava M.R. Štefánik Airport (BTS); Czech Airlines, ✆ **+42 (0) 239 007 007,** www.csa.cz/en/portal/homepage/cz_homepage.htm.

Slovenia: Ljubljana Airport (LJU); Adria Airways, ✆ +386 1 369 10 10, www.adria.si/en/index.cp2.

By Car

Public transportation in Eastern Europe generally is excellent and a good way to cover a lot of territory inexpensively. However, access to a car is a must if you want to see remote attractions or if you don't have time to wait for train or bus connections. If you plan to rent a car, reserve it before you leave home. Rates are lower and you are likely to get a better choice of cars. Look for a weekly rate with unlimited mileage. Expect to pay $50 and up per day for an economy car with manual transmission and unlimited mileage. Often cars at that price point are not air-conditioned or low-mileage models, either. Gas, parking, and insurance are always extra.

Note: Be sure you examine and document any scratches, broken equipment, or interior stains when taking possession of your car. You could be charged for the damage when you return the car if you haven't pointed it out ahead of time and noted it on your contract.

By Train

Train travel in Eastern Europe is comfy, pleasant, and fairly efficient. Almost all major population centers (with the exception of Dubrovnik, Croatia) are linked by rail service. Overnight trains serve a double purpose: They get you to your destination and save the cost of a night in a hotel. If you use this option be sure to ask if you have to make a separate reservation for the berth in addition to the reservation for your transport. The **Thomas Cook European Timetable** (www.thomascook.com) gives an inclusive listing of train schedules and tells you when you have to book in advance or pay extra for things like a pillow. In general, train travel in Eastern Europe is more expensive than bus travel and sometimes fares are comparable with airfares within the country. Not all countries in Eastern Europe honor rail passes. Hungary is the only country covered in this book that accepts the Eurailpass. However, Bulgaria, the Czech Republic, Romania, and Hungary sell single-country rail passes. ***Note:*** Intercountry rail travel is becoming less of a hassle in Eastern Europe as national rail lines are beginning to align their schedules to make connections and border crossings easier. However, you might run into a glitch (and a long layover) unless you do meticulous planning ahead of time. Intracountry travel usually is problem-free.

By Bus

Bus travel is a way of life in all of Europe, including Eastern Europe. Usually international buses are equipped with luxuries such as reclining seats, air-conditioning, and even television. Buses tend to be the best for reaching smaller towns and remote sites, and sometimes they are the only option for reaching mountainous villages and tiny hamlets. You rarely have to reserve a seat in advance, but you can buy a ticket in advance at a main bus station or from the driver when you board. Buses work well for travel between cities in a single country and for access to areas trains can't access. Every major city in Eastern Europe has a well-developed commuter system that involves buses, trams, and sometimes sophisticated metro systems.

5 MONEY & COSTS

CURRENCY

While most of the countries in this guide are in various stages of becoming members of the European Union, Slovenia is the only one that had replaced its local currency with the euro at publication time. Nonetheless, hotel, attraction, and restaurant prices in Eastern European countries have been quoted in both euros and local currency for years, a practice that sometimes confuses tourists. No matter how prices are listed, most establishments will accept payment in the local currency, and you'll get a more favorable conversion rate if you pay with local cash. In addition, **countries such as Bulgaria and Romania**

Local Currency

For specifics about each country's currency and conversion rates, please see the "Money" sections in the individual country chapters.

still are a mostly cash economy, so carrying local currency there is a necessity. ***Note:*** Concessions in most Eastern European airports usually accept U.S. dollars and euros as well as local currency, but it's always useful to have the local currency on hand.

If prices in this book are quoted in the local currency, we provide the conversion rate to U.S. dollars and British pounds; if prices are quoted euros, we provide the conversion rate in U.S. dollars only. For real-time exchange rates of any currency, check **www.xe.com/ucc** or **www.oanda.com**.

ATMS

In Eastern European cities, the easiest and best way to get cash away from home is from an ATM (automated teller machine), commonly referred to as a "bancomat" in Eastern Europe. The **Cirrus** (**© 800/424-7787;** www.mastercard.com) and **PLUS** (**© 800/843-7587;** www.visa.com) networks span the globe; look at the back of your bank card to see which network you're on, then call or check online for ATM locations at your destination. Be sure you know your personal identification number (PIN) and daily withdrawal limit before you depart. ***Note:*** Remember that many banks impose a fee every time you use a card at another bank's ATM, and that fee can be higher for international transactions (up to $5 or more) than for domestic ones (where they're rarely more than $2). In addition, the bank from which you withdraw cash may charge its own fee. For international withdrawal fees, ask your bank. ***Note:*** In some rural areas, ATMs may not be available and/or reliable. This is especially true in Bulgaria and Romania. For details, please see the "Money" sections in the individual country chapters.

CREDIT CARDS

Credit cards are another safe way to carry money. They also provide a convenient record of all your expenses, and they generally offer relatively good exchange rates. You can withdraw cash advances from your credit cards at banks or ATMs, provided you know your PIN. Keep in mind that you'll pay interest from the moment of your withdrawal, even if you pay your monthly bills on time. Also, note that many banks now assess a 1% to 3% "transaction fee" on *all* charges you incur abroad (whether you're using the local currency or your native currency).

Visa, MasterCard, and Diners Club are the cards commonly accepted in hotels and upscale restaurants in the larger cities of Eastern Europe. Establishments in smaller towns and villages usually require payment in cash, but even if they do accept credit cards, they will often offer a discount for cash payments.

TRAVELER'S CHECKS

You can buy traveler's checks at most banks in the U.S. in denominations of $20, $50, $100, $500, and sometimes $1,000. Generally, you'll pay a service charge ranging from 1% to 5%. However, in most Eastern European countries where mom-and-pop businesses thrive, cash is king and traveler's checks aren't always accepted. Even when they are, a service fee is tacked on them, which makes them a very expensive payment option.

If you want to use traveler's checks despite the drawbacks, you can buy them at almost any bank. **American Express** offers U.S. dollar denominations of $10, $20, $50, $100, $500, and $1,000 and tacks on service charges ranging from 1% to 4%. By phone, you can buy traveler's checks by calling ✆ **800/807-6233.** American Express cardholders should dial ✆ **800/221-7282;** this number accepts collect calls, offers service in several foreign languages, and exempts Amex gold and platinum cardholders from the 1% fee.

Visa offers traveler's checks at Citibank locations nationwide, as well as at several other banks. The service charge ranges between 1.5% and 2%; checks come in denominations of $20, $50, $100, $500, and $1,000. Call ✆ **800/732-1322** for information. AAA members can obtain Visa checks for a $9.95 fee (for checks up to $1,500) at most AAA offices or by calling ✆ **866/339-3378.**

MasterCard also offers traveler's checks. Call ✆ **800/223-9920** for a location near you.

American Express, Thomas Cook, Visa, and **MasterCard** also offer **foreign currency traveler's checks,** which are useful if you're traveling to one country, or to the euro zone; they're accepted at locations where dollar checks may not be.

If you do choose to carry traveler's checks, keep a record of their serial numbers separate from your checks in the event that they are stolen or lost. You'll get a refund faster if you know the numbers.

6 HEALTH

STAYING HEALTHY

Staying healthy during a trip to Eastern Europe requires common sense and an ounce of prevention. No vaccinations are necessary to visit the region and digestive upsets are visitors' biggest health challenges. It is safest to stick with bottled water everywhere.

General Availability of HealthCare

Hospitals and pharmacies are available in all Eastern European countries, but the quality of treatments and drugs varies widely, even within a single country. Consult individual country chapters for specific information.

If you plan to visit forested areas in the summer or if you choose to consume unpasteurized dairy products, you put yourself at risk for tick-borne infections. According to the Centers for Disease Control and Prevention (CDC), tick-borne encephalitis, a viral infection of the central nervous system, has been reported in Russia, the Czech Republic, Hungary, Poland, and Slovenia, so take precautions against tick bites if you visit these countries.

In general, the CDC warns travelers not to eat food purchased from street vendors or undercooked food to reduce risk of hepatitis A and typhoid fever. Do not drink beverages with ice if the water supply is suspect. Avoid unpasteurized dairy products. Don't swim in fresh water to avoid exposure to waterborne diseases. Don't handle animals, especially monkeys, dogs, and cats, to avoid bites and rabies and plague. Do not share needles for tattoos, body piercing, or injections. HIV and hepatitis B are global hazards. Avoid poultry farms, bird markets, and other places where live poultry is raised or kept.

Contact the **International Association for Medical Assistance to Travelers (IAMAT;** ✆ **716/754-4883,** or 416/652-0137 in Canada; www.iamat.org) for tips on travel and health concerns in the countries you're visiting, and for lists of local, English-speaking doctors. The United States **Centers for Disease Control and Prevention** (✆ **800/311-3435;** www.cdc.gov)

provides up-to-date information on health hazards by region or country and offers tips on food safety. The website **www.trip-prep.com**, sponsored by a consortium of travel-medicine practitioners, may also offer helpful advice on traveling abroad. You can find listings of reliable clinics overseas at the International Society of Travel medicine (www.istm.org).

What to Do If You Get Sick Away from Home

If you suffer from a chronic illness, consult your doctor before your departure. Pack **prescription medications** in your carry-on luggage, and carry them in their original containers, with pharmacy labels—otherwise they might not make it through airport security. Carry the generic names of prescription medicines, in case a local pharmacist is unfamiliar with the brand name. Have prescriptions translated into the local language before you leave home.

For travel abroad, you may have to pay all medical costs upfront and be reimbursed later.

We list **additional emergency numbers** in the individual country chapters.

7 SAFETY

STAYING SAFE

The U.S. Department of State's Consular Information Program provides consular information sheets, travel warnings, and public announcements. Travel Warnings are issued when the State Department recommends that Americans avoid travel to a certain country. Public Announcements are issued as a means to disseminate information quickly about terrorist threats and other relatively short-term conditions that pose significant risks to the security of American travelers. Free copies of this information are available by calling the Bureau of Consular Affairs at ✆ **202-647-5225** or via the fax-on-demand system: ✆ **202/647-3000.** Consular Information Sheets and Travel Warnings also are available on the Consular Affairs Internet home page at http://travel.state.gov.

Croatia, the Czech Republic, Hungary, Poland, Slovakia, and Slovenia are generally safe for tourists, though you should exercise the same caution you would in any unfamiliar city and always be aware of your surroundings when walking in less trafficked areas or at night.

Bulgaria, Romania, and Russia are less safe, and visitors should take precautions to keep their valuables secure from pickpockets and others who prey on the unaware in major cities. Corruption is widespread in these developing countries and visitors should be skeptical about policemen who stop you and demand payment for fines levied for bogus charges. If you are confronted with a policeman demanding cash on the spot to pay a fine assessed for an alleged infraction, you should insist on going to the nearest police station to pay. Before you go out, put jewelry and laptops in the hotel safe if you will be gone for the day and don't need them. Never leave any valuables or documents, including passports, in your hotel room when you are gone.

DEALING WITH DISCRIMINATION

Discrimination in Romania is usually reserved for members of the Roma minority (Gypsies) and for children with HIV. Bulgaria is slowly coming into compliance with E.U. antidiscrimination guidelines, but it, too, denies equal treatment to Roma (and women in general). The Russian constitution states that everyone is equal before the law and prohibits discrimination on the basis of race, ethnicity, national origin, or language, but there is no provision for punishment of anyone who breaks the law. In Russia, most discrimination is aimed at former Soviet citizens and select minorities, including the Roma. In the other Eastern European countries covered in this book, discrimination is largely based on internal conflicts and aimed at ethnic groups within the various countries.

8 SPECIALIZED TRAVEL RESOURCES

TRAVELERS WITH DISABILITIES

Most disabilities shouldn't stop anyone from traveling, and there are more options and resources available than ever before for travelers with disabilities. However, accommodations for such travelers in Eastern European countries are sporadic at best and usually concentrated in upscale establishments in larger cities.

If disabled access is an issue, it's best to book through a travel agency that caters to those with this concern. Many travel agencies offer customized tours and itineraries for travelers with disabilities. Among them are **Flying Wheels Travel** (✆ **507/451-5005;** www.flyingwheelstravel.com), **Access-Able Travel Source** (✆ **303/232-2979;** www.access-able.com), and **Accessible Journeys** (✆ **800/846-4537** or 610/521-0339; www.disabilitytravel.com). **Avis Rent a Car** has an "Avis Access" program that offers such services as a dedicated 24-hour toll-free number (✆ **888/879-4273**) for customers with special travel needs; special car features such as swivel seats, spinner knobs, and hand controls; and accessible bus service.

GAY & LESBIAN TRAVELERS

In the Catholic countries of Eastern Europe (Croatia, Poland, Slovakia, and Slovenia) where religious beliefs repudiate homosexuality, gay and lesbian travelers won't find many establishments that lay out the welcome mat for them. For the most part there is a macho mentality about sexuality in all the countries covered in this guide, and it is a sensibility that is not gay-friendly but not gay-hostile either. Thus, resources for gay and lesbian travelers are few or hidden in these nations. The Czech Republic and Slovenia are the most tolerant of the countries covered in this book. ***Note:*** In one recent instance, a hotel owner on the Croatian island of Hvar attempted to promote a week designed to appeal to gay and lesbian travelers, much to the chagrin of the local townspeople. The event was marred by many local protests. However, some organized tours to Eastern Europe might exist for this group. The **International Gay and Lesbian Travel Association (IGLTA;** ✆ **800/448-8550** or 954/776-2626; www.iglta.org) is the trade association for the gay and lesbian travel industry, and offers an online directory of gay- and lesbian-friendly travel businesses; go to the website and click on "Members."

Many agencies offer tours and travel itineraries specifically for gay and lesbian travelers. Among them are **Above and Beyond Tours** (✆ **800/397-2681;** www.abovebeyondtours.com); **Now, Voyager** (✆ **800/255-6951;** www.nowvoyager.com); and **Olivia Cruises & Resorts** (✆ **800/631-6277;** www.olivia.com).

Gay.com Travel (✆ **800/929-2268** or 415/644-8044; www.gay.com/travel or www.outandabout.com) is an excellent online successor to the popular ***Out & About*** print magazine. It provides regularly updated information about gay-owned, -oriented, and -friendly lodging, dining, sightseeing, nightlife, and shopping establishments in every important destination worldwide.

The following travel guides are available at many bookstores, or you can order them from any online bookseller: ***Frommer's Gay & Lesbian Europe*** (www.frommers.com), an excellent travel resource to the top European cities and resorts; ***Spartacus International Gay Guide*** (Bruno Gmünder Verlag; www.spartacusworld.com/gayguide) and ***Odysseus: The International Gay Travel Planner*** (Odysseus Enterprises, Ltd.); and the ***Damron*** guides (www.damron.com), with separate, annual books for gay men and lesbians.

FOR FAMILIES

Families are very important in Eastern Europe, but if you're traveling with children, don't expect any special treatment. You might get reduced rates for children under 12 when you visit museums, a reduced extra-person rate for the child in your hotel room, and a few kiddy menus here and there in restaurants, but other than that there are no financial breaks for the younger set. You'll find most young visitors at the beach, on the ski slopes, or in the museums of Eastern Europe.

Recommended family travel Internet sites include Family Travel Forum (**www.familytravelforum.com**), a comprehensive site that offers customized trip planning; Family Travel Network (**www.familytravelnetwork.com**), a comprehensive site offering sound advice for long-distance and international travel with children; and Family Travel Files, (**www.familytravelfiles.com**) which offers an online magazine and a directory of off-the-beaten-path tours and tour operators for families. If your destination is Croatia, then check out *Frommer's Croatia with Your Family.*

SENIOR TRAVEL

Many museums and attractions in Eastern Europe offer free or reduced rates to people of retirement age. However, few hotels offer age-based discounts and no restaurants offer the early-bird specials so popular with the over-50 set in the U.S. However, members of **AARP** (formerly known as the American Association of Retired Persons), 601 E St. NW, Washington, DC 20049 (© **888/687-2277;** www.aarp.org), may get discounts on hotels, airfares, and car rentals if these are linked to a U.S.-based company. AARP offers members a wide range of benefits, including *AARP The Magazine* and a monthly newsletter. Anyone over 50 can join.

Many reliable agencies and organizations target the 50-plus market. **Elderhostel** (© **877/426-8056;** www.elderhostel.org) arranges study programs for those aged 55 and over. **ElderTreks** (© **800/741-7956;** www.eldertreks.com) offers small-group tours to off-the-beaten-path or adventure-travel locations, restricted to travelers 50 and older. Recommended publications offering travel resources and discounts for seniors include: the quarterly magazine ***Travel 50 & Beyond*** (www.travel50andbeyond.com); ***Travel Unlimited: Uncommon Adventures for the Mature Traveler*** (Avalon); ***101 Tips for Mature Travelers,*** available from Grand Circle Travel (© **800/221-2610** or 617/350-7500; www.gct.com); and ***Unbelievably Good Deals and Great Adventures That You Absolutely Can't Get Unless You're Over 50*** (McGraw-Hill), by Joann Rattner Heilman.

WOMEN & SINGLE TRAVELERS

Solo women can travel safely in most of Eastern Europe, but like any other solo travelers, they might find it difficult to book any room at a single-room price. In fact, solo travelers may pay a premium to get a room. On package vacations, single travelers often are hit with a "single supplement" to the base price. To avoid it, you can agree to room with other single travelers or find a compatible roommate before you go, from one of the many roommate-locator agencies.

Travel Buddies Singles Travel Club (✆ **800/998-9099;** www.travelbuddies worldwide.com), based in Canada, runs small, intimate, single-friendly group trips and will match you with a roommate free of charge. **TravelChums** (✆ **212/787-2621;** www.travelchums.com) is an Internet-only travel-companion matching service with elements of an online personals-type site, hosted by the respected New York–based Shaw Guides travel service. The **Single Gourmet Club** (www.single gourmet.com/chapters.php) is an international social, dining, and travel club for singles of all ages, with club chapters in 21 cities in the U.S. and Canada. Many reputable tour companies offer singles-only trips. **Singles Travel International** (✆ **877/765-6874;** www.singlestravelintl.com) offers singles-only trips to places like London, Fiji, and the Greek Islands. **Backroads** (✆ **800/462-2848;** www.back roads.com) offers more than 160 active-travel trips to 30 destinations worldwide, including Bali, Morocco, and Costa Rica.

For more information, check out Eleanor Berman's latest edition of ***Traveling Solo: Advice and Ideas for More Than 250 Great Vacations*** (Globe Pequot), a guide with advice on traveling alone, either solo or as part of a group tour.

Note: In macho countries like Romania, Bulgaria, and Russia, a woman traveling solo may encounter harassment or other difficulties. In addition, it is not wise for a woman to travel alone at night in these places.

Check out the award-winning website Journeywoman (www.journeywoman.com), a "real-life" women's travel-information network where you can sign up for a free e-mail newsletter and get advice on everything from etiquette and dress to safety; or the travel guide ***Safety and Security for Women Who Travel*** by Sheila Swan and Peter Laufer (Travelers' Tales, Inc.), offering common-sense tips on safe travel.

9 SUSTAINABLE TOURISM

Sustainable tourism is conscientious travel. It means being careful with the environments you explore, and respecting the communities you visit. Two overlapping components of sustainable travel are **ecotourism** and **ethical tourism.** The **International Ecotourism Society (TIES)** defines ecotourism as responsible travel to natural areas that conserves the environment and improves the well-being of local people. TIES suggests that ecotourists follow these principles:

- Minimize environmental impact.
- Build environmental and cultural awareness and respect.
- Provide positive experiences for both visitors and hosts.
- Provide direct financial benefits for conservation and for local people.
- Raise sensitivity to host countries' political, environmental, and social climates.
- Support international human rights and labor agreements.

You can find some eco-friendly travel tips and statistics, as well as touring companies and associations—listed by destination under "Travel Choice"—at the **TIES** website, www.ecotourism.org. Also check out **Ecotravel.com,** which lets you search for sustainable touring companies in several categories (water-based, land-based, spiritually oriented, and so on).

While much of the focus of ecotourism is about reducing impacts on the natural environment, ethical tourism concentrates on ways to preserve and enhance local economies and communities, regardless of location. You can embrace ethical tourism by staying at a locally owned hotel or shopping at a store that employs local workers and sells locally produced goods.

Responsible Travel (www.responsibletravel.com) is a great source of sustainable travel ideas; the site is run by a spokesperson for ethical tourism in the travel industry. **Sustainable Travel International** (www.sustainabletravelinternational.org) promotes ethical tourism practices, and manages an extensive directory of sustainable properties and tour operators around the world.

In the U.K., **Tourism Concern** (www.tourismconcern.org.uk) works to reduce social and environmental problems connected to tourism. The **Association of Independent Tour Operators (AITO;** www.aito.co.uk) is a group of specialist operators leading the field in making holidays sustainable.

10 PACKAGES FOR THE INDEPENDENT TRAVELER

Package tours are simply a way to buy the airfare, accommodations, and other elements of your trip (such as car rentals, airport transfers, and sometimes even activities) at the same time and often at discounted prices.

One good source of package deals is the airlines themselves. Most major airlines offer air/land packages, including **American Airlines Vacations** (✆ 800/321-2121; www.aavacations.com), **Delta Vacations** (✆ 800/221-6666; www.deltavacations.com), **Continental Airlines Vacations** (✆ 800/301-3800; www.covacations.com), and **United Vacations** (✆ 888/854-3899; www.unitedvacations.com). Several big **online travel agencies**—Expedia, Travelocity, Orbitz, Site59, and Lastminute.com—also do a brisk business in packages.

Travel packages are also listed in the travel section of your local Sunday newspaper. Or check ads in the national travel magazines such as *Arthur Frommer's Budget Travel Magazine, Travel + Leisure, National Geographic Traveler,* and *Condé Nast Traveler.*

For more information on package tours and for tips on booking your trip, see Frommers.com.

11 ESCORTED GENERAL-INTEREST TOURS

Escorted tours are structured group tours, with a group leader. The price usually includes everything from airfare to hotels, meals, tours, admission costs, and local transportation.

Despite the fact that escorted tours require big deposits and predetermine hotels, restaurants, and itineraries, many people derive security and peace of mind from the structure they offer. Escorted tours—whether they're navigated by bus, motorcoach, train, or boat—let travelers sit back and enjoy the trip without having to drive or worry about details. They take you to the maximum number of sites in the minimum amount of time with the least amount of hassle. They're particularly convenient for people with limited mobility and they can be a great way to make new friends.

On the downside, you'll have little opportunity for serendipitous interactions with locals. The tours can be jam-packed with activities, leaving little room for individual sightseeing, whim, or adventure—plus they often focus on the heavy traffic sites, so you miss out on many a lesser known gem.

Abercrombie & Kent Private Journeys (✆ **800/554-7016;** www.abercrombiekent.com) is U.S.-based and internationally recognized as a luxury travel company. A&K started as an African safari specialist in 1962 and now offers escorted and independent trips to more than 100 countries, including Russia and central and Eastern European nations.

Vega International Travel Service (✆ **800/FLY-THERE** [359-8437]; www.

Discovery on Foot

Classic Journeys (✆ **800/200-3887;** www.classicjourneys.com) is a specialty tour operator that offers unique, upscale escorted vacations to a variety of locations around the world. Their three Eastern Europe excursions run through Croatia's Dalmatian Coast, Istria, and the area from Prague to Budapest. It's up to you to arrange airfare from your home country; the package price is for the in-country experience, though Classic Journeys will help with flight details and extra hotel nights if you ask. The basic fee covers a local guide, first-class hotels, most meals, and all tips, admission fees, tours, and transfers. Tours average 10 people per adventure and the itineraries emphasize culture, history, and walking. We've found that Classic Journeys carefully plans every detail to spare guests unpleasant surprises, but the plan is also flexible in case the group decides there is something they really want to see or do. Classic Journeys can arrange family-oriented experiences or culinary trips, too.

vegatravel.net) specializes in travel to Eastern Europe for individuals and corporations. Vega also arranges pilgrimage tours to such popular Catholic shrines as Međugorje in Bosnia and Czestochowa in Poland.

You can also get recommendations for reputable tour operators with expertise in the area you want to visit from the **American Society of Travel Agents** (✆ **859/226-4444;** www.ntaonline.com).

For more information on escorted general-interest tours, including questions to ask before booking your trip, see Frommers.com.

12 SPECIAL-INTEREST TRIPS

Here are a few companies offering activity-specific trips in Eastern Europe.

- **Globus** (✆ **866/755-8581;** www.globusjourneys.com) offers vacations to Eastern Europe in a variety of styles. Choose family-oriented, religious pilgrimage, culinary, or other vacation styles from this 75-year-old company.
- **Smithsonian Journeys** (✆ **877/338-8687;** www.smithsonianjourneys.org) puts together meticulously researched educational trips designed to maximize the time you spend in the places that command the most interest. Itineraries include "behind-the-scenes" visits that enhance the cultural and educational experience. Tour leaders are often internationally recognized experts in their fields. Smithsonian's Eastern European destinations include Slovenia, Prague, Budapest, Moscow, and St. Petersburg.
- The **Coordinating Committee for International Voluntary Service (CCIVS)** (www.unesco.org/ccivs) is a good place to look for opportunities to immerse yourself in an Eastern European culture and help the people there at the same time. CCIVS helps match aspiring volunteers with organizations that need their help in a country of interest.

VOLUNTEER & WORKING TRIPS

Volunteer travel has become increasingly popular among those who want to venture beyond the standard group-tour experience to learn languages, interact with locals, and make a positive difference while on vacation. Volunteer travel usually doesn't require special skills—just a willingness to work hard—and programs vary in length from a few days to a number of weeks. Some programs provide free housing and food, but many require volunteers to pay for travel expenses, which can add up quickly.

For general info on volunteer travel, visit **www.volunteerabroad.org** and **www.idealist.org**. Before you commit to a volunteer program, it's important to make sure any money you're giving is truly going back to the local community, and that the work you'll be doing will be a good fit for you. **Volunteer International** (www.volunteerinternational.org) has a helpful list of questions to ask to determine the intentions and the nature of a volunteer program.

13 STAYING CONNECTED

TELEPHONES

For information on making calls, see the "Planning Your Trip to . . ." section of each individual country chapter.

CELLPHONES

The three letters that define much of the world's wireless capabilities are GSM (Global System for Mobiles), a big, seamless network that makes for easy cross-border cellphone use throughout Europe and dozens of other countries worldwide. In the U.S., T-Mobile, and AT&T Wireless use this quasi-universal system; in Canada, Microcell and some Rogers customers are GSM, and all Europeans and most Australians use GSM.

If your cellphone is on a GSM system, and you have a world-capable multiband phone such as many Blackberry, Motorola, Sony Ericsson, or Samsung models, you can make and receive calls across civilized areas around much of the globe. Just call your wireless operator and ask for "international roaming" to be activated on your account. Unfortunately, per-minute charges can be high—usually $1 to $1.50 in Western Europe and up to $5 in places like Russia and Indonesia. Be sure you bring your AC charger, a converter, and an adaptor plug and check with your provider to be sure your converter is safe for the phone's delicate electrical circuits. A car charger can be useful, too.

It's handy to buy an "unlocked" world phone from the get-go. Many cellphone operators sell "locked" phones that restrict you from using any removable SIM card other than the one they supply. Having an unlocked phone allows you to install a cheap, prepaid SIM card that you can purchase and use in your destination country. (Show your phone to the salesperson; not all phones work on all networks.) You'll get a local phone number and dramatically lower calling rates.

Getting a locked phone unlocked can be a hassle, but it can be done. Call your cellular provider before you leave and say you'll be going abroad for several months and want to use the phone with a local provider.

For many, **renting** a phone is a good idea. While you can rent a phone from any number of overseas sites, including kiosks at airports and at car-rental agencies, we suggest renting the phone before you leave home. North Americans can rent one before leaving home from **InTouch USA** (✆ 800/872-7626; www.intouchglobal.com) or **RoadPost** (✆ 888/290-1606 or 905/272-5665; www.roadpost.com). InTouch will also, for free, advise you on whether your existing phone will work overseas; simply call ✆ **703/222-7161** between 9am and 4pm EST, or go to **http://intouchglobal.com/travel.htm**.

Buying a phone can be economically attractive, as many nations have cheap prepaid phone systems. Once you arrive at your destination, stop by a local cellphone shop and get the cheapest package; you'll probably pay less than $100 for a phone and a starter calling card. Local calls may be as low as 10¢ per minute, and in many countries incoming calls are free.

INTERNET & E-MAIL

With Your Own Computer

More and more hotels, cafes, and retailers are signing on as Wi-Fi (wireless fidelity) "hotspots." Mac owners have their own networking technology: Apple AirPort. **T-Mobile Hotspot** (www.t-mobile.com/hotspot) serves up wireless connections at more than 1,000 Starbucks coffee shops nationwide. **Boingo** (www.boingo.com) and **Wayport** (www.wayport.com) have set up networks in airports and high-class hotel lobbies. iPass providers (see below) also give you access to a few hundred wireless hotel lobby setups. To locate hot spots that provide **free wireless networks** in cities worldwide, go to **www.personaltelco.net/index.cgi/WirelessCommunities**.

For dial-up access, most business-class hotels throughout the world offer dataports for laptop modems, and a few thousand hotels in the U.S. and Europe now offer free high-speed Internet access. In addition, major Internet service providers (ISPs) have **local access numbers** around the world, allowing you to go online by placing a local call. The **iPass** network also has dial-up numbers around the world. You'll have to sign up with an iPass provider, who will then tell you how to set up your computer for your destination(s). For a list of iPass providers, go to www.ipass.com and click on "Individuals Buy Now." One solid provider is **i2roam** (✆ **866/811-6209** or 920/235-0475; www.i2roam.com).

Wherever you go, bring a **connection kit** of the right power and phone adapters, a spare phone cord, and a spare Ethernet network cable—or find out whether your hotel supplies them to guests.

Like Western Europe, Eastern Europe is on 240V electrical circuits. You'll need at least one two-pronged adaptor plug and a current converter unless your electronic gear operates on dual voltage (120V and 240V).

Tip: To find public Wi-Fi hotspots wherever you are in Eastern Europe, go to **www.jiwire.com**; its Hotspot Finder holds the world's largest directory of public wireless hotspots.

14 TIPS ON ACCOMMODATIONS

Accommodations in Eastern Europe cover a spectrum as broad as the region is vast. See individual country chapters for specifics on individual accommodations categories for that country.

No matter where you travel in Eastern Europe or what kind of accommodations you plan to use, it is a good idea to make a reservation for your first night in the country well in advance of your arrival.

CAMPING

Pitching a tent is the least expensive accommodations in Eastern Europe and it is also one of the most popular. Campgrounds can range from a monastery backyard (Brač, Croatia) to an elaborate affair with bungalows, cabins, and amenities like a theater, tennis courts, and gourmet restaurants. Camping facilities are also usually away from any town center, but they often have waterfront property. Some camp facilities are set aside for naturists (read: nudists) and others are geared to people who stay for the entire summer. Reservations are accepted at most campgrounds and the better ones fill up quickly. Depending on the country and campground category, these facilities usually close in the winter months and some are open in July and August (high season) only. It's best to make arrangements ahead of your arrival. ***Note:*** In Eastern Europe it is illegal to camp out anyplace but a recognized campground.

PRIVATE ACCOMMODATIONS

Eastern Europe's underground economy runs on the private accommodations industry. When booking this option, you'll find everything from a room in an elderly woman's apartment where you share her bathroom with her to a detached multilevel villa on a family estate. It's safest to book a private stay from a local tourist agency, but you will pay a commission. If you use the agency, you also will have the option of inspecting the room and asking for another choice if you don't like it. You also can agree to rent from one of the many "entrepreneurs" who haunt ferry landings and train and bus stations to find guests for their spare rooms. This option is less expensive than an agency-booked place, but you could find that it is inconveniently located or substandard by the time you get there. Almost all private accommodations require cash payment and almost none includes breakfast or any other meals.

Note: If you are staying in a private home in Russia you'll have to pay a rental agency to register your visa with a hotel.

House Swapping

House swapping is becoming a more popular and viable means of travel; you stay in their place, they stay in yours, and you both get an authentic and personal view of the area, the opposite of the escapist retreat that many hotels offer. Try **HomeLink International** (www.homelink.org), the largest and oldest home-swapping organization, founded in 1952, with over 11,000 listings worldwide ($75 for a yearly membership). **HomeExchange.org** ($49.95 for 6,000 listings) and **InterVac.com** ($68.88 for over 10,000 listings) are also reliable. Many travelers find great housing swaps on Craigslist (www.craigslist.org), too, though the offerings cannot be vetted or vouched for. Swap at your own risk.

HOSTELS

Most hostels in Eastern Europe are part of the national Youth Hostel Association (YHA), an arm of Hostelling International (HI; www.iyhf.org), but you don't have to be young to use them. Hostels provide beds in dorm-type rooms, the use of a communal bathroom, and sometimes the use of kitchen facilities. Hostels vary widely in quality and amenities and some even accept reservations.

HOTELS

Eastern Europe rates its hotels via the star method, though there is little consistency within the method or within any given country either. A three-star hotel in Slovenia is likely to be much more luxurious and comfortable than a three-star hotel in Bulgaria, for example. Ratings sometimes are ambiguous between cities in the same country, too. However, a few generalizations are possible. Hotels in Eastern Europe almost always include breakfast in the price; single rooms can cost as much as a double because guests are charged by the room, not the number of people (and some hotels do not book "singles"); many hotels require multiday bookings and refuse single-night reservations, especially during high season; and many hotels require that you book an all-inclusive room rate and that you take your meals there.

AGRITOURISM

Farmhouse stays are a growing trend in Eastern Europe. In reality these are just a rural version of private accommodations. Usually you'll be staying on a working farm and staying in rooms that mirror the resident family's rooms. Often you can help feed the animals, take a walk in the fields, and enjoy a huge farmer's breakfast made from the earth's bounty. That sometimes means getting up with the chickens, too.

Note: If you stay on a farm in Eastern Europe, you have to identify yourself to Customs when you return to the U.S. to avoid transport of dangerous bacteria.

For apartment, farmhouse, or cottage stays of 2 weeks or more, **Idyll Untours** (✆ **888/868-6871;** www.untours.com) provides exceptional vacation rentals for a reasonable price—which includes air/ground transportation, cooking facilities, and on-call support from a local resident. Best of all: Untours—named the "Most Generous Company in America" by Newman's Own—donates most profits to provide low-interest loans to underprivileged entrepreneurs around the world (see website for details).

15 TIPS ON DINING

Eastern European food is often maligned by Westerners who imagine that they will be dining exclusively on bread, potatoes, meat, and cabbage during a stay in that region. Yes, Eastern European food can be heavy, especially in places like Russia and Romania, where the temperature can fall to arctic levels and stay there for a long time. But this region's cuisine also can be surprisingly light and sophisticated, like the delicate truffle dishes in Istria (Croatia) and other regional specialties.

When looking for a restaurant, avoid places that display menus translated into seven languages. These are bound to offer diluted versions of wonderful regional foods or awful interpretations of "foreign" dishes. Instead, look for small mom-and-pop places filled with locals having a good time. Alternatively, you can make quite a good meal from local bakeries and markets where everything from caviar to laundry detergent is sold.

Dining is relatively inexpensive wherever you go in Eastern Europe. You'll find wonderful fish, Italian-style fare, and local wine in Slovenia and Croatia's coastal cities, spicy goulash stews in Hungary, and excellent beer in Poland and the Czech Republic. If you're lucky, you'll also be able to sample a few homemade liqueurs, usually potent brews made from plums, cherries, or other fruits.

One thing is for sure: You won't go hungry in this land where eating is a social event, a sport, and a way to celebrate life.

4

Bulgaria

By Karen Tormé Olson

Bulgaria, which was founded in 681 A.D., is the oldest state in Europe, but its roots reach far deeper into the past. In tombs adorned with frescoes and bas-reliefs in the Valley of the Kings, archaeologists continue to discover beautifully worked golden objects buried with Bulgaria's Thracian forebears, some dating to 3000 B.C. Uncovering the countless burial mounds that dot central Bulgaria is a process started in earnest just a decade ago. In that short time, it has become clear that Bulgaria once was home to the world's most sophisticated goldsmiths. The discoveries also have prompted local claims that it was here, in the shadow of the Balkan Mountains, that Europe's first civilization was born.

Traversing Bulgaria's mountain ranges, which are carpeted with ancient forests and carved by mineral-rich rivers, you can see why the country's sophisticated warrior-artists chose to settle in its fertile plains. Bulgaria is a fascinating country, with a temperate climate that is more southern European than eastern. It is this gentle climate, along with a sweeping, sandy beach bordering the Black Sea coastline, that continues to attract new visitors, the vast majority of whom arrive in high summer.

Most of Bulgaria's unique treasures lie hidden in the ancient tombs of the Valley of the Kings; in the mixture of Bulgarian Renaissance architecture and ancient Roman ruins lining the cobbled streets of Plovdiv; in the medieval university town of Veliko Tarnovo that rises precipitously from limestone cliffs above the winding Yantra River; and in the architectural museum towns snuggled deep in Bulgaria's mountains. It is particularly the latter, their narrow cobbled lanes and alleys lined with 19th-century stone-and-timber homes, that define Bulgaria as an undiscovered gem.

Getting to the villages is an adventure as you snake along empty roads edged with high embankments billowing with red poppies and white elder flowers. You'll inevitably pass women in patterned headscarves tilling fields by hand, and wizened old men driving horse-drawn carts piled with hillocks of hay so huge you can't see their wheels. It's Bulgaria at its unspoiled best, a cache of natural beauty and ancient history, comfortable accommodations, and fresh cuisine in surroundings that show few signs of the so-called advances of the 21st century. It's no surprise that Bulgaria's tourism is on the increase, albeit it slowly, with 7.7 million visitors now including this unpolished Balkan jewel in their Eastern European itineraries. With a lack of tourism infrastructure, shockingly uneven service levels, and a foreign alphabet, Bulgaria may not be the easiest destination to master, but armed with this chapter, it will provide some of the most authentic experiences Eastern Europe has to offer.

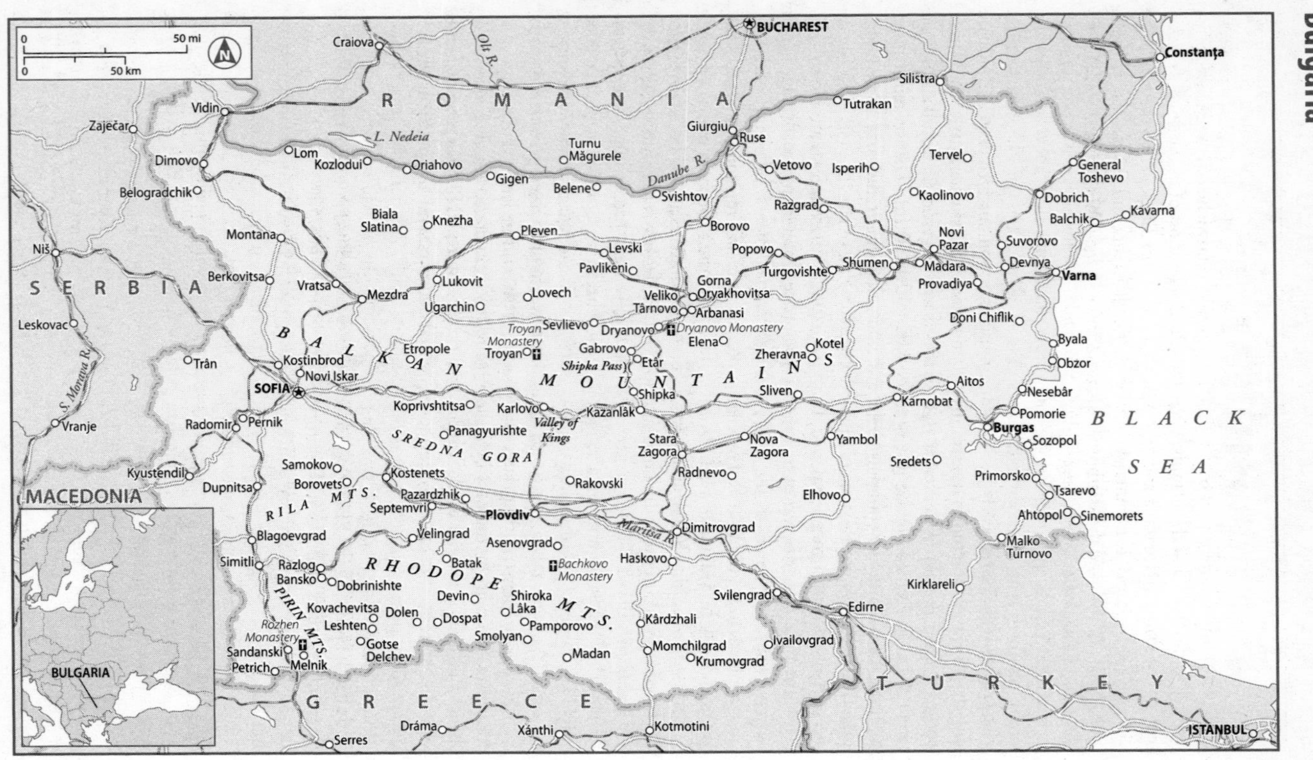
0
50 mi
0
50 km
BUCHAREST
Craiova
Olt R.
Constanța
Silistra
ROMANIA
Vidin
Zaječar
L. Nedeia
Lom
Kozlodui
Oriahovo
Gigen
Turnu Măgurele
Belene
Danube R.
Giurgiu
Ruse
Tutrakan
Vetovo
Isperih
Tervel
General Toshevo
Kaolinovo
Dobrich
Dimovo
Belogradchik
Svishtov
Razgrad
Balchik
Kavarna
Biala Slatina
Knezha
Borovo
Montana
Pleven
Levski
Popovo
Novi Pazar
Suvorovo
Niš
Pavlikeni
Shumen
Madara
Devnya
Turgovishte
Varna
Berkovitsa
Vratsa
Lukovit
Gorna Oryakhovitsa
Provadiya
SERBIA
Mezdra
Lovech
Veliko Târnovo
Ugarchin
Arbanasi
Leskovac
Doni Chiflik
Troyan Monastery
Sevlievo
Dryanovo
Dryanovo Monastery
Elena
Kotel
Byala
Etropole
Troyan
Gabrovo
Zheravna
Kostinbrod
Trân
Novi Iskar
BALKAN MOUNTAINS
Shipka Pass
Etâr
Obzor
S. Morava R.
SOFIA
Sliven
Aitos
Shipka
Nesebâr
Koprivshtitsa
Karlovo
Kazanlâk
Karnobat
Pomorie
Vranje
Radomir
Pernik
Valley of Kings
Panagyurishte
Burgas
BLACK SEA
Stara Zagora
Nova Zagora
Yambol
Sozopol
SREDNA GORA
Samokov
Sredets
Kyustendil
Kostenets
Radnevo
Primorsko
Borovets
Dupnitsa
Rakovski
MACEDONIA
Pazardzhik
Elhovo
Tsarevo
RILA MTS.
Septemvri
Plovdiv
Ahtopol
Sinemorets
Dimitrovgrad
Maritsa R.
Blagoevgrad
Velingrad
Asenovgrad
Malko Turnovo
Simitli
Razlog
Batak
Bachkovo Monastery
Haskovo
Bansko
RHODOPE MTS.
Dobrinishte
Kirklareli
Devin
Shiroka Lâka
Svilengrad
Kovachevitsa
Dolen
Dospat
Edirne
PIRIN MTS.
Leshten
Pamporovo
Kârdzhali
Rozhen Monastery
Gotse Delchev
Smolyan
Momchilgrad
Ivailovgrad
Sandanski
Madan
Krumovgrad
BULGARIA
Petrich
Melnik
TURKEY
GREECE
Dráma
Xánthi
Kotmotini
ISTANBUL
Serres

THE LAY OF THE LAND

Bulgaria is in the eastern part of the Balkan Peninsula, sandwiched between Greece and Turkey to the south and the Danube River (which denotes most of its border with Romania) to the north. Macedonia and Serbia lie to the west, the Black Sea to the east. More than half the country is mountainous, with the Sredna Gora and Balkan ranges slicing the country in half, and the southcentral plains (Valley of the Kings) flanked by the Pirin, Rila, and Rhodope mountain ranges.

THE REGIONS IN BRIEF

Bulgaria's capital, **Sofia,** is by far the country's most populous area, with 1.2 million citizens. But the southern mountain ranges 90 minutes away are where the country really starts to strut its stuff. The eternally snowcapped and majestic **Rila** and **Pirin** peaks dominate the region, stopping just short of 3,000m (9,840 ft.). These mountains are home to the country's most popular hikes and skiing opportunities as well as the hottest mineral spring in Europe—a scalding 216°F (102°C). East of the Rila and Pirin lies the **Rhodope** range, with gorges and valleys covered in virgin forest and dotted with mountain villages. Touring this region by car is a must for any traveler serious about seeing the "real" Bulgaria.

Sredna Gora and the Balkan mountain ranges east of Sofia run through central Bulgaria, creating the Danubian plains of the north, while their southern slopes drop into the evocative-sounding **Valley of the Kings** (aka Valley of Roses after the rose farms there that produce some of the world's best-quality attar). **Kazanluk** is the unofficial capital of the region, but **Plovdiv,** Bulgaria's second-most populous city (pop. 340,000), has a gorgeous historic center and makes a far better base for exploring.

Veliko Tarnovo is a short drive north from Plovdiv and just as captivating. Once Bulgaria's medieval capital, it is in the central Balkan range and a good stopover on your way to **Varna,** Bulgaria's third largest city (pop. 300,000, but larger during summer). Varna marks the beginning of a highly commercialized concrete ribbon of resorts that line the 380km (236-mile) Black Sea coastline, broken by the UNESCO-listed village of **Nessebar,** with its numerous Byzantine-influenced churches, and laid-back **Sozopol.**

SUGGESTED ITINERARY: BULGARIA IN 1 WEEK

The following tour covers the best of Bulgaria, but at a cracking pace. If you want to relax along the way, extend it by 3 days, with 2 nights each in Sofia, Plovdiv, and Veliko Tarnovo. If you're really pushed for time, 4 days, with a night each in Sofia, Kovachevitsa, Plovdiv, and Veliko Tarnovo, works.

Day 1: Arrive in Sofia

Spend the afternoon decompressing. Have an espresso in one of the open-air bars near the City Garden and book a table for dinner at Beyond the Alley. If you have the energy, tackle the walking tour (p. 72) or at least visit the Russian churches. Get to bed early so you're ready to rise at dawn.

Day 2: Melnik ★★

Have your driver meet you at your hotel at 5:30am (an hour later in winter) to catch the morning service at Rila Monastery—the best way to experience this UNESCO-listed site, with no tourists to detract from its spirituality. Snack on doughnuts and yogurt from the monk-run bakery outside the gates or take an early lunch at Drushliavitsa (above the monastery). Then head south to the tiny winegrowing village of Melnik. Visit Kordopulov's house, sample wine with "Six Fingers," and dine at Mencheva Kushta. See p. 82.

Day ❸: Leshten/ Kovachevitsa ★★★

Visit Rozhen Monastery, then—conditions allowing—head to Leshten via the mountain road that leads to Gotse Delchev, or travel via Bansko. Stop for lunch in Leshten. Stay in one of the Leshten cottages, or head deeper into the mountains to overnight at Kovachevitsa (note that it's worth exploring this heritage village, about a 20-min. drive from Leshten, even if you're not spending the night there). See p. 83 for the Rozhen Monastery; see p. 89 for Leshten.

Day ❹: Plovdiv ★★★

Travel to Plovdiv, stopping to explore the village of Dolen and Bachkovo Monastery along the way. Take a late lunch at Vodopada (p. 96) or push on to Plovdiv. That evening, stroll the cobbled streets of Old Plovdiv. Dine and stay at Hebros.

Day ❺: Veliko Tarnovo ★★

Set off early for the Kazanluk tomb (make prior arrangements to view the original), then head over the Shipka pass to visit the Icon and Woodcarving museums in Tryavna. If you have time, visit Etura, the open-air ethnographic museum nearby. Spend the night at Gurko (p. 100) in Veliko Tarnovo.

Day ❻: Varna ★

Travel to Varna (about 4 hr. away), via the Madara Horseman. Varna is a party city, so once you've checked out the Thracian treasures in the Archaeological Museum, blow off some steam at one of the many clubs and bars that line the beachfront.

Day ❼: Koprivishtitsa ★★★/Sofia

If you're up for a drive, take the coastal road south (just under 3 hr.) to lunch at a sea-facing restaurant in the fishing port of Sozopol, then head west to overnight at Koprivishtitsa (about 4 hr. from here), one of the country's prettiest heritage villages. Enjoy your last Bulgarian meal at Bashtina Kushta. Ask your driver to drop you off at the airport the following day, allowing around 90 minutes' traveling time, plus check-in time. Alternatively, spend your final night in Sofia and do some last-minute shopping before your flight the next morning.

BULGARIA TODAY

Just 6 months before Bulgaria's admission to the European Union (Jan. 1, 2007), E.U. Enlargement Commissioner Olli Rehn criticized the country's laggard performance on some key criteria for joining the E.U. Key among them were that no progress had been made dealing with corruption and the powerful underground barons who control as much as 25% of the Bulgarian economy and wield a troubling political influence, and the existence of human and drug trafficking activity in Bulgaria. The ultimatum was clear, and a month later Bulgaria's politicians delivered a task list that promised "zero tolerance" in the offending sectors. Bulgaria's reforms have had some success, and it still is having difficulties with corruption and other issues. How sustained efforts to implement the reforms will play out remains to be seen.

Tourism increasingly is becoming Bulgaria's most important economic engine. One area that *could* affect the country's tourism industry adversely is its atrocious infrastructure and the absence of any planning or design standards for building along the Black Sea Coast. Resorts and condos in that prime tourism region have been built and overbuilt while highly leveraged by banks. Like many real-estate ventures in the same situation in the 2008 U.S. market, some Black Sea developments are in financial trouble. Add to that a worldwide decline in tourism linked to oil prices, currency fluctuations, rising prices (because of Bulgaria's E.U. integration), and subpar service standards in Bulgaria's tourism industry (Bulgarians are learning), and a potential slowdown in the country's economic growth is not an unrealistic prediction.

Bulgaria's complicated and shifting political landscape is another factor that will have great influence on how long it will take Bulgaria to right its ship of state.

Currently, Bulgaria is managed by a fragile coalition between three very disparate parties: the toothless, class-based BSP; the hugely resented Movement for Rights and Freedoms, predominantly supported by ethnic Turkish minorities of the south; and the newly popular Citizens for European Development of Bulgaria (Grazhdani za Evropeysko Razvitie na Bulgaria, or GERB, which means "Coat of Arms" in Bulgarian). The Nationalist Movement Simeon II party (headed by the ex-prince who stands in the shadow of his Italian cousin's corruption trial for drug and human trafficking) still exists, though it has barely 5% of the populist support and popular opinion is that the former king only arrived on the scene to reclaim his family lands, which likely were misappropriated from the people a century ago anyway.

How these factions will carve up power is an unknown, but it is clear that the key challenge for government remains how best to achieve structural reforms that will have a lasting effect, not only on corruption, but productivity and accountability, so that ordinary Bulgarians—too many of whom still live beneath the breadline—can experience the kind of living standards long enjoyed by their wealthier cousins to the west.

A LOOK AT THE PAST

Fragments and tools uncovered near the coast (on view in Varna's fascinating Archaeological Museum) date human habitation here back some 10,000 years, but these pale in significance when viewing Bulgaria's most exhilarating archaeological finds: the Thracian treasures, known as "the oldest gold in the world," proving that a highly sophisticated civilization flourished in Bulgaria from 3000 B.C. to 200 B.C.

What little we know of the Thracian tribes was recorded by the Greeks, who described them as "savage, bloodthirsty warriors," and appropriated a few of the Thracian gods, including Dionysus and Orpheus, for themselves. Weakened by infighting, Thracian numbers were reduced and finally absorbed by the Romans, who arrived in droves in the 1st century, only to be turned out during the 5th century by the Bulgars. In 681 Khan Asparoukh claimed the First Bulgarian Kingdom, a region comprising latter-day Serbia, Macedonia, and parts of northern Greece. But Bulgaria remained a cultural backwater until 855, when the saintly brothers Cyril and Methodius created the Glagolic alphabet (later simplified into Cyrillic) primarily to translate the Bible into their indigenous tongue, but thereby creating an independent literary tradition for Slavic communities as far afield as Russia.

In 1018 Bulgaria fell to the Byzantines, who ruled for almost 170 years before the Bulgarians wrested it back. This launched the second Bulgarian Kingdom in new capital Veliko Tarnovo, from where they ruled the Balkans from the Adriatic to the Aegean. Jealous of its strategic position, the Ottomans invaded in 1398, ushering in a 500-year tenure that came to be known as the "Yoke of Oppression." A groundswell of nationalism, which spawned the flourishing 19th-century design and art that came to be known as "National Revival" or "Bulgarian Renaissance" style (the best examples found in Plovdiv and Koprivishtitsa), led to the 1876 April Uprising. Following its brutal squashing, Russia finally came to the rescue, helping to oust the Ottomans in 1877. For that act, the

When Yes Means No & No Means Yes

It's worth noting that traditionally Bulgarians shake their heads from side to side when saying yes *(da)*, and nod when saying no *(ne)*. This quirky characteristic is dying out, but definitely worth knowing when asking, or answering, a question in rural areas.

Bulgarians remained permanently in Russia's debt, erecting numerous monuments and churches, like the Alexander Nevski in Sofia, as proof of their "special relationship."

This may explain why Bulgaria so meekly accepted the Soviet "invasion" after World War II (during which Bulgaria sided with Hitler in the mistaken hopes of finally reclaiming the territory it lost in World War I). Ostensibly an independent Communist state, Bulgaria in reality once again found itself dominated by an outside power, this time under the "yoke" of the hard-line dictator Todor Zhivkov, who ruled until 1989, when he was quietly removed from power.

Bulgaria's first free elections were held in January 1990, when the Bulgarian Socialist Party was voted into power. Predictably, the poorly managed transition to a free market economy resulted in hyperinflation (579% in 1996), and by the end of the millennia Bulgaria was at the mercy of the International Monetary Fund (IMF), which introduced austere reforms. In 2001 Bulgarians, ill disposed to their fledgling democracy and overwhelmed by the return of their tsar-in-exile, voted with their hearts. Simeon Saxe-Coburg Gotha, who fled after World War II at age 9, was placed at the helm a few months after his return, but the gray, characterless tsar did little to improve the fortunes of the country or the average person.

Bulgaria still is managed by a fragile coalition (see "Bulgaria Today," above), and it still lacks strong, selfless leadership. Voter sentiment is highly positive over Boiko Borissov—Sofia's mayor and Todor Zhivkov's former security chief—and the improvements that finally have been made in the capital. Borissov's popularity is strong enough for the local press to speculate on his presidential ambitions even though he has many ties to past regimes. The ideal of an accountable, transparent leader with no tentacles into the shadowy past is clearly not one held by all. Without economic reform, real freedom remains elusive.

BULGARIAN PEOPLE & CULTURE

Bulgarians can be both insufferably rude and unbelievably charming. According to World Value Surveys (WVS), the Bulgarian culture is "collectivist," meaning that good service and quality goods are traditionally reserved for "in-group" members, and that nepotism may be seen as a value, while individual pride, competitiveness, and initiative may be suppressed. These findings play out in the service industry; you may be shocked by the brusque or downright hostile treatment you'll receive in certain shops, hotels, or restaurants. Ironically, people you meet outside the service industry are often far friendlier. Things improve in the countryside, where curiosity and warmth are the order of the day, and simple requests may not be understood but are met with smiles and an invitation to sample a glass of home-brewed *rakia.* According to the WVS, Bulgarians, like most East Europeans, are fatalists, which helps explain their passive attitude to the endemic corruption and political cul-de-sac they seem to find themselves in.

Despite 4 decades of Communism and its atheistic philosophy, 86.6% of Bulgarians are members of the Bulgarian Orthodox Church. There also is a significant minority of Muslims living in the south, including the so-called Pomaks in the Rhodope—Bulgarians forced under the Ottoman rule in the 16th century to convert to the Islamic faith. The tiny minority Gypsies (or Roma, descendants of Indian refugees) are still victims of serious discrimination. Parts of the traditional rural society remain untouched by the advent of the 21st century (at the end of 2005 only 27% of the population had a bank account; over 60% had ever had dealings with a bank), and while the tradition of the extended family living under one roof is still common, patterns are changing. Many young Bulgarians are opting to remain childless or are migrating west to more lucrative jobs, but most say they have every intention of returning. And despite the problems Bulgaria faces, it's not hard to see why.

BULGARIAN CUISINE

If you're expecting a steady diet of stodgy East European stews, think again: While the pretentious may brand Bulgarian food "peasant" cuisine, it is the best-kept secret this side of the Balkans, with an emphasis on fresh seasonal produce, and healthy, unfussy preparation methods. Influenced by the 500-year Turkish occupation and the country's proximity to Greece, Bulgarian cuisine features plenty of spices (many of which are indigenous), and predominantly chicken, pork, and veal, often baked with cheese or yogurt, and piles of fresh vegetables. Perhaps the answer to why Bulgarian fare is so delicious (and hard to export) lies in the quality of the Bulgarian soil, which some say is imbued with a special bio-energy (Bulgarian herbs are considered the highest quality in Europe), a result of the country's mineral-rich rivers and streams.

Bulgarians almost always start their meal with a simple salad accompanied by a shot (or two) of *rakia,* the local grape- or plum-based liquor. Meat—chicken or pork, usually chargrilled over coals or baked in an earthenware pot with vegetables—follows, with a side order of potatoes or bread. *Chubritsa,* a unique Bulgarian spice, usually is on the table to perk up a meal should you deem the flavors too bland.

Besides the wonderful quality of the cuisine, there is the price: You need not pay more than 3€–5€ ($3.80–$6.35) for a meal, and about as much for a good-quality red wine to accompany it. Wine lovers will do well to order reds made with Mavrud or Melnik, both grape varieties unique to Bulgaria (white wines fare less well).

LANGUAGE

The biggest challenge for new visitors is not just an unfamiliar language but also a new alphabet. When trying to find your way around the cities, make sure you have a good map and a Cyrillic decoder. If you get lost, seek advice or directions from the youngest, hippest looking person on the street; older citizens tend to speak no English and asking if they do usually affronts. You will find yourself a little more lost outside main centers where English speakers are rare. However, this is more than compensated by sincere friendliness, and rural folk will usually make a real effort to assist in any way they can. Speaking even just a few phrases of Bulgarian can thaw a strained atmosphere or—outside the city—have you seated and trying out a bowl of homemade bean soup with your delighted host. Here are a few phrases to help you on your way. Words, when written with Latin alphabet, are done so phonetically to aid pronunciation, but make for variations in spelling, even in place names (for example, Triavna = Tryavna).

English	Bulgarian	Pronunciation
Please	**Molya**	*Mall*-yuh
Thank you	**Blagodarya**	*Blago*-darya
Thanks (informal)	**Mersi**	*Mer*-see
Good day	**Dobur-den**	*Do*-bar-den
Hi! (informal)	**Zdravei!**	*Zdra*-vay!
How are you?	**Kak si?**	*Kuck*-see?
I am fine	**Az sum dobre**	Az sum *dob*-reh
Okay	**Dobre**	*Dob*-reh
Where is . . . ?	**Kude . . . ?**	*Ku*-deh
How much?	**Kolko struve?**	*Kol*-koh *struh*-vah
Do you sell . . . ?	**Prodavate li . . . ?**	*Prodava*-te li
Can I have . . . /? Do you have . . . ?	**Mozhe li . . . /? Imate li . . . ?**	*Moh*-zhe li/*Ima*-teh li
I like/love . . .	**As obicham . . .**	As *obi*-cham
Sorry	**Proshtavaite**	*Proshta*-va-ee-teh
I want . . .	**Az iskam . . .**	Az *iz*-kam
Bank/ATM	**Bankata/Bankomata**	*Bunk*-ata/*Banko*-ma-tah
Menu/the bill	**Menu/Smetkata**	*Men*-u/*Smet*-katah
Coffee	**Café**	*Cah*-feh
Milk	**Mlyako**	*Mlya*-ko
Water (ice)	**Voda (led)**	Vo-*da (led)*
Wine (red/white)	**Vino(cherveno/byalo)**	*Vie*-noh(*cherve*-no/*bya*-loh)
Beer	**Bira**	*Bee*-ra
Side orders	**Garnitura**	*Garnee*-too-rah
Bread	**Hlyab**	*Hlya*-b
Pharmacy	**Apteka**	Ap-*tech*-ah
Doctor/dentist	**Lekar/Zubolekar**	*Le*-kar/Za-bo-*le*-kar
I am ill	**Bolen sum**	*Bo*-len *sum*

2 PLANNING YOUR TRIP TO BULGARIA

VISITOR INFORMATION

With limited funds and a (somewhat understandable) suspicion of any centralized bureau, a state-funded tourism body for Bulgaria does not at present exist, nor does a tourism-oriented ethos. There are, however, a number of websites professing to be independent travel advisors. Of these, www.discover-bulgaria.com is the best for general information. Sofia-based **Zig Zag** (**✆ 02/980 5102;** www.zigzagbg.com) is an excellent independent advice bureau and offers a range of services. If you're particularly interested in monasteries, **Alder Travel** specializes in tours to these (**www.alder-tansport.com** or

Tour Guides on Call

With English-speaking guides and useful leaflets rather thin on the ground, there is a welcome service launched by local cellphone operator Globul. Look for large brown signboards at popular sites headed with "CALL AND LEARN MORE ABOUT . . . "; dial the number and a recorded voice provides you with background information about the site. Cost of the call is 1.20lev ($1.50/95p), 30% of which goes toward upkeep of the site; information lasts about 3 minutes.

www.bulgarianmonasteries.com). Other recommended tour operators offering general information on their websites are **www.andantetravels.com** and **www.alexandertour.com**. For up-to-date political and economic news on Bulgaria, check out **www.sofiaecho.com**, the country's English-language weekly newspaper, staffed by a group of enthusiastic expats and opinionated Bulgarians.

ENTRY REQUIREMENTS

Documents

Citizens of the U.S., Canada, Australia, New Zealand, and the U.K. may visit visa-free for 30 days in any 6-month period, as long as their passport is valid for 3 months beyond their stay. Travelers can import an unlimited amount of cash, but if it exceeds 4,000€/$5,080, the sum must be declared, as it is against the law to export more than you import. The quotas for duty-free import and export of goods for noncommercial use are generally the same as in E.U. countries; note that valuable antiques, artworks, or coins need a permit issued by the Ministry of Culture.

Upon arrival visitors are supposed to register with the local police within 5 days—most hotels will do this paperwork for you, providing you with a registration slip, which you should keep with your passport for when you depart. Officially you are liable to be fined should the authorities demand to see this before you leave the country, but as a short-term visitor you are unlikely to encounter any problems, and there is talk of phasing this out.

Embassies

The **U.S. embassy** is at 16 Kozyak St. (© 02/937 5100 or 02/963-2022; http://bulgaria.usembassy.gov). For citizens of the **U.K.,** head to 9 Moskovska St. (© 02/9343-9222; www.british-embassy.bg). The **Canadian** consulate can be reached at © 02/943-370, while the **Australian** consulate can be reached at © 02/946-1334.

MONEY

Regardless of what the tourist literature may tell you about credit cards being widely accepted, please note that outside of Sofia, they certainly are not. *Always carry cash.* The local currency is known as the lev or leva (BGN). One lev is made up of 100 stotinki (in denominations of 10, 20, and 50). The national currency currently is tied to the euro at a fixed rate of almost 2lev = 1€. Euros are almost universally accepted; the dollar, being a less stable rate, is less popular (conversions here are worked at a 1€=$1.27 and $1=1.24lev rate). Banks are the best place to exchange other currency, or draw money on your cards (exchange bureaus charges are usually higher). There are plenty of functioning

Major Festivals in Bulgaria

The Bulgarian calendar features numerous festivals throughout the year, particularly in the rural areas, but the following are worth noting. The **Kukeri Festival** is visually arresting: Villagers don terrifying outfits to ward off the demons that stalk the earth. It is celebrated in the southwest on **New Year's Eve, January 1,** or **January 14** (and sometimes in March; see box "Scary Monsters: Freddy, Eat Your Heart Out" on p. 78). **Velikden (Easter)** is the most important holiday in the Orthodox Church, and services with huge attendances are deeply moving. The main service takes place on Saturday night when priests emerge from behind the iconostasis with blazing candelabra and the congregation follows. The whole group walks around the church three times in celebration of the resurrection. The hugely popular but overrated **Festival of Roses** is celebrated in **early June** in the town of Kazanlak. The **Sofia Music Weeks** usually take place **late May** to **early June** and are a must for classical music lovers, as is the **symphonic musical festival** held in Plovdiv in **mid-June.** Jazz is added to the lineup for the **Varna Summer Festival (mid-June to mid-Aug)** and Sozopol's **Appollonia Festival (early Sept).**

ATMs in cities and medium-size towns. As credit cards are usually not accepted outside of the big cities (and even where they are, it's worth knowing that MasterCard and Visa are more widely so), it is probably ideal to carry a combination of euro traveler's checks and card(s) to make periodic ATM transactions—look out for the latest FNB machines, as these now allow a 400lev ($253/£157) withdrawal in one go (and three in succession). At press time, the exchange rates for 10lev roughly equaled $8.09 or £4.05. Many hotels list rates in euros—in those instances, we only list euro and U.S. dollar amounts at an exchange of 1€ to $1.27.

WHEN TO GO

With four clearly defined seasons, what you do depends on what time of the year you visit, and—given altitude ranges from sea level to 2,000m (6,560 ft.)—where in Bulgaria you're heading. The best time to visit from a scenic and cuisine point of view is June, when the markets are full of fresh produce; or during September for the fall colors. July and August tend to be hot, sometimes uncomfortably so (average is around 86°F/30°C, but the temperature can be in excess of 104°F/40°C). This is when people traditionally flee Sofia and Plovdiv, seeking respite in the cooler mountain villages and on the crowded coast. Bulgaria is not worth visiting in winter unless you go for the snow; skiing season runs from December to March.

HOLIDAYS

Shops, museums, and banks are closed January 1 (New Year's Day), March 3 (Liberation of Bulgaria), Easter Sunday and Easter Monday, May 1 (Labor Day), May 6 (St. George's Day), May 24 (Saints Cyril and Methodius Day, aka Day of Slavonic Education and Culture), September 6 (Unification Day), September 22 (Independence Day), and December 24, 25, and 26 (Christmas).

GETTING THERE

By Plane

Bulgaria has three international airports: Sofia, Varna, and Bourgas, but most visitors arrive at Sofia, currently served by 17 airlines from 47 European and Middle Eastern cities, with a brand-new terminal that opened in 2006. At present travelers from North America cannot fly directly to Bulgaria; the most frequent connections are usually through London or Frankfurt. ***Tip:*** Wizz Air (www.wizzair.com) offers flights from most destinations across Europe into Bulgaria, but a round-trip flight from London's Luton Airport to Sofia can cost as much as 385£ ($622) including taxes. In addition, charter flights into Varna and Bourgas usually are available during the peak summer season; others fly into Plovdiv to coincide with the skiing season, but beware of the taxes and fuel add-ons on any carrier that calls itself a "low-cost" airline.

By Train

Rail travel is very time-consuming (traveling from Budapest via Serbia takes 17–24 hr.; via Romania, it's closer to 60), and trains and infrastructure in Bulgaria are not well maintained. There is also the wearing potential of a trip ruined by thieves or hustlers. Should you still favor the romance of rail, you will at least (assuming you're a citizen of the U.S., Canada, Australia, New Zealand, or the U.K.) not need a transit visa through Serbia or Romania. For information on a Eurail Selectpass, which allows travel between three to five Eastern European countries, check out www.eurail.net, though note that these passes seldom end up being real value for the money. Popular routes are the Trans-Balkan, which connects Budapest with Thessalonniki, stopping in Sofia (there's also a stop near Veliko Tarnovo), and the Bulgaria Express, which connects Sofia with Moscow; and the daily Sofia-Belgrade line. In summer you can travel from Bucharest, Budapest, Bratislava, and Prague to Varna and Bourgas.

By Bus

Buses are generally newer and cleaner than trains, and most major cities in Germany, as well as Budapest, Prague, and Vienna, have regular bus service to Sofia. However, due to distances and poor roads (and occasionally tedious and lengthy delays at border crossings), this can be a time-consuming way to travel. Most of the bus journeys from western Europe pass through Serbia; as above, no transit visa is required. For information about bus service from Sofia's relatively slick International Railway Station, call © **02/952-5004.**

By Car & Ferry

Visitors traveling from western Europe by car either will take a ferry from Italy to Greece, then head due north; pass through Serbia, where special car insurance is required; or traverse Romania, where road conditions are poor. The ferry crosses the Danube from Vidin. Insurance is compulsory: It either can be taken out beforehand or on the Bulgarian border.

GETTING AROUND

By Car

To see the real Bulgaria, you'll have to get off the beaten track, and this means hiring a car and driver because most directional and street signs are written in Cyrillic. If you have time to get lost, numerous car-rental companies are available (and presently all you'll need is your national driver's license). To get the best deal, surf around and compare the big-name global brands with the highly reputable www.avtorent.com (10-group cars from 14€–52€/$18–$66, including unlimited mileage and insurance), www.md-rent.com, and www.vickyrent.com. The speed limit in the country is 50 to 60kmph (31–37 mph) in populated areas, 80kmph (50 mph) on minor roads, and 120kmph (74 mph) on highways; note that you'll need to display a 5€ ($6.35) per week vignette/decal (from OMV or Shell gas stations).

To rent a car with a driver, contact **Rent-Cars-With-Driver** (✆ **359 02828/68 67** or 359 0888/68 48 48 (mobile); http://rentacarsdriver.dir.bg) or **Alexander Tours** (✆ **359 2 983 52 58;** www.alexandertour.com), which is a Sofia-based full-service agency that provides air-conditioned cars and drivers who are also knowledgeable guides. You can book one of their standard tours (seacoast, UNESCO sites, and the like) or design your own itinerary. Contact Aneliya Gospodinova at office@alexandertours.com to book. Ask for the services of their superguide Toma Georgiev. If you use Plovdiv as your base, Toma, who lives in Plovdiv, is available for private day tours to Veliko Tarnovo, Rila Monastery, the Black Sea Coast, and many other destinations. The charge per day is 70€ ($89) plus 15€ ($19) per 100km (62 miles), and includes travel in an air-conditioned Ford Focus and guide services, plus return to Plovdiv or drop-off at your destination. Contact Toma directly at ✆ **359-887-863-591** or at toma@ivelconsult.com.

Alternatively, **Surprise Tours** is a one-man company run by the charming Svetlio (✆ **088/7485174;** svelte@mail.bg). Svetlio charges 70€ ($89) per day and 8€ ($10) per 100km (62 miles) to drive you anywhere in his (non-air-conditioned) Passat. While not an official guide, he is knowledgeable and he is at your beck and call 24 hours. If you want an air-conditioned or 4×4 vehicle, there is an additional fee. Day trips to Rila, Koprivshtitsa, Melnik, Plovdiv, and Veliko Tarnovo cost 80€ to 85€ ($102–$108). A tip is welcome (and usually earned), but not expected.

By Bus

This is the best way to get around if you have decided against hiring a car, as the proliferation of private companies like ETAP and Grup (www.etapgroup.com) and Biomet (www.biomet-bg.com) has meant that buses are smart, clean, reliable, and user-friendly. This is particularly true if you are traveling and making all your bookings from Sofia. The recently renovated Central Bus Station (http://tis.centralnaavtogara.bg) has an information desk staffed by helpful English speakers, and also boasts an easy-to-use self-help computer system, providing timetables and exact prices charged. There are regular buses (almost hourly) to Plovdiv, Varna, and Veliko Tarnovo; getting to smaller towns like Bansko and Koprivshtitsa will require advance planning.

By Train

Train travel is not recommended at present. Not only is infrastructure old, leading to potential delays, but cars are often grimy and fellow passengers, usually heavy smokers, are plucked from Sartre's depiction of hell. Bus travel is by comparison well organized, relatively comfortable, and faster. That said, national train carrier Bulgarian State Railways (BDZh) connects most towns in Bulgaria (with the exception of those located in mountainous Rhodopes and Pirin) and hosts a friendly website, so travelers use the rail system relatively easily (though note that outside of Sofia you'll still have to deal with signboards in Cyrillic, and no on-board indication that you've arrived at your destination); for timetables check http://bdz.creato.biz/en or www.bdz.bg. For information contact Sofia's Central Railway Station at ✆ **02/932-3333.**

By Plane

Air travel is a tad indulgent, given that Bulgaria is relatively small (it takes 4–5 hr. to drive from Sofia to the coast), but if you need to get from one side of the country to the other fast, a few airlines connect Sofia with the coast (see Varna "Essentials," later in this chapter).

TIPS ON ACCOMMODATIONS

Unless you're staying in one of the few five-star hotels in Bulgaria, do not expect western standards of service. In small towns you probably will be better off dealing with a family proprietor, but there you'll often struggle to find someone who speaks English. Bulgaria's star ratings are misleading; take one off from most establishments and you'll have a much better idea of what you're in for. Decor trends are firmly stuck in the last century (only a handful of hotels across the country could be described as modern boutique), and rooms generally are bare, with cheap prefab pine furniture and laminate flooring. Note that Bulgarian hotel descriptions often refer to suites as "apartments," but do not assume that this means a kitchenette or dining area. Bathrooms are usually tiny shower rooms: a large cubicle with a toilet and basin with shower overhead, sans doors or shower curtain but with a drain in the middle of the floor. If you're lucky, the toilet paper will remain dry.

On the bright side, places are almost always impeccably clean and incredibly cheap (hoteliers are no longer allowed to charge foreigners a higher price than locals). Websites worth investigating are **www.hotelsbulgaria.com** and **www.hotels-in-bulgaria.com**, though neither features opinionated reviews. If you're more interested in B&B/guest-houses/family hotels, the Bulgarian Association for Alternative Tourism (BAAT), offers a fabulous booklet with a single photograph and brief description of each entry, along with useful advice on how to plan your trip. To find out where to get a booklet, check **www.baat.org**. ***Tip:*** In small towns you may have problems making a booking, particularly if you want a particular room, as so few people speak English; use Surprise Tours booking service—send your entire Bulgaria itinerary to svelte@mail.bg and all your bookings will be made for a one-time fee of 20€ ($25).

TIPS ON DINING

Bulgarians are not very adventurous when it comes to dining, and restaurants—be they upscale, traditional *mehanas* (taverns), informal diners, or sidewalk cafes—tend to serve the same menu, with small regional differences, throughout the country. Food varies between good and incredibly delicious; location and price are not good predictors of quality or what arrives on the plate. A much better bet is to look for places that attract what clearly is a local clientele, despite the ubiquitous plastic chairs and/or lack of obvious ambience. In fact, the only bad meal you're likely to come across is in an upscale (and empty) restaurant featuring a fancy fusion menu.

One of the best things about Bulgarian restaurants is that they don't define lunch or dinner time—most open at around 11am and you can order anything anytime after this. Note that plates are served as they are ready, so don't expect courses to arrive at the same time. Also, if you eat at a *mehana,* portions are often small; for a full meal, choose a few items. Service is sometimes atrocious, but don't take it personally and make sure you check the bill carefully. A 10% tip is expected, but a service charge is often included. Most places have an English translation of the menu, but descriptions are general, making the choice, given the enormous length of most menus, difficult. If lost, order any of the following stalwarts, featured on every menu across the land: **Tarator** (cold cucumber and yogurt soup, with chopped garlic, walnuts, and dill); ***shopska*** **salad** (cucumber, tomatoes, spring onion, and red pepper, topped with grated white cheese, not unlike feta in taste, and an olive); ***kebapche*** or ***kufte*** (respectively, finely spiced barbecued sausage or meatball, often cumin-dominated, and prepared over coals), ordered with "garnish" (potatoes or vegetables, and/or bread—ask for the bread grilled), or try ***parlenka,*** the local pizza, or ***patatnik,*** a Rhodopean specialty in which the potatoes are grated and pan-baked with onions, egg, goat's cheese, and herbs); ***shopski*** **cheese** (a creamy cheese, tomato, onion, egg, and mild chili pepper bake); **mish mash** (a surprisingly delicious egg, cheese, and red-pepper mix); or ***burek*** (red peppers or zucchini stuffed with a feta-type cheese, spices, and egg). Other typical items on the menu include *kavarma* (individual casseroles of meat, at its best melt-in-the-mouth tender, baked with garlic, onion, peppers, and mushrooms in a traditional earthenware pot), *sarmi* (vine leaves stuffed with rice and tender spicy minced pork and covered in dill-infused strained or thick yogurt), and *moussaka* (a Greek dish of minced meat with eggplant). Bulgarian breakfast is comprised of *banitsa* flaky pastry stuffed with salty white *cheese*, and espresso or *boza,* made from fermented millet; the latter is an acquired taste.

TIPS ON SHOPPING

Bulgarians are gifted artisans. Low prices only add to the temptation, so make sure you arrive with plenty of space in your suitcase. Crafts worth buying include the uniquely painted earthenware table- and cookware; wooden carvings; spices (*chubritsa* in particular); *rakia* (the grape- or plum-based brandy, enjoyed as an aperitif with salad); red wine (even when it's dirt cheap it's good, but if you're after something special look out for anything produced by Damianitza, particularly Red Ark and No Man's Land); carpets; and embroidered clothing and tablecloths (the traditional red tablecloths you find in almost every restaurant are as cheerful as gingham). Icons are sold on every street corner and in churches, but most are prints pasted on to timber blocks. For a beautifully painted icon you're best off purchasing direct from a master, like the two working out of Etura (see under "Veliko Tarnovo & Environs," later in this chapter). Clothing produced locally is very cheap but looks it; better bargains are imported from Turkey. Shops tend to close on Saturday afternoons and on Sundays. Most important (again!), bear in mind that outside of Sofia, shops usually don't accept credit cards. Of those that do, MasterCard and Visa are more widely accepted. A useful website if you're looking for something specific is www.need.bg/en, a comprehensive Bulgarian business catalog.

Fast Facts Bulgaria

Addresses Note that streets in Bulgaria are called *ulitsa;* squares are *ploshtad;* and a boulevard is *bulevard. Sveta,* usually prefacing a church, means Saint, and some places have no address at all.

Area Code The area code is **359.**

Banks You'll find banks and ATMs almost everywhere in the city centers and on the main roads running through most towns. Cash is still the most widely used form of payment; make sure you've withdrawn from these before visiting small villages in the mountains.

Business Hours Shops usually open weekdays 9 or 10am to 7pm, and Saturdays 9am to 1pm. On Sundays, most shops are closed. Banks, shops, and sites in rural towns often take a midday break between 12:30 or 1pm and 2pm, and close at 5pm. Most museums are closed on Mondays.

Car Rentals All major international car-hire agencies are represented. See "Getting Around: By Car," p. 55.

Climate Summers have a mean maximum temperature of 86° to 95°F (30°–35°C), while winters range between mean maximum of 50° and 59°F (10°–15°C). Hottest months are July and August. For local weather forecast call ✆ **175.**

Directory Assistance For telephone numbers call ✆ **144** or 02/987-3131; information on long-distance calls can be obtained at ✆ **0123.**

Drugstores While these are found in most towns, most are staffed by people who do not understand English. If you do not have a prescription in Bulgarian or a guide, ask your concierge or host to assist you.

Electricity Local current is 220 volts. Outlets take plugs with two round prongs, typical to continental Europe.

Emergencies Ambulance ✆ **150;** fire ✆ **160;** police ✆ **166;** traffic police ✆ **165;** roadside assistance **91 146;** crime hot line ✆ **02/982-2212.**

Hospitals If you are involved in an accident in Sofia, ask to be taken to Hospital Vita (www.vita.bg), located at 9 Dragovitza St. (✆ **02/943-4398** or 02/846-5376). For nonsurgical procedures, head for IMC Medical Centre, located at 28 Gogol St., where staff is on call 24 hours (✆ **02/944-9326** or 0886 532 551; imc@gbg.bg).

Internet Access Bulgaria has good Internet services in major cities; outside that, cybercafes are sparse. If it's important, choose a hotel that offers Internet connection.

Maps See "Lost? Just Count the Blocks . . .," p. 61.

Newspapers & Books You can pick up the *Sofia Echo,* the weekly English-language paper, at most newspaper stands in Sofia. English books outside the capital tend to be the schlock crime genre or highbrow classics catering to the student population. When in Sofia, head for the Book Market on ploshtad Slaveikov (open daily, weather permitting) for used novels, or pop into nearby Dom na Knigata, on ul Graf Ignatieve (✆ **02/981 7898;** Mon–Sat 8am–8pm, Sun 9am–6pm).

Police While corruption and Mafiosi-style crime makes headlines, you're unlikely to become a victim. *Politsia* can be contacted at ✆ **166.**

Post Office Post offices are located throughout the country, and usually are open from 8:30am to 5:30pm Monday to Saturday, but opening hours can be unpredictable in small towns. The main post office is in Sofia, at 6 Gen Gurko St. (✆ **02/9496442/46**). There is also an Internet cafe here.

Restrooms Public restrooms are generally not great, and many charge a small fee for their use and for toilet paper despite the fact that they are often Turkish-style "squat pots." Better to head into the nearest restaurant.

Telephone Calling home from Bulgaria can be costly. Hotels often quadruple phone charges. Pay phones demand a prepaid phone card, typically sold in small kiosks by a person not likely to speak English (though some hotels stock them).

Intrafonica Bulgaria offers easy-to-use GSM cellphone rentals; review the packages on the Net (www.intrafonica.com), make your choice, and fax the order form and copy of your passport. They will provide you with a local GSM cellphone number within 48 hours, then deliver the phone to your hotel on the first night of arrival. Bulgaria's code is ✆ **359.**

Tipping Leave 10% to 15% for all good restaurant and bar service.

Safety & Crime Bulgaria is one of Europe's safest countries, with a below-average crime rate; all you need to guard against is pickpockets and petty theft.

Time Zone Bulgaria is 2 hours ahead of GMT.

Water Bulgaria's tap water is not only potable but delicious.

3 SOFIA

Sofia, capital of Bulgaria, is a fascinating city. It's as run-down as you would expect from a country that suffered under Communist rule, and it continues to be short on civic pride due to the high levels of corruption, a poor judicial system, and Oliver Twist–like bands of street thieves. But step away from the traffic-choked boulevards and drab gray concrete towers and into the cobbled streets east of the central square, and you'll find the hard edges of the city softened by untended but verdant parks and towering trees filled with the unexpected sound of birdsong.

One of the most recent capitals of Europe (it was declared the country's administrative center in 1879), Sofia has little to show for its 2,000-year-old origins: Aside from the 4th-century Rotunda of Sveti Georgi, Sofia's oldest structure, most of the city's historic buildings date no earlier than the 18th and 19th century. Even then there is a lack of great architectural beauty, and the corresponding absence of a major tourist draw. But Sofia's attraction does not lie in checking off a list of must-see sites. Rather, Sofia's charm lies in wandering its streets at will or stopping to drink the occasional espresso at an open-air bar/cafe in and around the city's parks. While Sofia traditionally has been regarded as nothing more than a gateway to Bulgaria's beautiful hinterland, itineraries increasingly are featuring 2-night stays in this city, which is gradually evolving into a sexy south-European destination, a testament to the veracity of the city's motto: "Grows but never ages."

GETTING THERE

By Plane

Sofia International Airport lies 10km (6¼ miles) east of the city center—to find out times and details of flights from 47 cities across Europe and Middle East on any specific day, take a look at www.sofia-airport.bg, or call ✆ **02/937 2211/12/13.** You can arrange a 10€ ($13) pickup from **Surprise Tours** by sending an e-mail or text message with your flight details to Svetlio to ✆ **088/7485174** or svelte@mail.bg a few days in advance. Alternatively, exchange a small amount of money (exchange bureau facilities are located in the area before border control in Arrivals Hall, but rates are not great) and head for the **OK Supertrans** counters in the Arrivals Hall to book one of their cabs for around 5€ to 7€ ($6.35–$8.90). If you're on a really tight budget, 1lev (81¢/50p), plus

Tips — Lost? Just Count the Blocks . . .

Thank heavens for Sveti Kirov, creator of www.map-guide.bg, a series of free maps that include the Map&Guide Sofia (also Bulgaria, Plovdiv, Varna, Nessebar, Bourgas, Sunny Beach, and Golden Sands). Not only are the top attractions very clearly marked as three-dimensional drawings on the map, but every street is named and the street numbers are indicated on every block, as are the tram lines (with tram numbers that run on them). So with a little concentration, even those with no sense of direction will not get lost. Maps are distributed by advertisers featured; track down the full list by looking at the website, or just head for the Sheraton or Radisson. Reception staff are usually happy to hand over a copy even if you're not staying there.

an additional .50lev (40¢/25p) for every suitcase, buys you a ticket on bus no. 84, departing daily every 10 to 15 minutes (5am–11pm) and will drop you at Eagle Bridge on bulevard Vasil Levski, near Sofia University (a 10-min. walk from the central square, pl Sveta Nedelya). Minibus no. 30 will take you a little closer, to bulevard Maria Luisa, but drivers may not speak English, and once there you'll probably be stymied by the Cyrillic road signs, so it's best to fork out for a taxi or transfer.

By Bus

The new **Central Bus Station** (✆ **02/813-3202;** www.centralbusstation-sofia.com) is located next to the train station, but it is much more sophisticated—we're talking clean toilets, self-help computer terminals, and an information desk at the entrance staffed with efficient English-speakers. **Group** (or Grup), **Biomet,** and **ETAP** are recommended operators but are by no means the only reputable companies; for more information on timetables for buses arriving from abroad and onward internal travel, call ✆ **090021000.** Given that you'll be burdened with luggage, it's a rather long (at least 1.5km/1 mile) walk to where most of the recommended hotels are. Use the taxi booking office at the main exit or catch tram no. 1 or 7 from the platform at the subterranean underpass opposite the train station forecourt (.70lev/57¢/28p), can be purchased from the driver); these will drop you off at **ploshtad Sveta Nedelya,** the central city node (look out for the winged figure of Sofia and the Sheraton on your right), and walk east or west from there.

By Train

Arriving at the grim Central Railway Station on Maria Luiza Boulevard (✆ **02/931 1111** or 02/932 3333; www.bdz.bg for train schedule information) is not the best introduction to the city. The station is a huge, impersonal, and run-down space offering the usual: coin-operated left luggage lockers, money exchange kiosks, ATMs, dodgy fast food/bar outlets, and ubiquitous station pickpockets.

CITY LAYOUT

Surrounding inner-city "old" Sofia is a large sprawling sea of run-down tenements, Communist-era high-rise buildings, and green suburban areas that lap right up to the foothills of distant Mt. Vitosha. Other than two major sites of interest, both located in the hillside suburb of Boyana, there is no real reason to venture beyond the central city, where everything is within easy walking distance. Both the central rail and train stations are located just over 1km (1/2 mile) north of **ploshtad Sveta Nedelya,** the traffic-choked central city "square" (it's more of an oval). The nodus that connects **Bulevard Knyaginya Maria Luiza,** a busy, bustling road, is intimidating for pedestrians. Narrower and slightly more laid-back **Bulevard Vitosha** is the city's most renowned shopping street. Together these are the main north-south arteries of the city, effectively carving the central city in two. To the east lies the "golden brick road"—historic **Tsar Osvoboditel,** which is lined with government buildings, including the former Royal Palace, opposite which lies the City Garden, the real heart of the city. In fact, the majority of city's sites and most of the best hotels and restaurants lie east of Bulevard Maria Luiza. You may be tempted to stick to this side of Sofia, but it's worth crossing bustling Maria Luiza, if only to find yourself in the **Zhenski Pazar** ("ladies market"), where women pick out the best fruit and vegetables while catching up on the day's gossip. This is the closest Sofia ever gets to Bulgaria's rural roots.

GETTING AROUND

On Foot

The best way to get around the city center is on foot. You can walk to every site and restaurant with the exception of the Boyana church and the National History Museum. See the walking tour below. Make sure you have sensible shoes—many of the streets are cobbled; still more are potholed.

By Taxi

All registered taxis are yellow and must operate by meter. You can hail a taxi from the street or call; make sure the meter is on or ask the price upfront (best to have established with your concierge or host what the going rate should be), as taxi drivers are notorious for charging foreigners many times the going rate. Taxi drivers also tend to be quite aggressive, so try not to get into an argument—just take down the license and registration details surreptitiously and ask your embassy to report the driver to ✆ **0800 18018** or 02/988 5239 (the latter used to report any criminal activity). According to reliable sources, the best (read: honest) taxi service is offered by just three taxi companies: 91119, 92180, and 92121. These are the taxis' phone numbers and how you identify them. Others will charge 10 to 20 times more than the standard fare. ***Tip:*** *Never, ever* take a taxi from the Sheraton if you want to avoid exorbitant overcharges. Instead, walk a block in either direction along Maria Luiza/Vitosha to taxis parked at the curb. Also, drivers and even dispatchers often speak only Bulgarian, so it's best to get your concierge or host to assist and have your destination written in Cyrillic.

By Tram or Bus

Traveling by tram, bus, and metro is incredibly cheap—a single ticket (interchangeable for all three) is 1lev (81¢/41p); a day pass is 3lev ($2.43/£1.50). Tickets are purchased from news dealers or booths near stops; remember to validate the ticket once on board or you could be fined 5lev ($4.05/£2.50) by a plainclothes official skulking on board. All public transport operates daily between 5:30am and 11pm. However, the difficulty of traveling by bus or tram (the metro line currently services only the western suburbs, of no interest to tourists) is knowing where to get off. Unless you have a helpful Bulgarian on board, you may overshoot your stop. Stick to a combination of walking and taxis unless you know your landmarks.

VISITOR INFORMATION

The **National Information and Publicity Centre,** on ploshtad Sveta Nedelya (✆ **02/987 9778;** www.bulgariatravel.org; Mon–Fri 9am–5pm), has plenty of brochures but staff is not trained or well traveled, so help is pretty substandard. **Zig Zag,** 20V Stamboliyski Blvd. (entrance on Lavele St.; ✆ **02/980 5102;** www.zigzagbg.com; Mon–Fri 9am–6:30pm), is an independent agency that specializes in good-quality B&B and guesthouse bookings (in Sofia as well as in certain rural destinations) as well as car rental (from 35€/$44 per day). They also offer very good-value themed trips, including monasteries and mountain village hikes focusing on rare fauna and flora; adventure tours in the mountains; or just a walking tour of Sofia. For personal advice on an itinerary, contact Nevyana at nevyana@zigzagbg.com.

If you're looking for up-to-date city listings and general information about Sofia, there are three excellent in-depth booklets distributed free through Zig Zag and a number of hotels: *Sofia in Your Pocket* (www.inyourpocket.com), *The Insider's Guide* (www.insidesofia.com), and *Sofia City Guide* (www.sofiacityguide.com). If you want to know what's on during your stay, take a look at www.programata.bg. Plenty of tour operators offer guided day trips (from 8:30 or 9am–6pm) to the country's top attractions (all remarkably close to the city). **FairPlay International JSC** (✆ **02/943 4574;** www.fpitravel.com) comes highly recommended by concierges; day trips include 3-hour or full-day Sofia tours, Rila Monastery, Koprivishtitsa, Melnik, Plovdiv, and Veliko Tarnovo.

Fast Facts Sofia

Banks With more than 40 banks now vying for trade, ATMs are spread throughout the city center and you'll have no problem withdrawing money.

Internet A number of places offer Internet services. **Site** (✆ **02/986-0896**) is conveniently located on 45 Vitosha Blvd., or head for **Internet Café,** Garibaldi on 6 Graf Ignatiev St. (next to KFC; www.garibaldicafe.net).

Medical **IMC International Medical Centre,** 28 Gogl St. (✆ **0944 9326,** 0944 9317, or 0886 532 551), has English-speaking doctors who make house calls, as well as pediatricians and gynecologists. For dental help, try **Dentail Center,** VI 5 Ivan Vazov (✆ **02/987-8422**), or **Denta Plus,** 41 Graf Ignatieff (✆ **02/981-0366**).

Pharmacy For information on the closest pharmacy dial ✆ **178.** A good 24-hour pharmacy is **BD Pharmel-Em** at 10 Yano Sakazov Blvd. (✆ **02/943-3972**); alternatively, try **Apteca** at 160 G. Rakovski (✆ **02/986-7984**).

Restrooms Public restrooms are best avoided. See details in "Restrooms" in "Fast Facts: Bulgaria" (p. 59).

WHERE TO STAY

Sofia's hotel scene has come a long way recently with an improved selection across all price categories. Anyone expecting western standards of service and decor will, however, have to pay more. Of the few five-star hotels, the best are featured below—given that the city center sights are great to see as a walking tour, it makes sense to stay strolling distance from the center, and to this end all the options featured below are exactly that. It's worth bearing in mind that with most hotels aimed at serving the business community, weekend rates often are significantly cheaper than Monday through Thursday.

Note: Ask if the rates you are quoted include 20% VAT; the city tax is negligible.

Expensive

Crystal Palace ★★ It's a layer-cake of glass and steel atop a historic 19th-century building, but facade aesthetics aside, the Crystal Palace is one of the most elegant hotels in Sofia and it offers some of the best service. Rooms are sunny and large and furnishings are period reproductions. Room nos. 503 and 504 are the only standard category rooms with balconies and views of Doctor's Garden across the street, but even if you don't snag those, the creature comforts at even basic levels make this a comfortable choice.

14 Shipka Ulitsa. ✆ **02/948 9488.** Fax 02/948 9490. www.crystalpalace-sofia.com. 63 units. From 190€ ($241) double; from 240€ ($305) suite. Rates include breakfast and VAT. AE, DC, MC, V. **Amenities:** Restaurant; fitness center; Internet access; conference center; nonsmoking rooms. *In room:* A/C, SAT/TV, minibar, hair dryer, safe.

Les Fleurs ★★ Don't let the floral theme of this August 2007 addition to Sofia's hotel scene fool you: Les Fleurs isn't a fussy tribute to botany but rather a haven of daring style and artistic flair. No two guest rooms are alike, thanks to offbeat-shaped spaces with ceiling-to-floor hanging glass-bead lamps, dark hardwood floors, flatscreen LCD TVs, and bathrooms outfitted with clear cylindrical shower chambers that resemble the transporters in *Star Trek.* Add clamshell-shaped tubs, a generous stash of Lanvin toiletries, and a wall of windows and you have accommodations that truly are boutique. ***Bonus:*** The top-floor rooms have balconies that look out on the city and the first-floor corridor is adorned with sculpture and a purple ostrich-feathered easy chair you have to see to believe. ***Another bonus:*** The chichi Le Bouquet restaurant ★★ on the lower level is a place to see and be seen.

21 Vitosha Blvd. ✆ **02/810 0800.** Fax 02/810 0801. www.lesfleurshotel.com. 31 units, including 2 suites. From 150€ ($191) double weekdays, 130€ ($165) weekends; from 290€ ($368) suite weekdays, 270€ ($343) weekends. Weekend rates require a minimum 2-night stay. Rates include breakfast and VAT. AE, DC, MC, V. **Amenities:** Restaurant; lobby bar; Wi-Fi; boutiques; nonsmoking rooms; elevator. *In room:* A/C, SAT/TV, minibar, hair dryer, safe.

Radisson SAS Grand Hotel ★★ This hotel is certainly not grand, but when it comes to personal, sincere service, the Radisson is a hands-down winner—from the man who opens the door to the mother figure who presides over breakfast (incidentally the biggest and best in Bulgaria), to the wonderful snacks offered in the top-floor business center, you'll feel well and truly pampered. The facility, however, is an ugly, semicircular building on Narodno Sabranie square, but ideally placed: The pretty Parliament buildings, which are lit up at night, are opposite and the iconic Alexander Nevski Cathedral is a little farther beyond that. The reception area spills over into Flannagan's, a popular pub that attracts a raucous crowd of expats and Bulgarians on weekends. Pay the extra 10€ ($13) for a superior room, identical to a standard but with a Parliament view. ***Tip:*** Ask for the highest floor available.

4 Narodno Sabranie Sq., Sofia 1000. ✆ **02/933 4334** or 02/933 4333. Fax 02/933 4335. www.radissonsas.com. 136 units. Mon–Thurs 155€–190€ ($197–$241) superior double, 280€ ($356) suite; Fri–Sun 135€–170€ ($171–$216) superior double, 230€ ($292) suite. AE, M, V, DISC. Rates include breakfast. **Amenities:** Restaurant; bar; health and fitness center; travel desk; business center; conference center; 24-hr. room service; laundry service; dry cleaning. *In room:* A/C, TV, Internet connection, minibar, hair dryer, safe.

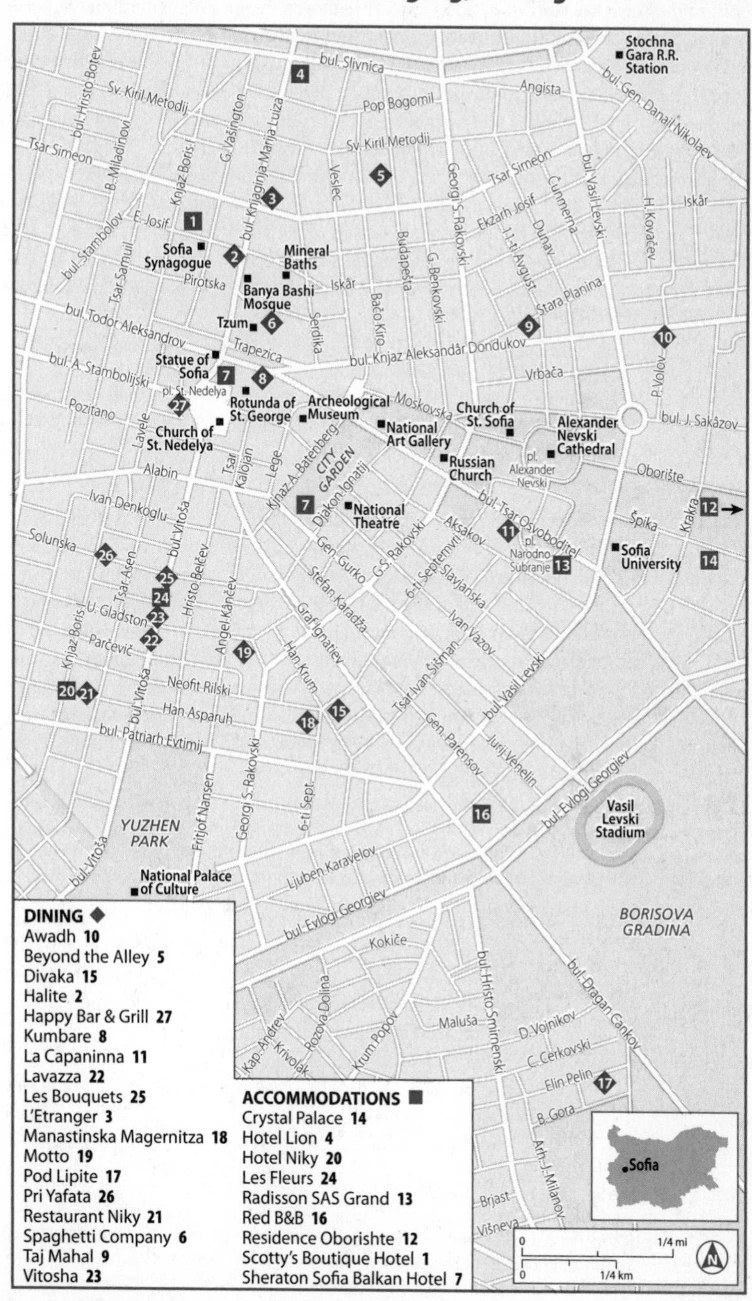
Stochna Gara R.R. Station
bul. Slivnica
bul. Gen. Danail Nikolaev
Angista
Pop Bogomil
Sv. Kiril Metodij
Tsar Simeon
bul. Hristo Botev
B. Miladinovi
Knjaz Boris I
G. Vašington
bul. Knjaginja Marija Luiza
Veslec
Georgi S. Rakovski
Ekzarh Josif
11-ti August
Dunav
Čumerna
bul. Vasil Levski
H. Kovačev
Iskâr
bul. Stambolov
E. Josif
Tsar Samuil
Sofia Synagogue
Mineral Baths
Pirotska
Banya Bashi Mosque
Budapešta
G. Benkovski
Stara Planina
Tzum
Serdika
Bačo Kiro
bul. Todor Aleksandrov
Trapezica
bul. Knjaz Aleksandâr Dondukov
Vrbača
P. Volov
bul. A. Stambolijski
Statue of Sofia
pl. St. Nedelya
Rotunda of St. George
Archeological Museum
Moskovska
Church of St. Sofia
Alexander Nevski Cathedral
bul. J. Sakâzov
Pozitano
Church of St. Nedelya
Lavele
National Art Gallery
Russian Church
pl. Alexander Nevski
Oborište
Alabin
Tsar Kalojan
Lege
Knjaz A. Batenberg
CITY GARDEN
Djakon Ignatij
National Theatre
bul. Tsar Osvoboditel
Ivan Denkoglu
bul. Vitoša
Aksakov
Špika
Krakra
Solunska
Hristo Belčev
Gen. Gurko
G.S. Rakovski
6-ti Septemvri
pl. Narodno Subranje
Sofia University
Tsar Asen
Slavjanska
U. Gladston
Stefan Karadža
Ivan Vazov
Angel Kânčev
Graf Ignatiev
Parčevič
Han Krum
Tsar Ivan Šišman
bul. Vasil Levski
Knjaz Boris I
Neofit Rilski
Han Asparuh
Gen. Parensov
Jurij Venelin
bul. Patriarh Evtimij
bul. Evlogi Georgiev
Vasil Levski Stadium
Fritjof Nansen
Georgi S. Rakovski
6-ti Sept.
YUZHEN PARK
bul. Vitoša
Ljuben Karavelov
National Palace of Culture
BORISOVA GRADINA
Kokiče
Kap. Andrev
Krivolak
Rozova Dolina
Krum Popov
Maluša
bul. Hristo Smirnenski
bul. Dragan Cankov
D. Vojnikov
C. Cerkovski
Elin Pelin
B. Gora
Arh. J. Milanov
Brjast
Višneva
Sofia
0 1/4 mi
0 1/4 km
N
DINING
Awadh 10
Beyond the Alley 5
Divaka 15
Halite 2
Happy Bar & Grill 27
Kumbare 8
La Capaninna 11
Lavazza 22
Les Bouquets 25
L'Etranger 3
Manastinska Magernitza 18
Motto 19
Pod Lipite 17
Pri Yafata 26
Restaurant Niky 21
Spaghetti Company 6
Taj Mahal 9
Vitosha 23
ACCOMMODATIONS
Crystal Palace 14
Hotel Lion 4
Hotel Niky 20
Les Fleurs 24
Radisson SAS Grand 13
Red B&B 16
Residence Oborishte 12
Scotty's Boutique Hotel 1
Sheraton Sofia Balkan Hotel 7

Sheraton Sofia Hotel Balkan ★★★ Housed in the Presidency, which is one of Sofia's landmarks dating from 1886, this is the only hotel in Sofia with a real sense of history. Shadowing the 4th-century Rotunda, and sandwiched between the Presidential Palace and the central square that feeds into Vitosha (the city's best-known shopping street), the Sheraton is also in the heart of things, perhaps too much so, given that it also overlooks the traffic-choked and alienating intersection between Tsar Osvoboditel and Maria Luiza. The rooms and suites are undeniably elegant, with decor in keeping with the historic nature of the building. Only the rooms on the first floor, with their wonderfully high ceilings, give any real indication of the grand proportions of the building, though rooms on the fifth floor have the best views. The Sheraton is pricey, however, and its position as the first choice among well-heeled visitors is slowly being eroded by better-value competitors who know how much guests appreciate such perks as including breakfast with the daily rate.

5 Sveta Nedelya Sq., Sofia 1000. ✆ **02/981 6541** or 02/981 8787. Fax 02/980 6464. www.luxurycollection.com/sofia. 188 units. 320€–370€ ($406–$470) double; 420€–435€ ($533–$552). Breakfast 19€ ($24). AE, DC, MC, V. **Amenities:** 2 restaurants; cafe; bar; fitness center; concierge; business center; salon; 24-hr. room service; butler service; executive lounge; laundry; dry cleaning; free airport pickup. *In room:* A/C, TV, minibar, Internet connection, hair dryer, safe.

Moderate

Residence Oborishte ★★ (Value) This elegant establishment—a converted private residence dating from the 1930s—is more guesthouse than hotel, with a tiny public area and limited facilities, but the rooms are great. The seven suites are spacious and tastefully appointed in royal colors, and two of them have fireplaces (useful when Sofia has a bout of cold weather). The staff isn't huge, but there are always at least two people on hand to offer you a complimentary welcome drink, arrange for breakfast to be served in your room (good idea as the breakfast room is poky), or arrange a candlelit dinner (given prior notice); the free pickup service from the airport is also useful. Located near Doctor's Gardens, the most prestigious residential area in Sofia, this is about 10 minutes' walk from Alexander Nevski Cathedral and the city center.

63 Oborishte St., Sofia 1000. ✆ **02/814 4888** or 02/814 4878. Fax 02/846 8244. www.residence-oborishte.com. 9 units. Mon–Thurs 90€–160€ ($114–$203) double; Fri–Sun 80€–130€ ($102–$165) double. No credit cards. Rates include breakfast. **Amenities:** Breakfast room; bar; complimentary use of nearby fitness center; laundry; dry cleaning. *In room:* A/C, TV, Internet connection, minibar, safe.

Scotty's Boutique Hotel ★ It's not really a hotel, let alone boutique, but step inside what appears to be a pretty residence and you've found yourself a really good-value B&B/guesthouse that is gay-friendly and has a funky offbeat character. And—as it's diagonally opposite the Old Synagogue—it's right on the walking tour. Rooms are cheaply furnished but with more imagination than anything comparable in this price category. The six double deluxe rooms (75€/$95), named after famous cities, all have balconies with synagogue views (Sydney and San Francisco are particularly appealing). Doubles and singles are quite a bit smaller; ask for a room with a balcony. Bathrooms for all the rooms are appropriately billed as "shower cubicles." There are no real public spaces, and the reception area is up a flight of stairs. Note that breakfast (served only on request, and delivered to the room) costs an additional 5€ ($6.35).

11 Ekzarh Iossif St., Sofia 1000. ✆ **02/983 6777** or 088/983 6777. Fax 02/983 3229. www.geocities.com/scottysboutiquehotel. 16 units. 55€–75€ ($70–$95) double. AE, DC, MC, V. **Amenities:** Fitness facilities nearby; guided tours; car rental and pickup service on request. *In room:* A/C, TV, Internet connection, minibar, tea- and coffeemaking facilities.

Inexpensive

Niky ★★ Finds One of the best-kept lodging secrets in Sofia, Niky's rooms often are monopolized by a cadre of repeat visitors who make reservations months in advance, and no wonder. The hotel, which bills itself as "Sofia's first all-suite hotel," has a great location 2$^1/_2$ blocks west of Vitosha, friendly service, and fairly priced oversize rooms that inspire loyalty. Add to that the garden restaurant Niky (reviewed below) that is a stand-alone destination in its own right, and you have a winner. The majority of Niky's rooms actually are condolike, with kitchenettes, microwaves, and bathtubs, and all have modern furnishings, free Wi-Fi, and updated bathrooms. Be sure to secure your booking at least 2 months in advance.

16 Neofit Rilski Ulitsa. ✆ **02 952 3058.** Fax 02 951 6091. www.hotel-niky.com. 22 units. From 40€ ($51) double; from 55€ ($70) suite. Rates include breakfast and VAT. AE, DC, MC, V. **Amenities:** Restaurant; Internet access. *In room:* A/C, SAT/TV, minibar.

Red B&B Finds If you're looking to meet the city's intelligentsia rather than foreign hostel dwellers, this B&B is without a doubt the top budget option in Sofia. Once home to one of Bulgaria's most famous sculptors, Andrey Nikolov, it was for 3 decades a meeting place for Bulgarian bohemians, and in the autumn of 2004 again opened its doors as a Centre for Culture and Debate (www.redhouse-sofia.org). Accommodations are basic—red-walled rooms have quirky furniture pieces (room nos. 4 and 6 have queen-size beds; nos. 1 and 2 have double beds; the rest are single) but are pretty bare, and none are en suite. Rooms on the first floor (three bedrooms) share a toilet and bathroom, while those on the third floor (three bedrooms) share two toilets and a shower. Friends traveling together should look at the three-bedroom apartment (sleeps five) for 100€ ($127). The Centre also hosts fascinating debates, dance performances, film screenings, and "freely improvised music experiment." There are shared kitchen facilities and a rooftop terrace where you could eat, but right next door are two cafe/restaurants.

15 Ljuben Karavelov St., Sofia 1000. ✆/fax **02/988 8188.** www.redbandb.com. 7 units. 40€–50€ ($51–$64) double; 3-bedroom suite 100€ ($127). No credit cards.

WHERE TO DINE

Sofia's dining scene is wonderful. You can choose between the fine-dining atmosphere of evocative-sounding places like Beyond the Alley, Behind the Cupboard (Sofia's best restaurant; see below) and House with the Clock (located in the pretty 19th-century villa at 15 Moskovska St., right next to the British Embassy). Or, if you're in a more laid-back mood, hang out in trendy bar-restaurants like Motto (reviewed below) and watch the city's media and model types schmooze, or go rustic for around 5€ ($6.35) at any number of unpretentious places that fill up in the evenings with students and office workers.

Restaurants that serve Bulgarian food are generally speaking superior to "foreign" cuisine types (with the exception of Turkish, Greek, or Armenian restaurants, like the excellent Egur Egur, where cuisine is very similar to Bulgarian). If you feel like Italian, **La Capaninna,** on Narodno Subranie Square (next door to Radisson SAS, with same lovely parliament views; ✆ **02/980 4438**), is a very good alfresco option, as is the more cafe-style **Club Lavazza** at 13 Vitosha Blvd. (✆ **02/987-3437**)—the latter is also the best place in town for a coffee (Lavazza, of course), with plenty of cigar-chomping bad boys to make it feel like a truly authentic Italian joint. If you're in the mood for Indian, **Taj Mahal,** Ulitsa 11-i August 11, is rated the best (✆ **02/987 3632**), though newcomer **Awadh,** 41 Cherkovna, is making real inroads (✆ **02/943 3001**). Cozy **L'Etranger,** 78 Tsar Simeon St. (✆ **983 1417**), is the city's best French bistro, in one of Sofia's most cosmopolitan areas, but still a wonderfully intimate affair with only seven tables personally tended by owners Oliver and Mitana. **Tambuktu,** 10 Aksakov St. (✆ **02/988 1234**), a chain specializing in fish dishes, is also highly rated by locals, though the garish signage did not encourage exploration on our part.

With the exception of Pod Lipite and Awadh, all the restaurants listed here are within walking distance of the hotels reviewed above, though you might want to take a taxi at night rather than risk getting lost. And don't forget to carry cash if credit cards aren't listed—given how inexpensive dining is at these places, it needn't be much.

Expensive

Le Bouquet ★★ INTERNATIONAL/BULGARIAN This trendy dining destination in the Les Fleurs Hotel (reviewed above) is a perfect example of a restaurant on the cutting edge. Even so, it has its silly excesses, like a 6m-wide (20-ft.) semicircular marble staircase subtly lit with fiber optics that descends into the restaurant from the lobby so seamlessly (and without handrails) that you could unknowingly take a header leaving the reception desk. But the menu is well thought out and the wine list robust, so opt for the glass elevator, which will safely transport you to the ultramodern space. Le Bouquet's ambitious menu lists dishes like rabbit filet on a bed of iceberg lettuce and carrots, beef filet with gooseliver and king prawns, or scallops poached in Roederer champagne. Bring your 401K to pay the steep prices (for Bulgaria).

21 Vitosha Blvd. ✆ **02 810 0800.** Fax 02 810-0801. www.lesfleurshotel.com. Entrees 12lev–45lev ($9.70–$36/£6–£22). DC, MC, V. Reservations essential. Daily 7:30am–midnight.

Moderate

Beyond the Alley, Behind the Cupboard ★★★ INTERNATIONAL/BULGARIAN It's not just the name that's quirky; located in an attractive Art Nouveau house in an interesting up-and-coming area just north of the cathedral, the decor at this fabled restaurant is equally eccentric. You are greeted in the garden by a classic Bulgarian water fountain sprouting some 20 taps; and an antique cupboard filled with childhood mementos (changed seasonally) is in the lobby. Even the bathroom is a surprise, so don't miss it (and look up)! Food is a mix of French/Italian but with Bulgarian influence—the "village salad," for instance, comprises fresh vegetables topped with Rhodope cheese matured in a juniper casks, while the balls of Itchera goat's cheese, coated and deftly fried in slivered almond coats, is superb. With a large cellar updated annually, the wine list is also a superb introduction to one of Bulgaria's best-kept secrets. Small wonder that this is a personal favorite for the editor of *Bacchus,* Bulgaria's revered food and wine magazine and host to the likes of Bill Clinton and Catherine Deneuve. In short, if you have time for only one restaurant in Sofia, head to Beyond the Alley.

31 Budapeshta St. ✆ **02/983 5545.** www.beyond-the-alley.com. Reservations essential at night. 13lev–25lev ($11–$20/£6.80–£12). 7% service charge is added to bill. MC, V. Daily noon–midnight.

Kumbare ★ GREEK Sofia is just 100 miles from Greece and this pretty restaurant on the south side of the Sheraton Sofia is as authentic as they come. Enjoy the best grilled octopus we've ever tasted at a table inside the pleasant pale green, yellow and white taverna or outside under big white umbrellas and two leafy oaks. Complement the octopus with *tirosalata* (cheese salad), crusty Greek bread, and a nice *retsina,* but be wary of the cost because everything is a la carte and a bit overpriced, probably because of the restaurant's proximity to the ritzy Sheraton.

14 Saborna (behind Sveta Nedelya Church south of the Sheraton Sofia). ✆ **02/981 1794.** www.kumbare.com. Entrees 11lev–35lev ($8.90–$28/£5.50–£17). DC, MC, V. Daily 11am–midnight.

Motto ★ CAFE Motto attracts a really cool crowd, and that includes the staff. If you're not in the mood for eating, this is just the place to lounge around with a cocktail or a glass of wine (some of Bulgaria's famous reds are available here by the glass). In inclement weather you'll have to sprawl in the stylish dining hall, but if it's balmy head to the green garden furnished with modern timber couches and tables and chairs. Those in search of a romantic spot, be warned: It's laid back at lunch but can get very crowded and loud at night. Light meals include a tasty avocado-and-veal salad, chili con carne with tortilla chips, burritos, and spinach rolls with stewed tomatoes and celery. If you really want to fill up, there's a heavier selection (duck breast roasted in red wine and forest mushroom jam, or chicken breast stuffed with prosciutto, cheese, spinach, and cream). Whether it's a light cafe-style burger or slightly more challenging main, the kitchen delivers—maybe not immediately when it's at full buzz, but who cares when you're entranced by the beautiful people there.

18 Aksakov St. ✆ **02/987 27 23.** www.motto-bg.com. Main courses 8lev–25lev ($6.50–$20/£4.05–£12). AE, MC, V. Daily 10am–1am.

Niky ★★★ Value BULGARIAN Niky is the kind of unpretentious, earthy dining spot that puts guests at ease in a whimsical setting, then wows them with fabulous food at a fair price. The restaurant, which is part of the Hotel Niky (see above), has indoor tables, but for the full experience, sit in the partially covered garden, which is open year round thanks to a wood-burning fireplace. In summer, the garden is festooned with a great array of flora and fauna, including caged parakeets, a parrot, and five tortoises that dominate the garden's water features. Niky specializes in salads and grilled meat and we suggest that you try everything, including the huge *shopska* salad, a skewer of grilled meat, and perhaps a *sache,* an earthenware dish of meat baked with vegetables. Wash it all down with a glass of Bulgaria's Kamenitza beer.

16 Neofit Rilski Ulitsa. ✆ **02 952 3058.** Fax 02 951 6091. www.hotel-niky.com. Entrees 7lev–19lev ($5.65–$15/£3.50–£9.30). MC, V. Daily 11am–midnight.

Pod Lipite ★★★ BULGARIAN This is possibly the best Bulgarian-themed restaurant in the city. Step inside and you've left the city for a classic, rural, timber-beamed *mehana,* four rooms decorated with traditional weavings, musical instruments, and farm implements. Outside in the courtyard replete with fountain are more rustic tables, each with the traditional ceramic spice dish containing pepper, salt, and other spice mixtures (used regularly in Bulgaria like salt and pepper) such as *chubritsa, lyut,* and *sharena sol,* so you can spice to taste. This is the place to try Bulgarian food. There's a great selection of salads, delicious breads (try the *louchnik*—a wedge of bread filled with lightly seasoned caramelized onions), followed by a selection of delicately spiced charcoal-grilled meats (or one of the zucchini, eggplant, and/or pepper-and-cheese dishes, or "leaf" rolls, if you're no carnivore). The food is excellent, the live music in the evenings is good, and the waiters know what they're talking about. No wonder it's been going strong since 1926.

1 Elin Pelin St. ✆ **02/866 5053.** Reservations essential. 8lev–20lev ($6.50–$16/£4.05–£9.90). No credit cards. Daily noon–1am.

Inexpensive

Divaka ★★ BULGARIAN Open 24/7, Divaka ("Savage") serves up amazingly large and delicious portions to young Sofians in search of the best bargain this side of the Balkans. The decor is no nonsense—rough tables and benches in three small rooms with timber archways, as well as a tiny outside area round the back—and service is at best

Moments **Feeling Devout**

The best time to experience any of Sofia's Orthodox Churches is when the domes are filled with the sonorous sounds of chanting, and the candelabras are ablaze with the flickering flames lit by the devout for the living and the dead. Religion is alive and thriving in Bulgaria, and the ritual and huge and varied community it serves—from young vamps in figure-hugging jeans and snakeskin boots, to aged widowers in black bent over walking sticks—can affect even the most jaded traveler. Note that candles for the dead are placed on the floor, while candles for the living are around eye height. Daily liturgy usually takes place at 8am and 5pm; at Alexander Nevski the Saturday vigil occurs at 6:30pm, while the Sunday evening Mass is at 9:30pm.

described as indifferent, but the food is really good. The Divaka *sarmi* a deliciously spiced mix of rice and minced pork meat, rolled in vine leaves and covered in a creamy dill and garlic sauce, is out of this world, as is the Hungarian Good Woman, finely spiced strips of grilled pork and sliced vegetables, served with hunks of fresh lemon (the serving is big enough for two), or Savage Leg with Savage Sauce, a grilled chicken leg baked with *lukanka* (spicy Bulgarian sausage), cheese, mushrooms, and onions. There's also a huge choice of Bulgarian salads (big portions), and the vegetarian shish kabob is a hit with noncarnivores.

41A 6th Septemvri St. ✆ **02/986 6971.** Main courses 5lev–8lev ($4.05–$6.50/£2.50–£4.05). No credit cards. Daily 24 hr.

Manastinska Magernitza ★★★ BULGARIAN Dom Perignon was a monk, but who knew monks ate this well? Manastinska Magernitza, literally "Monastery Kitchen," is in an elegant 19th-century house on a quiet street. Every room is decorated with traditional Bulgarian rugs and fabrics, and the atmosphere is wonderfully laid back. The owners have collected traditional recipes from 161 Bulgarian monasteries and there is plenty on the menu you won't find elsewhere, like Plakovsjka Hayverna, peeled garlic mashed with salt and oil, lemon, bread and walnuts; and Haryana Tartan, nettle and spinach stew, cooked with walnuts, garlic, cheese, and butter. Almost empty at lunch, Manastinska Magernitza is better visited at night.

67 Hans Aspire Ulitsa. ✆ **02 980 3883.** www.magernitsa.com. Entrees 8lev–12lev ($6.50–$9.70/£4.05–£6). MC, V. Daily 11am–2am.

EXPLORING SOFIA

Sofia has enough museums, churches, and street life to set aside at least 1 day to explore it. If you're based in the central city, all of Sofia's attractions can be viewed in a walking tour, outlined below, with only the Boyana Church and National History Museum requiring a 20-minute taxi journey. Both are located in the suburb of Boyana. It's best to hire a taxi to travel to Boyana Church and ask your driver to wait. The viewing of the tiny church won't take more than the 10 minutes each visitor is allowed, and the taxi driver then can drop you off at the National History Museum (just over 2km/1¼ miles away), a visit that could take up 3 hours, depending on your interest.

Boyana Church ★★★ It's an unassuming 11th- and 13th-century building surrounded by lush vegetation, but UNESCO-listed Boyana Church evokes awe in art historians who struggle to explain how the three-dimensional facial expressions in the frescoes covering the interior came to be painted during the 13th century, since this innovation was ushered in by Italian Renaissance painters over a century later. It's a tourist-friendly spot. Upon payment you are provided with an English-speaking guide who will point out the emotive profiles and movements, and the introduction of realism into the choice of latter-day fashion and fabrics. The guide also will identify the models, including Kalogen and his wife, Desislava, the Sofia landlord and patron who commissioned the building of the 13th-century extension. With any luck you'll be the only ones in the church, as tour groups make for a claustrophobic experience. The church has not functioned as such since 1954.

1–3 Boyansko Ezero St. (20 min. from the city center, or hr.-plus journey on tram 9 to Hladilnika followed by bus 64 to Boyana). ✆ **02/959 0939.** Admission 15lev ($12/£7.45). Daily 9:30am–5:30pm.

A Great Day Trip: The Village of Koprivshtitsa

The most popular day trip from Sofia is Rila Monastery (p. 78) but an equally rewarding destination lies 110km (68 miles) east from Sofia: the architectural museum town **Koprivshtitsa,** one of Bulgaria's most beautiful villages, with almost 400 superb examples of the National Revival building style that swept through the country in the 19th century. Then populated with merchants and tax collectors who imported many of the artisans from Plovdiv to build homes that signified their wealth, tiny Koprivshtitsa also birthed a few of the key revolutionaries who, tired of the living under the corrupt Ottoman Empire, staged the April Uprising of 1876—a rebellion that was brutally squashed but signaled to the rest of Bulgaria, and the Russians, that the country was ready to liberate itself from the "Yoke of Oppression."

There are six house museums for which you purchase a single ticket from the museum administration office (daily 10am–6pm) on the main square. Note that most of the house museums are closed on Mondays (the exception being Oslekov House, which opens in the morning). Of the six, the most impressive are **Lyutov House** and **Oslekov House,** the latter's grand facade painted with images of Rome, Venice, and Padua. **Kableshkov House** is a far humbler abode, but of historic interest as the birthplace of rebel leader Todor Kableshkov (b. 1851): Todor launched his disastrous uprising on April 20—ahead of schedule, due to a traitorous spy—by sending the Ottoman authorities notice in the famous "Bloody Letter," written in the blood of a dead Turk.

If you opt to overnight in town, try **Bashtina Kushta** ("Father's House"), a modern 14-room family-run inn at the edge of town, 32 Hadzhy Nencho Palaveev St. (✆ **359 07184 30 33;** www.fhhotel.info) for 31€ ($46) per double (MC, V), or at the rustic, historic Dahlia at 12 Peter Jilkov St. (✆ **359 07184 30 65;** www.dahlia.hit.bg) for 19€ ($30) per double (no credit cards). Rates for both include breakfast. ***Tip:*** For other meals, be sure to try the authentic, mouth-watering cuisine at Bashtina Kushta.

National History Museum ★★★ Built by the Communist dictator Todor Zhivkov, the building alone is worth the journey: A fabulous brooding presence at the foot of Vitosha, the "Palace" (it has no bedrooms; only huge entrance areas and massive meeting halls) has a wealth of '70s design detailing, and clearly no expense was spared in ensuring that the proportions suitably awed and intimidated all who came to seek an audience. The massive collection is no less impressive; the most interesting offerings are displayed on the halls on the second floor, dating from "Prehistory: 6th to 2nd millennia B.C." (Hall 1) and "Bulgarian lands from the end 6th century B.C. to 6th century A.D." On the third floor you'll find the slightly dull and badly labeled "Third Bulgarian Kingdom 1878–1946" in Hall 5, and various temporary exhibitions in the remainder. If you're pushed for time, head straight for Hall 2 to view the Thracian-era armor and jewelry, the biggest display outside Varna's Archaeological Museum. Then take a look in Hall 3, if only to admire its magnificent ceiling and views of the overgrown yet stylized gardens that flow into the mountain wilderness.

16 Vitoshko Lale St., Boyana (10km/6¼ miles south of town near the ring road/Okolovrusten put); 20-min. from city or 40-min. journey on trolleybus 2. ✆ **02/955 7604.** www.historymuseum.org. Admission 10lev ($8/£4.95). Tours 20lev ($16/£9.95). Daily 9:30am–5:30pm.

WALKING TOUR CATHEDRALS TO MARKETS

START: **Alexander Nevski Cathedral.**

FINISH: **Zhenski Pazar.**

TIME: **With one or two stops you're looking at around 4 hours.**

The best time to do the tour is on a Saturday or Sunday, when the churches are at their most atmospheric, and the City Park is filled with quirky Bulgarians and buzzing cafes. Note that Monday sees most of the museums closed.

❶ Alexander Nevski Cathedral ★★ & Icon Museum ★★★

It makes sense to start at the gold-domed Alexander Nevski Cathedral, iconic emblem of the capital, and largest in the Balkans. Built in memory of the Russian soldiers who died during the 1877 to 1878 war that helped Bulgaria lift the Ottoman "Yoke of Oppression," it was designed by a Russian architect and named after the patron saint of the Russian "Tsar Liberator." The sheer scale of the richly decorated interior—said to hold 7,000 people—deserves a visit, particularly during one of the services. Don't miss the crypt, which houses the **Icon Museum.** Charting the history of Bulgarian iconography from the end of the 4th century to the end of the 19th-century National Revival period, this selection of beautiful paintings—far superior to anything to in the rest of the National Gallery's collection—is an absolute must-see. Also on the A. Nevski Square (to the right with the cathedral behind you) burns the Eternal Flame of the Unknown Soldier, lit in 1981 in memory of all those who lost their lives in war. Just beyond this is the entrance to:

❷ Church of St. (Sveta) Sofia ★★

Established in the 5th century, St. Sofia (daily 9am–6pm) is the city's oldest Eastern Orthodox church, and gave the city its name during the 15th century. Recently restored, it has undergone various incarnations (including as a mosque during Ottoman rule, abandoned after two earthquakes

1 Alexander Nevski Cathedral
2 Church of St. Sofia
3 Russian Church of St. Nicholas
4 Ethnographic Museum & National Art Gallery
5 Archeological Museum
6 Rotunda of St. George
7 St. Nedelya Church
8 Statue of Sofia
9 Banya Bashi Mosque
10 Sofia Synagogue
11 Zhenski Pazar

toppled the minaret and cost the then-imam two sons), but a few remnants of its ancient past remain. Look for the fragment of original Roman mosaic flooring in the right-hand aisle. The simple red brick interior—austere by Orthodox standards—is beautiful, and the church has become a popular venue for weddings. From here you can stroll around the stalls set up on the square (see "Shopping," below), or proceed directly south down Rakovski Street then turn west into Tsar Osvoboditel, turning your back on the statue of the Russian tsar Alexander II on horseback, and head along its yellow bricks to the:

❸ Russian Church of St. Nicholas ★★★

Hastily built from 1912 to 1914, apparently to serve the needs of a neurotic Russian diplomat who felt that Bulgarian Orthodox traditions bordered on the heretic, the Russian Church (Tsar Osvoboditel 3; daily 8am–6:30pm) is not as grand as Alexander Nevski, but the small interior is huge on atmosphere, with weekends seeing plenty of devoted worshippers milling around to bow or kiss the various icons. A path to the left leads to the crypt, where Sofians deposit their prayers in the box next to the marble sarcophagus of Archbishop Serafim, head of the Russian church in Bulgaria in the early 20th century. Continue along Tsar Osvoboditel. The grand yellow building on the right is the former Royal Palace, built in 1873 for the governor during the Ottoman occupation, and today housing the:

❹ Ethnographic Museum ★ and National Art Gallery

The National Art Gallery (Tues–Sun 10am–6pm) is a disappointment, with mediocre art and very unfriendly staff—hardly worth the 3lev ($2.45/£1.50) admission; certainly not if Plovdiv, where most of Bulgaria's best artists seem to have originated or congregated, is part of your itinerary. But in the east wing you'll find the Ethnographic Museum (same hours and admission), which has a wonderful display of folk arts and crafts, and explanations on traditional rites. It's a little haphazard, and at times displays look a little like a high-school project, but this is a worthwhile half-hour, particularly if you want to do a little souvenir shopping (see "Shopping," below). Opposite the palace is the City Garden, overlooked by the beautiful baroque Ivan Vazov National Theatre. Take a walk in the gardens and stop at one of the cafe-bars, or keep heading down Tsar Osvoboditel to the:

❺ Archaeological Museum ★★

Housed in what used to be the 15th-century "Bujuk" ("Big") mosque, this is a lovely, light, and airy space with well-displayed exhibits, and it's small enough to tour in 20 minutes. The collection comprises Thracian (don't miss the 400 B.C. gold burial mask upstairs), Greek, Roman, and medieval Bulgarian artifacts. Though not nearly as impressive as the National History Museum, this is a must if you don't have the time to catch a cab to Boyana. Opposite the entrance is the Presidency, administrative quarters of the president (and where the Changing of the Guard occurs daily on the hour). Head around to the left into a courtyard where, shadowed by the Sheraton, you'll see the:

❻ Rotunda St. George

Built by the Romans in the 4th century, the rotunda (daily 8am–5pm) became a church in the 6th century. The 12th- to 14th-century frescoes inside the central dome are worth a glance, but in comparison to Sofia's churches, the UNESCO-protected building feels pretty soulless.

❼ St. Nedelya Church ★

This 19th-century church was largely destroyed by a bomb in 1925—intended to blow up Tsar Boris III. His life was spared by an accident of timing, but 200 of his subjects were not that fortunate. Like the Russian church, Sveta Nedelya is hugely popular, and as a result one of the most atmospheric churches in Bulgaria during services. From here head north, crossing the "Largo" (use the underpass) to emerge on the other side at TZUM, Sofia's Communist-era shopping mall, which is surrounded by roads and a half submerged 14th-century church. The indifference of its location dates back to Ottoman times, when grounds around churches were excavated to symbolically "lower" them. Also surrounded by busy roads is the:

❽ Statue of Sofia

Erected in 2001, the 24m-high (78-ft.) statue created by Georgi Chapkanov and Stanislav Konstantinov holds the symbols of fame and wisdom in her hands; her head bears the crown of Tjuhe, Goddess of Fate. Walk north along Maria Luiza Boulevard, and on the right you will see the:

❾ Banya Bashi Mosque

Built in 1576, its minarets still call the city's small Muslim population to prayer. Women should bring a head covering to enter and all visitors must wear modest clothing and leave their shoes outside. The mosque is named after the city's Baths, currently being restored. In front of the Baths is a large paved area with a tapped spring where locals fill bottles with fresh mineral water. Note that the water flowing from the fourth tap is piping hot. Opposite is the Halite, built in 1909 as the city's food market and useful if you feel like a snack. From here you can either stroll along Pirotska Street, Sofia's only pedestrianized shopping street, or head 2 blocks down Ekzarch Josif Street to:

⑩ Sofia Synagogue

Built between 1905 and 1909, this beautiful synagogue is the largest in the Balkans. It once served a community of some 25,000 descendants of the Sephardic community who, expelled by Catholic rulers in Spain in 1492 and Portugal in 1497, found refuge in Bulgaria under the decidedly more tolerant Islamic rulers. Today the community has dwindled to a handful, as most chose to leave for Israel during the Communist era. The vast majority of Bulgaria's Jews survived World War II despite the fact that the country sided with Hitler. Under immense pressure from local civic leaders, Tsar Boris III refused to deport Bulgarian Jews, fobbing off Nazi demands by forcing the Jews to disperse within the countryside. Many Bulgarians believe this cost him his life—he died mysteriously in 1943, and rumor has it that he was poisoned by the Nazis. Having stepped inside to admire the massive Viennese chandelier (weighing in at 1,700 kilograms/3,750 lb.), saunter to the:

⑪ Zhenski Pazar ★★★

This multicultural street (A2, A3 Stefan Stambalov St.), known as "Women's Market," is a world away from the nearby City Garden and its metropolitan pavement cafes. Here heavyset women in headscarves peruse large piles of colorful fruits and vegetables, bargain for Troyan ceramics (the cheapest prices you'll find anywhere), or pick up domestic essentials from the tiny shops and Turkish stalls that line the fresh produce market. It's a great place to wander and pick up a bag of sweet cherries or a freshly baked *banitsa* (traditional Bulgarian pastry), but do watch your valuables.

SHOPPING

Most visitors head for **TZUM,** a relatively small shopping mall opposite the Sheraton, or the boutiques lining **Vitosha Boulevard,** Sofia's main shopping street. **Hristo Botev Street** runs parallel to Vitosha, and has better bargains, like **Decade** (no. 16), stocking locally produced cotton leisure wear, and **Rumi Factory Outlet** (no. 23), where you can pick up relatively cheap Bulgarian leather products. Inveterate shoppers should also include a wander down **Graf Ignatief** and **Tsar Ivan Shishman** streets. Fashionistas looking for local designs make a beeline for the bohemian creations at **Atelie Mirela Bratova** (no. 4), peruse the collections at **Magazine No 10** (no. 4) or, if you prefer a more quirky take, keep going to **525** (no. 525).

Pirotska (near TZUM, opposite the mosque) is another popular shopping street, and it's a more pleasant experience than Vitosha Boulevard. Stroll down here or head north after a few blocks to get to the **Zhenski Pazar** (see walking tour above).Stepping into this open-air market after Vitosha and Pirotska feels like time travel, with the clientele picking through heaps of fresh produce a century away from their high-heeled counterparts perusing the racks in glitzy boutiques.

Bulgarian Folk Crafts

Alexander Nevski Square Flea Market If the weather is fine, this open-air arts and crafts flea market in front of the cathedral and St. Sofia Church is the best place to browse for bargain-priced icons (though not equally so; don't buy at the first stall). Also on offer are embroidered tablecloths, Russian dolls, knitted socks, handmade toys, ceramics, various carved items, and so-called antiques (coins, uniforms, medals), many dating from the Communist era.

Centre of Traditional Folk Arts and Crafts Conveniently located on the ground floor of the Ethnographic Museum (also an outlet on Paris St.), and open daily, this has the entire range of crafts produced throughout the country. Not always the best prices, but markups aren't huge, and you're sure to find something to suit even the smallest budget—from painted dolls with rose oil capsules to sachets with traditional Bulgarian spices. 2 Aleksandur Batenberg. ✆ **989 5210.** 2nd location at 4 Paris St.; ✆ **02/989-6416.** www.bulgariancrafts.hit.bg.

Chushkarcheto Carpet House Incredibly professional and hard to beat when it comes to selection of predominantly Chiprovtsi carpets. And if none of the ready-made kilims or rugs suits you, you can have one tailor-made to your design and color specifications, then have it shipped. 38 G.S. Rakovski St. ✆ **02/983-6609.** www.tchukilim.com.

Traditzia This "charity gallery" is a great place to shop for a wide variety of crafts (kilims, knitted or silk accessories, paintings, dolls, tea towels, greeting cards, jewelry, and so on), not least because by shopping at Traditzia you directly support artists from far-flung poverty-stricken regions, as well as the mentally and physically challenged. Staff are friendly. 36 Vasil Levski Blvd. (across the road from Downtown Hotel). ✆ **02/981-7765.** www.traditzia.bg.

SOFIA AFTER DARK

Sofia's music, opera, and dance seasons are at their peak during the spring and early summer, but by mid-July most of the city's actors and artists have, like the rest of the population, deserted the sweltering capital and migrated to the coast, taking the city's cultural life with them. This also affects the general nightlife scene, which quiets down in Sofia when it takes off on the coast. To find out what's on during your stay, take a look at **www.programata.bg**, pick up one of the free seasonal or monthly guides, or purchase a copy of the weekly English newspaper, *Sofia Echo.*

Theater performances are almost always in Bulgarian, so stick to music concerts or opera. Tickets are extremely affordable relative to what you'd pay in a western European city, and while performances don't usually star top-end performers, there always are foreign imports with impeccable credentials. The monolithic **National Palace of Culture (NDK),** 1 Bulgaria Sq. (✆ **02/916 6208;** www.ndk.bg), built in 1981 (ostensibly to mark the year Bulgaria turned 1,300), is the place to be during the **Salon Des Arts Sofia,** which usually runs mid-May to mid-June; as does the International **Sofia Music Weeks Festival,** hosted in the Bulgaria Hall and Bulgaria Chamber Hall, home to the Bulgarian philharmonic orchestra, 1 Aksakov St. (✆ **02/987 7656**). Described as "the jewel in Sofia's cultural crown," the **Sofia National Opera,** 1 Vrabcha St., off Rakovski Street (✆ **02/981 1549**), is where the city's most talented artists and guest performers from all over Europe play out the great opera and ballet classics. See what's on while you're there by logging onto www.operasofia.bg/index.php. If you're looking for a more avant-garde experience, check out the hip and happening **Red House Centre for Culture and Debate** (www.redhouse-sofia.org; p. 67).

The Sofia nightlife scene is low-key but vibrant, with plenty of nightclubs and trendy bars in the city. The following three are staples, but it's worth mentioning that Brilliantine, 3 Moskovska St., is hugely popular, attracting a diverse and interesting crowd, as does gay-friendly Chillout Café, 6 Baba Nedelya St., just behind the NDK.

Apartament 52 LOUNGE BAR This is the apartment of Boris, who usually hangs out in the kitchen (he's the one in the easy chair, with the Maltese poodle on his lap).

This is also where drinks are dispensed, including a startling array of freshly squeezed juice combos, most with health-giving additives like ginseng and ginkgo. The rest of the rooms are furnished with comfortable couches on which couples catch up with friends, and loners curl up with books or the Internet (there's a free Internet station, as well as a computer with iPod). Open daily 10am to 2am. 52 Parchevich St. ✆ **02/887 753454.**

Chervilo BAR CLUB If you want to know where the Sofian eye candy likes to hang out, head for multiple-bar Chervilo. It's not just that the bar girls and boys are disaffected and gorgeous; or that the interiors are superstylish; or that the music thumps until sunrise; or even that your party "colleagues" are rich, attractive, interesting, or all three (strict "face control" at the wrought-iron gates, but English-speaking foreigners always welcome). Chervilo is housed in the attractive buildings that are part of the Military Club on Tsar Osvoboditel, and it's easy to find on foot. There is a 5lev–15lev cover charge. Open daily 10pm to 4am. 9 Tsar Osvoboditel Blvd. ✆ **359 2981 66 33.** www.chervilo.com.

Toba & Co CAFE BAR If it's a balmy evening, this is a super Parisian-style cafe-bar hangout before or after supper (House with the Clock is diagonally opposite), with pretty tables and wooden chairs set up in the cast-iron pavilion in the garden behind the Royal Palace. It's principally a bar, but after 10pm a DJ pumps up the atmosphere with groovy sounds, and no one will mind if you raise your hands and swing your hips while sashaying over to the bar. Open daily 9am to 6am. 6 Moskovska St. ✆ **02/989 4696.**

4 THE RILA, PIRIN & RHODOPE MOUNTAINS

Sofia might be the country's commerce center, but the headiest rush is to be had while traveling into the mountainous landscape that defines much of southwestern Bulgaria. From the soaring snowcapped peaks of the Rila and the Pirin ranges, which flow almost seamlessly into the forested flanks of the Rhodope, the scenery is balm for stressed city dwellers' souls. No wonder that St. John of Rila, Bulgaria's most famous hermit, retreated to a cave in these mountains for 20 years before emerging to establish Bulgaria's finest spiritual sanctuary in the shadow of these peaks. Rila Monastery, the physical embodiment of the skills and crafts spawned by Bulgaria's 19th-century renaissance, is the country's most popular inland attraction, and it makes a wonderful day trip from Sofia. But the monastery is far from the only or even best attraction in this region.

Farther south, in the foothills of the Pirin's mountainous border with Greece, lies the tiny village of Melnik. This is the country's best-known wine-producing area (Churchill apparently got through World War II armed with cases of Melnik wine), but the village itself is lined with tall, whitewashed buildings and it is a delight. It also is the ideal base from which to visit nearby Rozhen monastery, at first glance not as impressive as the larger Rila, but since Rozhen monks still outnumber tourists, it is perhaps the most atmospheric sanctuary in Bulgaria. Northeast lies Bansko, Bulgaria's premier ski resort, but unless you're here for the skiing, head straight through (or, if road surfaces allow, via Melnik) to the real gems of this region: the Rhodopean villages denoted as architectural museums, where cobbled lanes meander past 19th-century stone-and-timber homes, their wrinkled owners basking on benches in the sun. Kovachevitsa and Leshten in particular offer the best places to stay and eat in rural Bulgaria and they are essential stops on the itinerary.

Scary Monsters: Freddy, Eat Your Heart Out

While the majority of Bulgarians are traditional Orthodox, plenty still ascribe to more pagan animistic rituals. At no time is this more evident than during the annual *kukeri* and *survakari* rites, designed to repel evil spirits and promote fertility and still practiced in certain villages and cities in the southwest with great fervor on New Year (or Jan 14). During a 30-day period known as the "dirty days" or "Mrasni Dni," when the days that denote the new and old year mingle, it is believed that the gates to both heaven and hell are temporarily left open, allowing demons carrying illness and evil to walk the earth. A group of selected villagers or townsfolk, each playing specific roles, don terrifying masks and girdles sagging with huge bells. Armed with wooden guns, swords, or axes, they stalk the streets, entering homes to sound off the demons with loud clanging bells and smoke, and "killing" the evil harbingers by sweeping through rooms with their swords.

During the fertility rites the *kukeri* leader, who on occasion carries a large red phallus, simulates sexual encounters with the women in the village to ensure that everything (and everyone) is ready to be "fertilized" in the new year, something that would no doubt see him slapped with a sexual harassment case in the west but that is accepted here with much hilarity. You can see the best, most frightening examples of *kukeri* masks, as well as plenty of photographs, in Sofia's ethnographic museum (see above), or arrange to see a real "Festival of the Kukeri"—the largest (and most accessible) is held in Pernik, when some 3,500 revelers dress up to participate in this ancient ritual during the last weekend in January (every even-numbered year). Pernik, 30km (19 miles) southwest of Sofia, is a short bus or train trip away.

PLANNING YOUR JOURNEY IN THE SOUTHWEST

Day trips to one or two of the destinations below simply do not do justice to this region, the most beautiful in Bulgaria. There are very few direct bus or train connections between Sofia and most of these destinations. Here, more than anywhere else, you have to hire a car, preferably with a driver, and traverse the gorgeous mountain passes and villages at your own pace. (See "Getting Around," earlier in this chapter). Ideally you should set aside 3 or 4 nights, though it is possible to cover the area in 2, overnighting first in Melnik, and the following night in Leshten or Kovachevitsa, before moving on to Plovdiv.

RILA MONASTERY ★★★

120km (74 miles) south of Sofia

Bulgarian monks knew how to pick prime real estate, and Rila is no exception. Accosted by thundering water charging over large boulders—two rivers, the Rilksa and Drushlyavitsa, flank the monastery—and the startling sight of thick alpine forests rising above you like cliffs, you know you are in one of the most beautiful places in Bulgaria. And that's before you step inside the country's biggest monastery.

Rila was included in the UNESCO World Heritage List in 1983 as "a characteristic example of the Bulgarian Renaissance, symbolizing an awareness of a Slavic cultural identity following centuries of occupation." The original sanctuary was founded in the 10th century by the followers of Ivan Rilski "the Miracleworker," aka St. John of Rila, who lived in a tiny cave about a 30-minute walk from the monastery. Revered by kings and subjects alike, the monastery was a cultural and religious refuge during centuries of foreign rule, but it was during the 1830s that the monks gave physical expression to its powerful position within the Bulgarian psyche, building a four-floor residential building within fortresslike stone walls to house 300 monks and provide guest rooms for its many donors. In fact, most of what you see today was built between 1834 and 1837 (predated only by the 14th-c. brick tower that rises in the middle of the inner courtyard, and the small 14th-c. church (1343) that stands next to the tower; this had a belfry added in 1844).

Despite the impressive surroundings, it is the church they call "the Nativity of the Virgin" that draws the visitor's eye, with its porch entirely covered in rich decorative frescoes. Step inside and the interiors are equally beautiful, with an intricately carved and glittering gilt iconostasis beckoning devotees closer. This is one of the finest examples of the art of the woodcarvers of Samokov, a nearby town that is famous (like Tryavna) for producing Bulgaria's finest artists. Here you'll find a silver box with the hand of St. John of Rila (see "Kissing the Bones of a Well-Traveled Saint," below). Farther to the left, kept in a drawer, is a 12th-century icon of the Virgin. In a chapel opposite, underneath a simple wooden cross, lies the heart of Tsar Boris III. The king, who had refused to hand over his Jewish subjects, died on his way back from a trip to Berlin in 1944, prompting speculation that he had been poisoned by the Nazis. The murals were painted by many artists, including Dimitar and Zahari Zograf, the Samakov brothers who were to become the most famous icon painters of the 19th-century National Revival. Zahari is in fact the better known, perhaps because he was arrogant (or sensible) enough to sign his work. He eventually courted enormous controversy by painting himself into some of his murals. The exterior murals are particularly absorbing, with the most awful damnations heaped upon sinners, apocalyptic images that look inspired by the diabolical imagination of Hieronymus Bosch, and must have done plenty to herd the illiterate into the Orthodox fold.

After viewing the church, move on to the renovated monastery museum (daily 8am–5pm; 5lev/$4.05/£2.50), which houses a number of interesting artworks and relics, the most fascinating of which is Raphael's Cross: Carved from a single piece of wood, the 81cm-high (32-in.) cross features no less than 104 religious tableaux with 1,500 tiny figures, a 12-year labor of love that cost the monk Raphael his eyesight. After this you can visit one of the monk's cells and the massive cauldrons in the "kitchen"—look up and you realize you've stepped into what is effectively the world's largest chimney. If you have a few hours, set off on the 4km (2.5-mile) walk through the forest above the monastery to St. John of Rila's original hermitage, a fairly nondescript cave unless you try to work your way up through the fissure known as "Miracle Hole." In days of yore, those who could not achieve this relatively simple feat were thought to be tainted with sin and sent home to atone.

Essentials: Getting There & Getting a Meal

Rila Monastery (✆ **07054/2208**), about 90 minutes south of Sofia, is an easy day trip from the capital by car or tour bus, and serviced by numerous tour operators. **Zig Zag** (✆ **02/980 5102;** www.zigzagbg.com) offers the best-value day trip (58€/$74). The trip

Kissing the Bones of a Well-Traveled Saint

John of Rila (aka Ivan Rilski) died in 946 at 66. His devoted, grieving followers virtually defiled his corpse, which was sent to Sofia. Stolen as plunder by the Hungarian king Bela III in 1183, the relic (or what remained of it) was returned 5 years later (apparently it had made a Catholic bishop blind after the bishop denied the bones were those of a saint), only to then make its way to Veliko Tarnovo in 1194. St. John of Rila finally came home in 1469, but his respite was short. A century later his right hand was removed and toured Russia, distributing miracles and earning funds for the monastery. St. John's left hand is now kept in the church, and is believed to have healing powers—you can ask one of the monks to draw back the velvet cover to reveal the glass box under which the yellowed bones still miraculously gleam, but note that you will then have to kiss it as a sign of respect. Wads of cotton wool, kept on a pedestal nearby, are said to be imbued with healing power because of their proximity to the hand. Pilgrims who take a piece to place near a source of pain apparently experience real relief.

is in a private car with a guide, and a maximum of four others. If you don't want to share the experience, book with Surprise Tours (see details below), which will take you to the monastery for 80€ ($102). If you're not hassled by traveling in a large impersonal group book with **FairPlay International JSC** (✆ **02/943 4574;** www.fpitravel.com; 25€/$32, lunch and guide included). Note that there are no direct public buses from Sofia. Using this travel method may require an overnight stay. Except for the new Gorski Kut Hotel (below), none of the accommodations options, including the spartan and less-than-spotless monastery cells, make for a happy holiday experience.

Dining is the exception, as the monk-run bakery just outside the monastery sells the best Bulgarian doughnuts and delicious yogurt. If you're ready for a full meal, keep space for these as a takeout dessert and grab a table at the **Gorski Kut** restaurant (✆ **359 07/054 2170;** www.gorski-kut.com; daily 8:30am–11pm). Nikolay Davidkov and his wife Tsveta have wowed diners for more than 10 years with Gorski Kut's fabulous and affordable (2.50lev–13lev/$2–$11/£1.25–£5.50) dishes, including fried trout, bean soup, salads, and egg dishes in this restaurant on a bluff overlooking the Rilska River about 5km (3 miles) from the monastery. In 2007 the couple opened the Gorski-Kut Hotel, a delightful 12-unit property adjacent to the restaurant (doubles from 72lev/$58/£36; suites from 107lev ($87/£54 with breakfast). The rooms are bright and airy and, Nikolay says, they have heaters instead of air-conditioners because of the cool mountain air.

Above the monastery, **Drushliavitsa** restaurant (daily 8am–11pm) is perched above the complex to the one side of its namesake river, with a small outdoor terrace. This is another great place to eat in the area, serving fresh trout, the mildly spiced local sausage *(kebabche),* and wonderful firm yellow-fleshed potato chips. Bread is baked fresh daily by the monastery bakery. Despite being next to Bulgaria's top inland attraction, the most expensive item is 5lev ($4.05/£2.50).

Tips: Monastery gates open at dawn and close at dusk; try to get here at 7am (or 8am, depending on time of year) to catch the early-morning service. There's a good chance you'll be the only visitor here, watching a ritual that has been witnessed daily by these walls for 200 years. On Thursdays the morning service is dedicated to St. John; the beautiful liturgical chanting that accompanies the service dates from the 15th century. Avoid the weekends when the natural tranquillity of the monastery is all but ruined by the huge number of visitors. The same goes for the two main festivals celebrated on August 18 (St. John's birthday) and October 19 (his feast day).

MELNIK ★★

186km (115 miles) from Sofia

Once a thriving outpost, Melnik boasted a population of 20,000 predominantly Greek citizens (it's a mere 15km/9 1/3 miles from the border with Greece) before the Second Balkan War of 1913. It's hard to believe when you first turn into the sandstone gorge to see the tiny village that today is home to a mere 270.

Set amid numerous pyramid-shaped sandstone outcroppings that create a jagged mountainous backdrop, Melnik is officially designated as a historical reserve. Semiarid, with a mixed Mediterranean and mountainous climate, is ideal winemaking territory, with a *terroir* (a group of vineyards or vines from the same region) that nurtures the dusky and robust flavors of the unique Bulgarian red-grape variety known as Melnik Broad Vine. It also has soft sandstone that allows for cool cave cellars.

Populated by a handful of born-and-bred locals, the village admittedly is focused on the tourist buck, with at least half the homes transformed into places to stay or eat. But the townspeople are justifiably proud of their village, and there's no ugly tourist tat. This, together with the fact that Melnik is not en route to any other major attraction, has left the most popular destination in southern Pirin unspoiled.

Essentials: Getting There & Getting Around

FairPlay International offers day trips to **Melnik** from Sofia for 49€ ($62), 180€ ($229) with your own car and driver/guide; both prices include lunch. **Surprise Tours** offers a car and driver for 80€ ($102). **Intersport** arranges day trips to Melnik and Rozhen from Bansko for 30€ ($38), lunch included (see "Bansko," below); the same company also offers a 2-day guided walk from Bansko to Melnik, with an overnight stop and dinner on the Tevnoto Lake, the highest in Pirin; the price is 50€ ($64) all inclusive. Melnik is not connected by train, and if you travel by public bus you will need to change in Sandanski, a potentially difficult enterprise when drivers and most passengers are unlikely to speak English. Note that Melnik has no information bureau, ATM, or bank, so be sure you have enough cash before you leave your last destination or make a withdrawal in Sandanski, the last big town before Melnik.

Where to Stay

Should Bolyarka be full, you'll find that **Despot Slav** is a close runner-up. Decor is busier, but room size and rates are virtually identical (**© 0743/248** or 089 9984406). A really good alternative if you are watching your budget (and possibly preferable, because it is so personally run that it feels more like a private home than a hotel) is **Uzunova Kushta** (**© 0889 450849,** 0887 321446, or 07437/270). It's also a mere 20lev ($16/£9.90) per person, breakfast included.

Hotel Bolyarka ★ This humble hotel is the poshest in Melnik, with a stone-walled lobby bar dressed with slightly incongruous faux Regency-style furniture. Rooms are pretty small as are the bathrooms, but this is as good as it gets in the village. Most of the best rooms feature a balcony (the one off room 107 has a good view). Alternatively ask for a corner room, like no. 207, which is slightly bigger (note that there is no elevator, so if you're carrying heavy luggage, the second floor probably is not a good idea for only

TP on the Go

Before I left for Bulgaria in the summer of 2008, I was warned by someone who had just returned to take toilet paper. Apparently, he had not visited Belovo, a town in southern Bulgaria at the western end of the Thracian Plain. Locals know Belovo as the toilet paper capital of Bulgaria, a name it richly deserves. The town's main street is lined with roadside stands selling not produce but huge bundles of pastel-colored toilet paper stacked 1.8m (6 ft.) high on the sidewalks. It's not because the people of Belovo have a TP fetish; rather, it's because Belovo is home to a paper mill that produces toilet paper and other paper products distributed throughout Bulgaria.

1 night). Apartments are slightly larger and worth the extra cost (not so the "luxury" apartments, which are tasteless). The best restaurant in town (see below) is directly opposite.

Main St. ✆ **07437/383,** 07437/368, or 0888 455045. Fax 07437369. www.bolyarka.hit.bg. 21 units. 60lev ($49/£30) double; 80lev ($65/£40) apt; 130lev ($105/£65) luxury apt. Rates include breakfast. **Amenities:** Restaurant; bar; fitness room; sauna; small conference room; room service; massage; laundry; cellar. *In room:* TV, minibar, fireplaces (apt only).

Where to Dine

Ask any local to recommend the best place to eat, and without fail they all answer **Mencheva Kushta.** Ask proprietor Mladen Menchev for *his* recommendation, and he points up to **Varvara** (✆ **088 799 2191** or 07437/388), the bustling *mehana* just below the **Kordopulov House.** Views from up here (you look down and across the village) are certainly sublime, as is the aroma that wafts across from the terrace as you enter or leave the Kordopulov House. But if you're only in town long enough for one meal, make sure it's the *kavarma* or *meshaniza* prepared by Mr. Menchev's cooks.

Mencheva Kushta ★★★ BULGARIAN This unassuming little *mehana,* housed in a 200-year-old building, may not look exceptional, but what comes out of the kitchen is. The Mencheva's chicken *kavarma* is one of the best examples of this traditional cooking method (essentially slices of chicken, onion, tomatoes, and red pepper, oven baked with egg in an earthenware ceramic pot), as is the "*meshaniza* of melnik," with wonderfully tender meat and crunchy vegetables. A 100% family affair (patriarch Mladen Menchev is aided by his wife and three children and two daughters-in-law), it was one of the first restaurants to open in Melnik in 1993. Before that, Mladen was a waiter, unable under the old Communist rules to establish his own restaurant. But the years of serving tables paid off: Mladen is now the proud proprietor of Melnik's most successful restaurant. In the evenings Jan and Elana, a young couple dressed in traditional garb, provide wonderful live music, based on their travels into the far-flung communities of the Pirin mountains.

Main St. ✆ **07437/339** or 0889406861. www.melnik-mehana.com. 2.50lev–10lev ($2–$8.10/£1.25–£5). MC, V. Daily 10am–11pm.

Exploring the Village & Surroundings

The 18th- and 19th-century homes that line the dusty main road feature a simplified version of the National Revival architectural style prevalent elsewhere in Bulgaria. They typically are built with fortress like stone foundations that can stretch as high as two stories, sometimes into the sandstone slopes into which caves were dug to store huge barrels of wine. The whitewashed walls tower above this stone base, their facades punctuated with shutters, usually closed to ward off the summer heat. It's a lovely look that is unique to Melnik.

Once you've strolled along the main street, head uphill to visit the main attraction: the stately home (at least it must have been in 18th-c. Melnik) of the **Kordopulovs** (✆ **07437/265;** daily 10am–9pm; 2lev ($1.65/£1). Said to be the biggest National Revival house in Bulgaria, with 24 windows (many of the panes multicolored stained glass, giving it an Eastern-influenced look), Melnik's grandest home was built in 1754 by Kordopulov, a rich trader of Greek descent. After walking through the large airy rooms, you descend into the cool cellar where Kordopulov stored 250 to 300 metric tons of wine in a cave system that took him 12 years to carve. You can do a wine tasting here (not even vaguely in the league of Melnik's finest, but very drinkable and similar in taste to what most of the local villagers produce as their house wine) before exiting and making your way to Mitko's cave (see "Drinking Wine with 'Six Fingers' Manolev," below). Aside from this and a visit to Rozhen Monastery, perhaps the best reason to venture this far south lies at the Mencheva Kushta (see above), one of the best dining experiences in Bulgaria.

Rozhen Monastery ★★ Rozhen is in no way comparable to Rila in terms of size or setting, but approaching the low-slung building there is not a tourist stall in sight. Enter and it is as if you've stepped into another world, a silent, serene place where nothing bad ever happens—ironic, given how often the monastery has been pillaged since it was founded by Alexius Slav in 1220. Within the small courtyard, which is surrounded by a two-story timber structure, is the Church of the Birth of the Holy Virgin. Like Rila, it attracts pilgrims seeking miraculous answers to their prayers, all the while warning them about the consequences of sinning by means of a vivid mural depicting demons tossing

Moments Drinking Wine with "Six Fingers" Manolev

Even though the region is famous for its red wines, there is no wine shop dedicated to promoting the winemakers in the village, nor is it possible for individuals to arrange a wine tasting with the region's best producer, **Damianitza Cellar** (www.melnikwine.bg), which caters to groups only. But, if you're not a wine snob, there is a delightful wine-tasting experience to be had in a 250-year-old cave overlooking the village. As you leave Kerdopulova Kushta, take the high path that curves along the hill in the direction of town to find **Mitko Manolev** (✆ **0887 545 795**), aka "Six Fingers," brooding over his barrels. He will offer you a tasting of his wines direct from the barrel (1lev/80¢/40p), all the while ranting about how the E.U. regulations will be the ruin of independent winemakers. Mitko will bottle your wine of choice (two types of red, both close cousins to grape juice, but without preservatives and slightly sparkling). The wine may not be entirely to your liking but worth purchasing, if only to watch Mitko personally fill, cork, and label the bottles, the most personally handled wine you're likely to purchase anywhere.

fleeing sinners into the gaping mouth of the Serpent. While Rozhen is one of the smallest of Bulgaria's monasteries, it is in relatively good condition, with well-tended gardens and orchards, proof of how much it is loved by the monks. There is a strong sense here that this is very much a living monastery into which you are intruding as a tourist rather than a pilgrim, so be sensitive to noise levels. Also note that it is strictly forbidden to photograph the monks or the inside of the church.

7km (4⅓ miles) by road from Melnik, via Karlanovo. Free admission. Daily dawn–dusk.

BANSKO

150km (93 miles) from Sofia

Sprawling at the base of the Pirin, Bansko is Bulgaria's fastest-growing winter resort, with a cumulative 65km (40 miles) of marked ski runs and brand-new lifts to ensure that the resort continues to attract the lion's share of foreigners to the slopes of Bulgaria's "Alps." Besides the range of runs—ideal for a group comprising beginners, intermediate, and experienced skiers—Bansko is also the only Bulgarian ski resort that is centered around a historic old quarter, a tangle of cobbled streets lined with thick stone walls and metal-studded gates that guard half-timbered double-story homes. Many of these are now atmospheric *mehanas,* their windows aglow with crackling fires in winter and the sound of lilting traditional songs wafting out along with the delicious aroma of Bulgarian fare, served up at such reasonable prices that even those forced to go half- or full-board by hotels during peak season can afford to junk these (generally awful) meals and head into the old quarter for a decent spread. But if you're not high up in the mountains or settled around a table in the village heart, the picture is a little less pretty, as Bansko's innate charm is increasingly compromised by the unprecedented growth seen in the last few years. Every season sees more concrete poured into foundations that creep beyond the "official" building line as developers try to deliver on the promise of "uninterrupted views," with prospects for the hotels left in the wake of their greed ever-diminishing. The only justice is that eventually these developers will have to face the butt end of the new kids on the block. The exception to this is the pricey Kempinski, which is situated on the western side where flower-edged balconies provide views of the Pirin, interrupted only by skiers flashing down the slopes.

Essentials: Getting There & Getting Around

Surprise Tours offers direct transfers to Bansko (just under 3 hr.) for 75€ ($95). If you're counting every stotinka, take the **public bus.** The 3-hour journey from Sofia to Bansko will cost a mere 8lev ($6.50/£4.05), as does the 3½-hour bus trip from Plovdiv. Buses pull into Ul Patriarch Evitimi, on the northern outskirts; it's a 10-minute walk from the old quarter and about 25 to 40 minutes to the new developments upslope, where most of the "better" hotels are located. If this is your destination, make sure you prearrange a transfer. Around the corner from the bus station you'll find the small **train** station. Bansko's only rail connection (via narrow-gauge track) is with Septemvri, which in turn lies on the Sofia-Plovdiv line. The journey between Bansko and Septemvri is wonderfully scenic as it trundles through forest-clad mountains and valleys of timeless bucolic beauty, but at 5 hours, the ride is inconveniently long. However, if you catch the earliest train (there are three a day; get your host to check most recent times), this could be the best way to reach Plovdiv, allowing you to take in some Pirin and western Rhodopean scenery without going to the expense of renting a car. Alternatively, you can experience two-thirds of the journey by booking with Intersport (see details below), which will put you on the train, pick you up from the Velingrad station, and take you to Bansko by road.

The **tourist information** center is located off the central square (pl Vaptsarov) just north of the old quarter, but opening hours are in reality inconveniently flexible (✆ **07443/5048;** Mon–Fri 9am–1pm and 2–5pm).

For a wide variety of 1-, 2- and 3-day guided hiking or biking excursions in the Pirin National Park (ranging from 39lev–149lev/$32–$121/£20–£75), or 1-day rafting (99lev/$80/£50) and rock-climbing expeditions (49lev/$40/£25), contact **Intersport** (✆ **088 878 8859;** www.intersport-bansko.bg). Intersport also offers sightseeing excursions to Melnik and Rozhen Monastery, Leshten and Kovachevitsa, and Dancing Bear Park; all of these include all transportation, a guide, and lunch, and cost only 59lev ($48/£30).

Where to Stay

You have two lodging choices in Bansko: You can stay in a B&B in the old quarter, where facilities are basic but atmospheric and close to the best restaurants in town (note that these may be a little *too* close in high season, when evening festivities can continue until quite late). Or you can base yourself in the new part of town, where the main benefit is the proximity to the gondola (a 15- to 25-min. walk if you're based in the old quarter).

The selection below includes the best available in 2008, but note that developments continue apace. If you're in Bansko for an extended skiing trip, you may get a far better package deal in a hotel not listed here. The hotel and service might prove forgettable, but the price may be just right. For details on agents who can arrange lodgings, see the last entry of this section. Expect to pay double the summer rate during winter, and triple over the peak time (usually the period just before Christmas and a few days into Jan). Hotels and even B&B owners are reluctant to divulge winter rates early (supply and demand being the order of the day), so be prepared for some fluctuations to rates quoted below. Children age 4 and under usually stay free.

Old Quarter

There are plenty of places to stay in the old quarter, but **Dedo Pene** (✆ **0888 795970,** or 937/299-5643 in the U.S.; www.dedopene.com; 50lev/$41/£25 double) is one of the coziest. The 1820 home is a bit eclectic, so its 10 rooms vary quite a bit, as do their prices, but all share a wonderfully authentic, rustic, and cozy atmosphere, with traditional furnishings and fittings (including the lovely basins—traditionally used to carry water from the well), and wood- and coal-burning fireplaces. Room nos. 1 and 4 have lovely views of the distant Pirin; others look out onto the red-tiled roofs of the old quarter. Make sure you request a room with a view. A close contender, and a little cheaper (in every way) is **Dvata Smurcha,** 2 Velyan Ognev (✆ **07443/2632;** 16lev–18lev/$13–$15/£8.05–£9.30 per person, including breakfast). It is located a few steps away from the brilliant **Baryakova** *mehana* (see "Where to Dine," below) and named after the two pine trees in its well-tended garden. The friendly proprietor speaks virtually no English but is all smiles, and offers five spotless en suite rooms, most with balconies. The old part of the house (over 100 years) has rooms with balconies that provide lovely views of the Pirin, while rooms in the newer part are slightly bigger and fresher, with garden views. If you fancy staying in a museum of sorts, another good option is **Hadzhiruskovite** *kushti,* 33 Pirin St. (✆ **07443/8422;** 15lev–18lev ($12–$15/£7.45–£9.30 per person). Once home to the man who designed the village church's bell tower, which still calls the faithful to worship every Sunday, and until recently the property of the Union of Bulgarian Architects, it is a truly authentic example of Bansko's 19th-century residences: It is almost totally original, with solid stone walls and heavy woodwork. Note that just the two rooms on the second floor (nos. 5 and 6) are worth booking. These have enough light (rooms below are dark) and open onto a wide veranda with rustic tables and chairs that overlook the untended stone-walled garden. The charming Marin (enough English to get by), makes a delicious home-brewed *rakia* (brandy). If he knows you know, he's sure to offer.

"New" Bansko

The four-star **Hotel Perun** (✆ **0749/88477;** www.hotelperunbansko.com) is very much a Kempinski wannabe, but without the class, staff, or view. Nonetheless, it is a rather smart-looking alpine edifice, a 10-minute walk from the gondola (or you can use the hotel's shuttle bus service), and has after Kempinski, the second-best facilities in town (okay, Hotel Strazhite has a bowling alley, but you don't want to be stuck with *that* decor). It's also the best value for your money, even in high season when rooms range between 60€ and 170€ ($76–$216). Families should book the Double Deluxe rooms with two separate rooms, each with its own bathroom. If you can forego hotel facilities and are planning to stay for more than a couple of days, **Todorini Kuli** apartments (✆ **0888 441005;** www.todorinikuli.com) are the best deal in "new" Bansko, offering excellent value and a great location directly opposite the Kempinski (50m/165 ft. from the gondola). Apartments are pretty characterless, but they are newish, so finishes look fresh and equipment functions well. Couples should book room no. 2, the biggest; families should opt for a one-bedroom apartment, with separate bedroom and open-plan lounge with fireplace, dining room, and kitchen—no. 15 is a good option. Rates, depending on size and season, range between 10€ and 82€ ($13–$104).

Kempinski Hotel Grand Arena ★★★ "Excellent position, great staff; pricey though," reads one review, and that just about sums up the Kempinski. This five-star hotel has set the bar high, bringing the joys of a grand foyer bar, a wellness center, and a huge indoor pool to Bansko. Typical of many chain hotels, rooms are bland but large and luxurious with balconies from which to enjoy the town's only truly unobstructed mountain views. It also offers various dining options, admittedly overpriced given what's available a 15-min. walk downhill. The location is unbeatable, and thankfully this is one that will remain so: The hotel is almost butted up against the gondola station so it is ski-in, ski-out. ***Note:*** Under no circumstances should you accept a room facing town; book a full mountain-facing room, and stick to your guns. Specify if you want a nonsmoking room.

96 Pirin St., Bansko. ✆ **0749/88888.** Fax 0749/88560. www.kempinski-bansko.com. 159 units. Deluxe and executive rooms 220€–270€ ($279–$343) double; 310€–470€ ($394–$597) suite. Rates include breakfast. Check for summer specials. AE, DC, MC, V. Valet parking and garage. **Amenities:** 2 restaurants; bar; 2 lounges; outdoor and indoor pools; tennis court; fitness center; Jacuzzi; steam room and sauna; Kneipp wading basin; kids' club; concierge; conference center; shops; salon; babysitting; laundry; dry cleaning; solarium. *In room:* A/C, TV, wireless Internet connection, minibar, hair dryer, safe.

Roka Villa ★★ Finds If you care about design, this is the top choice in town though it is a hike to the gondola. (Use the hotel's shuttle service). A modern boutique hotel the likes of which Sofia has yet to see, Roka Villa is clad almost entirely in a mesh of thin gray strips of timber. It's not quite the antithesis of the cutesy alpine chalet look, but it still alerts the passerby that something different lies within. From the black-walled and gray slate reception, where casually strewn white boulders from the nearby river make a stylish, organic statement, to the lobby bar, which looks more like a club than a hotel watering hole, Roka Villa is as edgy as it gets in Bulgaria, never mind Bansko. Rooms are divided into Small Double (very small, but adequate), Standard Double (some with balconies), Deluxe Double (the best-value category; ask for no. 349 or 351, or one with a balcony facing the mountain), Double "Brod" room, and Deluxe Maisonette. There is also a Standard Maisonette, with an unworkable floor plan, to be avoided at all costs. Extra-tall dark-timber headboards are etched against dark-red walls. Glass dividers are used in the smaller rooms, which incidentally have just one bedside light. That is irritating if you're both readers. The basement spa is equally stylish, though the design is a little cold.

37B Glazne St., Bansko. ✆ **0749/88337.** Fax 0749/88446. www.villaroka.com. 99 units. Summer 56lev–66lev ($45–$53/£28–£17) double, 76lev ($62/£38) double deluxe, 84lev ($68/£42) double "Brod," 92lev ($75/£46) double "Brod" deluxe and deluxe maisonette; winter 150lev–180lev ($122–$146/£76–£91) double, 210lev ($170/£105) double deluxe, 213lev ($173/£107) double "Brod," 250lev ($203/£126) double "Brod" deluxe and deluxe maisonette. No credit cards. Rates include breakfast and dinner. **Amenities:** Restaurant; bar; spa center (pool, sauna, steam, solarium, range of treatments; Internet access); shuttle service to gondola; room service; laundry. *In room:* TV, minibar.

Where to Dine

There are more than 40 atmospheric *mehanas* in the old quarter, all offering basically the same Bulgarian menu, but make sure you don't miss **Baryakova,** generally rated the best of the lot (see below). However, **Dedo Pene** is also excellent, with a warren of cozy rooms leading to a small central courtyard (see "Where to Stay," above). If you've tried these and you're looking for something new, **Molerite 1972** (✆ **07443/8494**) is another highly rated restaurant, this time just outside the old quarter on Glazne Street (look out for the two large barrels).

Baryakova ★★★ Like most *mehanas,* this is an extended-family affair in an old 19th-century building covered in traditional decorations (dark timber beams and tables; bright red embroidered table cloths), but the quality of the food is a cut above. There are a number of specialties—tender pork leg, grilled over coals; ceramic hot plate with sizzling strips of meat and vegetables; the "three meats" (strips of chicken, pork, and veal), cooked with sauerkraut in a pot and served with rice. The latter is Banska Kapama, a local delicacy, as is Banski Staretz, a local "dry" sausage (like salami, but not as fatty and uniquely spiced). Order this with white cheese and fresh bread as a starter. Note that Baryakova is open evenings only, and that the family takes a month off in summer but cannot say in advance which month this will be.

Velyan Ognev (just off central sq. Vuzrazhdane, in Old Town). ✆ **0889 534582,** 0899 670734, or 0899 653377. Main courses 4.80lev–15lev ($3.90–$12/£2.40–£7.45). No credit cards. Daily 5pm until late.

Exploring Bansko

Bansko's attraction list is predictably small and centered within its old quarter, where cobbled lanes spread out from ploshtad Vuzrazhdane, the square marked by the statue of Father Paisii, author of the *Slav-Bulgarian History,* one of the books that helped launch the National Revival. On the mountain side of the square is the **Church of Sveta Troitsa.** It's pretty ordinary except for the high walls, which were erected to hide the major extensions commissioned by the wealthy elite during the early 19th century, a time when the Ottoman rulers had put a lid on further Orthodox development. The then-mayor of Bansko paid for this defiance with 5 years in prison. Behind the church is the **Neofit Rilski House Museum** (daily 9am–noon and 2–5pm; 3lev/$2.45/£1.50), birthplace of one of Bulgaria's great scholars (he was the first to translate the New Testament into Bulgarian) and another key player in the National Revival. Other than this there is the nearby Rilski Convent, housing a small **Icon Museum,** Yane Sandanski (Mon–Fri 9am–noon and 2–5pm; 3lev ($2.45/£1.50), and the **Velyanova Kushta Museum,** 5 Velyan

At Last, a Break for "Dancing" Bears

Bear sightings are notoriously rare in the wild; if you're keen to see one up close, head to the Dancing Bear Park at Rila Mountain, just outside of Bansko (tours every hour daily from 10am–6pm Apr–Sept; 10am–4pm Oct–Nov; no tours Dec–Mar; donations welcome), where formerly abused ursines get a new lease on life. Founded by the Vier Pfoten organization, which is supported by animal rights crusader Brigitte Bardot, the park is a sanctuary for bears that were once used for a particularly barbaric form of entertainment: Cubs were placed on a hot plate while music was turned up so that they appear to "dance." Once a widespread form of "entertainment," the cruel practice was thankfully banned in Bulgaria in 2002. Sadly, the bears still get up on their paws and dance involuntarily, perhaps associating human visitors with the demands of their former owners.

Ognev (same hours as convent), home to the man who carved the iconostasis in the Church of Sveta Troitsa, and today furnished with typical 19th-century items that provide insight into the relatively humble lifestyle of Bansko's hoi polloi. A little farther north from the old quarter is ploshtad Nikola Vapstarov, where the annual **Bansko International Jazz Festival** is held in August. You can visit the **Nikola Vapstarov House** (same hours as convent; 3lev/$2.45/£1.50), where the revolutionary poet was born. It's pretty dull except for a few crafts on sale in one of the adjacent rooms and the occasional art exhibition held in the hall downstairs.

THE ARCHITECTURAL RESERVE VILLAGES OF RHODOPE ★★★

If you like nature enhanced by 18th-century rural architecture, traveling from Bansko through the Rhodope mountains to Plovdiv will likely be the highlight of your sojourn in Bulgaria. It's not just the scenic beauty or the long, empty roads, but the romance of seeing fields tilled by horse-drawn plows, and women and men in traditional garb reaping the produce that will end up delighting your palate at a roadside restaurant. Exploring the mountain villages (the best of which are Leshten, Kovachevitsa, Dolen, and, to a lesser extent, Shiroka Luka and Gela) is like stepping into a living museum, where old folk sit mutely on benches in the sun against stonewalled, timber-framed homes, just as their ancestors have for over 300 years. Alleys and lanes in these villages are impassable by car—potholed, and sometimes thick with dung and mud—so you must explore the villages on foot (wear sturdy shoes), stumbling onto images of novel beauty: An old woman walking her goat like a dog greets another bent under a huge stack of hay. A gaggle of teenage girls move their hips to a badly tuned radio, giggling at a passing boy on a powder-blue Communist-era motorbike as a girl comes thundering past on horseback, riding with no bridle or saddle, her long brown hair streaming behind her. A camera is essential; extra film or memory card is recommended.

Essentials: Getting There & Getting Around

Seeing the best this region has to offer involves traveling up roads that are effectively cul-de-sacs. You will have to accept a fair amount of doubling back as you travel east to Pamporovo, one of Bulgaria's top three ski resorts, before heading north to Plovdiv. The only tourism bureau is in Shiroka Luka, which has the efficient **Rhodopi tourist center**

(✆ **03030/233;** www.bulgaria-trips.info/Shiroka-Laka/Shiroka-Luka.html; daily 8:30am–noon and 1–6:30pm) servicing the region. Staff provides you with maps and recommendations on places to stay, as well as more information on the annual *kukeri* carnival held every March, and the **International Bagpipe Festival** (www.gaidaland.com).

Where to Stay & Dine

Kapsazov's Kushta ★★★ Finds Relaxing in the immaculate stonewalled garden, watching swallows dive-bomb the pretty pool or just gazing up at the forested slopes that surround the house, is a delight; but it is at the dining table that you really know you've gone to heaven. The angel in the kitchen is Sofia Kapsazov—she has written a cookbook on traditional Bulgarian cooking and also hosts regular cooking courses. After tasting one of her meals you'll wish you had the time to sign up for one of her lessons. Dinners are enjoyed communally, either outside in the main dining room upstairs, or in the huge kitchen (where you can watch Sofia work her magic). There's every chance you'll get a chance to mingle with an interesting crowd, particularly if you stay over weekends. Book months in advance, even though the Kapsazovs plan to convert three more houses in the future.

15-min. drive north from Leshten. Booking office P.O. Box 656 BG, Sofia 1000. ✆ **099 403089** or 048/969676. 5 units. 55€ ($70) per person. No credit cards. Rates include breakfast and dinner. **Amenities:** Cooking courses; mushroom and herb picking; hiking.

Leshten Cottages ★★ Finds Leshten is where you'll find the little Bulgarian country cottage you never knew you wanted. Built on a steep hillside in the southwestern Rhodope mountains, Leshten's views—rolling forested hills, the snowcapped Pirin range—are the best in Bulgaria, no mean feat given the competition. Once a bustling village, the original population slowly dwindled to nothing, but the village was saved from ruin by the industrious Misho Marinov, who has renovated 15 of the 18th-century houses, retaining their original character and furnishing them with traditional rugs and blankets. The result is a collection of absolutely charming cottages, all with the creature comforts you need for a thoroughly relaxing stay. (If you're looking for a romantic option, book the tiny clay Mali-style en suite home, the only one Misho has built virtually from scratch.) Most have shaded balconies furnished with rustic timber tables and benches from which to drink in the magnificent view. Some, like Popskata, even have small, walled-off private gardens.

And while the cottages are well equipped for self-catering, why cook, when the best restaurant for miles is a stroll down the lane? **Krachma ★★★** (literally, "restaurant") is a tiny building on the main road through town, marked by the red-and-white gingham tablecloths you'll see under the spreading canopy of a magnificent old tree with wine corks dangling from its branches. Tug one and tinkling bells summon the waiter. The Kofte Leshten Style is superb—a single tender cut of pork rather than a patty, delicately flavored—order it with *ljutenitza* (mashed red peppers, leek, and spices) and chips—the latter a deep yellow color, waxy and rich in flavor; even the plain cucumber salad, remarkably sweet, is superb. It's hardly surprising to hear that all the produce is grown on Misho's farm. ***Tip:*** Across the road from the restaurant is a gallery. Pop in to see the art on display. With any luck you'll bump into the Bulgarian poet Boris Christov (his wife is the artist), a fascinating character who is passionate about Leshten. Boris has a created a photographic catalog of the village history in a small book, *Leshten,* which is on sale here, along with CDs that expound his "personal mythology about the universe."

Leshten is 40km (25 miles) from Bansko (40 min.). ✆ **07527/552** or 0899 990 776. 15 units. 60lev ($49/£30) room; 120lev ($98/£61) house. No credit cards. **Amenities:** Restaurant. *In room:* TV, kitchen, backgammon, fireplace.

Outdoors in the Rila, Pirin & Rhodope Mountains

Hiking

The most rewarding hike in the country is the Rila Seven Lakes trail, a moderate 2- to 4-day walk (5–6 hr. per day). It is well signposted, but if you would prefer an English-speaking guide and prebooked meals and accommodations, **Zig Zag** (see Sofia "Visitor Info," earlier in this chapter) can arrange it. Their 4-day Rila hike (180€/$229) also includes a visit to Rila Monastery and Mount Malyovitza—at 2,729m (8,951 ft.) not much smaller than nearby Mount Mussala (2,925m/9,594 ft.), the latter the highest summit in southeast Europe. Zig Zag also offers a 4-day guided hike in the Rhodope for 250€ ($318) per person (minimum two participants) as well as hikes that combine kayaking on Rhodope rivers and dams.

In Pirin, the most highly rated trail is the Bansko-to-Melnik hike. Almost on a par is the hike from Mt. Vihren (Pirin's highest point at 2,914m/9,558 ft.) to Tevnoto Lake, the highest water in Pirin. Both 2-day hikes are offered by **Intersport** (www.intersport-bansko.bg), which charges 50€ ($64) per person, all-inclusive (see "Bansko: Essentials: Getting There & Getting Around," earlier in this chapter, for details).

Skiing

Bulgaria has three main winter resorts: **Borovets,** the oldest, is in the Rila Mountains, but attracts the younger end of the market with the cheapest package deals. Skiing in the Rhodope range is centered around **Pamporovo,** attractively situated in forested surroundings but with no retail or nightlife, while in the Pirin it is **Bansko** that is turning into the fastest developing winter resort in southeastern Europe. Combining the most sophisticated lifts in the country, the longest ski season (mid-Dec to mid-Apr some years), and a 19th-century village heart that is full of character, Bansko is likely to be your first port of call for skiing (see "Bansko," above). However, given the uncontrolled construction that is slowly overtaking this town, less developed Pamporovo may be a better bet. Here the best hotel—and with no attractive heart to the resort, you do want to stay in a hotel with the best facilities in town—is the **Hotel Orlovetz** ★★ (✆ **03021/9000** or 03021/8511; pamporovo@bsbg.net). In 2008, 3 nights in a very spacious double room with wonderful mountain views cost 200lev ($162/£100) per night, including breakfast (less per day with a longer stay). The hotel also has an excellent and equally reasonably priced range of treatments to deal with aching après ski muscles.

If you would prefer to have everything booked by one operator, from accommodations and equipment rental to instructor and passes, take a look at **www.BulgariaSki.com**, the biggest source of information on skiing and snowboarding in Bulgaria. Booking here is often very cost-effective. A 6-day ski package including instruction, equipment, and lift tickets, costs 263€/$334).

Caveat: While they are fairly inexpensive, none of Bulgaria's resorts comes close to the standards set by European and American resorts, and not only from an infrastructure point of view, the reason they didn't make the 2014 Winter Olympics short list. That is something you will notice if you cannot ski for a day or two due to foul weather.

5 PLOVDIV & THE VALLEY OF THE KINGS

Plovdiv: 147km (91 miles) from Sofia; 190km (118 miles) from Veliko Tarnovo

Five thousand years ago the central plains of Bulgaria, stretching from the foothills of the Balkan mountains to the heartlands of the Rhodopes, once were home to the Thracian tribes, said to be Europe's first civilization, whose gold- and silversmith techniques were the most sophisticated of ancient times. The area is referred to as the "Valley of the Kings" and it is rich in archaeological finds. The UNESCO-listed Kanaznluk Tomb is the most famous, but the most popular destination in the region is a city described during Thracian times as "the biggest and most beautiful town in all of Thrace." Gorgeous Plovdiv still is the jewel in Bulgaria's crown, with a long and varied history that is vastly more palpable than Sofia's.

Plovdiv was known to the ancient Greek writers as Eumolpiade. The original settlement was invaded by Philip II of Macedon (father of Alexander the Great) in 342 B.C., and he renamed it Philippopolis in honor of himself. Initially, Plovdiv was a frontier town and the city's strategic position on the Belgrade-Constantinople trade route ensured that it flourished under Roman rule. There is still ample proof of those times, most notably the Roman theater, said to be the largest outside of Italy. Location also ensured that Plovdiv would be invaded (and renamed) no fewer than six times.

Plovdiv experienced its second heyday during the late 17th to 19th centuries, when the town's most affluent merchants flashed their wealth by building beautiful town houses in the best urban examples of the style known as National Revival (also referred to as Bulgarian Baroque). Declared an architectural-historical reserve in 1956, the cobbled streets of Old Plovdiv meander past Roman ruins, imposing mosques, cool church courtyards, and the beautifully painted facades and terraced architecture of these National Revival homes. They offer a crash course in local history, while the sheer beauty of the color combinations and geometric lines provide even the most amateur photographer with striking images to show off back home.

It may be Bulgaria's second-largest city, but Plovdiv likes to lay claim to the title of "Cultural Capital." Certainly its art galleries far outclass Sofia's, and in the spring and early summer the Old Town's streets also exude a vibrant, sophisticated atmosphere: Behind the walls of Kuyumdzhioglu House you may hear the tinkling of a piano—a recital in the gardens—while a few blocks farther an orchestra sets up for an evening concert in the ruins of the Roman amphitheater. Old Plovdiv is a pleasure to explore for a few hours or over 2 to 3 days. It is also an ideal base for a trip to nearby Bachkovo Monastery, Bulgaria's second-biggest monastery; or farther south into the Rhodopes to view quaint villages like Shiroka Luka and Gela (see section above); or northeast to the Valley of the Kings and the Kazanluk Tomb, which can be viewed as a day trip from Plovdiv; or as a staging post in your journey from Plovdiv to Veliko Tarnovo or the Black Sea Coast.

ESSENTIALS

Bulgaria's most beautiful city planned to open the doors to its first tourism bureau only at the end of 2006, but as of the summer of 2008 that still had not happened. Alternatively, take a look at the semi-useful site www.plovdivcityguide.com. Astral Holidays (www.astralholidays.bg) is one of the city's most established independent travel agencies, but its advice on hotels and restaurants still is lacking. For current info on what's playing in town, pick up the monthly *Plovdiv Visitor's Guide* or *Programata* (www.programata.com).

Plovdiv is best visited in spring and early summer (July–Aug can be unbearably hot) or autumn. Try to avoid the Plovdiv Fairs (early May and mid- to late Sept; for exact dates see www.fair.bg), or at least book your accommodations long in advance as space is limited and prices inflated then.

GETTING THERE

The Sofia-Istanbul highway that links Sofia with Plovdiv is in tiptop condition, so the journey by car takes 70 to 90 minutes, making it a possible day trip from Sofia. Plenty of tour operators offer the itinerary, but an even better option is to skip Sofia and treat Plovdiv as your base.

There are three bus terminals. **Yug** is the main terminal on Hristo Botev, where buses connecting Plovdiv with Sofia pull in almost hourly (the trip is just over 2 hr.; 10lev/$8.10/£5 one-way). Buses also travel to Assenovgrad, from where you can catch another bus to Bachkovo, Varna (7 hr.), Bourgas (4 hr.), and Istanbul (6 hr.).

GETTING AROUND

The city is divided into two sections: the 18th- and 19th-century open-air architectural reserve that is Old Plovdiv, sprawled across the three remaining hillocks of ancient Eumolpiade, and "New" Plovdiv, spread around the foothills. With its meandering cobbled lanes, Old Plovdiv—and even the smattering of sites in New Plovdiv, along pedestrian Knyaz Aleksandur I Street—is best explored on foot, with all the top sites and hotels listed within walking distance of each other.

WHERE TO STAY

Plovdiv's hotel scene has improved in the last few years with the Novotel reinvigorated by a splashy 2006 renovation and the opening of the brand new Alafrangite in June 2008. (The Alafrangite's owner, Ivan Kolev, managed the Timontium for 27 years and is owner/manager of the Alafrangues restaurant next door.) If the hotels below are full (with the exception of the Trimontium and Novotel, they are all quite small), look at the **Hotel Bulgaria** at the edge of Knyaz Aleksandur I Street (✆ **032/633 403**). Its location adjacent to the main shopping/dining area couldn't be more convenient, but the facility itself is a dank, Communist-era hulk. Desk personnel speak English and are very helpful, however, and you won't need a car to explore the *korso* (promenade) or Old Town. Go to www.hotelbulgaria.net for information. The Bulgaria's doubles start at 160lev ($130/£81) and include breakfast in the dreary basement dining room that reeked of insecticide when we visited.

If you don't need the big-hotel vibe, a better deal is the tiny five-room hotel right on Old Plovdiv's borders (technically part of it), and a stone's through from the Dzhumaya Mosque: The aptly named **Hotel-Bar Central** (✆ **032/622 348;** www.hotel-bar-central.com; 40€/$51 double) is wonderfully convenient, albeit understaffed. It's a slim building, with each room taking up an entire floor, and floor-to-ceiling tinted glass walls provide a sense of space. If you'd prefer to wake up surrounded by the wonderful architecture of Old Plovdiv's National Revival homes, **B&B Old Town** offers a great location and two lovely old-fashioned rooms with carved ceilings and wall frescoes. The surly manager does not speak English but the website makes for easy bookings, and this is a perfect place to flop into after a hard day's sightseeing—around the corner from Arena, the outdoor cafe/bar overlooking the Roman theater (✆ **032/265679** or 0887 420 185; www.bulguide.com/bedbreakfast; 35€–55€/$45–$70, depending on room and season).

Alafrangite ★★ (Finds It's hard to say how good the Alafrangite will be, as it had just started its "soft" opening when we visited in June 2008, but if the attention to detail evident while the hotel in the Three Hill neighborhood of Old Plovdiv was working out the kinks is any indication, the Alafrangite will be a standout. From the granite-floored lobby to the rooftop garden to the peach-and-taupe color scheme, construction of the Alafrangite (translated as "in the French style") clearly was a labor of love. Most rooms have a view of the hotel's garden or rooftop terrace, but others look out on surrounding trees. There are lots of windows, which give the rooms and public spaces an open feel. All rooms have showers, not tubs, but the suites have bidets. Breakfast is served in the beautiful lobby or on the terrace, and the best part is that it is catered from the Alafrangues restaurant next door (see below).

17 Kiril Nektariev St. ✆ **359 032/26 95 95.** Fax 032/23 61 88. www.restorant-alafrangite.org/home_en.html. 16 units, including 2 suites. From 58€ ($74) double; from 75€ ($95) suite. AE, DC, MC, V. Rates include breakfast and taxes. **Amenities:** Restaurant (next door); bar; rooftop garden terrace; free garage. *In room:* A/C, cable TV, Wi-Fi, minibar, hair dryer.

Hebros ★★★ (Value This little gem on a quiet cobbled street in the heart of Old Plovdiv is so completely head, shoulders, and feet above the competition that it's almost worth arranging your trip around room availability here. Once the place where top Communist party members relaxed when visiting Plovdiv, the opulence of the materials and craftsmanship displayed in this typical National Revival home are matched by the furnishings. You'll find Bulgarian and Italian antiques throughout; windows draped in heavy velvet or edged with lace; dark varnished floors invariably dressed with rich Oriental rugs; walls decorated with traditional frescoes or timber clad. Despite a lack of hotel facilities, including a proper reception (most just enter through the restaurant), the most important aspects are taken care of: helpful staff, excellent restaurant, and a charming atmosphere and location.

51 A.K. Stoilov St., Plovdiv 4000. ✆ **032/260180** or 032/625929. Fax 032/260252. www.hebros-hotel.com. 10 units. 95€ ($121) double. Rates include breakfast. MC, V. **Amenities:** Restaurant; Jacuzzi; sauna; room service; laundry. *In room:* A/C, TV, Internet connection, minibar, hair dryer.

Old Town Residence ★★ (Value If your budget cannot stretch to the Hebros, or it is full, the Residence is one of the best-value deals in town, but be warned: You may have to put up with some rather surly service. Rumored to be the Plovdiv holiday home of some heavies who built it with ill-gotten gains, this hotel is styled on the neoclassical grand mansions of late-19th-century Old Plovdiv, but there's no mistaking New Money, with its penchant for chandeliers, reproduction furniture, white marble, and bits of gold leaf. Rooms are quite grand, rates are good, and the location—also in the heart of Old Plovdiv, but with views of the city sparkling at your feet—unbeatable. This is a great place to watch Plovdivians at play. The restaurant is also highly rated.

11 Knyaz Ceretelev St., Plovdiv 4000. ✆ **032/632389** or 032/620789. residence@abv.bg. 6 units. 50€–75€ ($64–$95) double; 40€ ($51) studio. MC, V. **Amenities:** Restaurant; room service; laundry. *In room:* A/C, TV, hair dryer, fireplace.

Plovdiv Novotel ★★★ There's nothing special about the Novotel's exterior architecture. In fact, it is quite ugly. But a clever 2006 renovation has transformed the interior of the once-sterile behemoth overlooking the Maritza River and Old Town into an attractive, ultra-modern destination hotel that is elegant, user-friendly, and brimming with guest perks. From the first floor shops and watering holes to the indoor bowling alley, the Novotel has become more than just a place for guests to lay their heads: It's also a place where they can relax and have fun. Public spaces buzz with activity and gleam with creative lighting, artwork and color. Guest rooms all have been redecorated in a subdued Scandinavian style with tubs and showers in the bathrooms and a menu of amenities that you'd expect in a luxury hotel. The classy ★★ Four Seasons restaurant, one of three in the hotel, is a standout.

2 Zlatiu Boiadjiev St. (P.O. Box 647). ✆ **359 032/934 481.** Fax: 032/934 346. www.icep.bg. 330 units, including 9 suites. Doubles from 120€ ($187); suites from 180€ ($280); presidential suite 360€ ($560). AE, DC, MC, V. **Amenities:** 3 restaurants; cafe; 3 bars; night club; indoor pool; tennis courts; bowling alley; spa; excursions; guarded parking; playground; beauty salon; rental car agency; shops; meeting rooms. *In room:* A/C, SAT/TV, radio, minibar, room service, ironing board, valet service, hair dryer, Internet connection.

Trimontium Princess Hotel ★ No list of Plovdiv hotels would be complete without including the Trimontium: A grand structure looming over Tsentralen Sq., this hotel is rated by some as the city's best, and currently it is the hotel of choice for top-end tour operator Abercrombie & Kent. No doubt it's a good bet if you have a group too large for the Hebros, but it's a letdown if you're expecting something grand as its name. Rates are currently a bargain and it does have all the facilities you'd expect from a large hotel (including a new pool—a great boon in summer, when Plovdiv can be sweltering). But rooms are furnished with items that appear to have been acquired at a bargain sale on office furniture. You can only wonder how it is possible for a hotel that was renovated a decade after the 1980s to be so entirely gauche. The aptly named Panoramic Floor bar is a great place to be during Happy Hour with its white leather chairs teetering on tiny timber feet and the view of the city below.

Kapitan Raicho St. 2, Plovdiv 4000. ✆ **032/605000** or 032/605080. www.dedeman.com. 158 units. 35€–55€ ($44–$70) double; rates vary depending on room size and season (high season June 1–Oct 1). Rates include breakfast. AE, DC, MC, V. **Amenities:** 2 restaurants; bar; fitness room; sauna; hairdresser; business center; casino. *In room:* A/C, TV, Internet, minibar, hair dryer.

WHERE TO DINE

Plovdiv's dining scene is not as stimulating as Sofia's, or even Varna's, but there certainly is plenty of choice, particularly along pedestrian Knyaz Aleksandur I Street, where cafes and pizzerias spill out onto the street. For a more intimate atmosphere you're better off grabbing a table in one of the cool walled courtyards in Old Plovdiv. Besides the places discussed below you will find two good options on 4th January Street: **Janet** (no. 3; ✆ **032/626 044** or 032/634 149) and **Ulpia** (no 17; ✆ **032/65 3747**), both serving typical Bulgarian fare in wonderful 19th-century National Revival homes.

Alafrangue ★★★ BULGARIAN When you climb the narrow, winding stone staircase bordered by lush greenery that leads to Alafrangues, become very aware that you're in a 19th-century National Revival house in Old Plovdiv. Midway, you might pick up the sound of soft chamber music and the delicious aroma of grilling meat, but when you reach the gorgeous courtyard restaurant that is protected by graceful trees and grape arbors, you'll know for sure that you're in a place where you'll experience real Bulgarian hospitality. Settle in at a terrace table or take a seat in the cozy dining room, which is rich with woodcarvings and Bulgarian artifacts. Either way, you'll be treated to some of the best preparations of Bulgarian national dishes and grill in Plovdiv. Choose the lamb, rabbit, or even tripe from the menu, which is thoughtfully translated into English. Portions are huge and all dishes at this family-run spot are served with sublime homemade bread. End you meal with Turkish coffee with figs, which appear as a small dab of jam on your saucer.

17 Kiril Nektariev St. ✆ **359 032/26 95 95.** Fax 032/23 61 88. www.restorant-alafrangite.org. Entrees 5.20lev–13lev ($4.20–$11/£2.60–£6.80). MC, V. Daily 11am–11pm.

Four Seasons ★★ CONTINENTAL A big wine list, an inventive menu, and clever partitioning make this newly renovated (2007) restaurant on the lower level of the Plovdiv Novotel a special occasion destination for locals and hotel guests alike. Try the pork with Roquefort port sauce, shark baked in egg white, or one of the traditional Bulgarian dishes executed with a modern twist. The wine list offers wines from many countries as well as the best Bulgarian vineyards, but only three are offered by the glass. This is a white-tablecloth restaurant, but you won't blanche when you get the check.

2 Zlatiu Boiadjiev St. ✆ **359 032/934 481.** Fax 032/934 346. www.icep.bg. Entrees 6lev–29lev ($4.85–$24/£3–£15). AE, DC, MC, V. Daily 11am–11:30pm.

Hebros ★★★ INTERNATIONAL Voted the best restaurant in the country a few years back, Hebros restaurant is, like the hotel, a little gem, with a cozy semisubterranean room and pretty terraced courtyard. The menu features a few traditional Bulgarian dishes, like the ubiquitous (and surprisingly delicious) mish mash—peppers and tomato baked with egg and white cheese in an earthenware pot—but this is probably a good place to take a break from Bulgarian cuisine. Try one of the specialties, like tender rabbit cooked with plums, tomatoes, and shallots. Local wines are recommended by the glass with each respective dish, so this is also a great place to be introduced to new Bulgarian wines.

51 A.K. Stoilov St. ✆ **032/260180** or 032/625929. Main courses 17lev–19lev ($14–$15/£8.70–£9.30). MC, V. Daily 11am–11pm.

Puldin ★★ BULGARIAN Roman fortifications march through sections of this labyrinthine Revival-era house. Don't dally in the first courtyard you enter, furnished with frilly wrought-iron chairs, nor at the fancy "ritual" dining hall, but descend into the cellarlike basement (where rough-hewn timber tables, covered with traditional red tablecloths, contrast with the rather kitschy lit mural, below which water trickles over large boulders) and step outside into the courtyard that lies beyond, where a violin-and-piano-playing duo usually are entertaining diners, and tables are shaded by trees and vines. If it's hot, order a mixture of cold appetizers (eggplant, roasted peppers, and mushrooms are all delicious). If you're famished, try the grilled pork "sword" (big enough for two), or the pork filet, roasted with peppers, tomatoes, apple, and herbs.

3 Knjaz Tsereletev St. ✆ **032/631 720.** Main courses 5.50lev–16lev ($4.45–$13/£2.80–£8.05). AE, DC, MC, V. Daily 11am–11pm.

EXPLORING PLOVDIV

Plovdiv's meandering layout, dead-end streets, and dearth of signs require a flexible approach for any walking tour of the architectural-historical reserve. Old Plovdiv is a wonderful place to get lost; just make sure you're armed with a camera to chart your journey. Plovdiv's steep, cobbled Old Town streets (Ulitsa Knyaz Seretelev, Ulitsa Tsanko Lavrenov, especially) are lined with gorgeous National Revival houses. Try to cover a few of these, but go wherever your eyes lead you: A street like Kiril Nektariev has no museums, but boasts some of the best facades. You easily can cover its prettiest streetscapes in a morning, unless you're keen to examine a few of the opulent interiors or view the artworks housed in some of these splendid houses. In that case, plan a full day or two.

Bachkovo Monastery ★★★ Bulgaria's second-largest monastery is, like Rila, a UNESCO-listed monument, and while the natural environment does not impose the sense of grandeur that surrounds its more famous sister, Bachkovo's artworks alone make this a must-see if you are in the region. Founded in 1083 by two Georgian brothers, the complex was razed during the Ottoman invasion. Today the oldest buildings are the Refectory (1601) and the principal Church of the Assumption of Our Lady (Sveta Bogoroditsa), the latter built in 1604 (though the Sveta Troitsa, a church about 600m/1,968 ft. from the gates, dates from the 14th century, it is usually locked). Sveta Bogoroditsa is filled with beautiful frescoes and murals, but what draws local pilgrims is its 14th-century Virgin Mary icon—said to be a portrait painted by the apostle Luke. Pilgrims believe it has miraculous properties. Besides Sveta Bogoroditsa, the complex also has two smaller churches: Church of the Archangels (13th–14th c.), located next to the main church, and Church of St. Nikolai (1834–37), in the adjoining courtyard. The latter is worth visiting for the murals, said to be the first documented work by Zahary Zograf and featuring a portrait of the artist in the upper-left-hand corner of the *Last Judgment* mural that dominates the porch. You also can enter the refectory (4lev/$3.25/£2), where you will find murals of the great Greek philosophers. The monastery is still home to men in flowing black cassocks and gray beards, but today they are vastly outnumbered by tourists and pilgrims lined up to see the icon or to fill their plastic water bottles with the delicious mineral water that runs continuously from the monastery's piped spring.

Tip: The walkway to the monastery gates is lined with dozens of small stalls selling tourist knickknacks as well as Rhodopean specialties and fast foods. On weekends it can be annoying with blaring music and thronging crowds. For a more convivial atmosphere and decent service, keep heading downhill to the restaurant **Vodopada (© 359 0896 021 053)**. You can't miss the huge outdoor terrace situated around a waterfall and trout-filled pond, and the food is excellent. There is no English menu, but ask for Lily, the can-do English-speaking waitress, and order the house specialties: marinated mushrooms, followed by charcoal-grilled fresh trout or spit-grilled lamb.

30km (19 miles) south of Plovdiv, clearly signposted off the main road connecting Assenovgrad and Smolyan. © **03327/277.** Monastery and restaurant daily 7am–8pm. Admission to the monastery grounds is free; admission to the refectory is 4lev ($2.60/£1.70). A guided tour of the refectory is an additional 5lev ($3.25/£2.10). Restaurant does not take credit cards.

Kazanluk Thracian Tomb ★★★ Kazanluk, center of the rose-growing plains that surround it, was until recently more strongly associated with the overrated Festival of Roses, which takes place here every June. But the past decade has seen an increasing number of Thracian vaults excavated from beneath the burial mounds scattered throughout the surrounding countryside, and the area is increasingly referred to as the Valley of the Kings (see "Thracian Tombing: Exploring the Graves of Europe's First Civilization," below). The first tomb discovered was in Kazanluk in 1944, when soldiers were digging out an air-raid bunker on what then were the outskirts of town. The Kazanluk Tomb is listed by UNESCO, but it was off limits to the general public before 2006. An exact replica was built in 1978 and this comprises the main museum, staffed and open daily. To view the original you need to call ahead to make arrangements. Be sure to do this if you can because standing in the small domed chamber (approached through a slim corridor-like antechamber—very *Temple of Doom*) is an incredible experience. The ceiling frescoes, dating from the late 4th century B.C., are so close you almost can touch them.

Thracian Tombing: Exploring the Graves of Europe's First Civilization

The area around the otherwise sleepy town of Kazanluk is dotted with an estimated 1,500 burial mounds, or *mogili.* With each excavation, more is revealed about the advanced craftsmanship of the Thracians—one of the most recent, in August 2006, was a 5,000-year-old dagger made from a superior alloy of gold and platinum.

You can arrange a private tour of some of these tombs through Kazanluk-based **Iskra Historical Museum** (✆ **0431/63762;** Mon–Fri 9am–5:30pm; 15lev/$12/£7.45 per tomb includes an English-speaking guide; if you have problems, ask to speak to Dr. Kosyo Zarev, director of the museum).

The seated man with his arm entwined around that of a pale woman presumed to be his wife is thought to be the nobleman who was buried here.

Tyulbe Park (300m/984 ft. from town center). Tomb replica daily May–Oct 9am–5pm. Admission 5lev ($4.05/£2.50). To view the original call ✆ **0431/63762.** 20lev ($16/£9.90).

Koulata Ethnographic Museum Complex ★★ Located on cobbled Mirska Street in the oldest part of the small town of Kazanluk, this museum complex is near the Kazanluk Thracian Tomb. The complex is made up of 18th- and 19th-century Bulgarian National Revival buildings, which have been restored and open to visitors as a museum since 1976.

Ulitsa Nikola Petkov 18. ✆ **359 04312/17 33.** Mon–Fri 9am–5pm mid-May to mid-Oct. Winter hr. erratic. Inquire at the Iskra Museum. Admission 2lev ($1.30/85p).

Accommodations & Dining

If all this ancient history has built up an appetite, or if you decide to hang around Kazanluk for more than 1 day (and you will if you are visiting more than one tomb), try the following establishments.

Balgaran ★★★ Value BULGARIAN/SERBIAN Twenty-four hectares (60 acres) might sound like a lot of space for a restaurant, but Balgaran, which opened in 2007, makes good use of every inch. From its mini-ethnographic museum to the resident farm animals/petting zoo to the multilevel seating arrangement, Balgaran does everything on a grand scale—except for its prices. There's an oven large enough to roast a whole pig, a space that could accommodate a dozen or more Bulgarian ember dancers, and seating for 800 guests. Even the menu has a dizzying array of offerings. If you are up for it, try the *cheverme,* lamb and pork roasted on a spit (5.80lev/$4.70/£2.90 per 250g).

Starite Lozia. ✆ **359 431/6 49 20.** www.balgaran.com. Entrees 5.55lev–23lev ($4.50–$18/£2.80–£11). No credit cards. Daily 11am–11pm.

Hadji Eminova Kushta ★ It's part of the Ethnographic Museum Complex (see above), an authentic house "museum" with a choice of four rooms along the porch. All are traditionally furnished and feature wonderful carved ceilings. Bathrooms are clean but old, dating from 1976 when the municipal authorities installed them (showers are okay but tubs are unusable). Ask for no. 11 or 14, both of which are spacious. Note that Mr. Dimitros, the charming manager, speaks very little English.

Ulitsa Nikola Petkov 22. ✆ **0431/62595.** 25lev–50lev ($20–$41/£12–£25) double.

Hotel Zornica ★ If you can get past the bubble-gum-pink leather furniture in the lobby, the Zornica is a comfortable place to stay in Kazanluk. Zornica was updated in 2006 and it's bright, pleasant, and loaded with more than the usual amenities for its class, such as both indoor and outdoor swimming pools, an English garden, and saunas. Guest bathrooms have showers, not tubs, but that's a small inconvenience when you consider the price. Currently laptop users can connect to cable in the lobby, but the owners are planning to put Wi-Fi in every room.

Tiulbeto Park, 6100 Kazanluk. ✆ **359 0431/63939.** For information e-mail info@zornica-bg.com. 51 units, including 9 suites. From 110lev ($89/£55) double; from 135lev ($109/£68) suite. MC, V. Free parking. **Amenities:** Restaurant; bar; indoor and outdoor pools; Internet access; lobby safe. *In room:* A/C, cable TV, minibar, hair dryer.

6 VELIKO TARNOVO & ENVIRONS

Veliko Tarnovo 220km (136 miles) from Sofia; 226km (140 miles) from Varna

Veliko Tarnovo was capital of Bulgaria's Second Kingdom from 1185 to 1396, and it was glorified in European circles as "the third city after Rome and the second after Constantinople." Today it is more tiny university town than city, and while it does not have the obvious architectural splendors of more famous Plovdiv, it is in some ways an even more charming destination, surrounded by a natural environment that remains within view even when you're in its urban heart. The imposing medieval citadel of Tsarevets, perched on its own hill from where it glowers down upon the inhabitants it once enclosed, is the town's top sight. From there the lazy Yantra River curls into the guiding arms of the white limestone cliffs from which narrow red-roofed buildings rise precipitously along one bank to overlook the densely vegetated and virtually unpopulated hillsides opposite. It is this undulating green backdrop that gives the place its charm, but it is during the languid summer evenings that the city really comes into its own. Sitting on the cantilevered balcony of one of the city's restaurants as the setting sun turns the narrow dwellings stacked below a soft, pale pink, watching as thousands of birds swoop and dive into the gorge below, you almost could be in a cliff-top village in the Italian Riviera's Cinque Terre, only here the seagulls are swallows, the sea is a tangled forest, and there is hardly a tourist in sight.

The old part of Veliko Tarnovo is pleasant to stroll, but besides enjoying the innate beauty of its geography and the town's particular brand of National Revival architecture—dominated here by Viennese Secession–style wrought-iron balconies—Veliko's chief draw is as a base for (or stopover to) the many day trips that lie within a comfortable radius. They include Tryavna, home to Bulgaria's finest icon and woodcarving museums; Etura, a pretty outdoor ethnographic museum where you also can shop for crafts; the impressive Madara horseman, another of Bulgaria's UNESCO-listed sights; the quaint architectural museum town of Arbanassi; the historic Shipka Pass, gateway to Kazanluk and its famous tomb; as well as 10 nearby monasteries.

ESSENTIALS

GETTING THERE With no stops, Veliko Tarnovo is a 2½-hour drive by car from Sofia. It is not economical to travel by **train** as there is no direct line to the central station (trains from Sofia and Varna pull into Gorna Oryahovitsa, 13km/8 miles north of Veliko Tarnovo, where scheduled trains then connect you to the city, an unwieldy arrangement). By contrast traveling to Veliko Tarnovo by **bus** is fast, convenient, and inexpensive. From

Sofia the journey takes no more than 3 hours, costs 11lev ($8.90/£5.50) one-way (an additional 11lev/$8.90/£5.50 onward to Varna), with buses departing, on average, every 2 hours. Private buses from Sofia and Varna, including those belonging to highly efficient ETAP, pull in at the centrally located tower-block Hotel Etar on Ivailo Street (no matter how convenient the location, do not be tempted to overnight in these overpriced rooms). Buses also arrive here from Plovdiv, a 4-hour journey (13lev/$11/£6.80).

GETTING AROUND The main sites are centered in the old part, which is tiny. In fact, the entire city is so small that you can drive from side to side in about 15 minutes. To get to nearby Arbanassi, order a taxi (5lev/$4.05/£2.50). You can get to Tryavna very easily by bus from the Zapad Bus Terminal, 4km (2½ miles) west of the center; the journey takes around 2 hours. For the other recommended day trips it's best to rent a car. The Tourism Information Centre (see below) can arrange one for 35lev ($28/£17) a day. Bus travel to these destinations is complicated, involving two to three changes with drivers who don't speak English. If you're up for this, speak to the tourism officials for bus schedule details.

VISITOR INFORMATION Veliko Tarnovo has a reasonably helpful Tourism Information Centre, with an English-speaking staff that not only dispenses brochures (including the free city guide; www.veliko-tarnovo.net) but can, if pressed, provide reasonably qualitative advice on where to stay and dine. Be sure also to pick up a copy of *The Frontier Times.* The center is conveniently located just behind the bus terminal, at Hristo Botev Street (✆ **062/622148;** www.velikoturnovo.info; Mon–Sat 9am–6pm Apr–Sept, Oct–Mar closed Sat).

WHERE TO STAY

Ironically enough, Veliko Tarnovo has better standards of accommodations than more famous Plovdiv.

Dryanovo Monastery (Moments) You can stay in most active monasteries for around 10lev ($8.10/£5) per person, but while the locations are almost always sublime, living conditions in the monasteries are often austere (no hot water; shared bathrooms) and, well, less than hygienic. Not so at Dryanovo Monastery. Besides the dormitory rooms (open to men only), the monks have renovated a small wing with en suite rooms for those who expect a little more than a thin mattress—each room has two single beds and a cell-like window that—when open—allows the gushing sound of the river coursing past the fortified walls below to lull you to sleep. Shower rooms are clean (if a tad musty), and don't expect more than a bar of soap by way of toiletries, and a towel only slightly larger than a facecloth. But it's a wonderful thing to witness a long-bearded ascetic in a black cassock enter your name into a massive ledger that has the names of countless pilgrims over the years. If you're happy to forgo this sight there is an even better option within the monastery grounds: **Komplex Vodopadi** is a renovated wing that sports larger, more comfortably furnished rooms (and women are allowed here), with balconies overlooking either the monastery or the river—at exactly the same price, this is the bargain of the Balkans. The other reason this monastery stay is so worthwhile is the restaurant, conveniently located just outside the monastery gates, with tables on a terrace right on the river. **Andaka** scores high on service and food, too—the chicken *kavarma* (chicken, onions, mushrooms, and tomatoes roasted and baked in a ceramic dish) is extremely tasty (if on the small side); best of all, they also open for breakfast.

Dryanovo, 24km (15 miles) south of Veliko Tarnovo. Monastery rooms ✆ **067/6238;** Komplex Vodopadi ✆ **0899147848.** 25lev ($20/£12) double. No credit cards. **Amenities:** Restaurant. *In room:* No phone.

Grand Hotel Yantra ★★ The Yantra definitely is worth consideration for its views, facilities, and decent guest rooms. It is a good value when you consider what you get besides a room (slick spa and wellness center, indoor swimming pool, and wonderful lobby lounge with superb views of the Tsarevets fortress). Despite a 2005 overhaul, however, guest room decor looks as if it were deliberately chosen to be blah, but if you book a suite with a balcony overlooking the fortress, all fashion faux pas are forgiven. Even if your room has a less-than-perfect vantage point, Yantra's restaurant has the best views in the house, including ringside seats for Tsarevets' weekly light and sound show. The only drawbacks are that most of the Yantra's rooms only have a small square hole through which to enjoy this picture-perfect view, and the hallways are downright dingy, especially the carpets. ***Tip:*** The Yantra's spa has a long list of services (including honey and chocolate massages) and the ground-floor souvenir shop is loaded with treasures.

Velchova Zavera Sq. 2. ✆ **359 62/600 607.** Fax 62/606 569. www.yantrabg.com. 71 units, including 11 suites. From 150lev ($122/£76) double on Tsarevets side; from 170lev ($138/£86) suite on Tsarevets side. Rates include breakfast, taxes, and use of the pool and fitness center. **Amenities:** Restaurant; cafe; lobby bar; indoor pool; spa; casino; lobby safe. *In room*: A/C, SAT/TV, Internet connection, minibar, hair dryer.

Hotel Bolyarski ★★★ (Finds) When you drive past the Bolyarski it looks like a well-kept small hotel with a good location. Don't let the hotel's five-story face to the world fool you. The Bolyarski, which was newly built and opened in early 2007, has another persona—the trendy one. With a 15-story, cliff-side wall of glass that looks down on the valley's spectacular scenery and bit of clever architectural engineering, the hotel actually is built 15 stories high into the mountainside, something that can't be seen from the street. That means most rooms are carved into rock below street level and they have great views of the Yantra River and the Monument of the Assens, but that's not all. Bathrooms are loaded with a stash of toiletries and those that have tubs also have Jacuzzis. Creature comforts aside, the Bolyarski's crowning glory is the alfresco barbecue restaurant At the Top on the 15th floor; it is done up in classic Bulgarian folk style and features Bulgarian grilled foods, thanks to a huge brick oven/grill that fills the air with tantalizing aromas. The only negatives are the big-screen TVs in the lobby terrace bar and restaurant that are perpetually tuned to MTV-like stations.

53A Stefan Stambolov St. ✆ **359 62/613 200.** Fax 62/613 222. www.bolyarski.com. 69 units. From 130lev ($105/£53) double with view; from 180lev ($142/£73) suite with view. Rates include breakfast and taxes. MC, V. **Amenities:** Restaurant; lobby bar/cafe; piano bar; spa; Wi-Fi in public spaces; lobby safe. *In room:* A/C, SAT/TV, free Wi-Fi, minibar, hair dryer.

Hotel Gurko ★★★ This geranium- and vine-covered, timbered three-story hotel is located on historic Gurko Street and it is as traditional and charming as they come: Almost all rooms open onto balconies with great views of the hillside and the Yantra River below. Every guest room in this National Revival–era home is spotless and comfortable. Most have double beds, and all have en suite tubs and flatscreen TVs. General use of color and furnishings (plenty of solid timber) is traditional Bulgarian, with some beds covered in traditional bedspreads. This is one of the best options in town: an authentic family-run outfit, cheerful and efficient, with a tavern ★★ on the ground. Wi-Fi is free but the signal doesn't reach all rooms. No matter. You can use your laptop in the lobby, the restaurant, and even on the benches across the street that overlook the valley, and the Gurko has a complimentary computer station reserved for guests without laptops. ***Tip:*** If you stay for more than 3 days, the Gurko staff will do your laundry and ironing free of charge.

33 Gurko St. ✆ **062/627838** or 0888 352 941. www.hotelgurko.hit.bg. 20 units. 55€ ($70) double. No credit cards. Free parking. **Amenities:** Restaurant/bar; excursions; free use of Internet-connected computer and free Wi-Fi for laptops; room service; laundry; elevator. *In room:* A/C, TV, Internet, free Wi-Fi in most rooms, minibar, hair dryer, safe.

Studio Hotel ★★★ Value This stylish hotel is one of the few true boutique hotels in Bulgaria and proves (like the Rako Villa in Bansko) that 21st-century decor and design trends have finally, albeit belatedly (Studio opened in 2006) arrived in Bulgaria a stone's throw from the Cathedral and the Tsarevets fortress. Some of the rooms have great views; book over the weekend in season and catch the light show from your bed. The renovators skillfully gutted an old late-19th-century building, leaving the exterior intact. It's not a cutting-edge concept, but the combination of an old facade hiding an übermodern interior is exhilarating. The palette is restrained (predominantly black, white, and gray) but playful, as evidenced by the plentiful touches of red (like the gorgeous '70s-retro bedside lights in bright red, set against baroque-patterned black-and-white wallpaper). Bathroom fittings are predictably sleek and modern (possibly the best showers in Bulgaria) and the whole experience one of restrained luxury.

4 Todor Lefterov St. ✆ **062/604010** or 062/604009. 13 units. 66€ ($84) double. AE, DC, MC, V. **Amenities:** Restaurant; lobby bar; bar terrace; room service; laundry. *In room:* A/C, TV, Internet connection, minibar.

Tsarevets ★★ The hotel, built in 1891 for the grand Bulgaria Insurance Company, is currently is under U.K. ownership/management. It is also well located in the old part of town—a minute's walk from the Tsarevets fortress gates, 5 minutes from Rakovski Street. It's a small, intimate place, with comfortably furnished, compact rooms. Downside: Showers are on the small side (it's hard to take a shower without wetting the toilet paper).

23 Chitalistna St., Veliko Tarnovo. ✆ **062/601885** or 062/605655. www.tsarevetshotel.com. 9 units. 65€ ($83) double. MC, V. **Amenities:** Breakfast room/lobby bar; concierge and booking service; Internet access; room service; laundry; dry cleaning. *In room:* A/C, TV, minibar, safe, hair dryer.

WHERE TO DINE

The best restaurants all offer wonderful views of the terraced city as it tumbles down to the Yantra below. To make sure you have a table on the edge of the terrace (and believe us, you're on the edge), ask your hotel or driver to book 1 or 2 days in advance, and call again to confirm. If neither Ego nor Shtastlivetsa has a table on the terrace, try **Rich,** 1 Yantra St., located down a flight of steps opposite the Stambolisky monument (✆ **062/27980**). It is owner managed, an exceptionally good value, and it has superb views from the terrace. Whichever restaurant you choose, make sure you end up on cobbled Rakovski Street at **Stratilat,** Veliko Tarnovo's most happening cafe, and collapse in a wicker chair for a postprandial espresso.

At the Top ★★★ The Bolyarski's (see above) signature restaurant is on the hotel's uppermost level, a location that takes advantage of its position overlooking the Yantra Valley and the Veliko Tarnovo Art Museum. But it is the restaurant's concept as an informal alfresco barbecue spot that makes it so inviting. Tables are scattered about the half-covered terrace, which is dominated by a huge brick oven/grill at one end. You can make your meal as simple or as elaborate as you wish, with entrees running the gamut from single skewers of grilled chicken to a hungry-man portion of barbecued veal (800g). ***Tip:*** There is live music most nights.

53A Stefan Stambolov St. ✆ **359 62/613 200.** Fax 62/613 222. www.bolyarski.com. Entrees 8.50lev–80lev ($6.90–$65/£4.30–£40). MC, V. Mon–Fri 4pm–1am; Sat–Sun 11am–1am.

Ego ★ (Value BULGARIAN/PIZZA This cavernous space, with large doors that slide away to the outdoor terrace perched above the Yantra, is just the ticket as the sun goes down, provided you can get a seat in the small alfresco space. Ego has a huge menu (85 salads alone), everything is fresh, and service is fast and friendly, but waitresses speak little to no English and eating in the non-air-conditioned indoor dining room can be unpleasant. If you stop by in summer, opt for the refreshing Tambaktu salad, mango with greens, chopped cucumber, and crumbled blue cheese; or the tasty Ego, a bulgur wheat salad served with peeled and roasted tomatoes, peppers, and eggplant, and finely chopped parsley, garlic, onion, garlic, and walnuts. As is the case at Shtastlivetsa, salad portions are huge, so you'll struggle to find the space for the huge array of good pizzas or traditional Bulgarian offerings on the menu.

17 Stefan Stambalov. ✆ **062/601804.** Reservations for the terrace essential. 2.90lev–11lev ($2.35–$8.90/£1.45–£5.50). No credit cards. Daily noon–11pm.

Gurko Mehana ★★ Gurko isn't at cliff's edge like some of its more glamorous sisters, but alfresco diners have a view of the City Art Museum and Monument of the Assens as well as surrounding cliff-side buildings from the tables that spill outside the stucco and brick dining room onto the sidewalk. All tables are set with red Bulgarian cloths and menus have English translations. Try the Thracian Salad of lettuce, garlic, walnuts, corn, and the best yogurt in Bulgaria. The veggie sache is a mélange of sautéed potatoes, mushrooms, tomatoes, eggplant, zucchini, onion, and carrots baked on a flat earthenware plate that comes to the table sizzling. Add traditional Bulgarian bread (flat grilled pita with butter drizzled on top) and one of the five locally brewed beers on the menu and you have a feast. ***Tip:*** The Gurko is bordered by a cobblestone street, so foot and auto traffic can sometimes be distracting.

33 Gurko St. ✆ **62/627 838.** Fax 62/603 039. www.hotel-gurko.com. Entrees 5.50lev–25lev ($4.45–$20/£2.80–£12). No credit cards. Daily 10am–11:30pm.

Shtastlivetsa ★★ (Value BULGARIAN/PIZZA Walk along Stefan Stambolov, which leads to the old part of town, and look for a restaurant without an empty table and you've found Shtastlivetsa. The locals love this place as much for its huge portions and delicious food as for its prices. It's hardly surprising that Shtastlivetsa serves to a packed house almost every day, despite the opening of another branch at 7 Marno Pole St. For a Bulgarian take on pizza, try the "country bread" with two types of cheese, walnuts, bacon, and apricots; salads are even bigger than Ego's (we're talking a full pound, minimum). The house specialty is meat cooked "in a sache," which is a meat-vegetable combination prepared in or on traditional earthenware. Dishes can be ordered as 450g or 750g (1 lb. or 1½ lb.)—specify the smaller (unless you're sharing) or the waiter probably will "assume" you've ordered the larger portion, which comes with a larger service charge.

79 Stefan Stambalov. ✆ **062/600656.** Reservations for the terrace essential. 5lev–15lev ($4.05–$12/£2.50–£7.45). AE, DC, MC, V. Daily 11am–11pm.

EXPLORING VELIKO TARNOVO ★★★

Touted as the city's top attraction, **Tsarevets fortress** (✆ **062/636 828;** Apr–Sept daily 8am–7pm; Oct–Mar daily 9am–5pm; 5lev/$4.05/£2.50) must have been an incredible sight when the medieval walls that girdle the hill enclosed a royal palace, 18 churches, and over 400 houses, but there's not much left of these grand origins. Besides climbing one of the watchtowers for the views, or heading over to Execution Rock to shudder at the hopefully swift justice meted out to the king's itinerant subjects, the main attraction is the hilltop Patriarch's Church of the Ascension. Declared the "mother of all churches" in the Bulgarian Kingdom in 1235, it was restored in 1981 to commemorate Bulgaria's 1,300th birthday. Interiors are covered with starkly modern murals, executed in an almost monochromatic palette by a student of Svetlin Rusev, one of Bulgaria's most influential expressionists. It's a total contrast to the usual church interior. While a daytime wander around the fortress (plan to get here early or late, rather than during the draining midday heat) is mildly satisfying, the power that Bulgaria's once-impregnable capital exerted over southeastern Europe for 200 years is better captured by the stunning 40-minute **sound and light show ★★★**, when the fortress comes alive in the changing shadows, and stirring music charges through the battlements. The show, held once a week during summer (usually on a weekend night at around 9pm) or whenever a tour group hits town, is best enjoyed from the Assen II Square in front of the main entrance.

Once you've explored the Tsarevets fortress, stroll down to the view the **Churches of Assenova** or "Assen's Quarter," the medieval-era part of town that straddles the banks of the Yantra as it winds through the saddle between Tsarevets and Trapezitsa hills. The area was pretty much destroyed by an earthquake in 1913, but a few of the churches have been restored, the most impressive being the **Sveti Dimitrius of Thessaloniki ★★**, where the *bolyari* (local nobleman) Assen and his brother Peter declared war on their Byzantine oppressors. The beautiful brickwork alternates bands of color with two kinds of brick, mortar, and stone and ceramic inlay for additional texture. It is typical of church construction during medieval times, which was heavily influenced by the Byzantine style, and you'll see more of this in UNESCO-listed Nessebar on the Black Sea coast. Located on the other side of the river is the recently restored **Church of the 40 Martyrs ★★**. Frescoes here date from the 12th and 14th centuries, but the two pillars with inscriptions are what fascinate historians: One has an 8th-century inscription that reads: "Man dies, even though he lives nobly, and another is born. Let the latest born, when he examines these records, remember he who made them. The name of the Prince is Omurtag, the Sublime Khan." Four hundred years later, Tsar Ivan Assen—inspired by the Khan's column—ordered that his victories be inscribed on a similar pillar to let people know how his "benevolence" spared many.

Heading back into town, stop to photograph the pretty facade of the **Museum of the National Revival and Constituent Assembly.** Built in 1872 by the prolific master builder Kolyu Ficheto, who left an indelible imprint on the region (the statue in front is of him), it originally was a Turkish police station, where the 1876 April Uprising rebels were tried. A mere 3 years later the Ottomans finally were defeated and the First Bulgarian Constitution was proclaimed by Bulgaria's newborn parliament in these halls. Exhibits are captioned in Bulgarian, so there is no real reason to enter here or the adjacent **Archaeological Museum.** Either take a look at the **Church of SS Konstantin I Elena** (also built by Kolyu Ficheto), or wander picturesque **Gurko Street.** Besides admiring the tall, narrow 18th- and 19th-century homes (you can enter the **Sarafkina House** at no 88; Wed–Mon 9am–6pm; 4lev/$3.25/£2), the street has wonderful river views. On the opposite bank, perched in front of its own tiny hillock, is the **Monument of the Assens.** This phallic sculpture is a symbol of the city and it commemorates the powerful kings of the Second Kingdom: Assen I, Peter, Kaloyan, and Ivan Assen II, under whose reign the Bulgarian Medieval State reached its zenith. Behind it is the 19th-century building that houses the **City Art Museum,** which is not worth visiting. The other street worth wandering is **Rakovski Street.** It's almost as pretty as Gurko and was once the main trading street. Today it still is lined with well-preserved shops, now touting tourist souvenirs and various artworks of dubious quality. A short stroll farther is the **House of the Little Monkey,** so named for the stone "monkey" attached to the facade of the first floor (centered between the arches), and another building by Kolyu Ficheto featuring his trademark *Fichevska kobilitsa*—the undulating wave that characterizes the roofline of his domestic architecture.

DAY TRIPS FROM VELIKO TARNOVO

With the exception the Madara Horseman and Zheravna, which can be seen en route to Varna or on a day trip from Ruse, most of the following can be combined into 1 day trip (though you'll have to choose one monastery). Note that if you're traveling from Plovdiv, you will be heading up the Shipka Pass to get to Veliko Tarnovo, and could cover Etura and Tryavna, possibly overnighting at Draynovo.

Arbanassi ★★

Located within sight of Veliko Tarnovo on a high plateau 4km (2½ miles) to the northeast, the village of Arbanassi was settled some 300 years ago, and showcases rather severely fortified Bulgarian architecture, with solid stone walls and thick nail-studded gates designed to repel accidental fires or planned incursions. The solidity and sheer size of the houses was both a celebration and a display of wealth, albeit in a rather discreet, austere form. To view the interiors, visit **Kostantsaliev House** (just behind the Kokona fountain; daily 9am–6pm; 4lev/$3.25/£2). But Arbanassi's main attraction is its 15th-century **Church of the Nativity** ★★★ (turn left at the fountain; 4lev/$3.25/£2), with its opulent and glittering interior, a stark contrast to the plain exterior.

Despite the heavy fortification, the village was regularly sacked by Turkish outlaws and the inhabitants gradually were forced to ameliorate with the city that lay shimmering below. Today the carefully restored town has a sleepy feel, with most of the houses either owned by wealthy city dwellers who descend but once a year, or by hoteliers, a situation that leaves the streets virtually empty unless swollen by foreigners. The view of Veliko Tarnovo from the terrace of Arbanassi "Palace," one of the Communist dictator Todor Zhivkov's many holiday homes, is spectacular.

Izvora Mehana ★★ Izvora is one of those restaurants that has so much going on you want to linger long after the meal is over just to check it out. Set in the garden of a hotel by the same name, Izvora is an informal alfresco "folk" tavern (there is also indoor seating) with heavy wood tables, colorful tablecloths, a menu of knock-your-socks-off traditional Bulgarian dishes, plus a garden with water features and assorted birds and barnyard animals scattered about the premises. If you are with a group, service can be family style with waiters bringing huge wooden trays laden with grilled meats and vegetables. Or, you can opt for conventional service. In any case, try the Hunter's Rabbit, tidbits of rabbit, ham, potatoes, carrots, mushrooms, onions, and pickled cucumbers, all cooked together on a clay dish.

5029 Arbanassi. ✆ **359 62/601 205.** Fax 62/601 206. www.izvora.com. Entrees 8lev–23lev ($6.50–$19/£4.05–£12). AE, MC, V. Daily 11am–midnight.

The White House ★★ (Finds) Arbanassi resident Ginka Stefanov is a retired teacher and her husband Todor a retired economist, and they operate a semi-agri B&B that gives guests the opportunity to live as Bulgarians do and to dine on meals prepared from the produce grown in Ginka's bountiful vegetable garden out back. Don't expect the Ritz; rather, immerse yourself in genuine Bulgaria in the company of two of the country's most gracious hosts. Each of the four rooms is comfortable and each has a different floor plan.

You will have to get used to showers without stalls: To shower, you just pull a cord in the en suite bathroom and hot water from the tank on the wall washes over you and into the drain in the floor.

5029 Arbanassi, opposite the entrance to Holy Nativity Church. ✆ **359 62/631 342.** 4 units. From 45lev ($36/£22) double. Breakfast is an additional 5lev ($4.05/£2.50) per person. Other 3-course meals with wine are available starting at 15lev ($12/£7.45) per person. No credit cards. *In room:* TV.

Tryavna, Etura & Environs ★★★

Tryavna ★★★ was established by refugees who escaped the fall of Tarnovo 400 years ago, but the old town's predominantly timber buildings, 140 of which are listed, date from when the village established the official Guild of Master Builders and Woodcarvers in 1804. Start wandering from the charming old town square, where village elders play card games under a spreading tree. The **tourism office,** 22 Angel Kunchev St., is just off the main square and it is useful for a map (✆ **359 0677/22 47;** Mon–Fri 9am–noon and 2–5pm). ***Note:*** All the museums (except the Icon, which opens an hr. later) are open daily 9am to 6pm in summer and 8am to 5pm in winter, and charge 2lev ($1.60/£1). The museums are also all located on the same street: P.R. Slaveikov Ulitsa. Of interest on the town square are the **Church of Archangel Michael** where the lovely iconostasis was painted by the local Vitanov family, Tryavna's most talented icon painters(Kapitan Dyado Nikola Place; ✆ 359 0577 34 42; daily 7am–7pm) and the 1839 **Old School.** But the real reason you're here is to see the museum of woodcarving, so head over the bridge to stroll down gorgeous cobbled **Slaveykov Street.** (Note the house on your right as you cross the bridge; owned by **Zograff Inn,** the two recently renovated rooms overlooking the river are by far the best deal in town; call ✆ **0677/4970;** ask for no. 21, a steal at 50lev [$40/£25]; www.bgglobe.net/zograf.html).

More or less in the center of Slaveykov, clearly marked, is the **Woodcarving Museum,** aka Daskalov's House (Ulitsa Slaveykov 27a; ✆ **359 0677 21 66;** Apr–Sept daily 9am–6pm; Oct–Mar daily 8am–4:30pm). On the first floor you can compare two of the most singularly beautiful ceilings, the result of a competition between Master Dimitur Zlatev and his then apprentice, Ivan Bochukovetsa. Upstairs is another amazing feat: carved portraits by Master Gencho Marangozov of Bulgarian heroes commissioned by another wealthy trader for his Patriotic Room.

From here it's an uphill hike to the **Tryavna Icon Museum** ★★ (Ulitsa Breza 1; ✆ **359 0677 237 53;** Apr–Oct daily 10am–6pm; Nov–Mar daily 8am–noon and 12:30–4:30pm), but well worth the effort. The most impressive work is in the first-floor room on the right, which contains the work of the Vitanov and Zachariev families. Inspired by the work on display here, you may want to take home a quality icon. Head for nearby **Etura** ★★★ (Apr–Oct daily 9am–6pm; Nov–Mar daily 8am–5pm; 6lev/$4.85/£3), an outdoor ethnographic museum where various crafts are produced by masters using traditional 19th-century methods. The Icon Studio is where you'll find Plamen Malinov and Rossen Donchev plying their trade and you'll pay more for one of their icons than you do for one on the streets, but both are acknowledged to be masters (this is a prerequisite for having any workshop in Etura). In a lovely location on the banks of a burbling stream (which powers much of the equipment), this will be one of your most delightful shopping expeditions in Bulgaria—unless you don't have cash, because no one here takes credit cards. Be sure to stop for lunch at the **Domestic Revival Tavern,** the ethno village's signature restaurant (no phone; entrees 5.20lev–18lev/$4.20–$15/£2.60–£9.30; no credit cards; Apr–Oct daily 11am–6pm, Nov–Mar 11am–5pm). Picnic tables are set in the garden out front under big leafy trees and covered with embroidered

Bulgarian tablecloths and little dishes of *chubritsa.* Bulgarian singers add to the folksy vibe, which is continued on the menu. Try a pepper *burek,* a filo dough purse filled with chopped, seasoned peppers; or *tarator,* a soup made of yogurt, cucumbers, onions, and dill. Whatever you order, don't miss the crusty round loaves of bread, which are baked in one of Etura's crafts exhibitions and served with *lyutanitza,* a seasoned red-pepper purée. It's directly across from the waterfall washtub.

Surrounding Monasteries ★★★ Twenty monasteries were built around Veliko Tarnovo during its zenith as capital of the Second Kingdom; 10 are within a half-hour drive. One of the closest is pretty **Preobrazhenski Monastery.** Follow the winding forest road that branches off the highway heading north to the Danube city of Ruse, and suddenly the trees clear to provide glorious uninterrupted views of the hills and valleys beyond. This sublime spot is where the Jewish wife of Ivan Aleksandur decided to celebrate her conversion to Christianity by building **Preobrazhenski,** meaning "Transfiguration," in 1360. Still officially "active," but guarded only by a monk, the monastery itself is largely in ruins, but the church frescoes are undergoing restoration. Don't miss Zahari Zograf's *Wheel of Life* on the south wall. Directly across the valley, also surrounded by dense vegetation, you can see the **Sveta Troitsa Convent.** There are other gems, like the **Kapinovo, Kilifarevo,** and **Plakovo** monasteries, but if you're looking for a lunch or dinnertime venue, head into the gorge that protects laid-back **Dryanovski Monastery,** as much for its peaceful riverside location and friendly monks, and stop for lunch at **Andaka,** the lovely riverside restaurant (see "Where to Stay," above). And if you have decided to include Etura in your itinerary, be sure to fill up a bottle with the sweet-tasting water from nearby **Sokolovski,** meaning "the Falcons"—appropriate, given the views.

Shipka Pass and Church ★ About 60km (37 miles) south of Veliko Tarnovo, on the road to or from Kazanluk, you will traverse the historic Shipka Pass, scene of the most momentous battle between Russian-Bulgarian and Turkish forces in 1877, a battle that decided the fate of the war and delivered a decisive blow to the Ottomans. There are two monuments to mark the battle. One is the rather stern six-story **Freedom Monument** (daily 9am–5pm; 2lev/$1.60/£1), which requires a fair degree of stamina—it's a steep flight of stairs just to the entrance, then many more to reach the top to take in the awesome views of the Balkan Mountains; and the Valley of the Kings (including Kazanluk—a tiny, sprawling insect nest below). More accessible is the picture-perfect gold-domed **Church Monument.** Located at the foot of the pass, this—like Alexander Nevski in Sofia—commemorates the Bulgarian and Russian lives lost during the 1877 to 1878 War of Liberation.

Zheravna ★★★ The charming architectural museum town of Zheravna is a contrast to Arbanassi and more authentic, thanks the town's local population (about 700). Depending on road conditions, this seldom-visited village lies 2 to 3 hours from Veliko Tarnovo, making it more suitable as an overnight stop on your way to the coast rather than as a day trip. But if you have not had a chance to explore the little museum towns scattered in the Pirin and Rhodope mountains, this is a must-see on your itinerary. A hodgepodge of cobbled streets lined with gorgeous 17th-century timber homes shaded by trees and sometimes covered with vines makes Zheravna pure, undistilled rural bliss. The most comfortable place to overnight is **Hotel Liv** (**© 088 978 3971;** www.hoteliv.com; 50lev/$40/£25 double, including breakfast), two 300-year-old homes recently renovated by Ivan and Vanya, who came here on holiday and fell in love with the village.

Madara Horseman ★★ Lying just over the halfway mark between Veliko Tarnovo and Varna, the UNESCO-listed Madara Horseman, a 95m-high (312 ft.) relief sculpture, was carved into the cliff more than 1,200 years ago. At least, the Greek inscriptions next to the carving date from the 8th century. Some believe the horseman predates these by many more hundreds of years, and is in fact the rider-god so revered by the Thracians. The relief is best viewed early morning (opens daily at 8am), or as the suns starts to set (closes 7pm in summer; 5pm in winter) when shadows help sharpen the lines of the horseman, whose steed appears to be trampling a lion, aided by his greyhound. The **Madara National History Archaeological Reserve** (admission 4lev/$3.25/£2) also comprises the remains of 8th- and 9th-century monasteries (also those of a 14th-century rock monastery), and you can take the cliff path up to the plateau above, where there are more ruins, this time of a 5th-century fortress, and wonderful views.

7 VARNA & THE BLACK SEA COAST

449km (278 miles) east of Sofia

Long the premier summer destination for the Eastern bloc, this heavily developed coastline is now a playground to hordes of package tourists from the West, keen to dance the night away at the numerous makeshift summer clubs along the coast. But when the sun rises and the shadows drawback to reveal the development that lines some of the beaches, it's a cluttered sight.

Bulgaria's once pristine coastline has been overdeveloped north of St. Konstantin, though between there and Varna the landscape just looks like prosperous resort property. But despite the crowds, a trip that incorporates a few days on the Black Sea Coast can be a good experience. Besides blowing off steam on the coastal capital's beachfront, it's worth coming this far just to view the "oldest gold in the world" in Varna's Historical Museum, which compares favorably with the National History Museum in Sofia as the most fascinating museum in the country. Afterward, head south to stroll past Byzantine churches and charming 19th-century timber houses in the UNESCO-listed village of Nessebar. Admittedly, Nessebar's cobbled streets can get clogged with day-trippers, but this is an excuse to head south to the gorgeous old town of Sozopol, with its plethora of seaside restaurants. Time your visit for lunch and, mesmerized by semitranslucent twinkling sea views, you'd be forgiven for thinking you were on the Riviera . . . only better, you realize, when the bill arrives.

ESSENTIALS

GETTING THERE From late April to October you can reach Varna by **plane,** either flying from Sofia or even direct to **Varna airport** (24-hr. flight information ✆ **052 573 323;** www.varna-airport.bg) or to **Bourgas airport** (www.Bourgas-airport.com). Most travelers, however, arrive by **road,** traveling from Sofia via Veliko Tarnovo or heading directly east to Bourgas and then turning north to Varna or south to Sozopol. Bank on spending around 5 hours in a car, 6 if you're traveling by bus (24lev/$19/£12). Buses arrive at the Central Bus Station (✆ **052/448 349**) on 158 Vladislav Varnenchik Blvd. For **trains** add at another 2 hours (✆ **052/630 414;** www.bdz.bg).

GETTING AROUND The easiest way to get around the main attractions in Varna, located within the compact area of its Sea Gardens and Maria Luiza and Suborni streets, is on foot. If you need a cab to explore farther afield, call Lacia at ✆ **052/500-000,** or

Maxa at ✆ **052/303 030** or 0888 308 050. If you have flown in, you can rent a car from one of the many reputable car-rental companies in town (www.avis.bg, www.hertz.bg, www.toprentacar.bg). If you wish to catch a bus to or from Nessebar (1½–2 hr. ride south), purchase your ticket from ETAP (at most of the larger hotels) then head to 7 Dobrovoltsi St. (✆ **052/448-349**).

VISITOR INFORMATION The **Regional Tourism Information Centre** is located at 36 Tsar Osvoboditel Sq. (✆ **052/602907;** www.tourexpo.bg; Mon–Fri 9am–7pm, Sat 9am–1pm).

WHERE TO STAY

Budget travelers need look no further than **Hostel Kushtata** (✆ **052/639660/1;** www.hostelkushtata.com). Centrally located, with seven bright, light en suite double rooms in a pale-yellow, century-old house overlooking a quiet leafy lane (only 50m/164 ft. from the beach) it's more B&B than hostel, with added extras like bicycles and room service, and good value at just 30€ ($38) per room.

Aqua Hotel ★ This businessman's hotel is close enough to Varna's shopping plazas and the sea to be convenient and far enough away to be out of the action. If you don't mind a 20-minute walk and are on a budget but need efficiency and perks, this is the place for you. Rooms are frugally done in blue utilitarian particleboard furniture, but bathrooms are lavishly tiled even if they just have showers. Breakfast in the first-floor dining room is a generous buffet of cheeses, cereal, yogurt, fruits, meats, and hot entrees of eggs and sausages. There is a nice ration of electrical outlets in each room and the free wireless is a boon.

12 Devnya St. ✆ **359 52/63 90 90.** Fax 52/63 13 90. www.aquahotels.com. 78 units, including 8 suites. From 170lev ($138/£86) double June–Sept, from 150lev ($122/£76) Oct–May; from 220lev ($178/£110) suite June–Sept, from 200lev ($162/£100) Oct–May. Rates include breakfast, taxes, and hotel insurance. MC, V. Free parking. **Amenities:** Restaurant; cafe; bar; fitness center; lobby safe. *In room:* A/C, SAT/TV, free Wi-Fi, minibar, hair dryer.

Grand Hotel Musala Palace ★★★ A grand old turn-of-the-20th-century hotel, this is a small, intimate boutique option with every one of its five stars well deserved. Rooms are inspired by the deep, rich comfort of a country club, with decor touches ranging from Louis XV–style wingback chairs to Regency-style curtain drapery, plus a few antiques and gilt-framed mirrors thrown in for good measure. Bathrooms, too, reflect the fact that the hotel was recently renovated. Standard rooms are very comfortable, but if it's a special occasion or money is no object, this is one place where it's worth splurging on a deluxe or studio. The hotel is in the center of town and strolling distance from the seafront, recommended restaurants, and archaeological museums. The only possible drawback is that once you are comfortably ensconced in your room you could be in a landlocked capital anywhere in Europe.

3 Musala St., Varna 9000. ✆ **052/664100.** Fax 052/664196. www.musalapalace.bg. 24 units. Fri–Sun 150€–185€ ($191–$235) double, Mon–Thurs 190€–230€ ($241–$292) double; 205€–250€ ($260–$318) suite, depending on day. Rates include breakfast. AE, DC, MC, V. Valet parking. **Amenities:** Restaurant; lobby bar/cafe terrace; wellness center and fitness center; transport services; business services; room service; laundry; dry cleaning. *In room:* A/C, TV, Internet connection, minibar, hair dryer, safe.

Hotel Odessos ★★ Value Location, location, location is the mantra for the Hotel Odessos, which occupies real estate just across from the portal to the Sea Garden and Varna's beach. The Odessos was built in the Socialist Drab style, and thanks to continuous renovation over the last 5 years, it is now a curious mix of capitalist comfort and

Communist cramping. However, the Odessos's sea-facing rooms can't be beat for the view and you can be comfortable here even if you and your luggage have to take separate elevators to your floor. ***Tip:*** All sea-view rooms have balconies and bathtubs and the two-bedroom, two-bath apartment is a roomy steal for family vacations.

1 Slivnica Blvd. ✆ **359 52/640 300.** Fax 52/630 403. www.odessos-bg.com. 94 units, including 4 suites. From 140lev ($113/£70) sea-view double; from 255lev ($207/£128) sea-view suite. MC, V. Free parking. **Amenities:** Restaurant; cafe; excursions; gift shop; hairdresser; room service; elevator; lobby safe. *In room:* A/C, SAT/TV, hair dryer.

Hotel Panorama ★★ The Panorama is perfectly positioned: walking distance from the sea, restaurants, and shopping, and it has an architectural design that gives most rooms a view of the water. Built in 2004, Panorama's guest rooms are equipped with all the aesthetics and conveniences required in the electronic age. The only drawback is the rather indifferent staff.

31 Primorski Blvd. ✆ **359 52/62 60 31.** Fax 52/62 60 33. www.panoramabg.com. 57 units. From 175lev ($142/£88) double; from 240lev ($194/£120) suite. Rates include breakfast and taxes. **Amenities:** Restaurant; bar; fitness room; garage; valet services; elevator. *In room:* A/C, SAT/TV, free LAN Internet access, minibar, hair dryer, bathtub.

WHERE TO DINE

Sofia may be the cuisine capital of Bulgaria, but when it comes to informal dining, Varna blows the socks off its big sister. Cafes and snack bars line the evening *korso* that stretches from Nezavisimost Square to the Slivnitsa before it spills onto the beach. Here, sandwiched between the city's Sea Gardens and the long curve of its sandy beach, is a wide ribbon of makeshift beach restaurants and bars that curve out from the harbor, finally petering out some 5 to 8km (3–5 miles) north. You can wander along and simply stop at the first place that takes your fancy: The backdrop—a deep sandy beach, lapped by the gentle waters of the Black Sea—is hard to beat. Rated the best fish restaurant by locals, **BM Zaliva** marks the southern tip of the beach. It's a great informal dive (plastic chairs; toes in the sand) where you could opt for a simple sesame-encrusted hake, a hunk of breaded shark, a meaty pan-fried red mullet, or the pricey turbot, fried in garlic and olive oil. But if you've had enough of the thumping beachfront scene, make sure you sample one of the following.

Bistro Europe ★★ Classic preparations and uncomplicated recipes are part of the philosophy that guides the selection of Bistro Europe's menu items. It looks like just another sidewalk cafe on restaurant-lined Slivnitsa Street, but Bistro Europe is much more. Try a slice of quiche or 1 of 10 mussel preparations for a light supper, or choose one of the plates with lots of veggie garnishes. Dining here is a pleasant no-brainer.

11 Slivnitsa. ✆ **359 52/60 39 50.** www.lagarde.bg. Entrees 6lev–26lev ($4.85–$21/£3–£13). MC, V. Daily 8am–midnight.

Kopitoto ★★★ *Finds* BULGARIAN "Folk restaurant" might be the best way to describe Kopitoto, which is located about 10 minutes north of Varna in St. Konstantin on the road toward Sunny Beach. The restaurant is huge and the best part is the outdoor garden section, which is a mass of dark-wood bench tables in alcoves and others set under an arbor of roses and grape vines. Bulgarian bells and other folk objects are used in the decor and there is a fire pit in the center that provides ashes for the nightly "ember dance" during which dancers stomp around on warm ashes to music. Entertainment aside, you should go to Kopitoto (translated as "horse hoof") for traditional Bulgarian food like *satch,* a combination of chicken, mushrooms, turkey, onion, yellow cheese, peas, corn, and chili cooked on a shallow earthenware plate, or *zapekanka,* a similar ingredient combination baked in an earthenware pot.

St. Konstantin and Helena Resort 5km (3 miles) south of Varna. ✆ **359 52/98 87 68.** http://kopitoto.net/eng.html. Entrees 7.90lev–25lev ($6.40–$20/£3.95–£12). No credit cards. Daily 10:30am–midnight.

Mr. Baba ★★★ Finds SEAFOOD Artist/teacher Stella Canfield, a Bulgarian national who divides her time between her homes in Seattle and Bulgaria and sponsors groups on painting trips to Bulgaria, told us that she takes all her visitors to Mr. Baba, her favorite restaurant in Varna. Mr. Baba's tables are in an atmospheric, wooden schooner permanently anchored in the harbor and the seafood couldn't be fresher. It is the ambience that makes everything taste so good, especially if you ask for an outside table on the upper deck with views of the beach and sea. The menu lists a nice array of salads, a long repertoire of grilled seafood, and even crocodile with prosciutto and pepper. A tall but entertaining tale about the Mr. Baba responsible for the restaurant's recipes is printed on the menus.

On the beach at Morska Gora (about a block south of the Panorama Hotel). ✆ **359 052/615 629.** Entrees 7.90lev–45lev ($6.40–$36/£3.95–£22). MC, V. Daily 8am–midnight.

Orient ★★ Value TURKISH "Poor quality prepared food will not be paid" [sic] says the menu, then, "In the event you're met unkindly or without a smile you have the right to require another waiter." This unpretentious restaurant, watched like a hawk by the large and friendly Turkish proprietor, treats the customer as king, and backs it up by the most wonderful food. The array of breads—stuffed or coated like pizzas with cheeses, olives, and meats—is fabulous, as are the roasted vegetables, stuffed with delicately spiced meats. Menus are illustrated with clear photographs and brief English descriptions, so ordering is relatively easy, though the huge list of mouthwatering choices does not preclude this from being a lengthy, drawn-out process.

1 Tzaribrod St. ✆ **052/602 380.** www.orientbg.com. Main courses 2.50lev–10lev ($2–$8.10/£1.25–£5). No credit cards. Daily 8am–11:30pm.

Prodadena Nevesta ★★★ Value BULGARIAN/INTERNATIONAL Owned by local photographer Nikolai Hristakiev, this restaurant located opposite the registry office in an old timber house is a popular choice with Varna foodies, who clamber upstairs to the cozy, wood-paneled rooms, almost every inch covered with bookshelves and wine racks (550 different labels on offer). There is no English menu, but some of the staff speak English and will ask you what you feel like eating. They might run through favorites like the bean soup, redolent with Bulgarian mint, and point out rarities like the very traditional but usually homemade *poparasis serena,* crusty bread with white cheese, butter, sugar, red pepper, and paprika. If you're really hungry, try the mixed grill served with fresh cucumber, tomato, and home-cut potato chips (ask for the latter to be fried with garlic and dill); or the pork loin slow fried with bacon, gherkins, and mushrooms, then slow baked with cheese.

1 Kralo Marko St. ✆ **0888 641 440.** Main courses 5lev–10lev ($4.05–$8.10/£2.50–£5). MC, V. Daily 11:30am–midnight.

EXPLORING VARNA

Driving into Varna, so-called "pearl" of the Black Sea, you can be forgiven for wondering what you're doing in this run-down port surrounded by ugly Socialist-era architecture and visually cut off from the sea by an overgrown and unkempt garden, but stay a day or two and Varna's cosmopolitan vibe starts to creep under your skin. Varna is Bulgaria's

Finds The Art of Travel

Artist Stella Canfield was born in Bulgaria, but in 1985 she moved to the U.S., where she enjoyed a successful career as a painter and teacher. Today, the personable Stella divides her time between a house in Coupeville, Washington, and her country home near Varna, from which she organizes "Adventure Artist Tours" in Bulgaria. Stella says the tours let participants "absorb the essence of these ancient cultures, while you document the entire adventure with your own drawings and paintings." Stella says the tours attract artists and nonartists alike, all of whom get to know Bulgarian people as they set up their easels at harbors, in front of churches, and wherever they see beauty. Proceeds from the trips help support an orphanage near Stella's Varna home through the Stellar Arts Foundation, which she founded as a way of giving back. The cost of Stella's 14-day, 2008 escorted tour in Bulgaria was $2,850 (£1,425), and it included (besides painting instruction) accommodations, transfers, sightseeing and entrance fees, breakfast, lunch, and six dinners. For more information contact Stellar Arts Foundation, Adventure Artist's Tour, P.O. Box 1676, Coupeville, WA 98239 (✆ **360.678.0838;** www.stellararts.org).

main naval and commercial shipping port. It is adjacent to the coastal resorts of Golden Sands, St. Konstantin, and Albena and it has an interesting edge, sharpened by the huge annual influx of foreigners and young Sofiates in summer. Most come to Varna for the overcrowded beaches and pedestrian walkways, and they inject energy into the endless disco beat. This in itself is not reason enough to include the Black Sea capital on your itinerary, but Varna's real draw, even if you're not a history buff, is its archaeological museum (see below).

If you still have energy after visiting the museum, you could take the short stroll west to the city's other notable site: the huge gold-domed **Assumption of the Holy Virgin Cathedral,** on ploshtad Mitropolitska Simeon. From here, you can explore the **Open Market** opposite, coming out at Rousse Street, where there is an excellent souvenir shop, the **Bulgarian Art Shop,** 19 Rousse St. (✆ **052/622299**). Head down Rousse to view the neo-baroque **Opera House** (✆ **052/650-555;** www.operavarna.bg) on **Nezavisimost Square,** center of the city's cultural life since 1932. It offers a host of shows, including a few modern and traditional ballets, and plenty of operas and operettas during the **International Music Festival Varna Summer,** held at the end of July (though shows start mid-June). Having checked what's showing that night, amble down to view the city's 1,700-year-old **Roman Thermae,** at ul Khan Krum and San Stefano (Tues–Sun 10am–5pm; 3lev/$2.45/£1.50), one of the largest ancient Roman ruins in Bulgaria.

Varna Archaeological Museum ★★★ Nothing brings home just how ancient Bulgaria's history is than wandering through the 21 rooms of this museum, viewing exhibits that are not only inconceivably old but also unbelievably sophisticated. Flint tools, some dating from 10,000 B.C., provide proof of just how long ago Bulgaria was inhabited. But it is when you enter the halls that exhibit artifacts from the 294 graves uncovered in the Varna Eneolithic Necropolis that you realize this region was one of the great cultural centers of the ancient world. Besides the complicated burial rituals (corpses were carefully arranged in various positions, and there also were numerous "symbolic" graves), there is the sheer quantity of gold found, providing an exceptionally rich inventory of goldsmith techniques 6,200 years ago. But even more jaw-dropping is the gold dating from the 3rd and 4th century B.C., in which the skills of the goldsmiths had developed to the extent that the fine features and billowing drapery of a figurine of Victory so tiny—a gold jewelry item found in the tomb of a Thracian woman—can only fully be appreciated when studied with a magnifying glass.

41 Maria-Luiza Blvd. ✆ **052/681 030** or 052/681 011. www.varna-bg.com/museums/archaeology/enexhibit. Admission 10lev ($8.10/£5). Tues–Sun 10am–5pm.

NESSEBAR ★★

A rocky "island" connected to the mainland by a short isthmus, Nessebar boasts the finest collection of 19th-century timber homes on the coast, as well as the largest collection of Byzantine-influenced churches. Exploring the tiny port is a wonderful experience if you stick to Old Nessabar. Both Old and New Nessabar are resort towns with all the pluses (facilities and attractions) and minuses (overcrowding and commercialism) that entails.

Only 850m (2,788 ft.) long and 350m (1,148 ft.) long, Nessebar is easy to cover and should take no more than a couple of hours—you can pick up a map from the **Archaeological Museum,** 2 Mesembria (Mon–Sat 9am–noon and 1–5pm; 3lev/$2.45/£1.50), which is to the right of the Byzantine town gate (A.D. 500). Inside you'll find some of the best bits taken from the surrounding churches as well as a few ancient exhibits, like the 3,000-year-old stone anchor and the 200 B.C. statue of Hecate, goddess of witches and fertility. A short stroll down Mesembria brings you to the 14th-century **Pantokrator Church ★★**. Of the 11 churches in Nessebar, this stone-and-redbrick church is the best preserved and has by far the prettiest, most photogenic exterior but, like most of Nessebar's churches, it serves as a gallery showcasing mediocre artists. Take the left-hand fork north to pass Church of St. John the Baptist, stopping to enter **Sveti Spas** (Church of the Saviour; Mon–Fri 10am–5:30pm, Sat–Sun 10am–1:30pm; 3lev/$2.45/£1.50). Built in 1609, this is one of only two churches that have frescoes well enough preserved to warrant a small admission; the other is **St. Stefan Church ★★** (daily 9am–6pm; 3lev/$2.45/£1.50). To the north and west of Sveti Spas is a meandering network of narrow cobbled lanes that spreads to the shore, along which you'll find the remaining five churches—the only one worth entering is **Sveta Bogoroditsa** for a brief view of its icons and carved bishop's throne. More or less in the center of Old Nessebar you can't miss the ruins of **St. Sofia Church,** built in the late 5th and early 6th century, and today surrounded by shops and tables where you can catch a quick espresso and a sandwich.

Where to Stay

If you need to spend the night (Nessebar is only 90 min. from Varna), the most atmospheric places lie within the old quarter. **Trinity ★★** (✆ **0554/46700;** www.trinity-nessebar.com) is a small, custom-built, modern hotel built in traditional timber-and-stone style. It is a good option, with professional service standards and rooms done in tasteful modern neutrals. Ask for a double room (all are twin-bedded) with a balcony and sea view, preferably on the second floor—nos. 9 and 10 are best. At 100lev to 150lev ($81–$122/£50–£76) double (studios from 120lev/$97/£60), Trinity is a good-value option, particularly compared with Varna hotels in the same price category. Virtually neighboring Trinity, cozy **Monte Christo** (✆ **0554/42055;** www.montecristo-bg.com;

95lev–125lev/$77–$101/£48–£62 double), with its more old-fashioned styling, is an equally good choice. For the best views book no. A8.

Alternatively, check out **St. Stefan Hotel,** 11 Ribarska St. (✆ **55/443 603;** fax 55/443 604; www.infotour.org). Meticulous attention to detail and genuine concern about guests' needs make this gem in the heart of Old Nessebar the best hotel in town. St. Stefan, which opened in 2000, is across the street from the church of the same name, one of only two churches in town with knockout, centuries-old icons inside. Each guest room is a different shape because this is a timbered house with irregular spaces. Ask for a room facing the sea and you will be rewarded with a fabulous view. Ask for no. 401, a suite, and you will get that plus room to spread out and the sounds of music from the nearby amphitheater if you open your window. Doubles start at 110lev ($89/£55) June through September, and 85lev ($69/£43) other times. Plan to add 5% if you use a credit card.

Where to Dine

There are a many places to eat in Nessebar, but be warned: The city's restaurateurs don't have to work at their cuisine standards to fill their tables, and some don't. Try one of the places below and you can't go wrong.

Kapitanska Sreschta (Captain's Table) ★ SEAFOOD Just head for the small fishing boat harbor and look out for the life-size statues in nautical T-shirts at the Captain's Table. "Fish on a tile" is a recommended house specialty, as are mussels, prepared and served in any way you can think of. This is one of the quieter, most scenic dining spots in Nessebar.

Chaika St. ✆ **0554/42124.** 5.90lev–20lev ($4.80–$16/£3–£9.90). Daily 11am–midnight.

Zornitza ★★★ (Finds SEAFOOD/BULGARIAN There is no better setting for dining in Old Nessebar than Zornitza, a terraced restaurant that opens to the sea breezes and view. Add to that an attentive, friendly staff and superb food and you have a can't-miss combination. Menus are tourist-friendly, with selections translated into four languages and it *is* a popular stop for tour groups, but the food doesn't suffer because of it and the prices haven't been jacked up to gouge foreigners either. Try the fried salmon with dill or the veal with mushrooms, or one of the grilled meat skewers, but don't miss the bread filled with garlic and white cheese topped with yellow cheese. It's a cross between pizza and calzone that will make your taste buds dance. ***Tip:*** Zornitza has a sister restaurant, Sevina, next door with the same view and menu, and both are open year round.

End of Ribarska St. at the water. ✆ **359 55/445 231.** www.zornitza.info. Entrees 8.90lev–24lev ($7.20–$19/£4.45–£12). MC, V. Daily 9am "till the last customer leaves."

8 THE DANUBIAN PLAIN

Bulgaria's Danubian Plain stretches from the northern Balkan range to the Danube River Valley with a patchwork of gold and green topography that is a colorful overlay on the plain's gentle hills and valleys. Almost nothing man-made interrupts the ever-changing patterns until you get to the river and the Austro-Hungarian-flavored town of Ruse. Nonetheless, even before you get to that sparkling Bulgarian river town, there are a few must-see gems sprinkled among the wheat and sunflower fields that cover almost 325km (200 miles) of northern Bulgaria.

RUSE

325km (200 miles) northeast of Sofia

Bulgarians refer to Ruse as "Little Vienna," a moniker that aptly describes the atmosphere of this Danubian town on the country's northern river border. Yes, Ruse has its share of ugly concrete towers, but that visual insult is overshadowed by the gorgeous Art Nouveau–style homes and public buildings that dominate its downtown. Unlike the dour, silent, heads-down demeanor of people on the streets of Sofia, there is a palpable *joie de vivre* among the folks on the streets of Ruse that is contagious. Perhaps it's because Ruse once was a transit city for travelers going from Central Europe to Istanbul, or perhaps it's because of the city's vibrant cafe society, several important cultural attractions, hotels, and restaurants that actually cater to the customer, and one of the most interesting, active promenades in Bulgaria. Whatever the reason, Ruse is a place where you can almost feel people shedding their stress as they mingle on the *korso.* It's a place where you will feel relaxed and welcome to become part of the party. If only the city fathers would clean up the riverfront.

Getting There & Getting Around

Ruse is accessible by train or bus, though we don't recommend that you ride the rails to Ruse or spend any time in its derelict-looking train station. Both terminals are about 2km (1¼ miles) south of the center on Borisova Ulitsa and you can catch a trolley (nos. 1, 11, 12, or 18) at either that goes to Ploshtad Svoboda (Liberation Sq.), the city's main gathering place. Avoid the unscrupulous taxi drivers if you can. If you are looking for accommodations, steer clear of "entrepreneurs" advertising rooms for rent and go to Dunav Tours, just southwest of Liberation Square, pl Han Kubrat 5 (© **359 082/223 088;** Mon–Fri 9am–12:30pm and 1–5:30pm), to secure private accommodations. Or try one of the options recommended below.

Where to Stay

Ruse has a variety of accommodations options. Be sure you choose a place that has either been recently renovated or recently built, and stay within walking distance of Liberation Square if you can.

Cosmopolitan Hotel ★★★ (Finds The level of sophistication, service, and value in this full-service hotel that opened in March 2008 is in another stratosphere in contrast to the service in the rest of Bulgaria. From the moment you walk into the lobby with its frosted-glass-art reception desk and view of the spectacular mosaic waterfall on the terrace, you know you're in a special place. Guest rooms are done with an eye to convenience and luxury, with flatscreen plasmas, bathtubs, in-room Wi-Fi, and the liberal use of original artwork. Even if you don't book it, check out the knockout two-story suite with its leather couch and loft bedroom. Add a world-class spa with Turkish steam bath and infrared sauna, a rooftop pool and terrace, the Cosmopolitan World Cuisine restaurant (see below), and a plethora of complimentary services, and you have a runaway winner.

1–3 Dobri Nemirov. © **359 82/80 50 50.** Fax 82/80 50 57. www.cosmopolitanhotelbg.com. 60 units, including 7 suites. From 80€ ($101) double; from 130€ ($165) suite. Rates include breakfast, VAT, parking, and use of the spa swimming pool. DC, MC, V. Parking 20lev ($16/£9.95) per day. **Amenities:** Restaurant; lobby bar; bar; Wi-Fi; room service; valet service; spa; elevator. *In room:* A/C, SAT/TV, minibar, hair dryer, Pierre Cardin toiletries in the suites (house brands in other rooms).

Hotel Princess Anna ★★ Finds Ruse's History Museum was steps from the Danube when the museum closed in 2001 and the riverbank land was a little seedy when the building reopened in 2003 as Hotel Princess Anna. An extensive renovation transformed the 19th-century edifice into a gracious yellow-and-white confection of a hotel, but the riverfront has deteriorated even further. That shouldn't stop you from staying at the Anna: Ruse's fabulous esplanade is just a few minutes away, as is a huge selection of shops and restaurants. You also could book one of Anna's rooms, order room service, and kick back to enjoy the complimentary Wi-Fi, bathrooms with tubs, generous array of toiletries, and a huge selection of TV channels.

7000 Ruse. ✆ **359 82/825 005.** Fax 82/825 522. www.annapalace.com. 30 units, including 6 suites. From 70€ ($89) double; from 120€ ($152) suite. Rates include breakfast, VAT, and tourist tax. Free parking. **Amenities:** Restaurant; 2 bars; room service; valet service; elevator; reception safe. *In room*: A/C, SAT/TV, free Wi-Fi, minibar.

Where to Dine

If you can't find a place to eat (and drink) from among the many choices lining all sides of Liberation Square, you aren't looking very hard. Almost all of these offer excellent cafe food for the money and almost none take credit cards or employ English-speaking staff. To experience a Bulgarian restaurant the way Bulgarians do, try the Friendly House listed below. If you are looking for something a little more sophisticated, try one of our other recommendations.

Cosmopolitan World Cuisine ★★★ Finds INTERNATIONAL/BULGARIAN When you walk into the gleaming Cosmopolitan Restaurant with its designer linens and clever indoor architecture, you'll think "classy." And when you see the menu with its very fair prices, you won't believe your good fortune. Add to that gorgeous outdoor terrace seating among plants and the sound of water tumbling down a towering blue mosaic fountain, and you might think you're dreaming. Sink into one of the comfy rattan chairs and order the risotto Milanese or the king prawns tempura from an international menu that includes Italian, Chinese, Spanish, and Japanese dishes, plus traditional Bulgarian fare. Cosmopolitan also offers a huge selection of salads for lighter appetites and a decadent dessert menu full of guilty pleasures.

1–3 Dobri Nemirov. ✆ **359 82/80 50 50.** Fax 82/80 50 57. www.cosmopolitanhotelbg.com. Entrees 2.45lev–11lev ($2–$8.90/£1.25–£5.50). MC, V. Daily 9:30am–midnight.

The Friendly House ★ Value BULGARIAN GRILL If you want to go native, Friendly House is the ticket. The menus are in Bulgarian only and none of the staff speaks English. However, it's worth getting out of your comfort zone for a casual meal at this inside/umbrella table restaurant on Ruse's Liberation Square opposite the Liberty statue. You also can make a pretty accurate choice from the illustrated menu, which features lots of salads and several pork and chicken dishes: Everything is pictured in living color. Beware: The menu is inexplicably peppered with racy photos of beautiful women.

Ruse Esplanade opposite the Liberty statue. No phone. Entrees 3.60lev–8.40lev ($2.90–$6.70/£1.45–£3.40). No credit cards. Daily 9:30-midnight.

Princess Anna Restaurant/Terrace Restaurant ★ BULGARIAN Grilled meats star at this surprisingly versatile hotel restaurant. Dine in the Hotel Princess Anna's (see above) pleasant first-floor dining room or on its flower-bedecked terrace, but be sure to try some of the grilled meats on the menu. The mixed pork grill (six cuts of pork on offer) is especially good and the pancake desserts make a nice finish. We liked the version with orange syrup. ***Tip:*** Hotel guests get a 10% discount in the restaurant.

 7000 Ruse. ✆ **359 82/825 005.** Fax 82/825 522. www.annapalace.com. Entrees 4.50lev–17lev ($3.65–$14/£2.25–£8.70). MC, V. Daily 7:30am–11pm.

Exploring Ruse & Environs

There are plenty of sites to explore within shouting distance of Liberation Square, so you don't need to go too far to get a taste of what Ruse has to offer. Walk a couple of blocks east and you'll find the **Church of the Holy Trinity (Sveta Troitsa),** a 17th-century beauty with a baroque facade and Russian bell tower that was added in 1878. Stop there to see the icons. Keep going east to the **Park of the Men of the Revival (Park n Vuzrozhdentsite)** to see the **Ruse Pantheon,** a mausoleum honoring the 100th anniversary of Bulgaria's liberation from Ottoman rule and housing the remains of Bulgarian heroes of the 19th century. In 2001 the Pantheon was "Christianized" when a cross was placed on its dome and a chapel added inside. It's open from 9am to noon and from 2 to 5pm Monday to Friday (4lev/$3.25/£2).

If you are staying in Ruse or in transit to somewhere else, detour to the **Rock Churches of Ianovo** ★★. The Rusenski Lom River valley is a steep, rocky, canyonlike furrow that cuts through the land to give the Rusenski Lom River a way to the Danube. At Ianovo (18km/11 miles) south of the valley you'll begin to see signs leading to the rock monasteries that were carved into natural caves occurring in a steep cliff. Follow the signs for 3km (1¾ miles) from the road to the entrance and then to the stairway leading up to the church. There are more than 60 of these stony chambers in the hills above Ianovo, but this, the Tsurkvata Cave, is the only rock church in Bulgaria open to the public. The climb up the steep stairs can be challenging if you are out of shape, but there is a handrail. At the top, you'll pay a 4lev ($3.25/£2) admission charge, plus an extra 2lev ($1.60/£1) if you want to take pictures of the frescoes painted on the chambers' walls and ceiling. There also is a short trail behind the church cave to a "panoramic rock" where you can take spectacular photos of the valley below. The church is open from 9am to 1pm and from 2 to 6pm daily.

Pliska ★ Pliska is a dig in progress. You'll see the remains of Bulgaria's first capital (681–893 A.D.) and a new hotel under construction, but the hotel is intended for the archaeologists who are painstakingly uncovering the stone fortress complex. The museum on premises is worth the entry charge: Captions are in English and the exhibits explaining the area's history are very well done. The infrastructure and museum were part of a European Union–funded PHARE project, and it shows: A small snack bar, clean restrooms, paved walkways, and a parking lot were included in the plans. ***Tip:*** The Pliska ruins are off the beaten path. Unless you are a ruins fan with a great imagination, you can skip it.

3km (1¾ miles) east of the village of Pliska. Daily 9am–5pm. 4lev ($3.25/£2) admission for the museum.

Sveshtary Tomb (Ginina Mogila) ★★★ *Moments* Bulgaria boasts more than 1,000 Thracian tomb finds in several locations, but viewing this UNESCO-protected burial site 95km (59 miles) southeast of Ruse near the village of Sveshtary is a unique, thrilling experience. Sveshtary's 3rd-century B.C. Ginina Mogila, discovered in 1982, is a must-see for anyone interested in ancient history because it is not a replica like the Kazanluk "tomb," which was recreated for tourists (p. 96); rather it is the real deal, the actual burial place of a person thought to be a Thracian ruler. The statuary and frescoes in the burial chamber where the bones of three people and five horses, two stone burial "beds," and numerous artifacts were found are magnificent. Be sure you call ahead for reservations because the number of people allowed inside the climate-controlled space each day is limited. Thanks to a European Union project that helps preaccession nations (PHARE), there are an excellent photo display in the anteroom museum, a visitor center, and a snack bar on premises. No photos are allowed in the tomb and you will have to don paper foot covers to enter. There also are two other tombs undergoing restoration in the immediate area, but these don't come close to Ginina Mogila. Be sure you ask for an English-speaking guide when you call for reservations. ***Tip:*** After you see the tomb, take the path that goes down for 2km (1¼ mile) beyond the tombs to Pette Pursta, a natural spring running alongside **Demir Baba Tekke,** a shrine to a 16th-century Muslim holy man. Tie a colored ribbon to one of the shrine's window frames or on one of the nearby bushes for good luck. The shrine is 3km (2 miles) west of Sveshtary.

1km (¾ mile) west of Sveshtary. ✆ **359 08/335 279.** 10lev ($8.10/£5) per person. Mar–Nov Wed–Sun 9:30am–4:30pm. Maximum of 9 people allowed in at a time.

5 Croatia

by Karen Tormé Olson & Sanja Bažulić Olson

Germans, Italians, Austrians, and Hungarians have been aware of Croatia's charms for more than a century and, until very recently, these groups comprised the bulk of the country's summer visitors. That changed after the 1991 war with Serbia. Even after hostilities ended, safety concerns and the notion that there was nothing left worth seeing kept foreign travelers away. Today, tourism is almost back to prewar levels, but negative perceptions persist. The reality is that Croatia is safe and welcoming for tourists, which is clear after the shortest sojourn.

As Croatia moves toward membership in the European Union, travelers from the around the world are flocking to the country's knockout coastline, ancient ruins, medieval hilltop castles, and abundant natural wonders. Tourism is—and always has been—one of Croatia's most important sources of revenue, but that doesn't mean this dynamic country is overrun with visitors, even when the annual summer influx of visitors from nearby European nations is at its peak. No matter how thick the crowds, in Croatia it still is possible to find a secluded cove where it seems you are the only person on earth, or a room in a private home where the landlord welcomes you like a long-lost friend.

Croatia's natural beauty is reason enough to visit, but for those who want to combine an active vacation with breathtaking scenery, adventure travel options abound. Whether you prefer kayaking on swift rivers, rock climbing the formidable Velebit limestone walls, windsurfing off islands like Brač, spelunking in the subterranean caves that honeycomb the karstic landscape, or scuba diving off Vis, Croatia is an ideal venue. For those drawn to more sedate pursuits, Croatia offers numerous resorts along its many stretches of "riviera," plus quaint agri-inns in the rural interior, where meandering wine roads are dotted with places to linger. For those who like to wander, there are leisurely day trips to offshore islands or pilgrimages to a plethora of religious sites. History buffs will revel in the castles, museums, ruins, and churches scattered about the countryside. The past is a living thing in Croatia, where every building, park, and hill has a story that adds to the lore of this ancient land.

Since gaining independence in 1991, Croatia has been working through economic, social, and political issues, and the country hopes to obtain full membership in the European Union by 2011. Meanwhile, Croatia is moving forward with renovation, road building, and restoration, three Rs of progress that are closely tied to the current tourism boom. Be sure to bring a sense of wonder and plenty of film—Croatia is a country of many colors and a magnificent work in progress.

1 GETTING TO KNOW CROATIA

THE LAY OF THE LAND

Croatia is a crescent-shaped country that borders Slovenia in the northwest, Hungary in the north, Serbia in the northeast, Bosnia-Hercegovina to the east along almost the entire

AUSTRIA
HUNGARY
ROMANIA
ITALY
SLOVENIA
SLAVONIA
PANNONIAN PLAIN
DINARIC ALPS
DALMATIA
ISTRIA
BOSNIA AND HERZEGOVINA
SERBIA
MONTENEGRO
ALBANIA
ADRIATIC SEA
VELEBIT MTS.
Kvarner
Kvarnerić
Sava R.
Drava R.
Danube R.
Tisza R.
Vrbas R.
Bosna R.
Drina R.
Una R.
Cortina d'Ampezzo
Maribor
Čakovec
Varaždin
Koprivnica
Pécs
Szeged
Subotica
Timişoara
Krapinske Toplice
Ljubljana
Udine
Vittório Veneto
Sombor
Bjelovar
Vrbovec
Zagreb
Virovitica
Samobor
Ivanič Grad
Daruvar
Osijek
Našice
Vukovar
Novi Sad
Treviso
Trieste
Sisak
Karlovac
Đakovo
Vinkovci
Ilok
Nova Gradiska
Slavonski Brod
Padua
Venice
Chioggia
Umag
Opatija
Rijeka
Ogulin
Pazin
Poreč
Crikvenica
Rovinj
Labin
Krk
Senj
Plitvice N.P.
Otočac
Bihać
Banja Luka
BELGRADE
Pula
Cres
Rab
Tuzla
Gospić
Pag
Zenica
Ravenna
Knin
Zadar
Sarajevo
Kraljevo
Cesena
Rímini
Dugi Otok
Biograd
Goražde
Kornat
Šibenik
Sinj
Žirje
Trogir
Split
Ancona
Mostar
Šolta
Brač
Makarska
Hvar
Ploče
Metković
Vis
Korčula
Pelješac
Nikšić
Lastovo
Mljet
Dubrovnik
Cavtat
Podgorica
CROATIA
0
50 mi
0
50 km
N

length of the Dalmatian coast, Montenegro in the extreme south, and the Adriatic Sea to the west. Croatia covers about 56,542 sq. km (21,831 sq. miles) and is slightly smaller than West Virginia, with a varied topography of mountainous regions, flat plains, lowland basins, and hilly terrain. The country's 1,168 islands account for 4,085 sq. km (1,577 sq. miles) of its 5,835 sq. km. (3,079 sq. miles) of coastline, but just 50 of the islands are inhabited.

THE REGIONS IN BRIEF

DALMATIA Croatia's southernmost region lies on the eastern Adriatic coast between **Pag Island** in the northwest and the **Bay of Kotor** in the southeast. Dalmatia's climate is Mediterranean with wet, mild winters and long, hot, dry summers. The width of inland Dalmatia ranges from 50km (31 miles) in the north to just a few kilometers wide in the south. Dalmatia is divided into four counties whose capital cities—**Zadar, Split,** and **Dubrovnik**—are popular tourist destinations. Dalmatia and its islands account for most of the seacoast, Croatia's main tourist draw.

INLAND CROATIA From **Zagreb** east to the Danube River, inland Croatia is home to treasures that include protected nature preserves, picturesque villages, and historic cities. Some, like Mt. Medvednica north of Zagreb, are close to urban areas and public transportation, while others are remote wetlands. The region is dotted with notable castles, cathedrals, and historic sites that are interspersed with villages, rolling wooded hills, long flat plains, lush vineyards, and farmland. Inland Croatia shares a border with Slovenia and Hungary in the north and with Bosnia-Hercegovina in the south. The Danube accounts for much of the eastern border with Serbia.

ISTRIA Croatia's westernmost region is the country's most visited, perhaps because it is the most accessible to visitors from continental Europe. Istria is a triangular peninsula that juts into the northern Adriatic across the bay from Venice. The region includes the islands of the **Brijuni Archipelago,** made famous by Yugoslav dictator Josip Broz Tito, who received countless celebrities and heads of state at the residence and wildlife park he established there. In addition, clusters of smaller islands and islets lie just off Istria's southeast coast. The region is adjacent to **Rijeka** in the east and is separated by just a few miles of Slovenia from Italy (Trieste) at its northwest corner. Istria's west coast is lined with pretty Venetian-influenced towns like **Rovinj** and **Poreč,** while its southernmost city, **Pula,** is home to magnificent Roman ruins. Medieval castles, woodland churches, and charming villages are surrounded by vineyards and olive groves in the interior, where the forests also support thriving hunting and truffle-gathering industries.

KVARNER GULF The northern coastal region that borders the Kvarner Gulf and neighboring islands comprise this region, Croatia's closest to central and western Europe. Location and a mild climate have made Kvarner a popular tourist destination for western Europeans since the heyday of the Austro-Hungarian empire. The Kvarner Gulf region includes the islands of **Krk, Cres, Lošinj, Rab, Unjie,** and **Susak,** as well as the **Opatija Riviera,** one of the country's busiest tourist centers.

THE ISLANDS Croatia's 1,168 islands account for much of its fabled seacoast. Even though just 50 of them are inhabited, each of its Adriatic islands from Istria to Dubrovnik has a unique personality. From the sultry **Brijuni** cluster off Istria in the north to remote **Vis** off Dubrovnik in the south, Croatia's islands are some of the country's strongest tourist draws. **Cres** and **Lošinj** in the Kvarner Gulf are characterized by rocky hills that overlook secluded azure bays, while to the east **Rab** is a living museum of Venetian architecture; its neighbor, **Pag,** is a dichotomy of stark, barren landscape and a bustling weekend-getaway center.

Farther south, the **Kornati Archipelago** off Zadar is a diver's paradise. **Hvar, Korčula, Brač, Vis,** and **Mljet** are Croatia's southernmost islands. Hvar has acquired a reputation as a sun-drenched celebrity playground, while Korčula is proud of its architecture and art. Brač is notable for the white stone mined in its quarries and the wind-sea collaboration that makes it a Shangri-La for watersports enthusiasts. Brač's major tourist center is **Bol,** which is home to photogenic **Zlatni Rat (Golden Horn)** beach, a thin peninsula that changes shape with the sea current and always draws a huge international crowd. **Vis** is a mecca for extreme watersports, and **Mljet** is the legendary island whose beauty so mesmerized Odysseus that he stayed for 7 years.

SUGGESTED ITINERARY — THE DUBROVNIK AREA IN 10 DAYS

Tourist routes through Croatia can be as disparate as land is from sea. Don't make the mistake of thinking that you can cover everything in a week or even a month. Rather, start from a hub and concentrate on sites within a hundred miles or so. Save other parts of the country for future trips. Connections, especially along the Dalmatian Coast south of Split and to the southern islands, can be inconvenient and time consuming, so plan carefully. Here is our suggestion for an introduction to southern Dalmatia.

This tour uses Dubrovnik as a starting point and base and allows 3 days to explore Old Town and the area in its immediate vicinity. Follow that with some island hopping, and end your tour in Split.

Day 1 Dubrovnik's Old Town ★★★

Start by orienting yourself to Old Town's sites by taking the walking tour detailed later in this section, and save the walk around the top of Old Town's wall for an early evening stroll. When you descend, enjoy a fish dinner at a restaurant overlooking the Old Harbor or the sea.

Day 2 Explore Mljet

Book a day trip to mystical Mljet with one of the numerous island excursion outfits that that have booths at the Old Harbor near Dubrovnik's Ploče Gate. Pack wine and cheese for a picnic in the island's forest. Dinner in Dubrovnik.

Day 3 Visit Cavtat

Take the bus or water taxi to Cavtat and explore its churches and museums or laze on the beach. Catch any remaining Dubrovnik sites during a predinner walk.

Day 4 Get Out of Town

Drive or book an excursion to the Pelješac Peninsula ★. Stop at Ston to climb the town's 14th-century ramparts and reward yourself with a lunch of oysters from the area's shellfish beds. Continue to Orebič through Pelješac's wine country, stopping to taste new vintages here and there. Dinner/overnight in Orebič.

Day 5 Head for Hvar ★★★

Book an excursion to Korčula ★★★ (p. 156). Spend the day exploring Marco Polo's alleged birthplace and take the late fast boat to Hvar. Have dinner at one of the courtyard restaurants off St. Stephen Square and overnight at Hotel Riva ★★ (p. 152).

Day 6 Explore Hvar

Explore Hvar Town ★★★ (p. 153) and Stari Grad in the afternoon. Return to the Riva and catch a concert at the Franciscan cloister and dinner at a restaurant on the harbor. Overnight at the Hotel Riva.

Day 7 Get Beached

Book transportation to Bol on Brač and spend the day swimming and sunbathing off Golden Horn (Zlatni Rat) beach ★★ (p.156). Tour the waterfront shops before dinner at a restaurant on the waterfront. Overnight in Bol.

Day 8 See Split ★★★

Book a ferry for the short ride from Brač to Split. After checking in to the Hotel Vestibul Palace ★★★ (p. 157), explore what's left of Diocletian's Palace ★★★ (p. 161) and the Old Town within its walls. Overnight in Split.

Day 9 Travel Back in Time

Take a bus 19km (12 miles) northwest to Trogir (or book a guided excursion) and take the day to explore this medieval town on a small island connected to the mainland by a bridge. Return to Split after dinner.

Day 10

If you have time, take a bus to the Roman ruins of Salona 6.4km (4 miles) outside Split and immerse yourself in the past. Return to Split for the flight home.

CROATIA TODAY

Croatia still is rebuilding its image more than a decade after the end of the Homeland War (Domovinski rat) in 1995, and it is determined to take its place at the world table. Signs of economic recovery are everywhere: From packed hotels on the coast to thriving boutiques and restaurants in Zagreb, Croatia is adopting a more sophisticated, savvy posture. Its government is working to reduce foreign debt, boost the economy, and promote the country's natural wonders while it waits for full membership in the European Union.

A LOOK AT THE PAST

Recorded Croatian history begins around 1200 B.C., when people occupying the region that is now Croatia, Bosnia, Albania, and Serbia formed a coalition of tribes known as Illyrians. The Greeks arrived in the 4th century B.C. and traded oil, wine, salt, metals and other commodities with the Illyrians. In the 3rd century B.C., a 60-year series of wars ended with the Romans on top and the creation of the province of Illyricum.

The spread of Roman colonies across Croatia continued until A.D. 9, when the Adriatic coast and interior lands were annexed by Tiberius to create three Roman provinces: Dalmatia (Adriatic seacoast), Noricum (northern territory/Austria), and Pannonia (Hungary), where the Romans built fortresses, roads, bridges, aqueducts, and sparkling new cities—such as Pola (Pula), Jader (Zadar), Salona (Solin) near Split, and Epidaurum (Cavtat). At the end of his reign, Roman Emperor Diocletian built his lavish "retirement home" in Split, where it remains as one of the best-preserved vestiges of the Roman era.

From the end of the 4th century until the 7th century, Croatia suffered a series of barbarian invasions. But it was the warlike Asian Avars who allegedly brought the Slavic Croats—ancestors to today's Croatians—to the area while sacking everything in their path along the way. Eventually the Croats organized into two dukedoms—Pannonia in the north and Dalmatia in the south—which evolved into two distinct cultures, central European and Dalmatian.

Croats continued to live under a series of foreign and Croatian administrations until A.D. 924, when the country was united under Tomislav I, the first King of Croatia. He was followed by King Petar Krešimir IV and King Dmitar Zvonimir, but after Zvonimir's death in the 11th century, the monarchy withered and Croatia and Hungary formed a common kingdom guided by a parliament (Sabor). During this time, free cities (Dubrovnik, among others) were founded along the coast, increasing trade and political strength in the region.

A Tatar invasion in 1242 diverted the government's attention to the country's defense, but ultimately, Hungarian King Bela IV outmaneuvered the Tatars and retained control. Venice, however, remained determined to control Istria and Dalmatia, and ultimately access to the sea; they finally achieved that goal in 1409. During the 15th century the Ottoman Turks advanced on Croatian lands and a series of battles and deaths put Ferdinand I of Habsburg on Croatia's throne and the Habsburg Empire took control.

In 1808 Napoleon captured several coastal towns, uniting Dalmatia with parts of Slovenia and Croatia. When Napoleon was defeated in 1815, control of Dalmatia once again reverted to the Habsburgs, and Austria created the Kingdom of Illyria, an administrative unit designed to thwart Hungarian nationalism and unification of the south Slavs. Dalmatia, however, was not part of this reorganization, as Austria decided to keep it as a vacation playground. At the same time, Croatian leaders pushed nationalism by promoting the Croatian language and culture; they formed a Slavic kingdom under the Habsburgs' noses.

Hungary challenged Austria during the revolution that was sweeping across Europe in 1848, and Croatia sided with Austria while calling for self-determination. Austria yielded to the pressure and raised Josip Jelačić to the position of ban (viceroy) of Croatia. Jelačić immediately suspended relations with Hungary and declared war, but his Austrian allies reasserted their authority over Croatia after defeating the Hungarians. Austria ended absolute rule over Croatia in 1860 and Croatia returned to Hungarian influence in 1868.

In 1906, Serbs and Croats again came together to create the Croat-Serb Coalition and immediately came under attack by Vienna, which feared that the groups' cooperation with each other would reduce the Austrian influence.

In 1908, Austria-Hungary annexed Bosnia and its diverse population of Catholic Croats, Orthodox Serbs, and Muslims. This move thwarted the Serbian goal of creating a Serbian state and reignited tensions between Croats and Serbs. On June 28, 1914, Austrian Archduke Franz Ferdinand and his wife were assassinated in Sarajevo, and less than a month later Austria-Hungary declared war on Serbia. Germany sided with Austria; and Russia, France, and Great Britain countered by forming an alliance of their own, putting Croatia and Serbia in opposite corners.

On December 1, 1918, after the Austro-Hungarian Empire had been defeated, the Serb leadership broke rank and created the Kingdom of Serbs, Croats, and Slovenes. In 1927, its name was changed to the Kingdom of Yugoslavia (South Slavia).

Yugoslavia tried to remain neutral at the start of World War II, but pressure to support the Axis side was great, and on March 25, 1941, Yugoslavia's leader aligned the country with the Nazis. Within 2 days the pact was nullified, but Germany would not let the cancellation stand. On April 6, they bombed Belgrade and invaded: It took them just 10 days to defeat the Yugoslav army.

A resistance movement was organized almost immediately after the German invasion, but it was divided between the pro-Serbian Četniks and the pro-Communist Partisans led by Josip Broz, better known as Tito. The Allies recognized Tito's Partisans as the official resistance and funneled all foreign aid to the Communist group, which helped liberate Belgrade. When the war ended in 1944, more than 1.7 million Yugoslavs had died, about 10% of the country's population.

After the war, Tito's Communist Party won the Yugoslav election, but Tito was not in lockstep with Stalin and declared Yugoslav nonalignment in 1948, which allowed him to function as a cafeteria Communist.

The country endured a Soviet blockade in the 1950s under Tito, but Tito's local site-management policy allowed tourism to flourish along the Adriatic coast. He also gave each of Yugoslavia's six republics—Croatia, Serbia, Slovenia, Bosnia/Herzegovina, Macedonia, and Montenegro—control over its own internal affairs.

Tito died on May 4, 1980, at the age of 88, leaving the Yugoslav state without a strong successor. To complicate matters, the region's economy was deteriorating in the wake of the 1970s oil crisis, a huge national debt, and the disappearance of foreign credit sources. Yugoslavia began to crack along national, religious, and ethnic lines.

In 1987, Slobodan Milošević emerged as a proponent of Serb superiority while working toward installing a Communist government in Yugoslavia. Two years after Milošević's debut as a champion of Serbs, the Berlin Wall came down, leaving him holding an unpopular position while the rest of Europe raced off in the opposite ideological direction.

In May 1989 the Croatian Democratic Union (HDZ), led by former general and historian Franjo Tuđman, became one of the first non-Communist organizations in Croatia, and in less than a year it began campaigning for Croatia's secession from Yugoslavia. Months later, free elections were held in Croatia and Tuđman was sworn in as president within weeks. He promptly declared Croatian statehood, a preliminary stage before independence, and a constitution was written that declared the Serbs in Croatia a national minority rather than a unique nation within the republic, a move that fomented outrage in the Serb community.

In 1991, Milošević began gathering support for a greater Serbia, which was to include all the areas of Croatia and Bosnia/Herzegovina where Serbs were in residence. Hostilities broke out in 1991 with Milošević and Serb forces from all over Yugoslavia pouring into Croatia. During the violence, cities such as Dubrovnik, Vukovar, and Osijek suffered heavy damage; thousands of Croatians were forced to leave their homes; thousands more were killed. Hostilities raged until peace was restored in 1995, but it was 3 more years before the last Serb military units left Croatia.

In April 2001, Slobodan Milošević was arrested and charged with corruption in connection with the war. In November of that year the UN War Crimes Tribunal charged him with genocide stemming from his alleged activity during the 1992 to 1995 Bosnian campaign. Milošević died in 2006 while in U.N. custody at the Hague before his trial could be concluded.

CROATIAN PEOPLE & CULTURE

After centuries of occupation by foreign powers, the 4.5 million citizens of Croatia are embracing their hard-won independence in a big way and reasserting their nationalism. Croatians living on the Venetian-influenced Dalmatian coast and in the central European interior are reveling in their heritage by reviving customs, traditions, and even national dishes that were put aside during the foreign domination. Many of these traditions revolve around religious holidays and saints' feast days and the village church once again is a center of community for Croatians, 90% of whom are Roman Catholic, 4% Serbian Orthodox, and 1% Muslim.

The 1991 to 1995 war devastated Croatia's economy, but the country is no charity case. Croatians see themselves as an active part of modern Europe with ties to western Europe. When Croatia still was part of Yugoslavia, Tito recognized and cultivated global relationships throughout his watch as the country's leader. Unlike other people under Communist influence at the time, Yugoslavians (including Croatians) were allowed to work and travel abroad and to own property. In addition, Croatia welcomed tourists from all over the world, a tradition that is now one of the country's most important sources of income. Modern Croatians value progress, family and friends, good food and wine, nice clothes, vacations on the coast, the environment, the country's historical treasures—and, most of all, freedom.

CROATIAN CUISINE

Dining is a national sport in Croatia and food is good throughout the country. However, besides consistent quality and an ever-present offering of grilled meat and fish and pizza from north to south, each region of the country prides itself on specific traditional dishes.

Cuisine in **continental Croatia** is more substantial than in other regions. Smoked meats and *prgica* (smoked cheese) are popular in regional markets, while *sarma* (ground meat in sour cabbage leaves), and *krvavice* (blood sausage with sauerkraut) are main meal staples. *Štrukle* (phyllo filled with fresh cheese, apples, cherries, or other fruit) and *palačinke* (crepes filled with honey and walnuts or jam) are common desserts. In **Gorski Kotar & Lika** in southwest central Croatia, homemade cheeses, fruit brandies, and spit-roasted lamb and pork are favorites. Look for *janjetina* (lamb) baked under a bell-shaped lid *(peka)* or roasted over an open grill.

Istria and the **Kvarner Gulf** regions boast the most diverse cuisine in Croatia. In the Kvarner, try *Creska janjetina* (lamb from the island of Cres) and *škampi* (shrimp dishes) or try any of the game stews infused with bay leaves that grow in the mountainous part of Cres island. On Pag, sample *Paški sir* (Pag cheese), a unique salty sheep cheese infused with herbal notes because of the animals' diet of local vegetation; lamb; and *pršut* (prosciutto). In Istria, any dish with *tartufe* (truffles) is worth a try. *Istarski fuži sa gulasom od divljači* (pasta with game goulash) is sublime. Istria is also the source of some of Croatia's best wines. The main meal in **Dalmatia** typically starts with *pršut* and *Paški sir* scattered with olives and drizzled with pungent olive oil. *Kamenice* (oysters) from the shellfish beds of Ston on the Pelješac Peninsula are prized, as is anything from the sea.

LANGUAGE

Language can be the most daunting aspect of a trip to Croatia for any English-speaking tourist. Signs in Croatian look like gibberish to English speakers, and conversations sound like it, too. Even with a dictionary, it is difficult to understand what is being said and it is even more difficult to figure out how to form the words for a response. Croatians realize that theirs is a complicated language; consequently, most are fluent in at least one other language, usually German, Italian, or English. However, Croatian words are fairly easy to pronounce if you remember to give sound to every letter, place the accent on the first syllable, and pronounce the letter "j" as a "y," "c" as "ts," "š" as "sh, " "ž" as "zhh," and "di" as "dj." If you try to learn to say and recognize at least a few rudimentary words and phrases in this Slavic variant, you will be richly rewarded for your efforts.

English	Croatian	Pronunciation
Yes	**Da**	dah
No	**Ne**	nay
Good	**Dobro**	*doe*-broe
I don't understand	**Ne razumijem**	nay ra-*zoo*-mee-yem
Where is . . . ?	**Gdje je . . . ?**	*gd*-yay yay. . .
How much/How many?	**Koliko?**	koe-lee-koe
Good day	**Dobar dan**	*doe*-bar dahn
Hi/bye	**Bok**	boke
Thank you	**Hvalas**	*huh*-vah-lah
Goodbye	**Doviđenja**	doe-vee-*djen*-ya
Please	**Molim**	*moe*-leem
I understand	**Razumijem**	rah-*zoo*-mee-yem
I don't understand	**Ne razumijem**	nay rah-*zoo*-mee-yem
Where is the . . . ?	**Gdje se nalazi . . . ?**	ga dyay say *nah*-lah-zee
Entry	**Ulaz**	*oo*-lahz
Exit	**Izlaz**	*eez*-lahz
Toilets (men)	**Toilets (muskarci)**	moosh-*kar*-tsi
Toilets (women)	**Toilets (žene)**	*zhe*-neh
Hospital	**Bolnica**	bole-nee-tsu
Police	**Policija**	poe-*lee*-tsee-yah
Prohibited	**Zabranjeno**	zah-brah-*nyay*-noe

2 PLANNING YOUR TRIP TO CROATIA

VISITOR INFORMATION

The home Web page of the **Republic of Croatia** (www.hr/index.en.shtml) offers potential visitors numerous links to the country. The **Croatian National Tourist Board website** (www.croatia.hr) contributes specifics about trip planning and focuses on transportation and accommodations.

The **Croatian National Tourist Board** has a U.S. office at 350 Fifth Ave., Ste. 4003, New York, NY 10118 (© **212/279-8672**); and a U.K. office at 2 Lanchesters, 162–164 Fulham Palace Rd., London W6 9ER (© **020/8563-7979**)

ENTRY REQUIREMENTS

DOCUMENTS All foreigners need a valid passport for entrance to Croatia. Citizens of the U.S., U.K., Australia, Canada, New Zealand, Israel, Ireland, and Singapore do not need visas for tourist/business trips of fewer than 90 days within a 6-month period. For a stay over 90 days, a visa should be obtained in advance. South Africans do require a visa. For more information on visas, go to **www.croatiaemb.org**. For information on getting a passport, see "Getting Your Passport in Order" in chapter 3.

EMBASSIES In the U.S.: 2343 Massachusetts Ave. NW, Washington, DC 20008 (✆ 202/588-5899; fax 202/588-8937; public@croatiaemb.org). In Canada: 229 Chapel St., Ottawa, Ontario, K1N 7Y6 (✆ 613/562-7820; fax 613/562-7821; croemb.ottawa@mvp.hr). In the United Kingdom: 21 Conway St., London, W1P, 5HL, U.K. (✆ 44 20 7387-2022; fax 44 20 7387-0936; consular.dept.London@mvp.hr). In Australia: 14 Jindalee Crescent, O'Malley Act, 2606, Canberra (✆ 61 2 6286-3544; croemb@bigpond.com). In New Zealand: 131 Lincoln Rd., Henderson/P.O. Box 83200 Edmonton, Auckland (✆ 64 9 836-5581; fax 64 9 836-5481; cro-consulate@xtra.co.nz).

MONEY

The official currency of Croatia is the **kuna (kn),** which comes in notes of 5, 10, 20, 50, 100, 200, 500, and 1,000 kn. One kuna equals 100 lipa, and coins with values of 1, 2, 5, 10, 20, and 50 lipa and 1, 2, 5, and 25 kuna are in circulation. To convert prices in kunas to current prices in U.S. dollars, go to www.xe.com/ucc.

EXCHANGE At press time, the exchange rate was 4.9 Croatian kuna to 1 U.S. dollar. With Croatia's anticipated E.U. membership in progress, many Croatian businesses are beginning to express their prices in euros and kuna, though euros are not yet widely accepted. ATMs (aka bancomats in Croatia) have been installed in almost all towns and are the most convenient and economical way to obtain Croatian currency. Foreign currency can be changed at post offices, banks, exchange offices, and at some hotels and travel agencies, but beware of service charges, which can be as high as 3%. Any Croatian bank will handle credit card cash advances.

CREDIT CARDS Most stores, hotels, and upscale restaurants in larger cities accept credit cards, but establishments in small towns generally do not. Most small businesses and market vendors do not accept traveler's checks.

Note: Many restaurants, hotels, and shops offer a discount for cash payments.

WHEN TO GO

July and August are high season on the Croatian coast and islands. This is when the coast is at its best—and worst: Hotel rooms are the priciest, restaurants the busiest, and crowds can be overwhelming. However, Zagreb and other interior cities can be bargains in summer because many citizens head for the coast. The downside is that some Zagreb restaurants and shops may be closed for vacation. In May, June, September, and October, coastal weather is usually mild, the sea warm, and prices lower, but some establishments might be shuttered and some ferry routes might be canceled or on reduced schedules.

Weather in Croatia is divided into two miniclimates. Northern Croatia has a Continental climate, with average temperatures ranging from near freezing in January to about 70°F (21°C) in August. The coastal areas have a more Mediterranean climate, with average temperatures ranging from the mid-40s in January to 100°F (38°C) or above in August. Spring and autumn are pleasant and mild along the coast; inland winters can be cold and snowy.

HOLIDAYS

Public holidays are New Year's Day (Jan 1), Easter (variable), Labor Day (May 1), Corpus Christi (June 15), Anti-Fascist Resistance Day (June 22), Victory Day and National Thanksgiving Day (Aug 5), Assumption Day (Aug 15), Independence Day (Oct 8), All Saints' Day (Nov 1), and Christmas (Dec 25–26). In addition, many towns celebrate their patron saint's day as a public holiday.

Major Festivals in Croatia

The festivals mentioned here are just a few celebrated every year. Inquire at the Croatian National Tourist Office or at local tourist offices for event contact information and for an updated calendar.

On **January 7,** Croatia's Eastern Orthodox Christians celebrate **Christmas** and take a day off from work. Dubrovnik celebrates its patron saint on **February 3** with a parade and lots of revelry to honor **St. Blaise.** From **mid-July to mid-August,** the **Split Summer Festival** takes over the city's historic core with exhibitions, concerts, dance, theater, and especially opera performed in the Peristil. Well-known international artists perform during the **Dubrovnik Summer Festival, from early July to late August.** For **3 weekends in October,** Lovran outside Opatija celebrates **Marunada,** a tribute to everything chestnut-related. **Martinje** (St. Martin's Day) is a church feast day, but **November 11** is also the day when the new wine is blessed and "tested" in unlimited amounts in almost all grape-growing regions of Croatia.

GETTING THERE

BY PLANE The biggest problem for North American tourists visiting Croatia is getting there. At press time, there were no direct flights to Croatia from anywhere in North America. Travelers from this part of the world must get to Zagreb, Split, Rijeka, or Dubrovnik with (usually) a Croatia Air (www.croatiaairlines.hr) connection from a European hub such as Amsterdam, Berlin, Brussels, Düsseldorf, Frankfurt, Moscow, Munich, Paris, Prague, Rome, Sarajevo, or Vienna. A number of Europe's discount carriers, such as Ryanair, easyJet, Wizz Air, and SkyEurope, serve Croatia via cities such as London and Venice, but some of these routes are seasonal, always crowded, and heavily taxed.

Note: Airline schedules are not always aligned for Croatia connections and logistics can require an overnight stay in the connecting city. If your itinerary requires an overnight stay, you might have to pick up your luggage and go through Customs in the connecting city, then repeat the process when you check in for the second leg of your journey.

BY TRAIN Croatia has international railway links with Slovenia, Hungary, Italy, Austria, Switzerland, Slovakia, France, Germany, and Bosnia/Hercegovina. There are trains to and from other European countries, but traveling any of these routes can be extremely time consuming. Getting from Paris to Zagreb, for example, takes 18-plus hours, while a trip from Frankfurt to Split will take almost 24 hours. If you must travel to Croatia from another European city by rail, check schedules and fares and get details on rail passes at **Rail Europe,** www.raileurope.com. Croatian rail travel usually requires train changes because the track gauge is different from that used on Eurail routes. Check **Croatia Railways** (www.hznet.hr).

BY FERRY Ferry travel is the most common way to access Croatia's islands and coastal towns. Four lines serve major Croatian ports from Bari, Ancona, Pescara, and Venice in Italy. Other lines operate seasonal routes. Information for all ferry lines listed below is available at www.cemar.it.

Note: Not all ferries operate daily routes to all destinations, so you need to check arrival/departure information carefully.

Jadrolinija has three international routes—Ancona-Zadar and Ancona-Split daily, and once-a-week service between Bari and Dubrovnik. Round-trip, weekend, deck passage for two adults and a vehicle runs 220€ ($279) for the overnight trip between Bari and Dubrovnik, while the fare for two in an external cabin with shower and toilet plus a vehicle is 692€ ($879).

Blue Line International (www.blueline-ferries.com) operates daily overnight service between Ancona and Split. Round-trip deck accommodations for two people and a car cost 268€ ($340), while a deluxe cabin for two with a vehicle runs 596€ ($757) during the summer. For weekend departures from late July through late August add 25%. **SNAV** operates several routes between Italy and Croatia, including an international connection to popular Hvar Island. Prices and schedule information are available from April through September on the cemar.it website (above).

Venezia Lines travels between Venice and cities such as Rovinj and Pula on Istria's western coast. Schedule and fare information is available at the website listed above or at www.venezialines.com from April through September.

BY CAR The highways that connect Croatia to Slovenia, Hungary, Bosnia-Hercegovina, and Serbia-Montenegro are good and getting better. This is especially true of the span between Ljubljana and Zagreb, a 2-hour journey. It takes about 5 hours to reach Zagreb (362km/225 miles) from Budapest, Hungary, while visitors from Italy and Austria cross an excellent stretch of road in Slovenia to get to Croatia's borders.

BY BUS International bus travel in Europe can be comfortable but time consuming, as the escalating price of fuel has catapulted this travel option out of the "cheap" category. Regular international buses connect Croatia with neighboring European countries and those well beyond its borders, including the U.K. (www.nationalexpress.com). If time is money for you, consider that while round-trip bus fare between London and Split costs just 200€ ($254), the trip takes about 38 hours, and almost 60 hours to return.

GETTING AROUND

BY PLANE Croatia Air has a near monopoly on flights that travel among Croatia's seven airports (Zagreb, Split, Dubrovnik, Rijeka, Pula, Zadar, and Brač), and unless one of these cities is your final destination, you'll have to transfer to some other mode of transportation to finish your trip.

Note: Domestic flights booked on Croatia Air from outside the country cost nearly twice as much as flights booked at a Croatia Air office in the country, unless they are part of a multicity international ticket.

BY BUS Almost every town in Croatia has a bus station, and the network of bus routes makes this form of transportation an excellent, economical option for travel *within* Croatia. Express routes on updated highways facilitate travel among major cities and buses stop at almost every village in the country, though schedules might be inconvenient for those with limited time.

BY FERRY Ferry/catamaran travel is a way of life on Croatia's coast. There is no other way to get to the islands (except Pag and Krk, which are linked to the mainland via bridges). Jadrolinija, Sem Marina, and SNAV are the major ferry operators. In summer, ferry schedules are beefed up to handle increased traffic, but not necessarily aligned to make connections and island hopping convenient. In winter some lines reduce their schedules. Whenever there is a *bura,* the fierce northwestern wind that sometimes hammers the area, ferries may be sidelined.

Note: When planning your trip, do not underestimate the time it takes to travel by ferry. Besides calculating time for the water crossing, build in time to get to the ferry port, wait in line (which can be hours), and get to your final destination. Check schedules carefully as not all routes operate every day.

BY CAR Driving is the best method for seeing the real Croatia—even the islands. However, car rental and fuel, with a subcompact starting at about 245kn ($50/£31) a day and gas selling at unprecedented high prices, can be expensive. During July and August it is important to reserve a rental car before you arrive.

Croatia's main highways *(autocestas)* are well marked, and well maintained. Secondary roads vary in quality and can range from excellent to unmarked dirt tracts. Gas stations are readily available near the larger cities. They usually are open from 7am to 7pm every day and until 10pm in the summer.

Note: It's a good idea to get a Croatia road map that locates gas stations across the country before you start a long trip. These usually are available at the stations themselves. See www.ina.hr and www.hak.hr for details.

BY TRAIN **Croatian Railways** (www.hznet.hr) is an efficient way to travel between Zagreb and the northern and inland parts of the country. All of Croatia's major cities except Dubrovnik are connected by train service.

TIPS ON ACCOMMODATIONS

Thanks to its longtime popularity as a vacation spot for European travelers, Croatia has an ample supply of accommodations, but the types and quality vary widely. Hotels are the most expensive option, in the shortest supply, and often in need of updating despite labels like "luxury" and "modern." All the best resort hotels fill up fast, so be sure to reserve early. Some hotels require full-board bookings of no fewer than 7 days in summer and those that do book on a daily, B&B basis often tack on a surcharge of as much as 50% per day. ***Note:*** Some hoteliers will offer a discount if you pay with cash.

Private accommodations are an economical alternative and can range from grand apartments to a bed in a dormlike room. Private accommodations can be booked through local agencies, online, or secured through individuals who solicit customers at ferry ports and train and bus stations. Private accommodations often require a minimum multinight stay. Payment is almost always on a cash basis.

Campsites generally have loads of amenities and prime locations near the sea. They can accommodate backpackers or families with RVs, but they fill up quickly in summer and reservations are a must. Croatia also has almost two dozen FKK (nudist) camps as well as some bare-bones hostels in the larger cities. Rates for all kinds of accommodations, including campsites, in the coastal areas are highest in July and August—sometimes double the usual rates.

TIPS ON DINING

Croatian cuisine, like the country itself, is regional in character and divided into coastal and interior styles, with fish and pasta the prevalent offerings in Dalmatia and Istria, grilled meat the entree of choice in the interior, and anything laced with paprika the specialty in Slavonia, the country's easternmost region. Meals at most Croatian restaurants are excellent values, but the smaller, family-run establishments known as *konobas* generally are the best buy because much of the food and wine is family produced, prepared, and reasonably priced. Whether you choose a restaurant that aspires to be "gourmet," an intimate ma-and-pa place, or a meal cobbled from the town market and corner *pekara* (bakery), you should try local specialties like *ćevapčići* (spicy grilled beef or pork meatballs), *blitva* (Swiss chard boiled and served with potatoes, olive oil and garlic), and *burek* (a heavy pastry filled with cheese, meat, or fruit). Fish is often sold by the kilogram in restaurants and the average portion is about 250 grams (9 oz.). Service is almost always included in the menu prices, though leaving loose change as a tip is appreciated. Credit cards are accepted at many upscale restaurants, but even some of the fancier dining rooms offer a discount for cash.

Note: In Dubrovnik, many restaurants no longer build gratuities into the cost of a meal, though almost all charge a *couvert,* which is a cover charge attached to the bread basket. If you don't want bread, refuse it before it lands on your table and you'll avoid the *couvert.*

TIPS ON SHOPPING

Unless you are looking for regional items such as Pag lace, Hvar lavender oil, naive art oil-on-glass paintings by artists from the Hlebine school, or Rijeka *Morčići* (ceramic and gold jewelry depicting a Moorish woman in a turban), you'll find that most clothing, shoes, jewelry, and textiles sold in Croatia are imported and expensive. **Town markets** are the best sources for local specialties like homemade *rakija* (brandy), lavender sachets and soap, as well as T-shirts and beachwear. **Grisia Street** in Rovinj and **Tklčićeva Street** in Zagreb are just two examples of town sites where you can find clusters of ateliers, galleries, one-of-a-kind jewelry, crafts, and clothing by Croatian designers. Department stores are open from 8am to 8pm weekdays and 8am to 2 or 3pm Saturdays. Many grocery stores are open Sunday mornings and most town markets are open daily from 7am to noon or beyond.

Fast Facts Croatia

American Express **Atlas Travel** (www.atlas-croatia.com) is the agent for American Express in Croatia, with offices in most major cities.

Business Hours Banks and post offices generally are open from 7am to 7pm Monday to Friday without midday breaks. Public offices are open Monday to Friday from 8am to 4pm. During the tourist season, post offices are generally open until 9pm, including Saturday. Shops and department stores stay open from 8am to 8pm and to 2pm Saturday without a break.

Drugstores *Ljekarna* are open from 8am to 7pm weekdays and until 2pm on Saturday. In larger cities, one pharmacy in town will be open 24 hours.

Electricity Croatian electricity is 220V, 50 Hz; the two-prong European plug is standard.

Embassies & Consulates **U.S.:** Andrije Hebranga 2, Zagreb; ✆ 01-66-12-200. **Australia:** Krsnjavoga 1, Zagreb; ✆ 01-48-36-600. **United Kingdom:** Vlaska 121, Zagreb; ✆ 01-45-55-310; also Obala hrvatskog narodnog preporoda 10, 21000, Split; ✆ 021-341-464.

Emergencies Police ✆ **92.** Fire ✆ **93.** Ambulance ✆ **94.** Roadside assistance ✆ **987.** (When calling from abroad or by cellphone, call ✆ 385 1 987.) General information ✆ **981.** Information about local and intercity numbers ✆ **988.**

Information about international numbers ✆ **902.** Weather forecast and road conditions ✆ **060/520-520.**

Language Most residents of major Croatian cities speak English. Most American movies and programs broadcast on Croatian TV are in English with Croatian subtitles.

Liquor Laws The minimum age for purchasing liquor is 18, but there is no minimum age for consuming it. Croatia recently abolished its zero-tolerance law for all regarding drinking and driving. If you are 24 and under, the 0.0% limit still applies, but for those over 24, the legal limit now is 0.5% blood alcohol. Package liquor (wine, beer, spirits) can be purchased in markets, wine stores, at some souvenir shops, and at almost every gas station.

Mail It costs 3.50kn (61¢/35p) to send a postcard back to the U.S., and 5kn (a little more than $1/60p) to send a letter weighing up to 20 grams (3/4 oz.). It takes 10 days to 2 weeks for postcards to arrive in the U.S. from Croatia and up to a month for regular mail and packages. Other carriers are available (DHL, FedEx, UPS) in major population centers, but the cost is prohibitive (around 245kn/$50/£31 per lb.).

Restrooms There are no free-standing public restrooms in Croatia, but most restaurants and public buildings have them.

Smoking There are no restrictions on smoking in restaurants or public places in Croatia, though many hotels offer nonsmoking guest rooms.

Taxes Croatia's VAT is 22%. Refunds of VAT are made to foreign nationals when they leave the country for goods purchased in Croatia for amounts over 500kn ($102/£63). Salespeople will provide a tax refund form when you make a purchase over 500kn. There is a 10% nonrefundable tax on excursions and hotel rooms. For further information, go to www.carina.hr.

Time Zone Croatia is 1 hour ahead of Greenwich Mean Time, 6 hours ahead of New York (EST), and 9 hours ahead of Los Angeles (PST). Daylight saving time is observed from late March to late September, when clocks are advanced 1 hour.

Tipping Tipping is not yet widely expected in smaller Croatian restaurants, but a 10% to 15% gratuity is often expected at upscale restaurants and larger cities. Otherwise, it is considered polite to leave any coins from your change. A 10% tip for other service providers (taxi drivers, hotel personnel, and others) is the norm, as is a tip for anyone who helps you carry luggage.

Water Tap water is potable throughout Croatia.

3 DUBROVNIK

It would take a legion of Hollywood's most creative architects to design a set as perfect as Dubrovnik, and it would take an army of diligent stagehands to build it. Yet even after being devastated by Serb shells during the Homeland war, this "city made of stone and light" is as enchanting as the shimmering sunsets that ricochet off its 14th-century ramparts. In short: The Dalmatian UNESCO World Heritage city is stunning. The only telltale reminder of the war is the brighter color of the terra-cotta roof tiles used to replace those damaged in the attacks. You might find a few bullet scars, but the "Pearl of the Adriatic" is as lustrous as it was 5 centuries ago, when it was a major sea power bustling with prosperous merchants and aristocrats.

Dubrovnik (nee Ragusa) began as a Roman settlement, but from the Middle Ages on it was a prize sought by Venice, Hungary, Turkey, and others who recognized the city's logistical value as a maritime port. *Libertas* (liberty) has always been uppermost in the minds of Dubrovnik's citizens, and through the ages, their thirst for independence kept would-be conquerors at bay.

In 1667, a catastrophic earthquake did to Dubrovnik what foreign invaders could not: It brought the city to its knees. The quake killed more than 5,000 people and destroyed most of the city's structures. But Dubrovnik recovered and was quickly rebuilt in the new baroque style of the times, only to be shattered again 3 centuries later—this time from the skies in a 1991 to 1992 siege during Croatia's war with Serbia. The hostilities decimated tourism throughout Croatia, but nowhere was the impact more devastating than in Dubrovnik, where visitors vanished. Crowds once again have returned to this charming city nestled between the Adriatic and Dinaric Alps, and it has regained its former status as a vacation destination par excellence.

GETTING THERE

Accessing Dubrovnik by any means except air can be inconvenient and expensive. Even driving there from elsewhere in Croatia is challenging because of the city's position between the mountains and sea and the lack of modern roads in the area. Ferry routes to Dubrovnik often include multiple stops at various islands, and train service is nonexistent. It's wise to build in extra travel time when you visit Dubrovnik.

BY PLANE Croatia Airlines (www.croatiaairlines.hr) operates daily flights to Dubrovnik from select European cities. Dubrovnik International Airport (Zračna Luka; www.airport-dubrovnik.hr) is at Čilipi, 18km (11 miles) from the city center.

Croatia Airlines operates shuttle buses to and from Dubrovnik Airport, and they are coordinated with incoming flights, even the late ones. Buses supposedly leave the main terminal in Dubrovnik at Gruž Port 90 minutes before each Croatia Airlines flight, but there is no posted schedule. You don't have to be a Croatia Airlines passenger to ride, however. Cost is 35kn ($7.15/£4.45) one-way and it takes about 25 minutes from the airport to the Pile Gate. Taxis also serve the airport and rides are metered at 25kn ($5.10/£3.15) and 8kn ($1.65/£1) per kilometer. A one-way trip between the airport and Dubrovnik costs about 250kn ($51/£31), but it could be more if you don't settle on the price and terms before you get in the cab. The taxi company's website (www.taxiservicedubrovnik.com) tells you not to pay if the driver doesn't turn on the meter, but arguing about that could get ugly.

BY FERRY The government-run ferry line Jadrolinija connects Dubrovnik with islands and cities up and down the coast, including Hvar, Split, and Zadar. Local ferries also run to the Elafiti Islands and Mljet, and excursion boats go just about everywhere. Buy tickets and obtain schedule information at Jadrolinija's Dubrovnik office in Gruž (© **020/418-000**) or at Jadroagent at Radića 32 (© **020/419-000**).

BY CAR The A-1 *autocesta* between Zagreb and Split opened in June 2005 and was extended another 27km (16 miles) to Omiš in 2007. However, the leg of the highway that continues on to Dubrovnik still is in the planning phase and not expected to open until 2010. Consequently, if you travel by car from Omiš to Dubrovnik, you still have to take the much slower E-65 for the entire 190km (115-mile) trip, which can take as long as 4 hours. If you drive straight from Zagreb to Dubrovnik, it will take approximately 7 hours—more during summer gridlock—so plan to take your time for this trip.

BY BUS Daily buses operate between the Dubrovnik ferry port at Gruž and Zagreb, Zadar, Split, Šibenik, Rijeka, Orebić, and Korčula, as well as Mostar and Sarajevo in Bosnia and the pilgrimage city of Međugorje in Hercegovina. The Dubrovnik bus terminal is at Put Republike 19 (✆ **020/357-020**).

BY TRAIN There is no train service to Dubrovnik.

NEIGHBORHOODS IN BRIEF

The area within Dubrovnik's walls is known as **Old Town,** and most of the city's attractions are there. Besides historic buildings, you will find restaurants, cafes, shops, and services in and around this pedestrians-only zone. **Ploče** is the neighborhood outside Old Town's Eastern Gate. Most of the city's upscale hotels are on beachfront property, as is Banje, the city's most pleasant beach. **Lapad** is a suburban promenade lined with hotels and restaurants backed by a residential area set on a peninsula west of Old Town. Lapad has some beach area, but its main attraction is a cluster of (relatively) moderately priced hotels. A 15-minute ride on the no. 6 bus connects Lapad with Old Town at the Pile Gate. At some indeterminable point, Lapad ends and **Babin Kuk** begins. Babin Kuk has hotels in various price ranges plus access to rocky coves with what optimists call beaches (read: major pebbles/rocks, no sand), scores of restaurants, shops, and public bus routes that connect it to Dubrovnik.

GETTING AROUND

There are no trains or trams in Dubrovnik, but the Libertas city bus system is fairly efficient (www.libertasdubrovnik.hr). If you are staying within comfortable walking distance of Old Town, everything important is accessible on foot.

BY BUS Buy one-way tickets from a the driver for 10kn ($2.05/£1.25) and save 2kn (40¢/25p) if you buy at a news kiosk or at your hotel. All buses stop at the Pile Gate and continue on to outlying hotels, the ferry port, and beyond. Schedules and route maps are available at the Tourist Information Center in Old Town across from the Franciscan Monastery.

BY TAXI Taxi stands are at the airport, bus station, and the Pile Gate. Taxis can be called locally ✆ **020/424 343** (Pile Gate), ✆ **020/423 164** (Ploče), ✆ **020/418 112** (ferry port), ✆ **020/357 044** (bus station), and ✆ **020/435-715** (Lapad). Rides start with 25kn ($5.10/£3.15) on the meter and go up 8kn ($1.65/£1) per kilometer. If you agree to a meterless ride, negotiate a price beforehand to avoid rip-offs and unwanted excursions.

ON FOOT Negotiating the busy streets outside the walls can be confusing, especially at night. But once you are in the vicinity of Old Town, you can devise your own walking tour using the suggestions in this book. You also can employ a private guide to accompany you on a walk, or you can book a guided Old Town walking tour through the tourist office or through a private tourist agency.

BY CAR Congestion and parking make driving in Dubrovnik stressful, and Old Town is pedestrianized anyway, but if you rent a car for excursions to nearby Pelješac or Ston, car-rental companies at the airport include **Hertz** (✆ **01/484 6777;** www.hertz.hr), **Budget** (✆ **020/773 290;** www.budget.hr), and **Thrifty** (✆ **020/773 3588;** www.thrifty.com). Be sure to reserve a car in advance to ensure availability.

BY BICYCLE Agency Korkyra (✆ **385 (0)20 716 295;** Iva Vojnovica 79; www.dubrovnik-rent.com/dubrovnikrent.html) rents 8-speed bikes by the hour, day, or week.

VISITOR INFORMATION

The agencies below represent a partial list that can help with Dubrovnik information and bookings.

Atlas Travel at Ćira Carića 3 (✆ **020/442-222**) operates multiple excursions out of Dubrovnik and can book hotels and private accommodations, air and ferry tickets, adventure sports experiences, and a variety of custom services. The **Dubrovnik Tourist Office** is across the street from the Hilton Imperial on the road leading to the Pile Gate, and at several other locations around town. The Pile Gate location at Starčevića 7 (✆ **020/427-591**) is also an Internet center where you can check your e-mail or connect with home. **Elite Travel** at Vukovarska 17 (✆ **020/358-200**) runs specialized tours such as the UNESCO World Heritage Croatia Tour, which visits the country's protected cultural and natural sites; a horseback tour of Konavale; and a canoe safari on the Trebezit River, among others.

Note: If you have the resources, consider booking an English-speaking private guide who not only can plan a custom itinerary for you, but also can arrange transport, transfers, and admittance to otherwise inaccessible sites. **Jelena Delić** (✆ **91/531-8782;** damale3@hotmail.com) is one of the best.

Fast Facts Dubrovnik

American Express **Atlas Travel,** Ćira Carića 3 (✆ **020/419-119;** fax 020/442-645; www.atlas-croatia.com), is the American Express agent in Dubrovnik. Atlas-Amex also has an office at Brsalje 17 (✆ **020/442-574**), open from 8am to 7pm Monday through Saturday.

ATMs Croatian banks operate bancomats at Stradun, Lapad, Gruž, Cavtat, and the post office across from the Hilton Imperial.

Banks Banks generally are open from 7:30am to 7pm Monday through Friday and from 7:30 to 11:30am Saturday. Some banks close for lunch.

Business Hours Most grocery and department stores are open from 7:30am to 8pm. Nongovernment offices work 8:30am to 5pm Monday through Friday.

Credit Cards Credit cards are generally accepted at hotels and larger restaurants, but be sure to ask before you order as the policy can change in tourist season.

Emergencies To call for an ambulance, dial ✆ **94;** fire, dial ✆ **93;** police, dial ✆ **92.**

Hospital Go to the **Dubrovnik General Hospital** (✆ **020/431-777**).

Pharmacy Pharmacies work morning and afternoon Monday through Friday, and Saturday mornings. Almost all accept credit cards.

Telephone Public telephone boxes use phone cards available from newspaper stands and post offices.

Time Zone Dubrovnik is on Central European Time (GMT plus 1 hr.). Daylight saving time starts at the end of March and ends September 30.

Weather Daily forecasts are available at www.dubrovnik-online.com/english/weather.php.

WHERE TO STAY IN DUBROVNIK

Note: Some owners refuse to rent for fewer than 3 or 7 days, especially during July and August. If you find one that rents by the night, expect a 20% to 50% surcharge.

Very Expensive

Bellevue ★★★ The Bellevue closed late in 2005 to undergo an extensive renovation, and the result is a clifftop beauty with jaw-dropping views of Dubrovnik and the sea. Natural materials that include Dalmatian stone and olive wood are featured in the decor throughout the hotel, and there's even a palm tree growing up from the restaurant to the reception area. Guest rooms are done in a sailboat motif; all walls are hung with original works by Croatian artists and all have a view of the Adriatic (88 have balconies, too). The hotel also has a full complement of amenities that includes a private theater room for movie screenings.

Pera Cingrije 7. ✆ **020/330-000.** Fax 020/330-100. www.hotel-bellevue.hr. 93 units. Doubles with sea view and balcony from 642€ ($815); suites from 927€ ($1,177). AE, DC, MC, V. Rates include breakfast. **Amenities:** 2 restaurants; 2 bars; indoor pool; spa; car rental; business center; Wi-Fi/LAN access; retail shops; valet service; private beach; screening room; garage. *In room:* A/C, SAT/TV, minibar, hair dryer, safe, Jacuzzis in suites.

Hilton Imperial ★★★ The Hilton is steps from the Pile Gate and combines the grace of its 1897 predecessor with stylish architectural detail and genteel luxury. The original Imperial (and its guesthouse across the street) sheltered refugees during Croatia's civil war and took direct mortar hits. Hilton wisely preserved what it could from the old Imperial—stone staircases, the lobby footprint—and the result is spectacular. Rooms are spacious and done in earth/sun color schemes with spacious bathrooms that include tubs and showers. Hilton staff members are trained in guest relations and extend the same courtesies to Brioni-suited businesspeople and backpackers alike, an anomaly in Croatia's resident-tourist relationship.

Marijana Blažića 2 (Pile Gate). ✆ **020/320-320.** Fax 020/320-220. www.hilton.com. 147 units. From 299€ ($380) double; from 365€ ($464) executive plus. AE, DC, MC, V. Parking 28€ ($36) per day for guests. **Amenities:** Restaurant; piano bar; pool; sauna; steam bath; nonsmoking rooms; room for those w/limited mobility. *In room:* A/C, TV, Internet connection (25€/$32 per day), minibar, hair dryer, safe.

Hotel Excelsior ★★★ The Excelsior enjoys a location that is walking distance from Old Town and steps from the sea. It was built in 1913, expanded in the 1960s, updated in 1998 and 2006, and completely renovated for the 2008 season. Guest rooms, whether in the old or new parts of the hotel, are well appointed, but the rooms overlooking the sea are stunning because they offer breathtaking views of Dubrovnik's wall and lookout towers.

Frana supila 12, Ploče. ✆ **020/353-300.** Fax 020/414-214. www.hotel-excelsior.hr. 164 units. From 540€ ($686) double with sea view and balcony; from 685€ ($870) suite. AE, DC, MC, V. Rates include breakfast. Half board available. Parking free for hotel guests. **Amenities:** 2 restaurants; piano bar; indoor pool; sauna; Internet access; rooms/facilities for those w/limited mobility. *In room:* A/C, TV, fax, Internet connection, minibar, hair dryer, safe.

Dubrovnik Lodging, Dining & Attractions

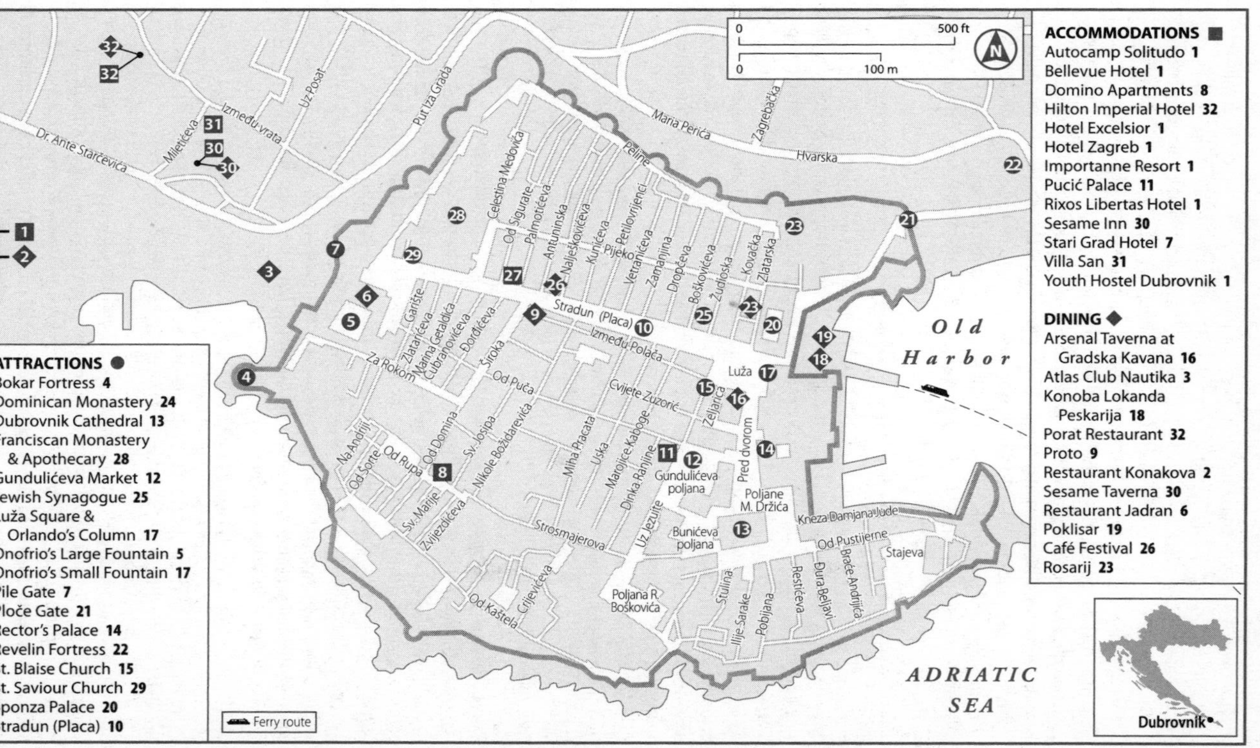

Coming Attractions

Dubrovnik's luxury accommodations pool soon will grow dramatically, thanks to the Rezidor Hotel Group, parent of the Regent Esplanade in Zagreb (p. 190). Rezidor has unveiled plans for a megaresort in Orašac, a picturesque village about 13km (8 miles) north of Old Town. Orašac has been targeted as a prime location for development because it is situated on a gorgeous coastal location and it is home to historical buildings that include a 15th-century church and a 16th-century palace. The Rezidor facilities will be home to a 408-unit Radisson SAS hotel/apartment complex and a luxurious 128-unit Regent hotel. The new hotels will be in the center of the Sun Garden Resort and will include a sports center, several outdoor swimming pools, numerous restaurants, and retail opportunities. A late 2009 opening is projected for the Radisson, and an early 2010 date is on tap for the Regent.

Importanne Resort ★★ Three hotels—the Neptun/Importanne Suites, the Ariston, and the upscale Villa Elita—now make up Importanne Resort, a cluster complex that opened in spring 2007 on the Lapad Peninsula 10 minutes from Dubrovnik's Old Town. The facilities are mostly renovated and offer accommodations to suit a wide demographic that includes both families and tycoons. Villa Elita is the poshest (and most expensive) of the lot, with a stratospheric tariff that *does* include the use of one of several luxury cars, use of a speedboat, and valet service.

Kardinala Alojzija Stepinca 31. ✆ **020/440-100.** Fax 020/440-200. www.importanneresort.com. 158 units (Importanne Suites), 116 units (Ariston), 6 units (Villa Elita). Luxury doubles in the Neptun 216€–12,000€ ($274–$15,240) for Villa Elita (up to 12 people). AE, DC, MC, V. Free parking. **Amenities:** 3 restaurants; beach bar; 2 seawater pools; spa; room service. *In room:* A/C, SAT/TV, Internet access, minibar, hair dryer, safe, balconies in most rooms.

Pucić Palace ★ (Overrated) The legendary haunt of well-heeled visitors to Dubrovnik combines the ambience of a Renaissance palace with contemporary comforts, but it falls short of what you'd expect for the hefty room rates. Furnishings are top-quality and bathrooms are lined with nonskid tiles and tasteful mosaics and loaded with toiletries, but we're talking tiny showers here. The hotel maintains a yacht in the harbor for guest use and offers extravagant in-room add-ons like a bottle of Dom Perignon (430€/$632) or hot chocolate cake (22€/$32 per piece); the terrace has a great view of the city; and you *are* staying in a historic monument; but you'll have to decide for yourself if those things offer enough value per dollar.

Ulica Od Puča 1, Old Town. ✆ **020/326-200,** or 020/326-222 reservations. Fax 020/326-223. www.thepucicpalace.com. 19 units. June–Sept from 673€ ($632) double; from 1,129€ ($1,659) suite. Other times from 430€ ($632) double; from 870€ ($1,278) suite. AE, DC, MC, V. Rates include breakfast. **Amenities:** Restaurant; bar; concierge; 24-hr. room service. *In room:* A/C, TV, minibar, safe.

Rixos Libertas ★★★ The opening of this exclusive property was delayed several times since 2004, when the Turkish hotelier bought the crumbling landmark Libertas Hotel and its real estate 15 minutes from Old Town's north gate. Nearly 4 years and $103 million later, Rixos unveiled the result of its Pygmalion project, which has transformed the former refugee shelter into a 14-story temple of glass, steel, and stone. The new Libertas opened in 2007; it is terraced into a cliff overlooking the Adriatic and it is loaded with every conceivable amenity. From stylish rooms outfitted with high-grade furnishings; large, upscale bathrooms; computers and plasma TVs, to a long menu of watersports, gourmet restaurants, and a two-story, full service spa, Dubrovnik's newest luxury address has it all. ***Tip:*** Look for Internet specials when booking—rates are among Dubrovnik's steepest.

Liechtensteinov Put 3. ✆ **020/333-720.** Fax 020/333-723. www.rixos.com. 315 units. From 390€ ($495) double; from 750€ ($953) suite. AE, DC, MC, V. Rates include breakfast. Free parking. **Amenities:** 3 restaurants; 5 bars; patisserie; cigar bar; nightclub; indoor and outdoor pools; spa; kids' program; designer retail outlets; laundry; rooms for those w/limited mobility; nonsmoking rooms; casino. *In room:* A/C, SAT/TV, Wi-Fi and broadband Internet access, minibar, room service, hair dryer.

Expensive

Domino Apartments ★ One of these six vintage luxury apartments is tucked into a tiny courtyard at the end of Siroko Street. Others are located in nearby historic buildings. Each is the equivalent of a luxury condo rental. The larger apartments have living rooms, while the smaller ones are really studios with kitchenettes. Furniture and appliances are modern; window views are of neighboring buildings; and the apartments can get noisy when local restaurants are busy. A rental office is in the Fendi store at ground level in the Hliđina Street property.

Hliđina 4, Old Town. ✆ **020/324-940.** Fax 020/324-824. www.dominoapartments.com. 6 units. July–Sept 250€ ($318); Oct–June 200€ ($254). Breakfast is not included. AE, DC, MC, V. *In room:* A/C, TV.

Hotel Stari Grad ★★ Value The tiny Stari Grad is a bargain when you consider that it is a cultural monument and just one of two hotels within Old Town's walls. The mansion opened as a hotel in 2002, and each room is comfortable, cozy, and augmented by bathrooms equipped with hydromassage showers. The view of Lokrum and Cavtat from the fifth-floor terrace is dynamite.

Od Sigurate br. 4, Old Town. ✆ **020/322-244.** Fax 020/321-256. www.hotelstarigrad.com. 8 units. July–Sept from 211€ ($268) double; Oct–June from 122€ ($155) double. Rates include breakfast. 10% surcharge for stays of 3 days or fewer. AE, MC, V. **Amenities:** Restaurant; babysitting; safe-deposit box; valet. *In room:* A/C, TV, dataport, minibar, hair dryer.

Moderate

Hotel Zagreb ★★ Finds A fabulous restoration has turned this salmon-colored 19th-century mansion with white trim into a showplace hotel on the Lapad promenade. Each guest room is unique, and staying here is like staying in a grand Habsburg home, complete with shaded garden and sprawling lawn. Some of the staff speak English; all are very helpful.

Šetalište Kralja Zvonimira 27, Lapad. ✆ **020/436-146.** Fax 020/436-006. 24 units. July to mid-Sept from 1,320kn ($270/£167) double; mid-Sept to June from 800kn ($164/£102) double. **Amenities:** Restaurant; bar. *In room:* TV, hair dryer.

Sesame Inn ★★ The Sesame Inn is a boutique hotel attached to a restaurant (p. 141). The entire package blends convenience, history, and gourmet dining for anyone who is lucky enough to book one of the inn's four modern rooms. The 200-year-old Dalmatian stone house has been updated with handsome white bathrooms, stylish furniture, and windows that overlook a fragrant garden and sunny terrace. Add to that reasonable (for Dubrovnik) rates, the hosts' (Ercegović family) cordiality, and the inn's position 150m (492 ft.) from the Pile Gate, and you have a perfect base from which to explore Old Town Dubrovnik.

Don Frane Bulića 4. ✆ **020/412-910.** www.sesame.hr. 4 units. July–Aug from 144€ ($183) double; Sept–June from 114€ ($145) double. No credit cards. Rates include breakfast and taxes. 20% surcharge for stays of 3 days or less. **Amenities:** Restaurant; terrace.

Villa San ★★ Private apartments and rooms are Dubrovnik's best moderately priced accommodations options, and Villa San can't be beat for convenience. Villa San is situated above a bank behind the Pile Gate bus stop, 90m (300 ft.) from the beach and steps from the water taxi to Lokrum. The property is managed by the Ahmić family, and it comprises four apartments ranging in size from "mini" to "penthouse." The latter is on the top floor and can sleep eight in three bedrooms, kitchen, living room, and two bathrooms, one with a Jacuzzi.

Tiha 2, near Old Town. ✆ **020/411-884.** www.villa-san.com. 4 units. July–Sept from 90€ ($114) double; Oct–June from 60€ ($76) double; from 180€ ($229) penthouse July–Aug and New Year's, from 120€ ($152) Sept–June. 20% deposit required. No credit cards. Free parking. *In room:* A/C, TV, some balconies.

Inexpensive

Autocamp Solitudo ★★ The bathrooms here are excellent and the camp is within .5km (1/4 mile) of the sea and many sports facilities, but it is 24km (15 miles) from Dubrovnik proper. Unless you're set on camping, a private room closer to town might be a better logistical choice.

Vatroslava Lisinskog 17, Babin Kuk. ✆ **020/448-686.** Fax 020/448-688. www.babinkuk.com. 238 campsites. Apr–Oct 15 site with electricity and 2 persons 31€ ($39). Price includes registration fee and VAT. 20% deposit required to hold reservation. AE, DC, MC, V. Dogs allowed in some areas. **Amenities:** Restaurant; market; pool; excursions; laundry; facility adaptations for those w/limited mobility.

Youth Hostel Dubrovnik ★ This hostel stays open all year long and it is just a 10-minute walk from the bus station and 15 minutes from Old Town. The hostel has a fine reputation, but you must be a member of a hostelling association to stay in these dorm-style accommodations near one of Dubrovnik's hottest nightlife areas.

Vinka Sagrestana 3, near Old Town. ✆ **020/423-241.** Fax 020/412-592. www.hfhs.hr/home.php?lang=en. 19 units with 82 beds. July–Aug bed-and-breakfast 16€ ($20) per person; rest of year bed-and-breakfast from 12€ ($15) per person. No credit cards. **Amenities:** Restaurant; TV room; membership kitchen.

WHERE TO DINE

It's hard to get a bad meal in Dubrovnik, but it's even more difficult to get a meal that's not overpriced or that bucks the grilled meat/fish or risotto/pasta formula.

Expensive

Porat ★★ CONTINENTAL/DALMATIAN The Hilton and its restaurant, Porat, opened to great fanfare in May 2005, and so far, neither has been a disappointment. Porat's elegant dining room and pretty terrace offer a menu of local dishes enhanced by creative twists and sauces. Try crispy skinned sea bass filet with candied lemon from the lava-stone grill, or beef tenderloin and tomato-shallot marmalade. Duck breast is on the menu, which is unusual in Dalmatia.

In the Hilton Imperial. Marijana Blažića 2. ✆ **020/320-320.** Fax 020/320-220. www.hilton.com. Reservations required for dinner. Dinner entrees 140kn–190kn ($29–$39/£18–£24); lunch and breakfast entrees 70kn–120kn ($14-$25/£8.70–£16). AE, DC, MC, V. Daily 7–10:30am, 12:30–2:30pm, and 7–11pm.

Moderate

Arsenal Taverna at Gradska Kavana ★ CROATIAN This upscale spot became a delightful addition to Dubrovnik's restaurant scene when it reopened in November 2005 on the Old Harbor near the Ploče Gate. Walk through the Arsenal Wine Bar across from

St. Blaise Church off Luža Square and claim a table on the terrace. The menu is typical of Dubrovnik with lots of fish dishes, but it also has a better-than-average selection of grilled meats and an extensive but pricey selection of Croatian wines. A plus: Appetizers include *paški sir,* a specialty sheep's milk cheese from the island of Pag, and *kulen,* a spicy sausage from Slavonia in eastern Croatia. Service can be slow, but who wants to hurry through a meal when the twinkling lights of Dubrovnik are the backdrop?

Pred Dvorom 1, Old Town. ✆ **020/321-065.** Entrees 70kn–140kn ($14–$29/£8.70–£18). AE, DC, MC, V. Daily 9am–2am. Kitchen closes at 11:30pm.

Restaurant Konakova ★★ Value DALMATIAN This second-floor terrace restaurant in Lapad packs them in every night. Like most other Dubrovnik dining spots, specialties are seafood, grilled meat, pizza, and pasta, but equal care is given to all dishes. Little touches like complimentary fish pâtés with the bread add value and make Konakova an even bigger bargain.

Šetalište Kralja Zvonimira 38, Lapad. ✆ **020/435-105.** Entrees 45kn–120kn ($9.20–$25/£5.70–£15). AE, DC, MC, V. Daily noon–midnight.

Rozarij ★★ Finds DALMATIAN SEAFOOD Rattan tables outside this tiny eatery are arranged on steps around the entrance. Rozarij is on a hard-to-find corner of restaurant-clogged Prijeko (at Zlatarska), but its impeccable seafood is worth searching out. Try shrimp with white risotto or mixed *buzzara,* a combination of mussels and scampi in a fragrant court bouillon.

Prijeko 2, Old Town. ✆ **020/321-257.** Entrees 50kn–120kn ($10–$31/£6.20–£19). No credit cards. Daily 11am–midnight.

Sesame Taverna ★★ DALMATIAN This dining room doesn't have a seaside location, but it does have stone walls, a vaulted ceiling bathed flickering candlelight, and a menu of beautifully presented dishes. Sesame Taverna is just west of the Pile Gate, and it as romantic as it gets, especially outside on the upstairs terrace. Try the chicken Elafiti with rosemary and olives, or any of the dishes with truffles accompanied by a reasonably priced bottle of wine.

Din Frane Bulića 7, west of the Pile Gate. ✆ **020/412-910.** www.sesame.hr. Entrees 50kn–125kn ($10–$26/£6.20–£16), more for seafood sold by the kilo. AE. Daily 8am–11pm.

Inexpensive

Café Festival ★ SANDWICHES It can get warm in the afternoon sun at tables under the nautical blue awning outside this smart cafe near the Pile Gate, so go inside to try the salads, pastas, fancy drinks, and homemade pastries. Café Festival is ideal for a light lunch or a cool drink.

Stradun bb, Old Town. ✆ **020/420-888.** Entrees 15kn–45kn ($3.05–$9.20/£1.90–£5.70). AE, DC, MC, V. Daily 8am–11pm.

Konoba Lokanda Peskarija ★ Value FISH/RISOTTO Turn left from Zlatarska at the east end of the Stradun and go through the wall opening to the Old Harbor. Entertainment is all around you: Watch walkers atop the wall, see boats dock and take off, observe chefs working in an open kitchen that looks like a beach bar, and watch hopeful diners standing around waiting for your table. Prices are low, main courses are limited to a few fish dishes and risottos, but portions are huge. The octopus salad and black risotto are standouts.

Gorica Svetog Vlaha 77. Old Town. ✆ **020/324-750.** Entrees 40kn–65kn ($8.15–$13/£5.05–£8.20). No credit cards. Daily 8am–2am. Kitchen noon–midnight.

Restaurant Jadran DALMATIAN Turn right after walking through the Pile Gate to Jadran, a touristy but solid restaurant with both a garden setting and an indoor dining room. The restaurant is in the former Convent of the Poor Clares, and the menu has all the usual Dalmatian entrees plus the occasional omelet and salad. Jadran is a good place for a quick bite before or after you embark on the walk around the city wall.

Paska Milićevića 1, Old Town. ✆ **020/323-403.** Fax 020/323-403. Entrees 19kn–49kn ($3.90–$10/£2.40–£6.20). AE, DC, MC, V. Daily 10am–midnight.

EXPLORING DUBROVNIK

Dubrovnik sprawls well beyond the city walls, but just about everything worth seeing is within the Old Town enclosure.

City Wall ★★★ No visit to Dubrovnik is complete without a walk along the top of its wall, a work of artful fortification built in medieval times that frames the historic city. As you make the 2km (1¼-mile) circuit around the wall, which is 25m (82 ft.) high and 6m (20 ft.) thick at some points, you'll see greater Dubrovnik and its landmark red-tile rooftops from every conceivable angle. You'll be voyeur to residents going about their lives and tourists swimming in the Adriatic off the wall's base, or dining at restaurants on rocky outcroppings that abut the wall's foundation.

You can access the wall at three points: just inside the Pile Gate, near the Maritime Museum/John's Fortress, and near the Dominican Monastery at the Ploče Gate. The entire circuit takes about an hour, longer if you're inclined to stop and gape at the spectacular scenery, but you can do a half walk, too. If you start at the **Pile Gate** entrance, you'll walk up a steep flight of stairs through an arch topped by a statue of St. Blaise. If you want to do the entire 360-degree stroll, continue straight up toward the **Minčeta Tower,** which is recognizable by its distinctive "crown." If you decide on the partial walk, halfway up the stairs you'll have to do a 180 from the stairs via a small landing to reach the wall, and you'll exit near **St. John's Fortress** on the south side. The 16th-century **Revelin Fort** is on the eastern side of the wall above the Ploče Gate; and the 15th-century **Bokar Fortress,** which guarded against sea incursions, is at the southwestern corner across from the 12th-century **Lovrijenac Fortress.**

Old Town. 50kn ($10/£6.30) adults; 10kn ($2/£1.25) children 5–14; free children 4 and under. Audio rental 40kn ($8/£4.95). July–Aug daily 9am–7:30pm; hours vary other times.

Stradun District

Old Town's western gate, the **Pile Gate ★★★**, is its busiest point of entry, largely because buses from the city, airport, and ferry terminals deposit their passengers there. A stone bridge leads to the outer gate, guarded by a statue of St. Blaise; during the summer, honor guards in period costume stand there mornings and evenings greeting tourists. The

The Heat

When Dubrovnik's temperature is above 80°F (27°C)—the average temperature May through September—tackle the wall when it opens at 9am, or wait until after 5pm. Besides being atop a high roof, you'll be standing on an unshaded stone path that absorbs the sun's heat from dawn to dusk and you'll be "cooked" from above and below. At the very least, wear a hat and take a large bottle of water.

Fun Facts **Getting Stoned**

When you leave St. Saviour Church for the Franciscan monastery next door, keep your eyes downcast and you'll see a 12-×12-inch stone with a carved face and smooth top protruding about 6 inches above the street. You'll also see a crowd watching people attempting to stand on the stone for a few seconds. Legend says that guys who can stay on the stone known as the "Mask" long enough to remove their shirts will have good luck. (Girls also try this but are entitled to the luck without removing their shirts.)

interior gate was built in the 15th century and it, too, has a statue of St. Blaise—this one by Ivan Meštrović, Croatia's premier sculptor.

When you enter Old Town through either the Pile Gate or the Ploče Gate, you will find one of **Onofrio's Fountains** ★★★. Both were constructed in the 15th century so visitors could wash away plague before they entered the city. The fountains provided clean, cold water via an aqueduct from the Dubrovnik River (Rijeka Dubrovačka), 11km (7 miles) away, but their efficacy as germ killers is questionable. The larger fountain at the Pile Gate looks like a domed vat decorated with 16 stone heads, the only ornamentation remaining from the original, thanks to the 1667 quake and the 1991 to 1992 siege. Water from the Luža Square fountain flows through a more ornate device with detailed sculpture work. People fill water bottles and soak bandannas in the cold water, especially in summer when Dubrovnik is steamy.

The **Stradun** (aka Placa) ★★★ is Dubrovnik's main thoroughfare. It runs from the Pile Gate through Old Town to the Ploče Gate and is paved with limestone buffed to a smooth, shiny surface by tourist footfall. The Stradun is lined with neat, uniform buildings housing shops, restaurants, and entryways to alley-size streets. Historical pictures show that Dubrovnik's pre-1667-earthquake buildings were far more ornate than the present structures.

Franciscan Monastery ★★ A small **apothecary** inside the 14th-century monastery complex has been in business in 1317 and claims to be the oldest working pharmacy in Europe. It has a fascinating display of ancient lab equipment, mortars, measuring implements, and decorative containers used over the centuries. The monastery itself is accessed via a narrow passage from **St. Saviour's Church;** the complex's **Romanesque cloister** is the monastery's most compelling feature (the post-quake Renaissance cloister is open to Franciscans only). The lower cloister's open wall of double columns (topped with human, animal, and plant carvings) frame a tranquil open garden area where you can imagine monks enjoying the contemplative life. The complex also is home to a **15th-century well,** the single-nave **St. Francis Church,** a **bell tower,** and the **monastery museum,** whose library contains ancient writings, music manuscripts, gold and silver objets d'art, and other items that illuminate Dubrovnik's history.

Monastery museum 20kn ($4.05/£2.50) adults; 10kn ($2/£1.25) children. July–Aug 9am–6pm daily; erratic hours other times of the year.

St. Saviour Church ★ The Renaissance-Gothic facade of this small church faces the large Onofrio Fountain inside the Pile Gate. St. Saviour was built in the early 16th century and it is one of the few structures not damaged in the 1667 quake.

Between the Pile Gate and the Franciscan Monastery at Stradun 2. Daily 9am–7pm.

Who Is St. Blaise?

Legend says that St. Blaise once saved a child from choking on a fish bone. Roman Catholics know the Armenian physician and martyr as the patron saint of people with throat problems. However, the people of Dubrovnik revere St. Blaise (Sv. Vlaho) as the hero who saved their city from a sneak attack by Venetian galleys in the 10th century. According to legend, Venetian ships dropped anchor off Lokrum to pick up fresh water for their journey, but the fleet was actually surveying the city in preparation for a takeover. St. Blaise (martyred by Diocletian in 316 B.C.) appeared to the cathedral's priest in a dream and told him about the nefarious plot, thus thwarting the attack. Ever since, St. Blaise has been immortalized in sculpture, art, and other media as the city's protector.

Luža Square

The eastern end of the Stradun opens into busy **Luža Square** ★★★, which is an Old Town crossroads where tourists stop at **Onofrio's Little Fountain,** explore exhibits in **Sponza Palace,** meet friends at the **city bell tower,** take a *bijela kava* break at the **Gradska Kavana,** or sit on the steps of **St. Blaise Church.** Luža Square is also where Dubrovnik's Summer Festival kicks off.

The likeness of a warrior is chiseled into the stone **Orlando's Column** ★★ in the center of Luža Square and represents the legendary hero who reputedly was Charlemagne's nephew. The column was erected in 1419 and once served as the city's forum for public proclamations, notices, rallies, and punishments. In 1990 a flag with the city's LIBERTAS motto was flown above the column, which became a rallying point for Dubrovnik's freedom fighters.

As you approach Luža Square from the Stradun, you'll see the arches of the 15th-century **Sponza Palace** ★★ (✆ **020/321-032;** free admission) on your left. Today the Sponza is a venue for art exhibits and concerts. A 30m (100-ft.) bell tower next to the palace tolls the hour.

St. Blaise is Dubrovnik's patron saint, and **St. Blaise Church** ★★★, on Luža Square, open 8am to 7pm daily, was built between 1706 and 1714 on the site of a ruined 14th-century church. St. Blaise's wide staircase and terrace are popular with weary tourists who settle there for a break, much the same as pigeons congregate on the square itself. Inside, you'll find a silver-plated statue on the main altar depicting St. Blaise holding a 15th-century model of the city as it was before the 1667 earthquake.

The original **Dubrovnik Cathedral (Church of the Assumption)** ★★★ was built between the 12th and 14th centuries atop the ruins of a Byzantine basilica at Poljana Marina Držica. According to legend, a grateful King Richard the Lionhearted financed it to give thanks after being shipwrecked and rescued in Dubrovnik. It was severely damaged in the 1667 earthquake and rebuilt in the au courant baroque style, making it the third church to be constructed on this site. The cathedral's **treasury** (10kn/$2/£1.25; Mon–Sat 9am–5:30pm, Sun 11am–5:30pm) holds the skull, arm, and leg of St. Blaise, plated with gold and stashed behind a marble altar topped by .9m-high (3-ft.) panels of glass.

The original 13th-century **Rector's Palace** was destroyed in 1435 when gunpowder stored inside exploded. The palace was rebuilt only to blow up again 28 years later. The current **palace** ★★ resides on the original site just south of Luža Square at Pred Dvorom 3 (✆ **020/321-497;** admission 15kn/$3/£1.90). Upstairs rooms now house the **City Museum (Gradski Muzej).** Classical concerts are held in its courtyard during the Summer Festival.

The 14th-century **Dominican Monastery and Museum** ★★★ at Sv. Dominika 4 (museum admission 10kn/$2/£1.25) are behind the Sponza Palace off a narrow passageway leading to the Ploče Gate. Don't miss the museum, whose art collection includes a reliquary containing the skull of King Stephen I of Hungary.

Old Harbor (Stara Luka) District

West of St. John's Fortress and to the right of the Rector's Palace is **Gundulić Square,** where a raucous **market** ★ selling fruits, vegetables, cheeses, homemade wine, recycled water bottles filled with *rakija* (fruit brandy), and other produce is open for business every morning.

The **Jesuit Steps** ★★, a long set of baroque stairs off Gundulic market, are reminiscent of Rome's Spanish Steps. They lead up to the **Jesuit Church of St. Ignatius of Loyola** ★★★, Dubrovnik's largest house of worship. The stairs were severely damaged in the 1991 to 1992 siege, but have been restored. They end at the 1658 **Jesuit College,** where many of Ragusa's greatest scholars were educated.

The **Ploče Gate** ★★★ is at the eastern end of the Old City and, like the Pile Gate, it has inner and outer sections. The 15th-century portal is approached via a stone bridge.

BEACHES

Croatians loosely define beaches as any place the sea meets the land, and while some beaches may have names, many are little more than rocks used for sunbathing and diving platforms. One "beach" around the corner from the old port is a must-see, if not a must-**swim area** ★★★ where those who are confident swimmers routinely take a dip from a **rocky ledge.** There is even a water polo setup for tournaments and a cliffside bar (**Buža I** ★★★) where spectators watch the show.

Dubrovnik's main public beach, **Banje,** exists as a beach club (see below). Bobin Kuk's **Copacabana Beach** is a pebble-and-concrete affair with a view of the graceful Dubrovnik bridge and part of the Elafiti Islands. It is one of the few Dubrovnik beaches with facilities for kids, sports enthusiasts, and swimmers with disabilities. A lift on the concrete part of the beach gives seniors and people with disabilities easy access to the water. A beach bar and restaurant provide refreshments, and at night the bar becomes a cocktail lounge/disco. **Lapad Bay** is another popular spot for beachgoers and many hotels there have built stairs leading to the flat concrete slabs they call beaches.

The **Eastwest Beach Club** ★★★ at Frana Supila bb (✆ **020/412-220**) is situated on Dubrovnik's public pebble beach **(Banje)** about 46m (150 ft.) from the entrance to the Ploče (Eastern) Gate. The club has a restaurant with a view, a cocktail bar with dance floor, watersports, a pebble beach with crystal-clear water, attendants, and the unique baldachin, which is a "bed" on the beach that looks like a raised four-poster hung with gauzy curtains. You can rent the baldachin for 200kn ($41/£25) per day.

START:	**Brsalje Square outside the Pile Gate, the west entrance to Old Town.**
FINISH:	**St. Blaise Church/Luža Square.**
TIME:	**Anywhere from 30 minutes to 3 hours, depending on how much time you spend exploring side streets, in churches and museums, shopping, or dining.**
BEST TIMES:	**Mornings from 8am to noon before the sun is overhead; evenings after 6pm and until the last bar closes. This when the promenade starts and segues into a fashion show for the young and beautiful.**
WORST TIMES:	**Noon to sundown or whenever the temperature rises above 95°F (35°C).**

Walking around the top of Dubrovnik's wall is a stroll no visitor should miss, but once you've made the circuit, you'll realize that there's much more to Dubrovnik than the red-tile roofs visible from the ramparts. A walk up and down both sides of the Stradun is an ideal way to become acquainted with the city's charms. Old Town's smooth limestone path originally was a canal separating Old Ragusa from the mainland, and walking its length is a good way to get your bearings and become familiar with the attractions between the Pile Gate and the Ploče Gate. There is a high concentration of important sites on and just off the Stradun, and the pedestrian thoroughfare is always crowded. Lots of narrow side streets radiate up and out from the Stradun and intersect with cobbled streets that are packed with religious sites, historic architectural spots, shops, restaurants, a few courtyards, and even some residences.

Start your tour outside the Pile Gate in Brsalje Square next door to the Atlas Travel Agency and between the Nautika restaurant and Dubravka Kavana cafe:

1 Brsalje Square

Rendezvous in this leafy park, but before you enter Old Town, walk away from the street to the low balustrade. You'll have an unobstructed view of the sea and **Fort Lovrijenac** (aka Croatia's Gibraltar) to the right and the 16th-century **Bokar Fortress** to the left. Lovrijenac is built on a high, rocky peninsula that juts into the sea, and it is Dubrovnik's oldest defensive structure. These days it is used as a theater for Shakespearean productions and for performances during **Dubrovnik's Summer Festival.** Croatian native and television star Goran Višjić of *ER* fame is a frequent performer there. Bokar was used as a prison in the 19th century.

Return to the street, turn right, and approach the:

2 Pile Gate

This is the busiest portal to Old Town and it is really two gates you approach across a wooden drawbridge that once was pulled up each night to protect the city. Note the statue of St. Blaise carved into a niche above the opening of the 16th-century outer gate, and another statue of the city's patron (by **Ivan Meštrović**) inside the even older (15th c.) inner gate. Occasionally musicians and vendors hang out in the courtyard between the gates to catch people on their way out.

Step through the inner gate and stop a moment to orient. Walk through and note:

3 Onofrio's Large Fountain & the Wall Walk Entrance

Walk inside the Pile Gate, and to the left you'll see a steep stairway that leads up to the **Minčeta Tower** at the top of the wall. This is one of three access points to the wall. To the right is **Onofrio's Large Fountain,** a tall concrete dome that during the Middle Ages was a collection point for water that flowed into the city from the **Dubrovnik River** 12km (7½ miles) away via an aqueduct. The fountain was more ornate when it was completed in 1444,

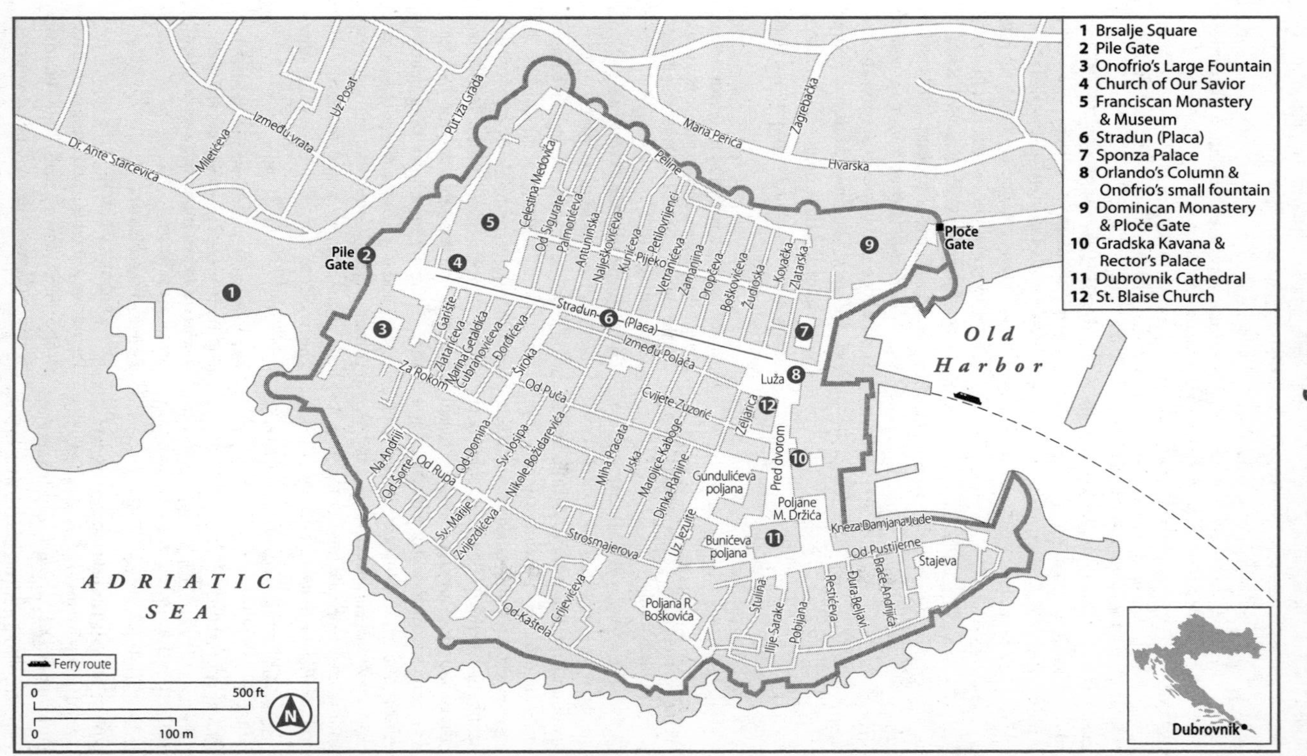
1 Brsalje Square
2 Pile Gate
3 Onofrio's Large Fountain
4 Church of Our Savior
5 Franciscan Monastery & Museum
6 Stradun (Placa)
7 Sponza Palace
8 Orlando's Column & Onofrio's small fountain
9 Dominican Monastery & Ploče Gate
10 Gradska Kavana & Rector's Palace
11 Dubrovnik Cathedral
12 St. Blaise Church
Old Harbor
ADRIATIC SEA
Pile Gate
Ploče Gate
Dubrovnik
Ferry route
0
500 ft
0
100 m
N
Stradun (Placa)
Luža
Pred dvorom
Poljane M. Držića
Gundulićeva poljana
Bunićeva poljana
Poljana R. Boškovića
Uz Jezuite
Između Polača
Cvijete Zuzorić
Zeljarica
Široka
Od Puča
Za Rokom
Od Domina
Sv. Josipa
Nikole Božidarevića
Miha Pracata
Uska
Marojice Kaboge
Dinka Ranjine
Strosmajerova
Od Rupa
Od Šorte
Na Andriji
Sv. Marije
Zvijezdićeva
Od Kaštela
Crijevićeva
Stulina
Ilije Sarake
Pobijana
Restićeva
Đura Beljavi
Braće Andrijića
Od Pustijerne
Kneza Damjana Jude
Stajeva
Garište
Zlatarićeva
Marina Getaldića
Cubranovićeva
Đorđićeva
Celestina Medovića
Od Sigurate
Palmotićeva
Antuninska
Nalješkovićeva
Kunićeva
Pijeko
Petilovrijenci
Vetranićeva
Zamanjina
Dropčeva
Boškovićeva
Žudioska
Kovačka
Zlatarska
Peline
Hvarska
Zagrebačka
Maria Perića
Put Iza Grada
Uz Posat
Između vrata
Miletićeva
Dr. Ante Starčevića

but the iron embellishments were destroyed in the 1667 earthquake.

Stay left. The first building on your left is:

❹ Church of Our Saviour

This tiny church was built as a memorial to the victims of a 1520 earthquake, but it became a symbol of strength when it became one of the few buildings to survive the 1667 quake that destroyed most of the city. Today it is used for concerts and exhibits.

Walk on a few steps to:

❺ The Franciscan Monastery/ Museum

Before you explore this building with its columned cloister and ancient pharmacy, note the small stone protruding from the bottom left of the church's front (p. 143) and the people who keep jumping on it. This building, with its garden, architectural features, pharmacy, and museum exhibits is worth a visit (p. 143).

Exit the monastery and begin your Stradun stroll in earnest to investigate the:

❻ Stradun Shops & Side Streets

The Stradun (aka Placa) runs to the clock tower and the **Ploče Gate.** All the buildings along the way are almost identical in style, a result of post-quake construction in the 17th century. Note the arches that frame a combo door and window. The sill was used as a counter over which business was conducted. If you are up for a detour, head up **Žudioska Street** to visit the second-oldest synagogue in Europe and its original 17th-century furnishings.

Continue along the Stradun past Zlatarska Street to the:

❼ Sponza Palace

As you approach Luža Square, note the graceful Renaissance arches of the **Sponza Palace** (p. 144), which used to be Dubrovnik's Customs House. Today it houses the **Memorial Room of the Dubrovnik Defenders,** a visual tribute to the more than 300 people who were killed from October 1, 1991, to October 26, 1992, while defending Dubrovnik against Serb attacks. Multimedia images of the destruction and photos of the young people who died in the conflict are moving reminders of the devastation that swept Croatia at that time.

Exit the palace and walk up to Orlando's Column in the center of Luža Square and pause at:

❽ Orlando's Column & Onofrio's Small Fountain

Orlando's Column (p. 144) will be in front of you as you exit the Palace and the **Clock Tower** will be to your left. Note the statue's forearm, which was Old Ragusa's standard of measurement (512mm/20 in.). The **Clock Tower** features a pair of bronze men that move up to strike the bell on the hour. The **Town Hall** is the large building to the right of the Clock Tower, and **Onofrio's Small Fountain** is in front of that.

Turn left from the front of Orlando's Column and walk through the passageway between the Sponza Palace and the Town Hall. Turn left and head to the Dominican Monastery:

❾ Dominican Monastery, the Old Port & the Ploče Gate

The Dominican Monastery is a complex that includes a large church, cloisters, and a museum. The original 14th-century church was destroyed in the 1667 quake and this one was rebuilt in the 17th century. There are some interesting paintings inside, and the church also doubles as a concert venue during the Summer Festival. The cloisters are a must-see, with courtyard gardens and interesting stonework (p. 145).

Exit the monastery and left onto Svetoga Dominika. Continue on to explore the Old Harbor, Ploče Gate, and Revelin Fortress and/or retrace your steps and return to Luža Square:

❿ Gradska Kavana & the Rector's Palace

As you return from the Dominican Monastery, the Town Hall and **Gradska Kavana (Town Cafe)** will be on your left. You can break for a cold drink or coffee and sit at tables facing the square, or go inside and grab a spot on the terrace overlooking the Old Harbor. The **Town Theater** is also in this building. The Venetian-Gothic **Rector's Palace** (p. 145) is adjacent to the Gradska Kavana complex, fronted by pillars made of marble from Korčula and topped with interesting carvings. The interior is used for summer concerts.

Exit the Rector's Palace and turn left:

⓫ Dubrovnik Cathedral

Note the minimalist gray marble altar that was installed when Roman Catholicism ruled that the priest should face the people during Mass. Its block style is incongruent with the rest of the church's baroque design. Don't miss the church **treasury** (p. 144), which is loaded with priceless relics, including the skull of St. Blaise and a piece of the True Cross.

Exit the cathedral and walk around to the rear, and walk up Androvićeva to the Jesuit Steps and Jesuit Church of St. Ignatius of Loyola (p. 145), or turn left and walk past the Rector's Palace to return to Luža Square.

⓬ St. Blaise Church

This 18th-century baroque church (p. 144) is a tribute to Dubrovnik's patron saint. Inside, the altar is the main draw with its statue of the saint holding a model of the city of Dubrovnik as it was before the 1667 quake. Outside, the church's wide steps are a popular resting/meeting place for tourists.

From St. Blaise you can return to the Pile Gate and inspect the shops along the south side of the Stradun, explore what you've just seen in greater depth, or venture up the steep side streets to discover more sights between the Stradun and the walls.

SHOPPING

You won't need to worry about going over your Customs limit when shopping in Dubrovnik. There are few stores that offer anything uniquely Croatian, and those that do are often overpriced. Goods from Stradun shops are especially costly, so stick to shops on the side streets and limit yourself to souvenir shirts and costume jewelry. If you just can't go home empty-handed, consider a bottle of wine from **Vina Miličić** on the Stradun (✆ **020/321-777;** daily 9am–8pm) or a piece of hand-embroidered linen from **Tilda** at Zlatarska 1 (✆ **020/321-554**). History buffs will want to visit **War Photo Limited** at Antuninska 6 (✆ **020/322-166;** daily 9am–9pm), a source for limited-edition prints of scenes from the 1991 war and other conflicts. Don't forget the **duty-free shop at Dubrovnik Airport** (✆ **020/333-773**), where you can get almost everything available in town without paying tax.

DUBROVNIK AFTER DARK

Dubrovnik's after-hours scene has an early and a late shift. From about 8 to 11pm the common activity for babes-in-arms to seniors is strolling the Stradun with an ice-cream cone. But at 11, there's a changing of the crowd as the early birds file out and 18- to 20-somethings flow in dressed in outfits that rival the costumes worn in *Dirty Dancing.* Follow the throbbing music blaring from jam-packed side streets where nightly block parties convene after the restaurants close, and you'll experience Dubrovnik cafe society's second shift.

For a disco experience, try **Fuego** outside the Pile Gate at Pile Brsalje 11, open daily 11pm to 6am; or **Troubadour Hard Jazz Cafe** at Bunićeva Polijana 5 (✆ **020/323 476**), open daily 9pm to 2am. There's also the **Night Club Revelin** in the Revelin Fortress at the wall (✆ **020/322-164**), which is one of the "in" places, and **Night Club Orlandinjo** in the Dubrovnik Palace in Lapad (✆ **020/430-000;** daily 10pm to 2am). Those with tamer tastes can take in a movie at **Sloboda,** a theater accessed via the mall entrance to the Arsenal Wine Bar (✆ **020/321-425**); hours vary.

4 EXCURSIONS FROM DUBROVNIK

Dubrovnik may be Croatia's best-known destination, but the islands off its coast and the Pelješac Peninsula have unique charms.

ELAFITI ISLANDS, CAVTAT & LOKRUM

Vivado Travel Agency (© **020/486-471;** www.dubrovnik-online.com/vivado) and others operate ticket kiosks at the Old Harbor near the Ploče Gate. They offer daily fish picnic excursions (250kn/$51/£32) to the **Elafiti Islands** (**Koločep, Šipan,** and **Lopud**), sleepy family resorts with minuscule sandy beaches. Koločep has **Hotel Villas Koločep,** the only hotel on the island, which was renovated in 2006. Rooms go for 116€ ($147) for an air-conditioned double that includes access to free Internet, the pool, and a sandy beach. Lopud's **Grand Hotel** is an abandoned ruin, but the island has a bank of restaurants and several historic churches. Šipan is completely skipable. Consider sampling the Elafitis on a 7-hour boating adventure that includes an onboard grilled-fish lunch followed by a quick post-meal stroll of each island and you'll cover everything worth seeing.

Cavtat (pronounced *sahv*-taht) is (17km/11 miles) southeast of Dubrovnik and reachable by bus, water taxi, or organized tour. Besides its beach and harbor, Cavtat is home to several museums, galleries, and churches. Don't miss the **Račić family mausoleum** in the town graveyard, which is decorated inside and out with sculpture by **Ivan Meštrović,** who worked in Cavtat in the 1920s. To see the artwork inside the mausoleum, call © **020/478-646** and a custodian will show up to open the tomb for 5kn ($1/60p) per person. Afterward, stop at **Restaurant Leut,** Trumbičev Put II (© **020/479-050;** daily 9am–midnight), for a light lunch.

Lokrum is the island closest to the Dubrovnik coast (1km/½ mile), and water taxis make the 15-minute crossing every half-hour from the Old Harbor from 9am to 5pm daily for 35kn ($7.10/£4.40) round-trip. The last boat back to Dubrovnik leaves Lokrum at 6pm. A change of pace is the main reason for visiting Lokrum, and you have your choice of swimming in a small salt lake, sunbathing on a concrete slab "beach," exploring church ruins, or wandering in the woods. The island's nature park was conceived by Archduke Maximilian Habsburg, who bought the island before he became emperor of Mexico in the mid–19th century.

PELJEŠAC PENINSULA ★

Vineyards, rugged terrain, a few medieval sites, good beaches, and sparse crowds are the draws for this finger of land that protrudes into the sea half an hour north of Dubrovnik. The peninsula is just 65km (40 miles) long, but the roads twist across hills and valleys, making the drive to the peninsula's tip challenging.

Ston and **Mali Ston** are the peninsula towns closest to the mainland, and if you venture no farther than that, you'll be rewarded with great photo ops, thanks to Ston's 14th-century walls, which snake up the hill behind the town like a mini Great Wall of China. Ston is also the center of Croatia's **oyster and mussel production** as well as an established working **salt pan.**

The peninsula beyond is wine country, where dozens of family vineyards are terraced onto the hills and planted in the valleys. Mike Grgić of California winemaking fame has a small winery at **Trstenik.** It is one of many operated by Croatia's big-name vintners. Many vineyards also have tasting rooms, small restaurants, and even retail outlets where you can sample and buy the latest vintages. At the tip of Pelješac, **Orebič** is home to one of the country's best beaches and one of its more interesting waterfront promenades. Orebič is also a great spot to set up home base for island hopping.

5 THE REST OF SOUTHERN DALMATIA

Southern Dalmatia is a relatively narrow expanse of land, but it is fringed by hundreds of islands. To get the most out of a trip to this region, first-time visitors should settle on a few nearby locations that offer multiple attractions—watersports, historic architecture, and/or natural wonders—*after* checking out transportation options and travel times between them.

Warning: Ferry schedules, mountainous roads, and circuitous routes characteristic of this region can make the time it takes to travel even short distances deceiving. Booking a guided tour that hits the highlights while leaving ferry connections and logistical problems to an expert is another option.

HVAR ISLAND/HVAR TOWN ★★★

St. Tropez, Majorca, Aspen, and other glamour destinations don't have anything on Hvar, the glitzy island playground patronized by celebrities, the idle rich, and the average visitor.

The island is a hilly piece of real estate with very rocky terrain, a few vineyards, and patches of wild lavender between abandoned stone structures and sparsely populated villages. The island's principal population centers are **Hvar Town, Stari Grad, Vrboska, Jelsa,** and **Sucuraj,** towns that have ferry/catamaran ports. Hvar Town is the island's tourism epicenter.

Getting There & Getting Around

Jadrolinija operates service to Stari Grad and Sucuraj, and buses connect from there to Hvar Town and Jelsa. Jadrolinija (✆ **021/741-132**) has offices in both Hvar Town and Stari Grad and can provide prices and schedules. Sem Marina runs a daily boat to Hvar Town from Split via Korčula, and tourist agencies operate other island hoppers. A bus will take you from Hvar Town to Stari Grad and back, but if you want to see anything else, a car is necessary. Hvar Town is closed to vehicular traffic from the bus station to the Riva, which is clogged with pedestrians until after nightfall when the main square, **Trg Sveti Stjepana,** becomes the central mob scene.

Visitor Information

Hvar Town's principal **tourist office** is at Trg Sv. Stjepana bb (✆ **021/741-059;** fax 021/742-977; www.tzhvar.hr). Stari Grad's is at Nova Riva 2 (✆ **021/765-763;** www.hvar.hr). Both can provide literature and maps, but if you want accommodations in Hvar Town, go to **Pelegrini Travel,** steps from the boat landing (✆ **021/742-743;** pelegrini@inet.hr; 8am–10pm Mon–Sat and 6–8pm Sun). Pelegrini also books through travel agencies in Split.

During July and August, there is the potential for a reservation snafu, so be sure you have confirmed—and preferably paid for—accommodations before you arrive. **Atlas Travel** (✆ **021/741-670**), on the west side of the Hvar Town harbor next to the renovated (Sept 2006) **Adriana Hotel,** is an excellent place to book excursions.

Tips **bb**

bb in a street address means *bez broja* (without number). This address designation is quite common in Croatia, particularly if the place is a well-known church or restaurant. If you see an address listed with a street name followed by bb and you are having trouble finding it, simply ask a local for directions.

Where to Stay

There are no hotel bargains in Hvar Town. Innkeepers have been scrambling to expand and renovate since the island became all the rage, and the result is that prices are escalating faster than improvements. Moderately priced private accommodations exist, but in the summer, you must book for 4 days or more just to get a reservation.

Very Expensive

Adriana ★★★ After a 2-year-long renovation, the Adriana emerged in 2007 as Croatia's first and only member of the Leading Small Hotels of the World. Adriana deserves the recognition after its transformation from package hotel to stylish luxury destination. The rooftop terrace has a heated indoor/outdoor seawater pool plus bar and lounge area. Guest rooms are done in soft neutral colors and natural materials with wood floors and touches of rattan. They are spacious and full of light, which makes for a relaxing ambience. Bathrooms are big and ergonomic and stocked with plenty of toiletries. ***Note:*** Adriana's Sensori Spa is its showpiece. Besides the usual beauty and massage services, the spa offers boutique services like a VIP suite for couples, an olive leaf and salt scrub, and a sea mud wrap.

Fabrika bb. ✆ **021/750-200.** Fax 021/750-201. www.suncanihvar.com. 59 units including 9 suites. From 350€ ($445) double; from 380€ ($483) suite. Rates include breakfast. **Amenities:** Restaurant; cafe; 2 bars; pool; spa. *In room:* A/C, SAT/TV, free Wi-Fi, LAN connection (charge), minibar, hair dryer, safe, some patios.

Hotel Riva ★★ Riva wins the ugly-duckling-to-swan award, and it's *still* all about location. Anyone who stays at this hotel about 9m (30 ft.) from the pier where passengers disembark has a bird's-eye view of the waterfront action and since 2006, they also have plush surroundings: A 6-month-long renovation has turned this historic building into a chic, hip place to stay, dine, and socialize. Rooms still are small because of the building's protected status, but now they have ultramodern bathrooms, flatscreen TVs, slick designer colors, and walk-out patios. The hotel's terrace is home to a Mediterranean restaurant that serves nouveau interpretations of Dalmatian cuisine and a cocktail space where you can schmooze the night away.

Riva bb, Hvar Town. ✆ **021/741-820.** Fax 021/741-147. www.suncanihvar.com/riva. 54 units, including 8 suites and 1 twin. Mid-July to Aug from 275€ ($349) double, from 325€ ($413) suite, from 370€ ($470) Riva suite; Sept to mid-July from 214€ ($272) double, from 238€ ($302) suite, from 295€ ($375) Riva suite. Rates include breakfast. AE, DC, MC, V. **Amenities:** Restaurant; bar, spa access; Wi-Fi in public areas; terrace dancing. *In room:* A/C, SAT/TV, free Wi-Fi, hair dryer, safe, some patios.

Expensive

Hotel Podstine ★ The Podstine is nestled amid palm and citrus trees next to its own beach, which is a flat concrete strip with a view of the **Pakleni Islands.** The hotel is a 30-minute climb from Hvar Town center, but it offers shuttle service (20kn/$4/£2.50

one-way). Guest rooms are clean but showing their age, and most have private balconies. The shaded terrace is a tranquil place to kick back with a glass of wine.

Pod Stine, Hvar Town. ✆ **021/740-400.** Fax 021/740-499. www.podstine.com. 40 units. Mid-July to late Aug from 1,900kn ($389/£241) sea-side double; Sept to mid-July from 1,085kn ($222/£138) sea-side double. AE, DC, MC, V. Guarded parking. **Amenities:** Restaurant; bar; excursions; bike, scooter, and car rental; room service 11am–11pm; diving center. *In room:* A/C, TV, minibar.

Moderate

Hotel Palace Overrated Hvar's grande dame is situated behind the 16th-century **loggia** that once graced the town's ducal palace. The Palace was built in the early 20th century, and time has not been kind to its elegant features. Despite soaring ceilings and architectural splendor, guest rooms are small, dated, and without air-conditioning. If you open the window to get a sea breeze, you'll hear the noise on the square or Riva, and that can last until sunrise. The Palace underwent an exterior face-lift and minor interior renovation in 2008, but it still has major wrinkles.

Trg Sveti Stjepana bb, Hvar Town. ✆ **021/741-966.** Fax 021/742-240. www.suncanihvar.hr. 73 units. Mid-July to Aug from 163€ ($207) seaview double, from 193€ ($245) seaview suite; Sept to mid-July from 88€ ($112) double. AE, DC, MC, V. Rates include breakfast. **Amenities:** Restaurant; bar; pool. *In room:* TV.

Where to Dine

Most of the restaurants lining Hvar Town's harbor serve pizza, pasta, and grilled fish. However, some dining spots tucked into the narrow, unnamed side streets are bastions of distinctive cuisine. **Roots** ★ in the Hotel Riva (✆ **021/741-820**) gets points for its casual-chic terrace and creative offerings, but as beautiful as the food and surroundings may be, this glitzy dining room sometimes tries too hard to be "gourmet," especially with its designer pizza toppings: Raspberry vinaigrette, shrimp, and goat cheese might work on salads, but it turns pizza crust into a soggy mess. Roots also offers weekly theme menus (Tex-Mex), and a long list of grossly overpriced wines and exotic cocktails.

Lucullus ★★★, off the main square (✆ **021/742-498**), specializes in a light version of slow food, leisurely dining with well-prepared seafood and Dalmatian specialties served in a convivial atmosphere. Wood-grilled pizza is on the menu, but try the island lobster *brodeto* or *peka*-grilled meat (available if ordered 3 hr. in advance, it is cooked over a fire, under an earthenware lid). Lucullus also has a few rooms to rent. The affable owner of the **Golden Shell** ★★ at Petra Hektorovica 8 (✆ **098/1688-797**) cheerfully chortles that slow food is the opposite of fast food, but that doesn't begin to explain this Croatian style of dining. The slow-food approach paces courses made from the freshest ingredients to allow diners time to savor their meals. Start with Dalmatian ham and goat cheese in olive oil, and follow with steak stuffed with goat cheese and capers. Food is an art form here.

Gostiona Kod Matkovića ★, at 55 Godina Tradicije (✆ **021/741-854**), is a homey restaurant set in a small courtyard. It has a nice selection of seafood and meats, including spit-roasted lamb, but wine choices are limited to the house white or house red. **Macondo** ★★, at Groda bb (✆ **021/742-850**), is a seafood restaurant off St. Stephen's Square that spills into a nameless alley. Portions are huge; prices are moderate. You won't be able to resist the *gregada,* a garlicky seafood stew.

Exploring Hvar Town

Hvar Town is a languid mix of sensual countryside and 13th-century attractions on a harbor where mega-yachts come to mate. Sun, sea, and a trendy social scene pull in a glittering passel of visitors.

The 13th-century **St. Stephen's Square (Trg Sveti Stjepan)** ★★★ is Hvar Town's central stage. It is bookended by **St. Stephen's Cathedral** ★ (daily 7am–noon and 5–7pm) in the east and a small harbor in the west. The square is lined with restaurants, cafes, and galleries, and a **16th-century well** sits in the center of the paved space, which was redone in the late 18th century.

The **Venetian Loggia** ★★★ has suffered several insults to its historical pedigree: It was damaged by the Turks in 1571, repaired, then used as a cafe from the late 19th century to as recently as the early 1970s. The adjacent clock tower was built in the 19th century on the site of a ducal palace that was heavily damaged in the same assault that hit the loggia.

The 15th-century **Franciscan Monastery** ★ is south of the town center along the path skirting the sea. Enter through a cloister, where concerts are held every 2 days during the season. There also is a nice museum with a collection of sacral art and an idyllic garden with a view of the sea (daily summer 10am–noon and 5–7pm; winter daily 10am–noon). Performance times and prices vary. The adjacent church, **Our Lady of Mercy,** also dates from the 15th century (✆ **021/741-123;** 10kn/$1.75/£1.10). The 16th-century **Fortress (Fortica)** ★★ that overlooks the town offers a sweeping view of Hvar Town's rooftops and its harbor. Inside is a spooky dungeon, displays of amphorae, and a small cafe on the roof, north of Hvar Town center (✆ **021/741-816;** admission 10kn/$2/£1.25). It's open summer daily 8am to midnight, and by appointment only in winter.

Note: The walk up to the fortress is a challenging trek during the day, but at night it can be treacherous because the steps/path leading to the site are not lighted.

Hvar Town's Beaches

Hvar Town has both a public pebble beach and a slab beach west of the center that are usually crowded with sunbathers from the nearby package Hotel Amfora. There are a few small patches of pebbles below the Franciscan church, and lots of flat rocks and concrete slabs at other seaside spots. If you want privacy, for a mere 10kn ($2/£1.25), you can hop a taxi boat to nearby **Pakleni Otoci,** a cluster of pine-forested, uninhabited islands whose coastlines are alternately rimmed with rocks and little pebble beaches.

Watersports

Southern Dalmatia is home to some of the best conditions in Europe for windsurfing, kite boarding, jet-skiing, sailing, diving, and swimming. At the **Viking Diving Center** next to the Podstine Hotel (✆ **021/742-529**), you can rent equipment, get instruction, and even book rooms. Cost of a single dive is 220kn ($45/£28), a package of 5 days and 10 dives 1,720kn ($350/£217), or a full-day trip with cave diving 490kn ($100/£62). Equipment rental is extra. **Dive Center Hvar** near Hotel Amfora (✆ **021/741-503**) runs trips to the island of **Vis,** which recently has become the darling of extreme-sports enthusiasts. DCH also supports other watersports such as water-skiing, snorkeling, kite boarding, windsurfing, and banana boating. It rents boats, kayaks, and equipment. Prices run from 250kn ($51/£32) for a single dive including equipment to an all-inclusive certification course for 2,360kn ($481/£298).

6 SPLIT

Split marked its 1,700th birthday and the completion of Diocletian's magnificent palace (A.D. 305) in 2005. Diocletian deliberately chose this site for his retirement home because it provided the best of both country and city. The emperor's Split digs were just 6km (4 miles) from Salona, the provincial center of power, close enough to allow him to periodically stick his finger in affairs of state while living in his seaside palace, which was the size of a small city.

Today's Split is a transportation hub for the Dalmatian coast. Despite Old Town, whose borders are defined by the palace footprint, Split lacks the glamour of other Dalmatian destinations, though most travelers who head for Dubrovnik or the islands pass through or make connections there. Nonetheless, Split has developed into one of the most accessible cities in Croatia.

GETTING THERE

BY PLANE Split's **airport** (✆ **021/203-171;** www.split-airport.hr) is 26km (16 miles) northwest of the city center between Kaštela and Trogir. Flights from cities in Croatia and from many European hubs land there regularly. Service is more frequent in the summer, and a shuttle moves passengers between the airport and the bus station, Obala Kneza Domogoja 12 (✆ **021/203-305;** 30kn/$6.10/£3.80 each way).

BY CAR The Zagreb-Split *autocesta* cuts through mountains and bypasses country roads and has reduced the 5-hour travel time between Zagreb and Split by an hour since it opened in May 2005. Except for weekends in July and August, the 364km (226-mile) drive from Zagreb to Split takes less time than the 213km (132-mile) coastal drive from Split to Dubrovnik. ***Note:*** In 2007, another 27km (16 miles) of highway opened between Split and Omiš, but the Sveti Rock tunnel just north of Split is still just one lane in each direction and bottlenecks can be miles long on summer weekends.

BY BOAT International, local, and island carriers move in and out of Split's ferry port almost constantly, and daily catamaran service to the islands of Brač, Hvar, Vis, and Korčula originates there. Split also is an international port for ferries, making overnight runs to and from Ancona, Italy. Contact the local Jadrolinija office (✆ **021/338-333**), Sem Marina (✆ **021/338-292**), or Adriatica (✆ **021/338-335**) for schedules and prices. **SNAV,** an Italy based transit company, runs high-speed ferries (4 hr. or less) to Ancona from early June to mid-September (✆ **021/322-252**).

BY BUS Local bus routes include Split and its suburbs, Salona, Klis, Omiš, and Trogir, while multiple lines travel to Zagreb, Zadar, Rijeka, Dubrovnik, and destinations beyond several times a day. International buses provide daily service to Slovenia, Germany, and Italy, and weekly service to Austria and England. Schedule and fare information is available at ✆ **021/338-483.**

BY TRAIN Split's main train station is next to the bus terminal at Obala Kneza Domogoja 10 near the town center. It runs between Split and Zagreb, Knin, and Šibenik. There is also an overnight train between Split and Zagreb. Call the **Split train station** (✆ **021/338-535**) or the **national train office** (✆ **060/333-444;** www.hznet.hr) for schedule and fare information.

CITY LAYOUT & GETTING AROUND

Split's historic core is bounded by Obala Hrvatskog Preporoda (Riva) in the south, Marmontova Street in the west, Kralja Tomislava in the north, and Hrvojeva in the east; Old Town's main square, Narodni Trg, is almost in the center of the rectangle.

Most of Split's important sights are within the palace walls or nearby. The walled city is limited to pedestrians; even the street skirting the Riva outside the walls is closed to motorized vehicles. There are a few sights worth taking in beyond the historic core—the

Korčula & Brač

The islands of **Korčula** ★★★ and **Brač** ★★ are among the most popular day-trip destinations from Split. **Korčula Town** ★★★ is the big draw on Korčula, while **Bol** and its **Golden Horn (Zlatni Rat)** beach ★★ pull tourists to Brač. Spend your day exploring Korčula Town's medieval streets, soaking up the sun and international atmosphere on Bol's shape-shifting beach, or riding the waves on a wind board off either island.

Korčula Town: After you climb the **Grand Staircase** that leads across the town's only remaining **wall,** you'll think you've fallen in a worm hole to the past. Marco Polo's alleged birthplace is crisscrossed with picturesque stone structures that house restaurants, museums, families, and offices laid out on streets that branch off from the enclave's major north-south thoroughfare (Korčulaskog Statuta). You can spend hours exploring these narrow offshoots and never know exactly where you are in time or space, and you can spend hours more hiking or biking around the island. At its widest point, Korčula is just 8km (5 miles) wide and it is just 32km (20 miles) long.

Note: The approach to Korčula Town from the sea makes for one of the best vacation pictures ever if snapped in the morning.

Korčula Town's well-preserved walled core and medieval attractions, plus the city's claim that it is the birthplace of legendary explorer **Marco Polo,** are the island's main draw. Seasonal visitors also come to Korčula to see the **Moreška Sword Dance,** a summer spectacle that recalls a battle between Christians and "infidels" that was fought over a woman. Finally, the island is an excellent source of olive oil and wine, most notably white wines (Pošip, Grk).

Brač: Croatia's third-largest island (Krk and Cres are numbers one and two, respectively) and its **Golden Horn** (**Zlatni Rat)** beach ★★ are magnets for those who love sun and surf. Brač is one of Croatia's least-developed populated islands, but it is much more than that. This rugged land about an hour's ferry ride from Split also is famous as a windsurfer's paradise, the source of the stone that built Diocletian's palace, the White House in Washington, D.C., and the Reichstag in Berlin. Brač also has a reputation as the source of Bolski Plavac and other highly regarded wines. Brač is really a two-town island because only **Supetar** on the northern shore and **Bol** on the southern shore are easily accessed by tourists.

Meštrović Gallery in Marjan, the public beach at Bačvice. Both are reachable via bus or taxi. Taxi stands are at each end of the Riva (in front of the town market and in front of the Bellevue Hotel). If you don't see a cab, call ✆ **970.**

VISITOR INFORMATION Split's official **Tourist Information Center** is near the Silver Gate/Peristil (✆ **021/342-666;** www.visitsplit.com) behind the cathedral in the former chapel of St. Rocco. There is also an information center across from the ferry port at Obala Hrvatskog Narodnog Preporoda 7 (✆ **021/348-600**).

WHERE TO STAY

Hotel rooms are scarce in Split, and reasonably priced rooms are almost nonexistent, though private accommodations are fairly easy to secure.

Very Expensive

Atrium Hotel ★★ Dark reflective glass, marble, black and white leather, and artifacts on loan from a local museum exude sophistication in the lobby of this 101-room beauty that opened in 2007. Guest rooms are light and airy, oversize, and lavishly outfitted with ultramodern baths, desks, and high-speed Internet access. The hotel also had the foresight to put in an underground garage that comes in handy in parking-challenged Split. ***Warning:*** Atrium's setting in the shadow of a cluster of brand-new, garishly painted apartment high-rises in Brodarica, 15 minutes from the Old Town, could be a turnoff for some.

Domovinskog Rata 49a. ✆ **021/200-000.** Fax 021/200-100. www.hotel-atrium.hr. 101 units, including 2 suites. From 1,425kn ($290/£180) double; from 1,800kn ($366/£227) suite. Rates include breakfast and VAT. AE, DC, MC, V. **Amenities:** Restaurant; bar; indoor pool; spa; garage. *In room:* A/C, SAT/TV, high-speed Internet, minibar, hair dryer, safe.

Hotel Vestibul Palace ★★★ Clever 21st-century architects carved this intimate boutique hotel into the space next to what was Diocletian's boudoir. The hotel opened in 2006 and the interior uses high design to meld glass with the ancient stone palace walls. The result is spectacular. Most of the bathrooms have tubs, but those without have high-tech showers and black-marble fixtures. Each room is different but each incorporates some detail of the palace, with modern comforts like flatscreen TVs. ***Tip:*** Room no. 7 has a spectacular view of the square below.

Vestibula 4. ✆ **021/329-329.** www.vestibulpalace.com. 7 units. July–Aug from 272€ ($345); suites from 405€ ($515). Other times doubles from 217€ ($275); suites from 308€ ($390). Rates include breakfast and VAT. AE, DC, MC, V. **Amenities:** Restaurant; excursions, parking 14€ ($18) per day. *In room:* A/C, SAT/TV w/ LCD screen, minibar, hair dryer, Wi-Fi.

Le Meridien Lav ★★ Le Meridien Lav, the only internationally affiliated hotel in the Split area, was unveiled in fall 2006, and the facility's metamorphosis from package hotel to exclusive resort is a mixed success. The 381-unit hotel has been positioned as a seafront destination, and it certainly has the real estate for that boast. Inside, however, vestiges of the Lav's socialist roots live on and detract from the ambience. For example, the hotel's **Spalatum** restaurant ★★ has an ambitious menu executed by a talented chef, but the room is a brightly lit cavern with the feel of a workplace cafeteria. The Lav's staff is mostly courteous and helpful, but we did encounter some serious service lapses that should not occur at this pricing level. Le Meridien has the potential to become a true first-class resort, but it still is a little rough around the edges. The hotel is in Podstrana, 6km (3¾ miles) from Split's Old Town (20 min.) and 40 minutes from Split-Kastela International Airport.

Grljevač 2a, 21312 Podstrana. ✆ **021/500-500.** Fax 021/500-705. www.lemeridien.com/split. 381 units, including 15 suites. From 425€ ($540) seaview double; from 650€ ($826) seaview suite. Rates include VAT. Breakfast 30€ ($38) per person. Free parking. **Amenities:** 2 restaurants; cafe; pub; 2 bars; nightclub; indoor and outdoor pool; tennis courts; spa; children's program; Wi-Fi in public areas (fee); shops; laundry service; nonsmoking rooms; rooms and access for those w/limited mobility; private beach; marina; casino. *In room:* A/C, SAT/TV, broadband Internet access (45kn/$9/£5.60 per hr. or 145kn/$30/£19 per day), minibar, safe.

Expensive

Hotel Peristil ★★ The Peristil opened in April 2005, putting guests in literal touch with history: The Peristil is just inside the **Silver Gate** and shares a wall with the palace. Outside, guests can breakfast on the limestone terrace; inside, they can listen to music from the annual **Split Summer Festival** from any of the rooms when the windows are open. Guest rooms are comfortably sized and hung with original artwork; most have showers rather than tubs; rooms are equipped with dial-up Internet access; and **Restoran Tifani** (see below) downstairs is a delight.

Note: If you are lucky enough to get room no. 302, you can hear the music *and* see the Silver Gate and Domnius Square below.

Poljana Kraljice Jelene 5. ✆ **021/329/070.** Fax 021/329-088. www.hotelperistil.com. 12 units. July–Aug from 162€ ($206) double; rest of year from 120€ ($152) double. Rates include breakfast. AE, MC, V. **Amenities:** Restaurant; bar. *In room:* A/C, TV, Internet access, hair dryer.

Moderate

Hotel Adriana ★★ The Adriana's accommodations are really rooms over its popular **restaurant** (see below), and include 2 apartments. If you can snag a booking, you will be in an ideal location for sightseeing. Guest rooms are plain but comfortable, especially those with a sea view.

Preporoda 8. ✆ **021/340-000.** www.hotel-adriana.hr. 9 units; 2 apts. Mid-Apr to mid-Oct from 1,200kn ($147/£78) double. 1,400kn ($242/£128) apt. Mid-Oct to mid-Apr doubles from 750kn ($135/£87); apt from 900kn ($160/£105). AE, DC, MC, V. **Amenities:** Restaurant. *In room:* A/C, TV, minibar.

Inexpensive

Hotel Jupiter ★ Value The Jupiter is located next to the 1,700-year-old Temple of Jupiter near Narodni Trg and in the middle of Split's nightlife action. Jupiter actually is a guesthouse, but it is an excellent place to bunk if you don't mind sharing a bathroom. Jupiter had a 2005 overhaul and the spartan rooms and bathrooms gleam.

Grabovčeva Širina 1. ✆ **021/344-801.** www.hotel-jupiter.info. 25 units. 250kn ($51/£31) per person. No credit cards. **Amenities:** Cafe/bar; TV room. *In room:* A/C in double and triple rooms, fans in singles.

WHERE TO DINE

It isn't difficult to find a place to eat in Split, but finding a restaurant other than a pizzeria or *konoba* is challenging. However, Split's dining scene is improving as new hotels open and bring more tourist traffic to town.

Very Expensive

Restoran Boban ★★★ DALMATIAN Boban is one of the finest restaurants in Split with a reputation that goes back to its founding in 1973. Both the dining room and outdoor terrace are beautiful settings for Boban's consistently excellent food and quality wine list that includes such Croatian labels as Grgić, Zlatanotok, and Dingač.

Hektorovićeva 49. ✆ **098/205-575.** www.restaurant-boban.com. Entrees 10€–45€ ($13–$57). AE, DC, MC, V. Mon–Sat 10am–midnight; Sun noon–midnight.

Spalatum ★★ DALMATIAN (Le Meridien Lav) Spalatum is Latin for "Split" and the restaurant's menu showcases locally produced foods. Spalatum tries to be both glitzy restaurant and family friendly buffet, but the result is that neither effort is spectacular: A floor-to-ceiling glass wall showcases the city of Split and the chef has talent, but Spalatum's overall ambience is too institutional, even for a hotel as large as the Lav. Don't let that deter you from dining there, though. Try the trio of Dalmatian lamb, olive oil poached tuna, or the trio of chocolate crème brûlée. For early risers, the breakfast buffet is full of options.

Grljevačka 2a. 21312 Podstrana. ✆ **021/500-500.** Fax: 021/500-705. www.lemeridien.com/split. Entrees 85kn–350kn ($15–$62/£10–£41.) AE, DC, MC, V. Daily 6:30–10:30am for breakfast, 12:30–3:30pm for lunch, and 6:30–10:30pm for dinner.

Expensive

Caffe Restaurant Vestibul ★★ This restaurant in the classy Hotel Vestibul is open for breakfast and dinner only, but it is worth putting on your schedule if only to dine surrounded by history. Vestibul's food is Dalmatian and prepared with elegant simplicity to match the hotel's mood. Try the excellent grilled fish at dinner.

Iza Vestibula 4. ✆ **021/320-329.** Fax: 021/329-333. www.vestibulpalace.com. Breakfast 40kn-110kn ($7–$20/£4.75–£13.) and dinner entrees 80kn–150kn ($14–$27/£9.50–£18). AE, DC, MC, V. Daily from 7–10am for breakfast and 7–10pm for dinner.

Restoran Šumica ★★★ SEAFOOD Šumica is an upscale dining spot near Bačvice Beach southeast of Old Town. It has one of the most romantic atmospheres of any restaurant in Split and serves pristinely fresh seafood. Choose the house specialty of tagliatelle with scampi and salmon, a bottle from Šumica's excellent cellar, and a table on the outdoor terrace under the pines.

Put Firula 6. ✆ **021/389-897.** Fax 021/389-894. Entrees 80kn–300kn ($14–$53/£9.50–£36), more for seafood sold by the kg. AE, DC, MC, V. Daily 10am–midnight.

Moderate

Adriana ★★ DALMATIAN This sprawling restaurant on the Riva near Old Town is always crowded, perhaps because the food is fairly priced or perhaps because of the Adriana's prime location for people-watching. Either way, the seafood risotto is great and there is live music on weekends and sometimes on weekdays during the summer.

Obala Hrvatskog Preporoda. ✆ **021/344-079.** www.dalmatianet.com/adriana/indexhrv.htm. Entrees 45kn–160kn ($8–$28/£5.30–£19). AE, DC, MC, V. Daily 8am–11pm.

Fun Facts Mining Silver

The Silver Gate (Srebrena Vrata), which leads inside the palace gates from the Pazar market, is a relatively new site in Split's Old Town. For centuries the gate was hidden behind a brick wall; it was discovered and excavated in the 1950s.

Away from the center, the **Meštrović Gallery ★★★** at Šetalište Ivana Meštrovića 46, Marjan (✆ **021/358-450;** 15kn/$3/£1.85), was built as a home/atelier for Croatian sculptor Ivan Meštrović and his family. Traveling exhibitions from Croatia and other locations are periodically on display here. Walk up the road to Šetalište Ivana Meštrovića 39 to visit the 16th-century **Kaštelet,** a summer house purchased and remodeled by Meštrović in 1939 as a showcase for his "Life of Christ" reliefs. There is no charge to enter Kaštelet if you have a ticket to the main gallery. From mid-July to mid-August, the **Split Summer Festival ★★★** takes place at **Croatian National Theater,** in the **Peristil,** at other Old Town squares, and at other venues. Contact the Croatian National Theater at Gaje Bulata 1 (✆ **021/585-999**) for information and tickets.

Restoran Sarajevo ★★ CROATIAN Grilled meat dominates the menu at this old-style dining room housed in a space framed by vaulted arches that were constructed at the beginning of the last millennium. Try the *ražnjići,* chunks of grilled meat skewered on tiny swords. The mixed-grill plate is excellent, too, but be warned that one of the grilled meats is liver. Service can be slow.

Domaldova 6. ✆ **021/347-454.** Entrees 62kn–150kn ($11–$27/£7.50–£18). AE, DC, MC, V. Daily 9am–midnight.

Inexpensive

Kalumela ★ HEALTH FOOD If you get the munchies and you're tired of pizza and grilled meat, Kalumela can supply organic whole-grain sandwiches and pastries as well as the usual health-food-store staples.

Domaldova 7. ✆ **021/348-132.** Entrees 40kn–70kn ($7–$12/£4.75–£8.30). AE, DC, MC, V. Mon–Fri 8:30am–1pm and 5:30–8:30pm; Sat 9am–1pm; closed Sun.

Konoba Varoš ★★ DALMATIAN This place close to the town center is creatively draped with fishnets, creating a cozy, comfortable atmosphere in a restaurant that charges decent prices. You'll see lots of locals here, which usually is a sign of a good restaurant in Croatia.

Ban Mladenova 7. ✆ **021/396-138.** Entrees 60kn–80kn ($11–$14/£7–£9.50). AE, DC, MC, V. Daily 11am–midnight.

Luxor ★★ SANDWICHES You can't get much closer to the palace walls than this cafe in the Peristil, across from the cathedral. In fact, the place shares a wall with the ancient structure. If you choose to sip your biela kava while sitting on the steps outside, be sure to take a peek at the dining room, which recently has been restored.

Kraj Sv. Ivana 11. No phone. Sandwiches 35kn–65kn ($6–$12/£4.30–£7.70). AE, DC, MC, V. Daily 9am–midnight.

Pizzeria Galija ★ Value This tiny place serves some of the best pizza in Split and it is one of the best bargains, too. Galija is off the tourist track on the western edge of town, but it is a worthwhile detour if you just want a relaxing beer and pizza. *Note:* You have to buy pizza whole here, so take a friend.

Kamila Tončića 12. ✆ **021/347-932.** Pizza from 26kn–100kn ($4.60–$18/£3–£12). AE, DC, MC, V. Daily 10am–11pm.

Time Traveling Near Split

Immerse yourself in Croatia's past by taking a day trip to the enchanting Renaissance town of **Trogir** just 19km (12 miles) from Split or to the ruined city of **Salona**, the Roman Empire's former seat of power in the region just 6.4km (4 miles) away from the city. Trogir is a vibrant, well-preserved town with a medieval flavor that is full of restaurants, hotels, and entrancing stone architecture. That includes formidable **Kamerlengo Castle,** which offers a theater and a splendid view of the harbor. Salona is Trogir's polar opposite, a stony vestige of history that is little more than a rocky blueprint of Roman grandeur. Walk on the Salona amphitheater's leveled foundation or nose around the crumbling walls that once embraced the Emperor Diocletian's "office" and you may begin to hear the sound of gladiator clashes as the wind sweeps through the decaying city.

Skipper Club Grill ★ CROATIAN/PIZZA The view from this informal dining spot above the ACI Marina is nothing short of spectacular. Whether you are at an umbrella table on the deck or at a table next to the windows in the air-conditioned dining room, you can see the harbor below, the Split skyline, and everything in between. Skipper specializes in pizza (34 kinds) but the huge, freshly made salads and pasta dishes are satisfying, too. Be sure to ask for bread. Skipper's variety is a cross between pita and nan and it comes to the table hot and freshly baked.

Uvala Baluni bb. ✆ **021/398-222.** Entrees 35kn–60kn ($6–$11/£4.30–£8) AE, DC, V. Daily 7am–midnight.

EXPLORING SPLIT

Diocletian's Palace is Split's marquee attraction, and the **Riva** outside its walls is one of Croatia's busiest promenades. ***Note:*** Many of the Riva's alfresco cafes now offer shade with your *biela kava;* the city has erected huge, free-standing white canvas awnings over blocks of tables along the entire span.

The Cathedral of St. Domnius ★★★, at Kraj Sv. Duje 5 (✆ **021/342-589;** 5kn/ $1/60p), was also Diocletian's mausoleum, an elaborate domed structure that Christians converted to a church in the 7th century. The original stone structure was framed by 28 granite and marble columns that Diocletian supposedly looted from Greek and Egyptian temples during one of his campaigns. Because of its proximity to the **Silver Gate,** the

Diocletian's Palace ★★★

Historians say Diocletian (A.D. 245–316) was born in a village near Salona, which at the time was the nerve center of the Roman government in Dalmatia. His palace was a heavily protected enclave that included a military installation, and its footprint covered nearly 3 hectares (10 acres) and encompassed the emperor's apartments, several temples, and housing for soldiers and servants.

Diocletian moved into the limestone palace in A.D. 305 after a reign of 21 years, and according to some historians, he had commissioned construction of the palace 12 years earlier, in A.D. 293. The names of architects Filotas and Zotikos are engraved on palace foundation stones.

In the years immediately following the emperor's death in 316, the palace was used as government office space, but it inadvertently became a haven for refugees in the early 7th century when the Avars and Slavs attacked and destroyed Salona, sending that city's citizens to nearby islands and later to the security of the palace walls, which were 2m (6 ft.) thick and nearly 30m (100 ft.) high at points.

This huge influx of refugees overcrowded the palace compound, and the new settlement spread outside its walls. Successive rulers, including the Byzantine emperors, the Croatian kings, the Hungarian-Croatian kings, and the Venetians, accommodated by building structures within and outside the complex, a practice that effectively destroyed the palace's Roman character and left little more than the original walls and vestiges within them.

Zipping Through Zadar

During World War II, Zadar was almost destroyed by Allied forces, though it was mostly rebuilt during the postwar Yugoslavia era. The city took another devastating hit when it was isolated by Serb forces and reduced to rubble in the 1991 war. Today, Zadar is fiercely nationalistic, an exceptional mix of new and old architecture, and home to diverse cultures.

Thanks to the new A1 *autocesta* between Zagreb and Split, it takes just 3 hours to cover the 285km (177 miles) between there and Croatia's capital. Frequent bus service, an airport, a train station, and a generous ferry schedule also make Zadar accessible. However, despite tourist-friendly touches like multilingual signs in front of notable sites, Zadar has not yet become a prime stop for visitors, but its Old Town is worth at least a day of your time.

Start at **St. Donatus Church** ★★★ and the **Roman Forum** ★★★ in its front yard. Look around the St. Donatus's unusual interior with a circular center and watch kids ride their Big Wheels over the Forum's ancient stones. Peek into the 11th-century **Church of St. Mary** ★★ across the street and stop in at the **Benedictine Convent** next door to see its **Gold and Silver of Zadar** exhibit ★★★, one of the best reliquary and religious-art collections anywhere. Have the freshest of fish dinners at **Foša**'s ★★★ open-air dining room in the shadow of the city's walls. If you have time (and room), top off the experience with a frozen treat from **Slastičarna Donat** ★★★ off **Obala Kralja Petra Krešimira IV,** the city's promenade, and pause to watch its nonstop street theater. Finally, sit on the marble seaside steps off the promenade and dangle your toes in the sea while you revel in the haunting melody of Zadar's mesmerizing **Sea Organ.** It's an experience you won't soon forget.

cathedral is a popular meeting place and its courtyard hosts performances during **Split's Summer Festival** ★★★ in July and August.

The **cathedral treasury** ★ above the sacristy contains a valuable cache of gold and silver. From there you can climb the **bell tower** ★ for 10kn ($2/£1.25) from 8am to 8pm in summer and whenever it is open in winter.

Narodni Trg (People's Square) ★★ is west along Krešimirova (formerly the Decumanus) through the Silver Gate. West of Narodni Trg you'll find the indoor fish market (**Ribarnica;** Kraj Sv. Marije; 7am–1pm Mon–Sat, 7–11am Sun). You'll smell it before you see it. Continue west to **Marmontova Street** ★, a brick-paved pedestrian thoroughfare that forms Old Town's western border. Here you will find international retail outlets (Tommy Hilfiger, Benetton) and a set of McDonald's golden arches. Just south of the walls along Marmontova you'll run into the aging **Bellevue Hotel** and the **Prokurative,** a horseshoe-shaped set of neoclassical government buildings on **Trg Republike.** Split's **Ethnographic Museum** in Diocletian's former apartment in the south part of the palace adds an extra dimension to the displays. The museum at Severova 1 also houses the church of St. Andrew de Fenestris and the former convent of St. Clare.

Braće Radić Trg (Voćni Trg or Fruit Square) ★ is smaller than Narodni Trg and dominated by Ivan Meštrović's sculpture of author **Marko Marulić,** who wrote "Judita," the first narrative poem in Croatian. Marulić (1450–1524) is revered as the father of Croatian literature and his statue shows him with—what else?—a book.

7 ISTRIA & THE KVARNER GULF REGION

Istria is a triangle-shaped peninsula at the northwestern end of Croatia that protrudes just far enough into the Adriatic to catch the seductive Mediterranean climate, while the Kvarner Gulf Region lies directly east of there. Three sides of Istria are lined with beaches and busy marinas, which in turn are festooned with Venetian-style towns that look just as they must have when tall trading ships sailed in and out of their harbors. Kvarner interior towns have an Austro-Hungarian bent.

GETTING THERE & GETTING AROUND

BY PLANE Istria's airport is at Pula, about 5km (3 miles) northwest of the center of town, and it is served by Croatia Airlines (www.croatiaairlines.hr). There is also a smaller airport for private planes and charters near Vrsar in the middle of the western coast. Shuttle buses and taxis (60kn–70kn/$12–$14/£7.45–£8.70) run between Pula's airport and the town center.

BY BOAT VeneziaLines runs catamarans from Venice to Umag, Poreč, Rovinj, Pula, and Rabac; and from Rimini to Pula. Check the website (www.venezialines.com) or call ✆ **041/24-24-000** from 9am to 6pm Venice time to book tickets or for detailed schedule information. Sem Marina at Boktulijin Put bb (✆ **021/352-444**) runs a ferry between Pula and Zadar with a stop at Mali Losinj.

BY BUS Autotrans (✆ 052/741-817; www.autotrans.hr) runs four daily buses from both Rijeka and Zagreb to Pula, and to major cities such as Umag, Poreč, and Rovinj on the coast. Most interior towns are connected to the coastal cities by at least one bus per day, but travel by bus to inland Istria can be inconvenient.

BY TRAIN Trains connect Pula to Zagreb (7 hr.) and to Rijeka (2½ hr.), plus other coastal towns. However, if you want to see inland Istria, a car is a necessity.

BY CAR Auto travel is by far the most flexible way to see Istria beyond the coast and the only sensible way to see the interior. There are car-rental agencies in most of the major population centers.

VISITOR INFORMATION

Istria has an efficient tourist association with information offices in almost every town from Pula on the coast to Oprtalj in the interior highlands. The association and its website (www.istra.com) provide information ranging from maps of the region's olive-oil roads to an up-to-date schedule of events.

PULA

This bustling city of 65,000 people at Istria's southern tip is 265km (165 miles) southwest of Zagreb and 720km (447 miles) northeast of Dubrovnik. Pula is a working port as well as a repository of some of the best Roman ruins in Europe.

Getting There & Getting Around

Tourists can make both regional and international ferry connections in Pula, which has a large number of bus routes to Zagreb and Rijeka, Rovinj, Vrsar, and Poreč, plus the gateway city of Trieste in Italy and coastal towns in Slovenia. Pula is a walkable city and its local bus system can get you almost anywhere you need to go. If you want to explore the hills and valleys of the Istrian interior, you'll need a car.

Visitor Information

The **Tourist Information Office** at Forum 2 (✆ **052/219-197;** www.pulainfo.hr; 9am–8pm Mon–Sat, 10am–6pm Sun and holidays) opposite the Temple of Augustus provides maps, brochures, and lists of events in Pula and around Istria.

Private agencies like **Activatravel Istra** at Scalierova 1 (✆ **052/215-497**) book special-interest tours, including truffle-hunting excursions (in season). Several of the Pula's hotels and private accommodations are handled by **Arena Turist** in the Riviera Hotel at Splitska 1 (✆ **052/529-400;** www.arenaturist.hr; 7am–8pm Mon–Sat, 8am–1pm Sun). **Atlas Travel** at Starih Statuta 1 (✆ **052/393-040;** www.atlas-croatia.com) is open from 7am to 8pm Monday to Saturday, 8am to 1pm Sunday. Atlas books excursions, finds private accommodations, and is Pula's American Express agent. **Istra Sun-Way** at Kandlerova 34 (✆ **052/381-329;** email kaktus@pu.htnet.hr) is open from 8am to midnight and books tours to the interior, so you can see some of the smaller inland towns without renting a car. **Istra Line Travel Agency,** located on the outskirts of Old Town at Partizanska 4 (✆ **052/427-062;** fax 052/432-116; www.istraline.hr), is one of several agencies that can book private accommodations. Istra Line specializes in apartment rental but they also can book individual rooms.

Where to Stay

There are very few hotels in the center of Pula, but private accommodations are plentiful. Most hotel and beach options are south of the center in on the **Verudela Peninsula,** at **Pješčana Uvala,** or at **Stoja,** reachable on the no. 1, 3, and 7 buses.

Valsabbion ★★★ is a boutique hotel 5.6km (3½ miles) south of the center at Pješčana Uvala IX/26 (✆ **052/218-033**), with a stylish blend of comfortable rooms, beach, an award-winning **restaurant** (see below), and spa services that help guests switch off stress. Room prices, which start at 159€ ($202) for a premier double and 214€ ($272) for a suite, do not include breakfast, which can be added for 10€ ($13). Half board is pricey, but you'll never forgive yourself if you miss the opportunity to eat as many meals as possible here.

Book early because rooms go fast at **Scaletta** ★★ at Flavijevska 26 (✆ **052/541-025**), a family-run hotel in central Pula that is one of the cheeriest, best-run hotels in town. Guest rooms start at 750kn ($153/£95) for a double and they are done in soft colors; bathrooms are roomy and gleaming. Scaletta is within walking distance of the Arena and Old Town and its **restaurant** (see below) has been recognized as one of the seven best in Istria. The downside is that access to reception requires stair-climbing and the breakfast room is a little too cozy.

Autocamp Stoja ★★ (✆ **052/387-144**) is about 3.2km (2 miles) southwest of the center in suburban Stoja and has 670 spaces for tents plus a bank of mobile homes that sleep up to five people each. A mobile home with air-conditioning starts at 114€ ($145) with a minimum 7-day stay. There are a beach, shops, a market, a restaurant, and sports equipment for use on the property or in the waters off the peninsula, which are some of the best for swimming and watersports.

Pula Youth Hostel ★ at Zaljev Valsaline 4 (✆ **052/391-133**) is in a tranquil setting 4km (2½ miles) south of the center on Valsaline Bay and reachable via the no. 2 bus from Giardini near the Sergi Arch. Rooms start at 98kn ($20/£13) per bed and are dorm-style, with four to six beds per room; rates include breakfast.

Where to Dine

There is no dearth of decent restaurants in central Pula, but most of the better (upscale) restaurants are in the suburbs south of the center.

Expensive

Valsabbion ★★★ CREATIVE MEDITERRANEAN Unique, superb, a don't-miss experience: This is dining at Valsabbion, where Istrian specialties meet artistic sensibilities and expert preparation. Even a simple lunch can be spectacular with the Petit Delice or Taste of Istria samplers of Istrian cheeses, tapenades, or fish mousses and olives accompanied by house-made breads. Dinner is the *pièce de résistance* here, and if you can't make up your mind between the scampi rolled in Istrian ham or the chicken breast in vermouth sauce with grapes and artichokes, then try the degustation menu with 11 small portions of Valsabbion's best recipes. ***Tip:*** Book a table on the VIP terrace, a breezy, canopied deck across the street from the hotel that has a view of the bay and a cachet of exclusivity. Splurge on the 12-course tasting menu. You'll feast on tasting portions of such innovative dishes as scallop wrapped in squid ink pasta or potato soup in a ring of spices. There is a 15% surcharge for the terrace and the author's tasting was 475kn ($97/£60) per person (without wine.)

Pjescana Uvala IX/26. ✆ **052/218-033.** Fax 052/383-333. www.valsabbion.net. Reservations required. Entrees 90kn–120kn ($18–$25/£11–£16). AE, DC, MC, V. Daily 10am–midnight.

Moderate

Bistro Kupola ★ Value CROATIAN A magnificent view of the imposing Sergi Arch dominates the Kupola's second-floor terrace. Music from the street and concerts at the nearby amphitheater float up to the outdoor tables above Pula's T-Mobile headquarters, adding a little extra to the dining experience. Service is polite and helpful, though food is a bit tourist-driven, but why not? This is the kind of spot that demands a look-see from anyone new to Pula. Try tagliatelle Alfredo, which is sprinkled with shaved truffles; or go for spaghetti with a generous helping of seafood. The house red is an excellent Plavac Zlatni.

Trg Portarata 6. ✆ **098/211-666.** Entrees 50kn–140kn ($10–$29/£6.20–£18). No credit cards. Daily 8am–midnight.

Scaletta ★★ Value CROATIAN The lovely Scaletta is a gastronomic delight with surprisingly sophisticated cuisine that incorporates unusual combinations of ingredients like ostrich in orange sauce with mozzarella and potatoes. The dining room has soft lighting, a marble fireplace, an attractive open bar, and a menu with lots of grilled meats and fish.

Flavijevska 26. ✆ **053/541-025.** Fax 052/541-599. www.hotel-scaletta.com. Reservations recommended. Entrees 60kn–220kn ($12–$45/£7.45–£28). AE, DC, MC, V. Mon–Sat 10am–11pm.

Vela Nera ★★ CREATIVE SEAFOOD You can watch your ship come in from Vela Nera's terrace or from the windows of its dining room perched steps away from the Sandy Bay harbor. Either way, you'll be treated to knowledgeable service and inspired cuisine. Vela Nera is more casual than Valsabbion, but no less satisfying. Try the risotto Vela Nero for an unusual taste sensation. It's made with peaches, scampi, and sparkling wine.

 Pješčana Uvala bb. © **052/219-209.** Fax 052/215-951. www.velanerahr. Reservations recommended. Entrees 50kn–150kn ($10–$31/£6.20–£19). AE, DC, MC, V. Daily 8am–midnight.

Inexpensive

Jupiter ★★ PIZZA Pizza is the specialty at this popular place near the Forum. Jupiter has several terrace levels of dining and a huge number of pizza topping choices. Pretty good pasta, too.

Castropola 38. © **052/214-333.** Small pizza 15kn–40kn ($3–$8/£1.85–£4.95). No credit cards. Daily 9am–11pm.

Exploring Pula

Pula's most interesting sites are its Roman ruins, and of those the best is the 1st-century **Roman Amphitheater ★★★** at Flavijevska bb (© **052/219-028**). Admission is 20kn ($4/£2.50) adults and 10kn ($2/£1.25) students, with an audio guide available for 30kn ($6/£3.70). It's open daily 8am to 9pm. The amphitheater closes at 4pm concert days and is most impressive. The Emperor Augustus (31–14 A.D.) started construction of the amphitheater (aka Arena) in 2 B.C.; it was finished in A.D. 14, during the rule of Vespasianus. Though smaller than Rome's Coliseum, the Arena's outer wall is almost entirely intact. Inside, vestiges of the structure's original fittings are still visible, though its stone seats were removed in medieval times to complete other building projects. The chambers under the Arena have been restored and now house a **museum ★★★**. During the summer, the Arena is a concert site attracting such big-name stars as Andrea Bocelli, and it is the site of the **Croatian Film Festival** (July).

The 1st-century **Temple of Augustus ★★★** at Trg Republike 3 (no phone; admission 4kn/80¢/50p adults, 2kn/40¢/25p children; daily in summer 10am–1:30pm and 6–9pm; closed in winter) is dedicated to Octavianus Augustus, the first emperor of Rome. It is on a square that once was the city's Forum, and it was converted to a church after Christianity became the religion of choice in Croatia. It also was used for grain storage and was severely damaged during World War II. A small museum inside has exhibit captions in English, Italian, and Croatian.

The **Sergi Arch ★★★** opens to Trg Portarata off Sergijevaca and stands in a busy shopping area. Walk through the Sergi Arch and bear left until you get to Carrarina, where you will encounter the **Hercules Gate ★★**, dating from the mid–1st century. It is decorated with a relief of its namesake mythical hero.

Church of St. Fosca (Sveti Foška)

The only directional sign to this unremarkable 7th-century church is a hand-painted sign leading to a gravel strip off the main road to/from Fažana in the direction of Barbaringa. According to locals, the church, which has one interesting fresco, is built on a field of positive energy that allegedly is responsible for healing a wide range of ailments from headaches to arthritis. The first of these healings was noted in the late 17th century, but the Catholic Church has not acknowledged the validity of any claims of miracles at the site. Despite that, people from all over the world visit this tiny church in a meadow to seek their own miracles and to pray to the saint who was betrayed by her father and martyred at 15 because she wouldn't renounce Christianity.

Historically significant finds from all over Istria are displayed in Pula's **Archaeological Museum** ★★ at Carrarina 3 (✆ **052/218-603;** admission 12kn/$2.45/£1.50 adults, 6kn/$1.20/75p children; summer Mon–Sat 9am–8pm Sun, and holidays10am–3pm; rest of the year Mon–Fri 10am–3pm, closed Sat–Sun) which once was an Austrian secondary school. Be sure to visit the outdoor sculpture garden decorated with scattered pieces of history. Also note the **Roman Twin Gates** and the **Roman Theater** in back of the garden.

ROVINJ

Rovinj is one of the most photographed cities in Croatia because from the air, its location on a promontory makes it look like a fairy-tale village suspended on a pillow of bright blue sea. At ground level, it is the quintessential fishing village. In fact, central Rovinj was an islet until the 18th century when the channel separating it from the mainland was filled in. Today, Rovinj's Old Town is a protected monument and one of Istria's most visited sites. The town has preserved the best of its architectural and cultural legacy by allowing development while keeping industry on the mainland, where a tobacco factory and cannery still play major roles in the local economy. Old Town Rovinj is a tangle of steep pedestrian streets that are paved with sea-salt-polished cobblestones and marked with signs in Italian and Croatian. These narrow, winding passages are lined with galleries, quaint shops, and excellent restaurants. Most lead to the town's highest point, where **St. Euphemia Church** and the tallest campanile in Istria dominate the skyline. Add to that a strong Italian personality, a thriving fleet of small fishing boats, a smattering of Venetian-style piazzas and houses, numerous restaurants and cafes with atmospheric rock walls and pounding waves, and you have a town that's both vibrant and historical.

Getting There & Getting Around

Rovinj is half an hour or 25km (16 miles) north of Pula and linked by well-marked roads if you are traveling by car. There is frequent bus service between Rovinj and Pula, as well as service to and from Croatian cities that range from Osijek to Dubrovnik and international service to select cities in Italy, Germany, and Slovenia. The main bus station is at Trg Na Lokvi 6 (✆ **052/811-453;** www.tzgrovinj.hr).

Rovinj is a wonderful walking city. To visit the Old Town, you'll have to leave your car in the city lot at the north end of town where fees are a modest 6kn ($1.20/75p) per hour. You can rent a bike at the lot's exit for 100kn ($20/£12) per day or 5kn ($1/60p) per hour if you don't want to rely on walking or if you want to try Rovinj's picturesque bike trail. Local buses serve areas outside the Old Town area, as do taxis.

Visitor Information

The **Rovinj Tourist Information Office** is at Pino Budičin 12 (✆ **052/811-566;** fax 052/816-007; www.tzgrovinj.hr). It is open from 8am to 9pm daily mid-June to mid-September; and from 8am to 3pm Monday to Saturday the rest of the year. Located just off the main square at the harbor, it dispenses brochures, maps, and information on accommodations, the town, and its history.

Where to Stay

There are very few hotels in Rovinj's city center and not many in the surrounding area either, considering the number of tourists who visit each year. However, private accommodations are abundant and usually very nice. Stop at any tourist agency, some of which set up kiosks on the road into town so you can book a room on arrival. Not only will these agencies find you a place to sleep, they also will lead you to it so you can see if it suits before you pay.

Very Expensive

Eden Hotel ★★ Every room (renovated in 2004) has a couch and a balcony. The balconies overlook green space or lawn where guests can sunbathe or dine. The lunch buffet is set on a terrace under the hotel eaves where there is often live music at night. Bathrooms, balconies, and public spaces were renovated in 2006.

I Adamovića. ✆ **052/800-250.** Fax 052/800-215. www.maistra.hr. 325 units. Aug from 204€ ($259) double, 310€ ($394) suites (minimum 7 nights); rest of year from 158€ ($201) double, 227€ ($288) suite. 50% reduction for children 2–11; free for children 1 and under. 20% surcharge for stays of 3 or fewer days. Rates include half board for doubles and breakfast for suites. AE, DC, MC, V. **Amenities:** Restaurant; bar; 2 pools; Internet; babysitting 10am–5pm (included in room rate). *In room:* A/C, TV, minibar, hair dryer, safe.

Villa Angelo d'Oro ★★★ This 17th-century bishop's palace in the Old Town was renovated in 2001 and has been kept in superb condition ever since. Each room is unique in size and decor with plush period furniture and fresh colors. Bathrooms have modern fixtures, though most have showers rather than tubs. Guests can treat themselves to one of the best views in the city from the open-air balcony off the third-floor library before or after they dine in the hotel's **restaurant ★★★**. Parking is .5km (1/4 mile) from the hotel, but the staff will shuttle guests to and fro.

Via Svalba 38–42. ✆ **052/840-502.** www.rovinj.at. 25 units. Mid-July to mid-Sept from 1,520kn ($310/£192) double, 2,220kn ($455/£282) suite; rest of year from 1,049kn ($215/£133) double, 1,811kn ($371/£230) suite. 50% discount for children 3–11; free for children 2 and under. Rates include breakfast. Half board available on request for 185kn ($38/£24) per person. AE, DC, MC, V. Limited free parking. **Amenities:** Restaurant; terrace dining; Jacuzzi; wine cellar; solarium; library. *In room:* A/C, TV, minibar, hair dryer.

Expensive

Hotel Park ★★ From the front, this 1972 structure looks like another impersonal tourist hotel. The Park might offer packages, but it is surprisingly user-friendly. Rooms are done in yellows and blues in modest but comfortable style. The Park also has a long list of guest amenities and services as well as a spectacular view of St. Catherine Island and Old Town Rovinj from the balcony off its lobby. The Park is conveniently located 2 minutes from Zlatni Rt-Punta Corrente Nature Park and 5 minutes from Old Town. Despite its size, the hotel fills up from May to October. Call no later than April for reservations.

IM Ronjigova. ✆ **052/811-077.** Fax 052/816-977. www.maistra.hr. 237 units. Aug from 177€ ($225) double, from 231€ ($293) suite; rest of year from 138€ ($175) double, 177€ ($225) suite. 50% discount for children 2–11; free for children 1 and under. Rates include breakfast and are based on stays exceeding 3 days. 20% surcharge for stays of 3 or fewer days. Half board available on request. AE, DC, MC, V. Closed 2 months each year, usually mid-Dec to mid-Feb. **Amenities:** Restaurant; bar; ice-cream parlor; 3 pools; excursions; kids' programs; Internet; salon; babysitting; exchange office. *In room:* A/C, TV, hair dryer.

Villa Valdibora ★★ The four apartments in this 18th-century town house could not be more unique or more convenient to Old Town Rovinj. Oil paintings, antiques, and Old World service are juxtaposed with ultramodern bathrooms, electronics, and comforts. This is a perfect place to stay to explore Rovinj and environs.

Silvana Chiurca 8. ✆ **052/845-040.** Fax 052/845-050. www.valdibora.com. 4 units. July–Aug from 200€ ($254) apt (2 persons), from 130€ ($165) other times. Rates include breakfast. AE, DC, MC, V. Pets allowed. **Amenities:** Bike use; laptop rental; room service; valet service; daily housekeeping. *In room:* A/C.

Where to Dine

Restaurants that line the Rovinj waterfront are touristy and predictable, and prices are a bit inflated. However, all serve respectable seafood and excellent pizza and pasta. Venture a little farther afield for menus that go beyond the expected.

Very Expensive

Amfora ★★★ SEAFOOD The fish is fresh and the ambience cheerful in this beautiful restaurant that overlooks the marina and Old Town. Amfora is a cut above most waterfront dining both in its cuisine and service—and that is also reflected in its prices. However, if you want first-class seafood, Amfora can't be beat. Try the salted sea bass or a risotto and pair it with one of the restaurant's excellent wines.

A. Rismondo 23. ✆ **052/816-663.** Entrees 90kn–175kn ($19–$36/£12–£22). AE, DC, MC, V. Daily 11am–midnight. Closed early Jan to early Mar.

Angelo d'Oro ★★★ ISTRIAN During the summer, the restaurant moves to a lovely walled garden, and in winter it settles in an imaginatively styled room inside. Either way, the cuisine is creative and beautifully presented. Try the cream of potato soup with truffles or a grilled fish dish. Don't miss a tour of the stone wine cellar, where you can taste Istrian wines and local specialties such as Istrian ham or cheese.

Via Svalba 38–42. ✆ **052/840-502.** www.rovinj.at. Reservations recommended. Entrees 90kn–165kn ($19–$34/£12–£21). AE, DC, MC. Daily 7pm–midnight.

Expensive

Konoba Veli Jože ★ ISTRIAN This rather dark dining room is so loaded with Croatian tchotchkes that they spill over to the outdoor tables, The food is first-rate and really representative of traditional Istrian cuisine. Try the *fuži* with truffles for a taste of the distinctive Istrian pasta and celebrated specialty. Or dig into one of Veli Jože's lamb or fish dishes, which are a bit expensive but worth the extra cost.

Svetog Križa 1. ✆ **052/816-337.** Entrees 30kn–120kn ($6–$25/£3.75–£16). AE, DC, MC, V. Daily 10am–3am.

Taverna da Baston ★★ ISTRIAN/SEAFOOD A warm welcome will make you feel at home at this bustling place next door to Rovinj's fish market. Dark brick walls are hung with fishing nets, and local music provides background. Try any of the superfresh fish dishes or the handmade gnocchi with truffles.

Svalba 3. ✆ **098/982-63-95.** Entrees 50kn–150kn ($10–$31/£6.20–£19). AE, DC, MC, V. Prices include tax, *couvert,* and service. Daily 6am–midnight.

Moderate

Calisona ★ ITALIAN Calisona, across from the town museum, can get very busy at lunch, partly because of its location and nicely shaded tables, and partly because of its reasonably priced food. Pizza, spaghetti, and risotto are the specialties at Calisona, though there are some grilled fish and meat dishes such as veal medallions, too. The menu is multilingual.

Trg Pignaton 1. ✆ **052/815-313.** Entrees 30kn–100kn ($6–$21/£3.75–£13). AE, MC, V. Daily 8am–midnight.

Gostonica Cisterna ★★ Value ITALIAN Inside, stone walls and old farm implements create a rustic ambience. Outside, 12 tables with pink tablecloths beckon passersby to see what smells so good. The seductive aroma will usually be fish on the restaurant's grill or risottos simmering on the stove. Cisterna is in a small courtyard at the bottom of Grisia near the Balbi Arch—easy to miss if you're not looking for it.

Trg Matteotti 3. ✆ **052/811-334.** Entrees 35kn–100kn ($7–$21/£4.35–£13). AE, DC, MC, V. Daily 8am–3pm and 6pm–midnight.

Inexpensive

Stella di Mare ★★ Value PIZZERIA/SPAGHETTERIA This laid-back restaurant is so close to the water that sea spray occasionally mists over outdoor tables when waves hit the rocky shoreline. Views of old Rovinj, boats in the harbor, gulls catching dinner, and the roiling sea are incomparable from the restaurant's blue-and-white umbrella tables. A few seafood dishes complement the pizza and pasta offerings. For a local treat, try *koki sa jajem* pizza, a crispy crust topped with cheese, tomato, prosciutto, and an egg (added raw but baked into the mix).

Croche 4. ✆ **091/528-88-83.** Pizzas 28kn–45kn ($6–$9/£3.75–£5.60); pasta from 35kn ($6/£3.75). AE, DC, MC, V. Daily 8am–midnight.

Exploring Rovinj

Rovinj is a browser's paradise, with lots of places to explore on its narrow, winding streets. Rovinj is also an aesthetic gem, and its beauty is readily apparent from a distance and close up. Most sites worth exploring are in the Old Town, plus places farther afield like **Zlatni Rt-Punta Corrente Nature Park** ★★, a densely forested park just steps from the Hotel Park (see above). Zlatni Rt is rimmed with rocky beaches and full of hiking paths. **Limska Draga Fjord** ★★★ is a flooded karstic canyon less than 16km (10 miles) north of Rovinj. It looks like a ribbon of clear blue-green water framed with forested walls on two sides. At least two caves with evidence of prehistoric habitation have been discovered there, and several local legends say that pirates used the inlet as a base for surprising merchant ships. Excursions to Limska Draga leave from Rovinj daily and often can be

Finds Grisia Street Standouts

Rovinj's main street is really a steep, cobbled passageway that runs from the main square all the way up to St. Euphemia Church. It is lined with shops and galleries and buildings that still sport vestiges of the town's medieval roots. **Galerija Peti-Božić** at no. 22 is one of the most pleasant and most interesting. This tiny shop specializes in Croatian naive art created by Marija Peti-Božić, who has shown her work in galleries and museums in Zagreb and elsewhere in Europe. Most of Peti-Božić's work is oil on glass, typical of the Hlebine School. The shop is run by the artist's jovial husband, who will proudly rattle off his wife's accomplishments as well as wrap your purchases securely for travel.

Another Grisia Street shop worth a stop is no. 37, where award-winning artist **Olga Vicel** creates naive art in another medium—embroideries using silk thread on linen. Framed pieces run 50€ to 500€ ($64–$635). Galerija Peti-Božić, Grisia 22 (✆ **091/578-65-28**), is usually open Easter through October 8am to 10pm daily. (Call to confirm open hours.)

August is officially the month of Grisia's art celebration; during this month, shops and restaurants remain open as long as there are people in the streets.

booked directly at seaside or from any travel agency in town for about 200kn ($40/£25) per person.

Balbi Arch ★★ Enter Old Town from the main square through the 17th-century Balbi Arch, which leads up to Grisia, Rovinj's most interesting street. The arch is on the site where one of the town's seven gates once stood; it is carved with a Turk's head on one side and a Venetian's head on the other.

St. Euphemia Church ★★ The baroque church dedicated to Rovinj's co–patron saint is the third iteration of the shrine built in her honor. The present church was built atop Rovinj's highest hill in the early 18th century and the adjacent **bell tower** was built 50 years earlier and is one of the highest campaniles in Istria. It is topped with a copper statue of St. Euphemia that includes a palm and a wheel, symbols of her martyrdom. The people of Rovinj made St. Euphemia a patron saint along with St. George after the stone sarcophagus containing her body mysteriously showed up on their shores following its disappearance from Constantinople in A.D. 800.

Petro Stankovića. ✆ **052/815-615.** Daily summer 10am–3pm; only during Mass other times.

POREČ

"Something for everyone" could be Poreč's motto. The seaside resort 67km (42 miles) north of Pula offers everything from a UNESCO World Heritage basilica complex to endless shopping opportunities to slick resort hotels so crammed with activities and services that you think you're in DisneyWorld. Poreč courts tourism, supports tourism, and profits from tourism, but the town and surrounding area still manage to intrigue, perhaps because they are a seamless blend of medieval heritage, a well-oiled service industry, idyllic vineyards and olive groves, and blatant commercialism. Old Town's immaculate cobblestone streets, precisely clipped plantings, multilingual signs, plus enough jewelry stores and gelaterias for every tourist in Croatia are the draw.

It's no mystery why visitors love Poreč: It has a sophisticated tourism infrastructure that lets everyone have a good time without feeling hassled. Poreč is conveniently connected to transportation for exploring the Istrian Riviera or interior.

Getting There & Getting Around

Poreč is just 42km (26 miles) north of Rovinj and a stop on Istria's coastal bus route. (Go to www.autotrans.hr and click on the "Istra-Promet" button at the bottom of the page for schedules and timetables.) If you are driving, allow 45 minutes for the trip from Rovinj because you will have to go around the Limski Fjord. Poreč's Old Town is easy to navigate on foot, though its end-to-end shopping opportunities might slow you down. City buses serve the Lanterna complex south of town (the bus station is .5km/¼ mile from the town center) as well as nearby spots like Tar, but a car is necessary if you want to stay in one of the charming family-run inns outside the center or if you want to explore the surrounding area.

Visitor Information

Poreč knows how to make visitors feel at home. The **Poreč Tourist Information Office,** Zagrebačka 11 (✆ **052/434-983;** www.istra.com/porec), can provide maps and brochures as well as leads on available accommodations and events. It is open 8am to 10pm Monday to Saturday all year and 9am to 1pm and 6 to 10pm Sundays during July and August. **Atlas Travel Agency,** Eufrazijeva 63 (✆ **052/434-983;** www.atlas.hr), can arrange excursions, hotels, private accommodations, and airline reservations. It is also the local American Express agent. **Di Tours ★★**, Prvomajska 2 (✆ **052/432-100;** fax 052/431-300; www.di-tours.com), is one of many private tourist agencies in town, but it has a huge inventory of rooms and apartments in Poreč and vicinity. In August, it offers doubles with shower from 28€ ($36), apartments from 45€ ($57). During the rest of the year, doubles start at 12€ ($15), apartments from 16€ ($20).

Where to Stay

Poreč is the most visited city in Istria, and it has a wide inventory of accommodations. Most hotels are managed by Riviera, but there is a lot to choose from, especially if you opt for a small hotel outside the center.

Expensive

Diamant ★★★ (Value) Guest rooms are huge and more like suites in this beautifully restored (2003) hotel less than a mile from Poreč's center. Most rooms have balconies and glass doors that are tinted and shaded, plus two bathrooms, one with a tub, and the 10th floor is all suites. The Diamant is also notable for its effort to make the entire hotel accessible to travelers with disabilities. Service is personal and helpful, more typical of small boutique establishments than huge package hotels. The same is true of the hotel's special bike tour that stops at local wineries, farms, olive groves, and monuments, and features a gourmet picnic.

Brulo. ✆ **052/400-000.** Fax 052/451-206. www.riviera.hr. 244 units. End of July to mid-Aug from 221€ ($280) double, 331€ ($420) suite; rest of year from 96€ ($122) double, 158€ ($201) suite. Rates include breakfast and dinner. 20% surcharge for stays of 3 days or fewer. AE, DC, MC, V. **Amenities:** 2 restaurants; bar; Internet cafe; juice bar; 2 pools; hot tub; whirlpool; kids' program; excursions; massage; solarium. *In room:* A/C, TV, minibar, hair dryer.

Hotel San Rocco ★★★ A haven for lovers of quiet, relaxation, and fine cuisine complete with its own swimming pool, this 12-room boutique hotel in Brtonigla was named the best small hotel in Croatia in 2007, and no wonder. The San Rocco caters to guests who want to be near the sea, but not amid the hustle and bustle of Poreč, which is less than 15 minutes away. The air-conditioned rooms in the 100-year-old, renovated stone house have sumptuous beds under wood-beamed ceilings and big bathrooms, some with tubs and turbo-massage showers. In addition, the hotel restaurant (see review below) has a way with local ingredients. ***Tip:*** If you can't get to Istria and the San Rocco, you still can get a feel for the hotel and its setting at **Istrian Charms,** a Zagreb boutique that sells San Rocco olive oil and other Istrian products. The store also offers a virtual tour of the hotel and restaurant on a flatscreen TV and you can book a room at the hotel on the spot.

Srednja Ulica 2, Brtonigla, 52474. ✆ **052/725-000.** Fax 052/725-026. www.san-rocco.hr. 12 units. Mid-June to mid-August and Christmas week from 185€ ($235) premier doubles; rest of year from 165€ ($210) premier doubles. Rates include breakfast and taxes. 35% discount for singles occupying a double room. Parking. **Amenities:** Restaurant; bar; pool; sauna; Wi-Fi in bar area; elevator; access for those w/limited mobility; wine cellar. *In room*: A/C, SAT/TV, minibar, hair dryer, safe.

Moderate

Neptun ★ Neptun has a great location facing the sea. It was built in 1968, renovated in 1995, and improved every year since, though air-conditioning was not part of the plan. Some rooms have dynamite harbor views, as does the rooftop cafe, which is closed during very hot weather. Bathrooms are adequate but have showers and no tubs. Reception is very helpful and pleasant and also handles details for guests of the hotel's two annexes.

Maršala Tita 17. ✆ **052/408-800.** Fax 052/431-351. www.riviera.hr. 145 units. July 30 to mid-Aug from 153€ ($194) double, 275€ ($349) suite; rest of year from 74€ ($94) double, 134€ ($170) suite. Rates include breakfast. AE, DC, MC, V. Half board available. Discounts for children in the same room as parent. **Amenities:** Restaurant; bar. *In room:* TV, minibar, hair dryer.

Inexpensive

Bijela Uvala ★★★ Located between Funtana and Poreč, this environment-friendly campground uses solar power and practices ecologically oriented camp management: The camp also offers a large pebble beach with paved sunning areas and lots of programs to amuse the kids.

52440 Poreč. ✆ **052/410-551.** Fax 052/410-600. www.plavalaguna.hr. July–Aug campsite with tent, car, and 2 people 27€ ($34) per day; rest of year from 14€ ($18). AE, DC, MC. Closed Nov–Mar.

Lanternacamp ★★★ If you must stay at a huge campground, Lanternacamp is one of the best, with more than 3,000 spaces for tents and/or campers. Lanterna wisely provides plenty of amenities such as electricity and water hookups, superclean bathrooms, supermarkets, a laundry, a pool, and activities for kids. The camp is 13km (8 miles) from Poreč.

52440 Poreč. ✆ **052/404-500.** Fax 052/404-591. www.riviera.hr. From 35€ ($44) per night for campsite and 2 people. AE, MC, V. Closed Nov–Mar.

Villa Filipini ★ Value This family-run place 10 minutes from Poreč opened in 2003 and is done in pine to resemble a rustic farmhouse. Mom serves breakfast and Dad is the accountant/handyman, while their son manages the desk and waits on diners in the inn's **restaurant** (see review below). Guest rooms are exceptionally clean and comfy, with French doors that open to the terrace. Upper-floor suites have balconies. You can meet the family's world-champion Istrian hunter in its home at the dog kennel behind the hotel. ***Warning:*** The rooms can get a bit toasty until the evening breeze cools them.

Filipini 1B. ✆ **052/463-200.** www.istra.com/filipini. 8 units. July–Aug from 77€ ($98) double, from 153€ ($194) suite; rest of year from 54€ ($69) double, 108€ ($137) suite. All rates computed on a per-person basis and include breakfast. Half board available. AE, DC, MC, V (only when phone connections work). Limited free parking. **Amenities:** Restaurant; bar; tennis court; bike rental; laundry service. *In room:* TV, Internet access.

Where to Dine

Dining in Old Town Poreč tends to be a one-note experience: Almost all the restaurants rely on pizza, pasta, and grilled seafood for their menu mainstays. If you want to taste authentic grilled lamb or more unusual Istrian preparations, your best bet is to get out of (Old) Town.

Very Expensive

Cardo ★★ SEAFOOD Fish on ice is displayed in a glass case for all to see outside this classy terrace restaurant. A gnarled olive tree and soft lights surrounding the terrace create a romantic mood for diners at the outdoor tables, which are always full. Try the salmon piquant or noodles with mussels, either of which is perfect with a glass of Istrian Malvasia.

Cardo Maximus 6, Old Town. ✆ **052/255-164.** Entrees 35kn–330kn ($7.15–$69/£4.40–£43). AE, DC, MC, V. Daily Apr–Nov 1 noon–midnight.

Gostonica Istria ★★ Locals rave about the seafood at Gostonica Istria, a typical indoor/outdoor coastal place where people-watching from the terrace is a side dish. Istria's multi-language menu makes it easy to order. You'll get expertly prepared, authentic

 Istrian cuisine such as minestrone, fuži, and spiny lobster with noodles. Service is accommodating even if the prices are a little high.

Msgr. Bože Milanovića 30. ✆ **052/434-63.** Fax 052/451-482. Entrees 65kn–190kn ($14–$39/£8.70–£24). AE, DC. Daily noon–midnight.

Restoran San Rocco ★★★ (Finds) ISTRIAN The chef at this restaurant in the San Rocco Hotel (see above) in Brtonigla, 5km (3 miles) from Poreč, specializes in three- to five-course tasting menus that rely on local ingredients creatively presented. Typical offerings include octopus salad with olive oil foam and pork breast with pistachios. Pairings with local wines from San Rocco's well-stocked cellar are suggested for each course, but boost the tariff considerably. A la carte options are available, but prices are available only on request.

Srednja Ulica 2, Brtonigla 52474. ✆ **052/725-000.** Fax 052/725-026. www.san-rocco.hr. Tasting menu 290kn–510kn ($60–$106/£37–£66). AE, DC, MC, V. Daily 1pm–10pm.

Sv Nikola ★★★ Nikola is one of the extremely chic dining spots on the "high style" segment of Poreč's waterfront where large private yachts like to congregate. Food is well prepared and beautifully presented, but pricey. Try the tagliatelle Altijež, ribbons of al dente pasta with scallops, langoustines, and a white-wine reduction.

Obala Maršala Tita 23. ✆ **052/423-018.** Entrees 80kn ($17–$33/£11–£20), more for seafood sold by the kilo. AE, DC, MC, V. Daily 1–10pm.

Expensive

Distinguished Guest ★★ MEDITERRANEAN High fashion meets the waterfront at this chic restaurant dressed up like a French salon with chandeliers and black and cream furniture. DG's broad selection of seafood and meat dishes is complemented by an outstanding wine list. Dine alfresco and enjoy the entertainment of the yacht lineup and the nightly promenade along the wharf. ***Note:*** By day diners can gaze at St. Nicholas Island from DG's terrace tables.

Obala Maršala Tita 20. ✆ **052/433-810.** Entrees 70kn–140kn ($15–$29/£9.30–£37). AE, DC, MC, V. Daily noon–midnight; closed Nov 1–Dec 20.

Peterokutna Kula ★★ SEAFOOD Built into a pentagonal, 15th-century tower, this place has all the earmarks of another tourist trap—position on one of the highest traffic corners in town, old stone walls, steep steps—but it delivers first-rate food in a unique location. The spectacular view of the city from a rooftop five floors up (no elevator) is perfect garnish for PK's impeccably fresh food. The seafood assortment platter is a luscious collection of the shrimp, orada, mussels, and calamari at a very reasonable price. Service is friendly and prompt, a wonder since the kitchen is on the first floor. ***One caution:*** No credit cards are accepted and the occasional sea gull lands tableside to beg for leftovers.

Decumanus 1. ✆ **052/451-378.** Entrees 55kn–110kn ($11–$23/£6.80–£14). No credit cards. Daily noon–midnight.

Restaurant Villa Filipini ★★ (Finds) ISTRIAN Pastas are handmade and the kitchen is imaginative in this tiny restaurant in one of Istria's rural small hotels. Seating on the outdoor terrace gives the impression that you're dining in a forest. The chef bases his dishes on what is fresh in the market and choices can include green gnocchi with mixed cheese–and-walnut sauce, or ravioli filled with fresh cheese in herb butter. Fish dishes and sauces are particular strengths, as are the excellent wine list and creative sweet treats such as gelato on fresh cheese with sage honey–and-chocolate sauce.

Filipini 1B. ✆ **052/463-200.** www.istra.com/filipini. Entrees 40kn–150kn ($8.15–$31/£5.05–£19). AE, DC, MC, V. Daily noon–11pm.

Restoran Marconi ★★ ISTRIAN The delightful, shaded garden area of this bistro next to the cathedral is a great place to enjoy a light afternoon snack or early supper. And why not? Its palazzo setting was built by Italian nobles 500 years ago. Pizzas are flavorful, oozing with rich mozzarella; the seafood salad is loaded with squid, shrimp and mussels; and the seafood risotto is just as packed with the same ingredients. Save room for rich ice cream for dessert.

Eufrazijeva 24. ✆ **052/431-922.** Entrees 48kn–125kn ($10–$26/£6.20–£16); pizzas 30kn–50kn ($6.10–$10/£3.80–£6.20). MC, V. Daily 7am–11pm May–Oct.

Moderate

Old Pub Cotton Club ★ PIZZA/PASTA The burgundy awnings make Cotton Club look like a tourist trap, but serious food is prepared here. Try the tortellini *mille voglie* (with clams) or the tortellini with *pršut,* pumpkin, cream, and truffles. Pasta and pizza are emphasized, with nine tagliatelle preparations, 20 kinds of pizza, several risottos, good drinks, ice creams, and live music weekend evenings.

Trg Slobode 5. ✆ **052/453-293.** Fax 052/432-074. Entrees 40kn–110kn ($8.15–$23/£5.05–£14. No credit cards. Daily 9am–1am.

Ulixes ★ ISTRIAN The atmosphere at Ulixes is softened by indirect lighting on its brick courtyard walls, olive trees, soft music, and cats that beg for handouts from diners. When you order, however, stick with fish dishes, which are competently prepared, or try a pasta like *fuži* with game. Portions are on the small side, even for Croatia.

Decumanus 2. ✆ **052/451-132.** www.istra.com/ulixes. Entrees 40kn–110kn ($8.15–$23/£5.05–£14). DC, MC, V. Daily noon–midnight.

Inexpensive

Barilla ★ PIZZA/PASTA This casual restaurant *is* related to the pasta in the blue box you can get in American grocery stores. There is (understandably) a huge pasta menu supplemented with a few grilled meat/fish selections, but dine at Barilla for the 31 kinds of pizza baked in a brick oven.

Eufrazijeva 26. ✆ **052/452-742.** Small pizza 40kn–60kn ($8.15–$12/£5.05–£7.60). DC, MC, V. Daily noon–midnight.

Stari Saloon ★★ Value Bistro/Pizzeria This pizza joint is in a courtyard framed by buildings, but that doesn't stop people from jamming the restaurant nightly. Instead of sizing its pizza as small, medium, or large, Stari Saloon lists pie diameters in centimeters. Extra-large pizzas are a whopping 75cm (29 in.) across and served on a wooden disk the size of a small tabletop. Pizza prices start at 55kn ($11/£6.95).

Ribarski Trg. ✆ **052/453-228.** Entrees 35kn–110kn ($7–$23/£4.35–£14). AE, DC, MC, V. Daily 10am–11pm.

Exploring Poreč

Poreč's Old Town is small but packed with treasures, chief of which is the Euphrasius Basilica and its stunning **mosaics.** The rest of Old Town's attractions pale in comparison but are interesting enough to warrant a walk-through.

Baredine Cave ★★★ Excursions to these limestone caverns are among the most popular in Poreč. Just 7km (4½ miles) northeast of town on the road to Višjan, the caves are filled with stalactites and stalagmites. Entry fees cover the services of a guide, who takes you on a 40-minute tour of the underground halls and galleries and inevitably tells the story of the cave's legendary ill-fated lovers, who died while looking for each other in the subterranean maze.

Nova Vas 52446. ✆ **052/421-333.** www.istra.com/baredine. 45kn ($9.15/£5.70). July–Aug daily 9:30am–6pm; May–June and Sept daily 10am–5pm; Apr and Oct daily 10am–4pm; Nov–Mar for prearranged groups only.

Euphrasius Basilica Complex ★★ UNESCO has put this collection of early Christian and Byzantine architecture on its World Heritage List, and you should put them on your "must-see" agenda, too. The basilica is the last of four churches that were built between the 4th and 6th centuries, one on top of the other. An atrium, a baptistery, a bell tower, and a bishop's palace also comprise the complex, which is entered through the arches of the atrium. Even if you aren't into visiting churches, make an effort to see the complex's spectacular **gem-studded mosaics ★★★** as well as the symbolic early Christian fish mosaic.

Summer daily 7:30am–8pm. Other times during Mass only. Bell tower daily 10am–7pm, 10kn ($2/£1.25).

St. Nicholas Island ★★★ Poreč's better beaches are off this island, which is a short boat taxi ride away from the harbor.

Taxi boats leave the dock every half-hour.

Trg Marafor ★★ The remains of two Roman temples (Mars and Neptune) are the highlight of Marafor, which once was the site of a Roman forum. Today, Marafor is home to several sleek cocktail bars and jazz clubs. One, **Lapidarium,** is tucked into a courtyard strewn with ancient artifacts. Jazz concerts fill the courtyard during the season.

NOVIGRAD (CITTANOVA)

You might have a hard time keeping your eyes on the road if you drive the short stretch between Poreč and Novigrad in the early morning when the sun is hitting the water: During this time of day the landscape is bathed in a sheen of gold that gives it a mesmerizing, unearthly beauty. The scenic drive takes you just 18km (11 miles) north of Poreč. Once in Novigrad, you will immediately sense that this town is more relaxed than most coastal tourism destinations.

Visitor Information

The **Tourist Office** in Novigrad can provide maps, brochures, and information on area accommodations and events. It is located at Porporella 1 (✆ **052/757-075;** www.istra.com/novigrad) and is open daily, from 8am to 8pm in spring and summer, and 8am to 3pm Monday through Saturday the rest of the year.

Getting Around

Novigrad is fairly compact and easy to negotiate on foot. It doesn't take more than an hour to see the entire town unless you can't resist trying out one of the many access points to the sea. Most of the action and attractions are at the waterfront, including Sts. Pelagia and Massima Church.

What to See & Do

Much of Novigrad's Old Town buildings have been replaced or redone, so there is little original architecture there, but the town has a comfortable feel and is a good place to wander around for a few hours, especially the rock walk around the city that takes the place of a beach. The town's breakwater creates a calm swimming area, but access areas for stronger swimmers also are built into the open-sea side.

Be sure to stop in at the **Sts. Pelagia and Massima Church** ★. Built in 1882, it has a beautiful ceiling and unusual elevated gallery behind the ornate marble tabernacle. There is also an intricately carved wooden pulpit inside the church and a soaring bell tower outside. In 2007, there was a new hotel in town (Nautica) as well as a new harbor. Both opened in 2006. ***Tip:*** Photographers will want to use the **citi loggia** at the end of Belvedere Street as a frame for images of the sea.

Where to Stay

Novigrad is an unabashed seaside resort and it is relatively new for an Istrian town—its medieval architecture was destroyed by the Turks in the 17th century and rebuilt in the prevailing Venetian style. However, there is something remarkable about accommodations options there. Novigrad does have its share of blah package hotels, but it also has a couple of places that are charmingly boutique and one that is downright decadent, a nice change from the monotonous in-your-face tourist-trap look of Umag to the north and the mind-boggling vacation options in Poreč to the south.

Cittar ★★ At first glance, the Cittar looks as if it's a castle protected by a high wall, but look again. The hotel was built in 1991 behind one of the few sections of the medieval city wall that still stands, and the wall out front was constructed at that time as a grand entryway. Behind it is the lovely Cittar with a gorgeous, leafy terrace and enclosed sunroom off reception that give the hotel the air of a Tuscan palazzo. The friendly staff and resident cocker spaniel add to the illusion. Guest rooms are a good size and beautifully decorated in earth tones and wood. They come with comfortably large bathrooms that make the Cittar a fine home away from home.

Prolaz Venecija 1. ✆ **052/757-737.** Fax 052/757-229. www.cittar.hr. 14 units. Aug from 114€ ($145) double; rest of year from 78€ ($99) double. Rates include breakfast. Half board available. 30% discount for children 7–10; 50% discount for children 2–6. **Amenities:** Restaurant; elevator; limited free parking. *In room:* A/C, TV, minibar.

Nautica ★★★ Open since summer 2006, this is Novigrad's nod to luxury lodging—38 rooms and 4 suites dressed in mahogany and brass. Nautica is small enough to be exclusive and large enough to incorporate every conceivable amenity, all within a red-violet-hued building, a color that somehow works against the blue sea. The rooms have huge beds, tons of storage, and immense bathrooms that include tubs, bidets, and German-made toiletries. The hotel's restaurant (see below) and bar are sophisticated, spacious exercises in teak and brass with sprawling outdoor seating areas overlooking the marina. There is a large, free parking lot for guests' cars and 365 berths in the harbor for those who choose to arrive in their multimillion-dollar yachts.

Sv. Antona 15. ✆ **052/600-400.** Fax 052/600490. www.nauticahotels.com. 42 units, including 4 suites. Summer from 238€ ($302) double with a sea view, from 330€ ($419) suite; rest of year from 143€ ($182) double, from 270€ ($343) suite. Rates include buffet breakfast, use of spa and pool, and parking. AE, DC, MC, V. **Amenities:** Restaurant; cafe; bar; indoor pool; fitness center; sauna; shops; room service; valet; yacht harbor; ATM. *In room:* A/C, SAT/TV, Wi-Fi or broadband Internet access, minibar, hair dryer, safe, balcony.

Torci 18 ★ The oddly named Torci 18 (it's actually at Torci 34) has rooms that are simple, clean, and convenient. This is a good option that falls between the moderately priced Cittar and the private accommodations in Novigrad. The Cittar does not provide many luxuries, but you're not sharing a bathroom, either. Breakfast prepared in Torci 18's kitchen and served on the terrace is a big plus.

Torci 34. ✆ **052/757-799.** Fax 052/757174. www.torci18.hr. 12 units. July–Aug from 60€ ($76); rest of year from 50€ ($64) double. AE, DC, MC, V. **Amenities:** Restaurant; bar; terrace. *In room:* SAT/TV.

Where to Dine

Novigrad has several excellent restaurants, but most are more expensive than the pizza/pasta places in Poreč. The best bars overlook the sea.

Restaurant Navigarre ★★★ ISTRIAN The signature restaurant of the Hotel Nautica (see above) opened in 2006 as a crisp, shipshape venue for serious food. Diners can choose either light meals or "slow" food, both inside the brass-and-teak-fitted dining room and outside on the terrace under huge burgundy umbrellas. The menu, which is in five languages including Russian, features creative dishes based on local produce, including lamb, octopus, and veal prepared (with 3-hr. notice) under the *peka.* For a lighter meal, try homemade tagliatelle with *pršut* and peas or the more complex gnocchi with scallops and truffles. For dessert, the Florentine cream cake is to die for.

Sv. Antona 15, 52466 Novigrad. ✆ **052/600-400.** Fax 052/600-490. www.nauticahotels.com. Reservations recommended. Entrees 75kn–180kn ($15–$37/£9.30–£23). AE, DC, MC, V. Daily 7am–11pm.

Restoran Torci 18 ★★ Finds ISTRIAN It's hard to say if Torci 18 is a restaurant with pansion or a pansion with restaurant, because the two are seamlessly blended into a solid building with dark-wood beams, gardens, and glass under the old walls overlooking the sea. Menu choices are fairly predictable but well prepared. (You know the fish is fresh as can be when you see women cleaning the morning's catch with clamshells on the restaurant's beach side.) Pastas require a two-portion minimum and lobster is sold by the kilo. Atmosphere is gratis. ***Tip:*** Don't leave without buying a bottle of Torci 18's homegrown olive oil.

Torci 34. ✆ **052/757-799.** Fax 052/757-174. www.nautico.hr. Entrees 50kn–85kn ($10–$17/£6.30–£11) (more for fish sold by the kilo). AE, DC, MC, V. Daily noon–3pm and 6–10pm.

INLAND ISTRIA

It isn't easy being green in a region where seawater blue is the dominant color, but the Istria's emerald interior hints at the unspoiled nature and unique experiences that await those who venture into this often overlooked part of Croatia. As you exit the deep blackness of **Učka Tunnel** in the east or as you drive away from the golden brightness of the **Istrian Coast** in the west, you realize that this is territory that feeds the senses—all of them. In **Green Istria** you can take time to breathe the perfumed air, listen to the bird chatter, touch the rough stone of a medieval castle, or savor the taste of local wines. You can climb a hill to listen to cool jazz at **Grožnjan;** travel the wine road through Momjan; watch films under a night sky in **Motovun;** or soak in hot spring waters at **Istarske Toplice.** Inland Istria is where you can marvel at still-vibrant 15th-century frescoes in a woodland church near tiny **Beram,** or tramp through the woods outside **Buzet** while following a couple of dogs hunting truffles.

This is where you can feast on an elaborate dinner in an award-winning restaurant in **Livade** and wake up the next morning to a breakfast of home-smoked ham, homegrown fruit, and homemade cheese in the kitchen of the rural farmhouse where you spent the night. During the day, you can nose around Glagolitic artifacts in tiny **Hum** or explore the historic walled city of **Roč.** This is a place where you can immerse yourself in the land

and the lives of the people who live there, a place where you can wander without ever feeling lost.

Getting There & Getting Around

No matter how you get to Istria you will need a car to thoroughly explore its inland attractions—unless you opt for a guided excursion.

Most towns in inland Istria are small; in fact, one of them, **Hum,** bills itself as the smallest in the world. The main attractions in Istria's inland communities can be readily accessed by walking, but many are extremely hilly and must be approached on foot over irregular cobblestone streets, which can be difficult for some. To get to **Motovun,** for example, you have to leave your car at the bottom of a steep street and walk more than a quarter of a mile uphill. Some inland towns are remote, and driving is the only practical way to cover the distance between them.

Visitor Information

Every town in Green Istria has its own tourist information center, though those in the smaller towns have very limited hours and are difficult to find. To help visitors get the most out of a trip, the **Istria County Tourist Association** has produced attractive publications on farmhouse stays, cultural itineraries, wine roads, olive-oil roads, and truffle-hunting opportunities. These are available through the association, whose main offices are in Poreč at Pionirska 1 (✆ **052/452-797;** fax 052/452-796; tzzi-po@pu.hinet.hr), and in Pula at Forum 3 (✆ **052/215-799;** fax 052/215-722). The association also maintains a website with English-language links to almost every town: **www.istra.com.**

MOTOVUN, ROČ & HUM

Motovun is one of Istria's better-known interior towns, perhaps because it hosts the **Motovun Film Festival** (www.motovunfilmfestival.com; early Aug, but dates are variable), hot-air balloon competitions, and a festival celebrating truffles and wine. It also doesn't hurt that this hilltop town is just 20 minutes east of Poreč and home to the delightful **Hotel Kaštel** (see below).

One of the most compelling reasons to stop at nearby **Roč** is its location at one end of the **Glagolitic Alley.** A string of 10 outdoor sculptures that dot the road between Roč and Hum was erected between 1977 and 1981 to celebrate and preserve Glagolitic script, which was devised in the 9th century by Saints Cyril and Methodius. It is an alphabet that consists of 34 letters that have both meanings and a numerical value. For example, a letter "K" also means "how" and it represents number 40. This script was used in Croatia until the 15th century and in Dalmatian, Istrian, and Kvarner regions until the end of 19th century.

Even though there aren't any explanations on most of them, the sculptures (dedicated to Glagolitic scholars) are interesting to look at. Today Roč is primarily known as a center of Glagolitic literature, and every year the town puts on the **Small Glagolitic Academy** to keep the traditional writing alive. Private rooms are available in Roč (there are signs on the road), and there is a decent *konoba.* The short strip of road that links Roč and Hum is just 6.4km (4 miles) long, but it is a historic corridor because of the commemorative Glagolitic sculptures along the way. Even though Hum's claim to fame is its status as the world's smallest town, from the looks of tourism in the present-day village, that could be changing. Hum has spiffed up in the last 3 years and it is quite appealing. Only about 20 permanent residents live within its well-preserved walls, which enclose two small streets and two churches (one dating from the 12th c.).

Getting There & Getting Around

Istria's intercity buses (www.autotrans.hr) serve Motuvun, Roc, and Hum, but service can be slow and erratic. Renting a car or booking a guided excursion are the most efficient ways to see these tiny treasures. The important sites in all these towns can be easily accessed on foot.

Visitor Information

Information on all three towns and their festivals is available at the **Istria County Tourist Offices** in Pula and Poreč and in each town's local bureau. Motovun's tourist office is at Andrea Antico bb (✆ **052/681-642**); the **Tourist Information Office** in Buzet serves Roč and Hum. It is at Trg Fontana 7/1 in Buzet (✆ **052/662-343;** www.tzg-buje.hr) and can provide information on private accommodations, including farmhouse stays, camping, and events.

Where to Stay & Dine

Besides the Hotel Kaštel in Motovun, the only accommodations in these villages are in private homes, making this an ideal area to try a farmhouse stay and to savor the flavors of Istria at a local dining establishment.

Hotel Kaštel ★★ in Motovun at Trg Andrea Antico 7 (✆ **052/681-607**) provides panoramic views of the Mirna valley, and each guest room offers a different perspective. Guest rooms, which start at 113€ ($144) for a double with a balcony in July and August (from 98€/$124 rest of the year), were refurbished in 2003 and are equipped with modern bathrooms that don't destroy the character of the 17th-century structure, which once was a palace. If you call ahead, the hotel will pick you up at the bottom of the street leading into Motovun so you don't have to drag your luggage uphill.

Barbacan Enoteque & Restaurant ★ on the main walkway into Motovun at Barbacan 1 (✆ **052/681-791**) is pricier than most, but it's also more interesting. Start with the pâté of veal sweetbreads with truffles or the truffled chicken broth. Entrees include filet of beef with black truffle butter, and risotto Montonese with saffron garlic and truffles.

Restoran Kaštel ★★, in Motovun at the Hotel Kaštel at Trg Andrea Antico 7 (✆ **052/681-607**), serves unusual Istrian dishes as well as a signature dessert that's not on the menu. Try the *frkanci* with venison goulash. The pasta, which is a hybrid gnocchi/noodle, is handmade by Istrian home cooks just for the hotel. Ask for the special chocolate truffle for dessert—it's the size of an egg.

You'll feel like you're in Mom's kitchen in **Ročka Konoba** ★★ in Roč (✆ **052/660-005**), a rustic dining room with a great view of the rolling countryside. Local specials such as *fuži,* spicy Istrian sausage, hearty soups, and fragrant homemade bread are on the menu.

The line was literally out the door when we visited the Hum institution **Humska Konoba** ★★, and no wonder. The tiny dining room at Hum 2 (✆ **052/660-005**) puts local flavor in the food and atmosphere in this wood-and-stone building. If you dare, sip home-brewed *biska,* a grape brandy–based aperitif flavored with white mistletoe and other herbs. Forget about cholesterol; dig into a meal of home-smoked meat with sauerkraut and have *krostole* (doughnuts) for dessert.

Vrh ★★ technically is in Buzet, but it's really in the Istrian hills at Vrh 2. Buzet. (✆ **052/667-123**). Get directions at the Buzet tourist office to this delightful spot on the road between Ponte Porton and Buzet. Vrh's menu is standard Istrian with dishes such as *fuži* with truffles or gnocchi with game. Sausages are house made, *peka*-baked meat is a specialty, and nettle pâté is a delicacy. Try Vrh's house label wine, and, if you're staying nearby, a glass of local grappa, which is renowned all over Croatia.

THE KVARNER GULF

Experiencing the diverse charms of the Kvarner Gulf region requires a strategically orchestrated campaign, but once you decide on a plan, it's fairly simple to visit the major mainland towns along the Kvarner coast from Opatija to Senj. It's more challenging to coordinate ferry connections to, from, and between the Kvarner islands.

Rijeka

142km (88 miles) SW of Zagreb; 615km (382 miles) NE of Dubrovnik

No matter which part of the Kvarner Gulf region you choose to explore, you'll probably go through Rijeka, which is at the southern end of the Zagreb-Rijeka *autocesta.* There are no beaches or resorts on Rijeka's shores, so most people breeze past on their way to somewhere else without a thought to stopping. Rijeka's magnificent collection of 19th-century buildings and monuments *could* use a good power washing and a little paint, but the city has many attractions worth investigating.

Getting There & Getting Around

BY CAR Almost all roads in Croatia eventually lead to Rijeka, but you can drive there from Zagreb in less than 2 hours on the Zagreb-Rijeka *autocesta* (A-6) from the north. A-6 also connects to the A-1 *autocesta* from Split in the south. From Ljubljana in Slovenia, take E-70 via Postojna and connect with local Rte. 6 at Illirska Bistrica. You will encounter a border crossing at Rupa (***warning:*** occasionally there is some hassle here, so be sure your documents are in order) and follow E-61 to Rijeka. Ferries from several nearby islands stop at Rijeka and dock near the Riva, south of the center. A schedule and prices can be obtained from www.jadrolinija.hr, or call © **06/032-13-21** for schedule and price info.

BY TRAIN Except for fast-train service between Zagreb and Split, rail service in Croatia can be cumbersome, but the train stations usually are something to see. That's especially true of the terminal in Rijeka, which is straight out of 19th-century Hungary. Trains that stop there connect with Opatija and other Croatian towns and with some European hubs, too. For a schedule, check the HZ website, www.hznet.hr, which has routes and prices in English. Or you can call the central office, Željeznički Kolodvor (© **060/333444**), though you might not be able to find anyone who speaks English. The station's ticket office is open daily from 9am to 4pm and from 5:30 to 8:45pm. At other times you can buy tickets on the train.

BY BUS Buses to and from Rijeka connecting with other parts of Croatia run frequently and fares are affordable. A one-way ticket to Zagreb costs 1.50€ to 16€ ($1.90–$20) depending on the route. Buses also connect with other cities in Europe. The main bus hub is at Trg Žabica 1 and is open from 5:30am to 9pm (© **060/302 010** reservations and information). You can also buy tickets on board the bus, but getting a seat is uncertain in summer.

BY PLANE You can get to Rijeka by air, though the airport is actually near **Omišlj** on **Krk Island** 24km (15 miles) south of the city. After you deplane, you can get to town on the Autotrolej bus, which lets you off at the station at Jelačić Square for 2€ ($2.55) one-way. Or you can grab a taxi outside the airport and pay as much as 31€ ($39) for the

Rijeka's Morčićl

This ceramic-and-gold rendering of a black woman in a turban has become a symbol of Rijeka and a distinctive design for jewelry, where the baubles are made. The colorful Mořić is mostly used in earrings, though the image of a Moorish woman is a popular mask worn by revelers during Rijeka's huge pre-Lenten carnival. There are many legends about the Morčić, including tales of victory over the Turks thanks to a woman's prayers, but in reality, the Mořić probably is a vestige of 17th- and 18th-century European fashion, which was mad about anything Asian. As earrings, Morčić were worn by upper-class married women, sailors, fishermen, and only-sons (in the right ear) to ward off evil spirits.

same ride. Call the Rijeka airport (© **051/842-040**); for flight info, call © **05484-21-32** or check www.rijeka-airport.hr.

Getting Around

Navigating Rijeka and the surrounding area is fairly easy, whether you wander around the center or go farther afield. City bus tickets can be purchased at **Tisak** kiosks (newsstands) or from the bus driver, and fares depend on how far you are going. You can go to **Lovran** for 2.50€ ($3.20), or to the nearby 'burb of **Trsat** for less than 1.50€ ($1.90). Walking is the favorite travel mode in Rijeka, and maps and other information about restaurants, shows, and monuments can be obtained at the **tourist office** at Korzo 33 (© **051/335-882;** www.tz-rijeka.hr).

Taxis are plentiful and you can hail one off the street that will take you anywhere within the city limits, but you should always confirm the fare with your driver before getting in the car. Buses are also abundant and make regular runs from 5am to 11:30pm daily.

Where to Stay & Dine in Rijeka

Despite its position as the third-largest metropolis in Croatia, Rijeka has few standout hotel and dining options, but you won't go wrong with the selections below.

The 125-year-old **Grand Hotel Bonavia** ★ at Dolac 4 (© **051/357-100**) in the city's Old Town was completely redone in 2000, with big-city amenities and a covered dining terrace. The standard rooms are a bit tight for 162€ ($206) for a double, but for an extra 20€ ($25) you can get a notably larger space or even a suite (317€/$403) with a view. Some rooms have balconies; all have roomy tiled bathrooms.

The brand new **Bitoraj Hotel** ★★ at Sveti Kirž 2 in Fužine, half an hour from Rijeka (© **051/835-019**), opened in August 2007, shortly after the fantastic Bitoraj restaurant (see below) moved into its new quarters on the main floor of a new building. Guest rooms are done with lots of wood and soft colors with big windows for natural light. Most rooms have showers, but some have tubs. The best thing about the rooms is their position above the restaurant. The **Continental Hotel,** at Šetalište Andrije Kačiča-Miošiča (© **051/372-008**), looms over the park in Rijeka's center, but its exterior is far more elegant looking than the 42 units inside. Doubles, while clean and plain, offer few extras and go for 62€ ($79), while suites cost 105€ ($133). Public areas are a bit shabby, but the hotel does have a nice terrace and the coffeehouse serves great desserts.

The **Bitoraj Restaurant** ★★★, at Sveti Križ 1, Fužine (first exit on the Rijeka/Zagreb tollway; ✆ **051/835-019**), is a 30-minute drive from Rijeka, and the 75-year-old restaurant will transfer you to a completely different mind and food set from that of the Adriatic coast. In 2007, Bitoraj moved to a beautiful new space that includes a pansion (see above), but thankfully the owners didn't change anything about the restaurant's exceptional food. The menu offers a huge selection of meals heavy on meat and forest products, and you will be able to choose from exotic appetizers and main courses available few other places. From bear and deer ham, to Bitoraj's signature dish of young wild boars baked under a lid on an open fire *(peka),* to great desserts, all dishes utilize the best ingredients the surrounding woods can offer. The ambitious **Bonavia Classic** ★ at Dolac 4 (✆ **051/357-100**), in the Grand Hotel Bonavia (see above), has a menu that combines the best of Croatian produce with inspired preparations. Begin with piquant octopus soup before you try the Riga, a salad of bitter greens and lobster. Splurge on the Symphony Bonavia, a mélange of beef, veal, and pork filets grilled and accented with gorgonzola.

Order a *plat du jour* at unpretentious **Zalogajnica Grandis Placa** at Zagrebačka 16 (✆ **051/331-981**) and you won't be hungry for a week. ZGP specializes in such classics as stew, goulash, and casseroles. You can see what the locals eat without emptying your wallet.

Exploring Rijeka

The wide pedestrian street called **Korzo** ★★ originally was constructed along the town walls and today is lined with stores, cafes, restaurants, and even an enclosed mall. However, most stores close at 1pm on Saturday and don't reopen until Monday morning, making the area pretty dead on weekends.

The bright yellow **Gradski Toranj (City Tower)** ★ above the city gate was one of the few structures left standing after the powerful 1750 quake, but it was renovated and tinkered with for 140 years or so after the seismic event, which further altered its appearance. The clock was added in 1873 and the dome on its top in 1890. Walk through the portal below the Tower to **Trg Ivana Koblera,** where you will run into the **Stara Vrata (Roman Gate),** Rijeka's oldest surviving structure. The Stara Vrata once served as the portal to the Roman Praetorium, which was Rijeka's military command center. Much of Rijeka's Old Town (Stari Grad) was demolished to make way for modern infrastructure, but you still can see remnants of the ancient city of **Tarsatica** that once stood in what is now in the vicinity of **St. Vitus Church** ★★ at Trg Grivica 11 (✆ **051/330-879**). According to legend, when a disgruntled 13th-century gambler threw a rock at the crucifix on St. Vitus's main altar, the rendering of Christ's body on the cross began to bleed and the gambler was swallowed up by the earth except for his hand.

Opatija

Less than 16km (10 miles) west of Rijeka, Opatija and its adjacent villages are everything Rijeka is not—vibrant, welcoming, clean, and full of clear-water beaches, breathtaking views, comfortable accommodations, and excellent restaurants.

Opatija started as a fishing village with a church and a population in the low double digits. But in the mid–19th century, the mild climate and spectacular seashore caught the fancy of **Iginio Scarpa,** a wealthy Italian businessman who built the lavish **Villa Angiolina** (named after his late wife), surrounded it with a jungle of exotic flora from around the world, and invited all his aristocratic friends for a visit. Privileged Europeans were so taken with Villa Angiolina and Opatija that one by one they erected villas of their own, each bigger and more ornate than the next, thus cementing Opatija's reputation as a winter playground for the wealthy.

Getting There & Getting Around

BY CAR If you've driven to Rijeka, it's only another 20 minutes to Opatija via the coastal highway.

BY BUS The bus (no. 32) stops in front of the Rijeka train station and travels the length of the Riviera to Lovran every 20 minutes for 10kn ($2/£1.25) one-way.

Once in Opatija, walking throughout the town and to nearby villages is customary.

Where to Stay & Dine

The lemon-drop-yellow **Bristol** ★★, at Maršala Tita 108 (✆ **051/706-300**), reopened in late June 2005 after an extensive renovation that ended 2 decades of being closed to the public while it sheltered Slavoninan Croats who were displaced by the 1991 war. Happily, the Bristol is now a sophisticated, tasteful showpiece with doubles starting at 156€ ($198). The exceptional English-speaking staff will help guests find a restaurant, book a bike tour/picnic, and everything in between.

The **Hotel Astoria** ★★, at Maršala Tita 174 (✆ **051/706-350**), was built in 1904 as Villa Louise in Austrian-Mediterranean style. Today the hotel's atmosphere is more Guggenheim Museum with touches of whimsy. Guest rooms, which start at 150€ ($191) for a double, are sleek and comfortable with artwork, vases filled with lucky bamboo, and a generous-size flatscreen TV.

Despite Viennese architect Carl Seidl's artful 1924 reconstruction of the property, **Villa Ariston**'s ★ guest rooms, which start at 810kn ($165/£102) for a double, are disappointingly cramped, dim, and in need of updating. The presidential suite, however, has a fabulous balcony and an unsurpassed view of the garden. It is rumored that Coco Chanel and JFK slept in the inn at Maršala Tita 179 (✆ **051/271-379**), but not together.

Walking up the long, wide staircase to the **Hotel Imperial**'s front door at Maršala Tita 124/3 (✆ **051/271-577**) makes you feel like you're approaching a monument, and once inside, the impression sticks. The hotel was built in 1885 and resembles a fine old opera house—crystal chandeliers, soaring ceilings, long corridors, heavy velvet curtains, and a dining room fit for a royal banquet. Guest rooms, which start at 585kn ($119/£74) for a double, have updated bathrooms and period furniture, but they are dark and tired-looking even if they have balconies.

The Hotel Park ★★ is a blue-and-white confection at M. Tita 60 in Lovran (✆ **051/706-200**), next to the historic East Gate that leads to Old Town. The Park has a long history as a hotel, but its new era began in July 2005 after an extensive makeover. Today it is a comfortable accommodations option with lots of amenities away from the hustle and bustle of Opatija's nightlife and doubles from 1,124kn ($229/£142). Bathrooms are spacious and most have showers only that must have been installed by Paul Bunyan: The fixtures are a good 2.1m (7 ft.) up the wall. **Preluk** ★ (✆ **051/622-249**) is a campground 4.8km (3 miles) north of Opatija near Volosko, and for 109kn ($22/£14) for two people and a car and tent site, it is particularly well-situated bargain for those who love watersports.

Amfora ★★★, at Črnikovica 4 (✆ **051/701-222**), in Volosko about 1.6km (1 mile) away from Opatija's main drag, is one of the best restaurants on the Opatija Riviera. Try the savory black risotto done to creamy perfection and full of tender pieces of squid—it's an Adriatic specialty.

Le Mandrać ★★★ at Obala Frana Supila 10, Volosko (✆ **051/701-357**), bills itself as a "fish restaurant for the new millennium." Its ultramodern decor and stylized food presentations certainly follow that theme, but the restaurant is much more. The menu is imaginative and changes frequently to take advantage of available fresh, seasonal ingredients, which the chef combines in unusual pairings. If you have the time (and the money), try the "tasting" menu, which allows diners to sample small servings of a wide range of dishes such as poached egg with Istrian ham and nettle, or fudge with pear ice cream and rosemary.

Plavi Podrum ★★, at Obala F. Supila 4, Volosko (✆ **051/701-223**), sits under crisp blue awnings on the waterfront terrace steps away from Mandrać. Plavi Podrum offers creative cuisine like green-tea tagliatelle with scampi, shrimp, wild asparagus, and nettle without sky-high prices or formality. The wine list is solid, but the bar also pours a wide selection of Scotch and Irish whisky. **Slatina ★**, at Maršala Tita 206 (✆ **051/271-949**), is a local hangout on an enclosed porch, and it dishes up huge portions of Slav specialties like *šopse* salad, a mix of chopped cukes, tomatoes, onions, and peppers covered with shaved sheep cheese, and *tavće gravće* (beans in a paprika sauce), a dish that will make you turn up your nose at canned pork and beans forever.

Bellavista ★★, at Stari Grad 22 in Lovran (✆ **051/292-123**), is in a building that has been a restaurant for 40 years, but this iteration of the atmospheric space just past the historic East Gate entrance to Old Town opened in June 2007 with a new look and a new owner. Ask for one of the tables along the removable windows that look out to sea, but no matter where you sit, you will be rewarded with a fine meal and warm ambience. For a treat, try the salt-baked fish, which is sold by the kilo. Or sample any of the homemade pastas like ravioli with spinach and truffles. Bellavista pays special attention to wines, too, and offers tasting plates of food that match select varietals.

The Kvarner Islands

Croatia's largest island, **Krk** (pronounced "Kirk" with a strong Scottish burr), is also the country's most developed, especially in the north where the island is connected to the mainland via a mile-long toll bridge that sometimes is congested with commuters who live on Krk but work in Rijeka. Much of **Rab**'s coast resembles a strip-mined mountainside devoid of vegetation and inhospitable to intelligent life. The southwestern side of the island, however, is a very different story. Tranquil beaches and coves, green spaces, and a beautifully kept medieval Old Town belie travelers' first impressions. **Cres** and **Lošinj** are really a single island, separated only by a 48m-wide (30-ft.) man-made channel that has been bridged by roadway. Despite their proximity and historical link, these islands couldn't be more different. Cres stretches 60km (40 miles) from tip to tip and is twice as long as Lošinj. Both islands are covered with biking and hiking trails, but it is Cres that is a haven for campers who like to rough it and for hikers who like a challenge. Lošinj, on the other hand, is the island of choice for yachters and tourists looking for relaxing cafes and beaches.

The Opatija Riviera is also loaded with affordable pizza places and cafes, most of which are along Maršala Tita and the Lungomare.

Exploring Opatija

Promenading on **Šetalište Franza Josefa ★★★** in the evening is an art form in Croatia in general and in Opatija in particular, and this 12km (7¼-mile) flagstone walkway along the shore from **Volosko ★★** (2km/1¼ miles north of Opatija) to **Lovran ★★** (5.6km/3½ miles south of Opatija) is the granddaddy of them all. It runs past **Villa Angiolina ★★**, the villa that started it all, and that is now a popular venue for weddings when it isn't being used for art exhibits and other cultural events. It's open daily June to September from 10am to 9pm.

Nightlife

Opatija rocks until around 11pm, which is closing hour for most restaurants and bars. Until then, you can sip a glass of wine, have a beer, or get rowdy at **Hemingway's** on the promenade or at any restaurant or cafe along the way. However, the most nighttime action is on the **Lungomare** and **Maršala Tita**—and it is alcohol-free. On any given evening it looks like all of Croatia is out taking a stroll, rollerblading, or pausing to watch break dancers and mimes. An ice-cream cone is the party treat of choice.

8 ZAGREB

Because visitors to Croatia tend to use Zagreb as a stopover rather than a destination, many of the city's charms are overlooked. It takes patience to discover Zagreb, and it takes knowledge about the past to understand its Balkan soul.

ARRIVING

BY PLANE Zagreb is the entry point for most visitors to Croatia, but there are no direct flights from the U.S., Canada, or Australia. Croatia Air, the national airline company, connects Zagreb with many European hubs as well as with other Croatian cities. **Pleso International Airport** (**© 385 01/626-5222**) is 16km (10 miles) south of the city center, and Croatia Air operates a shuttle every 30 minutes from 5:30am to 7:30pm between the airport and Zagreb's main bus station for 30kn ($6/£3.75) one-way. The ride takes half an hour (**© 385 01/615 79 92**). Taxi fares to the city center run between 150kn and 250kn ($26–$51/£16–£32). ***Note:*** Croatia Air's luggage weight limits may differ from those of other international carriers, so if you are not checking your luggage directly through to Zagreb, you should query Croatia Air on this policy, which is subject to seasonal changes.

Note: When returning to the U.S., be aware that Croatia Air does not allow battery-operated devices in checked luggage, so remove them before checking your bag.

BY BUS Zagreb's bus station is a bright, efficient hub with restaurants, shops, a post office, and local connections to the city center. A 24-hour *garderoba* (luggage storage area) charges 1.20kn (25¢/15p) per hour, or 29kn ($6/£3.60) per day. ATMs are located near the ticket office, as is an exchange that is open from 6am to 10pm daily. Frequent buses link Zagreb and all of Croatia's main cities, which in turn hook up with local lines that run to virtually every village in the country.

BY TRAIN The 19th-century **Zagreb train station (Glavni Kolodvor)** facing Trg Kralja Tomislava on the city's green horseshoe was renovated in 2004 and is now a pink confection adorned with cherubs and other statuary. It is close to bus and tram connections into the city center, which is a 10-minute walk with several hotels along the way. A 24-hour *garderoba* is available for 10kn ($2/£1.25) per day. A restaurant with a lovely terrace overlooks the park. There are ATMs, exchange facilities, and an information center (daily 6–10am, 10:30am–6pm, and 6:30–10pm).

Catch the no. 5, 6, or 13 tram in front of the Kralja Tomislav monument to get to Trg Bana Josip Jeličića. Routes may vary, so watch for handwritten signs listing changes taped up at bus stops.

BY CAR Driving in Zagreb can be stressful. Most streets are marked by small ornamental signs on plaques affixed to building walls at intersections, so you can't see the sign until you're past the intersection. Many buildings in Zagreb do not display street numbers at all, or if they do they can't be read unless you are on top of them. To complicate matters, there is a tangled network of one-way and pedestrian streets. Add to that perpetual street construction and a parking dearth, and you have a driver's nightmare inside the city limits.

VISITOR INFORMATION

The **Zagreb Tourist Information Center,** Trg Bana Jelačića 11 (© **01/481-40-51;** www.zagreb-touristinfo.hr; Mon–Fri 8:30am–8pm, Sat 9am–5pm, and Sun and holidays 10am–2pm). It sells the **Zagreb Card** for 90kn ($18/£11), which covers 72 hours of city transportation (including the Sjleme cable car), a 50% discount at most museums and galleries, and discounts at participating businesses. There is a second Tourist Information Center at Trg Nikole Šubića Zrinskog 14 (© **01/492-16-45**).

The **Zagreb County Tourist Association,** Preradovićeva 42 (© **01/487-36-65;** www.tzzz.hr), is invaluable for information about excursions from Zagreb. Hours are 8am to 4pm Monday to Friday.

Croatia Airlines has an office at Trg Nikole Šubića Zrinskog 17 (© **01/481-96-33**). It is open 8am to 7pm Monday to Friday and 8am to 3pm Saturday. Tours to sites and cities in Zagreb and throughout Croatia can be arranged through **Atlas Travel,** Zrinjevac 17 (© **01/481-39-33**), Croatia's largest agency. Atlas is also Croatia's American Express agent. **Generalturist,** at Praška 5 (© **01/480-55-55;** www.generalturist.com), books flights, excursions, and other trips.

CITY LAYOUT

Zagreb is nestled between **Mount Medvednica** and the **Sava River.** It is a sprawling city, but almost every attraction of note is within 2.4km (1½ miles) of **Trg Bana Jelačića,** the city's main square. The area north of the Trg Jelačića includes **Gornji Grad (Upper Town)** and its Gradec and Kaptol neighborhoods, which are perhaps Zagreb's most picturesque areas. **Donji Grad (Lower Town)** south of Trg Jelačića includes Zagreb's central green spaces known as the Green Horseshoe and runs south to the main train station. You can walk to most points of interest from Trg Jelačića, or hop on the public tram system for 6.50kn ($1.30/80p) per ride. After that, only a smattering of sights is worth seeking out. **Mount Medvednica Nature Park** and its **Sjleme Peak** in the hills north of town can be accessed from the square by taking tram no. 14 to the end of the line and then tram no. 15 to its terminus. From there you can get a cable car to Sjleme's top. **Mirogoj Cemetery** is also north of the center and can be reached via the no. 106 bus from the cathedral. **Novi Grad (New City)** is an area of bland apartment towers and industry south of the Sava; except for **Jarun Lake** just north of the river and the airport,

Tips Using Croatian Telephones

To call Zagreb from the United States, dial the **international prefix 011,** then Croatia's country code, **385;** and then Zagreb's city code, **1.** Then dial the actual phone number.

To call the U.S. from Zagreb, dial the **international prefix 00,** then the U.S. country code, **1;** then the area code and number. Other country codes are as follows: Canada, **1;** the United Kingdom, **44;** Ireland **353;** Australia, **61;** New Zealand, **64.**

To call from one city code to another within Croatia: Dial the Croatian city code, including the zero, followed by the phone number.

To make a local call, simply dial the phone number—no codes necessary. Local calls cost about 5kn ($1/60p) per minute.

To use a prepaid phone card, call the service, key in the code on the back of the card, and call the number. It's a good idea to have a prepaid phone card for emergencies because most pay phones don't take currency and you'll need a card to use them. You can buy prepaid cards in denominations of 50, 100, 200, and 500 units at most newspaper kiosks, at post offices, and at some tobacconists. Calls are based on unit-per-minute rates, and the farther away you call, the more each unit costs and the faster you use up your units. You can also buy prepaid cards at **Nexcom,** Zavrtnica 17 (✆ **01/606-03-33**); or at **Voicecom,** Ilica 109 (✆ **01/376-01-23;** www.voicecom.hr).

To use a mobile phone, you can buy a SIM card for 400kn to 600kn ($82–$123/£51–£76) from **VIP** (✆ **091**) or **T-Mobile** (✆ **098**). You can also buy pay-as-you-go SIM cards from news kiosks in smaller denominations. If you have a GSM-equipped phone, it will register and readjust to T-Mobile in Zagreb, provided you activate its international capabilities with your service provider in the U.S. before you leave. To call the U.S., hold down the zero key until a plus sign appears in the display. Then dial 1 plus the area code and number. Be aware that you will pay for roaming charges besides the call, which are extremely expensive because the call has to bounce from Croatia to the U.S., and back to Croatia again.

there isn't much to see here. **Maksimir Park** is an elegant wooded zone east of the center. It can be reached via tram nos. 4, 7, 11, and 12.

GETTING AROUND

BY TRAM OR BUS Zagreb's electric tram system is quick, efficient, and reliable, and it runs 24/7. Tram routes cover central Zagreb and connect to buses that serve outlying areas and suburbs. Most lines eventually end up at the main train station, Trg Ban Jelačića, or both.

Tickets can be purchased at Tisak news kiosks for 8kn ($1.65/£1) or on board for 10kn ($2/£1.25). Tickets are good for 90 minutes each way and must be validated with a time stamp at the orange machines on board. Random control checks keep cheaters in check and if you are caught without a ticket or with an unvalidated ticket, the fine is 150kn ($31/£19) on the spot, more if you don't have the money in hand.

Note: Keep a tram/bus route map with you whenever using the system so you can locate the routes' end streets and determine if the vehicle is going in your direction. Almost none of the tram and bus operators speak English.

BY TAXI Taxis are expensive in Zagreb and charge a 19kn ($4/£2.50) flat fee plus 7kn ($1.45/90p) for every 3/5 of a mile. A 20% surcharge is added on Sunday and at night, which makes taxis a very expensive way to travel. However, if you must use a cab, you can call one at ✆ **01/668-25-05.** It's a good idea to try to negotiate a price for your trip before you hop in.

ON FOOT Walking is by far the best (and healthiest) way to see Zagreb. Crime is low and you can safely get to almost any museum or restaurant in the central town within half an hour by walking.

Fast Facts Zagreb

American Express American Express services are available through **Atlas Travel** at Zrinjevac 17, 10000 Zagreb (✆ **01/481-39-33;** fax 01/487-30-49). There is also an Amex office at Lastovska 23 (✆ **01/612-44-22**).

ATMs & Currency Exchange You can withdraw cash using American Express, Diners Club, Maestro/MasterCard, Cirrus, and Visa at ATMs (bancomats) installed all over Zagreb. Change money or traveler's checks at most banks, exchange offices, and travel agencies for a 1.5% or greater fee. The fee is even higher if you change money at a hotel. **A-Tours** at the main bus station (✆ **01/600-86-66**) is the exchange office with the longest hours. It is open from 6am to 10pm every day.

Business Hours Most banks open at 9am and stay open until 7pm or later Monday to Friday, and 9am to 1pm on Saturday. The airport branch of Zagrebačka Bank is open on Sunday. Offices generally are open from 8am to 5pm; some have Saturday hours, usually until 1pm. Store hours vary, with many closing from 2 to 5pm or some other interval during the day, but smaller stores open at 9am and close 8pm Monday to Saturday and are closed all day Sunday. Stores in larger malls are open 7 days a week, but most don't reopen after the weekend until 2pm on Monday so employees can restock shelves.

Emergencies For police dial ✆ **92;** for an ambulance, ✆ **94;** and to report a fire, ✆ **93.** For road assistance, dial ✆ **987;** for the **Croatian Auto Club,** dial ✆ **01/464-08-00.**

Internet Access Croatia has embraced computer technology in a big way, and Internet access is easy to find. Try **Ch@rlie's** in the shadow of the Hotel Dubrovnik at Ljudevita Gaja 4a (✆ **01/488-02-33**). The staff is helpful and you can catch up on e-mail for 10kn ($2/£1.25) per hour while you sip an espresso. Hours are 8am to 10pm daily. **Sublink Cybercafe** is close to Trg Jelačića at Nikole Tesle 12 (✆ **01/481-13-29**). You can e-mail, print, copy, or scan for 14kn ($2.60/£1.60) per hour.

Mail Mail letters at any yellow *posta* box, but if you need to buy stamps or send a package, the Central Post Office is at Jurišićeva 13 near the Jadran Hotel (✆ **01/481-10-90**). Hours are 7 to 9pm Monday to Friday, 8am to 4pm Saturday.

Newspapers & Magazines Very few news kiosks sell English-language newspapers, and those that do sell out quickly. *The International Herald Tribune* is the easiest to find and costs 20kn ($4/£2.50). Many hotels print faxed copies of U.S. and other English-language newspapers for a fee.

Pharmacies Need an aspirin? In Zagreb (and all of Croatia) you'll have to go to a pharmacy *(ljekarna)* to buy some. No drugs of any kind are sold anywhere except at a pharmacy. There are several 24-hour *ljekarna* in Zagreb. Two are at Trg Jelačića (✆ **01/481-61-54**) and at Ilica 301 (✆ **01/375-03-21**).

Safety Zagreb enjoys relatively low crime rates, and it's safe to ride public transportation at night and to walk through high-traffic areas. Police presence on Zagreb streets is subtle and you'll rarely see a uniformed officer, but they're there. Exercise the same precautions you'd take in any big city.

WHERE TO STAY

There are few moderately priced and virtually no bargain hotels in Zagreb. In fact, unless you go with private accommodations, most options are at the extreme ends of the price—and quality—list.

Very Expensive

Dubrovnik ★★ "Rms w vu" should be the motto of this modern-looking glass-and-metal tower off Trg Jeličića, where many of the hotel's rooms look down on the Croatian hero's statue in the main square. Opened in 1929 as the Hotel Milinov, the hotel changed its name to Dubrovnik, added more than 150 rooms in a new glass-and-aluminum wing in 1982, and completed a total renovation in 2003. ***Note:*** The business suite (1,600kn/$327/£203) includes a rooftop terrace.

Gajeva 1., P.P. 246, 10000 Zagreb. ✆ **01/487-35-55.** Fax 01/486/35-06. www.hotel-dubrovnik.hr. 274 units. From 1,300kn ($265/£164) double; from 1,500kn ($307/£190) suite. Rates include breakfast. Special 9-hr. "daily rest" rate 50% the regular room rate. AE, DC, MC, V. Limited free parking. **Amenities:** Restaurant; cafe; bar; business center; salon; room service; nonsmoking rooms; valet; rooms for those w/limited mobility. *In room:* A/C, TV, wireless/dataport, minibar, hair dryer, safe.

Palace ★★ The Secessionist-style hotel just 5 minutes from Trg Jeličića was built as a private residence in 1891 and converted to a hotel in 1907, which makes it the oldest in Zagreb. If you're looking for a convenient place to stay that has character and a bit of history, the Palace is the ticket. Rooms are in tune with 19th-century sensibilities; some have been updated for modern guests.

Trg JJ Strossmayera 10, 10000 Zagreb. ✆ **01/481-46-11,** reservations 01/492-05-30. Fax 01/481-13-58. www.palace.hr. 123 units. From 1,250kn ($256/£159) double; from 1,680kn ($343/£213) junior suite; from 2,300kn ($470/£291) suite. 20% discount on weekends. Rates include breakfast. AE, DC, MC, V. Limited free parking. **Amenities:** Restaurant; bar; room service; babysitting; nonsmoking rooms. *In room:* A/C, TV, Internet, minibar, hair dryer.

The Regent Esplanade ★★★ The elegant Esplanade has attracted well-heeled guests since its opening in 1925 as a stop on the Orient Express, and now a painstaking renovation has seamlessly added new-world creature comforts to the historic hotel's old-world opulence. Add to that service that is second to none, and the result is one of the most beautiful and best-run hotels in Croatia. Amenities are first class and augmented with little luxuries such as fresh flowers, twice-a-day housekeeping, and cushy slippers

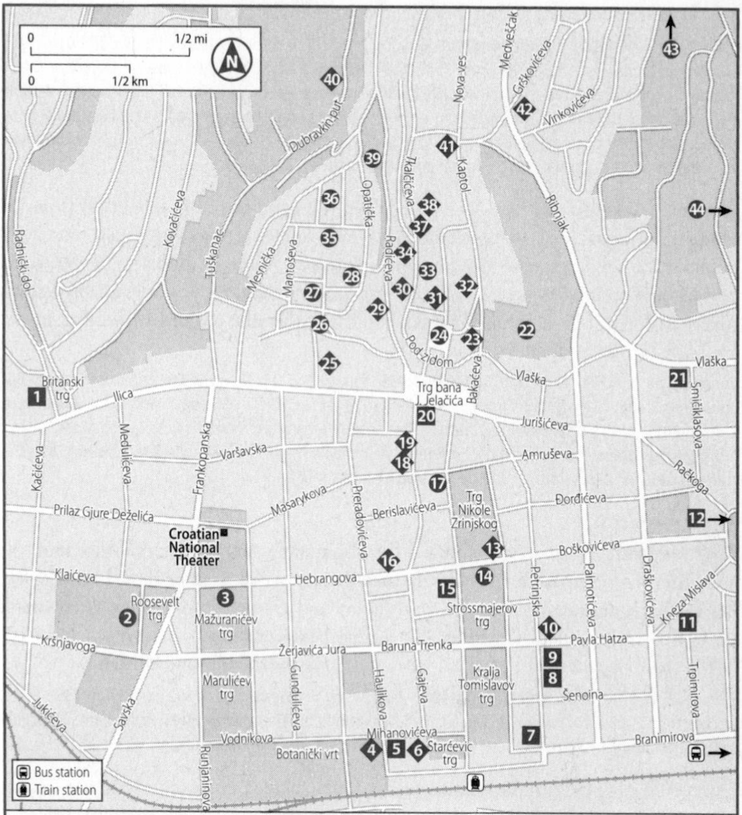

ACCOMMODATIONS ■
Best Western Astoria **9**
Central **7**
Dubrovnik **20**
Ilica **1**
Jadran **21**
Palace Hotel **15**
Regent Esplanade **5**
Sheraton Zagreb **11**
Sliško **12**
Zagreb Youth Hostel **8**

DINING ◆
Agava Trattoria **29**
Bagueri **34**
Baltazar **41**
Boban **19**
Capucine Spaghetteria **32**
Dubrovkin Put **40**
Gallo **16**
Kaptolska Klet **23**
Kod Žaca **42**
LeBistro **6**
Leonardi **30**
Nokturno **31**
Panino **37**
Paviljon **13**
Pinguin Sandwich Bar & Grill **18**
Pod Gričkim Topom **25**
Purger **10**
Restoran Ivica I Marica **38**
Zinfandel's **4**

ATTRACTIONS ●
Atelier-Ivan Meštrović **36**
Burglars' Tower (Kula Lotrščak) **26**
Cathedral of the Assumption of the Virgin Mary **22**
Croatian Museum of Naïve Art **27**
Dolac Market **24**
Ethnographic Museum **3**
Kamenita Vrata **28**
Mimara Museum **2**
Mirogoj Cemetery **44**
Mt. Medvednica **43**
The Museum of the City of Zagreb **39**
St. Mark's Church **35**
Strossmayer Gallery of Old Masters **14**
Tkalčićeva Ulica **33**
Zagreb Archeological Museum **17**

ideal for padding around on the bathroom's heated marble floor. Liberal use of wood and brass in both private and public areas, a chic **Croatian fusion restaurant** (see review below), and a staff ready to fulfill every need have brought back the hotel's glory days.

Mihanovićeva 1, 10000 Zagreb. ✆ **800/545-4000** from the U.S., or 01/456/66-66. Fax 385 01/66 020. www.regenthotels.com. 209 units. From 154€ ($196) double; from 309€ ($392) suite. AE, DC, MC, V. Breakfast buffet not included but available for 22€ ($28) per person. Pets allowed at 20€ ($25) per day. **Amenities:** 2 restaurants; terrace dining w/live music; bar; sauna; salon; concierge; room service; valet service; casino; club floor; nonsmoking rooms; 2 rooms for those w/limited mobility. *In room:* A/C, TV w/pay movies, wireless connection/dataport, minibar, hair dryer, trouser press, safe.

Sheraton Zagreb ★★★ The glass-and-metal front of this hotel not far from the train station makes it easy to spot among Zagreb's vintage architecture. Guest rooms and public spaces are bright and airy, and all bathrooms are fitted with bathtubs and toiletries. Most hotel services are available 24/7 and the restaurant staff is remarkably knowledgeable. There isn't a thing management hasn't thought of, and everything in the Sheraton Zagreb is superbly executed.

Kneza Borne 2, 10000 Zagreb. ✆ **01/455-35-35.** Fax 01/455/30/35. www.sheraton.com/zagreb. 306 units. From 240€ ($305) double; from 390€ ($495) suite. AE, DC, MC, V. Guarded parking lot. **Amenities:** 2 restaurants; pastry cafe; piano bar; pool; sauna; concierge; salon; room service; valet service; casino; nonsmoking rooms; rooms for those w/limited mobility. *In room:* A/C, TV, wireless/dataport, minibar, coffeemaker, hair dryer, iron/ironing board, trouser press, safe.

Expensive

Best Western Astoria ★★ Value Location and a 2005 renovation that took the hotel from frayed to fabulous make the Astoria one of the most underrated in Zagreb. Besides being midway between the train station and Trg Ban Josip Jeličića, guest rooms are loaded with modern amenities like heated bathroom floors and French toiletries. Public spaces have a spiffy, polished look, and service is friendly and efficient.

Petrinjska Ulica 71, 10000 Zagreb. ✆ **01/484-12-22.** www.bestwestern.com. 102 units. From 135€ ($171) double; from 202€ ($257) suite. AE, DC, MC, V. Rates include breakfast. **Amenities:** Restaurant; nonsmoking rooms; Internet; rooms for those w/limited mobility. *In room:* A/C, TV, minibar.

Central ★ The Central's location across from Zagreb's main train station is convenient to transportation, but rooms facing the street can be noisy when trams rumble by. The quality of the Central's rooms' decor is Wal-Mart, and most have showers rather than tubs, but they have decent amenities following a 2002 renovation.

Branimirova 3, 97, 10000 Zagreb. ✆ **01/484-11-22.** Fax 01/484-13-04. www.hotel-central.hr. 76 units. From 780kn ($159/£99) double; from 1,400kn ($286/£177) suite. AE, DC, MC, V. Rates include breakfast. **Amenities:** Restaurant (breakfast only); adjacent casino. *In room:* A/C, TV, dataports and minibars in some rooms, Internet connection, hair dryer.

Moderate

Hotel Ilica The Ilica is set back from the far end of Zagreb's main shopping street and it is priced lower than almost all other hotels in the central city. Guest rooms are adequate, but the suites are over-the-top kitsch that incorporates a lot of gilt and plastic (there is a full-size refrigerator in the living room of one of them). The no. 6 tram stops in front of the hotel and Britanski Trg and its Sunday antiques market are steps away.

Ilica 102, 10000 Zagreb. ✆ **01/377-76-22.** Fax 01/377-77-22. www.hotel-ilica.hr. 24 units. From 83€ ($105) double; from 124€ ($157) suite and apt. Rates include breakfast. AE, DC, MC, V. Limited free parking. **Amenities:** Restaurant; nonsmoking rooms; rooms for those w/limited mobility. *In room:* A/C, TV.

Jadran ★ Thanks to a 2003 renovation, the once shabby Jadran is now a pleasant, affordable choice just 5 minutes from the city center. Decor in guest rooms and public areas has been turned up a notch, and both are reasonably modern, though the rooms are not exactly spacious. The Jadran's main advantages are its location and easy access to public transportation.

Vlaška 50, 10000 Zagreb. ✆ **01/455-37-77.** Fax 01/461-21-51. www.hup-zagreb.hr. 49 units. From 726kn ($149/£92) double. AE, DC, MC, V. Rates stay the same all year and include breakfast. Limited free parking. **Amenities:** Restaurant. *In room:* A/C, TV, hair dryer.

Sliško ★ (Value The Sliško is a solid no-frills hotel in back of the main bus station. Opened in the mid-1990s, the Sliško has just enough amenities to make it comfortable, and a pricing scale to prevent wallet welts. Rooms are furnished in utilitarian modern and some are small, but all are clean and affordable; pricing is according to the number of beds used. The first-floor restaurant is thoughtfully glassed off from the smoky bar.

Supilova 13, 10000 Zagreb. ✆ **01/619-42-23.** Fax 385 01/619-42-10. www.slisko.hr. 18 units. From 531kn ($109/£68) double; from 776kn ($159/£99) suite (4 beds). AE, DC, MC, V. 10% discount for cash. Rates include breakfast. **Amenities:** Restaurant; bar. *In room:* A/C, TV.

Inexpensive

Fulir Backpackers' Inn ★ (Value A couple of large, brightly painted second-floor rooms make up the Fulir, but this hostel just off Trg Jelačića is loaded with personality. Its founders are college friends who opened Fulir in 2006 to mimic the kinds of places they liked to stay when they were traveling. It's clean, safe (someone is always on duty), affordable, and centrally located. The owners explained that the Fulir space once was owned by one of their grandmothers and that it is in a historic building. There is a kitchen for guests' use and lockers where they can keep their valuables when they are out and about. ***Note:*** There is no age limit for guests and Fulir's doors are open from 8am to 10pm. If you need to leave early or get back late, you can notify the person on duty to let you out or in.

Radiceva 3A. ✆ **01/483-08-82** or 098/193-05-52. www.fulir-hostel.com and www.myspace.com/fulir hostel. 2 rooms with 16 beds (1 with 12 and 1 with 4). 145kn ($30/£19) per person. **Amenities:** Kitchen, TV room, lockers, bike storage.

Zagreb Youth Hostel The lobby looks like a homeless shelter intake area, and the scent of insecticide is in the air as you approach reception. However, it's one of the few bargain accommodations in Zagreb and as such, its off-putting details can be overlooked. Accommodations range from six-bed, dorm-style rooms to doubles with private bathrooms. The only amenities are vending machines in the lobby, but the ZYH is 5 minutes from both the city center and the train station.

Petrinjska 77, 10000 Zagreb. ✆ **01/484-12-61.** Fax 01/484-12-69. www.hfhs.hr. 215 beds, most in multibed dorm-style rooms with shared bathrooms, 10 doubles with private bathroom. From 350kn ($72/£45) double; from 110kn ($23/£14) bed. 5kn ($1/60p) discount for people 26 and under. AE, DC, MC, V. Check-in is 2pm; checkout is 9pm.

Private Accommodations

Evistas ★★ This accommodations matchmaker is low profile but high on service. Evistas specializes in finding private apartments and *sobes* (rooms) in private homes for frugal travelers staying in Zagreb, but it also locates and books city youth hostels, rooms on the coast, and suites in posh hotels.

Šenoina 28, 10000 Zagreb. ✆ **01/483-95-54.** evistas@zg.htnet.hr. Mon–Fri 9am–1:30pm and 3–8pm; Sat 9:30am–5pm.

WHERE TO DINE

Eating is a social occasion in Croatia, and Zagreb is full of good restaurants, although the range of cuisine choices is narrow.

Very Expensive

Paviljon ★★ CROATIAN Paviljon's setting on the Green Horseshoe flanked by some of Zagreb's best museums gives the restaurant a cultured aura, and its formality and old-school decor give it the patina of class. The terrace looks out over a park area toward the main train station and Tomislav Trg, and inside the dining room is all elegance with a cherrywood floor and a fireplace. However, it is the restaurant's well-executed menu featuring Croatian interpretations of classic dishes that steals the show. Start with goose-liver in Cumberland sauce or smoked tuna carpaccio, and follow with roast duck with red cabbage and figs for an unusual taste combination. Wines are on the high end, but when you're serving top Croatian names like Grgić, it's understandable.

Trg Kralja Tomislava 22. ✆ **01/45-54-066.** Fax 01/434-659. www.restaurant-paviljon.com. Entrees 65kn–125kn ($13–$26/£8.05–£16). AE, DC, MC, V. Mon–Sat noon–midnight. Bar opens at 10am.

Pod Gričkim Topom ★★★ CROATIAN Location, location, location draws a crowd at this traditional-style restaurant on the Strossmayerovo Šetalište, steps midway between Trg Bana Jelačića and Gornji Grad. Bread and tiny balls of Croatian pâté start most meals, which could be anything from grilled meat to pasta. Try the monkfish, which comes with *blitva,* the Croatian version of chopped spinach. Desserts are decadent and the wine list is loaded with fairly priced Croatian choices.

Zakmardijeve Stube 5. ✆ **01/483-36-07.** Entrees 130kn–250kn ($27–$51/£17–£32). AE, DC, MC, V. Daily 11am–midnight.

Zinfandel's ★★★ FUSION By day, diners have a view of lovely Fountain Square through the window-walls of this sophisticated dining room in the Regent Esplanade (see review above), which is the source of the best breakfast buffet on the planet. A little later, Zinfandel serves a casual but wonderfully diverse lunch menu. However, it is at night that things get really creative with dishes such as duck and venison casseroles served with a salad of walnuts, oyster mushrooms, and cranberries; or lamb filet wrapped in zucchini.

Mihanovićeva 1. ✆ **01/456-66-66.** Main courses 70kn–210kn ($16–$43/£9.90–£27); barbecue 120kn ($24/£15) per person. AE, DC, MC, V. Dinner daily 6–11pm.

Expensive

Agava Trattoria ★★ (Value) ITALIAN Set above Tkalčićeva on a terraced hill, diners at this trendy spot have a bird's-eye view of the action, whether they sit on the handsome outdoor deck or in the dining room behind tall glass windows. The food here tends to be Italian, but there are some Croatian specialties and salad and pasta choices, too. Try the Coquilles St. Jacques and cashew salad and end with the divine figs and plums in red wine sauce with vanilla ice cream. ***Note:*** There may be "reserved" signs on all the tables. Don't let that dissuade you. Our waiter quipped that the signs were there "for people who eat here."

Tkalčićeva 39. ✆ **01/482-98-26.** Entrees 30kn–120kn ($6.15–$25/£3.80–£16). AE, DC, MC, V. Daily noon–11pm.

Baltazar ★★ CROATIAN Grilled meat is the focus of this pleasant dining spot with a nice terrace, north of the cathedral on Kaptol. Baltazar is in what may be the city's trendiest neighborhood, but the food holds with tradition. This is the place to try Croatian schnitzel and any national dish you've wanted to try. Service is superb.

Nova Ves 4. ✆ **01/466-69-99.** www.morsko-prase.hr. Entrees 55kn–125kn ($11–$26/£6.80–£16). AE, DC, MC, V. Mon–Sat noon–midnight.

Gallo ★★★ ITALIAN Food is art at this beautiful, unpretentious restaurant behind the facade of an unremarkable building a few blocks from the city center. Homemade pasta in countless shapes and a rainbow of colors dries behind glass near the restaurant entrance. The menu is mostly fish with interesting preparations such as tuna with polenta and red-wine sauce, or beef soup with ravioli. There are a stylish stone terrace, a casual dining room, and a formal space where crystal and silver set the tone.

Andrije Hebranga 34. ✆ **01/481-40-14.** Fax 01/481-40-13. www.gallo.hr/all.asp. Reservations recommended at dinner. Entrees 60kn–120kn ($12–$25/£7.45–£16). AE, DC, MC, V. Daily 11:30am–midnight.

Kod Žaca ★★ CROATIAN COUNTRY This is a terrific place for veal, beef, ostrich, turkey, pork, horse, and chicken and the sauce of your choice—mushroom, truffle, pepper, or cheese. The portions are generous and all meat dishes are accompanied by either homemade gnocchi or croquettes. With its old-country decor and only 10 small tables inside, Kod Žaca provides a cozy atmosphere in which to dine and feel relaxed.

Grškovićeva 4, just steps up from where Ribnjak changes to Medveščak. ✆ **01/468-4178.** Reservations recommended. Entrees 60kn–120kn ($12–$25/£7.45–£16). No credit cards. Daily noon–2am.

Moderate

Boban ★ This boisterous cellar restaurant named after a Croatian soccer star is two flights below Boban's bar and way below it in noise level. Food is straightforward Italian with a few Croatian-inspired dishes such as venison salami and vegetable-stuffed pancakes with béchamel. The food isn't gourmet and prices won't break your vacation budget, but you won't be wowed by creativity either. Service can be slow when all the tables are full—and that's usually all night, every night.

Gajeva 9. ✆ **01/481-15-49.** www.boban.hr. Entrees 30kn–80kn ($6.15–$16/£3.80–£9.90). AE, DC, MC, V. Daily 10am–midnight.

Capucine Spaghetteria ★ (Value) PIZZA/ITALIAN Endless variations of spaghetti, pizza, and other Italian fare are on the menu at this noisy hangout across the street from Zagreb Cathedral. Pizza is ultrathin-crusted European style, and toppings are mostly fresh ingredients, unless you opt for unusual varieties such as the (untried) Nutella version. The restaurant also has daily blackboard specials for 15kn to 30kn ($3.05–$6.15/£1.90–£3.80), including a horse-meat burger.

Kaptol 6. ✆ **01/481-48-40.** www.capuciner.hr. Entrees including pizza 15kn–60kn ($3.05–$12/£1.90–£7.45). AE, DC, MC, V. Mon–Sat 10am–1am; Sun noon–1am.

Kaptolska Klet ★★ CROATIAN A huge array of steaks complements an amazing list of Croatian home recipes such as goulash and roasted lamb or pork at this attractive spot across from Zagreb's cathedral. There's a menu for dieters (including ostrich filet) and one for vegetarians, too. The folk-culture ambience on the terrace and inside seems more touristy than functional, but there's nothing ersatz about the food.

Kaptol 5. ✆ **01/481-48-38.** Fax 01/481-43-30. www.kaptolska-klet.com. Entrees 35kn–80kn ($7.15–$16/£4.40–£9.90). AE, DC, MC, V. Daily 11am–11pm.

LeBistro ★★ FRENCH/CROATIAN This glassed-in meet-and-eat place in the Regent Esplanade specializes in classic French preparations such as baked escargot, but there is also a touch of nouveau in simple dishes such as bass with wilted Swiss chard and garlic confit. Le Bistro boasts that it serves the best *zagorski štrukli* (cheese baked in phyllo with cream sauce) in town and even offers a frozen version to take home, but we found the dish rather bland, even with sugar on top.

Mihanovićeva 1. ✆ **01/456-66-66.** Main courses 40kn–100kn ($8.15–$20/£5.05–£12). AE, DC, MC, V. Daily 10am–11pm.

Nokturno and **Leonardi** ★★ PIZZA/PASTA At first glance it's hard to tell where Nokturno begins and its next-door neighbor Leonardi ends. Both are crammed in a space on the side of an alleyway; both have similar menus; and both have the same opening hours. Nokturno is always jammed with patrons, while Leonardi isn't quite so busy, but the pace there is slower, too. It is Nokturno's interpretation of pizza that attracts crowds with its crispy crust and fresh ingredients. Whichever restaurant you choose, you can't miss.

Nokturno: Skalinska 4. ✆ **01/481-33-94.** Small pizzas 18kn–30kn ($3.65–$6.15/£2.25–£3.80); other dishes 20kn–45kn ($4.05–$9.20/£2.50–£5.70). AE, DC, MC, V. Daily 9am–1am. Leonardi: Skalinska 6. ✆ **01/487-30-05.** Small pizzas 15kn–35kn ($3.05–$7.15/£1.90–£4.45); other dishes 28kn–65kn ($5.70–$13/£3.55–£8.20). AE, DC, MC, V. Daily 9am–1am.

Pinguin Sandwich Bar ★★★ **Finds** SANDWICHES Get in line with the locals who mob this tiny made-to-order sandwich shack at all hours. The huge menu is entirely in Croatian, but order takers understand some English, and most sandwiches are illustrated with color photos. Try the Rustico, a tasty combo of mozzarella, pancetta, oregano, olives, tomatoes, herbed mayo, and any of half a dozen condiments between two fresh-made pitalike rectangles of olive bread. Don't try to eat these Croatian subs while walking down the street or you'll wear them.

Nikola Tesle 7. No phone. Sandwiches 13kn–20kn ($2.65–$4.05/£1.65–£2.50). No credit cards. Mon–Sat 24 hr.; Sun 5pm–midnight.

Purger ★ **Value** CROATIAN It's easy to overlook Purger, a nondescript storefront near the Omladinski Hostel near Zagreb's center, but you shouldn't, especially if you're on a budget. The interior is "cute" but nothing fancy, and the menu is loaded with tantalizing homemade dishes at a fair price.

Petrinjska 33. ✆ **01/481-0713.** Entrees 30kn–90kn ($6.15–$18/£3.80–£11). AE, DC, MC, V. Mon–Sat 7am–11pm.

Restoran Ivica I Marica ★★ CROATIAN VEGETARIAN This kitschy dining spot on busy Tkalčićeva has introduced a novel concept—Grandma's Croatian preparations made healthier with whole grains and seasonal local products. Inside, the restaurant has lots of wood and homey touches. What you can see of the kitchen reveals colorful tole-painted flowers on all the cabinets. The menu at this woodsy place named after Hansel and Gretel (in Croatian, of course) is no less fascinating. Begin with whole-grain flatbread accompanied by local fresh cheese or olives and tomatoes. Then move to *integral sujnudle* (boiled dumplings with hunter sauce or mushroom sauce). Fish is on the menu, as are moussaka with eggs and soya ham, plus four varieties of *štrukli. **Note:*** Servers wear traditional national dress.

Tkalčićeva 70, 10000 Zagreb. ✆ **01/482-89-99.** Fax 098/317-092. ivicaimarica@adriazdravahrana.hr. Entrees 39kn–70kn ($8–$14/£4.95–£8.85). AE, DC, MC, V. Daily noon–11pm.

EXPLORING ZAGREB

The best—and in some cases the only—way to see Zagreb is on foot. Gornji Grad (Upper Town) is full of historic buildings and churches, restaurants, boutiques, monuments, and entertainment venues. Donji Grad (Lower Town) is strong on museums, parks, historic architecture, and shopping. Other sights are a short bus or tram ride from the center of town. Whatever you do, don't miss **Trg Bana Jelačića (Jelačić Square)** ★★★, where the Ban's statue stood for nearly 80 years until World War II, when the square was renamed Republic Square. The statue was removed and stored in pieces after it was determined that the monument had become a rallying point for Croatian nationalists, who were a threat to the ruling Communist Party. It wasn't until 1990 that the statue was returned to its original home, and the square to its original name.

Kaptol

Dolac ★★★ market at Dolac bb (Mon–Fri 6am–2pm; Sat 6am–3pm; Sun 6am–noon) is a lively open-air enterprise north of Jelačić, where colorful Croatian products create a vibrant mosaic every day, especially on Friday and Saturday. Opened in 1930, it is Zagreb's most popular open-air market and some say one of the best in Europe. Fruits, vegetables, plants, and textiles are on the upper level, while meat, cheese, olives, herbs, and more are in the covered area below. Fish and cheese are in separate spaces to avoid olfactory overstimulation.

To the left of Dolac as you face the stairs leading to it, a cobblestone street called **Tkalčićeva Ulica** ★★★ winds up a steep incline into the belly of the upper city. It is lined with boutiques, bars, restaurants, and galleries in rehabbed 19th-century mansions, interspersed with renovation projects. Tkalčićeva is also home to Zagreb's cafe society, and every evening the tables along this thoroughfare are full.

The Cathedral of the Assumption of the Virgin Mary ★★★, at Kaptol 31 (✆ **01/481-47-27;** free admission), is topped by 105m (345-ft.) twin spires that seem perpetually covered with scaffolding. Work began on the exterior in 1990 and is ongoing, but it can't spoil the grace and beauty of the Herman Bollé masterpiece, which has become a symbol of Zagreb. Inside, the cathedral glows following a refurbishment that was completed in 1988. Note the 18th-century marble pulpit and the sarcophagus of the controversial Blessed Alojzije Stepinac behind the main altar. A Meštrović relief showing Stepanic kneeling before Christ marks the Croatian icon's grave.

Ivan Meštrović (1883–1962)

Some say Ivan Meštrović is Croatia's greatest sculptor of religious art since the Renaissance. Meštrović was born in 1883 to a peasant family in Vrpolje and spent most of his childhood in Otavice, a tiny, impoverished village in the rocky, mountainous interior of Dalmatia. In the early 1920s, Meštrović settled in Zagreb, where he transformed a 17th-century house (Meštrović Atelier) into his home and studio. After World War II, he immigrated to New York, where he became a professor of sculpture at Syracuse University. In 1955 he moved to a similar position at the University of Notre Dame in South Bend, Indiana, where he lived until his death in 1962. Throughout his career, Meštrović was a prolific artist. His works are on display in museums, public places (including Chicago's Grant Park), and at Notre Dame.

Heart of the Matter

The shiny red hearts on display in nearly every Zagreb souvenir shop are actually *licitar,* honey dough similar to gingerbread that is shaped in wooden molds, hardened, and coated with edible red lacquer and decorated with flowers, swirls, and other trim. The colorful hearts traditionally were used as love tokens by young men, who gave them to their girlfriends as an expression of love. Today, the decorated cookies still are given as a sign of affection, but they also are given as special-occasion gifts or as remembrances.

Gradec

Gradec is the second arm of central Zagreb's civic triumvirate. Less commercial than Kaptol, Gradec is packed with interesting museums and monuments.

Kamenita Vrata ★★ is a steep walk up a long flight of stairs to Radićeva from Tkalčićeva and a few minutes more up a cobblestone path. Kamenita Vrata was one of four entrances to the walled city of Gradec. Today it is the only gate that survived a devastating 1731 fire. Just inside is a small, dark area that houses the **Chapel of God's Mother ★★**, where a **painting of the Virgin and Child ★** is installed in an alcove behind a baroque grid. According to legend, the painting is the only thing that survived the fire and it is revered as a miraculous sign. There are a few pews in the dark chapel where people come to pray.

The **tile mosaic ★★★** depicting the Croatian, Dalmatian, and Slavonian coats of arms is **St. Mark's Church**'s most recognizable feature. Inside, the church at Trg Svetog Marka 5 (✆ **01/485-16-11**) is rather ordinary, except for a beautiful Meštrović crucifix. Hours are variable and posted on the door, but not always observed by the folks who have the key to the church. Call to be sure it's open.

Think Grandma Moses–interprets-Croatia when you approach the **Croatian Museum of Naive Art ★★** at Ćirilometodska 3 (✆ **01/485-19-11**), a baroque mansion that houses works by such Croatian masters as Ivan Generalić and Ivan Lacković. The enchanting museum focuses on the Hlebine School and its 1,500 colorful, historical, and sometimes irreverent but utterly charming works.

Atelier-Ivan Meštrović Foundation ★★★ comprises the artist's studio and his 17th-century house at Mletačka 8 (✆ **01/485-11-23**), which are the settings for a vast array of his sculptures and models. Renderings of famous people, religious icons, and just plain folks are exhibited inside and outside in the garden. Not only are finished works on display, but also sketches, models, and photographs, most notably a small study of the Grgur Ninski sculptures in Split and Nin in Dalmatia.

The Museum of the City of Zagreb ★, at Opatička 20 (✆ **01/485-13-64**), is situated in the renovated former convent of the Order of St. Clare. Displays illuminate life in Zagreb from medieval times to the present through weaponry, religious objects, furniture, ethnic costumes, an incredible collection of photographs documenting the city through the years, and scale models of Zagreb at various times in its history. Captions are multilingual. There is also an nice restaurant on the premises open from noon to midnight.

A cannon is fired at **Kula Lotrščak (Burglars' Tower) ★★**, a vestige of Gradec's fortifications at Strossmayerovo Šetalište 9 (✆ **01/485-17-68**), every day at noon, supposedly to commemorate a Croat victory against the Turks. You can climb the tower to get a fabulous view of the city . . . or just to say you did.

Lower Town (Donji Grad)

A mixture of Greek, Macedonian, and Croatian artifacts fills glass cases throughout the **Zagreb Archaeological Museum** ★ at Trg Nikole Šubića Zrinskog 19 (✆ **01/487-31-01**), a monument to prehistoric times. But it is the mummies and funerary exhibits that draw the most oohs and ahs in the northernmost section of Zrinevac. Skeletal remains and the Bronze Age baubles are exhibited as they would have looked *in situ.* There is no museum map or audio guide available, but occasional English-language histories and titles are available. The highlight of the collection is the "Zagreb mummy" and its bandages, which are actually a linen book in Etruscan script.

Bishop Josip Strossmayer began collecting art when he became bishop of Đakovo. He secured funds to build the beige 19th-century building at Trg Nikole Šubića Zrinskog 11 (✆ **01/489-51-17**), where the **Strossmayer Gallery of Old Masters** ★★ opened in 1884 to house his vast collection of mostly religious art. Today it is also home to the fabled **Baška Tablet,** which is the oldest known example of Glagolitic script in existence, and perhaps Croatia's most important artifact. The tablet is displayed under glass in the ground-floor lobby without any conspicuous sign or fanfare. Entry to the gallery is on the third floor, though no signs direct you there.

The **Ethnographic Museum** ★★★ at Mažuranićev Trg 14 (✆ **01/482-62-20**), south of Trg Maršala Tita, is loaded with a dizzying array of traditional aprons and tunics from all parts of Croatia, as well as collections of agricultural artifacts such as olive- and grape-growing implements and winemaking items. Most of the museum's collections were acquired in the 19th and 20th centuries and cover the full spectrum of how people worked and lived in Old Croatia. Don't miss the gingerbread collection.

Croatian-born Ante Topić Mimara was a lifelong collector who bequeathed his treasures to his country. While there has been some controversy about the provenance of some of the works, the **Mimara Museum**'s vast portfolio is impressive. The museum at Rooseveltov Trg 5 (✆ **01/482-81-00**) opened in 1987, but displays are surprisingly unsophisticated and the lighting design does not show the works to advantage. Captions are in Croatian only.

After decades of neglect, a renovated **Bundek Park** ★★ in Novi Zagreb reopened to the public in May 2007. The park's gravel-beach lakes, bike paths, gardens, and children's playground all were redone, and the result is a serene urban green space that attracts families, joggers, and events such as flower and art shows. Bundek's transformation from overgrown eyesore to city showplace is just the first phase of "Zagreb on the Sava," the city's initiative to develop the banks of the Sava River for recreation and tourism. Bundek is less than a block from the city's new **Museum of Contemporary Art** on Avenija Dubrovnik and across from the **Zagreb Fairgrounds.** Admission is free.

Farther Afield

Ski, hike, or bike on **Mount Medvednica (Bear Mountain),** 20 minutes north of the Zagreb's center, where cafes, ski rental shops, warming huts, caves, and a **medieval fortress** ★★ of Medvedgrad await. If you drive, the turns up to the top are rather steep, but you don't have to worry about oncoming traffic because the road up is one-way, as is the road down. Take the cable car (✆ **01/458-03-94**) to the top for 11kn ($2/£1.25) or back down for 17kn ($3.45/£2.15). It's open daily 8am to 8pm.

Note: Be sure you pay attention when driving or biking back to Zagreb: There is a road that goes to the back side of the mountain and ends up in the Zagorje region.

Fun Facts Let There Be Light

At night, Zagreb's Gradec neighborhood glows under the light of gas lamps. At promptly 7pm in the summertime, all 267 of the street fixtures are individually lighted by an old-fashioned lamp lighter.

Many of Croatia's heroes and common folk are buried in fascinating **Mirogoj Cemetery ★★★**, but this is no Arlington or Shady Lawn. Mirogoj is a mix of architecture that includes soaring domes; a neo-Renaissance arcade; and trees, flowers, and gravestones adorned with Christian crosses, Jewish six-pointed stars, socialist five-pointed stars, and slender five-sided Muslim headstones—people of all faiths and nationalities are interred here without segregation. To get to Mirogoj, take the no. 106 bus from Kaptol opposite the cathedral or the no. 14 tram from Trg Jelačića toward Mihaljevac. Exit at the fourth stop. The cemetery is open daily 8am to 8pm.

Organized Tours

Almost everything worth seeing in Zagreb is within walking distance of the main square or a short tram or bus ride away. However, if you want to inject some whimsy into your sightseeing, try one of the city's 2-hour-long costumed walking tours. A guide dressed like a famous person from Zagreb history will show you around and perhaps throw in little-known facts about the city and its sites. You can buy tickets at the Tourist Information Center at Andrijevićeva 12 (✆ **01/370-35-53**) for 95kn ($20/£12) per person. Tours leave from the TIC daily at 10am and 4pm.

SHOPPING

Zagreb's economy is recovering after years of being in the dumps following occupations by foreign governments and the 1991 war. But the country has not yet been admitted to the European Union and E.U. investment hasn't kicked in. Except for the action at Dolac market, shopping isn't very exciting in Zagreb, and serious bargain hunters will be disappointed in the prices and what's available. The number of stores that sell good-quality garb is increasing, but as a rule, clothing is either imported and very expensive, or cheaply made and still expensive, depending on its country of origin. However, there are a few retailers worth checking out.

If you stay in Zagreb more than a couple of days, you're likely to need one of the handmade umbrellas from **Cerovečki,** Ilica 50 (✆ **01/484-74-17;** Mon–Fri 8:30am–8pm, Sat 8:30am–3pm). **Marks and Spencer,** Nova Ves 11 (✆ **01/468-61-99**), in Kaptol Center, specializes in traditional style and conservative casual wear. Hours are Monday to Saturday 9am to 9pm. Also at King Cross shopping mall in Jankomir, **Algoritam,** Gajeva 1 (✆ **01/481-86-72**), has a large selection of English-language books and magazines as well as reading materials in other languages. Hours are Monday to Friday 8am to 9pm, and Saturday 8am to 3pm. Dalmatian ham, prosciutto, *Paški sir* (distinctive cheese made on the island of Pag), and olive oil and wine from Istria and other parts of Croatia are sold at **Pršut Galerija,** Vlaška 7 (✆ **01/481-61-29**). Hours are Monday to Friday 8am to 8pm, and Saturday 8am to 2pm. **Lazer Rok Lumezi,** Tkalčićeva 53 (✆ **01/481-40-30**), likes to collaborate with his customers on designs so he can match his jewelry creations to the personality of the person who will wear them. Hours are 9am to 8pm Monday to Friday, and 9am to 3pm Saturday. The branch of **Turbo Limaž,** Ljudevita Gaja 9a (✆ **01/481-15-48**) in Zagreb, is fine for picking up something to amuse the kids. Think Toys "R" Us, only smaller. Hours are 8am to 8pm Monday to Friday, and 8am to 3pm Saturday.

ZAGREB AFTER DARK

Nightlife in Zagreb is varied but not obvious. Besides the usual complement of bars and cafes, there are casinos, jazz clubs, discos, cinemas, and comedy clubs to occupy even die-hard night owls. Lately, **Jarun Lake,** 4km (2½ miles) southwest of the center, has become hot year-round, with "branches" of almost all of Zagreb's popular bars setting up water-side shops there.

Boban This bar/restaurant is owned by one of Croatia's top soccer players and it's always packed to the max with a noise level to match. There is also outside seating where promenading in resplendent finery is a sport for both sexes. Open daily 7am to midnight. Ljudevita Gaja 9. ✆ **01/481-15-49.** www.boban.hr.

Casino City A comfortable gambling house beneath the Regent Esplanade with roulette tables, card tables, slot machines, and a VIP area for serious gamblers, Casino City offers free entrance for Esplanade guests. Open daily 8pm to 4am. Mihanovićeva 1. ✆ **01/450-10-00.**

Club Casino Vega A high-powered establishment in the Sheraton where games include blackjack, roulette, slot machines, and poker. Open daily 8pm to 7am. Draškovićeva 43. ✆ **01/461-18-6.** Fax 01/461-19-25. casinovega@post.htnet.hr.

Jackie Brown This spot in Kaptol Centar is aimed at a sophisticated crowd that enjoys the finer things in life—cool jazz, vintage Armagnac, and classic cars. Open daily 8am to 1am. Nova Ves 17 (Kaptol Center). ✆ **01/486-0241.**

Khala The decor here is reminiscent of a Far Eastern harem, and the effect screams "extremely chic and wealthy." Brown wicker chairs and couches fitted with white linen cushions are always filled with beautiful people sipping exotic drinks while murmuring into cellphones and keeping an eye on their Porsches parked at the curb. Open daily 10am to 2am. Nova Ves 11 (Kaptol Center). ✆ **01/486-02-41.**

Maraschino ★ Named after the famous cherry juice from the coast that is also available in a potent fermented version, Maraschino carries the fruit theme to its drink menu. The crowd here is young and casual, and the music is loud and funky and occasionally live. Open 8am to 1am Monday to Saturday, and 9am to 1am Sunday. Margaretska 1. ✆ **01/481-26-12.**

9 PLITVICE LAKES NATIONAL PARK

Plitvice Lakes National Park, 137km (85 miles) south of Zagreb, is Croatia's most touted natural wonder: Its majestic waterfalls, lakes, and forests have earned it a place on the UNESCO register of World Heritage Sites and made it Croatia's biggest tourist attraction outside the Adriatic Coast and islands. The park's most compelling features are the waterfalls that interconnect 16 clear turquoise lakes, which are set in dense forests of beech, fir, and spruce. Anywhere you go in this nearly 4,800-hectare (11,850-acre) reserve, the water is crystal clear and teeming with fish, thanks to deposits of travertine (powdery white limestone rock) under the water. It is the constant distribution of travertine that is responsible for buildups of underwater mounds, and thus the waterfalls. The park is also rich with caves, springs, flowering meadows, a gorge that looks like a green branch of the Grand Canyon, and several animal species including deer, wolves, wild boar, and the increasingly rare brown bear.

Plitvice became a national park in 1949. One of the Serb-Croat war's first casualties was a park policeman who was killed in an incident that is sometimes cited as the flashpoint for the 1991 war. The park was occupied for most of the war by Serb troops, and during that time, its offices and hotels were trashed, but the park itself was undamaged. Since then, the hotels and other buildings have been restored and in the last 10 years visitors have returned in droves.

GETTING THERE & GETTING AROUND

BY CAR From Zagreb (trip time about 2 hr.), take the Zagreb-Rieka *autocesta* to Karlovac. Then follow the signs to Plitvice via the old road to Split (E-71).

BY BUS Catch a bus at the main station in Zagreb (2½ hr.), from 8:20am to 1:45am for 48kn to 64kn ($10–$13/£6.20–£8.05) one-way, depending on the time of departure, bus line, and other factors. Check schedules online at www.akz.hr, but you must call for reservations (✆ **060/313-333**) and stop at the main office at Avenue Marin Držića 4 in the town center to get a ticket.

Plitvice is off the old road (E-71) between Split and Zagreb. Almost every town and every hotel in the country either runs tours or connects visitors with tours that include Plitvice or focus on it. There is even a separate **Plitvice Tourism Office** in Zagreb at Trg Kralja Tomislava 19 (✆ **01/461-3586**).

Note: Make sure your bus stops at Plitvice and that it doesn't take the new highway and bypass the park on the way to Split; this is a possibility since the Zagreb-Split leg of the A-1 *autocesta* opened in June 2005.

VISITOR INFORMATION

There are two entrances to the park, Ulaz 1 and Ulaz 2, each of which has a tourist information office, gift shop, and snack shop. The tourist office at Ulaz 1 is open daily from 8am to 8pm during July and August, from 9am to 5pm April to June and September, and from 9am to 4pm October to March. The office at Ulaz 2 is open daily from 8am to 7pm July and August, and from 9am to 5pm April to June and September. Tickets are 85kn ($18/£11) per day for adults and about 40kn ($8/£4.95) for seniors and kids 7 to 18. Children 6 and under are free. Prices listed here are for high season and are lower other times. Enter at Ulaz 2 to begin your tour (if you are visiting anytime except Oct–Mar), because that entrance puts you in the middle of the property and gives you more options for exploring the park. Ulaz 2 is also the site of the park's three hotels (Jezero, Plitvice, and Bellevue).

WHERE TO STAY & DINE

Private accommodations abound all around Plitvice. The hotels below are operated by the park and within walking distance.

Rooms are small, the restaurant is big at the **Hotel Jezero** ★ (✆ **053/751-400**), and everything else is generic looking. However, the food is surprisingly good and the location couldn't be more convenient to the park. Doubles start at 114€ ($145).

The Jezero's sister hotels, **Plitvice** (✆ **053/751-100**) and **Bellevue** (✆ **053/751-700**), are farther away from the park and have fewer services. Doubles at the two start at 82€ ($104) and 75€ ($95), respectively.

Hundreds of dining spots pepper the road to and from Plitvice, most offering spit-roasted lamb or pig and other local specialties. You can stop for a bite or buy your roasted meat by the kilo and picnic in the woods. There are a few sandwich concessions within the park itself as well as hotel restaurants, but there is only one free-standing restaurant within walking distance of the park hotels. But if you stay at one of the park hotels, try **LičKuča** ★★ at Ulaz 1 (✆ **053/751-023**), a touristy but interesting restaurant with a wood-burning stove large enough to roast a whole cow and a menu laden with authentic Lika dishes.

EXPLORING PLITVICE

Plitvice is hiker heaven, but even couch potatoes can see most of Plitvice's features by combining walking with riding on the park's ferries and buses. Ulaz 2 is roughly in the middle of the park, so if you start there, you can easily get to **Prošćansko,** the park's highest and largest lake, which is ringed by a hilly green landscape. No waterfalls here, as you are at the top of the cascade. From Ulaz 2 it is a quick downhill walk to a ferry, which will take you toward paths flanked by waterfalls you can almost touch. ***Note:*** Don't try this. Swimming is forbidden, as is walking on the travertine.

Follow the signs to the foot of **Veliki Slap (Big Waterfall),** where slender streams of water zoom off the vertical granite face into **Korana Gorge.** Veliki Slap is the most dramatic waterfall in the park, and sometimes it seems that everyone is rushing to get there. However, there are smaller falls, series of falls, and clusters of falls in other parts of the park that are impressive, too.

6 The Czech Republic

by Hana Mastrini

Here, the last 1,000 years of triumphs in art and architecture have collided, often violently, with power politics and conflicts.

1 GETTING TO KNOW THE CZECH REPUBLIC

THE LAY OF THE LAND

The Czech Republic borders Germany to the north and west and Austria to the south. Slovakia to the east (which joined with the Czechs at the end of the Austro-Hungarian Empire in 1918 to form the Republic of Czechoslovakia) split with its Slavic neighbor in 1993 to form the independent Czech and Slovak republics in the "Velvet Divorce."

About 10.3 million people inhabit the Czech lands of Bohemia and Moravia, with 1.2 million living in the dozen districts comprising the capital, Prague, metropolitan area.

THE REGIONS IN BRIEF

Of the two regions which make up the Czech Republic, the most well known is Bohemia. It is the land that gave Europe its favorite moniker for a free spirit: "Bohemian." Despite being beaten into submission by successive Austrian, German, and Soviet hegemony, that spirit has lived on. In the 14th century, Prague was the seat of the Holy Roman Empire under Charles IV. So Bohemians maintain their collective historical memory that they, too, at least briefly ruled the world. Even under the domination of the Austrians, Bohemia's industrial base was world-class, and in the peace between the big wars, independent Bohemia, especially Prague, created some of the greatest wealth on earth.

While Bohemia is the traditional home of a beer-favoring populace and the seat of Czech industrial muscle, the less-visited kingdom of Moravia to the south and east has spawned a people more attuned to the farmland and the potent wines it creates. Here, winemaking is taken as seriously as it is in most other European grape-growing regions. Many wine bars throughout Moravia serve the village's best straight from the cask, usually alongside traditional smoked meats.

SUGGESTED CZECH ITINERARY:

The Best of Prague in 1 Day

In order to digest enough of Prague's wonders, do what visiting kings and potentates do on a 1-day visit: Walk the Royal Route (or at least part of it). From the top of the castle hill in Hradčany, tour Prague Castle in the morning. After lunch begin your slow descent through the odd hill-bound architecture of Lesser Town (Malá Strana).

Then stroll across Charles Bridge, on the way to the winding alleys of Old Town (Staré Město). You can happily get lost finding Old Town Square (Staroměstské

P O L A N D
G E R M A N Y
A U S T R I A
S L O V A K I A
B O H E M I A
M O R A V I A
S U D E T Y M O U N T A I N S
C A R P A T H I A N M T S.
B O H E M I A N F O R E S T
E R Z G E B I R G E
Oder R.
Elbe R.
Vltava R.
Morava R.
Danube R.
Legnica
Görlitz
Wrocław
Dresden
Gera
Chemnitz
Zwickau
Częstochowa
Opole
Děčín
Liberec
Jablonec nad Nisou
Teplice
Ústí nad Labem
Česká Lípa
Turnov
Litoměřice
Chomutov
Most
Mladá Boleslav
Jičín
Náchod
Bytom
Gliwice
Katowice
Hof
Karlovy Vary
Žatec
Louny
Mělník
Sokolov
Hradec Králové
Jeseník
Kladno
Poděbrady
Cheb
Krnov
Mariánské Lázně
PRAGUE
Beroun
Kolín
Pardubice
Ústí nad Orlicí
Šumperk
Opava
Kutná Hora
Ostrava
Karviná
Bielsko-Biała
Havířov
Stříbro
Plzeň
Konopiště
Svitavy
Šternberk
Příbram
Frýdek-Místek
Havlíčkův Brod
Žďár nad Sázavou
Votice
Olomouc
Hranice
Nový Jičín
Domažlice
Prostějov
Valašské Meziříčí
Tábor
Přerov
Klatovy
Jihlava
Blansko
Kojetín
Vsetín
Písek
Vyškov
Kroměříž
Sušice
Strakonice
Zlín
Žilina
Telč
Třebíč
Brno
Otrokovice
Jindřichův Hradec
Regensburg
Uherské Hradiště
České Budějovice
Třeboň
Hodonín
Znojmo
Český Krumlov
Břeclav
CZECH REPUBLIC
Landshut
Passau
0
50 mi
0
50 km
Linz
St. Pölten
VIENNA
Bratislava

nám.), stopping at private galleries and cafes along the way. From Old Town Square take Celetná street to Ovocný trh, and you get to Mozart's Prague venue, the Estates' Theater. Dinner and your evening entertainment are all probably within a 10-minute walk from anywhere in this area.

The Best of Prague in ❷ Days

On your second day, explore the varied sights of New Town, Old Town, the Jewish Quarter, and Lesser Town—what you didn't have time for the day before. Just wander and browse. Throughout Old Town you'll find numerous shops and galleries offering the finest Bohemian crystal, porcelain, and modern artwork, as well as top fashion boutiques, cafes, and restaurants. While the shops aren't that much different from those in other European cities, the setting is.

From Old Town, it's just a short walk across Charles Bridge to Lesser Town. This was once the neighborhood for diplomats, merchants, and those who served the castle, with narrow houses squeezed between palaces and embassies. Finish the day by getting a riverside view of the city and Charles Bridge from Kampa Park.

The Best of the Czech Republic in 1 Week

The Czech lands offer many historic and cultural monuments. Castles and châteaux dominating the picturesque natural landscape represent the most important part of Czech attractions. Below, I give you one example out of many possible itineraries.

Days ❶ & ❷: Arrive in Prague

Spend the first 2 days as recommended above. Then rent a car from one of the rental agencies recommended on p. 220. Keep in mind that the speed limit is 90kmph (56 mph) on two-lane highways and 50kmph (31 mph) in villages.

Day ❸: Český Krumlov ★★★

Leave for this romantic destination in southern Bohemia early in the morning, when the roads aren't too crowded. This will also allow you time to stroll around the city. Take Hwy. D1 and then E55. The trip takes about 2½ hours. Once there, visit the castle first, then just wander, and finally relax in a local restaurant. Spend the night in one of the recommended hotels or pensions. But book early, as Krumlov is the most popular Czech destination after Prague. See details on p. 262.

Day ❹: České Budějovice, Castle Hluboká nad Vltavou ★★

On this day start heading for Plzeň via České Budějovice, the home of Budvar beer. Upon arrival at České Budějovice, have a quick stroll around one of central Europe's largest squares, where you can also have lunch. In the early afternoon, take Hwy. E49 and then Hwy. 105 north for 30 minutes (this includes parking time) to the tiny town Hluboká nad Vltavou, where you'll see a castle fashioned after the Windsor Castle in England towering above the green meadows. For more information see p. 266.

Next, take Hwy. E49 to Plzeň. You'll get there in about 2 hours. Spend the night there. See p. 266.

Day ❺: Plzeň

Explore Plzeň's center in the morning, when it is the least crowded. If you're interested in the beer-making process, visit the Pilsner Breweries in the early afternoon. Just outside the factory is a restaurant that serves traditional Czech food. See p. 267 for more details.

After your break, hit the road again. Hwy. E49 will take you to the most popular Czech spa town, Karlovy Vary, in about 1 hour. Spend the night there.

Day ❻: Karlovy Vary ★

This town was built for relaxation, which makes it the perfect place to end your Bohemian week.

Start slowly with a stroll around the city's historic center. Then, get your "cup" and taste the mineral waters which make this destination so famous. Finally, book yourself a massage or other individual spa treatment at one of the recommended spa complexes. Find out more about Karlovy Vary on p. 258.

Day ❼: Karlovy Vary to Prague

It's time to return to Prague. Take Hwy. E48. You should reach the capital in 2 hours. Be warned that this two-lane highway is one of the busiest in the country.

THE CZECH REPUBLIC TODAY

Although it was under Communist rule until 1989, Prague was ready for prime time and First World competitive pressures when the Czechs joined nine other countries to become new members of the European Union in May 2004.

The first decade of a return to capitalism is well past, and the city has taken on the familiar air of a European metropolis that makes a good living from tourism. The most-visited castles and cathedrals are now surrounded by entrepreneurs trying to make back the bucks (or koruny) denied to them under Communism—and they're trying to make them back as quickly as possible.

Prague is a city rebuilding its face and its spirit. It's trying to keep up with the massive new flood of cars and visitors and is getting used to the pros and cons of its renewed affluence.

THE CZECH PEOPLE & CULTURE

Prague has once again become a well-heeled business center in the heart of central Europe. Nostalgic and successful Czechs say it is capitalism, not Communism, that comes most naturally here.

If you talk to a Praguer long enough, the conversation will often turn into a lecture about how the country had one of the world's richest economies, per capita, between the world wars. Forty years of Communism, a Praguer will say, was just a detour. The between-wars period, lovingly called the First Republic, recalls a time when democracy and capitalism thrived, and Prague's bistros and dance halls were filled with dandies and flappers swinging the night away, until the Nazi invasion in 1939 spoiled the party.

The First Republic motif has been revived in many clubs and restaurants, and you can see hints of this style in Czech editions of top Western fashion magazines.

Since the 1989 Velvet Revolution, Praguers have been obsessed with style. Many people—especially the *novobohatí* (nouveau riche)—rushed out to buy the flashiest Mercedes or BMW they could find with the quick money gained from the restitution of Communist-seized property.

In the evening, you can find a typical Bohemian playing cards with friends at the neighborhood *hospoda* or *pivnice* (beer hall) or debating at a *kavárna* (cafe). Most likely, though, the typical Czech will be parked in front of the TV, as the country maintains one of the highest per-capita nightly viewing audiences in Europe.

CZECH CUISINE

Czech menus are packed with meat, and the true Czech experience can be summed up in three native words: *vepřo, knedlo, zelo*—pork, dumplings, cabbage. When prepared with care and imagination, Czech food can be hearty and satisfying. Plus, with new restaurants pouring into the city, it's getting easier to eat lighter in Prague.

Besides being the center of extracurricular activity, pubs *(hospody)* are the best places to get fulfilling, inexpensive meals, not to mention the best brews—Pilsner Urquell, Budvar, Staropramen (some call them "liquid bread"). Selections are typically the same: sirloin slices in cream sauce and dumplings *(svíčková na smetaně),* goulash *(guláš),* roast beef *(roštěná),* or breaded, fried *hermelín* cheese *(smažený sýr).*

Reservations aren't usually accepted, but you might see tables reserved for regulars known as *štamgast.*

LANGUAGE

Bohemia, through good times and bad, has been under a strong Germanic influence, and throughout a great deal of its history, German was the preferred language of the power elite. The Czech language, however, stems from the Slavic family, which includes Polish, Russian, Slovak, and others, though German has altered many Czech words. Czech uses a Latin alphabet, with some letters topped by a small hat called a háček to denote Slavic phonic combinations like "sh" for *š,* "ch" for *č,* and, everyone's favorite, "rzh" for *ř.* Slovak differs slightly from Czech, but Czechs and Slovaks understand each other's language.

USEFUL WORDS & PHRASES

English	Czech	Pronunciation
Hello	**Dobrý den**	*doh*-bree den
Good morning	**Dobré jitro**	*doh*-breh *yee*-troh
Good evening	**Dobrý večer**	*doh*-bree *veh*-chair
How are you?	**Jak se máte?**	*yahk* seh *mah*-teh
Very well	**Velmi dobře**	*vel*-mee *doh*-brsheh
Thank you	**Děkuji vám**	*dyek*-ooee vahm
You're welcome	**Prosím**	*proh*-seem
Please	**Prosím**	*proh*-seem
Yes	**Ano**	*ah*-no
No	**Ne**	neh
Excuse me	**Promiňte**	*proh*-min-teh
How much does it cost?	**Kolik to stojí?**	*koh*-leek taw *stoh*-ee
I don't understand.	**Nerozumím.**	*neh*-roh-zoo-meem
Just a moment.	**Moment, prosím.**	*moh*-ment, *proh*-seem
Goodbye	**Na shledanou**	*nah* skleh-dah-noh-oo
I'm looking for . . .	**Hledám . . .**	*hleh*-dahm . . .
a hotel	**hotel**	*hoh*-tel
a youth hostel	**studentskou ubytovnu**	*stoo*-dent-skoh *oo*-beet-ohv-noo
a bank	**banku**	*bahnk*-oo
the church	**kostel**	*kohs*-tell
the city center	**centrum**	*tsent*-room
the museum	**muzeum**	*moo*-zeh-oom
a pharmacy	**lékárnu**	*lek*-ahr-noo
I have a reservation.	**Mám zamluvený nocleh.**	mahm *zah*-mloo-veh-ni *nohts*-leh
My name is . . .	**Jmenuji se . . .**	*meh*-noo-yee seh . . .

2 PLANNING YOUR TRIP TO THE CZECH REPUBLIC

VISITOR INFORMATION

INFORMATION OFFICES **E-Travel,** a private Prague-based firm, has developed a fantastic set of websites, including **www.travel.cz** for general Czech tourist and accommodations information and **www.apartments.cz** for booking private apartments online. Start any trip planning here.

The former Communist-era state travel agency, **Čedok,** is now privatized so its only U.S. office has long since closed its doors, but you can contact English-speaking staff through its London or Prague offices or via the Internet. In the United Kingdom, the address is 314–22 Regent St., London W1B 3BG (✆ **020/7580-3778;** www.cedok.co.uk). You can call the Prague main office for advance bookings at Na Příkopě 18, Praha 1 (✆ **224-197-632;** www.cedok.cz).

INTERNET INFORMATION Those hooked up to the Web can find updated information in English on the official Czech Foreign Ministry site at **www.czech.cz**. For general tips, check out the Prague Information Service at **www.pis.cz** or **www.prague-info.cz**. And for the latest city lights and sights, try the weekly *Prague Post* website at **www.praguepost.com**.

ENTRY REQUIREMENTS

Documents

American, Canadian, Australian, and New Zealand citizens need only passports and no visa for stays less than 90 days. Their passports must be valid for a period of at least 90 days beyond the expected length of stay in the Czech Republic.

Nationals from the European Union (United Kingdom, Ireland) can travel to the Czech Republic with passports (validity is not limited) and they are allowed to stay for an unlimited period of time.

Children inscribed in their parents' passports can travel with their parents up to the age of 15. Once the child has reached the age of 15, a separate passport is necessary.

For more information, go to **www.czech.cz**. A full list of the Czech embassies and consulates abroad is available on **www.mzv.cz**.

Embassies

The **U.S. Embassy,** Tržiště 15, Praha 1 (✆ 257-022-000), is open Monday to Friday from 8am to 4:30pm. The **Canadian Embassy,** Muchova 6, Praha 6 (✆ 272-101-800), is open Monday to Friday from 8:30am to 12:30pm and 1:30 to 4:30pm. The **U.K. Embassy,** Thunovská 14, Praha 1 (✆ 257-402-111), is open Monday to Friday from 8:30am to 12:30pm and 1:30 to 5pm. You can visit the **Australian Honorary Consul,** Klimentská 10, Praha 1 (✆ 296-578-350), Monday to Friday from 9am to 1pm and 2 to 5pm. The **Irish Embassy** is at Tržiště 13, Praha 1 (✆ 257-530-061) and is open Monday to Friday from 9am to 1pm and 2 to 5pm. The **New Zealand Honorary Consul** is located at Dykova 19, Praha 10 (✆ 222-514-672), and visits here are by appointment.

MONEY

The basic unit of currency is the **koruna** (plural, **koruny**) or crown, abbreviated **Kč.** Each koruna is divided into 100 **haléřů** or hellers. In this guide, I quote the koruna at about $0.0666 in U.S. dollars: $1 buys 15Kč, and £1 buys 25Kč. Even though the Czech Republic is now a member state of the European Union, it has not accepted the euro as its currency—yet. You will see in Prague's hotels and restaurants prices listed in euros anyway, so European visitors can easily and quickly compare. At this writing, 1 euro buys 25Kč. These rates may vary substantially when you arrive, as the koruna often gyrates wildly in the open economy.

For up-to-the-minute currency conversion go to **www.xe.com/ucc**.

In the Czech Republic, hundreds of new storefront shops provide exchange services but, if possible, use credit cards or bank cards at ATMs (don't forget your PIN). In both cases, rates are better and the commissions are lower. If you must exchange at a storefront shop, beware of fees, which can go as high as 10% of the transaction.

Chequepoint has outlets in heavily touristed areas and keeps long hours, sometimes all night, but its business practices are sometimes questionable. Central Prague locations are 28. října 13 and Staroměstské nám. 21 (both 24 hr.); Staroměstské nám. 27 (daily 8am–11:30pm); and Václavské nám. 32 (daily 8am–11pm).

If you can't use your credit card at an ATM, stick to larger banks to make your trades; there's usually a 1% to 3% commission.

American Express, MasterCard, and Visa are widely accepted in central Prague, but shopkeepers outside the city center still seem mystified by plastic. The credit card companies bill at a favorable rate of exchange and save you money by eliminating commissions. You can get cash advances on your MasterCard, Visa, or American Express card from **Komerční banka,** at its main branch, Na Příkopě 33, Praha 1 (✆ **222-432-111**); or at most any of its branches, which now have 24-hour ATMs.

The American Express branch at Václavské nám. 56, Praha 1, provides the lost/stolen card service on ✆ **222-800-237.** For more information and facts go to p. 215.

WHEN TO GO

Spring, which can occasionally bring glorious days, is best known for gray, windy stints with rain. The city and the countryside explode with green around the first of May, so if you're depressed by stark contrasts and cold-weather pollution, plan your trip for between May and October. The high summer season brings a constant flow of tour buses, and people-watching (of practically every culture) is at its best. Most Praguers head for their weekend cottages in high season, so if you're looking for local flavor, try another time.

September into October is one of my favorite periods, as cool autumn breezes turn trees on the surrounding hills into a multicolored frame for Prague Castle. The crowds are thinner and the prices are better.

A true lover of Prague's mysticism should aim to come in the dead cold of February. It sounds bizarre, but this is when you can best enjoy the monochrome silhouettes, shadows, and solitude that make Prague unique. You'll never forget a gray, snowy February afternoon on Charles Bridge. The only drawback of a winter visit to Prague, if you forget about the cold and occasional snow, is that castles and other attractions in the provinces are closed (though not Prague Castle).

HOLIDAYS

Official holidays are observed on January 1 (New Year's Day); Easter Monday (Mar/Apr); May 1 (Labor Day); May 8 (Liberation Day, from Fascism); July 5 (Introduction of

Major Festivals in the Czech Republic

Febiofest (www.febiofest.cz), held in **late March,** is one of the largest noncompetitive film and video festivals in central Europe. The **Prague Spring Music Festival** is a world-famous 3-week series of symphony, opera, and chamber performances (www.festival.cz); it takes place from **mid-May to early June.** The **Slavnost Pětilisté Růže (Festival of the Five-Petaled Rose),** held annually the **third weekend in June** to mark the summer solstice, gives residents of Český Krumlov the excuse to dress up in Renaissance costumes and parade through the streets (www.ckrumlov.cz).

Early July's **Karlovy Vary International Film Festival** (www.iffkv.cz) predates Communism and has regained its "A" rating from the international body governing film festivals. The **Moravian Autumn International Music Festival** (www.mhf-brno.cz) in Brno is dedicated to symphonic and chamber musical works and takes place in **late September/beginning of October.**

Christianity); July 6 (Death of Jan Hus); September 28 (St. Wenceslas Day); October 28 (Foundation of the Republic); November 17 (Day of Student Movements in 1939 and 1989); December 24 and 25 (Christmas); and December 26 (St. Stephen's Day).

On these holidays, most businesses and shops (including food shops) are closed, and buses and trams run on Sunday schedules.

GETTING THERE

By Plane

About two dozen international airlines offer regularly scheduled service into Prague's **Ruzyně Airport.** The only U.S. carrier flying direct to Prague is Continental via its New York/Newark hub using a code-sharing arrangement with the Czech national carrier **ČSA Czech Airlines** (© **800/223-2365;** www.czech-airlines.com). ČSA also flies to Prague from Toronto and Montreal. Germany's **Lufthansa** (© **800/645-3880;** www.lufthansa-USA.com) has frequent connections to Prague with flights from New York and San Francisco via their Frankfurt hub.

By Train

Train fares in Europe are lower than those in the United States. Czech tickets are particularly inexpensive, but prices are rising. Because European countries are compact, it often takes less time to travel city to city by train than by plane. Prague is about 5 hours by train from Munich, Berlin, and Vienna. Direct trains to Prague depart daily from Paris (via Frankfurt) and Berlin (via Dresden).

You should also check the schedule for the ultramodern, high-speed, passenger-only train that travels from London St. Pancras International Station to Europe, the **Eurostar,** at www.eurostar.com or by calling © **08705-186-186.**

For more information on traveling on České dráhy (Czech Railways), see www.cd.cz.

TRAIN PASSES *Note:* The Czech Republic is not covered by the Eurailpass, though the **European East Pass** and the **Austrian Czech Railpass** are accepted. The republic does have two country-specific pass options.

CZECH FLEXIPASS This pass entitles you to any 3 to 8 days of unlimited train travel in a 15-day period. It costs $125/£78 for first class and $86/£53 for second class.

PRAGUE EXCURSION PASS This pass provides one round-trip excursion on the Czech National Railways from any Czech border to Prague (note that you don't have to return to the same border town on the way out from Prague). It is valid for 7 days, and stops in other places in the Czech Republic are allowed on the way to and from Prague, but your entire journey must be completed within 1 calendar day. The pass costs $104/£64 for first class or $78/£48 for second class. Travelers 12 to 25 years old can get a **Prague Excursion Youth Pass,** which costs only $87/£57 for first class and $70/£43 for second class.

All of the passes above must be purchased in North America before you leave on your trip. You can buy them on the phone or online from **Rail Europe** (✆ **877/257-2887** in the U.S., or 800/361-RAIL [361-7245] in Canada; www.raileurope.com).

If you're visiting more countries in Eastern Europe, you might want to get the **European East Pass,** which combines travel in Austria, the Czech Republic, Hungary, Poland, and Slovakia. It costs $284/£176 (first class) or $199/£123 (second class), and you can use it for 5 days of unlimited train travel in a 1-month period.

Many rail passes are available in the United Kingdom for travel in Britain and Europe. However, one of the most widely used of these passes, the InterRail card, isn't valid for travel in the Czech Republic.

By Bus

Throughout Europe, bus transportation is usually less expensive than rail travel and covers a more extensive area. European buses generally outshine their U.S. counterparts. In the Czech Republic, buses cost significantly less than trains and often offer more direct routes. **Europabus,** c/o DER Tours/German Rail, 11933 Wilshire Blvd., Los Angeles, CA 90025 (✆ **800/782-2424** or 310/479-4140), provides information on regular coach service. **Busabout London Traveller's Centre,** 258 Vauxhall Bridge Rd., London, SW 1V 1BS (✆ **0207-950-1661;** www.busabout.com), is a British operator specializing in economical bus tours of Europe. Bookings can be made online.

If you're coming from London, **Eurolines** (✆ **08705-143-219;** www.eurolines.co.uk) runs regular bus service from London to Prague at about $204/£126 round-trip. Coaches are equipped with toilets and reclining seats, and trips take about 30 hours. By law, drivers are required to stop at regular intervals for rest and refreshment.

By Car

You definitely shouldn't rent a car to explore Prague. But if you want to see the countryside, driving can be a fun way to travel. Czechs, who learned to drive in low-powered Škodas, still run up your tailpipe before passing, even though many now drive beefier BMWs and Opels. The combination of high-speed muscle cars, rickety Eastern bloc specials, and smoky cargo trucks crawling along can make driving on two-lane highways frustrating. But a car will make it easier to find a budget hotel or a comfortable spot to camp.

GETTING AROUND

By Car

A liter of gasoline costs about 32Kč ($2.13/£1.32), cheaper than in Western Europe. Gas stations are plentiful, and most are equipped with small convenience stores.

Czech Rail Online

Czech Rail has a useful though somewhat complicated website in English, German, and Czech at **www.cdrail.cz**. To check the timetable, go to **www.jizdnirady.cz** or **www.idos.cz**.

Except for main highways, which are a seemingly endless parade of construction sites, roads tend to be narrow and in need of repair. Especially at night, you should drive only on major roads. If you must use smaller roads, be careful. Also, there is a new rule—each car in use must have its **headlights** on at all times. For details on car rentals, see p. 220.

If you experience car trouble, major highways have emergency telephones from which you can call for assistance. There's also the **ÚAMK,** a 24-hour motor assistance club that provides service for a fee. They drive bright-yellow pickup trucks and can be summoned on main highways by using the SOS emergency phones located at the side of the road every kilometer or so. If you are not near one of these phones or are on a road that doesn't have them, you can contact ÚAMK at ✆ **1230.** This is a toll-free call.

By Train

Trains run by České dráhy (Czech Railways) provide a good and less expensive alternative to driving. The fare is determined by how far you travel: 50km (31 miles) cost 64Kč ($4.26/£2.64) in second class or 96Kč ($6.40/£3.95) in first class. First class is not usually available, or needed, on shorter trips.

It's important to find out which Prague station your train departs from, since not all trains leave from the main station, though all major stations are on metro lines. Check when you buy your tickets. Trains heading to destinations in the north usually depart from **Nádraží Holešovice,** Vrbenského ulice, Praha 7 (✆ **224-615-865**), above the Nádraží Holešovice metro stop at the end of the red metro line (line C). Local trains to the southeast are commonly found at **Smíchovské Nádraží,** Nádražní ulice, Praha 5 (✆ **224-617-686**), on the yellow metro line heading west from the center. Most trains to west and south Bohemia and Moravia leave from **Hlavní Nádraží (Main Station),** Wilsonova 80, Praha 1 (✆ **224-224-200**), at the metro stop of the same name on the red metro (line C) in the center. Train stations in Prague are now better at providing information, especially in English. There are also timetables for public use that allow you to plan your trips.

By Bus

The Czech Republic operates a pretty decent bus system, and because trains often follow circuitous routes, buses can be a better, though slightly more expensive, option. State-run ČSAD buses are still relatively inexpensive and surprisingly abundant, and they offer terrific coverage of the country. Like train passengers, bus passengers are charged on a kilometer basis, with each kilometer costing about 1.20Kč (8¢/5p). Make sure, however, that you buy your tickets early, especially on weekends, and get to the proper boarding area early to ensure you get a seat.

Prague's main bus station, **Central Bus Station—Florenc,** Křižíkova 5, Praha 8 (for bus connection information call ✆ **900-144-444;** www.florenc.cz), is above the Florenc metro stop (line C). Unfortunately, few employees speak English here, making it a bit tricky for non-Czech speakers to obtain schedule information. To find your bus, you can try the large boards just next to the office where all buses are listed. They're in alphabetical order, but sometimes it's tough to find your destination since it may lie in the middle of a route to another place. If you have some time before you depart Prague, your best bet for bus information and tickets is to visit **Čedok,** Na Příkopě 18, Praha 1 (✆ **800-112-112** or 224-197-111; www.cedok.cz), open Monday to Friday from 9am to 7pm, Saturday 9:30am to 1pm.

By Bike

Central European Adventure Tours, Jáchymova 4, Praha 1 (✆/fax **222-328-879;** http://cea51.tripod.com), rents touring bikes and arranges whatever transport you need for them. The best biking is outside Prague, on the tertiary roads and paved paths in the provinces. They will suggest routes and provide maps. A 1-day guided biking trip around Karlštejn Castle and Koněpruské Caves costs 680Kč ($45/£28). Call ahead to make arrangements. Tickets and information are also available at the PIS office, Rytířská 31, Praha 1.

TIPS ON ACCOMMODATIONS

Note that in Prague you can find the best value in the center of the city by staying in one of the numerous pensions or hotels near náměstí Míru. Don't be afraid to rent a room away from the old quarters of town, especially if it's close to a metro stop. The farther away from the center, the lower the rates will be, and the metro connections are fast and affordable. Always know the latest market exchange rates when budgeting your stay, and build in some padding for any potential surge. The exact rate at many hotels depends on the daily koruna/euro exchange rate.

TIPS ON DINING

Stick to Czech and European cuisines; ingredients for other dishes are more rare and expensive. The more the menu varies from pork, cabbage, and dumplings (with the exception of pizza), the higher the price will be. And remember that the farther from the Castle or Old Town you go, generally the cheaper your meal will be. Go for the beer and eat where you drink it. The food won't be stunning but will be filling and usually cheap. Watch out for on-table treats like almonds, olives, and appetizers. Some restaurants gouge customers by charging exorbitant amounts for them.

BEST BUYS

Fine crystal has been produced in the Bohemian countryside since the 14th century. In the 17th and 18th centuries, it became the preferred glass of the world's elite, drawing royals and the rich to Karlovy Vary to buy straight from the source. Today, the quality remains high, and you can still purchase contemporary glass for prices that are much lower than those in the West. Antiques and antiquarian books and prints are widely available and are distinctive souvenirs, sold by specialist Antikvariáts. Since beer is a little heavy to carry home and the local wine isn't worth it, take home a bottle of **Becherovka,** the nation's popular herbal liqueur from Karlovy Vary. You'll find the distinctive green decanter in shops; it costs about 400Kč ($27/£17) per liter.

Fast Facts The Czech Republic

Area Code The area codes for each city are combined with the local numbers. Local phone numbers consist of 9 digits, which must be dialed from anyplace within the Czech Republic.

Business Hours Most **banks** are open Monday to Friday from 8:30am to 6pm. Business **offices** are generally open Monday to Friday from 8am to 6pm. **Pubs** are usually open daily from 11am to midnight. Most **restaurants** open for lunch from noon to 3pm and for dinner from 6 to 11pm; only a few stay open later. **Stores** are typically open Monday to Friday from 9am to 6pm and Saturday from 9am to 1pm, but those in the tourist center keep longer hours and are open Sunday as well.

Currency Exchange Banks generally offer the best exchange rates, but **American Express** is competitive and doesn't charge commission for cashing traveler's checks, regardless of the issuer. Don't hesitate to use a credit card; card exchange rates often work to the traveler's advantage.

Electricity Czech appliances operate on 220 volts and plug into two-pronged outlets that differ from those in America and the United Kingdom. Appliances designed for the U.S. or U.K. markets must use an adapter and a transformer (sometimes incorrectly called a converter). Don't attempt to plug an American appliance directly into a European electrical outlet without a transformer; you'll ruin your appliance and possibly start a fire.

Emergencies Dial the European Emergency Number ✆ **112,** or you can reach Prague's **police** at ✆ **158** and **fire** services by dialing ✆ **150** from any phone. To call an **ambulance,** dial ✆ **155.**

Language Berlitz has a comprehensive phrase book in Czech. A clever illustrated **Web tutorial** is found at **www.czechprimer.org**.

Liquor Laws There's no law against teenagers drinking alcohol, but it can only be sold to those who are over 18. Any adult selling liquor to younger person can be prosecuted. Pubs and clubs can stay open 24 hours.

Mail Post offices are plentiful and are normally open Monday to Friday from 8am to 6pm. Mailboxes are orange and are usually attached to the sides of buildings. If you're sending mail overseas, make sure it's marked PAR AVION so it doesn't go by surface. If you mail your letters at a post office, the clerk will add this stamp for you. Postcards to the U.S. cost 12Kč (80¢/40p), to any E.U. country 11Kč (73¢/36p). Mail can take up to 10 days to reach its destination.

Police Dial the European Emergency Number ✆ **112** from any phone in an emergency. For Czech police dial ✆ **158.**

Restrooms You'll find plenty of public restrooms. Toilets are located in every metro station and are staffed by cleaning personnel who usually charge users 5Kč (33¢/16p) and dispense a precious few sheets of toilet paper.

Be aware—even though restrooms at the city's train stations are staffed, you need to get your toilet paper yourself, from a dispenser on the wall, before you actually enter the restroom. The charge here is 6Kč (40¢/20p).

Restaurants and pubs around all the major sights are usually kind to nonpatrons who wish to use their facilities. Around the castle and elsewhere, public toilets are clearly marked with the letters WC.

Safety In Prague's center you'll feel generally safer than in most Western cities, but always take common-sense precautions. Be aware of your immediate surroundings. Don't walk alone at night around Wenceslas Square—one of the main areas for prostitution and where a lot of inexplicable loitering takes place. All visitors should be watchful of pickpockets in heavily touristed areas, especially on Charles Bridge, in Old Town Square, and in front of the main train station. Be especially wary on crowded buses, trams, and trains. Don't keep your wallet in a back pocket and don't flash a lot of cash or jewelry. Riding the metro or trams at night feels just as safe as during the day.

Taxes A 19% **value-added tax (VAT)** is built into the price of most goods and services rather than tacked on at the register. Most restaurants also include the VAT in the prices stated on their menus. If they don't, that fact should be stated somewhere on the menu. There are no VAT refunds for the Czech Republic.

Telephone & Fax For **directory inquiries** regarding phone numbers within the Czech Republic, dial ✆ **1180.** For information about services and rates abroad, call ✆ **1181.** Dial tones are continual high-pitched beeps that sound something like busy signals in America. After dialing a number from a pay phone, you might hear a series of very quick beeps that tells you the line is being connected. Busy signals sound like the dial tones, only quicker.

There are two kinds of **pay phones** in normal use. The first accepts coins and the other operates exclusively with a phone card, available from post offices and news agents in denominations ranging from 50Kč to 500Kč ($3.35–$33/£2.05–£21). The minimum cost of a local call is 4Kč (25¢/15p). Coin-op phones have displays telling you the minimum price for your call, but they don't make change, so don't load more than you have to. You can add more coins as the display gets near zero. Phone-card telephones automatically deduct the price of your call from the card. These cards are especially handy if you want to call abroad, as you don't have to continuously chuck in the change. If you're calling the States, you'd better get a phone card with plenty of points, as calls run about 20Kč ($1.35/80p) per minute; calls to the United Kingdom cost 15Kč ($1/60p) per minute.

A fast, convenient way to call the United States from Europe is via services like AT&T USA Direct. This bypasses the foreign operator and automatically links you to an operator with your long-distance carrier in your home country. The access number in the Czech Republic for **AT&T USA Direct** is ✆ **00-800-222-55288.** For **MCI CALL USA,** dial ✆ **00-800-001-112.** Canadians can connect with **Canada Direct** at ✆ **00-800-001-115,** and Brits can connect with **BT Direct** at ✆ **00-800-001-144.** From a pay phone in the Czech Republic, your local phone card will be debited only for a local call.

Tipping Rules for tipping aren't as strict in the Czech Republic as they are in the United States. At most restaurants and pubs, locals just round the bill up to the nearest few koruny. When you're presented with good service at tablecloth places, a 10% tip is proper. Washroom and cloakroom attendants usually expect a couple of koruny, and porters at airports and train stations usually receive 30Kč ($2/60p) per bag. Taxi drivers should get about 10%, unless they've already ripped you off, in which case they should get a referral to the police. Check restaurant menus to see if service is included before you leave a tip.

3 PRAGUE

GETTING THERE

By Plane

Prague's **Ruzyně Airport** (✆ **220-111-111;** www.csl.cz) is located 19km (12 miles) west of the city center. Its new, airy, and efficient departures and arrivals terminals have lost the Communist-era feel and have many added amenities. There's a bank for changing money (usually daily 7am–9pm), car-rental offices (see "Getting Around," below), and information stands that can help you find accommodations if you've arrived without reservations.

GETTING DOWNTOWN You can make your way from the airport to your hotel by taxi, airport shuttle bus, or city bus.

Official airport taxis are plentiful and line up in front of the arrivals terminal. Alas, the Volkswagen Passats queued directly outside the terminal's main exit all belong to the same cartel sanctioned by the airport authority. (See "Getting Around" below for details.) The drivers are getting more pleasant but are still often arrogant and dishonest. Negotiate the fare in advance and have it written down. Expect to pay about 700Kč to 800Kč ($46–$53/£29–£33) for the 20 or so minutes to the city center, depending on the whims of the syndicate. If you want to save money, find other travelers to share the expense.

CEDAZ (✆ **220-114-296;** www.cedaz.cz) operates an **airport shuttle bus** from the airport to náměstí Republiky in central Prague. It leaves the airport daily every 30 minutes from 6am to 9pm and stops near the náměstí Republiky metro station. The shuttle costs 120Kč ($8/£4.95) for the 30-minute trip.

Even cheaper is **city bus no. 119,** which takes passengers from the bus stop at the right of the airport exit to the Dejvická metro station (and back). The bus/metro combo costs only 26Kč ($1.75/£1.10), but the bus makes many stops. Travel time is about 40 minutes.

By Train

Passengers traveling to Prague by train typically pull into one of two central stations: Hlavní nádraží (Main Station) or Nádraží Holešovice (Holešovice Station). Both are on line C of the metro system and offer a number of services, including money exchange, a post office, and a luggage-storage area.

At both terminals you'll find **AVE Ltd.** (✆ **251-551-011**), an accommodations agency that arranges beds in hostels as well as rooms in hotels and apartments. It's open daily from 6am to 11pm. If you arrive without room reservations, this agency is definitely worth a visit.

Hlavní nádraží, Wilsonova třída, Praha 2 (✆ **224-224-200**), is the grander and more popular station. From the train platform, you'll walk down a flight of stairs and through a tunnel before arriving in the ground-level main hall, which contains ticket windows, a useful **Prague Information Service** office that sells city maps and dispenses information, and restrooms. Also useful is the **ČD center** (✆ **840-112-113;** www.cd.cz) run by the Czech Railways. It provides domestic and international train information as well as currency exchange and accommodations services. It is open daily 7 to 11am, 11:30am to 2pm, and 2:30 to 5:45pm. Visa and MasterCard are accepted. An information window is open 3:15am to 12:40am (the train station is closed 1–3am). ***Warning:*** The station's basement has luggage lockers for 60Kč ($4/£2.50) per bag per day, but they aren't secure and should be avoided.

Nádraží Holešovice, Partyzánská at Vrbenského, Praha 7 (✆ **224-615-865**), Prague's second train station, is usually the terminus for trains from Berlin and other points north. Although it's not as centrally located as the main station, its more manageable size and location at the end of metro line C make it almost as convenient.

Prague has two smaller train stations. **Masaryk Station,** Hybernská ulice (✆ **221-111-122**), is primarily for travelers arriving on trains originating from other Bohemian cities or from Brno or Bratislava. Situated about 10 minutes by foot from the main train station, Masaryk is near Staré Město, just a stone's throw from náměstí Republiky metro station. **Smíchov Station,** Nádražní ulice at Rozkošného (✆ **224-617-686**), is the terminus for commuter trains from western and southern Bohemia, though an occasional international train pulls in here. The station has a 24-hour baggage check and is serviced by metro line B.

By Bus

The **Central Bus Station–Florenc,** Křižíkova 4–6, Praha 8 (✆ **900-144-444** for timetable info), is a few blocks north of the main train station. Most local and long-distance buses arrive here. The adjacent Florenc metro station is on both lines B and C. Florenc station is relatively small and doesn't have many visitor services. Even smaller depots are at **Želivského** (metro line A), **Smíchovské nádraží** (metro line B), and **Nádraží Holešovice** (metro line C).

CITY LAYOUT

The river **Vltava** bisects Prague and provides the best line of orientation; you can use **Charles Bridge** as your central point. From the bridge, turn toward **Prague Castle,** the massive complex on the hill with the cathedral thrusting out. Now you're facing west.

Up on the hill is the Castle District, known as **Hradčany.** Running up the hill between the bridge and the castle is the district known as Lesser Town (**Malá Strana,** literally the "Small Side,"). Turn around, and behind you on the right (east) bank is **Old Town** (**Staré Město**), and, farther to the south and east, **New Town** (**Nové Město**). The highlands even farther east used to be the royal vineyards, **Vinohrady,** now a popular neighborhood for expatriates with a growing array of accommodations and restaurants. The districts farther out are where most Praguers live, and have few attractions.

MAIN BRIDGES, SQUARES & STREETS You'll best enjoy Prague by walking its narrow streets, busy squares, and scenic bridges. After **Charles Bridge (Karlův most),** the other two bridges worth walking are **Mánes Bridge (Mánesův most),** which provides a stunning low-angle view of the castle, especially at night, and the **Bridge of the Legions (most Legií),** which links the National Theater to Petřín Hill.

On the left bank coming off Charles Bridge is **Mostecká Street,** and at the end of it sits the cozy square under the castle hill, **Malostranské náměstí.** On the hill outside the main castle gate is the motorcade-worn **Hradčanské náměstí,** on the city side of which you'll find a spectacular view of spires and red roofs below.

On the east side of Charles Bridge, you can wind through most any of the old alleys leading from the bridge and get pleasantly lost amid the shops and cafes. The tourist-packed route through Old Town is **Karlova Street.** Like Karlova, almost any other route in Old Town will eventually lead you to **Old Town Sq. (Staroměstské náměstí),** the breathtaking heart of Staré Město. A black monument to Jan Hus, the martyred Czech Protestant leader, dominates the square. The tree-lined boulevard to the right behind Hus is **Parisian Blvd. (Pařížská),** with boutiques and restaurants; it forms the edge of the Jewish Quarter. Over Hus's left shoulder is **Dlouhá Street,** and in front of him to his left is the kitschy shopping zone on **Celetná.** Across the square to Hus's right, past the clock tower of Old Town Hall (Staroměstská radnice), is **Železná Street,** which leads to Mozart's Prague venue, the Estates' Theater. Farther to Hus's right is the narrow alley **Melantrichova,** which winds southeast to **Wenceslas Sq. (Václavské náměstí),** site of pro-democracy demonstrations in 1968 and 1989.

GETTING AROUND

By Public Transportation

Prague's public transportation network is one of the few sound Communist-era legacies and is still remarkably affordable. In central Prague, metro (subway) stations abound. Trams and buses offer a cheap sightseeing experience but also require a strong stomach for jostling with fellow passengers in close quarters.

TICKETS & PASSES For single-use **tickets,** there are two choices. You can ride a maximum of five stations on the metro (not including the station of validation) or 20 minutes on a tram or bus, without transfers (on the metro you can transfer from line A to B to C within 30 min.), for 18Kč ($1.20/75p); children 6 and under ride free, 6- to 15-year-olds for 9Kč (60¢/35p). This is usually enough for trips in the historic districts. Rides of more than five stops on the metro, or longer tram or bus rides, with unlimited transfers for up to 75 minutes (90 min. on Sat, Sun, public holidays, and after 8pm on workdays) after your ticket is validated, cost 26Kč ($1.75/£1.05).

A **1-day pass** good for unlimited rides is 100Kč ($6.65/£4.15); a **3-day pass,** 330Kč ($22/£14); and a **5-day pass,** 500Kč ($33/£20).

You can buy tickets from yellow coin-operated machines in metro stations or at most newsstands marked TABÁK or TRAFIKA. Hold on to your validated ticket throughout your ride—you'll need to show it if a ticket collector (be sure to check for his or her badge) asks you. If you're caught without a valid ticket, you'll be asked, and not so kindly, to pay a fine on the spot while all the locals look on, shaking their heads in disgust. The fine is 700Kč ($46/£29).

BY METRO Metro trains operate daily from 5am to midnight and run every 2 to 6 minutes. On the three lettered lines (A, B, and C, color coded green, yellow, and red, respectively), the most convenient central stations are Můstek, at the foot of Václavské náměstí (Wenceslas Sq.); Staroměstská, for Old Town Square and Charles Bridge; and Malostranská, serving Malá Strana and the Castle District. Refer to the metro map for details.

BY ELECTRIC TRAM & BUS The 24 electric tram (streetcar) lines run practically everywhere, and there's always another tram with the same number traveling back. You never have to hail trams; they make every stop. The most popular trams, nos. 22 and 23 (aka the "tourist trams" and the "pickpocket express"), run past top sights like the National Theater and Prague Castle. Regular bus and tram service stops at midnight,

Tips A Warning about Walking

Unless you're in great shape or are a devoted walker, you should gradually prepare for your trip with a walking program to build up the muscles in your legs and feet for the inevitable pounding they'll take. And make sure to do this while wearing the comfortable shoes you plan to bring. Prague is a city of hills, steep staircases, and cobblestone streets that require strong legs and shock-absorbing shoes. Take your time and go at your own pace.

after which selected routes run reduced schedules, usually only once per hour. Schedules are posted at stops. If you miss a night connection, expect a long wait for the next.

Buses tend to be used only outside the older districts of Prague and have three-digit numbers.

Both the buses and tram lines begin their morning runs around 4:30am.

By Taxi

I have one word for you: ***Beware.***

You can hail taxis in the streets or in front of train stations, large hotels, and popular attractions, but many drivers simply gouge visitors. In the late 1990s, the city canceled price regulations, but instead of creating price competition, it started a turf war between cabbies vying for the best taxi stands. The best fare you can hope for is 25Kč ($1.65/£1.05) per kilometer and 30Kč ($2/£1.25) for the starting rate when you phone a taxi company. It will get more expensive when you stop a taxi on the street. Rates usually aren't posted outside on the taxi's door but on the dashboard—once you're inside it's a bit late to haggle. Try to get the driver to agree to a price and write it down before you get in. Better yet, go by foot or public transport.

If you must go by taxi, call reputable companies with English-speaking dispatchers: **AAA Taxi** (© **14014** or 222-333-222; www.aaataxi.cz); **ProfiTaxi** (© **844-700-800;** www.profitaxi.cz); or **SEDOP** (© **271-722-222;** www.sedop.cz). Demand a receipt for the fare before you start, as it'll keep them a little more honest.

By Car

Driving in Prague isn't worth the money or effort. The roads are frustrating and slow, and parking is minimal and expensive. However, a car is a plus if you want to explore other parts of the Czech Republic.

RENTAL COMPANIES Try **Europcar Czech Rent a Car,** Pařížská 28, Praha 1 (© **224-811-290;** www.europcar.cz). There's also **Hertz,** Karlovo nám. 28, Praha 2 (© **225-345-031;** www.hertz.cz). **Budget** is at Ruzyně Airport (© **220-113-253;** www.budget.cz) and in the Hotel InterContinental, náměstí Curieových, Praha 1 (© 222-319-595).

By Bike

Though there are no special bike lanes in the city center, and smooth streets are unheard of, Prague is a particularly fun city to bike when the crowds are thin. Vehicular traffic is limited in the city center, where small, winding streets seem especially suited to two-wheeled vehicles. Surprisingly, few people take advantage of this opportunity; cyclists are largely limited to the few foreigners who have imported their own bikes. The city's ubiquitous cobblestones make mountain bikes the natural choice. Check with your hotel about a rental.

VISITOR INFO

If you want to arrange accommodations before you come, Prague-based **E-travel.cz** offers handy English websites. The general site at www.travel.cz provides booking for hotels and practical touring information, while at www.apartments.cz, you can book a private apartment in a wide range of prices and areas. Once in the city, you can find E-travel.cz near the National Theater at Ostrovní 7, or call its 24-hour call center (✆ **224-990-990;** fax 224-990-999). Especially for those arriving by train or air, **AVE Travel** (✆ **251-551-011;** www.avetravel.cz) can arrange accommodations or transfers inside these terminals. It has outlets at the airport, open daily from 7am to 10pm; at the main train station, Hlavní nádraží, open daily from 6am to 11pm; and at the north train station, Nádraží Holešovice, open daily from 7am to 9pm.

The **Prague Information Service (PIS),** Staroměstské náměstí 1, Praha 1 (✆ **12-444;** www.pis.cz), at the City Hall, provides tips and tickets for upcoming cultural events and tours. It can also help you find a room. From April to October, it's open Monday to Friday from 9am to 7pm and Saturday and Sunday from 9am to 6pm. During the rest of the year, it's open Monday to Friday from 9am to 6pm and Saturday and Sunday from 9am to 5pm. There is also a PIS office at Rytířská 31, Praha 1, and inside the main train station.

Čedok, at Na Příkopě 18, Praha 1 (✆ **800-112-112** or 224-197-111; fax 224-216-324; www.cedok.cz), was once the state travel bureau and is now a privatized agency. Its entrenched position still gives it decent access to tickets and information about domestic events, and the staff can book rail and bus tickets and hotel rooms. Čedok accepts major credit cards and is open Monday to Friday from 9am to 7pm, Saturday 9:30am to 1pm.

Fast Facts Prague

American Express For travel arrangements, traveler's checks, currency exchange, and other member services, visit the city's sole American Express office at Václavské nám. 56 (Wenceslas Sq.), Praha 1 (✆ **222-800-237**). It's open daily from 9am to 7pm.

Bookstores The largest English-language bookshops are the **Globe,** Pštrossova 6, Praha 1 (✆ **224-934-203;** www.globebookstore.cz), and **Big Ben Bookshop,** Malá Štupartská 5, Praha 1 (✆ **224-826-565;** www.bigbenbookshop.com).

Currency Exchange There's an American Express office in Prague (see above).

Komerční banka has three convenient Praha 1 locations with ATMs that accept Visa, MasterCard, and American Express: Na Příkopě 33, Spálená 51, and Václavské nám. 42 (✆ **800-111-055,** central switchboard for all branches; www.kb.cz). The exchange offices are open Monday to Friday from 8am to 5pm, but the ATMs are accessible 24 hours.

Unicredit (former Živnostenská banka), Na Příkopě 20, Praha 1 (✆ **224-121-111;** www.ziba.cz), has an exchange office open Monday to Friday from 10am to 9pm and Saturday from 3 to 7pm.

Chequepoint keeps the longest hours but offers the worst exchange rates. Central Prague locations are 28. října 13, Václavské nám. 48, and Železná 2 (all 24 hr.).

Doctors & Dentists If you need a doctor or dentist and your condition isn't life-threatening, you can visit the Polyclinic at Národní, Národní 9, Praha 1 (✆ **222-075-120**) during walk-in hours Monday to Friday from 8:30am to 5pm. For emergency medical aid call the mobile phone (✆ 720-427-634). The **Medicover Clinic,** Vyšehradská 35, Praha 2 (✆ **224-921-884**), provides EKGs, diagnostics, ophthalmology, house calls, and referrals to specialists. Normal walk-in hours are Monday to Saturday from 7am to 7pm.

For **emergency medical aid,** call the **Foreigners' Medical Clinic,** Na Homolce Hospital, Roentgenova 2, Praha 5 (✆ **257-272-146,** or 257-272-191 after hours).

Hospitals Particularly welcoming to foreigners is **Nemocnice Na Homolce,** Roentgenova 2, Praha 5 (✆ **257-272-174**). The English-speaking doctors can also make house calls. See "Doctors & Dentists," above, for more information. In an emergency, dial ✆ **155** for an ambulance.

Internet Access One of Prague's trendiest places is the **Globe** ★, Pštrossova 6, Praha 1 (✆ **224-916-264;** www.globebookstore.cz), a cafe-cum-bookstore that provides Internet access. You can browse for 1.50Kč (10¢/5p) per minute. Its new location is open daily from 10am until midnight.

Check your e-mail and surf at the very centrally located new Internet cafe **Internet Café Spika,** Dlážděná 4, Praha 1 (✆ **224-211-521;** http://netcafe.spika.cz). It is open Monday to Friday 10am to 11pm and the connection charge is 20Kč ($1.35/65p) per 15 minutes. The **Bohemia Bagel,** Masná 2, Praha 1 (✆ **224-812-560;** www.bohemiabagel.cz), has about 15 PCs in a pleasant setting for 2Kč (13¢/6p) per minute; it is open daily from 7am to midnight on Monday to Friday, 8am to midnight on Saturday and Sunday. Another place to access the Internet is **Cyber Cafe-Jáma** at V jámě 7, Praha 1 (✆ **224-222-383;** www.jamapub.cz). It is open daily 11am to 1am.

Laundry & Dry Cleaning **Laundry Kings,** Dejvická 16, Praha 6 (✆ **233-343-743**), was Prague's first American-style, coin-operated, self-service laundromat. Each small load costs about 70Kč ($4.60/£2.85). An attendant can do your wash for 180Kč ($12/£7.45) in the same day. Laundry Kings is open Monday to Friday from 7am to 10pm and Saturday and Sunday from 8am to 10pm.

Laundryland, Londýnská 71, Praha 2 (✆ **222-516-692**), offers dry cleaning as well as laundry service and charges about the same as Laundry Kings. Located 2 blocks from the Náměstí Míru metro station and close to the I. P. Pavlova metro station, it's open daily from 8am to 10pm.

Lost Property If you lose any of your personal property, luggage, or other belongings, try your luck at the Lost Property Office at Karolíny Světlé 5, Praha 1 (✆ **224-235-085**).

Luggage Storage & Lockers The **Ruzyně Airport Luggage Storage Office** never closes and charges 60Kč ($4/£2.50) per item per day. Luggage lockers are available in all of Prague's train stations, but they're not secure and should be avoided.

Mail The **Main Post Office (Hlavní pošta),** Jindřišská 14, Praha 1 (✆ **221-131-111**), a few steps from Václavské náměstí, is open 24 hours. You can receive mail, marked POSTE RESTANTE and addressed to you, care of this post office. If you carry an American Express card or Amex traveler's checks, you would be wiser to receive mail care of **American Express,** Václavské nám. 56 (Wenceslas Sq.), Praha 1 (✆ **222-800-237**).

Pharmacies The most centrally located pharmacy *(lékárna)* is at Václavské nám. 8, Praha 1 (✆ **224-227-532**), and is open Monday to Friday from 8am to 6pm. The nearest emergency (24-hr.) pharmacy is at Palackého 5, Praha 1 (✆ **224-946-982**). If you're in Praha 2, there's an emergency pharmacy on Belgická 37 (✆ **222-519-731**).

Transport Information The **Prague Information Service,** near Wenceslas Square, Rytířská 31, Praha 1 (✆ **12444;** www.pis.cz), is open daily from 9am to 7pm April to October, and 9am to 6pm November to March. PIS can help you get where you are going on local transport (while the travel agencies Čedok, E-Travel.cz, and AVE Travel are all good for intercity connections; see "Visitor Info," above). Train and bus timetables can also be viewed at www.jizdnirady.cz or at www.idos.cz. All metro stations now have much better maps and explanations in English. You will find more on Prague's public transportation at www.dpp.cz.

WHERE TO STAY

The range of accommodations in Prague widened significantly during the '90s. Today you can choose the opulence of the Four Seasons Hotel, the coziness of an innovative B&B, or a more spartan stay in a hostel.

Many hotels and pensions are old properties reconstructed to a higher standard, including refined interiors and tiled bathrooms with modern fixtures. The concept of easy access for travelers with disabilities has been slower to emerge, however.

HOTELS Full-service hotels have begun to catch up with Western standards in the face of competition, but rooms are still more expensive than those in many European hotels of similar or better quality. The staff, while much more attentive than they were soon after the revolution, still often act as if you are invading their turf.

The selection is growing, but because there's not much room to build in the historic center, newer properties tend to be farther out. Notable exceptions are given below.

PENSIONS These guesthouses with few services are cheaper than hotels, but when compared to similar Western B&Bs, they're still relatively expensive. Some have found a niche offering a quaint stay in a quiet neighborhood.

Several local agencies offer assistance. The leader now is Prague-based **E-Travel.cz** (www.travel.cz or www.apartments.cz). Its office is near the National Theater at Ostrovní 7 (✆ **224-990-990;** fax 224-990-999). Another agency, especially good for those arriving late by train or air, is **AVE Travel Ltd.** (✆ **251-091-111;** www.avetravel.cz). It has outlets at the airport, open daily from 7am to 10pm; at the main train station, Hlavní nádraží, open daily from 6am to 11pm; and at the north train station, Nádraží Holešvice, open daily from 7am to 8:30pm.

Prague Lodging & Dining

ACCOMMODATIONS ■

Andante **39**
Betlem Club **27**
Corinthia Towers Hotel **46**
Dům krále Jiřího **25**
Flathotel Orion **45**
Four Season Hotel **28**
Hotel Aria **5**
Hotel Ametyst **44**
Hotel Evropa **30**
Hotel Jalta **31**
Hotel Josef **17**
Hotel Neruda **4**
Hotel Paříž **18**
Hotel Savoy **2**
Mandarin Oriental Hotel **6**
Palace Hotel **24**
Pension Museum **33**
Pension Větrník **1**
Prague Marriott Hotel **20**

DINING ◆

Ambiente Pasta Fresca **21**
Bellevue **26**
Bohemia Bagel **13**
Bonante **41**
Dahab **14**
Don Pedro **36**
Globe **35**
Hergetova Cihelna **10**
Hradčany Restaurant **2**
Grand Café **1**
Kampa Park **9**
Kavárna Obecní dům **19**
Kavárna Slavia **28**
Kogo **22**
La Degustation **15**
Lahůdky Zlatý kříž **29**
Le Café Colonial **11**
Osmička **42**
Ovocný bar Hájek **32**
Pizzeria Rugantino **12**
Potrefená husa **37**
Radost FX Café **40**
Red Hot & Blues **16**
Restaurant U Čížků **38**
Rybí trh **36**
Saté **3**
U Malířů **8**
U Modré kachničky **7**
Velryba **34**

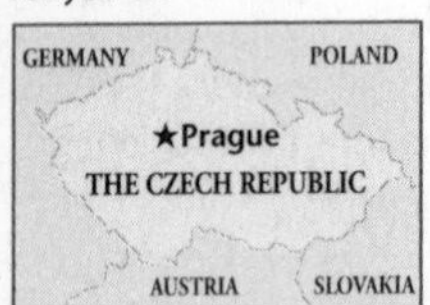

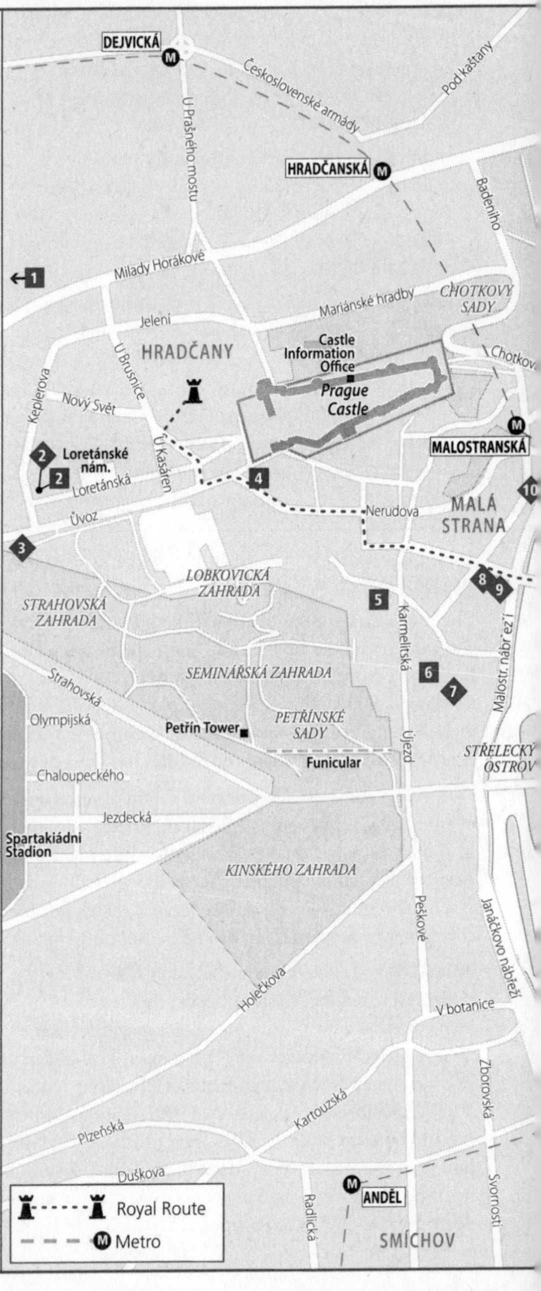

DEJVICKÁ
Československé armády
Pod kaštany
U Prašného mostu
HRADČANSKÁ
Badeniho
Milady Horákové
CHOTKOVY SADY
Mariánské hradby
Jelení
HRADČANY
U Brusnice
Castle Information Office
Prague Castle
Chotkova
Keplerova
Nový Svět
Loretánské nám.
Loretánská
Ke Kasáren
MALOSTRANSKÁ
Úvoz
Nerudova
MALÁ STRANA
LOBKOVICKÁ ZAHRADA
STRAHOVSKÁ ZAHRADA
Karmelitská
Malostr. nábřeží
SEMINÁŘSKÁ ZAHRADA
Strahovská
Olympijská
Petřín Tower
PETŘÍNSKÉ SADY
Újezd
STŘELECKÝ OSTROV
Funicular
Chaloupeckého
Jezdecká
Spartakiádni Stadion
KINSKÉHO ZAHRADA
Peškové
Janáčkovo nábřeží
Holečkova
V botanice
Zborovská
Kartouzská
Plzeňská
Duškova
ANDĚL
Radlická
SMÍCHOV
Svornosti

Royal Route
Metro

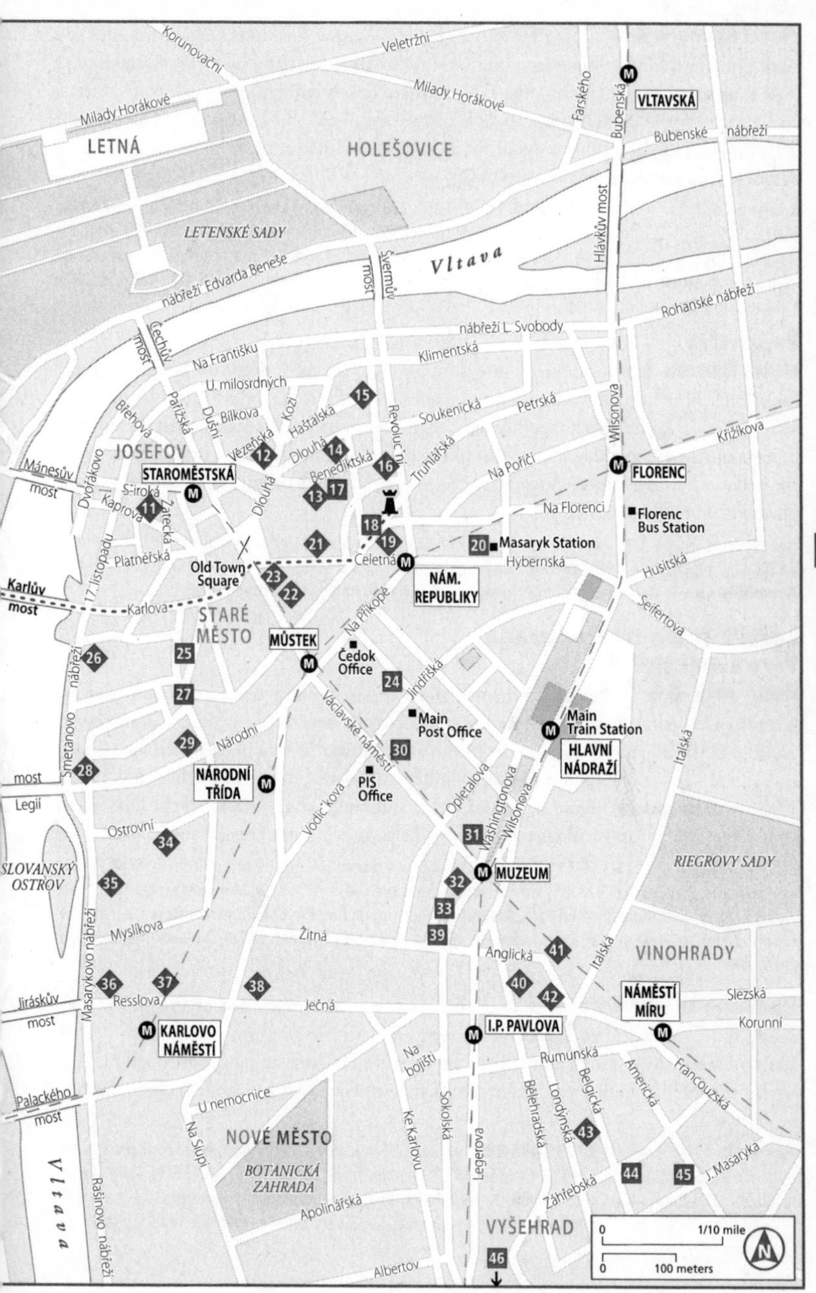
LETNÁ
HOLEŠOVICE
LETENSKÉ SADY
Vltava
VLTAVSKÁ
JOSEFOV
STAROMĚSTSKÁ
Old Town Square
STARÉ MĚSTO
MŮSTEK
NÁM. REPUBLIKY
FLORENC
Florenc Bus Station
Masaryk Station
Čedok Office
Main Post Office
PIS Office
Main Train Station
HLAVNÍ NÁDRAŽÍ
NÁRODNÍ TŘÍDA
SLOVANSKÝ OSTROV
MUZEUM
RIEGROVY SADY
VINOHRADY
NÁMĚSTÍ MÍRU
KARLOVO NÁMĚSTÍ
I.P. PAVLOVA
NOVÉ MĚSTO
BOTANICKÁ ZAHRADA
VYŠEHRAD
1/10 mile
100 meters

Hradčany

Very Expensive

Hotel Savoy ★★★ Just a few blocks from the castle, the Hotel Savoy welcomes you with a modern lobby. The guest rooms are richly decorated and boast every amenity as well as spacious marble bathrooms. The beds are consistently huge, which is in contrast to the customary central European style of two twin beds shoved together. The pleasant staff provides an attention to detail that's a cut above that at most hotels in Prague. Its Hradčany restaurant is excellent (p. 231).

Keplerova 6, Praha 1. ✆ **224-302-430.** Fax 224-302-128. www.hotel-savoy.cz. 59 units. From 7,485Kč ($499/£309) double; from 10,050Kč ($669/£415) suite. Rates include breakfast. AE, DC, MC, V. Tram: 22 or 23. **Amenities:** Restaurant; bar; "relaxation" center w/small set of exercise machines; sauna; whirlpool; concierge; business services; salon; 24-hr. room service; massage; laundry. *In room:* A/C, TV, VCR, DVD, dataport, minibar, hair dryer, safe.

Expensive

Hotel Neruda ★★ Squeezed into a long row of curiosity shops on Nerudova street is a strong contender for the best boutique hotel in Malá Strana—the Hotel Neruda. This refurbished 20-room villa has combined a high level of modern elegance with the original accents of its 14th-century shell. Most of the fixtures—from the fresh new bathrooms to the beds and dining tables—suggest a bold sense of Prague's promising future, but enveloped within its Renaissance past.

Nerudova 44, Praha 1. ✆ **257-535-557.** Fax 257-531-492. www.hotelneruda-praha.cz. 20 units. From 3,870Kč ($258/£160) double. Rates include breakfast. AE, DC, MC, V. Tram: 22 or 23 to Malostranské nám. **Amenities:** Cafe-restaurant; concierge. *In room:* A/C, TV, VCR, minibar, hair dryer, safe.

Lesser Town (Malá Strana)

Very Expensive

Hotel Aria ★★ This music-themed hotel is just around the corner from the St. Nicholas Cathedral. Each of its four floors is tastefully decorated by Versace designers to evoke a different genre of music. The rooms and bathrooms vary in their size and layout, and all are kept to the same exceptionally high standard evident throughout the hotel. There is an impressive library of CDs, DVDs, and books about music off the lobby, and a full-time resident musicologist available to help you choose a concert in the city.

Tržiště 9, Praha 1. ✆ **225-334-111.** Fax 225-334-666. www.ariahotel.net. 52 units. From 7,380Kč ($492/£305) double; 9,225Kč ($615/£381) suite. Rates include breakfast. AE, MC, V. Metro: Malostranská, then tram 12, 22, or 23 to Malostranské nám. **Amenities:** Restaurant; bar; exercise room; courtesy car from the airport; 24-hr. business center; 24-hr. room service. *In room:* A/C, Internet, DVD/CD player, minibar, hair dryer, safe.

Mandarin Oriental Hotel ★★ This latest addition to the list of Prague's luxury design hotels offers superior accommodations and service in a top-notch spot in Malá Strana. Smart, sleek design underlines the relaxing Far East ambience throughout this former Dominican monastery. Large rooms are well equipped and some include impressive views.

Nebovidská 459/1, Praha 1. ✆ **233-088-888.** Fax 233-088-668. www.mandarinoriental.com/prague. 99 units. 8,610Kč–18,655Kč ($574–$1,243/£356–£771) double; from 22,960Kč ($1,529/£948) suite. Rates include breakfast. AE, MC, V. Metro: Malostranská. **Amenities:** Restaurant; bar; tea lounge; spa-relaxation center; business center; 24-hr. room service. *In-room:* A/C, TV, CD/DVD player, Internet, minibar, safe.

Expensive

Best Western–Hotel Kampa On the edge of the park where troops once camped along the banks of the Vltava, the Kampa occupies what was a 17th-century armory. The rooms are comfortable enough if you don't expect first-class surroundings. The best ones boast a park view—request one of these when booking or checking in. There's a restaurant, but you'd be better off visiting one of those nearby, like Kampa Park under Charles Bridge (p. 240).

Všehrdova 16, Praha 1. ✆ **257-404-444.** Fax 257-404-333. www.euroagentur.cz. 84 units (shower only). From 4,410Kč ($294/£182) double. Rates include breakfast. AE, DC, MC, V. Metro: Malostranská, then tram 12, 22, or 23 to the Hellichova stop. **Amenities:** Restaurant w/garden; bar; room service; laundry service; dry cleaning. *In room:* TV, minibar, hair dryer, safe.

Old Town (Staré Město) & Josefov

Very Expensive

Four Seasons Hotel ★★★ This addition to Prague's short list of luxury hotels is its most impressive. Located in an imposing position on the banks of the Vltava River right next to Charles Bridge, the Four Seasons provides an elegant base for exploring Old Town and enjoying the symphonies at the nearby Rudolfinum, while taking in a wonderful panoramic view of Prague Castle across the river.

Its executive suites and guest rooms are nicely appointed. The best have sweeping views and sunken marble tubs. In the tasteful and lower-priced Art Nouveau wing, comfortable doubles can be booked for less than 4,500Kč ($300/£186), but the street-side views are much less impressive.

All rooms are fitted with fine solid wood furniture, some with antique pieces, others with more modern avant-garde accents.

Veleslavínova 2a, Praha 1. ✆ **221-427-000.** Fax 221-426-000. www.fourseasons.com. 162 units. From 7,590Kč ($506/£314) double; from 16,710Kč ($1,113/£690) suite. AE, DC, MC, V. Metro: Staroměstská. **Amenities:** Restaurant; bar; health club; concierge; business services; 24-hr. room service; laundry; dry cleaning overnight. *In room:* A/C, TV, CD, DVD player, dataport, minibar, hair dryer, safe.

Expensive

Hotel Paříž ★★ At the edge of náměstí Republiky and across from the Municipal House, the 100-year-old Paříž provides a rare chance to put yourself back in the gilded First Republic. The high-ceilinged guest rooms are done in a purplish theme; they aren't plush but are comfortable and adequately equipped, with more modern furnishings than the lobby would suggest. It's the ground floor that really maintains an authentic period elegance.

U Obecního domu 1, Praha 1. ✆ **222-195-195.** Fax 224-225-475. www.hotel-pariz.cz. 94 units (74 with tub/shower combination, 20 with shower only). 3,315Kč ($221/£137) double; 5,895Kč ($393/£243) suite. AE, DC, MC, V. Metro: Náměstí Republiky. **Amenities:** Restaurant; cafe; concierge; business services; 24-hr. room service; babysitting; laundry; dry cleaning. *In room:* A/C, TV, minibar, hair dryer, safe.

Moderate

Dům U krále Jiřího The "House at King George's" perches above two pubs on a narrow side street. The rooms are pretty bare but have a bit more charm than they used to. The ceilings are high, and the dark wooden furniture is another improvement. Ask for a room in back if you want to deaden the clamor of the pubs below. Breakfast is served in the wine cellar, which lacks character despite a recent remodeling.

Liliová 10, Praha 1. ✆ **221-466-100.** Fax 221-466-166. www.kinggeorge.cz. 11 units. From 2,500Kč ($166/£102) double or suite. Rates include breakfast. AE, MC, V. Metro: Staroměstská. *In room:* TV, minibar, fridge, safe.

Expensive

Palace Hotel ★★ The Palace has long been the quintessential Prague address for visiting dignitaries and celebrities like Steven Spielberg, the Rolling Stones, and Britain's Prince Charles. The 1903 Art Nouveau building offers a more stoic "Viennese" approach to the era's architectural fashion than the more ornate Paříž (see above). The lobby boasts accents like buttery-wood paneling and furniture with subtle flowered upholstery, but the overall effect is that of contemporary wealth sampling the past rather than building a museum to it. The staff makes a point of remembering guests' names and provides excellent service.

The soothing, delicately colored guest rooms are some of the largest luxury accommodations in Prague, each with an Italian marble bathroom.

Panská 12, Praha 1. ✆ **224-093-111.** Fax 224-221-240. www.palacehotel.cz. 124 units (tub/shower combination). From 3,690Kč ($246/£152) double; 4,515Kč ($301/£186) suite. Rates include breakfast. AE, DC, MC, V. Metro: Můstek. **Amenities:** 2 restaurants; cafe; concierge; business services; 24-hr. room service; laundry service. *In room:* A/C, TV, VCR, minibar, safe.

Moderate

Andante (Value) This best-value choice near Wenceslas Square is tucked away on a dark side street, about 2 blocks off the top of the square. Despite the less-than-appealing neighborhood, this is the most comfortable property at this price. It lacks the character of the old Hotel Evropa (see below) but is better cared for. With modern beds and good firm mattresses, as well as high-grade Scandinavian furniture and colorful decorations, the rooms gain in comfort what they lose in adventure. They offer plenty of space and white, well-kept bathrooms with tub/shower combinations, some with shower only.

Ve Smečkách 4, Prague 1. ✆ **222-210-021.** Fax 222-210-591. www.andante.cz. 32 units (some with shower only, some with tub only). 2,250Kč ($150/£93) double; 3,075Kč ($205/£127) suite. Rates include breakfast. AE, MC, V. Metro: Muzeum. **Amenities:** Restaurant; tours arranged w/the reception desk; business services; limited room service. *In room:* TV, minibar, hair dryer, iron, safety box available at the reception desk.

Inexpensive

Hotel Evropa Born in 1889 as the Hotel Archduke Stephan, the Evropa was recast in the early 1900s as an Art Deco hotel. However, this is yet another classic that has seen much better days. Though the statue-studded exterior, still one of the most striking landmarks on Wenceslas Square, has recently been polished, the rooms are aging; most don't have bathrooms, and some are just plain shabby. The best choice is a room facing the square with a balcony.

The hotel's famous cafe, a wood-encased former masterpiece that no longer glows, furthers the theme. Still, this is an affordable way to stay in one of Wenceslas Square's once-grand addresses.

Václavské nám. 25, Praha 1. ✆ **224-215-387.** Fax 224-224-544. www.evropahotel.cz. 90 units, 20 with bathroom (tub only). 1,950Kč ($130/£81) double without bathroom; 4,000Kč ($266/£165) double with bathroom. Rates include continental breakfast. AE, MC, V. Metro: Můstek or Muzeum. **Amenities:** Restaurant; concierge; safe; luggage storage.

Pension Museum (Value) Located just across the National Museum, the pension offers clean and comfortable rooms with modern furniture. Do not be put off by the busy road in front, however. There are actually only two rooms facing it, and the new double-glazed windows block the noise very well. The private cozy courtyard garden serves as an oasis for relaxation, which is otherwise hard to find around Václavské náměstí, the city's most lively shopping area.

Mezibranská 15, Praha 1. ✆ **296-325-186.** Fax 296-325-188. www.pension-museum.cz. 12 units with bathroom (shower only). From 1,970Kč ($131/£81) double; 2,440Kč ($162/£100) suite. Rates include breakfast. AE, MC, V. Metro: Muzeum. **Amenities:** Atrium garden; concierge; Internet; laundry; luggage storage. *In room:* A/C, TV, Internet, minibar, hair dryer, safe.

Near Náměstí Republiky/Banking District

Expensive

Hotel Josef ★★ The Josef stands as the new home for tasteful minimalism in the new Bohemia. British-based architect Eva Jiřičná brings a new study on the interior use of glass to her native land with its own long history of the glazier's craft.

There is a daring and dramatic effect in every room. Superior rooms are so bold as to offer transparent bathroom nooks, shower stalls, and washrooms with a full view of grooming activities for your partner to absorb in the main sleeping chamber.

Rybná 20, Praha 1. ✆ **221-700-111.** Fax 221-700-999. www.hoteljosef.com. 110 units. From 5,415Kč ($361/£224) double. Breakfast 345Kč ($23/£14). AE, DC, MC, V. Metro: Náměstí Republiky. **Amenities:** Restaurant; health club; concierge; car rental; courtesy limo; business center; room service; babysitting; laundry. *In room:* A/C, TV, DVD, CD player, dataport, minibar, hair dryer, safe.

Prague Marriott Hotel ★ (Kids) The Marriott provides just what you would expect—a high standard. The large rooms have bright colors, tasteful, homogenized furniture, and comfortable beds as well as phones, faxes, laptop connections, and other services. The bathrooms are spacious and immaculately maintained. In an effort to attract families, the Marriott offers Sunday family brunches in the Brasserie Praha, where kids are welcome and PC games are available.

V Celnici 8, Praha 1. ✆ **222-888-888.** Fax 222-888-889. www.marriott.com. 328 units. 6,135Kč ($409/£254) double; 7,155Kč ($477/£296) executive-level double; from 9,615Kč ($641/£397) suite. Rates for suites and executive rooms include breakfast. AE, DC, MC, V. Valet parking 510Kč ($34/£21) per day. Metro: Náměstí Republiky. **Amenities:** Restaurant; cafe; bar; indoor swimming pool; well-equipped fitness center; gym; spa rooms; whirlpools; saunas; concierge; fully equipped business center; salon; 24-hr. room service; laundry; dry cleaning. *In room:* A/C, TV, dataport, minibar, hair dryer, safe.

Vinohrady

Expensive

Hotel Ametyst The most expensive full-service hotel in an affordable part of town, the Ametyst is less expensive than hotels of similar quality in the older districts, but you can get a better deal at one of the nearby pensions. On a quiet back street about 5 blocks from náměstí Míru, it's spotless and decorated in a warm contemporary style. The top-floor rooms are especially bright and cheery, with pitched ceilings and balconies overlooking the peaceful residential neighborhood.

Jana Masaryka 11, Praha 2. ✆ **222-921-921.** Fax 222-921-999. www.hotelametyst.cz. 84 units (some with tub only, some with shower only). 4,605Kč ($307/£190) double. Rates include breakfast. AE, DC, MC, V. Metro: Náměstí Míru. **Amenities:** 2 restaurants; bar; small fitness center; sauna. *In room:* TV, minibar, hair dryer, safe.

Inexpensive

Flathotel Orion (Kids) The best family value close to the city center, the Orion is an apartment hotel, with each unit sporting a well-equipped kitchen. All accommodations have either one bedroom (sleeps two) or two bedrooms (sleeps up to six). The spacious guest rooms are comfortable but not very imaginative, bordered in pale blue with leather armchairs and dark wooden bed frames without much on the walls. The beds vary in the firmness of their mattresses. The bathrooms are small, basic white, and modern, as are the kitchens. In this friendly neighborhood, fruit and vegetable shops and corner grocery stores can be found around náměstí Míru, just up the street.

Americká 9, Praha 2. ✆ **222-521-706.** Fax 222-521-707. www.okhotels.cz/en/hotel-orion. 26 apts with bathroom (tub/shower combination). 2,290Kč ($152/£94) 1 bedroom; 2,590Kč ($172/£107) 2 bedrooms. Breakfast 160Kč ($11/£6.80). AE, MC, V. Metro: Náměstí Míru. **Amenities:** Sauna; tours and activities arrangements at reception; room service; laundry; dry cleaning. *In room:* TV, kitchen, fridge, coffeemaker.

Elsewhere in Prague

Expensive

Corinthia Towers Hotel ★ Kids Opened in the mid-1980s, this hotel was one of the last "achievements" of Communist central planners. The medium-size rooms used to be like those in a 1980s upper-middle-range Sheraton, but have undergone renovation. They are fitted with solid furniture and the beds have firm mattresses, but the decoration is pretty bland. The bathrooms are reasonably sized and have tub/shower combinations.

The hotel is American in its approach, with an AMF bowling alley in the basement. Though the city center isn't within walking distance, the Vyšehrad metro station is just below the hotel entrance.

Kongresová 1, Praha 4. ✆ **261-191-111.** Fax 261-225-011. www.corinthia.cz. 583 units. 3,120Kč ($208/£129) double; from 5,070Kč ($338/£209) suite. Rates include breakfast. AE, DC, MC, V. Metro: Vyšehrad. **Amenities:** 2 restaurants; cafe; well-equipped fitness center w/pool, sauna, exercise machines; game room; concierge; activities desk; salon; 24-hr. room service; babysitting; laundry; bowling alley. *In room:* A/C, TV, minibar.

Inexpensive

Pension Větrník Value Kids A mostly scenic half-hour tram ride (or metro-tram combo) from the city center takes you to this romantic, secret, country hideaway. After getting off the tram, walk back behind a bunch of large concrete dorms to find a painstakingly restored 18th-century white windmill house. Once you buzz at the metal gate, Miloš Opatrný will greet you. Lush gardens and a tennis court lead to a quaint guesthouse with a stone staircase and spacious rooms with big beds, open-beamed ceilings, and modern amenities. The plain bedcovers and odd-shaped table lamps could stand some improvement, however. The bathrooms are roomy, with stand-up showers, and the windows are shuttered and boast flower boxes.

U Větrníku 40, Praha 6. ✆ **220-612-404.** Fax 220-513-390. www.pensionvetrnik.wz.cz. 6 units (4 with shower only, 2 with tub/shower combination). 2,100Kč ($140/£87) double; 3,150Kč ($210/£130) suite. Rates include breakfast. MC. Metro: Line A to Hradčanská station, then tram no. 1 or 18 to Větrník. **Amenities:** Private lighted tennis court in the courtyard. *In room:* TV, hair dryer.

WHERE TO DINE

Whenever someone mentions this country's heavy food, Czechs delight in the fact that obesity is much more of a problem in the United States. Statistically they're right. It seems that the walking-hiking-biking lifestyle of Czechs goes a long way toward keeping their waistlines trim.

As for **main courses,** no self-respecting Czech restaurant could open its doors without serving at least some version of the three national foods: *vepřo, knedlo,* and *zelo* (pork, dumplings, and cabbage). The **pork** *(vepřové maso)* is usually a shoulder or brisket that is baked and lightly seasoned, smoked, or breaded and fried like a schnitzel *(řízek).* Unlike German sauerkraut, the **cabbage** *(zelí)* is boiled with a light sugar sauce. The **dumplings** are light and spongy if made from flour and bread *(houskové knedlíky),* or dense and pasty if made from flour and potatoes *(bramborové knedlíky).* This "VKZ" combo cries out for an original **Budweiser (Budvar), Kozel,** or **Pilsner Urquell** to wash it down.

There's usually a good selection of indigenous freshwater fish, such as trout, perch, and carp, the Christmas favorite. Since the country has no coastline, you'll find most **seafood** at the more expensive restaurants, but a growing selection of salmon, sea bass, shark, and shellfish is shipped in on ice.

As for **dessert,** try a *palačinka,* a crepe-thin pancake filled with chocolate, fruit, or marmalade and whipped cream. Another favorite is *ovocné knedlíky,* whole dumplings filled with strawberries, apricots, or cherries, rolled in butter, topped with powdered sugar and cream.

Hradčany

Expensive

Hradčany Restaurant ★ INTERNATIONAL Matching the crisp English setting of the hotel in which it resides, the Austrian-managed Hradčany is the most elegant choice this side of the castle. The menu lists vary depending on the season. At this writing, they offer delicious roasted veal with corn or tasty rump steak with pistachio crust.

In the Hotel Savoy, Keplerova 6, Praha 1. ✆ **224-302-150.** Reservations recommended. Main courses lunch 450Kč–650Kč ($30–$43/£19–£27), dinner 590Kč–790Kč ($39–$52/£24–£32). AE, DC, MC, V. Daily noon–3pm and 6–11pm. Tram: 22 or 23, 2 stops past Prague Castle.

Inexpensive

Saté INDONESIAN The Saté has made quite a business out of simple Indonesian dishes at low prices. It's just down the street from the Castle Square (Hradčanské nám.) and past the massive Černín Palace. The unassuming storefront near the Swedish Embassy doesn't stand out, so look closely. The pork saté comes in a peanut sauce along with a hearty *mie goreng* (traditional Indonesian fried noodles).

Pohořelec 152/3, Praha 1. ✆ **220-514-552.** Main courses 42Kč–220Kč ($2.80–$15/£1.75–£9.10). No credit cards. Daily 11am–10pm. Tram: 22 or 23.

Lesser Town (Malá Strana)

Very Expensive

U Malířů ★ FRENCH Surrounded by Romance-age murals and gorgeously appointed tables in three intimate dining rooms here, you're faced with some tough choices. Half-baked salmon filets swim in caper sauce, tiger shrimps come with oranges, lamb steak is glazed with red-pepper sauce, and baked quail bathes in Sherry. If you want a truly old-world evening of elegant romance and French specialties, U Malířů is worth it.

Maltézské nám. 11, Praha 1. ✆ **257-530-000.** www.umaliru.cz. Reservations necessary. Main courses 480Kč–2,390Kč ($32–$159/£20–£99); fixed-price menus 1,190Kč ($79/£49) and 1,790Kč ($119/£74). AE, DC, MC, V. Daily 7pm–2am. Metro: Malostranská.

Moderate

Hergetova Cihelna ★ INTERNATIONAL/PASTA/CZECH This addition to a list of Prague's top dining experiences quickly became a popular spot on the riverbank. The interior is divided into a restaurant, cocktail bar, cafe, and music lounge, and the modern furniture is simple and comfortable. From the large summer terrace you can experience one of the most exciting and unforgettable views of the river and Charles Bridge. The food is a good standard; I enjoyed their homemade Czech potato soup with forest mushrooms and garlic called *bramboračka* and Czech *svíčková* (sirloin) served in a cream sauce with dumplings and cranberries.

Cihelná 2b, Praha 1. ✆ **296-826-103.** www.cihelna.com. Main courses 215Kč–695Kč ($14–$46/£8.70–£29). AE, MC, V. Daily 11:30am–1am. Metro: Malostranská.

Kampa Park ★★ CONTINENTAL/SEAFOOD The best thing about Kampa Park is the summertime riverside view from its patio below Charles Bridge. In high season, the terrace is lively, with grills churning out solid portions of beef, pork, ribs, halibut, sea bass, and other barbecued favorites. Desserts like the fresh strawberry cappuccino have won raves. During colder weather, this left-bank chalet is even more sublime, as candlelit tables provide glimpses of the stone bridge through the windows.

Na Kampě 8b, Praha 1. ✆ **296-826-102.** www.kampagroup.com. Reservations recommended. Main courses 345Kč–795Kč ($23–$53/£14–£33). AE, DC, MC, V. Daily 11:30am–1am. Metro: Malostranská.

U modré kachničky ★ CZECH/CONTINENTAL/WILD GAME At the "Blue Duckling," on a narrow Malá Strana street, is my choice for the most innovative attempt at refining standard Czech dishes into true Bohemian haute cuisine. The menu is loaded with an array of wild game and quirky spins on Czech village favorites. Starters include lightly spiced venison pâté and gooseliver on toast. You can choose from five different duck specialties. And, the ubiquitous *palačinky* crepes are thin and tender and filled with fruit, nuts, and chocolate. There is an even more popular sister to the first "kachnička," at Michalská 16, Praha 1.

Nebovidská 6, Praha 1. ✆ **257-320-308.** www.umodrekachnicky.cz. Reservations recommended for lunch, required for dinner. Main courses 290Kč–690Kč ($19–$46/£12–£29). AE, MC, V. Daily noon–4pm and 6:30–11:30pm. Metro: Malostranská. Sister restaurant: ✆ 224-213-418. Reservations recommended. Main courses 240Kč–685Kč ($16–$46/£9.90–£28). AE, MC, V. Daily 11:30am–11:30pm. Metro: Můstek.

Inexpensive

Bohemia Bagel (Kids) BAGELS/SANDWICHES Bohemia Bagel emerged in 1997 as the answer to the bagel-less morning blues. The roster of golden-brown, hand-rolled, stone-baked bagels is stellar. There's plain, cinnamon raisin, garlic, onion, poppy, tomato basil, cheese, or apple and nut providing a sturdy but tender frame for Scandinavian lox and cream cheese or maybe jalapeño-cheddar cheese.

On the website www.bohemiabagel.cz, you can order bagels and other food for at least 500Kč ($33/£20) to be delivered in Praha 1 within an hour.

Lázeňská 19, Praha 1 (Malá Strana). ✆ **257-218-192.** www.bohemiabagel.cz. Bagels and sandwiches 30Kč–145Kč ($2–$9.65/£1.25–£6). No credit cards. Daily 7:30am–11pm. Metro: Malostranská. Tram: 12, 20, 22, or 23 to Malostranské náměstí.

Old Town (Staré Město)

Very Expensive

La Degustation ★★★ CONTINENTAL/CZECH One of the city's best dining spots. Three different seven-course menus are served, with a focus on diners' sampling an array of both food and wine. The *Boheme Traditionnelle* menu finds inspiration in old Czech cookbooks and raises the level of Czech classic cuisine served in restaurants here. Each dish is accompanied by an excellent selection of wines. This unique experience is definitely worth the money.

Haštalská 18, Praha 1. ✆ **222-311-234.** www.ladegustation.cz. Reservations recommended. Fixed-priced menu 2,400Kč ($160/£99). AE, MC, V. Mon–Sat 5pm–midnight. Metro: Staroměstská.

Expensive

Bellevue ★★ INTERNATIONAL With its excellent view of Prague Castle, the Bellevue is my perennial top choice. The ambitious owners have put all their energy into the intelligent menu: beef, nouvelle sauces, well-dressed fish and duck, delicate pastas, and artistic desserts. For a tamer but extraordinary treat, try the filet of fallow deer. Al dente pastas share a plate with lobster-and-spinach purée, garlic and herbs, or tomatoes and olives. Desserts feature hot bitter chocolate tart, or wild berries in port and cognac served with vanilla and walnut ice cream.

Smetanovo nábřeží 18, Praha 1. ✆ **222-221-443.** www.zatisigroup.cz. Reservations recommended. Main courses 490Kč–890Kč ($33–$59/£20–£37). AE, DC, MC, V. Daily noon–3pm and 5:30–11pm; Sun brunch 11am–3pm. Metro: Staroměstská.

Rybí trh SEAFOOD That strange smell wafting from deep inside the courtyard behind Týn Church is the most extensive selection of fresh seafood in Prague, served at the "Fish Market." From starters like oysters on the half shell and jumbo shrimp to main choices like monkfish, salmon, eel, shark, and many others, you select your favorite fish and method of preparation at the bright counter near the entrance.

Týnský Dvůr 5, Praha 1. ✆ **224-895-447.** www.rybitrh.cz. Reservations recommended. Main courses 299Kč–1,500Kč ($20–$100/£12–£62). AE, MC, V. Daily 11am–midnight. Metro: Můstek.

Moderate

Ambiente Pasta Fresca ITALIAN What this outlet on Celetná offers is location, location, location, and usually enough tables to satisfy the endless tourist rush hour. In a candlelit basement trattoria, the menu is limited to pastas—albeit served about 50 different ways—salads, a few meaty entrees, and garlic bread if you're still hungry.

Celetná 11, Praha 1. ✆ **224-230-244.** www.ambi.cz. Reservations recommended. Main courses 158Kč–580Kč ($11–$39/£6.80–£24). AE, MC, V. Daily 11am–midnight. Metro: Můstek.

Kogo ★★ Value ITALIAN This modern, upscale trattoria has become the local Italian favorite for the many brokers and bankers who work nearby. Tucked away on a side street adjacent to the Estates' Theater, Kogo manages to combine the warmth and boisterousness of a family restaurant with a high culinary standard in its pastas, meaty entrees, and desserts.

Kogo has a second location in the atrium of the newly reopened Slovanský Dům shopping and culture center at Na Příkopě 22 (✆ **221-451-259**).

Havelská 27, Praha 1. ✆ **224-214-543.** www.kogo.cz. Reservations recommended. Main courses 190Kč–480Kč ($13–$32/£8.05–£20). AE, MC, V. Daily 9am–midnight. Metro: Můstek.

Red Hot & Blues ★ Kids AMERICAN/CAJUN/MEXICAN Tex-Mex regulars plus burgers and nachos are on the menu here. Sunday brunch, best enjoyed in the small courtyard, includes tangy huevos rancheros on crispy tortillas. The casual French Quarter feel makes this a family-friendly choice. From 7 to 10:30pm you can hear live jazz.

Jakubská 12, Praha 1. ✆ **222-314-639.** Main courses 119Kč–479Kč ($7.95–$32/£4.95–£20). AE, MC, V. Daily 9am–midnight; Sat–Sun brunch 9am–4pm. Metro: Náměstí Republiky.

Inexpensive

Pizzeria Rugantino ★ Kids PIZZA/PASTA Pizzeria Rugantino serves generous iceberg salads and the best selection of individual pizzas in Prague. Wood-fired stoves and handmade dough result in a crisp and delicate crust. The Diabolo with fresh garlic bits and very hot chilies goes nicely with a salad and a pull of Krušovice beer. The constant buzz, nonsmoking area, heavy childproof wooden tables, and lots of baby chairs make this a family favorite.

Dušní 4, Praha 1. ✆ **222-318-172.** Individual pizzas 100Kč–250Kč ($6.65–$17/£4.10–£11). No credit cards. Mon–Sat 11am–11pm; Sun noon–11pm. Metro: Staroměstská.

Value Inexpensive Meals on the Run

The Czech-style delicatessen **Lahůdky Zlatý Kříž,** Jungmannovo nám. 19 (entrance from Jungmannova 34), Praha 1 (✆ **221-191-801**), offers the typical Czech snack food *chlebíčky*—a slice of white bread with ham or salami and cheese or potato salad. You have to eat standing up, but prices are pure Czech. Or take it with you and go eat in the cozy garden behind the corner of this building (enter from the square). It's open Monday to Friday from 6:30am to 7pm and Saturday from 9am to 3pm. No credit cards are accepted.

Ovocný bar (fruit bar) **Hájek** at Václavské nám. 52, Praha 1 (✆ **222-211-466**), upstairs from an ice-cream stall, welcomes all for coffee and delicious desserts, ice cream, and fruit salads priced from 13Kč to 90Kč (85¢–$6/55p–£3.70). This sweet oasis has been popular with the locals for decades. It's open Monday to Saturday 9am to 8pm, Sunday 10am to 8pm.

If you are visiting Prague's Vinohrady quarter, you can't avoid its main square, náměstí Míru, with St. Ludmila's Church. On the right side of the church, when facing it, near the metro entrance, there is usually a stand with the **best hot dog** in Prague. The dog is topped with ketchup or two kinds of tasty Czech mustard and served on a fresh white roll. It costs 14Kč (93¢/46p) and it is available Monday to Friday from 9:30am until the supply for that day runs out.

If you're craving a snack, try one of the cafes in the **Paneria** chain found around the city. These bakeries serve freshly baked baguettes with toppings of your choice, crunchy panini, or sweet scones. One location is at Národní 18, Praha 1 (✆ **224-933-055**), open Monday to Friday 7am to 7pm, Saturday and Sunday 8am to 7pm.

New Town (Nové Město)

Moderate

Restaurant U Čížků ★ Value CZECH One of the city's first private restaurants, this cozy cellar-cum–hunting lodge on Charles Square can now be identified by the long line of German tour buses parked outside. The fare is purely Czech, and the massive portions of game, smoked pork, and other meats will stay with you for a while.

Karlovo nám. 34, Praha 2. ✆ **222-232-257.** Reservations recommended. Main courses 120Kč–290Kč ($8–$19/£4.95–£12). AE, MC, V. Daily 11:30am–10:30pm. Metro: Karlovo nám.

Inexpensive

Potrefená husa (The Wounded Goose) Value CZECH/INTERNATIONAL This outlet on the river in New Town has its own open fireplace (roaring in the colder months), and discreetly placed TVs. The most interesting offerings on the menu are the thick homemade soups—mainly vegetable based—served in *chléb* (whole, hollowed-out round bread loaves), and yes, it's cool to eat the bread after the soup is done. There are also standard grilled meats, pastas, salads, and plenty of varieties of beer on draft or in bottles.

Resslova 2, Praha 2. ✆ **224-918-691.** www.pivovary-staropramen.cz. Main courses 100Kč–300Kč ($6.65–$20/£4.10–£12). AE, MC, V. Daily 11:30am–1am. Metro: Karlovo nám.

Vinohrady

Expensive

Bonante (Value) INTERNATIONAL Bonante is especially great for shunning the cold of an autumn or winter evening near the roaring fire in the brick-cellar dining room. There are several vegetarian and low-calorie chicken-based selections on the menu. Jazz combos play on most nights from a small stage in the corner. When reserving, ask for a table within view of the fireplace.

Anglická 15, Praha 2. ✆ **224-221-665.** www.bonante.cz. Reservations recommended. Main courses 105Kč–295Kč ($7–$20/£4.35–£12). AE, MC, V. Daily 11am–11pm. Metro: I. P. Pavlova or Náměstí Míru.

Inexpensive

Osmička ★ (Value) (Kids) CZECH/INTERNATIONAL Osmička is an interesting hybrid in Vinohrady on a side street a few blocks above the National Museum. At first sight, the "Number 8" reveals a tourist-geared cellar restaurant with tawny eclectic colors, local art for sale on the walls, and a menu dominated by Italian standbys, fresh salads, and a variety of sandwiches. But once a Czech sits down, he or she quickly recognizes the neighborhood secret: This is still a good ol' Bohemian *hospoda* with *vepřo-knedlo-zelo* and other indigenous fare at local prices—served on new solid wood furniture by nicer-than-normal staff.

Balbínova 8, Praha 2. ✆ **222-826-888.** Main courses 54Kč–328Kč ($3.60–$22/£2.25–£14). MC, V. Mon–Fri 11am–midnight; Sat noon–midnight. Metro: I. P. Pavlova or Náměstí Míru.

Radost FX Café ★★ (Value) VEGETARIAN En vogue and full of vegetarian offerings, Radost is a clubhouse for hip new Bohemians, but it attracts plenty of international visitors, too. The veggie burger served on a whole-grain bun is well seasoned and substantial. Sautéed vegetable dishes, tofu, and huge Greek salads round out the health-conscious menu. The dining area is a dark rec room seemingly furnished by a rummage sale of upholstered armchairs, chaise longues, and couches from the 1960s. Guests eat off coffee tables. Too cool.

Bělehradská 120, Praha 2. ✆ **224-254-776.** www.radostfx.cz. Main courses 60Kč–285Kč ($4–$19/£2.50–£12). AE, MC, V. Daily 11:30am–5am. Metro: I. P. Pavlova.

Cafe Society

Old Town (Staré Město) & Josefov

Today, most of Prague's cafes have lost the indigenous charm of the Jazz Age or, strangely enough, the Communist era. During the Cold War, the venerable Café Slavia, across from the National Theater, became a de facto clubhouse in which dissidents passed the time, often within listening range of the not-so-secret police. It's here that Václav Havel and the arts community often gathered to keep a flicker of the Civic Society alive.

Grand Café CAFE FARE The biggest draw of this quaint cafe, the former Café Milena, is a great view of the Orloj, an astronomical clock with an hourly parade of saints on the side of Old Town Square's City Hall. With a new management came wider selection of main courses as well as higher prices. Make sure you get a table at the window.

Staroměstské nám. 22, Praha 1 (1st floor). ✆ **221-632-520.** www.grandcafe.cz. Cappuccino 89Kč ($5.95/£3.70); main menu 190Kč–490Kč ($13–$33/£8.05–£20). AE, MC, V. Daily 10am–midnight. Metro: Staroměstská.

Kavárna Obecní dům ★★ CAFE FARE An afternoon here feels like a trip back to the time when Art Nouveau was the newest fashion, not history. The reopening of the entire Municipal House in 1997 was a treat for those who love this style of architecture, and the *kavárna* might be its most spectacular public room. Witness the lofty ceilings, marble wall accents and tables, altarlike mantel at the far end, and huge windows and period chandeliers. Coffee, tea, and other drinks come with pastries and light sandwiches.

In the Municipal House, náměstí Republiky 5, Praha 1. © **222-002-763.** www.vysehrad2000.cz. Cakes and coffees from 50Kč–135Kč ($3.35–$9/£2.05–£5.60). AE, MC, V. Daily 7:30am–11pm. Metro: Náměstí Republiky.

Kavárna Slavia ★ CAFE FARE You'll most certainly walk by this Prague landmark, so why not stop in? The restored crisp Art Deco room recalls the Slavia's 100 years as a meeting place for the city's cultural and intellectual corps. The cafe still has a relatively affordable menu accompanying the gorgeous riverfront panoramic views of Prague Castle.

Národní at Smetanovo nábřeží, Praha 1. © **224-218-493.** Coffees and pastries 20Kč–40Kč ($1.35–$2.65/85p–£1.65); salad bar and light menu items 40Kč–120Kč ($2.65–$8/£1.65–£4.95). AE, MC, V. Daily 8am–midnight. Metro: Národní třída.

Velryba CAFE FARE This is the city center's cafe for young intellectuals. Journalists and actors set the mood in this bareish basement on a back street off Národní třída, where the emphasis is on good friends and hard talk. Pretty decent pasta dishes are served.

Opatovická 24, Praha 1. © **224-912-391.** Light meals 62Kč–135Kč ($4.15–$9/£2.55–£5.60). No credit cards. Daily 11am–midnight. Metro: Národní třída.

New Town (Nové Město)

Globe ★ LIGHT FARE A mainstay for younger English-speaking expats, the Globe is split into a fairly well-stocked bookstore and a usually crowded literary cafe serving pastas, sandwiches, salads, and chewy brownies along with stiff espresso. This cafe offers several terminals for Internet connections costing 1.50Kč (10¢/5p) per minute.

Pštrossova 6, Praha 1. © **224-934-203.** www.globebookstore.cz. Salads, sandwiches, pastas, and desserts 50Kč–145Kč ($3.35–$9.65/£2.10–£6). No credit cards. Daily 10am–midnight. Metro: Národní třída.

Vinohrady

Kavárna Medúza CAFE FARE With the feeling of an old attic, the Medúza, near several Vinohrady hotels and pensions, has a comfortable mix of visitors and students. The cappuccino comes in bowls, not cups, and the garlic bread hits the spot.

Belgická 17, Praha 2. © **222-515-107.** Cappuccino 25Kč ($1.65/£1); pastries/light meals 39Kč–95Kč ($2.60–$6.35/£1.60–£3.95). No credit cards. Mon–Fri 10am–1am; Sat–Sun noon–1am. Metro: Náměstí Míru.

Value Saving Money on Entrance Fees

If you like museums, galleries, castles, and churches, you may consider getting a **Prague Card.** This pass is valid for 4 days and allows you to visit up to 55 top attractions in the city, including the Prague Castle.

The price is 740Kč ($49/£30) adults and 490Kč ($33/£20) students 25 and under, and you can buy it at the Čedok office or the PIS information center at Rytířská 31, Praha 1. For more information and the whole list of sights go to www.praguecard.biz.

EXPLORING PRAGUE

While Prague's classical music and the Czech Republic's unmatched beer are among some of the better reasons to visit, the primary pleasure for many is simply strolling Prague's winding cobblestone streets and enjoying the unique atmosphere. Only by foot can you explore the countless nooks and crannies. It would be hard to think of another world capital where there is so much in such a compact area.

Prague Castle (Pražský Hrad) & Charles Bridge (Karlův Most)

The huge hilltop complex known collectively as **Prague Castle (Pražský Hrad)** ★★★, on Hradčanské náměstí, encompasses dozens of houses, towers, churches, courtyards, and monuments. A visit to the castle can easily take an entire day or more, depending on how thoroughly you explore it. Still, you can see the top sights—St. Vitus Cathedral, the Royal Palace, St. George's Basilica, the Powder Tower, and Golden Lane—in the space of a morning or an afternoon.

If you're feeling particularly fit, you can walk up to the castle, or you can take metro line A to Malostranská or Hradčanská or tram no. 22 or 23.

TICKETS & CASTLE INFORMATION Tickets are sold at the **Prague Castle Information Center** in the second courtyard after you pass through the main gate from Hradčanské náměstí. The center also arranges tours in various languages and sells tickets for individual concerts and exhibits. The castle is located at Hradčanské náměstí, Hradčany, Praha 1 (✆ **224-373-368;** fax 224-310-896; www.hrad.cz). Admission to St. Vitus Cathedral and the grounds is free. A combination ticket for a tour of the Royal Palace (including "The Story of Prague Castle" permanent exhibition, St. George's Basilica, Powder Tower, Golden Lane, Daliborka Tower, and the Prague Castle Picture Gallery), without a guide costs 350Kč ($23/£14) adults, 175Kč ($12/£7.45) students; the short tour (Royal Palace, St. George's Basilica, Golden Lane, and Daliborka Tower) costs 250Kč ($17/£8.50) adults, 125Kč ($8.35/£5.20) students. For guided tours (groups of five and more), supplement 100Kč ($6.65/£4.10) per person and hour (4 hr. minimum) only Tues–Sun 9am–4pm. All tours are free for children 5 and under. Tickets are valid for 2 days. The castle is open daily 9am to 6pm (to 4pm Nov–Mar). By metro, exit at Malostranská, then take tram no. 22 or 23, up the hill two stops.

Touring St. Vitus Cathedral (Chrám sv. Víta) ★★★

St. Vitus Cathedral (Chrám sv. Víta), named for a wealthy 4th-century Sicilian martyr, isn't just the dominant part of the castle, it's the most important section historically.

Built over various phases beginning in A.D. 926 as the court church of the Premyslid princes, the cathedral has long been the center of Prague's religious and political life. The key part of its Gothic construction took place in the 14th century under the direction of Mathias of Arras and Peter Parléř of Gmuend. In the 18th and 19th centuries, subsequent baroque and neo-Gothic additions were made. The **Golden Portal** entrance from the third courtyard is no longer used; however, take a look above the arch. The 1370 mosaic *The Last Judgment* has been painstakingly restored with the help of computer-aided imagery provided by American art researchers.

Of the massive Gothic cathedral's 21 chapels, the **St. Wenceslas Chapel (Svatováclavská kaple)** ★ stands out as one of Prague's few must-see indoor sights. Midway toward the high altar on the right, it's encrusted with hundreds of pieces of jasper and amethyst and decorated with paintings from the 14th to the 16th centuries. The chapel sits atop the gravesite of Bohemia's patron saint, St. Wenceslas.

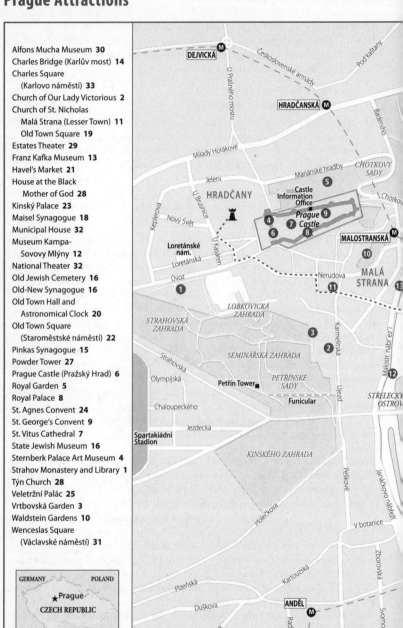

Prague Attractions

Alfons Mucha Museum **30**
Charles Bridge (Karlův most) **14**
Charles Square
(Karlovo náměstí) **33**
Church of Our Lady Victorious **2**
Church of St. Nicholas
Malá Strana (Lesser Town) **11**
Old Town Square **19**
Estates Theater **29**
Franz Kafka Museum **13**
Havel's Market **21**
House at the Black
Mother of God **28**
Kinský Palace **23**
Maisel Synagogue **18**
Municipal House **32**
Museum Kampa-
Sovovy Mlýny **12**
National Theater **32**
Old Jewish Cemetery **16**
Old-New Synagogue **16**
Old Town Hall and
Astronomical Clock **20**
Old Town Square
(Staroměstské náměstí) **22**
Pinkas Synagogue **15**
Powder Tower **27**
Prague Castle (Pražský Hrad) **6**
Royal Garden **5**
Royal Palace **8**
St. Agnes Convent **24**
St. George's Convent **9**
St. Vitus Cathedral **7**
State Jewish Museum **16**
Sternberk Palace Art Museum **4**
Strahov Monastery and Library **1**
Týn Church **28**
Veletržní Palác **25**
Vrtbovská Garden **3**
Waldstein Gardens **10**
Wenceslas Square
(Václavské náměstí) **31**

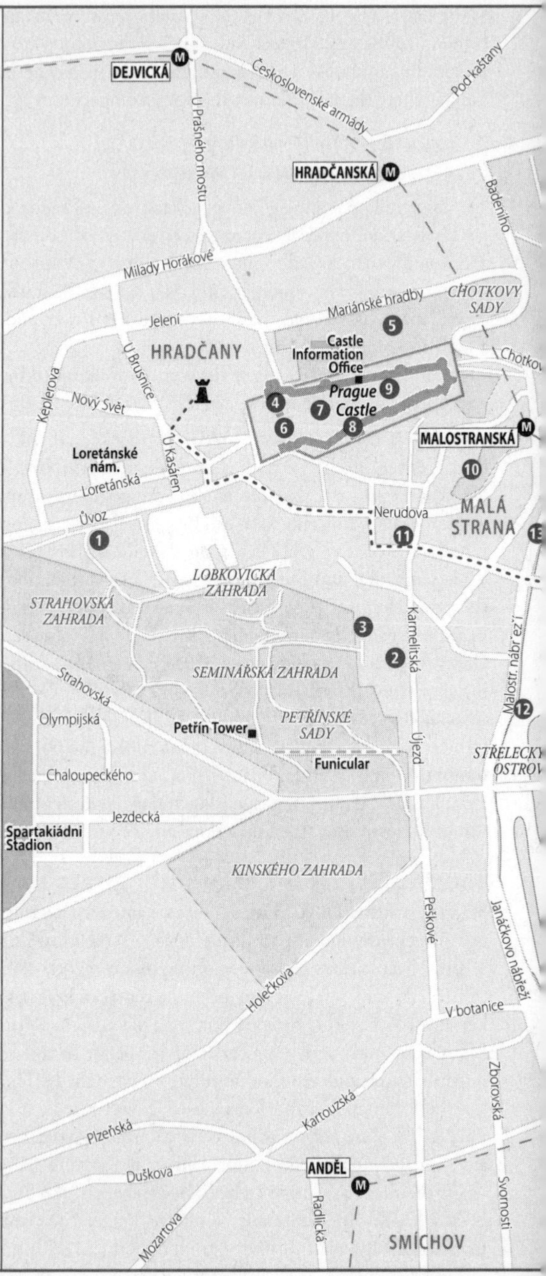

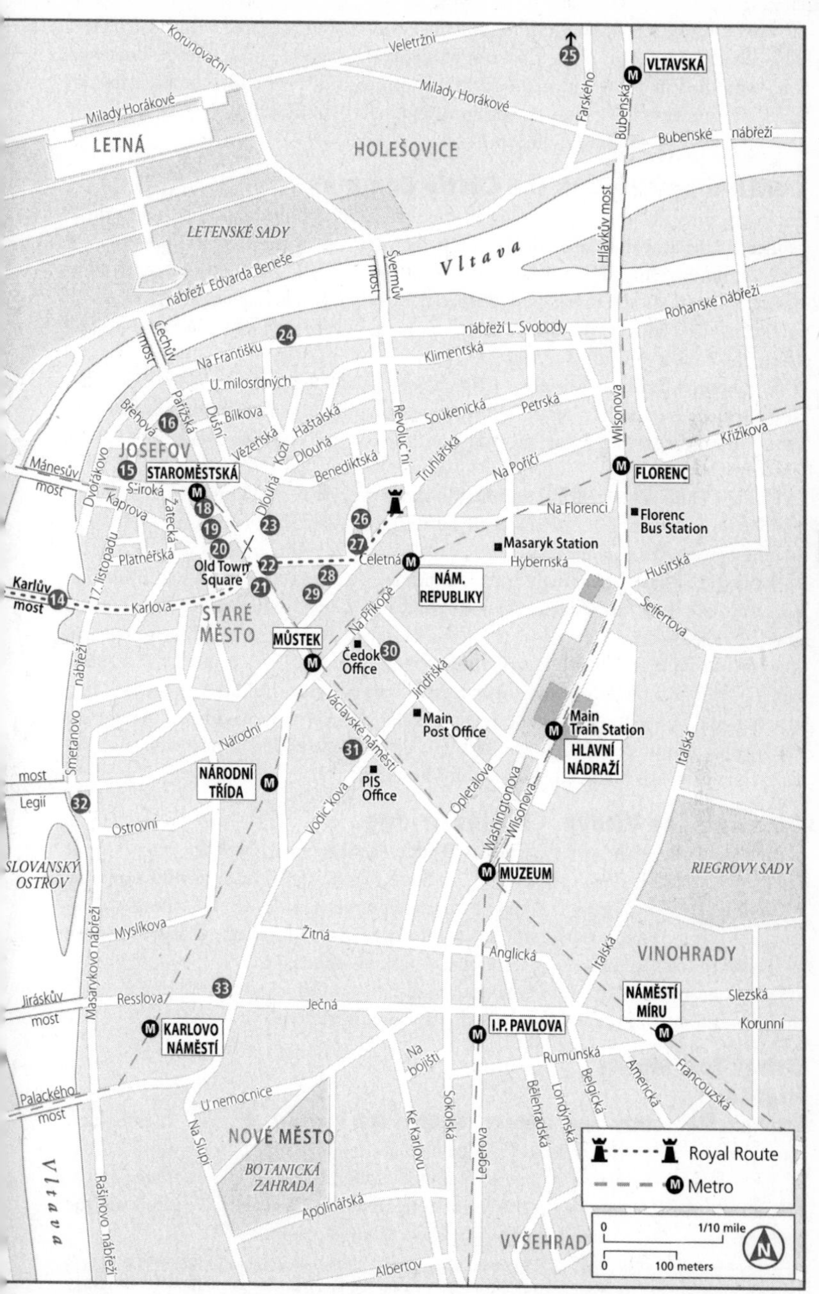

Korunovační
Veletržní
25
VLTAVSKÁ
Milady Horákové
Milady Horákové
LETNÁ
HOLEŠOVICE
Farského
Bubenská
Bubenské nábřeží
LETENSKÉ SADY
Hlávkův most
Vltava
Švermův most
nábřeží Edvarda Beneše
Rohanské nábřeží
Čechův most
nábřeží L. Svobody
24
Na Františku
Klimentská
U milosrdných
Břehová
Pařížská
16
Dušní
Bílkova
Vězeňská
Kozí
Haštalská
Dlouhá
Revoluční
Soukenická
Petrská
Wilsonova
Křížikova
JOSEFOV
Mánesův most
15
STAROMĚSTSKÁ
Dvořákovo
Široká
Benediktská
Truhlářská
Na Poříčí
FLORENC
Kaprova
Žatecká
18
19
20
Dlouhá
23
26
27
Na Florenci
Florenc Bus Station
Masaryk Station
17. listopadu
Platnéřská
Old Town Square
22
Celetná
Hybernská
NÁM. REPUBLIKY
Husitská
Karlův most
14
Karlova
21
28
29
STARÉ MĚSTO
Na Příkopě
Seifertova
MŮSTEK
Čedok Office
30
nábřeží
Jindřišská
Smetanovo
Národní
Main Post Office
Main Train Station
HLAVNÍ NÁDRAŽÍ
Václavské náměstí
31
Italská
most
Legií
32
NÁRODNÍ TŘÍDA
PIS Office
Opletalova
Washingtonova
Wilsonova
Vodičkova
Ostrovní
SLOVANSKÝ OSTROV
MUZEUM
RIEGROVY SADY
Masarykovo nábřeží
Myslíkova
Žitná
Anglická
VINOHRADY
Italská
Jiráskův most
33
Resslova
Ječná
NÁMĚSTÍ MÍRU
Slezská
KARLOVO NÁMĚSTÍ
I.P. PAVLOVA
Korunní
Na bojišti
Rumunská
Belgická
Americká
Francouzská
Palackého most
U nemocnice
Sokolská
Bělehradská
Londýnská
Na Slupi
Ke Karlovu
Legerova
NOVÉ MĚSTO
BOTANICKÁ ZAHRADA
Vltava
Rašínovo nábřeží
Apolinářská
Royal Route
Metro
VYŠEHRAD
0
1/10 mile
0
100 meters
N
Albertov

Just beyond this, the **Chapel of the Holy Rood (Kaple sv. Kříže)** leads to the entrance of the underground **royal crypt.** In the early 1900s, the crypt was reconstructed, and the remains of the kings and their relatives were replaced in new sarcophagi. The center sarcophagus is the final resting place of Charles IV, the favorite Bohemian king who died in 1378 and is the namesake of much of Prague. In the back row are Charles's four wives (all in one sarcophagus), and in front of them is George of Poděbrady, the last Bohemian king, who died in 1471.

Continuing through the Castle Complex

For more than 700 years, beginning in the 9th century, Bohemian kings and princes resided in the **Royal Palace (Královský palác),** located in the third courtyard of the castle grounds. Vaulted **Vladislav Hall (Vladislavský sál),** the interior's centerpiece, hosted coronations and is still used for special occasions of state such as inaugurations of presidents. The adjacent Diet was where kings and queens met with their advisors and where the Supreme Court was held.

St. George's Basilica (Kostel sv. Jiří), adjacent to the Royal Palace, is Prague's oldest Romanesque structure, dating from the 10th century. It also houses Bohemia's first convent. No longer serving a religious function, the convent contains a gallery of Gothic Czech art.

Golden Lane (Zlatá ulička) and Daliborka Tower ★ is a picturesque street of tiny 16th-century houses built into the castle fortifications. Once home to castle sharpshooters, the houses now contain small shops, galleries, and refreshment bars. In 1917, Franz Kafka is said to have lived briefly at no. 22; however, the debate continues as to whether Kafka actually took up residence or just worked in a small office there. The rounded tower that rises above Deer Moat is Daliborka Tower, which was a prison from 1496, when it was built as part of the city fortifications, until 1781. It's named after a young knight, Dalibor, who gave refuge to some rebellious peasants. Dalibor was the jail's first prisoner, and he spent his time in captivity playing the violin. Legend has it that during his long imprisonment, people would stand beneath the tower to hear him play sad songs. Sadly, he was eventually executed for his crime.

Crossing the Vltava: Charles Bridge

Dating from the 14th century, **Charles Bridge (Karlův most) ★★★**, Prague's most celebrated structure, links Prague Castle to Staré Město. For most of its 600 years, the 510m-long (1,673-ft.) span has been a pedestrian promenade, though for centuries walkers had to share the concourse with horse-drawn vehicles and trolleys. Today, the bridge is filled with folks walking among artists and busking musicians.

The best times to stroll across the bridge are early morning and around sunset, when the crowds have thinned and the shadows are more mysterious.

Other Top Sights

Hradčany

Strahov Monastery and Library (Strahovský klášter) ★ The second-oldest monastery in Prague, Strahov was founded high above Malá Strana in 1143 by Vladislav II. It's still home to Premonstratensian monks, a scholarly order closely related to the Jesuits, and their dormitories and refectory are off limits. What draws visitors are the monastery's ornate libraries, holding more than 125,000 volumes.

Strahovské nádvoří 1, Praha 1. ✆ **233-107-711.** www.strahovskyklaster.cz. Admission 80Kč ($5.35/£3.30) adults, 50Kč ($3.35/£2.10) students. Daily 9am–noon and 1–5pm. Tram: 22 or 23 from Malostranská metro station.

Lesser Town (Malá Strana)

Church of St. Nicholas (Chrám sv. Mikuláše) ★★ Moments This church is one of the best examples of high baroque north of the Alps. However, K. I. Dienzenhofer's 1711 design didn't have the massive dome that now dominates the Lesser Town skyline below Prague Castle. Dienzenhofer's son, Kryštof, added the 78m-high (256-ft.) dome during additional work completed in 1752.

Malostranské nám. 1, Praha 1. ✆ **257-534-215.** www.psalterium.cz. Daily 9am–5pm (4pm in winter); concerts are usually held at 5pm. Admission 60Kč ($4/£2.50) adults, 30Kč ($2/£1.25) students. Concerts 450Kč ($30/£19). Metro: Line A to Malostranská.

Old Town (Staré Město)

Estates' Theater (Stavovské divadlo) Completed in 1783 by wealthy Count F. A. Nostitz, the neoclassical theater became an early symbol of the emerging high Czech culture—with the Greek theme *Patriae et Musis* (the Fatherland and Music) etched above its front columns. In 1799, the wealthy land barons who formed fiefdoms known as the Estates gave the theater its current name.

Wolfgang Amadeus Mozart staged the premier of *Don Giovanni* here in 1787 because he said that Vienna's conservative patrons didn't appreciate him or his passionate and sometimes shocking work. They also wanted mostly German opera, but Praguers were happy to stage the performance in Italian. "Praguers understand me," Mozart was quoted as saying.

Czech director Miloš Forman returned to his native country to film his Oscar-winning *Amadeus,* shooting the scenes of Mozart in Prague with perfect authenticity at the Estates' Theater.

Ovocný trh 1, Praha 1. ✆ **224-901-448.** www.nd.cz. Metro: Line A or B to Můstek.

Old Town Hall (Staroměstská radnice) & Astronomical Clock (Orloj) Kids Crowds congregate in front of Old Town Hall's Astronomical Clock *(orloj)* to watch the glockenspiel spectacle that occurs hourly from 8am to 8pm. Built in 1410, the clock has long been an important symbol of Prague. According to legend, after the timepiece was remodeled at the end of the 15th century, clock artist Master Hanuš was blinded by the Municipal Council so that he couldn't repeat his fine work elsewhere. In retribution, Hanuš threw himself into the clock mechanism and promptly died. The clock remained out of kilter for almost a century.

Staroměstské nám., Praha 1. ✆ **724-508-584.** www.pis.cz. Admission to tower 60Kč ($4/£2.50) adults; 40Kč ($2.65/£1.65) students, children 9 and under, and seniors. Mar–Oct Mon 11am–6pm, Tues–Sun 9am–6pm; Nov–Feb Mon 11am–5pm, Tues–Sun 9am–5pm. Metro: Line A to Staroměstská.

Josefov

Within Josefov, you'll find a community that for centuries was forced to fend for itself and then experienced horrific purges under Nazi occupation in World War II. Although more than 118,000 Jews were recorded as living in the Czech lands of Bohemia and Moravia in 1939, only 30,000 survived to see the end of the Nazi occupation. Today, the Jewish community in the entire country numbers about 3,000 people, most of whom live in Prague.

The **Jewish Museum in Prague** (www.jewishmuseum.cz) is the name of the organization managing all the Jewish landmarks in Josefov. It provides guided package tours with an English-speaking guide as part of a comprehensive admission price. The package includes the Ceremonial Hall, Old Jewish Cemetery, Old-New Synagogue, Pinkas Synagogue, Klaus Synagogue, Maisel Synagogue, and Spanish Synagogue. From April to

October, tours leave on the hour starting at 9am with the last tour at 5pm, but there must be at least 10 people in a group. Off season, the tours are between 9am and 4:30pm. The package costs 490Kč ($32/£20) for adults and 330Kč ($22/£14) for students, free for children 5 and under.

The Maisel Synagogue now serves as the exhibition space for the **Jewish Museum.** In October 1994, the State Jewish Museum closed; the Torah covers, 100,000 books, and other exhibits once housed there were given to the Jewish community, who then proceeded to return many items to synagogues throughout the country. The Nazis destroyed much of Prague's ancient Judaica during World War II. Ironically, those same Germans constructed an "exotic museum of an extinct race," thus salvaging thousands of objects, such as the valued Torah covers, books, and silver now displayed at the Maisel Synagogue.

Old Jewish Cemetery (Starý židovský hřbitov) ★ Just 1 block from the Old-New Synagogue, this is one of Europe's oldest Jewish burial grounds, dating from the mid–15th century. Because the local government of the time didn't allow Jews to bury their dead elsewhere, graves were dug deep enough to hold 12 bodies vertically, with each tombstone placed in front of the last. The result is one of the world's most crowded cemeteries: a 1-block area filled with more than 20,000 graves. Among the most famous persons buried here are the celebrated Rabbi Loew (Löw; d. 1609), who created the legend of Golem (a giant clay "monster" to protect Prague's Jews); and banker Markus Mordechai Maisel (d. 1601), then the richest man in Prague and protector of the city's Jewish community during the reign of Rudolf II.

U Starého hřbitova; the entrance is from Široká 3. ✆ **222-317-191.** Admission 290Kč ($19/£12) adults, 190Kč ($13/£8.05) students, free for children 5 and under. Apr–Oct Sun–Fri 9am–6pm; Nov–Mar Sun–Fri 9am–4:30pm. Metro: Line A to Staroměstská.

Old-New Synagogue (Staronová synagóga) ★ First called the New Synagogue to distinguish it from an even older one that no longer exists, the Old-New Synagogue, built around 1270, is Europe's oldest remaining Jewish house of worship. The faithful have prayed here continuously for more than 700 years, carrying on even after a massive 1389 pogrom in Josefov that killed over 3,000 Jews. Its use as a house of worship was interrupted only between 1941 and 1945 because of the Nazi occupation. The synagogue is also one of Prague's great Gothic buildings, built with vaulted ceilings and retro-fitted with Renaissance-era columns. It is not part of the Jewish Museum, so you can visit this synagogue separately.

Červená 2. ✆ **222-317-191.** Admission 200Kč ($15/£9.30) adults, 140Kč ($9.35/£5.80) students. (If part of the package for Jewish Museum, 490Kč/$32/£20 adults, 330Kč/$22/£14 students.) Free for children 5 and under. Sun–Thurs 9:30am–5pm; Fri 9am–4pm. Metro: Line A to Staroměstská.

Museums & Galleries

Many fine private art galleries showing contemporary work by Czech and other artists are in central Prague, within walking distance of Staroměstské náměstí. Although their primary interest is sales, most welcome browsing.

As for public museums and galleries, note that many museums are closed on Monday.

National Gallery Sites

The national collection of fine art is grouped for display in the series of venues known collectively as the **National Gallery (Národní Galerie).** Remember that this term refers to several locations, not just one gallery.

The most extensive collection of classic European works spanning the 14th to the 18th centuries is found at the Archbishop's Palace complex in the **Šternberský palác** across from the main gate to Prague Castle.

Veletržní Palace houses most of the country's 20th-century art collection and now also shows the important national revival works from Czech artists of the 19th century. Much of the rest of the national collection is divided between Kinský Palace on Old Town Square and the Gothic collection at St. Agnes Convent near the river in Old Town.

The key Prague sites within the national gallery system are listed below.

Hradčany

St. Agnes Convent (Klášter sv. Anežky České) A complex of early Gothic buildings and churches dating from the 13th century, the convent, tucked in a corner of Staré Město, began exhibiting much of the National Gallery's collection of Gothic art in 2000. Once home to the Order of the Poor Clares, it was established in 1234 by St. Agnes of Bohemia, sister of Wenceslas I. The Blessed Agnes became St. Agnes when Pope John Paul II paid his first visit to Prague in 1990 for her canonization.

U Milosrdných 17, Praha 1. ✆ **224-810-628.** www.ngprague.cz. Admission 100Kč ($6.65/£4.15) adults, 50Kč ($3.35/£2.10) children. Tues–Sun 10am–6pm. Metro: Line A to Staroměstská.

St. George's Convent at Prague Castle (Klášter sv. Jiří na Pražském hradě) Dedicated to displaying traditional Czech art, the castle convent is especially packed with Gothic and baroque Bohemian iconography as well as portraits of patron saints. The most famous among the unique collection of Czech Gothic panel paintings are those by the Master of the Hohenfurth Altarpiece and the Master Theodoricus.

Jiřské nám. 33. ✆ **257-531-644.** www.ngprague.cz. Admission 130Kč ($8.65/£5.35) adults, 80Kč ($5.35/£3.30) students, free for children 5 and under. Tues–Sun 9am–5pm. Metro: Line A to Malostranská or Hradčanská.

Šternberk Palace (Šternberský palác) ★ The jewel in the National Gallery crown (also known casually as the European Art Museum), the gallery at Šternberk Palace, adjacent to the main gate of Prague Castle, displays a wide menu of European art throughout the ages. It features 5 centuries of everything from Orthodox icons to Renaissance oils by Dutch masters.

Hradčanské nám. 15, Praha 1. ✆ **233-090-570.** www.ngprague.cz. Admission 130Kč ($8.65/£5.35) adults, 80Kč ($5.35/£3.30) students and children. Tues–Sun 10am–6pm. Metro: Line A to Malostranská or Hradčanská.

Old Town (Staré Město)

Kinský Palace (Palác Kinských) The reconstructed rococo palace houses graphic works from the National Gallery collection, including pieces by Georges Braque, André Derain, and other modern masters. Pablo Picasso's 1907 *Self-Portrait* is here and has virtually been adopted as the National Gallery's logo.

Staroměstské nám. 12, Praha 1. ✆ **224-810-758.** www.ngprague.cz. Admission 100Kč ($6.65/£4.15) adults, 50Kč ($3.35/£2.10) students. Tues–Sun 10am–6pm. Metro: Line A to Staroměstská.

National Gallery (Veletržní Palace) This 1925 constructivist palace, built for trade fairs, was remodeled and reopened in 1995 to hold the bulk of the National Gallery's collection of 20th-century works by Czech and other European artists. Three atrium-lit concourses provide a comfortable setting for some catchy and kitschy Czech sculpture and multimedia works. Alas, the best cubist works from Braque and Picasso,

Rodin bronzes, and many other primarily French pieces have been relegated to the second floor.

Veletržní at Dukelských hrdinů 47, Praha 7. ✆ **224-301-111.** www.ngprague.cz. Admission 160Kč ($11/£6.85) adults, 80Kč ($5.35/£3.30) students. Free for children 5 and under. Tues–Sun 10am–6pm. Metro: Line C to Vltavská. Tram: 17.

Other Museums & Galleries

Malá Strana

Museum Kampa–Sovovy mlýny ★ This building on Kampa island served for most of its history, due to the location, as a mill. Throughout the centuries it was struck by floods, fires, and destructive wars. In September 2003, the Sovovy mlýny was opened as a museum of modern art by Czech-born American Meda Mládková and her foundation. She has been collecting works of Czech and central European artists since the 1950s. Her dream reached its pinnacle when she presented the permanent exhibition of František Kupka's drawings and Otto Gutfreund's sculptures.

U Sovových mlýnů 503/2, Praha 1. ✆ **257-286-147.** www.museumkampa.cz. Admission 120Kč ($8/£4) adults, 60Kč ($4/£2) students, free for children 5 and under. Daily 10am–6pm. Metro: Malostranská.

New Town (Nové Město)

Alfons Mucha Museum (Muzeum A. Muchy) ★ This museum opened in early 1998 near Wenceslas Square to honor the high priest of Art Nouveau, Alphonse (Alfons in Czech) Mucha. Though the Moravian-born, turn-of-the-20th-century master spent most of his creative years in Paris drawing luminaries like actress Sarah Bernhardt, Mucha's influence can still be seen throughout his home country. The new museum, around the corner from the Palace Hotel, combines examples of his graphic works, posters, and paintings, and highlights his influence in jewelry, fashion, and advertising. Those who remember the 1960s and 1970s will flash back to one of Mucha's most famous works, the sinuous goddess of Job rolling papers.

Panská 7, Praha 1. ✆ **224-216-415.** www.mucha.cz. Admission 120Kč ($8/£4.95) adults, 60Kč ($4/£2.50) students and children. Daily 10am–6pm. Metro: Můstek.

Historic Squares

The most celebrated square in the city, **Old Town Square (Staroměstské nám.) ★★★**, is surrounded by baroque buildings and packed with colorful craftspeople, cafes, and entertainers. In ancient days, the site was a major crossroads on central European merchant routes. In its center stands a memorial to Jan Hus, the 15th-century martyr who crusaded against Prague's German-dominated religious and political establishment. It was unveiled in 1915, on the 500th anniversary of Hus's execution. The monument's most compelling features are the dark asymmetry and fluidity of the figures. Take metro line A to Staroměstská. The square and Staré Město are described in more detail in the walking tour below.

One of the city's most historic squares, **Wenceslas Square (Václavské nám.) ★★**, was formerly the horse market (Koňský trh). The once muddy swath between the buildings played host to the country's equine auctioneers. The top of the square, where the National Museum now stands, was the outer wall of the New Town fortifications, bordering the Royal Vineyards. Unfortunately, the city's busiest highway now cuts the museum off from the rest of the square it dominates. Trolleys streamed up and down the square until the early 1980s. Today the half-mile-long boulevard is lined with cinemas, shops, hotels, restaurants, casinos, and porn shops.

The square was given its present name in 1848. The pedestal of giant statue of St. Wenceslas has become a popular platform for speakers. Actually, the square has thrice been the site of riots and revolutions—in 1848, 1968, and 1989. At the height of the Velvet Revolution, 250,000 to 300,000 Czechs filled the square during one demonstration. Take metro line A or B to Můstek.

The rapid influx of visitors, the post-Communist wage growth, and a new consumer economy fueled by the shopping habits of the Czech nouveau riche have resulted in expensive boutiques and specialty shops popping up like mushrooms in Prague.

For those looking for a piece of Czech handwork, you can find some of the world's best crystal and glass, often at shockingly low prices. Antiques shops and booksellers abound, and the selection of classical, trendy, and offbeat art is immense at the numerous private galleries. Throughout the city center you'll find quaint, obscure shops, some without phones or advertising.

WALKING TOUR: OLD TOWN (STARÉ MĚSTO)

Although this tour is far from exhaustive, it takes you past some of Old Town's most important buildings and monuments. Go to náměstí Republiky 5, at the metro station. Begin at the:

1 Municipal House (Obecní dům)

From the beginning, this ornate Art Nouveau building has been an important Czech cultural symbol—the document granting independence to Czechoslovakia was signed here in 1918. The **Prague Symphony** performs in Smetana Hall, the building's most impressive room, with a gorgeous stained-glass ceiling.

With your back to the Municipal House main entrance, walk around to your right under the arch of the:

2 Powder Tower (Prašná brána, literally Powder Gate)

Once part of Staré Město's system of fortifications, the Powder Tower was built in 1475 as one of the walled city's major gateways. The tower marks the beginning of the **Royal Route,** the traditional path along which medieval Bohemian monarchs paraded on their way to being crowned in Prague Castle's St. Vitus Cathedral.

Continue through the arch down Celetná Street (named after *calt,* a bread baked here in the Middle Ages) to the corner of Ovocný trh, where you'll find the:

3 House at the Black Mother of God (Dům U Černé Matky boží)

At Celetná 34, this building is important for its cubist architectural style. Cubism, an angular artistic movement, was confined to painting and sculpture in France and most of Europe. As an architectural style, cubism is exclusive to Bohemia.

With your back to the House of the Black Mother of God, cross Celetná into Templová, walk 2 short blocks, and turn left onto Jakubská. At the corner, on your right, you'll see:

4 St. James's Church (Kostel sv. Jakuba)

Prague's second-longest church contains 21 altars. When you enter, look up just inside the church's front door. The object dangling from above is the shriveled arm of a 16th-century thief.

Return to Celetná and continue walking about 90m (295 ft.). On the right, below the towering spires, is:

5 Church of Our Lady Before Týn (Kostel paní Marie před Týnem–Týnský chrám)

This is one of the largest and prettiest of Prague's many churches. Famous for its twin spires that loom over nearby Staroměstské náměstí, the church was closely connected to the 14th-century Hussite movement for religious reform. Note the tomb of Danish astronomer Tycho de Brahe (d. 1601), near the high altar.

Exit the church and continue a few more steps along Celetná, which opens up into:

6 Old Town Square (Staroměstské náměstí)

Surrounded by baroque buildings and packed with colorful cafes, craftspeople, and entertainers, Staroměstské náměstí looks the way an old European square is supposed to look.

Old Town Square has also seen its share of political protest and punishment. Protestant Hussites rioted here in the 1400s. In the 1620s, the Catholic Habsburg rulers beheaded 27 Protestants here and hung some of the heads in baskets above Charles Bridge. A small white cross has been embedded in the square near the Old Town Hall for each of the beheaded.

To begin your walk around the square, go straight toward the massive black stone monument in the center. Here you'll find the statue of:

7 Jan Hus

Jan Hus was a fiery 15th-century preacher who challenged the Roman Catholic hierarchy and was burned at the stake for it. The statue's pedestal has been used as a soapbox by many a populist politician trying to gain points by associating himself with the ill-fated Protestant.

From here, turn around and walk left toward the clock tower.

8 Old Town Hall (Staroměstská radnice)

Try to time your walk so you can pass the hall and its **Astronomical Clock** at the top of the hour. It may be an understated show, but each hour a mechanical parade of saints and sinners performs for the crowd watching below (p. 241). If you have time and your knees are up to it, try making the steep, narrow walk up to the top of the tower for a picturesque view of Old Town's red roofs.

Walking past the right side of the clock tower toward the northwest corner of the square, you'll come to:

9 St. Nicholas Church (Kostel sv. Mikuláše)

This is the 1735 design of Prague's baroque master architect K. I. Dienzenhofer. The three-towered edifice isn't as beautiful or as ornate inside as his St. Nicholas Church in Lesser Town, but the crystal fixtures are worth a look.

From the front of the church, walk behind the back of the Hus monument, through the square, to the broad palace with the reddish roof and balcony in front. This is:

10 Kinský Palace (Palác Kinských)

From the rococo balcony jutting from the palace's stucco facade, Communist leader Klement Gottwald declared the proletariat takeover of the Czechoslovak government in February 1945. Italian architect Lurago designed the building for Count Goltz. It was later taken over by the Habsburg Prince Rudolf Kinský in 1768. It now houses a fine modern art collection in the **National Gallery** complex of palaces (p. 243).

Next to this is the:

11 House at the Stone Bell (Dům U kamenného zvonu)

The medieval Gothic tower was built in the 14th century for the father of Charles IV, John of Luxembourg.

From here, head back toward Old Town Hall, but then about midway to the tower, turn left toward the square's south end and begin walking down Železná. Continue down this car-restricted walking zone about 300m (984 ft.); then, on the left you'll see the pale green:

12 Estates' Theater (Stavovské divadlo)

Mozart premiered his opera *Don Giovanni* in this late-18th-century grand hall.

Make sure to walk down Rytířská in front of the theater to get a full view of this beautifully restored building.

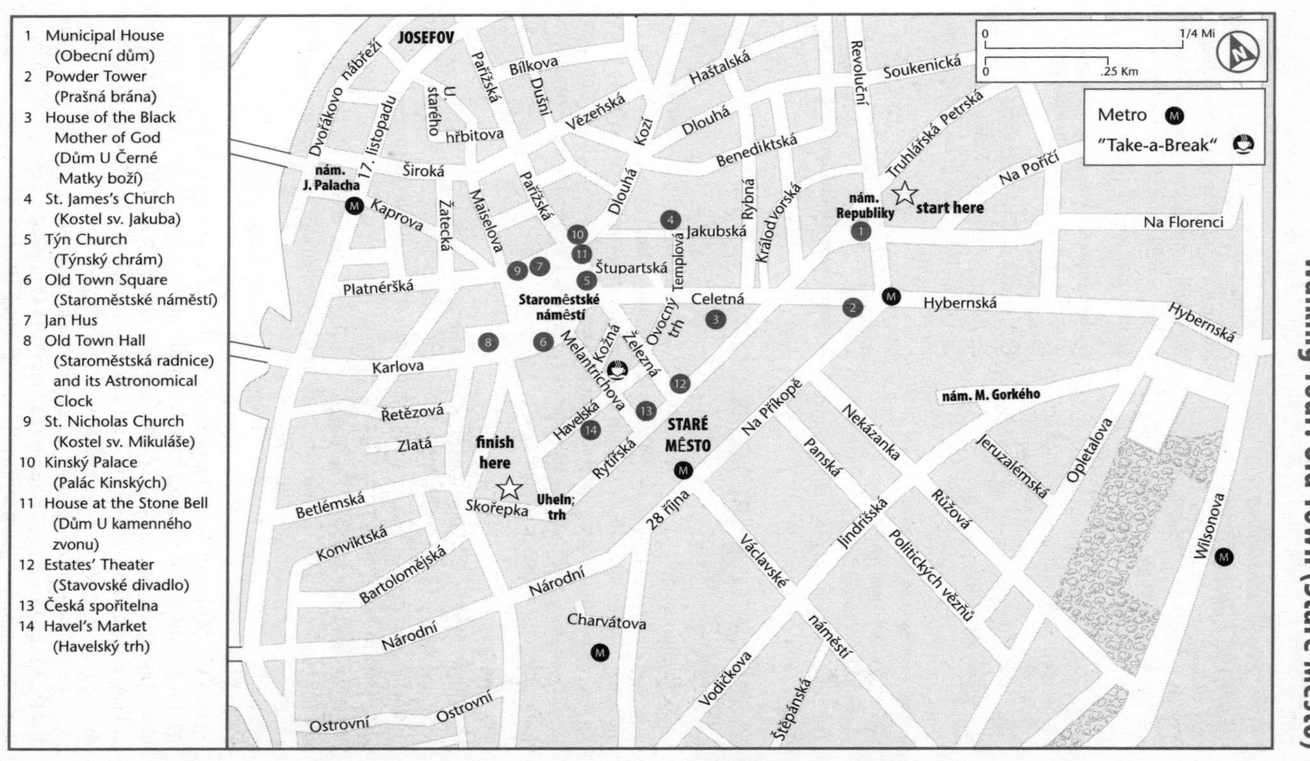

1 Municipal House (Obecní dům)
2 Powder Tower (Prašná brána)
3 House of the Black Mother of God (Dům U Černé Matky boží)
4 St. James's Church (Kostel sv. Jakuba)
5 Týn Church (Týnský chrám)
6 Old Town Square (Staroměstské náměstí)
7 Jan Hus
8 Old Town Hall (Staroměstská radnice) and its Astronomical Clock
9 St. Nicholas Church (Kostel sv. Mikuláše)
10 Kinský Palace (Palác Kinských)
11 House at the Stone Bell (Dům U kamenného zvonu)
12 Estates' Theater (Stavovské divadlo)
13 Česká spořitelna
14 Havel's Market (Havelský trh)

From the front of the theater, walk about 10 steps back up Železná and take the first left on Havelská.

> **13 TAKE A BREAK**
> At Havelská 27, you can stop for a tasty pasta, lasagna, tiramisu, or thick Italian espresso at the **Kogo** (p. 233). There are tightly packed tables inside, but if the weather is nice, sit in the more comfortable archway. Hours are daily from 9am to midnight. Salads and appetizers start at 160Kč ($11/£6.80). You won't be disappointed by their homemade pasta, from 192Kč ($13/£8.05).

Continue down Havelská. On the left you'll see:

14 Czech Savings Bank (Česká spořitelna)

The 1894 building was originally intended to be a bank, but after the 1948 coup it was seized by the government and turned into a repository for Communist propaganda. After the 1989 revolution, the building was returned to the bank, which restored the intricate friezes and frescoes depicting bankers' propaganda of early Czech capitalism. This is the largest Czech savings bank and worth a peek.

Your next destination is the popular street market that overtakes the remainder of Havelská Street. Simply continue on to:

15 Havel's Market (Havelský trh)

At this popular local meeting place, you'll find vegetables, fruit, drinks, soaps, toiletries, artwork, and leather goods. Prices here are generally lower than in most shops. Have fun browsing.

The nearest metro is Můstek, line A or B.

SIDE TRIP TO KARLŠTEJN CASTLE ★★★

29km (18 miles) SW of Prague

By far the most popular destination in the Czech Republic after Prague, Karlštejn Castle is an easy day trip for those interested in getting out of the city. Charles IV built this medieval castle from 1348 to 1357 to safeguard the crown jewels of the Holy Roman Empire. Although the castle had been changed over the years, with such additions as late Gothic staircases and bridges, renovators have removed these additions, restoring the castle to its original medieval state.

Essentials

GETTING THERE The best way to get to Karlštejn is by **train** (there's no bus service). Most trains leave from Prague's Main Station (at the Hlavní nádraží metro stop) hourly throughout the day and take about 45 minutes to reach Karlštejn. The one-way, second-class fare is 46Kč ($3/£1.85).

VISITOR INFORMATION The ticket/castle information booth (✆ **311-681-370**) can help you, as can any of the restaurants or stores. The castle itself has a website that you can visit at www.hradkarlstejn.cz.

Exploring the Castle

Since Karlštejn's beauty lies more in its facade and environs than in the castle itself, the 20- to 30-minute walk up the hill is, along with the view, one of the main features that makes the trip spectacular. It's an excursion well worth making if you can't get farther out of Prague to see some of the other castles. When you finally do reach the top, take some time to look out over the town and down the Well Tower.

To see the interior of the castle, you can choose from two tours. The 50-minute **Tour 1** will take you through the **Imperial Palace, Hall of Knights, Chapel of St. Nicholas, Royal Bedroom,** and **Audience Hall. Tour 2,** which lasts 70 minutes, offers a look at the **Holy Rood Chapel,** famous for the more than 2,000 precious and semiprecious

Moments A Romantic Getaway

If the air and noise of Prague start to grate on your nerves, or if a quiet, romantic, overnight trip to a castle in the country sounds like the perfect getaway, head for the **Romantic Hotel Mlýn (Mill Hotel)** ★, 267 18 Karlštejn (✆ **311-744-411;** fax 311-744-444; www.hotelmlynkarlstejn.cz).

On the river's edge on the bank opposite the castle, the Mlýn is exactly what its name says—a mill. Converted into a hotel and recently reconstructed, this reasonably priced country inn takes you away from the hustle and bustle of traveling. Its 28 rooms are a little on the small side, but they're quaint and nicely decorated with rustic furniture. At the outdoor patio bar and very good restaurant, you can relax and enjoy the soothing sounds of the river. Service here is a cut above what it is at the other hotels in the area. If you are here for lunch or dinner when the outdoor grill has been fired up, take advantage of it. Use the hotel also as a base for bike and canoe trips along the river. The staff can help you with local tennis courts and reservations for a round of golf.

Rates are 2,500Kč ($167/£104) for a single and 3,100Kč ($206/£128) for a double. MasterCard and Visa are accepted. To get to the hotel, take the bridge across the river that leads to the train station and turn left at the first street. If you cross the rail tracks, you've gone too far.

inlaid gems adorning its walls; the **Chapel of St. Catherine,** Karel IV's own private oratory; the **Church of Our Lady;** and the **library.**

Note that you need to make a reservation to visit the Holy Rood Chapel on Tour 2 (✆ **274-008-154;** fax 274-008-152; www.hradkarlstejn.cz). The shorter Tour 1 costs 220Kč ($15/£9.30) adults, 120Kč ($8/£4.95) students, 20Kč ($1.35/85p) children 5 and under. Tour 2 with the Holy Rood Chapel costs 300Kč ($20/£12) adults, 150Kč ($10/£6.20) students, free for children 5 and under. The castle is open Tuesday to Sunday: May, June, and September 9am to noon and 12:30 to 5pm; July and August 9am to noon and 12:30 to 6pm; April and October 9am to noon and 1 to 4pm; and November, December, and March 9am to noon and 1 to 3pm.

SHOPPING AREAS

The L-shaped half-mile running from the middle of **Wenceslas Square** around the corner to the right on **Na Příkopě** and to the Myslbek Center has become Prague's principal shopping street. In this short distance you'll find three multilevel shopping gallerias.

A handful of fine private **art galleries** is concentrated on the stretch of **Národní třída** running from just east of the National Theater to Wenceslas Square. The wide tree-lined Pařížská, from Old Town Square to the Hotel InterContinental, is flanked with top-level boutiques, travel agencies, and airline offices, as well as eclectic local shops.

In the streets surrounding **Old Town Square,** you'll find a wide variety of expensive shops with bizarre nooks offering woodcarvings, garnets, handmade toys, and typical Czech glass and porcelain.

In **Malá Strana,** you'll find artists and craftspeople selling their jewelry, prints, handicrafts, and faux Red Army surplus on Charles Bridge.

Hours & Taxes

Prague's centrally located shops rely on tourist business and keep fairly long hours. Most are open Monday to Friday from about 9am to 6pm and Saturday from 9am to 1pm, and sometimes much later. Many open on Sunday as well, though usually for a shorter time. Note that some small food shops that keep long hours charge up to 20% more for all their goods.

Prices for goods in shops include the government's 19% **value-added tax (VAT).** All tourists from **outside the E.U.** can save up to 16% of this tax. To make use of this concession, buy from stores with the TAX FREE sign. To qualify, the purchase price must exceed 2,000Kč ($133/£82), including the VAT, in 1 day in one store.

SHOPPING A TO Z

Antiques

Antique-Andrle Vladimír A wide selection of antique porcelain and ceramics, jewelry, and clocks distinguishes this shop. There's also a large selection of small antique sculptures and other accessories. Open Monday to Saturday from 10am to 7pm and Sunday from 10am to 6pm. Křížovnická 1, Praha 1. ✆ **222-311-625.** Metro: Staroměstská. www.antiqueandrle.cz.

Art Galleries

The Czech Museum of Fine Arts This museum presents works of contemporary Czech and other Eastern European artists. Coffee-table books and catalogs with detailed descriptions in English and color reproductions usually accompany well-planned exhibitions. Open Tuesday to Sunday from 10am to 6pm. Husova 19 and 21, Praha 1. ✆ **222-220-218.** www.cmvu.cz. Metro: Národní třída or Můstek.

Crystal & Glass

Cristallino ★ This store offers one of the largest assortments of Bohemian crystal and glass, as well as some porcelain and jewelry. Designs come from top Czech glass makers and vary from classic patterns to modern glassware. Open daily 9am to 8pm April to December, 9am to 7pm January to March. Celetná 12, Praha 1. ✆ **224-225-173.** www.cristallino.cz. Metro: Můstek.

Moser ★★★ Value The Moser family began selling Bohemia's finest crystal in central Prague in 1857, drawing customers from around the world. Even the king of Siam made a special trip to the Karlovy Vary factory in the 1930s to pick his place settings. The dark-wood showroom upstairs is worth a look if only to get the feeling of Prague at its most elegant. Open Monday to Friday from 9am to 8pm, Saturday and Sunday from 10am to 7pm. Na Příkopě 12, Praha 1. ✆ **224-211-293.** www.moser-glass.com. Metro: Můstek. 2nd shop at Malé nám. 11, Praha 1. ✆ 224-222-012. Metro: Můstek.

Department Stores & Shopping Malls

Obchodní Centrum Nový Smíchov ★★ This modern shopping mall built on the defunct site of one of the city's most famous factories is Prague's new temple to post-Communist consumption. In just a few minutes' metro ride from Old Town or Malá Strana, you can find some items cheaper than in Western Europe. Open daily 9am to 9pm (shops); 7am to midnight (Tesco department store); 11am to 11pm (restaurants and entertainment). Plzeňská 8, Praha 5. ✆ **251-511-151.** www.novysmichovoc.cz. Metro: Anděl.

Palác Flora ★ This addition to the city's shopping malls is located in the residential area of Vinohrady. The modern building has been erected right above Flora metro

Value An Open-Air Market

On the short, wide street perpendicular to Melantrichova, between Staroměstské náměstí and Václavské náměstí, **Havel's Market (Havelský trh),** Havelská ulice, Praha 1 (named well before Havel became president), features dozens of private vendors selling seasonal homegrown fruits and vegetables at the best prices in the city center. Other goods, including detergent, flowers, and cheese, are also for sale. It's open Monday to Friday from 8am to 6pm. Take metro line A or B to Můstek.

station, so it is easily accessible from the center. Inside you will find a wide selection of shops, restaurants, and cafes and an entertainment center that includes 3-D and 2-D cinemas. Boutiques and fashion shops occupy the second floor. Open Monday to Friday 9am to 9pm, Saturday and Sunday 10am to 9pm. Vinohradská 149, Praha 3. © **255-741-712.** www.palacflora.cz. Metro: Flora.

Tesco The best reasons to shop at Tesco are the gifts (including fine Leander rose porcelain), snacks on the ground floor (like a Little Caesar's pizza), and a fine grocery store in the basement. Open Monday to Friday from 8am to 9pm (food department from 7am), Saturday from 9am to 8pm (food department from 8am), and Sunday from 10am to 8pm (food department from 9am). Národní třída 26, Praha 1. © **222-003-111.** Metro: Národní třída.

Garnets

Český Granát Value This shop has an excellent reputation for good-quality jewelry at reasonable prices. Traditional, conservative earrings and pendants are spiked with some interesting and unusual designs. Most pieces are set in 24-karat gold or gold-plated silver. Open Monday to Saturday from 10am to 7pm and Sunday from 10am to 7pm. Celetná 4, Praha 1. © **224-228-281.** Metro: Můstek.

Gifts & Souvenirs

Botanicus ★★ Finds This chain of natural scent, soap, and herb shops is an amazing Anglo-Czech success story. Started by a British botanist and Czech partners on a farm northeast of Prague, Botanicus has found 101 ways to ply a plant into a sensuous gift and a lucrative trade. There are several outlets throughout Prague, with this one close to Old Town Square probably most convenient for tourists. Open daily from 10am to 6:30pm. Týn 3 (Týnský Dvůr), Praha 1. © **234-767-446.** www.botanicus.cz. Metro: Můstek.

Dům Porcelánu Praha Value Traditional Czech "onion" *(cibulák)* china is the calling card for this representative shop of the porcelain factory in Dubí near the German border. The folksy blue-on-bone cobalt onion patterns have become a familiar sight in country kitchens around the world. Open Monday to Friday from 9am to 7pm, Saturday from 9am to 2pm, and Sunday from 2 to 5pm. Jugoslávská 16, Praha 2. © **221-505-320.** www.cibulak.cz. Metro: Náměstí Míru or I. P. Pavlova.

Music

Bontonland Megastore Selling everything from serious Bohemian classics to Seattle grunge, the store is in the Koruna Palace, which is open Monday to Saturday from

 9am to 8pm and Sunday from 10am to 7pm. Václavské nám. at Na Příkopě 1, Praha 1. ✆ **224-473-080.** www.bontonland.cz. Metro: Můstek.

PRAGUE AFTER DARK

For many Czechs, the best nighttime entertainment is boisterous discussion and world-class brew at a noisy pub. Visitors with a penchant to blend in with the locals can learn a lot about this part of the world with an evening at the corner *hospoda.* Many are fascinated just by a quiet stroll over the ancient city's cobblestones lit by the mellow lamps of Charles Bridge and Malá Strana. Others seek the dark caverns of a fine jazz club or the black light and Day-Glo of a hot dance club.

But Prague's longest entertainment tradition, of course, is classical music.

A safe bet is Mozart's ***Don Giovanni,*** usually presented about twice a month in its original 2-centuries-old home, the **Estates' Theater.** This production, which has modern accents, can be choppy, but the beautifully restored setting makes even a mediocre performance worth attending.

Serious music lovers are better off at one of the numerous performances of the **Czech Philharmonic** at the Rudolfinum, the **Prague Symphony Orchestra** at Obecní dům, or top **chamber ensembles** at salons and palaces around the city. A pipe organ concert heard while sitting in the pews of one of the city's baroque churches can be inspirational.

TICKETS Events rarely sell out far in advance, except for major nights during the Prague Spring Music Festival or a staging of *Don Giovanni* in the high season. To secure tickets before arriving, contact the travel bureau **Čedok** in Prague, at Na Příkopě 18, Praha 1 (✆ **224-197-640;** www.cedok.cz). You can also contact the Prague ticket agency **Ticketpro,** Václavské nám. 38, Praha 1 (✆ **296-329-999;** www.ticketpro.cz).

Large, centrally located ticket agencies are **Prague Tourist Center,** Rytířská 12, Praha 1 (✆ **296-333-333**), open daily from 9am to 8pm; and **Bohemia Ticket,** Na Příkopě 16, Praha 1 (✆ **224-215-031;** www.bohemiaticket.cz), open Monday to Friday from 10am to 7pm, Saturday from 10am to 5pm, and Sunday from 10am to 3pm.

The Performing Arts

While performances of Mozart's operas at the Estates' Theater are probably the visitor's best overall choices because of the setting, the **National Opera,** performing in the gold-crowned 19th-century National Theater, remains the country's best-loved company.

The **Prague State Opera (Státní opera Praha),** in the aging State Opera House near the top of Wenceslas Square, has reorganized after its 1992 split with the National Opera and now concentrates primarily on Italian classics, though a few Czech favorites are included each season.

Classical Music

This small capital boasts three full orchestras, yet all are financially strapped, so the repertoire tends to be conservative, with most concerts providing popular time-tested works. You can get information about all of them at the ticket agencies listed above. Tickets range from 100Kč to 600Kč ($6.65–$40/£4.15–£25) during the regular season and up to 2,000Kč ($133/£82) for the opening night of the **Prague Spring Festival.** You can find dozens of concerts by the full orchestras or chamber groups each month, but the pickings are thin in July and August, when the musicians are on their holiday.

Classical Concerts Around Town

When strolling, you'll undoubtedly pick up or be handed lots of leaflets advertising chamber concerts in churches, museums, and other venues. These recitals and choral arrangements usually have programs featuring a classical and baroque repertoire, with an emphasis on pieces by Czech composers. The quality varies, but the results are usually enjoyable. Tickets range from 100Kč to 350Kč ($6.65–$23/£4.15–£14) and can be purchased at the churches' entrances or sometimes from hotel concierges.

Landmark Theaters & Concert Halls

The Czech Philharmonic at Rudolfinum (Moments) Named for Prince Rudolf, the beautifully restored Rudolfinum has been one of the city's premier concert venues since it opened in the 19th century. The Rudolfinum's Small Hall mostly presents chamber concerts, while the larger, more celebrated Dvořák Hall is home to the Czech Philharmonic. Alšovo nábřeží 12, Praha 1. ✆ **227-059-227.** www.rudolfinum.cz. Metro: Staroměstská.

Estates' Theater (Stavovské divadlo) ★★ In a city full of spectacularly beautiful theaters, the massive pale-green Estates' still ranks as one of the most awesome. Built in 1783, this is the only 18th century theater in the world that's still in its original condition. The Estates' was home to the premiere of Mozart's *Don Giovanni,* which was conducted by the composer himself. Simultaneous English translation, transmitted via headphone, is available for plays staged here. Ovocný trh 1, Praha 1. ✆ **224-901-448.** www.nd.cz or www.mozart-praha.cz. Metro: Line A or B to Můstek.

National Theater (Národní divadlo) ★★ This neo-Renaissance building overlooking the Vltava River was completed in 1881. The theater was built to nurture the Czech National Revival—a grass-roots movement to replace the dominant German culture with that of native Czechs. To finance it, small collection boxes with signs promoting "the prosperity of a dignified national theater" were installed in public places. Almost immediately upon its completion, the building was wrecked by fire; it was rebuilt and opened in 1883 with the premiere of Bedřich Smetana's opera *Libuše.* Národní 2, Praha 1. ✆ **224-901-448.** www.nd.cz. Metro: Národní třída.

Prague Symphony Orchestra–Smetana Hall (Smetanova síň) ★ Named for the popular composer and fervent Czech nationalist Bedřich Smetana (1824–84), Smetana Hall is located in one of the world's most distinctive Art Nouveau buildings. Since its 1997 reopening after the building's painstaking reconstruction, the ornate and purely exhilarating Smetana Hall has hosted a series of top-notch events. In the Municipal House (Obecní dům), náměstí Republiky 5, Praha 1. ✆ **222-002-336.** www.fok.cz. Metro: Náměstí Republiky.

State Opera House (Státní opera) ★ First the "New German Theater" and then the "Smetana Theater," the State Opera was built in the 1880s for the purpose of staging Germanic music and drama. Based on a Viennese design, the Renaissance-style theater was rebuilt after suffering serious damage during the bombing of Prague in 1945. Over the years, the auditorium has hosted many great names, including Richard Wagner, Richard Strauss, and Gustav Mahler. Wilsonova 4, Praha 2. ✆ **224-227-266.** www.opera.cz. Metro: Muzeum.

The Club & Music Scene

Where else in the world but Prague can you boogie in a crumbling underground former cinema like the Roxy, then stop off for the herbal wonder liqueur Becherovka in a Romanesque stone cellar? A good source on the latest club spaces, raves, and parties is

Think (www.think.cz), a free monthly usually found at Radost (see below). Also try the Czech Techno site (www.techno.cz/party). Things don't really get started until after 11pm.

Rock & Dance Clubs

Duplex Club & Café ★★ Located right in the heart of Wenceslas Square, this is one of Prague's more exclusive clubs. From the roof terrace, visitors enjoy a magnificent view of the city's very center. Prague's best DJs perform inside the club itself, where cool lighting and high-tech sound set the right atmosphere. Yes, it was here that Mick Jagger had his 60th birthday party during the Stones' fourth concert in Prague. Prices are reasonable. It's open daily 10:30pm to 3am (Fri–Sat until 5am). Václavské nám. 21, Praha 1. ✆ **224-232-319.** www.duplex.cz. Admission 150Kč ($10/£6.20). Metro: Můstek.

Radost FX ★ Finds The Radost tries so hard to catch the retro 1960s and 1970s crowd that it has become a cartoon of itself, yet it remains popular with a mixed straight, gay, and model crowd. The rec-room interior of the ground-floor lounge is great for a chat and a drink. The series of downstairs rooms gets filled with rave and techno mixes. The crowd is very attractive and style-obsessed, and the bouncers have been known to boot those who don't look the part. Open daily from 10pm to 5am. Bělehradská 120, Praha 2. ✆ **224-254-776.** www.radostfx.cz. Cover 100Kč–250Kč ($6.65–$17/£4.15–£11). Metro: I. P. Pavlova or Náměstí Míru.

Roxy Another reincarnation of a dead cinema, the Roxy pushes the boundaries of bizarre in its dark, stark concrete dance hall down Dlouhá Street near Old Town Square. The balcony allows the artsy crowd to people-watch amid the candlelight. The club is ultra-deconstructionist. Acid jazz, funk, techno, salsa, and reggae are among the tunes on the playlist from the recorded or live acts. The Roxy is the longest late-night romp in town, open daily from 7pm to 5am. Dlouhá 33, Praha 1. ✆ **224-826-296.** www.roxy.cz. Cover 50Kč–250Kč ($3.35–$17/£2.10–£11). Metro: Náměstí Republiky.

Jazz

Prague attracts all the serious underground bands you'd expect in a famed capital of Bohemian living. International global fusion groups turn up, and so do some of the top talents of the jazz and funk world, especially during the Prague International Jazz Festival.

AghaRTA Jazz Centrum ★ Upscale by Czech standards, the AghaRTA regularly features some of the best music in town, from standard acoustic trios and quartets to Dixieland, funk, and fusion. Hot Line, the house band led by AghaRTA part-owner and drummer Michal Hejna, regularly takes the stage. Bands usually begin at 9pm. Open daily from 7pm to midnight. Železná 16, Praha 1. ✆ **222-211-275.** www.agharta.cz. Cover 100Kč ($6.65/£4.15). Metro: Můstek.

Metropolitan Jazz Club There never seems to be anyone under 30 in this sophisticated downstairs jazz club, fitted with ceramic-topped tables and red-velvet chairs. It's home to a house trio that plays several nights a month, and Dixieland and swing bands fill the rest of the calendar. Concerts begin at 9pm. Open Monday to Friday from 11am to 1am and Saturday and Sunday from 7pm to 1am. Jungmannova 14, Praha 1. ✆ **224-347-777.** Cover 100Kč ($6.65/£4.15). Metro: Můstek.

Pubs

Good pub brews and conversations are Prague's preferred late-evening entertainment. Unlike British, Irish, or German beer halls, a true Czech pub ignores accoutrements like cushy chairs and warm wooden paneling, and cuts straight to the chase—beer. While some Czech pubs do serve a hearty plate of food alongside the suds, it's the brew, uncommonly cheap at usually less than 30Kč ($2/£1.25) a pint, that keeps people lingering for hours.

U Fleků One of the original microbreweries dating from 1459, U Fleků is Prague's most famous beer hall, one of the few pubs that still serves only its own beer. It's a huge place with a maze of timber-lined rooms and a large, loud courtyard where an oompah band performs. The ornate, medieval-style wood ceilings and courtyard columns are charming but not very old. Tourists come here by the busload, but disparaging locals who don't like the German atmosphere avoid the place. The pub's sweet dark beer is excellent and not available anywhere else; however, the sausages and goulash are overcooked and overpriced. For musical entertainment at the Cabaret Hall (daily from 8pm) there is a cover charge of 100Kč ($6.65/£4.15). Open daily from 9am to 11pm. Křemencova 11, Praha 2. ✆ **224-934-019.** www.ufleku.cz. Metro: Národní třída.

U medvídků (At the Little Bears) This 5-centuries-old pub off Národní třída was the first in town to serve the original Budweiser, Budvar, on tap. It also serves typical Czech pub food, including *cmunda,* potato pancakes topped with sauerkraut and cured meat. It's smoky inside, but it's easier to breathe here than at most local pubs. Open daily from 11:30am to 11pm. Na Perštýně 7, Praha 1. ✆ **224-211-916.** www.umedvidku.cz. Metro: Národní třída.

The Bar Scene

The city has acquired a much wider selection of bars in recent years to complement its huge array of beer pubs. The competition has brought out a variety of watering holes—from country to French, from straight to gay to mixed—that match the offerings in most any major European capital.

Baráčnická rychta (Small Homeowners Association) In the heart of Malá Strana, just off Malostranské náměstí, you can find and taste a little bit of old-fashioned good times. Sample good Czech food with Czech beer. Open daily noon until 1am. Tržiště 23, Praha 1. ✆ **257-532-461.** www.baracnickarychta.cz. Metro: Malostranská.

Chateau/Enfer Rouge Hidden on a small Old Town back street, this loud and lively ground-floor place has twin bars, plank floors, and a good sound system playing contemporary rock. It sells four types of beer on tap and features regular drink specials. It's busy and fun—if you avoid the headache-inducing concoctions from the frozen drink machine. Open Monday to Thursday noon to 3am, Friday noon to 4pm, Saturday 4pm to 4am, Sunday 4pm to 2am. Jakubská 2, Praha 1. ✆ **222-316-328.** www.chateaurouge.cz. Metro: Náměstí Republiky.

Jáma (the Hollow) ★ This place has been popular for several postrevolutionary years. It feels a lot like an American college pub; Czech and international food is served and Czech beer is on tap. Open daily from 11am to 1am. V Jámě 7, Praha 1. ✆ **224-222-383.** www.jamapub.cz. Metro: Můstek.

Není Pivo Jako Pivo: There's No Beer Like Beer

This seemingly absurd local proverb makes sense when you first taste the cold golden nectar *(pivo)* from its source and realize that you've never really had beer before. While Czechs on the whole aren't religious, *pivo* still elicits a piety unseen in many orthodox countries. The golden Pilsner variety that accounts for most of the beer consumed around the world was born here and has inspired some of the country's most popular fiction, films, poetry, and prayers.

For many Czechs, the corner beer hall (*hospoda* or *pivnice*) is a social and cultural center. Regulars in these smoke-encrusted caves drink beer as lifeblood and seem ill at ease when a foreigner takes their favorite table or disrupts their daily routine. For those wanting to sample the rich, aromatic taste of Czech lagers without ingesting waves of nicotine, dozens of more ventilated pubs and restaurants have emerged since the Velvet Revolution. Alas, the suds at these spots often cost as much as five times more than those in the standard *hospoda.*

While always informal, Czech pubs observe their own unwritten code of etiquette:

- Large tables are usually shared with strangers.
- When sitting, you should first ask *"Je tu volno?"* ("Is this place taken?"—yeh *two* vohl-no). If it's not, put a cardboard coaster down in front of you to show that you want a beer.
- Don't wave for a waitperson—it'll only delay the process when he or she sees you.
- When the waitperson does finally arrive and sees the coaster in front of you, simply nod or hold up fingers for the number of beers you want for you and your companions.
- If there's a choice, it's usually between size—*malé* (mah-*lay*) is small, *velké* (vel-*kay*) is large—or type—*světlé* (svyet-*lay*) is light, *černé* (cher-*nay*) is dark.
- The waitperson will make pencil marks on a white slip of paper that remains on your table.
- If your waitperson ever comes back for a second round, order enough for the rest of your stay and ask to pay. When he or she returns, say, *"Zaplatíme"* ("We'll pay," zah-plah-*tee*-meh) . . . you might not see him or her again for a long time.

According to brewing industry studies, Czechs drink more beer per capita than any other people. The average Czech downs 320 pints of brew each year; the average American drinks about 190. Of course, a Czech *hospoda* regular

Gay & Lesbian Clubs

Prague's small gay and lesbian community is growing in its openness and its choices for nightclubs and entertainment. Go to http://prague.gayguide.net for more information. You should also see the review for **Radost FX Café** on p. 235.

will drink the year's average for a family of six. Pub regulars do not wonder why the Czech national anthem is a song that translates as "Where Is My Home?"

Several widely held Czech superstitions are connected with drinking beer. One says that you should never pour a different kind of beer in a mug holding the remnants of another brew. Bad luck is sure to follow. Some believe that the toast—usually *"Na zdraví!"* ("To your health!")—is negated if anyone fails to clink his or her mug with any of the others at your table and then slams the mug on the table before taking the first chug.

Czech beer comes in various degrees of concentration, usually marked on the label or menu. This is not the amount of alcohol, though the higher degree does carry a higher alcohol content. The standard premium 12-degree brew contains about 5% alcohol, though each label varies. If you want something a little lighter on the head, try a 10-degree, with 3.5% to 4% alcohol content.

The never-ending debate over which Czech beer is best rages on, but here are the top contenders, all readily available in Prague. (Each pub or restaurant will usually flaunt its choice on the front of the building.)

- **Pilsner Urquell:** The original Pilsner lager. A bit bitter but with a smooth texture that comes, the locals say, from the softer alkaline waters that flow under Pilsen. Urquell is mostly packaged for export and often seen at beer boutiques across the Atlantic.
- **Budvar:** The original "Budweiser," this semisweet lager hails from České Budějovice, a town also known by its German name, Budweis. The clash with U.S. giant Anheuser Busch over the "Budweiser" trademark kept the American giant from selling Bud in much of Europe for years. There's little similarity in the taste of the two—you decide. Busch wanted a stake in the Budvar brewery, but the Czech government balked at a deal in 1996.
- **Staropramen:** The flagship of Prague's home brewery is a solid choice and is easiest to find in the capital. Now that Britain's Bass owns Staropramen, they're marketing a hybrid called Velvet, a cross between a Czech lager and an Irish ale. It's worth a try.
- **Kozel:** This is a favorite with the American expat community, with a distinctive namesake goat on the label. It has a spicy taste and full body. Light beer it is not.
- **Krušovice:** From a tiny brewery in the cradle of the western hop-growing region, this brew, commissioned by Rudolf II 4 centuries ago, used to be hard to find in Prague, but no longer. Lighter but not fizzy, it has just a hint of bitterness.

Friends Its atmosphere of an old bar is combined here with a comfortable setting, a super sound and video projection system, new dance floor, and private lounge. Free Wi-Fi Internet connection available. Open Sunday to Thursday 6pm to 3am, Friday and Saturday 6pm to 5am. DJ parties start at 10pm Wednesday through Saturday. Bartolomějská 11, Praha 1. ✆ **226-211-920.** Metro Národní třída.

Tingl Tangl A popular nightclub attracting a mixed gay, straight, foreign, and local crowd near Charles Bridge, Tingl Tangl offers the most extensive cabaret shows in Old Town, with comical drag queens featured during the weekend and Wednesday shows. Open daily from 8pm to 5am. Karolíny Světlé 12, Praha 1. ✆ **224-238-278.** Cover charges 250Kč ($17/£11) for show nights. Metro: Národní třída.

4 BOHEMIA

Though Bohemia has historically been undivided, there are clear-cut distinctions in the region's geography that make going from town to town easier if you "divide" it into sections. After exploring Prague, decide which area you'd like to see first and then plan accordingly.

Once the religious hotbed of the country, south Bohemia (where you'll find Český Krumolov) was a focal point of the Hussite wars that eventually ravaged many of its towns and villages. Though the days of war took their toll, the region still features fine examples of architecture from every era. West Bohemia (see Karlovy Vary below), home to the country's spa towns, is one of the few places where a full-blown tourist infrastructure is already in place.

KARLOVY VARY (CARLSBAD) ★

120km (74 miles) W of Prague

The discovery of Karlovy Vary (Carlsbad) by Charles IV reads like a 14th-century episode of the TV show *The Beverly Hillbillies.* According to local lore, the king was out huntin' for some food when up from the ground came a-bubblin' water (though discovered by his dogs and not an errant gunshot). Knowing a good thing when he saw it, Charles immediately set to work building a small castle in the area, naming the town that evolved around it Karlovy Vary, which translates as "Charles's Boiling Place." The first spa buildings were built in 1522, and before long, notables like Albrecht of Wallenstein, Peter the Great, and later Bach, Beethoven, Freud, and Marx all came to Karlovy Vary for a holiday retreat.

After World War II, Eastern bloc travelers discovered the town, and Karlovy Vary became a destination for the proletariat. On doctors' orders, most workers would enjoy regular stays of 2 or 3 weeks, letting the mineral waters ranging from 110° to 162°F (43°–72°C) from the town's 12 springs heal their tired and broken bodies. Even now, a large number of spa guests are here by a doctor's prescription.

Today, some 150,000 people, both traditional clientele and newer patrons, travel to the spa resort every year to sip, bathe, and frolic, though most enjoy the "13th spring" (actually a hearty herb-and-mineral liqueur called Becherovka) as much as—if not more than—the 12 nonalcoholic versions. Czechs will tell you that all have medical benefits.

Getting There

At all costs, avoid the train from Prague, which takes over 4 hours on a circuitous route. If you're arriving from another direction, Karlovy Vary's main train station is connected to the town center by bus no. 11.

Taking a bus to Karlovy Vary is much more convenient. Frequent express **buses** make it from Prague's Florenc bus station in 2¼ hours at a cost of 140Kč ($9.35/£5.80). From Karlovy Vary's Dolní nádraží (bus station) take a 10-minute walk or local bus no. 4 into

Karlovy Vary's spa center. Note that you must have a ticket to board local transport. You can buy tickets for 12Kč (80¢/50p) at the bus station stop, or from the bus driver, which will then cost you 16Kč ($1/60p). For timetable information go to www.jizdnirady.cz.

The nearly 2-hour **drive** from Prague to Karlovy Vary can be very busy and dangerous due to undisciplined Czech drivers. If you're going by car, take Hwy. E48 from the western end of Prague and follow it straight through to Karlovy Vary.

Visitor Information

Infocentrum města Karlovy Vary is located near the main Mlýnská kolonáda, on Lázeňská 1 (✆ **355-321-176**). It's open Monday to Friday from 9am to 7pm, and Saturday and Sunday from 10am to 6pm. Alternatively, you'll find information on www.karlovyvary.cz.

Where to Stay

Some of the town's major spa hotels accommodate only those who are paying for complete treatment, unless for some reason their occupancy rates are particularly low. The hotels I've listed below accept guests for stays of any length.

Expensive

Grandhotel Pupp ★★ Well known as one of Karlovy Vary's best hotels, the Pupp, built in 1701, is also one of Europe's oldest hotels. Its public areas boast the expected splendor and charm, as do the renovated guest rooms. The best ones tend to be those facing the town center and are located on the upper floors; these have good views and sturdy wooden furniture. Some rooms have amenities such as air-conditioning, television, minibar, and safe, though not all do. The hotel also has a stylish casino (midnight–4am).

Mírové nám. 2, 360 91, Karlovy Vary. ✆ **353-109-630.** Fax 353-226-638. www.pupp.cz. 110 units. Note that there are no rates in local currency; hotel charges at a converted rate upon checkout. $516 (£319) double deluxe; from $666 (£413) suite; $2,486 (£1,541) presidential apt. Rates include breakfast. AE, DC, MC, V. Valet parking. **Amenities:** 4 restaurants; bar; cafe; pool; golf course; tennis courts; health club; limousine/taxi service; salon; room service (6am–midnight); same-day laundry; casino.

Moderate

Hotel Embassy ★ On the riverbank across from the Pupp, the Embassy has well-appointed rooms, many with an early-20th-century motif. Set in a historic house, the rooms are medium size with medium-size bathrooms. The staff here really helps make this hotel worthy of consideration, as does the proximity to the pub, which serves up some of the best goulash and beer in the city.

Nová Louka 21, 360 01 Karlovy Vary. ✆ **353-221-161.** Fax 353-223-146. www.embassy.cz. 20 units. 3,130Kč ($208/£129) double; 3,788Kč ($252/£156) suite. AE, MC, V. **Amenities:** Pub; lobby bar; indoor golf; pool table. *In room:* TV, minibar, safe.

Inexpensive

Hotel Astoria In the heart of the historic town, the restored Astoria mainly caters to spa guests but, unlike many of its competitors, it is big enough to usually have several rooms available for nontreatment visitors. The staff can be a little gruff at times, but the rooms are big, with satellite TV an added bonus. The restaurant serves standard Czech fare.

Vřídelní 92, 360 01 Karlovy Vary. ✆ **353-335-111.** Fax 353-224-368. www.astoria-spa.cz. 100 units. Note that there are no rates in local currency; hotel charges at a converted rate upon checkout. $80 (£50) double. AE, MC, V. **Amenities:** Restaurant. *In room:* TV, fridge.

Spa Cures & Treatments

Most visitors to Karlovy Vary come for a spa treatment, a therapy that lasts 1 to 3 weeks. After consulting with a spa physician, you're given a specific regimen of activities that may include mineral baths, massages, waxings, mudpacks, electrotherapy, and pure oxygen inhalation. After spending the morning at a spa or sanatorium, you're usually directed to walk the paths of the town's surrounding forest.

The common denominator of all the cures is an ample daily dose of hot mineral water, which bubbles up from 12 springs. This water definitely has a distinct odor and taste. You'll see people chugging it down, but it doesn't necessarily taste very good. Some thermal springs actually taste and smell like rotten eggs. You may want to take a small sip at first. Do keep in mind that the waters are used to treat internal disorders, so the minerals may cleanse the body thoroughly—in other words, they can cause diarrhea.

You'll also notice that almost everyone in town seems to be carrying "the cup." This funny-looking cup is basically a mug with a built-in straw running through the handle. Young and old alike parade around with their mugs, filling and refilling them at each thermal water tap. You can buy these mugs everywhere for as little as 60Kč ($4/£2.40) or as much as 230Kč ($15/£9.30); they make a quirky souvenir. ***But be warned:*** None of the mugs can make the warmer hot springs taste any better.

The minimum spa treatment lasts 1 week and must be arranged in advance. A spa treatment package traditionally includes room, full board, and complete therapy regimen; the cost varies from about $56 to $140 (£35–£87) per person per day, depending on season and facilities. Rates are highest from May to September and lowest from November to February.

Where to Dine

Expensive

Embassy Restaurant CZECH/CONTINENTAL On the ground floor of the Embassy Hotel, this is one of the oldest restaurants in town. It offers an intimate dining room with historic interior. Here you'll find many traditional Czech dishes with slight twists that make them interesting. The grilled loin of pork covered with a light, creamy, green-pepper sauce makes a nice change from the regular roast pork served by most Czech restaurants.

Nová Louka 21. © **353-221-161.** Reservations recommended. Soups 55Kč–85Kč ($3.65–$5.65/£2.25–£3.50); main courses 175Kč–985Kč ($12–$65/£7.45–£40). AE, V. Daily 11am–11pm.

Moderate

Hospoda U Švejka CZECH This addition to the pub scene plays on the tried-and-true touristy *Good Soldier Švejk* theme. Luckily, the tourist trap goes no further, and once inside, you find a refreshingly unsmoky though thoroughly Czech atmosphere. Locals and tourists alike rub elbows while throwing back some fine lager for 55Kč ($3.35/£2.10) per half liter, and standard pub favorites such as goulash and beef tenderloin in cream sauce.

For information and reservations in Prague, contact **Čedok,** at Na Příkopě 18, and also at Václavské nám. 53, Praha 1 (✆ **224-197-632;** fax 224-213-786; www.cedok.cz). Many hotels also provide spa and health treatments, so ask when you book your room. Most will happily arrange a treatment if they don't provide them directly.

If you're coming for just a day or two, you can experience the waters on an "outpatient" basis. The largest balneological complex in town (and in the Czech Republic) is the **Alžbětiny Lázně-Lázně V,** Smetanovy sady 1145/1 (✆ **353-222-536;** www.spa5.cz). On their menu are all kinds of treatments, including water cures, massages, a hot-air bath, a steam bath, a whirlpool, and a pearl bath, as well as use of their swimming pool. You can choose packages of different procedures between 90Kč and 600Kč ($6–$40/£3.70–£25). It's open Monday to Friday 8am to 3pm for spa treatments; the pool is open Monday to Friday 9am to noon and 1 to 9pm, Saturday 9am to 9pm, and Sunday from 9am to 6pm.

The **Sanatorium Baths III,** Mlýnské nábřeží 7 (✆ **353-225-641**), welcomes day-trippers with mineral baths, massages, saunas, and a cold pool. It's open Monday to Friday 7am to 2pm for spa treatments; the swimming pool and sauna are open Monday to Friday 3 to 6pm and Saturday 1 to 5pm.

The Castle Bath (Zámecké Lázně), Zámecký vrch (✆ **353-222-649**), is a new spa and wellness house located in a reconstructed site at the foot of the Castle Tower (Zámecká věž) in the old city center. Visitors are welcome Monday to Friday from 7:30am to 7:30pm and Saturday to Sunday 8:30am to 7:30pm to enjoy individual spa treatments. A single entry for 2 to 4 hours costs between $30 and $76 (£19–£47).

Stará Louka 10. ✆ **353-232-276.** Soups 35Kč ($2.35/£1.45); main courses 135Kč–319Kč ($9–$21/£5.60–£13). AE, MC, V. Daily 11am–10pm.

Inexpensive

Cafe Eléfant COFFEE/DESSERT Who needs to travel all the way to Vienna? Since this is a cafe in the true sense of the word, all you'll find are coffee, tea, alcoholic and nonalcoholic drinks, desserts, and enough ambience to satisfy the hordes of Germans who flock to this landmark.

Stará Louka 32. ✆ **353-223-406.** Cakes and desserts 40Kč–120Kč ($2.65–$8/£1.65–£4.95). AE, MC, V. Daily 10am–10pm.

Shopping

Crystal and porcelain are Karlovy Vary's other claims to fame. Dozens of shops throughout town sell everything from plates to chandeliers.

Ludvík Moser founded his first glassware shop in 1857 and became one of this country's foremost names in glass. You can visit the **Moser Factory,** kapitána Jaroše 19 (✆ **353-449-455;** www.moser-glass.com; bus 1, 10, or 22), just west of the town center. Its glass museum is open Monday to Friday 8am to 5:30pm and Saturday 9am to 3pm.

There's also a **Moser Store,** on Tržiště 7 (✆ **353-235-303**), right in the heart of new town; it's open Monday through Friday from 10am to 7pm, Saturday and Sunday 10am until 6pm). Dozens of other smaller shops also sell the famed glass and are as easy to find in the Old Town as spring water.

ČESKÝ KRUMLOV ★★★

167km (104 miles) S of Prague

If you have time on your visit to the Czech Republic for only one excursion, seriously consider making it **Český Krumlov.** One of Bohemia's prettiest towns, Krumlov is a living gallery of elegant Renaissance-era buildings housing charming cafes, pubs, restaurants, shops, and galleries. In 1992, UNESCO named Český Krumlov a World Heritage Site for its historical importance and physical beauty.

Getting There

From Prague, it's a 2-hour drive down Hwy. 3 through Tábor.

The only way to reach Český Krumlov by train from Prague is via České Budějovice, a slow ride that deposits you at a station relatively far from the town center (trip time: 3 hr., 50 min.). Six trains leave daily from Prague's Hlavní nádraží; the fare is 336Kč ($22/£14) first class, 224Kč ($15/£9.30) second class. If you are already in České Budějovice and you want to make a trip to Krumlov, several trains connect these two cities throughout the day. The trip takes about 57 minutes and costs 46Kč ($3/£1.85). For timetables, go to **www.jizdnirady.cz.**

The nearly 3-hour **bus** ride from Prague usually involves a transfer in České Budějovice. The fare is 136Kč ($9/£5.60), and the bus station in Český Krumlov is a 15-minute walk from the town's main square.

Visitor Information

Right on the main square, the **Information Centrum,** náměstí Svornosti 2, 381 01 Český Krumlov (✆ **380-704-622;** fax 380-704-619; www.ckrumlov.cz), provides a complete array of services, from booking accommodations to reserving tickets for events, as well as a phone and Internet service. It's open daily, in July and August from 9am to 8pm; in June and September from 9am to 7pm; in April, May, and October from 9am to 6pm; and from November to March from 9am to 5pm.

Exploring the Chateau

Reputedly the second-largest castle in Bohemia (after Prague Castle), **Český Krumlov Château** was constructed in the 13th century as part of a private estate. Throughout the ages, it has been passed on to a variety of private owners, including the Rožmberk family, Bohemia's largest landholders, and the Schwarzenbergs, the Bohemian equivalent of the Hilton family.

There are three guided tours. Tour I begins in the rococo **Chapel of St. George,** and continues through the portrait-packed **Renaissance Rooms,** and the **Schwarzenberg Baroque Suite,** outfitted with ornate furnishings that include Flemish wall tapestries, European paintings, and also the extravagant 17th-century **Golden Carriage.** Tour II includes the **Schwarzenberg portrait gallery** as well as their 19th-century suite. Tour III presents Castle's **Baroque Theater.** Tours last 1 hour and depart frequently. Most are in Czech or German, however. If you want an English-language tour, arrange it ahead of time (✆ **380-725-110;** tourist.service@unios.cz). The guided tours cost 160Kč ($11/£6.80) adults, 80Kč ($5.35/£3.30) students (Tour I); 140Kč ($9.35/£5.80) adults and 70Kč ($4.65/£2.90) students (Tour II); 180Kč ($12/£7.45) adults, 90Kč ($6/£3.70) students (Tour III). The tickets are sold separately. The castle hours are from Tuesday to Sunday: June to August 9am to 6pm; and April, May, September, and October 9am to 5pm. The last entrance is 1 hour before closing.

Once past the main castle building, you can see one of the more stunning views of Český Krumlov from **Most Na Plášti,** a walkway that doubles as a belvedere to the Inner Town. Even farther up the hill lie the castle's riding school and gardens.

Where to Stay

With the rise of free enterprise after the fall of Communism, many hotels have sprouted up or are getting a "new" old look. PENSION and ZIMMER FREI signs line Horní and Rooseveltova streets and offer some of the best values in town. For a comprehensive list of area hotels and help with bookings, call or write to the Information Centrum listed above in "Visitor Information."

Expensive

Hotel Růže (Rose Hotel) Once a Jesuit seminary, this stunning Italian Renaissance building has been turned into a well-appointed hotel. Comfortable in a big-city kind of way, it's packed with amenities and is one of the top places to stay in Český Krumlov. The rooms are clean and spacious, but the promise of a Renaissance stay dissipates quickly. For families or large groups, the larger suites, which have eight beds, provide good value. For the adventurous or those with the right haircut, try one of the cells, where the Jesuit monks used to stay.

Horní 154, 381 01 Český Krumlov. ✆ **380-772-100.** Fax 380-713-146. www.hotelruze.cz. 71 units. 3,800Kč–7,100Kč ($253–$473/£157–£293) double; 5,300Kč–9,600Kč ($353–$640/£219–£397) suite. Rates include breakfast. AE, MC, V. **Amenities:** Restaurant; bar; pool; health club. *In room:* TV, minibar, hair dryer.

Inexpensive

Pension Anna Kids Along "pension alley," this is a comfortable and rustic place. What makes this spot a favorite are the friendly management and homey feeling you get as you walk up to your room. Forget hotels—this is the kind of place where you can relax. The owners even let you buy drinks and snacks at the bar downstairs and take them to your room. The suites, with four beds and a living room, are great for families and groups.

Rooseveltova 41, 381 01 Český Krumlov. ✆/fax **380-711-692.** www.pensionanna.euweb.cz. 8 units. 1,250Kč ($83/£51) double; 1,550Kč–2,250Kč ($103–$150/£64–£93) suite. Rates include breakfast. No credit cards. **Amenities:** Bar. *In room:* TV.

Pension Na louži ★ Smack-dab in the heart of the Inner Town, the small Na louži, decorated with early-20th-century wooden furniture, is a charming change from many of the bigger, bland rooms found in nearby hotels. If the person at reception starts mentioning names without apparent reason, don't worry; it's not a language problem. Management has given the rooms human names instead of numbers. The only drawback is that the beds (maybe the people for whom the rooms were named were all short) can be a little short for those over 2m (6 ft.).

Kájovská 66, 381 01 Český Krumlov. ✆/fax **380-711-280.** www.nalouzi.cz. 7 units. 1,350Kč ($90/£56) double; 1,700Kč ($113/£70) triple; 2,300Kč ($153/£95) suite. No credit cards. **Amenities:** Restaurant/bar.

Where to Dine

Moderate

Krumlovský mlýn CZECH This restored mill house, which history dates back to the 16th century, is a restaurant, antiques shop, and exhibition in one. Large wooden tables and benches are part of the thematic restaurant on the ground floor, where a traditional Czech menu is served. The terrace on the bank of the Vltava River above the water channel here is a super place to sit in the summer.

Široká 80. ✆ **380-712-838.** www.krumlovskymlyn.cz. Main courses 150Kč–425Kč ($10–$28/£6.20–£17). No credit cards. Daily 10am–10pm.

Inexpensive

Hospoda Na louži CZECH The large wooden tables encourage you to get to know your neighbors at this Inner Town pub, located in a 15th-century house. The atmosphere is fun and the food above average. If no table is available, stand and have a drink; tables turn over pretty quickly, and the staff is accommodating. In summer, the terrace seats only six, so dash over if a seat empties.

Kájovská 66. ✆ **380-711-280.** Main courses 58Kč–158Kč ($3.85–$11/£2.40–£6.80). No credit cards. Mon–Sat 10am–11pm; Sun 10am–10pm.

ČESKÉ BUDĚJOVICE

147km (91 miles) S of Prague

This fortress town was born in 1265, when Otakar II decided that the intersection of the Vltava and Malše rivers would be the site of a bastion to protect the approaches to southern Bohemia.

Today, České Budějovice, the hometown of the original Budweiser brand beer, is now more a bastion for the beer drinker than a protector of Bohemia.

Getting There

If you're **driving,** leave Prague to the south via the main D1 expressway and take the cutoff for Hwy. E55, which runs straight to České Budějovice. The trip takes about 1½ hours.

Daily express **trains** from Prague make the trip to České Budějovice in about 2½ hours. The fare is 306Kč ($20/£12) first class or 204Kč ($14/£8.70) second class. Several express **buses** run from Prague's Florenc station each day and take 2½ hours; tickets cost 120Kč ($8/£4.95).

Visitor Information

Tourist Infocentrum, náměstí Přemysla Otakara II. 2 (✆ **386-801-414**), provides maps and guidebooks and finds lodging. It is open Monday to Friday 8:30am to 6pm, Saturday until 5pm, and Sunday 10am to 4pm. In winter it is open Monday and Wednesday 9am to 5pm; Tuesday, Thursday, Friday 9am to 4pm; and Saturday 9am to 1pm. There is a good website about the city; go to **www.c-budejovice.cz** for information.

Exploring the Town

You can comfortably see České Budějovice in a day. At its center is one of central Europe's largest squares, the cobblestone **náměstí Přemysla Otakara II**—it may actually be too large, as many of the buildings tend to get lost in all the open space. The square contains the ornate **Fountain of Sampson,** an 18th-century water well that was once the town's principal water supply, plus a mishmash of baroque and Renaissance buildings.

Moments A Renaissance Pub Endures

Most visitors don't venture far enough into the castle to experience this place during the day or night. That's their loss, for I've experienced one of my finest dining experiences in the Czech Republic at **Krčma Markéta,** Zámek 62 (✆ **380-711-453**).

To get here, walk all the way up the hill through the castle, past the Horní Hrad (Upper Castle) and past the Zámecké divadlo (Castle Theater). Walk through the raised walkway and into the Zámecká zahrada (Castle Garden), where you'll eventually find this Renaissance pub.

When you go inside, you'll feel as if you've left this century. Unfortunately, one of the pub's main draws, former owner Robin Kratochvíl, is gone. The new owners have traded in Kratochvíl's big-enough-to-turn-a-Volkswagen tongs for a set of racks where the meat cooks; they brought in sets of plates, as opposed to the original wooden blocks on which food used to be served; and there is even a menu now. But still go up to the fire and see what's roasting; usually there's a wide variety of meats, including succulent pork cutlets, rabbit, chicken, and pork knees, a Czech delicacy. When the plate comes, don't wait for the vegetables—there aren't any (though vegetarian dishes are available). Before the night is over, you'll probably find yourself talking to someone else at the pub's large wooden tables.

Krčma Markéta is open April to October Tuesday to Sunday from 6 to 11pm, and main courses cost 75Kč to 155Kč ($5–$10/£3.10–£6.20).

One block northwest of the square is the **Black Tower (Černá věž),** which you can see from almost every point in the city. Consequently, its 360 steps are worth the climb to get a bird's-eye view in all directions. The most famous symbol of České Budějovice, this 70m-tall (236-ft.) 16th-century tower was built as a belfry for the adjacent **St. Nicholas Church.** It is open Tuesday to Sunday (daily July–Aug) from 10am to 6pm; admission is 20Kč ($1.35/85p).

Where to Stay

Hotel Bohemia The Bohemia really isn't a hotel but a small pension in the city center, as you'll discover when you walk into the lobby and think that you've stepped into someone's house. The staff makes you feel like one of the family, with their attentive service, and the rooms are pleasant despite being a little small.

Hradební 20, 370 01 České Budějovice. ✆/fax **386-360-691.** 18 units. 1,790Kč ($119/£74) double. AE, MC, V. **Amenities:** Restaurant. *In room:* TV, minibar.

Where to Dine

U královské pečeti (at the Royal Seal) ★ CZECH This typical Czech-style pub serves up hearty food at reasonable prices. It offers a tasty goulash as well as *svíčková* or game dishes. Located in the Hotel Malý Pivovar, this is a very good choice for a Czech food experience.

In the Hotel Malý Pivovar, ulice Karla IV. 8–10. ✆ **386-360-471.** Soups 30Kč ($2/£1.25); main courses 65Kč–290Kč ($4.30–$19/£2.65–£12). AE, DC, MC, V. Daily 10am–11pm.

Keeping Up with the Schwarzenbergs: Visiting a 141-Room English Castle

Only 8km (5 miles) north of České Budějovice lies **Hluboká nad Vltavou ★★** (✆ **387-843-911;** www.zamekhluboka.cz). Built in the 13th century, this castle has undergone many face-lifts over the years, but none that left as lasting an impression as those ordered by the Schwarzenberg family. As a sign of the region's growing wealth and importance in the mid–19th century, the Schwarzenbergs remodeled the 141-room castle in the neo-Gothic style of England's Windsor Castle. No expense was spared in the quest for opulence. The Schwarzenbergs removed the impressive wooden ceiling from their residence at Český Krumlov and reinstalled it in the large dining room. Other rooms are equally garish in their appointments, making a guided tour worth the time, even though only about a third of the rooms are open to the public.

The castle is open daily May to August from 9am to 5pm (last tour at 4pm); April, September, and October, hours are Tuesday to Sunday from 9am to 4:30pm (last tour at 3pm). There is a lunch break between noon and 12:30pm. Tours in English cost 160Kč ($11/£6.80) adults, 80Kč ($5.35/£3.30) students.

If you're driving to Hluboká from České Budějovice, take Hwy. E49 north and then Hwy. 105 just after leaving the outskirts of České Budějovice.

The town's new **Information Center** at Masarykova 35 (✆ **387-966-164;** www.hluboka.cz) will provide you with maps, souvenirs, and answers to your questions.

PLZEŇ (PILSEN)

88km (55 miles) SW of Prague

"Zde se narodilo pivo." The phrase ("the birthplace of beer") greets you at almost every turn. And they aren't kidding. Some 400 years ago, a group of men formed Plzeň's first beer-drinking guild, and today beer is probably the only reason you'll want to stop at this otherwise industrial town. Unfortunately for the town, its prosperity and architecture were ravaged during World War II, and few buildings were left untouched. The main square, náměstí Republiky, is worth a look, but after that there's not much to see.

Getting There

A fast **train** from Prague whisks travelers to Plzeň in just under 2 hours without you having to witness the mayhem caused by Czech drivers. Trains between the two cities are just as plentiful and fit most every schedule. The train costs 210Kč ($14/£8.70) first class or 140Kč ($9.35/£5.80) second class.

It is an easy 45-minute cruise by **car** on the new Hwy. D5, which leaves Prague from the west.

Visitor Information

Trying to be as visitor-friendly as possible, the **City Information Center Plzeň,** náměstí Republiky 41, 301 16 Plzeň (✆ **378-035-330;** fax 378-035-332; www.plzen-city.cz), is packed with literature to answer your questions. It is open daily 9am to 6pm.

Fun Facts Plzeň's Claim to Fame

Founded in 1295 by Václav II, Plzeň was and remains western Bohemia's administrative center. King Václav's real gift to the town, however, wasn't making it an administrative nerve center, but granting it brewing rights. So more than 200 microbreweries popped up, one in almost every street-corner basement. Realizing that the brews they were drinking had become mostly inferior by the late 1830s, rebellious beer drinkers demanded quality, forcing the brewers to try harder. "Give us what we want in Plzeň, good and cheap beer!" became the battle cry. In 1842, the brewers combined their expertise to produce a superior brew through what became known as the Pilsner brewing method. If you don't believe it, look in your refrigerator. Most likely, the best beer in there has written somewhere on its label "Pilsner brewed."

Touring the Beer Shrines

Pilsner Brewery (Plzeňské Pivovary), at U Prazdroje 7, actually comprises several breweries, pumping out brands like Pilsner Urquell and Gambrinus, the most widely consumed beer in the Czech Republic. The 1-hour tour of the factory (which has barely changed since its creation) includes a 15-minute film and visits to the fermentation cellars and brewing rooms. The tour starts at 12:30, 2, and 4pm daily. Tours cost 130Kč ($8.65/£5.40); the price includes a dozen beer-oriented postcards and a tasting of freshly brewed beer. (For details on other tours, call © **377-062-888** or log onto www.prazdroj.cz, or e-mail visits@pilsner.sabmiller.com.)

If you didn't get your fill of beer facts at the brewery, the **Beer Museum (Pivovarské muzeum)** © **377-235-574;** www.prazdroj.cz) is 1 block away on Veleslavínova 6. Inside this former 15th-century house, you'll learn everything there is to know about beer but were afraid to ask. Admission is 80Kč ($5.33/£3.30), and hours are daily 10am to 6pm (to 5pm Jan–Mar).

Where to Stay

Hotel Central As you look around the historically beautiful old town square, one thing stands out: the Hotel Central. This rather sterile building is across from St. Bartholomew's Church. The surly staff notwithstanding, the hotel is good and surprisingly quiet despite its central location. Ask for one of the rooms facing east; they have a nice view of the church as the sun rises.

Náměstí Republiky 33, 301 00 Plzeň. © **377-226-757.** Fax 377-226-064. www.central-hotel.cz. 77 units. 2,200Kč–2,800Kč ($146–$186/£91–£115) double. AE, MC, V. **Amenities:** Restaurant; cafe; bar; exercise room; sauna; solarium. *In room:* TV, minibar, safe.

Where to Dine

Pilsner Urquell Restaurant CZECH In the same building that houses the brewery's management, this pub has remained true to those who supply it with beverages by cooking hearty, basic Czech meals, though it is a little pricier than Na Spilce across the way. Because the brewery workers make up the majority of customers here, don't expect a multilingual menu or staff.

U Prazdroje 1 (just outside the brewery gates). ✆ **377-235-608.** Soups 25Kč ($1.65/£1); main courses 65Kč–219Kč ($4.35–$15/£2.70–£9.30). AE, MC, V. Mon–Sat 10am–10pm.

5 MORAVIA

Having seen its fair share of history, Moravia conjures up a different image than Bohemia: Here, too, castles and picture-perfect town squares exist. But the people and slower lifestyle set Moravia apart.

BRNO: THE REGION'S CAPITAL

224km (139 miles) SE of Prague; 128km (79 miles) N of Vienna

Since Brno came of age in the 19th century on the back of its textile industry, the city's architecture, for the most part, lacks the Renaissance facades and meandering alleys of other towns. Indeed, the main square, náměstí Svoboda, bears this out. But spend a day or two here, and the beauty of the old city center will become apparent.

Getting There

Driving to Brno is a trade-off. Take the E50—also named the D1—freeway that leads from the south of Prague all the way. The drive shouldn't take more than 2 hours. But the scenery is little more than one roadside stop after another.

Brno is the focal point for **train** travel in Moravia and most points east, making it an easy 2¾-hour trip from Prague. **Trains** leave almost every hour; the majority leave from Hlavní nádraží (Main Station). The fare is 243Kč ($16/£9.90) first class or 160Kč ($11/£6.80) second class. **Buses** leave Prague's Florenc station to Brno every hour. The trip takes 2½ hours and costs 140Kč ($9.35/£5.80).

Visitor Information

The **Turistické Informační Centrum (TIC),** Radnická 8, Brno (✆ **542-211-090;** www.ticbrno.cz), provides a plethora of information on accommodations, plus what's on in Brno and how to see it. It's open Monday to Friday from 9am to 6pm, Saturday and Sunday 9am to 5:30pm.

Strolling Around Brno

The Old Town holds most of the attractions you'll want to see, so it's probably best to start at the former seat of government, the Old Town Hall on Radnická 8. Built in the 13th century, the **Old Town Hall** is a hodgepodge of styles—Gothic, Renaissance, and baroque elements melding together, demonstrating Brno's development through the ages.

Just south of the Old Town Hall is **Cabbage Market (Zelný trh),** a farmers' market since the 13th century.

Another block closer to the train station, on Kapucínské náměstí, are the **Church of the Sacred Cross (Kostel Nalezení svatého Kříže)** and the **Capuchin Monastery (Kapucínský Klášter;** ✆ **542-213-232**).

Dominating **Zelný trh** at its southwest corner is the **Moravian Regional Museum,** Zelný trh 8, Brno (✆ **542-321-205;** www.mzm.cz), housed in the Dietrichstein Palace.

The museum displays a wide array of stuffed birds and wild game, as well as art, coins, and temporary exhibits. Admission is 50Kč ($3.35/£2.05) adults, and 25Kč ($1.65/£1) students and children. It's open Tuesday to Saturday from 9am to 5pm.

From the museum, head up Petrská Street to the **Cathedral of Saints Peter and Paul.**

Take a break at **Denisovy sady,** the park behind the cathedral, and prepare to climb the hill to get to **Špilberk Castle.** It was built in the 13th century, and the Hussites controlled the castle in the 15th century. The Prussians saw the castle's position as an excellent lookout when they occupied it in the early 17th century. And the Nazis turned it into a torture chamber during their stay, executing some 80,000 people deep inside the dungeons. At Špilberk's **Brno City Museum** (✆ **542-123-611;** www.spilberk.cz), you can see several new permanent exhibitions such as "Jail of Nations" or "History of Brno" and others. Admission to all exhibitions, casemates, and the lookout tower is 160Kč ($11/£6.80) adults, 90Kč ($5.60/£3.45) students. It's open May to September Tuesday to Sunday from 9am to 6pm, October and April Tuesday to Sunday from 9am to 5pm, and November to March Wednesday to Sunday 10am to 5pm.

Where to Stay

Note that prices, even in the high season, often double during major trade fairs and the Motorcycle Grand Prix.

Expensive

Grandhotel Brno ★ Ever since it was taken over by the Austrian chain Austrotel in the mid-1990s, the Grandhotel has lived up to its name. Its rooms are spacious and well appointed, though some located at the front get a little noisy due to the major street running past with its never-ending stream of trams; ask for a room that has windows facing north, away from the commotion.

Benešova 18–20, 657 83 Brno. ✆ **542-518-111.** Fax 542-210-345. www.grandhotelbrno.cz. 110 units. 3,300Kč ($220/£124) double; 6,150Kč ($256/£159) suite. AE, DC, MC, V. Parking 150Kč ($10/£6.20). **Amenities:** 2 restaurants; nightclub; room service (7am–3am); 24-hr. laundry; casino. *In room:* TV, minibar.

Moderate

Holiday Inn The very modern Holiday Inn Brno, on the fairgrounds, caters mainly to the trade-fair crowd, so be warned that prices may jump steeply when events are scheduled. Everything, from the rooms to the restaurant to the bars, looks eerily similar to their counterparts in other Holiday Inns around the world. Still, the beds are more comfortable than most, and the staff is very friendly and speaks English.

Křížkovského 20, 603 00 Brno. ✆ **543-122-111.** Fax 543-246-693. www.hibrno.cz. 205 units. 3,700Kč ($246/£153) double; 4,200Kč ($280/£174) suite. AE, DC, MC, V. Parking 150Kč ($10/£6.20) per day. **Amenities:** Restaurant; bar; pool; coin-op laundry. *In room:* TV, minibar, hair dryer, iron, trouser press.

Inexpensive

Penzion na Starém Brně Built into the stables below the castle is a restaurant that has now added a small and very cheap pension. Though a little out of the center, lying halfway between the exhibition grounds and the main square, this spot is very clean and quiet. The rooms are sparsely furnished with rustic pieces and hardwood floors, but since they are relatively small, that's okay.

Mendlovo nám. 1, 639 00 Brno. ✆ **543-247-872.** Fax 541-243-738. www.penzion-brno.com. 7 units. 950Kč ($63/£39) double. MC, V. **Amenities:** Restaurant. *In room:* TV.

Where to Dine

Moderate

La Braseria ★ ITALIAN They say that when in Rome, do as the Romans do. So when in Brno, follow this saying and do what the Romans do—come here. Their authentic Italian cuisine (sorry, dumpling aficionados) is too zesty to be passed up. Try the chicken in green-peppercorn sauce for a delicate change. The restaurant is located between the fairgrounds and the center, about a 10-minute walk from either.

Pekařská 80. ✆ **543-232-042.** Reservations recommended. Soups and antipasti 25Kč–210Kč ($1.65–$14/£1–£8.70); *primi piatti* 55Kč–215Kč ($3.65–$14/£2.25–£8.70); *secondi* 85Kč–300Kč ($5.65–$20/£3.50–£12); pizzas 50Kč–150Kč ($3.35–$10/£2.10–£6.20). AE, DC, MC, V. Daily noon–midnight.

Modrá Hvězda (Blue Star) CZECH The Blue Star is one of the few moderately priced restaurants in Brno where you can get good-quality food well into the night. The pepper steak is the favorite and, as you can tell, anything from the grill is your best bet.

Šilingrovo nám. 7. ✆ **542-215-292.** Soups 25Kč–45Kč ($1.65–$3/£1–£1.85); main courses 99Kč–299Kč ($6.60–$20/£4.10–£12). MC, V. Daily 11am–1am.

TELČ ★

149km (92 miles) SE of Prague; 86km (53 miles) W of Brno

As you pass through towns on your way here, you may be tempted to pass up Telč, dismissing it as yet another "small town with a nice square." Don't. Those who make the trip to Telč strike gold. Telč is one of the few towns in Europe that can boast of not being reconstructed since its original edifices were built. It now enjoys the honor of being a United Nations (UNESCO) World Heritage Site.

Getting There

Located about halfway between České Budějovice and Brno, Telč can be reached by taking Hwy. 23. **Driving** from Prague, take Hwy. D1 in the direction of Brno and exit at Jihlava, where you pick up Hwy. 38 after going through the town. Then head west on Hwy. 23. It's a 2-hour drive from Prague.

Visitor Information

At the **Informační Středisko,** náměstí Zachariáše z Hradce 10 (✆ **567-112-407;** www.telc-etc.cz or www.telcsko.cz), you'll find a wealth of information concerning accommodations, cultural events, guided tours, and even hunting; brochures are in Czech, German, and English.

Special Events

The **Holidays in Telč (Prázdniny v Telči),** a season of concerts, recitals, and fairs, runs from the end of July to the middle of August. For details, contact the **Informační Středisko** (or go to www.prazdninyvtelci.cz).

Where to Stay

Hotel Celerin The most upscale hotel on the square, the Celerin has medium-size rooms; the best ones overlook the square. If you're looking for location, this is the place to stay. Looking out over the square at night when it's bathed in light will remind you why this town is so treasured. Travelers with disabilities will find the staff here helpful, and some rooms are fully accessible.

Náměstí Zachariáše z Hradce 43, 588 56 Telč. ✆ **567-243-477.** Fax 567-213-581. www.hotelcelerin.cz. 12 units. 1,600Kč ($106/£66) double. Rates include continental breakfast. AE, DC, MC, V. **Amenities:** Restaurant; bar. *In room:* TV, fridge.

Where to Dine

U Černého Orla (At the Black Eagle) ★ CZECH If it looks as though all visitors in town are trying to get in here, it's because they are. The Black Eagle is worth the effort. This is one of the few restaurants in Telč that can be trusted to serve good food consistently. Crowd in at any free space and enjoy a wide range of Czech meals.

Náměstí Zachariáše z Hradce 7. ✆ **567-243-222.** Reservations recommended. Soups 20Kč ($1.35/85p); main courses 50Kč–190Kč ($3.35–$13/£2.10–£8.05). AE, MC, V. June–Sept daily 7am–10pm; Oct–May Tues–Sun 7am–10pm.

7

Hungary

by Dr. Ryan James

It never occurred to me when living in Modesto, California, that some day I would be living in Budapest, Hungary, and have the opportunity to write for Frommer's. After graduating with a doctorate in International and Multicultural Education in 2000, with over 25 years of teaching experience at that point, it was time to make a major move. Moving to Hungary was not in the plan at the time; moving to the East Coast of the U.S. was, but finding that "right fit" university position was not in the cards.

We rented our house, sold the cars and the furniture, and started traveling across the U.S. to say good-bye to friends and family. We were set to leave the country on September 14, 2001, for London.

On the morning of September 11, I woke extra early, remembering I had forgotten to order our rail passes. I was on the phone with Rail Europe ordering the tickets when the agent asked for my address. When he heard the New Jersey address, he responded, "Oh, can you see New York City from where you are?" Those words are burned into my memory. Thinking he was naïve, I chuckled and said no, but we are not that far away, and inquired why he asked that question. He said he had the radio on at his desk and heard a plane flew into one of the Twin Towers. As soon as I finished the call, I turned on the television, horrified over the events that followed.

We were not able to start our journey until September 24, but even then we were skeptical about leaving the country. We landed in London with our BritRail and Eurail FlexiPasses in hand, traveling all over England, Scotland, Wales, Ireland, the Netherlands, Belgium, and Germany.

In 1998, we had spent a week in Budapest only to be overwhelmed with the sheer range of architectural styles—everything from Romanesque and Gothic to Hungarian Art Nouveau with Zsolnay ceramic roofs. Not a single street lacked a visual banquet to be savored. History learned and long forgotten came to life before our eyes. When we reached Cologne, it was December and getting too cold to be hotel hopping and dragging luggage that held a year's supply of living necessities.

Suddenly, Budapest, which had spun its spell on our souls, beckoned us back. First, there was the allure of spending a winter defrosting in the city's famed therapeutic thermal baths. Also, Budapest is both a convenient walking city and one with superior public transportation. That gave us plenty of options for investigating a plethora of museums, cafes, or cultural venues within easy access. The world famous Liszt Ferenc Academy is just one of the many excellent places to hear music, while the opera house is breathtakingly opulent. Our choice was simple.

Each day, we grew to appreciate the city exponentially—beauty is not something one needs to seek out in Budapest, as the city itself is a feast for the eyes. By serendipity, we were both offered university positions. I was hired at Eőtvős Loránd University, the largest university in Central Europe, in the American Studies department.

As the saying goes, the rest is history, and I did find that perfect university fit.

1 GETTING TO KNOW HUNGARY

A QUICK OVERVIEW

Hungary joined the European Union in the spring of 2004; however, they will not use the euro until 2012. Hungary will shortly have its fifth democratic election since the fall of Communism. As politics go, each election seems to bring into power a different party, which dismantles what the previous one assembled only to start from square one once again. Hence, Hungary does not seem to make major inroads into accomplished development. During Communism, Hungary was the "model" of what Communism could aspire to, but now many older people wish for the old days when they perceive that their lives were better off. Due to the economy, in many ways their lives were better off than they are now.

THE REGIONS IN BRIEF

Budapest, the capital, has close to one-third of the country's population of 10 million people. Life is faster in Budapest than other cities in the country, but still a slower pace than many major cities. The city needs time for savoring and one should plan more than a few days here. Every part of the city has a sumptuous buffet spread out to be soaked in. A stroll down Andrássy út, listed as a UNESCO World Heritage Site, will fascinate you with the diverse architecture, the new high-end shopping, and farther up, the museums and embassies leading directly to Heroes' Square. It is also the path of the first metro in continental Europe and the second in the world, built for the millennium celebration in 1896. For the most up-to-date listing of events in the capital, pick up a free copy of *Funzine* magazine, published every 2 weeks. If you need a break from the capital, venture off to some of the smaller—but no less interesting—cities. Szentendre, an old Serbian village, is only 45 minutes from Budapest. Szeged is the proud paprika capital of the world. Pécs has a Roman past from 2,000 years ago.

SUGGESTED ITINERARIES

For most people, visiting Hungary begins with Budapest. With that in mind, these itineraries are samples of a detailed 2-day tour of Budapest, followed by various side-trip optional ideas.

Day 1

On your first day in Budapest, start at Deak ter, or anywhere in Inner City.

❶ Inner City & Central Pest ★

Budapest, a city where wide boulevards intersect with some narrow streets, reminds you that this was once part of the Austrian-Hungarian Empire. Wide boulevards were well suited for accommodating carriages for royals and others of wealth. This is definitely a walking city, so start in the center city wandering the grand boulevards to admire the architecture. Make sure you look up. So many interesting features on buildings are not at eye level.

Depending on your travel tastes, you may want to visit a few museums and highlights of the area. You may find the Greek-looking **Hungarian National Museum** ★★ (p. 312) especially appealing or the **Budapest Holocaust Memorial Center** ★★ (p. 312). As you wander through the area, remind yourself of two facts: Unlike Prague, much of Budapest was bombed during World War II. Many historic buildings are being replaced with boutiques, apartment complexes, or restaurants. Others are being renovated to their former glory, but in my opinion, certainly not enough. History is being replaced by sterility of the new and modern.

Váci utca is the perennially favorite shopping and walking street of Budapest. Having developed after the regime changes in 1989, it has blossomed with many international stores, and some Hungarian ones as well. For examples of Hungarian crafts, visit the **Vali Folklór** folk craft shop (p. 335), the **VAM Design Gallery**, and various clothing stores (avoid the touristy cafes here).

Walk from Váci utca to the Danube Promenade and stroll along the river. Following the no. 2 tram line, you will be making your way to Kossuth tér for:

2 Parliament ★★★

Budapest's exquisite Parliament building is the second largest in Europe after England's Westminster. I have done the tour six times—it's that good. The main facade faces the Danube. Designed by Imre Steindl and completed in 1902, the building mixes neo-Gothic style with a neo-Renaissance dome reaching 96m (315 ft.), significant since the country's millennium occurred in 1896 and the conquest of the kingdom of Hungary was in 896. St. Stephen's is also 96m (315 ft.) high for the same reasons. It is by far one of my favorite buildings in Budapest. After climbing a grandly ornamented staircase, there is a hexadecagonal (16-sided) central hall with impressive chamber leading from here. The fabled Hungarian crown jewels of St. Stephen are on display. Unfortunately, you can enter only on guided tours (the 45-min. tour is worthwhile for the chance to go inside). See p. 315 for tour times and information.

3 FREEDOM SQUARE (SZABADSAG TÉR) ★

This beautifully maintained park is the home of a large obelisk statue that commemorates when the Soviet Union liberated Hungary at the end of World War II. It is the last remaining memorial to the Soviet Union in the city. You may want to rest in the park or have a coffee at Farger's Café at Zoltán u. 18, right on the square. You will be directly across from the U.S. Embassy.

Walk back to Parliament and then south about a quarter of a mile toward the historic Chain Bridge, which you will see in the distance:

4 Chain Bridge ★

Known by a couple of names, the Széchenyi Bridge or the Chain Bridge, the bridge holds the distinction of being the first permanent crossing to link Buda and Pest in 1849 when it opened. The 19th-century Hungarian reformer Count István Széchenyi provided the idea and funding when he could not cross by boat to see his dying father. Designed by William Tierney Clark, an Englishman, the bridge was one of the largest suspension bridges of its time when it opened in 1849. ***Note:*** You might duck into the **Four Seasons Hotel Gresham Palace ★★★** while you're here to view its breathtaking interiors (p. 295).

Walk across the Chain Bridge, and take the funicular up to the:

5 Castle District ★★

Castle Hill, a UNESCO World Cultural Heritage Site, consists of two parts: the Royal Palace itself and the so-called Castle District. Most of this area is a reconstructed medieval city, but the original castle was destroyed in World War II and replaced with the current Royal Palace. For a detailed, 3-hour itinerary of this area, see "Walking Tour: the Castle District," on p. 324.

There are many cobblestone streets, so choose your shoes carefully. You might stop into a few highlights, including the

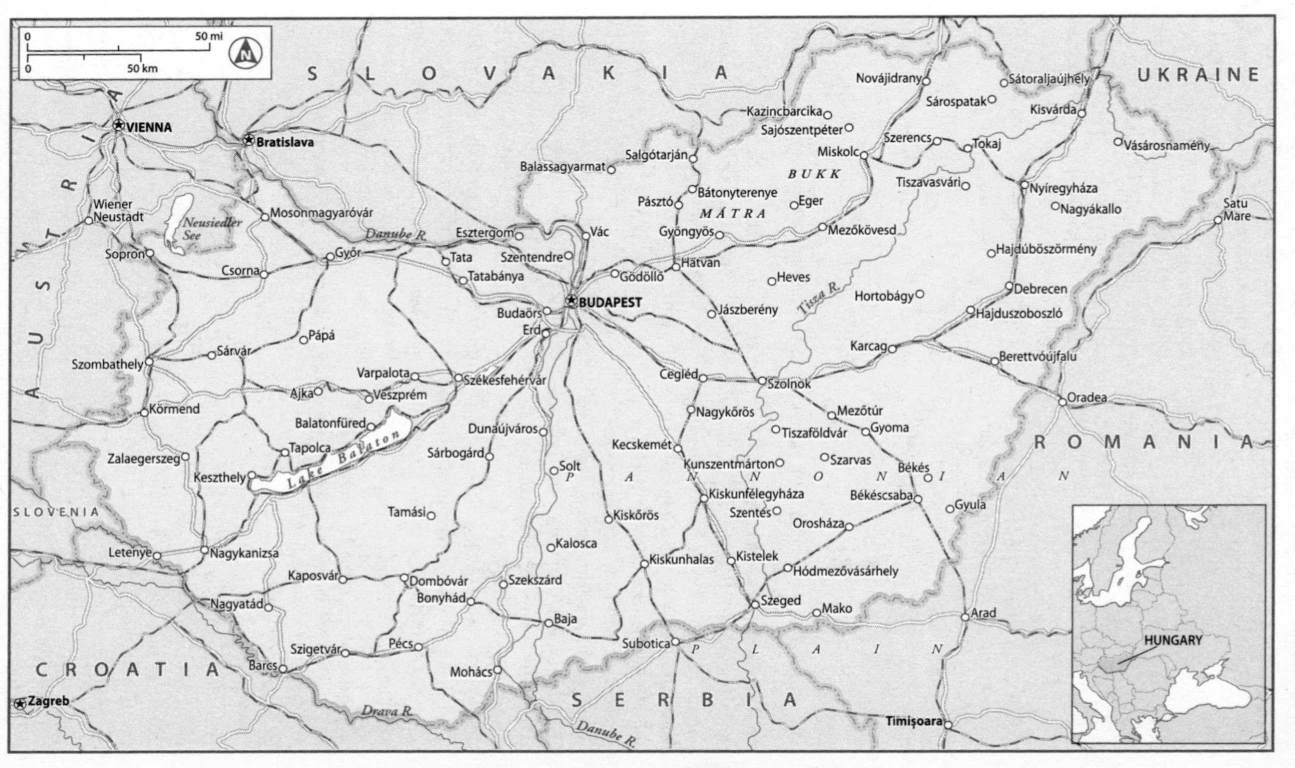
0
50 mi
0
50 km
SLOVAKIA
UKRAINE
AUSTRIA
ROMANIA
SERBIA
CROATIA
SLOVENIA
PANNONIAN PLAIN
VIENNA
Bratislava
BUDAPEST
Zagreb
Wiener Neustadt
Neusiedler See
Sopron
Csorna
Mosonmagyaróvár
Győr
Danube R.
Esztergom
Tata
Tatabánya
Szentendre
Vác
Budaörs
Érd
Balassagyarmat
Salgótarján
Kazincbarcika
Sajószentpéter
Bátonyterenye
Pásztó
MÁTRA
BUKK
Eger
Gyöngyös
Hatvan
Gödöllő
Mezőkövesd
Miskolc
Novájidrany
Sárospatak
Sátoraljaújhely
Kisvárda
Szerencs
Tokaj
Tiszavasvári
Vásárosnamény
Nyíregyháza
Nagyákallo
Satu Mare
Hajdúböszörmény
Heves
Tisza R.
Hortobágy
Debrecen
Hajduszoboszló
Jászberény
Karcag
Berettvóújfalu
Oradea
Pápá
Sárvár
Szombathely
Varpalota
Székesfehérvár
Ajka
Veszprém
Körmend
Balatonfüred
Lake Balaton
Tapolca
Zalaegerszeg
Keszthely
Dunaújváros
Sárbogárd
Solt
Cegléd
Szolnok
Nagykőrös
Mezőtúr
Tiszaföldvár
Gyoma
Kecskemét
Kunszentmárton
Szarvas
Békés
Kiskunfélegyháza
Békéscsaba
Gyula
Szentes
Orosháza
Tamási
Kiskőrös
Kalosca
Kiskunhalas
Kistelek
Hódmezővásárhely
Letenye
Nagykanizsa
Kaposvár
Dombóvár
Szekszárd
Bonyhád
Nagyatád
Baja
Szeged
Mako
Arad
Szigetvár
Pécs
Subotica
Barcs
Mohács
Drava R.
Timişoara
Danube R.
HUNGARY

Hungarian National Gallery ★ (p. 317) and the **Budapest History Museum** ★★ (p. 326).

RIVALDA CAFÉ & RESTAURANT ★

After a long day of walking and sightseeing, one option for a meal while still on the hill is the Rivalda Café & Restaurant. This restaurant is housed in a building that was once a monastery of Carmelite monks, but disbanded in 1786. The building was then given to the people of Buda by Joseph II to become a theater. Opened as a restaurant in 2000, Rivalda has saxophone or piano music nightly. I. Szinház u. 5-9; ✆ **1/489-0236.** See p. 309.

After dinner, you might head back to your hotel to relax for a bit so you'll be ready to:

7 Socialize at a Bar, Club, or Bistro

Budapest has a variety of lively nightlife possibilities suit every taste. You'll find all levels of partying available, whether you're looking for hardcore clubbing or just a pub for drinks with the locals. Clubs such as the **Old Man's Pub** (p. 344) has nightly music. It is quite popular for nighttime drinks and socializing; you'll find locals of all ages mingling here.

Day 2

For your second day in Budapest, start at the New York Palace Hotel.

1 New York Palace Hotel ★★

The New York Life Insurance Company originally commissioned the building, which opened on October 23, 1894. During the 1900s, the cafe was a center of intellectual life in the city, frequented by writers and journalists. After many years of remodeling and revitalizing the original eclectic style with a strong Italian renaissance influence, the Boscolo hotel chain reopened the cafe and the hotel in 2006. The detailed reconstruction is worth admiring and returning to in the evening when lit up.

Walk toward Oktogon, noting the grand turn-of-the-20th-century architecture of Pest. At Oktogon turn right and walk up to Andrássy u. 60:

2 House of Terror (Terror Háza) ★★

First the headquarters of the secret police of the Nazi Arrow Cross regime, it immediately turned into the headquarters for the Communist secret police when the Soviets liberated Hungary. This building is the setting of some of the most horrific days of 20th-century Hungary, which lasted for over 50 years. Hundreds were tortured and murdered in the basement by both regimes. For the Nazis their primary victims were Jews, but for the Communists, it was anyone who spoke out against the government.

The building was set up as a museum as a memorial to the victims of both Fascism and Communism as an everlasting reminder of the effect of oppressive regimes in Hungary. However, for political reasons, it has caused continual controversy since it opened, especially the building's overhang with the word TERROR stenciled out. When the sun projects through these letters, it is meant to symbolize the terror which was projected onto the people.

3 Andrássy Boulevard ★

Strolling up the majestic Andrássy Boulevard toward Heroes' Square and City Park, you are taking the UNESCO World Heritage Site tour. The boulevard is lined with trees and a wealth of beautiful apartment buildings; many are now used as embassies of various countries. In addition, there are restaurants and museums scattered along the way leading to Heroes' Square. This is Pest's greatest boulevard.

If you are ready for a break:

4 KOGART GALLERY AND RESTAURANT ★★★

Designed by Ignác Alpar, who also designed the Vajdahunyad castle in City Park, this historic building is now home to a beautiful cafe and restaurant. Take your coffee while reading a paper in English and sitting on leather sofas in a quiet corner of the room. If you are so inclined, the art gallery upstairs has rotating exhibits of superior quality. **Andrássy út 112;** ✆ **1/354 3830.** See p. 307.

Once you reach the end of Andrássy Boulevard, adjacent to the Museum of Fine Arts, the Múcsarnok, and City Park, you'll find:

5 Heroes' Square ★★★

Heroes' Square, as were many other monuments and buildings, was created for the millennium in 1896 (remember the reoccurring 96) which celebrated the arrival of the Magyar tribes in the Carpathian Basin in 896. The statues represent the chronology of some 1,000 years of Hungarian history. The seven statues on the left are Hungarian kings. On the right, they are famous Hungarians, but only one was a king. In 1896 during the famous world exhibition, this space was the apex of some 200 pavilions that made up the festivities. Many festivals are still held here.

To your left you will find the **Museum of Fine Arts** ★ (p. 313). The museum is the main repository of foreign art in Hungary, has one of central Europe's major collections, and is considered one of the most important art collections in Europe. Free 1-hour tours are offered by highly trained docents Tuesday through Friday at 11am and 2pm and on Saturday at 11am.

Walk through the park and you will arrive at:

6 The Széchenyi Baths ★★★

After a long day, you deserve to rest and relax. Nothing could be better after a day of touring than a soak in a thermal. This is one of the largest spa complexes in Europe and the first thermal bath on the Pest side. It is mixed men and women and bathing suits are mandatory. See the listing on p. 323.

Now head out for dinner. You can take the Yellow metro from Széchenyi and go one stop to Mexikói or choose a dining spot near the baths, but either way make a reservation.

7 Trófea Grill Étterem ★★★

You have had a full day of exercise, so treat yourself to the best Hungarian all-you-can-eat restaurant in the city. With over 100 choices from soups to desserts and everything in between, everyone is sure to leave satisfied.

8 Attend Some Nighttime Culture ★★

Spend an evening attending a concert at the **Ferenc Liszt Music Academy** (p. 337), or an opera at the **opera house** ★★★; both are Budapest's premier venues. The first is a more classical hall, while the opera house is magnificently beautiful inside. The fine arts are alive and well in Budapest, and a nighttime cultural event is the way to round out your short stint in the city. Note that performances usually start at 7pm, not the customary 8pm.

The Best of Hungary Side-Trip Options

After a taste of Budapest, perhaps now you want to experience other parts of the country and see how life differs. Since Budapest draws the most visitors to Hungary, I've opted to give you side-trip options from the city rather than full-week itineraries. All rail tracks lead to Budapest, so regardless of which direction you go, chances are you will have to return to Budapest when changing from one geographical area to another, making a full Hungarian tour both difficult and time consuming. Traveling by bus is even more time consuming and less comfortable. Driving a car can be downright dangerous if you're not used to European driving, not to mention the cost. Trains are easy and safe, and they usually cost less than 5,000 Ft ($27/£14) round-trip, depending on the destination.

This section lists four options for Hungarian side trips: **Szentendre** is an old Serbian village and is charming. It is only 20km (12 miles) from the bustle of the capital. **Vác** is a historic town only 34 km (21 miles) and a world apart when relaxing in the beautiful square or the Danube Park. **Pécs** is a booming cultural center and has been chosen as the **European Capital of Culture for 2010** by the European Union. It is home to the famous Zsolnay Porcelain Factory. **Szeged** is the paprika capital.

Option ❶: A Day in Szentendre ★★

After some time in Budapest, you might visit Szentendre (pronounced *Sen*-ten-dreh), just north of Budapest on the Danube and one of the most visited spots in all of Hungary. Take the HÉV (regional train) from Budapest's Batthyány tér metro for a 45-minute ride.

Visit the **Margit Kovács Museum** ★★★ and see the interesting collection of the late Margit Kovács. Primarily a ceramicist, her depictions of peasant life in Hungary are charming. Have a late lunch at the **Aranysárkány Vendéglő** ★, and take a walk along the river. Then spend your afternoon exploring the many shops, museums, churches, and galleries in town. Fő tér, the main drag, is enticing, but explore all the side streets of this small, manageable town. Try **Chez Nicolas Restaurant** ★★, Kígyó u. 10.

See the "Szentendre" section on p. 350.

Option ❷: A Day in Vác ★★★

Just past Szentendre along the Danube, but actually faster to reach, Vác has a direct train from Budapest, making the trip in as little as 25 minutes. Although this is a very historic little town, it also has one of the most beautiful Danube parks I have seen. All along the river is a wide promenade with winding walking and biking paths with play areas for children interspersed along the way. Vác is a town for strolling, since most of the historic sights can be seen from the outside, with a couple of exceptions. Starting at the main square, **Március 15 tér** ★★★ there is the historic **White Friar's Church** ★★ and the impressive statute and fountain of St. Hedwig on the side of the church. Directly across from the church is the **Memento Mori** ★★★, with the preserved crypts that were uncovered accidentally when the renovations took place on the White Friar's Church. Also on the square sit historic and interesting baroque buildings such as the **Cathedral of the Assumption.** At **Géza Király tér** is the Franciscan or **"Brown" Church,** which sits next to the castle, the oldest building in Vác. An Italian architect designed the synagogue on Eötvös utca in romantic style.

See the "Vác" section on p. 353 for more information.

Option ❸: 2 Days in Pécs ★★★

The popular Pécs is the most culturally vibrant Hungarian city outside of the capital—warm and arid, with lots of museums, galleries, and a large student population from the university.

Take an early morning InterCity train from Budapest's Déli Station to Pécs, a 3-hour ride. Walk down Káptalan utca, the street of museums housed in medieval houses. Visit the **Tivadar Csontváry Museum** ★ and the **Victor Vasarely Museum** ★, institutions that celebrate two of Hungary's most notable artists. In the **Zsolnay Museum** ★★★, housed in a Gothic residence, you will find displays of the finest pieces of award-winning porcelain, and even paintings. Then check out the hustle and bustle of the **Pécsi Vásár** ★★ flea market, where you can find traditional Hungarian wares. Head up on the hill for dinner at the **"Hunters' Lodge" Vadasztanya** ★★, where you can enjoy a fine Hungarian wine before checking in at the fun, centrally located **Hotel Főnix** ★★.

For a midmorning snack, stop for a coffee and pastry at the **Mecsek Cukrászda** before checking out Pécs' houses of worship, the **Pécs Cathedral,** the **Pécs Synagogue** ★, and the largest standing Turkish structure, the **Mosque of Pasha Gazi Kassim.**

See "Pécs: the 2,000-Year-Old City," on p. 369.

Option ❹: 2 Days in Szeged ★★

The southeastern Hungarian town of Szeged is the cultural center of the region. With a thriving university, it is overflowing with students. If you're in Hungary in the summer, come here for the **Szeged Summer Open Air Festival** ★★ in Dóm tér, which offers rock operas, classical music, ballet, and contemporary dance in July and August, making it the largest festival of its kind in Hungary.

From Budapest, take the train from Nyugati Station for a 2½-hour ride. Start off with a coffee and pastry at the famous **Virág Cukrászda.** Enjoy some of the impressive architecture; visit the **Votive Church of Our Lady of Hungary** ★★★, the cathedral built in Hungarian Ecclesiastic architecture.

Take a walk on the river's edge, then head back to **Kárász utca** ★★, the main walking street, which is usually bustling with students. Have a casual dinner on the terrace at the **Gödör Restaurant** or, for a more upscale meal, try **Göry Restaurant & Terrace** ★. Try to get a room at the reasonably priced and clean **Family Pension,** not far from the train station and Dóm tér.

See "Szeged: Hungary's Spice Capital," on p. 374.

HUNGARY TODAY

Regardless of being part of the European Union, Hungary is continually shifting its political focus. Political polarization has become a constant struggle between the left- and right parties and their supporters. Each party in power seems to antagonize enough people to have demonstrations to voice opposition. One ultra-right-wing group, the Hungarian Guard, has come into being . . . or some would say resurfaced. Their message is xenophobic, anti-E.U., and back to traditional Hungarian ways. Discussing politics with a Hungarian is not a good idea.

HUNGARIAN PEOPLE & CULTURE

Ethnic Hungarians make up about 90% of the population of Hungary. The population of the Roma (Gypsies) is 4%. The rest of the population is made up primarily of Germans, Slovaks, Croatians, and Romanians. Chinese immigrants and African refugees have settled primarily in the capital.

For the most part, Magyars are courteous and generally friendly toward foreigners, and they take great pride in their country. However, you may find customer service lacking the standards one would expect. If you know a Hungarian and are invited to his or her home, bring a small gift such as chocolate or wine. There are a few customs surrounding fresh flowers, so it is best to avoid them. It is always nice to learn a few key words of Hungarian as the effort will please most people.

HUNGARIAN CUISINE

Traditional Hungarian cuisine reflects the rich and varied flavors of many international influences. Since the first Magyars were nomadic people, they learned from the Turkish and other cultures with which they came into contact. Perhaps thanks to the fact that they were rarely in one place for too long, soup was an important staple of the Magyar lifestyle. A large pot called a *bogrács* is a cast-iron kettle that hangs on an iron rod over the fire and the pot used for cooking soups. It was easily transported as they moved from place to place, and with the soup sitting in the pot, it thickened over time as it was consumed over days. The *bogrács* is a very popular cooking utensil even today, and soups continue to be an important part of a meal.

Different parts of Hungary have their regional traditions and favorite recipes, but any good Hungarian restaurant in Budapest will incorporate some from each on its menu. Some restaurants will specialize in the more exotic fare such as deer, wild boar, or other nondomesticated animals. Regardless of what is on the menu, if it is a traditional Hungarian menu, you are guaranteed that the meal will be plentiful. Hungarian cooking uses a great deal of pork or goose fat, which adds incredible flavors to dishes that would not be possible without them. Sour cream, potatoes, or a form of pasta added enriches a dish.

The main course is generally a meat dish. Vegetarianism is slowly being recognized in Hungarian restaurants; many establishments now offer a vegetable plate entree, usually consisting of seasonal steamed and grilled vegetables or cheese plates. Hungarians look on vegetarians with suspicion, regardless of their nationality.

LANGUAGE

The Hungarian language, Magyar, has long been one of the country's greatest obstacles and continues to be as many business and tour websites, especially for smaller cities and villages, are in Magyar only. The problem is that Magyar is a complex and unusual language—it originated on the eastern side of the Ural Mountains, and along with Finnish and Estonian, it's one of Europe's few representatives of the Finno-Urgic family of languages. Fortunately for the modern-day traveler, and for Hungary's ascension into the E.U., many young people have taken their foreign language studies more seriously. Many young people speak English and most people in tourism venues do to some extent. Do not be daunted if you attempt some polite words and find you are faced with a confused Hungarian staring at you. The difference between an o and ó can change the meaning of the word, and the Magyar people are so unaccustomed to hearing strangers attempt their language, they get a bit befuddled with mistakes. At the least, try to learn the polite words and stick with them.

USEFUL WORDS & PHRASES

English	Hungarian	Pronunciation
Good day/Hello	**Jó napot**	*yoh* napoht
Good morning	**Jó reggelt**	*yoh* reg-gelt
Good evening	**Jó estét**	*yoh* esh-tayt
Goodbye	**Viszontlátásra**	*vee*-sont-lah-tahsh-ra
My name is . . .	**vagyok . . .**	*vodge*-yohk
Thank you	**Köszönöm**	*kuh*-suh-nuhm
You're welcome	**Kérem**	*kay*-rem
Please	**Legyen szíves**	*ledge*-yen *see*-vesh
Yes	**Igen**	*ee*-gen
No	**Nem**	*nem*
Good/Okay	**Jó**	*yo*
Excuse me	**Bocsánat**	*boh*-chahnat

English	Hungarian	Pronunciation
How much does it cost?	**Mennyi bekerül?**	*men*-yee *beh*-keh-roohl?
I don't understand	**Nem értem**	*nem* ayr-tem
I don't know	**Nem tudom**	*nem too*-dum
Where is the . . . ?	**Hol van a . . . ?**	*hohl* von a . . . ?
bus station	**busz állomás**	*boos ahh*-loh-mahsh
train station	**vonatállomás**	*vah*-not-*ahh*-loh-mahsh
bank	**bank**	*bahnk*
pharmacy	**patiká**	*paw*-tee-kah
tourist office	**turista iroda**	*too*-reesh-ta *eer*-ohda
restroom/toilet	**wc**	*vayt*-say

2 PLANNING YOUR TRIP TO HUNGARY

VISITOR INFORMATION

The tourism infrastructure has developed extensively over the years with strong support from the Ministry of Tourism. There are many high-quality hotels and restaurants; and it seems new ones are appearing every few months. Most cities have a tourism-related information office usually called **TourInform** (© **1/438-8080** or 06/80-630-800; www.tourinform.hu), a branch of the Hungarian National Tourist Office, at V. Sütő u. 2, Budapest; it's open daily from 8am to 8pm. You'll also find a branch office in the heart of Budapest's Broadway, at Liszt Ferenc tér 11 (© **1/322-4098;** fax 1/342-2541), open weekdays from 9am to 6pm. In the castle district, it is located at Szentháromság tér (© **1/488-0475;** fax 1/488-0474), open daily from 10am to 6pm. These offices distribute pamphlets on events and attractions that can be found in the area where you are visiting, and help you with finding appropriate accommodations and restaurants. The tourism authority, **Magyar Turizmus Rt.** (© **1/488-8701;** www.hungarytourism.hu), also has offices throughout the world, and it is their mandate to promote Hungary as a destination for tourism.

For general country information and a variety of pamphlets and maps before you leave home, contact the government-sponsored **Hungarian National Tourist Office,** 350 Fifth Ave., New York, NY 10118 (© **212/695-1212;** www.gotohungary.com). In London, the **Hungarian National Tourist Office** is at 46 Eaton Place, London SW1X 8AL (© **020/7823-1032**). The Hungarian National Tourist Office's main website, a great source of information, is **www.gotohungary.co.uk**.

Other sites with lots of helpful bits of information are the Internet sites of the printed periodicals ***Funzine*** at www.funzine.hu, the ***Budapest Sun*** at www.budapestsun.com, and the ***Budapest Times*** at www.budapesttimes.hu.

ENTRY REQUIREMENTS

DOCUMENTS Passports are required for all visitors from the U.S., Canada, Australia, and New Zealand. European Union nationals may enter the country using a valid national ID card. No visas are required for stays of less than 90 days. If you plan to stay longer, check with your embassy for more details (see below).

EMBASSIES The embassy of **Australia** is at XII. Királyhágó tér 8–9 (✆ **1/457-9777**); the embassy of **Canada** is at II. Ganz u. 12–14 (✆ **1/392-3360**); the embassy of the **Republic of Ireland** is at V. Szabadság tér 7 (✆ **1/301-4960**); the embassy of the **United Kingdom** is at V. Harmincad u. 6 (✆ **1/266-2888**); and the embassy of the **United States** is at V. Szabadság tér 12 (✆ **1/475-4400**). **New Zealand** does not have an embassy in Budapest, but the U.K. embassy can handle matters for New Zealand citizens.

MONEY

The basic unit of currency in Hungary is the **forint (Ft).** Coins come in denominations of 5, 10, 20, 50, 100, and 200 Ft. Banknotes come in denominations of 500, 1,000, 5,000, 10,000, and 20,000 Ft.

The U.S. dollar has weakened alarmingly over the past 4 years and inflation has hit. These factors combined have made Hungary only slightly less expensive for travelers than most Western countries.

As of this writing, the rate of exchange is US$1 = 185 Ft (or 100 Ft = US54¢), and this is the rate used to calculate all the U.S. dollar prices in this book. Of course, exchange rates fluctuate over time. Go to www.oanda.com/convert/cheatsheet to print out a "cheat sheet" for currency exchange rates to save using a calculator all of the time.

The best official rates for cash exchanges are at exchange booths located throughout the city center, but exchange booths in airports, train stations, and hotels almost uniformly offer a less favorable rate than others. ATMs (automated teller machines) are found in front of banks throughout the city and in major shopping malls. You may withdraw forints at the daily exchange rate from your home account through the Cirrus and PLUS networks. At most exchange booths and a few banks you will get a better rate when exchanging cash. Traveler's checks are almost impossible to cash.

If you are approached by someone on the street to exchange money, ignore the person or tell him or her to leave you alone. This is not only illegal if someone really has the cash, but many times, it is a scam. If caught exchanging money from anyone other than an authorized change booth or bank, you could be arrested.

The Hungarian forint is convertible back to other currencies; however, when you look at the rate board, the buy rate is never as good as the sell rate. It does not matter if it is an exchange booth or bank. This is standard procedure throughout the world. Coins are never accepted for exchange. Use them up before leaving.

Most people never think to use the airport ATMs, only to pay higher rates by exchanging some money at home first, to cover airport incidentals. You can exchange money at your local American Express or Thomas Cook office or at your bank. The American Express offices here closed over 3 years ago, although it was still listed on the website. To cash traveler's checks, you will have to search for a willing bank, a real rarity, or the Western Union office, where you will get an alarmingly low exchange rate, plus they charge commission of up to 2%.

WHEN TO GO

Budapest has a relatively mild climate most of the time. The annual mean temperature in Hungary is 50°F (10°C). Nevertheless, summer temperatures often exceed 80° to 85°F (27°–29°C), and sweltering hot, humid days are typical in July and August. January and February are the coldest months, averaging 30°F (–1°C), though temperatures can dip well below that on any given day. Be prepared for damp and chilly weather in winter. It may snow often, but rarely does it last more than 1 day and with no accumulation.

Spring is usually mild and, especially in May, wet. Autumn is usually quite pleasant, with mild, cooler weather through October.

HOLIDAYS

Hungarian holidays are January 1 (New Year's Day), March 15 (National Holiday), Easter Sunday and Easter Monday, May 1 (May Day), White Monday (which falls in May), August 20 (St. Stephen's Day), October 23 (Republic Day), November 1 (All Saints' Day), and December 25 and 26 (Christmas). Shops and banks are closed on all holidays; some museums stay open on some holidays.

GETTING THERE & GETTING AROUND

By Plane

Northwest Airlines (✆ 800/447-4747) and **Malév** (✆ 800/877-5429, 800/262-5380, or 800/223-6884), the former Hungarian state airline, offer nonstop service between North America and Budapest. Other leading carriers include **Lufthansa** (✆ 800/645-3880), **British Airways** (✆ 800/247-9297), **Delta Airlines** (✆ 800/241-4141), and **Austrian Air** (✆ 800/843-0002).

Budapest is served by two adjacent airports, **Ferihegy I** and **Ferihegy II,** both located in the XVII district in southeastern Pest. Ferihegy I is the airport that all budget airlines use, while Ferihegy II (which has a **Terminal A** and a **Terminal B**) serves the flagship carrier and other traditional airlines. There are several main information numbers: For airport information call ✆ **1/296-5959,** and for general information call ✆ **1/296-7000.** For ease of language, use the airport's English version website at www.bud.hu/english/transport for flight arrival information.

All arriving flights are international, since there is no domestic air service within Hungary. With the advent of the Schengen agreement, if you fly in from a Schengen zone country, you will no longer go through passport control in Budapest.

Ferihegy I was remodeled and enlarged just a few years ago. **Ferihegy II** is larger, but still not overwhelmingly large, so you will not have any fears of getting lost in it. In each airport, you will find accommodations offices, rental-car agencies, shops, and exchange booths, plus a TourInform desk.

By Train

Countless trains arrive in Budapest from most corners of Europe. Many connect through Vienna, where 18 daily trains depart for Budapest from either the Westbahnhof or Sudbahnhof station. Ten daily trains connect Prague and Budapest, while four connect Berlin with Budapest and one connects Warsaw with Budapest.

The train trip between Vienna and Budapest takes about 3 hours on an IC train. For more information on Vienna trains, contact the **Austrian National Tourist Board,** 500 Fifth Ave., Ste. 800, New York, NY 10110 (✆ **212/944-6885**); 11601 Wilshire Blvd., Ste. 2480, Los Angeles, CA 90025 (✆ **310/477-3332**); 30 St. George St., London W1R 0AL (✆ **020/7629-0461**); 2 Bloor St. E., Ste. 3330, Toronto, ON M4W 1A8 (✆ **416/967-3381**); or 1010 Sherbrooke St. W., Ste. 1410, Montreal, PQ H3A 2R7 (✆ **514/849-3708**).

Train travel within Hungary is generally very efficient; trains usually depart on time and, generally, arrive on time. You can access a full, user-friendly timetable on the Web, at **www.mav-start.hu**.

Hungarian ticket agents generally speak little English, so you will need to know some basic terminology in Hungarian. *Indul* means "departure" and *érkezik* means "arrival."

The timetables for arrivals are displayed in big white posters *(érkező vonatok),* while departures *(induló vonatok)* are on yellow posters. The relevant terms in the timetables are *honnan* (from where), *hova* (to where), *vágány* (platform), *munkanap* (weekdays), *hétvége* (weekend), *munkaszüneti nap* (Sat), *ünnepnap* (holiday), *gyors* (fast trains that stop only at major cities, as posted), and *IC* (inter-city, which stop only once or twice en route; you must reserve a seat for IC trains). Ticket terminology is as follows: *jegy* (ticket), *oda* (one-way), *oda-vissza* (round-trip), *helyjegy* (reservation), *első osztály* (first class), *másodosztály* (second class), *nem dohányzó* (nonsmoking), *ma* (today), and *holnap* (tomorrow).

A train posted as *személy* is a local train, which stops at every single village and town on its route. Always opt for a *gyors* (fast) or InterCity train to get to your destination in a timely manner. All InterCity trains (but no other domestic trains) require a *helyjegy* (seat reservation); ask for the reservation when purchasing your ticket; don't depend on the agent to offer it. On InterCity trains, you must sit in your assigned seat. A local trying to avoid the extra charge may be in your seat; show your reservation. All InterCity trains now comply strictly with a new law imposing constraints on smoking in public spaces; if there is a smoking car at all, it is in first class and only a single car, while the rest of the train is nonsmoking. If you want a seat in the smoking car, you need to ask for *dohányzó* when buying your ticket. The *gyors* train is typically an old, gritty, well-worn train with the classic eight-seat compartments. The InterCity, a state-of-the-art, clean, modern train without compartments, is said to travel faster, but my experience has been that there's seldom more than 30 minutes difference if that.

During the day, MÁV operates a call center called **MÁVDIREKT** (© **1/371-9449**). Purchase tickets at train-station ticket windows. You need at least an hour before departure time to make a reservation.

By Bus

Buses to and from western and eastern Europe and points in Hungary west of the Danube arrive at **Népliget** bus station. You reach this station by getting off at the Népliget metro stop on the Red line. Buses to and from the Danube Bend and other points north of Budapest depart and arrive at the **Árpád híd bus station** (© **1/320-9229** or 1/317-9886). Take the Blue line metro to Árpád híd. For domestic and international bus information, call © **1/219-8080,** though it can be difficult to get through to the bus stations over the telephone and then getting an English speaker will be a miracle. Your best bet is perhaps to gather your information in person or ask for assistance at the TourInform office (p. 281).

By Car

Several major highways link Hungary to nearby European capitals. The recently modernized **E60** (or M1) connects Budapest with Vienna and points west; it is a toll road from the Austrian border to the city of Györ. The **E65** connects Budapest with Prague and points north.

The **border crossings** from Austria and Slovakia (from which countries most Westerners enter Hungary) are hassle-free for the most part. Border control has ended for many points due to the Schengen agreement. In addition to your passport, you may be requested to present your driver's license, vehicle registration, and proof of insurance (the number plate and symbol indicating country of origin are acceptable proof). Cars entering Hungary are required to have a decal indicating country of registration, a first-aid kit, and an emergency triangle.

Driving distances are: from Vienna, 248km (154 miles); from Prague, 560km (347 miles); from Frankfurt, 952km (590 miles); and from Rome, 1,294km (802 miles).

By Hydrofoil

The Hungarian state shipping company **MAHART** operates hydrofoils on the Danube between Vienna and Budapest in the spring and summer months. It's an extremely popular route, so you should book your tickets well in advance. In North America or Britain, contact the Austrian National Tourist Board (see "By Train," above). In Vienna, you can contact MAHART, Handelskai 265 (✆ **43/729-2161;** fax 43/729-2163) or visit this website: www.besthotelz.com/hungary/hydrofoil/hydrofoil.htm.

From April 7 through July 2 the MAHART hydrofoil departs Vienna at 9am daily, arriving in Budapest at 3:20pm, with a stop in Bratislava when necessary (passengers getting on or off). From July 3 to August 29, two hydrofoils make the daily passage, departing Vienna at 8am and 1pm, arriving in Budapest at 1:30 and 6:30pm, respectively. From August 30 to November 1, the schedule returns to one hydrofoil daily, departing Vienna at 9am and arriving in Budapest at 2:30pm. The dates and times may change depending on water levels, so check with MAHART for the current information. Customs and passport controls begin 1 hour prior to departure. Eurailpass holders also receive a discount, as long as they buy the ticket before boarding. ISIC holders also receive a discount. The Budapest office of **MAHART** is at V. Belgrád rakpart (✆ **1/318-1880**). Boats and hydrofoils from Vienna arrive at the international boat station next door to the MAHART office on the **Belgrád rakpart,** which is on the Pest side of the Danube, between the Szabadság and Erzsébet bridges.

TIPS ON ACCOMMODATIONS

Budapest's accommodations run the gamut of categories, from beautiful, historic gems; those that have sprung from the ground up; and those that have remained the same from the beginning.

Accommodations rates in Budapest have risen considerably in the last few years, becoming more comparable to the rates of other European capitals. In high season or during the Formula 1 weekend in August, it can still be difficult to acquire your first choice of room. Make reservations and get written confirmation well in advance of your stay.

Bear in mind that many European standards call a room with two twin beds a double. If you want a double bed, you will need to request it specifically. Extra beds or cots are generally available also. Hungarian hotels often blur the use of the words "apartment" or "suite" to describe bedrooms with a living room in them or connected rooms including a bedroom and living room. Some have a kitchen, while others do not.

All hotels are required to charge a 12% value-added tax (VAT). Most build the tax into their rates, while a few tack it on top of their rates. When booking a room, ask whether the VAT is included in the quoted price. Unless otherwise indicated, prices in this book include the VAT.

Ibusz can help you make hotel arrangements throughout the city. The main reservations office is at Ferenciek tere 10 (✆ **36/1-485-2700;** fax 1/318-2805; www.ibusz.hu), accessible by the Blue metro line. This office is open year-round Monday through Friday 9am to 6pm.

TIPS ON DINING

There are many words used for eateries, while few of them have clear-cut boundaries. *Étterem* is the most common Hungarian word for restaurant and is applied to everything from cafeteria-style eateries to first-class restaurants. A *vendéglő,* an inn, is smaller and more intimate, often with a Hungarian folk motif; a *csárda* is a countryside *vendéglő* (often built on major motorways and around Lake Balaton). An *önkiszolgáló* indicates a self-service cafeteria, which is open for lunch only. *Büfés* (snack counters) are not like buffets in English. They are often found around the city and transportation hubs. A *cukrászda* is a pastry bakery, while a *kávéház* is a coffeehouse. Traditionally, many coffeehouses are places to sit for hours.

Other names on establishments that you will encounter are those whose primary function is to serve liquor, but some also serve meals or snacks. A *borozó* is a wine bar; these are downstairs off the street (they are likely to include in their name the word *pince* [cellar] or *barlang* [cave]), and generally feature a house wine. A *söröző* is a beer bar; these places, too, are often found in downstairs locations. Sandwiches are usually available in *borozós* and *sörözős.* Some are wonderful places, while others are dives where cheap drinks are served to the less economically advantaged.

Warning: Hungary is landlocked. Be careful what fish you order. See the "Where to Dine" section (p. 302) for more information.

Fast Facts Budapest

American Express Budapest's only American Express office closed its doors in 2005. They have replaced the office with a local toll-free number, so if you need assistance, call them at ✆ **06/800-1-7920.** It may look strange, but it works.

Banks In general banks are open Monday through Friday from 8am to 4pm. Some banks open a half-hour later on some days, but stay open an hour later that day.

Business Hours Most **stores** are open Monday through Friday from 10am to 6pm and Saturday from 9 or 10am to 1 or 2pm. Most stores are closed Sunday, except those in the central tourist areas. Some shop owners and restaurateurs also close for 2 weeks in August. On weekdays, food stores open early, at around 6 or 7am, and close at around 6 or 7pm. Convenience stores, called "nonstops," are open 24 hours and just about every neighborhood has at least one.

Doctors **First Med Center** (formerly called the American Clinic), I. Hattyu u. 14, fifth floor (✆ **1/224-9090;** www.firstmedcenters.com), is a private outpatient clinic with two U.S. board-certified physicians and several English-speaking Hungarian doctors.

Electricity Hungarian electricity is 220 volts, AC. With the exception of the U.K., the same adapter will serve you throughout Europe.

Emergencies Dial ✆ **104** for an ambulance, ✆ **105** for the fire department, and ✆ **107** for the police. ✆ **1/438-8080** is a 24-hour hot line in English for reporting crime.

Etiquette & Customs Old-world etiquette is still in vogue in Hungary with older people, but it is not always the same with the young generation. Those taught well hold doors open for women and readily give up their seats on the bus for those who need them. Since older people feel entitled, you may not receive any thanks for your efforts.

Internet Access In larger cities, there is no shortage of Internet cafes. Wi-Fi hot spots with free access are incredibly common, having been a competing point for businesses to draw customers. Look for hot spot stickers at cafes and restaurants.

Liquor Laws The legal drinking age in Hungary is 18. There is zero tolerance for drinking and driving.

Newspapers & Magazines For English-language current events and political news in Hungary, pick up the *Budapest Sun* or the *Budapest Times,* both weeklies. For fun and cultural events, I choose *Funzine.* It comes out every 2 weeks.

Police Dial ✆ **107** for the police.

Restrooms The words for toilet in Hungarian are *WC* (pronounced *vay*-tsay), *mosdó,* or *toalett. Női* means "women's"; *férfi* means "men's." Many American-type fast-food restaurants are charging for the use of their bathrooms unless you have your receipt from a purchase made that day.

Safety Hungary is one of the safest countries in Europe, and violent street crime is almost unheard of. However, you should always avoid political demonstrations and be aware of pickpockets, especially on crowded buses, trains, and trams. In Budapest, there always seem to be obnoxious drunks at night, but often they are foreigners who have come here to party. (***Note:*** Budapest is filled with underpasses. Be careful at night; you can always choose to cross a street aboveground if an underpass appears deserted.)

Smoking Smoking is forbidden in all public places (including all public transportation), except in most restaurants and pubs. Hungarians are smokers, making it part of the cafe or pub lifestyle. Although a 1999 law requires all restaurants to have a nonsmoking section, it is sometimes side by side with the smoking section. A few restaurants have gone nonsmoking. *Tilos a dohányzás* or *Dohányozni tilos* means "no smoking."

Taxes Taxes are included in restaurant and hotel rates, and in shop purchases. International travelers are entitled, upon leaving the country, to a refund of the 25% VAT on certain purchases once you have spent a specific amount at each store.

Telephone The country code for Hungary is 36. **To call to Hungary from abroad:** Dial the appropriate numbers to get an international dial tone (011 from the U.S.), then dial 36 (Hungary country code), followed by the appropriate city code (for Budapest, 1), followed by the six- or seven-digit telephone number. **To make international calls:** To make international calls from Hungary, dial 00 and then the country code (U.S. or Canada 1, U.K. 44, Ireland 353, Australia 61, New Zealand 64). Next you dial the area code and number. **To make a call from one Hungary area code to another,** first dial 06; when you hear a tone, dial the area code and number.

Time Zone Hungary is on Central European time, 2 hours ahead of Greenwich Mean Time and 6 hours ahead of Eastern Standard Time from March 26 to October 26; from October 27 to March 25 (during the equivalent of daylight saving time), the difference is 1 hour and 5 hours, respectively.

Tipping If a restaurant bill includes a service fee, as some restaurants do, it usually goes to the business. Adding another 10% to 15% for the server is appreciated.

Water Tap water is safe for drinking. Mineral water, which many Hungarians prefer to tap water, is called *ásványvíz.* Purified bottled water has pink labels for identification.

3 BUDAPEST

I have been living and working in Budapest since 2001 and the changes have been incredible, but may not be apparent to the casual visitor. The youth strive to become more European in their values, dreams, and goals while the older generations cling to the past. Young Hungarians are making their names known internationally in the film, music, and fashion arenas. Hungarians not being risk takers by nature, a few are breaking out of the box and succeeding while paving the way for others to follow.

ARRIVING

BY PLANE The **Airport Shuttle** (✆ **1/296-8555;** www.bud.hu/english) is a public service owned and operated by the Budapest Airport Authority. There is a clearly visible kiosk in each of the terminals. A round-trip fare is 4,390 Ft ($24/£13 per person) and one-way is 2,490 Ft ($13/£8.05 per person). The fares are the same for both airports. Depending on the number of people, you may find the taxi service to be less expensive.

Although in the past airport taxis were notorious for swindling tourists, the airport authority took steps to correct this situation. The airport now exclusively contracts with **Zóna Taxi** (✆ **1/365-5555**), making this the official taxi service of both airports. Their fares are fixed rates per cab, not per person, and adhere to predestined zones within the city.

It's also possible to get to or from the airport by public transportation; the trip takes about 1 hour total. Take the red-lettered **bus no. 93** to the last stop, Kőbánya-Kispest. From there, the Blue metro line runs to the Inner City of Pest. The cost is two transit tickets, which are 270 Ft ($1.45/90p) each; tickets can be bought from the automated vending machine at the bus stop (coins only) or from any newsstand in the airport. From **Ferihegy 1,** there are two bus options: **bus no. 93** and **bus no. 200.** I recommend bus no. 200 as it is a new route that is shorter with less stops, but with the same ending stop.

There is also an airport train, which runs from **Ferihegy 1** to **Nyugati** train station. The cost is 300 Ft ($1.60/£1) for one way. There are over 30 trains daily. If you arrive at **Ferihegy 2,** take either bus above to **Ferihegy 1** in order to catch the train.

BY TRAIN Budapest has three major train stations: **Keleti** pályaudvar (Eastern Station), **Nyugati** pályaudvar (Western Station), and **Déli** pályaudvar (Southern Station). The stations' names, curiously, have no correspondence to anything, so don't try to use any logic here. Each has a metro station beneath it and an array of accommodations offices, currency-exchange booths (which I recommend avoiding), and other services, including food. Under no circumstances should a traveler take a taxi from any of the train stations unless you have called the company yourself. This is the most-often-used scam for tourists, charging inflated prices and taking 20 minutes to get to a destination 5 minutes away.

Most international trains arrive at **Keleti Station** (✆ **1/314-5010**). An impressively elegant European train station on the outside, it is located in Pest's old and tired Baross tér, beyond the Outer Ring on the border of the VII and VIII districts. Various people will be offering rooms and taxis to travel-weary tourists, but a polite smile while you continue walking is all that is needed to tell them you are not interested. The Red line of the metro is below the station; numerous bus, tram, and trolleybus lines serve Baross tér as well.

Some international trains arrive at **Nyugati Station** (✆ **1/349-0115**), another classic designed by the Eiffel company and completed in1877. This is the site of the first Hungarian train station dating back to 1846. The current station is located on the Outer Ring, at the border of the V, VI, and XIII districts. The Blue line metro is beneath Nyugati. Numerous tram and bus lines serve busy Nyugati tér.

Few international trains, but some from Vienna, arrive at **Déli Station** (✆ **1/375-6293**); a modern ugly building, it borders on the depressing. It is the only station on the Buda side; the terminus of the Red metro line is beneath this train station.

MÁV operates a minibus that will take you from any of the three stations to the airport. However, the pricing system is complicated and depends on how many passengers are traveling, which station you are leaving from, and enough other variables to recommend calling a legitimate taxi service instead. If you are not dissuaded by this, then call the minibus at ✆ **1/353-2722.**

BY BUS The Népliget Bus Station is the city's recently opened modern main bus terminal on the Red metro line at the **Stadionok** stop. The Blue line goes to the much smaller **Árpád híd bus station** that caters to domestic bus service only.

CITY LAYOUT

To really appreciate the city and the layout, you will need a short history lesson. The city of Budapest came into being in 1873, making it relatively young in its present form. It is the result of a union of three separate cities: Buda, Pest, and Óbuda (literally meaning Old Buda), consisting of 23 self-governing municipal districts. Budapest is divided by the river Danube (Duna) with Pest, almost completely flat on the eastern shore, making up almost two-thirds of the city. On the western bank is Buda and farther yet, Óbuda, which are the hilly areas; these areas being much older settlements. The Danube River flows eastward, making some strange twists and turns, flowing through or forming part of a border of 10 European countries. It is the longest river in the European Union.

GETTING AROUND

By Public Transportation

Budapest has an extensive and efficient transportation system. If you have some patience and minimal skills with reading maps, you can easily learn the system. Public transportation, however, has its drawbacks due to the construction of a fourth metro line. There have been interruptions citywide that will continue until 2010 at the earliest. The biggest disadvantage, however, is that metros and tram routes shut down for the night at around 11:30pm (see "Night Service," below). Some areas of the city, most notably the Buda Hills, are beyond the reach of some night bus services. Taxis to the rescue. During rush hours, all forms of transport are crowded, making it best to plan your travel around these times. Most importantly, crowded public transport is the place where you are most likely to be targeted by Budapest's professional pickpockets.

FARES **All forms of public transportation** (metro, bus, tram, trolleybus, some HÉV railway lines, and cogwheel railway) in Budapest require the self-validation of prepurchased tickets *(vonaljegy),* which cost 270 Ft ($1.45/90p) apiece (children 5 and under travel free); single tickets can be bought at metro ticket windows and newspaper kiosks. There are also automated machines in most metro stations and at major transportation hubs, but I still don't trust them. I recommend buying a transport pass to avoid the trouble of constantly having to replenish your tickets. For 2,350 Ft ($13/£7.85) you can get a 10-pack *(tizes csomag).*

A transport pass does not require validation. They are available for 1 day *(napijegy)* for 1,550 Ft ($8.40/£5.20) and are good until midnight of the day marked. The other pass options are 3 days *(turistajegy)* for 3,400 Ft ($18/£11), 7 days for 4,000 Ft ($22/£14), and 14 days *(kéthétibérlet)* for 5,300 Ft ($29/£18). The 7- and 14-day passes need to be signed.

If your stay is even longer, there is a 30-consecutive-day pass *(30 napos bérlet)* at 8,250 Ft ($45/£28), which requires a photo. If you are going to be here for 4 to 5 days, the 7-day *(hetijegy)* pass is still a savings over individual tickets. Passes are more convenient than a handful of tickets. Honestly, these will save you money in the end. Dark-blue-uniformed inspectors check for valid tickets, particularly at the top the escalators to metro platforms. They may also approach you on trams or buses. On-the-spot fines of 6,000 Ft ($32/£20) are assessed to fare dodgers; pleading ignorance generally doesn't work. Risking a time-consuming altercation with metro inspectors is probably not worth it. Metro tickets are good for 1 hour for any distance along the line you're riding. Passes provide unlimited travel.

I do not recommend the **Budapest Card,** a tourist card that combines a 3-day *turistajegy* (transportation pass) with free entry to certain museums and other discounts; those discounts are marginal and you will not make up the cost.

SCHEDULES & MAPS All public transport operates on rough schedules, posted at bus and tram shelters and in metro stations. The schedules are a little confusing at first, but the column on the left is weekdays, the middle is Saturdays, and the right is Sundays and holidays. Make note of the last ride of the night or you will be waiting for a bus that is not coming until the wee hours of the morning.

The transportation map produced by the Budapest Transport Authority *(BKV térkép)* is sometimes available at metro ticket windows for a small fee. On the map's reverse side is a full listing of routes, including the all-important night-bus routes. There has been a shortage of these maps and it is uncertain whether they will continue printing them or not.

NIGHT SERVICE Most of the Budapest transportation system closes down between 11:10pm or midnight and 4:30am. There are, however, 31 night routes, a dramatic increase over years past. They're generally quite safe, though you may find a number of loud and inebriated youth or tourists traveling as well. For the most part, they are harmless. Night routes are posted at bus stops if that route has one. All night buses have a 9 as the first of a three-digit number. A few of them share the same numbers as buses on daytime routes or they may actually run different routes. You will need a special night-bus ticket for 350 Ft ($1.90/£1.15) to be purchased from the driver with exact change. A pass eliminates the need for additional tickets.

UNDERPASSES Underpasses are the way you cross most major boulevards in Budapest. Underpasses are often little underground cities with vendors, shops, and bakeries, some with bars. The most confusing part for a traveler—as well as some long-time residents—is which exit to use. Many of them have as many as five or six different exits, each letting you out onto a different part of the square or street, which can be quite disorienting. Signs direct you, often using the word *fele,* meaning "toward." The signs will also include the street(s) at the top of the stairs. I suggest that before you enter the underground, you take note of the landmarks on the corner of your destination, framing the direction you will need to follow once downstairs.

By Metro

The metro system is clean and efficient, with trains running every 3 to 5 minutes on weekdays and 6 to 8 minutes on weekends, from about 4:30am until about 11:10pm. There are currently three lines, with only the Red line going under the Danube to Buda. The three existing lines are universally known by colors, but numbers are also used: Yellow (1), Red (2), and Blue (3). You will see both the color and number on maps, and all signs are color-coded. All three lines converge at **Deák tér,** the only point where any of the lines meet.

The **Yellow (1) line** is the oldest metro on the European continent and second oldest in the world, having been built in 1894 as part of the Hungarian millennial celebration. Refurbished and restored to its original splendor, it is the most attractive and shortest metro line in the city. Yellow metro signs are different from those for the Red and Blue lines. They lack the M to signify metro. Instead, the aboveground stations have large yellow signs above the stairwells with the word *földalatti* (underground). Most of the stations entryways are painted yellow as a visual clue. Each station has two separate entrances, one for each direction. Confusingly, some of the stairwell entrances are in the opposite direction from the direction the train will be going.

The **Red (2)** and **Blue (3) lines** are modern metros, though the outside of the cars tend to look old and decrepit. To reach them you descend long, steep escalators; the Red line has the longest and steepest. If you are prone to vertigo, you may want to take care. The Red line runs from Örs vezér tere in eastern Pest, through the center, and under the Danube, finally ending at Déli Station. Nyugati Station is along the Blue line.

On the street, distinctive colored **m** signs of both the Red and Blue lines point out the stations. Validate tickets at automated boxes before you descend the escalator. When changing lines at Deák tér, you're required to validate another ticket (unless you have a special "metro transfer ticket"). The orange or red validating machines are in the hallways between lines, but are easy to miss, particularly if there are big crowds.

By Bus

There are almost 175 different bus *(busz)* lines in greater Budapest. Many parts of the city, most notably the Buda Hills, are best accessed by bus. Although buses are the most difficult to use of Budapest's transportation choices, with patience (and a BKV map) you'll be able to get around. With the exception of night buses, most lines are in service from about 4:30am to about 11:30pm. Some bus lines run far less frequently (or not at all) on weekends, while others run far more frequently (or only) on weekends. This information is posted at every bus stop.

Black-numbered local buses constitute most of the city's lines. Buses with red numbers are express buses that skip minor stops. Check the list at the stop to see if your destination is one of the stops. If the red number on the bus is followed by an E (there are only five routes with an E), the bus makes very few stops between terminals and is best avoided. Look for the sign on the front of the bus to see if it is a regular or express.

Tickets are self-validated onboard the bus by red boxes found by the doors. You can board the bus by any door, but manners dictate that you stand to the side of the door to allow disembarking passengers out before you start to board. Each time you change buses, you need a new ticket and have to validate it. Again, this is not necessary with a transport pass. Tickets cannot be purchased from the driver; see "Fares" above for more information.

By Tram

You'll find Budapest's 32 bright-yellow tram lines (known as *villamos* in Hungarian) very useful, particularly nos. 4 and 6, which travel along the Outer Ring (Nagykörút). Tram no. 2, which travels along the Danube on the Pest side between Margit híd and Boráros tér, provides an incredible view of the Buda Hills, including the Castle District. It is better than a tour bus. I especially recommend this route at night. Tickets are self-validated onboard. As with buses, tickets are valid for one ride, not for the line itself. ***Important:*** The red buttons near the tram doors are for emergency stops, not stop requests.

When a tramline is closed for maintenance, replacement buses are assigned the tram route. They go by the same number as the tram, with a V (for *villamos*) preceding the number. See "Fares" above for information on tickets.

By Trolleybus

Trolleybuses are electric buses that receive power from a cable above the street. There are only 16 trolleybus lines in Budapest, all in Pest. Of particular interest to train travelers is no. 73, the fastest route between Keleti Station and within a block of Nyugati Station. All the information in the "By Bus" section above applies to trolleybuses as well. See "Fares" above for information on tickets.

By HÉV

The HÉV is a suburban railway network that connects Budapest to various points along the city's outskirts. There are four HÉV lines; only the Szentendre line is of importance here.

Most hotels, restaurants, and sights in northern Buda and Óbuda are best reached by the HÉV (so indicated in the directions given). To reach Óbuda's Fő tér (Main Sq.), get off at the Árpád híd (Árpád Bridge) stop. For trips within the city limits, the cost is one transit ticket, self-validated as described above, or use a pass.

The HÉV suburban railroad connects Budapest's Batthyány tér with Szentendre. On the Pest side, you can catch the HÉV from the Margit Híd, Budai Híd Fő.Trains leave daily, year-round, every 20 minutes or so from 4am to 11:30pm (trip time: 45 min.). The one-way fare is 500 Ft ($2.70/£1.65); subtract 230 Ft ($1.25/80p) if you have a valid Budapest public transportation pass. The trip takes 45 minutes. This HÉV route runs regularly between 4am and 11:30pm.

By Cogwheel Railway & Funicular

Budapest's **cogwheel railway** *(fogaskerekű)* began running in 1874, becoming electrified in later years. It runs from Városmajor, across the street from the Hotel Budapest on Szilágyi Erzsébet fasor in Buda, to Széchenyi-hegy, one terminus of the Children's Railway (Gyermek Vasút) in 20 minutes. The cogwheel railway runs from 5am to 11pm, and normal transportation tickets (see "Fares," above; self-validated onboard) are used.

The **cable car** or **funicular** *(sikló)* connects Buda's Clark Ádám tér, at the head of the Széchenyi Chain Bridge, with Dísz tér, just outside the Buda Castle. The funicular is one of only two forms of public transportation serving the Castle District (bus nos. 10 and 16 are the other possibilities; see "By Bus," above). The funicular offers an extremely steep and short ride, but an excellent view. It runs at frequent intervals from 7:30am to 10pm daily (closed on the second Mon of the month). Tickets cost 700 Ft ($3.80/£2.35) to go up and 1,300 Ft ($7.30/£4.50) for a round-trip for adults, while children get a break at 400 Ft ($2.15/£1.35) up and 750 Ft ($4.05/£2.50) round-trip.

By Taxi

Budapest taxis fall into two general categories: legitimate and not. All legal taxis must have a yellow license plate and a yellow taxi sign on the roof. The fare to be paid at the destination consists of three basic parts: the base fee; the kilometer distance fare; and the waiting tariff, which is used if the taxi has had to stop or has to travel slower than 15kmph (9 mph) in traffic. Fares are due to rise in 2009, but government approval has yet to determine the amount.

The best rates are invariably those of the larger fleet companies. I particularly recommend **Tele5** (✆ **1/355-5555**). Other reliable fleets include **City Taxi** (✆ **1/211-1111**), **Volántaxi** (✆ **1/466-6666**), **Rádió Taxi** (✆ **1/377-7777**), and **Fő Taxi** (✆ **1/222-2222**). Call one of these companies from your hotel, ask a restaurant person, or ask whoever is in charge to call for you, even if there are other private taxis waiting around outside. You will seldom, if ever, wait more than 5 minutes for a fleet taxi unless you're in an extremely remote neighborhood (or in bad weather).

Dishonest drivers will ask you to pay for the return trip, ask to be paid in anything but forints, or quote you a "flat rate" in lieu of running the meter. The chances are slim that you will encounter this with any of the companies above. If you need extra room, request a station wagon by asking for a *kombi,* and in the summer you can also request an air-conditioned vehicle.

Tipping is usually not more than 10%. Hungarians usually round the bill up. If you think the driver has cheated you, then you should call the company and complain, as most will punish their members for untoward behavior.

By Car

I believe anyone wanting to drive in Budapest has a death wish. Not only are there crazy drivers, but you also will find a serious lack of stop signs or traffic lights on most streets. However, you may wish to rent a car for trips out of the city. Hertz, Avis, Alamo, National, and Budget have offices in the city and at the airport, but marginally better deals may be found by making arrangements directly and in advance on their websites. You are urged to reserve a rental car as early as possible. If you reserve from abroad, ask for written confirmation by fax or e-mail. If you don't receive a confirmation, it's wise to assume that the reservation has not been properly made.

I have sample quoted rates for an economy car currently listed by two agencies with these conditions: The driver must be 21 years old with no upper age limit and is the only authorized driver; the driver's license must be at least 1 year old; an International driver's license is required. Please note, I have had many negative comments from readers on their car-rental experiences.

Budget Car Rental, at both Ferihegy Airports or at I. Krisztina körút 41–43 in the Hotel Mercure Buda (✆ **1/214-0420**), requires a credit card deposit equal to twice the amount of the rental terms. A rental is a continuous 24-hour day. The renter is responsible for any damages and repairs needed. A typical economy car, such as a Ford Fiesta, rents for 15,000 Ft ($81/£50) a day for a 1- to 3-day rental, or 65,000 Ft ($351/£218) for a week. They also require a hold on a credit card of 255,000 Ft ($1,377/£854) as a deposit. This includes insurance, unlimited mileage within Hungary, and VAT.

Fox Auto Rent, XXII. Nagytétényi út 48–50, XXII Budapest (✆ **1/382-9000;** fax 1/382-9003; www.fox-autorent.com), rents the Fiat Panda for 12,000 Ft ($65/£40) per day for a rental of 1 to 3 days, and 65,000 Ft ($351/£218) for a week, insurance and mileage included. They also require a deposit of 100,000 Ft ($541/£335) on a credit card. Though located far from the city center, Fox will deliver the car to you at your hotel without charge between 8am to 6pm, but only if you book it directly through the number above. Rates are more expensive if booked online. Special arrangements need to be made directly with the office listed if you intend to drive outside of Hungary.

VISITOR INFORMATION

The tourism infrastructure has developed extensively over the years with strong support from the Ministry of Tourism. There are many high-quality hotels and restaurants; and it seems new ones are appearing every few months. Most cities have a tourism-related information office usually called **TourInform** (✆ **1/438-8080** or 06/80-630-800; www.tourinform.hu), a branch of the Hungarian National Tourist Office, at V. Sütő u. 2, Budapest; open daily from 8am to 8pm. You'll also find a branch office in the heart of Budapest's Broadway, at Liszt Ferenc tér 11 (✆ **1/322-4098;** fax 1/342-2541), open weekdays from 10am to 6pm. In the castle district, it is located at Szentháromság tér (✆ **1/488-0475;** fax 1/488-0474), open daily from 10am to 6pm.

The ***Budapest Sun*** (www.budapestsun.com) and ***Budapest Times*** (www.budapesttimes.hu), both English-language weekly newspapers, also have listings for concerts, theater, dance, film, and other events, along with restaurant reviews and the occasional interesting article; they are available at most hotels and many newsstands. ***Funzine*** magazine, a free au courant, hip publication, has all of the current cultural events with lots of visual information for travelers. It is available at hotels, restaurants, and the TourInform offices.

WHERE TO STAY

Seasons

Hotels and pensions in Budapest often use three seasons, but without conformity. **High season** is roughly from March or April through September or October. The week between Christmas and New Year's, Easter week, and the period of the Budapest Spring Festival (mid- to late March) are also considered high season. **Special season** is the weekend of the Grand Prix, which is the second weekend in August. The months of March (except the Budapest Spring Festival in mid- to late March) and October and/or November are usually considered **special season. Low season** is roughly November through February. Many of the larger hotels offer a holiday discount on their websites. Shop around for the best deal. Be aware that some accommodations on the Buda side may have transportation impeded due to the metro 4 construction, making it difficult to access downtown Pest.

Price Categories

Most accommodations in Budapest list their prices in euros as a hedge against forint inflation (though the forint has done well over the past few years). Hungary is not expected to adopt the euro until 2012. All hotels in Budapest accept payment in Hungarian forints as well as in foreign currencies. Where prices are quoted in euros, I provided a dollar conversion. The exchange rate as this book goes to press is 1€ equals US$1.27. Exchange rates fluctuate over time, of course, so the price of a room in dollars will change as the euro-to-dollar exchange rate changes.

All hotels are required to charge a 12% value-added tax (VAT). Most build the tax into their rates, while a few tack it on top of their rates. When booking a room, ask whether the VAT is included in the quoted price. Unless otherwise indicated, prices in this book include the VAT.

Note: I have found that the websites of small hotels are frequently neglected and out of date with respect to rates, so make sure to call or e-mail the hotel to confirm.

The Inner City & Central Pest

Very Expensive

Four Seasons Hotel Gresham Palace ★★★ This hotel is so remarkable, tour buses stop here. Walking into this Art Nouveau building, one of the most elegant and majestic properties in the city, it stands as one of the finest in the world. With the Chain Bridge directly opposite the front doors, it has a picture-perfect view of the Buda Castle, making this the most picturesque location of any hotel in the city. Built as the Gresham Life Assurance Company in 1906, it awed the world with the craftsmanship provided by the most acclaimed craftsmen available. Nearly destroyed by World War II, it was most recently restored so that every single piece of remaining decor has been brought back to its original glory. As is Four Seasons tradition, guests are pampered in every way possible. Mahogany furniture beautifully appoints all rooms. Each bathroom in every room is fitted with Italian and Spanish marble with deep-soak bathtubs. Due to the shape of the building, not all rooms within a category are the same size, but the little space differences will not be missed. The spa has a full range of services available. This hotel does not follow traditional seasons for its rates; bed-and-breakfast specials are on the website throughout the year.

V. Roosevelt tér 5–6, 1051 Budapest. ✆ **800/819-5053** in North America, or 1/268-6000. Fax 1/268-5000. www.fourseasons.com/budapest. 179 units. 320€–860€ ($406–$1,092) double; 1,050€–4,800€ ($1,334–$6,096) suite. 20% VAT not included. Children stay free in parent's room. Breakfast 7,200 Ft ($39/£24). AE, DC, MC, V. Parking 10,000 Ft ($54/£33) per day. Metro: Deák (all lines). **Amenities:** 2 restaurants; bar; indoor swimming pool; sauna; exercise room; concierge; airport transfer; business center; salon; 24-hr. room service; massage; laundry service; dry cleaning. *In room:* A/C, satellite TV, fax machine available, Web TV, high-speed Internet access for a fee, minibar, hair dryer, safe, robe, slippers, newspapers.

Le Meridien Budapest ★★★ Centrally located near Deák tér is Le Meridien, which was originally designed in 1913 for the Italian Adria Insurance Company; the building was completed in 1918. After World War II, the Budapest Police made this their home until 1997. The original structure is a protected monument, thus still has its austere exterior. The Duna Plaza Group bought the structure, reopening at the end of 2002. Elegant architectural details are evident in the lobby as well as the hallways, surrounded by wrought-iron railings. These overlook the stained-glass dome topping the breakfast area below. Guest rooms are beautifully appointed with French classical decor with a navy-and-beige color scheme, luxurious fabrics, and mahogany furniture. The suites are sumptuously grand, with some having artificial fireplaces, and range from extra large to huge. Bathrooms are high styled with marble floors and sink tops, and separate tubs and showers. On the eighth floor, you will find the spa and fitness room designed with a glass ceiling, filling the room with natural light. Le Meridian Budapest is a new Starwood Preferred Reward Program partner as of 2007.

V. Erzsébet tér 9–10, 1051 Budapest. ✆ **800/253-0861** in North America, 0845/6000-778 in Britain, or 1/429-5500. Fax 1/429-5555. www.lemeridien/budapest.com. 218 units. 399€–429€ ($507–$545) double; 499€–3,000€ ($634–$3,810) suite. VAT and city tax not included. Children 12 and under stay free in parent's room. Breakfast 27€ ($34). AE, MC, V. Parking 9,000 Ft ($49/£30) per day. Metro: Deák tér (all lines). **Amenities:** 2 restaurants; bar; indoor swimming pool; sauna; steam bath; exercise room; concierge; tour desk; business center; conference facilities; wireless Internet on conference floor; salon; 24-hr. room service; massage; babysitting; laundry service; currency exchange. *In room:* A/C, TV, stereo in suites, high-speed Internet for a fee (free in suites), minibar, coffee/tea, hair dryer, safe, PlayStations upon request.

ACCOMMODATIONS ■

Andrássy Hotel **29**
Art'Otel Budapest by Park Plaza **11**
Atrium Hotel **52**
Baross Hotel **44**
Berg Hotel **6**
BudaBaB **51**
Charles Apartment House **15**
City Ring Hotel **21**
Four Seasons Hotel Gresham Palace **45**
Hilton Budapest **8**
Hilton Budapest West End **22**
Hotel Zara **57**
Ibis Heroes Square **23**
Le Meridien Budapest **46**
NH Hotel **19**

DINING ◆

Aztek Choxolat Café **48**
Bajai Halászcsárda **3**
Blue Tomato Pub **20**
Café Eklektika **38**
Café Noé **50**
Centrál Kávéház **54**
Cotton Club **34**
Eden **5**
Frici Papa Kifőzés **41**
Gerlóczy Kávéház **47**
Govinda Vegetariánus Étterem **37**
Gundel **26**
Hemingway **17**
Két Szerecsen **40**
Kogart Restaurant **28**
Marquis de Salade **33**
Mátyás Pince **53**
Paprika Vendéglő **30**
Remiz **4**
Rétesvár **9**
Rivalda Café & Restaurant **12**
Shalimar **43**
Tabáni Terasz **14**
Taverna Dionysos **56**

ATTRACTIONS ●

Aquincum (Roman Ruins) **1**
Budapest Holocaust Memorial Center (Holokauszt Emlékközpont) **59**
Dohány Synagogue **49**
Ferenc Liszt Memorial Museum (Liszt Ferenc Emlékmúzeum) **36**
Fisherman's Bastion (Halászbástya) **7**
Gellért Baths **18**
Heroes' Square
Hősök tere (Heroes' Square) **24**
Király Baths **2**
Ludwig Museum of Contemporary Art (Ludwig Múzeum) **58**
Ethnographical Museum (Néprajzi Múzeum) **32**
House of Terror (Terror Háza) **35**
Hungarian National Gallery (Nemzeti Galéria) **13**
Hungarian National Museum (Nemzeti Múzeum) **55**
Hungarian State Opera House (Magyar Állami Operaház) **39**
Matthias Church (Mátyás Templom) **10**
Museum of Fine Arts (Szépművészeti Múzeum) **25**
Parliament **31**
Rudas Baths **16**
St. Stephen's Church (Szent István Bazilika) **42**
Széchenyi Baths **27**

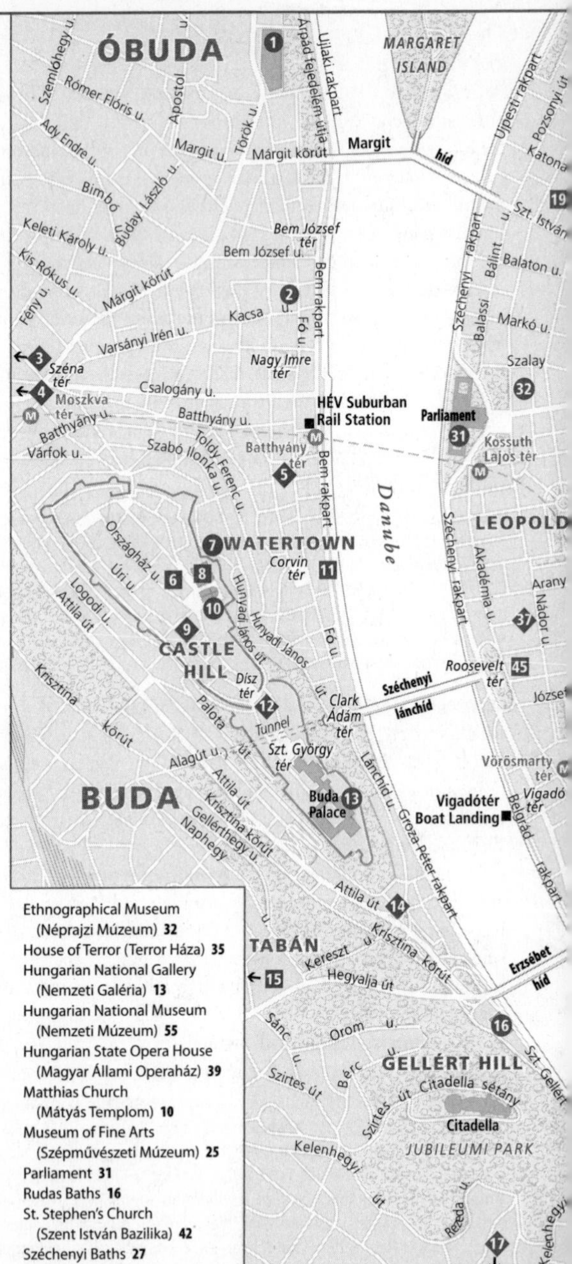

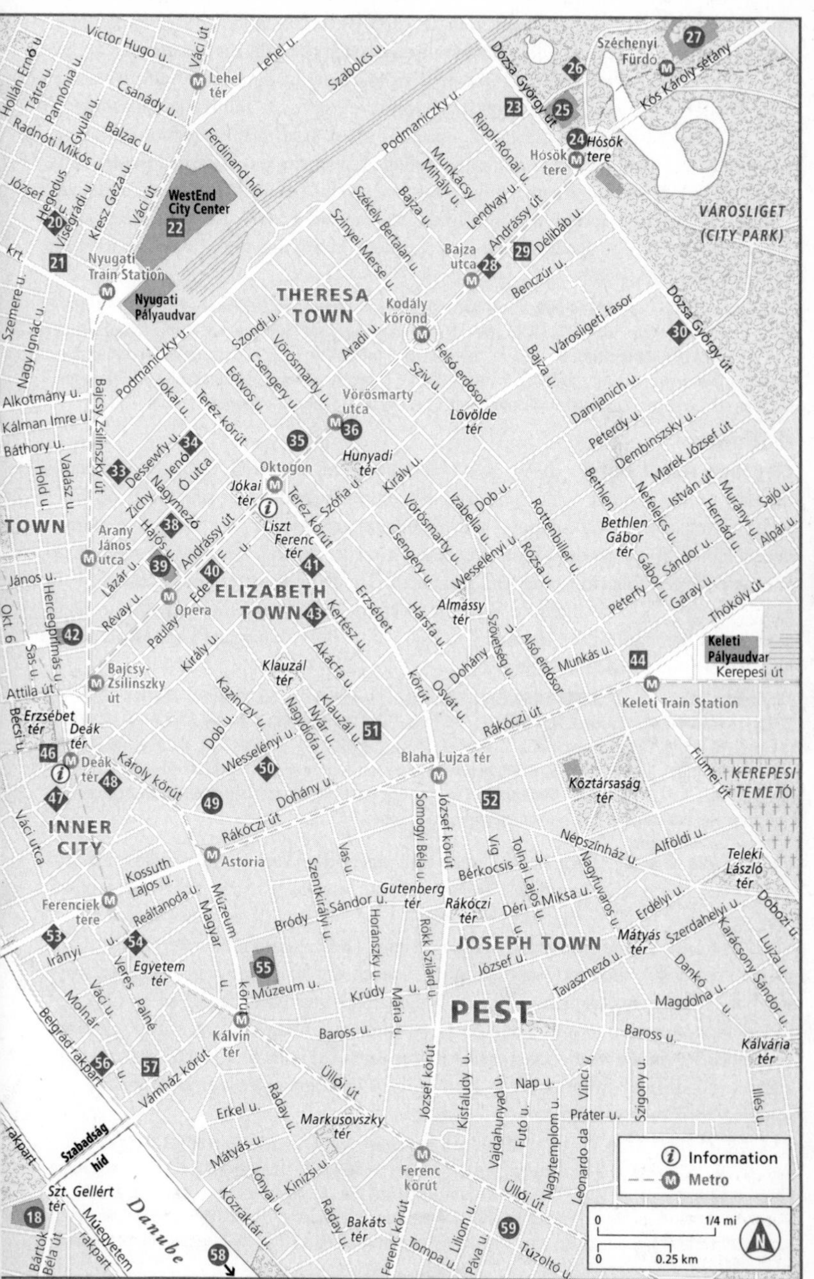
THERESA TOWN
ELIZABETH TOWN
INNER CITY
JOSEPH TOWN
PEST
TOWN
VÁROSLIGET (CITY PARK)
KEREPESI TEMETŐ
Danube
WestEnd City Center
Nyugati Train Station
Nyugati Pályaudvar
Keleti Pályaudvar
Keleti Train Station
Széchenyi Fürdő
Hősök tere
Oktogon
Deák tér
Astoria
Ferenciek tere
Kálvin tér
Blaha Lujza tér
Ferenc körút
Bajza utca
Kodály körönd
Vörösmarty utca
Opera
Arany János utca
Bajcsy-Zsilinszky út
Lehel tér
Andrássy út
Rákóczi út
Teréz körút
Erzsébet körút
József körút
Ferenc körút
Károly körút
Múzeum körút
Vámház körút
Dózsa György út
Üllői út
Szabadság híd
Information
Metro
0 1/4 mi
0 0.25 km
N

Expensive

NH Hotel ★★★ I don't usually associate modern elegance with a homey atmosphere, but this Spanish-owned chain has it. Built in 2003, directly behind the Vigszinház Theater, this hotel has taken a modern, minimalist approach that still has a warm welcoming feeling. Their use of textiles in the room decor in shades of browns and tans with rich dark wood, the variety of fabric from the drapes, the bed cover, and the fabric panels on the bed board add cozy warmth to the spacious room. Add to this the mottled brown and tan marble used in the bathroom, the feeling of quiet elegance is carried throughout. The eighth-floor exercise room is limited but beautifully executed with modern exercise equipment, changing rooms, and a solarium. At the end of 2007, they had solar panels installed on the roof to generate their own electricity; this is one of the most eco-friendly hotels in the city.

XIII. Vigszinház u. 3. ✆ **1/814-000.** Fax 814-0100. www.nh-hotels.com. 160 units. 131€–191€ ($166–$243) double. Breakfast 16€ ($20). AE, DC, MC, V. Secured parking 16€ ($20) per day. Metro: Nyugati (Blue line) or tram 4 or 6. **Amenities:** Restaurant; bar; exercise room; bikes; room service; free LAN connection; massage; laundry service; dry cleaning. In room: A/C, TV, LAN connection (cable available), Wi-Fi for a fee, minibar, coffeemaker, hair dryer, iron on request, safe, electric adaptors on request.

Moderate

City Ring Hotel ★★★ Being only 1 block away, this is perfectly located for the train traveler coming or going from Nyugati train station. Situated on the ring road, you have access to transportation, shopping, and restaurants just outside your door. The rooms, overwhelmed by the modern furniture, have a crowded feeling, but they are more than adequate, impeccably clean, and with great beds. The showers are on the small side. The rooms are in a different building from the reception area, so you have to cross a small corridor before reaching the elevator. The staff will assist with luggage for those in need. This is operated by Mellow Moods.

XIII. Szent István krt. 22. ✆ **1/340-5450.** Fax 1/340-4884. www.cityhotels.hu. 39 units. 19,000 Ft–27,000 Ft ($103–$146/£64–£91) double, 24,000 Ft–33,500 Ft ($130–$181/£81–£112) triple, 21,500 Ft–30,750 Ft ($116–$166/£72–£103) deluxe double; special season 31,500 Ft ($170/£105) double, 40,500 Ft ($219/£136) triple, 37,750 Ft ($204/£126) deluxe double. Rates include full breakfast. AE, MC, V. Metro: Nyugati (Blue line) or tram 4 or 6. **Amenities:** Dry cleaning next-day service; hair dryer and iron at reception, free use; safe deposit box; nonsmoking rooms. *In room:* A/C, TV, minibar.

Hotel Zara ★★★ Located on a small side street off of Váci u., the pedestrian shopping street, it is just 2 short blocks from the Great Market, where it is extremely quiet. Having opened in 2006, this small boutique hotel is a beautifully executed mix of eclectic styles from Murano glass lights to Thai designs. The standard rooms seem small at 18 sq. m (193 sq. ft.), since most of them sport a queen-size bed, a rarity in less than a five-star hotel, but roomy enough to be comfortable. Superior rooms are 23 sq. m (247 sq. ft.), giving more room to spread out. Each is furnished in Asian modern, with a soft pink and chocolate-brown theme (even the bathrooms are tiled in browns and beiges) creating a warm mood. Only five rooms to a corridor give an intimate feeling; there are distinct smoking and nonsmoking floors.

V. Só u. 6. ✆ **1/577-0700.** Fax 1/577-0710. www.zarahotels.com. 74 units. 95€–150€ ($121–$191) standard, 105€–165€ ($133–$210) superior; special season 165€ ($210) standard, 185€ ($235) superior. Children 12 and under stay free in parent's room. Rates include VAT, city taxes, and breakfast. AE, MC, V. Metro: Kálvin tér (Blue line). Parking 18€ ($23). **Amenities:** Restaurant; bar; Wi-Fi free in public areas; room service; laundry service; dry cleaning same day. *In room:* A/C, TV, free high-speed Internet access, minibar, safe.

Inexpensive

BudaBaB ★★ Value This small bed-and-breakfast has been owned and operated by two American ex-pats for 5 years. BudaBaB being small allows the owners who are in residence to provide as much time and attention to guests' needs as they want. Breakfast is included. It is within the historic Jewish ghetto area. The kitchen has a mural painted by American artist Scott Allen, who is becoming known for his murals around the globe. Smoking is allowed in common rooms, but not bedrooms. ***Full disclosure:*** This accommodation is owned and operated by the author of this chapter.

VII. Akácfa u. 18. ✆ **1/267-5240.** www.budabab.com. 2 units. Double 45€–55€ ($57–$70); triple 55€–70€ ($70–$89); quad 85€ ($108). Breakfast included. No credit cards. Metro: Blaha Lujza (Red line). **Amenities:** Communal kitchen; Internet access available; hair dryer and iron available; Wi-Fi; washing machine.

Central Buda

Expensive

Art'Otel Budapest by Park Plaza ★★★ In 2000, a German chain opened this as the first Art'Otel outside of Germany. Each property spotlights the work of one particular artist, thus you are staying in a gallery of modern art. At this hotel, the artist is Donald Sultan, an American modernist. More than 600 pieces of his work grace the hotel's walls from the lobby to the hallways and guest rooms. He designed everything from the carpets to the dinnerware. The modern side of the hotel is a seven-story building facing the Danube, with a walkway leading to four 17th-century, two-story, baroque town houses, which now serve as rooms, suites, and the Chelsea Restaurant. Rooms are modern and comfortable with Sultan designs throughout. Somewhere in each room, there is a bird on a perch designed by Sultan. Rooms on the top three floors of the new building facing the Danube command the best views, especially rooms ending with 19, 20, and 21, but with a higher price tag, while rooms in the old houses have higher ceilings, some unusual doors and locks from their original era, but no view.

I. Bem Rakpart 16–19, Budapest. ✆ **1/487-9487,** 800/814-7000 in North America, 0800/169-6128 in Britain. Fax 1/487-9488. www.artotels.hu. 164 units. 125€–155€ ($159–$197) double non-Danube view, 25€ ($32) Danube view supplement; 155€–185€ ($197–$235) executive suite; 185€–210€ ($235–$267) art suite. Lower weekend and Internet rates. VAT included. Children 12 and under stay free in parent's room. Breakfast 12€ ($15). AE, DC, MC, V. Parking 15€ ($19) per day. Metro: Batthyány tér (Red line). **Amenities:** Restaurant; bar; sauna; exercise room; concierge; business center; wireless Internet in public areas; salon; limited room service. *In room:* A/C, TV, dataport for a fee w/ISDN, wireless Internet for a fee, minibar, coffeemaker (in suites and executive rooms or by request in superior rooms), hair dryer, iron/ironing board on request, safe, robe, slippers.

Moderate

Charles Apartment House ★ From 1991, owner Károly Szombati has accumulated 73 apartments in a group of buildings in a less-than-eye-appealing Buda side neighborhood. The apartments are a 45-minute walk at a good pace or a 15-minute bus ride from downtown Pest. All of the apartments were refurbished in 2006; though they are pleasant enough, spectacular does not come to mind. The furnishings are comfortable, clean, and for the most part new with the last remodel. All apartments have full bathrooms and kitchens stocked with dishes, cups, and silverware. Some kitchens are part of the bedroom, while others have them in a separate room. Request an interior room for less noise. Only the deluxe rooms have air-conditioning. A nearby park has tennis courts and a track. The friendly, English-speaking reception is open 24 hours.

I. Hegyalja út 23. ✆ **1/212-9169.** Fax 1/202-2984. www.charleshotel.hu. 73 units. 57€–79€ ($72–$100) double, 72€–89€ ($91–$11) deluxe double, 77€–114€ ($98–$145) triple, 77€–138€ ($98–$175) apt for 1–4 people; special season 100€ ($127) double, 130€ ($165) deluxe double, 130€–160€ ($165–$203) triple and apt. Rates include breakfast. Internet specials. AE, DC, MC, V. Parking 2,500 Ft ($14/£8.70) per day. Bus: 78 from Keleti pu. to Zsolt u. stop, then a 200m (656 ft.) walk; no. 8 or 112 stop in front. **Amenities:** Restaurant; bar; bike rental; business center (600 Ft/$3.25/£2) half-hour; free Wi-Fi in building; babysitting; laundry service. *In room:* A/C, TV, minibar, hair dryer in deluxe rooms and by request for standard, safe.

The Castle District

Expensive

Hilton Budapest ★★★ This Hilton has the most enviable piece of real estate in Budapest, sitting right next door to Matthias Church with part of the Fisherman's Bastion behind it. The hotel's award-winning design incorporated both the ruins of a 13th-century Dominican church (the church tower is alongside of the hotel) and the baroque facade of a 17th-century Jesuit college, which makes up the hotel's main entrance. The ruins were carefully restored during the hotel's construction, and others are on view in the wine cellar where art gallery exhibitions are open to the public. The hotel completed renovations in 2007; the rooms are now a uniform rose, green, and beige color scheme, and are very large for standard rooms. The corner suites are beautifully decorated with separate sitting areas, a dining area, and bedroom with oversized windows for a spectacular view of the Bastion and Danube. The very elegant Baroque Room is three levels and has a fully equipped kitchen. Other suites are small apartments with everything one would need. Rooms with a view of the Danube are more expensive, while the other rooms overlook the distinctive architecture of the district. The lovely Dominican Courtyard is the site of summer concerts. Two floors are smoke-free rooms.

Hess András tér 1–3. ✆ **1/899-6600.** Fax 1/899-6644. www.hilton.com. 322 units. 90€–160€ ($114–$203) advanced purchase; 100€–170€ ($127–$216) value rate; 120€–220€ ($152–$279) flexible rate; Danube view supplement 30€ ($38); 60€ ($76) executive-floor supplement. VAT and tourist tax not included. 1 child per adult stays free in parent's room. Breakfast 27€ ($34). AE, DC, MC, V. Parking 25€ ($31) per day in public garage. Bus: 10 from Moszkva tér or 16 from Deák tér. **Amenities:** Restaurant; bar; exercise room; concierge; Wi-Fi in lobby; shops; business center; salon; 24-hr. room service; massage in room; babysitting; laundry service. *In room:* A/C, TV, Wi-Fi for fee in standard rooms, minibar, coffeemaker, hair dryer, iron/ironing board, safe.

Moderate

Berg Hotel ★★★ Finds An overlooked treasure on Castle Hill, this hotel sits on a corner directly across from St. Matthias Church, an excellent location. The multilingual staff is as friendly as they are talented with languages. The rooms are spacious and beautifully decorated in muted greens, rose, and beige with modern, comfortable furniture. The corner rooms are extra large, but any room would be comfortable. The blue-tiled bathrooms are simple, but sizeable. All rooms have a view of Trinity Square. Breakfast is served in a large, lovely, decorated room with many windows overlooking the square. There is no lift, but it is only two floors above the ground-floor entrance.

I. Szentháromság tér 7–8. ✆ **1/212-0269.** Fax 1/212-3970. www.burghotelbudapest.com. 26 units. 99€–115€ ($125–$146) double, 29€–39€ ($36–$49) extra bed; special season 175€ ($222), extra bed 39€ ($49). Children 13 and under stay free in parent's room. Rates include breakfast, VAT, and tourist tax. Parking 25€ ($31) per day in public garage. AE, DC, MC, V. Bus: 10 from Moszkva tér or 16 from Deák tér. **Amenities:** Bar; Wi-Fi in lobby; laundry service; dry cleaning. *In room:* A/C, TV, minibar, hair dryer, safe.

Outer Pest

Very Expensive

Hilton Budapest WestEnd ★★ Shop until you drop has new meaning with the hotel conveniently located in West End City Center and located next to Nyugati train station. This Hilton focuses on the business set, but it welcomes leisure travelers as well. Opened in 2000, it was a start-up player in the new group of five-star hotels. Each room is stylishly decorated with extra large beds and a large ergonomic lounge chair offering luxurious relaxation. The room color scheme of eggplant, dark green, and tans is standard throughout all rooms. Bathrooms have both a shower and a tub, as two separate units in separate areas in oversized bathrooms. The fourth-floor executive lounge (and its panoramic views) makes check-in quick and easy, and where the service includes snacks and drinks throughout the day. The chic and ultramodern Zita cafe on the ground level attracts many people from the area due to its lunch specials.

VI. Váci út 1–3, 1069 Budapest. ✆ **800/445-8667** in North America, 00/800/44-45-86-68 in Britain. Fax 1/288-5588. www.hilton.com. 230 units. 200€–280€ ($254–$357) double; 260€–405€ ($330–$514) suite. Lower weekend rates. VAT and tourist tax not included. Breakfast 27€ ($34). AE, MC, V. Parking 4,000 Ft ($22/£14) per day. Metro: Nyugati pu (Blue line). **Amenities:** Restaurant; bar; cafe; sauna; exercise room; concierge; car-rental desk; business center; secretary services; Wi-Fi for fee; 24-hr. room service; babysitting; laundry service; dry cleaning same day. *In room:* A/C, TV, dataport w/ISDN, minibar, coffeemaker, hair dryer, iron/ironing board, safe, robe, slippers.

Expensive

Andrássy Hotel ★★★ This hotel started as the Bauhaus orphanage for Jewish children in 1937, but has had many incarnations since. As the Andrássy Hotel, the most recent renovation was at the end of 2007. The new theme of decor combines relaxing grays, greens, and browns, with burnt-orange sofas and chairs adjoining contemporary blond-wood furniture, with modern Asian prints. The holistic mood is a Zen feel, making it perfectly relaxing. The enormous suites are marvelous, featuring double beds, plasma TV, stuffed chairs, an artificial fireplace, balcony, and spacious bathrooms with massage showers, Jacuzzi bathtubs, and vintage Budapest prints. Standard rooms also share the new designs, but the spacious suites are worth the splurge. Most rooms come with terraces. Situated in an exclusive embassy neighborhood, just a few minutes' walk will get you to Heroes' Square or to the nearest metro station. You won't find fitness facilities here, but guests can use those at a partner hotel located nearby. The refreshed image continues its worthiness of their exclusive luxurious boutique hotel status featured in Small Luxury Hotels of the World (www.slh.com)—one of two in Hungary. Ask about the special Budapest/Tokaj packages arranged with Gróf Degenfeld Castle Hotel, another member of the Small Luxurious Hotels of the World, on their vineyard in Tokaj.

VI. Andrássy út 111. ✆ **1/462-2100.** Fax 1/322-9445. www.andrassyhotel.com. 70 units. 109€–229€ ($138–$291) classic; 129€–259€ ($164–$330) superior; 149€–289€ ($189–$367) deluxe; 209€–329€ ($265–$418) junior suite; 239€–409€ ($304–$519) ambassador suite. AE, DC, MC, V. Parking 16€ ($20) per day. Metro: Bajza u. (Yellow line). **Amenities:** Restaurant; lounge; concierge; wireless Internet throughout hotel, Wi-Fi card provided if needed; 24-hr. room service; massage in room; laundry service; dry cleaning same-day service. *In room:* A/C, satellite TV, VCR and DVD on request, dataport, fax, minibar, hair dryer, iron on request, safe, 2 phone lines, snacks, bathrobes, slippers, umbrella.

Atrium Hotel ★★ Opened in March 2007, this ultra-modern hotel, part of the Mellow Mood chain, is a breath of fresh air, only 1 block from the Red metro. The greenish-gray walls mixed with the blues in the carpeting make the rooms feel airy and roomy, yet exude coziness. The extra-large built-in double closet is convenient for a long-term stay, as each room has copious storage for clothes. Each room has soundproof windows. Attention to detail has been obvious when converting this former post office to its current incarnation, a completely smoke-free hotel. The bed has a firm mattress; the pillows are scrunchable. The bathroom is tiled with complimentary colors maintaining the color scheme. I loved the indented shelf with recessed lighting that runs the length of the bathroom wall. The 2/3-length shower door unfolds, exposing the extra-large shower head.

VIII. Csokonai u.14. ✆ **1/299-0777.** Fax 1/215-6090. www.hotelatrium.hu. 57 units, 22 with double beds and 35 with twin beds. 31,200 Ft–39,000 Ft ($168–$211/£104–£131) double, extra bed charge 7,000 Ft ($38/£24); special season 46,800 Ft ($253/£157) double. Rates include full breakfast. AE, MC, V. Parking 4,320 Ft ($23/£14) per day. Metro: Keleti (Red line). **Amenities:** Bar; room service; in-room massage; babysitting; dry cleaning. *In room:* A/C, TV, Wi-Fi, minibar, fridge, coffeemaker, hair dryer, safe.

Moderate

Baross Hotel ★ For rail travelers, you couldn't ask for a better location; this hotel is located across the street from Keleti train station. A bonus is having the Red metro just outside, along with four bus lines. On the minus side, Baross tér is not the prettiest of areas. With that said, this hotel is a little gem in the rough and the area is trying hard to clean its face. Constituting three floors of a larger building, all of the basics needed are in clean, brightly lit green-colored rooms. Certainly large enough for two people to be comfortable, the double bed was ultrafirm; conversely, the pillows were filled with foam rubber chunks, making them too mushy. If you request a room with the courtyard view, you will have plenty of natural light with pleasant flowerpots hanging on the railings, giving a minigarden effect. The apartments have kitchenettes. Guests run the gamut from seniors to young travelers in this mellow hotel. Baross tér is a busy street, so a room on that side may be noisier late at night.

VII. Baross tér 15. ✆ **1/461-3010.** Fax 1/343-2770. www.barosshotel.hu. 48 units. 78€–98€ ($99–$124) double, 90€–114€ ($114–$145) triple, 100€–126€ ($127–$160) quad, 125€–200€ ($159–$254) apt; special season 145€ ($184 double), 165€ ($210) triple, 180€ ($229) quad, apt same as high season. Rates include full breakfast. AE, MC, V. Parking 2,000 Ft ($11/£6.80) per day. Metro: Keleti (Red line). **Amenities:** Coin-op Internet access available for a fee; hair dryer, iron, and safe deposit at reception, free use; nonsmoking rooms. *In room:* A/C, TV, minibar, safe.

Ibis Heroes' Square ★★ Formerly the Hotel Liget, it is an unusual modern designed building by the Hungarian architect Jozsef Finta. The location is excellent, across the street from the zoo, the Museum of Fine Arts, and Heroes' Square. Accor bought the property in 2007, immediately remodeling it in the company's new "poppy" theme. Poppy red with beiges and tans is throughout the hotel and the rooms. Each room is 20 sq. m (215 sq. ft.), furnished with modern sleek furniture and wood floors. The terra-cotta-beige walls and deep red curtains are quietly soothing. Bathrooms are equipped with showers only, no tubs at all. The focus is on the business and leisure traveler, but not families. They offer both smoking and nonsmoking floors. For the best view of the zoo across the street, request room no. 420.

VI. Dózsa György út 106. ✆ **1/269-5300.** Fax 1/269-5329. 139 units. 61€–74€ ($77–$94); special season 130€ ($165). Breakfast 8€ ($10). 3% city tax. AE, DC, MC, V. Metro: Hősök tere (Yellow line). **Amenities:** Restaurant; bar; bike rental. *In room:* A/C, TV, Internet connection, Wi-Fi for a fee, hair dryer, iron available on request, safe.

WHERE TO DINE

Budapest naturally features the more traditional eateries serving Hungarian specialties, but you will also find an incredibly diverse range of ethnic restaurants. Ethnic restaurants have sprouted on the scene in the last decade, with just about all ethnic groups represented. Of course, the best part of travel is sampling the cuisine of the culture and you will have ample opportunities to choose either traditional or nouveau Hungarian recipes. Traditional dishes rely heavily on goose fat and the portions are generous.

However, one warning: While this country is landlocked, many restaurants pride themselves of their fresh seafood delights. *I recommend staying away from imported seafood, as it has been frozen.* At traditional Hungarian restaurants, you will find the national local fish soup: **Szeged** or **Tisza** fish soups incite national pride and are prepared with river fish, usually carp or catfish.

WARNING The U.S. Embassy provides a list of restaurants that engage in "unethical business practices" such as "excessive billing," using "physical intimidation" to compel payment of excessive bills, and "assaulting customers" for nonpayment of excessive bills. However, it states that this list is not comprehensive. At all costs, you should avoid these establishments. The list includes **Városközpont,** Budapest V district, Váci u. 16; **La Dolce Vita,** Október 6. u. 8; **Nirvana Night Club,** Szent István körút 13; **Ti'Amo Bar,** Budapest IX district, Ferenc körút 19–21; **Diamond Club,** Budapest II district, Bimbó út 3; and **Pigalle Night Club,** Budapest VIII district, Kiss József utca 1–3. If women approach you for "directions" and they ask for you to buy them a drink, the red flags should shoot into the air. The embassy cannot offer assistance in these situations due to Hungarian laws that are ineffective. Buyer beware.

You can always check the embassy website for more information: http://hungary.usembassy.gov/tourist_advisory.html.

The Inner City & Central Pest

Expensive

Cotton Club ★★★ (Finds INTERNATIONAL I came across this restaurant accidently. The restaurant is beautifully decked in a 1920s and '30s theme, focusing on the music of those eras. The period furniture and lighting keep this hideaway looking like a place of nostalgia. The eating area is all nonsmoking, but you can indulge in the adjoining cigar room. I had the garlic soup, which was strong with the stinking rose, just how I love it. I would have preferred a bowl rather than a cup. The crispy duck legs were served with red cabbage and potato doughnuts. I could not have asked for better—the legs were meaty and crispy. The waiters could not be more accommodating. The band starts playing at 8:30pm on weekends and continues through the night with a vocalist who pours out the songs of yesteryear.

VI. Jókai u. 26. ✆ **1/354-0886.** www.cottonclub.hu. Reservations recommended. Main courses 2,290 Ft–6,990 Ft ($12–$38/£7.65–£23). Daily noon–1am. AE, MC, V. Metro: Opera (Yellow line).

Mátyás Pince ★★★ (Moments HUNGARIAN TRADITIONAL Art, history, or music buffs will love this restaurant established in 1904, named for King Matthias; the myths and legends of his reign grace the walls in magnificent style. The frescoes and stained glass decorating the dining areas were registered as national monuments in 1973. Music is provided by the Lakatos Dynasty, a famous Gypsy ensemble, every night but Mondays, from 7pm until closing, creating an all-around romantic experience. I sampled the cold blackberry soup, rich in creamy fruit flavor. The main entree was King Matthias's favorite menu of sirloin of beef on a spit, leg of duck, gooseliver wrapped in bacon, roast sausage, onion potatoes, steamed cabbage, and letcho. Beautifully presented, every morsel was delectable, and certainly fit for a king, or anyone aspiring to eat like one. The service is impeccable. The menu is extensive. The combination of a memorable meal with entertainment is priceless.

V. Március 15 tér 7–8. ✆ **1/266-8008.** www.cityhotels.hu. Reservations recommended. Main courses 2,700 Ft–7,900 Ft ($15–$43/£9–£27). AE, MC, V. Daily 11am–midnight. Metro: Ferenciek tere (Blue line).

Taverna Dionysos GREEK Feel like you have been transported to Greece at this authentic-looking Greek tavern, located on Pest's Danube embankment? They serve all of the typical Greek specialties you would expect if you were sitting at a tavern in a Greek village. The menu comprises an extensive fish selection, shrimp, and lobster, as well as *souvlaki* and other delicacies, all in a Mediterranean environment. The restaurant is located in a typical Greek whitewashed building, and you are served on blue-and-white tablecloths. We have found the food here to be on par with what we have had in Greece, but our only complaint is that the servings seem to get smaller as the years go by while the prices are going up. Weather permitting, sidewalk dining overlooking the Danube is available, but call in advance to reserve.

V. Belgrád rakpart 16. ✆ **1/318-1222.** Reservations recommended. Main courses 2,800 Ft–12,100 Ft ($15–$65/£9.30–£40). MC, V. Daily noon–midnight. Metro: Ferenciek tere (Blue line).

Moderate

Blue Tomato Pub ★★★ HUNGARIAN CONTEMPORARY Don't let the name fool you; this is a serious place for treating your taste buds with tasty morsels. The dark woody walls are plastered with old Americana and European advertisements, creating a cozy homespun atmosphere. The smoking section is fully segregated from the nonsmokers, a real plus in Hungary. The corn soup with bacon and almond slivers tempted me. Thick, creamy, and with chunks of bacon and many almonds, it was bowl-licking delicious. Ordering rib steak with fried onions and oven-roasted potatoes turned out to be a satisfying surprise. The steak pounded thin and covered with a mound of thin crispy onion rings was delectable. A fellow diner had walnut-coated, stuffed, fried chicken breast. The only thing I regretted was not having come here before now. Fantastic food at reasonable prices with good service is a winning combination.

XIII. Pannónia u. 5–7. ✆ **1/339-8099.** www.bluetomato.hu. Reservations recommended. Main courses 1,390 Ft–3,900 Ft ($7.50–$21/£4.65–£13). MC, V. Mon–Sat 11am–4am; Sun noon–midnight. Tram: 4 or 6 Jászai Mari tér.

Café Eklektika ★★ Value HUNGARIAN CONTEMPORARY A mellow mood is created at this eatery by the soothing vocals with a cabaret feel serenading in the background, the monthly changing art work on the walls, and the dependably excellent service. Sometimes we are seduced by rosé duck breast with mashed potatoes and cinnamon-plum ragout. Beside the changing menu offerings, there are weekly specials on a blackboard. Outside seating is available in good weather, but inside free unlimited Wi-Fi is your treat for the price of a coffee. No one will rush you out; this is a place to call home away from home.

V. Nagymező 30. ✆ **1/266-1226.** Reservations for dinner recommended. Main courses 1,390 Ft–2,890 Ft ($7.50–$16/£4.65–£9.90). Cash only. Mon–Fri 10am–midnight; Sat–Sun noon–midnight.

Gerlóczy Kávéház ★★★ Value HUNGARIAN CONTEMPORARY Two of us had coffee here once by accident, when caught unexpectedly in a sudden summer storm. Enjoying the atmosphere, we vowed to return. When we did, we did so without reservations in both senses of the word. With the tables in front occupied, the host noticed our dilemma; he appeared with another table and set it with two chairs. This was the start of a perfect dinner, which included a half portion of two different ciabattas. The smoked sheep cheese with grilled peppers and garlic was enormous; think slices grilled to a crusty coat, but soft on the inside. They left little room for the salad that came with it. The five huge pieces of grilled filet mignon of pork appeared with boiled potatoes formed into a ball with Swiss chard interlaced. Both dishes had us nabbing at each other's plate with sounds of pleasure in between; neither was overly spiced, allowing the natural flavors to express their character, making it sumptuous. The waiter returned to check on us enough times to provide great service, but not enough to be disruptive. Thank goodness for sudden storms.

V. Gerlóczy u. 1. ✆ **1/235-0953.** Reservations recommended. Main courses: cold entrees 890 Ft–1,980 Ft ($4.80–$11/£3–£6.80), hot entrees 1,680 Ft–4,200 Ft ($9.10–$23/£5.65–£14). MC, V. Mon–Fri 7am–11pm; Sat–Sun 8am–11pm. Metro: Deák tér (Red line).

Két Szerecsen (Two Brothers) ★★ Kids SPANISH Having opened 7 years ago, this restaurant only gets better with time. After a dramatic remodel, the interior is expanded. Now with equally large smoking and nonsmoking rooms, each sports deep-orange walls and pounded-metal lamps with multicolored glass pieces dangling. What may be disturbing are the many old advertising signs and posters, which are dated in their depiction of black men, who are shown in subservient roles; we learned, however, that two black men from Africa had a coffee shop here over 100 years ago, and the restaurant's name and decor are a tribute to them. If you are in the mood for tapas, a sampling from the 13 choices could make a complete meal. The regular menu is not extensive, but a number of daily specials add to imaginative choices. One example is the lasagna with peach and duck ragout, which I tried. The pasta layers alternate with julienned carrots, peach bits, leaf spinach, and then covered with a light duck sauce. The portions are very generous. Sitting outdoors under the huge tree blocking the sun is relaxing, and although it is on a trolleybus route, there are no fumes and little noise from the electric buses.

VI. Nagymező u. 14. ✆ **1/343-1984.** www.ketszerecsen.hu. Reservations recommended. Tapas 670 Ft–1,590 Ft ($3.60–$8.60/£2.25–£5.35); main courses 1,390 Ft–3,990 Ft ($7.50–$22/£4.65–£14); children's menu 1,100 Ft ($5.95/£3.70). AE, DC, MC, V. Daily 8am–1am. Metro: Opera (Yellow line).

Marquis de Salade ★★★ Moments AZERBAIJAN We discovered this restaurant on our first trip to Budapest in 1998 and loved it then. After almost 10 years, it has only improved. Enter on the street level, but the restaurant is downstairs in a cavelike atmosphere, decorated in Asian rugs on the walls and ceiling. Beyond the first dining area, there is another room for a group of six and yet another room in the back is suitable for a romantic interlude. The latter is more like a Pasha's den with low seating and many cushions. Our group started with the Marquis's Salads, a sampler platter of six different salads. Along with the bread, this about constituted a diversely sumptuous meal, but we plunged forward with entrees; the Adajab sandal, a luscious lamb stew with eggplant, tomato, and potato cooked in a clay pot, was excellent. The spices had all of us savoring the flavors and begging for more. This is a small intimate restaurant, so the service is impeccable.

VI. Hajós u. 43. ✆ **1/302-4086.** www.marquisdesalade.hu. Reservations recommended. Main dishes 2,500 Ft–3,900 Ft ($14–$21/£8.70–£13). No credit cards. Daily 11am–1am. Metro: Arany János (Blue line). Bus: 70 or 78 to Bajcsy-Zsilinszky út.

Shalimar ★★★ INDIAN One could, and many have, walked right by this unpretentious restaurant, located downstairs, due to the small outdoor sign. Being amongst the first Indian restaurants in the city, it has reinvented itself a number of times, but it remains a perpetual award winner in Budapest culinary competitions. What you find on the menu are typical items from Mughlai cuisine, from northern India. They are typically rich meat dishes in various sauces, grilled meats using an enormous array of spices cooked in a tandoori along with different breads. Newly redecorated with false backlit stenciled windows, it has a fresh new appearance. We have been here so often over the years, we have sampled almost everything on the very extensive menu: Pork Vindiloo, for example, is served in lavish red gravy made with a coconut milk base, or the Shahi beef korma, cooked in a cashew-and-almond-cream gravy, is excellent. Order different naan breads baked in a tandoor clay oven, fired with charcoal to enrich your meal. For a while, the portions shrunk, but they are doggie-bag size once again. They now have business lunch specials with a fixed menu.

VII. Dob u. 50. ✆ **1/352-0305.** Reservations recommended. Business lunch special 1,100 Ft–1,300 Ft ($5.95–$7.05/£3.70–£4.35); main courses 1,680 Ft–4,150 Ft ($9.10–$22/£5.65–£14). AE, MC, V. Daily noon–4pm and 6pm–midnight. Tram: 4 or 6 to Király u.

Inexpensive

Frici Papa Kifőzés ★ Value HUNGARIAN TRADITIONAL This is a restaurant with attitude, not for the decor, but from the staff. At times, they can be downright surly, but it does not keep the customers away; we think it actually makes for entertainment with the meal, if you know what to expect. This is a plain, down-home place with no frills and the prices reflect it. The daily offerings—from soup to desserts and everything in between—are posted with signs hanging from a pegboard near the front windows. Everything is a la carte; even catsup for the French fries will cost you extra. If you want to see the living definition of a surly waiter, ask yours for something again after he has delivered your meal and before you ask for your check. The portions are humungous and when something runs out, that is the end of it. We love the chicken with the bleu cheese sauce, and the mashed potatoes are the real deal. Lunch or an early dinner is best to ensure the full day's selection is available. After 7pm, you are taking your chances. Now take a deep breath and order everything you think you want.

VI. Király u. 55. No phone. Main dishes 559 Ft–600 Ft ($3–$3.25/£1.85–£2). Cash only. Mon–Sat 11am–9pm. Tram: 4 or 6 Király u.

Govinda Vegetariánus Étterem ★ INDIAN Once you descend the steep steps to enter this restaurant, you will find a simply decorated, ultraclean restaurant that is run by the local Hare Krishna group here in the city. Eliminate any negative thoughts, since the proceeds from this restaurant help to support their efforts in feeding the homeless of the city by setting up a monthly food giveaway. They serve delicious vegetarian food in a tranquil, smoke-free environment with Indian gods and goddesses looking over your shoulder. The operation is on a self-service system, where you can choose from different dishes, each at a set price. You can also choose from two daily menu options written on a blackboard, or a small or large sampler platter. Choices might include stuffed squash with Indian ragout and brown rice; or a potato-pumpkin casserole with garlic Roquefort sauce, steamed cabbage, and spinach soufflé. Perhaps you only want a soup (cream of cauliflower or lentil) and the salad bar. Unless you have a healthy appetite, we recommend the small sampler, which is ample. Seating is plentiful, but this place can be packed at lunchtime on weekdays, so you may have to wait in line. The English-speaking staff will explain each dish. There is a small shop in back, stocked with New Age and Eastern literature, clothes, candles, and incense. For those inclined, there is a meditation room also.

V. Vigyázó Ferenc u. 4. ✆ **1/269-1625.** Main courses 620 Ft ($3.25/£2); small sampler meal 1,450 Ft ($7.80/£4.85); large sampler meal 1,750 Ft ($9.45/£5.85); student menu 720 Ft ($3.95/£2.45). Cash only. Mon–Sat noon–9pm. Metro: Kossuth Lajos tér (Red line).

Beyond Central Pest

Very Expensive

Gundel ★ Overrated HUNGARIAN TRADITIONAL This is Budapest's fanciest, most famous, probably most expensive, and undoubtedly most overrated restaurant. Gundel reopened in 1992. The restaurant is the place for the Hungarian elite or others who need to see and be seen dining in the opulent dining room adorned with 19th-century paintings. Lamb and wild-game entrees are house specialties. The Gundel menu also includes four sets of gourmet choices with fixed prices. There are many other choices in the city for excellent meals, at a lower cost, and no jacket is required.

XIV. Állatkerti út 2. ✆ **1/468-4040.** www.gundel.hu. Reservations highly recommended. Jackets required for men in the evening. Lunch prix-fixe menus 3,500 Ft–4,700 Ft ($19–$25/£12–£16); Sun brunch buffet 5,800 Ft ($31/£19); children 5–15 2,900 Ft ($16/£9.90), 4 and under free; main courses 3,990 Ft–10,620 Ft ($22–$57/£14–£35); dinner prix-fixe menu 11,890 Ft–39,200 Ft ($64–$212/£40–£131). AE, DC, MC, V. Mon–Sat noon–4pm; daily 6:30–11pm; Sun brunch 11:30am–3pm. Metro: Hősök tere (Yellow line).

Expensive

Kogart Restaurant ★★ INTERNATIONAL Situated in the lower level of the Kogart Art Gallery, this restaurant emits an understated elegance. Paintings on the wall change on a rotating basis; the chairs are covered with beautiful print covers, the linens elegantly draped over the tables. One corner has a sitting area with leather sofas to wait for the rest of your party or relax with a drink. In summer, there is a terrace where the food is cooked on a grill. The sommelier assists with wine choices from the extensive list. Surprisingly, the menu is limited, but has a number of fish choices. The chicken with lasagna was an excellent choice. The cranberry crème brûlée turned out to be blueberry, but mouth-watering nevertheless. Although the restaurant is elegant, dress is sporty casual to more formal. Upstairs is the Kogart Art Gallery.

VI. Andrássy ut. 112. ✆ **1/354-3830.** www.kogart.hu. Reservations recommended. Main courses 2,390 Ft–5,590 Ft ($13–$30/£8.05–£19). AE, MC, V. Daily 10am–midnight. Metro: Bajza (Yellow line).

Moderate

Paprika Vendéglő ★★★ Finds HUNGARIAN TRADITIONAL If you want to escape to the Hungarian countryside to sample the cuisine without leaving the city, this is the place. This is by far my favorite restaurant in the city. The old-fashioned earthen oven, oversized cooking utensils, and the log cabin interior will mellow you in rustic comfort. The chairs and benches are also made of logs, adding to the country ambiance. Let yourself go hog wild and try the roasted wild boar with brandy or saddle of deer. My personal favorite is the leg of goose Vadazsdi style, oven roasted and served with red cabbage and parsley potatoes. Not feeling so adventurous? No problem; they have other poultry, beef, and pork dishes to choose from on a liberal menu. No matter what you order, the portion will be generous; don't hesitate to ask to have leftovers wrapped to take home. The wine list has a wide selection of Hungarian wines. Sometimes the service can be a bit slow, but this is a minor inconvenience. Menus are in English. There are separate dining areas for smoking and nonsmoking.

VII. Dozsa Gyorgy 72. ✆ **06/70-574-6508** mobile phone. Reservations recommended. Main courses 1,650 Ft–3,200 Ft. ($8.90–$17/£5.50–£11). MC, V. Daily 11am–11pm. Metro: Hősök tere (Yellow line) 4½ blocks from Heroes' Sq.

Expensive

Hemingway ★★★ Moments HUNGARIAN CONTEMPORARY Another city escape awaits you when visiting this restaurant, placed next to a small lake with plenty of trees. Having opened 9 years ago, this dining choice has never lost its popularity. The interior of the venue made us feel like we had joined Hemingway in one of his favorite getaways; the room is open and airy. Most of the tables sit on a platform, with the nonsmoking section in another room. The piano and bass duo adds to the relaxing *Casablanca* atmosphere. We started with one order of the grilled ewe cheese over a mixed olive oil salad; it was large enough for two. The thick slice of cheese was golden and the salad dressing excellent. For main courses, we recommend highly the Glenn Close pasta; spinach linguine with garlic, red peppers, cream sauce, and a touch of anise. The Mangalica pork was perfectly prepared with a tomato-brown sauce over mounds of fresh mashed potatoes. The white-chocolate mousse was presented beautifully, but it was a more sugar than chocolate. The waiter service was superior. In clement weather, eat outside on the terrace overlooking the water.

XI. Kosztolányi D. tér 2, Feneketlen tó. ✆ **1/381-0522.** www.hemingway-etterem.hu. Reservations recommended. Main courses 2,390 Ft–5,990 Ft ($12–$32/£7.50–£20). AE, DC, MC, V. Daily noon–midnight. Bus: 7 toward Buda to Kosztolányi Dezső tér and look for Feneketlen tó, which is a small manmade lake.

Moderate

Tabáni Terasz ★★★ HUNGARIAN TRADITIONAL We had to sneak a peek at the inside of this restaurant, since we sat outside on the large terrace shaded by umbrellas. The dishes are all prepared with a nice variety of vegetables, which is unusual for Hungarian cuisine. As traditional fare, the portions smother the dishes. The ewe cheese salad had nondescript iceberg lettuce, but the dressing was mild and tasty; the portions of cheese were generous enough to share. Chicken breast rolled around asparagus with Hollandaise sauce and tarragon potatoes featured an incredible three large pieces of chicken. In the off season, the interior dining is cozy and intimate. The inside consists of small rooms with tables and chairs and gives the feel of entering someone's home, decorated with wall hangings, some paintings, and other regional touches. It is a bit difficult to get to from the Pest side, but worth the effort.

I. Apród u. 10. ✆ **1/201-1086.** www.tabaniterasz.hu. Main courses 1,990 Ft–4,300 Ft ($11–$23/£6.80–£14). AE, MC, V. Daily noon–midnight. Bus: 86 to Döbrentei tér.

Inexpensive

Eden ★ Finds VEGETARIAN Vegans can celebrate, for this historic building houses the first and only vegan restaurant in Buda. The building was restored in 2001 and this vegan buffet restaurant opened. All ingredients are natural and fresh without any coloring, additives, or preservatives. After making your selection, you have the choice of sitting in the charming country-cozy dining room or in the atrium garden. Their selection of 12 juices freshly squeezed from fruits or vegetables will quench anyone's thirst. When you order, take note that the price for salad is by weight and the drinks are by volume.

I. Iskola u. 31, Batthyány Sq. ✆ **06/20-337-75-75** mobile phone. www.edenetterem.hu. 290 Ft–590 Ft ($1.55–$3.20/95p–£2). Cash only. Sun 11am–9pm; Mon–Thurs 7am–9pm; Fri 7am–6pm. Metro: Batthyány (Red line).

The Castle District

Moderate

Rivalda Café & Restaurant ★ HUNGARIAN CONTEMPORARY The building has much history to tell, once being a monastery and later a theater with casino in the 17th century. In the summer months, you will be pleased to be seated in the huge courtyard with wicker tables and chairs, hurricane lights and a pianist serenading diners while the stars shine in the sky. Peeking inside, we found the interior to be pleasingly decorated with Impressionist scenes from theater productions, actual theater lighting directed at the small stage at the end of the room, and gossamer hanging lucidly from the ceiling. Rivalda has a simple but varied menu, so we started with the pear-ginger soup and the lemon-chicken soup. We followed these with an Argentinean steak served with a baked potato and green beans, and rosé duck breast accompanied by couscous and mixed vegetables. The food was excellently prepared, the vegetables were al dente, but the menu was not as imaginative as we had been led to believe. Unfortunately, the surroundings are more theatrical than the dinner options.

I. Szinház u. 5–9. ✆ **1/489-0236.** www.rivalda.net. Reservations recommended. Main courses 2,300 Ft–4,950 Ft ($12–$27/£7.70–£17). AE, MC, V. Daily 11:30am–11:30pm. Bus: 16 from Deák or Várbusz from Moszkva tér.

The Buda Hills

Very Expensive

Bajai Halászcsárda ★ HUNGARIAN TRADITIONAL *Csárda* means a restaurant near a major traffic area, and this one is right next to a cogwheel and bus stop, making it easy to access. *Halász* means fisherman, and the interior is country style with heavy woods and fishing décor tastefully ornamenting the walls. However, in the Buda Hills, an extensive fish menu is a bit out of place, but here it is. The specialty is the traditional Bajai type of fish soup, which has a special pastry in it. But we bypassed anything fishy for the turkey stuffed with cheese and french fries. The five exceptionally large pieces of fried turkey were overflowing with cheese. It was moist and flavorful, but not exceptional. If you have a desire for fish dishes, this would be the place to go and other diners seemingly were enjoying their fresh-from-the-river tasty treats. There were a pianist and violinist serenading with American and Hungarian oldies. Every few songs, the pianist would belt out a song a la Piaf with a hauntingly romantic voice. The resident parrot's whistling in the background was a mixture of humor and annoyance.

XII. Hollós u. 2. ✆ **1/275-5245.** www.bajaihalaszcsarda.com. Reservations recommended. Main courses 2,900 Ft–5,400 Ft ($16–$29/£9.90–£18). AE, MC, V. Daily 11:30am–10pm. Bus 21 from Moszkva tér.

Moderate

Remiz ★★★ (Value) HUNGARIAN CONTEMPORARY *Remiz* is literally the place where trams spend the night, and such is the location of this restaurant. It can be an adventure to get to from the city center, but you will be well rewarded, especially in summer. This is when they crank up the barbecue outside in the gazebo for their ultimate special dish, spare ribs. Unlike any we have ever tasted, the two extra large racks of ribs, sans any sauce, were incredibly meaty and flavorful. This dish, unique to Hungarian menus, has been perfected here. A sea of diners is a common occurrence during the summer months, filling the tree- and umbrella-covered terrace with plates of ribs in front of them. The Italian garlic soup starter was excellent, as was the breaded eggplant Cesar salad with chicken. During the rest of the year, the tram-shaped restaurant is decorated with early-20th-century Budapest posters, creating a special atmosphere for delicious meals.

II. Budakeszi út 5. ✆ **1/275-1396.** www.remiz.hu. Reservations recommended. Main courses 1,980 Ft–3,980 Ft ($11–$22/£6.80–£14). AE, DC, MC, V. Mon–Fri 11am–11pm; Sat–Sun 9am–11pm. Bus: 158 from Moszkva tér (departs from Csaba u., at the top of the stairs, near the stop from which bus 10 departs for the Castle District).

COFFEEHOUSES—TRADITIONAL & MODERN

As part of the Austro-Hungarian empire, Budapest—just as in Vienna—has developed a coffeehouse culture where people of like minds meet to discuss politics, literature, or music. Each coffeehouse has its own story as to which literary movement or political circles favored the establishment. More than one claims the legend that someone stole the keys to the front door to keep their favorite cafe from ever closing. During the Communist times, these traditions evaporated into history, though a few of the coffeehouses did survive those strained times. With full freedoms returned, some have been restored to their previous glory, while other, more modern coffeehouses have sprung up to create a new legacy of java traditions.

The Inner City & Central Pest

Aztek Choxolat Café ★★ Finds If you are a fan of the movie Chocolat, you are in for one extraordinary treat. Being such a small place, you would never expect it to be a chocoholic's fantasyland, with a hot chocolate called Secret of the Mayas that offers a blend of six herbs and spices mixed in hot molten chocolate, our personal favorite. For the less adventurous there is chocolate with sour cherry and coriander, and 12 other combinations. If your taste buds run more to java than chocolate, there are also treats in store for you. The coffees here come in 20 combinations, many undiscovered by the big chains, but also in three sizes. If you supersize it here, you will be floating out. In agreeable weather, they have four tables in the passageway; otherwise, you will have to scramble for one of the three tables inside. And did I mention that all of their spices can be bought mixed for 400 Ft ($2.15/£1.15) a bag, to be added to your own cocoa when you return home? They also sell pralines in imaginative flavors and beautiful designs, placed in a lovely box ready for gift giving. You can enter the short passageway from either street; keep your eyes open, as it is sometimes easily missed.

V. Karoly krt. 22 or Semmelweiss u. 19. ✆ **1/266-7113.** Hot chocolate 400 Ft–750 Ft ($2.15–$4.05/£1.35–£2.50); coffee 280 Ft–750 Ft ($1.50–$4.05/95p–£2.50). Mon–Fri 7am–7pm; Sat 9am–2pm.

Café Noé ★ This is the only pastry shop to find a delectable treat called flódni, a layered pastry with apple, poppy seed, walnuts, and plum jam; it is an old Eastern European traditional pastry. Every pastry we sampled has been fresh and delectable. They also have diabetic pastry selections. Order a coffee, wander upstairs to their funky cafe area, and bring your laptop—the Wi-Fi is free here. They just started featuring local Hungarian artists' work, creating a gallery atmosphere. If it catches on, they will do a rotating art show. They have a second location called the Bulldog Cukrászda at Veres Pálne u. 31. You can also order a custom cake from their website and have it delivered to someone special in Budapest.

VII. Wesselényi u. 13. ✆ **1/321-7145.** www.torta.hu. Pastry 300 Ft–450 Ft ($1.60–$2.45/85p–£1.30), coffee 250 Ft–350 Ft ($1.25–$1.75/75p–£1). Mon–Fri 10am–6pm.

Centrál Kávéház ★★★ Coffeehouse culture is ingrained in Budapest history; this coffeehouse is one of the historic places where writers and artists gathered. Today it is a perfect replica of the original establishment, which opened in 1887. Although there is a superb restaurant here, the menu is limited, making it best known as a coffeehouse. Restored by one of Hungary's own millionaires, Imre Somodyt, to its former richness, it is a hot spot for tourists and locals alike. With its perfect location, you will find a mix of tourists, businesspersons, locals, and local celebrities. In the room at the right, at the right-hand corner of the smoking section, there is a table perpetually reserved for local writer Géza Csemer. He happened to be there on my visit so I confirmed it with the staff. While mellowing in this coffeehouse's calm green interior with lavishly attractive ceilings, and brass hanging lamps with glass shades, you can browse the free copies of various newspapers. A simple espresso at Central costs 420 Ft ($2.25/£1.40), but for the ambience it is worth the price. If you order a torta (a piece of cake) after 10pm, you will receive a 30% discount.

V. Károlyi Mihály u. 9. ✆ **1/266-2110.** www.centralkavehaz.hu. Main courses 1,490 Ft–3,790 Ft ($8.05–$21/£5–£13). AE, MC, V. Daily 8am–midnight. Metro: Ferenciek tere (Blue line).

Gerbeaud's (Overrated) Perhaps the most famous of the Budapest coffeehouses, Gerbeaud's is likely the most overrated also. Founded in 1858, it has stood on its current spot since 1870. There is no denying that the exterior and interior are lovely, but the pastries and coffee are no better than any other shop in the city. The extravagant prices they charge are for the window dressing, not the goods. If you are interested in the decor of the late 19th century, go in, peek, and then go to another pastry shop for your snack.

V. Vörösmarty tér 7. ✆ **1/429-9000.** www.gerbeaud.hu. Pastry 650 Ft–750 Ft ($3.50–$4.05/£1.85–£2.15), coffee 690 Ft–750 Ft ($3.70–$4.05/£1.95–£2.15). AE, DC, DISC, MC, V. Daily 9am–9pm. Metro: Vörösmarty tér (Yellow line).

The Castle District

Rétesbar ★★★ (Finds) To say that this little bakery has the absolutely best *rétes* (strudel) I have ever had is no exaggeration. Warm out of the oven, the flaky pastry was just enough to hold the warm cheese filling inside. It is melt-in-your-mouth scrumptious. They have a variety of other *rétes* and some other savory small pizza-type pastries. It's small, with no seating inside, but there are benches outside to sit and enjoy. It is a bit difficult to find; it is directly across from the TourInform office, right past the fountain in the brick alleyway *(köz)*. Tell them you saw them in Frommer's and you will be overpowered with the smile you receive.

I. Balta köz 4. No phone. Pastry 250 Ft–350 Ft ($1.25–$1.75/75p–£1). Coffee 350 Ft ($1.75/£1). Cash only. Daily 9am–8pm. Bus: 10 from Moszkva tér or 16 from Deák tér to Castle Hill. Funicular: From Clark Ádám tér to Castle Hill.

EXPLORING BUDAPEST

Historic Budapest is smaller than people realize when they first arrive. Since this is a great walking city, many attractions listed in this chapter are easily reached by foot from the city center. However, if you are short on time, public transport will get you there too. As you stroll from one place to the next, look up at the buildings even if you have to stop a minute. So many missed treasures are above normal view and go underappreciated by the masses. And bear in mind that most places will charge you an additional fee if you wish to take photos or use a video camera—individual listings for prices.

Museums

Museums are closed on Mondays, except where noted. Most museums only offer discounts to Hungarian or E.U. students and seniors, but it is worth asking anyway if you have an ID. Sometimes a lackadaisical worker with give it to anyone. Many also offer a family rate. Inquire at the ticket window.

Budapest Holocaust Memorial Center (Holokauszt Emlékközpont) ★★★ Opened in 2004 to coincide with the 60th anniversary of the Holocaust, it is the first government-funded Holocaust Memorial Center in central Europe. Architecturally, it is a combination of classical and modern creating asymmetrical lines. All of the distorted symmetry is intentionally symbolic of the warped, perverse history of the Holocaust. In the center is a refurbished eclectic-style synagogue that was originally designed by Leopold Baumhorn, a famous architect of synagogues at the turn of the 20th century. The space has a permanent exhibition, a research center, and an excellent bookshop. Temporary exhibitions span local and international interests. A large wall surrounds the courtyard, serving as remembrance for the Hungarian victims of the Holocaust. Engraved into the glass wall are the names of the victims.

IX. Páva u. 39. ✆ **1/455-3333.** www.hdke.hu. Admission 1,000 Ft ($5.50/£3.40) adults. No photos. Tues–Sun 10am–6pm. Metro: Ferenc körut (Blue line).

Ethnographical Museum (Néprajzi Múzeum) ★★ Kids One of the largest specialist museums in Europe, it contains over 139,000 Hungarian and 53,000 international art objects. Housed in the former Hungarian Supreme Court building, directly across Kossuth tér from the House of Parliament, the museum has the pleasure of being in a Renaissance, baroque, and neoclassical building. The lavish interior alone is worth a visit. A ceiling fresco of Justitia, the goddess of justice, by the well-known artist Károly Lotz, dominates the lobby. The permanent exhibition named "From Primitive Cultures to Civilization" needs a good dusting; nevertheless, it is fascinating. Its featured dioramas explore all periods of early Hungarian history.

V. Kossuth tér 12. ✆ **1/473-2400.** www.neprajz.hu. Admission 800 Ft ($4.50/£2.80) adults, 400 Ft ($2.25/£1.40) students. Photo 300 Ft ($1.50/95p), video 1,000 Ft ($5.40/£3.35). Tues–Sun 10am–6pm. Metro: Kossuth tér (Red line).

Hungarian National Museum (Nemzeti Múzeum) ★★ The Hungarian National Museum was founded in 1802, thanks to the numismatic, book, and document collections of Count Ferenc Szénchényi. One of my favorite buildings in Budapest, this enormous neoclassical structure was finished in 1846. It was here that the poet Sándor Petőfi and others of like mind are said to have roused the emotions of the people of Pest to revolt against the Habsburgs on March 15, 1848. If you look carefully, you will find a column on a plinth on the left side of the entrance that Mussolini gave to Hungary. The column was from the Forum in Rome. Due to its negative history, the plaque now states "A gift from the Italian nation." The permanent exhibit holds over one million pieces of Hungarian historical artifacts.

VIII. Múzeum krt. 14. ✆ **1/338-2122.** www.hnm.hu. Admission 1,000 Ft ($5.50/£3.40) adults, 500 Ft ($2.70/£1.65) students. Photo 3,000 Ft ($16/£9.90), video 5,000 Ft ($27/£17). Tues–Sun 10am–6pm. Metro: Kálvin tér (Blue line).

Ludwig Museum of Contemporary Art (Ludwig Múzeum) ★ Located in the Palace of Arts (Mûvészetek Palotája), which opened in 2005, overlooking the Danube. It is the most important collection of contemporary international and Hungarian art. The collection includes American, German, Russian, and French artists from the last 50 years and central European contemporary works from the 1990s. It includes several late Picassos and Andy Warhol's *Single Elvis,* as well as an eclectic mix of Hungarian works by artists like Imre Bukta, Beáta Veszely, and Imre Bak. This museum is worth visiting for an interesting temporary exhibition, mostly by alternative European artists, than it is for its permanent exhibits. Art experts have told me that this museum uses its funding to bring temporary exhibitions here, depleting finances to add to the permanent collections.

IX. Komor Marcell u. 1. ✆ **1/555-3444.** www.ludwigmuseum.hu. Admission 1,200 Ft ($6.25/£3.85) adults, 600 Ft ($3.25/£2) students. Free tours led by docents Thurs 6:30pm. No photos. Tues–Sun 10am–8pm; last Sat of the month 10am–10pm. Tram: 2 or 2A.

Museum of Fine Arts (Szépművészeti Múzeum) ★★★ During the 1896 millennial celebration of the Magyars settling and forming a nation in 896, the plans were proposed for the Museum of Fine Arts. Ten years later in the presence of Franz Josef, the king and emperor of Austria and Hungary, the Museum of Fine Arts opened at the left side of Heroes' Square. This was the last great monument built during the most prosperous period of Hungary's history. Designed in the Beaux Arts style, the main facade has three classical Greek temples connected by colonnades. The temples represent the grove of muses, a place of relaxation. There are eight sections in the museum: Egyptian Art, Antiquities, Baroque Sculpture, Old Masters, Drawings and Prints, 19th-Century Masters, 20th-Century Masters, and Modern Sculpture. Most great names associated with the old masters—Tiepolo, Tintoretto, Veronese, Titian, Raphael, Van Dyck, Brueghel, Rembrandt, Rubens, Hals, Hogarth, Dürer, Cranach, Holbein, Goya, Velázquez, El Greco, and others—are represented here. Delacroix, Corot, and Manet are the best represented 19th-century French artists in the museum. The overall collection consists of over 3,000 paintings, 10,000 drawings, and 100,000 prints. Trained docents offer a 1-hour guided tour in English, free of charge Tuesday through Saturday at 11am and 2pm, Saturday at 11am.

XIV. Hősök tere. ✆ **1/469-7100.** www.szepmuveszeti.hu. Admission 1,200 Ft ($6.25/£2) adults, 600 Ft ($3.25/£2) students. Photo 300 Ft ($1.50/95p), video 1,500 Ft ($8/£4.95). Tues–Sun 10am–5:30pm. Metro: Hősök tere (Yellow line).

National Jewish Museum and Archives (Nemzeti Zsidó Múzeum és Levéltár) Sitting to the left of the Dohány Synagogue (see below), the museum contains an excellent collection of Judaica, which survived the war by being housed in the basement of the National Museum. The permanent collection contains devotional objects for Jewish holiday celebrations, everyday objects, and a special room with an exhibit called the "History of the Hungarian Holocaust." Outside there is a plaque stating that Theodor Herzl, the founder of Zionism, was born on this spot. The museum is only four rooms, but it is a powerful display. Note that admission to the synagogue includes the museum.

VII. Dohány u. 2–8. ✆ **1/342-8942.** Admission 1,400 Ft ($7.50/£4.65) adults, 700 Ft ($3.75/£2.35) students. Photo tickets 500 Ft ($2.70/£1.65) for synagogue, museum free. Mon–Thurs 10am–4:30pm; Fri 10am–2:30pm; Sun 10am–5:30pm (except Jewish holidays); in winter doors close 30 min. earlier. Metro: Astoria (Red line) or Deák tér (all lines). Bus: 74.

House of Terror (Terror Háza) ★★ You will have to brace yourself before going into this historical building. All of the information in English is on copious sheets of paper in each room. This is the former headquarters of the ÁVH secret police; this building witnessed some of the darkest days of 20th-century Hungary and is now a chilling museum. The goal was to create a memorial to the victims of both Fascism and Communism in successive oppressive regimes in Hungary. Critics claim it misses the mark by putting more energy into the Communist times. The Nazis headquartered here in 1944, using the basement for torture and murder of suspected traitors and others they thought were undesirables. The Communist secret police wasted no time at all in taking over the building and continuing what the Fascists started. The fact that it is now a museum has caused much debate amongst locals, who feel it is glorifying the evil past. The artsy roof that overhangs its stenciled letters onto the street doesn't help the cause, given that Andrássy út is a World Heritage Site noted for its period look.

VI. Andrássy út 60. ✆ **1/374-2600.** www.houseofterror.hu. Admission 1,500 Ft ($8/£4.95) adults, 750 Ft ($4/£2.50) students. No photos. Tues–Fri 10am–6pm; Sat–Sun 10am–7:30pm. Metro: Oktogon (Yellow line).

Historic Squares & Buildings

Heroes' Square (Hősök tere) ★★★ Kids Located at the end of the grand World Heritage boulevard, Andrássy út, the square is the entryway into the best-known park in the city, City Park (Városliget). Like so many other things in the city, the square and the park were planned and built to celebrate the arrival and settling of the Magyars' forming a nation in 896. The tricky part at the time was that Hungary was part of the Austrian empire and was beholden to the emperor while celebrating its independence as a nation. The monument as viewed today was not completed until 1929; the collapse of the empire preceded it.

At the base of the center column are statues of the seven tribal conquerors on horseback. The one in the forefront is Árpád, the leading chieftain who led the six other Magyar tribal leaders in conquering the land. To the sides of the column in a colonnade, are seven heroes of Hungarian history on each side. Starting from the far left you will find King Stephen I, the country's first Christian king, followed by six other kings who followed him. On the right side, only the second statue is a royal, King Matthias Corvinus, who presided over Buda's golden age in the 15th century (sixth from right). Other statues found atop the colonnade are immediately to the left and right of the column, the chariots of peace and war. At the forefront top on the left and right sides are statues representing work and welfare, while on the other side glory and knowledge.

Take the metro to Hősök tere (Yellow line).

Hungarian State Opera House (Magyar Állami Operaház) ★★★ Built in a neo-Renaissance style, this is the most beautiful building of this style on Andrassy út. The architect was Miklós Ybl, the most successful and prolific architect of his time. He created what many agree is one of the most beautiful opera houses in Europe. It was completed 1884. As Hungary's most celebrated performance hall, the opera house boasts a fantastically ornate interior featuring frescoes by two of the best-known Hungarian artists of the day, Bertalan Székely and Károly Lotz. Both inside and outside are dozens of statues of such music greats as Beethoven, Mozart, Verdi, Wagner, Smetana, Tchaikovsky, and Monteverdi. You may enter the lobby where the ticket office is located without charge, but the only way to tour the interior is with a guided tour offered at 3pm and 4pm daily. A minimum of 10 people is required, and costs 2,500 Ft ($14/£8.70) for adults or 1,300 Ft ($7/£4.35) for students with an international ID card.

VI. Andrássy út 22. ✆ **1/331-2550.** www.opera.hu. Photo ticket 500 Ft ($2.75/£1.70), video same, with small cameras. Tours daily at 3 and 4pm. Metro: Opera (Yellow line).

Parliament ★★★ Budapest's great Parliament building, the second largest in Europe after London, is an eclectic design mixing the predominant Gothic revival style with a neo-Renaissance dome. It began in 1884, 16 years after Westminster, and was completed in 1902. Standing proudly on the Danube bank, visible from almost any riverside point, it has from the outset been one of Budapest's proud symbols, though until 1989 a democratically elected government had convened here only once (just after World War II, before the Communist takeover). Before entering, take note that the top of the building is 29m (96 ft.) high at its peak, commemorating the 896 conquest. St. Stephen's Basilica is the same height.

It used to be a bicameral parliament with an upper and lower house, but now is unicameral with the necessity of coalitions forming. As you walk up the imposing staircase, you are led under the dome with 16-sided hallway with 16 statues of rulers. In the center floor under the dome is a glass case with the "legendary" jeweled crown and scepter of King St. Stephen. Historical records have shown that the crown is of two parts and from two different eras, neither from King St. Stephen's time, but Hungarians want to believe it was Stephen's. Nevertheless, it is one of the oldest royal crowns in history. In St. Matthias Church on Castle Hill, there is a small but impressive museum dedicated to the crown (see Mátyás Templon, below).

V. Kossuth tér. ✆ **1/441-4415.** Tourist.office@parliament.hu. Admission by guided tour only; 50 min. tour in English 2,300 Ft ($12/£7.45) adults, 1,150 Ft ($6.20/£3.85) students. E.U. Passport holders get free admission. Tickets available at gate X. Prebook by e-mail or phone ✆ 1/441-4904 or -4415. Photography allowed at no charge. Tours year-round Wed–Sun at 10am, noon, 1, and 2pm. Closed when Parliament is in session, usually Mon and Thurs. Metro: Kossuth tér (Red line); Tram 2 and 2A Szalay u..

Churches & Synagogues

Dohány Synagogue ★★★ Built in 1859, this is the second-largest working synagogue in the world, after Temple Emanu-El in New York City, and the second-oldest large synagogue left standing. The oldest is the National Museum. The architect was non-Jewish Lajos Förster, who designed it with Romantic, Moorish, and Byzantine elements. The synagogue's interior is a mix of Orthodox and Reformed Judaism for the Hungarian Neolog Jewish denomination, which seems to exist only in Hungary. Due to this, many are surprised to see an organ in the loft. They have always had a non-Jewish organist to play it. The synagogue has a rich but tragic history; it was one of many detention areas for Jews during the Holocaust. The Jewish museum next door traces the origins of Hungarian Judaism and features exhibits of ceremonial Judaica throughout the centuries. The museum periodically puts on excellent temporary exhibitions. The Holocaust Memorial and Heroes' Temple in the courtyard are well worth visiting. Note that the Holocaust Memorial Museum is at a different location.

VII. Dohány u. 2–8. ✆ **1/342-8942.** Admission 1,400 Ft ($7.50/£4.65) adults, 700 Ft ($3.75/£2.35) students. Photo tickets 500 Ft ($2.70/£1.65) for synagogue, museum free. Mon–Thurs 10am–4:30pm; Fri 10am–2:30pm; Sun 10am–5:30pm, except Jewish holidays (closing time 30 min. earlier each day in winter). Metro: Astoria (Red line) or Deák tér (All lines). Bus: 74.

St. Stephen's (Church Szent István Bazilika) ★★ The country's largest church, this basilica took more than 50 years to build (the 1868 collapse of the dome caused significant delay) and was finally completed in 1906, which explains the differences in architectural designs. Szent István Square, a once-sleepy square in front of the church, was elegantly renovated in the autumn of 2002 and the entire church was given a good cleaning in 2003. The plaza area was converted along with several neighboring streets

Statues, What Statues?

By now, most people have forgotten that the city was littered with statues to Lenin, Marx, Engels, and the other representatives of the Communist times. If you have some recollection of them and wonder where they have disappeared to, here is your answer: In the aftermath of 1989, with the statues a constant reminder of difficult times, a plan was conceived for a **Socialist Statue Park (Szoborpark Múzeum),** since renamed **Memento Park.** The park is inconveniently located outside of the city, and to call it a park is bordering on a misnomer. From the outside, it looks like an old American fort, but as you enter, socialist marching music is playing on a loud speaker. The large, unkempt plot of dusty land has a circular exhibit of the statutes that were transplanted here. What little information is available on or near each statue is in Russian or Hungarian only, which is confusing; the majority of visitors are tourists and not Hungarians.

Located in the XXII district (extreme southern Buda) on Balatoni út (✆ **1/424-7500;** www.szoborpark.hu), the park is a memorial to an era, to despotism, and to hatred. The tiny museum gift kiosk sells Communist-era memorabilia, such as T-shirts with flamboyantly modern sayings, medals, and cassettes of Red Army marching songs. The park is open daily from 10am to dusk and admission is 600 Ft ($3.25/£2). To get to the park, take the black-lettered bus no. 7 from Ferenciek tere to Etele tér. Buy a separate ticket for the yellow Volán bus (to Érd) for a 20-minute ride to the park; ask the driver where to get off. It is not easily marked, basically just a roadside stop. The Volán bus is not a city bus; passes and transit tickets are not valid. Or, for a premium, you can take the new and convenient direct bus service from Deák tér for 3,950 Ft ($21/£13) or 2,450 Ft ($13/£8.05) for students (admission ticket to the park included). The timetable varies by season, but the 11am departure remains constant with an additional run at 3pm for July and August.

into a pedestrian-only zone, now surrounded with restaurants. As you wander into the church and to the left in the back chapel you can view St. Stephen's mummified hand, or you can wait until August 20, his feast day, to see it for free when it is paraded around the city. To get the box to light up to actually see it, you will have to spring for 100 Ft (55¢/35p).

V. Szent István tér 33. ✆ **1/318-9159.** www.basilica.hu. Church free admission; treasury 400 Ft ($2.15/£1.35); panorama tower 500 Ft ($2.70/£1.65). Photos free. Thorough guided tours ($11/£6.80) can be requested at the church. Church daily 9am–7pm, except during services; treasury daily 9am–5pm; Szent Jobb Chapel Mon–Sat 9am–5pm, Sun 1–5pm; panorama tower daily 10am–5pm. Metro: Arany János u. (Blue line) or Bajcsy-Zsilinszky út (Yellow line).

Buda: The Top Attractions

Matthias Church (Mátyás Templom) ★★★ Originally founded by King Béla IV in the 13th century, it is officially named the Church of Our Lady and a symbol of Buda's Castle District. It is popularly referred to as Matthias Church after the 15th-century King Matthias Corvinus, who added a royal oratory and was twice married here. The original church was built in stages that spanned from the 13th to the 15th centuries. Like other old churches in Budapest, it has a history of destruction and reconstruction, always refashioned in the architectural style in vogue at the time. Renovation has been an ongoing process as financial considerations allow, and it is currently covered with scaffolding. When I went to investigate, I was shocked to hear the planned end was 2012. Regardless, it is a church not to be missed, one reason being its Zsolnay ceramic tiles, which are uniquely iridescent red, thanks to a process developed at the Pécs-based ceramics factory in 1893. Do not miss the museum upstairs; often overlooked by travelers who do not realize it is there, it has an interesting history of the royal crown and a wonderful view of the church.

I. Szentháromság tér 2. ✆ **1/355-5657.** www.matyas-templom.hu. Admission 650 Ft ($3.50/£7.60) adults, 400 Ft ($2.15/£1.35) students. Photos free. Mon–Fri 9am–5pm; Sat depends on weddings; Sun 1–5pm. Metro: Moszkva tér, then bus 10; or Deák tér, then bus 16. Funicular: From Clark Ádám tér to Castle Hill.

Hungarian National Gallery (Nemzeti Galéria) ★ With a collection of over 10,000 art objects, this museum is not for the cultural faint of heart. The works cover the period from the beginning of Hungary as a nation to the present day. I have yet to see the entire collection, even with subsequent visits, as it is so easy to succumb to sensory overload; not everything is labeled in English. Hungarian artists have produced some outstanding work, particularly the period for which they are most famous, the late 19th century. Permanent exhibitions include medieval and Renaissance lapidariums; Gothic woodcarvings and winged altars; Renaissance and baroque art; and the works of Hungarian celebrities Mihály Munkácsy, László Paál, Károly Ferenczy, and Pál Szinyei Merse. Some other works to look for are sculptures by Isván Ferenczy and Miklós Izsó. József Rippl-Rónai's canvases are premier examples of Hungarian post-Impressionism and Art Nouveau (see *Father and Uncle Piacsek Drinking Red Wine* and *My Grandmother*), while Tivadar Csontváry Kosztka, the "Rousseau of the Danube," is considered by some critics to be a genius of early modern art.

Located in Buda Palace, wings B, C, and D, on Castle Hill. ✆ **1/375-5567.** Admission 800 Ft ($4.25/£2.65) adults, 400 Ft ($2/£1.25) students; dome 300 Ft ($1.50/95p). Photo ticket 1,500 Ft ($8/£4.95), video 2,000 Ft ($11/£6.80). Variable entrance fees for temporary exhibitions. Tues–Sun 10am–6pm. Bus: 10 from Moszkva tér or 16 from Deák tér to Castle Hill. Funicular: From Clark Ádám tér to Castle Hill.

Óbuda

Roman Ruins (Aquincum) ★★ When thinking of the conquests of the Roman Empire, rarely does Hungary pop into anyone's mind, but if you enjoy Roman history or ruins, this is a must. One of the largest archeological parks in the country, this area was the capital of the Lower Pannonian province in the 2nd century, where the Romans flourished for over 110 years. At the time, it was an important city in the Roman Empire, now named Óbuda. When you arrive by HÉV the suburban train, the stop is also called the Aquincum. You will see the ruined **Amphitheater of the Civilian Town.** It is open all of the time, but it is often a gathering place for the homeless, so you may want to view it from the fence, rather than wander amongst the ruins. Just a little farther down the road is the **Aquincum Park** with the **Aquincum Museum.** Don't be fooled from outside appearances; at first glance the park looks small, but once you enter you will realize you need a good half-day here to do justice to the 2,000-year-old history that is still intact. Each section has its own map of the buildings within each section, and it is in English. There are many special events, some recreating Roman history.

Gellért Hill (Gellért Hegy)

Towering 235m (770 ft.) above the Danube, Gellért Hill offers the city's best panorama on a clear day (bus: 27 from Móricz Zsigmond körtér). It's named after the Italian Bishop Gellért, who assisted Hungary's first Christian king, Stephen I, in converting the Magyars. Gellért became a martyr, according to legend, when vengeful pagans, outraged at the forced and violent nature of Stephen's proselytism, rolled Gellért in a nail-studded barrel to his death from the side of the hill. An enormous statue now stands on the hill to celebrate his history. On top of Gellért Hill, you'll find the **Liberation Monument,** built in 1947 to commemorate the Red Army's liberation of Budapest from Nazi occupation. The 14m (45-ft.) statue of the woman holding the palm leaf of victory is visible from just about any viewpoint along the river. To her sides are statues representing progress and destruction. Following the first election in 1990, there was much discussion as to whether the statue should be removed since the Soviet troops were more of an occupation rather than liberation. Also atop the hill is the **Citadella,** built by the Austrians shortly after they crushed the Hungarian uprising of 1848 to 1849. Views of the city from both vistas are excellent, but the Citadella is spectacular. Don't bother paying the extra to traipse up to the upper part; the view is not that much higher, so don't waste your money.

III. Szentendrei út 139. ✆ **1/454-0438.** www.aquincum.hu. Adult 900 Ft ($4.85/£3), student 450 Ft ($2.45/£1.50). Photos in the garden free, but photo or video ticket needed for exhibitions 500 Ft ($2.70/£1.65) or 1,500 Ft ($8.10/£5). Apr 15–30 and Oct Tues–Sun 10am–5pm; May–Sept Tues–Sun 9am–6pm. HÉV: Aquincum (direction Szentendre from Batthyány tér).

PARKS & GARDENS

Spending time in a park or any green space is a wonderful pastime for many of the city dwellers to have an escape when they cannot actually retreat from the city for some countryside getaway to recharge their mental batteries.

Popular **Margaret Island (Margit-sziget)** ★★★ has an interesting royalty related history going back to King Béla. He vowed that if he were successful in the Mongol invasion in 1242 to 1244, his daughter Margaret would be brought up as a nun. Well, he was, so she was sent to the island at the age of 10 to live a life of pious chastity. On the island, there are the ruins attesting to the religious who lived here. You can walk around what is left of the Dominican Convent where you will find signs mentioning St. Margaret, a 12th-century chapel, and a 13th- to 14th-century Franciscan church. Once called "Rabbit Island," the island was at one time infested with rabbits. No bunny was able to leave without a bridge connecting the island to shore at the time. The island has been open to the public since 1908, but visitors were charged a fee, double on Sundays. It was not until 1945 when it became free for all. The long, narrow island is a wonderful escape from the hectic city.

In the summertime, you will find the large fountain plays classical music every 20 minutes and all of the selections are posted on a pole nearby. The flower gardens are well kept, so it is not unusual to find crowds gathered on the lawn or benches surrounding it.

Connected to both Buda and Pest via the Margaret and Árpád bridges, only local buses are allowed, with few other exceptions. The island holds many attractions, including the Palatinus Strand open-air baths, the Alfréd Hajós Sport Pool, and the Open-Air Theater. In the warm season, a restaurant called the Holdudvar serves good food at reasonable prices and features outdoor movies, making it popular with the university set. Margaret Island remains a tranquil place for a city break within the city. Trams no. 4 or 6 are the best ways to reach Margaret Island, which stop at the entrance to the island midway across the Margaret Bridge, or you can take bus no. 26 from Nyugati tér, which continues through the length of the island.

City Park (Városliget)★ sits behind Heroes' Square and is just as popular as Margaret Island for lazy walks, picnics in the grass, and the many attractions located in and around the park. It was built in stages, but the first stage started in the mid-1800s. The famous Hungarian poet János Arany (of Arany János u. fame) wrote a poem called "Song of the City Park" in 1877. The park, along with Heroes' Square, has been privy to many demonstrations as well as celebrations during their long histories. The **Vajdahunyad Castle** located by the lake is stunning when lit at night. The lake is used for small boat rides in the summer. Nearby the lake, an area is flooded to freezing for ice skating in winter. The park also embraces **Animal Garden Boulevard (Állatkerti körút),** where the zoo, the circus, and the amusement park are all found. You will also find Széchenyi Baths (p. 323) on one outer rim of the park. The **Transport Museum** is off at the southern end of City Park, which is considerably less crowded, but also less landscaped, making it less attractive for a relaxation area. The nearby **Petőfi Csarnok** is the venue for a variety of popular cultural events, concerts, and the weekly flea market. The Yellow metro line makes stops at Hősök tere (Heroes' Sq.), at the edge of the park, and at Széchenyi fürdő, in the middle of the park.

FOR THE MUSIC LOVER

Ferenc Liszt Memorial Museum (Liszt Ferenc Emlékmúzeum) Located in the apartment in which Liszt spent his last years, this modest museum features several of the composer's pianos, including a child's Bachmann piano and two Chickering & Sons grand pianos. Also noteworthy are the many portraits of Liszt done by the leading Austrian and Hungarian artists of his time, including two busts by the Hungarian sculptor Alajos Stróbl. Concerts are performed here on Saturdays at 11am.

VI. Vörösmarty u. 35. ✆ **1/322-9804.** Admission 500 Ft ($2.75/£1.70) adults, 250 Ft ($1.25/80p) students. Photo 800 Ft $4.25/£2.65), video 1,600 Ft ($8.75/£5.45). Mon–Fri 10am–6pm; Sat 9am–5pm. Metro: Vörösmarty u. (Yellow line).

ORGANIZED TOURS

Boat Tours

Legenda Tours This private company was founded in 1990, offering several boat tours on the Danube, using two-story steamboats. The daytime tour, called "Duna Bella," operates daily at 2:30pm, year-round, with additional daily trips during the summer. The 2-hour ride includes a stop at Margaret Island, with an island walk. Tickets cost 3,800 Ft ($21/£13). The nighttime tour, departing daily at 8:15pm, called the "Danube Legend," is less than impressive. "Legend" tickets cost 4,700 Ft ($26/£16). On either trip, your ticket entitles you to two free glasses of wine, beer, or soft drinks. A shorter variation of the daytime tour, without the stop on the island, runs from mid-April to mid-October. All boats leave from the Vigadó tér port, Pier 7. Tickets are available through most major hotels, at the dock, and through the Legenda website, where they will give you a CD if you book two tickets online.

V. Vigadó tér Pier 7. ✆ **1/317-2203.** www.legenda.hu. Daily 2:30pm all year. Evening tour 8:15pm. Tram: 2.

MAHART The Hungarian state company operates a daily 2-hour daytime sightseeing cruise on the Danube, using two-story steamboats. Boats depart frequently from Vigadó tér (on the Pest waterfront, between the Erzsébet Bridge and the Chain Bridge, near the Budapest Marriott hotel) on weekends and holidays in the spring and every day in summer. In the low season, they sail October 1 to November 4 and March 30 to April 29. Rates are 2,990 Ft ($16/£9.90) for adults; students with an ISIC card pay 2,490 Ft ($14/£8.70); and children 6 to 15 pay 1,490 Ft ($8/£4.95). For something different, you might try an evening cruise, with and without dinner. If this floats your boat, they sail daily during high season; sailings are Friday, Saturday, and Sunday in low season. Buffet dinner and cruise is 5,990 Ft ($32/£20), or cruise only 2,990 Ft ($16/£9.90).

V. Belgrád rakpart. ✆ **1/318-1704.** www.mahartpassnave.hu. Call for times and reservations. Tram: 2.

Bus Tours

I highly recommend **See Budapest Tour** ★★★ (✆ **06/70-455-0356** mobile only; www.seebudapest.hu) for its personal service. You receive a 3-hour tour in a small-group comfortable minivan (for a minimum of 1 or a maximum of 12 people), with a guide who is energetic about touring. The tours are done in English only, with five stops: Heroes' Square, St. Stephen's Basilica, Royal Castle Quarter, Citadel, and finishing in downtown Pest. Being small groups, they do not rush you, allowing you time to take pictures or just stroll. The tour is rich in historical details, interesting stories, and practical information. The guides have a great knowledge of the city and welcome questions. Pick up anywhere in Budapest is free. Their office is located at V. Molnar u. 3. Adult tickets are 6,500 Ft ($35/£22), children 11 and under are 3,250 Ft ($18/£11); students with ISIC or Hostelling International cards receive a 15% discount. Tours take place daily at 10am and 2:30pm.

Specialty Tours

Barlangaszat If you have a craving for caving, then this tour company will fill that hole in your life. Spend 3 to 3½ hours traipsing through the second-longest cave of Hungary, the Pál-völgyi–Mátyás-hegyi cave system, mostly under Budapest. They have been providing this tour since 1994. Following a professional caving guide, you will explore the natural untouched cave system. The guides explain the formation of the Budai Mountains, the cave formations, and fossils along the way. They provide all of the

Walkabout

For dedicated walkers who want to see the city at their own pace, the new **Walker's Guide Tours** (www.walkersguide.travel) self-guided touring is certainly an asset. Their motto is "Think out of the bus." Rent a headset at the **TourInform** office (p. 281) or some participating hotels, and then choose from 12 different tours and five adventures covering 90 main attractions. Tours range from 3 hours (rental 3,000 Ft/$16/£10) to a full day (5,000 Ft/$27/£17). The colorful book of maps and pictures allows you to tour at your own pace and interests.

necessary equipment with the tour: overalls, helmet, and headlamp. A changing room is available at the cave entrance. Crawling, scrambling, and hunkering down will be done many times during the tour, but no previous experience in caving is needed. Minimum age is 6 years, but there is no upper age limit. It is not recommended for those who are claustrophobic or unable to squeeze through tight places. Three English tours are offered each week, or a special tour can be arranged for a minimum of five people.

No office. ✆ **06/20-928-4969** mobile only. www.barlangaszat.hu. 3,800 Ft ($16/£9.90). Meet at 3:45pm at Nyugati tér. Reservations mandatory by phone, Web, or Yellow Zebra Bikes at V. Sütő u. 2 location only.

Chosen Tours Since 1990, this company has specialized in tours showing Budapest through Jewish life and heritage. All of their guides are from the Jewish community and speak excellent English. A "Special City Tour" is by coach, lasting 3 hours with stops, and adds the focus of the Jewish connections with the usual history. The "Jewish Heritage Tour" is 3 hours as a combined coach and walking tour, taking you to Buda's extraordinary Jewish landmarks followed by a walk in Pest's Jewish quarter, where you visit and enter all the highlights and the hidden treasures. Each of the tours runs 9,250 Ft ($50/£31). The walking portion can be done separately at 6,500 Ft ($35/£22) per person. To combine both 3-hour tours over 2 days, the cost is 14,800 Ft ($80/£50). For private tours for a minimum group of four, add 1,850 Ft ($10/£6.20) to the rates above per person. They also have a tour to Szentendre with Jewish sights pointed out.

No office. ✆/fax **1/355-2202.** chosentours@yahoo.com. Reservations mandatory to arrange meeting.

SPA BATHING & SWIMMING: BUDAPEST'S MOST POPULAR THERMAL BATHS

The baths of Budapest have a long history, stretching back to Roman times. The thermal baths were popularized by the Turks, who started building them in 1565, giving them a place to bathe in case of a siege on the city. Budapest and other parts of Hungary are built over hot springs, making this a natural way of acquiring the mineral-rich waters for bathing. Hungarians and other Europeans are great believers in the medicinal powers of thermal bathing, with all of the thermals being medical clinics as well for the treatment of skin, muscular, and bone ailments. Time spent in a thermal bath will lift your spirits and drench you in culture. Most baths in Budapest have recently instituted a complicated new pricing system (dubbed the "refund system") that charges according to the time spent in the baths. You are required to pay for the longest possible duration (4 hr. or more) when you enter the bathhouse, but you are refunded money based on the actual time spent in the thermal area. You are given a chip card upon entry; keep careful track of the card because if you lose it, you are assumed to have stayed for the maximum time. The exception is the Király, which is still a set fee for entry and you are allowed 1½ hours and then are expected to leave. On Saturdays, it is limited to 1 hour.

Gellért Baths (Overrated) Once one of Budapest's most spectacular bathhouses, the Gellért Baths are located in Buda's Hotel Gellért, the oldest Hungarian spa hotel and a Secessionist-style hotel. Over the years, the baths have lost their luster and some of the tile work. Remodeling took place in 2007. I find the entry cost prohibitive, so I do not recommend this thermal. Foreigners, usually staying at the hotel, get free entry and are those most likely to frequent it. The staff is churlish. If you go, enter the baths through the side entrance. The exterior of the building is in need of restoration, but once inside the lobby, the details are lovely, but most of it stops here. In the summer months, the

Thermal Bathing 101

Thermal bathing is a social activity deep within the Hungarian culture, and each bath has its own set of rules. Employees tend to be unfriendly holdovers of the old system, who hold these civil service positions since the city still owns most of the baths. They do not speak English, and have little patience. Don't be intimidated; just plunge forth. It is a cultural experience you will not forget. Explore once inside and you will feel comfortable and confident within minutes. The best advice is to try to enjoy the foreignness of the experience, because, after all, this is the reason you are here.

The most inhibiting part may well be approaching the ticket window, with the long list of services and prices, often without English translations. Chances are you're coming to use one of the following facilities or services: *uszoda* (pool); *termál* (thermal pool); *fürdő* (bath); *gőzfürdő* (steam bath); massage; and/or sauna. There is no particular order in which people move from one facility to the next; do whatever feels most comfortable. Most of the thermals are also medical clinics; therefore, many services will not apply to you. Towel rental is *törülköző* or *lepedő*. Few places will provide a towel or sheet for drying off; if you don't want to rent one, bring your own. An entry ticket generally entitles you to a free locker in the locker room *(öltöző)*; or, at some bathhouses, you can opt to pay an additional fee for a private cabin *(kabin)*.

Remember to pack a bathing suit and a bathing cap if you wish to swim in the pools so you won't have to rent vintage 1970 models. Lukács requires a bathing cap for both sexes and for all thermals and pools. Long hair must be capped when bathing at the other facilities. In the single-sex baths (Rudas, Lukács, and Gellért), men are provided with a loin cloth; bathing suits are not permitted. At the Király, bathing suits are required. Bring what you need in a plastic grocery bag to the pools to avoid having to return to the locker. Shower before getting into a thermal or pool. Some of the waters are high in mineral content, so you will most likely want to shower well and shampoo your hair before leaving. Depending on the pool, you may find a strong sulphur smell, but remember: It will do glorious things for your skin.

Generally, extra services (massage, pedicure) occur after a bath. Locker room attendants appreciate tips, especially if you plan on returning. 200 Ft ($1.10/70p) is a nice tip, unless you have repeatedly returned to the locker, then make it a bit more. Masseurs and manicurists expect a tip in the 400 Ft to 600 Ft range ($2.15–$3.25/£1.30–£2). There are drinking fountains in the bath areas, and it's a good idea to drink plenty of water before, during, and after a bath. Bathing on an empty stomach can cause nausea and lightheadedness for those unaccustomed to the baths. Most bathhouses have snack bars in the lobbies where you can pick up a cold juice or sandwich on your way in or out, but you must eat it there. Stay hydrated.

outdoor roof pool attracts a lot of attention for 10 minutes every hour on the hour, when the artificial wave machine turns on. In general, you need patience to navigate this place, and the staff is not helpful. With Metro 4 construction happening in front of the hotel, it may be difficult to access.

XI. Kelenhegyi út 4. ✆ **1/466-6166.** Admission 3,100 Ft ($16/£10) for 4 hr. or more; a 15-min. massage is 2,500 Ft ($14/£8.40). Lockers or cabins are included. Admission to all pools and baths, without a cabin and only communal dressing rooms, is 2,800 Ft ($15/£9.30) adults and children, for 3 hr. or more. Prices and the lengthy list of services, including the complicated refund system, are posted in English. May–Sept daily 6am–7pm; Oct–Apr Mon–Sat 6am–7pm, Sun 6am–5pm, with the last entrance an hr. before closing. Tram: 47 or 49 from Deák tér to Szent Gellért tér.

Király Baths ★★ This is one of the oldest baths in Hungary, dating back to around 1563, when the Turkish built the baths so they could bathe and be ready for battle. Other legends say the Turks built them to get the Hungarians to bathe. Regardless of the reason, the Király Baths are still one of Budapest's most important architectural tributes associated with Turkish rule. Bathing under the octagonal domed roof with sunlight filtering through small round windows in the ceiling gives the water a special glow. This bath is time-limited; Monday through Friday, you are allowed to stay for only 1½ hours and on Saturday, only 1 hour, before being expected to leave. Bathing suits are required for both sexes, and take a towel with you. Women use the baths on Monday, Wednesday, and Friday from 7am to 5pm. Men are welcome on Tuesday, Thursday, and Saturday from 9am to 7pm.

I. Fő u. 84. ✆ **1/201-4392.** Admission 1,300 Ft ($7/£4.35). Metro: Batthyány tér (Red line).

Rudas Baths ★★ Close to the Erzsébet Bridge, on the Buda side, is the second oldest of Budapest's classic Turkish baths, built in the 16th century. These baths are for men only every day, except Tuesdays during the day or Friday and Saturday nights at 11pm. This is a new phenomenon, which started after the bath reopened after a year's remodeling in 2007. The centerpiece is an octagonal pool under a 10m (33-ft.) domed roof, with some of the small window holes in the cupola filled with stained glass, while others are open to the sky, allowing diffused light to stream in. Along the sides, there are four corner pools of varying degrees of temperature. During early mornings, the crowd is predominantly composed of older Hungarian men.

I. Döbrentei tér 9. ✆ **1/356-1322.** Admission 2,200 Ft ($12/£7.45), with refunds available up to 3 hr., swimming pool with locker 1,200 Ft ($6.50/£4). Mon–Fri 6am–8pm; Sat–Sun pool only 6am–2pm. Bus: 7, but not 7 Express, stops right in front on the Buda side.

Széchenyi Baths ★★★ One of the largest spa complexes in Europe, Széchenyi was also the first thermal on the Pest side. Located in the City Park, the Széchenyi Baths are the most popular with locals and travelers alike. From the outside, you'd never believe its enormity, but once inside it is humungous, with a variety of water temperature pools, including a whirlpool that spins you around. Crowds of bathers, including many families and tourists, visit the palatial unisex outdoor swimming pool, but due to its size, it never feels overcrowded. Turkish-style thermal baths are segregated and are located off to the sides of the pool. In warm weather, there is segregated nude sunbathing on the roof.

XIV. Állatkerti út 11–14, in City Park. ✆ **1/363-3210.** www.spasbudapest.com. Admission to the thermal baths 2,400 Ft ($13/£8.05), dressing cabins 400 Ft ($2.15/£1.35) extra. Massage available 3,500 Ft ($19/£12) for 30 min. Daily 6am–10pm; some pools close earlier on Sat–Sun. Metro: Széchenyi fürdő (Yellow line).

START: Roosevelt tér, Pest side of Chain Bridge or alternatively take bus no. 16 from in front of the Le Meridian Hotel.

FINISH: Tóth Árpád sétány, Castle District.

TIME: 3 to 4 hours (excluding museum visits).

BEST TIMES: Tuesday through Sunday.

WORST TIME: Monday, when museums are closed.

Castle Hill was not always the focal point of Hungarian rule and authority. The original capital was in Esztergom, where King Stephen was crowned and where the seat of the Hungarian Catholic Church is located. It was not until King Béla IV built a fortress here that it became something more than a hill. This district has had its share of devastation, the last time being the 1945 Soviet bombing the Nazi forces. With each reconstruction, the prevailing style shifted from Gothic to baroque to Renaissance. Castle Hill, a UNESCO World Cultural Heritage Site, consists of two parts: the **Royal Palace** (no longer a castle) and the associated Castle District, which is now a mostly reconstructed city reflecting a former time in history. The Royal Palace is home to the **Hungarian National Gallery** and the **Budapest Museum. The National Archives,** the equivalent to the Hungarian Library of Congress, is an attached building in the back. The Castle District is a small, tapered neighborhood with cobblestone streets and twisting alleys creating an old-world feel.

Views of the Castle Hill can be seen from all points on the river bank, but we will start from Pest's Roosevelt tér just past the Gresham Four Seasons Hotel, and walk on the:

1 Széchenyi Chain Bridge

The bridge was built in 1849, funded by Count Széchenyi. During World War II, the Nazis destroyed all of the bridges in the city to hold off the Allied forces. Rebuilt in 1949, the bridge opening ceremony was held 100 years to the day after its original inauguration.

Walk across the bridge. Arriving in Buda, you're now in:

2 Clark Ádám tér

Ádám Clark was a Scotsman engineer commissioned to build the bridge. After doing so, he stayed here with the Hungarian woman he met and married. This square was named for him.

From Clark Ádám tér, take the:

3 Funicular (sikló)

The funicular, an almost vertical elevator, will transport you up the 100m-long (328-ft.) track to the entryway of the Royal Palace. It went up and down in 1 to 2 minutes, but the public petitioned for it to be slowed down so the view could be enjoyed longer. If you are feeling energetic, you can also walk up the steep stairs to Castle Hill or take the winding trail.

Whichever method you choose, when you arrive at the top, turn and look left at the statue of the:

4 Turul

The turul is the Hungarian mythical bird that legends say appeared to Emese, telling her she was pregnant with a great leader of the nation, Álmos, the future father of Árpád.

You're at the main courtyard of the palace, with the entrance to the Hungarian National Gallery located farther down the path, but first go down the nearby stairs to see the statue of the fisherboys and past them to the:

5 Equestrian Statue of Prince Jenő (Eugene) Savoyai

On September 11, 1697, Prince Eugene and his 50,000 men caught the Turks while they were crossing the river Tiza, annihilating the Ottoman army. You

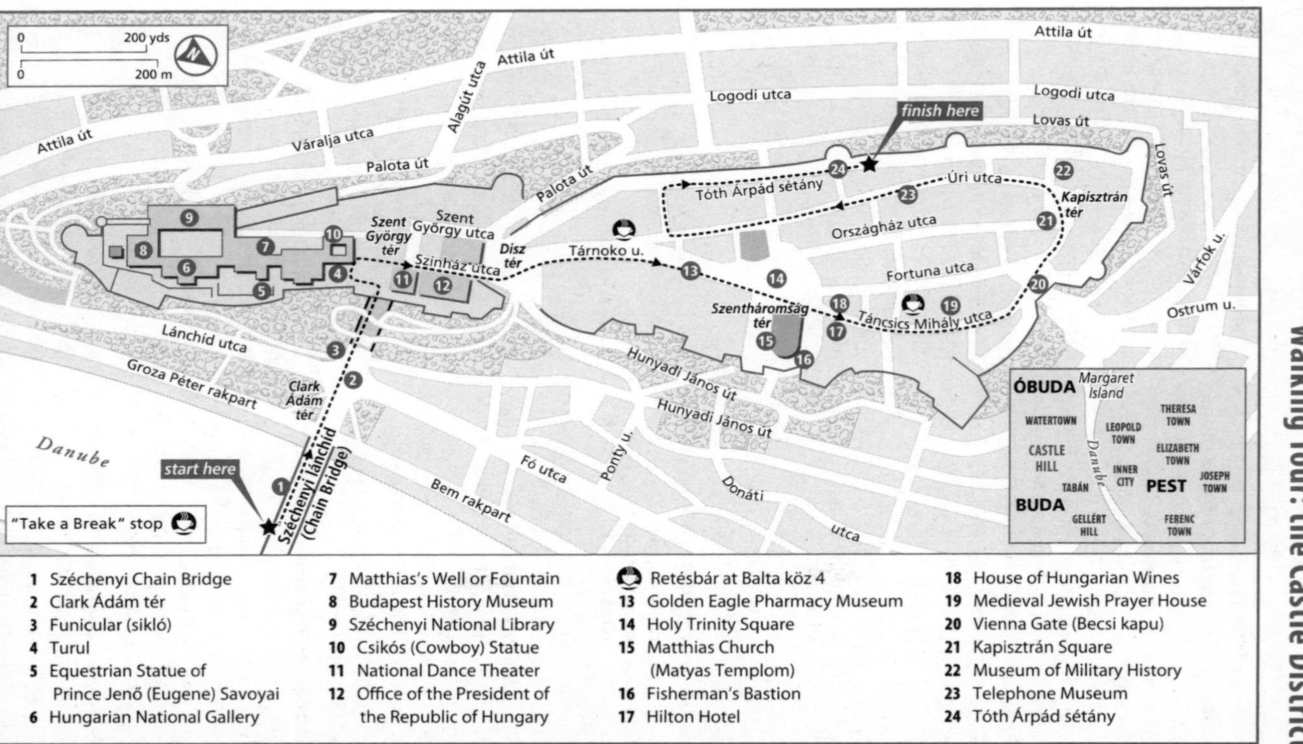
0 200 yds
0 200 m
N
Attila út
Alagút utca
Váralja utca
Palota út
Logodi utca
Lovas út
finish here
Tóth Árpád sétány
Úri utca
Kapisztrán tér
Országház utca
Szent György tér
Szent György utca
Disz tér
Színház utca
Tárnoko u.
Fortuna utca
Szentháromság tér
Táncsics Mihály utca
Várfok u.
Ostrum u.
Lánchíd utca
Groza Péter rakpart
Clark Ádám tér
Hunyadi János út
Ponty u.
Fő utca
Donáti utca
Bem rakpart
Danube
start here
Széchenyi lánchíd (Chain Bridge)
"Take a Break" stop
ÓBUDA
Margaret Island
WATERTOWN
CASTLE HILL
TABÁN
BUDA
GELLÉRT HILL
LEOPOLD TOWN
INNER CITY
THERESA TOWN
ELIZABETH TOWN
JOSEPH TOWN
PEST
FERENC TOWN
Danube
1 Széchenyi Chain Bridge
2 Clark Ádám tér
3 Funicular (sikló)
4 Turul
5 Equestrian Statue of Prince Jenő (Eugene) Savoyai
6 Hungarian National Gallery
7 Matthias's Well or Fountain
8 Budapest History Museum
9 Széchenyi National Library
10 Csikós (Cowboy) Statue
11 National Dance Theater
12 Office of the President of the Republic of Hungary
Retésbár at Balta köz 4
13 Golden Eagle Pharmacy Museum
14 Holy Trinity Square
15 Matthias Church (Matyas Templom)
16 Fisherman's Bastion
17 Hilton Hotel
18 House of Hungarian Wines
19 Medieval Jewish Prayer House
20 Vienna Gate (Becsi kapu)
21 Kapisztrán Square
22 Museum of Military History
23 Telephone Museum
24 Tóth Árpád sétány

might want to visit the National Gallery now or return after the walking tour.

The first museum is the:

❻ Hungarian National Gallery

This museum houses much of the greatest Hungarian art. ***Be warned:*** It seems to go on forever and not much is in English, though it is worth a look. If you are an art lover, you will be in heaven. The most important era in Hungarian art was the 19th century and the artists of that period.

Proceed through the courtyard to the:

❼ Matthias's Well or Fountain

This is one of my favorite fountains. Legend claims that King Matthias was on a hunting expedition when a fair maiden happened upon him. She, Ilona, not knowing he was the king, fell in love with him instantly and him with her. He has the deer he has just killed, his hunting dogs, and his servants with him. This is the most photographed statue in the city.

If you continue around the fountain and into the large courtyard, directly in front of you is the:

❽ Budapest History Museum

Boasting four floors, the exhibits contain prehistoric, ancient, Roman, and pre-Hungarian art, up to more current times. The highlights here are the Gothic rooms and statues that were uncovered by surprise when reconstruction and rebuilding of the Royal Palace was taking place.

Next, as we turn to leave the courtyard again, on our left we have the:

❾ Széchenyi National Library

The library was started through the initiative of Ferenc Széchenyi, the father of István, who had the Chain Bridge named for him. It was founded in 1802. It now houses the world's greatest collection of "Hungarica," with some four million holdings.

Now proceed to up the path, where you'll find the:

❿ Cowboy (Csikós) Statue

The horse wrangler is taming a wild horse. This statue originally stood in front of the Riding School in the former Újvilág terrace. It was moved here after being repaired in 1983.

As you continue walking past the funicular, you will find the:

⓫ National Dance Theater

First built as a cloister and church by an order of Carmelites in 1736, this building was turned into a theater when the order disbanded in 1787. Today it continues as the National Dance Theater.

Right next to the theater you will see the:

⓬ Office of the President of the Republic of Hungary

The classicist palace next to the theater was ordered by Count Vincent Móric, engaging the services of architects János Ámon and Mihály Pollack. It was the head office of the prime minister from 1887 to 1945. Now it is the office of the president of the Republic of Hungary.

TAKE A BREAK

The absolute best of Budapest *retes,* Hungarian strudel both sweet and savory are baked at this small shop, the Rétesvár at Balta köz 4. You can have a coffee or tea with a sumptuous pastry. They also have savory snacks. Sit on the bench in the *köz* (alley) and enjoy the rest.

Continue walking away from the palace area; you will pass an open-air tourist area selling crafts and folk goods, but I don't recommend your buying here. Next you will come to the:

⓭ Golden Eagle Pharmacy Museum (Arany Sas Patikamúzeum)

I love this museum, because it offers free admission, and the Renaissance and baroque pharmacy relics displayed are fascinating.

Just ahead on Tárnok utca is:

⓮ Holy Trinity Square (Szentháromság tér)

In this central square of the district is the highest point on the hill, where you'll find the Holy Trinity Column, or Plague Column. At 14m (46 ft.) high, it was erected in 1710 to 1713 in hopes of fending off another plague.

And the:

⓯ Matthias Church (Mátyás Templom)

Officially called the Church of Our Lady, this symbol of the Castle District is universally known as Matthias Church because the Renaissance monarch, Matthias Corvinus, one of Hungary's most revered kings, was the major donor of the church and was married twice inside it. Reconstruction that will last until 2012 is hiding its glorious exterior under scaffolding. Be sure to go in.

As we leave the church to the left is:

⓰ Fisherman's Bastion (Halászbástya)

An extraordinary staircase climbs up from the river to the top of the hill at the tail end of the 1800s. When reaching the top, there are the bastions, the ornaments, and the arcades of this gorgeous neo-Romanesque structure that was completed in 1901. It is not certain if this was the site of an old fish market or the fishermen's guild (hence the name).

Behind the Fisherman's Bastion is the:

⓱ Hilton Hotel

The Castle District's only major name hotel, the Hilton, through the work of architect Béla Pintér, incorporates one wall of the old Jesuit cloister built in late rococo and decorated in plaits along with the Gothic remains of a Dominican church dating back to the 13th century. The baroque facade of the 17th-century Jesuit college makes up the hotel's main entrance. The hotel has frequent art gallery shows in areas that demonstrate the melding of the old and the new. Admission is free. The Dominican Courtyard hosts summer concerts.

Across from the Hilton is the:

⓲ House of Hungarian Wines

If you like or love wine, you will want to come back to this place. For a set fee, you are set loose to try 60 different Hungarian wines from all regions of the country. You are given 2 hours to taste with snacks for palate cleaning along the way.

Now we head a few feet for a:

LUNCH BREAK

If you would like some down-home Hungarian cooking, stop at the Fortuna passage, just a short way from the House of Wine. Turn into the passage, but pass the first door, which goes to the Fortuna Restaurant, and look for the next door with a wooden sign that says ÖNKISZOLGÁLÓ VENDÉGLŐ. If you see stairs, you are in the right place. This is a cafeteria that is open only until 2pm. The food is great and inexpensive.

Because the entire length of each of the Castle District's north-south streets is worth seeing, the tour will now take you back and forth between the immediate area of Szentháromság tér and the northern end of the district. First, head down Táncsics Mihály utca, to Táncsics Mihály u. 7, the:

⓳ Medieval Jewish Prayer House

This building dates from the 14th century. In the 15th and 16th centuries, the Jews of Buda thrived under Turkish rule. This building belonged to the Jewish prefect. The synagogue was built in his home in the 16th century. The 1686 Christian reconquest of Buda was soon followed by a massacre of Jews. Many survivors fled Buda; this tiny Sephardic synagogue was turned into an apartment.

After exiting the synagogue, retrace your steps about 9m (30 ft.) back on Táncsics Mihály utca, turn left onto Babits Mihály köz, and then turn left onto Babits Mihály sétány. This path will take you onto the top of the:

⓴ Vienna Gate (Bécsi kapu)

This is one of the main entrances to the Castle District. If you have come from or are going to Moszkva tér by bus, you will use this gateway. The enormous neo-Romanesque building towering above Bécsi kapu tér houses the National Archives. Bécsi kapu tér is also home to a lovely row of houses (nos. 5–8).

From here, it is a 1-minute walk to:

21 Kapisztrán Square

Named for a companion of the Turkish conqueror János Hunyadi, here you will see the ruins of a Gothic church, which was erected in 1276 honoring Magdalen. During the Turkish invasion, it was alternately used by Catholics, Protestants, and then became a Turkish *djami.* The church was destroyed during World War II, leaving only the base walls, the tower, and one window of the sanctuary left to memorialize it.

You don't have to venture far. On the northwest corner of the square is the:

22 Museum of Military History

On the northwest side of the square, you can't miss noticing the Museum of Military History (Hadtörténeti múzeum). Besides a large collection of flags, military uniforms, and other military memorabilia, its collection displays Hungary's involvement in various wars. Admission is free if you want to breeze through.

Now take Úri utca back in the direction of the Royal Palace. In a corner of the courtyard of Úri u. 49, a vast former cloister, stands the small:

23 Telephone Museum

Sometimes the entrance to the courtyard changes from one side to the other, meaning it might be on the street parallel to Úri u. Press the bell for the attendant to open the door. The museum's prime attractions are the collection of old phones, the actual telephone exchange (7A1-type rotary system) that was in use in the city from 1928 to 1985, and the phone line cable system. I find it fascinating.

Walk back down Úri u. toward the tower and make the first left turn to bring you to the:

24 Tóth Arpád sétany

This promenade runs the length of the western rampart of the Castle District. This is a shady road with numerous benches. If you walk to the right, you will run into the Museum of Military History again, but it is worth the view over the wall to see the panorama of Buda's Rózsadomb (Rose Hill) district, Gellért Hill, and the small neighborhood of Krisztinaváros (Christine Town) situated just west of Castle Hill. It is named after Princess Christine, the daughter of Maria Theresa, who interceded for buildings to be erected in this area. Walking away from the museum along the wall, you find your way back to Korona Cukrászda, the pastry shop.

The walking tour ends here, where you can take the no. 16 bus down to Deák tér, or if you go around the corner, the no. 10 bus will take you down to Moszkva tér.

SHOPPING

MAIN SHOPPING STREETS The world of fashion and commercialization has bombarded the capital with a silent invasion. Each week, COMING SOON signs are appearing on storefront windows, promising yet other items of globalized fashion, but you can rest assured they are not for the average Hungarian. From famous designer labels like Louis Vuitton and Chanel, brand-name items, stylish secondhand shops, and, sad to say, As Seen on TV stores, Budapest offers a far wider array of shopping experiences than just a few years ago.

A popular yet overpriced shopping area for travelers is the **Castle District** in Buda, with its abundance of folk-art boutiques and art galleries. A healthy education about Hungarian wines from historical local viticulture regions can be found in the intimate labyrinthine cellar of the **House of Hungarian Wines,** but buy elsewhere for a better price. Most supermarkets carry an extensive selection of Hungarian wines.

Hungarians tend to do their serious shopping on Pest's **Outer Ring (Nagykörút),** which extends into **West End Center,** a shopping mall, located just behind the Nyugati Railway Station. Another favorite shopping street is Pest's busy **Kossuth Lajos utca,** off the Erzsébet Bridge, and its continuation, **Rákóczi út. Andrássy út,** from Deák tér to Oktogon, is popular for browsing or wishing, since it is the more upscale shopping street. Together with the adjacent **Liszt Ferenc tér** and **Nagymező utca,** Andrássy út is a popular hub for nightlife, with numerous coffee shops, bars, and restaurants (many change often). Nestled among the plethora of cafes and restaurants on the lively **Ráday utca,** you will often find small boutiques and shops where you can find unique presents and doodads. You can often pay by credit card in the most popular shopping areas.

HOURS Most stores are open Monday to Friday from 10am to 6pm and Saturday from 9 or 10am to 1pm or sometimes 2pm. Some stores stay open an hour or two later on Thursday or Friday. Sunday, most shops are closed, except for those on Váci utca. Shopping malls are open on weekends, sometimes as late as 7pm.

TAXES & REFUNDS Refunds on the 5% to 16.5% **value-added tax (VAT),** which is built into all prices, are available for most consumer goods purchases of more than 45,000 Ft ($243/£151) purchased in one store, in 1 day (look for stores with the TAX-FREE logo in the window). The refund process, however, is elaborate and confusing. In most shops, the salesperson can provide you with the necessary documents: the store receipt, a separate receipt indicating the VAT amount on your purchase, the VAT reclaims form, and the mailing envelope. The salesperson should also be able to help you fill out the paperwork. Use a separate claim form for each applicable purchase. If you are departing Hungary by plane, you can collect your refund at the **IBUSZ Agency** at Ferihegy Airport. You have to do this right after checking in but *before* you pass security control. Otherwise, hold on to the full packet until you leave Hungary and get your forms certified by Customs when you land. Then, mail in your envelope and wait forever for your refund. Two wrinkles: You must get your forms certified by Customs within 90 days of the purchase showing that it is leaving the country, and you must mail in your forms within 183 days of the date of export certification on the refund claim form. We have never found this to be any significant savings since there is a "service charge" for the service. Unless you are making grandiose purchases, you may want to save your time and energy for other things. For further information, contact **Global Refund (Innova-Invest Pénzügyi Rt.),** IV. Ferenciek tere 10, 1053 Budapest (✆ **1/411-0157;** fax 1/411-0159; www.globalrefund.com).

SHIPPING & CUSTOMS You can ship a box to yourself from any post office, but the rules on packing boxes are as strict as they are arcane. The Hungarian postal authorities prefer that you use one of their official shipping boxes, for sale at all post offices. They're quite flimsy, however, and have been known to break open in transit. The Hungarian post does not have a five-star rating on service, but they do rank four stars with misappropriating packages coming and going from the country.

Very few shops will organize shipping for you. Exceptions to this rule include most Herend and Zsolnay porcelain shops, Ajka crystal shops, and certain art galleries, which employ the services of a packing-and-shipping company, Touristpost. Touristpost offers three kinds of delivery: express, air mail, and surface. The service is not available directly to the public, but functions only through participating contracted shops. You need to consider whether the cost of shipping will still save you money by purchasing your fine porcelain and crystal in Hungary than at home.

Hungarian Customs regulations do not limit the export of noncommercial quantities of most goods, except collectibles. However, the export of some perishable food is regulated, but allowed if acceptable to the receiving country. The limit on wine and spirits is not limited at export if shipped, but may be limited by Customs at your destination. Shipping wine can be prohibitively expensive. For more on Customs, see p. 26.

Shopping A to Z

Antiques

Just about everywhere a traveler will venture, one will find shops carrying antique artifacts from keys to heirloom furniture; Budapest antique shops have something to please every shopping buff. When shopping for antiques, you should know that Hungary forbids the export of items that are designated "cultural treasures." All antiques over 50 years old need to follow a process. First, the antique must be shown to an expert for valuation purposes. To receive the valuation certificate, experts will need to see the object or a minimum of five photographs of it, and the charge of valuation is a percentage of the item's price. After you have the valuation certificate, you must then receive a permit issued by the appropriate official government office. If you are here for a short stay, take a picture and leave the item behind.

Anna Antiques Carefully packed from wall to wall, this beautiful shop presents a nice selection of furniture and pottery while also excelling in hand-embroidered textiles. Take your time learning more about the objects on display from the charming shop owner. V. Falk Miksa u. 18–20. ✆ **1/302-5461.** Tram 4 or 6 Jászai Mari tér.

Bardoni Eurostyle Antiques With its stay-a-while atmosphere, the store is decorated as a chic but congested living room. Bardoni carries characteristic Art Nouveau, Bauhaus, and Art Deco furniture and decorative items. V. Falk Miksa u. 12. ✆ **1/269-0090.** Tram 4 or 6 Jászai Mari tér.

BÁV (Bizományi Kereskedőház és Záloghitel Rt) Although it no longer has a monopoly on the sale of antiques, the state-owned trading house has staying power that other shops do not; thus, it can afford to continue its control over the antiques market in Hungary. BÁV people will tell you where to take an item for valuation, however, once it is purchased, they will only refund 60% of the paid price if their permission to export is denied, so it is best to take photographs first and then only purchase the item after receiving permission to export certificates. V. Bécsi u. 1. ✆ **1/277-2590.** Metro: Deák tér. Additional locations: V. Ferenciek tere 10 (✆ 1/318-3733; metro: Ferenciek [Blue line]) and II. Franken Leo u. 13 (✆ 1/315-0417).

Dunaparti Auction House and Gallery One of the largest galleries, with a wide range of antiques, paintings, porcelains, furniture, rugs, and lamps, this shop offers something for collectors and souvenirs hunters as well. V. Váci ut 36. ✆ **1/267-3539.** Metro: Vörösmarty (Yellow line).

Art Galleries

Budapest is home to a developing, yet often economically turbulent, art gallery scene. Many galleries open, seem to generate public enthusiasm, then just as quickly are vacant storefronts. Uniquely, some art galleries are also auction houses, and vice versa, but dedicated art galleries are trying their hand at independence. Many galleries are antiques-and-contemporary hybrid ventures that feature anything from fine art to vintage books.

Finds Contemporary Hungarian Art Lights the Spark

Sometimes foreigners can make a difference in the country they adopt as a home. Dianne C. Brown is one such example. After moving here in 1994 when her husband was transferred to Budapest, her interest in art and a university degree prompted her founding the **Friends of the Fine Arts Museum,** the first museum docent program in Europe. At the time, the museum was a place for research, but not an amicable place for visitors. Many of the holdings of the museum were shipped to Germany during the war, returned after a few years at the end of the war with the help of repatriated Hungarians who raised money and awareness of the importance of the pieces. The newly founded Friends organization sponsored events such as Open Day, allowing a behind-the-scenes look at the holdings which were not on display and how paintings were restored. Dianne continued to work with the group for 6 years, acting as its first president and continuing as a member of the board.

After a 14-year commitment to working with Hungarian art, she has again created an inspirational impact in the country's contemporary artists and their work. Dianne founded the **Sparks Gallery** and the **Art Factory** in 2005 and help to oversee them both. The studios are located in a Socialist-era industrial complex near the center of Budapest, a tremendously large space where artists can develop their style and their careers simultaneously. While the artists work in all mediums and styles, the common thread is a distinctly Eastern European emotional expressionism. Artists in residence are Zsolt Bodoni, Levente Herman, Dora Juhasz, Marta Kucsora, Mamikon Yengibarian, Ágnes Verebics, Krisztián Horváth, and Luca Korodi. Pieces of the work can be viewed at the Gresham Four Seasons Hotel, which has purchased work from the studio's artistic pool.

In addition to the Art Factory's vast studio and exhibition space, the facility also houses a newly built microgallery for photography, video, and works-on-paper. A small gallery and photo gallery is also at this location, open Saturday and Sunday noon to 3pm; viewing other times is by appointment and includes a studio tour. Contact Dianne Brown at ✆ **06/20-954-9941** (mobile phone) or e-mail her at dcbrown@starkingnet.hu. She welcomes visitors.

There are two Art Factory Gallery locations, and the easiest to get to is Art Gallery Factory II (✆ **1/302–5172**), at V. Markó u. 4. There is no nearby Metro, but you can take trams 2, 4, or 6 to the Jászai Mari tér stop. The Gallery is open Monday to Friday from 10am to 6pm, and on Saturdays from 11am to 2pm.

It is free to visit when the building is open, which is Monday to Friday 10am to 6pm and Saturday 11am to 2pm. Since this is a public space, the gallery is unattended, but the studio is nearby, making a tour convenient if arranged ahead.

A new generation of Hungarian collectors has developed, and significant interest from European and international collectors has really fueled the development of the Hungarian modern-art market. The market for antiques has also been on the rise as long forgotten objects from the Communist era have been removed from storage and are once again entering the market. Contemporary artists have made less headway in the past, but in the last few years, they are gaining recognition along with rewards for their efforts. Unless noted differently, all galleries are open Monday to Friday 10am to 5pm and Saturday 10am to 2pm.

Dorottya Gallery Albeit oppressively austere and small to some, this one-room gallery is associated with the Ernst Museum and compiles excellent contemporary installations, photographs, and media art. You don't even need to go in; you can see it all from the windows. They are open Monday to Saturday 10am to 6pm. V. Dorottya u. 8. ✆ **1/266-0223.** Metro: Vörösmarty tér (Yellow line).

Ernst Gallery The gallery features fine and applied arts from Hungary and around Europe. The Ernst Gallery, the most posh gallery in town, is run by a dynamic duo of the Austrian-born Ernst Wastl and his Greek-born wife, Eleni Korani. They put together exhibitions and discover "unknown" Hungarian artists, and whatever they put their hands onto ends up being the talk of the town. The gallery also exhibits and sells fine furniture and a wealthy collection of rarities including vintage art books, posters, and other curiosities. V. Irányi u. 27. ✆ **1/266-4016** or 1/266-4017. Metro: Ferenciek tér (Blue line).

Godot Gallery Located beside the cafe of the same name, Godot opened its door to the arty crowd in 1999 in order to present a new, dynamic space for contemporary Hungarian art. Exhibitions follow distinctly different themes, which makes it a gallery worth returning to, to see the works displayed. They are closed on weekends. VII. Madách I. u. 8. ✆ **1/322-5272.** Metro: Deák tér (all lines).

Kieselbach Gallery and Auction House Established and directed by art historian Tamás Kieselbach in 1994, the Kieselbach gallery functions as a gallery and auction house. It also puts on museum-type shows that present artworks from private collections at biannual nonselling exhibitions. The gallery specializes in paintings by Hungarian artists dating from the 19th and 20th centuries, which are becoming short in supply. Most are now off the market. They have a reputation for the documentation and display of artworks previously unknown to the public. V. Szent István körút 5. ✆ **1/269-3148.** Tram: 4 or 6 Jászai Mari tér.

Mû-terem Gallery and Auction House Established and directed by art historian Judit Virág and her husband, István Törö, this gallery also functions as an auction house. Similar to their main competitors, the Kieselbach Gallery, this gallery also puts on museum-type shows presenting artworks from private collections. Paintings by 19th- and 20th-century Hungarian artists are found here, a gallery that regularly produces record-setting prices for artists. Auctions are held twice a year. V. Falk Miksa u. 30. ✆ **1/269-3148** or 1/269-2210. Tram: 4 or 6 to Jászai Mari tér.

Bookstores

Bookstation This great store is a bit difficult to find, but worth the effort. All currently shelved books are inventoried on the computer and the staff will happily search for a book by title, author, or subject. The primary focus is used books in English. The bookstore is located in an *udvar* (courtyard). Cross the street from Keleti station and about a half a block up, look for the THÖKÖLY UDVAR sign on the top of the building.

Walk into the courtyard and it is at the back. If you get lost, it may still be open since hours are daily 10am to 7pm. VII. Thököly út. 18, Thököly Udvar. ✆ **1/413-1158.**

Pagony and Kispagony Children's Bookstores A bookstore devoted to children in my opinion is an exceptional idea. Not only will kids find books here, mostly in Hungarian, but they will also discover toys, presents, CDs, and DVDs. The children's reading area with the huge tree, many pillows, and other child-safe items make this an ideal place for kids to unwind. What better memory of their trip and something to show off to their friends than a Hungarian alphabet book? It just might inspire a future linguist. They have two locations. Pagony is open Monday to Friday 10am to 7pm and Saturday 10am to 2pm; Kispagony is open the same weekday hours, plus Saturday and Sunday 10am to 6pm. Pagony: XIII. Pozsonyi út 26. ✆ **1/239-0285.** Kispagony: II. Lövöház u. 17. ✆ 1/336-0384.

Red Bus Bookstore Red Bus is a paperback sanctuary with a large selection of classical literature, thrillers, and fiction by more British authors than the other bookstores. For as small as this shop is, it has stuffed an incredible amount of books into it, forcing the serious browser to spend considerable time here, especially since they don't have a computerized inventory. Nevertheless, the staff is helpful. They are open Monday to Friday 11am to 7pm and Saturday 10am to 2pm. V. Semmelweis u. 14. ✆ **1/337-7453.** Metro: Astoria or Deák (Red line).

Treehugger Dan's Bookstore Café Another tiny giant of a bookstore, run by an American expat eco-activist, this wisp of a store is loaded to the rafters with over 4,000 books, all in English. Have a cup of fair trade organic coffee or tea while shopping and receive a free hour of Wi-Fi Internet service besides. Dan has a computerized inventory and the staff is very helpful finding particular items. Dan will also do a book exchange if you want to lighten your load. The store is open Monday to Friday 10am to 7pm and Saturday 10am to 5pm. VI. Csengery u. 48. ✆ **1/322-0774.** 2nd location at VI. Lázár u. 16 (✆ 1/269-3843).

Fashion & Shoes

Here are just a few options, assuming since you'll discover many others as you wander through the city. For discount clothes, see "Markets," below.

Alberto Guardiani Shoes in the latest fashion trends for the sophisticated man or woman who demands excellent craftsmanship as well as style in a high end selection of shoes. Accessories are sold also. VI. Andrássy ut 34. ✆ **1/354-0054.** Metro: Opera (Yellow line).

Bagaria I don't carry a purse, but if these handbags and purses make a man take notice of them, they will certainly attract your attention. Venconi, a Hungarian designer, makes up 50% of the collection, while the rest are Italian designs. The colors and styles were bright, exciting, and original. The shop is back in the courtyard, so don't miss it. V. Váci u. 10. ✆ **1/318-5768.** Metro: Vörösmarty tér (Yellow line).

Emilia Anda Mixing organic materials like silk with plastic or paper, the noted young designer Emilia Anda's clothes make heads turn. Her studies in architecture paved the way for creating her inimitable lustrous get-ups, ones that stand out in the Hungarian fashion world. V. Váci u. 16/b. No phone. Metro: Vörösmarty tér (Yellow line).

Iguana Looking for some sparkling oversized grandma glasses, or perhaps crazy '60s or '70s cult accessories? A shrine for retro rats, the shop stocks rows of peace jackets, trousers, bags, and jewelry. Listen to or purchase some of their all-star euphoric second-hand CDs. Don't confuse this store with the restaurant of the same name. No nachos here. VIII. Krúdy Gyula u. 9. No phone. www.iguanaretro.hu. Metro: Kálvin tér (Blue line). Tram: 4 or 6.

Budapest's Youthful Designers

WAMP (Wasárnapi Művész Piac) is the Hungarian designers association that follows the example of the London and New York markets. Its main objective was to establish a regular forum for design and applied art products. Secondly, it wanted to create a more intense relationship between artists and potential buyers through interaction. Success has come for many artists in this organization when they have improved their craft through interactions with buyers or direct feedback from visitors.

Not every artist or craftsperson can get into WAMP; first you have to present a portfolio of your work and have it judged for quality of workmanship, design, and unique appeal. After passing that round, the artist is allowed to register in the WAMP database and sell at its sponsored functions.

The number of Hungarian designers associated with WAMP is quickly growing, with more than 90 artists exhibiting and selling their products in its first year of existence. Artists are realizing the uniqueness of the sponsored events as a seal of approval for their work. A wide range of design objects, such as jewelry, textiles, clothing, ceramics, glassware, children's toys, games, and cake design, is routinely presented. WAMP opens its market on variable Sundays of the month. During the warm months, it is held at Erzsébet tér (the former bus station) across from Le Meridian Hotel from 11am to 8pm. During the winter, the locations change, so check **www.wamp.hu** for current information.

For more information on the Budapest designer and fashion scene, you may want to try your luck with the Hungarian-only sites of the Budapest fashion scene: **www.bpfashion.hu**, **www.budapestfashionweek.com**, or **www.fashionweek.hu**.

Intvita Art Gallery You will also find this gallery listed under home decor below, because they have two locations with the same name, but very different products. This shop is filled with textiles; clothing, scarves, handbags, hats, and jewelry all made by Hungarian designers filling the shelves and racks. Notice the artistic wood walls and shelves while you are there. The owner handcrafted them himself and they are superb. This is at the end of the pedestrian street closer to the great market. V. Váci u. 61. ✆ **1/337-1248.** Tram: 47 or 49.

Katalin Hampel This Hungarian designer has her own unique designs to blend traditional Hungarian clothing with a modern flair. Katalin Hampel designs women's clothing marked by delicate precision of handmade embroidery, creating a new chic style. V. Váci u. 8. ✆ **1/318-9741.** Metro: Vörösmarty tér (Yellow line).

Louis Vuitton View the latest handbags, purses, and accessories by this famous designer at his own store directly across the street from the opera house. VI. Andrássy ut 24. ✆ **1/373-0487.** Metro: Opera (Yellow line).

Manu-Art Handmade by local designers, these warm clothes are likely to cheer up those who work in the cool outdoors. Odd fluffy sheep, crazy snails, or curlicue nonfigurative designs suit all ages. You'll find a second store in the busy Mammut mall (same phone number). V. Károly krt. 10. ✆ **1/266-8136.** Metro: Astoria (Red line).

Náray Tamás Situated in the posh Ybl Palace, across from the Central Kávéház, this elegant and spacious shop sells the creations of one of Hungary's most celebrated designers, Tamás Náray. The clothes are tasteful, but expensive. V. Károlyi Mihály u. 12. ✆ **1/266-2473.** Metro: Ferenciek tere (Blue line).

Retrock A group of young contemporary designers display their modern, exclusive, entrancing collections of clothes and accessories for women and men in a nostalgic atmosphere of the last century. I call this a den of discovery for those fashion aficionados who like living on the edge. Very popular with college students. V. Heinszlmann Imre u. 1. ✆ **06/30-556-2814** mobile phone only. Metro: Astoria (Red line).

Tisza Cipő A former Soviet-era brand, Tisza Shoes have been smartly resuscitated into a retro shoe brand that shot up on the must-have shoe list in Hungary and steadily is moving into the international market. It is now enjoying its laid-back high-end-segment market position. VII. Károly körút 1. ✆ **1/266-3055.** Metro: Astoria (Red line).

Za-Za This shop offers the imaginative creations of the hot young Hungarian designers of Magenta Clothing Company, who brag that they have a new line every 2 weeks. I cannot attest to this, but their display of clothes did get my attention. V. Váci u. 12. ✆ **1/267-0280.** Metro: Vörösmarty tér (Yellow line).

Folk Crafts

Hungary's famous folkloric objects are the most popular souvenirs among foreign visitors. The mushrooming number of folk art shops (*népművészeti háziipar*) have a great selection of handmade goods. Popular items include pillowcases, embroidered tablecloths, runners, wine cozies, pottery, and porcelain, dolls, intricately painted or carved eggs, dresses, skirts, and sheepskin vests. The main store, **Folkart Centrum,** is at V. Váci u. 58 (✆ **1/318-5840**), and is open daily from 10am to 7pm. One shop that has a wide selection and helpful staff is **Folkart Craftman's House** on the side street, Régiposta u. 12 right off of Váci u. (✆ **1/318-5143;** daily 10am–7pm). One outstanding private shop on Váci utca is **Vali Folklór,** in the courtyard of Váci u. 23 (✆ **1/337-6301;** weekdays 10am–5pm). A soft-spoken man named Bálint Ács, who travels the villages of Hungary and neighboring countries in search of authentic folk items, Communist-era badges, pins, and medals, runs this cluttered shop. His sales staff does not speak English, so don't try to ask questions.

Holló Folkart Gallery, at V. Vitkovics Mihály u. 12 (✆ **1/317-8103**), is an unusual gallery selling handcrafted reproductions of folk-art pieces from various regions of the country. It is open weekdays from 10am to 6pm and Saturdays 10am to 2pm. **Csók István Galéria,** located at V. Váci u. 25 (tel **1/318-2592**), is the perfect place for something a little more upscale, unique, but still affordable, so don't miss browsing. Although it is called a *képcsarnok* (picture gallery), it has a wonderful and exciting selection of ceramics, glass work, and other artistic media as well as pictures from some of Hungary's current artistic talent pool. They are open daily10am to 8pm.

Jewelry

Varga Design A wide and individualized handcrafted selection of jewelry is available in this shop by Miklos Varga, who after perfecting gold jewelry turned to silver and semiprecious stones. Each design is available in complete set of necklace, earrings, and other pieces. V. Harias köz 6. ✆ **1/318-4089.** Metro: Vörösmarty tér (Yellow line).

Markets

Warning: Markets in Budapest are very crowded, bustling places. Beware of pickpockets; carry your valuables under your clothing in a money belt rather than in a wallet.

FRUIT & VEGETABLE MARKETS (CSARNOK OR PIAC) There are five vintage market halls *(vásárcsarnok)* in Budapest, built in the 1890s. These architectural wonders of steel and glass were the first attempts to bring sanitation to the markets by giving sellers indoor protection from the elements. Those still in use as markets provide a measure of local color you find absent in any grocery store. Hungarian produce in season is reasonably priced and the fresh fruit in season makes for a handy snack during the day's travel.

The **Központi Vásárcsarnok (Central Market Hall)** is the largest and most spectacular market hall. Located on the Inner Ring (Kiskörút), just on the Pest side of the Szabadság Bridge, its impeccable reconstruction took place in 1995. This bright, three-level market hall is a pleasure to visit. Fresh produce, meat, and cheese vendors dominate the street level. Keep your eyes open for inexpensive saffron and truffles. We have had French guests who found truffles for 5€ ($6.35). The mezzanine level features folk-art booths, coffee and drink bars, and fast-food booths. The basement level houses fishmongers, pickled goods, a complete selection of spices, and Asian import foods, along with a large grocery store. Open Monday 6am to 5pm, Tuesday to Friday 6am to 6pm, and Saturday 6am to 2pm. IX. Vámház körút 1–3. ✆ **1/217-6067.** Metro: Kálvin tér (Blue line).

The recently restored **Belvárosi Vásárcsarnok (Inner City Market Hall)** is located in central Pest in the heart of the Lipótváros (Leopold Town), behind the Hungarian National Bank at Szabadság tér. It houses a large supermarket and several cheesy discount-clothing shops, in addition to a handful of independent fruit-and-vegetable vendors. Open Monday 6:30am to 5pm, Tuesday through Friday 6:30am to 6pm, and Saturday 6:30am to 2pm. V. Hold u. 13. ✆ **1/476-3952.** Metro Kossuth tér (Red line) or Arany János u. (Blue line).

The **Rákóczi tér Vásárcsarnok** was restored and reopened in 1991 after a fire ruined most of it. This is the least impressive of the markets, since there are mainly retail booths and few produce stands. Open Monday 6am to 4pm, Tuesday through Friday 6am to 6pm, and Saturday 6am to 1pm. VIII. Rákóczi tér 7–9. ✆ **1/313-8442.** Tram no. 4 or 6 Rákóczi tér.

The **Fény utca Piac** is on the Buda side behind the Mammut Mall. Formerly a nondescript neighborhood market, it underwent an ambitious reconstruction in 1998 in connection with the building of the Mammut shopping mall, to which it is attached. Unfortunately, the renovation has meant higher rental fees, which have driven out most of the small independent vendors. Except for a small area on the first floor designated for vendors, the new market retains little of the old atmosphere. Open Monday 6am to 5pm, Tuesday to Friday 6am to 6pm, and Saturday 6:30am to 1pm. II. Fény u. Metro to Moszkva tér (Red line).

Lehel tér Piac is another neighborhood market, whose reconstruction was completed in 2003, making it look like a beached ship. The market features a wide selection of fresh food and meats, and cheap Hungarian trademark products as well as rinky-dink clothing, kitchen appliances, and flowers. Open weekdays 6am to 6pm, Saturday 6am to 2pm. VI. Lehel tér. ✆ **1/288-6898.** Metro: Lehel tér (Blue line).

Music

Akt.Records Once known as Afrofilia, this cozy shop in the heart of Budapest stocks an impressive collection of minimal, hip-hop, electro, jazz, and folklore records. V. Múzeum körút 7. ✆ **1/266-3080.** Metro: Astoria (Red line).

Ferenc Liszt Music Shop (Liszt Ferenc Zeneműbolt) Budapest's musical crowd frequents this shop, located near both the Hungarian State Opera House and the Ferenc Liszt Academy of Music. Sheet music, scores, records, tapes, CDs, and books are available. The store carries an excellent selection of classical music, composed and performed by Hungarian artists. They have expanded the collections to include jazz recordings. Open Monday to Friday 10am to 6pm, Saturday 10am to 1pm. VI. Andrássy út 45. ✆ **1/322-4091.** Metro: Oktogon (Yellow line).

Fonó Budai Zeneház The Fonó Budai Zeneház entertainment complex is your source for Hungarian folk music. The complex features a folk music store and an auditorium for live folk performances *(táncház)*. It's open Monday and Tuesday 2 to 5pm, Wednesday to Friday 2 to 10pm, and Saturday 7 to 10pm. They have a summer camp for children and Argentine tango on Mondays in July; otherwise, they are closed July and August. XI. Sztregova u. 3. ✆ **1/206-5300.** Bus: 49V from Deák tér (5 stops past Móricz Zsigmond körtér).

Hungaroton The factory outlet of the Hungarian record company of the same name, this is definitely *the* place for classical-music buffs looking for Hungarian composers' recordings by contemporary Hungarian artists such as Zoltán Kocsis, Dezső Ránki, and András Schiff. Reasonable CD prices keep the Hungarian music alive. Open Monday to Friday 8am to 3:30pm. XII. Nagy Jenő u. 12. ✆ **1/202-2088.**

Selekta Located behind the impressive opera house, this shop—with an enticing chill-out interior—presents a broad spectrum of rhythmic Jamaican music, current dance hall, ska, hip-hop, and roots grooves. Open Monday to Friday noon to 8pm, Saturday noon to 4pm. VI. Lázár u. 7. No phone. Metro: Opera (Yellow line).

Wave On a small side street off Bajcsy-Zsilinszky út, directly across the street from the rear of St. Stephen's Basilica, Wave is a popular spot among young Hungarians looking for acid rock, rap, techno, and world music. Révay u. 4. ✆ **1/331-0718.** Metro: Arany János u. (Blue line).

Porcelain, Pottery & Crystal

Ajka Crystal Hungary's renowned crystal producer from the Lake Balaton region sells fine stemware and other crystal at great prices. Founded by Bernát Neumann in 1878, the company was privatized by FOTEX Rt. in 1990. Showcased are the company's brilliant yet simple crystal glasses, chalices, and crystal artwork. V. József Attila u. 7. ✆ **1/317-8133.** Metro: Deák tér (all lines).

Herend Shop Hand-painted Herend porcelain, first produced in 1826 in the town of Herend near Veszprém in western Hungary, is world renowned (check it out at www.herend.com). This shop, the oldest and largest Herend shop in Budapest, has the widest selection in the capital. They can arrange shipping through Touristpost. Even if you aren't a collector, it is interesting to come here to see some of Hungary's most famous product. The store is located in Pest's Inner City, on a quiet street just a few minutes' walk from Vörösmarty tér. Note: If you are heading to Veszprém, you may want to consider the Herend Factory (p. 358). All locations are open Monday to Friday 10am to 6pm, Saturday 10am to 2pm. József nádor tér 11. ✆ **1/317-2622.** Other locations at VI. Andrássy u. 16 (✆ 1/374-0006) and I. Szentháromság u. 5 (✆ 1/225-1051.)

Herend Village Pottery Some find the formal Herend porcelain styles stuffy or overly decorative; this is an alternative. Casually designed pottery may be the alternative, but know that this is not associated with the Herend porcelain company. The *majolika* (village pottery) is a hand-painted folklore-inspired way of making pottery. Choose from a wide variety of colors or patterns or have custom pieces made with names added, such as for a baby's first plate. All pieces are dishwasher and oven safe. Prices are reasonable here and with reorders are welcomed. The owners are very knowledgeable and eager to assist, but not pushy. Open Tuesday to Friday 9am to 5pm, Saturday 9am to 2pm. II. Bem rakpart 37. ✆ **1/356-7899.** Metro: Batthyány tér (Red line).

Wine, Spirits & Cheese

Budapest Wine Society Truly among the experts in wine, the Wine Society operates in four shops in Budapest. Founded by Tom Howells and Attila Tálos, the shop sells an immense amount of wines produced by over 50 local winegrowers. Drop in for free samples on Saturday at the Batthyány u. location, which is a much larger store with a wider selection. I. Batthyány u. 59. ✆ **1/212-2569.** Metro: Batthyány tér (Red line).

House of Hungarian Wines Taste your way through Hungary's 22 wine-growing regions in the convenience of one wine cellar. Upon payment of the entry fee, you are given a wine glass and a map of the cellar, where more than 50 wines are waiting to be tasted within a 2-hour time allotment. Snacks along the way are freely available to cleanse your palate, and if you need assistance, cellar masters are there to answer questions. Each month highlights a different region with growers from that area presenting their selections. They also arrange wine tours. They are open daily noon to 8pm. I. Szentháromság tér 6. ✆ **1/212-1030** or 1/212-1031. Fax 1/212-1032. www.winehouse.hu. Admission 4,000 Ft ($22/£14).

In Vino Veritas ★★ The gentleman who runs this store, which is almost like a wine supermarket, speaks English well and carries a vast assortment of wines and wine accessories from all over the country. You will notice their logo in many restaurant wine lists as the supplier of the wine and the list. They have hours Monday to Friday 9am to 8pm and Saturday 10am to 6pm. VII. Dohány u.58–62. ✆ **1/341-0646** or 341-3174. Metro: Blaha Lujza (Red line).

Pántlika Borház Not only does this store carry a vast selection of wines from all over Hungary, but the owner's knowledge of them is just as impressive. His English is good and he is willing to help make the right choice of wine for any occasion. Also in the store, you will find a nice selection of wine glasses, decanters, and other vino enthusiast accessories. Open Monday through Friday 10am to 6pm. VII. Dohány u. 30A. ✆ **1/328-0115.** Metro: Astoria (Red line).

BUDAPEST AFTER DARK

Budapest is definitely a cosmopolitan city with a tremendous variety of cultural events all throughout the year. There is no event that is unaffordable to the average tourist if you don't have your heart set on a particular section of a theater, but even then, seats are bargains as compared to New York, San Francisco, or London. At the Hungarian State Opera House, one of Europe's finest, tickets generally range from 300 Ft ($1.60/£1) for the nosebleed balcony to 10,900 Ft ($59/£37) for the ultraluxurious royal box once used by the Habsburgs. Almost all of the city's theaters and concert halls, with the exception of those hosting internationally touring rock groups, offer tickets for 1,000 Ft to 5,000 Ft ($5.40–$27/£3.35–£17). Of course, higher-priced seats are available also at the same venue if you want a closer view.

In some cases, it is wise to choose performances based on the venue. For example, you may not particularly be a fan of ballet, but if that is the only offering during your stay, you may want to consider less expensive tickets just to see the opera house up close and personal (alternatively, you could take the tour described on p. 340). You won't regret it; its splendor is superlative and it is best appreciated with any performance. The opera, ballet, and theater seasons run from September through May with some sporadic events in June, but most theaters and halls also host performances during the summer festivals. Bear in mind that none of them are air-conditioned and heat rises. If you are sitting in a balcony on a hot evening, you are going to be miserable. A number of the better-known churches and stunning halls offer concerts exclusively in the summer. While classical music is ingrained into the culture in Hungary, jazz, blues, rock, disco, and every other variation you left at home is here also. Stylish and unique new clubs and bars open and close regularly. The bar and club scene starts late and lasts until very early morning.

PROGRAM LISTINGS For the most up-to-date information, go to **www.jegymester.hu** and click on the English link. This site includes information for the opera house as well as the major theaters in the city. Complete schedules of mainstream performing arts are found in the free bimonthly ***Koncert Kalendárium,*** available at any of the TourInform offices or online at **www.koncertkalendarium.hu**, with a link for English. The ***Budapest Sun*** and ***Funzine*** (see "Fast Facts: Budapest," p. 286) also have comprehensive events calendars; the weekly ***Budapest Times*** includes cultural listings. ***Budapest Panorama,*** also a free monthly tourist booklet, only offers partial entertainment listings of monthly highlights.

TICKET OFFICES If you are looking for the easy way out, you can look at ticket availability online for purchasing opera, ballet, theater, or concert tickets for a number of different venues at www.jegymester.hu. It shows how many tickets are available with a seating chart to help you decide how much you want to spend for what seat. Their secure server allows you to make your purchase online. You can also prepurchase special museum exhibitions on this site, but it may require your printing an e-ticket. If you don't have Internet access, you can save time by going to the **Cultur-Comfort Ticket Office (Cultur-Comfort Központi Jegyiroda),** VI. Paulay Ede u. 31 (© **1/322-0000;** www.cultur-comfort.hu no English link). The office is open Monday through Friday 9am to 6pm. They sell tickets to just about everything, from theater and operettas to sports events and rock concerts. Schedules are posted for a variety of choices and they will show you a seating chart. If none of the cashiers speaks English, find a helpful customer who can translate for you. However, ticket agencies may not carry the entire price range of tickets. You may also find that agencies charge a commission (usually about 4%), especially for a popular performance.

For last-minute tickets or performances that are looking like they are sold out, try the venue box office for no-show tickets about 30 minutes before the performance. For **opera and ballet,** go to the **Hungarian State Opera Ticket Office (Magyar Állami Opera Jegyiroda),** VI. Andrássy út 22 (© **1/353-0170**), Mon–Fri 11am–5pm). Try **Concert & Media,** XI. Üllői út 11–13 (© **1/455-9000;** www.jegyelado.hu.), for classical performances as well as pop, jazz, and rock concerts. For just about everything from rock and jazz concert, opera, ballet performances, and theater tickets, try **Ticket Express,** VI. Jókai u. 40 (© **1/353-0692;** www.tex.hu), open Monday through Saturday from 10am to 7pm. Other Ticket Express offices can be found at V. Deák Ferenc u. 19 (© **1/266-7070**), open Monday through Saturday from 10am to 9m; VI. Andrássy út 18 (© **1/312-0000**), open Monday through Friday 9:30am to 6:30pm; and VIII. József krt. 50 (© **1/344-0369**), open Monday through Friday 9:30am to 6:30pm.

The Performing Arts

The major symphony orchestras in Budapest are the Budapest Festival Orchestra, the Philharmonic Society Orchestra, the Hungarian State Symphony Orchestra, the Budapest Symphony Orchestra, and the Hungarian Railway Workers' (MÁV) Symphony Orchestra. The major chamber orchestras include the Hungarian Chamber Orchestra, the Ferenc Liszt Chamber Orchestra, the Budapest String Players, and the Hungarian Virtuosi. Major choirs include the Budapest Chorus, the Hungarian State Choir, the Hungarian Radio and Television Choir, the Budapest Madrigal Choir, and the University Choir.

Budapest is now on the touring route of dozens of major European ensembles and virtuosos. Keep your eyes open for well-known touring artists.

Note: Most Budapesters tend to dress more formally when attending performances. However, where your seats are located will determine your dress code. If you are on the lower level, you should dress from semiformal to smart casual. In the upper regions, you can get away with jeans and a sweater. In wintertime, you are expected to check your coat and any bags. There is no getting around this, so don't try to argue with the attendant.

Opera, Operetta & Ballet

Budapest Operetta Theater (Budapesti Operettszínház) What is known as the Operetta Theater was designed by the famous Viennese architects Fellner and Helmer in 1894. When it was built, the giant stage of the auditorium faced two levels of intimate boxes arranged in a semicircle. A dance floor was included to provide a space adequately large enough for the waltz, polka, mazurka, plus the galop. Between 1999 and 2001, the theater was fully restored. The 100-year-old chandelier presides above the auditorium. The original lamp statues and supporting columns blend in with the newly added colored-glass windows, mirrors, and the period-style furnishings of the snack counter. Besides restoring the original ornamentation, a row of boxes in the circle were also rebuilt, while at the same time installing the most advanced European stage machinery. Today the theater not only boasts having 917 seats, but it also has air-conditioning in the auditorium. A highlight among Art Nouveau style buildings, the Operetta Theater hosts exquisite banquettes and balls. Performances of *Romeo and Juliette* are among the rotating Hungarian language standards. The off season is mid-July to mid-August. The box office is open Monday to Friday 10am to 2:30pm and 3 to 7pm, and Saturday 1 to 7pm. VI. Nagymező u. 17. ✆ **1/312-4866.** www.operettszinhaz.hu. Tickets 2,250 Ft–8,000 Ft ($12–$43/£7.55–£27). Metro: Opera or Oktogon (Yellow line).

Magyar Állami Operaház (Hungarian State Opera House) Definitely ranked as one of the most important buildings in Budapest, it was designed by Miklós Ybl, a famous Hungarian architect. He was also the designer of the basilica and the original Parliament, now the Italian institute. The opera house was completed in 1884 and is considered one of the most beautiful in Europe. When standing outside, on the first level, you can see the muses of opera: Erato, Thalia, Melpomene, and Terpsichore. There are also statues of Ferenc Liszt and Hungary's father of opera, Ferenc Erkel. The second level has statues of famous composers. In the lobby you will find it adorned with Bertalan Székely's frescoes; the ceiling frescoes in the concert hall itself are by Károly Lotz. Hungarians are great opera fans and many tickets are sold as season tickets. Regardless, if you don't wait until the last minute, you often will have a wide range of seats to choose from. The season runs from mid-September to mid-June. During the regular season, there are often matinees on Saturdays and Sundays at 11am. Regular performances start at 7pm, not the customary 8pm starting time. Summer visitors, however, can take in the approximately 10 performances (both opera and ballet) during the Summer Operafest, in July

The Millennium City Center

The **Millennium City Center** is situated on what was the last large available parcel of riverfront land in Budapest. On the 10 hectares (25 acres) of land, the plans have been to build a convention center in the southern section to include a 10,000 seat center for hosting conventions and sporting events, a casino, and a medicinal and recreational spa. A multifunctional exhibition hall will be adjacent to the Convention Complex while two international hotels will be built on the north side.

With the opening of the **Palace of Arts** ★★ in early 2005, the latest cultural complex created in the Hungarian capital includes a **National Concert Hall,** the **Ludwig Museum of Contemporary Art,** and the smaller **Festival Theater.** However, the plans for the rest of the center have yet come to fruition.

or August. Seating capacity is 1,289. The box office is open Tuesday through Saturday from 11am until the beginning of the performance, or to 5pm, and Sunday from 11am to 1 and 4pm until the beginning of the performances. Guided tours of the opera house leave daily at 3 and 4pm; the cost is costs 2,500 Ft ($14/£7) or 1,300 Ft ($7/£3.75) for students with an international ID card. VI. Andrássy út 22. ✆ **1/335-0170.** www.opera.hu. Tickets 300 Ft–10,900 Ft ($1.60–$59/£1–£37). Metro: Opera (Yellow line).

Classical Music

Matthias Church In my opinion, this is one of the most beautiful churches in Budapest, an icon in the center of the historic Castle district. This church is a neo-Gothic classic, named after Matthias Corvinus, the Renaissance king who was married here. Much to the dismay of many, the church is undergoing major renovations, which will last incredibly until 2012. Much or all of it is under scaffolding at all times. However, the church is a key location for excellent organ recitals, sacred music concerts for a cappella choir, orchestras, and at times folk concerts throughout the year. Ticket prices vary widely based on the offering, so the prices here are just a guideline. The ticket office is open Wednesday to Sunday 1 to 5:30pm. I. Szentháromság tér 2. ✆ **1/355-5657.** Tickets 1,000 Ft–7,000 Ft ($5–$35/£6.10–£22). Bus: 16 from Deák across from the Le Meridian Hotel or 10 from Moszkva tér. Or take the funicular or walk to the top of the hill.

Palace of Art The Palace of Art's National Concert Hall and Festival Theater concert and performing arts venues opened in 2005. The Palace of Arts was awarded the FIABCI Prix d'Excellence 2006 in the "specialized" category, which is the equivalent of an Oscar award for construction and real estate development. The main concert hall is the finest contemporary classical music venue in Budapest, and now hosts concerts from the most important orchestras from around the world. The scheduled events run the gamut and are not only classical music; their website has been beautifully created to be user-friendly. IX. Komor Marcell u. 1. ✆ **1/555-3001.** www.mupa.hu. Tram: 2 from downtown toward the Lágymányos bridge.

Liszt Academy of Music (Zeneakadémia) The Liszt Academy of Music, once known as the Royal National Hungarian Academy of Music, has five buildings around the city, but the primary one is at this location. With a seating capacity of 1,000, it is

Budapest's leading center of musical education and students come from around the world to study here. The academy was built in 1907 in its present form; the building's interior is decorated in lavish Art Nouveau style. The people are friendly, so don't hesitate to wander in just to look around at the extravagant decoration. Unfortunately, the Great Hall is not used in the summer months; the smaller Kisterem, also a fine hall, is used at that time. Student recitals are usually open to the public and are often free; however, major productions are the Hungarian and international performances. A weekly schedule is posted outside the Király utca entrance to the academy. The box office is open Monday to Friday from 10am to 8pm, and weekends 2 to 8pm. Performances are frequent. VI. Liszt Ferenc tér 8. ✆ **1/462-4600.** www.liszt.hu. Tickets 2,000 Ft–10,000 Ft ($11–$54/£6.80–£33). Metro: Oktogon (Yellow line).

Theater & Dance

Budapest has a varied and vivacious theater season from September through June, but most plays are in Hungarian only.

For international or Hungarian dance, music, or theater of the contemporary sort, the **Trafó House of Contemporary Art,** IX. Liliom u. 41 (✆ **1/215-1600** or 1/456-2040; www.trafo.hu), is the place to go. Having opened in 1998, this venue has offered a wide range of events that are extremely different and experimental, definitely not for the traditional thinker. Regardless, there have been performances I could have seen repeatedly and those for which I wanted to demand a refund, but it all equalizes in the end. If you happen to be here for any length of time, a season ticket of five performances is only 7,000 Ft ($38/£24). The beauty is that you can get two tickets for the same performance deducted from your five, to take a friend along. Prepare to get there early and stand close to the doors to the theater. It is open seating and like a cattle call when the doors open. We especially recommend some of the dance works by groups such as the French-Hungarian **Compagnie Pál Frenák** (www.ciefrenak.org); their men on ropes were unbelievably well done. Tickets cost 1,500 Ft to 2,000 Ft ($8–$11/£5–£6.80); the box office is open Monday through Friday from 2 until 8pm and weekends 5 to 8pm. Reserve or purchase tickets in advance on the website. Take tram no. 4 or 6 or metro to Ferenc Körut (Blue line).

One theater company that has been brought to my attention is the **Katona József Theater** at V. Petőfi Sándor u. 6. ((✆) **1/318-6599;** www.katonaj.hu). As a public theater, its main support is mainly provided the City of Budapest. An independent company was created here in 1982, after seceding from the National Theatre of Budapest. The troupe has extensive international connections, which are enhanced by its being a founding member of the Union of European Theatres. The company regularly embarks on international tours and to date has performed in more than 60 cities of the world. Both the productions as well as the artists have received numerous national and international awards.

For musical productions, especially those by Andrew Lloyd Webber, go to the **Madách Theater,** VII. Erzsébet krt. 29–33 (✆ **1/478-2041;** www.madachszinhaz.hu). However, I find it disconcerting to hear all of the songs redefined to accommodate the Hungarian language, so brace yourself for the experience. Built in 1961 on the site of the famous Royal Orpheum Theater, it has been restored to its former elegance. Their hit production since spring 2003 is *The Phantom of the Opera.* They have a love affair with the plays by Tim Rice and Andrew Lloyd Webber. You will find many of their plays rotating for years into 2009, with a few other American classics thrown into the mix. Ticket prices are 500 Ft to 10,000 Ft ($2.75–$54/£1.70–£33), but if you value your legs, you will not sit in the balcony where legroom is nonexistent. The box office is open daily from 3 to 7pm; performances are usually at 7pm. Take tram no. 4 or 6 to Wesselényi utca.

Affectionately called the wedding cake, a very ornate and striking theater is the **Vígszínház (Comedy Theatre of Budapest),** XIII. Szent István krt. 14 (✆ **1/329-2340;** www.vigszinhaz.hu). Here you will again only find productions in Hungarian, usually by Hungarians, but at times there will be international playwrights. The Vígszínház operates in the traditional repertory system, which is incredible to most foreigners; almost every evening a different performance is given, with the technical staff having to build and strike down the sets each day. The theater has a repertoire of actors who appear in numerous shows over the course of the month, having to learn the roles for each show. The repertory consists of 10 to 12 plays on the stages of the Víg's 1,100 seats. With a show almost every night, the theater stages numerous plays that pull in a delighted audience. The box office is open daily 11am to 7pm. Ticket prices are 900 Ft to 3,200 Ft ($4.75–$17/£2.95–£11). Take the metro to Nyugati pu. (Blue line).

An important venue of the world of contemporary performing arts in Budapest is the **MU Theatre,** XI. Körösy József u. 17 (✆ **1/209-4014;** www.mu.hu). Offering the work of contemporary choreographers and young dancers, this venue has similar events as the Trafó above. The box office is open Monday through Thursday 6pm till the beginning of the performance, and Friday through Sunday from 1pm until the start of the performance. Tickets cost 1,500 Ft to 2,000 Ft ($8–$11/£4.95–£6.80). Take bus no. 86, or tram no. 4 to Moricz Zsigmond körtér.

As the first children's and family theater in Budapest, the **Kolibri Pince (Hummingbird Cellar),** VI. Andrássy út 77 (✆ **1/351-3348**), a small theater with stage and seating for 60, offers entertainment for all age groups, but children are their main focus. Their repertoire includes adaptations and story musicals, as well as one-man shows and small theater pieces. Their other theater locations include the **Kolibri Fészek (Hummingbird Nest),** VI. Andrássy út 74, a room-theater where 50 to 70 children view the show sitting on pillows and chairs. The largest is the **Kolibri Színház (Hummingbird Theatre),** VI. Jókai tér 10, with a stage where puppet performances are usually held seating 220. Tickets cost 500 Ft to 2,000 Ft ($2.75–$11/£1.70–£6.80). Take the metro to Oktogon (Yellow line).

The Club Scene

Budapest has a hot club scene, but is volatile. Places open and close for business in the blink of an eye. To find out what is happening when you are ready to explore the nightlife, it is best to pick up a copy of ***Funzine,*** the English language guide, published every 2 weeks for up-to-date information. In order to help define the different categories of nightlife, I have tried to define an "average-age" guideline for the venues. Opening hours vary, but most clubs open hours before the partying begins, usually around 11pm, and they stay lively until closing time, which could be as late as 5am. Those with outside seating close earlier when restricted by district laws.

Barokko Club and Lounge Currently one of the hot spots on Liszt Ferenc tér, where seeing and being seen is of the utmost importance for those in their 20s and 30s when it really matters. Don't be fooled by the restaurant above; the club itself rocks. Open Sunday to Tuesday noon to 2am and Wednesday to Saturday noon to 3am. VI. Liszt Ferenc tér 5. ✆ **1/322-0700.** www.barokko.hu. Metro: Oktogon (Yellow line).

Cactus Juice Pub If you miss that Old West feeling, head here for a large drink selection with over 50 whiskey blends and a real party atmosphere. Light shows and special events are held on the weekends, with a DJ at other times. Open Monday to Thursday noon to 2am, and Friday and Saturday noon to 4am for those in their 20s, 30s, and pushing it a little older. VI. Jókai tér 5. ✆ **1/302-2116.** www.cactusjuice.hu. Metro: Oktogon (Yellow line).

E-Klub Meeting Hungarian guys or the young fashionable ladies is not a problem at this huge and hedonistic disco oozing with popularity. At one time, it was the E building of the Polytechnic University, hence the name. It has since moved to its current location and has been remodeled a number of times to stay current. They offer different special events for the party animals around the city. Guys have to pay 800 Ft ($4.30/£2.70) on Friday and 900 Ft ($4.85/£3) on Saturday for entry, but the ladies are always free. Drinks are cheap. Open for those in their teens to 20s on Friday and Saturday 10pm to 5am. X. Népligeti u. 2. ✆ **1/263-1614.** www.e-klub.hu. Metro: Népliget (Blue line).

Kulpung You may think you are walking into a car-repair shop when going to this club, because it was once. Still with a look of grunge, it is a hot spot for the university set who like their beer cheap, the music loud, and character over decor. Open daily 10am to 4:30am. Crowd: 20s and 30s. VI. Király u. 46. ✆ **30/636-8208** mobile phone only. No cover. Tram: 4 or 6 to Király.

Old Man's Music Pub ★★ Old Man's rotates the musical offerings nightly with jazz, blues, and soft rock. This place is often crowded, but since it is downstairs and only has one exit, I recommend you stand close to the door. It also gets very smoky and their drinks can be pricey. Open daily 3pm until the crowd leaves. Crowd: 30s and 40s. Akácfa u. 13. ✆ **1/322-7645.** www.oldmans.hu. Metro: Blaha Luzja tér (Red line).

Piaf Named after the French torch chanteuse, Piaf is infamous for its very late-night, after-hours parties. Some have said that you need a woman on your arm to gain entrance beyond the bouncer at the door, while others say they have heard people banging on the other side of the door to get out. Decked out like a brothel in red-velvet furnishings and low lights, part of its mystique is what happens once you are in and if you can survive the experience. In the downstairs dance floor, the spinning of oldies can get pretty heated, and the crowds can be quite wild. Open Sunday to Thursday 10pm to 6am, Friday and Saturday 10pm to 7am. Crowd: varied. VI. Nagymező u. 25. ✆ **1/312-3823.** Metro: Oktogon or Opera (Yellow line).

School Club Közgáz Touted as the biggest and most famous of the university pubs, this party place is located in the basement of Corvinus University. The disco floors are packed solid during weekends. Cheap drinks, all mix music, and the chance to test your singing with a karaoke tune, all add up for a ton of fun. Open Tuesday to Saturday 10pm to 5am. Crowd: 20s and 30s. IX. Fővám tér 8. ✆ **1/215-4359.** Cover 500 Ft ($2.70/£1.65) for men, free for women. Metro: Kálvin tér (Blue line). Tram: 2.

Trafó Bar Tango Associated with the dance venue by the same name and location, this club is housed in the basement. Trafó has a reputation for hosting the best of the best in alternative artists, from reggae to classic Indian music. The dance floor is not a reason to come here, but the small bar area is only the way station before heading to the relaxed, easygoing lounge where you can chill out with friends. Open daily 6pm to 4am or later, depending on performances. Crowd: varied. IX. Liliom u. 41. ✆ **1/215-1600.** www.trafo.hu. Cover 500 Ft–2,000 Ft ($2.75–$11/£1.70–£6.80). Metro: Ferenc körút (Blue line). Tram: 4 or 6 to Üllöi út.

The Pub Scene

Alcatraz Themed like its San Francisco namesake, the bar is a prison motif with waitstaff in prisoner uniforms. Sometimes their attitude is similar, also. Drinks are pricey, but the music is good and they pack them in. Being downstairs, they usually close June through August. Other months they are open Monday to Wednesday 6pm to 2am, and Thursday to Saturday 6pm to 4am. Crowds: 30s. VII. Nyár u. 1. © **1/478-6010.** www.alcatraz.hu. No cover. Metro: Blaha Lujza tér (Red line).

Balettcipő This colorful coffeehouse/bar, whose name translates to "ballet shoe," is on the side street of the opera house. The laid-back, open atmosphere makes it a favorite for Hungarians. The outdoor seating in suitable weather is an added draw. It has a simple cafe-style menu, perfect for a light dinner. Open Monday through Friday 8am to midnight, and Saturday and Sunday 10am to midnight. VI. Hajós u. 14. © **1/269-3114.** Metro: Opera (Yellow line).

Café Aloe A sizzling cellar bar, yet warm and friendly. The bar staff is attentive to guests' needs. This place is known among locals as the temple of good, inexpensive liquor. Open daily 5pm to 2am. VI. Zichy Jenő u. 37. © **1/269-4536.** Metro: Nyugati pu. (Blue line).

Café Bobek Named for a Communist rabbit, this is a cute little cafe bar where you can go for a quiet drink with friends. They also offer free Wi-Fi. Open Monday to Thursday 8am to 1am, Friday 8am to 3am, Saturday 11am to 3am, and Sunday 11am to 1am. VII. Kazinczy u. 51. © **1/372-9158.** Tram: 4 or 6 Király.

Café Csiga This small artsy cafe/pub is the perfect hiding place for a relaxing beer or a snack, where you can sit with your friends for hours. Set back on a corner off of a square, it is a bit difficult to find due to metro 4 construction right in front. However, the laid-back atmosphere, the country-style tables and chairs, and the funky artwork on the walls make it worth the effort. The daily offerings are written on the blackboard and change daily. The coffee is served hot, which is a plus in our book, and the staff actually smiles at you. Open Monday to Saturday 11am to 1am and Sunday 4pm to 1am (kitchen closes at 11pm and all day Sun). VIII. Vásár u. 2. © **1/210-0885.** Tram: 4 or 6 to Rákóczi tér.

Fehér Gyűrű It's been described as an unpretentious place for having a beer and a *pogácsa* (biscuit), where the university youth to the young working crowd like to hang out to talk. It is without overloud music drowning out conversations. Benches and plastic chairs provide extra seating if your crowd happens to grow as others join you. Open Monday to Thursday 1pm to midnight, Friday and Saturday 1pm to 1am, and Sunday 4pm to midnight. V. Balassi Bálint u. 27. © **1/312-1863.** Tram: 4 or 6 to Jászai Mari tér.

Janis Pub Named after the legendary Janis Joplin, this easygoing pub has an Irish theme with Guinness on tap, a selection of alcohols, live music nightly, and Janis Joplin artifacts for you fans out there. Open Monday to Thursday 4pm to 2am, Friday and Saturday 4pm to 3am, and Sunday 6pm to 2am. V. Királyi Pál u. 8. © **1/266-2619.** www.janispub.hu. Metro: Kálvin tér or Ferenciek tere (Blue line).

Paris, Texas Paris, Texas, has the distinction of being the first nightlife spot with the foresight to have opened up on the now-buzzing Ráday utca, the partial pedestrian-only street now lined with bars and cafes. The clientele runs the gamut during tourist season, but at other times, a predominately student-aged clientele lingers into the morning. This is a cozy place to drink and talk, but any food ordered comes from the Pink Cadillac nearby. The walls of three adjacent rooms are lined with old photographs, providing a window into the local culture of the 1910s and 1920s. In the summer, there is limited outdoor seating. They are open Monday to Friday 10am to 3am and Saturday and Sunday 1pm to 3am. IX. Ráday u. 22. ✆ **1/218-0570.** Metro: Kálvin tér (Blue line).

Pótkulcs Being a bohemian bar, Pótkulcs ("Spare Key") has no signs showing you the entrance, so you have to hunt for it. However, you will find an artsy-looking crowd of both travelers and locals. Beyond the rusty metal entrance, this large pub filled with rickety chairs, couches, and tables is a great place to socialize. Presenting the local artists-to-be, the pub features an eclectic mix of temporary art exhibitions and unique concerts. Open daily 5pm to 2:30am. VI. Csengery u. 65/b. ✆ **1/269-1050.** www.potkulcs.hu. Metro: Nyugati pu. (Blue line).

Szimpla Kert For cultural experiences, you cannot pass up Szimpla Kert. It is a beer garden, alternative cultural mecca. Located in an abandoned apartment courtyard that has not seen the wrecking ball, Szimpla Kert mixes junkyard aesthetics with such modernisms like Wi-Fi, a daytime cafe, and evenings of live music and indie film screenings. The dimly lit, couch-packed place, with small, open-to-the-sky rooms surrounding the courtyard, is a relaxing, pleasant place to unwind. Check your reality at the door. Open weekdays 10am to 2am and weekends noon to 2am. VII. Kertész u. 48. ✆ **1/342-1034.** Metro: Oktogon (Yellow line). Tram: 4 or 6 to Király u.

Szóda When I needed a Wi-Fi and caffeine fix at the same time, this was my favorite hangout. Redesigned a few times, it seems to look the same, with retro-futuristic leather, bench seats, and '50s-style chairs. The windows are filled with empty old-fashioned spritzer soda bottles. The underground bar and dance floor is a shelter for the whacky all-night dance rats. Note that the hours are open to interpretation, as they sometimes close during the day for no apparent reason or explanation. Open daily 8am to 5am. VII. Wesselényi u. 18. ✆ **1/461-0007.** www.szoda.com. Tram: 4 or 6 to Wesselényi u.

Vittula A hidden small new-wave cellar bar that looks like someone's basement that has not been cleaned of old storage items for 10 years, Vittula still seems to be a busy and popular place for youthful travelers, expatriates, and locals alike who come to listen to retro-funky vibes or live music by local youth talents. Some say there should be a warning label on the front door due to the unbearable smoke. Open daily 6pm to dawn. VII. Kertész u. 4. No phone. Metro: Blaha Lujza tér (Red line).

Hungarian Dance Houses

Hungarian folk music has many styles, sounds, and instruments, some specifically used with dances, while others are autonomous. Hand in hand with national identity, folk music has had a revival via the *táncház* (dance house). An evening of folk music and folk dancing can be a wonderful cultural experience during your stay. The events in a neighborhood community center certainly come with a higher recommendation than those offered as tourist events. When an American choreographer student was studying here, she pointed out that many of the dances were male-centered, with the ladies as window dressing. Perhaps some are, but others are definitely equally mixed. Listed below are a few of the best-known dance houses. The offering is dance instruction for an hour, and then several hours of dancing accompanied by a live band. You just might hear some of Hungary's best folk musicians in these simple dance houses. If you have two left feet, just go to watch and listen. Every festival has some folk dancing included, so if you are too inhibited to try these places, try to arrange your trip around some festival time. Most dance houses are open from September to June and close for the summer.

Authentic folk-music workshops are held at least once a week at several locations around the city. The leading Hungarian folk band is **Muzsikás,** the name given to musicians playing traditional folk music in Hungarian villages. They have toured the U.S., playing to great acclaim and host, but may not always be available at the *táncház.* However, live music is played every Thursday (Sept–May only) from 8pm to midnight (500 Ft/ $2.75/£1.70) at the **Marczibányi Square Cultural House (Marczibányi tér Művelődési Ház),** II. Marczibányi tér 5/a (✆ **1/212-2820**). Take the Red line metro to Moszkva tér.

In Buda, try the **Kalamajka Dance House (Belvárosi Ifjúsági Mûvelődési Ház),** V. Molnár u. 9 (✆ **1/371-5928**), reachable by metro 3 Ferenciek tere. On Saturday from 8pm to 1am for 500 Ft ($2.75/£1.70), you can dance until you drop. This is the biggest weekend dance, with dancing and instruction on the second floor, while jam sessions and serious *pálinka* drinking take place on the fourth. Béla Halmos leads the Kalamajka Band, who started the dance house movement in the 1970s. Usually traditional villagers give guest performances.

Every Monday, Friday, and Saturday from May to mid-October at 8.30pm, the touristy Folklór Centrum presents a program of Hungarian dancing accompanied by a Gypsy orchestra at the **Municipal Cultural House (Fővárosi Művelődési Ház)** at XI Fehérvári út 47 (✆ **1/203-3868**). This performance is one of the best of its kind in Budapest.

Most people who come to a *táncház* evening do so to learn the folk dances and the music that accompanies them, not for touristy reasons. However, this does not mean that tourists would not be welcome to learn the dances or to observe while hearing musicians practicing and partaking in a local scene at next to no expense. You have the opportunity to become part of the program instead of merely watching others perform.

Gay & Lesbian Bars

The bar scene, regardless of orientation, is volatile. Bars exclusively for gays have a difficult time staying in business, so you will find most of them mixed. Budapest's gay scene is largely male-oriented, with some progress in making it better for women. For reliable and up-to-date information, visit **www.budapestgaycity.net** or **www.gayguide.net**, or subscribe to the free Yahoo **Gay Budapest Information** group by sending an e-mail to gaybudapestinfo-subscribe@yahoogroups.com.

Note: Before Gay Pride July 2008, a number of gay venues were attacked with Molotov cocktails. This only seems to happen around Pride time.

Action Bar This is a well-hidden bar and can easily be overlooked. The hanging sidewalk sign is usually not even close to the entrance. Look for a large yellow A sign, and this is the entrance to this dark, often crowded basement bar. Most of the group consists of other tourists with a few locals mixed in, but exclusively men. You will receive a drink card which obligates you to drink the minimum of 1,300 Ft ($7/£4.35) or pay the difference when you leave. Make sure the bartender marks your card with every drink you order. There is a hefty fine for "lost" cards. Highlights are the spicy strip shows and go-go shows at 12:30 and 1:45am, busy dark video rooms, and a sizzling hot atmosphere, but it is empty until 11pm. Open daily 9pm to 5am. V. Magyar u. 42. ✆ **1/266-9148.** www.action.gay.hu. Metro: Kálvin tér (Blue line).

AlterEgo Another new club to make its way to the gay scene in 2007, this is regaled as a hip, jumping club for the younger set, but is small. Men and women are welcomed to their different events each night. Besides karaoke on Thursdays, they have guest singers and transvestite shows. Open Wednesday to Saturday 10pm until the sun rises again. VI. Dessewffy u. 33. © **06/70-345-4302** mobile only. Metro: Oktogon (Yellow line).

Capella Although labeled a gay club, with cross-dressing bar staff, this club draws a large nongay crowd. They offer cabaret-style shows and extravagant drag shows, which draw the curious heterosexuals at midnight and 1am. There are three levels to the bar. Some have reported that the cover charge changes sporadically and some customers have been overcharged, so proceed with caution and count your change carefully. Open Monday to Saturday 9pm to 5am. V. Belgrád rkp. 23. © **1/328-6231.** Metro: Fereciek tere (Blue line).

CoXx Club Once known as Chaos, it is a modern, metallic bar for sizzling gay men in the underground shelter. The entry level has an overpriced Internet cafe and a small art gallery, where you will be greeted and given your consumption card. In the winter, coat check is mandatory. Nothing happens here until midnight at the earliest. Open daily 9pm to 4am. VII. Dohány u. 38. © **1/344-4884.** www.coxx.hu. Drink minimum 1,000 Ft ($5.40/£3.35). Metro: Astoria or Blaha Lujza tér (Red line).

Habrolo Bisztro This is a small gay bar where locals hang out, so you can practice your Hungarian skills here. The staff from the former Angyal's bar has been here since its opening in 2006. Open Tuesday to Sunday 5pm to 5am. V. Szep u. 1/b. No phone. No cover. Metro: Astoria (Red line).

Le Café M Formerly the Mystery Bar, which was the first gay bar in the city, it changed its name for unknown reasons. It is a very tiny, but friendly place that draws a large foreign clientele. It is a great place to strike up a conversation and meet new people. Open Monday to Friday 4pm to 4am, Saturday and Sunday 6pm to 4am. V. Nagysándor József u. 3. © **1/312-1436.** www.lecafem.com. No cover. Metro: Arany János u. (Blue line).

More Entertainment

CASINOS Budapest has a couple dozen casinos. Many are located in luxury hotels: **Casino Budapest Hilton,** I. Hess András tér 1–3 (© **1/375-1001**); **Las Vegas Casino,** in the Atrium Hyatt Hotel, V. Roosevelt tér 2 (© **1/317-6022;** www.lasvegascasino.hu); and **Orfeum Casino,** in the Hotel Béke Radisson, VI. Teréz krt. 43 (© **1/301-1600**). Formal dress is required. Other popular casinos include **Grand Casino Budapest,** V. Deák Ferenc u. 13 (© **1/483-0170**); **Tropicana Casino,** V. Vigadó u. 2 (© **1/327-7250;** www.tropicanacasino.hu); and the most elegant **Várkert Casino,** on the Danube side, Ybl Miklós tér 9 (© **1/202-4244;** www.varkert.com). There are a number of smaller independent casinos around the city, but I do not recommend patronizing them.

MOVIES A healthy number of English-language movies are always playing in Budapest, but some are months-old releases. The best source of listings is the ***Budapest Sun*** or online at www.budapestsun.com. Movies labeled *szinkronizált, m.b.,* or *magyarul beszél* means that the movie has been dubbed into Hungarian; *feliratos* means subtitled. Tickets cost around 800 Ft to 1,800 Ft ($4.30–$9.75/£2.65–£6.05). Most multiplexes provide the option of seeing movies in their original language even if the movie itself was dubbed, but they are the most expensive theaters. For their addresses, check the *Budapest Sun* when checking the schedule. The art cinemas where English-language movies commonly play are **Corvin,** VIII. köz 1 (© **1/459-5050;** tram 4 or 6 to Ferenc krt.); **Európa,** VII. Rákóczi út 82 (© **1/322-5419;** bus 7 to Berzsenyi u.); **Művész,** VI. Teréz krt. 30 (© **1/332-6726;** tram 4 or 6 to Oktogon); **Puskin,** V. Kossuth L. u. 18 (© **1/429-6080;** metro to Astoria, Red line).

4 THE DANUBE BEND

The Danube Bend (Dunakanyar), a string of small riverside towns just north of Budapest, is a popular excursion spot for both Hungarians and international travelers. The name "Danube Bend" is actually a misnomer. It should be the Danube twist, turn, and twist again. The river doesn't actually change direction at the designated bend. The Danube enters Hungary from the northwest flowing southeasterly, forming the border with Hungary's northern neighbor, Slovakia. Just after Esztergom, about 40km (25 miles) north of Budapest, the river changes abruptly to the south. This is the start of the Danube Bend region. From here the river then sharply twists north again just before Visegrád, before going south yet again before reaching Vác. From Vác, it flows more or less directly south, through Budapest on toward the country's Serbian and Croatian borders. When looking at it on a map, it looks like a long snake after a seizure.

The small but historic towns along the snaking Bend—in particular, Szentendre, Vác, Visegrád, and Esztergom—are easy day trips from Budapest since they're all within a half-hour to a couple of hours from the city. The great natural beauty of the area, where forested hills loom over the river, makes it a welcome haven for those weary of the city. Travelers with more time in Budapest can easily make a long weekend out of a visit to the Bend.

GETTING THERE

BY BOAT From April to September, boats run between Budapest and the towns of the Danube Bend. A leisurely boat ride through the countryside is one of the highlights of a boat excursion. All boats depart Budapest's Vigadó tér boat landing, which is located in Pest between Erzsébet Bridge and Szabadság Bridge, stopping to pick up passengers 5 minutes later at Buda's Batthyány tér landing, which is in Buda and is also a Red line metro stop, before it continues up the river.

Schedules and towns served are complicated and change sometimes due to water levels of the river, so contact **Mahart,** the state shipping company, at the Vigadó tér landing (© **1/318-1704;** www.mahartpassnave.hu) for information. You can also get MAHART information from TourInform.

Round-trip prices are 2,085 Ft ($11/£6.80) to Szentendre, 2,235 Ft ($12/£7.45) to Visegrád, and 1,460 Ft ($7.90/£4.90) to Esztergom. Children 5 and under ride for free, children ages 6 to 15 receive a 50% discount, and students receive a 25% discount with the ISIC card.

The approximate travel time from Budapest is 2 hours to Szentendre, 3½ hours to Visegrád, and 5 hours to Esztergom. If time is tight, consider the train or bus (both of which are also considerably cheaper).

BY TRAIN For information and details on traveling by rail, see the "Getting Around" section on p. 283.

To Szentendre The HÉV suburban railroad connects Budapest's Batthyány tér station with Szentendre. On the Pest side, you can catch the HÉV from the Margit Híd, Budai Híd Fő stop on trams 4 or 6. Trains leave daily, year-round, every 20 minutes or so from 4am to 11:30pm (trip time: 45 min.). The one-way fare is 500 Ft ($2.75/£1.70); subtract 230 Ft ($1.25/75p) if you have a valid Budapest public transportation pass. The trip is 45 minutes.

To Vác An incredible 85 trains leave from Nyugati Station during the week and 58 on weekends, giving you lots of freedom on time of day to go. However, shoot for the train that leaves 5 minutes to the hour, since the trip is only 25 minutes. Other trains can take 45 minutes to 1½ hours for unknown reasons. The one-way fare is 525 Ft ($2.75/£1.70) each way. All of the trains are locals, so no reservation is needed.

To Visegrád There's no direct train service to Visegrád. Instead, you can take one of 28 daily trains departing from Nyugati Station for Nagymaros (trip time: 40 min.–1 hr.). From Nagymaros, take a ferry across the river to Visegrád. The ferry dock (RÉV **✆ 26/398-344**) is a 5-minute walk from the train station. A ferry leaves every hour throughout the day. The train ticket to Nagymaros costs 900 Ft ($4.75/£2.95); the ferryboat ticket to Visegrád costs 200 Ft ($1.10/70p) for adults and 100 Ft (55¢/35p) for students.

To Esztergom Twenty-five trains make the run daily between Budapest's Nyugati Station and Esztergom (trip time: 1½ hr.); IC trains are not available on this route. Train tickets cost 900 Ft ($4.85/£3).

BY BUS Approximately 30 daily buses travel the same route to Szentendre, Visegrád, and Esztergom, departing from **Budapest's Árpád híd bus station** (**✆ 1/329-1450;** at the Blue line metro station of the same name). The one-way fare to Szentendre is 375 Ft ($2/£1.25); the trip takes about 45 minutes. The fare to Visegrád is 750 Ft ($4.05/£2.50), and the trip takes 1¼ hours. To Esztergom, take the bus that travels via a town called Dorog; it costs 675 Ft ($3.65/£2.25) and takes 1¼ hours. The bus going to Esztergom via Visegrád takes 2 hours and costs 750 Ft ($4.05/£2.50); fare is determined by number of kilometers of travel, and this is a longer route. Keep in mind that all travel by bus is subject to traffic delays, especially during rush hour.

BY CAR From Budapest, Rte. 11 hugs the west bank of the Danube, taking you to Szentendre, Vác, Visegrád, and Esztergom. Alternatively, you could head "overland" to Esztergom by Rte. 10, switching to Rte. 111 at Dorog.

SZENTENDRE

21km (13 miles) N of Budapest

Szentendre (pronounced *Sen*-ten-dreh, meaning St. Andrew), 21km (13 miles) north of Budapest, has been populated since the Stone Age by Illyrians, the Celtic Eraviscus tribe, Romans, Lombards, Avars, and naturally, Hungarians. Serbians settled here in the 17th century, embellishing the town with their unique characteristics. Szentendre counts half a dozen Serbian churches among its rich collection of historical buildings.

Since the turn of the 20th century, Szentendre has been home to an artist's colony, where today about 100 artists live and work. The town boasts of its selection of 48 museums and monuments, but few people come here to visit the museums, distracted perhaps by the shopping opportunities. The hours posted are just a loose guide, meaning that museums do not have stable hours, even when posted on their door. Oftentimes a sign posted states it is closed for "technical reasons," but no future reopening date is given. Think of a museum as icing on the cake; if it is open, take the opportunity to visit it.

The town is an extremely popular tourist destination, with tour buses pouring people in the town for a few hours of exploring. This is sometimes a turnoff for other visitors, but the town is really is a treasure to be explored. To appreciate the rich flavor of the town, I recommend that you explore beyond the touristy shops and wander the streets looking at the architecture, the galleries, and the churches, if only from the outside. Dare to wander off main streets, where you will find hidden shops, beautiful old homes, and quiet little green spaces. Almost all of the streets are cobblestones, so choose comfortable footwear.

Essentials

One of Szentendre's information offices, **TourInform,** is at Dumtsa Jenő u. 22 (© **26/317-965**), with maps of Szentendre (and the region), as well as concert and exhibition schedules. The office can also provide accommodations information. The office is open April through October Monday to Wednesday from 9:30am to 6pm, and Thursday to Sunday 9:30am to 7:30pm; in the off season, it's open Monday to Friday from 9:30am to 5pm. To get here, just follow the flow of pedestrian traffic into town on Kossuth Lajos utca. Like all things in this town, they march to the beat of their own drummer, not always keeping with the schedule they give. If you arrive by boat, you may find the **Ibusz** office sooner, located on the corner of Bogdányi út and Gőzhajó utca (© **26/310-181**). This office is open April to October Monday through Friday from 10am to 6pm and weekends 10am to 3pm. From November to March, it's open weekdays only, 10am to 5pm.

Another good source of information, particularly if you are planning to stay in the region more than a day, is **Jági Utazás,** at Kucsera F. u. 15 (©/fax **26/310-030**). The staff here is extremely knowledgeable and dedicated. From planning hunting or horseback-riding excursions to helping you find the right pension room to recommending the best *palacsinta* (crepe) place in town, they seem to know it all. The office is open Monday to Friday 9am to 5pm and Saturday from 9am to 1pm in summer (closed Sat in winter).

Where to Stay

Róz Panzió ★, Pannónia u. 6/b (© **26/311-737;** fax 26/310-979; www.hotelrozszentendre.hu), has 10 units and a nice garden overlooking the Danube for breakfast when weather permits. Rooms are 12,000 Ft ($65/£40) for a double during off season and 13,000 Ft ($70/£43) in high season; breakfast is included. With their new website, you can book online and view videos. Parking is available.

Exploring the Museums & Churches

Barcsay Museum ★ The conservative Socialist dictates of the day restricted the work of artist Jenő Barcsay (1900–88). Nevertheless, in his anatomical drawings, etchings, and charcoal and ink drawings, Barcsay's genius shines through. I particularly like his pastel drawings of Szentendre street scenes.

Dumtsa Jenő u. 10. © **26/310-244.** Admission 400 Ft ($2.15/£1.35). Wed–Sun 9am–5pm.

Blagovestenska Church ★ The Blagovestenska church at Fő tér 4 is the only one of the town's several Serbian Orthodox churches that you can be fairly sure to find open. The tiny church, dating from 1752, was built on the site of a wooden church from the Serbian migration of 1690. A rococo iconostasis features paintings by Mihailo Zivkovic; notice that the eyes of all the icons are upon you.

Fő tér 4. No phone. Admission 250 Ft ($1.35/85p). Tues–Sun 10am–5pm.

Margit Kovács Museum ★★ This expansive museum features the work of Hungary's best-known ceramic artist, Margit Kovács, who died in 1977. This museum displays the breadth of Kovács' talents. Many appreciate her sculptures of elderly women and her folk art interpretations of village life. When the museum is full, people are required to wait outside before entering.

Vastagh György u. 1. ✆ **26/310-244.** Admission 700 Ft ($3.80/£2.35). Mar–Sept Tues–Sun 9am–5pm; Oct–Feb Tues–Sun 10am–4pm. Walk east from Fő tér on Görög u.

Marzipan Museum ★★ Interestingly, this is the most widely known museum in this village, claiming to be the only museum of its type in the world. Who could pass up this chance to see the 1.6m (5¼ ft.) long Hungarian Parliament made entirely in marzipan? Kids of all ages will love the Disney characters and the 1.8m (6-ft.) Michael Jackson, made of white chocolate. What they can create in marzipan and chocolate is amazing.

Dumsta Jeno u. 12. ✆ **26/311-931.** Admission 400 Ft ($2.15/£1.35). May–Sept daily 10am–7pm; Oct–Apr daily 10am–6pm.

Serbian Orthodox Museum ★★ The Serbian Orthodox Museum is housed next door to a Serbian Orthodox church (services are at 10am Sun) in one of the buildings of the former episcopate, just north of Fő tér. The collection here—one of the most extensive of its kind in predominantly Catholic Hungary—features exceptional 16th- through 19th-century icons, liturgical vessels, scrolls in Arabic from the Ottoman period, and other types of ecclesiastical art. Informative labels are in Hungarian and English. Entrance to the museum entitles you to visit the church, but a museum attendant unlocks the door for you and waits for you to leave again.

Pátriárka u. 5. ✆ **26/312-399.** Admission 500 Ft ($2.70/£1.70). May–Sept Tues–Sun 10am–6pm; Oct–Apr Tues–Sun 10am–4pm. Walk north from Fő tér on Alkotmány u.

Szántó Jewish Memorial House and Temple ★★★ (Moments) This is the first temple built in Hungary after World War II as a memorial to those from this area who died in the Holocaust. It is probably the smallest Jewish temple in the world. Professor József Sweitzer, the chief rabbi of Hungary, dedicated it on May 17, 1998. Men are given yarmulkes to wear when entering.

Albotmány u. 4. No phone. Free admission but donations accepted. Tues–Sun 11am–5pm.

Where to Dine

Aranysárkány Vendéglő (Golden Dragon Inn) ★ HUNGARIAN Located just east of Fő tér on Hunyadi utca, which leads into Alkotmány utca, the Golden Dragon is always filled to capacity. The crowd includes a good percentage of Hungarians, definitely a good sign in a heavily visited town like Szentendre.

Long wooden tables set with sterling cutlery provide a relaxed but tasteful atmosphere in this air-conditioned restaurant. You can choose from such enticing offerings as alpine lamb, roast leg of goose, Székely style stuffed cabbage (the Székely are a Hungarian ethnic group native to Transylvania), spinach cream, and venison steak. Vegetarians can order the vegetable plate, a respectable presentation of grilled and steamed vegetables in season. The cheese dumplings do a good job of rounding out the meal. Various traditional Hungarian beers are on draft, and the wine list features selections from 22 regions of the country.

Alkotmány u. 1/a. ✆ **26/301-479.** www.aranysarkany.hu. Reservations recommended. Main courses 2,400 Ft–3,600 Ft ($13–$20/£8.05–£12); special tourist menus for 3,300 Ft ($18/£11). AE, MC, V. Daily noon–10pm.

Chez Nicolas ★★★ FRENCH/HUNGARIAN Set away from the bustle of the square, this charming restaurant has intimate romantic dining with an outdoor terrace looking out to the river. For a more romantic experience, request the single balcony table.

You can choose from Hungarian or French dishes. The owner, Tamás Horváth, will be happy to explain the ingredients of each dish with you in his excellent English. We recommend the Pork Brasso with choice chunks of pork cooked smothered in paprika, oil, and potatoes. This is restaurant is a favorite of local residents.

Kígyó u. 10. ✆ **26/311-288.** Reservations recommended. Main courses 1,790 Ft–3,800 Ft ($9.75–$21/£6.05–£13). MC, V. Tues–Sun noon–10pm.

VÁC

34km (21 miles) N of Budapest

Just past Szentendre along the Danube, there sits this historic and lovely little town full of trees and wonderful little streets to explore. It dates back 9 centuries, but I have to admit that it took me 6 years and the writing of this book to explore this little beauty outside of Budapest. According to legend, there was a monk hermit, Laszlo, who lived in the forest in what is now known as Vác. He prophesied that Prince Géza would win the battle against King Soloman. The prince and the monk came upon a wondrous sight, a deer with candles on its horns. After seeing this, Géza decided to establish a church on this site, making it a bishopric.

Essentials

Trains leave every 30 minutes from Nyugati train station. The trip is only 30 minutes, making this an easy day trip from the city. Once you leave the Vác train station, there is only one street leading from it. Do not be disheartened by the mundane architecture of the little shops that fill the street. Walk straight down Széchenyi utca until you run into Március 15 tér, about a 15-minute walk; you will find a number of interesting buildings with history to share. TourInform is located at 17 Március 15 tér (✆ **27/316-160;** www.tourinformvac.hu). It is open 8am to 5:30pm daily. I will not cover places to stay, since the town is small and conveniently located to Budapest. If you have a desire to stay overnight, check with TourInform for accommodations information.

Exploring the Town

The beauty of this town is that you can see quite a bit for very little money at all. Starting with the main square at **Március 15 tér** ★★★, the center promenade was completely renovated in 2006 according to the design of architect László Sáros, a Ybl award winner (a coveted architecture prize). The huge square is a lovely area with places to sit and relax by the peaceful fountain, and the glass flooring that looks down into the most important museum in the city. The square was an important commerce center going back to the Middle Ages. The dominant building on the square now is **White Friar's Church** ★★ at Március 15 tér 24, built in the 18th century in baroque-rococo style, but the inside is highly decorated in bright colors. However, the statues are white. What makes this church extra special is what they found underneath it. In 1995, when doing reconstruction work on the church, workers discovered a secret crypt. The entrance to the crypt had been walled up 200 years ago. During the renovation, the crypt was found with several mummies inside. Final excavations found that by walling up the entrance, it created an ideal climate to maintain the integrity of the 262 coffins and their inhabitants. The exhibition is available to view at the **Memento Mori** ★★★ (✆ **27/500-750**) in the cellar of the house at Március 15 tér 19. The museum is open Tuesday to Sunday 10am to 6pm, but closed in the winter. Admission is 700 Ft ($3.75/£2.35), 350 Ft ($1.75/£1.10) for students with an I.D.

On the side of the church is a statue to **St. Hedwig,** with a three-stage fountain at her feet. St. Hedwig is the patron saint of the Danube and Vác is at the heart of it. St. Hedwig was born in 1373, the third and youngest daughter of the Hungarian-Polish King Louis the Great. She had a passion for helping the poor, the ill, the orphaned, and widows.

As you approach Március 15 tér 20, you will see the medieval building was once a private residence, renovated in baroque style and from 1170 operated as a hotel. The front is an eclectic style, and in September 2006 the **Wine Museum** was established here. It is open 10am to 5pm Monday to Friday. But what caught my attention was the **Chocloteria** in the same building. Operating as a cafe, they have a large selection of chocolates, pastries, coffees, and teas. They are open Monday to Thursday 9am to 8:30pm, Friday to Saturday 9am to 9:30pm, and Sunday 10am to 8:30pm. The building also houses a public gallery free to the public. Outside is the **Bell Pavilion,** with a glockenspiel that plays every hour.

Walking down the square first you will come to the **City Hall** located at Március 15 tér 11, considered the nicest baroque building in Vác. Above the front door is a wrought-iron balcony. On the frontage is a coat of arms of the town. Three statues sit above this, with the Greek goddess of Justice in the center and two reclining women on either side; one holds the nation while the other holds the family crest of an important family. Strolling down you will see the **Hospital of Mercy** and the **Greek Catholic Chapel** at Március 15 tér 7–9. The small chapel is worth a peek; though you cannot enter it, you can view it through the glass windows. Next, at Március 15 tér 6, you will find the **András Chazár Education Institute for Deaf-Mutes.** This was the first school of its kind in Hungary, established in 1802. At one time, the school was a bishopric palace, a school for religious orders, a cloister, and then a girls' school. Across from this, you will find the former **Palace of the Great Provost,** Március 15 tér 4, a medieval house rebuilt in baroque style in the second half of the 18th century. The front is decorated with ionic offsets, and a triangular frontal piece at the top. It houses the clerical art collection of the former owner. If you continue down the square, you will come to the **Vienna Town Gate,** a modern stone structure closing off the square.

Leave the square to find other treasures in this little town. The **Triumphal Arch ★★**, the oldest baroque arch in Europe outside of France, sits at Köztáraság utca.

The **Cathedral of the Assumption** on Konstantin tér has an elegant facade designed by Isidore Canevale. It is the only building in Hungary inspired by Parisian revolutionary architecture. The interior decorated with the paintings of F. A. Maulbertsch, is a treasure. At Géza Király tér is the **Franciscan or "Brown" Church,** which sits next to the castle, the oldest building in Vác, which faces the Danube waterfront park. The synagogue on Eötvös utca is a special building in the town. Abbis Cacciari, an Italian architect, built it in 1864 in Romantic style.

A walk along the Danube will be a delightful, peaceful time. The entire riverside is lined with trees and an extremely wide promenade; it boasts winding walking paths intertwined with resting areas, and separate, chestnut tree-lined sidewalks that run alongside the street. Garden patches are dotted here and there, where the flowers add color and beauty to the large boulevard. For children, there are a number of play areas, including swings, playhouses, and other child-safe ways to work off extra energy.

Where to Dine

Vácz Remete Pince ★★★ HUNGARIAN CONTEMPORARY Given that it was a warm sunny autumn day when we stopped in, my friend and I sat on the terrace outside of this restaurant next to the sloped garden filled with flowers. The menu was plentiful with choices, plus the food was creatively presented in a beautiful manner. Many Budapest restaurants could take a lesson. Be warned, though, that the portions are huge. We ordered side salad to share and could barely finish it with the entrees presented to us. Peeking inside, the two large rooms are decorated in dark-wood furniture, with artificial greenery around the arched doorways, giving a cozy, homey feel.

Fürdő lépcső 3. ✆ **27/302-199.** Reservations recommended in summer. Main courses 1,290 Ft–2,490 Ft ($7–$14/£4.35–£8.70). MC, V. Daily noon–10pm.

VISEGRÁD

45km (28 miles) NW of Budapest

Halfway between Szentendre and Esztergom, Visegrád (pronounced *Vee*-sheh-grod) is a sparsely populated, sleepy riverside village, which makes its history all the more fascinating and hard to believe. The Romans built a fort here, which was still standing when Slovak settlers gave the town its present name in the 9th or 10th century. It means "High Castle." After the Mongol invasion (1241–42), construction began on both the present ruined hilltop citadel and the former riverside palace. Eventually, Visegrád boasted one of the finest royal palaces ever built in Hungary. Only one king, Charles Robert (1307–42), actually used it as his primary residence, but monarchs from Béla IV in the 13th century through Matthias Corvinus in the late 15th century spent time in Visegrád and contributed to its development. Corvinus expanded the palace into a great Renaissance center known throughout Europe.

Essentials

For information on getting to **Visegrád,** see "The Danube Bend: Getting There" on p. 349. **Visegrád Tours,** RÉV u. 15 (✆ **26/398-160**), is located across the road from the RÉV ferryboat landing. It is open daily 8am to 5:30pm; from November to March they conduct business from the associated hotel next door.

Where to Stay

Good accommodations can be found at **Honti Panzió and Hotel,** Fő u. 66 (✆ **26/398-120;** www.hotels.hu/honti). Double rooms run 11,000 Ft to 12,000 Ft ($59–$65/£37–£40) for the *panzio* (guesthouse) and 13,000 Ft to 15,000 Ft ($70–$81/£43–£50) in the hotel. All rates include breakfast and VAT, but a 300 Ft ($1.60/£1) tax per person per night is not; parking is provided.

Exploring the Palace & the Citadel

Once covering much of the area where the boat landing and Fő utca (Main St.) are now found, the ruins of the Royal Palace and the Salamon tower are all that remain today for visitors to explore. The entrance to the open-air ruins, the **King Matthias Museum** ★★, is at Fő u. 27 (✆ **26/398-026**). Admission is free. The museum is open Tuesday to Sunday from 9am to 5pm. The buried ruins of the palace, having achieved a near-mythical status, were not discovered until this century. The Salamon Tower is open Tuesday to Sunday from 9am to 5pm May through September.

The **Cloud Castle (Fellegvár)** ★★★ (✆ **26/398-101**), a mountaintop citadel above Visegrád, affords one of the finest views you'll find over the Danube. Admission to the Citadel is 800 Ft ($4.30/£2.65). It is open daily from 9:30am to 5:30pm. The City Bus, a van taxi that awaits passengers outside Visegrád Tours, takes people up the steep hill for a steep fare of 2,000 Ft ($11/£6.80) apiece. If you stay less than 30 minutes, you can ride down for 1,000 Ft ($5.40/£3.35); otherwise, it is again 2,000 Ft ($11/£6.80). Note that it is not a casual walk to the Citadel; consider it a day hike and pack accordingly with bottled water.

Where to Dine

Nagyvillám Vadászcsárda (Big Lightning Hunter's Inn) HUNGARIAN This restaurant is set on a hilltop featuring one of the finest views of the Danube Bend. Although vegetarians may struggle with a menu comprised mainly of meat and game dishes, it is nevertheless an extensive menu infusing Mediterranean influences with Hungarian recipes using 12 varieties of wild forest mushrooms. If you can, reserve a window table to maximize the glorious view, making this a unique dining experience.

Fekete-hegy. ✆ **26/398-070.** Main courses 1,700 Ft–4,500 Ft ($9.50–$24/£5.90–£15). Daily noon–11pm.

Renaissance Restaurant ★★ Kids HUNGARIAN This restaurant specializes in authentic medieval cuisine. Food is served in clay crockery without silverware, only a wooden spoon. Guests are offered Burger King–like paper crowns to wear. The decor and the lyre music enhance the fun, albeit openly kitschy atmosphere. This is perhaps the only restaurant in the whole country where you won't find something on the menu spiced with paprika, since the spice wasn't around in medieval Hungary. If you're big on the medieval theme, come for dinner on a Thursday (July–Aug), when a six-course "Royal Feast" is served following a 45-minute duel between knights, but it is available for groups of not less than 30 people. However, if you call, they will include you in a group if one is scheduled. It's open daily, from noon to 10pm. Tickets for this special evening are handled by the restaurant directly or Visegrád Tours (see above). If you are a vegetarian, you are out of luck! The duel gets underway at 6pm sharp.

Fő u. 11 (across the street from the MAHART boat landing). ✆ **26/398-081.** Set menu 4,500 Ft ($24/£15). Daily noon–10pm.

5 THE LAKE BALATON REGION

First settled in the Iron Age, the Balaton region has been a recreation spot since at least Roman times. From the 18th century onward, the upper classes erected spas and villas along the shoreline. Not until the post–World War II Communist era did the lake open up to a wider tourist base. Many large hotels along the lake are former trade union resorts built under the previous regime.

Lake Balaton may not be the Mediterranean, but it is the largest freshwater lake in Europe. For many years, it has attracted German and British tourists in droves as well as other Europeans, but others in smaller numbers, who filled the beaches to worship the sun on the lake's shore. In the past few years, though, the love affair has faded replaced by the beaches of Croatia as the best choice for a water resort. Hungary has instituted a fierce marketing campaign to redevelop the lake's regional favor with tourists, since many of the small towns depend on tourism for their survival. One company is developing a large watersports center and a three-star hotel, and a wellness center in **Balatonfenyves** should be completed by this book's printing. This region does not see many North American travelers at the best of times, but even less now.

Hungarians naturally are proud of area, defending this spot as one of the best in Europe; many city dwellers own summer homes there. With that said, there are still many other places to see and enjoy, even if you are not a sun and water person. I do caution you to check the health of the lake's waters near the time of your planned trip. Some years, the water level has been too low to support the many watersports it has become famous for, and at other times, there have been outbreaks of algae covering the water's surface in many tourist areas. The mosquito population can be fierce, so be wary of the pesticide spraying done in the area.

In the best of times, throughout the long summer, swimmers, windsurfers, sailboats, kayaks, and cruisers fill the warm and silky smooth lake, Europe's largest at 50 miles (80km) long and 10 miles (15km) wide at its broadest stretch. Around the lake's 197km (315 miles) of shoreline, vacationers cast their reels for pike; play tennis, soccer, and volleyball; ride horses; and hike in the hills.

On the south shore, Siófok was established as a resort in 1891. It is considered to be one of the most important tourist centers in the region, but it is frequented mostly by the youthful generation or those who love to party. Beachside hotels overflow all summer long with youthful party people playing disco music that pulsates into the early morning hours. My students have warned me about having people stop here if they are post-college age. Even for some of them, it is too rowdy to be enjoyable. The most popular venue is the Coca-Cola House, where there is nonstop music and dancing until dawn, making it the popular choice for the party animal who really doesn't care about the water adventures. According to my students, Budapest youth take the train to **Siófok,** party until the very wee hours, and then return to Budapest on the first train the next morning.

On a positive note, the town itself has an open-air exhibition with sculptures and monuments on public squares, including the work of the contemporary Hungarian sculptor Imre Varga, who was born here.

For those of us who are post-college, post-party-until-the-morning light, and family oriented, the better choice may be the graceful north shore, and it's the region we cover in this section. ***Note:*** Here and there, you will find little villages neatly tucked away in the rolling countryside, where the grapes of the popular Balaton wines ripen in the strong sun. Due to the needs of tourism, the area is becoming more and more commercialized, with the small food vendors being pushed aside by modern restaurants.

EXPLORING THE LAKE BALATON REGION

Getting There & Getting Around

BY TRAIN From Budapest, trains to the various towns along the lake depart from Déli Station. A few express trains run from Keleti Station and hook around the southern shore to Keszthely only. All towns on the lake are within 1½ to 4 hours of Budapest by a *gyors* (fast) train, though the trip will take much longer on a *sebes* (local). The *sebes* trains are interminably slow, stopping at each village along the lake. Unless you're going to one of these little villages (sometimes a good idea, though we cover only the major towns in this section), try to get on a *gyors.*

BY CAR From Budapest, take the M7 motorway south through Székesfehérvár until you hit the lake. Rte. 71 circles the lake.

If you're planning to visit Lake Balaton for more than a day or two, you should consider renting a car, which will give you much greater mobility. The various towns differ enough from one another that you may want to keep driving until you find a place that really sparks your interest. Without a car, this is obviously more difficult. In addition, wherever you go in the region, you'll find that private rooms are both cheaper and easier to get if you travel a few miles off the lake. Driving directly to the lake from Budapest

Herend: Home of Hungary's Finest Porcelain

About 16km (10 miles) west of Veszprém lies the sleepy village of Herend. What distinguishes this village from other villages in the area is the presence of the Herend Porcelain factory, where Hungary's finest porcelain has been made since 1826.

Herend Porcelain began to establish its international reputation as far back as 1851, when a dinner set was displayed at the Great Exhibition in London. Artists hand-paint every piece, from tableware to decorative accessories. Patterns include delicate flowers, butterflies, and birds.

The **Porcelanium Visitors Center** features the newly expanded **Herend Museum** (© **8/826-1801;** www.museum.herend.com), which displays a dazzling collection of Herend porcelain. It is open daily from April to October 9am to 4:30pm, and Tuesday to Saturday from November to March, 9:30am to 3:30pm. Admission is 1,500 Ft ($8.10/£5) for adults and 500 Ft ($2.70/£1.70) for students. The Porcelanium Visitors Center also has a coffeehouse and upscale restaurant. Food is, naturally, served on Herend china.

At the **factory store** (© **8/852-3223**), you might find patterns that are unavailable in Budapest's Herend Shop. The factory store is open October to May Monday to Friday 9:30am to 4pm, Saturday 9:30am to 2pm. In summer, hours are Monday to Friday 9:30am to 6pm, Saturday and Sunday 9:30am to 4pm. Herend is easily accessible via bus from the Veszprém bus station—the destination HEREND should be indicated on the front of the bus you want. The ride takes 15 minutes and costs 300 Ft ($1.60/£1); the bus leaves every 15 minutes.

will take approximately an hour and 30 minutes, depending on where along the lake you start out and, of course, traffic. During the summer season, traffic can be congested.

BY BOAT & FERRY Passenger boats on Lake Balaton let you travel across the lake as well as between towns on the same shore. The boat routes are extensive and the rates are cheap, but the boats are considerably slower than surface transportation. All major towns have docks with departures and arrivals. Children 3 and under travel free, and those 4 to 12 get half-price tickets. A single ferry *(komp)* running between Tihany and Szántód lets you transport a car across the width of the lake.

All boat and ferry information is available from the **BAHART** office in Siófok (© **84/310-050** or 84/312-144; www.balatonihajozas.hu). Local tourist offices all along the lake (several listed below) also have schedules and other information.

BY BUS Once at the lake, you might find that buses are the best way of getting around locally. Buses will be indispensable, of course, if you take private-room lodging a few miles away from the lake.

Where to Stay

Because hotel prices are unusually high (especially for Hungary) in the Balaton region, and because many local families rent out a room or two in summer, I especially recommend **private rooms** as the lodging of choice in this area. Most are clean and will give you the opportunity to get to know the local population. You can reserve a room through a local tourist office (addresses are listed below under each town) or you can just look for the ever-present SZOBA KIADÓ (or ZIMMER FREI) signs hanging on most front gates in the region. When you take a room without using a tourist agency as the intermediary, prices are generally negotiable. In the height of the season, you shouldn't have to pay more than 8,000 Ft ($43/£27) for a double room within reasonable proximity of the lake.

Many budget travelers pitch their tents in **lakeside campgrounds** all around the lake. Campgrounds are generally quite inexpensive, and their locations are well marked on maps. All the campgrounds have working facilities, but are probably not as clean as many people appreciate.

VESZPRÉM ★★

116km (72 miles) SW of Budapest

Just 16km (10 miles) from Lake Balaton, **Veszprém** (pronounced *Vess*-praym) surely ranks as one of Hungary's most charming and vibrant small cities, and it's the ideal starting point for a rail tour of Lake Balaton's northern shore. History and modern living are delightfully combined in this little city. The self-contained and well-preserved 18th-century baroque Castle District spills effortlessly into a typically modern city center, distinguished by lively wide-open, pedestrian-only plazas.

The history of Veszprém, like the scenic Bakony countryside that surrounds it, is full of peaks and valleys. According to local legend, Veszprém was founded on seven hills, like Rome. The seven hills are Várhegy (Castle Hill), Benedek-hegy (St. Benedict Hill), Jeruzsálem-hegy (Jerusalem Hill), Temetőhegy (Cemetery Hill), Gulyadomb (Herd Hill), Kálvária-domb (Calvary Hill), and Cserhát.

King Stephen I defeated the armies of his chief opponent, Koppány, near Veszprém in an effort to make Hungary a Christian nation. Hence, Veszprém became the seat of the first Episcopal See in 1009. This was the favorite city of King Stephen's queen, Gizella. The city is often called the "City of Queens." The long Turkish occupation caused its total destruction during the course of the Habsburg-Turkish battles, and the subsequent Hungarian-Austrian independence skirmishes. The reconstruction of Veszprém commenced in the early 18th century, though the castle itself, blown up by the Austrians in 1702, was never rebuilt. The baroque character of that era today attracts thousands of visitors who pass through each year.

Essentials

GETTING THERE Seventeen trains depart Budapest's Déli Station daily for Veszprém, with some taking as little as 1 hour and 45 minutes on one of the two IC trains. (It's a 2½-hr. trip if you take a regular train.) Tickets cost 2,160 Ft ($12/£7.45) for an IC train including the supplement, while on other trains the fare is 1,770 Ft ($9.55/£5.90) and the trip is longer.

If you're **driving,** take the M7 to the lake, then take Rte. 71 to Rte. 72 leading into the city.

VISITOR INFORMATION **TourInform,** Vár u. 4 (✆ **88/404-548**), is open in summer Monday through Friday from 9am to 6pm, and Saturday and Sunday 10am to 4pm; in winter, weekday hours are 9am to 5pm (closed weekends). **Ibusz,** Rákoczi u. 6 (✆ **88/565-540**), is open Monday to Friday from 8:30am to 4:30pm. Both offices provide information, sell city maps, and help with hotel and private-room bookings.

Where to Stay

You'll pay some 2,500 Ft ($13/£8.05) for a double room in a private home in Veszprém, and you can find a list of accommodations at www.veszpreminfo.hu. The room price usually does not include breakfast. You can book a private room through either of the tourist offices mentioned above.

Péter-Pál Panzió ★★ (✆ **8/832-8091;** www.hotels.hu/peter_pal_panzio) is conveniently located on Dózsa György u. 3; it's a 5-minute walk from the center of town. Don't be put off by the grungy building facade. Inside are 12 tidy but very small rooms, all with twin beds, a shower-only bathroom, and a TV. Insist on a room in the rear of the building, as the pension sits close to the busy road. Rates are 8,900 ($48/£30) double. Breakfast is included and is served in the garden in summer. Call ahead for reservations.

Hotel Villa Medici ★★, Kittenberger u. 11 (✆/fax **8/859-0070;** www.villamedici.hu), is a modern, full-service hotel set in a small gorge on the edge of the city, next to Veszprém's zoo park. There are 24 double rooms and two suites; each has a bathroom with shower and the usual hotel amenities. Rates are 24,300 Ft ($131/£81) for a double room and 32,900 Ft ($177/£110) for a suite. Breakfast is included. The hotel also features a sauna, a small indoor swimming pool, and a salon. Check the website for package deals. The reception staff speaks English and they will make tour arrangements. Major credit cards are accepted. Take bus no. 4 from the train station to the stop in front of Veszprém Hotel, and then change to bus no. 3, 5, or 10. These buses will take you as far as the bridge overlooking the gorge. You can walk from there.

Where to Dine

Veszprém does not have many dining options, but you should be able to find a satisfying meal at the following places:

Cserhát Étterem ★ (✆ **8/842-5441**), housed in the huge structure that is Kossuth u. 6, is an old-style *önkiszólgáló* (self-service cafeteria). You'll find this very popular cafeteria behind some clothing stores; go up the winding staircase inside the building. Hearty traditional meals are available for less than 500 Ft ($2.70/£1.70). The menu changes daily; it's posted on a bulletin board on the wall inside the restaurant upstairs. It's open Monday to Friday from 10am to 6pm and Saturday 10am to 3pm.

For something more upscale, **Villa Medici Étterem** (owned by the same people who own the hotel), at Kittenberger u. 11 (✆ **8/859-0072**), is *the* place. It's expensive for Hungary but worth it. Main courses here are between 3,250 Ft and 5,200 Ft ($18–$28/£11–£17). Villa Medici serves Hungarian/continental cuisine daily from noon to 11pm.

Exploring the City

Most of Veszprém's main sights are clustered along Vár utca, the street that runs the length of the city's small but lovely Castle District.

Housed inside the 18th-century canon's house, the **Queen Gizella Museum,** Vár u. 35, has a fine collection of religious (Roman Catholic) art. Admission is 300 Ft ($1.60/£1) for adults and 150 Ft (80¢/50p) for students. It's open daily from 10am to 5pm May to October 15.

At Vár u. 16, the vaulted **Gizella Chapel,** named for King Stephen's wife, was unearthed during the construction of the adjoining Bishop's Palace in the 18th century. Today, it houses a modest collection of ecclesiastical art, but is best known for the 13th-century frescoes that, in various states of restoration, decorate its walls. Admission is

200 Ft ($1.10/70p) for adults, 100 Ft (55¢/35p) for students. Open May 2 to October 15, hours are Tuesday to Sunday 10am to 5pm.

For a wonderful view of the surrounding Bakony region, climb the steps to the narrow observation deck at the top of the **Fire Tower** at Óváros tér. Though the foundations of the tower are medieval, the structure itself was built in the early 19th century. Enter via the courtyard of Vár u. 9, behind Óváros tér. Admission is 300 Ft ($1.60/£1), 250 Ft ($1.35/85p) for students. It's open daily from 10am to 6pm March 15 to September 30.

In addition to Roman relics uncovered in the surrounding area, the **Laczkó Dezső Museum** (✆ **88/564-310**), near Megyeház tér, features local folk exhibits (art, costumes, tools, utensils, and so on). There are also exhibits about the legendary highwaymen of the region, celebrated figures from 19th-century Bakony who share some characteristics with the legendary outlaws of the American West. Admission is 670 Ft ($3.60/£2.25) and children 340 Ft ($1.85/£1.15). From mid-March to October 14, it is open daily 10am to 6pm; otherwise it's daily noon to 4pm. To get to the museum, walk directly south from Szabadság tér, where the old and new towns converge.

The **Veszprém Zoo (Kittenberger Kálmán Növény és Vadaspark)** is located at Kittenberger u. 15 (✆ **88/566-140**). It's open daily in summer 9am to 6pm until September 30, then daily from 9am to 4pm until the end of February. Admission is 1,100 Ft ($5.95/£3.70) for adults, 750 Ft ($4.05/£2.15) for children. The zoo is set in a small wooded valley at the edge of the city center and boasts 550 animals from 130 species. It may not be the most joyful zoo you have been to.

BADACSONY & SZIGLIGET

160km (100 miles) SW of Budapest

If you are here for an extended stay or just want some country experiences, then these are recommended areas. Nestled in one of the most picturesque corners of Lake Balaton is Badacsony, an area which includes four villages noted for their beautiful vistas and some the best wines of Hungary. The Badacsony area is dotted with wine cellars, and the tradition of viticulture and winegrowing dates back to the Celtic and Roman times. Other than wine tasting, Badacsony boasts walking trails where you can study the diverse basalt forms and the former quarry walls. You'll also find a 4km-long (2.5-mile) circular trail, starting from the Kisfaludy House on the southern side of Badacsony Hill. Contact **Botanikai tanösvény Badacsony** (✆ **87/461-069;** www.bfnpi.hu) for guided tours.

One of the better-known vintners in Hungary is Huba Szeremley, whose Badacsony wines have consistently been winners in Italy, France, and Hungary. The best way to find out about Szeremley's regular wine tastings is to visit his restaurant, **Szent Orbán Borház és Étterem,** Badacsonytomaj, Kisfaludy S. u. 5 (✆ **87/432-382;** www.szeremley.com), open daily from noon to 10pm.

The **Borbarátok Panzió ★★**, Badacsonytomaj, Római út. 78 (✆ **87/471-000;** www.borbaratok.hu), is a family-owned and -operated restaurant and hotel. They serve traditional Hungarian fare and they offer a wide variety of programs, including wine tasting, harvest, fishing, and walking tours. During the summer months, they offer different music programs each night of the week. Main courses at the restaurant run from 1,700 Ft to 3,200 Ft ($9.20–$17/£5.70–£11). The restaurant is open daily 11:30am to 11pm in high season, and in low season daily 11:30am to 10pm.

Szigliget

Halfway between the Tihany peninsula and Keszthely is the lovely tiny village of Szigliget (pronounced *Sig*-lee-get), a picturesque Hungarian lake village with some magnificent castle ruins and an easy stopover point for rail travelers.

GETTING THERE Five daily trains leave from Veszprém's rail station that will get you to **Badacsonytördemic-Szigliget Station.** The trip can take as short as 2¾ hours or as long as 4½, depending on the train you catch and how many connections you need to make (there is no direct train service). InterCity trains (you must make a reservation!) are available for at least part of the route, but, in this case, won't get you to Szigliget any faster than some of the *gyors* trains because you have to make a number of connections.

It is a 20-minute bus ride to Szigliget from the train station. Each arriving train is met by a bus, which stops on the platform right outside the station building. The destination of the buses is Tapolca. You get off the bus at the stop near the beach in the village center (the village itself is tiny and easily traversed on foot).

VISITOR INFORMATION **Natur Tourist** (✆ **8/334-6063**), in the village center, is open daily 9:30am to 6pm from April 15 to September 15, and can help book private rooms. There are also ZIMMER FREI signs along the roads.

Where to Stay

Szőlőskert Panzió (✆ **8/746-1264**), on Vadrózsa utca, might be the best option for a stay, given its close proximity to the beach, which is just 400m (1,300 ft.) away. Situated on the hillside amid lush terraces of grapes, the pension is open only in summer. A double is 8,500 Ft ($46/£29) and includes breakfast.

Top Attraction & Special Moments

Szigliget is marked by the fantastic ruins of the 13th-century **Szigliget Castle,** which stand above the town on **Várhegy (Castle Hill).** In the days of the Turkish invasions, the Hungarian Balaton fleet, protected by the high castle, called Szigliget home. You can hike up to the ruins for a splendid view of the lake and the surrounding countryside; look for the path behind the white 18th-century church, which stands on the highest spot in the village.

If you really enjoy hiking, you might take a local bus from Szigliget (the station is in the village center) to the nondescript nearby village of **Hegymagas,** about 5km (3 miles) to the north along the Szigliget-Tapolca bus route. The town's name means "Tall Hill," and from here, you can hike up **Szent György-hegy (St. George Hill).** This marvelous vineyard-covered hill has several hiking trails, the most strenuous of which goes up and over the rocky summit.

The lively **beach** at Szigliget provides a striking contrast to the quiet village. In summer, buses from neighboring towns drop off hordes of beachgoers. The beach area is crowded with fried-food and beer stands, ice-cream vendors, a swing set, and a volleyball court.

Szigliget is also home to the **Eszterházy Wine Cellar,** the largest wine cellar in the region. After a hike in the hills or a day in the sun, a little wine tasting just might be in order. Natur Tourist (see above) can provide you with the best directions, as getting here can be a bit confusing. Tours of the cellar are offered only for organized groups; others can drop in and sample the wares. It's open Monday to Friday noon to 8pm, Saturday 3pm to 10pm. There's no admission charge.

An Excursion to the Thermal Lake in Hévíz

If you think the water of Lake Balaton is warm, just wait until you jump into the lake at **Hévíz** ★★ (pronounced *Hay*-veez), a resort town about 8km (5 miles) northwest of Keszthely. Here you'll find the largest thermal lake in Europe and the second largest in the world (the largest is in New Zealand), covering 50,000 sq. m (538,195 sq. ft.).

The lake's water temperature seldom dips below 85° to 90°F (29°–32°C)—even in the most bitter spell of winter. Consequently, people swim in the lake year-round. You are bound to notice the huge numbers of German travelers taking advantage of the waters. Hévíz has been one of Hungary's leading spa resorts for over 100 years, and it retains a distinct 19th-century atmosphere.

While the lakeside area is suitable for ambling, no visit to Hévíz would be complete without a swim. An enclosed causeway leads out into the center of the lake, where locker rooms and the requisite services, including massage, float rental, and a *palacsinta* (crepe) bar, are housed. ***Note:*** There is no shallow water in the lake, so take care.

Hévíz is an easy 10 minutes by bus from Keszthely (there's no train service), and costs 200 Ft ($1.10/70p). Buses (labeled HEVIZ) depart every half-hour or so from the bus station adjacent to the train station (conveniently stopping to pick up passengers in front of the church on Fő tér). The entrance to the lake is just opposite the bus station. You'll see a whimsical wooden facade and the words *tó fürdó* (Bathing Lake). Your day ticket costs 2,800 Ft ($15/£3.10), but less for stays from 3 to 6 hours, and entitles you to a locker; insert the ticket into the slot in the locker and the key will come out of the lock. Keep the ticket until exiting, as the attendant needs to see it to determine how long you've stayed.

LAKE BALATON'S SOUTHERN SHORE

If you're in that youthful energy category of spending long days in the sand and surf and then want to follow it up by spending long nights being the party animal, then the town of Siófok at the southern shore of Lake Balaton is where it is at. After all, a million Hungarian students can't be wrong. Or could they?

Siófok, located at the lake's southeastern end, is known as the capital of Lake Balaton; it is also the largest resort town on Lake Balaton. Siófok's railway station was completed in 1863; thus it is considered the birth year of Siófok as a holiday resort, with Budapest now connected by rail to the resort town. In 1865 Siófok, a settlement of not more than 200 houses with 1,500 inhabitants, was permitted to attain the status of market town. As the saying goes, the rest is history. It started to become overrun with holidaymakers during the summer season.

Siófok is the star attraction for the young, active crowd of mostly students and teenagers who flood the town's beaches from sunrise to sunset and then move en masse to the town's discos until the sun rises yet again. Large, modern, expensive hotels line the shore in Siófok, and more are in various stages of development. If you are looking for a quiet beach experience, you will not find it here, but you will find windsurfing, tennis, and boating. English will be at a premium. Though many younger Hungarians may speak English to some degree, they are not as tempted to indulge when surrounded by their fellow native speakers. This could be an isolating experience and difficult within the town.

While this city is no cultural capital, the architecture of some of the older buildings is impressive. Note the old railway station, and the many villas around the Gold Coast (Aranypart). You will also find some important contemporary buildings, notably the Evangelical Church, designed by one of Hungary's most appreciated architects, **Imre Makovecz.**

Siófok has also partaken in the major marketing campaign that includes all of the popular resorts of Lake Balaton. It is trying to bring back the throngs of visitors who have abandoned the lake for rediscovered beaches along Croatia's coastline. Due to the development of tourism, the prices have made this destination less of a bargain, and travelers wanted more for their money. Ironically, Siófok is being rejuvenated by constructing new wellness centers that cater to rejuvenations procedures, plus the allure of the warm-water springs of Hungarian fame. These facilities will be year-round operations in an attempt to stimulate the economy of the region, but the prices they intend on charging may be counterproductive.

For more information on the southern shore, contact the **TourInform** (✆/fax **84/310-117;** www.siofokportal.com) office in Siófok, right below the immense water tower in the center of town. Another site for planning your trip is www.siofok.com.

Where to Stay

Siófok is wall to wall with tourists during the summer months, mostly Hungarians. You will find a wide variety of accommodations options, from large hotels or resorts on the Gold Coast to the east of the center of town, or the Silver Coast (Ezüstpart), to the west. Additional accommodations can be found on the city's website at www.siofokportal.com.

We recommend pampering yourself at a wellness center for a few days. The **Hotel Azúr★★**, Vitorlás u. 11 (✆ **84/501-400;** www.hotelazur.hu), is one of the most comfortable, plush, and welcoming hotel and wellness centers in town at the moment, but heavy competition is being built continually. It has 222 air-conditioned rooms, many with balconies. The pools are large; it has a nice fitness room, sauna, massage club, Finnish saunas, beauty salon, and thermal pools. The whole complex is extremely tasteful. Rates are 140€ ($182/£113) in summer and 88€ ($115/£71) in winter for a double room. Breakfast and all taxes are included.

The **Hotel Residence★**, Erkel Ferenc u. 49 (✆ **84/506-840**), with its 56 rooms, also has an extensive list of services, including massages, gyms, baths, and aromatherapy. It is located 150m (492 ft.) from the beach. Rates are 125€ ($163/£101) in summer and 105€ ($137/£85) in winter for a double room with breakfast included. Note that the room rate has a 15% additional fee for Friday and Saturday night during high season. The hotel has a good-size indoor swimming pool, a sauna, a massage club, Finnish saunas, a beauty salon, and thermal pools.

Where to Dine

Try the **Sándor Restaurant** (✆ **84/312-829;** www.sandorrestaurant.hu), on Erkel F. u. 30, popular with locals for large portions of contemporary Hungarian food. If you're looking for more traditional Hungarian fare, in the spring time, with live Gypsy music, try the **Csárdás Restaurant,** at Fő u. 105 (✆ **84/310-642**). The menu contains Hungarian fish and meat dishes, but they also have international and vegetarian options.

6 NORTHEASTERN HUNGARY

Northeast of the Danube Bend is Hungary's hilliest region, with the country's highest mountain, Matra Hill, rising to 1,000m (3,280 ft.). It also contains the country's smallest village, the place where the first Hungarian language bible was written, and the oldest railway, from the 19th century. Here you can visit the preserved medieval village of Hollókő; see remnants of the country's Turkish heritage in Eger, also known for its regional wines and the region of the famous Tokaji aszú wines; and explore the 23km (14-mile) cave system in Aggtelek.

HOLLÓKŐ: A PALÓC VILLAGE FROM THE PAST

102km (63 miles) NE of Budapest

The village of Hollókő (pronounced *Ho*-low-koo, meaning "raven stone") is one of the most charming spots in Hungary, hidden in the Cserhát hills. Legend has it that the lord of a castle kidnapped a beautiful maiden, whose nurse was a witch. The nurse made a pact with the devil for the girl's return. The devil's servants disguised themselves as ravens, and took the stones of the castle away. The castle of Hollóko was built on top of the rock. Village history dates back to the 13th century; after the invasion by the Mongols, the castle was built on Szár hill. This UNESCO World Heritage Site is a perfectly preserved but still vibrant Palóc village with only 400 residents. The rural Palóc people speak an unusual Hungarian dialect, and they have some of the more colorful folk customs and costumes still used for daily wear. They have been able to preserve their folkways partially due to their isolation. If you're in Hungary at Easter time, by all means consider spending the holiday in Hollókő. Hollókő's traditional Easter celebration features townspeople in traditional dress and Masses in the town church.

Essentials

GETTING THERE There is only one direct **bus** to Hollókő, which departs from Budapest's central bus station, Stadionok Bus Station (✆ **1/382-0888**). It departs weekends only at 8:30am and takes about 2½ hours to reach the town if there is no traffic—but be warned, it could take as long as 3½ hours if there is, without breaks and no bathroom. The one-way fare is 1,750 Ft ($9.50/£5.90). Alternatively, you can take a bus from Árpád híd bus station in Budapest (✆ **1/412-2597**) to Szécsény or Pásztó, where you switch to a local bus to Hollókő; there are four daily, but the trip will be longer. By car from Budapest, take the motorway M3 as far as Hatvan, then along the main road turn off onto Rte. 21 in the direction of Salgótarján until you come to the junction for Hollókõ. From here, it is a 17km (11-mile) drive.

VISITOR INFORMATION The best information office is the **Foundation of Hollókő,** at Kossuth Lajos út. 68 (✆ **32/579-010;** www.holloko.hu). It's open in summer Monday to Friday 8am to 8pm and weekends 10am to 6pm; in winter, it's open Monday to Friday 8am–5pm and weekends 10am to 4pm. You can also get information through **Nograd Tourist** in Salgótarján (✆ **32/310-660**) or through **TourInform** in Szécsény, at Ady Endre u. 12 (✆ **32/370-777;** www.szecseny.hu).

Seasonal Events

At **Easter time** ★, everyone in the village puts on ornamented folk clothes for the 2-day celebration (Easter Monday is a holiday), reviving the old Easter traditions. Folklore programs fill the day with displays of folk articles for purchase, artisans' presentations, food specialties, and games for children. On the last weekend in July, folk groups of Nógrád county and from other counties gather to perform on the open-air stage of the village for the **Palóc Szőttes Festival★** . On the second Sunday of October for the **Vintage Parade,** the young people of the village walk along the main street in ornamented folk clothes, demonstrating that grape picking is over.

Exploring Hollókő

A one-street town, Hollókő is idyllically set in a quiet, green valley, with **hiking trails** all around. A restored 14th-century castle is perched on a hilltop over the village.

In the village itself you can admire the 14th-century wooden-towered church and the sturdy, traditional peasant architecture (normally seen only in stylized open-air museums, such as the one near Szentendre (p. 350), and observe the elderly women at work on their embroidery (samples are for sale). You can also visit the **Village Museum** at Kossuth Lajos u. 82, where exhibits detail everyday Palóc life starting in the early 20th century. Official hours have it open Tuesday through Sunday from 10am to 4pm, but it is closed in winter. Like everything else in town, though, the museum's opening times are up to the whims of the caretakers. Entry is 150 Ft (80¢/50p).

Where to Stay

If you miss the only direct bus back to Budapest, you will need a place to stay. In Hollókő, traditionally furnished thatch-roofed **peasant houses** are available for rent on a nightly or longer basis. You can rent a **room in a shared house** (with shared facilities), or rent an **entire house.** The prices vary depending on the size of the room, house, and the number of people in your party, but 9,000 Ft ($49/£30) for a double room is average. Standard **private rooms** are also available in Hollókő. All accommodations can be booked in advance through the tourist offices in Hollókő or Salgótarján (see "Essentials," above). If you arrive without reservations (which is not advised), the address and phone number of a room finder are posted on the door of the **Foundation of Hollókő** above.

Where to Dine

Dining options are limited in tiny Hollókő. The **Vár Étterem,** Kossuth Lajos u. 95 (**© 32/379-029**), serves decent Hungarian food at very low prices. Try a dish prepared with the "treasure of the local forests," porcini mushrooms. There is indoor and outdoor seating. The menu is available in English, and the waiters are patient. The restaurant is open daily noon to 8pm, except Christmas Day.

EGER

126km (78 miles) NE of Budapest

Eger (pronounced *Egg*-air), is the third-most-visited city in the country and the most visited of northern Hungary. It is a small baroque valley city between the Matra and Bükk mountains. Eger's fame is based on three things: its castle, its wine, and the brave struggle of its 16th-century women. When the Turkish army attacked in 1552, there were only 500 equestrians and an equal number of soldiers inside the fortress. The battle against 80,000 Turks was a little imbalanced, to say the least. Those in the fortress, including the girls and women, stood up to the Turks to defend themselves in winning a remarkable victory. The exuberant triumph is documented with golden letters in Hungarian history. Today, you can visit the exhibitions of the István Dobó Fortress Museum within the walls of the castle.

Today Eger's landscape presents a harmonious blend of old and new. The ruined castle, one of Hungary's proudest symbols, dominates the skyline. Eger is convincingly known as the "City of Baroque"' in its historic city center many beautiful and valuable baroque and late-baroque buildings fill each street. If you wander beyond the confines of the old section, you'll find a small modern city.

One of the most widely known and prestigious wines produced in this city is the claret, Eger Bull's Blood. Its distinctive traits are spiciness, fieriness, and relatively high acidity. In the Valley of the Beautiful Women, the most important outer part of town, wine producers are always ready to receive travelers to offer and sell them wine. Many of the wineries are out of the center of town, making it difficult to access without a car.

If you don't want to rent a car, but want to enjoy the wines of the region, another option may be one of the festivals. Festivals in different seasons include: Eger Spring Festival, an art festival from all mediums in late March or early April; the Feast of Eger Bikavér, a wine and food extravaganza in July; Wine Tasting, when wine producers present the wines of Northeastern Hungary in August; Agria International Folk Dance Festival, a convention of folk dance troupes in August; and the Benediction of Wine on the day of St. John, the traditional celebration of new wine and wine exhibitions.

Essentials

GETTING THERE Eger is a 2-hour direct **train** ride from Budapest. Daily trains depart Budapest's Keleti Station every hour. Tickets cost 2,810 Ft ($15/£9.30).

If you're **driving** from Budapest, take the M3 motorway east to Kerecsend, where you pick up Rte. 25 north to Eger. There is a toll, and toll tickets will be going up in price in the near future, so check at all MOL Petrol stations.

VISITOR INFORMATION For information, visit or contact **TourInform,** at Bajcsy-Zsilinszky u. 9 (✆ **36/517-715**). The office is open in summer Monday through Friday from 9am to 6pm and on weekends from 9am to 1pm; off season, the office closes an hour earlier on weekdays and is closed on Sunday. For private-room booking, try **Egertourist,** at Bajcsy-Zsilinszky u. 9 (✆ **36/510-270**). This office is open Monday through Saturday from 10am to 6pm.

Exploring Old Eger

Eger's main sites are fairly concentrated, making them within easy walking distance of each other and of **Dobó István tér** ★★. Like many European cities and villages, life revolved around the town square; the one in the center of old Eger is particularly lovely. The **Minorite Church** sits on Dobó István tér, with many believing it to be one of the most beautiful baroque churches in Europe. It is in razor-sharp contrast with the nearby solemn edifice of the friary. One of the greatest masters of European baroque, Kilian Ignaz Dientzenhofer, designed the church.

Placed in the center of the square, there is an impressive statue of the town defender Dobó, flanked by a knight and a woman, created by Alajos Strobl, one of the country's leading turn-of-the-20th-century sculptors. Erected in the 1960s, Strobl's execution of the work did not hold back on his feelings of the battle against the Turks. Strobl's other work includes the statue of King Stephen on Buda's Castle Hill and the statue of poet János Arany in front of the National Museum in Pest.

The reconstructed ruins of **Eger Castle,** visible from just about anywhere in the city, are easily reached by walking northeast out of the square; take the path out of Dózsa György tér. You can wander around the grounds free of charge daily from 8am to 8pm in summer and daily 8am to 6pm in winter, or you can explore the two museums on the premises. Walking the ramparts is a lovely stroll in warm weather and provides a nice view of the old town area. The **István Dobó Castle Museum** (✆ **36/312-744**), as the name implies, has the castle history along with displays of some Turkish artifacts left behind. The **Eger Picture Gallery** has work from the same 19th-century Hungarian artists who are featured in the Budapest museum. The museums are open Tuesday through Sunday from 10am to 5pm, until 4pm in winter. Admission to each separate museum is 1,000 Ft ($5.40/£3.35).

Just to the west of the castle, on Harangöntő utca, is Eger's most visible reminder of the Turkish period, its **minaret** at Knézich u. 1 (✆ **36/410-233**). The minaret survived, though the mosque under it was annihilated in 1841. The minaret is 14-sided, 33m-tall (110 ft.), and in good enough condition that for an admission charge of 200 Ft ($1/60p), you can climb to the narrow top. It is open from April to the end of October, Tuesday to Sunday 10am to 6pm. If you suffer from claustrophobia, I warn against it. The scramble up is steep, on a cramped spiral staircase, but because the space is so narrow, you can't turn back if anyone is behind you. Those who are successful, however, are justly rewarded with a spectacular view.

You can't miss the massive **basilica** (✆ **30/337-2398**); it is the second-largest church in Hungary, the largest being Esztergom's basilica, and it competes in size with the basilica in Pest. You just need to walk a few blocks south on Eszterhazy tér and it is the only Classicist building in Eger. Ordered by Archbishop Pyrker József, the architect József Hild was one of the architects of St. Stephen's Basilica in Pest. He completed this church in 1837 in the grandiose neoclassical style of the time. It's open daily from 6am to 7pm. If you are visiting in the high season, wander in at 11:30am Monday through Saturday or at 12:45pm on Sunday for a free organ presentation. Admission is free to the church at other times.

Next, you will find the **Lyceum** at Eszterházy Sq. 1 (✆ **36/325-211**), built in late baroque style. Count Eszterházy Károly ordered it built as a university at the end of the 18th century; it is now a college. There is a definite distinction between a college and university in Hungary—colleges are vocational schools. It houses the nationally famous diocesan library *(kö nyvtár)* on the first floor, with an impressive ceiling fresco of the Council of Trent by Johann Lukas Kracker and József Zach. The only original letter written by Mozart in Hungary is on display here. You can visit March 1 to September 30 Tuesday through Sunday 9am to 3pm; the rest of the year, hours are on Saturday and Sunday only from 9am to 1pm. Admission for adults is 350 Ft ($2/£1.20). Entrance to the balcony is free. In the yard of the Lyceum during July and August, there are frequent concert performances, so ask at TourInform for the schedule and ticket information.

If you missed visiting a spa or bathhouse in Budapest, check them out in Eger. Northeastern Hungary is rich in thermal waters; ask at TourInform for a list of spas in the region.

Where to Stay

Eger has some lovely places to stay right in the center of the town. The **Hotel Korona** ★, Tündérpart 5 (✆ **36/310-287;** fax 36/310-261), is a clean, cozy establishment on an extremely quiet residential street just a few blocks west of Dobó István tér. The hotel has a wine cellar and a shaded patio where breakfast is served in good weather. There are 40 rooms, all with private bathrooms. A double room goes for 80€ to 110€ ($102–$140). Rates include breakfast and the sauna. Credit cards are accepted. Bus no. 11, 12, or 14 will get you there from the train station; get off at Csiky Sándor utca and you're practically at the doorstep.

Another guesthouse is near the beginning of the Valley of Beautiful Women and only a 15-minute walk from the historical center of the town, the **Bacchus Panzio ★**, located at Szépasszony völgy u. 29 (✆ **36/428-950;** www.bacchuspanzio.hu). This hotel offers double rooms for 43€ to 54€ ($55–$69) in high season and 37€–43€ ($47–$55) in low season. Breakfast is 5€ ($6.35).

For something peacefully removed from the downtown, try the **Garten Vendégház,** Legányi u. 6 (✆ **36/320-371;** www.gartenvendeghaz.hu). Operated by the Zsemlye family, this guesthouse is located on a quiet residential street in the hills overlooking the city. The view from the gorgeous garden is splendid. The price of a double room is 40€ ($51) in high season and 30€ ($38) in low season. Rates include breakfast in high season only, otherwise it is 5€ ($6.35).

Travelers on a tighter budget should consider renting a private room through Egertourist (see above) or TourInform. Rates in Eger are as low as 5,500 Ft ($30/£18) for a bed with a shared bathroom and as high as 11,000 Ft ($60/£37) for an apartment with bathroom and kitchen.

Where to Dine

The **Fehér Szarvas Vadásztanya (White Stag Hunting Inn) ★**, located next door to the Park Hotel at Klapka u. 8 (✆ **36/411-129**), a few blocks south of Dobó István tér, is one of Eger's best-known and best-loved restaurants. The menu offers a full range of Hungarian wild-game specialties. Award-winning regional wines are featured. A piano and bass duet plays nightly amid the kitschy hunting lodge decor. The restaurant is open daily from noon to 11pm, and reservations are recommended. Credit cards are accepted.

7 SOUTHERN HUNGARY

In southwestern Hungary, you will find the fertile Mecsek Hills; the city of Pécs is the major city of this hilly region. Pécs has been named a European Capital of Culture for 2010, when the spotlight will be highlighting its history and cultural life. On the other side of the Danube River, to the south and east, lies the mainly agricultural region of the Alföld (Great Plain), which begins not far outside of Budapest; this is the farmland of wheat and orchards. This is a broad, bleak, yet dramatic landmass that covers almost half of the country. The last remains of the Puszta are in this region, birthplace of many Hungarian folk legends, and this area is the land of the Hungarian cowboys, known as *csikós.*

PÉCS: THE 2,000-YEAR-OLD CITY ★★★

197km (123 miles) SW of Budapest

Pécs (pronounced *Paych*) is the largest and most beautiful city in the Mecsek Hill region. Although far from the Mediterranean Sea, it has a Mediterranean feel to it due to its generally warm and arid climate. Due to this, the hills in the region produce some of the country's premium fruit. Pécs is located just 32km (20 miles) from the Croatian border.

Sopiane, as the Romans named it, has over 2,000 years of history still visible to speak of its past. Still in evidence are the remnants of the Roman era, which date back to around 350 to 400 A.D. The early Christian burial chamber dating back to the 4th century is the most noteworthy of the remains.

The later period of the Turkish rule and their structures are even more evident. They occupied the city for over 140 years, from 1543. The Inner City Parish Church is an incredibly beautiful place of worship, with an interesting history. It is located at the top of Szechenyi Square in the city center and you may not recognize it as a church, because it looks like a mosque. The Turks used the stones from St. Bartholomew's church at the other end of the square to build the mosque of Pasha Gazi Kassim. When the Turks were eradicated from the city in 1686, Jesuits occupied the mosque, restoring it to a Catholic church.

Pécs continued to be a vibrant city through the Turkish occupation, in part because the greatest ruler of the Ottoman Empire, Suleiman II, made this his home. The Turks introduced a new culture with baths, decorative fountains, and drinking fountains being built. Some of the most important Turkish remains in the country are landmark reminders of this historic time in the city life, such as the Mosque of Pasha Gazi Kassim.

Walking up Janus Pannonius utca toward Széchenyi tér, about a block up the street, you cannot help but notice a small wrought-iron fence covered with padlocks to the point where there are padlocks hanging from padlocks in chains. The story goes that one young couple in love placed a padlock there as a token of their love. Others followed, and now the fence is at risk from toppling from the weight.

Essentials

GETTING THERE Ten **trains** depart daily from Budapest's Keleti Station; seven of these are InterCity trains, which are much faster than others. The fare is 3,750 Ft for a one-way or 6,450 Ft for a return. You will need a reservation for IC trains and this will be an additional 520 Ft. An InterCity train will get you there in 3 hours. The "fast" train *(gyors)* leaves from Deli Station; the trip is at least 3¾ hours, but you don't need a reservation and the train is not as nice.

If you are **driving** from Budapest, take the M6 south for approximately 3 hours (the distance is 210km/130 miles).

VISITOR INFORMATION Once you leave Budapest, English speakers are harder to find except in hotels and some restaurants. The best source of information in Pécs is **TourInform,** at Széchenyi tér 9 (✆ **72/213-315;** www.tourinform.hu). TourInform is open April to October Monday to Friday from 9am to 7pm and on weekends from 9am to 6pm; in winter, hours are Monday to Friday from 8am to 4pm. TourInform can provide a list of local private-room accommodations, though you'll have to reserve the room yourself.

If you want to have a room reserved for you, visit **Mecsek Tourist,** at Ferenciek u. 41 (✆ **72/513-370;** www.mecsektours.hu). The office is open Monday to Friday from 9am to 5pm; hours extend to Saturday in summer from 9am to 1pm.

You can also get city information online at **www.pecs.hu**. Look for the English button at the top.

Exploring Old Pécs

The old section of Pécs is really awe inspiring, with the differences in architecture side by side; there is lots of eye candy to satisfy anyone. One of Hungary's most incredible central squares is **Széchenyi tér** ★★★. Starting with the mosque at the top of a minor hill, it descends on down to St. Sebastian's Catholic Church, where there is an unusual fountain with Zsolnay porcelain sitting in front.

Old Pécs is has a reputation for its many museums and galleries; after Budapest, Pécs is comes in second as the cultural center in Hungary. Many of the museums are relatively small, unlike the many grand ones in Budapest, so you can conceivably visit three or four in a day without feeling overstimulated. We list several museums below, but there are others, some containing works by contemporary, and student artists. The Zsolnay ceramics factory was founded here in the late 19th century. It is not as well known internationally as its rival Herend, but just may be more popular domestically. You will find examples of Zsolnay all over the city incorporated into buildings, fountains, and other designs. The Zsolnay Museum, also listed below, is a must-see in Pécs.

Museums

Jakawali Hassan Museum This museum is housed inside a 16th-century mosque, the most complete Turkish temple in Hungary. The mosque stands with its minaret still intact (though, unfortunately, you can't ascend the minaret). At one time there was a religious house of the Dervishes and a religious college next door. Like the much larger mosque up in Széchenyi tér, this mosque was converted to a church after the Turks were driven from Pécs; however, in the 1950s the mosque was restored to its original form. The museum's main attraction is the building itself, although various Muslim religious artifacts are on display as well.

Rákóczi út 2. © **72/313-853.** Admission 250 Ft ($1.35/85p). Apr–Sept Thurs–Sun 10am–noon and 1–6pm.

Tivadar Csontváry Museum ★ Tivadar Csontváry Kosztka (1853–1919) had a mystic revelation where he believed that God told him to paint. He worked 20 years preparing his finances by opening a pharmacy. He did not start painting until he was 41 years old. His revelation was attributed to the fact he suffered from schizophrenia, which most likely also influenced his art. He is considered the first post-Impressionist artist of Hungary, thus shunned from the artistic community. He remained unknown during his lifetime. When he died, his family wanted to sell his paintings for the value of their canvas, not the work itself. Someone who realized their potential value bought the selection that is on exhibit, making wagon makers angry—they wanted the large canvas for their wagon making. There is a story told that at some time after Csontváry's death, Picasso saw an exhibition of his work and said, "I did not know there was another artistic genius in this century, beside me." This little museum houses a fine collection of Csontváry's work.

Janus Pannonius u. 11. © **72/310-544.** Admission 700 Ft ($3.80/£2.35). Photo ticket 300 Ft ($1.60/£1), video ticket 600 Ft ($3.20/£2). Apr–Oct Tues–Sat 10am–6pm and Sun 10am–4pm; Nov–Mar Tues–Sun 10am–4pm.

Victor Vasarely Museum ★ The late Victor Vasarely, internationally known father of "op art," was born in the house that this museum now occupies, though he left early on for France. This is one of two museums in the country devoted solely to Vasarely's work (the other is in Óbuda). While Vasarely's fame was achieved abroad, Pécs proudly considers him as a native son. In addition to Vasarely's pieces, the museum also displays the work of a few significant Hungarian artists whose work of geometric and kinetic styles are from the second part of the 20th century. Some international artists are also on display at different times.

Kaptalan u. 3. © **72/324-822.** Admission 700 Ft ($3.80/£2.35). Photo ticket 300 Ft ($1.60/£1), video ticket 600 Ft ($3.20/£2). Apr–Oct Tues–Sat 10am–6pm and Sun 10am–4pm; Nov–Mar Tues–Sun 10am–4pm.

Zsolnay Museum ★★★ This is one of a number of the small museums on Kaptalan utca, Pécs's "street of museums," and you shouldn't miss it. The Zsolnay Museum displays some of the best examples of Zsolnay porcelain, produced locally since 1852. There are vases, plates, cups, figurines, and even ceramic paintings. Once you've seen the museum, check out the Zsolnay fountain at the lower end of Széchenyi tér in front of St. Sebastian's Church.

Kaptalan u. 2. ✆ **72/324-822.** Admission 700 Ft ($3.80/£2.35). Photo ticket 300 Ft ($1.60/£1), video ticket 600 Ft ($3.20/£2). Apr–Oct Tues–Sat 10am–6pm and Sun 10am–4pm; Nov–Mar Tues–Sun 10am–4pm.

Houses of Worship

Mosque of Pasha Gazi Kassim ★★ The largest Turkish structure still standing in Hungary, this one-time mosque now houses a Catholic church. It was built in the late 16th century, during the Turkish occupation, on the site of an earlier church. The mix of religious traditions is evident everywhere you look, and the effect is rather pleasing. An English-language description of the building's history is posted on a bulletin board on the left-hand wall.

At the top of Széchenyi tér. ✆ **72/227-166.** Free admission. Apr 16–Oct 14 Mon–Sat 10am–4pm, Sun 11:30am–3pm; Oct 15–Apr 15 Mon–Sat 10am–noon, Sun 11:30am–1:30pm.

Pécs Cathedral ★ Originally built in the 11th century by Bishop St. Maurice, this four-towered cathedral has been destroyed and rebuilt more than once, like many buildings during wars. The Turkish used it as a mosque and topped it with a minaret. At the end of the 19th century, the present neo-Romanesque exterior was added. The interior remains primarily Gothic, with some baroque additions and furnishings. The frescoes by leading 19th-century artists Károly Lotz and Bertalan Székely are inside. Organ concerts are performed in the cathedral throughout the year; inquire at the cathedral (no English spoken) or at TourInform for the schedule.

The square in front of the cathedral and the beautifully landscaped park with a magnificent fountain beneath it is a popular gathering place, and occasionally the site of folk concerts, dances, and fairs.

On Dóm tér. ✆ **72/513-030.** Cathedral admission (includes treasury and crypt) 1,000 Ft ($5.40/£3.35). Apr 15–Oct Mon–Sat 9am–5pm and Sun 1–5pm; Nov–Mar Mon–Sat 10am–4pm and Sun 1–4pm. The church is not open to the public during weddings, which are often on Sat afternoons.

Pécs Synagogue ★ Pécs's grand old synagogue is incongruously situated in what is now one of the city's busiest shopping squares, Kossuth tér. The gentleman at the door speaks excellent English and is warm and inviting. Once inside, you will forget the outside world. Built in 1865 and consecrated in 1869, the synagogue has the original rich oak interior to this day. It was the third synagogue built in the city in Hungarian romantic style for a Neolog Jewish community. Sadly, it is the only surviving synagogue in the city after World War II. Prior to World War II, the synagogue had over 4,000 members, of whom only 464 survived the Holocaust. Every year, Pécs's small and aging Jewish community commemorates the 1944 deportations to Auschwitz on the first Sunday after July 4.

Regular services are held in the smaller temple next door at Fürdő 1 (there isn't a sign; go through the building into the courtyard and cross diagonally to the right) on Friday at 6:30pm from March to October.

Kossuth tér. 1–3. ✆ **72/315-881.** Admission 500 Ft ($2.70/£1.70). Mar–Oct Sun–Fri 10am–noon and 1–5pm. Closed Nov–Feb.

Where to Stay

You can book a private room through **Mecsek Tourist** (see "Essentials," above) or **Ibusz,** Király u. 11. (© **72/212-157;** www.ibusz.hu).

For the best little hotel right in the center of town, try the popular **Hotel Fönix** ★★, at Hunyadi út 2 (© **72/311-682**). This unique hotel's structure is reminiscent of a building from a children's fairy tale. It sits just off the top of Széchenyi tér across from the mosque. With only 14 rooms and 3 apartments, this adds to its charm, as does the fact that each room has oddly angled walls and partial dormer-type ceilings. Some of the rooms are a bit cramped, but all are clean with refrigerators and TVs, and the common facilities are well maintained. The three apartments have full facilities and their own entrance off the street. The staff is incredibly helpful and friendly. Double rooms run 9,590 Ft to 11,590 Ft ($52–$63/£32–£39), triples are 12,990 Ft to 14,990 Ft ($70–$81/£43–£50), and apartments range from 19,990 Ft to 29,990 Ft ($105–$162/£65–£100). Rates include breakfast, but not tourism tax of 200 Ft ($1.10/70p) per night per person. Call several days ahead to reserve a room. Credit cards are accepted.

If the Hotel Fönix is full, the management can book a room for you at a pension that they operate called **Kertész Panzió,** at Sáfrány u. 42 (© **72/327-551**).

Where to Dine

Palatinus Hotel Restaurant ★★HUNGARIAN The interior of this restaurant is incredibly decorated with a combination of Art Nouveau and other styles with Zsolnay porcelain tossed in here and there. The peacock Zsolnay fountain will have you wondering whether to eat or stare at the colors and design of the building. Eat, though—the food is excellent and so is the staff. Try the filet mignon slices with potato pancakes and stewed plums. I found it delectable.

Király u. 5, off main sq. © **72/889-400.** Reservations recommended. Main courses 1,700 Ft–3,500 Ft ($9.20–$19/£5.70–£12). AE, DC, MC, V. Daily 11am–11pm.

Coffeehouses & Ice-Cream Parlors

If you have a sweet tooth, there are opportunities to satisfy it all over town. Pécs offers numerous places to enjoy coffee and sweets. Try **Mecsek Cukrászda,** on Széchenyi tér 16 (© **72/315-444**), for a quick jolt of espresso and any number of luscious looking and inexpensive pastries. For people-watching on the pedestrian street, try **Caflisch Cukrászda** at Király 32 u. They also have a large selection of ice cream flavors. **Capri,** a very popular shop at Citrom u. 7 (© **72/333-658**), 3 blocks south of Széchenyi tér, serves up various sundaes as well as cones, but their choice of pastries is limited. You will want to sit on the terrace to enjoy your treats, because the garden is well kept and colorful and you can take in the incredible view of the Posta building on the next block. The Secessionist architecture is breathtaking as is the building to the left of it. Another place for sweets and ice cream is **Magda Cukrászda** ★★, at Kandó Kálmán u. 4 (© **72/511-055**). This is a bright, bustling neighborhood *cukrászda,* where the selection and quality of cakes and ice creams is superb (though ice cream is not sold during the winter). It is an out-of-the-way location, but if you have time on your hands, it is worth the walk. The store is open daily 10am to 8pm, in winter to 7pm.

Shopping

As you stroll through the city, you will be surprised at the number of pedestrian-only streets there are, making shopping in Pécs a pleasurable activity. Many of the stores are standard shops that you will have found in Budapest or any other large city, for that matter, thanks to globalization.

SZEGED: HUNGARY'S SPICE CAPITAL ★★

168km (105 miles) SE of Budapest

Historically, Szeged (pronounced *Seh*-ged) was destroyed on March 12, 1879, when a distant dyke collapsed and flooded the city. Locals were given financial aid collected in other European countries and sent to Szeged to help them rebuild; hence, there are streets named Rome, Brussels, Berlin, Paris, London, Moscow, and Vienna, honoring those contributions. After the catastrophic flood, Szeged was redesigned with the engineer's precision of a compass and ruler to become the most modern town of Hungary. Its broad avenues and boulevards along with its extravagant center won the Europa Nostra award, which is granted annually to outstanding heritage achievements.

It is the proud capital of the Great Plain in Csongrád County, an interesting little, but hospitable city, large by Hungarian standards with a population of 177,000. World famous for its paprika and salami *(Pick Szalami),* Szeged is also home to one of Hungary's major universities, the University of Szeged, as it was renamed in 2003. From 1962 until its renaming in 2003, the university was once József Attila University, named for a poet who did not gain fame until after his death. His statue was erected in front of the university's main building on Dugonics tér. There is another statue of him next to the Parliament building in Budapest on Kossuth tér, sitting on the steps of the embankment.

The people of Szeged, many of whom are students, love to stroll along the riverside, sit in cafes, and window-shop on the just reconstructed elegant **Karász utca**★★, the town's main pedestrian-only street. Dóm tér, a beautiful, wide square, is home to the **Szeged Open Air Drama Festival**★, which celebrated its 75th year in 2007. It is a popular summer-long series of cultural events, with the majority in Hungarian, but they have opened competition to the festival, so other languages may be represented in the future. **THEALTER**, an association of artists, was founded in 1991 with the mission to introduce and support the work of experimenting, innovative artistic communities. They bring the best artists from minority-marginal positions to Szeged to perform during the festival. There is an emphasis on introducing well-known groups from western Europe as well as local artists to create progressive schemes and ways of viewing artistic performances. Over the last 16 years, the Old Synagogue has become synonymous with THEALTER, forming a close alliance. THEALTER has presented more than 130 groups from 27 countries to Szeged, some of them making their premier performance in Hungary, here in the town of Szeged. For more information about these festivals, contact **TourInform.** This small city is a delightful travel destination for a day or two of visiting.

Essentials

GETTING THERE Over 30 **trains** depart daily from Budapest's Nyugati Station, of which 14 are InterCity. The fare for an IC train is 3,130 Ft ($17/£11) plus an additional fee for a seat reservation. All other trains cost 2,780 Ft ($15/£9.30). On all trains, the travel time is the same 2½ hours, so the only advantage of an IC train is perhaps cleanliness, but not cost effectiveness.

If you're **driving** from Budapest, take the M5 motorway south through Kecskemét and Kiskunfélegyháza.

VISITOR INFORMATION The best source of information, as usual, is **TourInform,** at Dugonics tér 2 (✆ **62/488-699;** www.szegedvaros.hu), located in the renovated 19th-century courtyard of the fine pastry shop Z. Nagy Cukrászda (reviewed below). The office is open Monday to Friday from 9am to 5pm. For private accommodations, stop in at Ibusz at Oroszlán u. 4 or call **62/471-177.**

MAHART, the Hungarian ferry line company, organizes boat tours up and down the Tisza River from April 1 through mid-October. For information, contact the MAHART boat station in Szeged at Felső Tisza-part or call ✆ **62/425-834.**

Exploring Szeged's Historic Center

Gróf Palace ★★ This is a piece of architecture worthy of a look. Located at the corner of Lajos Tisza körut and Takarektar utca is the Gróf Palace named after Dr. Arpad Grof, who had it built. His intent was to rent out apartments to "modern professionals or officials at certain career level positions, who are well situated and able to afford high rent." The building was designed by Ferenc J. Raichl and was built within 13 months starting in 1912. The greater part of the building is framed on two sides by slender towers, held up by two pillars, proudly supporting their carefully formed spires. While in the area, see the **Reök Palace** in Gaudian style at Lajos Tisza körut and Kölcsey utca, both incredible pieces of architecture.

Pick Museum ★★ This is a must for anyone interested in food or cooking. The museum contains the history of Pick brand salami and Szeged paprika, both world famous as Hungarian products that developed from this city. Follow the history and evolution of the manufacturing of salami production from the 1869 foundation to today. On the first floor, follow the history of paprika production, all with puppets in period dress.

Felső Tisza-part 10. ✆ 06/20-468-9185 mobile only. www.pickmuzeum.hu. Admission 480 Ft ($2.60/£1.60). Tues–Sat 3–6pm.

Synagogue ★ A tribute to the once-thriving Jewish community in Szeged, this synagogue was built in 1907. Created in a number of architectural styles, it is a monumental 49m (161 ft.) tall, moorish Art Nouveau building, the ornamented space between the right or left exterior curve of the arch and the enclosing right angle is done in Gothic style. Roman columns support the galleries. The most beautiful part is the dome, but everywhere you look will be awe inspiring. This is considered the masterpiece of architect Lipot Baumhorn, who was a disciple of Ödön Lechner and the most prolific and renowned synagogue architect in modern Europe. It occupies a full block, making it the second-largest synagogue in Hungary. The synagogue is fully functioning and holds services at 6pm every Friday.

If you find the synagogue closed when it should be open, go to the address that's posted near the entrance and the caretaker will open the synagogue for you.

Jósika u. ✆ **62/423-849.** www.zsinagoga.szeged.hu. Admission 300 Ft ($1.60/£1). Summer Sun–Fri 9am–noon and 1–5pm; winter Sun–Fri 10am–2pm. Closed for Jewish holidays. From Dugonics tér, walk right on Tisza Lajos körút, and turn left on Gutenberg u.

Votive Church Built by the residents after the restoration from the flood that destroyed the city, the square that it sits in is exactly the same size as Saint Mark Square in Venice. In the church is an unusual representation of the Madonna created in mosaic by Ferenc Márton over the baldachin of the high altar. It is nicknamed the "Madonna in a Fur Coat" because she is depicted wearing a richly decorated fur coat typical of this region, with red slippers typical of Szeged. There are many magnificent pieces of artwork throughout the church. It houses Europe's third-largest church organ, with 9,040 pipes. Masses are held here at 6:30 and 7:30am, and 6pm every day.

Also on the square is the oldest historic monument of the city: the Saint Demetrius Tower, with a foundation dating back to the 11th century. The lower, squared Roman-styled section and early Gothic upper sections date back to the 13th century.

On Dóm tér. Free admission. Mon–Sat 9am–6pm; Sun 9:30–10am, 11–11:30am, and 12:30–6pm.

Where to Stay

Private rooms can be booked through **Ibusz** at Oroszlán u. 3 (✆ **62/471-177**).

Dóm Hotel Located on the square near the cathedral, this hotel opened in 2004, offering lovely modern rooms with easy access to all major tourist sights. Two apartments with a separated living room and bedroom are available for two to four people.

Bajza u. 3–6. ✆ **62/423-750.** Fax 62/423-750. www.domhotel.hu. 15 units. 20,500 Ft ($110/£68) double; 30,500 Ft–33,900 Ft ($165–$183/£102–£113) apt. Breakfast included, but VAT and tourist tax extra. AE, V. **Amenities:** Sauna; safe. *In room:* A/C, TV, minibar.

Kata Panzió ★ This lovely little pension which opened in 1995 is in a quiet residential neighborhood, just a short walk from central Klauzál tér. It features plenty of common space and sunny balconies on each floor. Four double rooms, one triple, and one quad are available; all have private bathrooms.

Bolyai János u. 15 (btw. Gogol u. and Kálvária sgt.), 6720 Szeged. ✆ **62/311-258.** 6 units. 14,800 Ft ($80/£50) double; 20,500 ($110/£68) deluxe double and quad. Breakfast included. 300 Ft ($1.65/£1) tourist tax per person per night extra. No credit cards. Free parking. *In room:* A/C, TV.

Where to Dine

Bolero HUNGARIAN Like its musical name, the menu starts with overtures for starters and sequels for the entrees. This is a place for elegant dining and for a town this size, the prices reflect it.

Zárda u. 7. ✆ **62/540-656.** Main courses 2,280 Ft–4,990 Ft ($12–$27/£7.45–£17). Mon–Thurs 11am–10pm; Fri–Sat 11am–2am; Sun 11am–5pm.

Gödör ★ HUNGARIAN Located next to the Hero's Arch right in the center of the city is where you will find this little restaurant. University students, teachers, and tourists alike frequent it. From spring to late summer, you can enjoy the terrace seating while enjoying your meal.

Tisza Lajos krt. 103. ✆ **62/420-130.** Main courses 750 Ft–1,800 Ft ($4.05–$9.70/£2.50–£6). No credit cards. Mon-Sat 11am–10pm; Sun 11am–4pm.

Gőry ★ HUNGARIAN A varied menu offers something for everyone at this old-fashioned Hungarian restaurant.

Liszt u. 9. ✆ **62/422-157.** Main dishes 1,950 Ft–2,990 Ft ($11–$16/£6.55–£9.90). No credit cards. Daily 11am–11pm.

Kiskőrösi Halászcsárda ★ HUNGARIAN You'd do well to sample local fish and the famous Szeged fish soup at this authentic riverside restaurant. Paprika and onions are the spices of choice for hearty fish stews and bisques alike.

Felső Tisza-part 336. ✆ **62/495-698.** Reservations recommended. Main courses 700 Ft–1,200 Ft ($3.80–$6.50/£2.35–£4.05). MC, V. Sun–Thurs 11am–midnight; Fri–Sat 11am–2am.

Pagoda Étterem ★ CHINESE A favorite Chinese restaurant of the locals, this is a restaurant that will not overwhelm your dining with kitsch decor. The menu is extensive and the dishes are reportedly delicious.

Zrinyi u. 5. ✆ **62/312-490.** Main courses 840 Ft–2,800 Ft ($4.55–$15/£2.80–£9.30). AE, V. Tues–Sat noon–midnight; Sun–Mon noon–11pm.

Coffeehouses & Ice-Cream Parlors

Sándor Árvay and his son Kálmán created a patisserie, which became famous by the end of the 19th century because of the quality of their goods. It was nicknamed the "Gerbaud of Szeged." The Virágh brothers bought it in 1922, continuing the quality reputation and renaming it **Virág Cukrászda,** located on Klauzál tér. It is open daily from 8am to 10pm. This square has more than its share of pastry shops, with the **Kis Virág (Little Flower)** ★★, across the square, where you can get your pastries to go. The prices are slightly cheaper for take-away. Some say this has the best ice cream in town; in winter you can find it inside the Kis Virág. Their specialty is *rakott rétes* (layered strudel), which is the divine local version of the traditional Jewish pastry *flodni.* Kis Virág is open daily from 8am to 8pm. There are other, smaller shops on or near the square vying for attention, but these two are the main attractions.

Z. Nagy Cukrászda ★ on Dugonics tér, just off Karász utca (the pedestrian-only street) is yet another rivaling pastry shop. With its terrace in the courtyard, it makes a pleasure place to stop and relax. One cookie you might try is *Erzsi kocka,* walnut paste sandwiched between two shortbread cookies, dipped in dark chocolate. When the summer heat is beating down, head for the line of people waiting to be served at the most popular ice-cream shop, **Palánk,** on the corner of Tömörkény and Oskola utcas.

Szeged After Dark

Átrium Music Cafe at Kárász u. 9 (✆ **06/30-289-4466,** mobile only) is a lively place with a variety of different music styles each night, including jazz, funk, and soul, with specific ladies nights. **Szote Klub,** found at Dóm tér 13 (✆ 62/545-773), is a definite disco with DJs knocking out the tunes, but the action doesn't start until 9:30pm and goes into the wee hours, whenever the action slows down. The famous **Jate Klub** of the university opened its doors in 1973. Originally, it was an air-raid shelter located in the basement of the main building of the university. During the day, it operates as a cafe, and in the evening it hosts parties, concerts, and cultural, theatrical, and literary events. Divided into four sections, there are different events held in each. It is open Monday to Friday 10am to the end of the program, and, oddly enough, on Saturday from 10pm to the end of the program.

8

Poland

by Mark Baker

Poland is coming into its own as a vacation destination. During the first decade after the 1989 democratic revolutions in Eastern Europe, it seemed Prague and Budapest grabbed all the headlines. Now, travelers are looking for something farther afield, and with the advent of budget air carriers in Europe, travel to countries like Poland has never been cheaper or easier.

For some, a trip to Poland is an opportunity to reconnect with their Polish roots, a chance, perhaps, to sample some of their grandmother's pierogies in their natural setting. Others are attracted to the unique beauty of Kraków, which has rightfully joined Prague and Budapest as part of the trinity of must-sees in central Europe. Still others are drawn by Poland's dramatic and often tragic history. The absolute horrors of World War II, followed by the decades of Communist rule, have etched painful and moving monuments in the landscape. No country, with the possible exception of Russia, suffered as much as Poland during World War II. Millions of Poles, and nearly the entire prewar Jewish population of over three million, were killed in fighting or in concentration camps. The deeply affecting and sobering thoughts on seeing the camps at Auschwitz and Birkenau, near Kraków, will last a lifetime. Nearly equally moving are the stories of the Łódź and Warsaw Jewish ghettos, or the tragic story of the Warsaw uprising of 1944, when the city's residents rose up courageously but futilely against their Nazi oppressors.

There are triumphant moments too. In Warsaw, the entire Old Town has been rebuilt brick by brick in an emotional show of a city reclaiming its history. In Gdańsk, you can visit the shipyards where Lech Wałęsa and his Solidarity trade union first rose to power to oppose Poland's Communist government in 1980. It was the rise of Solidarity that helped to bring down Communism in Poland, and arguably sparked the revolutions that swept through all of Eastern Europe in 1989.

And Poland is not only history. To the south, below Kraków, rise the majestic High Tatras, one of Europe's most starkly beautiful ranges. To the north, the Baltic Sea coast, with its pristine beaches, stretches for miles. The northeast is covered with lakes that run to the borderlands with Lithuania and Belarus. In the east of the country, you'll find patches of some of Europe's last-remaining primeval forest, and a small existing herd of indigenous bison that once covered large parts of the European continent.

1 GETTING TO KNOW POLAND

THE LAY OF THE LAND

Poland is a mostly flat, sprawling country, covering some 312,000 sq. km (around 121,000 sq. miles). Its historical position, between Germany in the west and Russia in the east, has caused no end of hardship. Following World War II, the country's borders were shifted approximately 200km (120 miles) to the west, gaining territory at the

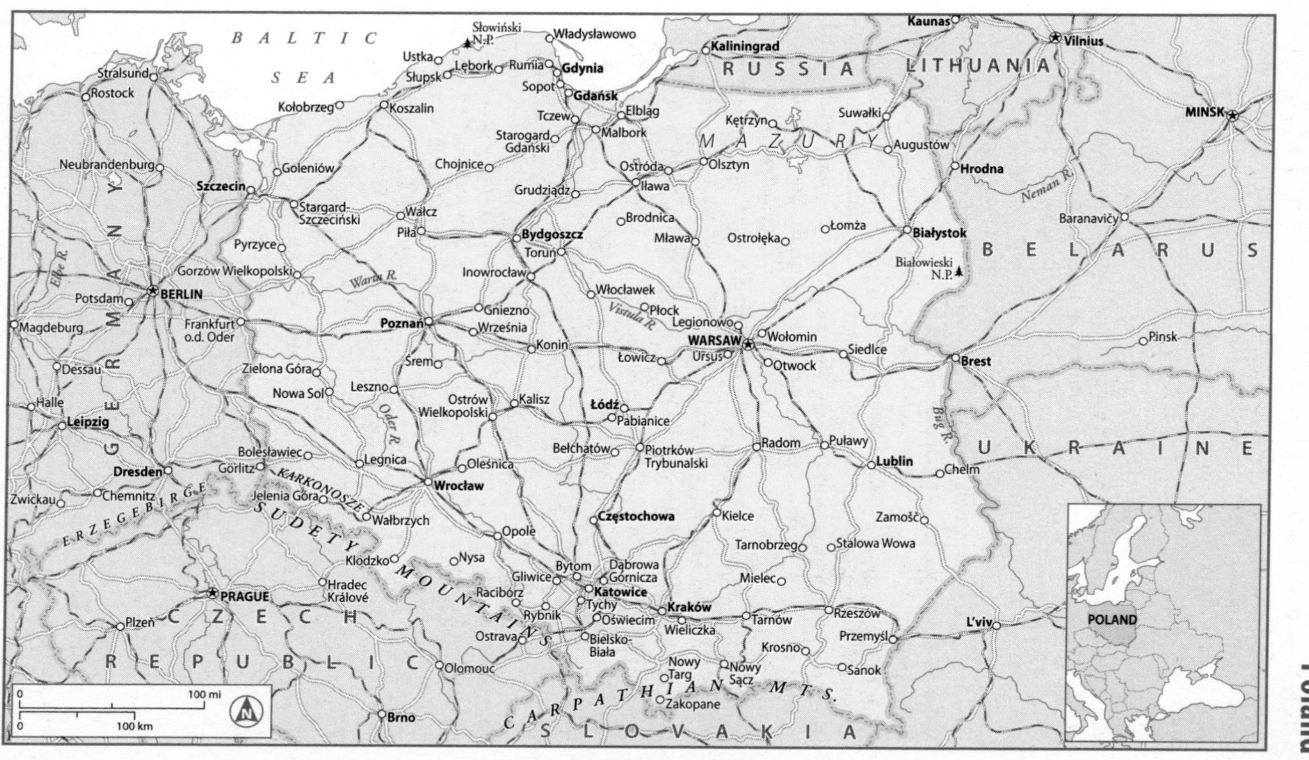
BALTIC SEA
RUSSIA
LITHUANIA
BELARUS
UKRAINE
SLOVAKIA
CZECH REPUBLIC
GERMANY
MAZURY
CARPATHIAN MTS.
SUDETY MOUNTAINS
KARKONOSZE
ERZGEBIRGE
POLAND
Kaliningrad
Kaunas
Vilnius
MINSK
Hrodna
Baranavičy
Pinsk
Brest
Białystok
Białowieski N.P.
Augustów
Suwałki
Łomża
Siedlce
Lublin
Chełm
Zamość
Stalowa Wowa
Puławy
Radom
Otwock
Wołomin
WARSAW
Ursus
Legionowo
Ostrołęka
Kętrzyn
Olsztyn
Ostróda
Iława
Mława
Brodnica
Elbląg
Malbork
Gdańsk
Gdynia
Sopot
Władysławowo
Rumia
Lębork
Słowiński N.P.
Ustka
Słupsk
Koszalin
Kołobrzeg
Tczew
Starogard Gdański
Grudziądz
Chojnice
Wałcz
Piła
Bydgoszcz
Toruń
Inowrocław
Włocławek
Płock
Gniezno
Września
Konin
Łowicz
Łódź
Pabianice
Piotrków Trybunalski
Bełchatów
Częstochowa
Kielce
Tarnobrzeg
Mielec
Tarnów
Rzeszów
Przemyśl
Sanok
Krosno
Nowy Sącz
Nowy Targ
Zakopane
Kraków
Wieliczka
Dąbrowa Górnicza
Katowice
Tychy
Oświęcim
Bielsko-Biała
Bytom
Gliwice
Rybnik
Racibórz
Ostrava
Olomouc
Opole
Nysa
Kłodzko
Wałbrzych
Wrocław
Oleśnica
Ostrów Wielkopolski
Kalisz
Śrem
Poznań
Leszno
Legnica
Jelenia Góra
Bolesławiec
Görlitz
Zielona Góra
Nowa Sól
Gorzów Wielkopolski
Pyrzyce
Stargard-Szczeciński
Goleniów
Szczecin
Frankfurt o.d. Oder
BERLIN
Potsdam
Neubrandenburg
Stralsund
Rostock
Magdeburg
Dessau
Halle
Leipzig
Dresden
Chemnitz
Zwickau
Plzeň
PRAGUE
Hradec Králové
Brno
L'viv
Vistula R.
Warta R.
Oder R.
Bug R.
Neman R.
Elbe R.
0 100 mi
0 100 km

expense of Germany and losing it to the then–Soviet Union. The country shares borders with the Czech Republic and Slovakia in the south, and Belarus and Ukraine to the south and east. Germany lies to the west. To the north, Poland borders the Baltic Sea and Lithuania. Poland also shares a long northern border with the Russian enclave of Kaliningrad, part of the former German province of East Prussia that the Soviet Union claimed after World War II, but which does not connect to the Russian mainland.

THE REGIONS IN BRIEF

Warsaw, the capital, lies in the easterly center of the country, the main city of a relatively flat region known as Mazovia. To the northeast, an interconnected series of rivers and lakes, known as the Mazurian lakes, stretches out to Kaliningrad and Lithuania. Much of this land was part of the German province of East Prussia and belonged to Germany as recently as World War II. South of Warsaw and Mazovia are the regions of Małopolska (Little Poland), often seen as the Polish heartland, and Kraków. Under Austrian occupation, Kraków was a leading city of the province of Galicia, which spreads east into present-day Ukraine. Below Kraków begins an area known as the Podhale, the foothills of the Tatras, and then farther south the mountains themselves. To the immediate west of Kraków lies the immense industrial region of Upper Silesia, including the central city of Katowice. Farther west, to Lower Silesia, the region becomes more agricultural. The capital of this area is Wrocław, the former German city of Breslau. North of Wrocław, starts the enormous regions of Wielkopolska (Greater Poland) and Pomorze (Pomerania)—the ancient borderlands between Germany and Poland and rich with the legacy of the Teutonic Knights.

SUGGESTED ITINERARY: POLAND IN 10 DAYS

Poland is a large country with small roads and generally slow trains. That means it's hard to cover ground quickly and it's best to keep travel plans relatively modest. The following itinerary is laid out for car travel, but with a little effort can be adapted to train and/or bus travel.

Days ❶–❷: Arrive in Warsaw

Get settled in and if you've got the energy, try to arrange for a city tour in the afternoon. Warsaw is sprawling and even if you're not an "organized tour" type of person, this is one place where it makes sense. Spend the second day with a more leisurely stroll of the Old Town. Don't pass up the chance to see the Museum of the Warsaw Uprising.

Days ❸–❹: Kraków

Drive or take the train to Kraków—either way it will take about 3 to 4 hours. Give yourself plenty of time to enjoy Poland's most popular travel destination. Dedicate at least a day for the Old Town and the Wawel castle area, and another for Kazimierz and the sights of the former Jewish quarter.

Day ❺: Kraków Day Trip

The former Nazi extermination camp at Auschwitz/Birkenau lies about 90 minutes west of Kraków by car; alternatively, you can book one of several Auschwitz day tours through the tourist information office. It's a must. If you're traveling with small children and looking for a more cheerful day trip, try the Wieliczka Salt Mines, easily reachable from Kraków by bus or train.

Day ❻: Wrocław

This formerly German city—and now firmly Polish—is a delight. Spend the day on the square and walking along the little lanes near the river. Unlike Kraków, there are no real must-sees here; simply take in the town at your own pace and recharge your batteries.

Day 7: Poznań or Toruń

You choose. Both are about 2 hours north of Wroclaw on the way to Gdańsk. Poznań is a bustling, medium-size city with great restaurants and decent nightlife. Toruń is smaller, with a beautiful little square and a couple of great boutique hotels, though the options in the evening are limited.

Days 8–9: Gdańsk

This Baltic seaport is one of the real highlights of any trip to Poland: a beautifully restored city, rich with history and natural beauty. Try to squeeze out an extra day if you can. Sopot makes an easy day trip (and especially good in hot weather since there's a beach). If you've got more time, visit the enormous Teutonic Knights' castle at Malbork to the south or the sand dunes at Słowiński National Park to the northwest.

Day 10: Warsaw

Warsaw and your gateway home is an easy few hours train journey from Gdańsk. By road, plan on at least 5 or 6 hours, owing to bad roads and heavy traffic. But if you've come this far by car, you know by now that it always takes a lot longer than it looks on the map!

POLAND TODAY

Poland's transformation since the fall of Communism in 1989 has been nothing short of phenomenal. What was until not long ago a downtrodden, debt-ridden, basket case of a country has turned itself around 180 degrees. Today, Poland is a proud member of the European Union and NATO. Its currency is stable, and its economy is one of the fastest growing in Europe. You'll see gleaming new office towers on the ever-changing Warsaw skyline. And throughout the country, you'll see evidence of an emerging prosperity that was unthinkable 10 to 15 years ago.

To be sure, alongside this newly emerging wealth, you'll run across many still-depressed areas—particularly in industrial cities like Łódź and in large parts of Warsaw itself. You'll also see greater numbers than you might expect of homeless people, public drunks, beggars, and simply those who have fallen through the cracks. Not everyone has benefited equally from the country's rapid transformation to a democratic political system and a free-market economy. Industrial workers, particularly those over the age of 50 for whom adapting to the changes proved more difficult, have been hardest hit. Young people, too, have found it difficult to cope with ever-rising living costs on very low wages. Many have left the country for places like the U.K. and Ireland, where they can earn more tending bar than they can working as young professionals at home.

But it's important to put this into some perspective. Just a little more than 2 decades ago, Poland was falling apart. The country was $30 billion in debt to international lenders. The air was unbreathable—particularly in Kraków, downwind from the enormous steel-mill complex at Nowa Huta. It wasn't unusual for Poles to spend hours standing in line simply to buy a piece of fruit or a bottle of imported shampoo. And membership in the European Union was unthinkable. Worst of all, perhaps, was the feeling of utter hopelessness, as if it were somehow Poland's fate to end up on the wrong side of history every time. That's been replaced by something better and infectious: a cautious optimism that maybe this time around the better times are here to stay.

A LOOK AT THE PAST

Nowhere in Europe will you feel recent history more strongly than in Poland. The country's unenviable position through the ages, between Germany in the west and Russia to the east, and without defensible natural borders, has meant Polish history has been one long struggle for survival.

The Poles first established themselves in the areas to the west of Warsaw around the turn of the first millennium, descendants of migrant Slav tribes that came to Eastern Europe around A.D. 700 to 800. In the first centuries following the first millennium, the early nobility forged a strategic union with an order of crusaders, the Teutonic Knights, to defend Polish interests from pagan Prussians to the west. The Knights built enormous castles over a wide swath of western Poland, and the Poles soon found themselves with a cunning and ruthless rival on their hands for the spoils of the Baltic Sea trade. In 1410, the Poles joined forces with the Lithuanians and others and managed to defeat the Teutonic Knights at Grünwald, in one of the great epic battles of the Middle Ages. That battle is still fondly remembered in Polish history books.

Poland's early capital was Kraków, but the seat of government was moved to Warsaw in the 16th century after union with Lithuania greatly expanded Poland's territory. In the 17th century, the Poles are generally credited with saving Europe in another epic battle, this one against the Ottoman Turks. Commander Jan Sobieski saved the day for Christian Europe, repelling the Turks at the gates of Vienna in 1683.

From this point on, Polish history runs mostly downhill. Poland was unable to resist the gradual rise of Prussia in the west and tsarist Russia in the east as great powers. The result was a series of partitions of Poland in the late 18th century, with parts of Polish territory eventually going to Prussia, Russia, and Habsburg Austria. For 125 years, Poland disappeared from the map of Europe.

Independent Poland was restored in 1918 after the collapse of Austria-Hungary and Germany in World War I. The interwar period was relatively rocky, but World War II was Poland's worst nightmare come true. Nazi Germany fired the first shot from Gdańsk harbor on September 1, 1939. Russia, under terms of a nonaggression pact with Germany, seized the eastern part of the country a few weeks later. In the ensuing battle between fascism and Communism, Poland was caught in the middle. Nearly a quarter of all Poles died in the war, including some three million Polish Jews. The Nazis used Polish soil for the worst of their extermination camps, at Auschwitz-Birkenau and Treblinka, among others. Poland's once-handsome capital of Warsaw was ordered razed to the ground by a Nazi leadership enraged by Polish resistance there. By the end of the war, nearly every one of the city's one million inhabitants had been killed or expelled, and 85% of the city lay in ruins.

Poland was reconstituted at the end of the war, but with radically different borders. Bowing to Stalin's demands, the U.S. and U.K. ceded vast tracts of formerly Polish territory in the east to the Soviet Union. In turn, the new Poland was compensated with former German territory in the west. The Polish borders were shifted some 200km (120 miles) westward. The ethnic German population was expelled and replaced by Poles transferred from the east of the country.

But the end of the war brought little relief. Poland was given over to the Soviet sphere of influence, and though Communism as an ideology held little appeal for most Poles, a series of Soviet-backed Communist governments uneasily led the country for the next 4 decades. The government managed to maintain order through massive borrowing on international financial markets, but mismanagement of the economy led to one crisis after another. In the end it was this desire for higher living standards—perhaps even more than a desire for political freedom—that led to the creation of the Solidarity trade union and the genesis of the anti-Communist movement. Solidarity began at the shipyards in

Gdańsk, but eventually spread to the rest of the country. The initial demands were for higher wages and more influence in managing the economy, but the challenge to the Communist leadership was clear. At around the same time, the Catholic Church had elevated a cardinal from Kraków, Karol Woytyła, to be pope. If Solidarity provided the organizational framework for Poles to resist, Pope John Paul provided the moral inspiration. In early 1989, the Poles held their first semifree election—a landmark vote that bolstered anti-Communist activists across Eastern Europe. By the end of that epic year, the Eastern bloc was free.

Since the end of Communism, Poland has made great strides, reducing its international debt while living standards have continued to rise. In 1999 Poland realized a longtime goal of joining the NATO military alliance, and in 2004 entered the European Union.

POLISH PEOPLE & CULTURE

Poles are typically highly educated and highly cultured, with a firm grasp of their country's long and rich tradition in literature, poetry, performing arts, and film. The strong role of culture in everyday life is not surprising given the country's tragic history. For the 125 years, until 1918, that Poland ceased to exist as a country, it was quite literally a shared culture that held the people together. In modern times, it was this common cultural heritage that helped people to weather the Nazi and Soviet occupations, and to endure 40 years of Communist rule after World War II. Don't be surprised if your Polish hosts ask you if you've ever heard of this or that Polish romantic poet or postwar film director. And don't be surprised if they appear disappointed if you can't immediately come up with some insightful comment. Part of this disappointment is the feeling that if Polish history hadn't been so brutal, many of these writers and intellectuals would be as well known today as their counterparts in western Europe.

You'll sense too a strong feeling of national pride. Poles are proud of their history. They're proud of their resistance, however futile, to the Nazi invasion in 1939, and of the tragic Warsaw uprising in 1944. And they're proud of their country's leading role in ending Communism in the 1980s. And today this pride extends to Poland's membership in the European Union. Poland was the largest of the new countries to enter the E.U. in 2004, and Poland has effectively used its size to carve out an influential role for itself in Brussels.

Americans are likely to feel particularly welcome. Poland's ties to the United States go back all the way to Tadeusz Kościuszko and the Revolutionary War. Today, Poles proudly cite Chicago as the second-biggest Polish city in the world after Warsaw (even though these days more young Poles are emigrating to Ireland and the U.K. than to the U.S.). Just about everyone has a cousin, uncle, or grandparent who lives or used to live in one of the 50 states.

POLISH CUISINE

Polish food has a hearty, homemade feel, and when it's done well, it can be delicious. The staple of Polish cuisine is probably the **pierogi,** a pocket of dough stuffed with anything from potato meal, cottage cheese, or cabbage to ground beef or even plums or strawberries. Pierogies are traditionally prepared boiled and served with fried onions (except of course the fruit-filled ones), though you may also find them baked or fried and topped with anything from sour cream to garlic sauce. Pierogies are extremely flexible. They can be eaten as a snack or as a main course, for lunch or for dinner. They also make a great option for vegetarians; just be sure to tell them to hold the bacon bits they sometimes pour on top. Pierogies prepared "Ruskie" style are meatless, stuffed with potatoes and cottage cheese. ***Placki,*** potato pancakes, are nearly as ubiquitous and delicious, and are often cooked with mushrooms or smoked meat.

Meals generally begin with an appetizer, cold ***(przekąski zimne)*** or hot ***(przekąski gorące).*** Among the former, herring ***(śledź),*** usually served in a sour-cream sauce and piled with chopped onions, is my favorite. Other popular cold starters include stuffed fish or pâté ***(pasztet).*** Hot starters can include pierogies or a piece of homemade sausage ***(kiełbasa).***

Soups ***(zupy)*** are a mainstay. ***Żurek*** is a filling, sourish rye broth, seasoned with dill and usually served with sausage and egg. ***Barszcz*** is a clear, red-beet soup, often served with a little pastry on the side. ***Bigos,*** known on menus in English as "hunter's stew," another national mania, is made from sauerkraut, and is something between a soup and a main course. Every Polish grandmother has her own version, and local lore says the homemade variety tastes best on the seventh reheating!

Main courses are less original, and often revolve around chicken, pork, or beef, though game (venison or boar usually) and fish (pike and trout are popular) are also common. Sides ***(dodatki)*** usually involve some form of potato, fried or boiled, or sometimes fried potato dumplings. More creative sides include buckwheat groats or mashed beets, the latter sometimes flavored with apple. Common desserts include fruit pierogies, apple strudel, the ubiquitous ice cream ***(lody),*** and pancakes, sometimes filled with cottage cheese and served with fruit sauce.

Mealtimes adhere to the Continental standard. Breakfast is usually taken early, and is often no more than a cup of tea or coffee and a bread roll. Hotels usually lay on the traditional buffet-style breakfast, centered on cold cuts, cheeses, yogurts, and cereals, but this is more than what a Pole would normally eat. Lunch is served from about noon to 2pm, though restaurants don't usually get rolling until about 1pm. Dinner starts around 6pm and can go until 9 or 10pm. After that, kitchens start closing down.

Snack foods run the gamut from Western fast-food outlets (McDonald's, KFC, and Pizza Hut are the most common) to kebob stands and pizza parlors. You'll find decent pizza in nearly every Polish city and town of any size. Look especially for ***zapiekanki,*** foot-long, open-faced baguettes, topped with sauce and cheese, and then baked. It's known affectionately as "Polish pizza."

As for drinking, Poles are best known for their vodka, but it's beer in fact that's the national drink. You'll find the major brands—Okocim, Lech, Tyskie, and Żywiec—just about everywhere. There's little difference among the majors, though Tyskie appears to be the most popular. Men take theirs straight up. Women frequently sweeten their beer with fruit syrup (raspberry is the most common) and drink it through a straw. Among the most popular vodkas, Belvedere and Chopin are considered top shelf, though increasingly imported vodkas are squeezing out the local brands. In addition, you'll find a range of flavored vodkas. Żubrówka is slightly greenish, owing to a long blade of bison grass from the east of the country in every bottle. Miodówka, honey-flavored and easy to drink in large quantity, is worth a try. Wine is much less common, and nearly always imported.

As for nonalcoholic drinks, Poles are traditionally tea drinkers, though coffee, increasingly sold as espressos and lattes in trendy coffee shops, is making inroads. Tea is normally drunk in a glass with sugar. The quality of the coffee has greatly improved in the past decade, but for some reason the dark, bitter liquid called "coffee" served at hotel and pension breakfasts is still often undrinkable.

LANGUAGE

Unless you're a scholar of Slavic languages (or you already speak some Polish), you'll find Polish nearly incomprehensible. There are relatively few English cognates, and the vexing combinations of consonants—"szcz" comes to mind—and accent marks (z's with dots and l's with lines through them?) will have you shaking your head after a couple of minutes of trying to puzzle it out. Fortunately, there are a fair amount of English speakers around, and nearly all hotels, tourist offices, and restaurants will be able to manage some English. German will also help, especially in areas of the south and west, close to the German border.

USEFUL WORDS & PHRASES

English	Polish	Pronunciation
Hello/good day	**Dzień dobry**	djeen *doh*-bree
Yes	**Tak**	*tahk*
No	**Nie**	nee-yeh
Hi! or Bye! (informal)	**Cześć!**	*chesh*-ch
Good evening	**Dobry wieczór**	*doh*-bree *vyeh*-choor
Goodbye	**Do widzenia**	*doh* vee-*djen*-ya
Good night	**Dobranoc**	doh-*brah*-nohts
Thank you	**Dziękuję**	djen-*koo*-yeh
Please/you're welcome	**Proszę**	*proh*-sheh
How are you? (informal)	**Jak sie masz?**	*yahk* sheh mahsh?
How are you? (formal)	**Jak sie pan (to a man)/ pani (to a woman) ma?**	*yahk* sheh pahn/ pahn-ee mah?
Fine	**Dobrze**	*dohb*-zheh
Do you speak English?	**Czy pan/pani mówi po angielsku?**	chee pahn/pahn-ee *moo*-vee poh ahng-*yel*-skoo?
I don't understand	**Nie rozumiem**	ne-yeh roh-*zoom*-yem
How much is it?	**Ile kosztuje?**	eel-eh kosh-*too*-yeh
Menu	**Jadłospis**	*jahd*-woe-spees
The bill, please	**Proszę o rachunek**	*proh*-sheh oh *rahk*-oo-nek
Cheers!	**Na zdrowie!**	nah-*zdroh*-vyeh
Bon appétit!	**Smacznego!**	smahch-*neh*-go
Open	**Otwarty**	*oh*-twar-tee
Closed	**Zamkniety**	*zahm*-knyeh-tee

2 PLANNING YOUR TRIP TO POLAND

ENTRY REQUIREMENTS

There are no special requirements for entering Poland. Passport holders from the U.S., Canada, and Australia can enter the country without a visa and stay for 90 days. Passport holders from E.U. member countries, including the U.K., do not need a visa. Poland is a member of the E.U.'s Schengen common border zone, meaning that—in theory at

Major Festivals in Poland

The calendar is filled with festivals of all kinds, with the most popular celebrations connected to religious dates or Poland's folk or cultural traditions. The annual Marian pilgrimages culminate in August at the Jasna Góra shrine in Częstochowa for the **Feast of the Assumption** on **August 15**. Warsaw, Kraków, Wrocław, and Poznań all host jazz, contemporary, and classical music festivals throughout the year. The best idea is to check in with the local tourist information offices when you arrive to see what's going on during the time you're there. Kraków's Kazimierz district hosts the increasingly popular **Jewish Cultural Festival** every year in **late June and July**. Klezmer music concerts, films, and cultural discussions highlight the agenda. Zakopane and the surrounding area is the epicenter of the country's folk fests, with the biggest draw being **Zakopane's Mountain Folklore Festival** in **August**.

least—if you are arriving from another E.U. country, you will not be asked to show a passport. Note that you are still obliged to carry your passport with you and show it if requested.

MONEY

The main unit of currency is the **złoty (zł),** which is divided into 100 **groszy (gr).** Bills come in denominations of 10zł, 20zł, 50zł, 100zł, and 200zł. The most useful coins are the 5zł, 2zł, and 1zł. You'll also see coins of 50 gr, 10 gr, 2 gr, and rarely 1 gr. At the time of this writing, 1 U.S. dollar was worth around 2.3zł, and 1 British pound about 3.7zł.

Though Poland is a member of the European Union, the country does not use the euro nor are there plans to introduce the euro any time soon. For convenience sake, some hotels will quote their rates in euros and accept euros as payment, but in general it's best to carry local currency.

You can change money in nearly any bank or exchange office, identified in Polish as *kantor.* You'll see them everywhere, but be sure to shop around for the best rates since they differ from shop to shop. You'll get a decent rate simply by using your credit or debit card in an ATM. In large cities and towns you'll see an ATM on nearly every block.

WHEN TO GO

Poland's climate is characterized by hot summers and dark, cold winters. Unless you're heading to the Tatras to ski, avoid travel from January to March. Many of the attractions are closed for the season, and the cold and snow make getting around difficult. Note that Kraków and Zakopane are both popular Christmas and New Year's destinations and hotel prices rise accordingly. Summer brings good weather, but more crowds as Poles take to the roads on their summer holidays. September and October are ideal, with fewer crowds and usually reliably good weather.

HOLIDAYS

Offices, banks, museums, and many stores are closed on the following holidays, though some stores and restaurants remain open: January 1 (New Year's Day), Easter Sunday and Monday, May 1 (State Holiday), May 3 (Constitution Day), Corpus Christi (falls on ninth Thurs following Easter Sunday), August 15 (Assumption), November 1 (All Saints' Day), November 11 (Independence Day), and December 25 and 26 (Christmas Day).

GETTING THERE

BY PLANE Warsaw remains the major air gateway to Poland, with extensive connections throughout Europe, and some nonstop flights to North America. See "Warsaw: Getting There," below, for more details. Kraków's Jan Pavel II Airport is also easy to reach from nearly any large airport in Europe. The advent of low-cost budget carriers in Europe in recent years has opened up several other cities to regular and convenient air travel, including Łódź, Poznań, Wrocław, and Gdańsk.

BY TRAIN The national rail network, PKP, is well integrated into the Europe-wide rail system. Warsaw lies on the main east-west line running from Berlin to Moscow. Kraków is accessible from Prague, Vienna, and points south, though some connections may require a change of trains at Katowice.

BY BUS International bus travel has become less popular in recent years due to the arrival of the budget air carriers, which often match the buses for ticket prices, but get you there much quicker. Nevertheless, the Polish national bus carrier works in cooperation with the trans-European carrier Eurolines, and large Polish cities are easy to reach by bus.

BY CAR Poland is easily accessible by car and Polish highways are integrated into the larger E.U. highway grid. If entering from an E.U. country (Germany, Czech Republic, Slovakia, and Lithuania) you no longer have to stop to show a passport. Standard border controls are still in effect if traveling to or from Ukraine, Belarus, or the Russian Federation.

BY SHIP It's possible to travel to Poland by ferry from two ports in Sweden, putting in at Gdańsk and Gdynia on the Baltic coast. See "Gdańsk: "Getting There," later in this chapter, for more details.

GETTING AROUND

BY CAR Car travel offers flexibility but can be slow and highly frustrating. Most Polish highways—even those connecting major cities—are of the narrow, two-lane variety and are usually clogged with trucks, buses, tractors, and even occasionally horse-drawn carts. For most stretches, plan on at least 2 hours driving time per 100km (62 miles) distance. And drive defensively. Polish drivers have an abysmal record when it comes to per capita accidents and fatalities. Poland follows normal Continental rules of the road, with priority given to cars on roundabouts and vehicles coming from the right at unmarked intersections. Note that drivers are required to keep headlights on at all times. The speed limit on (the few) four-lane freeways is 130kmph (80 mph). This drops to 90kmph (56 mph) on two-lane highways outside urban areas, and 50kmph (31 mph) or slower in built-up areas. Speed checks are common. Spot alcohol checks are also frequent. The blood/alcohol limit is 0.2%—approximately one beer.

BY TRAIN The Polish state railroad, PKP, has improved its service in recent years, and train travel is usually the quickest and best way to move between big cities or to cover long distances. PKP maintains a useful online timetable (but be sure to use Polish spellings for city names): www.rozklad-pkp.pl. The best trains are the InterCity (IC) trains, which link nearly all of the country's biggest cities. You'll see IC trains marked in red on timetables; these are more expensive than regular trains and require an obligatory seat reservation. Next best are express trains (Ex), which also require a reservation. Avoid other types of trains for longer distances. You can buy tickets at stations or directly from the conductor on the train, though you'll have to pay a surcharge of 8zł ($3.50/£2.15) for the latter. Fares are relatively low by Western standards. A second-class ticket from Kraków to Warsaw, for example, costs about 85zł ($37/£23). For overnight trips, you can usually book a couchette in a six-bunk car or a sleeper in a three-bunk car. Sleepers run about 120zł ($52/£32). Be sure to book these in advance if possible.

BY BUS Polski Express (www.polskiexpress.pl) maintains an extensive network of routes linking Poland's major cities. Prices and journey times are comparable to the trains and the service is highly useful if you can't find a convenient train connection. Within regions, buses are usually better than trains for getting around to smaller cities and towns. From Kraków, for example, buses are quicker and cheaper than trains for the popular day trip to Zakopane. In general, bus stations are almost always located near main train stations. Try to buy bus tickets in advance if you can, but it's usually possible to buy them directly from the driver. Watch to have exact change on hand, since drivers may not have enough cash to deal with large bills.

TIPS ON ACCOMMODATIONS

The past decade has seen a boom in hotel construction, but most of that has come in the high and high-middle ends of the market in order to cater to the growing amount of business travel to Poland. That means rates will probably be higher than you expect. On the good side, this dependence on the business traveler means that hotels often cut rates on the weekends to fill beds—it never hurts to ask at reception if the rate they are quoting is the best one available. Rates are often also lower if you prebook over a hotel's website. "Standard double rooms" are usually understood to mean twin beds; rooms with queen-size beds are often classified as "deluxe" and cost more. Most places now have nonsmoking accommodations, and a growing number of hotels are now mostly or entirely smoke-free. If you're traveling by car, note that parking is often not included in the price. Hotels will frequently offer guarded parking for a fee, usually for around 30zł ($13/£8.10). This is probably a good idea, especially in urban areas where there's a small but definite chance of a break-in.

In addition to hotels and pensions *(pensjonaty),* there's no shortage of people offering private accommodations in their homes or flats. This is more common in heavily touristed areas away from larger cities—in places like Zakopane, for example. Look for the signs saying *wolny pokoj* (free room) or *noclegi* (lodging) hanging from outside houses. Prices are much lower than hotels, but standards vary considerably. Always take a look at the room first before accepting.

TIPS ON DINING

Restaurant meals have greatly improved in the past decade. It used to be nearly impossible to find decent food outside of a private home, but entrepreneurs have seized on the growing numbers of businessmen and tourists. In addition to standard restaurants *(restauracja),* look for places with the word *karczma* (literally "inn") in the name. These are often done up in traditional, peasant style, with simpler cooking and a warmer atmosphere. Here and there you'll still see the occasional *bar mleczny,* or milk bar; these self-service canteens traditionally cater to students and are great for simple Polish meals like pierogies, potato pancakes, soups, and some meat dishes. Milk bars often have shorter opening hours, are nonsmoking, and don't serve alcohol.

Fast Facts Poland

Business Hours Stores and offices are generally open Monday to Friday 9am to 6pm. Banks are open Monday to Friday 9am to 4pm, and occasionally have morning hours on Saturday. Some larger stores have limited Saturday hours, usually 9am to noon. Museums and other tourist attractions are often closed on Mondays.

Doctors & Dentists In Warsaw, the LIM Medical Center, Al. Jerozolimskie 65/79, is centrally located in the Marriott complex and staffs a full range of English-speaking doctors and specialists (✆ **022/458-70-00**). For dentists, the Austrian Dental Center, Żelazna 54 (✆ **022/654-21-16**), comes highly recommended.

Electricity Polish outlets follow the Continental norm (220v, 50hz) with two round plugs. Most appliances that run on 110v will require a transformer.

Embassies In Warsaw, **U.S.:** ul. Ujadowskie 29/31 (✆ 022/504-27-84); **Canada:** ul. Matejki 1/5 (✆ 022/584-31-00); **U.K.:** Al. Róż 1 (✆ 022/311-00-00).

Emergencies In an emergency dial the following numbers: police ✆ 997, fire ✆ 998, ambulance ✆ 999, road assistance ✆ 981 or 9637 (Polish motoring association/PZM). The general emergency number if using a cellphone is ✆ 112. The number of English-speaking operators is small.

Internet & E-mail Internet cafes are ubiquitous throughout Warsaw, Kraków, and other large cities. Internet cafes generally charge around 6zł ($2.60/£1.60) per hour of Internet use. Many better hotels now set aside at least one public computer for guests to use. A growing number of hotels and cafes offer wireless Internet access.

Post Offices & Mail The rate for mailing a postcard abroad is around 3.20zł ($1.40/85p), but it's always best to have letters weighed at the post office in order to ensure the proper postage.

Safety Violent crime is relatively rare, but theft is a serious problem. Don't leave valuables in cars overnight. Watch your pockets and purses carefully. If you're traveling with a bike, don't leave it outside unattended (even if it's firmly locked). Many hotels and pensions will allow you to take your bicycle in with you to your room.

Telephones & Fax Poland's country code is 48. To dial Poland from abroad, dial the international access code (for example, 011 in the U.S.), plus 48, and then the local Poland area code (minus the zero). The area code for Warsaw is 022. To call long distance within Poland, dial the area code (retaining the zero) plus the number. To dial abroad from Poland, dial 00 and then the country code and area code to where you are calling. A call to the U.S. or Canada, for example, would begin 00-1.

Time Zone Poland is in the Central European Time zone (CET), 1 hour ahead of GMT and 6 hours ahead of the eastern United States.

Tipping In restaurants, round up the bill by a maximum of 10% to reward good service. Bellhops, taxi drivers, and tour guides will also expect a small amount in return for services rendered. A 5zł ($2.15/£1.35) coin is usually enough under any circumstance.

Toilets Public toilets are a relative rarity, so keep an eye out for clean restaurants and hotels. In smaller establishments there may only be one toilet shared by both men and women. You'll find pay toilets at train stations and highway service stations (of varying states of cleanliness). The fee is usually 2zł (85¢/55p). Some public toilets still use the older symbols to designate men's and women's facilities. For the record, men are upside-down triangles; women are circles (don't ask me why).

Water Tap water is generally potable and there are no specific health concerns. If in doubt, buy bottled water, which is cheap and widely available.

3 WARSAW

Poland's capital city—not often included on many tourist itineraries—deserves a fresh look. While it will never have the charm of Kraków or Gdańsk, there's a spirit of rebirth here that's immediately contagious. Some 85% of the city was destroyed during World War II, and nearly everything you see, including the charming and very "old" looking **Old Town (Stare Miasto),** has been around only for a few decades. The Old Town was faithfully rebuilt, brick by brick, in the aftermath of the war, according to paintings, photographs, architectural sketches, and personal memories. The reconstruction was so good that in 1980 UNESCO included the Old Town on its list of World Cultural Heritage sites.

Warsaw started life as a relatively small river town in the 14th century, but within a century it had become the capital city of the Duchy of Mazovia, ruling over small fiefdoms in central Poland. The city's fortunes steadily improved in the 16th century after the duchy was incorporated into the Polish crown and Poland formed a union with Lithuania. The union greatly expanded the amount of territory under Polish influence. In 1596, King Sigismund III decided to move the capital to Warsaw from Kraków, mainly because it was easier for noblemen to travel to more centrally situated Warsaw. The subsequent centuries saw alternating periods of prosperity and disaster. The Swedes even sacked the city in the 17th century. But in spite of it all Warsaw continued to grow wealthier.

The Polish partitions at the end of the 18th century relegated Warsaw to the status of a provincial town for the next 125 years. Initially, the Prussians ruled over the city, but the Congress of Vienna, in 1815, placed tsarist Russia in control. Despite the occupation, Warsaw thrived in the 19th century as a western outpost of the Russian empire. Finally, in 1918, after Germany's defeat and Russia's collapse in World War I, Warsaw was reconstituted as the capital of newly independent Poland.

Things went reasonably well for a time until World War II, when the city—like the rest of the country—was plunged into a modern-day Dante's Inferno. The Nazis occupied Warsaw in 1939 and held it for nearly the entire course of the war. The occupation was brutal; thousands of Warsaw residents were imprisoned or killed. Initially, it was the Jews who bore the brunt. The Nazis herded the city's entire Jewish population of about 300,000, as well as around 100,000 Jews from elsewhere around Poland, into a small ghetto area west of the Old Town. Nearly all of them eventually lost their lives to sickness, starvation, or—mainly—the gas chambers at Treblinka. In 1943, the Jews heroically rose up against their oppressors in the first of two wartime Warsaw uprisings. The uprising was quickly put down and what remained of the ghetto was completely destroyed.

A year later, in 1944, with the war going badly for the Germans, the Polish resistance fighters, the Home Army, called for a general uprising against the German occupiers. For weeks in August and September of that year, Warsaw residents fought pitched battles with the Germans throughout the city, initially recording some heroic victories. Part of the plan was to enlist the assistance of the approaching Soviet Red Army, who had advanced to the Warsaw suburb of Praga across the river. That assistance never came, and the Germans eventually crushed the uprising. Hitler was so enraged that he ordered the remaining population expelled and the city razed to the ground. By the end of the war, 85% of Warsaw lay in ruins, and two out of every three residents—nearly 900,000 people—had died or were missing.

The postwar years were bleak ones. Poland was cut off by the Soviet Union from Marshall Plan aid. With so much of the city destroyed, the Soviet-inspired planners could start from scratch. They widened the avenues to the proportions you see today and filled them with drab Socialist-Realist–style offices and apartment blocks. To be fair, some of these buildings aren't so awful. The area around the Plac Konstytucji, in particular, has some handsome postwar buildings. And of course the unmissable Palace of Culture and Science is the granddaddy of them all. It's a strictly love-it-or-hate-it affair, with many city residents falling squarely into the latter camp.

One notable exception to the postwar reconstruction was the Old Town. It was completely leveled—save for one building—by the Germans. But instead of rebuilding the Old Town in a modern Socialist-Realist style, like the rest of the city, Warsaw planners chose to reconstruct it exactly how it was—brick for brick, building for building. It's a moving story of reclaiming identity from history, and the results are phenomenal.

Since the fall of Communism, the city's fortunes have improved immensely. Warsaw, as the capital city, has grabbed more than its share of the country's newfound wealth, and the city skyline is looking more and more like a Sunbelt boomtown every day. The changes are every bit as dramatic on the cultural front. New clubs, theaters, performance spaces, and restaurants have opened their doors, and the city feels more vital now than it has in many, many decades.

GETTING THERE

BY PLANE Warsaw's Okęcie airport (✆ **022/650-42-20;** www.lotnisko-chopina.pl), also called Frederyk Chopin Airport, is 10km (6¼ miles) from the center. The airport is in the midst of a massive rebuilding phase. For the moment most international flights still arrive at the old terminal, Terminal 1. Domestic flights arrive at and depart from a smaller domestic terminal downstairs and around the corner from the main terminal. Most of the tourist services, including tourist information, rental cars, and ATMs, are located in Terminal 1—but this is likely to change as the new buildings come on stream. To get to the center, take bus no. 175, which makes the run in about half an hour. Use bus no. 611 at night. Tickets cost 2.40zł ($1/60p) and can be purchased at news agents or at Ruch or Relay kiosks. Taxi fare to the center averages 40zł ($17/£11)—the exact fare depending on the destination. Be sure to choose only cabs that are clearly marked and refuse any offers of rides or assistance you may get while inside the terminal or just outside the door. These are likely to be rip-offs.

BY TRAIN Major international and domestic trains arrive at and depart from Warsaw's Central Station, Warszawa Centralna, Al. Jerozolimskie 54 (✆ **022/94-36;** online timetable: www.rozklad-pkp.pl), located in the heart of the city in Śródmieście (just across the street from the Marriott Hotel). Centralna is, to put it mildly, confusing. It's a vast 1970s concrete jungle, filled with underground passageways that seemingly go nowhere and misleadingly marked stairways that will have you coming and going (and getting nowhere at all). Once you get off the train, head upstairs to the main hall, which has a helpful tourist information office, as well as train information and ticketing windows. Centralna is well served by taxis, trams and buses; the only trick is finding which stairway to use to locate the tram going in the direction you want to travel.

BY BUS Most international and InterCity domestic buses arrive at Warsaw's West Bus Station, Dworzec Autobusowy Warszawa Zachodnia (© **0300/30-01-30;** www.pks.warszawa.pl). The station is located just outside the city center (Śródmieście), about 2km (1¼ mile) to the west of Centralna train station along Al. Jerozolimskie. To travel between the bus and train stations, use bus no. 405, 517, or 127. Tickets cost 2.40zł ($1/60p) and can be purchased at Ruch or Relay news agents. A taxi ride to a central destination will cost about 20zł ($8.70/£5.40).

BY CAR As Poland's capital city, all roads lead to Warsaw. You'll have no problem finding your way here. You may be surprised, though, by how long it takes and, once you're here, by the sheer volume of traffic. Once you've found your hotel, stow the car and use trams and taxis.

CITY LAYOUT

Warsaw is cut in two by the Vistula River (Wisła), but nearly all of the interesting things to see and do lie on the river's western side. The heart of the city, and where you'll find most of the hotels, restaurants, and nightlife, is the central district known as Śródmieście. With its huge avenues and acres of space between buildings, it's not particularly pedestrian-friendly. But trams scoot down the rails at an impressive speed and can whisk you around in a few minutes. The center of Śródmieście is the intersection of Aleje Jerozolimskie (Jerusalem Ave.) and Marszałkowska street. The Old Town (Stare Miasto) lies about 2km (1½ mile) to the north. The best way to find it on foot is to follow the street Nowy Świat, which intersects with Al. Jerozolimskie, and continue along the "Royal Route," Krakowskie Przedmieście, which brings you to the Royal Castle and the start of the Old Town. To the south of Jerozolimskie, along the Al. Ujazdowskie, beginning at Plac Trzech Krzyży, you'll find Warsaw's embassy district, and some of the city's swankiest shops, cafes, restaurants, and nightclubs. Farther to the south lies the enormous residential district of Mokotów, home to some half of the city's two million people. Across the Vistula from the Old Town is the up-and-coming industrial district of Praga. This area has long been one of the poorest in Warsaw, but has seen a revival of sorts, spurred by Praga's rock-bottom rents.

GETTING AROUND

ON FOOT Warsaw is a big city, so walking is only an option within specific areas, such as the Old Town or in Śródmieście. For longer distances, you'll want to use public transportation or taxis.

BY TRAM Trams trundle down Warsaw's enormous avenues regularly from about 5am to 11pm, and are the best means for covering large distances quickly and cheaply. Tickets costs 2.40zł ($1/60p), and you can buy them from Ruch or Relay kiosks around town or almost any place near a tram stop that sells newspapers and cigarettes (ask for *bilety,* or tickets). You may have a hard time finding a place to buy a ticket in the evening, so buy several during the day and stock up. You can also buy reasonably priced long-term tickets: for 1 day (7.20zł/$3.10/£1.95), 3 days (12zł/$5.20/£3.25), and 1 week (24zł/$10/£6.50).

Riding without a ticket is possible but risky. Fines start at 120zł ($52/£32) if you're caught. The tram network will look highly confusing at first. Before trying to decipher the system on your own, ask at your hotel reception for specific directions and tram numbers.

BY BUS Buses supplement the tram network and run pretty much the same hours and use the same ticketing system. The bus layout is even more confusing than the trams, so get specific directions to your destination and write the numbers down.

BY METRO Warsaw has a small subway (metro) system, but you'll probably never use it or see it. There's only one line and it connects the center of town to the residential area of Mokotów. Tickets are the same as for the buses and trams, and must be validated before boarding the train.

BY TAXI Taxis are a cheap and reliable way of getting from point A to point B. Expect to pay around 20zł ($8.70/£5.40) for in-town destinations and around 40zł ($17/£11) to get to the airport. Dishonest drivers have been a problem in the past, but the situation is improving. Nevertheless, use only clearly marked cabs, and always make sure the driver has switched on the meter.

BY BIKE Biking is not an option on Warsaw's heavily trafficked, dirty, and dangerous roads. Marked bikeways are few and far between.

VISITOR INFORMATION

The **Warsaw Tourist Office** maintains three conveniently located information centers that can help with general directions, provide maps, and advise on hotels and restaurants. The main office is located in the **Warszawa Centralna Train Station** (**© 022/94-31;** www.warsawtour.pl; May–Sept daily 8am–8pm, Oct–Apr daily 9am–6pm). Two other branches are located at **Frederyk Chopin Airport** and at **Krakowskie Przedmieście 39,** along the royal route to the Old Town. Another helpful office is the **Warsaw Centre of Tourist Information,** Zamkovy 1/3 (**© 022/635-18-81**), situated just at the entrance to the Old Town near the Royal Castle. They also have maps and brochures, and can help with things like getting concert tickets and renting a car.

Marzurkas Travel, Długa 8/14 (**© 022/389-41-83**), offers daily 3-hour sightseeing trips with pickups from all of the major hotels. The 140zł ($61/£38) fee per person is steep, but if you've only got a day, it's the best way to cover ground (given the fact that Warsaw is so large and spread out). The tour includes the Old Town and Jewish ghetto area, and finishes up with a rousing church organ concert (but no lunch!). **Warsaw City Tours,** Marszałkowska 140 (**© 022/826-71-00**), offers a similarly priced 3-hour coach tour, with departures in the morning and the afternoon. You can book either at your hotel concierge.

Warsaw is blessed with a number of English-language publications that have cultural listings, restaurant reviews, and general information. Look out particularly for the cheeky monthly *Warsaw Insider* (available at hotels and some restaurants) and comprehensive *Warsaw in Your Pocket,* published every 2 months.

WHERE TO STAY

Hotels here can be frightfully expensive. Warsaw is skewed toward high-end four- and five-star corporate palaces—a reflection of the fact that most visitors are here to make money, not spend it. Nearly all of these are grouped in the skyscraper zone of Śródmieście and offer similarly high standards. Try looking for deals on the Internet and booking in advance. Many hotels slash rates on weekends.

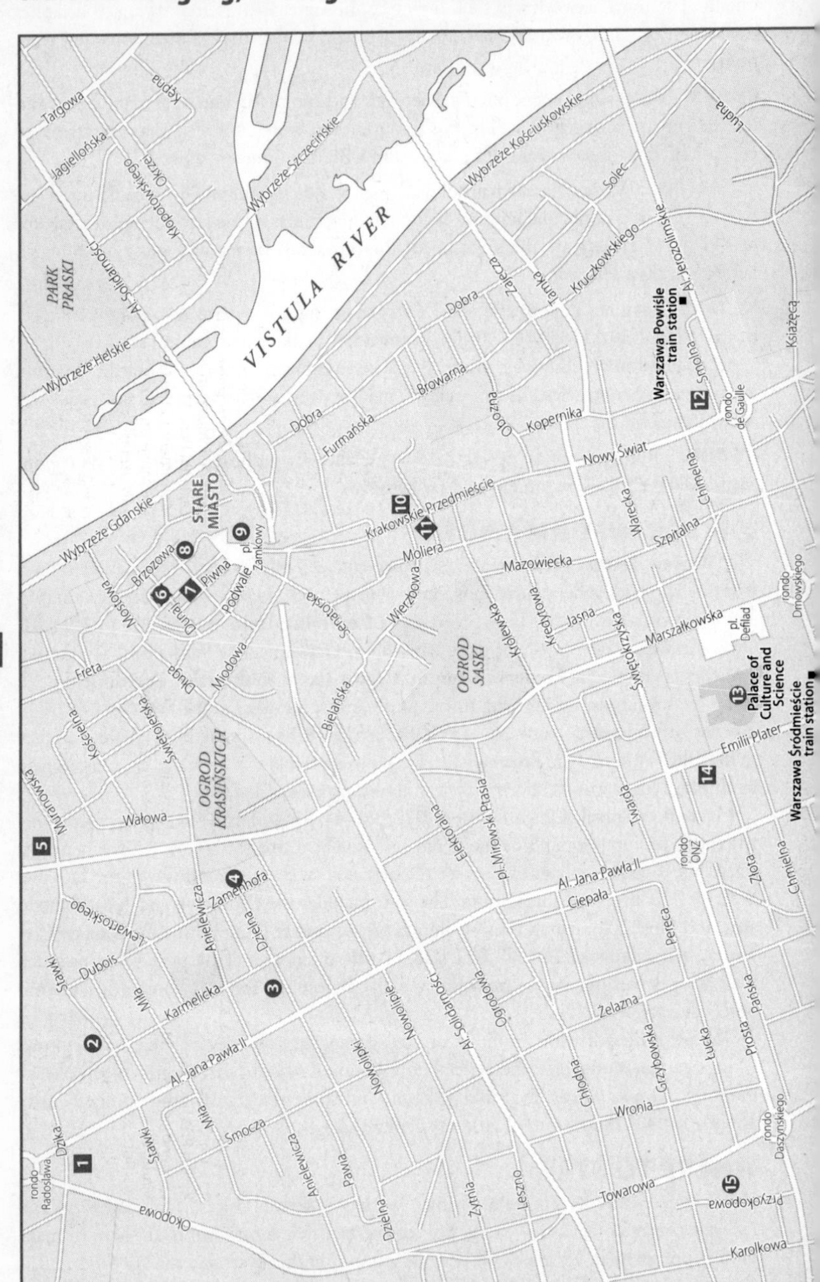
VISTULA RIVER
STARE MIASTO
PARK PRASKI
OGROD SASKI
OGROD KRASIŃSKICH
Palace of Culture and Science
Warszawa Powiśle train station
Warszawa Śródmieście train station
Wybrzeże Gdanskie
Wybrzeże Helskie
Wybrzeże Szczecińskie
Wybrzeże Kościuszkowskie
Al. Solidarności
Al. Jana Pawła II
Al. Jerozolimskie
Krakowskie Przedmieście
Nowy Świat
Marszałkowska
Świętokrzyska
Emilii Plater
Senatorska
Miodowa
Podwale
Piwna
Freta
Długa
Mostowa
Brzozowa
Dunaj
pl. Zamkowy
pl. Defilad
rondo ONZ
rondo de Gaulle
rondo Dmowskiego
rondo Daszyńskiego
rondo Radosława
Targowa
Jagiellońska
Okopowa
Towarowa
Karolkowa
Przyokopowa

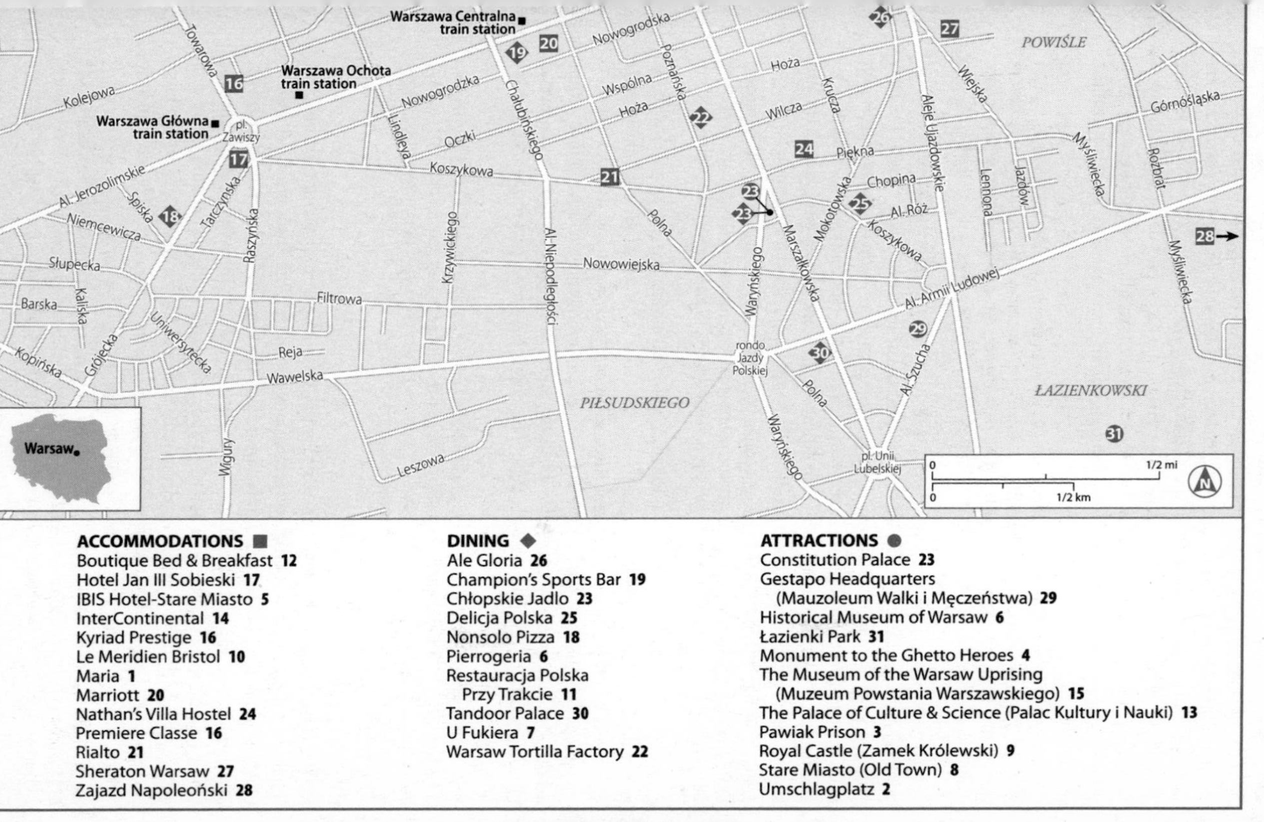
Warszawa Centralna train station
Warszawa Ochota train station
Warszawa Główna train station
pl. Zawiszy
Towarowa
Kolejowa
Nowogrodzka
Nowogrodzka
Poznańska
Wspólna
Hoża
Hoża
Wilcza
Krucza
Piękna
Aleje Ujazdowskie
Wiejska
POWIŚLE
Górnośląska
Rozbrat
Myśliwiecka
Myśliwiecka
Jazdów
Lennona
Chopina
Al. Róż
Koszykowa
Koszykowa
Mokotowska
Marszałkowska
Chałubińskiego
Lindleya
Oczki
Al. Jerozolimskie
Spiska
Niemcewicza
Tarczyńska
Raszyńska
Krzywickiego
Al. Niepodległości
Nowowiejska
Polna
Polna
Waryńskiego
Waryńskiego
Słupecka
Barska
Kaliska
Filtrowa
Uniwersytecka
Grójecka
Kopińska
Reja
Wawelska
Wigury
Leszowa
PIŁSUDSKIEGO
rondo Jazdy Polskiej
Al. Armii Ludowej
Al. Szucha
pl. Unii Lubelskiej
ŁAZIENKOWSKI
Warsaw
0
1/2 mi
0
1/2 km
N
ACCOMMODATIONS
Boutique Bed & Breakfast 12
Hotel Jan III Sobieski 17
IBIS Hotel-Stare Miasto 5
InterContinental 14
Kyriad Prestige 16
Le Meridien Bristol 10
Maria 1
Marriott 20
Nathan's Villa Hostel 24
Premiere Classe 16
Rialto 21
Sheraton Warsaw 27
Zajazd Napoleoński 28
DINING
Ale Gloria 26
Champion's Sports Bar 19
Chłopskie Jadlo 23
Delicja Polska 25
Nonsolo Pizza 18
Pierrogeria 6
Restauracja Polska Przy Trakcie 11
Tandoor Palace 30
U Fukiera 7
Warsaw Tortilla Factory 22
ATTRACTIONS
Constitution Palace 23
Gestapo Headquarters (Mauzoleum Walki i Męczeństwa) 29
Historical Museum of Warsaw 6
Łazienki Park 31
Monument to the Ghetto Heroes 4
The Museum of the Warsaw Uprising (Muzeum Powstania Warszawskiego) 15
The Palace of Culture & Science (Palac Kultury i Nauki) 13
Pawiak Prison 3
Royal Castle (Zamek Królewski) 9
Stare Miasto (Old Town) 8
Umschlagplatz 2

Very Expensive

LeMeridien Bristol ★ This is commonly regarded as Warsaw's nicest big hotel, and from the outside that may well be true. The sensitively restored Art Nouveau exterior and the period-piece details in the lobby and public areas are part of the city's architectural heritage. However, I'm not sure all the glitter rates prices that are at least $100 a night above the competition. Still, the location—right on the nicest part of the Royal Route—and the beautiful period details in the rooms and suites, offer compelling arguments for a stay here. Ask to check out several rooms before deciding, since each is furnished differently.

Krakowskie Przedmieście 42/44. ✆ **022/551-10-00.** www.lemeridien-bristol.com. 205 units. 1,000zł ($435/£270) double. AE, DC, MC, V. **Amenities:** 3 restaurants; swimming pool; health club; sauna; concierge; courtesy car; business center; salon; 24-hr. room service; dry cleaning; executive-level rooms; nonsmoking rooms. *In room:* A/C, TV, fax, dataport, minibar, coffeemaker, hair dryer, iron, safe.

Rialto ★★ High-style boutique hotel, with prices to match, for those who demand original Thonet chairs and William Morris furniture. The theme here is Art Deco, and each of the rooms has been meticulously designed, using a mix of authentic furnishings from that time and new creations. The rooms feature high-quality sound systems, DVD players, and flatscreen TVs. The hotel has a small fitness center and sauna, but guests have also access to the tony Sinnet racquet club for indoor tennis, squash, and swimming.

Wilcza 73. ✆ **022/584-87-00.** www.rialto.pl. 44 units. 700zł ($305/£189) double. AE, DC, MC, V. **Amenities:** Restaurant; fitness center; sauna; concierge; courtesy car; business center; 24-hr. room service; dry cleaning; executive-level rooms; nonsmoking rooms. *In room:* A/C, TV, dataport, minibar, hair dryer.

Sheraton Warsaw ★ This is a superb hotel from nearly any perspective, with an armload of amenities and an excellent location, just a short stroll from the trendy embassy district in one direction and the charms of Nowy Świat and the Old Town in the other. This Sheraton features the Tower Suites, an even more exclusive "hotel within a hotel." It's an excellent choice for business, since all the rooms come with several phones, dataports, and an extrawide desk. The fitness center too gets top marks (but no pool).

Ul. B. Prusa 2. ✆ **022/450-61-00.** Fax 022/450-62-00. www.sheraton.pl. 350 units. 600zł ($261/£162) double. AE, DC, MC, V. **Amenities:** 3 restaurants; state-of-the-art health club; sauna; concierge; courtesy car; business center; salon; 24-hr. room service; dry cleaning; executive-level rooms; nonsmoking rooms. *In room:* A/C, TV, fax, dataport, minibar, coffeemaker, hair dryer, iron, safe.

Expensive

Hotel Jan III Sobieski ★ This is a slightly cheaper version of the upscale business hotels, but still offering very high-quality accommodations. The lower prices are probably due to the hotel's location, slightly down from the heart of Śródmieście (but still an easy tram jaunt away). The hotel was one of the first luxury properties to open after the fall of Communism in 1989 and as such is showing its age a little. That said, the rooms are very nicely done in a muted contemporary look and soundproofed against the busy street below. The guest list includes Art Garfunkel, Carlos Santana, and Herbie Hancock (which shows they must be doing something right here).

Plac A. Zawiszy 1. ✆ **022/579-10-00.** Fax 022/659-88-28. www.sobieski.com.pl. 429 units. 560zł ($244/£151) double. AE, DC, MC, V. **Amenities:** 2 restaurants; health club and spa; concierge; business center; 24-hr. room service; dry cleaning; nonsmoking rooms. *In room:* A/C, TV, dataport, minibar, hair dryer.

InterContinental ★★★ The striking postmodern glass skyscraper is a nice addition to the Warsaw skyline, and the high style extends throughout the hotel, from the chic, muted lobby to the contemporary leathers and woods in the rooms. Just about everything you'd expect from the InterContinental chain; one advantage over the similarly appointed Sheraton is a two-story wellness center and pool on the 43rd and 44th floors (and the InterContinental is slightly cheaper to boot), though the room price does not include breakfast.

Ul. Emili Plater 49. ✆ **022/328-88-88.** Fax 022/328-88-89. www.intercontinental.com. 404 units. 520zł ($226/£140) double. AE, DC, MC, V. **Amenities:** 3 restaurants; swimming pool; health club; sauna; concierge; courtesy car; business center; salon; 24-hr. room service; dry cleaning; executive-level rooms; nonsmoking rooms. *In room:* A/C, TV, dataport, minibar, coffeemaker, hair dryer, iron, safe.

Marriott ★★ Of the big chains in town, this one offers arguably the best value. Maybe because the hotel has been established here the longest, since 1989, its rack rates are among the lowest of the four-star hotels. It is every bit as posh and comfortable as any of the others, and the hotel has worked hard in recent years to upgrade the rooms (and improve the bedding). Former guests include former U.S. President George W. Bush. For years, Warsaw residents have admired the hotel's rectangular skyscraper—like something out of the Dallas or Denver skyline—as a fitting capitalist foil to the Socialist-Realist wedding cake Palace of Culture just across the street.

Al. Jerozolimskie 65/79. ✆ **022/630-63-06.** Fax 022/830-03-11. www.marriott.com/wawpl. 518 units. 520zł ($226/£140) double. AE, DC, MC, V. **Amenities:** 3 restaurants; indoor pool; health club and spa; concierge; business center; 24-hr. room service; dry cleaning; nonsmoking rooms. *In room:* A/C, TV, dataport, minibar, coffeemaker, hair dryer, iron, safe.

Moderate

Boutique Bed & Breakfast ★ This unique B&B was the dream of a Polish expat living in Chicago who returned home after 1989. He wanted to create the best small hotel experience he could think of and has mostly succeeded. Each of the rooms is done up differently, but the emphasis is on high-quality traditional furniture and a decidedly homey ambience. The "Queen" and "King" apartments come with full kitchens and Internet access. Don't come expecting anonymity. The owner likes to take an interest in his guests and wax enthusiastically about his hometown. If you're looking for something more interactive than the standard hotel, this may be just right.

Smolna 14/7. ✆ **022/829-48-01.** Fax 022/829-48-02. www.bedandbreakfast.pl. 8 units. 350zł ($152/£94) double. AE, DC, MC, V. **Amenities:** Business center; nonsmoking rooms. *In room:* TV, kitchen (some rooms), fridge (some rooms), coffeemaker (some rooms), hair dryer.

IBIS Hotel-Stare Miasto ★★ Sometimes the IBIS hotel chain is a real lifesaver. The philosophy of a clean, modern, stripped-down business hotel at tourist rates is especially welcome in a city like Warsaw, where every other place seems to assume that the payroll department is footing the bill. The rooms and public areas are stark in keeping with the IBIS idea, but you won't find a nicer room at this price so close to the Old Town.

Muranowska 2. ✆ **022/310-10-00.** Fax 022/310-10-10. www.orbisonline.pl. 330 units. 279zł ($121/£75) double. AE, DC, MC, V. **Amenities:** Restaurant; nonsmoking rooms. *In room:* A/C, TV, dataport.

Kyriad Prestige ★★ This hotel is owned by the same chain as the Premiere Classe (see below), but the philosophy here is to offer top-end business services at moderate prices. Travelers accustomed to four-star luxuries can save substantial cash over the likes of the Sheraton and Marriott. The neighborhood is on the gray side, but a nearby tram can get you to the center in about 10 minutes. The rooms are large and comfortably furnished in contemporary styles. Excellent business services are offered, including several conference rooms, if you happen to be mixing business with pleasure.

 Towarowa 2. ✆ **022/582-75-00.** Fax 022/582-75-01. www.kyriadprestige.com.pl. 133 units. 359zł ($156/£97) double. AE, DC, MC, V. **Amenities:** Restaurant; spa; room service; nonsmoking rooms. *In room:* A/C, TV, dataport, minibar, hair dryer.

Maria ★ Arguably the best of the smaller, family-run hotels in town, the rooms at the Maria are on the austere side of modern, but several have hardwood floors and these tend to be smarter looking and more comfortable. The restaurant is light and cheerful, and the staff couldn't be more welcoming. The in-town location is convenient to the sights, especially to the former Jewish ghetto. The Old Town is about a 20-minute walk. The location, just off a major artery, is easy to get to if you're coming by car.

Jana Pawla II 71. ✆ **022/838-40-62.** Fax 022/838-38-40. www.hotelmaria.pl. 24 units. 350zł ($152/£94) double. AE, DC, MC, V. **Amenities:** Restaurant; nonsmoking rooms. *In room:* A/C, TV, dataport, minibar, hair dryer.

Zajazd Napoleoński There's been an inn on this site on the eastern side of the Vistula since at least the 18th century, when the location was ideal for the incoming carriage trade. The current building dates from the 19th century and is rich in period detail, including elegant crystal chandeliers and tiled flooring. One of the dining areas is done up in Biedermeier. The rooms can't match the style of the public areas but are large, with high ceilings and a solid feel. The location, a bit out of the action, helps to keep prices in check, yet the center is an easy tram ride away. A nice choice if you're looking for something other than an international chain and don't want to shell out for the Rialto.

Płowiecka 83. ✆ **022/815-30-68.** Fax 022/815-22-16. www.napoleon.waw.pl. 24 units. 330zł ($144/£89) double. AE, DC, MC, V. **Amenities:** Restaurant; concierge; courtesy car; business center; dry cleaning; nonsmoking rooms. *In room:* A/C, TV, dataport, minibar, hair dryer.

Inexpensive

Nathan's Villa Hostel ★★ Nathan's Villa shares the same owner and the same philosophy as the Nathan's hostel in Kraków. The idea is to combine some of the amenities of a decent hotel with the sociability of a hostel. Nathan is a likable American expat who wants to provide high standards at a fair price. Most of the clientele falls into the standard backpacker category, but the doors are open to all comers, young, old, and in-between. Several private doubles are on offer, so you don't have to sleep *en groupe.* Free laundry is one of several perks, and the central city location is ideal.

Piękna 24/26. ✆ **022/622-29-46.** Fax 022/622-29-46. www.nathansvilla.com. 19 units. 180zł ($78/£49) double. AE, DC, MC, V. **Amenities:** Laundry; nonsmoking rooms.

Premiere Classe ★★ (Value The theory behind this French hotel chain is to offer spotless, modern rooms with absolutely no frills at cut-rate prices. It's found a real niche in Warsaw, where decent, affordable rooms in the center are in short supply. The rooms themselves are microscopic—and I've seen Winnebagoes with bigger bathrooms—but they're very clean, cozy, and comfortable. Watch the add-on prices. Room rates do not include breakfast or parking.

Towarowa 2. ✆ **022/624-08-00.** Fax 022/620-26-29. www.premiereclasse.com.pl. 126 units. 189zł ($82/£51) double. AE, DC, MC, V. **Amenities:** Restaurant; nonsmoking rooms. *In room:* A/C, TV, Internet (wireless).

WHERE TO DINE

The dining scene is exploding—Warsaw is great for Polish food, and as a bustling city of two million, also good for just about any international cuisine you can think of. The best places tend to be in the central city, Śródmieście, especially south of Al. Jerozolimskie.

Dress is casual to neat-casual except in the more expensive places (where snappier dress is more appropriate, though rarely required).

Very Expensive

Ale Gloria ★★ POLISH Fusion food is catching on in Poland, but here it's defined a little differently. Instead of the usual "Asia meets the West" concept common in other places, in Poland it often means "traditional Polish food plus something wacky tossed in." For starters, try wild game pâté served with bitter orange sauce or stuffed carp in a raisin-wine gelatin. The mains are more down to earth, but still exhibit an occasional flight of fancy. One of the best is boar roulade served in a Bombay gin–and-honey sauce. The service is top-notch and the crowd is a mix of beautiful people and embassy types who can afford to dabble.

Plac Trzech Krzyży 3. ✆ **022/584-70-80.** Reservations recommended. Lunch and dinner items 60zł–80zł ($26–$35/£16–£22). AE, DC, MC, V. Daily noon–11pm.

U Fukiera ★ POLISH One of the fanciest meals in the city, served in an overwrought but undeniably intimate and romantic space on the Old Town's main square. Antique crystal, fresh flowers, and original art on the walls lend a special feel. The quality of the food is disputed. Some say it's the best in town, others that it's overrated (but still *quite* good). Not surprisingly for a traditional restaurant, the menu is heavy on game. For a different kind of starter try the white borscht with porcini mushrooms. The roast leg of venison in cream sauce won't disappoint. Dress up for this one.

Rynek Starego Miasta 27. ✆ **022/831-10-13.** Reservations recommended. Lunch and dinner items 50zł–90zł ($22–$40/£13–£25). AE, DC, MC, V. Daily noon–10pm.

Expensive

Delicja Polska ★★ POLISH Cozy, inviting space with excellent Polish food. The menu leans toward the traditional, but with the addition of something slightly unexpected. For a warm starter, try the pierogies stuffed with veal. Two of the best main course selections include the boar tenderloin with juniper sauce and beet root, and the veal cutlets marinated in bison grass. The intimate dining room makes it a destination choice for an evening meal. The easy-to-reach location is near Plac Konstytucji.

Koszykowa 54. ✆ **022/630-88-50.** Reservations recommended. Lunch and dinner items 30zł–60zł ($13–$26/£8.10–£16). AE, DC, MC, V. Daily noon–10pm.

Restauracja Polska Przy Trakcie ★★ POLISH Similar to but more traditional than Delicja Polska (see above), with an excellent location just off the Royal Route, midway between the Old Town and Al. Jerozolimskie and opposite the Le Meridien Bristol hotel. The specialty is roast pig, but the menu has a full range of Polish specialties. Casual enough for a quick lunch, but linens and candlelight at night make it a perfect splurge choice, too.

Krolewska 2. ✆ **022/827-01-98.** Reservations recommended. Lunch and dinner items 35zł–70zł ($15–$30/£9.45–£19). AE, DC, MC, V. Daily noon–10pm.

Tandoor Palace ★★ INDIAN One of the pleasures of a big city like Warsaw is the chance to branch out, culinarily speaking. This popular little place calls itself the "best Indian food in Poland," a claim of dubious merit (like boasting the "best burritos in Saskatchewan"). But no matter, the Indian food here is good. Try the yellow lentils with nan bread as a starter, followed by a spicy lamb curry. It's not cheap, though beloved by Warsaw's expats.

 Marszałkowska 21/25. ✆ **022/825-23-75.** Lunch and dinner items 27zł–60zł ($12–$26/£7.45–£16). AE, DC, MC, V. Daily noon–10pm.

Moderate

Champion's Sports Bar ★ AMERICAN Not unlike any other sports bar around the world, the big advantage here is location: smack dab in the center of town and right across the street from the train station—perfect if you've just come in from a long train ride and you're famished. Good burgers, salads, and bar-style food.

Al. Jerozolimskie 65/79. ✆ **022/630-51-19.** Lunch and dinner items 20zł–50zł ($8.70–$22/£5.40–£13). AE, DC, MC, V. Daily 11am–midnight.

Chłopskie Jadlo ★ POLISH I hesitated dropping this one in since it's a chain restaurant, but if you're dying to try decent Polish food and don't want to splash out lots of cash, this might be your best option. Chłopskie Jadlo has locations throughout the country. The idea is the same everywhere: good to very good traditional Polish food served with all the trimmings in a lively, informal, cottage-style atmosphere. It's a lot of fun, and the cost-value ratio may be the best in town.

Pl. Konstytucji 1. ✆ **022/339-17-17.** Lunch and dinner items 20zł–50zł ($8.70–$22/£5.40–£13). AE, DC, MC, V. Daily noon–11pm.

Inexpensive

Nonsolo Pizza ★★ ITALIAN This neighborhood Italian-run pizzeria has a traditional wood-fired oven and some of the city's best pizzas. The atmosphere is informal, and not a particularly great choice for a special night out, but it's fine for lunch or a quick meal. The pasta is great, too. It's especially convenient if you happen to be staying at the Sobieski, Premiere Classe, or Kyriad Prestige hotels (see "Where to Stay," above); it's an easy 5-minute walk from all of these along Al. Jerozolimskie heading away from the center.

Grojecka 20c. ✆ **022/824-12-73.** Lunch and dinner items 15zł–21zł ($6.50–$9.15/£4.05–£5.65). AE, DC, MC, V. Daily 10am–9pm.

Pierrogeria ★★ POLISH One of the most popular spots for pierogies, soups like *barszcz,* and other simple Polish dishes in the Old Town. Order your pierogies traditionally boiled or fried, and choose from a variety of sauces, including relative rarities like dill or garlic. The location makes it a great stop for an easy lunch while taking in the Old Town's sights—or a lunch choice after a morning bus tour.

Ul. Krzywe Kolo 30. ✆ **022/654-88-44.** Lunch and dinner items 15zł–20zł ($6.50–$8.50/£4.05–£5.25). MC, V. Daily noon–10pm.

Warsaw Tortilla Factory ★★ MEXICAN Very good, simple Tex-Mex offerings like burritos and fajitas—though they could be a little more generous with sides like salsa and sour cream! The atmosphere is casual, and the clientele is mostly young professionals and expats out for a fun night. Strong cocktails.

Wilcza 46. ✆ **022/621-86-22.** Lunch and dinner items 15zł–30zł ($6.50–$13/£4.05–£8.05). AE, DC, MC, V. Daily noon–10pm.

EXPLORING WARSAW

Warsaw is a large city, so plan your exploration in pieces at a time, moving between areas with trams or taxis. A good place to start a walking tour of the city is the **Old Town (Stare Miasto).** The beautiful baroque and Renaissance-style burghers' houses would be remarkable in their own right for their beauty and period detailing, but what makes these houses truly astounding is that they're only a few decades old. As one of the main centers of the 1944 Warsaw Uprising (see below), the Old Town bore the brunt of German reprisal attacks and the entire area, save for one building, was blown to bits at the end of 1944. After the war, to reclaim their heritage, the Polish people launched an enormous project to rebuild the Old Town exactly as it was, brick by brick. Many of the original architectural sketches were destroyed in the war, so the town was rebuilt from paintings, photographs, drawings, and people's memories. The reconstruction was so authentic that UNESCO in 1980 listed the Old Town as a World Heritage Site. Today, the Old Town is given over mostly to touts and tourists, but still rewards a couple of hours of strolling. Behind the old-world facades, the buildings themselves are modern apartment blocks. Spend a couple of hours walking here, taking in the central square, and the adjoining streets and alleyways. The **Royal Castle,** at the entrance to the Old Town, is also a replica, having been completed only in the 1980s. It's worth a stop to admire some rich period interiors and an excellent permanent art collection.

Continue your tour south along what's been known for centuries as Warsaw's Royal Route, following the now-swanky, cafe-lined streets of **Krakowskie Przedmieście** and **Nowy Świat.** As you walk, bear in the mind that these streets too saw intense fighting during World War II and were completely rebuilt from rubble after the war. Much of this area is dominated by Warsaw University, and the streets are often filled with students. By day, it's a great place to stroll and have a coffee; by night, you'll find plenty of clubs, bars, and restaurants.

Nowy Świat eventually empties into **Aleje Jerozolimskie (Jerusalem Ave.),** one of the main arteries of Warsaw's central city, **Śródmieście.** This is the heart of the city, and you'll find yourself spending a lot of time on this avenue, and the giant avenue that bisects it at the geographic center of Śródmieście, **Marszałkowska.** Heading west on Jerozolimskie, just beyond Marszałkowska, you can't miss the giant Stalinist wedding-cake **Palace of Culture and Science,** for years a symbol of the city's subjugation, firmly under the thumb of the Soviet Union. The 60-story structure was built in the 1950s as a "gift" (the kind you can't refuse) to the Polish people from Josef Stalin. What to do with the tower has bedeviled city planners since the fall of Communism in 1989. Suggestions have ranged from demolishing it to rehabbing it to its original purpose as a house of culture. The latter alternative appears to be winning out, and it looks as if the palace is here to stay. You can take an elevator to the 30th floor for some nice views of the city.

South of Jerozolimskie, following Marszałkowska, leads to a highly interesting complex of buildings built in the 1950s in an austere but still striking Socialist-Realist style. The most impressive—or hideous, depending on your taste in architecture—cluster of buildings lies on and around **Constitution Place (Plac Konstytucji).** Before the war, Marszałkowska was arguably the most fashionable avenue in Warsaw. It was totally destroyed by the Germans in reprisals for the Warsaw Uprising, and in the 1950s was widened and rebuilt in "Stalinist" style. Take a while to explore the area and the streets that branch off on both sides, noting the oversized reliefs of the proletariat heroes on the buildings. These days, this neighborhood is one of the trendiest in Warsaw and you'll see, sprouting here and there, hipster cafes and pubs that use the architecture in a newly ironic and humorous way.

Also south of Jerozolimskie, near the intersection with Nowy Świat, lies the city's most exclusive quarter and home to many government buildings, including the parliament (Sejm) and foreign embassies. It's also the preferred neighborhood for exclusive boutiques and fashion houses. Find **Three Crosses Square (Plac Trzech Krzyży)** and then follow the main boutique shopping street of **Mokotowska.** Make a note to come back here during the evening, when the street-side cafes start filling with life. A little farther on you'll find the city's favorite park for a stroll: **Łazienki Park.** The park is filled with little treasures, including a lake, lots of nice footpaths, and an overblown Art Deco statue honoring Poland's most famous composer, Frederyk Chopin (cultural aside: Chopin was born in Poland to a French father and a Polish mother). On Sundays in nice weather you'll find a regular Chopin-in-the-park concert; the music starts around noon. You'll also find here the very fine neoclassical summer palace of Poland's last king, Stanisław August Poniatowski.

You'll find the former **Jewish Ghetto** north of the city center, just to the west of the Old Town. Most of the ghetto, which in the early years of World War II held some 380,000 Jews, was destroyed in the war, and walking around today you'll find few clues to its former role. There are plans to build a Jewish cultural center and museum here, but those are still some years away. For now, the main sights are an evocative **Monument to the Ghetto Heroes** (ul. Zamenhofe), which recalls the heroic Jewish uprising in 1943, and a concrete-bunker-type memorial at the **"Umschlagplatz"** (ul. Stawki near the corner with ul. Dzika), the place where Jews were rounded up for train transports to the Treblinka extermination camp in the east of the country.

As in Kraków, Łódź, and other Polish cities, the tragedy of the Jews here is one of the most poignant stories of the war. Here in Warsaw, the Germans first started rounding up the city's enormous Jewish population in 1940. The ghetto's population swelled to nearly 400,000 people (the exact figure is not known) and conditions were appalling. An elaborate system of gates and staircases was built to allow Jews inside to move within the ghetto, but no one was permitted to enter or leave. The mass deportations and killings began in 1942. The Jews rebelled in April 1943 as news of the gas chambers reached the ghetto and residents realized they had no choice but to fight. The heroic rebellion, the "first" Warsaw uprising, not to be confused with the general Warsaw uprising a year later, was brutally put down by the Germans. The ghetto was liquidated shortly thereafter, and what remained was destroyed in the general uprising the next year. Nearly all of the city's Jews were killed in the uprising or the extermination camps, and today only around 2,000 Jews remain in Warsaw. Roman Polański's Oscar-winning film, *The Pianist,* recounts the story of the ghetto through the eyes of Władysław Szpilman, an accomplished piano player and one of the ghetto's best-known residents. Szpilman eventually escaped during a transport to the concentration camp and survived the war. He even returned to live out his life in Warsaw.

In addition to the major sights listed below, there are smaller museums to suit every interest, including, among others, one dedicated to Polish Romantic poet Adam Mickiewicz, Rynek Starego Miasta 20 (✆ **022/831-76-91**); to composer Frederyk Chopin, Okólnik 1 (✆ **022/827-54-73**); and to the horrific Katyń massacre in which an entire generation of Polish army officers—some 20,000 in all—was shot and killed by the Soviet Red Army in the Katyń woods, at ul. Powsińska 13 (✆ **022/842-66-11**).

Gestapo Headquarters (Mauzoleum Walki i Męczeństwa) ★★ Currently housing the Ministry of Education, from 1939 to 1945 this was the one place in town you absolutely didn't want to be summoned to for questioning. A small museum in the building's lower reaches shows the cells and interrogation rooms nearly untouched from how they were at the end of the war. The displays paint a vivid picture of the torture and killing that went on here—and the lengths to which the Nazis went to break the back of the Polish opposition.

Szucha 25. ✆ **022/629-49-19.** Free admission. Wed–Sun 10am–4pm.

Historical Museum of Warsaw ★★ A fascinating tour through the capital's ups and downs through the centuries. The exhibits paint an amazing contrast between the richness of the city up until World War II and the often-starker reality you see today. There are good displays on the Warsaw Uprising (though not as thorough as at the Warsaw Uprising museum). A moving film (English showings at noon) documents the destruction of the city during the war.

Rynek Starego Miasta 28/42. ✆ **022/635-16-25.** www.mhw.pl. Admission 6zł ($2.60/£1.60). Tues and Thurs 11am–6pm; Wed and Fri 10:30am–3:30pm; Sat–Sun 10:30am–4:30pm.

The Museum of the Warsaw Uprising (Muzeum Powstania Warszawskiego) ★★★ This relatively new museum, with its hands-on exhibits and high-tech imagery, has emerged as one of Warsaw's main tourist attractions. The museum, housed in a former transformer station for the trams, is a large and confusing space to navigate once inside. Try to follow the arrows on the suggested route, but don't despair if you find yourself ambling from one display case to another. Everyone else is doing the same.

A little history will help you to get your bearings. On August 1, 1944, at precisely 5pm, the commanders of the Polish insurgent Home Army, loyal to Poland's government-in-exile in London, called for a general uprising throughout the Nazi-occupied city. The Germans, at the time, were in retreat on all sides, having suffered reversals on the Western front, in France and Italy, and in the east, at the hands of the Soviet Red Army. By the end of July that year, the Red Army had moved to within the city limits of Warsaw and was camped on the eastern bank of the Vistula in the suburb of Praga. With the combined forces of the Home Army and the Red Army, it seemed the right moment to drive the Germans out and liberate Warsaw. Alas, it was not to be. The first few happy days of the uprising saw the Polish insurgents capture pockets of the city, including the Old Town and adjacent suburbs. But the Germans resisted fiercely, and the Red Army, for reasons that are not entirely clear to this day, never stepped in to help. The resistance lasted several weeks before Polish commanders were forced to capitulate in the face of rapidly escalating civilian casualties. Thousands of Warsaw residents died in the fighting and the subsequent reprisal attacks by German forces. The uprising so infuriated Hitler that he ordered the complete annihilation of the city. In the weeks following the uprising, Warsaw's buildings were listed in terms of their cultural significance and dynamited one by one. Some 85% of the city was eventually destroyed. As for the Russians, the accepted theory is that they viewed the Polish Home Army as a potential enemy and preferred simply to watch the Germans and Poles kill each other. To this day, many Poles have never forgiven the Russians for this decision.

The museum charts the full course of the uprising starting from the German invasion in 1939, through life in occupied Warsaw, and the events of 1944 and their aftermath. Don't miss the harrowing documentary films shown on the upper floors, with English subtitles, that tell the story from the inside. They were made by Polish journalists during the occupation and were shown in Warsaw cinemas while the fighting was going on.

Grzybowska 79. ✆ **022/539-79-33.** Mon, Wed, and Fri 8am–6pm; Thurs 8am–8pm; Sat–Sun 10am–6pm. Admission 4zł ($1.75/£1.10), free Sun.

The Palace of Culture and Science (Palac Kultury i Nauki) ★ Warsaw's landmark tower is a building many residents would like to see knocked down. The 1950s Socialist-Realist wedding cake was originally a gift from former Soviet leader Josef Stalin, but the symbolic intention was clear from the start. Stalin was marking his turf, and Poland was part of the Eastern bloc. Today, with Poland firmly within the European

Union and the Soviet Union a distant nightmare, public attitudes toward the "palace" have softened somewhat. What used to look tragic now looks undeniably comic, and it seems the building will continue in its role as a cultural venue for some time to come. You can ride to the top—30 stories—for a fine view over the city (but let's be honest here, 30 stories is not really that dramatic). The humdrum interior is also a bit of a disappointment. Save yourself the admission and, instead, admire the amazing exterior for free. You won't be able to take your eyes off of it.

Pl Defilad 1. ✆ **022/656-76-00.** www.pkin.pl. Daily 9am–8pm. Admission 20zł ($8.70/£5.40), reduced for groups of 10 or more.

Pawiak Prison ★★ Another frightening reminder of the horrific times of World War II. Something like 100,000 prisoners passed through the gates here during the nearly years of the Nazi occupation, when the prison was run by the Gestapo. Among the prisoners were political activists, members of the clergy, university professors, or simply anyone who could be suspected of opposing the Germans. Very few of the people imprisoned here got out alive. Most were sent to extermination camps, while around 40,000 people were actually executed on the grounds.

Dzielna 24/26. ✆ **022/831-92-89.** Free admission. Wed–Sun 10am–4pm.

Royal Castle (Zamek Królewski) ★★ The original residence of Polish kings and dating from the 14th and later the seat of the Polish parliament, the castle was completely destroyed in the Warsaw uprising and its aftermath. What you see today is a painstaking reconstruction that was finished only in 1984. Two tours are offered: "Route I" and "Route II." Of the two, the second is more interesting, passing through the regal apartments of Poland's last monarch, King Stanisław August Poniatowski, and to the Canaletto room, where the famed cityscapes of Warsaw by the Italian painter Bernardo Bellotto hang. These paintings, and others not on display, were of extreme value in rebuilding the Old Town from scratch after the war. The tour ends in the lavish ballroom, the largest room in the castle.

Pl. Zamkovy 4. ✆ **022/657-21-70.** www.zamek-krolewski.pl. Tues–Sat 10am–4pm; Sun 11am–4pm. Route 1 10zł ($4.35/£2.70), Route II 18 zl ($7.80/£4.85), Sun free admission.

Outside of Warsaw

Wilanów Palace ★★ Poles are rightfully proud of this baroque-era palace built to honor King Jan Sobieski. If you've seen Versailles near Paris or Schoenbruenn in Vienna, you'll get the idea immediately: Size matters. This enormous building has no less than 60 rooms, most stuffed with royal memorabilia and portraits of Polish monarchs and heavyweights—though some rooms, like the Etruscan Room, display oddities such as vases dating from the 4th century B.C. The garden surrounding the palace is a delight and well worth a walk around. The palace can be seen only with a guided tour. Take the hourly Polish tour if you're not particularly interested in all the details of all of the portraits; otherwise try to book an English tour in advance by calling the number below, or once there try to latch onto any English-speaking group you happen to see. To get there, take bus no. 116 from ul. Ujazdowskie. A taxi will cost about 40zł ($17/£11).

Ul. Stanisława Kostki Potockiego 10/16. ✆ **022/842-07-95** or e-mail rezerwacja@wilanow-palac.pl (to arrange tours). www.wilanow-palac.art.pl. Admission to the palace (with guided tour) 23zł ($10/£6.20); park 5zł ($2.20£1.35); free admission to the palace Sun, free admission to the park Thurs. May to mid-Sept Mon, Wed, and Sat 9:30am–6:30pm, Tues and Thurs–Fri 9:30am–4:30pm, Sun 10:30am–6:30pm; mid-Sept to Apr Mon, Wed–Sat 9:30am–4:30pm, Sun 10:30am–4:30pm.

SHOPPING

Not so long ago the idea of a shopping trip to Warsaw would have drawn laughs, with images of standing in line for bananas and knockoff jeans. But these days Warsaw can hold its own with any European capital, East or West, for food, fashion, or whatever you've got in mind. For clothing, most of the big international retail chains are clustered in **Śródmieście**—look especially along **Al. Jerozolimskie** and **Marszałkowska.** South of Jerozolimskie, especially in the area around the **Plac Trzech Krzyży,** you'll find the best of boutique shopping, with local Polish designers rubbing elbows with the likes of Escada and Hugo Boss. Trailing south from the Plac Trzech Krzyży you'll find the übertrendiest of Warsaw shopping streets, **Mokotowska,** with its low-rise mix of international boutiques, fashionable home-furnishing stores, and here and there still the occasional Polish deli or bakery. Mokotowska is currently home to the local branch of names like Commes des Garcons and Burberry, but check out also Polish shops and designers like Odzieżowe Pole, Mokotowska 51/53, and Finezja Studio, Mokotowska 63.

For more everyday shopping and particularly for picking up anything you might have forgotten at home, try the **Arkadia** mall, Ul. Jana Pawla II (✆ **022/331-34-00;** www.arkadia.com.pl), hailed locally as the biggest indoor shopping center in central Europe. You'll encounter hundreds of stores, with everything from high- and low-end fashions, home electronics, furnishings, and food. You're not likely to find many surprises, but the sheer scale of the place will shock. The mall also has a 15-cinema multiplex with a good bet to have several films in English.

For English-language books, try looking at **American Bookstore,** with a couple of central locations, at Koszykowa 55 and Nowy Świat 61 (✆ **022/234-56-37;** www.americanbookstore.pl). This place stocks a nice selection of Polish authors in translation, as well as books about the Holocaust, World War II, Solidarity, the fall of Communism, and other interesting topics.

For cheaper Polish-made products and low-cost souvenirs, try **Cepelia,** Marszałkowska 99/101 (✆ **022/628-77-57**), the local branch of a national group selling folk art, traditional fabrics, leather goods, ceramics, and woodworking. It's a nice place for a "Made in Poland" gift, though you may have to pick through some obviously touristy dross.

WARSAW AFTER DARK

Warsaw is a great after-dark town. The city's opera and classical music offerings are some of the best in the country, and the availability of relatively cheap tickets means the performances are accessible to just about anyone. The main opera venue is the **Teatr Wielki-Opera Narodowa,** Plac Teatralny 1 (✆ **022/826-32-88;** www.teatrwielki.pl). Here you'll find everything from the Italian classics to occasionally bolder works featuring Polish avant-garde composers. The theater box office is open Monday to Saturday 9am to 7pm, Sunday 10am to 7pm. For classical music, the first address is the **Filharmonia Narodowa,** the home of the National Philharmonic, Jasna 5 (✆ **022/551-71-49;** www.filharmonia.pl; tickets: bilety@filharmonia.pl). The box office is located at Sienkiewicza 10 and is open Monday to Saturday 10am to 2pm and 3 to 7pm. Try timing your arrival just before showtime to get cheaper last-minutes tickets.

There's no shortage of cafes, bars, and dance clubs. For cafes and little cocktail bars, try the strip along Krakowskie Przedmieście, Nowy Świat, and south of Al. Jerozolimskie to the area around Plac Trzech Krzyży. For clubs, most of the action is still in the central city, Śródmieście, though some of the trendier places are pioneering areas farther afield, like the still-somewhat-dingy (but getting cooler) suburb of Praga.

The Cinnamon Stylish, high-powered restaurant/disco/dance club, complete with velvet ropes and monkeys guarding the door. Draws a well-dressed, good-looking crowd, from 20s to 40s, with thick wallets (for him) and slinky dresses (for her). The party doesn't usually get rolling until after midnight. Plac Piłsudskiego 1. ✆ **022/323-76-00.**

Foksal 19 A truly beautiful cocktail bar with drinking the main pursuit on the main level and a *Boogie Nights*-inspired dance club upstairs. Similar in vibe and clientele to the Cinnamon, but the music is more interesting—not just the standard Ibiza dance tunes, but eclectic house and funk. Foksal 19. ✆ **0602/76-27-64.** www.foksal19.com.

Jazz HotL Part swanky restaurant and part funky jazz club, with a growing repertoire of good shows and a great location between Old Town and the central city. Decent choice for a low-key but enjoyable evening of music and conversation. Look for jazz on the weekends. Krakowskie Przedmieście 13. ✆ **022/826-74-66.** www.jazzhotl.pl.

Melodia A former swanky haunt in Communist times, it's now a dark-wood, upscale bar and restaurant, popular with the business crowd. Decent food and occasional jazz and other live performances. Good spot for a quiet drink. Nowy Świat 3/5. ✆ **022/583-01-80.** www.klubmelodia.pl.

Opium Pleasure Lounge A popular chill-out bar and music club, with a vaguely Middle Eastern, Persian theme. Popular with the beautiful crowd, and it doesn't really get going until very late. Open Wednesday through Saturday until 4am. Wierzbowa 9/11. ✆ **022/827-71-61.** www.opiumclub.pl.

Sheesha Bar Yet another late-night drinking spot offering those ubiquitous hookahs, and with a strong Middle Eastern, North African theme. Popular with students, and a nice spot to relax and converse. Sienkiewicza 3. ✆ **022/828-25-25.** www.sheesha.pl.

4 ŁÓDŹ

110km (65 miles) SW of Warsaw

Pronounced "woodge," Poland's second-largest city has traditionally been called the "Manchester of Poland," a reference to its rise in the 19th century as an industrial powerhouse, and to the vast textile mills here that employed tens of thousands of workers at the turn of the 20th century. For Americans, the hulking relics and depressed housing stock of a bygone industrial era will bring to mind the inner cities of Detroit, Buffalo, and Cleveland. Still, there's an energy and vitality here that many Polish cities lack, and if you're passing by, Łódź certainly merits a day of exploration. The city can be visited as a long day trip from Warsaw, but it's better approached as a destination in its own right. The prospect of some excellent restaurants and a couple of nice hotels sweetens the deal.

Łódź is relatively young as Polish cities go. It only came into its own in the 19th century, when German and later Jewish industrialists built large textile mills to exploit access to the vast Russian and Chinese markets to the east. Unlike Kraków or Wrocław, you'll search in vain here for a large market square, a Rynek, surrounded by gabled baroque and Renaissance houses. Instead, you'll find—amid the tenements and badly neglected housing stock—fine examples of the sumptuous neo-baroque and neoclassical mansions and town palaces favored by the wealthy 19th-century bourgeoisie.

By the start of the 20th century Łódź had grown from a village just a few decades earlier to a city of more than 300,000 people, and its factories, mansions, and civic institutions were among the finest in the country. It was a magnet for poor Poles from around the country, but above all it attracted Jews, drawn here by the relatively tolerant social climate and economic opportunity. At its height, the Jewish community numbered some 230,000 people, around a third of the city's immediate pre–World War II population.

But if the city's economic rise was rapid, its decline was precipitous as well. At the end of World War I, with the establishment of independent Poland, the city lost its privileged access to the Russian and Far Eastern markets. World War II, and the Nazi occupation, was an unmitigated disaster. While many of the buildings survived the war intact, nearly the entire Jewish population was wiped out—first herded into a massive ghetto north of the city center, and then shipped off train by train to the death camps at Chełmno and Auschwitz-Birkenau. For decades after the war, the story of the "Litzmannstadt" ghetto, as it was known at the time, was little known outside of Poland. Now, Jewish groups from around the world are getting the word out. You can tour much of the former ghetto as well as visit the Jewish cemetery, the largest of its kind in Europe.

The Communist period brought more ruin to the city. The once-profitable mills were run into the ground by inept state ownership. The city was blighted by some of the most insensitive Communist-era planning to ever come off the drawing board. The period since 1989 has seen a massive effort to transform the bleak postindustrial cityscape into a lively cultural center. And that effort is partially succeeding. The heart of the transformation is the city's main drag, Piotrkowska, a nearly 4km-long (2½-mile) pedestrianized strip, lined with restaurants, cafes, bars, clubs, and shops. By day, it's a place to stroll, window-shop, and take an open-air coffee. By night, it's arguably Poland's most intense street party, filled with raucous revelers swilling beer from cans as club music blares from behind nearly every door. Just to the north of the city center, the huge complex of former textile mills has now been transformed into Europe's biggest shopping and entertainment complex, Manufaktura.

Łódź also boasts one of Poland's best museums of modern art, and a clutch of other interesting museums, many housed in the mansions of the old industrial elite. For fans of international film, Łódź is home to the Poland's most highly regarded film school and the country's only Museum of Cinematography. Legendary Polish film directors Andrzej Wajda, Krzysztof Kieslowski, and Roman Polański, among others, all learned their craft here.

ESSENTIALS

GETTING THERE Łódź lies at the geographic center of modern Poland and is well served by roads, trains, and buses from around the country. Most trains arrive and depart from the main station, Fabryczna, at Pl. Salacińskiego 1 (✆ **042/94-36;** www.pkp.pl). Fabryczna is a 10-minute walk from the center of town. A taxi to the center will cost 10zł ($4.35/£2.70). Some trains also arrive at and depart from suburban Kaliska station, Ul. Unii Lubelskiej 3/5 (✆ **042/94-36**), or Widzew station, Słożbowa 8 (✆ **042/94-36**), so be sure to check your ticket. The main bus station, Pl. Salacińskiego 1 (✆ **042/631-97-06;** www.pks.lodz.pl), is situated just behind Fabryczna train station. This is also where Polski Express buses arrive. Several budget air carriers now fly to Łódź from various cities in the U.K. and continental Europe. Łódź's Władisław Reymont Airport, Gen. Stanisława Maczka 35 (✆ **042/688-84-14;** www.airport.lodz.pl), is a 10- to 15-minute drive southwest of the center. On arriving, take bus no. 55 to get to the main street Piotrkowska. A 30-minute bus ticket costs 2.40zł ($1.05/65p). A taxi into town will run about 30zł ($13/£8.10).

VISITOR INFORMATION The city of Łódź Tourist Information Center, Piotrkowska 87 (✆ **042/638-59-55;** www.cityoflodz.pl), is one-stop shopping for all you'll ever need to know. Here you'll find two helpful pamphlets for negotiating the city: *Łódź Tourist Attractions* and the *Łódź City Guide,* as well as the essential *Jewish Landmarks in Łódź.* The latter includes a (long) self-guided walking tour of the Łódź (Litzmannstadt) ghetto. The staff maintains a complete list of hotels and can help arrange transportation and restaurant reservations.

GETTING AROUND Łódź has an excellent public transportation system of buses and trams. Tickets cost 2.40zł ($1.05/65p) for a standard 30-minute trip and are available from news agents. There are no trams or buses, though, running down the main drag Piotrkowska, leaving walking (about 45 min. end to end at a brisk pace) or pedicabs as the only options for getting around. The pedicab rate is about 6zł ($2.60/£1.40). Łódź is flat as a board and perfect for cycling, but rentals can be hard to find. Ask at the Tourist Information Center. To reach the Jewish Cemetery and the Radegast station, take tram no. 1 or no. 6 to the end, or hail a cab. The taxi ride will cost about 15zł ($6.50/£4.05).

WHERE TO STAY

The better places are all clustered around the center at Piotrkowska, but the area can get noisy at night. Ask for a room away from the main street. Rates are generally high for what's offered, but many hotels offer steep discounts on weekends.

Campanile ★★★ Campanile is part of a French chain that aims for the high middle market and delivers with well-designed, clean, stylish rooms and a professional, hospitable staff. Similar to the IBIS down the street, but a step up in quality. Good location, just a couple of tram stops from Piotrkowska (or a 15-min. walk). Decent on-site restaurant. Excellent breakfast buffet (though it is not included in the room price).

Piłsudskiego 11. ✆ **042/664-26-00.** Fax 042/664-26-01. www.campanile.com. 104 units. Mon–Thurs 270zł ($117/£73) double; Fri–Sun 175zł ($76/£47) double. AE, DC, MC, V. **Amenities:** Restaurant; limited room service; nonsmoking rooms. *In room:* A/C, TV, dataport, minibar, hair dryer.

Grand Hotel ★ A faded turn-of-the-20th-century grande dame of a hotel that has fallen into benign neglect under the management of the former state-owned Orbis hotel chain. If you love those period Art Nouveau details, wide sweeping corridors, and generously sized rooms with high ceilings—and don't mind antiquated plumbing, indifferent service, and an inedible breakfast—then this is your place. The location is right at the heart of the pedestrian zone.

Piotrkowska 72. ✆ **042/633-99-20.** Fax 042/633-78-76. www.orbis.pl. 161 units. 360zł ($157/£97) double. AE, DC, MC, V. **Amenities:** Restaurant; limited room service; nonsmoking rooms. *In room:* TV, dataport, minibar, hair dryer.

Hotel Savoy ★ This likeably run-down turn-of-the-20th-century hotel is just down the street from the similar but more expensive Grand Hotel. The Savoy feels smaller than the Grand and more intimate, though it's plainer. Many of the older period elements have been stripped away through wars and countless, often thoughtless, renovations. Ask to see several rooms, since they all differ slightly in furnishings. Some are jewels of the schlock 1960s and 1970s, while others try to re-create a 1920s feel. Choose your mood. Ask for a room away from the deceptively quiet-looking courtyard. At 6am, it becomes a veritable beehive of heavy construction work. For fans of Austrian writer Josef Roth, this is the Hotel Savoy of Roth's novel of the same name.

Traugutta 6. ✆ **042/632-93-60.** Fax 042/632-93-68. www.hotelsavoy.com.pl. 70 units. 250zł ($109/£67) double. AE, DC, MC, V. **Amenities:** Restaurant; limited room service; nonsmoking rooms. *In room:* Some A/C, TV, hair dryer.

IBIS ★★ Similar to the Campanile and a good option whether you're here for business or pleasure. The hotel offers relatively rare local amenities like full conference facilities, Internet access, and a dedicated business center. It's also a good choice in midsummer, since it's one of a handful of hotels in town to offer in-room air-conditioning. Big weekend discounts.

Piłsudskiego 11. ✆ **042/638-67-00.** Fax 042/638-67-77. www.ibishotel.com. 208 units. Mon–Thurs 270zł ($117/£73) double; Fri–Sun 175zł ($76/£47) double. AE, DC, MC, V. **Amenities:** Restaurant; limited room service; nonsmoking rooms. *In room:* A/C, TV, dataport, minibar, hair dryer.

WHERE TO DINE

You'll find most of the restaurants, including all of the big Polish chains like Rooster, Sphinx, and Sioux, grouped along Piotrkowska. Skip the chains and try one of the special places listed below.

Anatewka ★★ JEWISH Fun, informal Jewish-themed restaurant; the kind of place where the chef comes out halfway through the meal to pour you a shot of kosher vodka on the house. The two tiny, crowded dining rooms feel more like the parlor of a Jewish aunt, with overstuffed chairs and walls crammed with Jewish bric-a-brac. A fiddler, while not quite on the roof, plays nightly from a little perch just below the ceiling. The food is very good. The signature Duck Rubenstein comes served in a tart sauce of cherries, seasoned with clove.

Ul. 6 Sierpnia 2/4. ✆ **042/630-36-35.** Lunch and dinner items 18zł–40zł ($7.85–$17/£4.85–£11). AE, DC, MC, V. Daily noon–11pm.

Ciągoty i Tęsknoty ★★★ *Finds* INTERNATIONAL Don't despair as the taxi heads out of town, past row after row of falling-down, Socialist-era housing projects. You're headed toward one of the best meals in Łódź, and one of the city's best-kept dining secrets. Perched between two ghastly apartment blocks is a little oasis of '50s jazz and fresh flowers. The menu is perched somewhere between home cooking and haute cuisine, with salads, pierogies, pasta dishes, and some seriously good mains centered on pork, chicken, and boiled beef. The tagliatelle with brie and fresh tomatoes is a creative vegetarian option. It's about 3km (2 miles) from the center of town, so a taxi (15zł/$6.50/£4.05) each way is the sanest option.

Wojska Polskiego 144a. ✆ **042/650-87-94.** Lunch and dinner items 24zł–40zł ($10–$17/£6.50–£11). AE, DC, MC, V. Mon–Fri noon–10pm; Sat–Sun 1–10pm.

Ganesh ★★ INDIAN I love Polish food, but sometimes you need a change of pace. This is excellent Indian cuisine, prepared informally in an open kitchen. The restaurant is small, so you might want to book ahead. Contains the usual mix of curry and tandoori dishes, with fresh nan bread and delicious *lassi* drinks. Tell the server if you'd like your food extra spicy or else it will come out on the bland side.

Piotrkowska 69 (in the passageway). ✆ **042/632-23-20.** Lunch and dinner items 15zł–30zł ($6.50–$13/£4.05–£8.05). No credit cards. Daily noon–10pm.

Presto ★ ITALIAN Much better than average pizzeria, serving doughy pies topped with a slightly sweetish red sauce and cooked in a traditional wood-fired oven. The menu includes the usual suspects, but pizza San Francisco breaks new ground with bananas, pineapples, and curry sauce. A more reliable choice might be Sparare, with bacon, mushrooms, and onions. Also offers a good range of salads and pasta dishes. Popular on Friday and Saturday nights because of its location in a little passageway just off of Łódź's main pedestrian walk. Service can be slow, so plan on a long evening.

Piotrkowska 67 (in the passageway). ✆ **042/630-88-83.** Lunch and dinner items 12zł–21zł ($5.25–$9.15/£3.25–£5.65). No credit cards. Daily noon–10pm.

Varoska ★ HUNGARIAN What could be better than having a traditional Hungarian *poerkoelt* (a thick stew) or a chicken paprika smack dab in the geographic center of Poland? If your taste buds need awakening after all of those pierogies, bite into one of those little red peppers that accompany every dish. The Hungarian potato pancake is a great and filling mix of pork goulash, sour cream, and snips of red pepper wrapped up in a fresh-baked potato pancake. The service is friendly, and the atmosphere somewhere between homey and intimate.

Traugutta 4. ✆ **042/632-45-46.** Lunch and dinner items 18zł–30zł ($7.85–$13/£4.85–£8.05). No credit cards. Daily noon–10pm.

EXPLORING ŁODŹ

To get your bearings, start out at one end of Piotrkowska (it doesn't matter which) and walk from end to end. This is where it all happens in Łódź. Feel free to meander down the various side streets. You'll find houses and buildings in all states of repair and disrepair. It's an urban-rehabbers dream, and someday this all might be trendy shops and boutiques. In addition to the numerous pubs, restaurants, and coffee bars, Piotrkowska is lined up and down with turn-of-the-last-century *neo*-this, *neo*-that architectural gems. The house at no. 78 marks the birthplace of renowned pianist Artur Rubinstein, the city's most famous local son.

The former textile mills, now the Manufaktura shopping mall, as well as the History of Łódź museum and the former Jewish ghetto, all lie to the north of the city center, beyond the terminus of Piotrkowska at the Plac Wolności, easily identified by the statue of Polish national hero Tadeusz Kościuszko at the center.

History of Łódź Museum ★ If you're intrigued by the city and want to know more, this is where to come. All about textiles, the history of the city's barons, a bit about Artur Rubinstein, and even information on Jewish Łódź, all housed in the sumptuous neobaroque palace of Łódź industrialist par excellence, Izrael Kalmanowicz Poznański.

Ogrodowa 15. ✆ **042/633-97-90.** www.poznanskipalace.muzeum-lodz.pl. Admission 7zł ($3/£1.90). Sat–Mon 10am–2pm; Tues and Thurs 10am–2pm; Wed 2–6pm.

Łódź Art Museum (Muzeum Sztuki w Łódźi) ★★ A must for fans of modern art, from the functionalist, constructivist 1920s to the abstract 1950s and pop-art, op-art 1960s. The collection includes works by Marc Chagall and Max Ernst. Skip the first two floors and head straight for the museum's prize pieces on the third floor, including several of the young rake Witkacy's amazing society sketches from the 1920s.

Więckowskiego 36. ✆ **042/633-97-90.** Admission 7zł ($3/£1.90). Tues–Wed and Fri 11am–5pm; Thurs noon–7pm; Sat–Sun 10am–4pm.

The Łódź Ghetto (Litzmannstadt) ★★ If one of your reasons for visiting Poland is to trace Jewish heritage, then you'll certainly want to explore what remains of the Łódź ghetto (known by its German name of Litzmannstadt), once the second-biggest urban concentration of Jews in Europe after the Warsaw ghetto. But be forewarned, not much of the former ghetto survived World War II and the area has been rebuilt with mostly prefab Communist housing blocks and shops. Much of a walking tour of the ghetto consists of weaving through drab and depressed streets, looking for hard-to-find memorial plaques and trying to imagine what life must have been like during what was a much different era.

The Litzmannstadt ghetto is one of the saddest and least well-known stories of the war. The Germans first formed the ghetto in 1940, after invading Poland and incorporating the Łódź area into the German Reich. In all some 200,000 Jews from Łódź and around Europe were moved here to live in cramped, appalling conditions. Next to the Jewish ghetto, the Nazis formed a second camp for several thousand Gypsies (Roma) brought here from Austria's Burgenland province. High fences and a system of heavily guarded steps and pathways allowed the detainees to move between various parts of the ghetto, but prevented anyone from entering or leaving. For a time, the ghetto functioned as a quasi-normal city, with the Jews more or less allowed to administer their own affairs in exchange for forced labor that contributed to the Nazi war effort. In 1944, with the approach of the end of the war, the Nazis stepped up their extermination campaign and began regular large-scale transports to death camps at Chełmno and Auschwitz. By the end of the war there were just a handful of survivors.

Begin the tour by picking up a copy of the brochure *Jewish Landmarks in Łódź,* available at the tourist information office on Piotrkowska. The walk starts north of the city center at the **Bałucki Rynek,** once the city's main market and the site of the German administration of the ghetto. You can find it by walking north along Piotrkowski, crossing the Plac Wolności, and continuing on through the park. From here the trail snakes along about 10km (6¹/₄ miles), ending at the **Jewish Cemetery (Cmentarz Złydowski),** the largest of its kind in Europe, and the **Radegast** train station, from where the transports to the extermination camps departed. The cemetery is open daily except Saturdays and has a small exhibition of photographs of Jewish life in Łódź and the ghetto. The Radegast station (about 15-min. walk north of the Jewish cemetery) has been restored to its appearance during the war, with three Deutsche Reichsbahn cattle cars ominously left standing on the tracks, the doors wide open.

After the war, a scattering of Jews returned to the city to try to rebuild a fraction of what they lost. Today, the Jewish population numbers just a few hundred from a pre–World War II population of nearly a quarter million.

Jewish Cemetery (Cmentarz Złydowski). Ul. Bracka. Free admission. Sun–Fri 10am–4pm.

Museum of Cinematography ★★ If you're a fan of international film, you'll want to stop by to pay tribute to Poland's panoply of great directors, including Roman Polański, Andrzej Wajda, and Krzysztof Kieslowski, all of whom studied and worked in Łódź. The museum's annual rotating exhibitions highlight the work of one of the directors, including stills and posters from the films and various memorabilia. The museum is housed in the former residence of one of the city's great capitalist barons, Karol Scheibler, and part of the fun is just poking around this incredible neo-baroque mansion.

Pl. Zwycięstwa 1. ✆ **042/674-09-57.** www.kinomuzeum.pl. Admission 5zł ($2.20/£1.35).Tues 10am–5pm; Wed and Fri–Sun 9am–4pm; Thurs 11am–6pm.

Radogoszcz Prison ★★ This former wartime Nazi detention and torture center for political prisoners holds fascinating exhibitions on Łódź during the German occupation, as well as photos and displays of the Litzmannstadt ghetto.

Zgierska 147. ✆ **042/655-36-66.** www.muzeumtradycji.pl/muzeum_tnr. Admission 2zł (85¢/55p).Tues and Thurs 10am–6pm; Wed and Fri 9am–4pm; Sat–Sun 10am–3pm.

SHOPPING

Łódź offers one of the most unusual shopping opportunities in Poland and possibly all of Europe. In an effort to revitalize the city, the former textile mills have been reconstructed and converted into an enormous shopping mall and entertainment facility, **Manufaktura,** Jana Karskiego 5 (© **042/664-92-60;** www.manufaktura.com; daily 10am–9pm), complete with a 15-screen multiplex, a climbing wall, Europe's longest fountain at 300m (984 ft.), and an on-site sandpit for beach volleyball. The 19th-century redbrick factory architecture is stunning and the restoration work a model for similar reconstruction efforts around the country. If you're a fan of urban rehab or just want to spend the day at the mall, stop by and take a look.

AFTER DARK

Łódź is a shot-and-a-beer town in the best sense of the term, and if you're looking for a spot to drink, carouse, and club, you needn't go any farther than Piotrkowska: 4km (2 1/2 miles) of restaurants, cafes, and bars that open early and close late. It might be the only city in Europe where you won't notice groups of drunken Brits on a stag party. The whole town, it seems, is on a stag-night blitz.

5 OLSZTYN & THE MAZURIAN LAKES

200km (124 miles) N of Warsaw

To the northeast of Warsaw, and stretching to the border with Russia (Kaliningrad) and Lithuania, lies an enormous expanse of lakes and interconnected waterways, the Mazurian lakes, that form one of the most popular summer vacation destinations for Poles. The medium-size city of Olsztyn (www.olsztyn.com.pl) is a pretty place in its own right, and makes for a good base for starting exploration of the lakes.

Olsztyn was founded in the 14th century by the Teutonic Knights, but passed into Polish hands a century later. It fell under Prussian control at the end of the 18th century and until World War II, the population was mostly German. Much of the city was destroyed during the war and its ethnic-German population expelled.

The lake district proper begins in Mrągowo, about 50km (30 miles) east of Olsztyn. The most popular, and arguably the nicest, lakeside town is Mikołajki (70km/432 miles from Olsztyn), just above Lake Śniardwy. Giżycko and Węgorzewo, to the north, are also comfortable lakeside resorts. One of the most popular activities in the lakes region is canoeing, and several organizers run multiday (1- and 2-week) paddle trips throughout the region, with the day spent out on the water and accommodations at night in simple bunks at canoe-rental outlets along the way. In summer, regular ferries also glide between the resorts. Olsztyn's helpful tourist information office (see below) can advise on lake outings.

ESSENTIALS

GETTING THERE Olsztyn lies on major Polish rail and bus lines and is easily accessible from nearly anywhere in the country. Figure on about 2 to 3 hours by bus or train from Warsaw. It's also a relatively easy though crowded drive from the capital. Figure on 3 hours of white-knuckle driving behind the wheel.

VISITOR INFORMATION Olsztyn's indispensable tourist information office, Staromiejska 1 (© **089/535-35-65;** www.warmia-mazury-rot.pl; daily 9am–5pm), is the first port of call for all kinds of information on exploring the lakes region. The office provides city and regional maps, as well as advice on where to stay and find rooms. They can also help arrange canoe and other boating trips as well as bike trips around the lakes.

Unfortunately, the staff speaks only halting English; German is more useful in this part of the country owing to the area's historical ties to Germany. You'll find the office just to the left of the big gate, called the High Gate, before you enter the Old Town.

GETTING AROUND Olsztyn's Old Town (Stare Miasto) is small, and once you've arrived from the bus or train station, walking is the best option. The bus and train stations are located about 1.6km (1 mile) from town. You can walk into town in about 20 minutes, or grab nearly any public bus, or a taxi (about 12zł/$5.25/£3.25).

For travel farther on to the lakes in the east, you have the option of taking either the train or the bus to resorts like Mrągowo and Mikołajki. Buses are often—but not always—the quickest option. The tourist information office can help with the latest transportation advice. The bus station itself maintains a relatively user-friendly timetable.

WHERE TO STAY

Olsztyn has a range of nice hotels, with most concentrated in and around the Old Town.

Expensive

Hotel Warmiński ★ A crisp and clean high-rise business hotel, nicely situated between the train station and the Old Town, about a 10- to 15-minute walk from both. The service is impersonal but efficient. Amenities include local rarities like a massage and fitness room, covered parking (for a fee), and in-room Internet access (LAN connection). The buffet breakfast is a treat, with a full range of Polish appetizers like salted herring, pâté, and homemade sausage on hand. The chef will whip up an omelet on the spot. The hotel occasionally runs special offers that include a buffet supper in the room price.

Kolobrzeska 1. ✆ **089/522-14-00.** Fax 089/533-67-63. www.hotel-warminski.com.pl. 133 units. 290zł ($126/£78) double. AE, DC, MC, V. **Amenities:** Restaurant; exercise room; limited room service; massage; dry cleaning; nonsmoking rooms. *In room:* TV, dataport, minibar, hair dryer.

Moderate

Hotel Kopernik ★ Nicer than the Gromada, and a decent low-budget pick if you can't get in at the Hotel Pod Zamkiem. The Kopernik began life as a Socialist-era block of houses or apartments, but a total makeover and a fresh coat of paint have given it a modern, efficient feel. The rooms are small, but are clean and the mattresses thicker than government-issue. The location is a bit out of the way, beyond the Old Town if you are approaching from the train and bus stations. Take a bus into the center and walk a couple of minutes, or take a taxi from the station for about 15zł ($6.50/£4.05). Rates are discounted about 20% on weekends.

Warszawska 37. ✆ **089/522-99-29.** Fax 089/527-93-92. www.kopernik.olsztyn.pl. 62 units. 225zł ($98/£61) double. AE, DC, MC, V. **Amenities:** Restaurant; nonsmoking rooms. *In room:* TV, hair dryer.

Hotel Pod Zamkiem ★★ *Finds* This is a nicely restored three-story Jugendstil villa, just a short walk from the castle. The villa once belonged to the head of the local stonemasons, and since 1989 has been on the registry of historic places. You'll love the high-beam ceilings, the dark-wood trim and the Secessionist/Art Nouveau detailing carved into the wood. The rooms can't match the high styling, but are cozy, and some are filled with antique wardrobes and beds. Once you've checked in, have a drink in the garden under 100-year-old trees. Room prices are discounted 20% on weekends.

Nowowiejskiego 10. ✆ **089/535-12-87.** Fax 089/534-09-40. www.hotel-olsztyn.com.pl. 15 units. 200zł ($85/£53) double. AE, DC, MC, V. **Amenities:** Restaurant. *In room:* TV.

Hitler's "Wolf's Lair"

Hidden among the beautiful Mazurian Lakes is a fascinating and creepy place that you should certainly seek out if you're in the area. Near the little town of Kętrzyn, north of Mrągowo, lies the bombed-out remains of Hitler's eastern command post, the Wolf's Lair ("Wolfschanze" in German, "Wilczy Szaniec" in Polish). It's best known as the site of a 1944 attempt on Hitler's life that nearly succeeded and might well have changed the course of history. The events provided the basis for the 2008 film *Valkyrie,* starring Tom Cruise.

The Wolf's Lair, in fact, was a large camp of reinforced-concrete bunkers, some with walls as thick as 8m (25 ft.). The top Nazi leadership, including Hitler and Hermann Goering, maintained their own personal bunkers. Additionally, there were bunkers for communications and troop commands, a train station, an airstrip, and even a casino bunker. Hitler was a frequent visitor to the Wolf's Lair from its initial construction in 1941 until 1944, when it was abandoned ahead of the Russian advance as the war drew to a close. In January 1945, the Germans dynamited the bunkers to prevent them from falling into enemy hands. This is what you see today. The bunkers have been preserved in their original "destroyed" state, and you're more or less free to walk among the jarring, jagged concrete ruins sitting incongruously amid beautiful forest.

The details of the assassination read like a spy thriller—or, in fact, an action movie. The would-be assassin, an officer of aristocratic bearing named Claus Schenk von Stauffenberg, by 1944 had come to see the war as unwinnable. He and other like-minded officers believed that if Germany had any hope of avoiding total annihilation, Hitler had to be stopped. On July 20, 1944, Von Stauffenberg was dispatched to the Wolf's Lair to brief the Fuehrer and other top Nazi leaders on troop levels on the Eastern Front. He arrived at the meeting with a time bomb hidden in his briefcase. Just before the meeting started, he placed

Inexpensive

Hotel Gromada A 1960s-era high-rise, just across from the train and bus stations, this is nevertheless an acceptable option if you're just passing through or arriving late and don't want to deal with transportation into the city. The inside is sterile, but cheerier and better maintained than the outside. The rooms are modern, small, and clean, with a kind of dormitory-for-grown-ups feel about the place.

Pl. Konstytucji 3. ✆ **089/534-63-30.** Fax 089/534-58-64. 96 units. 190zł ($80/£50) double. AE, DC, MC, V. **Amenities:** Restaurant. *In room:* TV.

WHERE TO DINE

The Old Town is filled with quick-bite and fast-food options, but if you have time for a real meal, try one of the places below.

Karczma Jana ★★★ POLISH Outstanding Polish food is served in a lovely cottage-style atmosphere in the Old Town just at the foot of the river. Don't expect lightning service, especially on the terrace in summer, but you wouldn't want to rush anyway. For something the briefcase near Hitler, activated the bomb, and immediately left the room. The resulting explosion eventually killed four people, but not Hitler. One of the generals had moved the briefcase just before it exploded, unwittingly saving the Fuehrer's life.

Von Stauffenberg quickly flew back to Berlin believing the assassination attempt had succeeded. Once Hitler recovered from his minor injuries, he ordered Von Stauffenberg's arrest and the rounding up of anyone and everyone who might have been involved in the plot. Von Stauffenberg was executed by firing squad later that night. The Nazis eventually arrested some 7,000 people on suspected involvement in the coup attempt, though many of these people had no prior knowledge of the plot and nothing to do it. In all, some 5,000 people were executed.

From Olsztyn you can get to the Wolf's Lair by taking a bus or train (about an hour in summer) to Kętrzyn, and then taking a bus from the combined bus/train station there 8km (5 miles) to the village of Gierłoż. You can also take a taxi from Kętrzyn station to Gierłoż. The fare will run about 30zł ($13/£8.10) one-way. If you're driving, follow the signs to Kętrzyn, picking up road 592 to the village of Gierłoż, following the signs to Wilczy Szaniec.

Once there you can buy a map of the grounds for 6zł ($2.60/£1.60) and walk the red- and yellow-marked paths that connect the ruins. If you're interested in learning more of the history, hire a private guide. Guides start at around 50zł ($22/£13).

Admission to Wolf's Lair (✆ **089/752-44-29;** www.wolfsschanze.home.pl) is 10zł ($4.35/£2.70), with parking costing 8zł ($3.50/£2.15). The site is open Tuesday through Sunday 9am to 6pm.

a little different, try the beef rolls, served with sides of spiced beets and buckwheat groats. On my last visit, the slow-cooked beef in a wine-mushroom sauce was superb. The kind of place where the waiter might bring a plate of pâtés as an *amuse-bouche.*

Kołłątaja 11. ✆ **089/522-29-46.** Lunch and dinner items 23zł–46zł ($10–$20/£6.20–£12). AE, DC, MC, V. Daily 11am–10pm.

Via Napoli ★ ITALIAN Very unlike your typical Polish pizza joint—meaning it's much more upscale (but not more expensive), with a clean, modern decor and a nicer range of salads, pizzas, and pastas. At the same time, the attitude is casual and reservations don't seem to be a problem. In summer, sit on the terrace in the back overlooking the river.

Okopowa 21. ✆ **089/527-99-99.** Lunch and dinner items 15zł–21zł ($6.50–$9.15/£4.05–£5.65). AE, DC, MC, V. Daily 11am–10pm.

Oh, Give Me a Home, Where the Bison Still Roam . . .

Primeval forests and wild herds of bison in Poland? That's right. Those buffalo heads on the sides of bottles of Żubr beer and fifths of Żubrówka vodka are not just marketing ploys. Poland is home to Europe's largest surviving herd of ancient bison. As in North America, bison were once ubiquitous on the landscape of Europe, but through overhunting and habitat encroachment, their numbers were sharply reduced. Now it's estimated Europe's herd has no more than a thousand or so animals—and many of them call Poland home.

You can see the bison at a remarkable national park that also holds some of Europe's last remaining parcels of primeval forest. The Białowieża National Park (Białowieski Park Narodowy; www.bpn.com.pl) covers some 1,000 sq. km (390 sq. miles) and since 1980 has been on the UNESCO list of World Natural Heritage Sites. In addition to around 250 head of bison, the park shelters large populations of deer, boar, elk, beaver, and wolf, as well as hundreds of species of birds and countless numbers of species of plant life. Something like 400 different types of lichen alone have been found in the park.

The park makes for a remarkable side trip. A separate nearby bison reserve (see location details below), also has on display large populations of horses, boar, and deer, and is great for kids.

The center of the action is the village of Białowieża, about 80km (50 miles) southeast of the industrial city of Białystok. Here you'll find the main park office as well as several decent hotels and restaurants for an overnight stay.

While much of the park is open to the public, the more valuable areas of primeval forest are restricted and can only be visited with a registered guide. You can hire guides (about 170zł/$74/£46 per group of up to 20 people) at the main park office. It's usually possible to hook on to an existing group to lower costs. The tour, on foot, takes about 3 hours and covers 3km to 4km (about 2 miles) of ground (liberally interspersed with lively stories about the park's origins and animal and plant life). You can also enter the park via horse-drawn cart. Expect to pay around 150zł ($65/£40) for a cart that holds four people.

The forest at Białowieża was known through the centuries as a prized hunting ground, and survived relatively intact for this very reason. It was a favored spot of the Polish and Russian nobility. The park had some rough years during World War II and immediately after, but appears to be thriving now.

The entrance to **Park Palacowy** is near the Best Western hotel in Białowieża. For a guide, call ✆ **085/682-97-00** (www.bpn.com.pl). The park is open Monday through Friday 8am to 4pm, and Saturday and Sunday 8am to 3pm.

The entrance to **Rezerwat Pokazowy Żubrów** (the bison reserve) is 4km (2 miles) from town along the road to Hajnówka. Hours are Tuesday to Sunday 9am to 5pm.

EXPLORING OLSZTYN

Much of the Old Town, the Stare Miasto, was destroyed during World War II. Though it was rebuilt in a traditional style, it retains a clean, cheerful 1960s-to-'70s feel, complete with surreal Socialist-era motifs on what were rebuilt to look like baroque and Renaissance buildings. The streets toward the Łyna River are particularly nice and atmospheric. Most of the sites in town center on the 14th-century **castle,** Zamkowa 2 (© **089/527-95-96;** www.muzeum.olsztyn.pl), originally constructed by the Teutonic Knights but thoroughly rebuilt since, tucked in behind the Old Town. You can climb to the top of the tower for a commanding view of the town and surroundings. A small museum (June–Sept Tues–Sun 9am–5pm; Oct–May Tues–Sun 10am–4pm) can fill you in on the region's Polish history, and there's a small room in the castle where the astronomer and jack-of-all-trades Nicholas Copernicus once lived. He once apparently commanded a Polish garrison here while under siege by the Teutonic Knights.

AFTER DARK

For a relatively small city, Olsztyn has a lively nightlife. Most of the better clubs and cafes are in the Old Town, on the streets around the main square and along the riverbank. The area is pretty small, so just take a walk and see if any places appeal. For good coffee or just a pleasant place to hang out, try the **Pryzmat Pub,** Okopowa 20 (© **089/527-06-25**). Another good spot for coffee or a quiet drink is **Awangarda,** Stare Miasto 23 (© **089/527-28-27**), next to the former cinema of the same name. The cozy "retro-rialto" interior, done up to look like an old cinema, is fun. One wall is given over to photos of Marilyn Monroe.

6 KRAKÓW

300km (180 miles) S of Warsaw

Kraków, the capital of the Polish region of Małopolska, is one of the most beautiful cities in central Europe and a highlight on any tour of the region. The city escaped serious damage during World War II and its only real regional rival for pure drop-dead beauty is the Czech capital, Prague. The formal perfection of its enormous central square, the Rynek Główny, as well as the charm of the surrounding streets and Wawel Castle, have always been known to Poles. (In fact, Kraków remains the number-one domestic tourist destination.) But now the word on Kraków has spread far and wide, and the city is firmly (and justifiably) established on the main central European tourism axis that includes Vienna, Budapest, and Prague.

That's good news for visitors. It means decent plane, rail, and bus connections from any point north, south, or west of the city. It also means that Kraków has some of the best restaurants and hotels in Poland, and is fully accustomed to catering to the needs of visitors.

Kraków's precise origins are unclear, but the city first rose to prominence at the turn of the first millennium as a thriving market town. The enormous size of the Rynek attests to Kraków's early importance, even if its exact origins are unknown. One story about Kraków's founding has it that a poor man named "Mr. Krak" started the whole thing by slaying a dragon that was ravaging the early inhabitants. Krak allegedly felled the beast by filling an animal carcass with sulfur (or lye) and tricking the beast to eat it. Naturally, so the story goes, he was awarded great wealth and a city, "Krak-ów," named after him.

Well, *maybe,* but the city of Brno, in the Czech Republic, for example, also has a similar myth about *its* early days. And it's hard to imagine there were that many dragons running around, as well as clever men with bags of sulfur on hand to finish the job. At any rate, what is clear is that by the time of the early Piast dynasty in the 11th century, Kraków was booming, and Wawel Hill, with its commanding view of the Vistula River, was a natural setting for a capital.

As befitting any medieval metropolis, Kraków had its ups and downs. In the 13th century, the city was razed to the ground by the central Asian Tartars, but was quickly rebuilt (and parts remain remarkably unchanged to this day). Kraków's heyday was arguably the mid–14th century when King Kazimierz the Great commissioned many of the city's finest buildings and established Jagellonian University, the second university to be founded in central Europe after Prague's Charles University. For more than 5 centuries, Kraków served as the seat of the Polish kingdom (it only lost out to the usurper Warsaw in 1596 after the union with Lithuania made the Polish-Lithuanian kingdom so large that it became difficult for distant noblemen to travel here).

Kraków started to decline around this time. Following the Polish partitions at the end of the 18th century, Kraków eventually fell under the domination of Austria-Hungary, and was ruled from Vienna. It became the main city in the new Austrian province of Galicia, but had to share some of the administrative duties with the eastern city of Lwów (which must have been quite a climb down for a former Polish capital!).

Viennese rule proved to be a boon in its own right. The Habsburgs were far more liberal in their views than either the Prussians or tsarist Russia, and the relative tolerance here fostered a Polish cultural renaissance that lasted well into the 20th century. Kraków was the base of the late-19th and early-20th-century Młoda Polska (Young Poland) movement, a revival of literature, art, and architecture (often likened to Art Nouveau) that is still fondly remembered to this day.

Kraków had traditionally been viewed as a haven for Jews ever since the 14th century when King Kazimierz first opened Poland to Jewish settlement. The Kraków district named for the king, Kazimierz, began life as a separate Polish town, but through the centuries slowly acquired the characteristics of a traditional Jewish quarter. By the 19th and early 20th centuries Kazimierz was one of the leading Jewish settlements in central Europe, lending Kraków a unique dimension as a center of both Catholic and Jewish scholarship.

World War II drastically altered the religious composition of the city and for all intents and purposes ended this Jewish cultural legacy. The Nazis made Kraków the nominal capital of their rump Polish state: the "General Gouvernement." The Nazi governor, and war criminal, Hans Frank, ruled brutally from atop Wawel Castle. One of the first Nazi atrocities was to arrest and eventually execute the Polish faculty of Jagellonian University. Not long after the start of the war, the Nazis expelled the Jews from Kazimierz, first forcing them into a confined ghetto space at Podgórze, about a half mile south of Kazimierz across the river, and later deporting nearly all of them to death camps. (As a historical aside: Frank was prosecuted at the Nuremburg trials and executed in 1946.)

Kraków luckily escaped major destruction at the end of the war, but fared poorly in the postwar decades under the Communist leadership. The Communists never liked the city, probably because of its royal roots and intellectual and Catholic pretensions. For whatever reason they decided to place their biggest postwar industrial project, the enormous Nowa Huta steelworks, just a couple of miles upwind from the Old Town. Many argue the intention was to win over the skeptical Kraków intellectuals to the Communist side, but the noise, dirt, and smoke from the mills, not surprisingly, had the opposite effect. The new workers were slow to embrace Communism, and during those wretched days of the 1970s, when a series of food price hikes galvanized workers around the country, the city was suddenly transformed into a hotbed of anti-Communist activism.

Kraków will be forever linked with its most famous favorite son, Pope John Paul II. The pope, Karol Woytyła, was born not far from Kraków, in the town of Wadowice, and rose up through the church hierarchy here, serving for many years as the archbishop of the Kraków diocese before being elevated to pope in 1978. If Gdańsk and the Solidarity trade union provided the industrial might of the anti-Communist movement, then Kraków and Pope John Paul II were the movement's spiritual heart. The pope's landmark trip to Poland in 1979, shortly after being elected pontiff, ignited a long-dormant Polish spirit and united the country in opposition to the Soviet-imposed government.

Kraków's charms are multidimensional. In addition to the beautifully restored Old Town, complete with its fairy-tale castle, there's the former Jewish quarter of Kazimierz. If you've seen Steven Spielberg's Oscar-winning movie *Schindler's List,* you'll recognize many of the film locations as you walk around Kazimierz. For anyone unfamiliar with the film (or the book on which it was based, Thomas Keneally's *Schindler's Ark*), Oskar Schindler was a German industrialist who operated an enamel factory during World War II. By employing Jews from the nearby ghetto, he managed to spare the lives of 1,100 people who otherwise would have gone to the death camps at Auschwitz. Schindler's factory, now closed down, is still standing (there are plans afoot eventually to open a museum). At the moment it's derelict and perhaps all the more fascinating for that.

Outside of central Kraków, there are several trips that merit a few hours or a full day of sightseeing. The most important of these is the former Nazi extermination camp at Auschwitz-Birkenau (in the town of Oświęcim, about 80km/50 miles to the west of the city). Also recommended is a trip to the unusual and unforgettable Wieliczka Salt Mines. And if you've got time and a penchant for modern architecture, check out the Nowa Huta steelworks and the amazing Socialist-Realist housing project built around the mills.

GETTING THERE

BY PLANE John Paul II International Airport (© **012/295-58-00;** www.lotnisko-balice.pl) is located in the suburb of Balice, about 10km (6¼ miles) from town. The airport has two terminals, a larger international terminal and a smaller domestic terminal at the back to handle flights within Poland. Most of the services, including rental-car outlets, ATMs, and restaurants, are located at the international terminal. The best way to get into town from the airport is to take Polish Railways' "Balice Express," regular train service to and from Kraków's main train station (regular departures on the half-hour). The price is 6zł ($2.60/£1.60) each way. To reach the small station from where the express train departs, you need to take a blue shuttle bus that departs from outside both terminals. You can also take a taxi into town, but be sure to use only clearly marked cabs and refuse any offers of a ride you might get from individuals inside the terminal or just outside the door. These are likely to be scams. Expect to pay about 65zł ($28/£17) to destinations in the center.

BY TRAIN Kraków's main train station, the Dworzec Główny, Pl. Kolejowy 1 (© **012/393-11-11;** www.pkp.krakow.pl), is about 20 minutes' walk from the center of the city. Kraków is well served by rail and departures for Warsaw and other major cities are frequent. The rail distance from Warsaw is about 3 hours. Note that travel to popular international destinations like Prague sometimes require a change of trains in Katowice.

BY BUS Kraków's central bus station, ul. Bosacka (© **012/393-52-52**), is located just behind the main train station and is an easy walk or relatively cheap taxi ride to the center of town. Nearly all buses, international and domestic, including Polski Express, use this station. This is also where buses to Zakopane and Oświęcim (Auschwitz) depart from. The station has two levels, so make sure you know which level your bus is using. There's a bank of ticket windows, but oftentimes you'll simply buy your ticket from the bus driver.

BY CAR Kraków lies on the main east-west highway, the A4, running through southern Poland. It's nearly a straight 3- to 4-hour shot on mostly four-lane highway from the German border, through the cities of Wrocław and Katowice. You'll have to pay a toll from Katowice, but for the speed and convenience (compared to other roads in Poland) it's a bargain. From other directions, including coming in from Warsaw to the north, you'll have to contend with much smaller roads and longer drive times. Once in Kraków, stow the car since it's unlikely to help you navigate the city's small, tram-clogged streets.

CITY LAYOUT

Kraków's Old Town is relatively compact and comprised of the main square (Rynek Główny) and the streets that radiate from it in all directions (bordered by what remains of the medieval town walls and the circular park, the Planty). Most of the main tourist sites are situated within a 10- or 15-minute walk from the square.

The Wawel castle district comprises a second major tourist destination and is a 15-minute walk south of the main square, following Grodzka Street.

The former Jewish ghetto of Kazimierz lies about a 25-minute walk south of the main square beyond the castle. To save time, it's possible to take a taxi from the Old Town to Kazimierz. Expect to pay about 15zł ($6.50/£4.05). A number of trams also make the run between the two.

GETTING AROUND

ON FOOT Much of Kraków is closed to traffic, so walking is often the only option. Distances are manageable.

BY TRAM Kraków is well served by a comprehensive tram network, and this is a quick and easy way to reach more far-flung destinations. Try to avoid tram travel at rush hour unless you enjoy getting pressed up against the doors like you're in the Tokyo subway. A ticket costs 2.50zł ($1.10/65p) and can be bought at newspaper kiosks around town. Validate your ticket on entering the tram and hold onto it until the end of the ride.

BY BUS Like trams, buses ply Kraków's streets every day from early morning until after 11pm or so and are a vital part of the city's transit network. You probably won't need to use the buses unless your hotel is well outside the city center. A ticket costs 2.50zł ($1.10/65p) and can be bought at newspaper kiosks around town. Validate your ticket on entering the bus and hold onto it until the end of the ride.

BY TAXI Taxis are relatively cheap and a dependable means of getting around. You can hail taxis directly on the street or at taxi stands around town. The fare for a typical hop, such as from the Old Town to Kazimierz, will average about 15zł ($6.50/£4.05).

BY BIKE Biking is becoming increasingly popular, and there are now bike lanes scattered around town, including a nice run along the Vistula river and through the park, the Planty, that rings the main square. That said, biking is a better bet for an hour or two of sightseeing rather than as a practical means for getting around. "Cruising Kraków" bike tours, ul. Basztowa 17 (✆ **0514/556-017**), offers fun and instructional 2-hour bike tours in season in the afternoons and evenings; the company also rents bikes and conducts longer trips in summer.

VISITOR INFORMATION

The city of Kraków maintains an extensive and helpful network of tourist information offices around town in all of the tourist hot spots, including an office in the former Jewish quarter of Kazimierz. Here you'll find some excellent brochures, including one called the *Tourist Information Compendium* and another *Two Days in Kraków.* They also have excellent free maps, a wealth of suggestions, and can help find and book hotel rooms. Note that the Kazimierz office is (inexplicably) closed on weekends. The main offices are located at the following addresses:

Town Hall Tower (Main Sq.) (✆ 012/433-73-10; daily 9am–7pm)
Św. Jana 2 (Old Town) (✆ 012/421-77-87; Mon–Sat 10am–6pm)
John Paul II International Airport/Balice (✆ 012/285-53-41; daily 10am–6pm)
Szpitalna 25 (Old Town) (✆ 012/432-01-10; Mon–Sat 9am–7pm, Sun 9am–5pm)
Józefa 7 (Kazimierz) (✆ 012/422-04-71; Mon–Fri 10am–4pm)

Several private companies offer walking and bus tours of the city, as well as themed tours, such as Jewish Kraków or Communist Kraków, and longer excursions to Zakopane, the Wieliczka Salt Mines, and Auschwitz-Birkenau. The tourist information office can advise. **Cracow City Tours,** Pl. Matejki 2 (✆ **012/421-13-33;** www.cracowcitytours.com), offers possibly the fullest range of options, including, among others, a John Paul II tour, a *Schindler's List* tour, and a Polish vodka-tasting night. **Crazy Guides,** Floriańska 38 (✆ **0500/091-200;** www.crazyguides.com), specializes in Communist theme tours, and offers both a "Communism" and a "Communism Deluxe" tour—the latter includes lunch in a Communist-era milk bar.

WHERE TO STAY

Kraków has some beautiful hotels, and if you've got the cash and want to splurge, you can do so in real style. Most of the stunning properties are located in the Old Town, along the streets running off the Main Square or tucked in a quiet park location off the Planty. A second cluster of decent places to stay is in Kazimierz. You won't find the five-star luxury class here like in the Old Town, but there are a number of nice three- and four-star properties that are, on balance, a little cheaper and quieter than their Old Town counterparts. As for location, both are excellent. An Old Town property puts you just a few steps away from the restaurants and cafes around the square, as well as Kraków's main museums and sites. On the other hand, if you're into bars, clubs, and trendy restaurants, then Kazimierz is where you want to be. Either way, the distances between the two are not great, just a 15-minute walk or short cab ride.

Rates are generally highest between April 1 and October 31, as well as over the Christmas and New Year's holidays. Room prices drop by 20% or more from November through March. The prices below are for a standard double room (twin beds) in high season (outside of the Christmas and New Year's holiday season).

Very Expensive

Amadeus ★ A fully modern hotel, working hard—and succeeding—at re-creating an 18th-century feel. For the room interiors, think Colonial Williamsburg, with intricately carved white woodworking in the beds and nightstands, chandeliers, and floor-to-ceiling floral print drapes. Mozart could actually drop by and feel quite at home. The service is top-notch and the location, just a couple feet off the main square, is ideal. A perfect choice if you want a hotel that will stick in your mind as long as Kraków's main square does.

Mikołajska 20. ✆ **012/429-60-70.** Fax 012/429-60-72. www.hotel-amadeus.pl. 22 units. 630zł ($274/£170) double. AE, DC, MC, V. **Amenities:** Restaurant; fitness club; sauna; limited room service; nonsmoking rooms. *In room:* A/C, TV, dataport, minibar, hair dryer.

Copernicus ★★ Widely considered the best address in town; certainly the best of the boutique-size properties. Managed by the international Relais & Châteaux chain, and the polish shows. You'll be charmed immediately by the enormous Renaissance atrium shooting to the ceiling, and the period detailing—from the 16th century—that extends throughout the hotel and to the wood-beamed ceilings in the rooms on the first and second floors. A fresco, the *Four Fathers of the Church,* dating from the year 1500, covers the wall in room no. 101. U.S. President George W. Bush and his wife, Laura, stayed here in 2003.

Kanonicza 16. ✆ **012/424-34-00.** Fax 012/424-34-05. www.hotel.com.pl. 29 units. 900zł ($391/£243) double. AE, DC, MC, V. **Amenities:** Restaurant; indoor pool; sauna; room service; nonsmoking rooms. *In room:* A/C, TV, dataport, minibar, hair dryer, safe.

Palac Bonerowski ★★★ Kraków's latest entry in the five-star category is a jaw-dropper: a sensitively restored 13th-century town house just off the main square. Many period elements, including some original stonework and carvings, have been preserved in the spacious rooms. The furnishings are tasteful and traditional, with cream-leather sofas and armchairs, and hardwood tables and chairs. The floors are polished parquet and oriental carpets. You can't miss the 15m-high (50-ft.) crystal chandelier running down the main staircase.

Sw Jana 1. ✆ **012/374-13-00.** Fax 012/374-13-05. www.palacbonerowski.pl. 8 units. 900zł ($391/£243) double. AE, DC, MC, V. **Amenities:** 2 restaurants; courtesy car; 24-hr. room service; nonsmoking rooms. *In room:* A/C, TV, dataport, minibar, hair dryer, safe.

Sheraton Kraków This is a relatively recent addition to the high-end corporate market, but is already setting standards as arguably the best business hotel in the city. Everything is conceived with comfort and convenience in mind all the way down to the high-tech fitness center's special "Cracow Experience" massage ("ideal after long sightseeing, travel, or work"). Unlike many Sheratons around the world, this one is actually in a very good location for sightseeing, close to the river and within an easy walk of the Old Town or Wawel Castle. Ask for a room with a view toward the Wawel.

Powiśle 7. ✆ **012/662-10-00.** Fax 012/662-11-00. www.sheraton.com/krakow. 232 units. 680zł ($296/£183) double. AE, DC, MC, V. **Amenities:** 3 restaurants; state-of-the-art health club; sauna; concierge; courtesy car; business center; salon; 24-hr. room service; dry cleaning; executive-level rooms; nonsmoking rooms. *In room:* A/C, TV, fax, dataport, minibar, hair dryer, iron, safe.

Expensive

Hotel Ester ★ One of just a handful of four-star hotels in Kazimierz, the Ester is probably the nicest overall hotel in the former Jewish quarter. The property was renovated a couple of years ago, and the rooms have that understated, white-linen feel that you sometimes get at a good boutique hotel. The staff is thoroughly professional. The hotel's Wi-Fi access extends to the public areas and onto the outdoor terrace. The location, at the heart of the former ghetto, is just a short walk away from the synagogues and major sites.

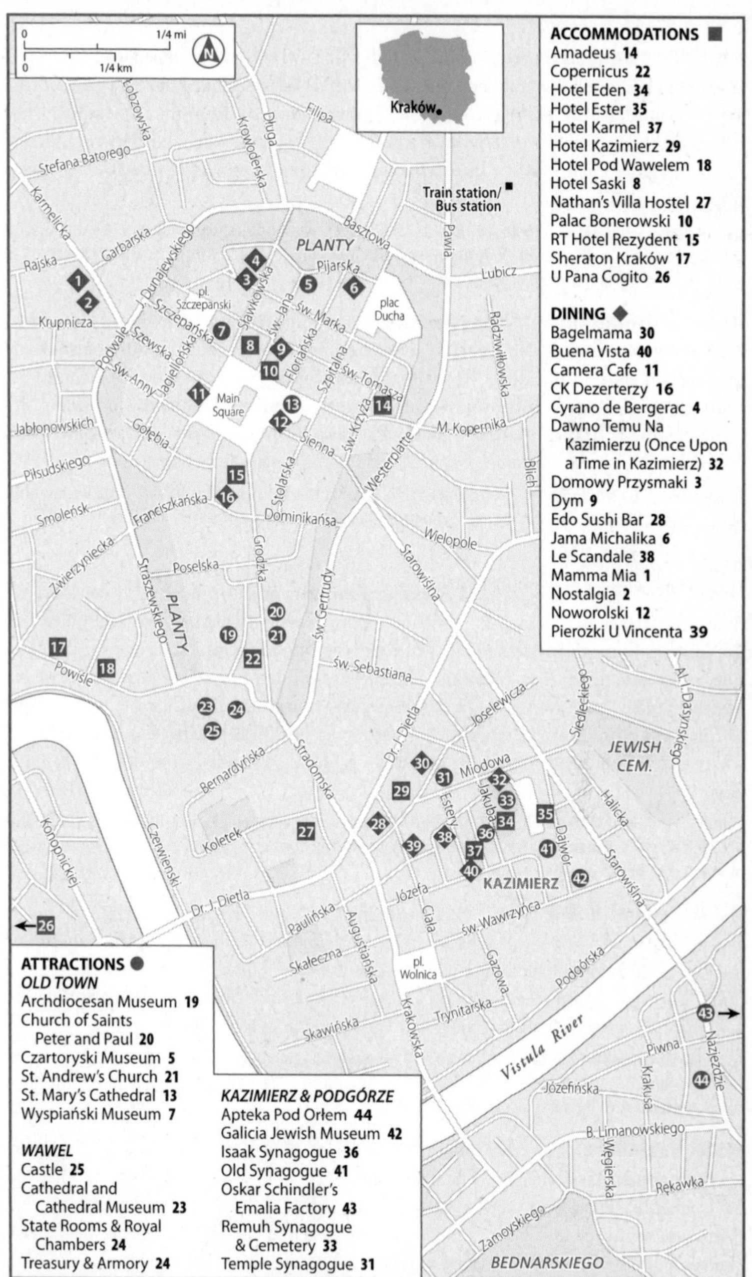
0 1/4 mi
0 1/4 km
N
Kraków
Train station/
Bus station
PLANTY
plac
Ducha
pl.
Szczepanski
Main
Square
JEWISH
CEM.
KAZIMIERZ
pl.
Wolnica
Vistula River
BEDNARSKIEGO
Stefana Batorego
Łobzowska
Krowoderska
Długa
Filipa
Karmelicka
Garbarska
Rajska
Krupnicza
Basztowa
Pawia
Lubicz
Pijarska
Sławkowska
św. Jana
św. Marka
Floriańska
Szpitalna
św. Tomasza
Szczepańska
Jagiellońska
Szewska
św. Anny
Podwale
J. Dunajewskiego
Radziwiłłowska
M. Kopernika
Jabłonowskich
Gołębia
Sienna
św. Krzyża
Westerplatte
Piłsudskiego
Stolarska
Franciszkańska
Smoleńsk
Dominikańska
Blich
Wielopole
Zwierzyniecka
Poselska
Grodzka
Starowiślna
Straszewskiego
św. Gertrudy
św. Sebastiana
Powiśle
Siedleckiego
Al. I. Daszyńskiego
Joselewicza
Dr. J. Dietla
Bernardyńska
Stradomska
Miodowa
Estery
Jakuba
Halicka
Konopnickiej
Koletek
Czerwienski
Dajwór
Józefa
Ciała
św. Wawrzyńca
Paulińska
Augustiańska
Skałeczna
Gazowa
Podgórska
Trynitarska
Skawińska
Krakowska
Piwna
Nadwiślańska
Krakusa
Józefińska
B. Limanowskiego
Węgierska
Rękawka
Zamoyskiego
ACCOMMODATIONS
Amadeus 14
Copernicus 22
Hotel Eden 34
Hotel Ester 35
Hotel Karmel 37
Hotel Kazimierz 29
Hotel Pod Wawelem 18
Hotel Saski 8
Nathan's Villa Hostel 27
Palac Bonerowski 10
RT Hotel Rezydent 15
Sheraton Kraków 17
U Pana Cogito 26
DINING
Bagelmama 30
Buena Vista 40
Camera Cafe 11
CK Dezerterzy 16
Cyrano de Bergerac 4
Dawno Temu Na Kazimierzu (Once Upon a Time in Kazimierz) 32
Domowy Przysmaki 3
Dym 9
Edo Sushi Bar 28
Jama Michalika 6
Le Scandale 38
Mamma Mia 1
Nostalgia 2
Noworolski 12
Pierożki U Vincenta 39
ATTRACTIONS
OLD TOWN
Archdiocesan Museum 19
Church of Saints Peter and Paul 20
Czartoryski Museum 5
St. Andrew's Church 21
St. Mary's Cathedral 13
Wyspiański Museum 7
WAWEL
Castle 25
Cathedral and Cathedral Museum 23
State Rooms & Royal Chambers 24
Treasury & Armory 24
KAZIMIERZ & PODGÓRZE
Apteka Pod Orłem 44
Galicia Jewish Museum 42
Isaak Synagogue 36
Old Synagogue 41
Oskar Schindler's Emalia Factory 43
Remuh Synagogue & Cemetery 33
Temple Synagogue 31

Szeroka 20. ✆ **012/429-11-88.** Fax 012/429-12-33. www.hotel-ester.krakow.pl. 32 units. 450zł ($196/£121) double. AE, DC, MC, V. **Amenities:** Restaurant; limited room service; dry cleaning; nonsmoking rooms. *In room:* A/C, TV, dataport, minibar, hair dryer, safe.

Hotel Pod Wawelem ★★ This was the first of what it is hoped will become a Kraków lodging trend: an unfussy, simple, yet still stylish boutique hotel in a great central location, not far from the river and about a 10-minute walk from the main square. The rooms are high-quality modern, with cheery light-colored walls and dark woods. In-room amenities include Wi-Fi Internet access. Ask for a room with a view toward Wawel Castle.

Na Groblach 22. ✆ **012/426-26-26.** Fax 012/422-33-99. www.hotelpodwawelem.pl. 47 units. 500zł ($218/£135) double. AE, DC, MC, V. **Amenities:** Restaurant; room service; sauna; nonsmoking rooms. *In room:* A/C, TV, dataport, minibar, hair dryer, safe.

RT Hotel Rezydent ★ Not quite the upscale boutique hotel that this place markets itself as, but a nice choice nevertheless given the absolutely top-notch location just off the main square and on the Royal Route that leads to Wawel and beyond. The rooms are relatively small, but with sturdy, stylishly modern furniture and hardwood floors. It's owned by the Polish RT chain of hotels, which also includes the similarly appointed and priced RT Regent in Kazimierz. Save 5% off the room rate by booking online.

Grodzka 9. ✆ **012/429-54-10.** Fax 012/429-55-76. www.rthotels.pl. 59 units. 380zł ($165/£102) double. MC, V. **Amenities:** Nonsmoking rooms. *In room:* Some A/C, TV, dataport, minibar, hair dryer.

Moderate

Hotel Eden ★ A good second choice in Kazimierz at this price level if you can't get in at the Karmel (see below). It's similar in many ways, well maintained and quiet, but not quite as immediately charming. The rooms are modestly furnished and on the plain side, more functional than inspiring. Uniquely, the Eden has a "salt grotto" spa in the basement. The idea is for you to sit in the special saline air for 45 minutes to reduce stress and heal a multitude of ills, ranging from asthma to tonsillitis to acne. Once you've cured whatever ails you, head around the corner to the local pub called (not kidding) Ye Olde Goat.

Ciemna 15. ✆ **012/430-65-65.** Fax 012/430-67-67. www.hoteleden.pl. 25 units. 300zł ($130/£81) double. AE, DC, MC, V. **Amenities:** Restaurant; spa; room service; nonsmoking rooms. *In room:* A/C, TV, dataport, minibar, hair dryer.

Hotel Karmel ★★★ (Finds) The most charming and inviting of Kazimierz's hotels and pensions. Maybe it's the quiet location, in a forgotten spot in the former ghetto, or the flowers hanging off the house windows, or the cute Italian restaurant on the ground floor. Something about the hotel says "home." Parquet flooring throughout. Splurge on a "comfort" room, with a big double bed and a couple of sofas in the room.

Kupa 15. ✆ **012/430-67-00.** Fax 012/430-67-26. www.karmel.com.pl. 11 units. 300zł ($130/£81) double; 340zł ($148/£92 "comfort room"). AE, DC, MC, V. **Amenities:** Restaurant; room service; nonsmoking rooms. *In room:* A/C, TV, dataport, minibar, hair dryer.

Hotel Kazimierz Probably the most popular hotel in Kraków's former Jewish quarter, but not necessarily the best. The plain lobby and public areas are redeemed somewhat by a beautiful, enclosed inner courtyard. The rooms, too, are nothing special, but are clean and comfortable. The location is superb, near the entrance to the former Jewish quarter, but also not far from Wawel and the Old Town. They sometimes lower the rates on weekends, so ask when you book.

Miodowo 16. ✆ **012/421-66-29.** Fax 012/422-28-84. www.hk.com.pl. 35 units. 280zł ($122/£76) double. AE, DC, MC, V. **Amenities:** Restaurant; room service; nonsmoking rooms. *In room:* Some A/C, TV, dataport, minibar, hair dryer.

Hotel Saski ★★ (Finds) Kraków residents might laugh at this hotel being labeled a "find" since it's one of the best-known hotels in the city, right off the main square. But what many don't realize is that it's at least 100zł ($44/£27) a night less than other hotels in its class and location (especially if you go for a double with a shared bath). So if you're looking for a glorious old hotel, with a tiled-floor lobby and chandeliers, in the center of town and don't want to shell out major cash, this is your place. Ask to see several rooms since they are all different—some are quite modern and border on the plain, while others are in high period style with quaint, old-fashioned beds and tables.

Sławkowska 3. ✆ **012/421-42-22.** Fax 012/421-48-30. www.hotel-saski.com.pl. 20 units. 310zł ($135/£84) double without bathroom, 410zł ($178/£111) with bathroom. AE, DC, MC, V. **Amenities:** Restaurant; room service; nonsmoking rooms. *In room:* Some A/C, TV, dataport, minibar, hair dryer.

Inexpensive

Nathan's Villa Hostel ★ The American owner of this well-run and highly regarded hostel just across from Wawel Castle says his aim is to combine the social aspects of a hostel with the amenities you'd expect from a hotel. And at this price he definitely gets it right. In addition to the standard 8- and 10-bed rooms typical for a hostel, Nathan's rents out private doubles. In summer most of the guests are backpackers, but during the rest of the year, the hostel fills up with people of all age groups looking to save money while not sacrificing on location or cleanliness. Perks include free laundry, an Internet room, and a DVD movie room.

Św. Agnieszki 1. ✆ **012/422-35-45.** www.nathansvilla.com. 20 units. 180zł ($78/£49) double. MC, V. **Amenities:** Bar; laundry service; nonsmoking rooms.

U Pana Cogito ★★ (Value) If you don't mind walking, this renovated villa complex, about 15 minutes by foot from the city center, represents real value. The modern rooms, done up in neutral beige and gold, have all of the personality of a standard Holiday Inn, but they're clean and quiet, with nicely done bathrooms and unexpected touches at this price point like air-conditioning in the rooms and full Internet access (both Wi-Fi and LAN connections).

Bałuckiego 6. ✆ **012/269-72-00.** Fax 012/269-72-02. www.pcogito.pl. 14 units. 250zł ($109/£67) double. AE, DC, MC, V. **Amenities:** Restaurant; nonsmoking rooms. *In room:* A/C, TV, dataport, minibar, hair dryer.

WHERE TO DINE

Most of the fancier and more established restaurants are in the Old Town on the main square or along the streets running off the square, particularly to the south. The newer, trendier, and sometimes better places are located in Kazimierz. One area in the former ghetto to look is along Plac Nowy; the other dining cluster, including most of the Jewish-themed restaurants, is along Szeroka. Except for the very pricey places in the Old Town, dress is mostly casual. That's particularly true of the Kazimierz locales, which cater to a largely student and young professional crowd. Note that though many restaurants claim to stay open until 11pm or midnight, on slow nights it's not unusual for kitchens to start closing down at 10pm. Go early to avoid disappointment.

Very Expensive

Cyrano de Bergerac ★ FRENCH It's such a pleasure to taste Polish food with a French twist when it's done this well. That means staples like game, pork, and duck, but with a nuance. The duck, for example, isn't served with apple or cranberry, but caramelized peach and cardamom instead. The pork knuckle is candied in honey—the glazing giving it a sweetish barbecue flavor. The brick exposed interior is stunning, with candlelight and white linens on the table. The service is polished, but can be slow on busy nights. Beware the prices on wines. Dress for this one and reserve in advance.

Sławkowska 26. ✆ **012/411-72-88.** Lunch and dinner items 40zł–90zł ($17–$39/£11–£24). AE, DC, MC, V. Mon–Sat noon–midnight.

Edo Sushi Bar ★★ JAPANESE One of the best sushi restaurants in central Europe is on a quiet corner in Kazimierz. The hushed, spare, modern decor puts the emphasis firmly on the food. Very fresh nigiri sushi and some creative maki rolls keep the crowds happy. Ask the guys behind the bar what looks good and settle in for a great meal.

Bożego Ciała 3. ✆ **012/422-24-24.** Lunch and dinner items 40zł–60zł ($17–$26/£11–£16). AE, DC, MC, V. Daily noon–11pm.

Expensive

Dawno Temu Na Kazimierzu (Once Upon a Time in Kazimierz) ★★★ JEWISH Finally, the kind of Jewish-themed restaurant that Kazimierz has long been waiting for. Relaxed and intimate, with the inevitable kitschy knick-knacks and homespun interior creating a warming—not distracting—effect (as with the other restaurants in the area). The food is great—especially recommended is the roast duck served with cherries.

Szeroka 1. ✆ **012/421-21-17.** Lunch and dinner items 24zł–40zł ($10–$17/£6.50–£11). AE, DC, MC, V. Daily 11am–10pm.

Nostalgia ★★ POLISH A meal here is like dining in the country home of a well-to-do friend—warm and inviting yet still refined and special. The atmosphere extends to the cooking as well: Polish staples like pierogies, pork, and game, but well turned out and served on fine china. This is a perfect balance between something like Cyrano de Bergerac (see above) and CK Dezerterzy (below), with the same attention to detail as the former, but with the more relaxed feel and prices of the latter. Reserve in advance to be on the safe side.

Karmelicka 10. ✆ **012/425-42-60.** Reservations recommended. Lunch and dinner items 20zł–40zł ($8.70–$17/£5.40–£11). AE, DC, MC, V. Daily noon–11pm.

Moderate

Buena Vista ★★ INTERNATIONAL/LATIN AMERICAN Casual tapas restaurant in Kazimierz serving excellent Spanish-style food, like paella served with chicken and spicy sausage. Full range of mojito drinks and tequila-based cocktails. In the evening, the bar area makes way for spirited salsa dancing. Highly recommended.

Ul. Jozefa 26. ✆ **0668/035-000.** Lunch and dinner items 20zł–35zł ($8.70–$15/£5.40–£9.45). AE, DC, MC, V. Daily noon–11pm.

CK Dezerterzy ★ POLISH A cozy, family-style tavern serving well-prepared traditional Polish cooking in a warm setting down a side street off the Rynek Główny. It's perfect if you've just arrived and want a hassle-free, good meal and don't want to stray too far from the hotel. The only possible drawback is that it's popular with guidebooks (like this one), so while you'll probably find many Poles on the night you're here and tucking into your *bigos* or pierogies, you may wind up next to a table of guests from your own hometown.

Bracka 6. ✆ **012/422-79-31.** Lunch and dinner items 15zł–30zł ($6.50–$13/£4.05–£8.10). AE, DC, MC, V. Daily 9am–10pm.

Le Scandale ★ INTERNATIONAL Great breakfast or light lunch spot right on Plac Nowy in Kazimierz. Decent bagels, eggs, and coffee served from 8am. On weekends, arrive early to snag one of those highly coveted square-side tables, perfect for people-watching while sipping your espresso. The menu is heavy on international munchies, like quesadillas, simple pastas, and sandwiches, but also does well with steaks and seafood.

Plac Nowy 9. ✆ **012/430-68-55.** Lunch and dinner items 15zł–24zł ($6.50–$10/£4.05–£6.50). AE, DC, MC, V. Daily 9am–11pm.

Mamma Mia ★★ ITALIAN Truly excellent wood-fired pizzas and a full range of pasta dishes, featuring the freshest ingredients. The refined space, not far from the main square, is perfect for business or pleasure, dressy or casual.

Karmelicka 14. ✆ **012/430-04-92.** Lunch and dinner items 15zł–30zł ($6.50–$13/£4.05–£8.10). AE, DC, MC, V. Daily noon–11pm.

Inexpensive

Bagelmama ★★ INTERNATIONAL Great bagels, as well as very good lentil soup, and even decent burritos, in a tiny shop just near to where Kazimierz starts if you're walking from Wawel and the Old Town. This is *the* place to go for that classic bagel breakfast with smoked lox, onions, and capers. ***Be forewarned:*** There are only three tables, so be prepared to wait or get takeout.

Podbrzezie 2. ✆ **012/431-19-42.** Lunch and dinner items 12zł–18zł ($5.20–$7.85/£3.25–£4.55). No credit cards. Tues–Sat 10am–9pm; Sun 10am–7pm.

Domowy Przysmaki ★ POLISH Informal lunch counter, with excellent pierogies and other lighter Polish fare, including very good soups. The perfect spot for a filling, cheap lunch or early dinner in the Old Town. Self-service.

Sławkowska 24a. ✆ **012/422-57-51.** Lunch and dinner items 6zł–12zł ($2.60–$5.20/£1.60–£3.25). No credit cards. Daily 10am–9pm.

Pierożki U Vincenta ★★ POLISH This tiny and inviting pierogi joint in Kazimierz serves every style of pierogi imaginable. The house version "Vincent" is stuffed with minced meat and spicy lentils and served with fried onions and bits of bacon. Other concoctions include Moroccan-inspired couscous pierogies and "Górale" pierogies stuffed with sheep's cheese. Try it with a cup of homemade beet soup.

Bożego Ciała 12. No phone. Lunch and dinner items 9zł–12zł ($3.90–$5.20/£2.45–£3.25). AE, DC, MC, V. Sun–Thurs noon–9pm; Fri–Sat noon–10pm.

Cafes

There is no shortage of cafes in Kraków catering to all tastes and budgets. You'll find the greatest concentration along the streets that radiate off the main square and around Plac Nowy in Kazimierz. In nice weather the entire Rynek Główny is transformed into a giant cafe.

Camera Cafe ★★ CAFE Laid-back, studenty cafe just off the Rynek Główny, with silent movies projected on the walls (hence the name). The specialty here is chocolate-based drinks, but they also serve excellent coffee and the standard offering of soft drinks.

 Wiślna 5. ✆ **012/429-37-40.** Light salads and sandwiches. Coffee drinks 7zł–10zł ($3.05–$4.35/£1.90–£2.70). No credit cards. Daily 9am–midnight.

Dym ★ CAFE Dark, relaxing space given over to arty and intellectual types. The name means "smoke," and indeed this is the place to come if you'd like to have a cigarette with your coffee or beer (and maybe a place to avoid if you don't).

Św Tomasza 13. ✆ **012/429-66-61.** No food. No credit cards. Daily 10am–midnight.

Jama Michalika ★ CAFE This cafe was the epicenter of all things cool in the early 20th century and a major meeting point for the Młoda Polska crowd. Alas, those days are gone, and now it's largely given over to tourists. The incredible Art Nouveau interior and the evocative period paintings are definitely worth a look. Beware the unfriendly cloakroom attendants (coat and hat check mandatory). You may have to wrestle a waiter to the ground to take your order.

Floriańska 45. ✆ **012/422-15-61.** Lunch and dinner items 12zł–27zł ($5.20–$12/£3.25–£7.30). AE, DC, MC, V. Daily 9am–midnight.

Noworolski ★★ CAFE Lovingly restored Art Nouveau interior recalls Kraków's elegant past. The perfect spot for a leisurely coffee and cake.

Rynek Główny 1. ✆ **012/422-47-71.** Lunch and dinner items 12zł–27zł ($5.20–$12/£3.25–£7.30). AE, DC, MC, V. Daily 9am–midnight.

EXPLORING KRAKÓW

A sensible plan for sightseeing in Kraków is to divide the city into three basic areas: the Old Town, including the Grand Square (Rynek Główny); the Wawel Castle compound (with its many rooms and museums); and "Jewish" Kraków, including the former Jewish quarter of Kazimierz and the wartime Jewish ghetto of Podgórze farther south. Ideally, leave a day devoted to each. If you're pressed for time, you could conceivably link the Old Town and Wawel in 1 day, while leaving Kazimierz for the next.

The Old Town

Kraków's Old Town is a pedestrian's paradise. It's hard to imagine a more attractive town core. It's a powerful argument for historical preservation and the value of vital urban spaces. The **Rynek Główny** by all accounts is a remarkable public space. This massive market square is ringed by stately buildings, creating a natural arena for public performances of all stripes.

The most striking building on the square is the beautiful Gothic cathedral of **St. Mary's**—its uneven towers evoking for Poles the very essence of the city. Be sure to stop here at some point precisely on the hour to hear a lone trumpeter play his plaintive wail from the open window of the highest tower. As you listen to him play, you'll hear the last note cut off in midblow. That's intentional and meant to recall the assault on the city by the Tartars in the 13th century. Legend has it that as the trumpeter at the time was calling the city's residents to arms, a Tartar marksman caught the trumpeter with an arrow right through his throat. (Judging from the height and size of the window, that Tartar must have been an excellent shot!)

At the center of the square is the **Cloth Hall,** the Sukiennice, which dates from the 14th century and served as the stalls of the town's original merchants. The original Cloth Hall burned down in the 16th century, and what you see today is a mostly Renaissance building, with neo-Gothic flourishes added in the 19th century. Today, it's still filled with marketers, hawking (mostly) cheap Polish souvenirs to the throngs of visitors. Just near the Cloth Hall stands the enormous **Town Hall Tower.** It's the last surviving piece of Kraków's original town hall, which was demolished in the early 19th century in an apparent bid to clean up the square. Today the tower houses a branch of the tourist information office, and you can climb to the top for a view over the Old Town.

Streets and alleys lead off the square in all directions. Of these the most important are **ul. Floriańska** and **ul. Grodzka,** both part of the famed Royal Route of Polish kings. Floriańska leads to the Floriańska Gate, dating back to the start of the 14th century. The gate was once the main entryway to the Old Town and part of the original medieval fortification system. Grodzka flows out of the square at the square's southern end and leads to the ancient Wawel Castle.

Archdiocesan Museum ★ This is essential viewing for fans of the late Pope John Paul II. He lived here as the archbishop of Kraków until his elevation to pope. Today, the museum has largely been given over to his legacy, with a fine collection of gifts presented to the pope by heads of state from around the world. You'll also see a nice collection of sacral painting and sculpture dating from the 13th century.

Kanonicza 19–21. ✆ **012/421-89-63.** Admission 5zł ($2.20/£1.35). Tues–Fri 10am–4pm; Sat–Sun 10am–3pm.

Church of Saints Peter and Paul ★ One of the most evocative of Kraków's many churches, chiefly because of the statues of the 12 disciples lining the front entrance. It's said that the Jesuits spent so much money building the front and facade that they ran out of money to finish the rest of the building (which if you look behind the facade you'll see is constructed from ordinary brick). The interior is less impressive, though still worth a peek in. Good spot for church concerts.

Grodzka 54. ✆ **012/422-65-73.**

Czartoryski Museum ★★ The Czartoryski family members were gifted art collectors, and this collection is one of the finest in central Europe. Two masterpieces are on display: Leonardo da Vinci's *Lady with an Ermine* and Rembrandt's *Landscape with the Good Samaritan.* Sadly, a third masterpiece, Raphael's *Portrait of a Young Man,* was taken by the Nazis and never recovered. The museum also houses a sizable collection of ancient art from the Middle East, Greece, and Egypt.

Św. Jana 19. ✆ **012/422-55-66.** www.muzeum-czartoryskich.krakow.pl. Admission 10zł ($4.35/£2.70); free Thurs. Tues, Thurs, and Sun 10am–3:30pm; Wed and Fri–Sat 10am–6pm.

St. Andrew's Church ★ It's hard to imagine a more perfect foil to the attention-grabbing Church of Saints Peter and Paul next door. This humble, handsome church dates from the 11th century and has been part of the city's history for some 900 years. Its simple Romanesque exterior is a tonic to the eyes. The interior, on the other hand, borders on the jarring, remodeled in baroque style in the 18th century.

Grodzka 56. ✆ **012/422-16-12.** Daily 7am–5pm.

St. Mary's Cathedral ★★★ The original church was destroyed in the Tartar raids of the 13th century, and rebuilding began relatively soon after. The hushed interior makes for essential viewing. The elaborately carved 15th-century wooden altarpiece, by the master carver Veit Stoss, is the immediate crowd pleaser. But the highlight of this church, at least for me, is not inside at all. It's the forlorn trumpeter in the high tower, playing his lonely hourly dirge to the defenders of the Kraków from the Tartar hordes—in order that the people below know the correct time.

Rynek Główny 4. ✆ **012/422-05-21.** Admission 6zł ($2.60/£1.60). Mon–Sat 11:30am–6pm; Sun 2–6pm.

Wyspiański Museum ★ Fans of Polish art will have heard of Stanisław Wyspiański, one of the originators of a turn-of-the-20th-century art movement known as Młoda Polska (Young Poland). The Młoda Polska movement, based largely here in Kraków and Zakopane, reinvigorated Polish culture in the years before World War I. You'll note parallels between Wyspiański's paintings and drawings and the Art Nouveau movements in Paris and Brussels, and Jugendstil in Vienna.

Szczepańska 11. ✆ **012/422-70-21.** www.muzeum.krakow.pl. Admission 8zł ($3.50/£2.15), free on Sun; Wed–Sat 10am–6pm; Sun 10am–4pm. Closed Mon, Tues.

Exploring Wawel Castle

Wawel Castle (www.wawel.krakow.pl) is Poland's pride and joy. With Warsaw having been flattened by the Nazis, this ancient castle, and former capital, rising 45m (150 ft.) above the Vistula, has become something of a symbol of the survival of the Polish nation. Understandably, for non-Poles Wawel has less significance, but is still a handsome castle in its own right and worth an extended visit.

The original castle dates from around the 10th century, when the area was first chosen as the seat of Polish kings. For more than 5 centuries, the castle stood as the home of Polish royalty. The original castle was built in a Romanesque style, and subsequently remodeled over the centuries, depending on the architectural fashions of the day. What you see today is a mix of Romanesque, Gothic, Renaissance, and baroque.

The castle fell into disrepair after the Polish capital was moved to Warsaw at the end of the 16th century, but its darkest days came during World War II, when it was occupied by Hans Frank, the Nazi governor of the wartime rump Polish state. The castle luckily escaped serious damage during the war.

Aside from the castle, the complex comprises a **cathedral,** including the **Royal Tombs,** the **Cathedral Museum,** the **Royal Chambers,** with an impressive collection of tapestries, and the **Treasury and Armory.** (There are actually more things to see, but these are the highlights.) It's a lot to see and the tourist office and guides will recommend putting in a whole day. But if castles are not your thing or your knowledge of Polish history leaves something to be desired, don't overdo it. Two to 3 hours are usually enough to see the main castle and cathedral complex.

The grounds are open to the public free of charge, but entry to the castle and various other sites requires buying separate tickets. Note that in high season, the number of visitors is restricted. To ensure you get to see what you want, phone ahead to the main ticket office (✆ **012/422-16-97**) to reserve at least a day in advance. Admission to the Royal Castle is 19zł ($8.25/£5.10). Hours are Tuesday to Saturday 9:30am to 4pm, Sunday 10am to 4pm.

Wawel Cathedral and Cathedral Museum ★★★ This is the spiritual home of the Polish state, testifying to the strong historical link between the Polish royalty and the Catholic Church. The chapels here, and the Royal Tombs below, hold the remains of all but four of Poland's 45 rulers (King Kazimierz the Great's tomb is in red marble to the right of the main altar.) Admission includes the tombs and the climb to the top of the Zygmunt Bell, which dates from the early 16th century. The bell is rung only occasionally to mark highly significant moments, such as the death of Pope John Paul II in 2005.

Wawel Hill. ✆ **012/429-33-27.** Admission to cathedral free; cathedral museum and royal tombs 10zł ($4.35/£2.70). Mon–Sat 9am–4pm; Sun 12:30–4pm.

State Rooms and Royal Chambers ★ The highlight of a visit to the State Rooms is 136 Flemish tapestries commissioned by King Sigismund August. The rooms hold vast collections of paintings, sketches, frescoes, and period furnishings. One of the more memorable rooms, on the top floor, is the Assembly Room, complete with the king's throne and a wooden ceiling carved with the likenesses of Kraków residents of the time. The splendor continues in the Royal Chambers (separate admission), with more tapestries and Renaissance decorations.

Wawel Hill. ✆ **012/422-51-55.** Admission to the State Rooms 14zł ($6.10/£3.80); Royal Chambers 19zł ($8.25/£5.15); Sun free. Tues–Sat 9:30am–4pm; Sun 10am–4pm.

Treasury and Armory ★★ Exhibitions of what's left of the Polish royal jewels, including the coronation sword. An impressive show of medieval fighting instruments, including swords and full complements of knights' armor.

Wawel Hill. ✆ **012/422-51-55.** Admission 14zł ($6.10/£3.80); Sun free. Tues–Sat 9:30am–4pm; Sun 10am–4pm.

Exploring Kazimierz

Kazimierz, the former Jewish quarter, is an absolute must that defies easy description. It's at once a tumbled-down, decrepit former ghetto, filled with the haunting artifacts of a culture that was brutally uprooted and destroyed a generation ago. It also happens to be Kraków's coolest nightclub district, filled with cafes, cocktail bars, and trendy eateries that would not be out of place in New York's SoHo or East Village. The juxtaposition is enlivening and jarring at the same time. To their credit, the Kraków city authorities have resisted the temptation to clean up the area to make it more presentable to visitors. Don't expect an easy, tourist-friendly experience. It's dirty, down at the heel, and at the same time thoroughly engaging.

Kazimierz began life as a Polish city in the 14th century, but starting from around 1500 onward it took on an increasingly Jewish character as Jews first decided to live here and then were forced to by edict. The original Jewish ghetto incorporated about the northern half of modern-day Kazimierz, bounded by a stone wall along today's Józefa Street. In the 19th century, the Jews won the right of abode and the walls were eventually torn down. Many elected to stay in Kazimierz, and the 19th century, through World War I and the start of World War II, is regarded as the quarter's heyday.

The Nazi invasion put an end to centuries of Jewish life here. The Nazis first imposed a series of harsh measures on Jewish life, and in 1941 forcibly expelled the residents across the river to the newly constructed ghetto at Podgórze. By 1943 and 1944, with the liquidation of the Podgórze ghetto, nearly all of Kazimierz's 60,000 Jews had been killed or died of starvation or exhaustion.

There's no prescribed plan for visiting the former Jewish quarter. The natural point of departure is the central **Plac Nowy,** once the quarter's main market and now given over to a depressing combination of fruit and flea market (no doubt with real fleas). The **tourist information center** maintains an office at Józefa 7 (✆ **012/422-04-71;** Mon–Fri 10am–4pm), and can provide maps and information. Look, too, for signposted routes marked **trasa zabytków żydowskych,** which includes all of the major Jewish sites. Visit the synagogues individually; each costs around 7zł ($3.05/£1.90) to enter. Don't expect gorgeous interiors; it's fortunate enough these buildings are still standing.

After you've toured the major sites, don't overlook the **Galicia Jewish Museum** on Dajwór Street, just beyond the main ghetto area. Check out, too, the **New Cemetery**

 (**Nowy Cmentarz**) at the far end of Miodowa Street, walking below a railroad underpass. This became the main Jewish cemetery in the 19th century, and the thousands of headstones are silent testimony to the former size of this community (Mon–Fri 10am–2pm).

Galicia Jewish Museum ★★ This often-overlooked museum, in a far corner of Kazimierz, is almost a must-see. The main exhibition features contemporary and often very beautiful photographs of important Jewish sites throughout southern Poland with an explanation of what happened there. The effect works beautifully. So much of the experience of visiting Poland is running across sites very much like these pictures and trying to piece together the history behind it. The lesson here is that nearly every place has a tragic story.

Dajwór 18. ✆ **012/421-68-42.** www.galiciajewishmuseum.org. Admission 12zł ($5.20/£3.25). Daily 10am–6pm.

Isaak Synagogue ★ This is considered the most beautiful synagogue in Kazimierz, dating from 1664. It was badly damaged during the Nazi occupation and has only been partially restored.

Kupa 16. ✆ **012/430-55-77.** Sun–Fri 9am–7pm.

Old Synagogue ★★ Home to an educational set of exhibitions of Jewish life in Poland. Dating from the early 16th century, this is the oldest surviving example of Jewish architecture in the country.

Szeroka 24. ✆ **012/422-09-62.** Tues–Sun 9am–4pm; Mon 10am–2pm.

Remuh Synagogue and Cemetery ★★ This synagogue dates from the middle of the 16th century and is still in active use. You can walk through the cemetery, which was used until the start of the 19th century, when the New Cemetery was opened.

Szeroka 40. ✆ **012/429-57-35.** Sun–Fri 9am–4pm.

Temple Synagogue ★ The relative grandeur of this synagogue best captures the wealth of Jewish life here before the war.

Miodowa 24. ✆ **012/429-57-35.** Sun–Fri 9am–4pm.

Podgórze

South of Kazimierz, across the Vistula River, lies the wartime Jewish ghetto of Podgórze. It was here, at today's **Plac Bohaterów Getta,** that thousands of the city's Jews were forcibly moved and incarcerated in March 1941. Much of the area has since been rebuilt, and walking the depressed streets today, you'll be hard-pressed to imagine what it must have been like for thousands of Jews to be pent up here with only the prospect of eventually being sent to the camps at Auschwitz or, more nearby, Płaszów. The ghetto was eventually razed in 1943 and the inhabitants murdered. Look for the **Apteka Pod Orłem** on the Plac Bohaterów Getta, which today houses a small but fascinating museum on the history of the ghetto. About a 15-minute walk from the square brings you to **Oskar Schindler's former enamel factory.** At press time, this was still abandoned but occasionally open to the public to walk around (this may change soon if plans go forward to open a museum or art gallery here).

Apteka Pod Orłem ★★ You'll find an enthralling collection of photographs and documents from life in the Podgórze ghetto, from its inception 1941 to its eventual liquidation 2 years later. The exhibition includes two films well worth watching. The first, an American documentary from the 1930s, shows Jewish life in Kazimierz. The second, a silent film taken by the Germans, shows the deportation process.

Plac Bohaterów Getta 18. ✆ **012/656-56-25.** Admission 4zł ($1.75/£1.10); free Mon. Mon 10am–2pm; Tues–Thurs and Sat 9am–4pm; Fri 10am–5pm.

Oskar Schindler's Emalia Factory ★★ An essential stop for anyone interested in the history of the Podgórze ghetto or in the film *Schindler's List.* Many of the scenes were filmed here and you'll have the distinct sense of déjà vu just arriving at the depressing scene. The factory is closed down, but occasionally the gates are open for an impromptu "museum." If you can get in, be sure to look through the guest book. More than once you'll see the signature of a former worker here along with the words "because of Oskar Schindler I am still alive." Gripping.

Lipowa 4. No phone. Free admission. Hours vary.

OUTSIDE OF KRAKÓW

Wieliczka Salt Mines ★★★ I must confess to a touch of claustrophobia, so I don't get much out of this trip to a subterranean salt mine, about 16km (10 miles) southeast of Kraków. But many people—including the folks at the UNESCO cultural heritage office—absolutely love it, so I'm bowing to popular will and giving it three stars. Salt has been mined in the area for centuries, and talented miners and artisans through the ages here have crafted some incredible chambers, bas reliefs, and statues from that once highly coveted white powder. The mine covers nine floors and goes to a depth of some 300m (nearly 1,000 ft.). The highlights include an enormous salt lake as well as St. Anthony's Chapel and the larger Chapel of St. Kinga. You can the visit the mine only via a guided tour. Polish language tours run throughout the day; English-language tours are less frequent, but still often enough (at least in summer) that you won't have to wait long (last English tour is at 5pm). In winter, it's best to time your arrival to the tour schedule (10am, 12:30, 3, and 5pm). The tours cover three levels of the mine and take about 2 hours. Be sure to pack a sweater since it's cool down there, and wear comfortable shoes. You can reach Wieliczka easily by train or a special minibus that leaves from the main train station. Several travel agencies in Kraków also offer guided tours as a day trip (see "Visitor Information," above).

Daniłowicza 10 (Wieliczka). ✆ **012/278-73-02.** www.kopalnia.pl. Admission 64zł ($28/£17) (includes foreign-language guided tour). Mid-Apr to mid-Oct daily 7:30am–7:30pm; mid-Oct to mid-Apr Tues–Sun 8am–5pm.

Nowa Huta ★ In the 1950s the Communist authorities decided to try to win over the hearts and minds of skeptical Cracovians by building this model Socialist community, just a tram ride away the Rynek Główny. They built an enormous steel mill (the name Nowa Huta means "new mill"), as well as rows of carefully constructed worker housing, shops, and recreational facilities for what was conceived of as the city of the future. It didn't quite work out as planned; Kraków intellectuals were never impressed by a steel mill, and the workers never really cottoned on to the Communist cause. But Nowa Huta is still standing and in its own way still looks great. Any fan of urban design or anyone with a penchant for Communist history will enjoy a couple of hours of walking around, admiring the buildings, the broad avenues, and the parks and squares. The structures have held up remarkably well, and indeed the area looks better now than it ever has. Part of the reason is that the mills are no longer running at anywhere near capacity, so the air is cleaner. And, ironically, capitalism has added a touch of badly needed prosperity, meaning the residents have a little money to maintain the buildings. Still, there's something undeniably sad, too; this grandiose project in social engineering has been reduced to little more than a curiosity (though more than 100,000 people still call Nowa Huta home). The shops that line the magnificent boulevards—once conceived to sell everything a typical family would need (even if the shops rarely had anything worth buying)—look forlorn; and many of them are empty. Aside from walking, there's not much to do, and little provision has been made for the visitor. You'll search in vain for a decent restaurant, so plan on eating back in Kraków.

The easiest way to reach Nowa Huta is take tram no. 4 or 15 from the train station about 20 minutes to the Plac Centralny stop. From here it's a short walk to the main square, renamed to honor former U.S. President Ronald Reagan. If you'd like a more in-depth tour, **Crazy Guides** (see "Visitor Information," above) offers guided visits to Nowa Huta, including travel in a Communist-era Trabant (an East German car, for those not in the know) for about 120zł ($52/£32) per person.

SHOPPING

Warsaw is better when it comes to high-end design and fashion, and Gdańsk is a better place to buy amber and jewelry. Still, Kraków is filled with interesting shops to peruse, especially for art, antiques, and trinkets. Most of the better stores are concentrated in the Old Town along the streets that radiate from the Main Square, especially ul. Św. Jana. Poke your nose in at the ancient books, maps, and old postcards at Stefan Kamiński, ul. Św. Jana 3 (© **012/422-39-65**). Sławkowska Street also has a nice grouping of art and antiques stores. **Atest,** Sławkowska 14 (© **012/421-95-19**), is one of the best. For some unusual modern Polish painting and sculpture, stop by **Galeria AG,** Dominikański 2 (© **012/429-51-78;** www.galeriaag.art.pl).

Kazimierz has emerged as a second shopping mecca; here, the emphasis understandably is on Judaica, but the little streets are filled with shops selling everything from trendy art and design to out-and-out junk.

For classic Polish souvenirs, including handicrafts, woodcarving, and (naturally) amber, first try the stalls at the **Cloth Hall (Sukiennice)** in the middle of the Rynek Główny. You'll have to pick through lots of dross, but hidden among the "Poland" T-shirts and mass-produced icons, you'll find some beautifully carved wood and amber chess sets, as well as locally produced cloth, lace, and leather goods.

For English-language books, Kraków is blessed with at least two treasures. The first is undeniably **Massolit,** Felicjanek 4 (© **012/432-41-50;** www.massolit.com), easily one of the best new and used English bookshops in Europe. Massolit is especially strong on Polish authors in translation, but has thousands of titles under all conceivable categories (plus a very cute cafe and a quiet, contemplative ambience highly conducive to reading and thinking). The other is **Austeria** in Kazimierz, next to the High Synagogue, Józefa 38 (© **012/430-68-89**). Here you'll find dozens of titles on Judaica, Polish history, and the Holocaust, as well as some incredibly beautiful photographs, posters, CDs, and reproductions of old maps.

Kraków is a good place to find that exclusive bottle of Polish vodka. Two stores stand out. **Szambelan,** Gołebia 2 (© **012/430-24-09;** www.szambelan.com.pl), and **F. H. Herbert,** Grodzka 59 (no phone). Szambelan is best known for its exotic bottle shapes, but both stores carry a nice range of the best straight and flavored vodkas, as well as an excellent selection of wines and other beverages.

KRAKÓW AFTER DARK

Kraków is the cultural hub of southern Poland, and as such supports an active program of live theater, dance, classical music, and opera. The **Cultural Information Center,** Św. Jana 2 (✆ **012/421-77-87**), is the first stop to find out what's on and see if tickets are available. The friendly staff can help guide you to the best events. The center for classical music is the **Philharmonic Hall,** Zwierzyniecka 1 (✆ **012/422-94-77;** www.filharmonia.krakow.pl; box office Tues–Sat noon–7pm). The city supports several opera companies, including the very good **Opera in Słowacki Theater,** Pl. Św. Ducha 1 (✆ **012/421-16-30;** www.opera.krakow.pl).

For drinking, dancing, and clubbing, both the Old Town and Kazimierz are natural areas to start a night crawl. The Old Town caters more to tourists and students from nearby Jagellonian University; in Kazimierz the scene is more diverse and a little older, with young professionals, artists, and hipsters of all sorts attracted to some of the best clubs in central Europe.

Old Town

Ministerstwo One of Kraków's best venue for DJs and house music (not to mention, the essential lava lamp decor!). The action starts late and runs until dawn. Good location, just off the Main Square. Open Tuesday through Saturday 11pm to 5am. Szpitalna 1. ✆ **012/429-67-90.** www.klubministerstwo.pl.

Nic Nowego I hesitated before including this modern Irish-themed bar, since it's so popular with tourists and is in every other guidebook. But if you're looking for a visitor-friendly place where English is spoken and the menu looks comforting and familiar, you could do far worse. In addition to decent cocktails and conversation, you'll find a nice array of burgers and sandwiches on the munchie menu. Breakfast is served daily, and the scrambled eggs and coffee here are probably a lot better than what your hotel or pension has planned for you. Open Monday through Friday 7am to 3am, Saturday to Sunday 10am to 3am. Św. Krzyża 15. ✆ **012/421-61-88.**

Pauza You'll have to look around a bit for this moody little cocktail bar, which now numbers among coolest drinking spots in the city despite few clues that it's even there. Order at the bar and head for the chill-out lounge in the back. Open daily noon to midnight. Floriańska 18/3. ✆ **0602/63-78-33.**

Rdza Another contender for best dance club in the Old Town. Choose fashionable dress to make it past the guys at the door, and then enjoy the trance, dance, and mood tunes, served up by some of the best Polish and imported DJs on offer. Attracts an early-20s to 30s crowd. Open daily 9pm to 4am. Bracka 3–5. ✆ **0600/39-55-41.**

Kazimierz

Alchemia One of the original bars/clubs to lead the Kazimierz renaissance in the late 1990s, when the former Jewish quarter morphed from a forgotten corner of Kraków to its current "party amid the past" feel. The old furniture, faded photos, and frayed carpets set a design tone that's still going strong. It's no longer the bar of the moment, but still a great place to get a feel for what Kazimierz is all about. Open daily 10am to 4am. Estery 5. ✆ **012/421-22-00.**

Les Couleurs/Kolory During the day, this Kazimierz locale is an innocent French-themed cafe, complete with good espresso and arty French posters on the wall. In the evening it morphs into a great little bar for an after-dinner beer or cocktail. Just boisterous enough to feel lively, but quiet enough to hear yourself talk. Open Monday to Friday 7am to 2am, Saturday to Sunday 9am to 2am. Estery 10. © **012/429-42-70.**

Mleczarnia Quiet, intimate, candlelit bar/cafe that's perfect for deep conversation or a low-key group outing. Highly recommended. Open Sunday to Thursday 9am to 2am, Friday to Saturday 9am to 3am. Rabina Meiselsa 20. © **012/421-85-32.**

Moment Popular bar that always seems to have a seat when the rest of Kazimierz is full to bursting. The theme is time and the walls are filled with clocks—maybe encouraging you to make this your moment. Open daily 9am to 1am. Józefa 34. © **0668/421-85-32.**

DAY TRIP: AUSCHWITZ-BIRKENAU

The concentration and extermination camps of Auschwitz and Birkenau lie about 80km (50 miles) to the west of Kraków, and can be seen visited in a day trip from the city. Getting to the camps is relatively easy. Both trains and minibuses cover the journey in 90 minutes and cost about 18zł ($7.85/£4.85) for a round-trip ticket. Trains leave from Kraków's main station and buses from the main bus station just behind the train station. Bus departures are more frequent and have the added advantage of dropping you at the entrance to the Auschwitz museum. Several tourist agencies run guided coach tours; these usually include transportation from Kraków's main square and an English-language guide once you've arrived at the camps. Ask at the tourist information office for details. By car it's an easy 90-minute drive along the main highway to Katowice, turning south at the Czarnów exit and following the signs first to Oświęcim and once in town to the "Auschwitz Museum."

Whatever you've heard or read about the death camps, nothing is likely to prepare you for the shock of seeing them in person. Auschwitz is the best known of the two, though it's at Birkenau, south of Auschwitz, where you really see and feel the sheer scale of the atrocities. The precise number of deaths at the camps is unclear, but well over a million people died in the gas chambers, or were hanged or shot, or died of disease or exhaustion. Most of the victims were Jews, brought here from 1941 to 1944 from all around Europe stuffed in rail cattle cars. In addition, thousands of POWs, including many Poles, Russians, and Gypsies (Roma), were exterminated here, too.

Most visitors start their exploration of the camps at Auschwitz, the first of three concentration/extermination camps built in the area (the third, Monowitz, is in a suburb of Oświęcim and not included on most itineraries).

Auschwitz got its start in 1940, when the Germans requisitioned a former Polish garrison town, Oświęcim, for the purpose of establishing a prisoner-of-war camp. The first groups of detainees included Polish political prisoners and Russian POWs. Conditions were appalling and in the first year alone, nearly all of the several thousand Russian POWs died of exhaustion and malnutrition. It was only later—in 1942, after the Germans adopted a formal policy of exterminating Europe's Jewish population—that Auschwitz became primarily a death camp for Europe's Jewry.

Admission to the Auschwitz museum is free, and you're allowed to roam the camp grounds at will, taking in the atrocities at your own pace. (If you're not employing a guide, pick up a copy of the Auschwitz-Birkenau guidebook available from the museum bookstore.) On entering the museum, you'll first have the chance of seeing a horrific 15-minute film of the liberation of the camp by the Soviet soldiers in early 1945. The film is offered in several languages, with English showings once every 90 minutes or so (if you miss a showing, you can always come back to see it later). After that, you walk through the camp gates passing below Auschwitz's infamous motto, "Arbeit Macht Frei"

(Through Work, Freedom). Once inside, the buildings and barracks are given over to various exhibitions and displays. Don't miss the exhibition at Block No. 4, "On Extermination." It's here where you'll see the whole system of rail transports, the brutal "selection" process to see which of the new arrivals would go straight to the gas chambers and which would get a temporary reprieve to work, as well as the mechanics of the gas chambers, the canisters of the Zyklon-B gas used, and, in one particularly gruesome window display, yards and yards of human hair used to make rugs and textiles.

Birkenau, also known as Auschwitz II, lies about 2km (1¼ miles) to the south. It's larger, more open, and even (if possible) more ghastly than Auschwitz. It's here where most of the mass gas-chamber exterminations took place at one of the four gas chambers located at the back of the camp. You can walk the distance between Auschwitz and Birkenau in about 30 minutes; alternatively take one of the museum's free shuttle buses that run hourly on the half-hour (less frequently in winter) from the front of the museum. A cab ride between the two camps will cost you about 15zł ($6.50/£4.05).

Birkenau appears almost untouched from how it looked in 1945. Your first sight of the camp will be of the main gate, the "Gate of Death." The trains ran through this entryway. The passengers were unloaded onto the platforms, where they were examined by SS doctors and their belongings confiscated. About 30 percent were chosen to work in the camp; the rest—mainly women and children—were sent directly to the gas chambers, just a short walk away. The scale is overwhelming—prisoner blocks laid out as far as the eye can see. There are no films here and few resources for the visitor. Instead, set aside an hour or so to walk around the camp to take it in. Don't miss the remains of the gas chambers situated toward the back, not far from the memorial to Holocaust victims. The Germans themselves attempted to destroy the gas chambers at the end of 1944 and early 1945 to cover up their crimes once it was apparent the war could not be won. Now, little remains. You can return to the main Auschwitz museum by foot, shuttle bus, or taxi, and from Auschwitz back to Kraków by bus or train.

7 THE REST OF MALOPOLSKA

ZAKOPANE

100km (62 miles) S of Kraków

Zakopane, in the foothills of the High Tatra mountains, is Poland's leading mountain resort. It's absolutely mobbed during the winter ski season, so advance preparations are in order if you're coming from late December through March. The summer hiking season is also busy, especially in August when the town hosts an annual folklore festival, though not quite as overrun as winter. During the rest of the year, it's possible to sense some of the beauty and rustic charm that first began drawing holidaymakers here in the 19th century.

Zakopane plays a role in Poland's literary and cultural history that may be unprecedented as far as mountain resorts go. In the late 19th and early 20th centuries, members of Poland's intellectual elite decamped here in a bid no less ambitious than to reinvent, or at least reinterpret, Polish culture. Many of the country's leading young writers, poets, painters, and architects gathered here and found something uniquely Polish in the unspoiled nature and solid mountain cottages of simple people.

The two World Wars and the decades of Communism that followed put an end to the Zakopane art colony, but some of that special, funky feeling remains. Certainly the huge wooden 19th-century houses here—known throughout Poland as the "Zakopane Style"—are some of the most beautiful you'll see anywhere, and in an among the trees and the gardens—and away from the crowds—you can still find traces of a uniquely Polish resort that feels very much of a different age.

Essentials

GETTING THERE Zakopane has a train station, but the bus is really the best and quickest way to get here. Several bus companies make the 2-hour trip from Kraków's main bus station to Zakopane's main station at near hourly intervals throughout the day. One of the leading bus companies in Zakopane is **Szwagropol,** ul. Kościuszki 19a (✆ **018/20-17-123;** www.szwagropol.pl). It offers 16 departures daily to and from Kraków. Tickets are 18zł ($7.85/£4.85) each way.

GETTING AROUND Central Zakopane is fairly compact and partly closed to car traffic, so walking is really the only option for getting around. The town itself, though, spreads out a couple of miles in both directions, so if you're staying outside of the center (and don't have a car), you'll have to rely on taxis or local buses to get around. The main taxi stand is conveniently located just outside the main bus and train terminals. Bikes are another option, but ask at the Tourist Information Office, since rental agencies change from season to season.

VISITOR INFORMATION When you arrive, you will be surprised by the sheer number of private tourist agencies offering everything from information to accommodation, lift tickets, and day trips. Zakopane's small **Tourist Information Center** (Centrum Informacji Turystycznej), Kościuszki 17 (✆ **018/201-22-11;** www.zakopane.pl), can help with general orientation questions and provide maps, but that's about it. For more hands-on service, including booking hotel rooms, walk across the street to **Tourist Punkt,** Kościuszki 20 (✆ **018/200-01-77;** www.tourist-punkt.pl). The helpful staff maintains lists of dozens of private rooms, pensions, and hotels at every price point. Simply describe what you're looking for and they will fix you up. Another private agency, **Zwyrtozłka,** two doors down toward town (Kościuszki 15, ✆ **018/201-52-12**), maintains a list of rooms. Both agencies can help arrange day trips, including excursions to Slovakia, as well as sell lift passes and advise on things like ski and bike rental.

Where to Stay

Hotel rates in Zakopane are high, and this is one town where you may want to consider staying in a pension or private room. These abound. If you arrive in town early, simply walk around and inquire where you see signs saying WOLNY POKOJE or NOCLEGI. Or to save time, try Tourist Punkt (see above). They maintain an extensive database of private accommodations (with photos) and will happily book you a room. Make sure to specify that you want to be in the center; otherwise they may try to place you in a far-flung corner of town. Expect to pay about 60zł ($26/£16) a person for a private room. Hotel and room rates rise considerably in the week between Christmas and New Year's. Aside from that, January, February, and August are the busiest times of the year, and prebooking is essential. The rates below are for summer and winter season, outside of the Christmas and New Year period.

Very Expensive

Hotel Belvedere ★★ This 1920s-era mountain resort is one of the classiest places to stay in Zakopane. The Jazz Age ambience is updated with extras like a Roman spa and a game room, as well as a bowling alley and other more modern pursuits. The in-house restaurant is top notch. The real advantage is the hotel's location, just where the mountains start about 2km ($1^1/_4$ miles) outside of the center. That makes it a 10- to 15-minute walk down to Krupówki, but means you can also escape the masses and enjoy the mountains if you want. One of the nicest hiking trails along the Biała river valley starts just above the hotel's doors.

Droga do Białego 3. ✆ **018/202-12-00.** Fax 018/202-12-50. www.belvederehotel.pl. 160 units. 690zł ($300/£186) double. AE, DC, MC, V. **Amenities:** Restaurant; indoor swimming pool; spa; bike and ski rental; concierge; business center; shopping arcade; salon; room service; dry cleaning; nonsmoking rooms. *In room:* A/C, TV, dataport, minibar, hair dryer, safe.

Hotel Litwor ★ A luxury hotel occupying a handsome mountain chalet that admittedly looks a little out of place in the middle of busy Krupówki Street. When it opened in 1999, the hotel claimed to be the first four-star hotel in this part of Poland. Certainly it's still one of the best in town, but the Belvedere offers more of a feeling of exclusivity, and the Grand Hotel Stamary is arguably smarter than both. The rooms are well proportioned and furnished in contemporary browns and blues. Ask for one with a view to the mountains. Wi-Fi Internet access is available throughout the hotel.

Krupówki 40. ✆ **018/202-02-14.** Fax 018/202-02-50. www.litwor.pl. 63 units. 600zł ($261/£162) double. AE, DC, MC, V. **Amenities:** Restaurant; indoor swimming pool; fitness room; spa; bike and ski rental; concierge; salon; limited room service; dry cleaning; nonsmoking rooms. *In room:* A/C, TV, minibar, hair dryer.

Expensive

Grand Hotel Stamary ★★★ Beautifully restored turn-of-the-century manor hotel that quickly whisks you away to those stylish 1920s and '30s with its elegant lobby and cocktail bar and wide corridors with dark-wood flooring. The period detailing extends to the rooms, furnished in browns and golds. The location is superb, just a short walk toward the center from the bus terminal. The main pedestrian street, Krupówki, is about 180m (600 ft.) down the street—near enough to be convenient but far enough from the commotion. The spa, with indoor pool and Jacuzzi, opened in 2007.

Kościuszki 19. ✆ **018/202-45-10.** Fax 018/202-45-19. www.stamary.pl. 53 units. 580zł ($252/£156) double. AE, DC, MC, V. **Amenities:** Restaurant; indoor swimming pool; fitness center; spa; dry cleaning; nonsmoking rooms. *In room:* A/C, TV, dataport, minibar, hair dryer.

Hotel Villa Marilor ★★ Occupying a sprawling cream-colored villa just across the street from the Grand Hotel Stamary and another contender for "nicest place to stay in Zakopane." Peace and quiet is what the hotel is offering here, and once you step onto the beautiful grounds you won't hear a sound. Everything feels refined, from the chandeliers and marble-topped desks in the lobby to the nicely sized rooms, furnished in late-19th-century style. The hotel offers special rooms for those with limited mobility. Wi-Fi Internet access is available throughout the hotel and in the garden.

Kościuszki 18. ✆ **018/200-06-70.** Fax 018/206-44-10. www.hotelemarilor.com. 20 units. 580zł ($253/£157) double. AE, DC, MC, V. **Amenities:** Restaurant; outdoor tennis court; fitness center, spa; concierge; business center; room service; dry cleaning; nonsmoking rooms. *In room:* A/C, TV, dataport, minibar, hair dryer.

Moderate

Hotel Gromada ★ Utilitarian, 1960s-era high-rise that offers amenities like a spa and fitness room at rates about half the competition. The rooms are boxy but clean and comfortable. Ask for a room away from the busy street. The location is central, just a couple steps off Krupówki. It tends to fill up fast, so try booking in advance. The reception says the hotel is due for a makeover, so some of the facilities may be updated by the time you arrive.

Zaruskiego 2. ✆ **018/201-50-11.** Fax 018/201-53-30. 55 units. 230zł ($100/£62) double. AE, DC, MC, V. **Amenities:** Restaurant; fitness room; sauna (w/salt grotto); nonsmoking rooms. *In room:* TV, hair dryer.

Inexpensive

Pensjonat Szarotka ★★ Finds This smallish, eccentric 1930s villa feels more in harmony with Zakopane's artistic past. The pension is not far from the Belvedere, about 2km (1¼ miles) out of the center of town, and close to the Biała valley hiking trail. The squeaky stairways, the cozy little reading room with a fireplace, and the evocative black-and-white photos on the wall will remind you of your grandmother's house. The lovely 1930s breakfast nook is a real treat. On the downside, the rooms are tiny and crammed together. (How did they carve 17 rooms out of this house?) Still, for the money, the atmosphere, and the location, it can't be beat.

Male Żywczańskie 16a. ✆ **018/206-40-50.** Fax 018/201-48-02. www.szarotka.pl. 17 units. 180zł ($78/£49) double. No credit cards. **Amenities:** Restaurant; nonsmoking rooms. *In room:* TV.

Where to Dine

Most of the restaurants are clustered along the main pedestrian area, Krupówki. The lower stretch is the loudest and most congested. If you're looking for something a little quieter, walk uphill along the street a couple of blocks and the crowds start to thin out. Restaurant meals are relatively cheap, and most of what's on offer in town is broadly the same. In addition to the places listed here, the restaurants in the Hotel Belvedere and Hotel Litwor are both highly regarded locally, though are somewhat more expensive.

Very Expensive

Otwarcze ★ POLISH The loudest and most popular of a number of similar faux-folk-style grill restaurants along the main pedestrian street. Rack after rack of yard-long shish kabobs on the grill, an ensemble of highlander musicians to set the mood, and waitstaff decked out like a Polish episode of *Little House on the Prairie.* Don't panic. It's just as kitschy for Poles as it is for everyone else, and the mood is definitely fun. The menu runs several pages long, but most people simply order the *szaszlyk* (shish kebob), a mix of grilled pork, sausage, and onions, served with grilled potatoes and a self-serve salad.

Krupówki 26–28 (just around the corner from the Kolorowe.) No phone. Lunch and dinner items around 35zł ($15/£9.45). No credit cards. Daily 11am–10pm.

Expensive

Kolorowe ★ POLISH Similar in attitude but perhaps slightly quieter and more civilized than the Otwarcze next door. A similar card, with mostly pork shish kabobs on the grill, and accompanying live music and waitresses in full peasant regalia. They also offer pizza and other dishes, but that's more of an afterthought. Stick with the grilled meats and enjoy.

Krupówki 26. ✆ **018/150-55.** Lunch and dinner items around 30zł ($13/£8.10). No credit cards. Daily 11am–10pm.

Moderate

Kalina ★★ POLISH The quietest and altogether most pleasant of the Polish-style restaurants on Krupówki and certainly worth seeking out. Here the folklore element is low-key. You won't always find live music, but as compensation you'll get a cook who pays more attention to what's on the plate and some alternatives to grilled pork, like decent pierogies and roast duck. The interior is done up in traditional cottage style, meaning intricately carved woodworking, wood-beamed ceilings, and a nice warm fire.

Krupówki 46. ✆ **018/201-26-50.** Lunch and dinner items 25zł ($11/£6.75). No credit cards. Daily 11am–10pm.

Pstrag Górski ★ SEAFOOD Popular little spot just off the main drag that specializes in grilled river fish, especially—as the name suggests—trout *(pstrag).* Good choice for a nice lunch or a light early meal. In addition to fish dishes, they also have a full range of grilled meats. In summer, eat on the covered terrace overlooking the throngs on Krupówki.

Krupówki 6. ✆ **018/206-41-63.** Lunch and dinner items 25zł ($11/£6.75). AE, DC, MC, V. Daily 11am–10pm.

Soprano ★★ ITALIAN If you're not in the mood for grilled meats and traditional food, you can still find pretty decent pizza around. Arguably the best is served here at Soprano, which offers the standard combinations, but also has healthier options like broccoli and fresh spinach toppings. Sit out on the terrace and enjoy the view, or have a quieter, candlelit pizza in the back.

Krupówki 49. ✆ **018/201-54-43.** Lunch and dinner items 23zł ($10/£6.20). No credit cards. Daily 11am–10pm.

Inexpensive

Pizza Dominium ITALIAN Not as good as Soprano, but cheaper and quicker. Dominium is a popular and successful Polish pizza chain going head to head with Pizza Hut. The locals may have the advantage with thick-crust pizzas and usually fresh ingredients. This branch is on Krupówki, but they also have a restaurant at 2,000m (6,560 ft.) on the peak at Kasprowy Wierch, if you happen to be in the neighborhood.

Krupówki 51. ✆ **018/206-42-11.** Lunch and dinner items 15zł ($6.50/£4.05). No credit cards. Daily 11am–10pm.

Exploring Krupówki

Krupówki merits about an hour's stroll end to end. Toward the northern end of Krupówki (downhill), follow Kościeliska to the left for a couple of blocks to see two of the town's most interesting sites. One is a tiny wooden church, the **Church of St. Clement;** the other is the adjoining **cemetery,** with some of the most ornately carved wooden headstones you're likely ever to see. Look especially for the highly stylized totem pole that marks the grave of Stanisław Witkiewicz (see below), the architect who first set off the local craze for all things wooden.

Museum of Zakopane Style (Muzeum Stylu Zakopańskiego) ★★ Just beyond the wooden church and cemetery is the Villa Koliba, home to a small museum dedicated to the Zakopane style of wooden homes and a tribute to the work of Polish architect Stanisław Witkiewicz. The villa dates from 1894 and was the first to be built in this style, roughly Poland's equivalent of the Arts and Crafts movement in the U.S. and Britain. One of the draws is simply the chance to walk around one of these big old houses, but there are plenty of interesting examples of ornately carved furniture and accessories. Upstairs, there's a small gallery of the freaky and fascinating 1920s society portraits by Witkiewicz's son, Witkacy. He was portraitist of choice for Poland's Lost Generation.

Kościeliska 18. ✆ **018/201-52-05.** Admission 7zł ($3/£1.90). Wed–Sat 9:30am–4:30pm; Sun 9am–3pm.

Tatra Museum (Muzeum Tatrzańskie) The main Tatra museum back in town is a disappointment. There's not much information in English, so you're not likely to get much out of this exhibition of the personalities and events that have shaped Zakopane and the Tatras down through the ages. Still, there are some interesting displays of folk architecture and costumes on the ground floor. Children will like the stuffed animals on the second floor.

Krupówki 10. ✆ **018/201-52-05.** www.muzeumtatrzanskie.com.pl. Admission 7zł ($3/£1.90). Tues–Fri 9am–4:30pm; Sun 9am–3pm.

Outside of Zakopane

Zakopane is a natural jumping-off point for active pursuits of all sorts. In summer, the activity of choice is hiking in the mountains. Good hiking maps are available at the tourist information offices and at nearly any hotel or kiosk. Many of the best trails begin just a short walk from town.

A good hike of about 4 hours of moderate to heavy exertion and some awesome views begins from the Hotel Belvedere and follows the yellow trail along the Biała Valley (Dolina Białego). After a 90-minute ascent, turn onto the black trail, following the signs for Stążyska Polana, and returning to Zakopane via the red trail along the Stążyska Valley. Another popular hike to a different part of the mountains is to follow the red trail to Morskie Oko, an Alpine lake in the far southern corner of Poland's share of the High Tatras. Most travel agencies in town offer packages that include transportation to the trail head to the east of Zakopane, but once you get off the bus you'll have to walk or take a horse cart (40zł/$17/£11) the 9km (5½ miles) uphill to the lake.

In winter, the most popular hill for skiing is Kasprowy Wierch, with several slopes of all difficulty levels starting from here. To reach it, take a bus from Zakopane to Kuźnice, and then by cable car to the peak.

Zakopane is also a good base for a rafting the Dunajec River, east of the Tatras along Poland's border with Slovakia. In nice weather, this is fabulous day out, especially for kids, on traditional timber boats, led by Górale mountain men kitted out in their folk garb. (For a longer description of the trip, see chapter 11, "Slovakia.") The boating center on the Polish side is at Sromowce Kąty. The Info-Tour travel agency, Kościeliska 11b (✆ **018/206-42-64**), is one of several agencies in Zakopane that arrange trips, including transportation, for about 100zł ($44/£27) a person.

Shopping

Krupówki is jammed wall to wall with souvenir shops, gold and silver dealers, and outdoor outfitters, all competing for your attention with a jumble of cafes, restaurants, pizza joints, and refreshment stands. Just about everything you might need, you'll find along this busy 5 or 6 blocks. Most of the gift and souvenir stores peddle in the same sorts of imported, mass-produced junk—wooden toys, T-shirts, hats and scarves, and mock traditional clothing that sadly have little connection to Zakopane. For something more authentic, try looking in at **Cepelia,** with two locations on Krupówki (nos. 2 and 48; ✆ **018/201-50-48**). Here you'll find locally produced carved wooden boxes, animal pelts, leather goods, and the odd knickknack or two. **Art Gallery Yam,** Krupówki 63 (✆ **018/206-69-84**), is about as funky as it gets in Zakopane. Check out the rotating exhibitions of contemporary Polish painters, some riveting modern Tatra landscapes, and other works that draw on the absurdist visual style of Polish art in the '70s and '80s.

One souvenir you won't be able to miss are those little rounds of sheep's milk cheese, **Oscypek,** that you see everywhere around town. The recipe apparently goes back some 500 years. The salty taste goes great with beer.

After Dark

Paparazzi The local version of a regional chain of cocktail bar/nightclubs occupies a beautiful creek-side location that is *the* after-hours spot in town for a cold beer or glass of wine. Paparazzi also offers passable versions of international dishes like chicken burritos and Caesar salads. Open daily noon to 1am. Ul. Gen. Galicy 8. ✆ **018/206-32-51.**

Piano Bar Just next to Art Gallery Yam, this bar draws on its artistic funkiness for a laid-back, hipster feel. Though it's just down a small alley from the Krupówki throng, it's a world away in attitude. Open daily 4pm to midnight. Krupówki 63 (in the little alleyway).

8 SILESIA

WROCŁAW

300km (180 miles) E of Kraków

Wrocław, the capital of Lower Silesia, known as Dolny Śląsk in Polish, is a surprisingly likable big city. Although it was extensively damaged during World War II and stagnated under Communism, it's bounced back in a big way. Part of the reason has been its western location, near the German border. This has made it easily accessible to prosperous German day-trippers, who pour over the border for a coffee and a strudel. It's also drawn outside investment, particularly from the Japanese, who are eager to reach the rich markets of western Europe while producing in low-wage Poland.

The heart of the city is a beautifully restored central square, the Rynek, and the playfully colorful baroque and Renaissance houses that line the square on all sides. On a warm summer's evening, the square comes to life, as it seems like the entire city descends for a glass of beer or a cup of coffee. Most of this area lay in ruins in 1945, when the Germans held out for months against an intense Russian barrage. But all that seems forgotten now. Only the presence of the battle-scarred redbrick Gothic churches evokes a sense of the scale of the destruction.

Wrocław was founded some 1,000 years ago by Slavs, but its population had become increasingly Germanized throughout the centuries. Until the end of World War II Wrocław was known as the German city of Breslau. The city came under Polish control with the defeat of Nazi Germany and the shifting of Poland's borders hundreds of kilometers to the west. The surviving Germans were driven out of the city, and Wrocław was repopulated by Poles—many coming from the east of the country, particularly the city of Lwów, which came under Soviet domination. Although the city was overwhelmingly German just a generation ago, about the only German you're likely to hear now are from the day-trippers ordering their coffee.

In spite of the border change and population shift, the city retains the unmistakable feel of a German provincial town, especially in the Rynek and the wonderfully atmospheric streets of the Old Town. Be sure to spend time as well along the Odra River, which passes just to the north of the Rynek, and the peaceful Ostrów Tumski, the "Cathedral Island" and home to the city's leading religious sites.

GETTING THERE Wrocław lies on the main four-lane highway (A4) linking the German border with the city of Kraków, so getting here from Germany or Kraków is easy. The stretch from Kraków to Katowice will cost a toll of 6.50zł ($2.85/£1.75) but is well worth the money. Rail and bus links are good between Wrocław and major Polish towns and cities. The train and bus stations are situated together, about 2km (1¼ miles) south of the central city. The main train station, Główny, is a spooky-looking multiturreted castle and a tourist site in its own right. To get to town from the station, walk 15 minutes or take a taxi.

GETTING AROUND You'll find yourself doing a lot of walking. The Old Town is relatively small and closed off to cars. Outside of the Old Town, tram and bus lines are extensive. Tickets cost 2.40zł ($1.05/65p), 2.80zł ($1.20/75p) for night buses, and are available from vending machines around town or newspaper kiosks. As for taxis, dishonest drivers have sometimes been a problem. Never get into an unlicensed taxi; use reputable firms when possible. **MPT Radio Taxi** (✆ **071/91-91**) and **Lux** (✆ **071/96-23**) are two of the best.

VISITOR INFORMATION Wrocław's helpful tourist information center is situated at Rynek 14 (✆ **071/344-31-11;** www.wroclaw-info.pl; daily 9am–9pm, 8pm in winter). In addition to the usual services of handing out maps and selling postcards, the staff can help arrange tours of the city, book hotel and restaurant reservations, help to sort out bus and train tickets, and even rent bikes. The office is also a good source of cultural information. To see what's on, pick up a free copy of *The Visitor,* updated every 2 months, at the tourist information office.

Where to Stay

Hotel prices have been rising in recent years in step with the growing economy and rising accommodations standards. You can beat the high cost by planning your visit on a weekend, when rates are cut by as much as 50%. There's a good cluster of hotels along Kiełbaśnicza, in the northern part of the Old Town near the university.

Very Expensive

Holiday Inn ★ Not long ago, this was arguably the best place to stay in Wrocław. It's still an exceptionally nice hotel, but for the money there are now equally comfortable places closer to the Rynek. The outlying location, however, is excellent if you are arriving by train or bus, since the hotel is just a short hop from both. For business, this is probably still the best address in town, given the extensive business center and conference facilities. And it's certainly still one of the few places around offering warmed bathroom tiles and bathtubs as standard.

Piłsudskiego 49/57. ✆ **071/787-00-00.** Fax 071/787-00-01. www.wroclaw.azurehotel.pl. 164 units. 520zł ($226/£140). AE, DC, MC, V. **Amenities:** Restaurant; exercise room; sauna; concierge; car-rental desk; business center; salon; room service; massage; executive-level rooms; nonsmoking rooms. *In room:* A/C, TV, dataport, minibar, hair dryer, trouser press (executive rooms only).

Expensive

Art Hotel ★ Occupying two renovated burghers' houses in Wrocław's art (and hotel) quarter, this is a welcome alternative to the chains. The funky, bright orange exterior will draw you in. The reception area is sleek and cool. Each room has been furnished individually in an eclectic mix of modern and traditional. The restaurant gets high marks from local critics.

Kiełbaśnicza 20. ✆ **071/787-71-00.** Fax 071/342-39-29. www.arthotel.pl 77 units. 500zł ($218/£135) double Mon–Thurs, 320zł ($139/£86) double Fri–Sun. AE, DC, MC, V. **Amenities:** Restaurant; exercise room; business center; salon; room service; massage; nonsmoking rooms. *In room:* A/C, TV, dataport, minibar, hair dryer.

Best Western Prima ★ To be sure, a clean and well-managed hotel, but feels overpriced given some of the newer properties on the market. Everything you would expect from the Best Western chain. The staff training is evident from the first encounter with the helpful reception desk. The rooms are upscale middle-market, with carpets and floral prints on the bedspreads (like a well-furnished suburban home). The hotel's Sir William restaurant comes highly recommended.

Kiełbaśnicza 16/19. ✆ **071/782-55-55.** Fax 071/342-67-32. www.bestwestern-prima.pl. 79 units. 400zł ($174/£108) double. AE, DC, MC, V. **Amenities:** Restaurant; exercise room; sauna; limited room service; nonsmoking rooms. *In room:* A/C, TV, dataport, minibar, hair dryer.

Hotel Patio ★★ Another renovated burgher's house on Kiełbaśnicza, but slightly cheaper than its rivals. The Patio is every bit as inviting as the Art and Best Western Prima hotels, but what you don't get for the price are a fitness room, sauna, and air-conditioning. The rooms, done in fresh colors, light woods, and whites, are a notch more inviting than the competition.

Kiełbaśnicza 24/25. ✆ **071/375-04-00.** Fax 071/343-91-49. www.hotelpatio.pl. 49 units. 360zł ($157/£97) double. AE, DC, MC, V. **Amenities:** Restaurant; limited room service; nonsmoking rooms. *In room:* TV, dataport, minibar, hair dryer.

Qubus Hotel ★★ This smallish and smart hotel just a short walk from the Rynek is oriented more toward visiting businessmen. Competes head-to-head with the Prima/Best Western but gets the nod for the in-house swimming pool and a more modern feel throughout. Qubus is a growing chain of high-quality hotels. Note that rooms are heavily discounted if you book over the Internet and reserve at least 7 days in advance. Rates fall another 25% on weekends.

Św. Marii Magdaleny 2. ✆ **071/797-98-00.** Fax 071/341-09-20. www.qubushotel.com. 87 units. 400zł ($174/£108) double (weekdays book in advance). AE, DC, MC, V. **Amenities:** Restaurant; indoor pool; sauna; limited room service; nonsmoking rooms. *In room:* A/C, TV, dataport, minibar, hair dryer.

Moderate

Hotel Zaułek ★ Decent in-town choice, given the excellent location and relatively low price. The hotel is run by a foundation for the University of Wrocław and does double duty hosting visiting professors and university guests. From the outside, the hotel looks like an aging housing complex, but on the inside it's neat, clean, and quiet. Free Wi-Fi is available throughout. The rooms are modestly furnished but perfect for a short stay.

Garbary 11. ✆ **071/341-00-46.** Fax 071/375-29-47. www.hotel.uni.wroc.pl. 12 units. 290zł ($126/£78) double. AE, DC, MC, V. **Amenities:** Restaurant; nonsmoking rooms. *In room:* TV, minibar, hair dryer.

Inexpensive

Centrum ★★ Value Technically classed as a hostel, but offers private singles and doubles of high quality at an excellent price. Not much in the way of hotel amenities, but clean rooms and hardwood floors in a bright, shiny space. Highly recommended if you're on a budget and pitch up in town on a weekday.

Św. Mikolaja 16/17. ✆ **071/793-08-70.** Fax 071/793-08-70. www.centrumhostel.pl. 12 units. 120zł ($52/£32) private double. AE, DC, MC, V.

Where to Dine

The Rynek is lined with restaurants, cafes, and bars from corner to corner. Most restaurants post their menus out front, so peruse the square and see what you're hungry for.

Very Expensive

Sakana Sushi Bar ★★ JAPANESE A standout Japanese sushi bar of the kind where you sit on stools and watch little boats of delicacies float by, selecting this one or that depending on your appetite—or, if you're like me, your wallet. Each plate has a different color, with white being the cheapest (starting at around 15zł/$6.50/£4.05) and heading north from there. Three plates makes for a filling meal, so if you choose carefully you can still keep it under budget, but what's the fun of that when the food is this fantastic?

Odrzańska 17/1a. ✆ **071/343-37-10.** Lunch and dinner 45zł–70zł ($22–$30/£14–£19). AE, DC, MC, V. Mon–Sat noon–11pm; Sun 1–10pm.

Expensive

Karczma Lwowska ★ POLISH/UKRAINIAN Named for the former Polish, now Ukrainian, city from where many current Wrocław residents originally hail. The menu features many hard-to-find specialties from eastern Poland, including Gołąbki Kresówki, peppers stuffed with spiced minced meat and mushrooms. In summer, dine on the terrace, or in winter in the evocative, tavern-style interior. Best to book ahead to avoid disappointment, especially on a warm summer's evening, when the terrace is filled to brimming.

Rynek 4. ✆ **071/343-98-87.** Lunch and dinner items 23zł–45zł ($10–$20/£6.20–£12). AE, DC, MC, V. Daily 11am–midnight.

Piwnicka Świdnicka ★★★ POLISH Choose at least one meal here at the city's best-known Polish pub. The local specialties, like beef roulade served with beet purée, are some of the best you'll taste, and the atmosphere—either on the terrace in summer or down in the cellar in winter—is festive and memorable. Great beer, too.

Rynek-Ratusz 1. ✆ **071/369-95-10.** Lunch and dinner items 23zł–45zł ($10–$20/£6.20–£12). AE, DC, MC, V. Daily 11am–11pm.

Moderate

Abrams' Tower ★★ MEXICAN/FUSION One of the most unusual restaurants you'll see, and worth a visit for that reason alone: a "Mexican-Fusion" restaurant with the city's best burritos and fajitas occupying the derelict tower of one of the city's medieval defense bastions. Dining is on three levels as you ascend the winding staircase higher. The top floor is the most atmospheric, with a mix of tables and a bank of trendy floor pillows, Moroccan-style. Both the Mexican and Asian-inflected dishes like Thai curry are excellent and good value.

Kraińskiego 14. ✆ **071/725-66-52.** Dinner items 28zł–40zł ($12–$17/£7.55–£11). AE, DC, MC, V. Daily 4pm–midnight.

Novocaina ★ ITALIAN A trendy entry on the Rynek that promises only the freshest ingredients, without preservatives or additives. And the Italian-influenced menu mostly delivers. The pizzas are cooked in a traditional cherrywood-fired oven and come out just right. The high points are the salads and sandwiches, making this a good lunchtime pick and popular with Wrocław's young professional crowd. Very good coffee and free Wi-Fi are two more good reasons to visit.

Rynek 13. ✆ **071/343-69-15.** Lunch and dinner items 25zł–40zł ($11–$17/£6.75–£11). AE, DC, MC, V. Daily 9am–11pm.

Inexpensive

Alladin's MIDDLE EASTERN A relative rarity in Poland is a decent Middle Eastern restaurant, and this one is one of the best you'll find. The big salads and falafel make for a welcome departure from heavier Polish food. Alladin's is close to the university and attracts an informal student crowd for both lunches and dinners.

Odrazańska 23. ✆ **071/796-73-27.** Lunch and dinner items 18zł–24zł ($7.85–$10/£4.85–£6.50). No credit cards. Daily 11:30am–10pm.

Hala Targowa ★ POLISH Not a restaurant per se, though there is a small good-value pierogi stand on the right-hand side as you enter the hall. The city's central market is a great place to pick up some fresh bread, cheeses, sausage, and fruit for a picnic lunch. The entrance is conveniently located just across from the bridge to the Ostrów Tumski (see below), with its acres of green grass, benches, and a pretty view over the city from across the river.

Piaskowa 17. ✆ **071/344-27-31.** Lunch and dinner items 10zł–20zł ($4.35–$8.70/£2.40–£5.40). No credit cards. Mon–Fri 8am–6:30pm; Sat 9am–3pm.

Rodeo Drive TEX-MEX One of the better Polish chain restaurants to emerge in the last few years, this one features "Texas-style" steaks, ribs, and burgers. Ordinarily, you could skip an American theme restaurant in favor of more authentic Polish fare, but in a land of mediocre burgers, this place really does stand out if you're in the mood. The portions are enormous, so even 6-foot-2 cowboys might be content with a "cowgirl" portion—even if the waitress does raise an eyebrow when you order it.

Rynek 28. ✆ **071/343-96-09.** Lunch and dinner items 20zł–35zł ($8.70–$15/£5.40–£9.45). AE, DC, MC, V. Daily 11am–10pm.

Exploring Wrocław

The main tourist attractions can be seen in a few hours of leisurely strolling. The natural place to start, and the best place to get your bearings, is the enormous **Rynek.** The Rynek is dominated (and that really *is* the right word in this case) by the enormous Town Hall, the Ratusz, at the center of the square. The Rynek is lined some of the most cheerful baroque and Renaissance facades to grace a Polish town square. On the northwest corner of the square is the foreboding, Gothic redbrick **St. Elizabeth Church (Kościól św. Elżbiety),** Wrocław's most impressive. You can climb the tower, but keep in mind it's over 90m (280 ft.) high. To the east of the Rynek is another evocative and beautiful church, the **Church of Mary Magdalene (Kościól św. Marii Magdaleny).** Just to the west of the Rynek, past the Tourist Information Office, is the smaller **Plac Solny,** the former salt market that's now given over to an enormous flower market. Off the square, the side streets in all directions merit a couple of hours of ambling. North of the Rynek, and along the Odra River, is the university district, where you'll find some of best nightspots. To the northwest of the Rynek, around Kiełbaśnicza, is Wrocław's arty district—formed amid some weathered but pretty blocks of buildings that survived the onslaught of World War II. Here you'll find a small street called the Old Shambles, "Stare Jatki." This was formerly the butchers' quarter, and is now filled with art galleries and coffee bars.

From the university district, follow the Odra River to right over a series of small, picturesque islands to the peaceful, restorative **Ostrów Tumski,** home to the city's cathedral and the spiritual heart of Wrocław. It's perfect for a picnic and a few hours of contemplative strolling.

National Museum (Muzeum Narodowe) ★ The National Museum is located just down from the Panorama Racławicka, and you can use the same admission ticket for entry to both. This museum is interesting primarily because it combines the collections of both the cities of Wrocław and Lwów, and is very strong on medieval painting and sculpture from both eastern and western Poland. That said, unless you're particularly interested in Poland or have some very specific historical knowledge, you're unlikely to get much from the very detailed holdings here.

Pl. Powstańców Warszawy 5. ✆ **071/372-51-50.** www.mnwr.art.pl. Admission 15zł ($6.50/£4). Wed–Sun 10am–4pm.

Panorama of the Battle of Racławice (Panorama Racławicka) ★★ This enormous 140m-long (450-ft.) "panorama" painting dates from the late 19th century and depicts the battle of Racławice on April 4, 1794, when a Polish force led by national hero Tadeusz Kościuszko defeated the Russian army. The battle came at a time when Poland faced threats from the east, west, and south, and aroused hopes that Poland might survive as a nation. Those hopes proved short-lived. A few months later, in November 1794, the Polish uprising was crushed, and Poland was later divided among Prussia, Russia, and Austria in the infamous Polish partition. The painting itself, executed while Poland was still partitioned, was a bold national statement at the time, and still evokes strong national sentiment. In the years following World War II, the painting was hidden from view lest its anti-Russian sentiments offend the Soviet overlords. After the rise of the Solidarity in the 1980s, the painting was finally unveiled to the general public in 1985.

Purkyniego 11. ✆ **071/344-23-44.** www.panoramaraclawicka.pl. Admission 20zł ($8.70/£5.40). Tues–Sun 9am–5pm.

Town Hall (Ratusz) ★★ One of Poland's largest and most awe-inspiring town halls. It was originally built in the late 13th century, but added on to and renovated time and time again down through the centuries. It's lost its administrative function and now serves a mostly decorative role—a place to situate a huge tower and hang an astronomical clock. The city museum inside is worth a quick peek, but more to see the inside of the building than to peruse the exhibits at length.

Rynek. ✆ **071/347-16-93.** www.mmw.pl. Wed–Sun 10am–5pm.

Outside Of Wrocław

If you have a couple of days to spare and are seeking relief from the city, Wrocław is a good jumping-off spot for exploring the Polish side of the **Sudeten (Sudety) mountains** that form the country's southern border with the Czech Republic. Both sides of the border are lined with little resort towns for hiking in summer and skiing in winter. The tallest peaks are in the 1,600m (5,248-ft.) range; most of the area is covered by the Karkonosze National Park, with its miles and miles of restorative hiking trails. The largest town in the region is picturesque **Jelenia Góra,** about 100km (62 miles) southwest of Wrocław. From Jelenia Góra it's just a short bus or car ride to the resorts of **Szklarska Poręba** and **Karpacz.** Both towns appear a bit scruffy and neglected, but the woods and hills themselves are beautiful. Several buses and trains daily make the trip from Wrocław to Jelenia Góra, with buses being slightly faster. By car, it's a 2-hour drive. If you're driving to the Czech Republic, the area is an easy stopover. The main Czech border crossing is only about 30km (18 miles) down the road from Jelenia Góra.

After Dark

Wrocław is renowned for its theater, long regarded as some of the most daring and experimental in the country. But for non-Polish speakers, this is likely to be of little interest. The Tourist Information Office at the Rynek is a good source of information on more accessible performances of classical music and opera. The **Wrocław Philharmonic,** Piłsudskiego 19 (© **071/342-24-59** box office; www.filharmonia.wroclaw.pl), is a good bet for an excellent concert in season on a Friday or Saturday night. The **Wrocław Opera,** Świdnicka 35 (© **071/344-57-79** box office; www.opera.wroclaw.pl), is one of the country's leading companies.

For culture of the lower-brow sort, Wrocław is a great drinking and party town. Its festive spirit, not surprisingly, is bolstered by tens of thousands of college students here. The university area has more than its fair share of beer gardens, cafes, and cocktail bars. For a good pub crawl, try the streets Ruska and Kuźnica that lead off from the Rynek. The Plac Solny is also lined with drinking spots and the Rynek itself is a major draw. What appear to be normal restaurants and cafes during the day transmogrify into everything from rowdy beer halls to ultrachill dance clubs after sunset.

Graciarnia ★ In spite of the foreboding location and doorway, this is a great spot if you're looking for a quiet beer or drink in the evening, a little bit away from the action. A self-described "chill zone" features antique furniture, a laid-back clientele, and very friendly servers. Open Monday to Friday noon to 2am, Saturday 5pm to 2am, and Sunday 5pm to midnight. Ul. K. Wielkiego 39. © **071/795-66-88.**

9 GDAŃSK & THE BALTIC SEA COAST

GDAŃSK

420km (250 miles) N of Warsaw

Gdańsk (www.gdansk.pl or http://guide.trojmiasto.pl) is a pleasant surprise. If you were expecting a dingy Baltic seaport, maybe reinforced by those foggy, black-and-white TV memories of Lech Wałęsa and embattled Solidarity dockworkers, you'll be in for a shock. Modern-day Gdańsk is a beautiful seaside town, with a lovingly restored Old Town and an easy, laid-back feel. On arrival, you'll immediately want to extend your stay, so plan on spending at least an extra day longer than budgeted.

Even for Poland, Gdańsk has a particularly twisted history that will play havoc with anyone who is even mildly geographically challenged. The city rose to prominence in the 16th and 17th centuries as one of the most important towns of the Hanseatic League, a grouping of prosperous seaport cities that controlled much of the trade in the North and Baltic seas. Because of its wealth, Gdańsk was hotly contested between German and Polish interests, though it managed to retain its status as a semi-autonomous city-state. After the Polish partition at the end of the 18th century, the city fell under Prussian rule and became firmly identified as "Danzig," its German name. Following Germany's defeat in World War I, the city's status became one of the thorniest issues facing the drafters of the Treaty of Versailles. They opted to create what they called the "Free City of Danzig"—neither German nor Polish—alongside a Polish-ruled strip of land that would effectively cut off mainland Germany from its East Prussian hinterland. Hitler was able to exploit very effectively the existence of this Polish "corridor" as part of his argument that the Treaty of Versailles was highly unfair to Germany. He even chose the port of Gdańsk to launch his war on Poland on September 1, 1939, when German gunboats fired on the Polish garrison at Westerplatte.

Gdańsk was thoroughly destroyed in World War II, with the Russians and Allied bombers effectively finishing off any destruction the Germans weren't able to complete themselves. But Gdańsk was luckier than many Polish cities in that the reconstruction after the war was uncommonly sensitive. And unlike the reconstruction of Warsaw's Old Town (which seemed mostly to benefit the tourists), Gdańsk's newly built Old Town feels thoroughly lived in and authentic. The main drag, Długa ulica, is gorgeous and the streets radiating from it are filled with life.

During the Communist period, Gdańsk rose to fame as the home of the Lenin Shipyards and the Solidarity Trade Union. It was here, now known as the Gdańsk shipyards, where very tense negotiations in August 1980 between Solidarity, led by a young, rakish Lech Wałęsa, and the government resulted in official recognition of the first independent trade union in Communist Eastern Europe. The government later reneged on the agreement and imposed martial law, but Gdańsk continued as a hotbed of labor unrest and strikes. Roundtable talks in the late 1980s saw the government agree to a power-sharing arrangement that in 1989 led to the first semifree elections and a nationwide political triumph for Solidarity. You can still see the shipyards, about a 15-minute walk north of the Old Town, and visit an inspirational museum, the Road to Freedom (Drogi do Wolności), that details those tense moments in 1980 and the eventual overthrow of Communism.

Gdańsk is the largest and southernmost of a string of three Baltic resorts known as the Trójmiasto (Tri-Cities). Sopot, about 6km (4 miles) farther along the coast, is smaller and more exclusive. Sopot was traditionally a retreat for the very wealthy, and while today it's probably better known as the Baltic party town par excellence, it still retains a whiff of old money. It's here, too, where you'll find the most easily accessible and acceptably clean beaches in summer. Gdynia, about 15km (10 miles) to the north, is the least impressive of the three. Gdynia began life as a relatively quiet coastal village, but it was built up in a hurry after World War I, when Polish authorities fashioned it into the country's busiest Baltic seaport. A convenient commuter rail line links all three towns, with departures in all directions several times an hour during the day.

Getting There

BY PLANE Port Lotniczy Gdańsk (also known as Lech Wałęsa International Airport), Słowackiego 200 (✆ **058/348-11-63;** www.airport.gdansk.pl), is about 8km (5 miles) west of the city. The airport has added several flights in recent years, and now has good direct connections to major European cities like London (Luton and Stansted), Frankfurt, and several Scandinavian cities, among others. To get to town from the airport, take bus B, which runs twice hourly during daylight hours to Gdańsk's central Główny train station. The trip costs 3zł ($1.30/80p) and you can buy tickets from the driver or the airport tourist information office (see below). Leave about 30 minutes for the journey (more during rush hour). A taxi into town will cost about 50zł ($22/£13). A taxi to Sopot will run about 60zł ($26/£16), and to Gdynia about 90zł ($39/£24).

BY TRAIN For most arrivals, Gdańsk's Główny train station (Dworzec PKP), Podwale Grodzkie 1l (✆ **058/721-54-15;** www.pkp.pl), is the first port of a call. The station is just a 5 minutes' walk (below a major highway) from the center of the city. Gdańsk is well served by the Polish state railroad, PKP, and fast InterCity train departures to Warsaw and other major cities are frequent. Fast and frequent commuter trains to Sopot and

Gdynia also depart from here. The station has several ATMs, a branch of the local tourist information office, and even McDonald's and KFC outlets if you turn up famished from a long train journey and need something quick to tide you over.

BY BUS The main bus station, Dworzec PKS, ul. 3 Maje 12 (© **058/302-15-32;** www.pks.gdansk.pl), is located just behind the train station. The Old Town is an easy walk, passing through the train station and then below the highway using the underpass. As Poland's Baltic hub, the city is a primary destination for domestic and international bus lines.

BY CAR Gdańsk is a traffic nightmare, so leave plenty of time to get here. The first problem is the major and seemingly permanent road construction, which has badly tied up routes coming from all directions. The main roads running south are the E75 to Toruń and the E77 to Warsaw. The E28 is the main route west toward Germany. Coming from the west, it skirts Gdańsk as it heads south. Once you arrive in the city, brace yourself for hour-long jams during the morning and evening rush hours. The drive from Warsaw, with traffic, may take as long 5 to 6 hours.

BY BOAT It is possible to arrive in Gdańsk by ferry from Sweden. Polferries (www.polferries.pl) offers regular service between the Swedish port of Nynaeshamm (60km/37 miles south of Stockholm) and Gdańsk's Nowy Port, Przemyslowa 1, 7km (4 1/3 miles) north of the center (© **058/343-00-78**). The ferries depart every second or third day at 6pm and arrive at noon. Returns from Gdańsk follow the same schedule. Tickets (one adult without car) run about $100 (£62) each way (in 2008, this was subject to an additional 20% fuel surcharge). Sleeping berths are extra and start at $20 (£12) for a modest bunk to nearly $200 (£124) for a luxury cabin for two. Stena Line (© **058/660-92-00;** www.stenaline.pl) runs a similar service from Gdynia's passenger ferry port to the picturesque Swedish city of Karlskrona and back. In summer, the ferries make the 10-hour journey twice daily at 9am and 9pm. Tickets (without car) run about $80/£50 each way.

City Layout

Confusingly, unlike other Polish cities, the heart of Gdańsk is technically not called Old Town, or **Stare Miasto.** There is a Stare Miasto, but it lies just to the north of the main center, the **Główne Miasto.** The Główne Miasto is where you'll find the main pedestrian walk, **ul. Długa (Long St.);** its extension, the **Długi Targ (the Long Market);** as well as the most interesting side streets, and the main pedestrian walk along the **Motława Canal.** Stare Miasto is about a 15-minute walk north, and it's here where you'll find the **Gdańsk shipyards.** Farther to the north, in the direction of Sopot, lies the still-skuzzy **Nowy Port,** as well as the far-nicer suburbs of **Wrzeszcz** and **Oliwa.** The former is home to many of the city's more affordable hotels and pensions. The heart of **Sopot** is about 6km (4 miles) to the north of Gdańsk's city center. **Gdynia** is about 15km (10 miles) farther to the north.

Getting Around

ON FOOT Much of central Gdańsk, including ul. Długa and the walkway along the canal, is closed to motor vehicles, so walking is the best option. The center is compact and easily walkable. To get to Sopot or Gdynia or places farther afield, however, you'll need to use public transportation.

BY TRAM Gdańsk has an efficient network of trams that whisk you from the center of the city to the suburbs of Wrzeszcz and Oliwa in a few minutes. Note that trams do not run to Sopot and Gdynia. Tickets cost 2zł (85¢/55p) for a short 15-minute ride and

2.80zł ($1.20/75p) for longer rides. You can buy tickets at Ruch kiosks, magazine counters, and from special vending machines.

BY BUS City buses are useful for getting to some of the pensions on Beethovena ul., but otherwise walking, trams, trains, and taxis should be sufficient. Ticketing is the same as for trams, with a single short journey of 15 minutes costing 2zł (85¢/55p).

BY TRAIN A quick and reliable local train service, the SKM (Szybka Kolej Miejska), links the main cities of the Tri-Cities: Gdańsk, Sopot, and Gdynia. Several trains an hour during the day depart from Gdańsk's main train station. The full journey up to Gdynia will take a little more than half an hour and costs 4.50zł ($1.95/£1.20). Buy your tickets at ticket windows or from special vending machines on the platforms and validate them before you board the train.

BY TAXI It's a good way to get to your hotel on arrival at the bus or train station, but you won't need taxis much once you've sorted out the public transportation system. Figure on fares of around 20zł ($8.70/£5.40) for journeys in town.

BY BOAT It's possible to go by ferry from Gdańsk to several local and regional destinations, including Westerplatte, Sopot, and Gdynia, as well as to the beaches on the Hel Peninsula farther afield. The main ferry landing, at Nabrzeże Motławy (✆ **058/301-13-23;** www.ztm.gda.pl), is along the canal. In summer months (May–Oct), take a fun ride on a mock pirate boat, the Galeon Lew, out to Westerplatte (Targ Rybny; ✆ **0601/629-191;** www.rejsyturystyczne.pl).

BY BIKE Gdańsk is navigable by bicycle, and several new bike lanes now connect the center with the suburb of Wrzeszcz and beyond toward Sopot. That said, the network is spotty and there are plenty of places where you'll still have to contend with stairways, sidewalks, heavy traffic, and clueless Polish drivers. Bikes, however, are a good way of getting around Sopot. An easy and tranquil 10km (6¼-mile) bike lane skirts the beaches from Sopot to the northern Gdańsk suburbs.

Visitor Information

The city's main tourist information office, at ul. Długa 45 (✆ **058/301-91-51;** www.pttk-gdansk.pl), is conveniently situated in the heart of the Główne Miasto on the pedestrianized ul. Długa. The office is badly overburdened in summer, but nevertheless an essential stop for maps, lists of hotels and pensions, and ideas of what to see and do. Pick up a copy of the map "Gdańsk, Stare Miasto," a large-format, easy-to-read guide to all of the major sights in the center of town. Also look for the free brochure *The Best of Gdańsk,* a comprehensive, self-guided walking tour, with explanations in English. The tourist office also hands out free copies of *Gdańsk, In Your Pocket,* an excellent overview of the city, including sections on Sopot and Gdynia. The tourist office maintains branches at the arrivals hall at Gdańsk airport and the main ticketing area of the train station.

Where to Stay

The lodging situation has improved in recent years, but accommodations are still tight in July and August, so prebooking is essential. Most of the expensive places, not surprisingly, are in the center, and you'll usually have to pay a premium for location. The cheaper places and pensions tend to be in the suburbs, like Wrzeszcz, about 3km (1¾ miles) north of the center toward Sopot.

Very Expensive

Hanza ★★ A clean, modern hotel along the river promenade, boasting an impressive roster of actors and politicians who regularly book here. The lobby and public areas have an understated, contemporary look. The rooms, in blue carpet and dark wood, are on the plain side, but very comfortable. Be sure to ask for a room with a view over the canal and the old town in the background (though these tend to fill up first). One big perk: It's one of the few hotels in the center to offer a full-service fitness club and sauna.

Tokarska 6. ✆ **058/305-34-27.** Fax 058/305-33-86. www.hotelhanza.pl. 60 units. 600zł ($261/£162) double. AE, DC, MC, V. **Amenities:** Restaurant; health club and spa; concierge; business center; limited room service; nonsmoking rooms. *In room:* A/C, TV, dataport, minibar, hair dryer.

Podewils ★★★ This small, old-fashioned villa across the river from the town center is widely regarded as the city's finest hotel, though for less money you get more amenities at the Hanza and a better view at the Królewski. Be sure to ask for a city view—not one that looks out onto the building site. That said, each of the rooms is meticulously decorated in beautiful antiques, and the professional staff will look after your every whim. Don't pass up the chance to have a meal or a glass of wine on the terrace overlooking the canal and the Old Town.

Szafarnia 2. ✆ **058/300-95-60.** Fax 058/300-95-70. www.podewils.pl. 10 units. 800zł ($348/£216) double. AE, DC, MC, V. **Amenities:** Restaurant; sauna; concierge; room service; nonsmoking rooms. *In room:* A/C, TV, dataport, minibar, hair dryer, safe.

Expensive

Kamienica Goldwasser ★ Value You couldn't ask for a better location at a better price. Seven nicely furnished apartments, right on the waterfront and above one of the city's nicest restaurants. Each apartment is furnished individually, in a tasteful mix of modern and traditional styles. Some rooms have fireplaces; ask to see a couple before choosing. That said there isn't much in the way of amenities or facilities. The reception is located inside the restaurant.

Długie Pobrzeże 22. ✆ **058/301-88-78.** Fax 058/301-12-44. www.goldwasser.pl. 7 units. 340zł ($148/£92) apt. AE, DC, MC, V. **Amenities:** Restaurant. *In room:* TV, dataport, hair dryer.

Królewski ★★★ This sleek, modern hotel is in a tastefully remodeled former granary just across the canal from Gdańsk's town center. If you can get it, ask for room no. 310—a corner double with drop-dead views of the riverside and all of Gdańsk's spires and gables. The rooms are tastefully modern, some with hardwood floors and bathtubs. The restaurant and breakfast room look out over the river, through a round little window like you're on a cruise. A special place.

Ołowianka 1. ✆ **058/326-11-11.** Fax 058/326-11-10. www.hotelkrolewski.pl. 30 units. 360zł ($156/£97) double. AE, DC, MC, V. **Amenities:** Restaurant. *In room:* A/C, TV, dataport, minibar, hair dryer.

Villa Eva Overpriced for what it is, but nevertheless a clean, comfortable hotel within relatively easy reach, via the tram, of the Old Town. The owners seem to be going for a "boutique hotel" ambience, but little things like the sparsely furnished rooms make it feel more like a high-end pension. The restaurant downstairs is very good, and a nice welcome if you arrive late and tired. The location, in the tony suburb of Wrzeszcz, is about 3km (1¾ miles) from the center (a 30-min. walk or a 10-min. tram ride from the train station).

Batorego 28. ✆ **058/341-67-85.** Fax 058/341-49-49. www.villaeva.pl. 15 units. 320zł ($139/£86) double. AE, DC, MC, V. **Amenities:** Restaurant. *In room:* TV, dataport.

Wolne Miasto ★ The first thing you'll notice is the beautiful antique reception desk. That sets the tone for a well-run, attractively appointed in-town hotel. The decor is a restrained traditional look, with rooms fitted out with red carpets and antique wardrobes. The restaurant dabbles in relative exotica like tapas dishes and gets good marks from local critics.

Św. Ducha 2. ✆ **058/305-22-55.** Fax 058/322-24-47. www.hotelwm.pl. 43 units. 410zł ($178/£111) double. AE, DC, MC, V. **Amenities:** Restaurant. *In room:* TV, dataport, minibar.

Moderate

Biała Lilia ★★ This lodging is somewhere between a small hotel and a pension. It offers excellent value, given the crisp modern furnishings and the in-town location, just across the bridge from the Green Door and the delights of Długa. After so many sterile contemporary rooms, it's nice to see one that actually looks inviting. The cream walls and dark-green carpeting lend a warmth that makes you want to linger. Ask the staff to show you the unique second-floor garden terrace out the back.

Spichrzowa 16. ✆ **058/301-70-74.** Fax 058/320-14-73. www.bialalilia.pl. 16 units. 290zł ($126/£78) double. AE, DC, MC, V. **Amenities:** Restaurant. *In room:* TV, dataport, minibar.

Kamienica Gotyk ★ (Finds) Ordinarily, you'd expect to pay a fortune for the location—in Gdańsk's oldest house on its loveliest street—but by some quirk of fate this charming little guesthouse is one of the more reasonably priced hotels in town. I guess the owners like to feel virtuous. Admittedly, there's not much in the way of services or amenities, and the room furnishings feel like an afterthought, but the location is unbeatable. If you can get in, don't hesitate to book it.

Mariacka 1. ✆ **058/301-85-67.** www.gotykhouse.eu. 6 units. 280zł ($122/£76) double. AE, DC, MC, V. *In room:* TV.

Inexpensive

Angela ★★ (Finds) Quieter than it looks, since the pension is perched back away from the busy suburban street. Once you walk back to where the house is you see a lovely garden setting and a very clean and well-run pension. The rooms are basic but good value in Gdańsk's overpriced hotel market. The breakfasts are the best in town. Take a cab on arrival to find the place; once you've checked in and gotten situated the receptionist can help you with the buses in and out of the center.

Beethovena 12. ✆ **058/302-23-15.** Fax 058/326-07-78. www.villaangela.pl. 19 units. 230zł ($100/£62) double. AE, DC, MC, V. **Amenities:** Restaurant. *In room:* TV, dataport.

Stemp-Tur Not nearly as nice on the inside as the Angela (and only limited English spoken), but the garden is a delight and the price is the best you'll find in overpriced Gdańsk. Johann Sebastien Bach Street, where the pension is located, is right out of a page of *Better Homes and Gardens* magazine. The only drawback are the beds—as rock hard as a driveway. Take a taxi to get here at first, and then use the bus for getting around after that.

Bacha 45. ✆ **058/306-35-30.** www.stemptur.com.pl. 5 units. 160zł ($70/£43) double. AE, DC, MC, V.

Where to Dine

With the possible exception of Kraków/Kazimierz, Gdańsk has some of the best restaurants in Poland. You'll find a mix of cuisines and some great Polish places at all price levels. Most are just a short walk from Długa.

Very Expensive

Gdańska ★★ POLISH Old-school fine dining with formal waitstaff, white linens, and the main dining room stuffed with knickknacks and bric-a-brac. A good choice for an evening of candlelight dining and raising a glass or two to the good life. The cooking is excellent if on the heavy side. The chef's specialty is roast goose, though the fish dishes are very good as well.

Św. Ducha 16/24. ✆ **058/305-76-71.** Lunch and dinner items 30zł–50zł ($13–$22/£8.10–£13). AE, DC, MC, V. Daily 11am–midnight.

Salonik ★★ POLISH Gdańsk is blessed with several natural "splurge" choices. The Goldwasser (see below) is a good one, and the elegant, upmarket "Salon," just down from the Neptune fountain on Długa, is another. The sign out front calls this a Polish restaurant, but they're not talking about pierogies and potato pancakes. Think more along the lines of duck breast in plum sauce or lamb medallions. The mood at lunch is less formal, and the street-side terrace is makes for a very memorable midday meal. In the evenings, you'll want to dress up a little to match the surroundings.

Długa 18/21. ✆ **058/322-00-44.** Lunch and dinner items 40zł–60zł ($17–$26/£11–£16). AE, DC, MC, V. Daily noon–11pm.

Expensive

Goldwasser ★★ INTERNATIONAL A local institution and well worth a splurge as much for the food as for the unbeatable riverside location and gorgeous interior. Here's also the place to sample Goldwasser, a slightly sweetish vodka flavored with, among other things, flakes of gold. Everything gets the thumbs up, but the fresh fish dishes come highly recommended, as do the homemade pierogies. In summer, sit outside on the terrace. In winter, warm yourself up in cozy, tavernlike surroundings.

Długie Pobrzeże. ✆ **058/301-88-78.** Lunch and dinner items 28zł–46zł ($12–$20/£7.55–£12). AE, DC, MC, V. Daily 10am–11pm.

Kansai JAPANESE Sushi hit the big time in Poland a few years ago, and it seems every large Polish city now has a decent sushi joint. Kansai is one of the best. Maybe it's the proximity to the sea and the high standards for seafood here generally, but the sushi tastes fresher than most, and the maki rolls go far beyond the standard tuna and salmon. The only drawbacks are the cost—but that goes with the territory—and the early closing time. Like most Japanese restaurants here, however, the atmosphere is stark bordering on sterile, and you wouldn't want to linger long after your sake anyway.

Oganta 124. ✆ **058/324-08-88.** Lunch and dinner items 30zł–50zł ($13–$22/£8.10–£13). AE, DC, MC, V. Daily noon–9pm.

Moderate

Estragon ★ INTERNATIONAL Trendy eatery combining high-quality international dishes and a stylish yet unpretentious atmosphere. The menu is a strong on what you might call "new Continental" cuisine: steaks, pork chops, and stuffed chicken breasts. The chicken stuffed with spinach is very nice and a lighter alternative to heavy Polish cooking. Vegetarians will welcome the soy burger on the menu. The unfussy presentation is reminiscent of something you might see in New York's East Village, and the cook serves up a reasonable and recommendable facsimile of a New York–style cheesecake.

Chlebnicka 26. ✆ **058/309-17-00.** Lunch and dinner items 20zł–40zł ($8.70–$17/£5.40–£11). AE, DC, MC, V. Daily noon–10pm.

Kreska ★ INTERNATIONAL A trendy and highly regarded modern restaurant, specializing in what it calls "fusion" food. In this case, judging by the menu, fusion refers to nothing more exotic than vegetarian lasagna, but no matter, the kitchen is trying and the results are mostly good. The stark and stylish decor draws a good-looking crowd in the evening. The kitchen really shines at lunch, though, when its freshly made sandwiches and salads are just what the doctor ordered. The spinach-stuffed pierogies are an inventive and welcome twist on a Polish classic.

Św. Ducha 2. ✆ **058/300-05-94.** Lunch and dinner items 25zł–40zł ($11–$17/£6.75–£11). AE, DC, MC, V. Daily 10am–11pm.

Targ Rybny (Fish Market) ★★ SEAFOOD One of the city's best places for fish—both grilled and fried. The location, on the city's Fish Market, a bit out of the center, is about a 15 minutes' walk from Długa ulica. For something different, try the pierogies stuffed with white fish. In summer, sit on the terrace overlooking the square called—appropriately enough—the "fish market."

Targ Rybny 6c. ✆ **058/320-90-11.** Lunch and dinner items 25zł–40zł ($11–$17/£6.75–£11). AE, DC, MC, V. Daily 11am–10pm.

Inexpensive

Napoli PIZZA Average pizzas at best, but quick, relatively cheap and boasting a super-convenient central location. A life-saver if you're traveling with kids whose interest in more sightseeing is starting to flag. Pizzas come conveniently sized in small and large, with small certainly adequate unless you haven't eaten in 3 days.

Długa 62/63. ✆ **058/301-41-46.** Lunch and dinner items 12zł–25zł ($5.20–$11/£3.25–£6.75). AE, DC, MC, V. Daily 11am–10pm.

Pierogarnia U Dzika ★★ POLISH A *pierogarnia,* as the word suggests, is a restaurant that specializes in pierogies. This one, centrally located around the corner from busy Mariacka street, is better than most and a good place to sample the little dumplings and a glass of beer to wash them down. The menu includes both standard stuffings liked ground beef, potato, and cottage cheese, and more inventive varieties. Pierogies "Wileńskie" are a nice change of pace, with buckwheat groats and bacon instead of the usual potatoes and cottage cheese. Servings are a large 10 pieces, enough for a full meal and then some.

Piwna 59/60. ✆ **058/305-26-76.** Lunch and dinner items 15zł–25zł ($6.50–$11/£4.05–£6.75). AE, DC, MC, V. Daily 11am–10pm.

Exploring Gdańsk

Central Gdańsk is one of the most pleasantly walkable cities in central Europe. You couldn't ask for a more strikingly beautiful and colorful main street than **ul. Długa,** the heart of the Główne Miasto. As you walk its length, from the **Golden Gate** at one end to **Długi Targ** and the magnificent **Green Gate** (which is not actually green) at the other, bear in mind that nearly everything you see was rebuilt after World War II. The focal point of Długa is the fountain of **Neptune,** the god of the sea. The fountain dates from 1549. You'll find the main tourist information office just opposite the fountain. The Green Gate was originally meant to house visiting royalty, but now it serves as an exhibition space and features the houses of former president and Solidarity leader Lech Wałęsa. Walk through the Green Gate and you'll find the **Motława canal** and a picture-perfect seaside promenade. Turn left on **Długie Pobrzeże** and continue up a few blocks, turning back into the city through St. Mary's Gate to **ul. Mariacka.** This is one of the most picturesque of the side streets that flank Długa and it's the heart of Amberville. In nearly every shop on the street you'll find gold, brown, and green amber broaches, pendants, necklaces, and earrings. At the western end of Mariacka you'll find the imposing redbrick monolith of the **Church of St. Mary,** reputedly the largest redbrick church in the world.

The Gdańsk shipyards are located north of the central city, about a 15 minutes' walk from Długa. The area is still fairly industrial and you'll need a good map or at least some perseverance as you meander along the old streets until you see the big 38m-high (125-ft.) piece of steel that marks the **Monument to the Fallen Shipyard Workers.**

Amber Museum ★★ A must for all fans of that beautiful ossified pine resin that helped make Gdańsk wealthy. On six floors of exhibits, you'll learn everything you'll ever need to know about amber, including how it's mined and processed, what it looks like under a microscope, and how it was used through ages, not just as jewelry but in art and medicine. If you're thinking of buying some amber while you're in Gdańsk, you might want to stop here first for an educational primer. One part of the exhibition is given over to fake amber, and how to identify the genuine article.

Targ Węglowy. ✆ **058/301-47-33.** www.mhmg.gda.pl. Admission 10zł ($4.35/£2.70). May–Sept Tues–Sat 10am–6pm, Sun 11am–6pm, Mon 11am–3pm; Sept–May shorter hr. and closed Mon.

Arthur's Court (Dwór Artusa) ★ One of the most impressive houses in the city was recently opened to the public after extensive renovation. The Arthur's Court, named for King Arthur, was founded as a meeting place for the town's wealthiest businessmen and leading dignitaries. The house dates from the 14th century, but was remodeled several times, including once in the 19th century when it was given its neo-Gothic look following the vogue of the time. One of the highlights inside is a 9m-high (30-ft.) Renaissance tiled oven. The exterior was demolished in World War II, but many of the interior pieces had been removed beforehand and survived the fighting.

Długi Targ 43/44. ✆ **058/767-91-00.** www.mhmg.gda.pl. Admission 8zł ($3.50/£2.15). May–Sept Tues–Sat 10am–6pm, Sun 11am–6pm; Oct–Apr shorter hr., closed Mon.

Central Maritime Museum ★ The best of four separate museums that highlight Gdańsk's history as a port city. Here you'll find more or less the A-to-Z compendium on Polish maritime history, from the turn of the first millennium to modern times. Some of the best exhibits are the detailed models of the ships, lots of old weaponry, and at the top some oil paintings of old boats. The museum is housed in three Renaissance-era granaries.

Ołowianka 9/13. ✆ **058/310-86-11.** www.cmm.pl. Admission 6zł ($2.60/£1.60). May–Sept daily 10am–6pm; Sept–May, shorter hr. and closed Mon.

Monument to the Fallen Shipyard Workers This enormous outdoor monument, some 40m (130 ft.) high, was built in 1980 to remember the 44 people who died during bloody anti-Communist riots of 1970. Its construction was one of the demands put forward by the striking workers in August 1980. The presence of the monument was keenly embarrassing to the Communist authorities. Solidarity leader Lech Wałęsa likened it to a harpoon driven into the side of a whale.

Plac Solidarności.

Roads to Freedom ★★★ A moving trip down memory lane of the anti-Communist struggle in Poland, starting with the riots in 1970 that tore the country apart to the rise of the Solidarity trade union later that decade, and finally to the historic agreement

Sopot

Don't pass up the chance to see Sopot, Gdańsk's answer to the Hamptons and Atlantic City all rolled up into one. Before World War II, Sopot was the haunt of the moneyed classes—a place where in order to properly summer you had to be somebody. After the war, during the Communist period, the resort lost some of its sheen. It was still regarded as exclusive, but the idea of a decadent seaside resort didn't fit well with the reigning ideological aesthetic. Since 1989, Sopot has mounted something of a comeback, cashing in on both its former allure and affirming its identity as Poland's top summertime party town.

Sopot's an easy 25-minute train ride from Gdańsk's main station. From the station, head down the steps to ul. Kościuszki, which leads you to town's main drag, ul. Bohaterów Monte Cassino, a long, sloping pedestrianized walk that takes you all the way to the pier.

From here there are several things to do. You can stroll the pier, the longest along the Baltic coast. It's possible to catch the ferry here to the Hel Peninsula or over to Gdańsk as alternative way to get back. Sopot's beaches, some of the nicest and most accessible in the Gdańsk area, fan off on both sides of the pier. To the right, a long, tree-lined walk, with a very nice bike path, skirts the beach and will take you all the back to the suburbs of Gdańsk. Should you feel the urge to cycle, Rowerownia in Gdańsk, Fieldorfa 11/3 (✆ **058/320-61-69**), rents by the hour or the day.

Bohaterów Monte Cassino is lined on both sides with restaurants and cafes; sometime around midevening—10pm or so—the mood shifts into party drive, and these very same places transform themselves into some of the Tri-Cities' most happening clubs.

in August 1980 that led to the union's official recognition by the then-Communist government. Solidarity was the first independent trade union to be recognized in the Eastern bloc; the move eventually paved the way for the first semifree elections in 1989 and finally the toppling of Communist regimes in Poland and throughout Eastern Europe. The exhibit begins with a mock-up of a typical empty grocery store during Communist times and then moves through a history of the anti-Communist opposition in Poland and the rest of Eastern Europe. The real draws, however, are the videos of the events as they unfolded during those tense times. One room features a short film of the days leading up to the August Agreement, and then to the tragic times a year later when the government reneged on the deal and imposed martial law. Another moving film looks at all of the revolutions in Eastern Europe. The Roads to Freedom exhibition was originally based at the Gdańsk shipyards but it's found a temporary home (until 2010) here in the basement of Solidarity headquarters in the center of the city.

Ul. Wały Piastowskie 24. ✆ **058/308-44-28.** www.fcs.org.pl. Admission 6zł ($2.60/£1.60). Daily Tues–Sun 10am–5pm.

St. Mary's Church ★★ This enormous redbrick church is reputedly the largest of its kind in the world. Its nave and 31 chapels can hold more 20,000 people. The church endeared itself to the people of Gdańsk in the years after the imposition of martial law in 1981, when members of the Solidarity trade union sheltered here. The church is more impressive from the outside than in; it was badly damaged during World War II and the frescoes inside were covered over in white. Note the astronomical clock on the outside; it not only tells time, but also gives the phases of moon, and shows the position of the sun and the moon in relation to the signs of the zodiac. If you're feeling up to it, climb the more than 400 steps to the top of the tower for an unparalleled view over the city. Podkramarksa 5. ✆ **058/301-39-82.** Admission 2zł (85¢/55p). Mon–Sat 9am–5:30pm; Sun 1–5:30pm.

Town Hall ★★ One of the country's finest town halls; the original building dates from the 14th century, but it was badly damaged during World War II and what you see today is a very nicely turned out reconstruction. The building is beautiful inside and out. One of the highlights inside is the Red Room (Sala Czerwona), truly red, with its sumptuous furniture and ceiling and wall paintings. At the center is a painting entitled *The*

Słowiński National Park

There's a remarkable landscape of wetlands and giant sand dunes, butted up against the Baltic Sea, about a 2 hours' ride or drive northwest of the Tri-Cities. The **Słowiński National Park** (daily 8am to dark) is unique enough to be included on the UNESCO's list of protected biospheres, and makes for a nice day out away from the bustle of Gdańsk and the Tri-Cities' crowded beaches.

The park begins about 2km (1¼ miles) west of the seaside resort of Łeba. Łeba itself is not much, but keep pressing on to see the park's two lakes and the enormous, shifting sand dunes that rise to a height of some 40m (131 ft.).

The park has something for everyone. The protected wetlands make it a great spot for birders, and in and among the more common species, you'll find rarer sorts like cranes and black storks. World War II history buffs will be interested in hearing how the Nazis used the unique sandy landscape as a training ground for Rommel's Afrika Korps. The Germans also conducted early experiments in rocketry here, and just west of the hamlet of Rabka, you'll find an early and eerie-looking launchpad and a small museum. And of course there are the amazing giant dunes themselves, stretching for a length of about 5km (3 miles). The dunes migrate up to 10m (33 ft.) every year. After you've hiked awhile into the center of the dunes, you'll swear you're in the Sahara. Poland feels far, far away.

Cars are restricted from entering the park area. In nice weather, walking is a pleasant option. But you can also rent bikes by the hour, or hitch a ride on a horse-drawn cart, electric trolley, or even a golf cart. To get here from the Tri-Cities, make your way north to Gdynia and take the bus for Łeba. If you're driving, follow the E28 highway in the direction of Słupsk, bearing right at Lębork. Allow at least 2 hours by bus or car along often-difficult roads.

 Glorification of the Unity of Gdańsk with Poland. Take a stroll through the city's historical museum here, noting the black-and-white photographs of Gdańsk in 1945 and its near total destruction in the war.

Długa 46/47. ✆ **058/767-91-00.** www.mhmg.gda.pl. Tues–Sat 10am–6pm, Sun 11am–6pm, Mon 10am–3pm; Oct–Apr closed Mon.

Westerplatte ★ Westerplatte is known to Poles as the place where World War II began. It was here on this far-flung peninsula on September 1, 1939, that the German gunboat *Schleswig-Holstein* first fired on a small garrison of about 180 Polish troops. The Poles, though badly outnumbered, held out valiantly, repelling 3,000 German soldiers for 7 days. There's not much to see out here (most of the exhibit is given over to a grassy park), but it makes a nice day's outing by boat (see above). A small museum outlines the history of those first few days of the war.

Sucharskiego 1. ✆ **058/343-69-72.** Tues–Sun 9am–4pm.

Outside Of Gdańsk

Hel Peninsula ★★ The first question in summer visitors usually ask is, "Where are the beaches?" If you've got little time, the best choice is probably Sopot, but if you've got a day to spare and the sun is shining, why not go for something a little more remote? The Hel Peninsula is a pencil-thin strip of land that juts into the Baltic north of Gdynia. It's far enough away from industrial Gdańsk to ensure some of the Baltic's cleanest water, and the sleepy fishing town of Hel is a delight in its own right. In summer, you can take the ferry out to Hel from Gdańsk, Sopot, or Gdynia. From Gdańsk, ferries depart from main ferry port along the Motława canal; figure on about 2 hours for the trip each way. Alternatively, there's train service from Gdańsk and Gdynia, and a quicker minibus from Gdynia's bus station.

Shopping

For centuries the center of the Baltic amber trade, Gdańsk is still *the* place to buy it. You'll find no shortage of amber dealers in town. The biggest concentrations are on the main street Długa and along quieter Mariacka, a couple of streets over. Before buying try to educate yourself a bit about quality amber. While the majority of the dealers are reputable, amber fakes abound so always watch carefully that you're buying the real deal. The **Amber Museum** (see "Exploring Gdańsk," above) is a good place to start to learn about amber. One legitimate gallery with some beautiful pieces is **L Galeria,** Mariacka 23/24.

Another purely "I got it in Gdańsk" gift is **Goldwasser** vodka. While the sweetish taste is not to everyone's liking, who could pass up flakes of gold in their cocktail? You can buy a gift box at the Goldwasser restaurant (p. 455).

Gdańsk After Dark

Most of the serious culture revolves around two venues: The **Frederyk Chopin Baltic Philharmonic,** Ołowianka 1 (✆ **058/320-62-62** [box office]; www.filharmonia.gda.pl), and the **State Baltic Opera,** Al. Zwycięstwa 15 (✆ **058/763-49-13;** www.operabaltycka.pl). The Philharmonic's main home is right across the Motława canal from the center of the city. Check the website or ask at the tourist information office on Długa. You can buy tickets at the Motława box office or at the specific performance venue up to 2 hours before the show. The opera maintains a lively program in season, with visiting and local companies. The quirky website is a good place to buy tickets to performances, or try the box office during office hours. Gdańsk's **Miniatura Theater,** Grunwaldszka 16 (✆ **058/341-12-09;** www.teatrminiatura.pl), maintains a lively and excellent repertoire of puppet shows and fairy tales aimed at children, but shows are almost exclusively in Polish.

The Główne Miasto is filled with cafes, bars, and clubs, with the best of these not necessarily on Długa, but on the side streets that parallel. Try the streets Św. Ducha, Piwna, and Chlebnicka. The embankment along Długie Pobrzeże is a nice spot for an evening stroll, with plenty of places along the way for a drink, a coffee, or a meal. That said, for serious partying, particularly in summer, Sopot is the place to be. Centrally located between Gdańsk and Gdynia, and with that seaside-chic thing going for it, it's a natural draw at night for the whole region.

Café Absinthe Fun and highly recommended bar where the emphasis is definitely on drinking, though not necessarily absinthe. Draws an eclectic crowd that seems to shares a love of chaos. Św. Ducha 2. ✆ **058/320-37-84.**

Costa Coffee A Starbucks knock-off that pours great espresso drinks and has free Wi-Fi. A lifesaver in the center of the city. Długa 5.

Faktoria In Sopot, probably the best gay dance club in the Tri-Cities. Draws a mix of gay and straight men and women for a big night out. Karaoke nights, special fashion shows, and the usual mix of disco, pop, and glam. Sportowa 1. ✆ **0600/447-369.**

Ferber Café Another central Gdańsk coffee bar that does double duty: a respectable Clark Kent by day serving tourists their espressos, and morphing into a party animal Superman at night, serving cocktails to the local glitterati. Długa 77/78. ✆ **058/301-55-66.**

Kamienica By day, the best place on Mariacka for that much-needed coffee or tea break. By night, a great little bar with a cozy feel and more-than-decent food. Mariacka 37/39. ✆ **058/301-12-30.**

Papryka Thoroughly enjoyable night out at a relatively laid-back Sopot bar and nightclub, where nearly everything—from the leather sofas to the walls—is bathed in warm, red hues. Great DJs and usually just quiet enough to converse under the music. Grunwaldzka 11. ✆ **058/551-74-76.**

DAY TRIP TO MALBORK CASTLE

The monumental Teutonic Knights castle at Malbork (or Marienburg, as it's known in German) lies just 60km (37 miles) south of Gdańsk and is an easy day trip by train or car. The castle, a UNESCO World Heritage Site, is a jaw-dropper—the biggest brick-built castle in the world.

The castle dates from the beginning of the 14th century and was intended to mark the capital of the Teutonic Knights' new northern European home. At the time, the Knights, an order of Christian crusaders fighting in the Holy Lands, had suffered a string of military defeats and were forced to retreat to Europe. They accepted an offer of land by a Polish duke, who was hoping to use the Knights' power to subdue pagan Prussians in the West. The Knights, always eager to subdue pagans, began construction of the Malbork castle in 1309. They were ruthless and highly disciplined, and soon came to rival the Polish kings for control over the vital Baltic Sea trade, including trade in amber. A century later, in 1410, the Poles—along with the Lithuanians and troops from other lands—joined forces to defeat the Knights at the epic Battle of Grünwald (sometimes called the Battle of Tannenberg in history books). This marked the beginning of the end of the Knights' reign in western Poland. They were eventually forced to abandon the

Malbork castle and were dispatched to East Prussia. (As a side note, the Knights still exist, but are devoted to wholly—and *holy*—peaceful pursuits, like running schools and hospitals.)

Following the Knights' defeat, the castle fell to the Polish kings, who used it as an occasional residence. After the Polish partition at the end of the 18th century the Prussians took control of Malbork and the castle, turning it into a military barracks. German control lasted until the end of World War II, when heavy fighting between Germans and Russians destroyed the town and left the castle in ruins. What you see today is the result of a long and steady restoration process that was completed only about a decade ago.

You can tour the castle individually or with a guide. There's an impressive amber display, lots of information about the Teutonic Knights and their militaristic lifestyle, and, of course, displays of medieval weaponry. Allow yourself 3 hours or more to give this incredible castle complex at least a cursory once-over.

By train, Malbork lies on the main Gdańsk–Warsaw line, meaning that departures from Gdańsk are frequent. By car, figure on about a 45 minutes' drive south along the E75/A1 highway.

Malbork Castle. ✆ **055/647-09-78.** www.zamek.malbork.pl. Admission 30zł ($13/£8.10). May–Sept Tues–Sun 9am–7pm; Oct–Apr Tues–Sun 9am–3pm.

TORUŃ

150km (93 miles) S of Gdańsk

Toruń is an exceedingly charming redbrick town with at least three things going for it: One is its claim to fame as the birthplace of Nicholas Copernicus in 1473. He was the first to postulate that the earth revolves around the sun (and not vice versa), setting the stage for later major advances in astronomy (and greatly ruffling the feathers of the Catholic Church in the process!). The second is Toruń's unrivaled stock of original baroque and Renaissance buildings, including some stunning redbrick churches. Unlike many Polish towns of its size, Toruń escaped major damage in World War II. This is a chance to see what Poland might have looked like had history turned out differently. The third is a number of very nice hotels, with at least one in each price category, including a beautiful and affordable boutique.

As with many cities in this part of Poland, Toruń began life as a stronghold for the Teutonic Knights, a German order that was originally invited in by the Polish kings to secure the area, but that later turned on its hosts and amassed its own empire. Tensions between the Knights and Toruń residents traditionally ran high, culminating in a moment of what must have been sheer madness in 1454, when the citizens stormed the Knights' castle just outside the Old Town and tore it apart brick by brick. Amazingly, the rubble is still there (looking not unlike it must have looked 555 years ago), and for the price of 5zł ($2.20/£1.35) you're free to walk around the ruins. The siege effectively ended the Knights' domination of the city.

Toruń later grew prosperous as a member of the Hanseatic League from trade along the Wisła River, but the town fell to the Prussians following the Polish partition at the end of the 18th century. Toruń was under German rule for the next 125 years, until the end of World War I. German troops occupied the city in September 1939 and stayed until February 1945, driven out by the Polish army. Thankfully, the town escaped heavy damage during the fighting.

Essentials

GETTING THERE Toruń lies on major bus and rail links, with frequent daily service to major cities. By road, it's equidistant from Poznań, Gdańsk, and Warsaw. Figure on 2 to 3 hours of driving time from each.

GETTING AROUND Toruń's historic area, comprising the Old and New Towns, is largely closed off to motor vehicles, so walking is the only option.

VISITOR INFORMATION The Toruń Tourist Information Center, Rynek Staromiejski 25 (✆ **056/621-09-31**), is centrally located on the Old Town Square and staffed by young, friendly English speakers. They can help find hotels, suggest restaurants, and bring you up-to-date on anything that might be going on in town of special interest.

Where to Stay

Toruń has some very nice hotels scattered in and around the Old and New Towns. Finding a room is usually not a problem outside of the busy summer months of July and August.

Expensive

Hotel Heban ★ Occupying two renovated town houses in the area just between the Old and New Towns. One building, much more atmospheric, dates from the 17th century, the other, plainer, is across the street and dates from the 19th century. The more modern building is pitched more toward business clients. For something really special, ask for room no. 3 in the older building—a picture-perfect double with hardwood floors and wood-beamed ceilings, and just waiting for a vase of beautiful flowers to complete the picture.

Małe Garbary 7. ✆ **056/652-15-55.** Fax 056/652-15-65. www.hotel-heban.com.pl. 22 units. 300zł ($131/£81) double. AE, DC, MC, V. **Amenities:** Restaurant. *In room:* TV, dataport, minibar, hair dryer.

Hotel Karczma Spichrz ★★ **Value** Beautifully renovated former granary near the river features rooms with traditional wood-hewn furniture and beamed ceilings. The location is ideal, between the river and the Old Town. The in-house restaurant, an upscale inn, has some of the best traditional Polish cooking in town. Highly recommended.

Mostowa 1. ✆ **056/657-11-40.** Fax 056/657-11-44. www.spichrz.pl. 19 units. 300zł ($131/£81) double. AE, DC, MC, V. **Amenities:** Restaurant. *In room:* TV, dataport, minibar, safe, hair dryer.

Moderate

Hotel Petite Fleur ★★★ **Finds** A boutique hotel occupying two stunningly renovated centuries-old burghers' houses. The reception area and cozy little reading room off to the side mix modern flair and traditional furnishings to good effect. The rooms on the top floor have wood-beamed ceilings. The chef in the hotel restaurant is French trained and serves up a mix of French and Polish specialties. You won't find this level of style and comfort at this price anywhere else in Poland.

Piekary 25. ✆ **056/621-51-00.** Fax 056/621-51-20. www.petitefleur.pl. 16 units. 270zł ($117/£73) double. AE, DC, MC, V. **Amenities:** Restaurant. *In room:* TV, dataport, hair dryer.

Inexpensive

Hotel Retman ★ **Value** Clean, quiet, family-run inn about a block away from the Old Town square. Rooms are on the small side, but nicely finished with dark woods and scrubbed clean. Unexpected amenities include in-room Wi-Fi. Limited street parking in front of the hotel.

Rabiańska 15. ✆ **056/657-44-60.** Fax 056/657-44-61. www.hotelretman.pl. 15 units. 230zł ($100/£62) double. AE, DC, MC, V. **Amenities:** Restaurant. *In room:* TV, dataport.

Where to Dine

Manekin ★ Sweet and savory crepes offer a nice budget alternative to pizzas and kabobs. The pancake with chicken, beans, and onions, topped with spicy tomato sauce, is filling without going overboard. Service is friendly and efficient. In summer you can eat on the terrace overlooking the Old Town Square.

Stary Rynek 16. ✆ **056/621-05-04.** Lunch and dinner items 10zł–15zł ($4.35–$6.50/£2.70–£4.05). No credit cards. Daily 11:30am–10pm.

Pizzeria Stara Browarna Exceedingly popular pizza joint, with good, filling pies and pasta dishes on offer. Friday and Saturday night finds the place crammed with teens and students; at other times, families predominate. Not great for a romantic dinner for two, but ideal for a quick, cheap bite on the run.

Mostowa 17. ✆ **056/622-66-74.** Lunch and dinner items 15zł–20zł ($6.50–$8.70/£4.05–£5.40). No credit cards. Daily 11:30am–10pm.

Pod Modrym Fartuchem/Masala ★★ This pleasant, traditional Polish inn is in a tiny baroque-facaded house on a corner just off the New Town Square. All of the classic Polish dishes, served in a refined but casual space. Also incongruously prepares decent if perhaps too mildly spiced Indian dishes. Sit outside near the square in nice weather.

Rynek Nowomiejski 8. ✆ **056/622-26-26.** Lunch and dinner items 20zł–30zł ($8.70–$13/£5.40–£8.10). AE, DC, MC, V. Daily 11:30am–10pm.

Exploring Toruń

Toruń is divided into a historic core and a modern city, comprising an Old Town (Stare Miasto) and a New Town (Nowe Miasto), each having its own square and connected to the other by the long Szeroka ul. You can easily take in the town in a couple of hours of leisurely walking. In addition to the sights below, be sure to stroll along the river for a great view of the town walls (especially pretty at night) and stop by the ruins of the former castle of the Teutonic Knights (ul. Predzamcze, between the Old and New Towns).

Gingerbread Museum (Muzeum Piernika) ★ Toruń is famous in Poland for the quality of its gingerbread *(piernik).* Here at this innovative, hands-on museum, you not only learn about gingerbread and its history, but you also get to bake your own gingerbread cookies!

Rabiańska 9. ✆ **056/663-66-17.** www.muzeumpiernika.pl. Daily 9am–6pm.

Nicholas Copernicus Museum (Muzeum Mikolaja Kopernika) ★★ If you're in Toruń, you've got to pay a visit to the birthplace of the man who banished the earth from the center of the universe. Copernicus's major work, "De revolutionibus orbium coelestium" ("On the Revolutions of the Heavenly Spheres"), was initially viewed as blasphemy by the Catholic Church, and it wasn't until his death in 1543 that the work was published. Copernicus's theories paved the way for a series of astronomical breakthroughs in the 16th and 17th centuries, including the work of Galileo, Tycho Brahe, Johannes Kepler, and Sir Isaac Newton. Copernicus was a jack-of-all-trades, and when he wasn't theorizing about the earth and the sun, he was working as a physician, a local administrator, and even as a commander defending Olsztyn castle against an onslaught of Teutonic Knights. You won't find an original copy of "De revolutionibus" here, but several rooms are filled with period artifacts and pictures.

Ul. M. Kopernika 15/17. ✆ **056/622-70-38.** www.muzeum.torun.pl. Tues–Sun 10am–5pm.

The Old Town Hall (Ratusz Staromiejski) Right in the center of the Rynek and the most impressive of a series of beautiful buildings that line the Old Town Square. You can climb the 42m (138-ft.) tower for a view over the city and across the river, and take in the town museum. Here you'll find a nice collection of stained glass and other crafts through the ages, and paintings of former prominent residents.

Rynek Staromiejski 1. May–Sept Tues–Sun 10am–6pm; Oct–Apr Tues–Sun 10am–4pm.

Shopping

Naturally enough, shopping in Toruń revolves around gingerbread. You'll find it available at shops around town. One excellent place to try is **Emporium,** ul. Piekarny 28 (✆ **056/ 657 61 08;** www.emporium.torun.com.pl). The young English-speaking owner is more than happy to tell you all about the history of gingerbread making in Toruń, and can even give you the recipe if you want to make it at home. He also stocks a range of other souvenirs unique to Toruń (T-shirts, statues of Copernicus, and so on) and runs a bicycle rental.

After Dark

After sunset it seems the whole town descends on the Old Town Square, near the Copernicus statue, and starts the evening promenade through the square and then down Szeroka, and then back. Most of the better clubs, bars, and cafes are along the strip. They're all fun and pretty much the same.

POZNAŃ

120km (75 miles) S of Toruń

Poznań, the main center of the province of Wielkopolska (Greater Poland), is a bustling city of 600,000 people. To Poles, it's regarded as the legendary birthplace of Poland, but to outsiders it's known more for its many annual trade fairs (making Poznań a cousin of sorts to Leipzig in Germany and Brno in the Czech Republic). The city lies on one of Europe's main east-west train lines, stretching from Paris and Berlin to Warsaw and Moscow, which makes getting here a snap. The city's principal attraction is its enormous and beautiful town square, the Stary Rynek, which when filled to brimming on a warm summer evening looks and feels not unlike a more down-to-earth version of Kraków's Rynek Główny or Prague's Old Town Square.

Poznań owes its traditional prosperity to its position along main transportation routes and astride the Warta River. During the Prussian occupation, when the town was known as Posen, it became one of the region's leading industrial centers, a position it retains until this day. The prosperity is evident in the sheer size of the square and in the many handsome buildings that stretch out in all directions.

In more modern times, Poznań has been known to Poles as the home of the 1956 anti-Communist riots, the first-ever show of resistance in the country to the Communist authorities. At the time, tens of the thousands of workers took to the streets to demand better working conditions and higher pay. The strikes turned violent and the government responded by calling in the soldiers and tanks. In all, some 76 civilians and 8 soldiers died in the fighting. The strikes were a major embarrassment throughout Communist Eastern Europe and pierced the veil of the Communist Poland as a "workers" state.

Most of the major sights can be seen in a few hours, but the presence of some nice hotels and good restaurants invites an overnight stay.

GETTING THERE Poznań's **Ławica International Airport,** Bukowska 285 (✆ **061/849-23-43;** www.airport-poznan.com.pl), is 7km (4⅓ miles) west of the city center. It's grown in importance in recent years and now has direct flights to a number of major European cities, including London (Gatwick, Luton, and Stansted), Brussels, Frankfurt, Munich, and Vienna. To get to town, you can get a taxi (about 25 zl/$11/£6.75 to the center) or the Express Line L bus (departures once an hour; buy tickets for 3.60 zl/$1.55/95p from a news agent) to the central rail station. By rail, Poznań lies on the main line connecting Berlin to Warsaw and points east. It's easy to hop off at Poznań in the morning, tour the town for a few hours, and then catch a later train in either direction. The **central train station,** Dworcowa 1 (✆ **061/866-12-12,** or 022/94-36 for information), is 2km (1¼ mile) from the town center, near the fairgrounds. It's a 15-minute walk, or a short tram or bus ride to the center. The **main bus station,** at Dworzec Autobusowy, Towarova 17/19 (✆ **061/664-25-25**), is near the train station. Poznań lies on major national and international bus routes. By car, Poznań lies on the main Berlin-Warsaw highway, the E30. Figure on about 3 hours or so to drive from Warsaw in normal traffic, and about 3 hours from Wrocław if you're coming up from the south.

GETTING AROUND Poznań has an efficient public transportation system of buses and trams, but if you're staying near the Stary Rynek, you'll be doing most of your travel by foot. Tickets can be bought at Ruch kiosks (or nearly anywhere they sell newspapers and tobacco) and cost 3.60zł ($1.55/95p) for a trip of 30 minutes, and 2zł (85¢/55p) for 15 minutes.

VISITOR INFORMATION The city's main **Tourist Information Center,** Stary Rynek 59/60 (✆ **061/852-61-56**), is conveniently located on the Old Town Square. The helpful staff gives out maps and brochures and can advise on rooms. Another good source of information is the **City Information Center,** Ratajczaka 44 (✆ **061/851-96-45;** www.cim.poznan.pl). The CIM is good on cultural activities and can sell tickets for concerts and performances.

Where to Stay

Poznań's hotel rates are reasonable except when an international trade fair is going on in town. Then, hotels unabashedly jack up the prices 30% to 40%. The summer months are normally safe, but during the rest of the year, there's usually a trade fair going on at least 1 week a month. The rates listed below are for standard doubles outside of fair times. Note that many hotels offer reduced weekend rates.

Very Expensive

Domina Residence ★ Designed more for corporate travelers than individuals, this hotel features 40 fully equipped apartments, complete with bedroom, living room, and kitchen. The kitchens haves fridges, stoves, microwaves, and full sets of pots and pans if you'd ever want to whip up a meal during your stay. The presentation is high end, with sleek modern furnishings, crisp uniforms for the staff, and lots of high-tech gadgetry throughout. Each of the apartments is slightly different, so ask to see a couple before deciding. Domina is popular during fair time.

Św. Marcin 2. ✆ **061/859-05-90.** Fax 0061/859-05-91. www.dominahotels.com. 40 units. 450zł ($196/£121) double. AE, DC, MC, V. **Amenities:** Concierge; business services; salon; nonsmoking rooms. *In room:* A/C, TV, fax, dataport, kitchen, fridge, coffeemaker, hair dryer, iron, safe.

Hotel Royal ★ The Royal is widely considered one of Poznań's best hotels, though with the option of the Brovaria (see below), the rates look a little high for what's on offer. The location is excellent, on one of the city's main arteries not far from the Stary Rynek. The hotel is tucked away in a little courtyard away from the street, so noise is not a problem. The Royal has a distinguished pedigree, dating from the turn of the 20th century, and was the first hotel in the city to open for business following World War II. The rooms are classy looking, with floral-print spreads and high-quality woods throughout. The reception desk is more than happy to book restaurant reservations or advise on city tours.

Św. Marcin 71. ✆ **061/858-23-00.** Fax 0061/858-23-06. www.hotel-royal.com.pl. 31 units. 420zł ($183/£113) double. AE, DC, MC, V. **Amenities:** Restaurant; concierge; business center; limited room service; dry cleaning; nonsmoking rooms. *In room:* TV, dataport, hair dryer.

Expensive

Hotel Brovaria ★★ For the money, probably the best bed (with a view) in town. The hotel's location, occupying three tastefully renovated town houses on the Stary Rynek, cannot be beat. The decor is a restrained modern—somewhere between 1930s "modern" and contemporary—with beige bedspreads and dark woods. The hotel's restaurant is one of the finest in the city, and the in-house pub even brews its own beer.

Stary Rynek 73/74. ✆ **061/858-68-68.** Fax 0061/858-68-69. www.brovaria.pl. 21 units. 360zł ($157/£97) double. AE, DC, MC, V. **Amenities:** 2 restaurants; limited room service; nonsmoking rooms. *In room:* TV, dataport, hair dryer.

Moderate

Hotel Stare Miasto ★★ (Finds A relatively new hotel and a great choice for the price; the rates are lower than you might expect for the quality of the facilities because of the hotel's location in a slightly dodgy, but still safe neighborhood, about a 10 minutes' walk from the Stary Rynek. The stylish reception area is open and airy. The rooms are on the small side, but nicely furnished in a contemporary look. The inevitable breakfast buffet is more inventive than most, and the chef will cook some eggs on the spot on request. The doubles are not uniformly furnished, so ask to see a couple of different styles before choosing.

Rybaki 36. ✆ **061/663-62-42.** Fax 0061/659-00-43. www.hotelstaremiasto.pl. 23 units. 300zł ($131/£81) double. AE, DC, MC, V. **Amenities:** Restaurant. *In room:* A/C, TV, dataport.

Inexpensive

Frolic Goats ★ (Value Though this is technically a hostel, the "Goats" offers a couple of attractive private singles and doubles that are an absolute steal given the location. The entryway into the hotel through a filthy corridor is not very promising, but things start to look up at the reception desk. The rooms themselves are adorable, with hardwood floors, old-fashioned beds, and clean white linens. The location is 3 minutes by foot to the main square.

Wrocławska 16/6 (entry from Jaskółlcza). ✆ **061/852-44-11.** www.frolicgoatshostel.com. 5 units. 200zł ($87/£54) double w/bath. AE, DC, MC, V. **Amenities:** Restaurant.

Hotel Lech A modern high-rise on a busy street, not far from the central square. The rooms are plain but clean. Not a bad deal, given the location and in-room amenities like free Internet access. Pulls in a lot of bus-tour packages, and even offers reduced rates for students. Avoid the restaurant downstairs; there's much better food just a short walk away.

Św. Marcin 74. ✆ **061/853-01-51.** Fax 0061/853-08-80. www.hotel-lech.poznan.pl. 79 units. 250zł ($109/£67) double. AE, DC, MC, V. **Amenities:** Restaurant. *In room:* TV, dataport, hair dryer.

Where to Dine

There's no shortage of restaurants along the Stary Rynek. Nearly every house along the perimeter of the enormous square offers some kind of food or drink, usually both.

Very Expensive

Dom Vikingów ★ INTERNATIONAL Similar in appearance to Bee Jay's (see below), but much more upmarket and with more attention paid to the food. Danish ownership explains the "House of Vikings" name, and also the appearance of Danish herring on the menu. The steaks and the imported wines are the draws here. The interior is divided into several different themes, including a cafe and sports bar. During the summer, the outdoor terrace is the place for afternoon coffee.

Stary Rynek 62. ✆ **061/852-71-53.** Lunch and dinner items 28zł–60zł ($12–$26/£7.55–£16). AE, DC, MC, V. Daily noon–11pm.

Expensive

Brovaria ★★ POLISH/INTERNATIONAL The first-floor restaurant of the Hotel Brovaria is one of the hippest spots in town and a real draw for locals and visitors alike. Many come for the home-brewed beer, which is hoppier and tangier than traditional Polish beer, and comes as both a standard Pilsner and recommendable honey-flavored lager. The menu is a balance of inventive international dishes and Polish standards with a view toward presentation and use of fresh ingredients. The roast duck with apple comes nicely crisped with a side of beets and potatoes, and is absolutely delicious.

Stary Rynek 73/74. ✆ **061/858-68-68.** Lunch and dinner items 25zł–50zł ($11–$22/£6.75–£13). AE, DC, MC, V. Daily noon–11pm.

Kresowa ★★ POLISH A little hard to find, tucked away in the maze of buildings at the center of the Stary Rynek, but well worth the effort. This is widely considered one of the top Polish restaurants in town, and a superb choice for the celebratory "we've arrived in Poznań" evening meal. The atmosphere is more formal than most, so smart-casual is the way to dress. The clientele includes a mix of businessmen, private parties, and Poles out for a special evening. The menu is heavy on Polish standards and meat dishes. The grilled salmon comes highly recommended. Try to book beforehand for Friday and Saturday nights.

Stary Rynek 3. ✆ **061/853-12-91.** Lunch and dinner items 25zł–45zł ($11–$20/£6.75–£12). AE, DC, MC, V. Mon–Sat 1–11pm; Sun noon–6pm.

Moderate

Bamberka ★★ POLISH Good choice for lunch on a sunny day on the Stary Rynek. Excellent Polish classics, including pierogies, stuffed cabbage leaves, potato pancakes, and the rest of it. The herring appetizer is particularly good—salty fish served in a sour cream sauce lightly sweetened with apple.

Stary Rynek 2. ✆ **061/852-99-17.** Lunch and dinner items 20zł–30zł ($8.70–$13/£5.40–£8.10). AE, DC, MC, V. Daily 11am–10pm.

Markowa Knajpa ★ POLISH Less formal than the Kresowa, but with similarly well-prepared local dishes. The decor is simple in keeping with the *knajpa* (bistro) theme, with stark, white walls, dark woods, and hardwood floors. The customer base includes mostly businessmen and young professionals. Czech Pilsner Urquell beer is on tap. Just a couple of blocks off the Stary Rynek.

Kramarska 15. ✆ **061/853-01-78.** Lunch and dinner items 20zł–30zł ($8.70–$13/£5.40–£8.10). AE, DC, MC, V. Daily noon–11pm.

Inexpensive

Bee Jay's ★ An enormous watering hole, sports-bar complex on the Stary Rynek. It's a popular spot for salads, sandwiches, quesadillas, and also the odd Indian entree. This food is more stick-to-your-ribs than stick-in-your-mind as a great meal, but if you're looking for something easy and relatively cheap, this is one of the best spots on the square.

Stary Rynek 87. ✆ **061/853-11-15.** Lunch and dinner items 15zł–30zł ($6.50–$13/£4.05–£8.10). AE, DC, MC, V. Daily 11:30am–2am.

Exploring Poznań

Naturally, any exploration of Poznań must start at the Stary Rynek, the city's cultural and commercial center for centuries. It's hard to find a livelier and sunnier town square than Poznań's—filled with color, people, and a range of performance art from early morning to late at night. At night, it's particularly beguiling. Most of the square is kept dark, with only the statues and some of the buildings lit up. Much of the square, and indeed much of the city proper, was destroyed in World War II, so many of the buildings here are faithful reconstructions of the originals.

West of the Stary Rynek, at the Warta River, is the small holy island of **Ostrów Tumski.** Legend has it this was the birthplace of the Polish nation. This is where Poland first accepted Catholic baptism in the 10th century; and one of the country's most celebrated cathedrals still stands here. To get there takes about a 10-minute walk from the main square.

Poznań's unofficial nickname could well be the "Museum City." In addition to the major museums noted below, the city has smaller museums dedicated to musical instruments, vintage cars, the Poznań army, and the work of Polish writer Henryk Sienkiewicz, who won the Nobel Prize for Literature in 1905, among others.

Cathedral ★★ The Basilica of Saints Peter and Paul retains its importance as one of the most revered churches in Poland. Excavations have revealed the presence of a church on this site for more than 1,000 years, since the Polish kings first accepted Catholicism in the 10th century. Architectural tinkering and rebuilding through the years, and the burning of the cathedral in 1945, have greatly altered its appearance, with the current appearance a mix of neo-Gothic and baroque. The remains of Poland's first kings, Mieszko I and Boleslaw the Brave, are in a chapel at the back of the altar.

Ostrów Tumski 17. ✆ **061/852-96-42.** Mon–Sat 9am–6pm.

National Museum ★★ An impressive art collection that's particularly strong on examples of the "Młoda Polska" art movement from the early years of the 20th century and some riveting abstracts from the 1950s and 1960s. An older wing holds extensive collections of Italian, Dutch, Flemish, and Spanish paintings.

Marcinkowskiego 9. ✆ **061/852-59-69.** www.mnp.art.pl. Admission 15zł ($6.50/£4). Tues–Sat 10am–5pm (Thurs 4pm); Sun 10am–3pm.

Old Town Hall (Ratusz) ★ Originally dates from the 14th century but extensively renovated in the 16th century in Renaissance style by the Italian architect Giovanni Quadro. Unfortunately, much of the building was destroyed in World War II, and little of the original structure remains. The best example of what remains is the early Gothic cellars, which today house the Historical Museum of Poznań. The museum is worth a look if you're interested in Poznań's development from the 10th century on. Entry to the museum also allows you to see the rich interior of the building itself. Outside the Town Hall, at noon, take a look at the clock to the see two mechanical goats butt heads. The goats apparently refer to a town myth that two animals once locked horns and drew the townspeople's attention to a fire that might have burned down the city.

Stary Rynek 1. ✆ **061/856-81-91.** Tues and Thurs–Fri 9am–4pm; Wed 11am–6pm; Sat–Sun 10am–3pm.

Zamek ★ This fascinating building will appeal to World War II buffs. The "castle" actually dates only from the beginning of the 20th century, and was built by the Germans to serve as a residence for the Kaiser on trips to the area (when Poznań, as Posen, was a German city). Between the two world wars, it was used by Poznań University, but after the Nazi invasion of 1939, work quickly began to refashion the building into an office for Adolf Hitler and a residence for the Nazi governor of this part of occupied Poland. The architect for the project was none other than Albert Speer. Work was completed in 1944, just shortly before the Germans were driven out of Poznań. For years, there was talk of tearing down the "castle," but today it's used as a cultural center. Visitors are free to walk the corridors during open hours.

Św. Marcin 80/82. ✆ **061/646-52-76.** www.zamek.poznan.pl. Daily 11am–7pm.

After Dark

The Zamek Cultural Center, Św. Marcin 80/82 (✆ **061/646-52-60;** www.zamek.poznan.pl), is a good first stop to check on what's on in Poznań. For events, buy tickets at the City Information Center/CIM, Ratajczaka 44 (✆ **061/851-96-45;** www.cim.poznan.pl).

For drinking and clubbing, you won't have to venture far from the Stary Rynek. To get started, check out **Dom Vikingów** or **Bee Jay's** (see "Where to Dine," above). For dancing, **Cute,** Wielka 27/29 (✆ **061/851-91-37**), is one of the city's best-known venues for house, techno, trance, and just plain dance. For a quieter night in summer, do like the locals and simply choose a table on the Rynek and watch the city walk by.

Romania

by Keith Bain

On a visit to Bucharest, Tolstoy noted that Romanians had a "sad destiny," his observation no doubt based on a strong sense of their troubled past—Romania's soul is tormented by history, its loveliness overshadowed by the reputations of malevolent personalities like Vlad the Impaler and Communist dictator Nicolae Ceauşescu. But while bloodthirsty men have worked their ugly politics here, and Communism has left its ruinous marks on the land, it remains a country of great beauty, one that (unlike its most misunderstood cultural export, Count Dracula) is shedding its curse and pulses with life and fascinating diversity. It is also a land of mighty, staggering contrasts.

While Bucharest buzzes with the frenzied energy of a world capital, somewhere in a field, a farmer wields a scythe, harvesting the grass his livestock will eat during the cold winters. In the context of the European Union (Romania became a full-fledged member in 2007) the contrast between urban and rural life is staggering. It is a country coated in forest and defined by the curved backbone of Carpathian peaks. Its natural treasures include the Alpine splendor of snowcapped mountains and the vast frontier wetlands of the Danube Delta, one of the last great wildernesses in Europe. And along with the rolling hills and soaring peaks, swathes of green and vast tracts of preindustrial landscape, there are enchanting castles, richly decorated churches, and rural villages where time moves at a surreal pace. All of this reflects the varied histories of a people who, for centuries, have struggled to create and hold onto a single, united state. Romania's past is riddled with intrigue and tales of war and political upheaval.

During its isolation under Communism, many of Romania's great treasures were unknown to the world, considered unimportant by a leadership hellbent on fulfilling its sociopolitical master plan. To the outside world, this was a dark and foreboding place, legendarily haunted by Dracula's eternal ghost, and tormented by Ceauşescu's living one. But while Ceauşescu's program of systemization tried to squash the past—the Communists built countless drab, gray apartments that still serve as cheap housing throughout the country—many lovely centuries-old towns and cities have maintained their historic grandeur, albeit faded and crumbling. Retaining their historic core, occasionally centered on dramatic fortresses and fleshed out by rambling cobblestone streets and narrow alleyways or ancient gateways leading to secret courtyards, Romania's baroque, Gothic, and Secessionist cities are well worth exploring, and while much work is needed to improve tourism infrastructure, the time to visit Romania is now. For Romania is on the verge of yet another revolution; this time riding the wave of E.U. membership with bolstered economic hopes, it's a revolution that will inevitably take its toll on the medieval lifestyle of many of its backwater communities. Romania, once a country weighed down by its troubled past, is poised for a formidable future.

1 GETTING TO KNOW ROMANIA

THE LAY OF THE LAND

Romania—just a bit smaller than the United Kingdom and roughly the size of the state of Oregon—is situated in the southeastern part of central Europe, and is made up, in roughly equal measures, of lowland, hilly, and mountainous terrain. It borders Hungary and Serbia to the west, Moldova and the Ukraine to the north and east, and Bulgaria to the south, with whom it shares, along with its northern neighbor Ukraine, a slither of Black Sea coastline to the east. Forming much of the border with Bulgaria and Serbia is the River Danube as it makes its way toward the Black Sea, where it forms one of Europe's largest wetlands, the Danube Delta.

THE REGIONS IN BRIEF

About one-third of the country comprises the **Carpathian Mountains,** or "Transylvanian Alps," a soaring back-to-front Nike swish that separates Transylvania from the country's two other main provinces, Wallachia, to the south, and Moldavia, to the east. Through the centuries, these three historically distinct regions have been fought over by invaders from all quarters, and they now make up the bulk of Romania, a unified nation for fewer than 100 years.

Transylvania has always been a great prize, ruled largely by the Hungarian Empire and also settled by Saxon immigrants who came to protect it on behalf of the Hungarians. Here, along with splendid medieval villages centered on fortified churches, are the country's most popular tourist destinations, located at the foothills of the Carpathians. **Wallachia** was the first Romanian province to gain independence from Hungary, and is known as the "Heart of Romania," with the centrally located capital, Bucharest, rapidly reestablishing itself in a bid to reclaim its former moniker as the "Paris of the East." **Moldavia,** which once included Bessarabia (now part of the Ukraine and the Republic of Moldova), was another former Hungarian principality, which achieved independence in the mid–14th century. Known primarily for its beautiful painted monasteries in the largely rural Bucovine region, Moldavia's sylvan scenery is a backdrop for villages trapped in time and imbued with great folkloric traditions.

Even better known for its ancient village life is the small region of **Maramureş,** in the northern part of Transylvania on the border with the Ukraine. Here, the sublime, unspoiled scenery shelters stunning wooden churches and a bucolic way of life. Occupying the western fringe of the country are **Crişana and Banat,** former Austro-Hungarian strongholds that now border Hungary and Serbia, respectively. Overdevelopment has blighted the Black Sea coastal resorts of the easternmost region of **Northern Dobrogea,** so much so that many local sun-seekers now head instead to the Bulgarian coast. Visitors still seeking a coastal sojourn should make for the Danube Delta, where the unique wetland ecosystem is an enchanting destination, particularly for birders.

SUGGESTED ITINERARY ROMANIA IN 10 TO 12 DAYS

The following itinerary can be adapted according to your preferences. For example, you can skip the Delta, or Maramureş, if you'd prefer just exploring Romania's cities and medieval towns.

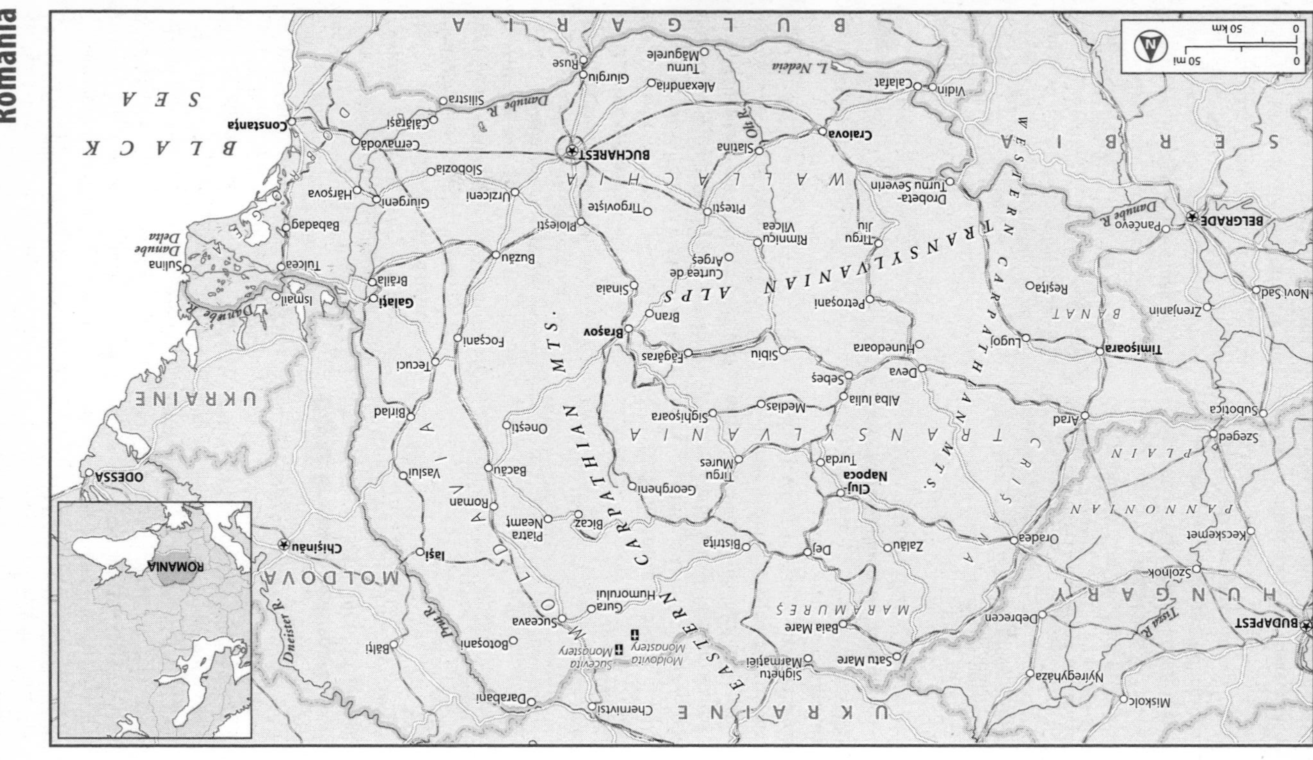
BLACK SEA
UKRAINE
MOLDOVA
HUNGARY
SERBIA
BULGARIA
ROMANIA
EASTERN CARPATHIAN MTS.
TRANSYLVANIAN ALPS
WESTERN CARPATHIAN MTS.
CRIS
TRANSYLVANIA
MOLDAVIA
WALLACHIA
MARAMUREȘ
BANAT
PANNONIAN PLAIN
Danube Delta
Danube R.
Dneister R.
Prut R.
Tisza R.
Olt R.
L. Nedeia
BUCHAREST
BUDAPEST
BELGRADE
Chișinău
ODESSA
Constanța
Sulina
Tulcea
Ismail
Babadag
Hârșova
Galați
Brăila
Cernavodă
Călărași
Silistra
Giurgeni
Slobozia
Urziceni
Buzău
Focșani
Tecuci
Birlad
Vaslui
Iași
Bălți
Botoșani
Darabani
Chernivtsi
Suceava
Sucevita Monastery
Moldovita Monastery
Gura Humorului
Piatra Neamț
Roman
Bacău
Onești
Bicaz
Bistrița
Georgheni
Brașov
Sinaia
Bran
Ploiești
Tirgoviște
Pitești
Curtea de Argeș
Făgăras
Sighișoara
Tirgu Mures
Medias
Sibiu
Rîmnicu Vîlcea
Slatina
Craiova
Alexandria
Giurgiu
Ruse
Turnu Măgurele
Calafat
Vidin
Drobeta-Turnu Severin
Tirgu Jiu
Petroșani
Hunedoara
Deva
Sebeș
Alba Iulia
Turda
Cluj Napoca
Dej
Zalău
Baia Mare
Satu Mare
Sighetu Marmației
Oradea
Arad
Timișoara
Lugoj
Reșița
Debrecen
Nyíregyháza
Miskolc
Szolnok
Kecskemet
Szeged
Subotica
Novi Sad
Zrenjanin
Pančevo
0 50 mi
0 50 km
N

Days ❶–❷: Bucharest

Arrange for your hotel to have a taxi pick you up at the airport and then experience the intoxicating energy of this heady, combustible capital: It's a city on the move. Make time for the Cotroceni Palace (call ahead to book a tour), the National Museum of Art, and the small but gorgeous Stavreolpolous Church, where it's also worth calling ahead if you'd prefer to learn something meaningful about Romanian Orthodox faith. It's also worth checking out the world's biggest example of architectural excess, Ceauşescu's megalithic Parliamentary Palace, but you'll probably need to devote an entire morning or afternoon, thanks to a rather annoying queuing-and-waiting procedure. Try to stay at the Rembrandt, a fabulous little hotel in the midst of the historic Lipscani District, or—if you don't mind forking out considerably more—check into the friendly, plush, no-nonsense K+K Elisabeta, right near the National Theater. At night, you'll be spoiled for choice—classy restaurants are opening faster than it's possible to keep track of, and there are dozens of bars that stay open until the wee hours. Start the night in the vicinity of the Romanian Athenaeum; if there's a concert on there, try to catch it.

Day ❸: Sinaia & Braşov

You can save time by catching the early morning train to Sinaia, where you can leave your luggage at the station before setting off for the guided tour of Peleş Castle, a fantastic introduction to modern Romanian history and a splendid example of just how far interior design can go with a big enough budget. After the castle, you can visit the local monastery before collecting your luggage and hopping on the first available train to Braşov, about an hour away. Braşov is centered on a wide-open medieval public square, surrounded by lovely architecture. You can view the whole historic center from Mount Tampa, getting to the top in a cable car. Visit the world-famous Black Church; in summer, you might catch a concert showcasing the brilliant acoustics and showing off the church's massive organ. But Braşov is great for just wandering around; there are lovely antiques stores, several fantastic restaurants, and great hidden alleyways. Don't miss the historic Schei neighborhood. Be sure to reserve a room in one of the small hotels recommended in the Braşov section under "Where to Stay."

Day ❹: Braşov to Sighişoara

Once you've had your fill of Braşov, take the train to the World Heritage citadel of Sighişoara. There's not much to do, except soak up the ambience of a walled, cobblestone, hilltop city. Explore its Church on the Hill, and climb to the top of the Clock Tower above the museum. Taste *tuică* (fruit brandy) made by Teo Coroian, and eat in the restaurant occupying the house where the real Count Dracula was born.

Day ❺: Sighişoara to Sibiu

Sibiu shared the title of European City of Culture in 2007 and got a thorough makeover in preparation—it's a beautiful mélange of medieval and baroque monuments, with churches, museums and pedestrian squares galore. Take your time exploring, and don't miss the great Transylvanian food at Crama Sibiul Vechi, which occupies a 500-year-old cellar.

Days ❻–❼: Maramureş

If you don't fancy spending 6 hours in a train, you can break the journey between Sibiu and Baia Mare—the main city in Maramureş—with a stopover in Cluj-Napoca, a prosperous city with a large student population and modern aspirations; explore the cafes around the lively town square, and visit the church lording over it.

The trip into Maramureş will take you back a hundred years or so. Arrange to stay with a local family for 1 or 2 nights to experience village life; with advance planning, DiscoveRomania (p. 488) will organize a driver to pick you up at the train station (or the airport) and can ensure that you have a guide throughout your stay in this, Romania's most bucolic region. Explore some of the gorgeous wooden churches scattered throughout the region, then visit the Merry Cemetery at Săpânţa and the anti-Communist museum in nearby Sighet.

Days 8–9: Moldavia's painted monasteries

From Maramureş, arrange to be driven all the way to Gura Humorului in the neighboring province of Moldavia, beyond the northern edge of the Carpathian Mountains. Spend what's left of the day exploring a few of the best of the painted monasteries of southern Bucovina—Voronet, Moldoviţa, Suceviţa, and Humor. Do whatever you can to spend the night at the beautiful green guesthouse, Casa cu Cerbi, in the tiny village of Voievodeasa, near Suceviţa. The following day, spend time idling in the villages, and catch up with more of the monasteries.

Days 10–12: Danube Delta

End your Romanian tour by getting back to nature. The Danube Delta is now home to the smartest resort in the whole country: Organize well in advance for staff at the Delta Nature Resort to arrange the long road transfer from Suceava. A day spent exploring the Delta will charge your batteries and prepare you for the trip back to Bucharest and then home.

ROMANIA TODAY

Existing impressions of Romania are usually a hangover from Ceauşescu's iron-fisted stranglehold: starving orphans, the systematic destruction of cultural monuments, and industrial plants spilling toxic waste. Indeed, Communism did a great deal to break the spirit of this nation. But the Romanian people broke the back of the regime in a small but bloody revolution that, back in 1989, was only the start of a long road to recovery. The transition from Communism has been uneven and uneasy; Ceauşescu's replacement is widely considered to have been just another Communist in disguise and insiders will tell you that he is a murderer responsible for the death of innocents during the overthrow of the Communist regime.

Chat with the locals, and you'll hear much about a country beleaguered by corruption (a 2006 World Bank report stated that 50% of businesses are troubled by the level of graft) and a general lack of confidence in political leaders, underscored by schizophrenic election results. Even after E.U. accession, corruption and red tape continue to dog its business environment. And while minister-level officials play dirty-tactic politics, people on the ground continue to experience widespread economic impoverishment, particularly in rural areas—about one-third of the workforce continues to earn a living through agriculture. Romania is seen as a source of cheap labor, and a number of foreign companies have set up shop here mainly to take advantage of these low-wage expectations. Many young people with skills and education, as well as those disheartened by limited work prospects at home, cross the border for better wages and opportunities; with E.U. accession, the drain of human resources has increased, and will likely continue until local wage prospects improve. Equally, locals complain, it is impossible to "get things done" in Romania, as a stultifying bureaucracy strangles entrepreneurial efforts.

In some ways, these ongoing problems are a residue of Communism, where the regime primarily served those who were connected to the seat of power, and a centralized public sector tended to curb anything resembling entrepreneurship. There was no such thing as foreign tourism, and therefore a general absence of service-industry culture. Jobs were there to be filled, not necessarily performed with any aplomb (if, indeed, at all), so the status quo—no matter how frustrating and dehumanizing—was fastidiously maintained.

Tips: Ceaşescu's Legacy on the Silver Screen

To get a feel for the kinds of social hardship endured under Ceaşescu's Communist stranglehold, rent Romania's 2007 Cannes Palme d'Or–winning film, *4 Months, 3 Weeks, and 2 Days,* directed by Cristian Mungiu. Raw, emotionally gripping, and at times shocking, the harrowing drama—shot on a shoestring budget—unapologetically depicts the misadventures of two students who try to procure an illegal abortion from a corrupt physician. Be warned: It will put you in touch with the psyche of Romania during the 1980s.

Some say that the twinning of Romanian bureaucracy with E.U. protocol presents even greater potential to subvert progress.

In 2009, Traian Băsescu enters his fifth year as president of Romania. Heading a large coalition, Băsescu has long professed to hold real democratic ideals and genuinely oppose corruption; he has been uncompromising in this regard to the extent that he has alienated his prime minister, who entered office a close ally of the president. Amongst his achievements have been the new government's imposition of one of Europe's most liberal tax systems, and wages are rising along with a slowly emerging middle class. But cultural problems persist in the form of corruption and red tape which continue to handicap the business terrain. Driven partly by the depreciation of the currency, rising energy costs, a nationwide drought affecting food prices, and a relaxation of fiscal discipline, inflation rose in 2007 for the first time in 8 years. Naturally, people on the ground blame E.U. membership, which perhaps came at a difficult time, when discussions about a global recession have sullied European optimism.

National elections in 2009 are likely to produce yet another set of disruptive results. Despite a desire for steady reform, Romania remains one of Europe's poorest nations, and while the spirit of development may be evident in projects in and around Bucharest, rural Romania still appears to stumble along at an altogether different pace. But the capital's transformation clearly signals the aspirations for a prosperous future and—despite ongoing public and media aspersions about corruption and political bungling—urban Romania seems hellbent on careening into full-blown capitalism and reaping the fruits of free-market enterprise. The rest of the country may well be better off for the time being, unaffected by the tidal wave of change.

A LOOK AT THE PAST

Romania's past is defined by violent conflict and war. Peace—and indeed nationhood—is new to a region that has been perpetually invaded for well over a millennium.

While Thracian tribes settled here about 3,000 years ago, Romanians trace their culture back to the Dacians. They were a highly regarded race, referred to by Herodotus as "the fairest and most courageous of men" because of their fearlessness in the face of death. Greeks colonized the territory near the Black Sea coast and developed the cities of Tomis (now Constanta), Istria, and Callatis (now Mangalia) from around 700 B.C., while the Dacian king Burebista controlled most of what is now Romania; he established a powerful kingdom between 70 and 44 B.C. By A.D. 100, the Dacian civilization had reached its zenith and the Romans now moved in, forcing its inhabitants to adopt the language of the conquerors. Rome was to rule Dacia for nearly 200 years before Christianity was adopted in the 4th century by the Daco-Romans, who fell subject to invasion by assorted

European and Asian tribes for the next 6 centuries. By the 11th century, when Magyar (Hungarian) armies invaded and occupied Transylvania, Romanians were the only Latin-speaking people in the eastern quadrant of the former Roman Empire. They were also the only Latin people still practicing the Orthodox faith.

While Transylvania's Romanian population was almost entirely subjugated by ruling Hungarians and their Saxon allies, the Middle Ages saw great (and bloodthirsty) local warriors in Moldavia and Wallachia—men like Stephen the Great, Vlad the Impaler, and Michael the Brave—fighting to maintain their sovereignty in the face of the ongoing Hungarian and Ottoman threat. In 1600, the Wallachian prince, Michael the Brave (Mihai Viteazul), even briefly united the three provinces, only to be defeated by the Turkish and Habsburg armies; Transylvania became a jewel in the burgeoning Austro-Hungarian Empire, while other bits of Romania were carved up and divided between different powers.

In 1848, Hungary took complete control of Transylvania, while Moldavia and Wallachia headed for unification, finally merging to become a fledgling Romania in the 1860s. A decision was made to give the new country a nonpartisan ruler, and so a German blue blood, Prince Karl of Hohenzollern-Sigmaringen, was chosen to sit on the throne of the new Romanian kingdom, created in 1881. He ruled as King Carol I until 1914, when he was succeeded by his nephew and adopted son, Ferdinand. During Ferdinand's rule, Romania joined World War I on the side of the Triple Entente in a successful effort to incorporate the lost Romanian provinces of Transylvania, Bucovina, and Bessarabia. In 1930, King Ferdinand I was succeeded by his son, Carol II. Ten years later, the Soviet Union annexed Bessarabia as well as northern Bucovina, while Germany and Italy forced Romania to give northern Transylvania to Hungary and southern Dobrogea to Bulgaria. Massive political turmoil and nationwide demonstrations caused the abdication of Carol II, leaving his 19-year-old son, Michael, to sit on the throne. With Carol II in exile, Marshall Ion Antonescu imposed a military dictatorship and Romania joined the Nazis, but the young Michael staged a royal coup in 1944 and quickly changed sides against the Germans.

In 1945, as part of the Yalta Agreement, Romania fell under direct Soviet influence; Red Army presence enabled the rapid strengthening of the country's Communists, who forced King Michael to abdicate in 1947. Less than 70 years after becoming a kingdom, Romania became a People's Republic and was under the direct, often excruciating, economic control of the U.S.S.R. until 1958. The notorious SovRom agreements exhausted the country's already limited resources, and Big Brother made taxing war-reparation demands. But the devastation was not limited to financial resources; during this time an estimated two million Romanians were imprisoned, mostly on spurious charges, and between 1948 and 1964, over 200,000 citizens died in Communist-related "incidents."

In 1968, an upstart Communist named Nicolae Ceauşescu publicly condemned Soviet intervention in Czechoslovakia, thereafter receiving kudos and economic assistance from the West. Apparently nobody noticed Ceauşescu's burgeoning megalomania until it was too late, when his obsessions turned toward national debt repayment and a catastrophic systemization of the economic and social structure with rapid industrial development, replete with concrete apartment blocks and toxic factories.

Amid the economic gloom, Ceauşescu created a monstrous police state and embarked on a program of cultlike self-glorification, which included the silencing of opponents and extreme and violent violations of human rights and civil liberties. So terrifying and pervasive was the dictatorship that women who suffered miscarriages were subjected to tormenting interrogation sessions, as an inability to carry full term was seen as an attempt to stymie Ceauşescu's plan to "grow" the nation's workforce.

Life increasingly unbearable, 1989 saw furious anti-Communist protests—sparked in Timişoara and then across the country—and Ceauşescu and his regime were finally toppled. Two years later a new democratic constitution was adopted, and the difficult transition toward a free-market economy was underway. But the road to recovery has been rocky due to the instability created by successive governments, a result of schizophrenic public support, marked by corrupt politicians, many of whom were active in the former regime. But after more than a decade of economic instability and decline, the new millennium finally seems to have ushered in an era of transformation, economic growth, and foreign investment. In October 2004, months before the E.U.-accession treaty was signed, the country was granted "functional market economy" status.

ROMANIAN PEOPLE & CULTURE

Many Romanians take pride in being "a Latin island in a Slavic sea," thinking of themselves as the most eastern Romance people, completely surrounded by non-Latin peoples. While often under the political and cultural dominance of the Ottoman Empire, it is Western culture that has come to predominate.

While Romanians are proud of their heritage, and take delight in recounting the names of great individuals—inventors, scientists, poets, discoverers, and leaders—they are not afraid to engage honestly with strangers about the challenges Romania faces. In fact, you'll hear a great deal on Romania's problems—its politics, its police, and in more or less the same breath, its rampant corruption—than about its burgeoning promise. Life under Ceauşescu may be a harder topic to broach, though, and use your own discretion when discussing matters such as religion and views on homosexuality. Almost 87% of the population belongs to the Romanian Orthodox Church, so exercise a basic respect for

Roma: Dancing to Their Own Tune

If there's one topic that stirs considerable debate and even anger among Romanians, it's the status of the Roma—or Gypsy—population, believed to be a widely disenfranchised 1.8 to 2 million, but counted at the polls as a mere 535,140 people at the last census. Many Romanians are overtly intolerant toward the Roma community, largely because of their associations with crime, vagrancy, and social disharmony. Many Roma live in ghetto-style environments at the fringes of villages and towns, earning a living through informal trade and begging. Rightly or wrongly, they are also held accountable for most of the petty crime in Romania. Hatred on both sides has sparked occasional violence. Nevertheless, the Gypsies are widely known for their savvy as well as their musical talent; although generally uneducated and unemployed, they carve out an existence and maintain strong cultural traditions; a few standout Gypsy musicians and bands have become international successes, for example. It's unfortunate that your strongest associations with this minority will most likely be through bright-eyed children asking for money or food on trains or selling kitsch at tourist hot spots.

conservative Christian values. Faith is very much a way of life rather than a once-a-week affair; many Romanians live a deeply religious life and you'll see Orthodox believers of all ages crossing themselves—passionately or casually—as they pass churches and other sacred places.

LANGUAGE

In all cities and towns you should have little trouble communicating in English, although Italian will occasionally serve you better. In villages, you may have difficulty communicating with older people, but young people who have attended school in the post-Communist dispensation usually understand English. Don't shy away from conversations that hinge on a vocabulary of just a few words.

Although there is a fairly sizeable Hungarian minority that continues to use its own language in schools and civil administration, a small Gypsy community that speaks Roma, and a few dwindling communities descended from the Saxons who settled in Transylvania centuries ago that speak German, Romanian is the official language.

Romanian is a Romance language, evolved from the Latin spoken in ancient times by the people in the eastern provinces of the Roman Empire. Structurally complex, it will sound familiar to if you speak or understand Italian, Spanish, French, or Portuguese. The language uses a Latin alphabet, with a few modified characters; these are â (also written as î, and pronounced "uh"), ă (pronounced "er"), ş (pronounced "sh"), and ţ (pronounced "ts").

Useful Words & Phrases

English	Romanian	Pronunciation
Hello	**Salut**	*sa*-luut
Good day	**Bună ziua**	boo-*na zyoo*-ah
Good evening	**Bună seară**	boo-*na sey*-rah
What's your name?	**Cum vă numiţ?**	*koom* vah noo-*mee*-tsee
Cheers (or Good luck!)	**Noroc!**	*noh*-rok
Yes/No	**Da/Nu**	da/noo
Thank you	**Mulţumesc**	mool-*tsoo*-mesk
I would like . . .	**Aş vrea . . .**	ash *vree*-ah . . .
Open/closed	**Deschis/închis**	*des*-kees /*iIn*-kees
Entrance/exit	**Intrare / Ieşire**	in-tra-*reh*/lesh-*eer*
Men's room/ ladies' room	**Bărbaţi/femei**	bar-*bah*-tee/*fem*-may
No entry	**Intrare interzisa**	in-trah-*reh* in-ter-stiza
How much?	**Cằt costă?**	kit kos-ta
Bon appétit	**Poftă bună**	pof-ta *boo*-na
Check, please	**Notă, vă rog**	*not*-a, *vah*-rog
Center (of town)	**Centru**	*sen*-true
Station	**Gară**	*ga*-ra

Fast Facts Romania

Addresses Str. (*strada*, or street), B-dul (*bulevardul*, or boulevard), and Şos. (*şosea*, or avenue) are abbreviations for different road types used throughout this chapter. *Calea* is another word used for avenue, and a *piaţa* is a square.

Airlines **Tarom** is the national carrier; local details appear throughout this chapter.

Area Code The international dialing code for Romania is **+40.**

ATM Networks All towns and cities across the country have ATMs where you can use your credit card to withdraw cash.

Banks & Currency Exchange As a rule, rather make use of ATMs to get cash; your bank will charge an international withdrawal fee, but you're saved the hassle of standing in a bank queue or dealing with any paperwork. Most banks and exchange offices advertise that they don't charge a commission on changing money, but don't expect a favorable rate on zero commission transactions. Check the international market price of the local currency regularly.

Business Hours Standard business hours are not yet the norm in Romania, although most shops open at 9 or 10am and close anywhere between 5 and 8pm during the week; in major cities, shops will be open Saturday mornings until 1pm. Sundays are generally reserved for family and home life. Most museums close on Mondays (and sometimes also Tues).

Car Rentals All major international car-rental agencies are represented in Romania; cars are relatively inexpensive, but you should consider a vehicle with off-road capacity if you're going to drive here with your nerves intact.

Drugstores Pharmacies are found in all cities and towns; you'll often find an outlet at city train stations.

Electricity Local current is 220 volts. Outlets take plugs with two round prongs, typical to continental Europe. Plug and power adapters are necessary for appliances requiring 110 volts.

Embassies & Consulates There is extensive foreign representation in Bucharest, with embassies for the U.S., U.K., Canada, and Australia (contact details are listed in the section on Bucharest, later in this chapter). New Zealanders should contact the embassy in Vienna in case of emergencies (✆ **0043/1/318-8505**).

Emergencies Dial ✆ **961** for general medical emergencies, including ambulance services. In case of fire, contact ✆ **981.**

Etiquette & Customs When visiting churches, women especially should avoid revealing clothing; shorts are generally not accepted in Orthodox churches. When attending an Orthodox liturgy, you can follow the protocol of other worshippers or observe from a distance; observe basic decorum.

Internet Access There are a few Internet cafes in cities and larger towns, but your best bet is to use Internet facilities in hotels.

Liquor Laws You can buy alcohol practically anywhere in Romania; drinking is legal in most public spaces, including trains and sidewalks. The legal age for drinking is 18. It is illegal to drive a car after drinking any amount of alcohol.

Local Law You are legally required to carry some form of identification on you at all times.

Mail It will take up to 2 weeks or more for a letter to reach the U.S. Post offices (look for signs that read POŞTA) are generally open weekdays 7am to 8pm, and Saturdays 8am to 1pm. To save time buy stamps through your hotel and ask reception to send your mail.

Maps You can access interactive maps at www.mapquest.com. Free maps of towns and cities are usually available at hotels and local tourist information offices.

Newspapers & Magazines Practically every city and large town has a slew of publications advertising and promoting entertainment and social events in the locality; these include ***24-Fun, Zile si Nopţi,*** and ***Şapte Serî.*** Local English newspapers are scant and more interesting for their quaint use of the language than for coverage of local or international events; Romania's first English daily is ***Nine O'Clock*** (www.nineoclock.ro). If you're interested in media, design, or architecture, look out for periodic publications by local publisher **igloo media** (www.igloo.ro).

Police Contact the police anywhere in Romania by dialing ✆ **955.** There are abundant complaints by locals about police corruption and also a laissez-faire attitude toward certain crimes; bribes are often expected. Generally, the same attitude is not extended to foreigners; a more likely problem may be an inability or unwillingness to understand English. If you have a police-related emergency, consider also contacting your embassy.

Restrooms Your general reaction to public toilets will be "yuck"; try to avoid these. In Bucharest, paid-for toilets in public gardens are increasingly acceptable.

Safety & Crime There is relatively little violent crime in Romania. Pickpockets may operate in crowded areas (like buses, trains, and stations), and tend to target the country's tourist hot spots. When sitting in bars, cafes, and restaurants, take care not to leave your handbag on the floor or over the back of your seat; similarly, don't leave valuables lying around. Be vigilant with your luggage on trains. Campers are vulnerable and should be cautious. Stray dogs pose a threat when hungry or provoked; some are infected with rabies; if bitten, seek medical assistance immediately.

Taxes & Service Charges An assortment of taxes may be added to your hotel bill; this will be clearly advertised and more often than not is included in the published tariff. VAT is mandatory, while there are a few state and local taxes which may apply, depending on where in the country you are. In a few towns, a small tax is added to the cost of museum tickets.

Telephones Romania's telecommunications are much improved and there is hardly an unconnected spot in the country. Mobile telephones are ubiquitous; the most convenient way to stay in touch is to purchase a SIM card when you arrive and top up with credit as you go. Public pay phones are orange and use magnetic cards, which can be bought from post offices and some hotels; you can purchase L10 ($4.30/£2.65) and L20 ($8.60/£5.35) cards. For an international operator, dial ✆ **971.** Most hotels now have direct international dialing from your room, although this is extremely pricey; those that have the facility usually have detailed dialing instructions in-room. Finally, for domestic calls, you can expect to hear a bizarre range of dialing tones, many of which sound convincingly like engaged or dead signals; often you should just wait to hear if your call is likely to be answered.

Time Zone During winter, Romania is 7 hours ahead of U.S. Eastern Standard Time, or 2 hours ahead of Greenwich Mean Time. During summer, daylight saving time puts Romanian clocks 1 hour forward, along with the rest of Europe.

Tipping Gratuities are neither mandatory nor expected in the majority of situations; expensive establishments are the exception, and in some upmarket city restaurants you're likely to be treated with abuse if you do not tip. Bear in mind, though, that Romanians in the service industry are paid appallingly. Consider giving a 10% tip in restaurants, and round up the fare for taxi drivers, if you feel you've been decently treated. Be aware of certain city taxi drivers who will just as soon assume that they can do the rounding up themselves; insist on getting your change, and then hand over whatever tip amount you've decided on.

Water One-third of Europe's naturally occurring mineral springs are found in Romania. Officially, tap water is potable and safe to drink, but most Romanians will tell you *never* to drink any water that isn't bottled.

2 PLANNING YOUR TRIP TO ROMANIA

VISITOR INFORMATION

Romania's **National Authority for Tourism** operates a website (www.romaniatravel.com) with extensive information about the country and latest developments. You can visit the website of the **Romanian National Tourist Office;** alternatively, try contacting their representatives in the **U.S.,** 355 Lexington Ave., 19th Floor, New York, NY 10017 (© **212/545-8484;** fax 212/251-0429; www.romaniatourism.com), or in the **United Kingdom,** 22 New Cavendish St., London WIM7LH (© **020/7224-3692;** fax 020/7935-6435; www.visitromania.com).

ENTRY REQUIREMENTS

American, Australian, Canadian, British, and New Zealand citizens require only a valid passport if intending to visit for 90 days or less; no visa is required. There is no entry or departure tax. Extensions of stays beyond 90 days can be obtained from the local passport office. No vaccinations are required.

Embassies & Consulates

In the U.S. Embassy: 1607 23rd St. NW, Washington, DC 20008; © **202/332-2879,** 202/232-4749, or 202/332-4852; fax 202/232-4748; www.roembus.org. Consulates: 200 E. 38th St., New York, NY 10016; © **212-682-9122;** http://newyork.mae.ro; and 11766 Wilshire Blvd. 560, Los Angeles, CA 90025; © **310/444-0043;** www.consulateromania.net.

In Canada Embassy: 655 Rideau St., Ottawa, Ontario, K1N 6A3; © **613/789-3709** or 613/789-5345; fax 613/789-4365; http://ottawa.mae.ro. Consulate: 555 Richmond

St., West Unit 1108, P.O. Box 210, Toronto, Ontario, M5V 3B1; © 416/585-9177 or 416/585-5802; fax 416/585-4798; http://toronto.mae.ro.

In the U.K. Embassy: 4 Palace Green, Kensington, London W84QD; © **020/7937-9666;** fax 020/7937-8069; http://londra.mae.ro. Visa section: M.E.I.C. House, 344 Kensington High St., London W14 8NS; © **020/7602-9833** or 020/7602-9662; fax 020/7602-4229.

In Australia 4 Dalman Crescent, O'Malley, Canberra ACT 2606; © **02/6286-2343;** fax 02/6286-2433; http://canberra.mae.ro.

In New Zealand There's an Honorary Consulate in Wellington: 53 Homewood Ave., Karori; © 04/476-6883; fax 04/476-6512; giffpip@xtra.co.nz.

Customs

You are entitled to carry the equivalent of $10,000 cash or traveler's checks on your person when entering Romania; any excess amount must be declared to Customs authorities. You may also bring personal goods and medicines, as well as publications, records and DVDs, slides, and other photographic materials, so long as these are for your personal use. In addition, you may freely carry other goods to the value of $150.

MONEY

Since January 1, 2007, the Romanian new *leu* (currency symbol: RON, plural *lei*)—called "new" because the country underwent currency reform in 2005—has been the only official currency, although in many tourist-oriented accommodations it is common to hear prices quoted in euros for the sake of convenience. Where prices are quoted in *lei,* the symbol "L" is used throughout this chapter. Romanian new lei notes come in denominations of 1, 5, 10, 50, 100, and 500. One *leu* is divided into 100 *bani,* and these come in coin denominations of 1, 5, 10, and 50 *bani.* At this writing, L1 was equivalent to 43¢ or 27p.

Although Romania is not expected to adopt the euro until 2014, many hotels prefer to give a straight euro quote; most of these establishments accept credit cards. MasterCard and Visa are accepted at just about all city hotels, restaurants, and shops, while American Express and Diners Club are less useful. Many outlets can only accept credit cards for which you have a PIN, which you'll be asked to punch in at the cash register; you'll then sign for the transaction as you would for a standard credit card purchase. Keep an eye on your credit card while it is being used for payment; there are frequent reports of illegal imprints being made by restaurant and store employees.

WHEN TO GO

Season, more than anything, is likely to influence the timing of your visit to Romania. Here, temperatures can be extreme; winters get nasty, with closure of certain attractions during the most bitterly cold times of the year, while ski destinations kick into gear from December to mid-March. If you fancy a white Christmas, December is a great time to experience a host of traditional celebrations, particularly in rural communities such as those found in Maramureş and Moldavia, as well as Transylvania. At the other extreme, midsummer can be grueling, with global warming taking its toll here (each July temperatures in some cities hit a stupefying 104°F/40°C; at the same time, in 2008, chilly conditions in the mountain regions were accompanied by extensive flooding). May and October are possibly the most beautiful months, unencumbered by extreme heat.

Major Festivals in Romania

Romanians love to party and have traditionally found many endearing reasons to celebrate; many of these celebrations are no longer observed, however. Festivals are generally determined by traditional folklore as well as by the Orthodox Church's important feasts; numerous local celebrations also add color to the lineup of festivals around the country. On **March 9, Forty Saints' Day** is celebrated as part of Lent in some rural communities where villagers bake *colaci,* special loaves of bread that are blessed and handed out as an act of charity. A popular spring festival is the **National Festival of Spring Agriculture Customs (Tanjaua de pe Mara)** held in **April/early May** in the Maramureş village of Hoteni; it remains a lively local party opportunity, with folk music, dancing, and much drinking. Also in **early May** (usually the first or second Sun), are the **Measuring of the Milk Festivals,** in the Apuseni Mountains, where shepherds compete to see whose sheep and goats are the biggest producers of milk; great carousing follows the ritual milking. On the **first Sunday in May,** the **Pageant of the Juni** in Braşov is one of the most accessible and splendid city festivals, drawing large crowds to see costumed youths parading with brass bands and culminating in spectacular Horăs (Round Dances). In summer, the **Girl Fair (Târgul de fete)** of Mount Găina takes place near Avram Iancu, in the Apuseni Mountains **(last Sun before July 20).** Traditionally an opportunity for shepherds to meet prospective brides, the festival is now a great opportunity to hear the country's finest traditional folk musicians perform live.

On **August 15,** Orthodox believers observe the **Feast of the Assumption of the Virgin Mary,** while in September it is the time of harvest festivals in numerous villages across the country. Saxons celebrate their heritage in the fortified town of Biertan, in Transylvania, on the **second Saturday of September.** The annual **Roma Festival** (a time of impressive celebration that draws Gypsies from across the country) is held in the Wallachia village of Costeşti **(first week of Sept).**

Braşov hosts an **International Jazz Festival** in **mid-May.** Pop fans can look out for the **Golden Stag Festival,** also in Braşov, in **mid-September;** running since 1968, the festival launched the international career of Julio Iglesias and has showcased the talents of Christina Aguillera and Ricky Martin. Drawing some major international film personalities, **TIFF (Transylvania International Film Festival)** happens in Cluj in **early June.**

HOLIDAYS

New Year (Revelion) is celebrated on January 1 and 2, while National Day—commemorating Transylvania's inclusion into greater Romania in 1918—is celebrated on December 1. Christmas (Crăciun) is officially observed on December 25 and 26, and both days are public holidays. Labor Day is celebrated on May 1, but businesses may shut down for more than just the 1 day. Determined according to the Julian calendar, Orthodox Easter is closely observed and while not an official public holiday, may influence opening and closing times. Most businesses and attractions are closed on these days.

HEALTH CONCERNS

Romania is free of risk when it comes to infectious diseases, malaria, and poisonous insects. Officially, tap **water** is potable and safe to drink, but there are accounts of water supplies in some areas being compromised, so it's essential to check with your host or hotel. Reports of rusty pipes in Bucharest are also a cause for concern, suggesting that you stick to bottled water. **Mosquitoes** frequent the Danube Delta as well as other low-lying areas during the hot summer months; bring insect repellent. Good **medical facilities** are available in cities and towns, but the quality of medical practitioners varies considerably; only visit a physician who has been recommended to you by a reliable source.

Smoking is banned in public spaces in Romania, and this law is slowly catching on; you will frequently have to put up with smoke in enclosed spaces, including restaurants and even the lobbies of five-star hotels. Most high-end hotels now have nonsmoking rooms.

GETTING THERE

By Plane

Delta (www.delta.com) is the only carrier offering nonstop flights from the U.S. to Romania; the flight from New York to Bucharest is under 9 hours. A good choice for flights from North America is Austrian Airlines (www.aua.com), which has flights from several U.S. and Canadian hubs, and onward connections to Bucharest, Sibiu, Timisoara, Baia Mare, Cluj, and Iaşi. Many national airlines, including Romania's official carrier, **Tarom** (www.tarom.ro), have direct flights from London and other major western European centers, including Amsterdam (KLM only), Athens, Bologna (Alitalia only), Düsseldorf (Lufthansa only), Frankfurt, Madrid, Milan, Munich, Paris, Rome, Vienna, and Zurich; most flights are under 2 hours. European capitals highlighted in other chapters in this book that are connected by air include Budapest, Ljuljana, Prague, Sofia, and Warsaw. Where possible, if you're traveling from North America, Australia, or New Zealand, you should shop around for an airline that offers direct connections from your country of origin through one of the European capitals; many of the bigger airlines have code-share agreements with Tarom, which means that times between connecting flights are reduced. If you're traveling from New York or Sydney, you are able to book your entire journey through Tarom, but departure dates are limited by the availability of partner airlines. If you're shopping around for a low-cost flight from within western Europe or the U.K., try **Blue Air** (www.blueair-web.com). Another option is **Wizz Air** (www.wizzair.com), a growing airline specializing in Eastern European destinations.

Most international flights arrive at Bucharest's **Henri Coanda International Airport** (still known by its pre-2006 name, **Otopeni**); however, Romania has several other international airports receiving flights from a growing number of European airlines. These airports are small and hassle-free and often their proximity to tourist-friendly destinations makes them a viable alternative for anyone wishing to avoid the capital altogether.

By Train

Trains are viable, but not necessarily cheap or speedy. **Romania's National Railway service** (www.infofer.ro) links with various international services, many of which include overnight sleepers in first- and second-class carriages. You can visit www.raileurope.com for details of schedules and reservations, but you'll have a much easier time simply making inquiries at a booking office in person.

By Bus

Nevertheless, Romania's principal cities are connected by bus services to most important European centers, including London, Paris, Rome, Frankfurt, Berlin, Budapest, Sofia, Vienna, Milan, Istanbul, and Athens.

By Car

If you drive a rental car into Romania, you will require a RoVinieta road toll license; these are available at border crossings, and can also be purchased at many gas stations. You will require proof that you have insurance for the car and you must carry all the vehicle registration documentation with you. Your existing driver's license should be acceptable for driving in Romania. Note that Romanian roads are often in a very dismal condition and driving is not recommended unless you have off-road capability.

GETTING AROUND

By Plane

Tarom, the national carrier, operates a timetable of flights between Bucharest and the country's smaller airports; the best deals can only be purchased online (www.tarom.ro). Romania's domestic airports are generally quiet and (with the exception of taxis) hassle-free; you can usually arrive for check-in within 30 minutes of your flight and have plenty of time to spare before takeoff.

By Train

Romania's rail network (CFR) is extensive and quite exhaustive. Trains are relatively comfortable and generally safe, although I've had first-hand experience of luggage being stolen—keep an eye on your bags at all times, and keep them secured and chained down while sleeping. In many of the newer trains, there is almost no difference between first and second class (except in the price). In the majority of cases, you will be assigned a specific carriage *(vagon)* and seat (the number beneath the date on your ticket). It's quite possible to plan all rail travel before leaving home, but you'll need considerable patience to deal with the online booking system. Go to the online timetable at www.infofer.ro or go to www.cfr.ro; click on "Train Schedule" to begin searching, bearing in mind that you must enter the Romanian spelling of your departure and destination cities.

CFR's services are categorized by the speed of the journey; the fastest trips are on InterCity (IC) trains; these are the most expensive. Next down the rung are Rapid (R) trains—slightly more economical but not quite as fast. Avoid Personal (P) trains, which stop at practically every village. While you can book your tickets online, nearly every town and city has a CFR office located in the center, where you can purchase domestic and international tickets in advance. Traditionally, tickets bought at the train station have only been made available 1 hour before the scheduled journey; this bureaucratic tradition seems to be fading, however, with tickets increasingly available several hours ahead of schedule. With the exception of very popular routes—such as those linking Bucharest with the coast during summer—it is relatively easy obtain train tickets even minutes before departure. The problem is that ticketing lines can be exasperating, with long waits (many travelers need to make elaborate purchases using state-discounted schemes that require time-consuming paperwork); you are advised to purchase tickets in a timely fashion—better still, have your hotel do it for you.

In Bucharest, you can make advance train bookings at either the **Agentia de Voiaj SNCFR,** Str. Domnita Anastasia 10–14 (✆ **021/313-2643**), up to an hour before departure, or at **Wasteels** at Gara du Nord station (✆ **021/317-0369;** www.wasteels.ro/en;

Mon–Fri 8am–7pm, Sat 8am–2pm), which is good for domestic as well as international trains.

By Bus

The size of the country along with the condition of most Romanian roads makes the thought of traveling overland in a large vehicle nothing short of nightmarish. Some companies run minibus services, but you'll still require a steady disposition.

By Car

You'll need nerves of steel to surrender to Romania's roads and culture of high-speed, aggressive driving; tarmac in some areas is in an unpredictable state of repair, signage is less than desirable, and local drivers are in a terrible hurry. Distances between some destinations, combined with heavy traffic, is another deterrent. You may, however, want to hire a car with a driver in order to get to attractions in some areas; to explore the villages of Maramureş and the painted monasteries in Moldavia, for example, this is a necessity, unless you are with an organized tour. If you have car trouble, contact the **Automobil Clubul Roman (ACR; ✆ 9271)**, Romania's version of the American Automobile Association.

TIPS ON ACCOMMODATIONS

In a country where the service industry was for a long time associated with spying on guests for the Communist government, service does not always meet expectations, but accommodations are steadily improving. Hotels are rated according to a star system, which is a moderately informative guide to the type of facilities you can expect to find. However, genuine quality often hides in the details, and there are many three-star properties that are more intimate and classy than their four- or even five-star neighbors. *Pensiunea* (basically, a family-run guesthouse or scaled-down version of a hotel) may be rated two or three stars (or "daisies"), because they offer meals and bedrooms with en suite facilities; in the same star category, however, you may find a much better villa which simply doesn't have an elevator.

When booking a room, note that a "double" usually refers to a twin-bedded unit; double-bedded guest rooms are frequently referred to as "matrimonials." To eliminate any misunderstanding, it's best to request a "matrimonial double," and top this with a request

Tips — Staying with the Locals

Homestays, *pensiunea,* and rural guesthouses are an excellent way of getting to grips with village or community life; in rural areas, there are an unprecedented number of agritourism schemes enabling you to stay with local families at low cost. Be warned, however, that life for some of these families may be fairly simple; you'll be expected to put up with similar conditions. Always check if there is regular hot water, electricity supply, and bathroom facilities (in this chapter, you'll find mention of any problems in this regard). For extensive homestay options across the country, contact **A.N.T.R.E.C. (National Association of Rural, Ecological and Cultural Tourism),** Str. Maica Alexandra 7, Bucharest (**✆ 021/223-7024;** fax 021/222-8001; www.antrec.ro), which has an excellent online booking system with helpful details of its network of guesthouses.

for a "king-size" bed, which will not really impact the size of the bed, but will ensure that you don't have two singles. And be suspicious of accepting accommodations when you're told that only the expensive suite is available as this is usually pure nonsense.

TIPS ON DINING

Meat is big in Romania, and you're generally expected to be a carnivore to cope with traditional Romanian cuisine that favors pork, but includes plenty of fish, widely considered a vegetable in these parts. Traditional staples include *mămăligă*, a polenta-type pottage made from cornmeal, and *sarmale,* parcels made with cabbage or vine leaves, stuffed with rice or meat. When you are treated to a multicourse meal, soup *(ciorbă)* is commonly served first, and the main dish is usually accompanied by some kind of salad *(salată)*. Specialties will vary from region to region, as will the tastes of similar dishes, prepared according to local traditions. Generally, most towns you visit will have restaurants, bistros, less formal taverns *(tavernă),* and wine cellars *(crama)* that double as atmospheric dining halls. Some of these places will have the formal stuffiness preferred in certain Eastern European circles, while down-home-looking eateries are often just fine for a homey, affordable meal. Most restaurants will also have a terrace *(terasă),* ideal in summer. Romania is also known for its potent homemade brandies, made from plums and other fruit; don't pass up the offer of a tot of ţ*uică* (or much stronger *palinca*), sure to raise your body temperature.

TOURS & TRAVEL AGENTS

DiscoveRomania ★★★, Str. Paul Richter 1/1, 500025 Braşov (✆ **0722/74-6262;** www.discoveromania.ro), is an excellent tour company that is also a founder member of the Association of Eco-Tourism in Romania (www.eco-romania.ro); hands-on owner Laura Vesa has a range of interesting and varied packages for travelers keen to discover the "real" Romania. To this end accommodations are generally with local families in small villages, and Laura can plan your visit around special festivals and events to deepen the experience. Nature lovers should inquire after the tour that combines 3 days animal tracking in the Carpathian Mountains with a night in a Moldavian wine-producing village and 2 nights in the Delta, in the fishing village of Uzlina.

Also putting together tours, this time for a clientele seeking sophisticated lodgings and looking for a touch of class and potentially specialized interests—like Jewish heritage, for example—is Eduard Popescu of **Medieval Tours** ★★★, Bd. Magheru 32–36, sc. C. ap. 17, 010337 Bucharest (✆ **021/326-6268** or 0721-161-323; www.medievaltours.ro). Eduard will not only tailor-make a tour that will bring Romania to life in an especially memorable way, but he'll also go above and beyond the call of duty to attend to special requests and unique interests. Fond of seeking out the undiscovered and not afraid to say it how it is, Eduard injects his tours with great charm and humor—if you want to discover the grown-up version of Romanian history and get under the country's skin whilst seeing its most alluring sights, this is an especially satisfying option.

For adventure tours and mountain activities, **Apuseni Experience** ★★★ (✆ **0259/47-2434;** www.apuseniexperience.ro) is one of the best outfits in Romania, based in the city of Oradea.

One of the best-known companies for Romanian exploration is U.K.-based **Transylvania Uncovered** ★★, 1 Atkinson Court, Fell Foot, Newby Bridge, Cumbria LA128NW (✆ **+44-1539-531258;** www.beyondtheforest.com), which offers dozens of specialized trips, such as the new "Secret Transylvania" tour. You might want to avoid their more gimmicky offerings, such as the "Ultimate Halloween Dracula Tours," however. The

Gay Romania

Homosexuality is no longer illegal in Romania, thanks largely to pressure from the E.U. to bring human rights practices in line with the rest of Europe. This represents the end of a long battle against nasty discrimination in legislation, but does not solve the problem of an inherently homophobic society. When the first Romanian gay pride march took place in Bucharest in 2005, it was in the face of tremendous, vocal opposition from the church, government, and the police, not to mention the city mayor; while the GayFest 2008 celebration certainly was colorful, it wasn't a showstopper event. Slowly, gay-friendly or exclusively gay clubs are emerging, but this is only in the larger cities; public displays of homosexual affection are not likely to attract a positive response.

company offers different travel and flight options, so you can match trips to your budget, and accommodations range from top hotels to stays on organic farms. Luxury travel outfit **Abercrombie & Kent** (✆ **1-800/554-7016;** www.abercrombieandkent.com) offers a 13-day "Highlights of Romania & Bulgaria" tour. U.S.-based **Quest Tours & Adventures** (✆ **1-800/621-8687;** www.romtour.com) has specialist tours to Romania, ranging in duration from the 2-day "Touch of Transylvania" tour to the 11-day "World Heritage" tour.

The online **Romanian Travel Guide** (www.rotravel.com) is a resource for virtual planners with links to local tour operators; you can book discounted accommodations at discounted rates through this service.

3 BUCHAREST

Caught up in a necromantic adventure with its elegant, faded past, Bucharest (Bucureşti) may not be to every traveler's taste (it was recently named Europe's most polluted city), but for those interested in experiencing the fast-paced, idiosyncratic flashiness of a city that's riding a tidal wave of change, it is certainly worth planning a few days here. A heady mix of beautifully old, blandly new, and somewhere ambiguously in between (the latter defined by the brash architecture of Ceauşescu-era behemoths), Bucharest seems to know that it's the capital of a nation on the move, a country finally ready to take its place in the European brotherhood.

Legend tells that Bucharest was named after a young shepherd, Bucur, who was so moved by the beauty of this spot on the eastern bank of the Dâmboviţa River that he built a church here, but these humble origins are since long lost in the shrouds of history. Strategically located, Bucharest grew wealthy off trade between the East and West, and entered its swinging heyday after it was crowned the nation's capital in 1862. Then came the World War II bombings, devastating earthquakes in 1940 and 1977, and Ceauşescu. The capital limped its way out of the 20th century, burdened with memories of devouring bulldozers, violent protests, and state-sanctioned massacres. Hard to believe that a mere decade later the pride and promise of the entire nation can be gauged in the strut and swagger of the city's youthful student population, their stride (and blood) quickened by new prospects and fortunes to be made with E.U. membership.

Bucharest today is once again a vibrant, culturally astute capital. Besides a sustained program of theater, music, and opera, it draws major international music acts that fill up the city's stadiums with up-for-it crowds: Since Romania joined the E.U., Kylie Minogue, the Rolling Stones, Metallica, Iron Maiden, George Michael, Massive Attack, and Lenny Kravitz are just a handful of the big names who have performed here, attracting energetic crowds, bound up in a perhaps worrisome embrace of all things Western. But while Ceauşescu might have torn out much of its antiquity, replacing century-old winding roads with pencil-straight boulevards, you can still get lost in the old soul of this riveting city. Playful curiosities, in which the past tangles with the future, remain—nuns reach into their habits to answer ringing cellphones; mafioso-wannabes show off in flashy new cars, racing past street-side Gypsies selling flowers; and men with scales on the sidewalks offer their services guessing your weight. And in antiques stores, treasures gather dust while locals stock up on symbols of modern consumerism. Luxury apartment blocks are going up fast, and at times it seems that the entire city is under renovation. There is much work yet to be done. You'll still notice swaths of endless dull gray concrete blocks, freckled with unsightly air-conditioners, flaking plaster, displaced windows, and hectic tangles of cabling stretched across every conceivable space. Aside from the people you meet, you'll often notice that the only color amidst all the inner city drabness exists in the form of myriad advertising billboards that cloak vast stretches of Bucharest's heart. The signs are all there; irrepressible Bucharest is shedding its skin and edging its way into the future. The journey is set to be a tough one.

GETTING THERE

BY PLANE International flights arrive at **Henri Coanda International Airport,** Şos. Bucureşti-Ploieşti (© **021/201-4050** or 021/204-1423), still generally referred to by its former name, Otopeni, which lies 16km (10 miles) north of the city and has a relatively small but moderately chaotic international terminal; the **information desk** (© **021/204-1000**) is located in the departures lounge. Note that all the taxis and even the shuttle services at the airport will overcharge you (20€–25€/$25–$32 instead of around 10€–12€/$13–$15) for the trip into the city; if you have a hotel reservation, have them arrange a transfer. A relatively reliable airport service is **Fly Taxi Company** (© **021/9440**), which charges a hefty L3.30 ($1.40/90p) per kilometer, or try one of the companies listed under "Getting Around," below. **Bus no. 783** stops outside the domestic terminal (downstairs from international arrivals) and heads into the city (40 min.) every 20 to 30 minutes; buy tickets (L7/$3/£1.85 round-trip from the booth just beyond the bus stop.

BY TRAIN Trains from various European capitals arrive at Bucharest's **Gara de Nord,** Piaţa Gară de Nord 1 (© **021/223-2060;** www.cfr.ro), a large, well-organized station that also has connections with almost every destination around the country.

BY BUS Think twice before tackling long-distance trips through Romania, and that includes any international journey toward Bucharest. If you must, then **Eurolines,** Str. Buzeşti 44 (© **021/230-5489;** www.eurolines.ro), is your best bet for the long, arduous journey from Paris, Madrid, Brussels, or Frankfurt.

CITY LAYOUT & NEIGHBORHOODS IN BRIEF

To the **north** of the city, broad tree-lined boulevards are home to fantastic, crumbling mansions, including foreign embassies and important diplomatic residences. Cobblestone side streets shelter gorgeous homes, many clad in layers of ivy and tucked behind overgrown gardens. It's a neighborhood with an opulent shabbiness, unencumbered by drab apartment blocks or concrete monstrosities; if there's one area in the city that's good for cycling or jogging, this is it. Two major roads, Şoseaua Kiseleff and Bulevard Aviatorilor, stretch from the lakes at the northern extremity of the city to **Piaţa Victoriei,** where security officers protect government buildings. The square is also close to the main train station, Gara de Nord, and near the important Museum of the Romanian Peasant.

From Piaţa Victoriei, **Calea Victoriei** leads southeast into the heart of **downtown Bucharest** with its heady urban feel; monuments and historic buildings stand cheek by jowl with more modern edifices, and there's a constant surge of energy.

Downtown has two notable centers. The first is **Piaţa Revolutiei,** bisected by Calea Victoriei; this where you'll find the Royal Palace (now the National Art Museum), and the Romanian Athenaeum, as well as smaller streets leading to all manner of restaurants, bars, and terraces. Southeast of here is **Piaţa Universitatii,** identifiable by the monstrous InterContinental Hotel and the austere National Theater building, both on one side of the busy intersection. Bulevard Regina Elisabeta becomes Bulevard Carol I as it slices through this point from west to east, while Bulevard Nicolae Bălcescu cuts through from the north. Farther south, **Strada Lipscani** is the main (now pedestrian) road of the city's historic district, known simply as Lipscani. To the east of Piaţa Universitatii are the lovely Cişmigiu Gardens, a small oasis in the middle of the big city.

South of the gardens is the notorious Palace of Parliament and the Centru Civic, where Ceauşescu demolished one-sixth of the old city to make way for a curtain of concrete blocks and pencil-straight boulevards. Principal among these is long, fat Champs-Élysées-style Unirii Boulevard, linking the parliamentary palace with Piaţa Unirii and studded with fountains, one for each county in Romania.

GETTING AROUND

BY TAXI Renowned for their unflinching rip-off tactics, Bucharest's taxis are actually a very affordable way of getting around the city. The onus is on you, however, to check that the fare is clearly displayed on the side of the vehicle (generally, L1–L3/45¢–$1.30/25p–80p per kilometer is acceptable, although some charge up to L7/$3/£1.85 for an air-conditioned ride); then make sure the driver uses the meter. A rated taxi company is **Grant** (✆ **021/9433**), upfront and honest; it's a good idea to call them well ahead of any important trips you need to make. Also reliable are Prof Taxi (✆ **021/9422**), Meridian (✆ **021/9444**), CrisTaxi (✆ **021/9461** or 021/9466), and Perrozzi (✆ **021/9631**).

BY METRO Completely underutilized by locals, the Metro can be a rather dull way to get around the city. Nevertheless, it is cheap and the network is simple enough to figure out with a brief glance at one of the maps posted in the underground stations. Buy tickets (each one is valid for two trips; L2.20/95¢/50p) at the booths adjacent to the passenger gates. Trains run between 5:30am and 11:30pm Monday to Saturday (with reduced hours on Sun), arriving every 5 minutes at busy times, but only three times an hour in slow periods.

ON FOOT In summer it's a punishing walk from one end of the city to the other, but if you're energetic you'll get a much better sense of the city and its people by strolling the sidewalks. This is also a great way to make architectural discoveries and find back-street neighborhoods that nobody ever mentions.

BY TRAM, BUS & TROLLEYBUS Public transport operates between 5am and 11:30pm Monday through Saturday, with shorter hours on Sunday, but you really need to know where you're going and get to grips with the network to make the trams and trolleybuses work for you. Bucharest's buses are cramped, hot, and stuffy, and you'll be more likely to fall prey to pickpockets on one of them than anywhere else. Tickets for all services (L1.10/45¢/25p) can be purchased at any of the many RATB kiosks around the city (look for BILETE signs), where you can also pick up a timetable (purchase Amco's *Public Ground Transport Map* if you're going to use public transport); timetables are also posted on streetlamps near bus stops (the central "station" is across the road from Hotel Ibis on Calea Griviţei). Remember to use the self-service machine to validate your ticket once you're on board, and good luck.

VISITOR INFORMATION

There is no official tourist information service in Bucharest; in most cases, your hotel will be able to point you in the right direction, and provide you with a map. Ask specifically for the listings publication, ***Bucharest in Your Pocket*** (www.inyourpocket.com), which has maps as well as details of hotels, restaurants, bars, and attractions. Bucharest's bookstores stock some good publications on the city and on major points of interest around the country.

Fast Facts Bucharest

Airlines The headquarters of the national carrier, **Tarom,** Spl. Independenţei 17 (© **021/303-4444;** www.tarom.ro; Mon–Fri 8am–7:30pm, Sat 9am–1:30pm), are at the **airport** (© **021/201-4979**). **British Airways:** Calea Victoriei 15; © **021/303-2222;** Mon–Fri 9am–5pm.

Ambulance In emergencies, dial © **973,** 961, or 021/243-1333. To summon **Puls,** a private ambulance service, dial © **021/224-0187** (Mon–Sat 7:30am–7:30pm; Sun 7:30am–1:30pm).

American Express Services are available through Marshal Turism (www.marshal.ro), at B-dul Unirii 20 (© **021/319-4444**) and B-dul Magheru 43 (© **021/319-4455**). Hours are Monday to Friday 9am to 6pm and Saturday 9am to 1pm.

Area Codes For Bucharest dial © **021** or 031; the latter is an additional dialing code for services offered by alternative telephony providers.

Banks & Currency Exchange Banks are the best place to exchange foreign currency. ATMs are everywhere and are the best way to obtain local currency, assuming that your credit card has a PIN or that your cash card has been enabled for international use.

Car Rentals Major companies include **Avis** (various branches; © **021/210-4344;** www.avis.ro), **Hertz** (© **021/222-1256;** www.hertz.com.ro), and **Europcar** (© **021/310-1797;** www.europcar.com). Standard car rental can be as low as 30€ ($38) per day for a cheap model with unlimited mileage. If you prefer something classier, try **Bavaria Rent a Car** (© **021/201-4534** or 0730-333-707; www.bavariarent.ro), specializing in BMWs, with tough models that will better handle some of Romania's more treacherous roads.

Drugstores Open round the clock, **Help Net** has branches at B-dul Unirii 24 (© **021/335-7425**), Calea 13 Septembrie 126 (© **021/411-9574**), B-dul Ion Mihalache 92 (© **021/224-44215**), and Str. Av. Radu Beller 8 (© **021/233-8984**).

Embassies The **U.S.** Embassy (Mon–Fri 8am–5pm) is at Str. Tudor Arghezi 7–9 (✆ **021/200-3300;** www.usembassy.ro). The Canadian Embassy (Mon–Thurs 9am–5pm; Fri 8.30am–2pm) is at Str. Tuberozelor 1–3 (✆ **021/307-5000;** www.dfait-maeci.gc.ca). The **U.K. Embassy** (Mon–Thurs 8:30am–5pm; Fri 8:30am–4pm) is at Str. Jules Michelet 24 (✆ **021/210-7200;** www.britishembassy.gov.uk/romania). Contact the **Australian Consulate General,** Str. Buzesti 14–18, Fifth Floor (www.dfat.gov.au) at ✆ **021/316-7558.** New Zealanders should contact the **New Zealand Embassy and Mission to the European Union** in Brussels (✆ **+32/2/512-1040;** www.nzembassy.com).

Emergencies Dial ✆ **961** in case of emergencies; for an ambulance, dial ✆ **961** or 973; and contact ✆ **981** in case of fire. See "Police," below.

Hospital Romania's best state-run facility is **Emergency Clinic Hospital (Spitalul de Urgenta),** Calea Floreasca 8 (✆ **021/230-0106** or 021/317-0171). A good private service is **Dr. Victor Babes,** Str. Mihai Bravu 281 (✆ **021/317-9503**), which is open daily from 8am to 8pm, and has a price list for all services on its website, www.cdt-babes.ro. A good chain of clinics is **Medicover** (emergency number ✆ **021/310-4040;** appointments **021/310-1599**), with three branches, at Calea Plevnei 96 (✆ **021/310-4410**), Str. Dr. Grozovici 6 (✆ **021/316-2155**), and Str. Grigore Alexandrescu 16–20 (✆ **021/310-1688**); they're open 8am to 8pm Monday through Friday and also Saturday morning.

Internet Access Most hotels now have Internet, and many have Wi-Fi.

Police Dial ✆ **955.** The most central police station is at Calea Victoriei 17 (✆ **021/311-2021**).

Post Office Bucharest's **main post office** is located at Str. Matei Millo 10, and is open Monday to Friday 7:30am to 8pm, and Saturday 8am to 2pm.

WHERE TO STAY

Bucharest is well geared to receive visitors with company expense accounts, with respected Western chains all represented here and offering most of the luxuries and comforts you might expect in other parts of the world. An increasing number of modest and better-priced accommodations are available, although you may miss some of the amenities offered by similarly priced properties back home (few have pools, for example). Budget hotels leave much to be desired. Since most hotels cater to business clients, weekend rates tend to offer better deals.

Hotels are spread across the city, but there are only about 4km (2½ miles) between the northernmost (Sofitel) and southernmost (Marriott Grand) hotels mentioned here. If you want to be in the heart of the city, there are plenty of hotels across the quality spectrum right in the center, within walking distance of major attractions. But bear in mind that Bucharest's attractions are spread out enough to make proximity to the center only a minor consideration when choosing your hotel.

Very Expensive

K+K Hotel Elisabeta ★★ Position, taste, service—what more could you want? Located bang in the heart of downtown Bucharest, K+K is right near the Teatrul National, and within walking distance from the Lipscani District and the Cişmigiu Gardens; there's even a Metro station just around the corner. It doesn't have an excess of hotel facilities but concentrates on the much more important business of service delivery. Staff is all exceptionally helpful—at breakfast (an excellent buffet that includes champagne), the waitresses may even offer unsolicited sightseeing advice. Guest rooms are of a generally high standard, with comforting touches like luxurious linens and flatscreen televisions; the only possible complaint is the relatively small size of the bathrooms. The convenient location also comes at a price; hotel planners had to carve this glamorous lodging out of a slightly seedy-looking side street; they've been steadily improving the neighborhood over the past 2 years, but some views out the back are still quite ugly, so make sure you book a street-facing room.

Str. Slănic 26, Bucharest. ✆ **021/311-8631.** Fax 021/311-8632. www.kkhotels.com. 67 units. 274€ ($348) business double; 308€ ($391) executive double; 515€ ($654) executive suite; 46€ ($58) extra bed. Rates include breakfast and taxes. AE, MC, V. **Amenities:** Bistro; bar; breakfast room; sauna; room service; laundry. *In room:* A/C, TV, Internet, minibar, tea- and coffeemaking facility, hair dryer, electronic safe, scale.

Novotel ★★ In the heart of the city, this postmodern structure consists of a massive wall of mirrored glass behind a reproduction of the old National Theater that once stood on this site. What this slick business hotel lacks in historic ambience, it more than makes up for with intelligent, helpful service. Receptionists—in gray and pink suits—double as concierges, and dish out meaningful, useful, personal advice. So, instead of hearing about all the usual tourist dives, you might actually be pointed toward a couple of local favorites. In this hotel, the crack staff actually make an effort to ask if they can be of assistance—the whole service philosophy seems to run contrary to the Romanian norm. Decor is pretty indicative of contemporary trends everywhere—plenty of straight lines, dark wood, upbeat lounge music, and vivid colors working to offset the IKEA-look furnishing. Guest rooms are hardly the stuff of radical innovation, but they're comfortable and thoughtfully laid out. All bathrooms come with tub *and* shower; toilets are in a separate room. Breakfast (18€/$23) is a particularly impressive buffet spread (attended to by model-like waiting staff); you can sip champagne as you gaze out through massive windows deep into the bowels of the city—the view makes for a startling contrast. ***Note:*** While the rack rates listed below are high, you'll find reductions when you book online, and weekends are considerably more affordable, too.

Calea Victoriei 37B, Bucharest. ✆ **021/308-8500.** Fax 021/308-8501. www.novotel.com. 258 units. 310€ ($394) Novation double; 350€ ($446) executive double; 390€ ($495) junior suite; 440€–790€ ($559–$1,003) suite. Rates exclude breakfast and taxes. AE, DC, MC, V. **Amenities:** Restaurant; bar; small indoor pool; fitness center; massage; hammam; business center; room service; laundry. *In room:* A/C, TV, Internet/Wi-Fi, minibar, tea- and coffeemaking facility.

Expensive

Hotel Amzei ★ (Finds Located just off Calea Victoriei and well positioned for some of the city's main sights and entertainment areas, this is a good attempt at a charming, borderline-luxury boutique hotel with a clear focus on the foreign tourist market. Guest rooms occupy four floors in an elegantly renovated early-20th-century mansion; decor is a marriage of modern-contemporary with some antique-look detailing, including plush furnishings and quality fittings; the beds in the standard rooms could be a touch larger, though. Still, bedrooms are wonderfully spacious with decent bathrooms (and tubs), and a full complement of modern amenities. While sleeping quarters are amongst the loveliest in the city, there are telltale signs that the whole project isn't entirely thought through, though, and you need to look beyond coarser details—like the Coca-Cola fridge (and nonstop TV) in the off-lobby lounge-bar, and the slightly claustrophobic basement

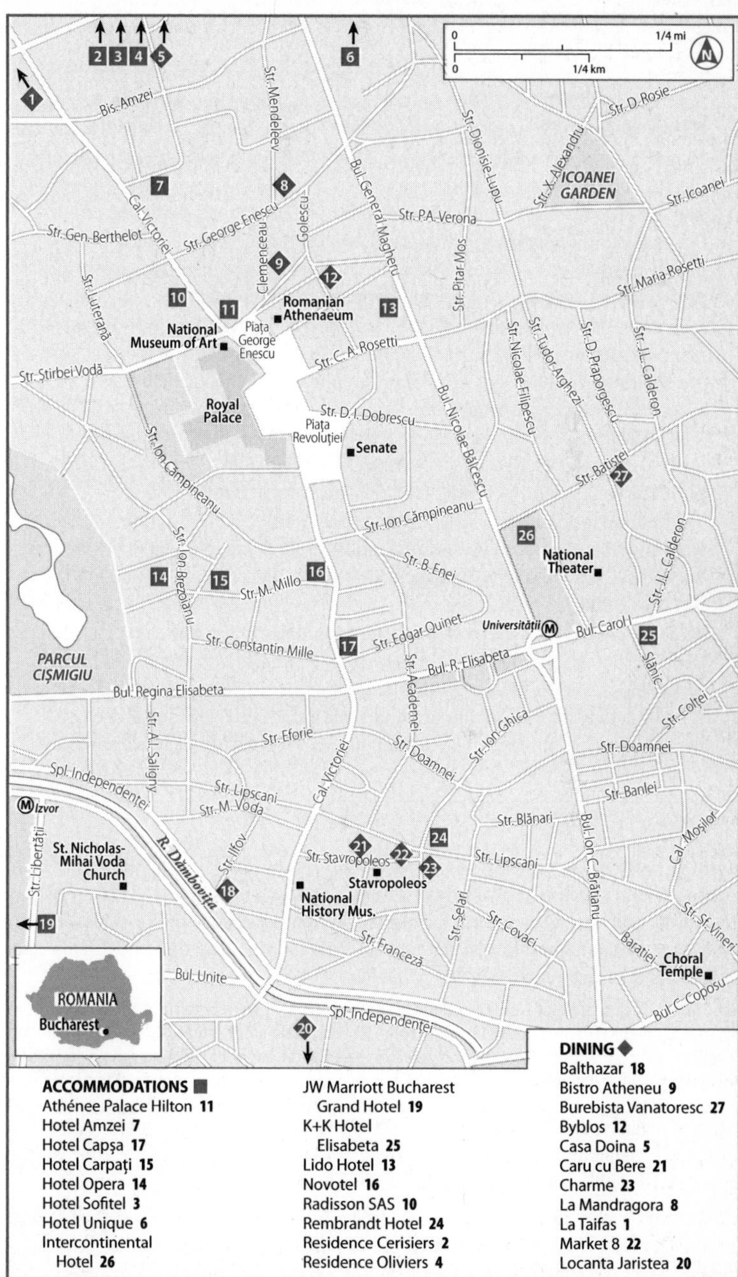
0 1/4 mi
0 1/4 km
N
Bis. Amzei
Str. Mendeleev
Str. D. Rosie
Str. Dionisie Lupu
Str. X. Alexandru
ICOANEI GARDEN
Str. Icoanei
Bul. General Magheru
Str. P.A. Verona
Cal. Victoriei
Str. George Enescu
Str. Gen. Berthelot
Golescu
Clemenceau
Str. Pitar Mos
Str. Maria Rosetti
Str. Luterană
Romanian Athenaeum
National Museum of Art
Piața George Enescu
Str. C. A. Rosetti
Str. Nicolae Filipescu
Str. Tudor Arghezi
Str. D. Praporgescu
Str. J.L. Calderon
Str. Știrbei Vodă
Royal Palace
Str. D. I. Dobrescu
Piața Revoluției
Senate
Bul. Nicolae Bălcescu
Str. Batiștei
Str. Ion Câmpineanu
Str. Ion Câmpineanu
National Theater
Str. B. Enei
Str. Ion Brezoianu
Str. M. Millo
Str. Edgar Quinet
Universității
Bul. Carol I
Str. Constantin Mille
Bul. R. Elisabeta
Str. Academiei
Slănic
PARCUL CIȘMIGIU
Bul. Regina Elisabeta
Str. A.I. Saligny
Str. Eforie
Str. Ion Ghica
Str. Colței
Str. Doamnei
Str. Doamnei
Spl. Independenței
Str. Lipscani
Str. M. Voda
Str. Banlei
Izvor
Str. Blănari
Cal. Moșilor
Str. Libertății
R. Dâmbovița
Str. Ilfov
Str. Stavropoleos
Str. Lipscani
St. Nicholas-Mihai Voda Church
Stavropoleos
National History Mus.
Bul. Ion C. Brătianu
Str. Șelari
Str. Covaci
Str. Sf. Vineri
Str. Franceză
Baratiei
Choral Temple
Bul. Unite
ROMANIA
Bucharest
Spl. Independenței
Bul. C. Coposu
ACCOMMODATIONS
Athénee Palace Hilton 11
Hotel Amzei 7
Hotel Capșa 17
Hotel Carpați 15
Hotel Opera 14
Hotel Sofitel 3
Hotel Unique 6
Intercontinental Hotel 26
JW Marriott Bucharest Grand Hotel 19
K+K Hotel Elisabeta 25
Lido Hotel 13
Novotel 16
Radisson SAS 10
Rembrandt Hotel 24
Residence Cerisiers 2
Residence Oliviers 4
DINING
Balthazar 18
Bistro Atheneu 9
Burebista Vanatoresc 27
Byblos 12
Casa Doina 5
Caru cu Bere 21
Charme 23
La Mandragora 8
La Taifas 1
Market 8 22
Locanta Jaristea 20

Hey, Big Spender! Staying in Bucharest's Glitziest Digs

Built between 1912 and 1914 on the site of an earlier inn, **Athénée Palace Hilton** ★★, Str. Episcopiei 1–3 (✆ **021/303-3777;** fax 021/315-3813; www.hilton.com), remains Bucharest's most celebrated hotel; its history smacks of glamour and intrigue—legend has it that staff would spy on important guests, and secret code words were frequently whispered in its halls and dining rooms. But today this is very much a top-quality Hilton-branded establishment, completely overhauled in 1997 with an eye to business and high-end travelers who prefer not to skimp on luxuries while connecting with some of the city's past—recent guests included the Rolling Stones, and it was here that world leaders could be spotted during the NATO Summit in 2008. Yet, while accommodations are pleasing (if reminiscent of hotel rooms anywhere), the location prime, and amenities extensive, I cannot imagine why you'd want to squander L1,960 ($843/£523) for a single night in a double room here. Neither breakfast nor taxes (12%) are included and bathrooms are small. Still, if you have cash to burn, the well-trained staff will probably help you put out the fire.

Although it doesn't have the historical pedigree, you'll find a more relaxed, vibrant, and contemporary atmosphere just across the road from the Hilton, at Bucharest's spanking new **Radisson SAS** ★★, Calea Victoriei 63–81 (✆/fax **021/311-9000;** www.bucharest.radissonsas.com; doubles from 335€/$425). It's a mammoth hotel, with 464 rooms, representing a major overhaul of the old Hotel Bucharest. Bedrooms are ultraplush, with large, inviting beds and sumptuous linens. There's plenty of fanciful, sometimes playful design detail—particularly in the lobby—and the vast atrium will induce vertigo in some. The hotel benefits from an outdoor pool, but still has to deal with the ugly backdrop of

breakfast room where electrical cabling all seems to stand out as though it's meant to be a design feature. Such is the sometimes brutal interpretation of Western luxury. Service treads a wobbly line between indifferent and overenthusiastic. Amzei opened in early 2008, so may yet mature into something splendid; in the meantime, book online for better rates than those listed below.

Piaţa Amzei 8, Bucharest. ✆ **021/313-9400.** Fax 021/313-9494. www.hotelamzei.ro. 22 units. L684 ($294/£182) double; L798 ($343/£213) junior suite. Rates include breakfast. AE, DC, MC, V. **Amenities:** Breakfast room; bar; sightseeing and car rental arranged; airport transfers; ticketing service; laundry. *In room:* A/C, TV, Internet, minibar, hair dryer, safe.

Hotel Capşa ★★ Beautiful chandeliers sparkle in the all-marble lobby of this historic hotel, signaling to all its long and distinguished pedigree. Established by Grigore Capşa in 1852, it was here that the first U.S. Embassy was housed between 1880 and 1884. Emperors, kings, statesmen, and Francis Ford Coppola have been guests here, and it still bears discreet references to significant political events that were decided in meetings held here by the country's leaders in times gone by. More graciously styled and better priced than a number of similarly comfortable Bucharest hotels, its guest rooms neighboring apartment blocks that loom quite jarringly over your potential sunbathing spot.

If for some reason you want to be near Ceauşescu's Palace of the People and, in fact, stay in the hotel he conjured up to accommodate his guests, consider reserving a room at the **JW Marriott Bucharest Grand Hotel** ★, Calea 13 Septembrie 90 (✆ **021/403-0000;** fax 021/403-0001; www.marriott.com/buhro; from L800/$344/£213 double, without breakfast or taxes), where you can expect the usual standard in-room amenities and hotel services. There's also the good chance of having important dignitaries as fellow guests (incidentally, George Dubya stayed here during the NATO talks); the Marriott is a typically huge and luxurious complex with myriad dining options, an expensive and extensive shopping mall, and the slight whiff of impersonal service (there are 407 guest rooms); public spaces are unlikely to make you feel much like you're on holiday with businessmen barking into their mobile phones as they pace around the lobby.

Part of another excellent international chain hotel (one that's also linked to the more centrally located Novotel; see below), located in the north of the city, and unfortunately attached to the World Trade Center, is **Hotel Sofitel** ★★, Montreal Sq. 10 (✆ **021/318-3000;** fax 021/317-2997; www.sofitel.com), with over 200 beautifully appointed rooms steeped in gracious luxury. There's plenty of space and an abundance of comforting extras; the bathrooms have tubs as well as separate showers. Every imaginable amenity is on hand and its marvelous Mediterranean restaurant, Les Oliviades, is one of the city's best. Doubles start at 240€ ($305), excluding breakfast and taxes, but go way up.

are spacious, with high ceilings and carpets, wall-mounted chandeliers, antique armoires, and plaster molded detailing. If it's important, specify whether you'd like a tub or shower. The real letdown here is lax service, deeply frustrating at times. Still, bear in mind that Capşa has good specials during quiet periods, so look out for last-minute deals (weekends—when service is at it's worst—also mean better rates).

Calea Victoriei 36, Bucharest. ✆ **021/313-4038.** Fax 021/313-5999. www.capsa.ro. 61 units. 230€ ($292) double; 260€ ($330) junior suite; 500€–685€ ($635–$870) suite. Breakfast and taxes extra. MC, V. **Amenities:** Restaurant; bar; fitness center; sauna; massage; hairdresser; room service; laundry; courier. *In room:* A/C, TV, minibar.

Lido Hotel ★ Operating since 1930, this grand old hotel is a good alternative if the Hotel Capşa is full, or has suddenly raised its rates substantially (Lido will happily provide discounts if you call ahead). Guest rooms, done out in faux-Venetian style with painted wood and a pale color palette, are comfortable enough but have a slightly faded feel; while these could do with a refurb the bathrooms are looking good, with combination tub/shower. One of the best reasons to stay here is the spectacle of city life from the tiny balconies overlooking busy General Mageru Boulevard—pure Bucharest (depending on your fancy, the housekeepers, who all seem to resemble supermodels and work in ridiculously short skirts, are another).

B-dul General Magheru 5, Bucharest. ✆ **021/314-4930.** Fax 021/312-1414. www.lido.ro. 119 units. 240€ ($305) double; 345€ ($438) suite. AE, MC, V. **Amenities:** Restaurant; brasserie; breakfast room; bar; fitness center; massage; Jacuzzi; sauna; salon; room service; laundry. *In room:* A/C, TV, minibar, hair dryer.

Moderate

Hotel Opera ★ This small hotel—right in the center of town—is one of the best options in the city in terms of location and price. Decorated with an assortment of music-related items, antiques, and lovely sepia photos of '50s Bucharest, Opera offers smart yet sensible lodgings, with spacious guest rooms. Bathrooms are equally comfortable; standard doubles have showers, so you'll need to book a more expensive unit if you prefer a tub. At weekends, when rates are reduced, it may be worth forking out a little extra for one of the junior suites, each named for a different opera. There's no in-house restaurant, but staff can point you in the direction of something suitable, or you can order meals to your room. If you're in the mood for company, you can join the locals who while away their time playing backgammon in the lobby bar.

Str. Ion Brezoianu 37, Bucharest. ✆ **021/312-4855/7.** Fax 021/312-4858. www.hotelopera.ro. 33 units. Weekday/weekend: 150€/130€ ($191/$165) double; 175€/150€ ($222/$191) executive double; 195€/150€ ($248/$191) junior suite. Rates include breakfast and VAT. AE, MC, V. **Amenities:** Breakfast room; lobby bar; fitness room; car rental; airport transfers; business lounge; room service; laundry. *In room:* A/C, TV, Internet, minibar, tea- and coffeemaking facility, hair dryer, safe.

Hotel Unique ★★ (Finds) Small, intimate, and contemporary, this boutique hotel opened in 2006, and has remained well under the radar. There are just four guest rooms and one suite per floor, but it's worth splashing out on the sumptuous penthouse apartment, which affords a panoramic view of the surrounding neighborhood. If that's taken, never mind; all the accommodations are still wonderfully spacious—and easy on the eye. Sleek, minimalist styling (white and blonde wood dramatically offset by touches of red or orange) defines each of the guest rooms. Not a huge array of facilities but the small, smart breakfast room and tiny garden terrace should suffice when you need to retreat from the city.

Piaţa Romana, Str. Caderea Bastiliei 35, Bucharest. ✆/fax **021/319-4591** or 021/311-8196. www.hotelunique.ro. 15 units. 133€ ($169) double; 165€ ($210) junior suite. Rates include breakfast and taxes. Weekend rates may be cheaper. Internet may offer lower rates. MC, V. **Amenities:** Breakfast room; coffee bar; terrace; airport transfers; limited room service (drinks only); laundry. *In room:* A/C, TV, DVD on request, Internet, minibar, tea- and coffeemaking facility, hair dryer, safe.

Rembrandt Hotel ★★★ (Value) Compact and chic, this Dutch-owned boutique hotel is the personal top choice in the city, with contemporary guest rooms, comfortable beds, and generally welcoming staff. It's also located slap-bang in the center of the city, across the road from the National Bank of Romania, another gorgeous city monument. Just 15 rooms are squeezed into an almost impossibly narrow slither of carefully restored downtown real estate, but the Rembrandt has, in just a few years, come to define the spirit of renewal and rejuvenation that Bucharest's historic Lipscani District is set to represent (although surrounding developments have been slower than anticipated). Accommodations are beautiful; simple and sleek, they're done out with wooden floors (***Caution:*** they're polished and slippery), hardy white linens, and Art Nouveau light fittings. If you don't mind having a slightly smaller room, note that there's one top-floor unit with a private balcony from which the spectacular views of the city stretch as far as

Room With a View

At the climax of the December 1989 Revolution, students from the **University of Bucharest** were among those who sat on busy University Square in protest, only to be driven over by tanks manned by those still loyal to Ceaușescu. The square is today still lorded over by the ugly frame of the **InterContinental Hotel,** B-dul Nicolae Bălcescu 4 (✆ **021/310-2020;** www.intercontinental.com), from where you can share the same view as the international press who witnessed the wholesale massacre of ordinary citizens barricaded in by the military. On the night of December 21, 1,000 helpless victims were killed here; a black cross marks the spot where the first victim fell in the early evening. Today, the areas in front of the **National Theater (Teatrul Naţional)** and the fountain in front of the University building are once again popular meeting points for students who find many diversions around or near this great physical and symbolic crossroads.

the Parliamentary Palace. Rembrandt is near a wide range of lovely restaurants, and is perfect for exploring the city on foot. ***Note:*** Rates drop by over 10% at weekends.

Str. Smârdan 11, Bucharest. ✆ **021/313-9315.** Fax 021/313-9316. www.rembrandt.ro. 15 units. 91€–101€ ($116–$128) tourist double; 114€–134€ ($145–$170) standard double; 142€–162€ ($180–$206) business double. Rates include breakfast and taxes. MC, V. **Amenities:** Bistro; bar; laundry. *In room:* A/C, TV, DVD and CD player, Internet, minibar, hair dryer.

Residence Oliviers ★★ Value Location aside (Residence is in the north of the city, within walking distance of the Arcul d'Triumf, but you will have to catch a cab to see other top sights), this is one of the best small hotels in Bucharest, and now one part of a small chain of boutique establishments. Wood-floor passages lead to carpeted guest rooms decked out in smart bamboo furniture (making them thoroughly unique in Bucharest) with wrought-iron beds; they're spacious and, by local standards, lovely. Public spaces are an eclectic combination of contemporary and neoclassical elements; there's a relaxed atmosphere that makes this Residence feel homey and inviting. The restaurant and the terrazzo-style dining area at the front of the hotel are popular meeting spots for locals and visitors. Even farther from the center, the newer hotel in a similar league is **Residence Cerisiers ★★**, Str. Alex. Constantinescu 33 (✆ **021/224-5044**), where a slightly higher rate (120€–150€/$152–$191 double) buys a more sophisticated look (and solid wood furniture), but also means extra travel time to the city's attractions.

Str. Clucerului 19, Bucharest. ✆ **021/223-1978.** Fax 021/222-9046. www.residencehotels.com.ro. 35 units. Weekdays/weekends: 130€/100€ ($165/$127) double; 150€/110€ ($191/$140) studio; 170€/120€ ($216/$152) suite. Rates include breakfast; taxes extra. MC, V. **Amenities:** 2 restaurants; bar; fitness center; travel services; airport transfers (free for stays of 2 nights or more); laundry. *In room:* A/C, TV, Internet, minibar.

Inexpensive

If you don't mind foregoing room service and the like, a good way to save money is to rent an apartment; just make sure you're not located too far from the action. **City Comfort** (www.citycomfort.ro) offers rentals that work out far cheaper than hotel stays; rates start at 39€ ($49) per night for a basic studio right in the center. Apartments vary, but are usually clean and modestly furnished; some have occasional cleaning service, air-conditioning, and even free Internet access.

Hotel Carpaţi Value Built in the 1920s, this six-floor hotel has assorted clean guest rooms, with or without en suite bathrooms; some have private showers but no toilet (and vice versa), while a few have their own bathroom *and* separate toilet. Rates vary according to the level of privacy and in-room amenities. The suites represent unbelievable value; they're disproportionately spacious, with old leather sofas, chandeliers, antique telephones, and bathtubs. They're let down by extremely soft mattresses, though. Rates include a simple breakfast and moody reception staff. This is one of Bucharest's most popular budget hotels, often filled with last-minute arrivals leading to complaints of reservations not being honored; if you decide to stay here, get your booking confirmation in triplicate. ***A final warning:*** Mind your head on the stairs, and don't come here looking for any sort of pampering.

Str. Matei Millo 16, Bucharest. © **021/315-0140.** Fax 021/312-1857. www.hotelcarpatibucuresti.ro. 40 units. 50€ ($64) twin with shared shower; 70€ ($89) en suite double; 85€ ($108) suite. Rates include breakfast. MC, V. **Amenities:** Breakfast area; laundry. *In room:* TV, some A/C, fridge.

WHERE TO DINE

If you just want to wander around looking for a restaurant, head for Str. Episcopiei, where the streets are lined with cafes and restaurants, including the charming Bistro Atheneu (reviewed below). A short stroll from here is **Byblos,** Nicolae Golescu 14–16 (© **021/313-2091;** www.byblos.uv.ro), a smart place to grab a drink and light lunch, like pizza, panini, bruschetta, and salad (including the delectable Byblos Salad—spinach leaves, pine-nut kernels, and Parmesan in a garlicky olive-oil dressing); at night Byblos is one of the city's more reliably classy dining venues, with reliably priced Italian fare.

Expensive

For upmarket Romanian fare, many locals with fat wallets (not to mention the grinning concierge at the ultrapricey Hilton) swear by **Locanta Jaristea** ★★, Calea George Georgescu 52 (© **021/335-3338**), a fine option if you're looking to splurge in the vicinity of the Parliamentary Palace. You'll dine in wonderfully decorous, traditional surroundings, with the knowledge that a meal here is accompanied by the sharpest service.

Balthazar ★★★ FRENCH-ASIAN One of the city's finest restaurants, this is a stunning example of Bucharest's contemporary aspirations; the owners describe the atmosphere as "sensual-chic," which pretty much sums up the elegant rusticity of the place. Start with Peking duck *blinis* (small Eastern European pancakes), tuna "cigars," or smoked eel on a bed of cheese. Mains include beef *pavé* smothered in the chef's secret Balthazar sauce and served with stuffed artichokes and tomatoes, lamb rib chops served with bamboo and a cherry sauce, and blue fin tuna steak with pineapple carpaccio, fennel, and bamboo salad. There's also sea bream with spinach mousse served with black tiger shrimp sauce. If you're after a lighter meal, opt for the Asian salad with black tiger shrimps and ginger sauce. The dessert menu is almost an occasion on its own: Who can decide between wild berry sorbet, chocolate surprise, and cheesecake served with ginger ice cream?

Str. Dumbrava Roşie 2. © **021/212-1460.** www.balthazar.ro. Reservations essential. Main courses L33–L79 ($14–$34/£8.80–£21). MC, V. Daily noon–midnight.

A Primer for Wine Lovers

Romania's best winegrowing regions are Dogrogea and Oltenia, a part of Wallachia. A good everyday red is Fetească Neagră, from the Banat's Val Duna region; similar to shiraz, it has the taste of dry, spicy plums. The La Cetate merlot is a reliable variety from Oltenia region; there's a hint of honey on the palate, accompanied by a lively, ripe tartness. But, if you really want to impress your sommelier, ask for a bottle of Romania's very best red, a cabernet sauvignon called La Catate Tezaur (or "treasure"); it's remarkably light despite being a big, robust, full-bodied wine. The 2002 is an exceptional vintage.

Casa Doina ★★ ROMANIAN/MEDITERRANEAN In Bucharest's leafy north, among the embassies and mansions, this classy establishment occupies a fine 18th-century villa with a gorgeous garden terrace for summer dining (which is also heated in winter); this is a favored place for the old school air-kissing crowd, where foreigners hobnob with the rich while chef Doru Dobre cooks up a storm for his sophisticated clientele. Start with polenta topped with bacon and shaved cheese, topped with an egg and served with sour cream, or have the in-house version of *sarmale,* sour cabbage leaves stuffed with meat and served (of course) with polenta. The menu is not too complicated, with plenty to keep both unadventurous and keen-to-experiment taste buds happy; chicken filet is stuffed with Roquefort and finished off with bacon and Parmesan; braised ducking is served with sauerkraut, and grilled duck liver with cherry sauce. Fresh fish is available at the daily market price; their swordfish is gently fried in olive oil. Finish off with nougat glace with egg custard and maple syrup.

Şos. Kiseleff 4. ✆ **021/222-3179.** www.casadoina.ro. Reservations recommended. Main courses L25–L50 ($11–$22/£6.80–£14). MC, V. Daily noon–1am.

La Mandragora ★★★ FRENCH FUSION Decadent decor and smart ideas about food have inspired a classy, edgy ambience at this lovely new restaurant that opened in a renovated house in June 2006. When we discovered it back then, we knew it'd be a hit, and now it's probably the best restaurant in the city, beloved by Bucharest's smarter diners. Lilac-colored walls, a glittering bar, and gathered drapes are the opening gambit for an evening of superb food. French dishes with a twist is how you might describe the divine creations of German chef Paul Peter Kopij, who plans seasonal innovations and additions to a cleverly sophisticated yet simple menu. Cream of carrot or shiitake mushroom soup, and beef carpaccio with beet and pine-nut salad are some of the starters likely to be on offer. Then there's breast of duck cooked in Guinness ale, while whatever fish is freshest from the daily market will be the favored seafood option. Best are the homemade ice creams; choose either La Mandragora's ice cream assortment, or crème brûlée with green-apple ice cream.

Str. Mendeleev 29. ✆ **021/319-7592.** Reservations essential. Main courses L24–L79 ($10–$34/£6.40–£21). MC, V. Mon–Sat 6pm–late; kitchen closes 11pm.

Moderate

Bistro Atheneu ★ ROMANIAN/ECLECTIC This atmospheric bistro, going strong since 1924, features bohemian decor that could have been culled from a flea market, with expired antique clocks, dangling bells, violins, and framed mirrors, even an ancient cash register. The kitchen may be relying a bit on its reputation, but it remains a reliable choice for wholesome, tasty meals at undaunting prices. The menu is chalked up daily (albeit illegibly and in Romanian—so you'll need to interact with the staff a bit); on offer will be the usual mainstays like grilled pork, grilled chicken, beef entrecôte, chicken livers, and lasagna. Romanian specialties include *sarmale* and *tochitura* (pork stew); if you're lucky (or you could inquire if the chef will prepare it), the delectable chicken breast, wrapped in bacon and prepared with smoked plum, cinnamon, red wine, and a secret brown sauce and finished with green basil, will be available.

Str. Episcopiei 3. ✆ **021/313-4900.** Main courses L19–L24 ($8.15–$10/£5.05–£6.40). MC, V. Daily noon–1am.

Burebista Vanatoresc ★ ROMANIAN This is pure unadulterated Romanian cuisine, but animal lovers (and vegetarians) should steer clear of this medieval-themed meat temple with decor straight out of a natural history museum. Animal trophies and stuffed birds peer down from the walls as you feast on dishes straight from the hunt: Specialties include bear paws and civet. Some more palatable items include spicy, crispy pork ribs; filet of wild boar in red-wine sauce; roasted wild pheasant with currant sauce; and flame-grilled beef filet with a red wine–and-brandy sauce. While there are promises of musical performances most evenings, it's not unlikely that you'll be listening to awful Western pop songs; be warned also that service can get extremely surly and sluggish.

Str. Batistei 14. ✆ **021/211-8929.** www.restaurantburebista.ro. Main courses L12–L74 ($5.15–$32/£3.20–£20); bear paws L466 ($200/£124) each. MC, V. Daily 11am–midnight.

Caru' cu bere ★★ ROMANIAN The "Beer Cart" restaurant is a Bucharest institution, and probably the most consistently photographed eatery in town, much loved for its dramatic traditional interior. A massive, cavernous, vaulted beer hall, heavily covered with original decorative details—painted floor tiles, fantastic stained glass windows, and walls padded with eye-catching memorabilia marking the restaurant's history since 1879. Adding to the attractiveness of the interior, there's a regular program of evening entertainment. And while it looks the part of a tourist haunt (and has a convoluted menu with English subtitles), the food is enduringly traditional and authentic; amongst the house specialties are a number of pork dishes with either cabbage or potatoes, and there are a range of regional items to choose from, too, so you can easily sup your way around the country. Order the sour tripe soup to start (and ask specifically for homemade bread to accompany this). Follow that up with something meaty, perhaps a platter of assorted grilled sausages *(platou cu cârnaţi)*, with a side order of pickled mushroom salad *(salată de ciuperci)*. Weekdays, ask about the specially priced lunchtime set menu (L22/$9.65/£5.95) consisting of a main dish accompanied by soup, salad, and dessert.

Str. Stavropoleos 5. ✆ **021/313-7560.** www.carucubere.ro. Main courses L15–L86 ($6.45–$37/£4–£23). MC, V. Sun–Fri 8am–midnight; Sat 8am–2am.

Charme ★ ITALIAN/ECLECTIC Laid-back hangout of Bucharest's entrepreneurial brat pack, this pleasant eatery centers on a long, lovely bar counter, and offers relaxed dining in a bright space in the Lipscani District. A self-consciously contemporary atmosphere (most of the indoor seating is on sofas or awkward, modish swivel chairs) is enhanced by good lounge music, and tall, friendly waiters. Dishes are simple, wholesome, and tasty: Take your pick of grilled lamb, *osso buco,* grilled swordfish, calamari with spicy ricotta cheese, lamb chops with black beer sauce, pasta with porcini mushrooms, or beef filet with a choice of mustard sauce, a rich Gorgonzola sauce, or fresh asparagus. Most of what's on the menu is under L25 ($13/£8), and your table will be supplied with fresh bread and olives to nibble on. It may no longer be flavor of the month (since opening mid-2006, several lookalike wannabes have popped up in the vicinity), but the location lends it great charm; grab a seat on the small wooden terrace and you'll easily spend an afternoon watching pedestrians come and go.

Smardan 12. ✆ **021/3111-1619.** Main courses L12–L59 ($5.15–$25/£3.20–£16). MC, V. Daily 9am–11pm. Lounge and bar until late.

Inexpensive

La Taifas ★★ Value ROMANIAN/INTERNATIONAL Restaurateur Gibi Anghelescu's atmospheric venture (this is the younger sibling of Bistro Atheneu) seems like the work of an Arabian Nights fantasist, with brightly colored walls and plenty of silver, copper, onion-dome, and filigree motifs; the name means "having a chat" and that seems to be what the cushioned, carpeted seating areas encourage you to do. All in all, an atmospheric, fun venue where there's often live music. The kitchen changes its mind daily, and items are chalked up on a board; best to simply ask for the favored dish of the day, but do ask about the mint cod *(cod cu mentă),* which is filleted and allowed to soak up the flavor from a bed of mint for 24 hours. La Taifas is also really good value, with a fabulous lunchtime special: L17 ($7.30/£4.55) for a three-course meal with a glass of wine (12:30–2:30pm).

Str. Gheorghe Manu 16. ✆ **021/212-7788.** Main courses L7–L30 ($3–$13/£1.85–£8.05). MC, V. Daily noon–1am.

Market 8 ★★ DELI Styled with a fun-loving designer's eye for contemporary flair, this lovely deli occupies a sidewalk corner in the Lipscani District. It opened mid-2005 to instant popularity, welcomed for its imaginative integration of lounge-bar with cafe-style delicatessen, brought to life with fanciful furniture (assorted, clever armchairs), a small gallery of carefully chosen books, paintings, and other objects d'arts, and purple walls painted with what can only be described as alien plant life. You can pop in to buy take-home eats, but you'd be missing out: Grab a seat in the eclectic-smart restaurant and, casual as service is, be prepared to be charmed by your waiter. There's an ever-changing menu of wholesome meals, such as pastas, pork schnitzel, or fragrant chicken prepared with cashews, but you can just as easily make do with a simple sandwich (try olive-encrusted ciabatta with eggplant, feta, crème fraîche, bacon, and mozzarella). Washed down with a cold Romanian beer, of course.

Str. Stavropoleos 8. ✆ **021/313-4167.** www.market8.ro. Main courses L12–L34 ($4.95–$15/£3.05–£9.05); sandwiches L11–L13 ($4.75–$5.60/£2.95–£3.50). MC, V. Mon–Sat 9am–midnight; Sun 11am–midnight.

EXPLORING BUCHAREST

City Tours & Guided Walks

For a personalized—and wonderfully personal—tour of the city (ideally followed by destinations farther afield), contact **Medieval Tours** (✆ **0721-261-323;** www.medievaltours.ro); Eduard Popescu will show you the major sights and reward you with an insider's history and perspective. **Cultural Travel & Tours** (✆ **021/336-3163;** www.cttours.ro) offers exactly what the name suggests. Tours of Bucharest start at 34€ ($43) per person (with at least two people sharing), and you can also arrange guided tours of any part of the country. Also offering personalized, culturally geared itineraries is the **Cultural Tourism Institute,** RoCultours; Str. Grigore Alexandrescu 108 (✆ **021/650-8145;** www.rotravel.com/cti), worth contacting in advance of your arrival.

Outlying Attractions

The majority of top attractions are located in the center of Bucharest, most of which can be covered on foot, but Bucharest's gems are not contained by its downtown heart. Marking the northern border of our sightseeing recommendations is Bucharest's very own **Arcul de Triumf (Arch of Triumph)** ★—if you haven't see it on your way from the airport, catch a cab to look at the 23m (70-ft.) archway (originally erected in 1922 to celebrate the outcome of World War I, and rebuilt in 1935), then head back into the city along leafy Şoseaua Kiseleff—parading through a mansion-filled upmarket residential neighborhood, lined with embassies, alighting in **Piaţă Victoriei,** more or less in the center of the city, where Şoseaua Kiseleff becomes **Calea Victoriei,** a lengthy concourse that continues south toward the **Centru Civic,** which marks the southern boundary of our sightseeing radius. This is where Ceauşescu's mad folly sought to reshape Bucharest entirely in drab concrete. Inspired by a trip to Communist Korea, he planned to outsize the Champs Elysee with a broad boulevard, and at its southern end, the infamous **Parliamentary Palace (Casa Populurui)** dominates the skyline, while its main balcony looks east, toward **Piaţa Unirii,** the city's very own characterless version of Times Square, with the huge **Unirea Department Store.**

Central & "Downtown" Bucharest

Kick off your tour (or end it) in the **Lipscani district,** the historic heart of Bucharest—thankfully ignored by Ceauşescu, the area is experiencing a steady (if longwinded) revival with trendy cafes, smart restaurants, and mammoth projects set to restore some of the city's most appealing architecture. Pedestrianized **Lipscani Street** and nearby **Covaci Street** are the main arteries of this district, but explore the side streets and you'll come across hidden treasures: antiques stores, fashionable boutiques, and hidden courtyards, not to mention a burgeoning party atmosphere and the lovely Stavropoleos church (see below). Sadly, you'll note that scores of buildings here are deemed unsafe—and likely to collapse in the event of an earthquake—and have been marked with big round warning signs. You're best off not venturing inside these.

From Lipscani you should turn north into **Calea Victoriei,** the long concourse that cuts through the center, along which most of this area's top attractions are ranged; unless of course you're a history buff, in which case you might want to turn south to visit the **National History Museum** at Calea Victoriei 12, though the grand facade of the former post office headquarters—a grand neoclassical monument built from 1894 to 1900—conceals a rather stultifying collection of historical artifacts that is only engaging in parts (www.mnir.ro; admission L7/$3/£1.85; Wed–Sun 10am–6pm). From here you continue north along Calea Victoriei to get to Bucharest's real heart, the place where—for millions of Romanians—reality and history changed forever at **Revolution Square.**

While it's always busy in some way or another, the space (which runs into George Enescu Sq.) somehow retains a somber, reluctant mood, as if the memory of what happened in 1989 still lingers, when Ceauşescu gave his last speech to an angry crowd from the balcony of the **Communist Party Central Committee building** before ordering soldiers to open fire and fleeing in his helicopter. Here, a headless statue commemorates heroes lost to the revolution, and nearby is the early-18th-century **Creţulescu Church.** To the far north of the square is one of the city's landmark hotels, the **Athénée Palace Hilton** (see the "Hey, Big Spender! Staying in Bucharest's Glitziest Digs" box, earlier in this chapter); also looking onto the square are the Ateneul Roman and National Museum of Art (see below).

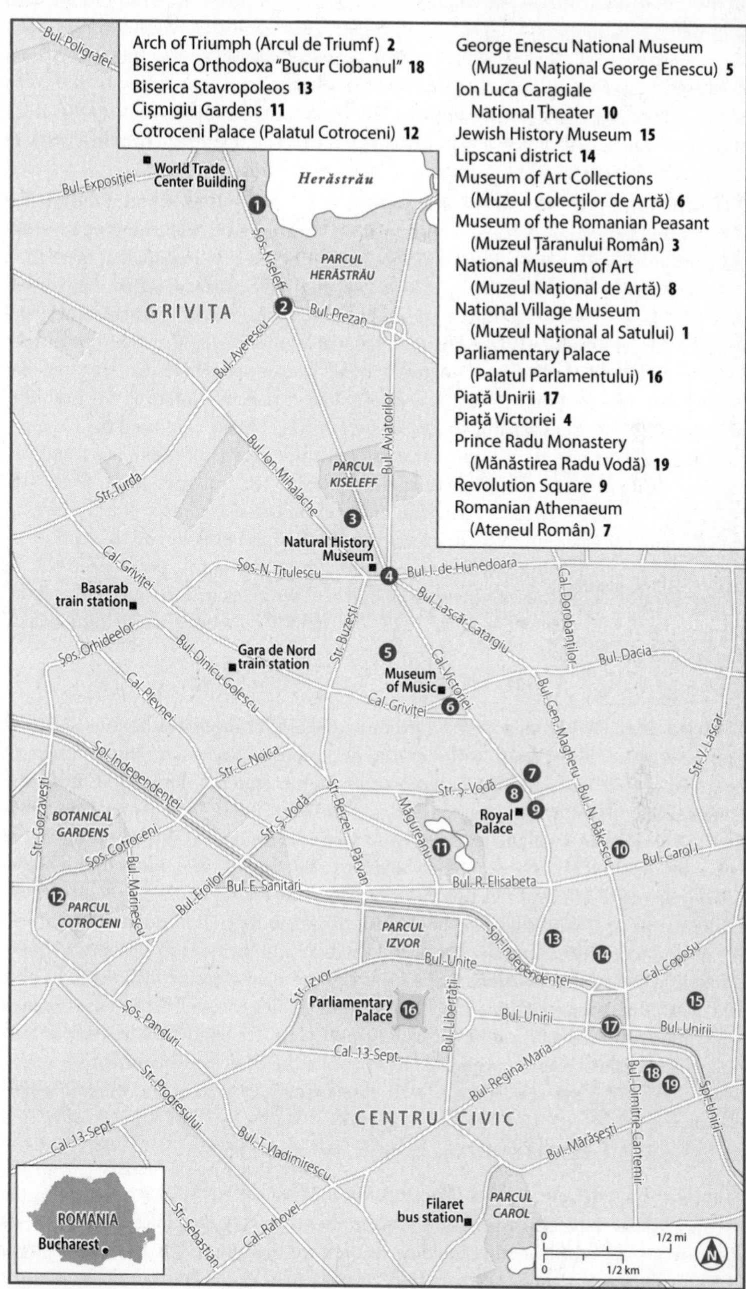

ROMANIA 9 BUCHAREST

Some distance north along Victoriei, it's worth the effort (manageable on foot) to get to the little-visited **Muzeul Naţional George Enescu** ★★, Calea Victoriei 141 (✆ **021/659-6365;** admission L4/$1.70/£1.05; Tues–Sun 10am–5pm). Amongst the most beautiful buildings in Bucharest, this superb Secessionist mansion was built in 1905 for Bucharest's then-wealthiest landowner, Gerge Cantacuzino. The entrance is flanked by sculpted lions and the interior—all stucco, polished wood, cherubs, and trumpeters—is now filled with personal artifacts of the country's greatest composer, as well as some of Enescu's valuable scores.

Ateneul Român (Romanian Athenaeum) ★★ Recognized as one of the loveliest architectural works in Bucharest, the Romanian Athenaeum is something of an urban fulcrum, marking out the cultural and social center of the city; inaugurated in 1888, it was designed by French architect Albert Galleron (who also conceived the shapely National Bank of Romania in the Lipscani District). Facing the Royal Palace and standing adjacent the **Athénée Palace Hilton** hotel, the lovely exterior is matched by interior frescoes and mosaics. You need to pay a small fee to whoever is manning the side entrance, and he'll let you see the grand foyer and remarkably intimate, yet beautiful, auditorium. Here, the wraparound fresco—which was covered up during the Communist era—tells the history of Romania, starting with the arrival of the Romans and culminating with the reign of King Ferdinand. See if you can spot Vlad Ţepeş (the inspiration for Count Dracula), dark and ominous on horseback, more or less above the stairs. The most wonderful way to experience the Athenaeum is to attend a concert in the 1,000-seat auditorium; intensify the experience by choosing a performance of the Philharmonic George Enescu, the city's premiere orchestra, named for the nation's greatest composer who debuted here in 1898. Apparently, the venue ranks third best in Europe for its acoustics.

Str. Benjamin Franklin 1–3. ✆ **021/315-2567** or 021/315-8798. Daily 1:30–4pm.

Biserica Stavropoleos ★★★ Dedicated to the archangels Michael and Gabriel, Stavropoleos (running parallel with Lipscani Str.) is one of Romania's most atmospheric churches, a small and gracious place of worship that is especially loved by its dedicated congregation, drawn by the enlightened and charismatic priest. Now restored as a monastery, Stavropoleos was built in 1724 by Ioanikie Stratonikeas (frescoed on the left as you enter the church), a Greek monk who came to Bucharest to raise funds for his hometown monastery. Today, it's in the hands of five hardworking nuns; they look after an impressive library with a collection of old manuscripts and spend time transcribing Cyrillic musical scores electronically. For one of the best introductions to Orthodox church symbolism, ask to see the exhibition of icons and liturgical objects which the nuns have laid out to simulate a traditional church plan; your guiding nun will explain the meaning of each icon and elaborate on its particular significance. Try to attend Mass here at least once; rites are held every morning (7:30am) when the choir consists of female voices, while on Wednesdays at 4:30pm, it's an all-male performance of the Byzantine-style chorus.

Str. Stavropoleos. ✆ **021/313-4747.** Free admission. Daily 7:30am–6pm.

Museum of Art Collections (Muzeul Colecţiilor de Artă) ★★ North of the Ateneul Roman is the Museum of Art Collections, occupying the Ghica Palace, or Casa Romanit, an early-19th-century building that housed the country's supreme court from 1883 until the Communist takeover. The art collections of the bourgeoisie were stored

Understanding the Orthodox Church

As you wander into an Orthodox church, you may think that the seemingly endless supply of beautiful frescoes and icons, and liturgical rites in which a priest keeps disappearing and reappearing from behind the iconostasis are nothing short of chaotic. You'd be wrong. There is meaning encoded in the design and layout of the artful interiors and rituals. Before entering, look above the door. You'll see Christ and several angels, generally along with the patron saint for whom the church is named. As you enter the *pronaos,* on the left are images of the church's builders and financiers, while on the right are frescoes of the leaders and royalty during the church's inception. Various important saints will occur throughout; those who practiced healing during their lifetimes will be holding a spoon, while those who were martyred are depicted with a cross. Humans painted with wings are said to have lived their lives like angels.

In the dome above the *pronaos,* you'll see the Holy Mother praying for you, watching you as you enter; prophets of the Old Testament surround her. Also in the *pronaos* is a free-standing icon depicting Romanian saints; worshippers press their lips to this upon arrival. Typically, men occupy the right side of the church, while women are on the left. The angels painted on the inside of the main dome over the *naos* are said to come down from the heavens to take part in the service. The altar at the front of the church is the reserve of the priest, and sometimes other men are permitted to enter; the altar is screened off from public view by an iconostasis (basically a giant partition), with a number of painted doors. The Royal Door is in the center, and is painted with the Annunciation (Gabriel, carrying a flower, informing Mary that she will be the mother of God); the emperor who was permitted to approach the altar traditionally used this door.

From left to right across the iconostasis are the four royal icons: the saintly church protector, then the Holy Virgin, Jesus Christ, and finally the patron saint, after whom the church is named. At Mass, the priest will repeatedly disappear through these doors, returning with different icons and incense burners strung with bells; the bells emulate the sounds of the cherubim, while some say the incense denotes Christ in the Virgin's womb (incense holder). Above the royal icons, a series of smaller panels depicts major Christian celebrations, or events from the life of Christ; the row above that depicts Jesus, flanked by Mary, St. John the Baptist, and all the Apostles. Above that is a row of prophets. The nuns at Stavropoleos will happily elaborate on details of their faith, should you show an interest.

here during the time when wealth was dangerously unfashionable. Today, the museum offers a condensed, manageable version of the extensive National Art Museum farther south, enjoyed in peace—don't be surprised if you are alone among a group of 20 museum attendants. At least that common attendance prior to the museum's closing for extensive renovations—it may come back to life as a revitalized, popular attraction. The collection includes a rich survey of notable 19th- and 20th-century Romanian artists, together with some good, if anachronistic, religious icons. Particularly lovely are sculptures by Bucharest-born artist Oscar Han (1891–1976), and the paintings by Nicolae Grigorescu (1838–1907). Other favorites include fabulous nudes by Nicolae Tonzita (1886–1940), Theodor Pallady's *Femei în peisaj* (six pale naked maidens frolicking in the bushes, 1920), and Iosif Iser's intense yet playful *Dancer in an Armchair,* directly opposite a series of cartoons by Marcel Iancu (1895–1984).

Calea Victoriei 111. ✆ **021/659-6693.** Admission L7 ($2.50/£1.35). Free admission 1st Wed of each month. Oct–Apr Fri–Wed 10am–6pm; May–Sept Fri–Wed 11am–7pm; last entry 30 min. before closing.

Museum of the Romanian Peasant (Muzeul Ţăranului Român) ★★ Occupying an early-20th-century building by Nicolae Ghica-Budeşti, the this museum is stocked full of furniture, farming equipment, costumes, crucifixes, tapestries, textiles, and some very beautiful religious icons; surprisingly, a great deal of the seemingly primitive technology on the first floor is what continues to be used—along with many of the lifestyle objects kept here—by rural communities to this day. During the Communist years, the building housed the Museum of the Communist Party and Romanian Revolutionary Workers Movement. On your way out, don't miss the basement exhibition (accessed via stairs next to the entrance) devoted to that time; the smell of mothballs adds a strangely appropriate atmosphere to a stirring display remembering Communism's collectivization scheme, highlighted by numerous unattractive busts of Lenin. Entitled "The Pest," the exhibit is a "memorial of the pain and hurt land-collectivization caused to the peasant world." Oddly, the main exhibit is a desk (from which collective control was exercised) littered with nutshells and onion peels. ***Tip:*** The souvenir shop here is worth browsing.

Şos. Kiseleff 3. ✆ **021/650-5360.** Admission L6 ($2.60/£1.60) adults; L2 (85¢/55p) students and children; audio guide L10 ($4.30/£2.65). Tues–Sun 10am–6pm; last entry at 5pm.

National Museum of Art (Muzeul Naţional de Artă) ★★★ Romania's National Museum of Art, opposite the Ateneul Roman, consists of three different collections, exhibited in part of the expansive former **Royal Palace** on Piaţa Revoluţiei. Of these, the most important are the **Gallery of Romanian Medieval Art** (almost exclusively devoted to icons, images, and carved objects related to religious pursuits), on the first floor, and the **Gallery of Romanian Modern Art,** above it. The latter provides a thorough overview of the evolution of 19th- and 20th-century painting and sculpture, working almost chronologically over two floors. It's an excellent place to discover the work of Gheorghe Tattarescu (1818–94), Theodor Aman (whose 19th-c. street scenes of popular tourist towns provide an excellent comparative study for some of the places you might visit), Karl Storck, Ioan Andreescu, sculptor Frederick Storck (look out for his fabulous *The Mystery,* 1925), the marvelous Impressionist Ştefan Luchian (1868–1916), and Theodor Pallady, who painted a great number of naked ladies. There's a lively selection of works by the Impressionists, abstract expressionists, and Cubists; Marcel Iancu's *Portrait of a Man* is a brilliant Cubist-inspired work, worth seeking out, as is—for different reasons—Jean Davis's *Portrait of a Woman,* which looks like a precursor for *Beavis and Butthead.* The most important work here is the handful of otherworldly sculptures by Constantin Brâncuşi (1876–1953); spend some time studying *Sleep* (1908), and then give your attention to *The Prayer* (1907), in which he renders a young female subject in an impossible kneeling position to stupendous effect. More wonderful sculpture includes Oscar Han's *The Kiss* (1924), and the only male nude on display, *Study of a Male Nude,* by Alexandru Plámádealá.

From the Romanian art collections, cross the courtyard to get to the less gripping **Gallery of European Art,** with its collection of 2,233 paintings, 578 sculptures, and 9,189 pieces of decorative art. Some astonishing lithographs are kept here, depicting amusing historical scenes as well as quite terrible images of death and disease.

Calea Victoriei 49–53. ✆ **021/313-3030.** European Gallery: 021/314-8119. www.mnar.arts.ro. Admission L10 ($4.30/£2.65). Combined ticket with Gallery of European Art L15 ($6.45/£4). Free 1st Wed of each month. Oct–Apr Wed–Sun 10am–6pm; May–Sept Wed–Sun 11am–7pm; last entry 30 min. before closing.

Southern Bucharest

Controceni Museum (Muzeul Cotroceni) ★★★ If you visit just one secular attraction in Bucharest, make it this one; the guided tour provides excellent historical insights and is a worthwhile survey of architectural trends in Romania. **Cotroceni Palace** (the official residence of the president, hence the tight security) was built by Carol I in the late 19th century, and became the loveless home of Ferdinand, his nephew and adopted heir, and the young Queen Marie (see "Quiet Escape to the Queen's Nest" in the "Varna & the Black Sea Coast" section of chapter 4), but has undergone many transformations since the initial designs were executed: During Ceauşescu's dictatorship it was used as the "Pioneer's Palace," where young leaders were schooled in the ways of Communism, and—after the devastating earthquake of 1977—restored as a guesthouse, although it never served this function. You will pass through a host of reception rooms, sleeping quarters, and private chambers, each styled to a particular theme: the German New Renaissance dining room, private dining quarters of Carol I in Florentine style; Oriental painting room used by Queen Marie and her children; the hunting room which showcases trophies hunted by King Ferdinand, as well as bearskin rugs hunted by Ceauşescu. Interestingly King Ferdinand's apartments are done out in a far more dainty, feminine style than Queen Marie's, whose quarters are quite austere—living proof of who wore the pants in this relationship. ***Note:*** You need to phone ahead and book one of the tours, and you must bring your passport as a security deposit; ask your taxi driver to wait for you, or order a cab in advance, as the museum entrance is on a busy road in the middle of nowhere.

B-dul Geniului 1. ✆ **021/317-3107/6.** Fax 021/312-1618. www.muzeulcotroceni.ro. Admission L12 ($5.15/£3.20) adults, L6 ($2.60/£1.60) students and children. Tues–Sun 9:30am–5:30pm.

Jewish History Museum (Muzeul de Istorie al Evreilor din România) ★ The Romanian military is known to have played a devastating role in the Holocaust, and this museum is a good lest-we-forget reminder of Bucharest's once-prominent Jewish community. The museum occupies a synagogue built in 1850 and is centered on a statue mournfully remembering the 350,000 Romanians who perished at Auschwitz. Today, you can still visit the **Choral Temple** (✆ **021/312-2169**), a redbrick synagogue on Strada Sf. Vineri to the east of the Old Town; built in 1857, it stands at the edge of an elegant neighborhood touched by the hand of 19th-century architect Marcel Iancu. Attended by the city's tiny, dwindling Jewish community, services are held 8am and 7pm daily, and at 8:30am and 7pm Saturdays.

Str. Mămulari 3. ✆ **021/311-0870.** Free admission. Sun–Wed and Fri 9am–1pm; Thurs 9am–4pm.

Mănăstirea Radu Vodă ★★ On a hill at the edge of the Dâmboviţa River, the church of the **Prince Radu Monastery** is set in a serene garden; built in 1613 and 1614, it replaced an earlier wooden structure. Bright, immaculate frescoes by Gheorghe Tattarescu were added in the 19th century. For a sublime experience, come for the liturgy,

Taking a Breather in the Big City

Bucharest has a number of lovely parks offering a few simple distractions from the mayhem of city life. Slap-bang in the center are the **Cişmigiu Gardens★★** (between B-dul Regina Elisabeta, Calea Victoriei, Str. Stirbei Vodă and B-dul Schitu Măgureanu), developed in the mid-1800s when indigenous Romanian flora was collected along with exotic varieties from Vienna. Hire a boat and row yourself around the miniature lake, or grab a table under one of the Heineken-sponsored umbrellas at **Ristorante Debarcader Cişmigiu** (✆ **021/25-8479**), where the food is expensive, but the views are free.

when worshipers kneel at the feet of the priest; as Mass is read and sung, you'll be hard-pressed to imagine that the Romanian language was not developed precisely for such heavenly devotions. Across the road from the monastery is the mid-18th-century **Biserica Orthodoxă "Bucur Ciobanul"★★** (✆ **0724-506-843;** 8am–6pm daily), reached via a steep stairway. Dedicated to the shepherd Bucur, attributed with the founding of Bucharest, the walls of this tiny church are covered in icons, executed in various styles and rendered on wood and glass. ***Note:*** Services can last between 1½ and 4½ hours, but worshippers (and observers) can come and go as they please.

Str. Radu Vodă 24A. Free admission. Daily 8am–1am. Liturgy daily 6 and 10:30pm; Mon–Fri 8am; Sat–Sun 8:30am.

Parliamentary Palace (Palatul Parlamentului) ★★★ No matter how much you prepare yourself for it, your first glimpse of this square concrete bulk with its classical facade and escutcheoned gateways is a jaw dropper. Ceauşescu infamously had a sixth of Bucharest flattened to make space for this project, and it kept 20,000 workers and 700 architects busy round-the-clock for 5 years during the main period of construction. Visiting the "House of the People," as it's known locally, is effectively to gaze at the physical manifestation of Ceauşescu's unyielding attempt to monumentalize his regime. Visitors buy a ticket from the tiny souvenir shop at the entrance; be prepared to wait for an English guide to appear and initiate a thoroughly long-winded security check. The tour is fascinating: You'll wander through redundantly spacious Soviet-style halls, passageways, and ballrooms, eyeing as you go an eye-popping collection of hand-woven carpets, miles of silk drapery, and patterned walls, floors, and ceilings fashioned from a million cubic meters of marble and tons of oak and cherrywood—all testament to massive squandering of the national coffers. Curiously, there is no air-conditioning (apparently Ceauşescu had a phobia in this regard), and the building is still only 90% complete; hysterically, Ceauşescu had a serious size complex; he had one of the stairways replaced several times because he found the steps too big for his little feet. By the way, don't believe all your guide tells you; one popular anecdote is that the balcony that looks toward Piaţa Unirii is where Michael Jackson greeted fans with the words "Hello Budapest"; Jackson actually performed at the National Stadium.

Calea 13 Septembrie 1. ✆ **021/311-3611** or 021/402-1426. Admission L15 ($6.45/£4) adults. Daily 10am–4pm. May close unexpectedly due to state functions.

NORTHERN CITY SIGHTS

National Village Museum (Muzeul Naţional al Satului) ★★ Showcasing Romanian rural architecture since 1936, this open-air museum is frequently referred to as one of the country's best (although Sibiu's is bigger); if you're not visiting any rural regions, it may well provide some insight into the simple, unencumbered lives led by those living in Romania's bucolic communities. Visitors roam through a selection of 85 different houses, huts, windmills, churches, and outhouses that have been collected from around the country to showcase the depth of variety and architectural beauty of ordinary homesteads and dwelling; most of the constructions are thatch-roofed and built of wood, clay, or mud. Divided by region, the museum's overgrown lawn-fringed concrete pathways take you from Transylvania to Dobrogea to Oltenia and Moldavia in a relatively short space of time. The audio guide is a useful tool for making sense of the different architectural styles, even if the voice recording is rushed. Be warned that although the museum opens at 9am, this is also the time for staff to start cleaning, and the majority of houses are unlocked for the public only after around 11am. Note that the souvenir shop is not as good as the one at the Peasant Museum.

Şos. Kiseleff 28–30. © **021/317-9110.** www.muzeul-satului.ro. Admission L6 ($2.60/£1.60) adults; L3 ($1.30/80p) students and children. Audio guide L8 ($3.45/£2.15), plus ID as deposit. Tues–Sun 9am–7pm; Mon 9am–5pm.

SHOPPING

Keep your eyes open on the streets; on the steps of old monuments and around inner city sidewalks (particularly near University Sq.), you'll spot casual traders selling collectibles, including books and old Romanian LP records. You can also browse for bargains at shops beneath the city surface in its subways.

ART, ANTIQUES & COLLECTIBLES Antiques lovers can have a lot of fun poking through Bucharest's innumerable *antichităti* stores. Typically, you'll find a mix of furniture, ornaments, knickknacks, and artworks that vary dramatically in value. You'll come across items that were salvaged during the Communist era, when homes and neighborhoods were destroyed, or things that have been kept in basements out of harm's way for decades. Start at **Hanul cu Tei ★★**, Str. Blanari 5–7 (© **021/313-0181;** www.hanulcutei.ro; Mon–Fri 10am–7pm, Sat 10am–2pm), an arcade in the heart of the Lipscani District; there are a range of stores and an extensive selection of artworks. Around here, you've every chance of finding street traders with something worthwhile to sell (old coins, fascinating prints, and unusual antique items). Also in the Lipscani area, you can admire antique furniture as well as smaller decorative items at **European Heritage,** Str. Şepcari 16 (© **021/315-9537;** www.european-heritage.com; Mon–Sat 10am–7pm, Sun noon–5pm). Stefan Vezure sells bronzes, porcelain, paintings, and sculptures as well as religious icons from his store, **Stef Art,** Str. Buzeşti 19 (© **0720/32-7338**).

For paintings, rare maps, and manuscripts, as well as antique photographs, visit **Galeria de Artă Zambaccian,** Str. Blănari 12 (© **021/315-3485**). If you'd like to visit an artist's studio, try **Iuliana Vîlsan,** Lascăr Catargiu 45 (© **0722/69-2892;** www.iuliana-vilsan.net), but call first to make an appointment. At **Atmosphere Deco,** Str. Eremia Grigorescu 5, you'll find smart antiques, paintings, and decorative trifles. Calea Victoriei can also be good for art purchases; you could pick up an interesting canvas or two at **Galateea,** Calea Victoriei 132 (© **021/317-3814**), a contemporary space hosting provocative exhibitions with work for sale. Nearby, the **Nemţoi Gallery ★★** (© **021/312-9800**) carries extraordinary glass sculptures by Ioan Nemţoi, who enjoys an international reputation.

BOOKS **Anthony Frost** ★★, Calea Victoriei 45 (✆ **021/311-5138**) is Bucharest's first proper English bookstore, located just off Revolution Square. **Cărtureşti** ★★★ is a fabulous bookstore chain with the best music collection in the city; head straight for the branch located on Strada Pictor Arthur Verona (✆ 021/317-3459; info@carturesi.ro). You'll find brilliant art books, coffee-table glossies, and also the most relaxingly atmospheric tea shop in town.

Also worth browsing is **Libraria Noi** ★★, B-dul Nicolae Bălecescu 18 (✆ 021/311-0700; www.librarianoi.ro), which is well stocked (with an extensive range of English books, including fashionable publications about Romania). You can also buy DVDs and CDs here (admittedly the selection is limited), but the real find is the little side-outlet with old maps, out-of-date prints, and lithographs, which you can paw through to discover that something special.

FASHION For all sorts of upmarket retail therapy, head for Calea Victoriei, where you'll find **Hugo Boss, Stefanel,** and **Guess,** next door to which is **Catwalk,** a stunning shoe boutique. Directly across the road from these, is **Musette** with fabulous ladies' shoes and accessories, and nearby **Man & Manetti** is an exclusive menswear store. The most fun clothing store we've come across in Bucharest is **ummagumma** ★ (✆ **0751/180180;** www.ummagumma.ro), tucked away in a small arcade at Calea Victoriei 122; owner Oana-Maria Toma stocks innovative, imaginative garments for young women and most of the designers are Romanian.

SOUVENIRS & HANDICRAFTS Rather pricey souvenirs and books can be purchased from this small shop at the end of your tour of the Cotroceni Palace, at **Cotroceni Magazin de Arta** ★; consider buying one of Ana Ponta's Dolls of Romania, lovely soft toys dressed in traditional costumes that are perfect as gifts for young children, or for collectors. The shop at the **Museum of the Romanian Peasant Shop** ★★, Şos. Kiseleff 3 (✆ 021/650-5360), is arguably the best place in the country to pick up authentic yet well-made handicrafts, traditional costumes, and folk art. A great memento for anyone with an interest in sports is a branded Steaua Bucharest football shirt from the country's most important club, at one of the **Nike** outlets in either the Unirea or Bucureşti mall.

BUCHAREST AFTER DARK

The best source for all entertainment happenings is ***Time Out Bucureşti*** ★★ (www.timeoutbucuresti.ro), which carries extensive listings and information; though published only in Romanian, with a little savvy you can figure it out and certainly make sense of the dates, times, and venues. The weekly publication is available at news agents and bookstores. The other reliable information source is the useful English-language ***Bucharest in Your Pocket*** ★★; though it only highlights major events, it lists just about every pub, club, bar, and disco in town. You can usually pick up a copy up from the larger hotels, often for free, or download it before leaving home at www.inyourpocket.com.

Live Music, Theater & Opera

Catch **classical concerts** by, among others, the George Enescu Philharmonic Orchestra at the sublime **Romanian Athenaeum** ★★★, Str. Benjamin Franklin 1–3 (✆ **021/315-8798**); the box office (✆ **021/315-6875**) operates Tuesday to Friday noon to 7pm, and before evening shows on Saturday and Sunday (4–7pm), and Sunday matinees (10–11am).

Opera buffs can take in occasional performances at the **Opera Română,** B-dul Mihail Kogălniceanu 70–72 (✆ **021/314-6980**); note that the box office is closed Monday.

Vice Advice for Guys

It's 10pm; the sun has just disappeared. You've finished a meal at a classy restaurant. Venturing onto the sidewalk, you're waiting while your partner powders her nose. Out of nowhere, a friendly, energetic man, no more than 22 years old, materializes: "Girls? You want girls? Wanna party with young girls?" Flabbergasted, you decline. "Not tonight? Take my number. Maybe tomorrow?" Prostitution is rife in Bucharest; the number of erotic clubs tucked between the churches and monuments is staggering, so it's easy to assume that anything and everything is up for grabs. Be warned: Prostitution is illegal. A system of bribes allows prostitutes to ply their trade even in top hotels; not surprisingly, the cops get the largest cut.

There's **jazz** at several venues around the city; one of the best-known spots is **Green Hours 22 Jazz Café,** Calea Victoriei 120 (✆ **0722-234-356;** www.green-hours.ro; 24 hr.), which has even spawned its own alternative record label; call beforehand to check what's on the program.

Major concerts, often by visiting international stars, are usually held at one of the city's two football stadiums, **Stadionul Dinamo** or **Stadionul National,** while slightly more intimate events are held at the **Arenele Romane** in Parcul Libertății (also called Parcul Carol I).

To find out what's showing (and whether it's in English) at the **Ion Luca Caragiale National Theater** ★, visit the box office, B-dul Nicolae Bălcescu 2 (✆ **021/314-7171;** Mon 10am–4pm, Tues–Sun 10am–7pm).

You can buy tickets for most live events by visiting **Bilete Online (Online Tickets)** at www.bilete.ro.

Bars & Clubs

Bucharest loves to party, and you'll find a busy watering hole any time, night or day. Cafes and bars are often interchangeable, adapting to the vicissitudes of the crowd or the time of day; the same place you visit for an early-morning espresso could turn out to be your late-night cocktail venue. Simply put: Bucharest has something for everybody.

Club Bamboo Grab a supermodel under each arm and strike a bourgeois pose; you'll probably need to drop names to get through the front door, but inside it's an anthropological study in excess and wealth. Apart from the unusually upmarket crowd, things are pretty mellow, with just enough action on the dance floor to keep things interesting. Open Thursday to Saturday 11:30pm to 6am. Str. Rămuri Tei 39. ✆ **0788-296-776.**

Embryo If for no other reason than to ogle the fantastic, near-futuristic design of this all-white bar, make an effort to get here and then see if the strutting clientele matches up to the decor. Str. Ion Oteteleşeanu 3. ✆ **0727-379-023.**

Expirat While this two-part club is something of a populist hangout, it's the upstart sibling around the corner—the **Other Side of Expirat**—that makes for a fun night out. The crowd is a little less restrained, not quite so obvious, and the no-nonsense contemporary design is offset by cool tunes courtesy of DJs spinning funky disco, electro, and electroclash. Open daily 5pm to 5am. Str. Ion Brezoianu 4/Str. Lipscani 5. ✆ **0726-804-142.**

Gaia ★★ With its fab decor, mirror balls, and hard-partying, fun-loving crowd, you can just about forgive the shameless display of Dom Perignon bottles. Come armed with your wallet bulging (credit cards also accepted) and prepare to rub shoulders with the trendiest crowd in town. Oh, and can you still say "Disco"? Open Thursday to Saturday 11pm to 6am. Str. Banul Antonache 40–44. ✆ **021/311-4242.**

Kristal Glam Club ★★ This is the one club that can be counted on to dish up top international DJs (Armand Van Helden, Carl Cox, Seb Fontaine, and the like), received with great enthusiasm by a highly energetic crowd. If progressive house is your scene, make a beeline for the front of the queue, or call ahead and book a table. Open Thursday to Sun 10pm to 5am. Str. J. S. Bach 2. ✆ **021/231-2136** or 0721-993-988. www.clubkristal.ro.

The Office ★ With a name this pretentious, you'd better dress for success; the crowd is hot and eager, yet decidedly loyal, given that the Office has pretty much outlived its sell-by date. Still, in terms of Bucharest's restless party scene, this remains a classic. Open Fri and Sat 10pm–4am. Str. Tache Ionescu 2. ✆ **0745 11 00 64.** www.theoffice.ro.

Queens Club This sweaty dance venue proclaims itself Romania's top gay club. There's only one way to test the theory: Go. Open Friday and Saturday 11pm to 5am. Str. Mihai Bravu 32. ✆ **0721-170-914.** www.queensclub.ro.

Salsa III ★ Want to see how Romanians tune in to their Latino roots? The dedicated salsa crowd (which seems to follow this club around as it reincarnates in different venues) certainly knows a thing or two about getting its groove on. Open Thursday to Sunday 8:30pm to 5am. Str. Mihai Eminescu 89. ✆ **0723-531-841.**

Tempo ★ One of the swanky places attracting Bucharest's chic crowd, Tempo is actually a restaurant, but its eye-catching decor— padded bar, glass tabletops balanced on short classical fluted columns, and trendy white-and-red theme—makes it a good spot for a sundowner or perpetual people-watching any time of day. Open daily 9am to 1am. Str. George Enescu 10. ✆ **0726-600-500.**

Tonka Soul Café ★ Open round the clock, the vibe changes according to the hour; great for early-morning coffee, it becomes a groovy hangout after dark and peaks after midnight when tunes get loud and the youngish crowd gets wild, ordering from a menu of cocktails and exclusively imported beers. Wooden deck chairs, orange cushions, flatscreen TVs, and contemporary art combine in a relaxed haven near the Amzei Market. Open daily 24 hours. Piaţa Amzei, Str. Biserica Amzei 19. ✆ **021/317-8342.** www.tonka.ro.

4 WALLACHIA

Wallachia, of which Bucharest is now the capital, is the traditional heart of Romania; in fact, locals refer to it as Ţară Românească—"The Romanian Land." Named for the landowner princes, the Wallachs (or Vlachs), who ruled southern Romania from the 14th to the 18th century, its key historical figures (including notorious Vlad Tepeş) were committed to defying Turkish control in one way or another. Proud claims insist that Wallachia was never actually part of the Ottoman Empire, enabling a distinctive post-Byzantine evolution in the arts and architecture that set it apart from the rest of the Balkans. Indeed, it was here that the uniquely Romanian architectural movement—known as the Brâncovenesc style—was developed by Constantin Brâncoveanu in the latter part of the 17th century; the best example of this being the beautifully frescoed Great Church at the Horezu Monastery.

Wallachia remains largely undiscovered, losing out to its famous northerly neighbor; most travelers get their "facts" directly from Dracula movies, associating the thrills of vampire tourism with Transylvania, whereas the "real" Count Dracula actually ruled Wallachia. Vlad the Impaler had his princely court in the city of Târgovişte, and any claims to a "Castle Dracula" really belong to the awesomely situated citadel at Poienari, north of the little town of Curtea de Arges, where there's another beautiful cathedral. Finally, north of Bucharest, on the Wallachia-Transylvania border, there is the ski resort of Sinaia, which boasts one of Europe's most beautiful palaces, Peleş, now the finest museum in the country.

SINAIA

135km (84 miles) N of Bucharest

Right near the Wallachian border with Transylvania, in the beautiful Prahova Valley at the foot of the Bucegi Mountains, Sinaia is regarded as the "Pearl of the Carpathians." When Romania became a kingdom in the late 19th century, this was chosen as the site of the royal summer palace, an absolute must-see on any Romanian itinerary. It's also an extremely popular weekend getaway for well-to-do city folk, and one of the country's most popular ski destinations, centered on Mt. Furnica.

Essentials

Sinaia is on a busy rail line between Bucharest (126km/78 miles) and Braşov (48km/30 miles); there are regular connections with both. If you plan a day trip from Bucharest, catch the morning InterCity train (between 9:45 and 10:15am) to Sinaia, and return to Bucharest on the 5:48pm. Another possibility is to stop in Sinaia and continue to Braşov by fast train at 3 or 6pm.

Sinaia is pretty much a walker's town. If you're self-driving, ensure that your hotel has parking (those reviewed here do), as traffic can get frustrating in busy periods. Taxis, buses, and maxitaxis are available for trips into the hills.

At the town hall, you'll find the **tourist information center,** B-dul Carol I 14 (**✆ 0244/31-1211**). Adventurous types can ask after hikes into the surrounding mountains; it may be worth hiring the services of a guide.

In winter, you can get information and hire equipment for snow-based activities from the aptly named ski school and shop, **Snow,** Str. Cuza Voda 2a (**✆ 0244/31-1198**); beginners can sign up for inexpensive private lessons. Experienced skiers have only to join the queues for the **cable car** (**✆ 0244/31-1674**) behind Hotel New Montana.

Where to Stay & Dine

Despite the influx of Bucharest's wealthy weekend-getaway crowd, there are sadly no really good accommodations options in Sinaia. There's also really only one noteworthy restaurant in town, and that's **Taverna Sarbului,** on Calea Codrului (**✆ 0244/31-4400;** daily noon–1am), which has the monopoly on satisfying hungry, ravenous carnivores. Things get incredibly busy—even medieval—as the waitstaff swoops around with feast-size portions of legendary meat dishes.

New Montana ★ A hefty bouncer stands watch at the entrance to this, Sinaia's smartest hotel; big, brash, and right in the center, New Montana seems a little out of place in this small town with its crumbling houses and mountain scenery. Built for Bucharest's wealthy weekend-getaway crowd, it's popular with loads of tourists who are bussed off for sightseeing trips from the front door. Inside, everything is shiny and modern, and more often than not it's Western hip-hop music that's playing in the bright lobby bar. Tight, gold-trimmed elevators whisk you up to your room, which are quite ordinary, despite soothing white cotton linens; bathrooms are slightly larger than the

Royal Romanian Bubbly

If you've got your own transport and are visiting Sinaia en route from Bucharest to Braşov, consider stopping off at the fabulously located **Rhein Wine Cellar** in Azuga, an attractive little town roughly midway between Sinaia and Braşov. Here, not only can you have a tour of the late-19th-century cellars and learn how Romania's most famous sparkling wine is produced, bottled, corked, and labeled, but you can also bed down for the night right above the cellar. **Pensiunea Rhein ★★**, Pivniţele Rhein, Azuga (✆ **0244/32-6560;** azuga@halewood.com.ro), has just a handful of spacious, attractive, wood-floored rooms, each named for a different Romanian grape variety, and done out in simple style with en suite showers, TVs, and wardrobes. Doubles cost L125 ($54/£33), or you could splurge on a junior suite for L155 ($67/£42); breakfast is extra. You can also ask in advance to sample one of their fixed-price lunch or dinner menus (around L47/$20/£10), hearty Romanian cuisine is served up alongside a selection of wines, including—of course—the same locally produced bubbly that for years was bottled exclusively for the Romanian royal household.

elevators, though. Ask for a room overlooking the main road; oddly, these are your best bet, since dogs bark perpetually at night round the back, where rooms don't have balconies.

24 B-dul Carol I, Sinaia. ✆ **0244/31-2751,** -2, -3. Fax 0244/31-2754. www.newmontana.ro. 177 units. 115€ ($146) double; 195€ ($248) junior suite; 245€ ($311) suite. **Amenities:** Restaurant; lobby lounge and pub; bar; health center w/pool. *In room:* TV, Internet, minibar, hair dryer.

Exploring Sinaia

In addition to the top sights in town, Sinaia is just 2km (1¼ miles) from the **George Enescu Memorial House (Casa Memorială George Enescu),** in Cumpătu (✆ **0244/31-1753;** Tues–Sun 9am–3pm; L6/$2.15/£1.35 adults), worth a visit if you have time. Built in the 1920s as a summer home for the country's great composer, it preserves antique furnishings, Enescu's piano, and also some poignant memorabilia; best of all, you'll get to hear recordings of his music as you explore the house, which—surprisingly, given that the Ottomans never got a look in—echoes the style of a Turkish Conac. On the way to or from the castle grounds you might want to take a brief look at **Sinaia Monastery ★**, Str. Mănăstirii 2 (✆ **0244/31-4917;** daily 9:30am–6pm; donation expected), where almost two dozen monks still actively worship at the pair of Orthodox churches, the smaller of which dates from 1695. The first Romanian-language Bible, written in Cyrillic script in 1668, is the prize exhibit in the monastery's little history museum.

Muzeul Naţional Peleş ★★★ Easily the most beautiful palace in Romania and one of the finest in Europe, magnificent Peleş Castle—the summer residence of Romania's first king, Carol I (it's his statue at the entrance)—looks from a distance like something out of *Harry Potter.* Begun in 1875 and inaugurated in 1883, it's a triumph of German neo-Renaissance architecture, with various modern conveniences added over time: This was the first palace in Europe to be completely served by electricity, the first to be centrally heated, and the first castle with a central vacuum-cleaning system. Peleş sports around 170 rooms, and the handful on public display are spectacular examples of "tasteful opulence"; the reception rooms, libraries, studies, bedrooms, and ballrooms are decorated with carefully selected works of extreme quality and value. Alongside the 2,000-strong collection of paintings are imported statues, chandeliers, exotic furniture, gigantic mirrors, and phenomenal hand-woven carpets; each room suggesting the ambience of a different country or region, and perfectly preserved. Although Ceauşescu claimed to have little regard for Peleş, he did use the palace to entertain; Nixon, Qaddafi, Ford, and Arafat were some of his notable guests here. While they no doubt got to experience the palace in a completely different light (you may, for instance, have to wait for the next available English tour), you will almost certainly be delighted by the guided hour-long tour, the best in the country.

Str. Peleşului 2. ✆ **0244/31-0918.** www.peles.ro. Admission L15 ($6.45/£4). Purchase a ticket and then ring the bell at the visitor's entrance. June–Sept Tues–Sun 10am–4pm; Oct–May Wed–Sun 9am–5pm; last ticket sold at 4pm. Hours subject to change.

Pelişor Peleş ★ The name literally means "Little Palace," and a visit here really does pale in comparison to the sensory overload at Peleş. It's said that Ferdinand (1865–1927), Carol's nephew and adopted son, commissioned this castle because he found Peleş too overwhelming; another, more likely story is that it was built for Marie, who didn't see eye to eye with the king. Built in German faux-medieval style in 1892, it's 200m (656 ft.) from Peleş, and its 70 rooms are filled with evidence of Marie's then-personal taste: a pastel-infused mixture of Celtic and Byzantine elements with an Art Nouveau sensibility, and plenty of turn-of-the-20th-century Viennese furniture and Tiffany glassware thrown into the mix.

Str. Peleşului. ✆ **0244/31-2184.** www.peles.ro. Admission L10 ($4.30/£2.65). June–Sept Tues–Sun 10am–4pm; Oct–May Wed–Sun 9am–5pm; last ticket sold at 4pm. Hours subject to change.

CURTEA DE ARGEŞ, POIENARI CITADEL & BEYOND

Although not all that easy to get to, Curtea de Argeş is worth the effort for its magnificent monastery as well as being home to Wallachia's oldest surviving church, built by the princes who ruled Wallachia from the adjacent palace during the 14th century. From **Curtea de Argeş,** heading north through the Argeş Valley, you'll come to the **Citadel of Poienari,** where you'll be able to say that you've finally caught up with the actual castle of "Count Dracula," or at least, what's left of it. From here, self-driving brave hearts can tackle the extraordinary **Tranfăgărăşan Highway,** a magnificent and challenging mountain pass (supposedly Europe's highest, reaching 2,034m/6,672 ft.) that wends its way over the Făgărăş Mountains and into Transylvania; due to extreme weather conditions the route is only open for 3 months of the year.

If you have the time and your own transport, it's worthwhile heading farther west to see the UNESCO-listed **Horezu Monastery,** particularly if you're here during the first week of September when the nearby village of **Costeşti** livens up for its annual **Roma Festival.** Attended by the self-proclaimed "emperor" of all the Roma people, it's a time of fierce celebration and deal making that draws Gypsies from across the country.

Some 200km (124 miles) west of Curtea de Argeş is **Târgu Jiu,** an unspectacular place were it not home to some of the magnificent outdoor sculpture of the great modernist, Constantin Brancuşi, who was born in a nearby village in 1876. The collection includes Brancuşi's most significant work, the *Endless Column,* considered one of the world's most important sculptures.

There are daily fast InterCity trains from Bucharest to Piteşti; from there, change for one of six connections to Curtea de Argeş. State buses and maxitaxis connect Bucharest and Curtea de Argeş more directly, if you're up for a bumpy ride. The town has been generously signposted, so it's easy to get to the sights. **Posada Tourism Agency** (✆ **0248/72-1109** or 0248/72-1451/2) in the Posada Hotel is your best bet for local information and for accommodations bookings.

Where to Stay & Dine

Besides offering the only **tourist information office** (✆ **0248/72-1109;** Mon–Fri 8am–4pm, Sat 10am–12:30pm) in town, **Hotel Posada,** B-dul Basarabilor 27–29 (✆ **0248/72-1451/2;** fax 0248/50-6047; www.posada.ro), is about your best bet for a decent night's stay in Curtea de Argeş; book a renovated superior room (L175/$75/£47) for the most comfortable stay, and don't forget your earplugs.

What to See & Do

The cathedral is the principal reason to be here, but time allowing you might want to take a wander through the ruins of the **Argeş Palace**—originally built in the 1300s by Wallachia's Hungarian founder, Radu Negru (or Basarab I)—and the **Princely Church,** Curtea Domnească; the latter is in fairly good shape and work has been done to reveal fantastic Byzantine frescoes long hidden under centuries of tacky restoration. Hours are Tuesday through Sunday 9am to 5pm (L6/$2.60/£1.60).

Mănăstirea Curtea de Argeş ★★★ This 16th-century Episcopal cathedral is considered one of the loveliest religious monuments in Wallachia, frequently compared to an elaborately decorated cake, made with marble and studded with mosaics. Several nasty stories surround the master builder and stonemason, Manole, responsible for the project. Tricked into building his own wife (who was very much alive at the time) into the walls of the church (a tradition meant to ensure that the victim's ghost would forever protect the building), Manole was left on the roof without means of escape, as the king wanted to ensure that no other similar church would ever be built. Insane with grief the poor man apparently tried to fly from the roof, only to crash and die on the spot now marked by the famous **Manole's Well.** The church was greatly restored and rebuilt in the late 19th century, and several members of the Romanian royal family, including Carol I and his wife, Elizabeth, are buried inside.

B-dul Basarabilor. Daily 8am–7pm.

Poienari Castle ★ Here's a cliff-top location to fuel the Dracula-obsessed imagination. The citadel—built by Vlad "The Impaler" Ţepeş, inspiration for the mythic bloodthirsty count (see "Vlad & the Epic Mythology of Count Dracula" below)—is about 5km (3 miles) north of the little village of **Arefu,** allegedly inhabited exclusively by descendants of villagers who long ago helped Vlad Ţepeş escape a decisive Turkish siege of the castle. Follow the road north out of Arefu (there is no public transport, by the way) until you come to a hydroelectric plant, next to which is the start of an exhausting 1,480-step climb up to the castle; be sure to buy something to drink at the little stall, since you'll be climbing for about half an hour. Tepeş built the castle as a defensive fortress against intruders from Transylvania; to save costs and punish his mortal enemies, the Turks, he had Turkish prisoners of war do all the work, subjecting them to hideous conditions as they toiled endlessly, often dying in the process. Clearly the enterprise was cursed, and a large chunk of the castle dropped off the cliff back in 1888; the same fate that befell

Vlad's wife 400 years earlier when she allegedly jumped to her death, Lady Macbeth-style, during the Turkish siege.

Cetatea Poienari. Admission L7 ($3/£1.85). Daily 9am–5pm.

5 TRANSYLVANIA

For horror fans, the name sits in the throat and is urged out with an unholy drawl, but—aside from the sheer Gothic drama of medieval towns and hilltop citadels—there's very little to evoke Transylvania's ominous association. Yes, Vlad Ţepeş was born in the fortress city of Sighişoara, and wolves do roam the Carpathians (in fact, they're considered a protective force in Romanian culture), but Transylvania's reality is more one of fairy-tale forests surrounding charming Saxon towns and fortified church steeples poking through the treetops.

A possession of the Hungarian king from the 10th century, Transylvania has been the source of a power struggle for 1,000 years. Hungary only gave up its territorial claims in 1996. Legend tells how the lost children of Hamelin emerged from a cave here; of course, that's a fanciful account of the arrival of Transylvania's Aryan German-speaking population, the Saxons. Settlers from the Lower Rhine, Flanders, and the Moselle region, these blue-eyed blondes were lured here in the 12th century by the Hungarian monarchy who promised them land and other liberties in return for protection against the Ottoman and Tartar threat. The Saxons established seven fortified cities, the Siebenbürgen, with outlying villages centered on fortified churches, serving as both spiritual and military protection. Today the major settlements of Braşov, Sighişoara, and Sibiu remain popular destinations, but there are dozens more Saxon villages throughout Transylvania that are remarkably untouched by modern life. The Saxon community has dwindled over the centuries, but Transylvania still includes a sizeable Hungarian minority tracing its ancestry to the Széklers, a clan of warriors accorded noble privileges for defending Hungary's eastern frontier.

Separating Transylvania from Wallachia in the south and Moldavia to the east are the Carpathian Mountains, where Anthony Minghella filmed *Cold Mountain,* a movie shot through with images of a sublime, beautiful wilderness. While you won't encounter any wolves, were- or otherwise, you will—as many trekkers discover—come across the odd shepherd or remote mountain village where smiles and frowns are your only tools of communication.

Near Braşov is Bran Castle, touted by the ill-informed as "Dracula's Castle." With a gorgeous medieval Saxon center, Braşov is also home to the ominously pretty Black Church, the biggest Gothic cathedral between Istanbul and Vienna. And if you are pining to rub shoulders with a real count, Transylvania may have the answer: Count Tubor Kalnoky offers some of the best lodgings in the country in the Hungarian farming community of Micloşoara.

BRAŞOV ★★★

168km (104 miles) NW of Bucharest

Also known by its Saxon name Kronstadt, Braşov grew to prominence from the 13th century when Germanic knights arrived and fortified their settlement with walls and watchtowers, and it became a prosperous trade center for the Austro-Hungarian Empire. Although it's hemmed in by the thick outer layer of a modern, industrial city, Braşov's

Vlad & the Epic Mythology of Count Dracula

Etched into popular consciousness by countless horror films, Count Dracula is best described as a mythical figure loosely based on blood-drinking rituals known to have occurred in certain Balkanic regions. However, Bram Stoker's anemic somnambulist is most fittingly linked with a Wallachian warlord nicknamed Vlad Ţepeş—Vlad the Impaler—in honor of his penchant for bloodletting and cruel tortures. In fact, his real-life atrocities were far more terrifying than anything conjured up by Bela Lugosi or Gary Oldman. As young boys, Vlad and his brother, Radu the Handsome, were sent to the Turks as hostages by their own father, who *was* nicknamed Dracul, or "Devil," because of a knightly order to which he belonged.

Undoubtedly witnessing all sorts of terrible tortures and abuses, and living in fear of his young life, Vlad remained in Adrianople until he was 17, when his father was assassinated by the Hungarians, and the Turks gave him an army in order to reclaim the Wallachian throne. It took him almost 10 years to finally capture the Wallachian throne convincingly and establish his court in Târgoviste. There he earned his reputation for dire cruelty; in one popular story, he set fire to a sealed castle filled with sick, poor, and destitute people, "to rid them of their troubles," as he callously put it. He ruthlessly did away with any perceived threat and enjoyed watching his victims die, often setting up banquets from which to observe the spectacle of suffering. Impalement was favored because the torment could go on for days, and he took great pleasure in mass executions; some estimates place the number of men, women, and children who died at his hands at 500,000.

Eventually, it was his brother, Radu the Handsome, who caused Vlad to flee to Hungary where he was first imprisoned, but then converted to Catholicism. After Radu's death, he once again took control of Wallachia, but was killed in 1476 in a battle with the Turks who displayed his head in Constantinople to prove to the world that he was indeed dead, while his body was supposedly buried at a monastery on the island of Snagov near Bucharest. Apparently, excavations there in 1931 found no sign of his coffin.

medieval and baroque heart is gorgeously well preserved, and seemingly sequestered from the world by mountains that surround it on three sides. A popular base for exploring legendary Bran Castle and hilltop Rasnov Fortress, Braşov also has its own ski resort, Poiana Braşov, which is a wonderful setting for summer hikes in the lovely, practically untouched Ardeal mountains.

Essentials

Braşov has no airport, but the city is extremely well served by trains from across the country; there are almost 20 per day pulling in from Bucharest, only 3 hours away on an InterCity train. The **train station** (✆ **0268/41-0233**) is about 3.5km (2 miles) from the heart of Braşov's old city; a taxi into town should cost around L5–L10 ($2.15–$4.30/£1.35–£2.65). You can purchase onward tickets from **CFR Agenţie de Voiaj,** Str.

The Bear Necessities

Unfortunately, you're unlikely to spot any of the 6,000 or so brown bears that roam wild in the Carpathians (nor wolves or lynx for that matter). Where bears do occur, however, are around the dustbins of certain Braşov suburbs, where they've learned to scavenge. This is partly out of laziness, and partly due to past environmental mismanagement. While the Carpathians can comfortably support 5,000 to 6,000 bears, during the Ceauşescu regime the population was purposefully grown to 10,000—to make the dictator's hunting trips more fruitful. Today, licensed hunting of around 600 bears per year helps keep numbers in check.

Republicii 53 (✆ **0268/47-0696;** Mon–Fri 8am–6pm, Sat 9am–1pm). Once you're in the historic part of the city, you should manage everything by foot or bus; you can get information on bus routes from the **tourist office** (✆ **0268/41-9078;** Mon–Sat 9am–5pm), conveniently located in the former **Council House (Casa Sfatului)** in the center of Piaţa Sfatului. Staff will also supply you with maps and information about the city, as well as advising on excursions to neighboring attractions, like Bran (just 30km/19 miles from Braşov) and Râşnov. A good introduction to the city as well as Romania itself is found at www.brasov.ro, well worth investigating before you leave home. To get to **Poiana Braşov,** take bus no. 20 from the Livada Postei stop; it leaves every half-hour and is a comfortable 20-minute journey.

Reserve at least 24 hours in advance to join **Braşov Walking Tours** (✆ **0727/38-1478**), which has a guided exploration of the city setting off from the tourist office; available in English, the 2½-hour tour costs 5€ ($6.35) per person, minimum of four people.

Where to Stay

Braşov's relatively new (late 2006) **Casa Wagner** ★, Piaţa Sfatului (✆ **0268/41-1253/4;** www.casa-wagner.eu), enjoys a prime position overlooking the main square, and with just 12 guest rooms—all relatively large and done out with antiques—is another of the better, more intimate options in town. So, if Bella Muzica or Casa Rozelor are full, you know where to turn.

Bella Muzica ★★ Right on Piaţa Sfatului, in a 400-year-old building, Bella Muzica is everything you want from a small hotel in a medieval town: Atmosphere, charm, and comfort are all here in equal measure. The designers used soothing earth tones punctuated by wood-framed watercolor paintings of buildings around Braşov, and ensured that contemporary comforts are combined seamlessly with the historical ambience. Furnishings are luxurious, but never grandiose, and while there's an antique theme, there's no sign of frilly excess. Guest rooms are carpeted and decently laid out in an approximation of what might be called "country antique style," and there's some exposed brickwork to remind you of the building's pedigree. Mattresses are on the thin side, and bathrooms aren't exactly enormous; if you want the tasteful ambience, but also value your space, opt for one of the apartments, or—even better—try getting a suite at Casa Rozelor (reviewed below). Note that there's no elevator, but there are rooms on the ground level if you'd prefer not to deal with stairs; the upstairs doubles are also smaller than those on the lower floor.

Moments Hobnobbing with Royalty: Romania's Finest Village Stay

In the predominantly Hungarian village of Micloşoara (known as Miklósvár in Hungarian), **Count Kalnoky's Estate** ★★★ (✆ **0742-202-586;** fax 0267/31-4088; www.transylvaniancastle.com) offers some of the finest accommodations in the country. The project is the brainchild of born-in-exile Count Tubor Kalnoky (a dead ringer for Ralph Fiennes), whose family left Romania in 1939 with the rise of fascism; after the fall of Communism, he spent nearly a decade in court fighting to get his family properties back from the government and has since set to work reclaiming his 750-year-old aristocratic heritage by restoring a series of houses scattered around the rural village; they've become luxurious and lovely cottagey guest rooms for visitors seeking an authentic treat in the heart of Transylvania. With a population of 500, Micloşoara's village life is confined to old people sitting on benches outside their homes, literally waiting for the cows to come home. These villagers are descendants of the Szeklers who came to Transylvania to defend their empire's eastern border.

At the main house—or "Hunting Manor"—there's a lounge with fireplace, and drawing rooms with books and antiques. There's also a 17th-century wine cellar, where dinners are usually served. Guest quarters are spread around the village, although you can stay in the old "serfs' house," near the main kitchen. Painted a fantastic blue, it's a favorite of regular visitors, so you'll need to reserve it in advance. Not that it really matters: Lodgings are all immaculate, with solid wooden floors, antique furniture, ceramic wood-burning fires, good lighting, comfortable beds, and wonderful modern bathrooms. There are no televisions or radios; instead, there's plenty of atmosphere and an in-room sauna. Accommodations

Piaţa Sfatului 19, Braşov. ✆ **0268/47-7956.** www.bellamuzica.ro. 22 units. L270 ($116/£72) double; L440–L540 ($189–$232/£117–£144) suite. Rates include breakfast. MC, V. **Amenities:** Restaurant; bar; breakfast room; laundry. *In room:* A/C (suites only), TV, Internet, minibar, safe, Jacuzzi (suites only).

Casa Rozelor ★★★ *Finds* Book now to stay in one of the five beautifully idiosyncratic, design-conscious apartments that have been fashioned from the hull of a 15th-century national monument, just a few steps from the center of the city. You'll not only enjoy absolute comfort, surrounded by a glorious collection of antiques, artworks, and bric-a-brac, but have a great deal of fun discovering the details of the interior design, executed by the artist-designer Mihai Alexadru. Incredibly spacious, yet made to feel like home, these apartments all have their own kitchen, dining area, lounge, and bedroom; each of the spaces—including the fabulous bathrooms—is unique and refreshingly original, an artful blend of classic or Deco elements with modern artworks and contemporary details (wonderful bathroom fittings, flatscreen TVs). They also have parquet flooring and exposed wood-beam ceilings; suite no. 6 is an upstairs-downstairs unit with its own spiral staircase leading to the bedroom where there's also a private terrace, while suite no. 5 is a massive second-floor open-plan space with another lovely balcony. Only opened in January 2006, Rozelor has made such an impression on in-the-know travelers go for 98€ ($124) double with breakfast, but rates go down the longer you stay, and there's an all-inclusive rate of 145€ ($184) per person per day.

To keep you busy between breakfast and dinnertime, the Count offers scheduled activities; spend the day with a shepherd, hang with a villager, ride on a cart, go horseback riding, or milk the cows; there are visits to neighboring villages, and the option of fishing or hiking. Tubor himself studied to be a vet, and birders should ask if he's available for a specialized tour. There are also various cultural excursions and explorations of local natural phenomena, including the nearby cave where the lost children of Hamelin supposedly made their reappearance. One drawback may be adhering to the daily program of organized events, so it's worth asking for a detailed schedule well in advance so you can request any tailor-made changes. Also note that dinner is communal; if you'd prefer privacy, make prior arrangements. In summer, it's worth requesting at least one outdoor dinner. If you've got your own car, this is a fantastic base from which to explore southern Transylvania, the only problem being the treacherous potholed road leading to the village itself. Alternatively, transfers are available from Bucharest or Braşov.

If Kalnoky's stay appeals, you can also opt to bed down at another royal guesthouse—at Prince Charles's 18th-century farmhouse in Viscri, another Transylvanian village, this time with a rich Saxon heritage. A well-known supporter of Romania's villages and its Saxon culture, the Prince of Wales bought the house in 2006, and—after painstaking restoration—it is now administered by Count Kalnoky's team. Rates are the same, but it's a far more intimate affair, with just three double bedrooms, two bathrooms, and a kitchen.

that two more units had to be created simply to keep up demand from regulars; they opened late 2008.

Str. Michael Weiss 20, Braşov. ✆ **0268/47-5212** or 0747/49-0727. Fax 0268/47-5212. www.casarozelor.ro. 5 units. 95€ ($121) double. Rates include breakfast and all taxes. MC, V. **Amenities:** Room service; breakfast served in room; massage; dry cleaning; laundry room. *In room:* TV, DVD player, Wi-Fi, kitchenette, hair dryer.

Residence Hirscher ★ *Finds* As if concealing its identity, this alternative to the traditional hotel is identified by nothing other than a single brass sign at the entrance of a stately late-19th-century Austro-Hungarian building; it's on Apollonia Hirscher Street, just a short stroll from the historic center of town, but feels far away from it all. Opened in late 2005, the sober neoclassical facade conceals modern interiors; with just 12 large apartments, each with a lounge, bedroom, kitchen, and dining area, it really is a "residence" rather than a hotel. With parquet flooring, decent furniture, and relaxed, neutral tones, this is a great option for anyone who values space, peace, and quiet. At press time, there were no hotel amenities, just daily servicing of apartments, a full-time reception, and the option of breakfast at nearby Casa Hirscher. There are plans, though, to upgrade the residence to a hotel in 2009, which may, unfortunately, also drive prices up.

Reşedinţa Hirscher, Str. Apollonia Hirscher 14, Braşov. ✆ **0368/40-1212** or 0726/74-6402. Fax 0368/40-1213. www.residence-hirscher.com. 12 units. 90€–105€ ($114–$133) double. DC, MC, V. *In room:* TV, Internet, kitchen, tea- and coffeemaking facilities.

Where to Dine

Bella Muzica ★★ MEXICAN/HUNGARIAN/ECLECTIC With a menu stretching the gamut of the globe—from fajitas and burritos to Romanian pork dishes—you'll be excused from initial confusion. Added to the dilemma of trying to figure out what inspired the kitchen's bold eclecticism is the setting—an underground cellar of beautiful vaulted brickwork, decorated with lanterns, bits of pottery, and lengths of rope, and each table outfitted with a red buzzer to alert your waiter. Accept the paradox and move on to the house specialties like the popular Outlaw's Steak *(friptura haiduceasca),* Banat-style escalopes of pork (served with egg and a tangy "brown" sauce); paprikash stew, made with chicken, pork and bacon; or the Kronstadt ragout. If you're lucky (and use your buzzer judiciously), you'll be offered free shots of Romanian plum moonshine *(palincă).*

Piaţa Sfatului 19. ✆ **0268/47-7946.** Reservations essential. Main courses L12–L49 ($5.20–$21/£3.20–£13). MC, V. Daily noon–11pm.

Butoiul Sasului ★★★ SAXON TRANSYLVANIAN/ECLECTIC In many ways, the "Saxon Barrel" may just be Braşov's least pretentious restaurant; the waiters are always smiling and helpful, and at night there's bound to be some great local music performed live—or perhaps table entertainment in the form of Braşov's top illusionist, Allin Blaine. The food is traditional Saxon Transylvanian, so there's plenty of sauerkraut and pork. Also available are two-person platters with hearty portions of spareribs *and* pork chops, or a mix grill plate of chops, smoked and salted meats, and sausages. If you want something cheap and down home, ask for the leg of pork with beans—it's simple, succulent, and very filling. There's also filet of cod and grilled trout if you're looking for something a little lighter. You can order a liter of house wine (from the restaurant's own vineyard) for L25 ($11/£6.80), and there are some pricier vintages from the Prahova Valley, which are well worth sampling. ***Note:*** Don't confuse this Saxon restaurant (in a cellar, reached via stairs from a courtyard off Str. Republicii) with the similarly named eatery upstairs: Ask for it by name.

Str. Republicii 53–55. ✆ **0268/41-0499** or 0745-315-936. Reservations recommended. Main courses L8–L59 ($3.45–$25/£2.15–£16); platters for 2 L36–L45 ($12–$14/£7.45–£8.70). MC, V. Daily 11am–midnight.

Casa Hirscher ★★ ITALIAN Occupying the back end of the famous "House of Trade" established by Apollonia Hirscher in 1545, this is a slightly upmarket bistro, with an outdoor courtyard. Outdoing the multifarious nearby venues flaunting Italian cuisine, dishes here are authentic and excellent. Try their homemade specialties: *tortelloni ripieni con melanzane* (pasta stuffed with eggplant, mussels, and pesto), or *tagliolini san Daniele,* made with sliced Italian ham, cream, Parmesan, and poppies. Fish lovers can choose from dorado, sole, trout, and pikeperch, all perfectly prepared, as is the beef filet with a cabernet sauce. There's also tasty roast deer, and melt-in-the-mouth oven-baked lamb, served with seasonal vegetables.

Piaţa Sfatului 12–14 (entrance on Str. Apollonia Hirscher). ✆ **0268/41-0533.** www.casahirscher.ro. Main courses L12–L55 ($5.15–$24/£3.20–£15). MC, V. Daily noon–midnight.

Sergiana ★ TRANSYLVANIAN Diners can choose from a variety of nooks and crannies in this cozy, partially subterranean eatery; waiters are decked out in camp Germanic outfits. Topping the list of popular dishes is deer calf with wildberry-and-hazelnut sauce, served with rice. Other recommendations for staunch meat eaters is the *Ceaunu lu Tuşa proptit în varză şi mălai,* a hearty plate of smoked sausages, ribs, and pork pastrami, served with polenta and sauerkraut, and all smothered with a healthy amount of freshly sliced garlic. You can forgo the sauerkraut in favor of a fresh salad. There's good wild boar stew, salmon prepared in wine, and a tasty pastry of pikeperch, served with grape and lemon sauce. Leave space for the sweet cheese dumplings, served with sour cream and jam. Order a bottle from the Murfatlar Winery from the fair-priced wine list.

Str. Mureşenilor 27. ✆ **0268/41-9775.** www.sergiana.ro. Main courses L9–L35 ($3.90–$15/£2.40–£9.30). MC, V (PIN required for credit card). Daily 11am–midnight.

Exploring Braşov

The city is centered on **Piaţa Sfatului** ★★, on which the city's most imposing monument, the **Black Church** (reviewed below), backs. A wide-open medieval square, Sfatului is the best place to succumb to Braşov's salubrious charms; throughout the day, people meet to plot their next move, be it dining at one of the always-packed restaurants, exploring the city's architectural heritage, or people-watching and chasing pigeons. Around the square a range of attractive Saxon buildings vie for attention. In the center of the square is the 15th-century yellow-and-white **Casa Sfatului (Council House),** now home to the city's tourist office as well as the **Braşov Historical Museum** (**Muzeul Judetean de Istorie Braşov;** ✆ **0268/47-2363;** Tues–Sun 10am–6pm); capping the building is the 58m-high (190 ft.) **Trumpeter's Tower,** originally used for meetings. West of the Council House, amid a long row of fabulous buildings, is **Casa Mureşenilor,** Piaţa Sfatului 25 (✆ **0268/47-7864;** Tues–Sat 9am–3pm), now memorializing the 19th-century political journalist and editor, Iacob Mureşianu. On the eastern side of the square is **Casa Hirscher.** Built between 1539 and 1545 by Apollonia Hirscher, the widow of one of the city's mayors, it was set up as a trading house for the merchant community, but is now a tourist restaurant, **Cerbul Carpaţin** (**Carpathian Stag;** ✆ **0268/44-3981**). And at the northern end of the square, next to the shamelessly located KFC, is a passage leading to the **Church of the Assumption of the Virgin,** tucked well away from public view; completed in 1899, the church tower was destroyed by earthquake in 1940, and only rebuilt in 1972.

From Piaţa Sfatului you can either wander south through the **Schei District** (described below), or head for the northwestern corner to take Strada Mureşenilor, which stretches past a number of restaurants and bars and soon reaches Bulevardul Eroilor, with the leafy expanse of Parcul Central on the far side. Turn right along Bulevardul Eroilor, passing the ugly facade of the Aro Palace Hotel to reach **Braşov's Art Museum** at no. 21 (Tues–Sun 10am–6pm), which includes a sizable collection of works by notable 19th- and 20th-century Romanian artists. Farther on is a **Memorial to the Victims of the 1989 Revolution;** behind this you'll see the bulky **District Council** building. Eroilor becomes Bulevardul 15 Novembrie, with Piaţa Teatrului spreading out in front of the **Sică Alexandrescu Drama Theater.** Turning right in front of the wooden memorial cross, however, you'll head into **Strada Republicii,** a charming car-free promenade lined with the city's most alluring shops and cafes, and a few decent restaurants; of particular note are the many antiques stores (the best being **Rams Antik** and **Antique Edy,** which has two branches). Although there are a few interesting diversions up the various side streets, Republicii eventually lands you back on Piaţa Sfatului.

Biserica Neagră ★★★ The 90m-long (295 ft.) and 21m-high (69-ft.) "Black Church" is the biggest Gothic cathedral between Istanbul and Vienna. Work started in

Bird's-Eye Views

Locals like to take romantic strolls along the promenade above the long section of defensive walls that still remains on the eastern edge of the city, at the foot of Mount Tâmpa. Midway along the promenade is the **Telecabina Tâmpa,** a cable car that delivers passengers to the top of the mountain, 995m (3,265 ft.) up, in 140 seconds (Mon noon–5pm, Tues–Fri 9:30am–6pm, Sat–Sun 9:30am–8pm; last ticket sold 30 min. before closing; L7/$3/£1.85 return). Ignore the restaurant (expensive and soulless) and take the path to the right and walk for around 10 minutes to the recently built **Terasa Belvedere** lookout point.

For more great photographic vantages of the city, head for the **Black Tower (Turnul Neagru),** part of the defensive walls, which once protected Brastov and which still hold vigil over the city from the face of Warthe Hill, west of Piaţa Sfatului (Tues–Sun 10am–6pm; last tickets 5:30pm; admission L4/$1.70/65p; photography L20/$8.60/£5.35). The tower includes a pretty drab medieval display; ignore this and take the steps leading to the top levels; the **view ★★** from the top of the Black Tower is spectacular (you can happily pass on the White Tower). Take the pathway behind the Black Tower up to **Promenade Warthe** for more great city views.

1383, but the building was destroyed during the Ottoman invasion of 1421 before it could be completed. It was finally finished in 1480, although there was more destruction between 1530 and 1630, when a total of 40 earthquakes hit the region. Originally a Catholic church, it became Lutheran during the Reformation. When a tragic fire swept through Braşov on April 21, 1689, the charred remains of the church (the baptismal font at the front of the church is one of the few thing that survived) afforded it its ghoulish name; today there is nothing dark about it, although the exterior is slightly ominous, even haunting. Inside, however, the church is overwhelmingly white and now horribly illuminated by awful modern light fittings. The 180 rugs you see hanging from the balconies—given to the church by merchants who returned after successful trade missions in the Middle East—make up the second-largest collection of its kind in the world; the bell in the clock tower is also the largest in Romania, weighing in at 6 tons. If you are a fan of church or choral music, look out for summer concerts (select evenings mid-June through Aug); this will be the best opportunity to hear the colossal 4,000-pipe organ and much-vaunted acoustics in action.

Biserica Neagră. Admission 1.10€ ($1.40). Mon–Sat 10am–6pm. Mass Sun 10am.

Schei District ★★ Follow Strada Porta Schei south and pass through the **Schei Gate** (1828), an archway leading to Braşov's oldest area, the neighborhood where the subservient Romanian community was sequestered during the racist rule of the Saxons. The neighborhood retains much of its historical character, defined by narrow streets and unimposing buildings; one of the loveliest is the Orthodox **Cathedral of St. Nicholas,** Piaţa Unirii (Mon–Sat 8am–6pm, Sun 9am–6pm), an eclectic merging of Gothic, Renaissance, and baroque elements. Established by the *voivodes* (landowners) of Wallachia, this is Transylvania's first Orthodox church, built 1493 to 1564 on the site of an earlier wooden building; it's lavishly adorned with frescoes and rugs. Near the church, behind the statue of an intellectual-looking man holding a scroll, is the **First Romanian School Museum ★ (Muzeul Prima Şcuală Românească,** Piaţa Unirii 1–2 (✆ **0268/44-3879;** daily 9am–5pm; 1.10€/$1.65), where the first Romanian Bible is kept, along with the first Romanian letter written using the Latin alphabet, and the country's first press, used in this building when it was a printing house. From the square, head farther

Will the Real "Dracula's Castle" Please Stand Up?

Part medieval fortress, part tourist con, **Bran Castle** Overrated (✆ **0268/23-8333;** www.brancastlemuseum.ro; Mon noon–7pm and Tues–Sun 9am–7pm May–Sept, Tues–Sun 9am–5pm Oct–Apr) is probably the best-known attraction in Romania, but its claim to fame is dubious indeed. Most people arrive in modest Bran village, just 30km (19 miles) from Braşov, expecting to find "Dracula's Castle," and many suckers leave oblivious to the truth: Vlad Ţepeş may have passed through Bran at some stage of his violent career, but he certainly never lived here (see "Vlad & the Epic Mythology of Count Dracula" earlier in this chapter). If anything, Bran Castle is very much a fairy-tale castle; perched upon a cliff, with whitewashed turrets and defensive bastions, it is somehow too quaint, too fragile, too pretty, to entertain thoughts of bats or monsters.

Completed in record time, between 1377 and 1382, Bran was built as a defensive outpost to protect Hungary's Transylvanian interests against the expanding Ottoman Empire; it also collected customs on goods moving between Wallachia and Transylvania. Control of the castle changed repeatedly over the centuries, until the people of Braşov gave it to the Romanian Royal family in 1920. At the request of Queen Marie, chief architect Karl Liman (who also worked for her at Pelişor in Sinaia) transformed the defensive fortress into a modern summer residence fit for royalty, complete with electric lighting and running water. Marie, who is featured in many photographic displays, undertook the interior design, styling the rooms much as they look today. There's certainly nothing scary here, unless you have a fear of crowds; try to arrive as early as possible to avoid the masses and walk through the castle at your leisure (alternatively, English guided tours are available; ask for availability), enjoying the fantastic views from the balconies, windows, and battlements.

Included in your ticket (L12/$5.15/£3.20 adults, L6/$2.60/£1.60 seniors and students, free for children 4 and under) is an ethnographic display of well-maintained (and usually locked) peasant homes at the foot of the castle hill. Not included is a visit to the superrevolting Haunted Castle and Skeleton's Tavern for kids that forms part of the tourist clutter of souvenir stalls near the ticket office. In 2006, the castle was officially returned to Princess Ileana's son, Dominic, a New York City architect. The jury is still out on what he will do with his inheritance, but so far there's been no indication that anyone's prepared to clear out the kitsch flea market around the entrance to Bran's extensive ground and restore some of the property's grandeur.

along Strada Prof. Vasile Saftu until you get to lovely **Church of the Holy Trinity (Biserica Sfânta Treime),** well off the beaten track, but memorable for its early-morning Mass (7:30am), attended by a congregation of retired locals; the interior is fantastically frescoed, and there's a small museum. The cemetery is where the city's Romanian serfs are buried. Schei also shelters the country's original **Romanian lyceum** on Strada Prundului, which hosted the first vernacular opera in 1882.

Schei, via Str. Porta Schei, south of Piaţa Sfatului.

Poiana Braşov

Braşov's fabulous little forest-fringed ski resort, **Poiana Braşov,** is situated on the slopes of the Postăvarul Massif, a fine year-round Carpathian Mountain getaway. It's beautiful in summer, when the mountains are perfect for extended hikes and when Romania's athletes come to train in open space and clean air. From December through March, it fills up with skiers; casual winter-sports enthusiasts will have an easy time of it. Experienced skiers won't be challenged, however; this is generally for beginners and anyone looking for a relaxing time on the slopes, although some of the pistes are rated difficult. There is limited off-piste skiing. There's a gondola service as well as two cable cars to get you to the summit of Cristianul Mave (1,690m/5,543 ft.) and Mt. Postavarul (1,802m/5,911 ft.), the two peaks here. Poiana Braşov offers ski instruction as well as a range of slope activities; for all the information you might need, visit www.ana.ro; alternatively, try www.skiresorts.ro. The best restaurant in town is **Coliba Haiducilor,** Strada Drumul Sulinarului (© **0268/26-2137**), with a lovely country atmosphere, warm log fire, and home-style cooking. If the salubrious atmosphere works its charms on you, ask the owners about their accommodations at **Casa Viorel,** Strada Poiana lui Stechil (© **0268/26-2431;** www.casaviorel.ro; doubles from 50€/$64). You can also organize accommodations through many agencies in Braşov; try to avoid staying at the larger hotels, which are soulless.

Braşov After Dark

With its wooden floors and exposed brickwork walls, **Festival '39 ★★**, Str. Mureşenilor 23 (© **0268/47-8664;** www.festival39.com; daily 10am–2am), is a classy little all-day bar; beautiful and unpretentious, it's decorated with dozens of framed antique photos and large picture windows that open onto a sidewalk—great for people-watching. For an evening drink, call to reserve a table.

SIGHIŞOARA ★★★

221km (137 miles) NW of Bucharest

Medieval Sighişoara is the only inhabited citadel of its kind in Europe; remarkably preserved, it's earned its place on UNESCO's World Heritage list. Of course, there's also plenty of hype around the fact that Vlad Tepeş (aka Count Dracula) was born here, but that's not the reason to make this excursion. Built in the 15th century, this hilltop fortress town is a gorgeous, tiny jumble of cobbled streets lined with medieval houses and towers jutting menacingly from the battlements—compact, yet with myriad ancient nooks and crannies, this is a wonderful place to explore, and easily better than the more popular Bran Castle.

Essentials

Sighişoara has a fairly good run of train connections with Braşov and Bucharest, and there is a fairly extensive range of services to and from other towns likely to be on your itinerary; you can for instance get a direct train here from Budapest, Vienna, and Prague. Sighişoara's **train station** is about 1km (²/₃ mile) from the old city, at one end of a quiet residential neighborhood outside the medieval center. When trains arrive, taxis turn up to drive visitors to their hotels; there is an access road leading from the lower city into the citadel. Although your hotel should be able to organize any onward travel, you can buy train tickets from the **CFR Agenţie de Voiaj,** Str. O. Goga 6A (© **0265/77-1886;** Mon–Fri 8am–4pm), in the lower part of town.

The **Cultural Heritage Info Center,** Str. Muzeului 6 (© **0788-115-511**) can assist you with just about anything; the efficient staff also dispenses maps and organizes tours.

Where to Stay & Dine

Casa Epoca ★★ Finds A stylishly spick-and-span guesthouse occupying a 15th-century Gothic building, Epoca has timbered floors, exposed wood-beam ceilings, and wrought-iron, wall-mounted electric candelabras. The gracious owner has gone to lengths to give character to the rooms, which are furnished with lovely wooden items, including reproduction medieval Saxon beds with firm mattresses and clean white linens (televisions are hidden away in a cupboard). All bathrooms have showers, except the apartment, which has a corner tub. The attic rooms are especially lovely. Breakfast is served in a fine vaulted brick cellar. ***Note:*** Unfortunately, at press time, Epoca was up for sale, and there's no telling what might become of it in the future.

Tips Getting Fortified in the Citadel

Palinca—homemade plum, apple, and pear brandy—is a fine Transylvanian tradition. In the heart of Sighişoara, you'll soon find your way to the homey little cellar of **Teo Coroian,** the local *palinca* distiller, at Str. Şcolii 14 (© **0265/77-1677**), where you can sample the powerful distillations and learn about the process from the man himself. Teo has hundreds of potent vintages for you to take home, and he's enlisted the help of various artisans to create bottles in an astounding range of shapes and sizes; combined with their spirited contents, they make good gifts. Teo also has comfortable en suite guest room in his home; these have modern en suite showers, and the rate (45€/$57) gets you breakfast and a help-yourself bar fridge filled with mineral water, beer, and—of course—plenty of homemade plum, pear, and apple brandy; also included are coffee and snacks, and the comfortable vibe of a small home.

Of the hotel restaurants, **Casa Wagner** (daily 8am–11pm) is the best, with a lovely wine cellar as well as a sheltered courtyard terrace round the back. If you've left Bran Castle disappointed, you may be interested in dining at **Casa Vlad Dracul,** the only restaurant in the country with any authentic link to the legend. History claims that Vlad Tepiş was born in this house in 1431. The medieval decor and candlelit tavern atmosphere do little to render the place "spooky," but the menu does, however, offer an unforgiving vampire bent: "Dracula House medallions," for example, are slithers of pork on bread, covered with a slop of garlic, mushroom, and tomato ketchup, that popular stand-in for blood.

Str. Tamplarilor 4, Sighişoara 545400. ✆ **0265/77-3232.** Fax 0265/77-2237. www.casaepoca.ro. 11 units. 45€–50€ ($57–$64) double; 68€–75€ ($86–$95) suite; 90€–100€ ($114–$127) apt. Rates include breakfast. No credit cards. **Amenities:** Bar; laundry; 24-hr. medical assistance; car rental; massage. *In room:* TV, minibar.

Casa Wagner ★ Perfectly sited in the center of the citadel, this good-value hotel is defined by its tasteful layout and Saxon antiques. While it doesn't have the long list of amenities offered at the tourist-oriented Hotel Sighişoara (virtually neighboring Wagner, though I suggest skipping it), you're likely to enjoy more personal attention from the staff. White-walled guest rooms are spacious, with wooden floors and simple, carefully selected furnishings. The finest rooms are in the annex across the road; these are large, wood-floored spaces, and include the Casa Wagner Suite, which features antique beds and a wonderfully frescoed ceiling; from here, guests love the views over the main square. Stairs leading to the rooms on the upper floors can be a bit taxing, so ask for a first-floor unit if you're not keen to lug luggage. Bathrooms are modern with a tub/shower combo. This hotel also has the best in-house dining options: Choose between the cozy cellar beneath the hotel, the courtyard-terrace round the back, or the more formal restaurant.

Piaţa Cetăţii 7, Sighişoara. ✆ **0265/50-6014.** Fax 0265/50-6015. www.casa-wagner.com. 32 units. 60€ ($76) double; 85€–95€ ($108–$121) suite. Rates include breakfast and VAT. MC, V. **Amenities:** Restaurant; bar; business services; room service; laundry. *In room:* TV, minibar.

Residence Fronius ★★★ Finds The early-2008 addition to Sighişoara's accommodations scene is one of the finest lodging options in the country: intimate, luxurious, and carefully run. Situated at the foot of the steps that lead up to the Church on the Hill, this ravishing property is the hard-earned result of 3½ years of careful restoration of one of the few houses that withstood the fire which ravaged the citadel in 1676—in fact, it's the oldest house on the street. Designers have left much of the original vaulted brickwork and wood beams exposed, and you can still see the indoor well which saved the house from the fire. Downstairs, you can lounge in leather armchairs, ordering drinks from the beautiful woodcarved antique bar (imported from Germany), or study the collection of intriguing artifacts used as classy decoration throughout. Upstairs, the seven bedrooms are immaculate, with wood floors, sumptuous king-size beds (or two ¾-beds), crisp white linens, and fabulous antiques that all come together stylishly (along with modern amenities, including plasma TVs) to create very elegant quarters; bathrooms are modern and beautiful. If you choose the right room (book no. 7 now), you won't even have to step outside to enjoy some of the best views in town. Some rooms are duplex style, with beds upstairs, above the neat little sitting areas, and there are three economical rooms in a separate house which are carpeted and only have showers.

Str. Şcolii 13, 545400 Sighişoara. ✆ **0265/77-9173.** www.froniusresidence.ro. 10 units. 120€ ($152) double; 70€ ($89) economy double. Rates include breakfast and taxes. Rates higher during Medieval Festival. MC, V. **Amenities:** Breakfast area; bar; access to fitness room, sauna, and massage at nearby Hotel Sighişoara; laundry. *In room:* A/C (some), TV, minibar (some), hair dryer.

Exploring Sighişoara

Part of its charm is that there's not much to do in Sighişoara; the citadel itself is the attraction. As you roam the streets, don't be surprised if déjà vu sets in; the town is tiny enough to be covered on foot in just a few minutes, but there's joy to be had in retracing your steps, as the architecture is affected by even the subtlest changes in light. Spend some time visiting the citadel's few churches and museums, which add context to the broader picture; try to climb the Clock Tower as early as possible, taking in the fantastic

The Saxon Churches of Transylvania

Fortified churches were the norm in medieval Europe, with the architectural form reaching its apotheosis in Transylvania under Saxon architects. Although there are scores of Saxon villages, many of which are worthy of a visit, Biertan (Birthälm) is home to one of the finest and largest of the Saxon churches. Situated within sylvan surroundings—low hills carpeted with orchards and vineyards—this UNESCO-listed church was built in the late-Gothic style during the first part of the 16th century; the village itself dates from 1283. The church occupies a hill in the center of town, its solid periphery walls and four watchtowers a reminder of how these religious buildings served a dual function as places of worship and defense against marauding enemies. At the foot of the hill, walls and archways and towers mark out further protective fortifications. A covered stairway allows access to the church, most of which is made of brick, plastered and painted throughout; 20th-century restoration work has revealed frescoes that have been partially restored. The stone pulpit, probably carved by a Braşovian named Ullricus, suggests a transition between Gothic and Renaissance periods. Between 1572 and 1867, Biertan was the residence of Transylvania's evangelical bishops, many of whose tombstones can be found inside the church. Biertan comes to life once a year in September when it plays host to a Saxon reunion, drawing a festive crowd of Transylvanian-born Germans.

The most convenient way to get to Biertan—or any of the Saxon villages—is on a guided tour with a knowledgeable expert; make arrangements through Sighişoara's **Cultural Heritage Info Center,** Str. Muzeului 6 (✆ **0788-115-511**), or contact **Peter Suciu** (✆ **0721-245-195**) of the new guiding organization Wunderlust directly. You'll spend a day traveling to three or four different villages (definitely request that Mălâncrav is included in your itinerary). Expect to pay around 30€ ($38) per person.

view of the city before the tourist hordes arrive (in fact, from up there you'll see the buses making their way up Strada Turnului, signaling that the historic town is open for business). Then visit the Church on the Hill, which seems ordinary from the outside, but is imbued with a fascinating energy. Wind down the day by grabbing a beer on Piaţa Cetăţii; there's sometimes a craft market and usually a lively atmosphere.

If you'd prefer a **guided tour** of the citadel (or to any of the Saxon villages in the region), contact **Peter Suciu** (✆ **0721-245-195**), a knowledgeable and exacting guide. Alternatively, you can hire an **audio guide** from the booth on Piaţa Cetăţii.

The Clock Tower & City Museums ★★ Surmounting the main entrance to the city, the whole **Muzeul de Istorie (History Museum)** is a climb up the Clock Tower (the city's defensive tower, most worthy of a fairy tale), so be prepared for some legwork. It's one of the more informative history museums, starting with a model of the town as it was in 1735. There is also a collection of surgical instruments that includes a bloodcurdling array of knives and saws, not to mention enema syringes that will make you grateful for being born into an enlightened age. The best exhibition room (reached via the short stairway next to the display of Dr. Josef Bacon, who founded the museum in 1899) includes several chromo-engravings of everyday life in 18th- and 19th-century Sighişoara. As you ascend the Clock Tower, you can check out different components of the elaborate clock mechanism, straining your neck along the way to get views of the city. From the top, the magical 360-degree view includes shingled rooftops, fairy-tale steeples, turreted guard towers, and—in the near distance—the encroachment of modern apartments. Polished metal plaques indicate distances to various capitals around the world; at this point, you're 7,431km (4,607 miles) from New York.

Back down on the ground, your combination ticket includes entrance to the tiny one-room **Torture Chamber Museum** (nearby, tucked into the city wall), which once served as the citadel's prison. Also nearby is the **Museum of Medieval Arms,** a curiously curated exhibition that includes African daggers and arrows among the more traditional assortment of European killing machines.

Piaţa Muzeului 1. ✆ **0265/77-1108.** History Museum and Clock Tower entry L5 ($2.15/£1.35); combined ticket for all museums L8 ($3.45/£2.15). Mon 10am–4:30pm; Tues–Fri 9am–6:30pm; Sat–Sun 9am–4:30pm.

Church on the Hill & Cemetery ★★ A covered stairway with nearly 180 steps leads up the hill to the Gothic-style Biserica din Deal, allegedly built in 1345 for the Saxon community; local guides will dispute this, however, claiming that this is simply the year when the church was converted to its Gothic form. There are a few surprises here, including a unique fresco in one of the archways in which the Holy Trinity is depicted as a three-faced entity, with the Holy Ghost depicted as female. Also unique is the Last Judgment fresco without any depiction of purgatory. Take the time to venture into the crypt beneath the church, where 30 tombs are cloaked in a cool atmosphere of vampiric calm.

Worth exploring for its weathered charm is the Saxon cemetery opposite the church doorway; strangely, the positioning of some of the gravestones clearly suggests that some of the dead have made attempts to escape. To the right of the cemetery entrance is the **Ropers' Tower.**

Biserica din Deal. Admission L5 ($2.15/£1.35). Times vary; usually 8am–8pm in summer.

SIBIU ★★★

274km (170 miles) NW of Bucharest

Sibiu hit the world stage in 2007 when it shared the "European City of Culture" title with Luxembourg. A thorough big-budget makeover rejuvenated its large medieval squares and elegant buildings, making it one of the most appealing places to explore in all Romania. An excellent example of the (usually smaller) fortified Saxon towns that dot the Transylvanian landscape, Sibiu was saved from destruction during the Communist era largely because Ceauşescu's son, Nicu, was the city's mayor. The medieval heart, surrounded by a sprawling city, is held together by stone-walled fortifications and the remains of the 39 guild towers that served as defensive watchtowers; within lie cobblestone streets, secret back alleys, crumbling stairways, and elegant monuments.

Built by the Saxons in the 12th century on the site of the Roman village of Cibinium, Sibiu is known to Germans as Hermannstadt and it remains home to Romania's largest German-speaking community, though now a meager 5,500. Originally designed to a concentric circular plan, with four walls dividing the residential zones according to class, this was Transylvania's ancient capital, with the Saxons ruling from the center and Romanians occupying the outermost ring. While it's often thought of as Romania's most welcoming and laid-back city, it's worth remembering that it was here, in the second half of the 19th century, that the Romanian nationalist movement first stirred, agitating against Transylvania's Magyarization; today, vestiges of Astra (the Transylvanian Association of Romanian Literature and Culture) can still be found, particularly at the Folk Museum just outside the city.

Essentials

Tarom, Str. Nicolae Bălcescu 10 (✆ **0269/21-1604;** Mon–Fri 8am–6pm), flies from Bucharest to Sibiu daily. Both Tarom and **Carpatair** (✆ **0269/22-9161**) have connections with German destinations, and Carpatair also flies to Timişoara. At press time, burgeoning budget carrier **Blue Air** (www.blueair.com) was launching various domestic and international services; you can also investigate **Austrian Airlines** (www.aua.com) for a direct international connection. For years, it has been difficult finding **train** connections to the city, and rail access remains limited. Nevertheless, Sibiu's **railway station,** Piaţa 1 Decembrie, is about .7km (1/2 mile) from Piaţa Mare, and is directly opposite the **bus station.** From the station, catch trolleybus no. 1 to get to the center, or use a **taxi** (✆ **0269/44-4444**). You can buy onward train tickets from **CFR's Agenţie de Voiaj office,** Str. Nicolae Bălcescu 6 (✆ **0269/21-6441;** Mon–Fri 7:30am–7:30pm).

For information and sightseeing services, head directly to the **Tourist Information Office,** Piaţa Mare 7 (✆ **0269/21-1110;** Mon–Sat 9am–5pm, Sun 10am–1pm); visit their website (www.sibiu.ro) before your trip. Alternatively, visit **Kultours** on the ground floor of Casa Luxemburg, Piaţa Mică 16 (✆ **0269/21-6854;** www.kultours.ro). They hand out a useful map, offer sightseeing trips, rent bicycles, rent rooms, and sell books, souvenirs, and postcards.

Where to Stay

Sibiu's accommodations scene has exploded thanks to the city's newfound fame. Still, there's only so much room for growth in the historical center, so most of the cushier options are located just beyond the old city walls. Although many people insist on staying at the historical "Roman Emperor" (below), it isn't exactly the classiest hotel in town. That distinction goes to the plush new **Ramada** ★★, Str. Emil Cioran 2 (✆ **0269/23-5505;** www.ramadasibiu.ro; doubles from 140€/$177), just outside the historical center. Its rooms are sumptuous and contemporary, with the best mattresses in town and just about every amenity you could hope for (including free Internet and large plasma TVs); all double rooms have tub/shower combos in the modern bathrooms. The chichi design throughout is relatively pleasing, and initial hiccups with service are steadily receiving attention. Book a room on the 12th floor, and insist on a view of the old city; don't forget to look out through the glass elevator as you're whisked up to your room.

Am Ring Hotel ★★ **Finds** Sibiu's new kid on the block—or rather, on the square—occupies a perfect position at the edge of Piaţa Mare. While it isn't perfect (service and public areas need some work), it's certainly a welcome addition, and guestrooms are especially impressive. Designers have gone for a classical in-room look and feel; each room is unique, with textured wallpapered walls (in dark shades with gold highlights) and restored 19th-century furniture. Some of the bedrooms are enormous, and a few have lovely views over the main square (the suites, however, may have absolutely no view); bathrooms have glass-encased showers on marble floors, while suites have Jacuzzi tubs. Some details miss the mark, however, and you may find that there's nowhere to put your toiletries, or that the minibar rests directly on the carpet, indicating a lack of attention of finer details. In the terrace, bar and dining areas, too, you may find the plethora of blaring televisions just a little taxing.

Piaţa Mare 14, Sibiu. ✆ **0269/20-6499.** 26 units. 110€ ($140) double; 130€ ($165) suite. MC, V. **Amenities:** Restaurant; bar; terrace cafe; laundry. *In room:* TV, minibar, hair dryer; Jacuzzi (suites).

Casa Luxemburg ★ Kids Run by Sibiu's best-located tourist agency, Luxemburg House occupies a great location in one of the city's famous original monuments at one end of Piaţa Mică—the city's medieval heart. You need to climb a tricky wooden stairway to get to the large rooms and suites on the second floor; these have modern furniture, parquet floors, and en suite showers. There is also an apartment with a kitchenette, but without the view over the square. Ironically, mattresses here are better than those at the Împăratul Romanilor, and this is a good option if you're traveling with children since it's possible to book a three- or four-bedded unit. There has been no attempt to capitalize on the history, and it's not luxurious, but a stay here does represent better value than the Emperor.

Piaţa Mică 16, Sibiu. ✆/fax **0269/21-6854.** www.casaluxemburg.ro. 6 units. L270 ($116/£72) double; L330 ($142/£88) triple; L360 ($155/£96) apt. MC, V. **Amenities:** Breakfast buffet; 24-hr. reception and tourist agency; sightseeing; car rental; souvenir shop. *In room:* TV, Wi-Fi, fridge (some), hair dryer.

Hotel Împăratul Romanilor Overrated The "Roman Emperor" hotel traces its history from 1555, when the city's first inn stood on this site in the heart of the medieval town. It considers itself the pride of Sibiu's hospitality industry, listing Johann Strauss, Franz Liszt, and various heads of state and royals among its guests, but this is a position it has earned more by default than anything else—indeed, many locals are a touch embarrassed by standards here. There are enough pieces of antique and reproduction furniture to evoke a sense of gracious living, but it lacks the bells and whistles of a definitively luxurious hotel—witness long passageways with much-scrubbed but still grubby-looking carpets, and mixed-bag guest rooms that combine faux-antique and modern to create a rather bland look. And in many respects, given the price, service is lax and e-mail bookings are unreliable. Unless you're gagging to rub shoulders with history, stay elsewhere.

Str. Nicolae Balcescu 2–4, Sibiu. ✆ **0269/21-6500.** Fax 0269/21-3278. www.imparatulromanilor.ro. 95 units. 120€ ($152) double; 135€ ($1713) studio; 165€ ($210) apt. Rates include breakfast. MC, V. **Amenities:** Restaurant; bar; lounge; fitness center; sauna; massage; 24-hr. room service; laundry. *In room:* TV, minibar.

Where to Dine

Built into the side of one of the city walls, reached via a set of steps between Strada Turnului and Piaţa Huet, is **Pivnita de vinuri "Weinkeller,"** Str. Tunrului 2 (✆ **0269/21-0319;** Tues–Sun noon–midnight), a wine cellar–cum-restaurant with traditional German dishes and light meals (like quiche Lorraine and cold meat-and-cheese platters) and an extensive wine list with vintage indicated on a map, so you'll learn a bit about where they've come from.

Crama Sibiul Vechi ★★★ Value TRANSYLVANIAN One of the top places in the country for authentic Transylvanian food, this unpretentious 100-year-old restaurant is loved by locals—and for good reason. Hidden away on a side street off Strada Nicolae Bălcescu, Sibiul Vechi occupies a late-15th-century cellar decorated in traditional "village style" and prides itself on the authenticity of the experience; waiters are in traditional costume getup, and even the plates and wine goblets are handcrafted. There's not much reason to study the menu: Without any hesitation (unless you're vegetarian), order the

Moments Sundowner Heaven

To catch the sun setting over Sibiu in style, head over to sweet and stylish **Café Wien★★**, just behind the Evangelical Cathedral. You can grab a table indoors, but on warm summer evenings, the terrace is perfect, and you might just get a free concert courtesy of the cathedral's choir, which sometimes performs in the adjacent square. Choose from a decadent menu of special coffees—the "Brukenthal" is prepared with a good dose of Amaretto—or ask after the homemade lemonade.

Shepherd's Bag *(traista ciobanului),* a chicken breast parcel stuffed full of sliced sausage, salami, and cheese, and served with grilled polenta—it's fantastic. Alternatives are more or less all meaty: peasant's stew (ladled into your bowl at the table), *muşchi de pork Sibiu* (pork filet, Sibiu-style), Transylvanian mixed grill, or even *creier pane* (deep fried brains in a light batter).

Str. Papiu Ilarian 3. ✆ **0269/21-0461.** www.sibiulvechi.ro. Main courses L9.50–L24 ($4.10–$10/£2.55–£6.20). MC, V. Daily 11am–midnight.

Exploring Sibiu

Sibiu's interesting bits stretch between **Piaţă Mică** in what is known as **"Lower Town,"** and **Piaţa Unirii,** situated at the junction of Sibiu's charming medieval heart and pulsing modern city. **Piaţă Mică** ("small" square), once the commercial center of the city—**Casa Artelor** at the northern end of the square originally dates from 1370 when it was a market hall—is surrounded on all sides by a lovely collection of buildings freshly coated in a palette of flash pastels. Of the prettiest is **Casa Luxemburg,** now occupied by several decent bars, a tourist shop, and guesthouse (see "Where to Stay," above), and right near the famous **Liar's Bridge**—so named because (among other fanciful reasons) it will apparently collapse if you tell a fib while standing on it; apparently no one has dared test the theory since it was constructed in 1859. The bridge links Piaţa Mică to adjacent **Piaţa Huet,** at the center of which stands the monumental **Evangelical Cathedral** (reviewed below). Piaţă Huet's southern end is in turn linked with **Piaţa Mare,** the "big" town square and once the social hub of the original walled city, where—among other crowd-pulling activities—executions were held. This marks the end of Lower Town.

Set aside an hour to explore the city's top attraction, located on Piata Mare—the **Brukenthal Palace,** with its famous art museum (reviewed below)—as well as the **Roman Catholic Cathedral,** built by the Jesuits (1726–33) in the baroque style (the statue out front memorializes the peasants who fought in the uprisings of 1848). Between the palace and the church is the gorgeously impressive headquarters of the **Banca Agricola,** and in the northwestern corner of the square, the **Council Tower** (1588).

Stretching southwest of Piaţa Mare is pedestrianized **Strada Nicolae Bălcescu,** established in 1492 and lined with shops, cafes, galleries, and a couple of side streets worth wandering for a sense of medieval back-alley life. Lined with Renaissance-style architecture, Strada Bălcescu eventually collides with modern Sibiu, a sudden time-shifting shock as you hit newly restored **Piaţa Unirii** (where you'll find Crama Sibiul Vechi, the city's highly rated restaurant). Along the southeastern periphery of the old center, much of the original defensive wall still stands, dotted with a few of its guild-sponsored watchtowers.

Upper Town's most attractive stretch is **Strada Avram Iancu,** which runs between the Council Tower building and the **Ursuline Church;** along the road is Sibiu's oldest residence, known as **Casa Bobel,** which has apparently retained the same appearance for half a millennium. Midway between the square and the church, you should come upon the steep **Pasajul Scolii (School Passage),** which leads to the cobbled depths of Strada Movilei.

The **Ursuline Church** is a huge edifice with a sculpted effigy of St. Ursula above the entrance; it was built in 1474 and was originally a Dominican monastery, but was closed in 1543 when the Reformation converted the Saxon population to Lutheranism; in 1733 it was taken over by the Ursuline nuns, who converted the original Gothic interiors to the baroque—get here at 8am to hear women in the church singing and chanting with great solemnity. Baroque flourishes define the city's **Franciscan Church** on Strada Şelarilor, situated in a quiet corner, and linked to Strada General Magheru by a narrow passageway. It was built in 1716 and the white-and-pastel interior includes such high kitsch as a Madonna statue framed by a rockery.

At the edge of the old city near the **Powder Tower** is the neoclassical **Sala Thalia** on Strada Cetăţii, the home of the State Philharmonic (established in 1788). Farther along Strada Cetăţii is the **Natural History Museum** (Tues–Sun 9am–5pm), founded in 1895.

Astra Museum of Traditional Folk Civilization ★★ Kids Rent a bicycle from Kultours and get directions for the 5km (3-mile) ride to this pleasant, well-organized outdoor museum in which traditional houses, farmsteads, and windmills are laid out in a fantastic simulation of Romanian village life. Occasionally, there are also demonstrations of various folk pastimes, and interactive events and festivals that kids especially will enjoy.

Calea Răşinarilor 14. ✆ **0269/24-2599.** L15 ($6.45/£4) adults; L4 ($1.70/£1.05) children. June–Sept Tues–Sun 10am–8pm; Oct–May Tues–Sun 9am–5pm.

Brukenthal Museum ★★ Baron Samuel von Brukenthal was an Austrian governor who played a significant role in Transylvanian history, and was also a significant patron for the development of homeopathic medicine. His Sibiu palace is of interest architecturally—it is one of Romania's great baroque monuments, built between 1778 and 1788—but it also hosts the country's oldest art gallery, with an extensive collection of works from the German, Austrian, and Flemish schools under stucco ceiling and chandeliers; vestiges of the original baroque styling remain, along with silk walls, white rococo stoves, and 18th-century Transylvanian marquetry furniture. Open to the public since 1817, the galleries are in dire need of better lighting (some of the paintings are almost nothing but glare and shadow). Nevertheless, there are a few good impressions of Transylvanian cities through the ages.

Also part of the National Brukenthal Museum are satellite galleries and exhibits, including the **Contemporary Art Gallery,** accessed on Strada Tribunei (L5/$2.15/£1.35), and the **History Museum (Muzeul de Istorie,** Str. Mitropoliei 2 (✆ **0269/21-8143;** L12/$5.15/£3.20; Tues–Sun 8:30am–4:30pm), with a collection of just about anything and everything stored up from Sibiu's historical heyday, housed in the 15th-century Primăriă Municipiului (also thoroughly renovated in 2006). Interesting as it all is, the views from the windows do beat the displays, however.

Piaţa Mare 4–5. ✆ **0269/21-7691.** www.brukenthalmuseum.ro. Admission L12 ($5.15/£3.20) adults, L3 ($1.30/80p) students. Tues–Sun 10am–6pm.

Evangelical Cathedral ★★ Work on this late-Gothic church began in 1320, and continued for 200 years. Gray-stone walls with curved vaulting form the interior stark;

Frosty Bedfellows

In winter, the Făgăraş Mountains hosts novelty accommodations at the eight-roomed, highly seasonal **Bâlea Lac Ice Hotel.** Situated at an altitude of 2,040m (6,500 ft.) and created with ice from Lake Bâlea, the star-shaped igloo of a hotel takes about 1 month to build and requires an indoor temperature of 37°F (–3°C). First built in early 2006 and only available until May (at the latest), the hotel's guest rooms feature sheepskin-covered ice beds and ice versions of Brancusi sculptures. Doubles are under 50€ ($64); book through Meridian Travel (www.ice.hotel.balea.lac.en.meridian-travel.ro).

at the back of the church, the 6,000-pipe organ is the biggest in the country. The north wall of the nave is studded with stone epitaphs, including that of Prince Mihnea the Bad (Vodă cel Rău), the son of Vlad the Impaler, who was assassinated on the church square in 1510 just after attending a service here. Also don't miss the fantastic 9m (30-ft.) fresco in the choir; known as the "Rosenauer Painting," it is a superb crucifixion scene rendered in 1445; above this, note the Hungarian royal insignia featuring a lion and Bohemian vulture; below the fresco are the first Christian Hungarian kings (Ludovic with an ax and Stephen with scepter). Rising to a height of 73m (239 ft.), the bell tower was built as part of the city's defense system when a pair of guards would keep watch and use flags to signal the arrival of enemy armies. You can join a **tower tour,** offered by a Kultours guide who'll be hanging around the entrance (in summer, daily 9am–7pm; L3/$1.30/80p), climbing a steep, thrilling 192 steps to get to the top, but it's worth it for the views.

Piaţa Huet. Daily, summer 10am–6pm; winter 11am–4pm. Organ concerts on Wed evenings June–Sept.

Orthodox Church ★ Marked by a pair of entrance towers, Romania's second-largest Orthodox church was built between 1902 and 1906, its sandy yellow-and-ocher-colored brickwork apparently a miniature copy of the cathedral of St. Sophia in Istanbul. The huge carved door bears a German symbol, while inside, incense wafts through a majestic space hung with fantastic chandeliers and glorious frescoes cover almost every inch.

Str. Mitropoliei 35. Daily 6am–8pm.

Sibiu After Dark

Most fun for idling at a terrace cafe is probably Piaţa Mică, and there are always watchable people trundling between Piaţa Mare and Lower Town. With its warren of nooks and crannies, **Kulturcafe ★★**, Piaţa Mică 16 (✆ **0788-154-475;** daily 9am–3am), is an atmospheric cellar-style venue in the basement of Casa Luxemburg; exhibitions of photographs or installation art often set the mood, while the music ranges from jazz or blues to retro and experimental electronica. German beer is served along with tequilas, cocktails, and "absolutely anything." In summer, there's a terrace out on Piaţa Mică. **Art Café ★**, Str. Filarmonicii 2 (✆ **0722-265-992;** daily 11am–midnight), is inside the building of the philharmonic; graffiti and musical instruments decorate the walls that embrace a bohemian bonhomie well into the night. The **Philharmonic** (✆ **0269/21-0264**) itself has been going since 1949, and lends the city of Sibiu a culturally glamorous air.

En Route to Maramureş

There's a long stretch between southern Transylvania and the northern frontier region of Maramureş; consider cutting the journey by stopping in Transylvania's capital city, **Cluj-Napoca.** A smart university town believed to be the most expensive place in the country to live, it's a cosmopolitan place, best measured by the popularity of its cafe culture; grab a seat at a venue around Piaţa Unirii and you'll find the place filled with supercool posers wearing D&G apparel and tearing around in sports cars, their faces hidden behind massive sunglasses. The best place to stay is **Déjà Vu** ★, Str. Ion Ghica 2, Cluj-Napoca (✆/fax **0264/35-4941/61;** www.deja-vu.ro; 67€–95€/$85–$121 double with breakfast), a great little Art Nouveau–style hotel in a quiet residential neighborhood near the historical center. The restaurant here is one of the best in town, and the staff extremely helpful.

HIKING & CLIMBING IN THE FĂGĂRAŞ MOUNTAINS

Between Braşov and Sibiu lie the lovely Făgăraş Mountains, a popular Carpathian hiking region, studded with glacial lakes and soaring peaks. Reachable during peak summer months from Wallachia along the high-altitude Transfăgărăşan Highway, there are other, less daunting routes accessed via Hwy. 1, running between Braşov and Sibiu. The region has plenty of overnight "cabanas," making the massif well suited to independent hikers. The main towns in the region are **Făgărăş** and **Victoria,** the latter the principal starting point for most hikers; it's just 10km (6¼ miles) south of the highway. There are great hikes toward Mount Moldeveanu (Romania's highest point at 2,543m/8,341 ft.), which is popular with climbers who can settle in for the night at **Cabana Podragu.** About 10km (6¼ miles) east of Victoria is the 17th-century **Brâncoveanu Monastery;** from the monastery, you can hike south, more or less along the Sâmbăta River, to reach **Cabana Valea Sambetei** (✆ **0269/31-5756**).

From **Cabana Bâlea Cascadă,** there's a cable car to take you up 1,968m (6,560 ft.), where you can explore glacial Lake Balea, where **Villa Paltinul** (✆ **269-524277;** www.balea-lac.ro), once a small hunting lodge for Nicolae Ceauşescu, is a convenient stopover for hikers; try to book the main bedroom. From the lake, you can also follow a trail to Negoiu Peak, the region's second-highest mountain.

Bear in mind that hiking in the Făgăraş Mountains can be challenging and technically difficult; you'll need to set aside several days to them justice. If you're looking for easier—although no less beautiful—hiking opportunities, make inquiries in Sibiu, and then head off (preferably by car; there are two daily buses, however) to the chair lift at **Păltiniş** (32km/20 miles away); from here there are seven different waymarked trails through shockingly lovely forested mountainside. The longest route follows a 12km (7½-mile) path that takes you Cindrel, where you'll discover glacial lakes and blissful peace and quiet. It's possible to get there and back in a single day; set off early, though, as the walk alone should take roughly 10 hours. The shortest walk from Păltiniş takes about 2 hours.

6 CRIŞANA & THE BANAT

Romania's westernmost regions, Crişana and the Banat, only became part of Romania in 1918, before which they formed part of a unique entity in the Austro-Hungarian crown. Many visitors who travel over land from Hungary drift in through the border at Borş to stop at Oradea, capital of Bihor county in the northern part of Romanian Crişana, before taking highway E671 to the Habsburg city of Timişoara. The principal city of the Banat is considered the country's most forward-thinking metropole—after all, it was here in Timişoara that the great Revolution of December 1989 was ignited, changing the course of Romanian history forever.

ORADEA

592km (367 miles) NW of Bucharest; 152km (94 miles) W of Cluj-Napoca

A small, prosperous city at the western limits of Romania, Oradea benefits from the marks left by the Austro-Hungarian Empire, best evidenced in the elaborate and sometimes dainty Secessionist architecture fringing its avenues and squares. A whiff of its former *fin de siècle* cosmopolitanism still hangs in the air, and the city has made great efforts to restore much of the visual glory of its historic center, a program that's been continuing since 2006. While Oradea is lovely for its restrained ambience (best experienced on foot), it is also convenient for adventures into the Apuseni Mountains, with its seamless meadows, karstic formations, spectacular caves, wildlife, and traditional communities.

Essentials

Tarom, Piaţa Republicii 2 (✆ **0259/23-1918;** Mon–Fri 6:30am–8pm, Sat 10am–1pm), has early-morning weekday flights from Bucharest to Oradea's **airport,** Calea Aradului (✆ **0259/41-6082**), situated 6km (3¾ miles) from the center. Shuttle buses run Tarom passengers to and from the airport free of charge.

Oradea's **train station,** on Piaţa Bucureşti, is 1km (⅔ mile) north of the center; there are always taxis out front. Book onward travel at the **CFR office** (Mon–Fri 7am–7pm) on the corner of Calea Republicii and Piaţa Ferdinand.

For the real lowdown on the city, visit the offices of **Apuseni Experience,** on the first floor at Piaţa Decembrie 4–6 (✆ **0259/47-2434**), specializing in adventure tours but happy to help visitors find their feet.

Where to Stay

A slightly cheaper alternative to those spots listed below, **Hotel Scorilo** (✆ **0259/47-0910;** www.hotelscorilo.ro; L200/$86/£53 double) scores low on taste (linoleum-covered headboards, melamine furniture, and wood-and-leatherette sofas) but high on service; it is situated in an old (1703) building near the Catholic Cathedral (and train station), and its in-house restaurant is the best dining option in town (see below).

Hotel Elite It doesn't quite live up to its name, but this is Oradea's classiest hotel, situated in a residential neighborhood, just a short distance from the historic center. Guest rooms are spacious, with simple, neat furnishings, decent-size bathrooms (with tub/shower combo), and comfortable beds; the best units enjoy views onto a tree-lined park. While the atmosphere is generally tranquil and laid back (a waistcoated barman hovering in the lobby all day waiting to take your order), handfuls of festive guests do sometimes occupy the terrace until the small hours, so things can get noisy. Helpful staff offers discreet service, and the restaurant is one of the best in town.

Str. I.C. Bratianu 26, 410051 Oradea. ✆/fax **0259/41-4924** or 0259/41-9759. www.hotelelite.ro. 30 units. 65€–95€ ($83–$121) double; 120€ ($152) deluxe. Rates include breakfast. AE, MC, V. **Amenities:** Restaurant; breakfast room; bar; Jacuzzi; sauna; room service; airport and train station transfers; car rental; laundry. *In room:* A/C, TV, Internet, minibar, hair dryer, safe.

Where to Dine

If you've tired of Eastern European meat and you're looking for a light southern Europe touch, **La Galleria** (✆ **0259/47-5490;** Mon–Sat noon–3pm and 7–11:30pm) is the finest Italian joint in town (you'll find it right near the State Theater). If not, you'll find plenty of low-key, down-home Romanian/Hungarian options along or around Strada Republicii. Alternatively, head for the small, agreeable restaurant at centrally located **Hotel Elite** (details above) where you could start with a salad of forest mushrooms and marinated vegetables, then move on to Moldavian-style pork, or Mediterranean-style orata fish, baked with tomato, olives, and oregano.

Scorilo's ★★ ROMANIAN/HUNGARIAN/ECLECTIC There's a stellar menu at this great little hotel restaurant just north of the center, and the venue is good, too: In winter you can dine in the cellar, while the summer terrace is lovely, and there's live music on weekday evenings. You will, however, have to come well prepared to eat meat: Wild boar, goose legs cooked in champagne, and traditional Hungarian stew made with pork *and* bacon and prepared with garlic and golden potatoes, are just a few of the favorites. If you can't decide, go all out and order the Hunter's Plate, and sample a large array of venison.

Hotel Scorilo, Parcul Petőfi 16. ✆ **0259/47-0910** or 0259/41-4681. Main courses L15–L66 ($6.45–$28/ £4–£18). MC, V. Daily 11:30am–midnight.

Exploring Oradea

Oradea has a fairly manageable center, its north and south divided by the Crişul Repede River, which flows through the city. The two main points of focus—**Piaţa Republicii** (north) and **Piaţa Unirii** (south)—lie on either side of the river, linked by one of several bridges. Running northeast from one corner of Piaţa Republicii is Calea Republicii, a long pedestrianized road lined with lovely buildings. Oradea's **Citadel** lies east of Piaţa Unirii, beyond the large Parcul Central, and behind a blight of modern concrete blocks.

Take a casual stroll down pedestrianized **Strada Republicii,** recently revamped and lined on both sides by an endless succession of Secessionist buildings, and you'll wish you were spending more time in the city, if only to browse the numerous shops and take plentiful breaks at the cafes. At its southern end, Republicii joins **Piaţa Regele Ferdinand,** where you can ogle the beautiful facade of the neoclassical **State Theater (Teatrul de Stat;** ✆ **0259/41-7864;** www.oradeatheatre.com), designed by Helmer and Fellner in 1900. Also worth a gander on this square is the facade of the **Art School (Scoala de Arte Oradea),** now the seat of the Philharmonic Orchestra.

Head south across the bridge over River Crişul Repede to reach wide-open and startlingly empty **Piaţa Unirii;** directly in front of you as you cross the river, is a Catholic church obscuring the view of a **statue of Mihai Viteazul,** the great Wallachian prince said to have passed through the city before the end of his reign (1593–1601). On your right is the **City Hall,** built in 1902 and 1903, and source of the hourly tolling of the city's bell. On your left, in the distance beyond the **statue of Mihai Eminescu,** you'll see the **synagogue,** decaying, but worth investigating (you may need to tip the "warder").

Adventures in the Apuseni Mountains

The Apuseni Mountains (the lowest-lying of the Carpathian range) are one of Romania's great adventure destinations, with opportunities not only for trekking and caving (there are some 7,000 caves in the region), but also river-based adventures, cycling, rock climbing, bird-watching, cross-country skiing, horse riding, and even dog sledding. The best way to experience this region—home to steadily increasing lynx and wolf populations, and high-altitude wetlands with carnivorous plants and rare orchid species—is with **Apuseni Experience** ★★★, no. 8, first floor, Piaţa Decembrie 4–6, Oradea (✆ **0259/47-2434;** www.apuseniexperience.ro), probably Romania's top mountain-adventure company. The company employs mostly specialists in their field, who will lead you on a variety of treks and caving adventures, including a visit to the country's longest (Vantului) cave and the Ciur Ponor cave system, with preserved prehistoric human footprints and a 3,500-year-old subterranean glacier.

Experienced cavers can arrange trips to underground waterfalls and lakes (including the Avenul din Sesuri, 217m/712 ft. below ground); less extreme treks, hikes, and bike trips take you into the heart of the so-called "Lost World" plateau to try your hand at shepherding, or tracking wolves and bears. During all of their trips, Apuseni Experience will introduce you to the culture of the local communities, or you can focus entirely on a cultural tour. Apuseni Experience is also involved in various internationally recognized projects aiming to preserve the region's unique heritage. While you can tailor-make your adventure, combining activities, there are also predetermined programs, with costs per head starting at around 65€ ($83) per day, all-inclusive. Accommodations are in mountain guesthouses, family homes, and rustic mountain chalets, or there's always the option of camping under the stars. To design an adventure that's to your taste, contact Paul Iacobaş (✆ **0745-602-301;** paul@apuseniexperience.ro), who started Apuseni Experience after 3 years with the U.S. Peace Corps.

Beyond the City Hall is the **library,** built in 1905; opposite is the renovated Art Nouveau "Black Vulture Palace," or **Palatul Vulturul Negru** (1907–09), which conceals a mall-like arcade and namesake hotel; bars, restaurants, and casinos occupy the warrenlike passageway under a wonderful stained-glass ceiling. Just down from the Black Vulture is Oradea's Orthodox **Moon Church (Biserica cu Lună);** built between 1784 and 1790, it is named for its unique mechanical lunar phase indicator.

To the east of Piaţa Unirii—beyond the central park, apartment blocks, and busy main road intersection—is Oradea's 13th-century **citadel,** much expanded in the 18th century, when it took its present five-cornered bastion-enhanced proportions. Situated just south of the Criul Repede, the crumbling fortress—home of the university's art department—is used for the odd upbeat event. Look out especially for medieval festivals held here in early July, when the citadel becomes a playground: There's a mix of folk, contemporary, and hard-core medieval music, and the best archers in the region compete in a serious test of mettle, dressed in Knights of the Round Table costumes of varying degrees of authenticity.

Roman Catholic Cathedral Looking more like an administrative building than the country's largest baroque church, this imposing edifice was built between 1752 and 1780; the attractive interiors are best experienced during Mass or when organ recitals are held here. Just next door is the **Episcopal Palace** (built in 1770), which previously housed the regional **Museum of the Crişana;** the museum will reopen at Str. Armatei Româna 1/A once its 400,000 artifacts have been relocated.

Str. Şirul Canoncilor.

TIMIŞOARA ★★★

562km (348 miles) W of Bucharest

Timişoara (pronounced tim-*uh*-schwara, and called "Temesvar" by Hungarians) is considered Romania's most cosmopolitan city, defined by its strong associations with western European culture and progressive aspirations: This was the first European city to install street lighting, and the first to run off hydroelectric power. You'd never guess that this peaceful place, with its languid parks and gardens and gorgeous, lively squares, was once a hotbed of military and political violence: Timişoara, regarded as the first free city of Romania, was for a long time one of the major military bases against the Ottoman Empire in its ongoing advance on central Europe. When the citadel did finally fall to the Turkish armies, it took 164 years of planned invasions, and more than one army, before the Habsburgs finally managed to toss out the Turkish occupiers. The Austrian stamp remains clearly evident in the city's urban design, appealing for its voluminous parks and squares, and mix of baroque, neoclassical, and Art Nouveau buildings.

Essentials

Tarom, B-dul Revolutiţiei 3–5 (© **0256/49-0150;** Mon–Fri 7am–7pm, Sat 7am–1pm), flies from Bucharest to Timişoara daily. You can skip Bucharest entirely by flying straight to Timişoara from London with a number of airlines, including Tarom, Malev, Austrian, Lufthansa, Alitalia, and low-cost carrier easyJet. There are also flights from other European cities, so it's worth investigating before booking yourself directly to the capital. Situated 13km (8 miles) from the city center, the **airport,** on Calea Lugojului (© **0256/49-1637**), has a free shuttle service into town for Tarom passengers; taxis and public buses are also available. **Avis** rents cars at the airport (© **0256/20-3234**) or in town (© **0256/30-9425**).

Trains from practically anywhere in Romania and a number of European cities pull in at **Gară Timişoara-Nord,** Str. Gării 2 (© **0256/49-1696**). Onward tickets can be purchased at the **CFR Agenţie de Voiaj,** Piaţa Vitoriei 2 (© **0256/49-1889**), on weekdays, but be warned that there is almost always a queue with lengthy waits.

For assistance with maps or queries about sights and accommodations, visit Timişoara's **tourist information center,** Str. Alba Iulia 2 (© **0256/43-7973**); this is also a good place to arrange excursions to outlying areas.

Where to Stay

La Residenza ★★★ Value This is one of the best hotels in Romania (and the country's only member of Small Elegant Hotels of the World); the preferred destination for business bigwigs and visiting celebs. Behind the shuttered walls is a family of hoteliers with a discreet sense of luxury; you're made to feel as though you are in your very own intimate and stylish home, with plenty of added comforts. Accommodations are elegant, combining distinctive old-world styling with Italian mattresses, Spanish drapes, and Belgian carpets; select antiques and lovely decorative elements work to create a remarkably unaffected sense of luxury. Standard (comfort) rooms are quite spacious, but for an extra 93L ($40/£25) you can book a massive suite; if you're up for a splurge the Garden Suite is tops. Public spaces are like an old country mansion; along with the fine furniture and artworks, the "living room" has a small library, plasma TV, chess set, fireplace, and piano. The garden, centered on a pool with its own pavilion, features apricot, fig, and quince trees that provide fruit for the homemade jams served at breakfast. The charming German owners (very much a family affair) are a great source on the city's best places to dine or shop.

Str. Independenţei 14, Timişoara. ✆ **0256/40-1080.** Fax 0256/40-1079. www.laresidenza.ro. 17 units. L450 ($194/£120) double; L550–L640 ($237–$275/£147–£171) suite. Rates include breakfast and taxes. MC, V. **Amenities:** Restaurant; bar; lounge; swimming pool; sauna; car rental; beauty treatments; room service; massage; laundry; library. *In room:* A/C, TV, Internet, minibar, hair dryer, safe.

Reghina Blue ★ This is a pretty reasonable four-floor hotel, with contemporary, modernist styling (though not that much cheaper than the entry level rooms at the vastly superior La Residenza). Guest rooms are functional, comfortable, and continue the modernist theme—plenty of straight, clean lines, offset by soft fabrics and the odd floral arrangement; they're carpeted with small balconies. Best of all, near the koi pond and Japanese garden (replete with white rabbits and turtles) is a gorgeous pool surrounded by a luxurious wooden deck. Staff can help with sightseeing.

Str. Cozia 51–53, Timişoara. ✆ **0256/40-7299.** Fax 0256/40-7298. www.reghina-blue.ro. 50 units. L320 ($138/£86) double; L1,000 ($430/£267) penthouse apt. Rates include breakfast. AE, MC, V. **Amenities:** Restaurant; bar; swimming pool; fitness center; sauna; business center; Wi-Fi; airport transfers; limited room service; laundry. *In room:* A/C, TV, Internet, minibar, hair dryer, safe.

Savoy Hotel ★ Value Built in 1935, the Savoy underwent a complete renovation in recent years; the original Art Deco facade was retained while creating a contemporary, minimalist interior. Designers have imbued the property with a low-key, tasteful ambience, thoroughly modernized public spaces using huge walls of glass to let in loads of light and elegant, spacious guest rooms imbued with a similarly minimalist aesthetic. With a fresh, modern makeover, the Savoy is one of the best-value places in the city, with more than sufficient comfort and staff (decked out in 1930s-style uniforms) who try hard to please. There's good dining in chef Gabriel Cretu's intimate restaurant, and the hotel isn't too far from the center, either, so it's ideal if you want to discover a few culinary favorites of your own.

Spl. Tudor Vladimirescu 2, Timisoara 300193. ✆ **0256/24-9900.** Fax 0256/27-5500. www.hotelsavoy-tm.com. 55 units. 87€ ($110) double; 107€ ($136) studio; 192€ ($244) suite. MC, V. **Amenities:** Restaurant; bar; terrace; fitness center; sauna; Internet; conferencing; room service; laundry. *In room:* A/C, TV, Internet, minibar, safe.

Where to Dine

Timişoara has a wide range of excellent restaurants, many of which were established by members of the city's Italian expat community. Da Toni is our top choice, but for high-profile dining (and celebrity prices), head to **Ristorante Al Duomo ★**, Str. Paul Chinezu 2 (✆ **0256/43-7199**), near the opera; the Italian chef has not only worked his way into the hearts of local diners, but also onto national television. Also worth a mention is **Pozzo dei Desideri ★★**, Str. E. Gojdu 6 (✆ **0256/22-9170**), owned by affable restaurateur

 Dana, who cooks a melt-in-the-mouth lamb. But if you want to be right near the action, head for **Casa cu flori (House of Flowers)** ★, Str. Alba Iulia 1 (© **0256/43-5080;** www.casaculflori.ro), an elegant restaurant serving Romanian specialties on the first floor of a house on the road linking Piaţa Victoriei with Piaţa Liberatii; the small terrace downstairs is ideal for watching the constant ebb of human traffic between these two popular spaces.

Da Toni ★★★ ITALIAN If you want to know where the Italian ambassador and his wife get a taste of home, come to this wonderfully relaxed but always bustling Tuscan eatery. A magnetic Italian named Toni, whose robust charms keep this lively eatery packed to bursting, serves authentic pizza and pasta. Toni's son, Oliviero, sells the best ice cream in town, so you know what to do for dessert. You'll need to catch a taxi to get here, but it'll be worth it.

Str. Daliei 14. © **0256/49-0298.** Main courses L12–L34 ($5.15–$15/£3.20–£9.10). MC, V. Daily noon–midnight.

Exploring Timişoara

To the southern end of the center, the Bega Canal forms a natural boundary between the old and newer parts of the city, surrounded on both banks by expansive **Parcul Central (Central Park),** favored by amorous students from the University of West Timişoara. North of the center are the **Botanical Gardens,** and nearby, tucked behind remnants of the city's ancient bastion walls, is the city's subdued open-air **market,** selling fresh farm consumables; visit the stalls in the middle for excellent honey as well as traditional herbal medicines. Near the market is Strada Gheorghe Lazăr, for a selection of good fashion outlets. Also in the vicinity is the **Great Synagogue,** Str. Mărăşeşti 6, which, at press time, was scheduled to reopen after extensive renovation. The city's main areas of interest, however, are its squares and pedestrianized boulevards, surrounded on all sides by architecturally idiosyncratic buildings that form an elegant backdrop to the public lives on display. All day long, people gather for drinks and gossip energetically; it's an atmosphere of complete civil flamboyance in a city largely remembered as the site of some of the most brutal political martyrdoms in recent Romanian history.

Piaţa Victoriei—lorded over by the delightful **Metropolitan Orthodox Cathedral** (reviewed below) at its southern end—is where the first blows of the great December 1989 Revolution were struck; you can still see bullet holes in some of the buildings, bizarre given the exuberant atmosphere of the square's high-society life. At the southern end, in front of the Orthodox Cathedral, is the **Luna Capitolina,** a monument to the victims of the revolution. At the north end is the city's 18th-century **National Theater and Opera House (Teatrul Naţional şi Opera Română),** Str. Mărăşeşti 2 (© **0256/20-1284**), not much to look at, but a fine place for an evening of culture (see "Timişoara After Dark," below). From the Orthodox Cathedral, it's an almost straight route north through Piaţa Victoriei, past the opera house and then along Alba Iulia into **Piaţa Libertătii,** "Liberty Square," the small square that is the city's historical center. This is where, in the early 16th century, the leader of the peasant uprising then raging across Transylvania was executed in public view before his followers were forced to eat pieces of his burned flesh. Now the public view is of languid sessions on cafe terraces, in full view of the baroque **Old Town Hall** (1734), housing the university's music school. Following the road north past the town hall, you will soon arrive at Piaţa Unirii, a large square surrounded by monumental, colorful baroque buildings and centered on a **column** erected in memory of victims of plague which struck in the 1730s. While you'll have your work

Touring the Revolution

In December 1989, after 45 years of Communism, ordinary Romanians had tired of the oppression, poverty, and enforced slavery to a system that controlled all facets of life. Ceauşescu had effectively cut his country off from the outside world, supplying citizens with only what little propaganda he deemed appropriate. While official reports spoke of industrial might and technological progress, in reality ordinary people were starving and those who spoke out were quickly silenced. In western frontier cities like Timişoara, however, media reports seeping in from nearby Hungary probably contributed to a more cantankerous social atmosphere. As the country prepared to celebrate another morbid Christmas, the long-awaited cries for change suddenly became roaring protests.

Over a period of 10 days, beginning with urgent gatherings in Timişoara, protestors demonstrated their opposition to the regime, destroying its symbols and burning effigies of Ceauşescu, and chanting "Down with Ceauşescu! Down with Communism! We want liberty!" The revolution is believed to have been sparked by a gathering at the **Tökés Reform Church (Biserica Reformată Tökés),** Str. Timotei Cipariu 1 (✆ **0256/49-2992**), south of the Bega Canal; here, on December 15, thousands of protestors rallied together to oppose the Securitate's planned eviction of Pastor Lászlo Tökés, a known opponent of the Ceauşescu regime.

In what many believe was a calculated opportunity, the small uprising quickly escalated, gaining momentum as it heaved toward **Piaţa Victoriei (Victory Square).** For 3 days, the rally continued, culminating in Ceauşescu's order to open fire. Look carefully for evidence of the event; you'll find bullet holes and plaques around the long, broad square now surrounded by relaxed cafes and boutiques. At one end of the square, across a busy road, the **Orthodox Cathedral** is where many young protestors lost their lives.

Near Piaţa Unirii is the **Museum of the December 1989 Uprising,** Str. Emanuil Ungureanu 8 (daily 8am–4pm; donations expected), which charts the events of the revolution through detailed exhibits, including photographs, paintings, and a 30-minute video, and dutifully looked after by Dr. Traian Orban, himself a survivor who was shot during the uprising. The museum is also where you can pick up a map indicating 12 significant points around the city that form a walking open-air museum, so you can literally tour the revolution.

cut out for you choosing which cafe or lounge-style terrace bar to arrange yourself at, it's worth first taking in some of the more noteworthy monuments, particularly the pale yellow **Serbian Orthodox Church** and—on the other side of the square—the **Roman Catholic Cathedral,** both built in the mid-1700s. At the southern edge of Piaţa Unirii, Strada Palanca leads east past the **Art Museum,** the **Dicasterial Palace,** and then finally to the **Banat Ethnographic Museum.**

Lounging by the River

A favorite venue for a late afternoon cocktail or early evening aperitif is **D'arc ★★**, which occupies a tranquil spot below the Podul Episcopiei bridge. To reach it, follow Boulevard Ferdinand I along the edge of the leafy park behind the Orthodox Cathedral; instead of crossing the bridge, go down the stairs (if you get lost, call ✆ **0722-891-085**). You can mellow out on one of the wood-and-cloth director's chairs on the riverside terrace, or sit on the deck built over the river itself. Cocktails run the gamut from mai tais to the "Angel's Tit," and there are superb alcoholic coffees, too. Café Brulot is made with cognac, Cointreau, and cream—perfect after dining out. Tunes are upbeat—lounge, ambient, and smooth electronic tracks—and there's a lively nighttime crowd. Incidentally, if you're up for something more rigorous, riverside D'arc is actually an extension of a popular club on Piaţa Unirii; go there if you're up for a bit of fun with a local crowd.

Metropolitan Orthodox Cathedral ★★ One of Romania's loveliest cathedrals, the 83m (272-ft.) towering Catedrala Mitropolitana Ortodoxa adds color to the skyline at the southern end of Piaţa Victoriei; combining neo-Byzantine and Moldavian architectural elements, its brick walls are an ornate patchwork of ocher and yellow bands, while the colored mosaic-style shingles on the turreted spires create dynamic geometric patterns. It's a young church (built 1936–46), but the atmosphere generated by its strong associations with the 1989 Revolution complements the somber spirituality of the interior, dominated by three gigantic chandeliers that float above the regular stream of worshippers. Since 1956, the cathedral has held the relics of St. Joseph the New (in a box to the right of the entrance). Joseph, the patron saint of the Banat, was born in Dalmatia in 1568 and became Metropolitan of Timişoara in 1658; he apparently had the gift of prophesy and could perform miracles, bringing on the rains which quelled a great fire that once threatened the city. In the basement, there's a **museum** (with irregular hours), exhibiting religious icons, some 500 years old.

B-dul 16 Decembrie 1989 and B-dul Regele Ferdinand I. No phone. Free admission. Dawn until late.

Timişoara After Dark

For event listings, pick up a free issue of ***24-Fun Timişoara,*** in Romanian with fragments of English, but which gives a fairly good idea of what's on and where.

Timişoara enjoys strong cultural associations and is proud of having independent German, Hungarian, and Romanian theaters; first up on the list of highlights is an opera or drama at the **National Theater and Opera House,** Str. Mărăşeşti 2 (✆ **0256/20-1284**). For an evening of classical music, head to the other end of Piaţa Victoriei to find the **State Philharmonic Theater (Filharmonia de Stat Banatul),** B-dul C.D. Loga 2 (✆ **0256/49-2521**), to the left of the cathedral. Tickets for both venues are available at **Agenţia Teatrală,** Strada Maraşe şti (✆ **0256/49-9908;** Tues–Sun 10am–1pm and 5–7pm), just around the corner from the opera house entrance. For jazz, the best place is **Jazz Club Pod 16 ★★**, Pod Piaţa Maria (✆ **0729-945-397;** www.jazzclubpod16.ro), which has something to look forward to every night of the week; look out especially for an outfit named Ţapinarii.

Komodo ★★, Str. Gheorghe Lazăr (✆ **0722-279-177;** daily 9am–late) is the city's best lounge bar, slickly designed for a chic crowd; there's a dance floor downstairs and the music varies from retro to house, but the atmosphere in the cocktail lounge is decidedly "Buddha Bar." To get your spirits up, order a Velvet Hammer or Playa Azul; caipirinhas and caipiroskas are the best in the Banat. Komodo occupies an unmarked building; look out for the round streetlights out front.

7 MARAMUREŞ

The northern county of Maramureş (pronounced mah-rah-*moo*-resh), situated on the Ukraine border, is widely regarded as a kind of living museum; lifestyles and culture have changed little in well over a century. Village life is surreal, defined by working horses, carts laden with hay, elaborately carved wooden gates, and people in traditional costumes. Aside from an otherworldly way of life, the most celebrated of the attractions here are the famous Maramureş wooden churches, a number of which are inscribed on UNESCO's World Heritage List. And as if wood-hewn churches in time-forgotten villages were not enough, Maramureş is also blessed with an idyllic setting, its backcountry roads providing surrender-to-the-moment journeys through valleys torn through majestic mountainscapes, the most famous perhaps being the Rodna Mountains, good for hiking and adventures far away from humanity.

Described here is a plan for exploration of the loveliest parts of Maramureş, discovering its traditional villages, a selection of churches, and two of the most idiosyncratic attractions in Romania, the Merry Cemetery of Săpânţa and the Prison Museum in Sighet. Enchanting as the region is, its bucolic rhythms won't be around forever, so prioritize a visit here soon.

ESSENTIALS

Tarom, B-dul Bucureşti 5 (✆ **0262/22-1624**), flies regularly from Bucharest to **Baia Mare,** the main city, and there are now also international connections via Vienna, thanks to **Austrian Airlines** (www.aua.com). The **airport** (✆ **0262/22-2245;** www.baiamare airport.ro) is 10km (6¼ miles) from the city at Tautii Magheraus village. There are also daily **train connections** from the capital and most other major centers, including Cluj, Oradea, Braşov, and Suceava; Baia Mare's **train station** is at Str. Gării 4 (✆ **0262/22-0995**). One train per day pulls in from Budapest. It's also possible to catch a train directly to **Sighetu Marmaţiei,** near the Ukraine border, although you're looking at a much longer journey. You can purchase onward tickets at the **CFR** office, Str. Victoriei 57 (✆ **0262/21-9113**).

For thorough assistance with the region, contact **MaramureşInfoTurism ★★**, Gheorghe Şincai 46, Baia Mare (✆ **0262/20-6113;** www.visitmaramures.ro); the small hardworking team can help you find your bearings and plan your stay.

Maramureş is best explored by car (or on bicycle), and you are better off having a driver who knows his way around; the region may be small, but it is certainly not signposted to make life easy for outsiders. If you need a taxi in Baia Mare, call **Stotax** (✆ **0262/953**) or **Gallant** (✆ **0262/942**).

All the villages are situated in two valleys in the eastern part of Maramureş, occupying a fairly compact region. These are the **Mara Valley** and the **Izei Valley,** both northeast of the district capital, **Baia Mare,** which is likely to be your point of arrival in Maramureş. Three days in the region, using a car and driver and staying at private homes in the villages (avoid the larger towns, which have little to recommend them aside from their small historic centers) will give you ample time. Arrange to be met at the airport or station by your driver, and head immediately for the Mara Valley and beyond (perhaps stopping briefly at Baia Mare's colorful outdoor market to pick up some fresh fruit, and perhaps a cheese that you can give to your host as a gift).

ORGANIZING YOUR MARAMUREŞ EXPERIENCE

For complete peace of mind, contact **DiscoveRomania** ★★★ (see "Tours & Travel Agents" at the beginning of this chapter). Laura Vesa will tailor-make a Maramureş holiday for you, arranging transport (about 50€/$64 per day) and accommodations (25€–30€/$32–$38 per person per day, half board) and incorporating fabulous experiences along the way. You can arrange everything via e-mail, and know that there's nothing to worry about; she will also let you know about local festivals so that you can plan your trip accordingly. DiscoveRomania is dedicated to eco-sensible sustainable tourism, so accommodations are mostly in village homes (three of these are reviewed below); if you insist on being in a city hotel, ask for one of the options in Baia Mare or Sighet that are suggested below. Iron out the details of your itinerary with Laura well in advance since your hosts may not speak English; this won't be a problem if you've arranged for a guide to accompany you, but if you're doing without a guide, it's best that your hosts understand all your needs while you're there.

If you leave your planning until your arrival in Maramureş, head for the **Mara Holiday Travel Agency** inside Baia Mare's Mara Hotel, B-dul Unirii 11 (✆ **062/22-6656**); on fairly short notice, they'll put together an itinerary and set you up with transport.

WHERE TO STAY & DINE

Village Stays

Homestays are a fine way of discovering the region and its people, and locals have discovered that they are an excellent way to supplement their incomes—in some villages, it seems as though every second house is open for business, offering beds and home-cooked meals; usually all rates include breakfast and dinner. Don't expect great luxury—these aren't hotels by any stretch of the imagination, but rather an opportunity to temporarily stay in a unique environment that in many ways hasn't changed in over a century. What has changed, of course, is the appearance of modern bathrooms, electricity, and many of the comforts that most urbanites take for granted. Granted, the back-to-basics experience isn't to everyone's taste, so if you're feeling less than adventurous, you may want to stick to the more modern rooms at Casa Popicu (below). Remember that the quality of accommodations may differ from home to home (a firmer mattress here, a larger shower room there), but ultimately, it is dealings with your convivial hosts that translate into memories. Besides the options described below, navigate to **www.visitmaramures.ro**, where you'll find details of many more agreeable options.

Casa Popicu ★★ The pace of life in Hoteni village is as relaxed and charmed as the couple who own this homestead; Ion Pop, nicknamed "Popicu" by his enchanting wife, Geţa, is one of Romania's most sought-after folk musicians, and is acknowledged internationally for his contribution to the preservation of traditional music. Popicu and Geţa have two wooden houses (including their original 150-year-old home) and a modern cottage each with guest accommodations; here, at the foot of the Gutai Mountains, they farm with bees, fish, and chickens, and share their garden with three lawn-mowing sheep and an obedient shepherd dog. Lodging options range from en suite rooms in the modern cottage, to rooms with shared bathrooms, and two-bedroom suites with private facilities. Most of the rooms enjoy a view over the surrounding farm landscape; some have private balconies. Geţa prepares hearty meals, served in the traditional dining room of the main house.

Hoteni Village 37A, Mara Valley. ✆ **0722-979-048** or 0262/37-4546. Reservations through DiscoveRomania (see "Tours & Travel Agents" at the beginning of this chapter). 11 units. 25€ ($32) per person per night. No credit cards. **Amenities:** Kitchen; dining room; living room w/TV and stereo.

Pensiunea Bebecaru (The Priest's House, Botiza) ★ Although it's known as the "Priest's House," these accommodations are firmly under the management of the priest's delightful wife, Victoria Bebecaru. The couple may not speak a word of English (Victoria does speak French), but they are warm and welcoming, and it's a bizarre honor to spend time with the village's spiritual leader (a man who incidentally also makes a potent plum *tuica,* which you'll sample at mealtimes). There are three upstairs rooms available in the priest's private home, a brick house stuffed full of books, handicrafts, animal skins, and family photos, but you'll probably want to opt for a room in their nearby guesthouse, fashioned out of wood in traditional Maramureş style. There are four twin-bedded rooms sharing three bathrooms. Accommodations are on the first floor, reached via a spiral staircase, while downstairs are themed artisan studios where Victoria works on her woolen handicrafts. You'll have just about everything you need for a relaxed escape from modernity, although you should first find out if the extensive flood-damage reparation work on the village has been completed—until then Botiza is a bit of a building site.

Botiza 743. ✆ **0262/33-4207** or 0262/33-4107. Reservations through DiscoveRomania (see "Tours & Travel Agents" at the beginning of this chapter). 6 units. 25€ ($32) per person per night. No credit cards. **Amenities:** TV; fishing; horseback riding.

Pensiunea Ileana Teleptean ★ Vadu Izei is practically on the southern edge of Sighet; development here has benefited tremendously from Belgian and French economic support, and you're likely to witness a blurring of traditional and contemporary lifestyles. Arguably the best guesthouse here is Casa Teleptean, owned and run by vivacious Illeana, who doesn't speak English, but is permanently beaming and busy. You'll recognize the house by its superb carved gateway and the collection of red pots that decorate the tree next to it. Topped by a beautifully carved roof, the three-story house offers neatly appointed, simple guest rooms with wooden floors, rugs, and beds covered with clean, patterned linens. Most of these have one bathroom between two rooms. On the second floor there are two carpeted rooms with en suite bathrooms (showers only); these also share a terrace with wonderful views. Also on the property is a traditional "honeymoon" apartment, filled with woolen blankets and tapestries. There's also a garden terrace area where Ileana serves excellent home-cooked meals; her children (who speak some English) are part of a traditional music group who often put on entertainment for guests. While here, visit the local **museum,** which is also the oldest house in the village, built in 1750. Another good option in Vadu Izei is the well-run **Traditional House Borlean** ★, Str. Zăvoi 689 (✆ **0262-33-0228;** www.vaduizei.ro), with three different traditional wooden houses set in a beautiful garden. The owner, Ioan Borlean, is famous for his paintings of religious icons on glass, and he can introduce you to several other artists working in the village.

Vadu Izei 506. ✆ **0262/33-0474** or 0742-492-240. Reservations through DiscoveRomania (see "Tours & Travel Agents" at the beginning of this chapter). 9 units. 25€ ($32) per person per night. No credit cards. **Amenities:** Dining area; traditional entertainment. *In room:* TV.

Pensiune Turlaş ★ Right on the main road that sweeps through the village of Săliştea de Sus, guests will discover a pretty, peaceable homestead steeped in flowers and various quaint ornamental details, many of them handcrafted in Maramureş. Magnificent views stretch out from what is essentially the back yard—a small garden between the medley of traditional houses that make up this family enterprise. Rooms are a mixed bag, with or without private showers, but each one a cozy reminder of just how the people of Maramureş have for so long kept things simple; plenty of pine, mountains of cushions, and piles of blankets to keep you warm. Traditional meals are prepared, and you can set your own times for breakfast and dinner (included). There's a swing chair in the garden as well as an inventive outdoor shower.

Sălıştea de Sus 195. ✆ **0262/33-8301** or 0740-008-373. www.agrotur.ro/turlas. 6 units. 25€ ($32) per person per night. No credit cards. **Amenities:** Dining room.

In Sighetu Marmaţiei

Casa Iurca de Câlineşti ★★ This gorgeous *pensiune,* next door to the Elie Wiesel Museum, is owned and operated by a noble family whose members trace their lineage from 1374; they've combined traditional elements such as carved doorways and craftwork furniture with modern comforts to create the best accommodations in Sighet. Neatly appointed twin-bedded guest rooms (there are no double beds) feature wooden floors and attractive country-style wooden furniture; they also have large bathrooms with showers. Room no. 5 has a small porch overlooking the wood-beam courtyard where costumed waiters serve local cuisine. There's also a themed indoor restaurant with a quaint fireplace and decorative touches, like exposed brick, clay jugs, and traditional cloth hangings, to create a village-dining-room atmosphere; this is easily the best place to dine anywhere in the region. The only drawback can be the noise generated by early morning traffic along the road out front, so you may wish to ask the titled owners about their swanky country house, where you can also arrange to stay.

Str. Dragoş Vodă, Sighetu Marmaţiei. ✆ **0262/31-8882.** Fax 0262/31-8885. www.casaiurca.ro. 5 units. 40€ ($51) double; 70€ ($90) apt. MC, V. **Amenities:** Restaurant; bar; laundry; traditional performances. *In room:* A/C, TV, Internet, minibar, hair dryer.

In Baia Mare

If you must stay in Baia Mare because of an early or late departure or arrival, there's a clutch of relatively decent hotels. Renovated to a relatively pleasing standard, **Hotel Rivulus,** Str. Culturii 3 (✆ **0262/21-6302;** www.hotelrivulus.ro; 64€/$81 double with breakfast), is right in the center of town. It's a slightly stiff business hotel with a no-nonsense atmosphere; nevertheless, the refurbished rooms are smart and comfortable, and have small private balconies. There's a decent restaurant and a popular terrace-cafe.

There's a variety of popular cafes and bars around the cobblestone town center, **Piaţa Libertăţii**—you could do a lot worse than **Corvin Medieval Restaurant** ★, worth a visit for the refreshingly naive-kitsch design (the whole place is decked out in faux-medieval memorabilia in a series of brick-vaulted rooms, with mannequins dressed in period costume; even the waitresses are styled as serving wenches) as well as the good Hungarian food. You'll sit on stiff Knights of the Round Table chairs and drink from large wine goblets as a bib is tied around your neck in true medieval feast style. After, shimmy on over to the **Barbarossa;** marked by two pirate statues at the entrance, this is possibly the most popular bar in town, with a hip, sexy crowd filling its outdoor tables.

WHAT TO SEE & DO

Baia Mare & the Mara Valley

Tracing its history from the early 1300s, when it grew as a gold-mining center and became a prized possession of the Hungarian royal family, Baia Mare (which means "Big Mine") is today better known for a range of 20th-century industrial-chemical disasters. Most recently, in January 2000, the Maramureş district capital was the site of the devastating Aurul Gold Mine cyanine-spill disaster, from which the greater European region is yet to recover. Baia Mare has for a long time had little to recommend it; there is a revolution afoot, however, and the town appears to be preparing for a revival. Keenest evidence of this is in and around its large cobblestone town center, **Piaţa Libertăţii,** which is now a perfectly pleasant place from which to admire the surrounding medieval and classical architecture, some of which dates from the 14th and 15th centuries.

That said, it's only once you've left Baia Mare, and passed through the dying mining town of Baia Sprie, that you'll lose your heart to Maramureş. Named for the Mara River, which runs from Baia Mare to Sighetu Marmaţiei, the **Mara Valley** is dotted with villages that epitomize the tranquil spirit of Maramureş, and where you'll discover many of the unique wooden churches that have brought architectural renown to the region. From Baia Sprie, the road forks; head south to reach the villages of **Plopiş** and **Şurdeşti,** both with UNESCO-protected wooden churches. From Şurdeşti, the road continues north through Cavnic and over the **Neteda Pass,** affording terrific mountainous views from 1,040m (3,411 ft.). The next village, also with a famous church, is **Budeşti.** From here, one of two northerly roads leads to **Ocna Şugatag,** a tiny former spa village, where salt was mined until 50 years ago. Most appealing of the villages in the vicinity is **Hoteni,** a total escape from the world and a perfectly positioned base from which to explore other parts of the Mara Valley. Be sure to visit Hoteni's wooden church and the nearby church at **Deseşti.** It's also worth making the effort to visit the hillside church in the village of **Călineşti.**

Festival Fever

Maramureş villagers are known for their traditional weekly neighborhood parties, known as *băută.* Of course, in the age of television, the party spirit is harder to sustain, but some traditional village festivals continue to hold out. In early May, Hoteni Village hosts the 2-week **Tânjaua de pe Mara** fertility festival to celebrate the completion of the spring plowing; folk music and dancing mark the occasion. In mid-July, Vadu Izea hosts the spectacular **Maramizical Festival,** a 4-day celebration of international folk music. In winter, it's Sighet that comes to life when the **Winter Customs Festival** hits town on December 27. The day is imbued with folkloric symbolism and good old-fashioned fun, and everyone dresses in traditional costumes and young men run through the streets wearing grotesque masks while cowbells dangle from their waists. For the when and where of Maramureş festivals, contact DiscoveRomania (see "Organizing Your Maramureş Experience," earlier in this chapter).

The Wooden Churches of Maramureş: A Field Guide

Traditional timber architecture defines the unique churches of Maramureş; built on a pebble-filled stone block base, they are a peculiar evolution of the Gothic style, based on the *Blockbau* system, using traditional techniques developed over generations by the stone- and woodcutters of the region. Oak or pine beams are assembled using V-, U-, or T-shaped joints, allowing solid but flexible constructions, with a high, steep double-pitched roof. That's the technical detail, anyway. In truth, their beauty lies in the organic textures of their darkly weathered wood, which have an almost liquid appearance, a shock of finely crafted dark chocolate assuming the shape of a church amid overgrown cemeteries.

These churches are particularly loved for their soaring bell towers, one of which has long been recognized as the tallest wooden structure in Europe. The churches were built to replace earlier constructions destroyed in 1717 during the Tartar invasions; barred from building permanent churches, their architects decided on the wooden solutions seen today. They may not be ancient, but their survival over the last few centuries does make them special, since they are without any real fortification. Briefly described here are a handful of the 93 wooden churches in Maramureş, each listed under the village in which it is found. All of these churches can be visited as excursions from accommodations recommended in either the Mara or Izei valleys. You'll more than likely find the churches locked; even if you are visiting without a guide, it should be quite easy to track down the key. Don't be afraid to approach one of the locals and then hint that you're looking for the key by saying *"chiea?"* (kay-yah) while indicating the church. You'll almost certainly receive a positive response.

Although nobody will say anything, it's only reasonable to leave a small donation at each church you visit. Try to see at least two of the churches in the following villages, but bear in mind that once you've visited two or three—unless you're a particularly big fan of church architecture—you'll have reached saturation point. Each village is also worth a look in its own right, so don't miss the chance to seek out the local watering holes and exchange a few words (or smiles) with people you might meet.

1. Smaller than most, the church at **Bârsana** (Izei Valley, 19km/12 miles from Sighet) was built in 1720 and was transferred to the present hilltop site in 1806, when a two-level portico was constructed and the painter Hodor Toader added the original interior frescoes; you'll notice the distinctive baroque and rococo influences on his work. Just outside the village are the salubrious grounds of the **Bârsana Monastery,** easily mistaken for Maramureş's very own Orthodox Disneyland. If you're curious, take a few minutes to wander around the manicured gardens and take a peek at the 16th-century church; most of the other monastic buildings were constructed after the fall of Communism.
2. The village of **Budeşti** (Mara Valley) is delightful; children charge around on bicycles, while grown-ups in traditional attire make conversation in the streets. Track down the local priest who has the key to the Church of St.

Nicholas and ask him to show you the frescoed interior. This is one of the most celebrated examples of the Maramureş style, built of oak in 1643; it is considered large—18m (59 ft.) long and 8m (26 ft.) wide. The earliest paintings date from 1762 by an artist named Alexandru Ponehalski, whose style you may recognize from one or two of the other churches.

3. While the church in **Călineşti** (Mara Valley) is not part of the World Heritage List consignment, and it's fairly well off the beaten track, it's well known to—and loved by—locals. The 14th-century church was apparently relocated to this site in 1665 because of a legend involving a girl named Călina; whenever she passed this spot her candle would start burning spontaneously—evidence that this is a place of miracles. Getting to the church involves a fairly stiff walk, possibly escorted by one of the ancient villagers. Once you're admitted to the church and the wooden shutters are opened, look out for the "Road to Heaven" fresco, represented by a ladder on which souls descend in order to be reunited with their bodies before the final judgment. Also look above the iconostasis for the slightly personified images of the sun and moon watching over Christ on the cross; the frescoes are the work of muralist Alexandru Ponehalski executed almost a decade before the frescoes you may have seen at Budeşti.
4. In **Deseşti** (Mara Valley), decorative motifs are cut into the wood of the exterior of the Church of the Holy Paraskeva, somehow transforming the entire construction into a sculptural artwork. The interior walls and curved ceiling are covered in frescoes executed in 1780 by the celebrated artist Radu Munteanu, then considered a leader in religious painting. For a better view at the paintings, climb the stairs to the balcony from where you can study the particularly splendid crucifixion scene at the front of the church. Built in 1770, the church—like most of the wooden churches—is now surrounded by tombstones in an overgrown graveyard.
5. Atop a hill in **Ieud Deal** (Izei Valley), the Church of the Nativity of the Virgin contains what are believed to be the best frescoes in all of Maramureş. Again, the artist is Alexandru Ponehalski, his technique having reached its apotheosis in 1782 when he embellished these walls with their rich iconography. Uniquely, this church is complemented by a free-standing bell tower.
6. Constructed in 1604, the church in **Poienile Izei** (Izei Valley) is one of the oldest. It's a firm favorite thanks to its late-18th-century interior frescoes, alive with fantastic cautionary images of bizarre, cruel tortures being carried out in hell. Look to the wall immediately on your left as you enter: Amongst other now-comical scenarios, you'll see a woman being punished for abortion (she has to eat her own offspring), and a man being tortured for falling asleep during a sermon.
7. Built at the pinnacle of the Maramureş architectural evolution (in 1767), the Church of the Holy Archangels in **Şurdeşti** (between Cavnic and Plopiş) is a must-see because of its exemplary synthesis of all the elements associated with the wooden churches; the interior was decorated by a team of three skilled painters. To get here, you need to cross the dramatic Neteda Pass (which reaches 1,040m/3,411 ft.) south of Budeşti, passing through the town of Cavnic along the way.

Sighetu Marmaţiei & Săpânţa

Sighet: 67km (42 miles) N of Baia Mare. Săpânţa: 12km (7½ miles) NW of Sighet

Close to the Ukraine border, Sighetu Marmaţiei (usually referred to as Sighet) is a relatively quiet market town, and the cultural center of Maramureş. Sighet is also home to one of the world's finest anti-Communism museums (reviewed below), also referred to as the Prison Museum; if you see only one thing here, make this it. Parts of the midtown **Ethnographic Museum,** Piaţa Libertăţii 15, pertain to the local way of life in a vaguely informative manner; included is a cornucopia of traditional costumes, exhibited alongside scarecrowlike effigies (one of which even has an erect corn cob phallus). Sighet is also remembered as the birthplace of Elie Wiesel, the Jewish writer who coined the termed "Holocaust" and won the 1986 Nobel Peace Prize. Wiesel himself now lives in Boston, but the house where he lived before the war has been converted into a museum, **Casa Elie Wiesel,** at the corner of Str. Dragoş Vodă and Str. Tudor Vladimirescu. Only one of the town's eight original synagogues still exists, serving the tiny Jewish population of 30; it's at Str. Bessarabia 10. For more information about the synagogue and other aspects of Maramureş's Jewish history, visit the adjacent **Jewish Community Center (✆ 0262/31-1652;** Tues–Sun 10am–4pm). Just outside of town, Sighet's **Village Museum** is another of Romania's many open-air exhibitions curating compendium-size collections of traditional homesteads; you'll get far more pleasure out of experiencing the villages firsthand.

Sighet is also very convenient for the nearby village of Săpânţa, where one of the country's most imaginative and unlikely attractions—a colorful cemetery (reviewed below)—is located.

Memorial Museum of the Victims of Communism and the Resistance ★★★ One of the most evocative museums in Romania, Sighet's Memorial Museum was built as a prison in 1897; in 1948 it became a political prison and remained as such until 1955. During that time, around 200 political prisoners—former leaders, academics, Catholic priests and bishops, and other enemies of the state—were detained, tortured, and kept hidden from public view; a quarter of these men died during their imprisonment. In 1997, the prison became a museum—alongside similar projects at Auschwitz and Normandy—dedicated to the memory of those who became victims of an authoritarian political regime. The 80 or so cells serve as exhibition rooms, each one shedding light on a different aspect of the tyrannies of Romania's 20th-century history, with particular focus on the atrocities of Ceauşescu as well as the abuses wrought on individuals and groups during the transition to Communism in the wake of World War II. Among the stirring exhibits is a corridor wall lined with 3,000 photographs of Romanian political prisoners. You'll see the tiny cell where 80-year-old former Prime Minister Iuliu Maniu died in 1953. Less important prisoners shared larger cells with up to 80 inmates. The so-called Black Cell was used for punishing inmates, who were often forced to stand chained and naked for "offenses" such as talking or looking at one another. The courtyard, one of two spaces where prisoners were allowed outside for 10 minutes per week, now houses a memorial chamber inscribed with the names of thousands of victims of Communism.

Str. Cornelieu Corposcu 4, Sighet. ✆ **0262/31-9424.** www.memorialsighet.ro. L5 ($2.15/£1.35) adults; L2.50 ($1.10/70p) students. Apr 15–Oct 15 daily 9:30am–6:30pm; Oct 16–Apr 14 Tues–Sun 10am–4pm. Last entry 30 min. before closing.

Săpânţa's Merry Cemetery ★★★ Apparently, the genealogical line from the ancient Dacians and the people of Maramureş is purer than elsewhere in Romania, as is evidenced in their cultural attitude toward death. The Dacians were often praised for their fearlessness in battle, which was linked to their belief in their supreme god, Zalmoxis, and in the afterlife. In contemporary Maramureş, villagers still don't see death as a tragedy; this pragmatic understanding of the relationship between life and the hereafter is exemplified in the unusual artistry practiced at Săpânţa's **Cimitirul Vesel,** or "Cheerful Cemetery," a zany collection of over 800 carved and colorfully painted wooden headstones surrounding the village church (built in 1886). The idea of marking the graves with anecdotal images and amusing epitaphs was that of Stan Ioan Pâtras, who died in 1977 and now occupying his own blue-marked grave facing the church entrance. Pătraş dedicated himself to creating grave markings that truly served the purpose of remembering those who lie buried here; the dedications either encapsulate the spirit of the life or describe the moment of death of the individual buried beneath it. Some simply describe the occupation of the buried person, while others come across as damning messages from beyond the grave; the poem on the tombstone of a baby girl reads: "Burn in hell, you damn taxi that came from Sibiu. As large as Romania is, you couldn't find another place to stop. Only in front of my house, to kill me." Pătraş's legacy continues today through Dumitru Pop who has been responsible for the headstones for 3 decades now; Pop runs a small **museum** dedicated to Pătraş, not far from the cemetery, where he will also demonstrate how the headstones are created.

Cimitirul Vesel, Săpânţa, 12km (7½ miles) northwest of Sighet. ✆ **0262/37-2127.** Cemetery and museum admission each L4 ($1.70/£1.05). Daily sunrise–sunset.

Izei Valley

Gorgeous Valea Izei is a hypnotically bucolic world between Sighet and the village of Moisei, farther east. Starting with **Vadu Izei,** 5km (3 miles) southeast of Sighet, an exploration of this lovely valley will transport you back in time where horse carts outnumber cars, traditional dress is more pervasive than modern attire, and the roads are lined with beautiful houses with thatched roofs and fantastic carved wooden gates, filled with elegant folkloric details. Practically every village also has its own exquisite wooden church worthy of exploration (although hunting down the key is often an adventure on its own). Beyond Vadu Izei are the villages of Onceşti and then **Bârsana,** site of a popular monastery and fabulous wooden church (see below). Farther south and east, the valley road passes through Roza Vlea and then splits; head southwest to the sprawling village of **Botiza,** where you can stay in the home of the local priest (see above), and hike (or drive) to the church of Poienile Izei, painted with horrific images of damnation and punishment. Back along the main road, it's a short journey to Ieud, known for the famous **Church on the Hill,** originally established in 1364, but rebuilt in the mid–18th century after destruction at the hands of the Tartars. Ieud's other, "lower" church is also worth a visit.

Each village usually has a dedicated market day, when everyone heads for the center to buy necessities and exchange gossip. You'll probably also encounter villagers practicing traditional crafts; here the age-old pastime of sitting on a bench in front of the house watching the world go by while spinning wool or simply waiting for the daily gossip is still in evidence. Of course, things are changing; satellite dishes signal a time when simple entertainments are being replaced by the tedium of television, and younger generations who set off to earn their fortunes in other parts of Europe are returning to build ugly concrete houses that will, if unchecked, blight this idyllic world forever.

Moments **Pottery from an Ancient Recipe**

The tiny village of Săcel in the southeast of the Izei Valley shelters one of the world's most unique teams of ceramicists. Working out of the same workshop that has been in his family for generations, **Tănase Burnar,** Str. Valea Bistriţei 297A, Săcel (© **0262/33-9438**), his wife, and two young sons make gorgeously simple red clay bowls, pots, and jugs using the same techniques that were developed in this region by the ancient Dacians. With clay dug out of the ground (from down to 17m/56 ft. beneath the surface) and then hand-cured, each piece is turned on a foot-powered wheel and, after drying, painted with the same ancient, organic zig-zag design—the special paint is also homemade from crushed stones. Later, each piece is polished by hand using smooth river stones and fired in a Roman-style kiln.

Remarkably, these traditional artisans use the same kiln—made of river rocks and built right into the ground beneath their house—that has served their ancestors for at least 500 years. Seeing the family in action is likely to be a highlight of your trip; these people keep the art alive purely for the love of it (although you can, of course, buy here, too). The best way to arrange a visit to the workshop is to call Tănase's son, who speaks lovely English, and will also talk you through the intriguing production process (© **0747-900-352**). Alternatively, contact MaramureşInfoTurism (© **0262/20-6113**) and ask for assistance visiting to the workshop.

8 MOLDAVIA & THE PAINTED CHURCHES OF BUCOVINA

Suceava: 439km (272 miles) NE of Bucharest and 150km (93 miles) NW of Iaşi

Achieving independence in the 14th century, Moldavia reached its apogee during the anti-Ottoman crusades with great defensive battles fought and won by Stephen the Great (who ruled 1457–1504) and his successor, Petrus Rareş. Military success ensured a cultural renaissance, evidenced in Moldavia's beautiful painted monasteries that have earned great artistic acclaim, and attract visitors from around the world. The most precious of these churches are all within a 60km (37-mile) radius of the city of Suceava; once the princely seat of the Moldavian rulers, but thoroughly ruined during Ceauşescu's reign, this is still a useful base from which to explore the churches. Mostly situated in remote rural villages in lush landscapes, the churches of these monastic complexes have almost all been painted—inside and out—with such brilliant and vivid frescoes that they have been accorded UNESCO World Heritage status and are amongst the world's great artistic treasures.

ESSENTIALS

Tarom has several flights per week from Bucharest to Suceava, but you might want to consider flying to Iaşi, the nearest city with daily connections to the capital, and then take a train to Suceava. Suceava is just 2 hours from Iaşi.

To rent a car, contact **Autonom Rent-a-Car** (www.autonom.ro) in Suceava at Str. Nicolae Bălcescu 2 (✆ **0230/52-1101**) or in Iaşi at Str. Ştefan cel Mare 8–12 (✆ **0232/22-0504**); you'll pay around 30€ ($38) per day for a cheap model with unlimited mileage.

WHERE TO STAY & DINE

Once an important Moldavian city, Suceava is one of those more severely impacted by Ceauşescu's industrialization program, its river poisoned by factory waste and its air polluted by unsavory gases, yet it remains an important tourism hub for excursions to the elegant painted monasteries in the surrounding countryside. Alternatively, you could base yourself in nearby Gura Humorului, a small town well geared for travelers, with privately run *pensiunes* by the bucket load. Better still, there are even more down-home places to stay in the immediate vicinity of some of the monasteries; these afford the best opportunity to sample the traditional Bucovine way of life.

In Suceava

If circumstance compels you to overnight in Suceava, there are more than a handful of hotels, none of them particularly alluring. Generally considered the best hotel in town, **Hotel Balada,** Str. Mitrolopiliei 3 (✆ **0230/52-2146** or 0230/52-0408; fax 0230/52-0087; www.balada.ro; L255/$110/£68 double), has clean, tidy rooms that, while not especially attractive, are functional in an old-fashioned sort of way. Unless you're dead set on the anonymity of a hotel, however, you'll have a better experience at smaller, family-run **Villa Alice,** Str. Simion Florea Marian 1 (✆/fax **0230/52-2254;** www.villaalice.ro). With rooms at less than half the price (L100–L190/$43–$82/£27–£51), hospitality here is a notch above that in the city's larger hotels; most importantly, it offers private tours to the monasteries. Guest rooms are simple, exceptionally clean, and have private balconies; they're also relatively comfortable, despite the kitschy gold bedspreads (and, in some cases, lime-green walls). In summer, it's worth paying a bit extra for a so-called "luxury room," which includes air-conditioning (and free Internet).

If you are stuck in Suceava with time for a meal, look no further than **Latino** ★, Strada Curtea Domnească (✆ **0230/52-3627**), across the road from the Armenian Monastery. Young waiters with Latin looks, long red aprons, and a willingness to go through the entire menu with you make this place a delight. Start by sharing an Aperitiv Latino—a platter of cheeses, Parma ham, and Italian salami, served with fresh bread. There's fine selection of pastas and pizzas, but those with a real appetite should consider splashing out for one of the duck *(raţă)* dishes, especially good with wild mushrooms.

Gura Humorului & Environs

Best Western Bucovina Club de Munte ★ While lacking any real sophistication or class, this thoroughly Western franchisee provides a range of comforts and is the full-service hotel best positioned for exploring the painted churches. Capped by a wood-timbered roof meant to echo traditional Bucovine architectural elements, it enjoys a commanding position overlooking Gura Humorului's main square. From the mezzanine, with its lobby bar, pool table, and token village souvenir ornaments, tiny elevators rise through eight floors of accommodations. Guest rooms are carpeted and decorated in unusual color combinations (yellow and green, or lime and ocher) and dark-wood furniture (including four-poster beds); bathrooms have showers and are small. Ensure that you reserve a "deluxe room with mountain view," and check twice (before arriving) that you

Moments A Night in the House of Stags

Guesthouses in villages and rural regions are now a dime a dozen in the Bucovine heartland—it is here that you will live, sleep, and dine in the cultural milieu you've really come to Romania to discover, a way of life so unencumbered by modernity and globalization that it's unlikely your hosts will communicate in English. What they will do, instead, is provide you with unerring hospitality and surprisingly fine comfort, all packaged in a manner that might be light-years away from the contemporary urban experience, but has a style and rustic sophistication that is unique and will be memorable for the right reasons.

Around 6km (4 miles) from Suceviţa monastery, in the teensy village of Voievodeasa, you'll come upon a striking, beautifully green wooden farmhouse. Built a few years back in traditional style, it's called "The House with Stags"—or **Casa cu Cerbi★★★** (✆ **0745-333-402;** carpathica@yahoo.com)—and offers a memorable chance to discover a traditional way of life, whilst enjoying relatively great comfort. The guesthouse features some large bedrooms—all with attached bathrooms (modern, with showers)—with plenty of simple, hand-painted traditional furniture, including good beds with wonderfully firm mattresses and handcrafted linens. Rugs and traditional ornaments bring atmosphere to a space that is beautifully modest and otherwise quite minimalist (no TVs or other modern distractions, but plenty of color in an immaculate, exceptionally attractive space). Thoughtful decorative touches include antique photographs and memorabilia representing the last hundred years of Romanian history. Clues to a more traditional way of life are nowhere more evident than in the handsome kitchen-cum–dining room—a giant ceramic-covered furnace keeps the room warm in winter, and guests sit down to enjoy miniature feasts at beautifully laid tables.

At dinner there'll be wine, water, and *palinca* (strong homemade brandy), and you'll be served with a smile by a kind old lady who might not speak a word of English but cooks up a storm. Your hosts are well-established guides, and can help you organize a thoroughly engaging tour of the region, or even farther afield. A night in this enchanting guesthouse costs 26€ ($33) per person, including breakfast and dinner.

have an upper-floor unit with balcony. Views from this—the closest thing to a skyscraper in these parts—are simply splendid.

Piaţa Republicii 18, Gura Humorului. ✆ **0230/20-7000.** Fax 0230/20-7001. www.bestwesternbucovina.ro. 130 units. 78€ ($98) double; 86€ ($109) deluxe with mountain view; 90€ ($114) VIP double; 120€ ($152) junior suite; 150€ ($191) VIP suite; 175€ ($222) presidential suite. AE, DC, MC, V. **Amenities:** 2 restaurants; bar; terrace; fitness center; sauna; Turkish bath; concierge; airport transfers; business facilities; Wi-Fi; room service; massage; mountain biking; hunting; fishing; horseback riding; skiing; rafting; safe. *In room:* TV, minibar, hair dryer.

Casa Elena A short drive from Gura Humorului, right near Voronet Monastery, Casa Elena is set in well-tended grounds with panoramic views of the Bucovina hillscape.

Reckoned to offer the best *pensiune*-style accommodations in the region (famous for having hosted three former presidents, including Iliescu, since it opened in 1999), the complex comprises five different "villas," each featuring a variety of rooms in different configurations. A stay here is pleasant enough, although—as with the nearby Best Western—you may find it packed out with tour groups, and the guest rooms are unspectacular, done out in a countrified approximation of modest luxury with strange color schemes and cheap wood furniture. Traditional touches have been used almost perfunctorily to develop some sort of aesthetic in the numerous public spaces (it's all built to quite a convoluted plan), but it's the convenience of the location rather than the design of the place that should draw you here. Be warned that the hot-water supply is inconsistent, and if you dine in one of the restaurants, you may find some of your choices unavailable. But if you succumb to the beauty of the surrounding lush landscape, you should soon forget its shortcomings.

Voronet, 3½ km (2 miles) from Gura Humorului. ✆/fax **0230/23-5326.** www.casaelena.ro. 35 units. 70€ ($89) double; 81€ ($103) apt. Rates include breakfast and taxes. MC, V. **Amenities:** 2 restaurants; bar; sauna; children's playground; airport transfers; Internet; meeting rooms; room service; laundry; cart and sleigh rides; billiards table; traditional performances. *In room:* TV, minibar, hair dryer.

EXPLORING THE PAINTED MONASTERIES ★★★

Among the great delights Romania has to offer (for some the greatest) are the monastic churches in the Bucovina region of Moldavia. With exteriors and interiors almost entirely covered in vivid frescoes of biblical tales—images rendering the word of God (and the clergy) accessible to the illiterate masses—these are considered so unique that the best preserved have been accorded UNESCO World Heritage status. Bluntly put, these well-preserved examples are nothing short of miraculous, given that their painted exteriors have faced exposure to extreme conditions, including snow and blinding sun, for 400 to 500 years.

Located within fortified monastic complexes designed to stave off enemy attacks, the churches were erected to thank God for victories in battles against the Turkish invaders; the frescoes that adorn the churches thus also honor their founders and, ironically enough, pay tribute to the violent warrior-leaders and womanizers, like Ştefan cel Mare (Stephen the Great), who fought to protect the land from marauding invaders. A cousin of Vlad the Impaler, Ştefan cel Mare was responsible for commissioning many of the churches; canonized in 1992, he not only slaughtered countless Turks, but left a trail of illegitimate children born of his voracious appetite for women.

Five monastic complexes are reviewed below, but there are many more that might be explored during a longer visit to the region; if you don't want to join an organized tour you will need to hire a car and driver or an English-speaking guide (see recommendations below). Note, too, that the five "monasteries" described here are actually inhabited by nuns rather than monks; nevertheless, they are all living religious monuments, and visitors should dress accordingly; don't show up with bare legs or shoulders (wraparound skirts are available for those ignorant of these strictly enforced rules). There's a small fee for photography (usually L6/$2.60/£1.60) within the monastic grounds, but cameras may not be used inside the churches. Opening times given here are for the summer; times may vary during colder periods, when monasteries close earlier.

Without too much of a rush, you can comfortably see all five monasteries reviewed below in 1 day. For a top-notch monastery tour, look no further than knowledgeable **Ciprian Şlenku** (✆ **0744-292-588;** monasterytour@yahoo.com), who will talk you through the history and cultural significance of each of the monuments you visit, tailoring an outing to match your schedule; he charges between 40€ and 100€ ($51–$127) per day, depending on your requirements. If he's not available, an equally rated guide is **Monika** (✆ **0723-782-328;** www.classhostel.ro). Besides operating a hostel in Suceava, this bright-eyed entrepreneur is on good terms with many of the nuns, which makes the visits even more special. Monika is also the most careful driver in Romania, and charges just L100 ($43/£27) per person for a full-day tour (excluding admission to monasteries).

If you'd prefer to go through a professional company, trips to the monasteries can be arranged through **Icar Tours,** Str. Vasile Alecsandri 10 (✆ **0230/52-3553;** www.icar.ro), an agency that's also useful for various other travel needs. **DiscoveRomania** (see "Tours & Travel Agents," earlier in this chapter) includes the Moldavian churches on one of its itineraries, and tours organized with this outfit will ensure that you enjoy the finest local homestays available.

Dragomirna Monastery ★★ Moments Fabulously situated amid rolling fields (a mere 15 min. by car from Suceava), these monumental defensive walls secured one of Bucovina's most elegant churches. While it's not on the UNESCO list and does not feature exterior frescoes, the combination of Georgian, Armenian, and Byzantine architectural elements has created a building that is akin to a beautiful stone spaceship, graced by a 42m (138 ft.) tower (undergoing many years of restoration). Pay your entry fee to the nun behind the souvenir counter in the entryway, where you can buy a decorative egg covered with beads studiously applied with beeswax by one of the 60 nuns who live here. Then venture into the nave. Unlike the other monastic churches, this one is very active, with Mass held from 8:30am until noon; try to come for this beautiful Orthodox ritual. Before leaving, ask the ticketing nun to show you the **museum of medieval art,** reached via the stairway near the entrance to the complex. Among various religious relics is the rather phallic **candle of consecration,** made from beeswax by Bishop Anastasie Crimca, who established the church between 1602 and 1609, when the candle was first lit.

12km (7½ miles) from Suceava. Admission L3 ($1.30/80p). Daily 8am–7pm.

Humor ★★★ Humor was built in 1530, the absence of a tower suggesting that it was not built by a royal leader but by High Chancellor Theodor Bubuiog at the request of Voivode Petru Rareş. Standout architectural elements include the floating Byzantine vault and the inclusion of Gothic window frames; the arcaded open porch was another innovation for the time, apparently inspired by local building traditions. Smaller than the other monastic churches, Humor's paintings are Byzantine, but include Gothic and Roman elements; the predominant color here is a dark red, made from the madder pigment. The exterior frescoes are less well preserved than those at Voronet, but what does remain is quite lovely. Badly faded on the southern wall is the siege of Constantinople, with the Virgin answering the prayers of the besieged. As you enter the church, angels peer down at you from above, perhaps preparing you for the sight of more horrors being visited upon the martyrs. In the adjacent "Woman's Room" there are numerous depictions of female saints. For spectacular views of the surrounding countryside and the village of Mănăstirea Humor, climb the fantastically narrow stairs in the tower (built in 1641) attached to the complex outer wall; the trip up is more fun than the Tower of London. Like Humor, this church was brought back into service only after the fall of Communism.

Roughly 5km (3 miles) north of Gura Humorului. Admission L3 ($1.30/80p). Daily 10am–6pm.

Moldoviţa ★★★ While it requires a fraction more effort to get here than to the slightly more commercial monasteries at Voronet and Humor, this is where you'll find some of the best preserved of all the monastery frescoes. Looked after by a group of 42 exceedingly friendly nuns (the oldest of whom, Mica Marina, is in her late 80s, and has been here since she was 14), the church was built by Petra Rareş, the illegitimate son of Stephen the Great, between 1532 and 1537, to replace an earlier church erected by Alexander the Good (Alexandru cel Bun). Notable here is the distinctive narrative style of the Byzantine technique; in many of the frescoes, you can discern two different points in time within a single frame. In other words, a single image is used to tell a story. Moldovita's exterior has been badly defaced—first by Turkish invaders who carved out the eyes of the frescoed characters in order to spare being judged by them, and later during the Austro-Hungarian occupation by Germanic visitors who carved their names into the porch walls. Inside, the first two rooms of the church are covered in representations of each day of the church calendar; if you can find a nun who speaks English, she may help you find the day of your birth and so identify the patron saint of your birthday. The museum, in one corner of the complex, houses Petru Rareş's throne, as well as the monastery's prized "Pomme d'Or" (Golden Apple) award from UNESCO.

Northwest of Gura Humorului. Admission L3 ($1.30/80p). Daily 10am–6pm.

Suceviţa ★★★ A host of angels greets you from the well-preserved southern wall of this gorgeously painted church, situated 32km (20 miles) north of Moldoviţa. Built a mere 410 years ago, Suceviţa once served as a fortified city-in-miniature for villagers who'd hide behind its massive walls during attacks; the fortifications and monastery grounds are certainly the largest. On the northern wall, Greek philosophers are represented as kings of knowledge; try to locate Plato—the coffin on his head symbolizes the fact that he was the first philosopher to speak about the soul, considered a Christian concept. The enclosed porch around the entrance is the most elaborately painted of all the churches. Pay attention to the zodiac signs above you as you enter, and notice the angels at the edges of the cycles, rolling up time. Inside, bloody accounts of the life, torture, and death of various saints—notably St. George—are depicted. In the second room, notice the Star of David on the lower curtainlike portion of the frescoes, an unusual symbolic reference to the Old Testament, not found in the three previous churches. Here, in the center of the iconostasis, is an exceptionally lifelike rendition of Christ. Another highlight is a curious tapestry woven by Ieremia Movila (whose father built the monastery); there are 10,000 pearls woven into the piece. The monastery is apparently haunted by the ghost of the artist who, while working on the western wall, tragically fell from the scaffolding; the frustrated spirit has since prevented the fresco from being completed. Nowadays, there's ongoing restoration of the interior frescoes, a painstaking process that often draws as much interest from visitors as the paintings themselves.

56km (35 miles) from Suceava. Admission L3 ($1.30/80p). Daily 8am–8pm.

Voronet ★★★ Revered for its *Last Judgment* fresco, Voronet is regarded by Romanians as the "Sistine Chapel of the East"; it remains marvelously preserved, despite being in disuse from the start of Habsburg rule in 1785 until 1991. Built by Ştefan cel Mare in 1488 after a victorious battle against the Turks, the construction took just 3 months and 3 weeks; frescoes were added in 1534 and 1535, during the reign of Stephen's illegitimate son Petru Rareş. The paintings here epitomize a Moldavian innovation in Byzantine painting, exemplified by the degree of chromatic harmony and a new humanism with religious scenes featuring recognizable aspects of the Moldavian people of the time, like the faces of the angels, purportedly based on Moldavian women. Look out also for archangels blowing the *bucium,* an instrument used by Romanian shepherds, and the portrayals of doomed souls—all have fierce faces and wear turbans, characterizing them as Turks. The exterior fresco work is characterized by the use of a spectacular blue, said to be of such originality that it has earned the sobriquet "Voronet blue."

But it is the marvelously preserved *Last Judgment* on the western facade that leaves you breathless; it's an excellent example of Christian art as a dire warning against paganism and wickedness. It's also a fascinating marriage of biblical and secular symbolism. Notice, for example, the inclusion of the wild animals being judged for tearing apart their human victims (pieces of which they now return), while amongst them a lone deer stands empty-handed since this animal represents innocence in Romanian folklore. Notice also how, at Christ's feet, important figures—kings and popes—struggle to get out of hell, while elsewhere people clamber to enter the Gates of Heaven. Near the seat of Judgment, Adam and Eve are depicted alongside various prophets and martyrs; they're separated from the "wicked" by a dove representing the Holy Spirit, while Moses (holding a scroll) points out their misdeeds. Below the dove, ugly demons try to steal souls, fighting among themselves as they torture sinners. On the southern wall is the *Tree of Jesse,* recounting Christ's genealogy. As you enter the church, you'll see the martyrdom of St. Sebastian, above you on your left; you'll also see numerous other martyrs suffering terrible tortures. Inside the church, the frescoes have been revitalized thanks to a thorough restoration job; works worth looking out for include *The Last Supper,* and, in the nave, a painting of Ştefan cel Mare with his wife and legitimate son, Bogdan.

4km (2½ miles) from Gura Humorului. Admission L3 ($1.30/80p). Tues–Sun 10am–7pm.

9 NORTHERN DOBROGEA: ROMANIA'S BLACK SEA COAST & THE DANUBE DELTA

Ancient Greek colonies were established in Dobrogea in the 7th century B.C., with the founding of Histria, 70km (43 miles) north of the regional capital Constanţa, Romania's major port city. Later, this became a Roman province, and a base for conquering the Dacians. From 1418, the region fell to the Turks and remained under Ottoman rule until they were expelled in 1878; Dobrogea was divided in two, the southern portion going to Bulgaria and Northern Dobrogea becoming part of Romania.

Today, there are two distinct regions comprising Northern Dobrogea. Like Bulgaria, the southern fringes along the Black Sea Coast have been totally colonized, turning the country's Riviera to near ruin. Now overdeveloped or steeped by the summer rush of both the moneyed elite and an unruly neobohemian crowd, there are few stretches of sand left unspoiled by tourist exploitation. The northern part of Dobrogea is known for its bird colonies, inhabiting the expansive Danube Delta, a wetland biosphere widely considered one of Europe's last true wildernesses.

BLACK SEA COASTAL RESORTS

Unfortunately, Romania's once lovely and fairly untouched seaside "Riviera on the Black Sea" has become developed and exploited to the point where domestic holidaymakers finally decided to boycott it, and visitor numbers dropped by about 50% in 2006. If you like getting caught up in the mayhem of a noisy, bloated string of resorts and beaches strewn with empty liquor bottles, music blaring from speakers across once-serene getaways, then by all means set off for one of the tiny villages within striking distance of Constanţa. Or you can join the bourgeoisie in their upmarket playground of Mamaia, a collection of fancy hotels and designer luggage, leaving almost no room to erect your beach umbrella. Beach reforms are planned, but they will take a few years to kick in; until such time, you're advised to save your sun-worshipping for elsewhere.

THE DANUBE DELTA ★★★

Heralded by some as the last great wilderness in Europe and the Continent's greatest wildlife sanctuary, the Danube Delta is a unique destination, affording nature experiences usually associated with Africa or South America. Only recently showing on the international tourist radar, this well-kept secret is developing into a top-class conservation area, protected by UNESCO as a World Heritage Site. Diversity is key; while there isn't the vast assortment of land animals and predator activity that one finds in Botswana's Okavango Delta, for example, the Danube is heaven for birders. Over 300 species of birds make their home in this unique ecosystem consisting of almost 250,000 hectares (617,500 acres) of waterways, lakes, reed beds, sand dunes, and subtropical forests as the 2,840km (1,761-mile) river splits into three main branches and flows into the Black Sea. And among the birdlife and the 1,150 species of flora are small fishing and farming communities that remain steeped in the culture of another, forgotten time. These include Russian, Lipovan, Greek, and Turkish communities with cultures and practices that are distinct from anywhere else in Romania.

Essentials

On the banks of the Danube, the ancient Greek port town of **Tulcea** might be considered the gateway to the Delta; although there's nothing in the town itself that should detain you, you're likely to pass through en route to destinations in the Delta proper. The fastest way to get to Tulcea from Bucharest is by **plane;** in 2008 Tarom began flying between Bucharest and Tulcea on Sundays and Thursdays (35 min.), and there are plans to increase the volume of flights in the future. Alternatively you can catch one of two daily InterCity **trains;** the journey is 4 hours (although at the time of writing this was actually 7 hr. due to railway works). Tulcea's **train station,** Strada Potului (✆ **0240/51-3706**), is right near the **bus station** (✆ **0240/51-3304**), which is attached to the **Navrom ferry terminal.**

Tulcea hosts the **Danube Delta Research Institute,** Str. Babadag 165 (✆ **0240/52-4550;** www.indd.tim.ro), useful if you're after hard facts about this unique biosphere. Tulcea is also home to the **Danube Delta Biosphere Reserve Headquarters,** Str. Portului 34A (✆ **0240/51-8945;** www.ddbra.ro), which hosts the **Information and Ecological Education Centre** (✆ **0240/51-9214;** www.deltaturism.ro), which can provide you with local and delta-related information; staff can also help you with accommodations, but note that they're only open weekdays.

All-inclusive Delta Experiences

In addition to the possibility of staying in small village guesthouses, there are a small handful of resorts that, mercifully, are striving to protect the natural resources of the region.

Delta Nature Resort ★★ Established in 2005, Romania's top-rated resort not only situates you on the edge of one of Europe's most unique natural environments, but also cushions you in luxury and offers a smorgasbord of activities to keep you entertained. In terms of Romania's burgeoning tourism market, this resort is something of a trendsetter, but doesn't necessarily afford guests with an authentic experience. Instead, thanks to its design, it's an earnest attempt to echo the style of the delta's fishing villages. There are 30 luxurious villas (rather closely packed together) high up on the banks of Lake Somova, an impressive location with great views over the water and reed beds, and as far as the Ukraine. Built from local wood and stone, each villa has a porch overlooking the wide-open expanse of the delta. Inside you have a private living room, plush bedroom, and fine contemporary bathrooms to match. Besides birding expeditions, some of the best cultural experiences in the country are to be had at a nearby monastery, where the nuns serve up delicious organic lunches, while traditional delta soups are served on some of the longer fishing and water-based excursions. More energetic guests can kayak or canoe their way across the waters, getting close to the pelicans and cormorants with one of the resident rangers, botanists, or naturalists. One downside is that all these outings and nature experiences are at additional cost, and quite pricey. Nature-loving purists may also be disturbed by the sense that the resort doesn't really blend all that seamlessly with the natural environment—passing traffic, day-trippers on adjacent public land, and even noisy groundstaff tend to intrude on the serene idyll from time to time. ***Note:*** Rates are between 45€ and 69€ more expensive on weekends; July, August and September are the priciest months, when the resort is also at its busiest.

Somova-Parches, Km 3, Tulcea. ✆ **021/311-4532.** Fax 031/710-0336. www.deltaresort.com. 30 units. 220€–415€ ($280–$527) deluxe double; 295€–490€ ($375–$622) premium double; 60€ ($76) extra person; 25€ ($328) extra child (5–12 years); children 4 and under free. Rates include breakfast and VAT. MC, V. **Amenities:** Restaurant; bar; pool; tennis; gym; Jacuzzi; sauna; bike hire; airport transfers (also from Bucharest); business center; gift shop; limited room service; massage center; laundry; library; boating; kayaking; fishing; birding; nature walks; quadbiking; table tennis; cultural tours; wine tasting; barbecue area; traditional performances. *In room:* A/C, TV, stereo, Wi-Fi, minibar, tea- and coffee-making facility, hair dryer, safe, fireplace.

Enisala Safari Village ★★ Far more intimate than Delta Resort, this rustic, smart little guest resort is in the old fortress village of Enisala, about 30km (19 miles) south of Tulcea, and less than 30 minutes from the Black Sea Coast. Enisala ("New Village") was once a Byzantine outpost, later colonized by the Genoese and the Ottomans. It's right near vast Lake Razim, and a couple of hours by motorboat from the very heart of the Danube Delta. Accommodations comprise thatch- or clay-tile roof cottages with white-washed walls and blue wooden shutters to mimic the rusticity of local village houses. Guest rooms are simple and bright, with patterned stone-tile floors and roll-down straw blinds. Different itineraries allow guests to get a varied experience of the region, and even spend a day venturing across the border, into Bulgaria, to see Queen Marie's Castle and sample traditional Bulgarian food and entertainment. Boats are available for lake and delta excursions, and guides take you hiking, bird-watching, and fishing. You can also explore the region by bike, motorbike, or quadbike. Staff will also arrange visits to the nearby Babadag mosque, the vineyards of Niculiţel, the ruins of the ancient Greek city of Histria, off-road trips to the Russian village of Slava Rusa, and the Slavonic monastery of Vovidenia, where you can arrange for a picnic. At night, fires are lit, and rugged types can opt to camp outdoors (in military tents). Dine outdoors at an open barbecue or experience a Byzantine-style evening in the wine cellar or in the intimate dinner lounge. It's small enough for guests to make the decisions, and pleasant enough to spend a couple of days.

Enisala, near 94 A, jud. Tulcea (Bucharest office: Str. Episcopiei 5, apt 18, Bucharest). ✆ **0722-300-200.** Fax 021/314-5837. www.safari.ro. 6 units. 138€ ($175) double, includes all meals; children 13 and under pay half. MC, V. **Amenities:** Dinner lounge; wine cellar; 2 terraces; barbecue area; sightseeing and organized trips; airport transfers; Internet; camping; bird-watching; photo safaris; Danube cruise; 4×4 trips; mountain biking; motorbiking; small archaeological museum. *In room:* A/C.

Homestays & Guesthouses in the Delta

If you'd like to mingle more intimately with the local people of the region, then there's no better way than arranging to stay in one of the villages deep in the heart of the delta. Unlike Delta Resort, for example, which is actually at the edge of the delta, the villages give you immediate access to this unique environment and allow you to sample life in places that have traditionally been pretty isolated from the outside world (although these days, local people are extremely familiar with the burgeoning tourist industry). Unfortunately, getting to the villages can be laborious, thanks to ferry schedules which may delay your journey by any entire day if you're not on the ball. Your best bet for securing a meaningful overnight experience in one of the delta's villages is through DiscoveRomania (see "Tours & Travel Agents" at the beginning of this chapter), which has access to the smartest guides in the area and will put you up in handpicked accommodations. The agency will also streamline your transport arrangements, which can be particularly tricky in this waterbound region.

10

Moscow & St. Petersburg

by Angela Charlton and Heather Coombs

Russia breathes superlatives: the world's biggest country; its largest supplier of natural gas and one of its largest oil producers; home of the planet's longest railroads and busiest subway system (Moscow's); and one of its deepest, biggest, and oldest lakes (Baikal, in Siberia). It even boasts balmy beach resorts (on the Black Sea), though the Kremlin and the snowcapped cupolas of its cathedrals seem truer reflections of this northern nation's might and mysticism.

There is much for travelers to experience in Russia's two most popular cities. In Moscow, the traditions of the Bolshoi Theater coexist with some of Europe's most cutting-edge DJs. In St. Petersburg, the Hermitage Museum is a fortress of fine art from around the world, and the Russian Museum overflows with works by local artists. Russia's tourism infrastructure is still underdeveloped, but Moscow and St. Petersburg are fast catching up with the changes brought by capitalism. Take along some pluck and flexibility and have a look at the best Russia has to offer.

1 GETTING TO KNOW MOSCOW & ST. PETERSBURG

MOSCOW & ST. PETERSBURG ORIENTATION

At Moscow's heart lies the Kremlin, from which the rest of the city has expanded in roughly concentric circles: the Boulevard Ring, the Garden Ring, and the Third Ring. The last circle, the Moscow Ring Road, is a bypass around the city limits. The Moscow and Yauza rivers curve through the city, delineating neighborhoods. Visitors are often struck by Moscow's broad boulevards and large swaths of green space.

St. Petersburg, like Moscow, is dense and territorially large, but not as unwieldy or overwhelming as its southern sister. Peter the Great built his dream city on a cluster of islands in the marshland of the Gulf of Finland. To make sense of this boggy site, he designed a network of canals and bridges, resulting in a city of remarkable logic and beauty. The Neva River folds around the city center, taking in water from the city's canals before flowing out to the Baltic Sea. The city's main land artery is Nevsky Prospekt, a 4km-long (2½-mile) avenue that slices across the city center.

MOSCOW & ST. PETERSBURG TODAY

Moscow is almost a country unto itself, a metropolis of 12 million people enjoying the fruits of Russia's booming oil economy. Despite Russians' innate conservatism, today's Moscow is a 24-hour city that pulses with change, from the ruthlessly competitive

restaurant and club scenes to the volatile financial markets and the clamor for the latest top-of-the-line cellphone.

St. Petersburg's reputation as Russia's intellectual and cultural center has not brought the city as much prosperity as today's Moscow enjoys, but Petersburg has better hotel choices and a restaurant scene nearly as vibrant as the capital's. Peter the Great's vision for the city lives on—even new buildings adhere to the symmetry and classicism of his day.

Although Russia as a whole is a graying country with a relatively low standard of living, Moscow and St. Petersburg are its glaring exceptions, and are experiencing a genuine economic boom that has brought them in line with the world's richest cities.

For tourists there's never been a better time to visit Russia. Surly Soviet service is giving way to smiling efficiency, new restaurants open in Moscow almost daily, and fashions are as fresh as in Milan. Cash machines are ubiquitous and English is increasingly widespread. Russia has, at last, opened its doors to the world.

A LOOK AT THE PAST

Russia's struggle for identity, association, and empire has defined it since the Vikings formed the state of Rus nearly 1,200 years ago. Blood and repression have marred this struggle, right up to the present.

Moscow has dominated the country's political, economic, and cultural life for most of the past 900 years; St. Petersburg, during the 2 centuries when it assumed the role of Russia's capital, thrust Russia at long last into the modern world.

The first Russian state was founded in Novgorod in the 9th century, and later shifted to Kiev, now the capital of Ukraine. The era of **Kievan Rus,** as it was called, saw the flowering of a major European entity, whose territories stretched across present-day Belarus, Ukraine, and much of western Russia. As Kievan Rus, the country gained a religion and an official language and developed the distinctive architectural styles seen across the region today.

Moscow became the seat of Russian authority in 1326. The Russian state was feeble, however, and fell to repeated invasion by Mongol Tatars from the east. The Tatars kept Russia's princes under their thumbs until Ivan III (Ivan the Great) came to power in the late 1400s. His reign saw Muscovite-controlled lands spread north to the Arctic and east to the Urals. Ivan the Great launched construction of the Kremlin's magnificent cathedrals and its current walls.

His grandson Ivan IV, the first Russian crowned "tsar," became better known as **Ivan the Terrible.** He instituted Russia's first secret police force, persecuted former friends as enemies, and killed his own son and pregnant daughter-in-law in a fit of rage. The country and his dynasty were devastated by the time Ivan IV died in 1584.

The ensuing decades were wrought with bloody, corrupt struggles that came to be known as the **"Time of Troubles."** At last the 16-year-old Mikhail Romanov, a distant relative of Ivan the Terrible, was elected tsar in 1613. Mikhail established a dynasty that would last until Tsar Nicholas II was executed by Bolsheviks 300 years later.

Although Russians through the ages have debated whether to look to western Europe or to their Slavic roots for inspiration, **Peter the Great,** who ruled from 1682 to 1725, had no doubts. Peter traveled to western Europe and upon his return moved to a swamp on the Baltic Sea, transforming it into a capital of columned, Italian-designed palaces along broad avenues and canals. St. Petersburg's beauty came at a great price: Thousands of people died fulfilling Peter's sometimes impossible building orders.

Russia's next exceptional leader was **Catherine the Great** (1762–96), a German princess who married into the Romanov family and conspired to oust her husband to attain the throne. She greatly expanded Russia's territory to the east and south, and her foreign policies won her and Russia great respect in the rest of Europe. Russia's aristocracy came to speak French better than Russian.

Russia's love affair with France collapsed under **Napoleon,** who gave Russia its biggest military challenge in centuries. The French made it into Moscow in 1812—but only after the Russians had set fires in the city, stripped it bare, and fled, leaving Napoleon's army without food and shelter on the eve of winter. The *Grande Armée* retreated, and the Russians' victorious drive into Paris 2 years later was immortalized in poems, songs, and children's rhymes.

Much of Russia's 19th century was defined by **prerevolutionary struggle,** and the tsars sought to stamp out dissent even where it didn't exist. The 1825 Decembrist uprising, led by reformist generals in the royal army, was quashed by Tsar Nicholas I, who then bolstered the secret police. Tsar Alexander II freed the serfs in 1861, but society remained unequal and most of the population was still poor and uneducated.

Nicholas II—the last of the Romanov tsars—assumed the throne in 1894 with few plans for reform. He stifled an uprising of striking workers in January 1905 on what is known as **Russia's Bloody Sunday.** Under pressure from the population, the tsar allowed the creation of a limited parliament, Russia's first ever, elected in 1906.

MOSCOW & ST. PETERSBURG

Fighting the Germans in World War I further weakened Nicholas's shaky hold on the country, and with revolution in the air, he abdicated in February 1917. An aristocrat-led provisional government jockeyed for power with revolutionary parties. Vladimir Lenin's extremist **Bolshevik Party** emerged the victor. Nicholas, his wife Alexandra, and their five children were exiled to Siberia and then executed in 1918, as civil war engulfed the nation. Years of chaos, famine, and bloodshed followed, before the Union of Soviet Socialist Republics was born.

After Lenin died in 1924, Josef **Stalin** worked his way to the top of the Communist Party leadership. Stalin crafted a dictatorship by gradually purging his rivals, real and imagined. His repression reached a peak in the late 1930s, with millions executed or exiled to prison camps across Siberia and the Arctic, referred to by their Russian initials GULAG, or State Agency for Labor Camps.

Stalin tried to head off war with Germany, but Hitler invaded anyway, plunging the Soviet Union into a war that cost the country 27 million lives, more losses than any nation suffered in World War II.

Genuine grief mixed with nervous relief gripped the country when Stalin died in 1953, as many feared that life without this frightening father figure would be even worse than with him. Nikita Khrushchev's eventual rise to power brought a **thaw;** political prisoners were released and there was a slight relaxation of censorship amid continued postwar economic growth. Soviet space successes during this time—including sending the first satellite, first man, and first woman to space—awed the world and fueled the Cold War arms race.

Long years of stagnation and tightened controls followed under Leonid Brezhnev. Then in the mid-1980s, **Mikhail Gorbachev**'s name became synonymous with the policies of ***glasnost*** (openness) and ***perestroika*** (restructuring) that he tried to apply to the Soviet system. But he underestimated how deeply the country's economy and political legitimacy had decayed. The reforms he introduced took on a momentum that doomed him and the Soviet Union.

The new Russia's heady and chaotic years under Boris Yeltsin were followed by a calmer, richer era under Vladimir Putin. However, while Putin stabilized Russia's huge economy he also disabled political opposition, stifled the media, and waged an internationally unpopular war in Chechnya. Putin retained considerable sway as prime minister after turning the presidency over to Dmitry Medvedev in 2008.

PEOPLE & CULTURE

Russians are among the most festive and giving people on the planet, always ready to put their last morsel of food and last drop of drink on the table to honor an unexpected late-night guest with toasts, more toasts, and laughter. Although the changes of the past 2 decades have been rough on Russians, they've adapted quickly—today's Russian university graduates know more languages, and more about financial markets and text messaging, than many of their Western counterparts.

Despite Russia's bloody history, it has produced some of the world's best science, music, and literature. In the 19th century, Alexander **Pushkin** became Russians' best-loved poet, with his direct, melodic use of the Russian language. Fyodor **Dostoevsky**'s fiction delves into innermost existential depths, and **Tchaikovsky**'s symphonies gave voice to the terror and triumph of war with France. They are just a few of the legions of cultural heroes who found renown in their uniquely Russian ways of expression.

Russians take great pride in their cultural heritage, and in the Soviet era nearly everyone, factory worker and collective farmer included, made regular visits to the theater, concert hall, or opera house. Russia's rigorous **ballet** traditions have relaxed little in the past 200 years, and that commitment to physical perfection carries over into every form of dance represented in today's Russia. For **classical music** fans, there's no better way to pay tribute to the homeland of Tchaikovsky, Rachmaninoff, Mussorgsky, Scriabin, Shostakovich, and Rimsky-Korsakov than to hear their works played in a Russian conservatory by their dedicated heirs.

CUISINE

Russia's culinary traditions run from the daylong, table-crushing feasts of the 19th-century aristocracy to the cabbage soup and potatoes on which generations of ordinary Russians were raised. Russian food is generally rich and well salted.

Traditional dishes include the Siberian specialty *pelmeni,* dumplings filled with ground beef, pork, or lamb and spices and boiled in broth (a bit like overstuffed ravioli). *Varenniki* are a larger, flatter version of these dumplings, filled with potatoes or berries. *Piroshki* are small baked pies filled with ground meat, cabbage, or fruit, and are eaten with your hands; *pirogi* are large dessert pies. Buttery *bliny,* thin crepelike pancakes, are spread with jam or savory fillings such as ham and cheese and rolled up. Tiny round *olady* are the pancakes eaten with caviar. Russian soups include the refreshing summer sorrel soup *zelyoniye shchi* or the winter stew *solyanka.*

Your trip to Russia will invariably involve a taste of **vodka,** the national drink. Most vodkas are distilled from wheat, rye, or barley malt, or some combination of the three. The Stolichnaya, Russky Standart, and Flagman brands are excellent choices. If you want to appreciate a good vodka the way Russians do, you should drink it well chilled and straight, preferably in 50g shots. Down it in one gulp, and always chase it with something to eat. Russians prefer pickles, marinated herring, or a slice of lard.

Local beers are improving rapidly; Baltika and Nevskoye are cheap and tasty choices. If you're feeling adventurous, try *kvas,* a thirst-quenching beverage made from fermented bread. Russians' drink of choice, however, is **tea** *(chai),* ideally served from a samovar: A small pot of strong tea base *(zavarka)* sits brewing on top and is diluted to taste with the hot water from the belly of the samovar *(kipitok).*

LANGUAGE

The Cyrillic alphabet scares off most tourists from trying to pick up any Russian, and that's a great shame. The 33-letter alphabet is not hard to learn, since many of the letters are the same as in English. Just knowing how to sound out those dizzying signs will make your trip through Russia a lot less mysterious and a lot more comfortable.

Most Russians in hotels, restaurants, and shops will speak some English, especially those of the younger generations. Any effort to speak Russian will be welcomed, and in smaller establishments even a few words of Russian may get you out of a bind or improve service. Below are some useful words and phrases.

USEFUL WORDS & PHRASES

English	Russian	Pronunciation
Yes/No	**Да/нет**	da/nyet
Hello	**Здравствуйте**	*zdras*-tvoo-tye
Goodbye	**до свиания**	da svi-*da*-nya
Thank you	**спасибо**	spa-*see*-ba

English	Russian	Pronunciation
Please/You're welcome	**пожалуйста**	pa-*zha*-li-sta
Excuse me	**извините**	eez-vee-*nee*-tye
Sorry	**простите, пожалуйста**	prah-*stee*-tye, pa-*zha*-li-sta
How are you?	**Как дела?**	kak deh-*la*
Fine, good	**Хороша**	kho-ro-*show*
Bad	**плохо**	*plo*-kha
Do you speak English?	**вы говорите по-анлийски?**	vy go-vo-*ree*-te po ang-*lee*-skee?
I don't speak Russian	**Я не говорю по-русски**	ya nee guh-vuh-*ryoo* pa-*roo*-skee
I speak a little Russian	**Я немного говорю по-русски**	ya ne-*mno*-go guh-vuh-*ryoo* pa-*roo*-skee
How much does it cost?	**склько стоит?**	*skol*-ka *sto*-eet?
Where is . . .	**где находитса . . .**	gde na-*kho*-dee-tsa . . .
the metro station	**станция метро**	*stan*-tsee-ya me-*tro*
the restroom/WC	**туалет**	tua-*let*
Pharmacy	**аптека**	ap-*teh*-ka
Currency exchange	**обмен валюты**	ob-*men* vah-*lyoo*-tee
ATM/cash machine	**банкомат**	bahnk-o-*mat*
Help!	**помогите**	pa-ma-*gee*-tye

2 PLANNING YOUR TRIP TO MOSCOW & ST. PETERSBURG

VISITOR INFORMATION

Hotels and tour desks are likely to have as much information as the official tourist offices (for addresses, see section 3, "Moscow," and section 4, "St. Petersburg").

Most hotels and many newspaper kiosks sell maps in English (ask for a *Karta na angliiskom,* pronounced *kar*-ta na ahn-*glees*-kom). See **www.yell.ru/map** for interactive maps of Moscow and St. Petersburg.

Useful websites include **www.infoservices.com**, featuring the Travelers' Yellow Pages for Moscow and St. Petersburg, with searchable telephone and address listings in English, including nearest metro station and opening hours.

There are numerous free listings magazines at nearly all hotels and many restaurants. Most are in English and Russian and are full of information.

ENTRY REQUIREMENTS

All visitors to Russia need a visa. Package tours usually take care of this, though you will need to give the travel agency your passport for submission to the Russian embassy. For independent travelers, visa applicants must provide proof of hotel reservations in an official letter from a hotel or travel agency. Travelers staying in private homes need an invitation from a Russian organization. Two places that offer this service for a fee are **www.waytorussia.net** and Sindbad's Hostel, **www.sindbad.ru** (✆ **812/332-2020**). Start the process several weeks before you leave. If you apply by mail, you will have to send your passport to the embassy.

While in Russia you need to **register your visa.** Most hotels will do this for you. If they don't offer this service, check with the visa agencies above.

Russian Embassy Locations Overseas

United States: Embassy: 2641 Tunlaw Rd. NW, Washington, DC (✆ 202/939-8907, 202/939-8913, or 202/939-8918; www.russianembassy.org).

Consulates: 9 E. 91 St., New York, NY (✆ 212/348-0926); 2790 Green St., San Francisco, CA (✆ 415/928-6878); 2322 Westin Bldg., 2001 6th Ave., Seattle, WA (✆ 206/728-1910).

Britain: 5 Kensington Palace Gardens, London W8 4QS (✆ 0870/005-6972; www.great-britain.mid.ru).

Canada: 52 Range Rd., Ottawa, Ontario K1N 8G5 (✆ 613/594-8488; www.rusembcanada.mid.ru).

Australia: 78 Canberra Ave., Griffith, Canberra, ACT 2603 (✆ 02/6295-9474; www.australia.mid.ru).

Ireland: 186 Orwell Rd., Rathgar, Dublin (✆ 01/492-3492; www.ireland.mid.ru).

CUSTOMS REGULATIONS

What You Can Bring Into Russia

Visitors can bring in most things other than weapons, drugs, and livestock. If you have cash in any currency worth more than $1,500; anything antique; or valuable jewelry, laptop computers, cameras, or other electronics, then fill out a Customs declaration form upon entry and go through the **Red Channel** at airport Customs. The declaration form will be stamped and returned to you, and you must present it again upon departure. You can take up to $10,000 if you declare it.

What You Can Take Home from Russia

Most souvenirs are safe to take home, except antiques, artwork, and caviar. The rules on artwork and antiques change frequently; they most often affect religious icons, old samovars, and artwork worth over $1,000. In some cases, the item cannot be exported; in others, export is permitted but only with Culture Ministry certification. Most vendors can complete the export certification for you. Tourists wishing to export anything valuable or anything made before 1960 (including books or Soviet memorabilia) should have the store certify it or clear it themselves with the **Russian Ministry of Culture's Assessment Committee** (in Moscow, ✆ **495/921-3258;** in St. Petersburg, ✆ **812/310-1454**). Applications are cheap (about $10), but export duties can run up to 100% and the process is tedious.

MONEY

Russia's **ruble** only recently became a "hard" currency, which means very few banks abroad will exchange them. If you're not queasy about carrying cash from home, change it at currency exchange booths. Booths in town are widespread, offer more competitive

Currency Confusion

Many hotels, restaurants, and chic shops list their prices in "monetary units" (abbreviated Y.E. in Russian). The unit is essentially another way of saying "dollars" or "euros" while adhering to Russian rules that forbid businesses from trading in any currency other than the ruble. Today the monetary unit is either pegged to the dollar, the euro, or somewhere in between. Restaurants and hotels will have a note at the front desk and on the menus or price lists indicating the current "monetary unit exchange rate" (for example: 28 rubles = 1 Y.E.). It's a good idea to have a small calculator handy for times like this. Even if the price is listed in dollar-pegged "units," however, you have to pay your bill in rubles.

rates than do hotels and airports, and do not charge commissions, though most buy only U.S. dollars and euros. Be sure to have crisp, new bills, as exchange booths often refuse well-worn or old notes.

The easiest way to get **cash** in Moscow and St. Petersburg is from an ATM. The **Cirrus** (✆ **800/424-7787;** www.mastercard.com) and **PLUS** (✆ **800/843-7587;** www.visa.com) networks span the globe, and most Russian ATMs accept both.

Credit cards are welcome in most Russian hotels and many restaurants, but many museums and train stations take only cash. Cards most commonly accepted in Russia are American Express, Visa, MasterCard, and Eurocard.

Few places in Russia accept **traveler's checks** outside major hotels and restaurants, and those that do usually only accept American Express.

Current exchange rates are around 24 rubles to the U.S. dollar and 47 rubles to the British pound.

WHEN TO GO

Frost tinged, wind whipped, ice glazed—snow blankets much of Russia for most of the year, and Moscow and St. Petersburg usually see flurries in May and September. Understandably, prices are lower September through May and tourist sites are less crowded. Hotel and airline rates spike around the New Year's holiday.

Most visitors favor **summer,** both in Moscow and subarctic St. Petersburg, with sunsets that linger until sunrise, balmy temperatures, and all-night activity that makes you forget that it's 3am and you haven't slept. Summer weather in both cities can be unpredictable, though, with spells of heavy heat (and rare air-conditioning) or drizzly cold. Bring layers and an umbrella no matter when you go.

Autumn is a few idyllic weeks in late September and early October when the poplars and oaks shed their leaves and the afternoon sun warms you enough to help you through the cooling nights. Spring, a few weeks in April, is slushy and succinct.

If a **winter wonderland** is your fantasy, Russia in December won't disappoint you. The northern sun shines softly low on the horizon, and snow masks garbage-strewn courtyards. Cross-country skiing fans can wind through forests within Moscow city limits or skate-ski along the frozen Gulf of Finland in St. Petersburg. However, many country palaces and other outdoor sites close in winter.

Businesses and government agencies slow down considerably because of vacations the first 2 weeks of January, the first 2 weeks of May, and much of August. These are calmer

Major Festivals in Russia

The biggest party of the year is undoubtedly **New Year's Eve.** After the Communists wiped Christmas off the official calendar, this date became the focus for gift giving and family celebrations. Since the fall of Communism, **Orthodox Christmas (Jan 7)** and **Easter** have reemerged as major religious holidays, marked by feasts and church services. **Maslenitsa** or Butter Week in **February/March** is traditionally a time to eat lots of buttery *bliny* and other rich foods before Orthodox Lent begins, and many towns stage raucous Maslenitsa festivals. Many still celebrate **Labor Day (May 1)** with parades under red Communist banners. **Victory Day** on **May 9** is still a major Russian holiday commemorating Hitler's defeat in World War II.

Cultural festivals include Moscow's **Easter Arts Festival** in **April/May,** featuring choral ensembles and bell ringing. St. Petersburg's **White Nights** in **late June/early July** are 2 weeks of all-night concerts, film festivals, and boat tours to celebrate the northern lights, when the sun never sets. The city's **White Days** festival in **late December** includes winter carnivals and a dense program of dance, opera, and orchestral performances.

times to visit Russia but can prove a nightmare if you have visa problems or other administrative needs.

Average temperatures in Moscow and St. Petersburg range from around 12°F (–11°C) in January to 66°F (19°C) in July.

HOLIDAYS

January 1 (New Year's Day), January 2, January 7 (Russian Orthodox Christmas), February 23 (Armed Forces Day), March 8 (International Women's Day), Monday following Orthodox Easter (which is not usually not the same day as Catholic/Protestant Easter), May 1 and 2 (Labor Day/Spring Festival), May 9 (Victory Day), June 12 (Russian National Day), November 4 (Unity Day), and December 12 (Constitution Day). December 25 is not a holiday in Russia. Commerce slows during holidays but doesn't shut down. Many museums and restaurants remain open but with limited hours.

HEALTH CONCERNS

No vaccinations are necessary to visit Russia, though there have been cases of diphtheria and cholera in provincial areas in recent years. Most visitors' biggest health challenges are digestive, either from St. Petersburg's bacteria-ridden water or dubiously prepared street food. Bottled water is cheap and widely available. HIV is a growing problem.

GETTING THERE

BY PLANE Russia's chief international carrier remains Aeroflot. Delta and American Airlines are the only major U.S. airlines that fly into Russia, though all major European carriers serve Moscow and St. Petersburg. You can often find good deals through British Airways, BMI, Air France, and KLM. For a cheaper option, try Eastern European airlines, such as Air Berlin, Poland's LOT, or Hungary's Malév; or Asian carriers such as Air India.

BY TRAIN Rail travel into and around Russia is romantic and often comfortable, but it's time consuming. The most direct train route from London to Moscow, for example, takes 48 hours. Customs procedures are unpredictable on trains. If you're traveling through Belarus or Ukraine you will need a transit visa; contact your nearest embassy or consulate for details.

BY CAR The country's vast expanse makes arriving by car a daunting proposition. Roads outside central Moscow and St. Petersburg are dismal, signage is poor and often only in the Cyrillic alphabet, and roadside services—including gas stations—are scarce. Be sure you have international documentation, including car registration and insurance, and an international driver's license. Your visa should indicate you are bringing a car into the country. Renting a car once you arrive is a more reliable and pleasant option.

BY BUS Several European tour companies offer bus trips to Moscow, usually from Germany; or to St. Petersburg, usually from Finland. The journey from Berlin to Moscow is long, about 2 days, and involves poorly maintained Russian highways and long waits at the borders. You will need transit visas if you travel through Belarus, as most Moscow-bound routes do. The Helsinki-to–St. Petersburg journey takes about 7 hours and is often included on Scandinavian-based tours.

PACKAGES FOR THE INDEPENDENT TRAVELER

Package tours are simply a way to buy the airfare, accommodations, and other elements of your trip at the same time and often at discounted prices. Tour companies to try are **Eastern Tours,** focusing on reasonably priced tours to Moscow, St. Petersburg, and Kiev (**© 800/339-6967;** www.traveltorussia.com); and **Cosmos Tours** (**© 800/276-1241;** www.cosmos.com). Most major airlines offer air/land packages, and several big online travel agencies—Expedia, Travelocity, Orbitz, Site59, and Lastminute.com—also do a brisk business in packages.

ESCORTED TOURS

Russia's tourism industry is only beginning to tap the travel possibilities across the world's largest country, and this makes an escorted tour—with a group leader, including airfare, hotels, meals, admission costs, and local transportation—quite appealing. The main drawback of an escorted tour is its high cost.

For general-interest tours, **Escorted Russian Tours** (**© 800/942-3301;** www.escortedrussiantours.com) provides a range of offerings focusing on Moscow and St. Petersburg, as do the U.K.-based **Russian Gateway** (**© 07050-803-160;** www.russiangateway.co.uk) and the Russian-based **www.tourstorussia.com.**

One popular excursion is a **cruise from St. Petersburg to Moscow.** It takes your boat about 10 days to wind through rivers and canals, with stops at the island monastery at Valaam, the fairy tale–like wooden village of Kizhi, lakes Ladoga and Onega, and the Volga river towns of Yaroslavl and Kostroma. **Russiana River Cruises** (www.russiana.co.uk) is a good place to start.

GETTING AROUND RUSSIA

BY TRAIN The most pleasant, romantic, and historical way to travel around Russia is by train. The Moscow–St. Petersburg route is the most frequented and best maintained. Travelers choose between a 8-hour night trip in a comfortable sleeping compartment, and a 5-hour day trip ($55–$95/£34–£59). Arranging train tickets before you arrive—for example, through a travel agent—is the safest way to go. Most hotels can arrange train tickets to major cities.

Commuter trains (called *elektrichki*) with hard benches and rock-bottom prices serve many of the country estates and other sights just outside the big cities.

BY PLANE Given Russia's size, plane travel is crucial for reaching more distant destinations. The Russian airlines Aeroflot and Rossiya (formerly Pulkovo) dominate the Moscow–St. Petersburg route, and prices for a one-way ticket run $60 to $100 (£37–£62). Flights on this route are on large, sturdy, and reliable Soviet-era jets and Western aircrafts, and the service is steadily improving. See www.aeroflot.ru, www.pulkovo.ru, or www.eastline-tour.ru. The new Russian low-cost carrier SKY EXPRESS has appeared on the market for domestic flights (www.skyexpress.ru).

BY CAR Renting a car can be a reasonable way to get around, but a strongly recommended alternative is to rent a car with a driver. It often costs no more than a standard rental. Companies to try include Avis (www.avis.com), Hertz (www.hertz.com), or Europcar (www.europcar.com).

BY BUS Russian-run tourist buses offer day trips to cities on the Golden Ring outside Moscow and several sights around St. Petersburg, and are generally comfortable. Vendors often hawk tours on loudspeakers at central spots such as St. Petersburg's Nevsky Prospekt metro station and Moscow's Red Square. Hotels can often arrange bus tours.

TIPS ON ACCOMMODATIONS

Luxury chains are well represented, and include Marriott, InterContinental, and Sheraton. Holiday Inn and Best Western are somewhat cheaper, but Moscow in particular has too few midrange hotel rooms to satisfy demand. Russia's star-rating system is an unreliable indicator of quality.

Several **Soviet-era hotels** used by package tours are undergoing renovations, and the higher prices charged for upgraded rooms are definitely worth it for the improved plumbing and service.

Russian **bed-and-breakfasts** usually occupy a single floor of an apartment building. Some were once communal apartments, but today they are renovated and quite comfortable. In St. Petersburg, **minihotels** are a very good option. They, too, often use converted apartment space but offer more services than most bed-and-breakfasts for a reasonable price.

Renting a **private apartment** for your stay is also popular, opening up more range in price and location than the hotel industry can. This is especially convenient during high seasons. The safest bet is to use a real-estate agency that services the apartment and is available for assistance at all hours in case of emergency.

If you're seeking a closer look at day-to-day Russian existence, or want to learn or practice Russian, a **homestay** can be a good option. The ideal homestay is an apartment with a family history and a family member eager to tell you about it. The best way to determine what you're getting into is to call your hosts before you reserve.

Shopping online for hotels is generally done by booking through the hotel's own website or through an independent hotel agency. Prices can vary considerably from site to site, and it pays to shop around. Two Russian-specialty sites to try are **www.bnb.ru** and **www.waytorussia.net**. Even the highest-end locations sometimes offer deep discounts through online or traditional travel agencies or their own websites, up to 60% off the official rate.

Neither Moscow nor St. Petersburg offers an official reservations service, and your chances of just showing up and getting a room are slim, even in hostels. It is strongly recommended to reserve in advance by phone or online.

Be sure to find out *before you reserve* whether your hotel or host can arrange your **visa invitation.** If not, you'll need to find a reputable travel agency to do that for you, which could cost up to $100 more and takes at least 2 weeks.

TIPS ON DINING

Restaurants generally serve continuously from lunch through dinner, and few are open before noon. Keep an eye out for **business lunches,** a good way to get a reasonably priced meal and quick service at midday.

Top-end hotels offer elaborate, all-you-can-eat **Sunday brunches,** replete with caviar and Russian delicacies. These hotels often offer a pleasant afternoon tea.

Try restaurants that specialize in Russian or fusion Russian-European cuisine, or sample the cuisines from other former Soviet republics: the Caucasus Mountains spices of Georgia, Azerbaijan, and Armenia. These cuisines have worked their way into Russian cooking over the centuries, and they boast a much richer selection of fruits, vegetables, and spices than Russia's cold climate can produce.

International chain restaurants, hotel restaurants, and those in the top price categories all have nonsmoking sections; elsewhere it's hit or miss.

TIPS ON SHOPPING

The chief challenge in finding unique souvenirs and gifts in Russia is determining whether you can export them. See "Customs Regulations," above, for the regulations of Russia's Culture Ministry, which affect Orthodox icons, samovars, and many artworks. Demand receipts when buying anything valuable, even items from open-air markets.

Moscow and St. Petersburg have no sales tax, but be clear with the vendor about which currency is being cited (see "Money," above). VAT is included in the price, but it is not refundable at the border as it is in some European countries.

Hotel gift shops are the most expensive places in town for souvenirs, and heavily touristed areas are a close second. Better bets are small crafts shops or **outdoor markets** farther from the center of town. For Orthodox icons and other church-related paraphernalia, the monasteries have the most authentic and attractive selection.

In general, vendors have become much more market savvy after a decade and a half of capitalism. That means the shocking bargains of black market days are long gone, but it also means that quality is more reliable and competition has livened up the selection of products available. Beware, as in all big cities, of con artists on the street trying to sell a "real" silver fox hat or tsarist medal hat for a suspiciously low price. Finally, avoid purchasing vodka from street kiosks—the rock-bottom prices often conceal liquids of dubious quality.

3 MOSCOW

Moscow has matured over a millennium into a richly layered, ever-expanding, and never-sleeping metropolis. Its sporadic growth has left it without a compact downtown, which means that great sights, hotels, and restaurants can be found in nearly any corner of the city. Its vast territory requires plenty of walking and rides on public transport.

VISITOR INFORMATION

Hotels or tour desks are generally the best source of information, although **Intourist,** formerly the government tourist agency, still has Moscow offices in the Kosmos Hotel at 150 Prospekt Mira (✆ **495/753-00-03;** www.intourist.ru) and on Leontyevsky Pereulok, #10 (✆ **495/753-00-03**). Pick up a copy of the free English-language daily ***The Moscow Times*** for weather, exchange rates, and entertainment listings. Most of the hotels listed carry copies. See also "Visitor Information" in section 2 in this chapter.

For general city tours and Kremlin tours, **Capital Tours,** 4 Ilinka Ulitsa, inside Gostiny Dvor (© **495/232-2442;** www.capitaltours.ru), is the best equipped and most friendly. Its Kremlin tours include the Armory and run Monday through Saturday at 10:30am and at 3pm, for $60 (£37) with admission. City bus tours run daily at 11am and 2:30pm for $32 (£20).

GETTING THERE

BY PLANE The international flights arrive at **Sheremetevo-2 Airport** (© **495/232-6565;** www.sheremetyevo-airport.ru), 30km (18 miles) north of downtown. An express train can take you to Savyolovsky Vokzal in Moscow in 30 minutes for 250 rubles ($10/£6.20). Taxis to the city center run at around $55 (£34). **Moscow Taxi** (www.moscow-taxi.com) and **Taxi Transparking** (© **495/578-8063**) offer good English-speaking services. Buses from Sheremetevo-2 stop at Rechnoi Vokzal metro station (bus no. 851C express) or Planernaya metro station (bus-taxi no. 49). The biggest European airlines, British Airways, Lufthansa, Emirates, and American Airlines now arrive at the bright, renovated **Domodedovo Airport** (© **495/933-6666** or 495/363-3064; www.domodedovo.ru), 50km (31 miles) south of the center. An **Aeroexpress** train runs direct to Paveletsky station, just south of the city center. The trip takes about 45 minutes and costs 150 rubles ($6/£3.70). Taxis from Domodedovo to the center take about an hour and cost at least $60 (£37). Licensed taxi companies include **Gorodskoe Taxi** (www.500-0-500.ru) and MV Motors (www.775-6-775.ru).

BY TRAIN The St. Petersburg–Moscow train route brings you into Leningradsky station, conveniently located on the Circle Line of the metro. Trains from western Europe generally arrive in Belorussky station, barely north of the city center and within walking distance of the hotels on busy Tverskaya street.

BY BUS Buses arrive at **Tsentralny Avtovokzal (Central Bus Terminal)** at 75 Schelkovskoe Shosse (© **495/468-0400**). The Schelkovskaya metro station is adjacent. Taxis from the terminal take about 30 minutes to reach the city center at a rate of $15 (£9.30).

BY CAR Take the vehicle to your hotel and inquire about secure parking. Don't drive around Moscow.

GETTING AROUND

BY PUBLIC TRANSPORTATION The **Moscow metro** is an attraction unto itself (p. 587), and well worth a visit just to view a few stations. Station entrances are marked with a letter M. Opening and closing times are roughly 5:30am to 1am daily. Tickets are sold in each station; 10 trips cost 155 rubles ($6.20/£3.85).

Three of the best **tram** lines (A, 3, and 39) run along the Boulevard Ring before crossing the Moscow River, offering a stunning view of the Kremlin. **Trolleybuses** are a good option for travel around the Garden Ring Road or along Novy Arbat Street. Trolley stops are marked with the letter T, and tram stops with the letters TP. Trams and trolleybuses run from 6am to midnight. Tickets for trams and trolleybuses cost 17 rubles (70¢/40p) from the driver.

BY TAXI Official taxis are hard to come by in Moscow, except at train stations and major hotels. Try **Moscow Taxi** (online only at www.moscow-taxi.com) or **www.taxi-t.ru** (© **495/**970-0778).

BY CAR The following agencies rent cars with and without drivers: **AM Rent,** 1 Partiyniy Pereyulok (✆ **495/506-7424;** www.amrent.ru); and **Budget Rent-a-Car,** Sheremetevo-2 Airport (✆ **495/578-7344**), and 23 1-aya Tverskaya-Yamskaya Ulitsa (✆ **495/931-9700,** ext. 117; www.budget.ru).

Fast Facts Moscow

American Express The main local office is at 17 Vetoshny Pereulok (a minor building of GUM; ✆ **495/543-9400;** Mon–Fri 9am–5pm).

Currency Exchange Exchange booths *(obmen valyuty)* are found in every hotel, at many restaurants, and near all major metro stations. Many are open 24 hours. Banks can give cash advances on a credit card in rubles.

Doctor The **American Medical Center Moscow,** 1 Grokholsky Pereulok (✆ **495/933-7700**), has Western-standard medical care and English-speaking staff.

Embassies **United States:** 21 Novinsky Bulvar; ✆ 495/728-5577; after-hours emergencies: 495/28-5025. **Britain:** 10 Smolenskaya Naberezhnaya; ✆ 495/956-7301. **Canada:** 23 Starokonyushenny Pereulok; ✆ 495/956-6666. **Australia:** 13 Kropotkinsky Pereulok; ✆ 495/956-6070. **Ireland:** 5 Grokholsky Pereulok; ✆ 495/937-5911.

Emergencies For fire, dial ✆ **01;** police ✆ **02;** ambulance ✆ **03.**

Internet Access Most hotel business centers offer Wi-Fi or online access. For Internet cafes, try 24-hour **Time Online** at Okhotny Ryad shopping center next to the Kremlin, 1 Manezhnaya Ploshchad (www.timeonline.ru), or **CafeMax** (see www.cafemax.ru for locations).

Postal Services The main international post office is at 26 Myasnitskaya (✆ **495/925-8623**). It's open daily 8am to 7:45pm. Several international shipping companies serve Russia, such as **FedEx** (✆ **495-788-8881**) and UPS (✆ **495/961-2211**), though their services are not cheap.

Telephone The city code for Moscow is 495. For international calls from Russia, dial 8, wait for a tone, then dial 10, then dial the country code. Access number for AT&T in Moscow is ✆ 755-5042; MCI is ✆ 747-3322; BT Direct you dial 8, wait for a tone then ✆ 10-80-01-10-1044; Canada Direct is also dial 8, wait for a tone then ✆ 10-800-110-1012.

WHERE TO STAY

The boom in Moscow hotel space since the Soviet Union's collapse has focused on luxury or business-class accommodations, and demand is high for midrange hotels.

Most of the better deals on hotels are found beyond the Garden Ring Road, well away from the main sights. If your hotel is near a metro station, that's a plus and can reduce travel time considerably. Rack rates listed here are in U.S. dollars, and do *not* include breakfast and the 18% VAT, unless noted. Most offer substantial discounts online.

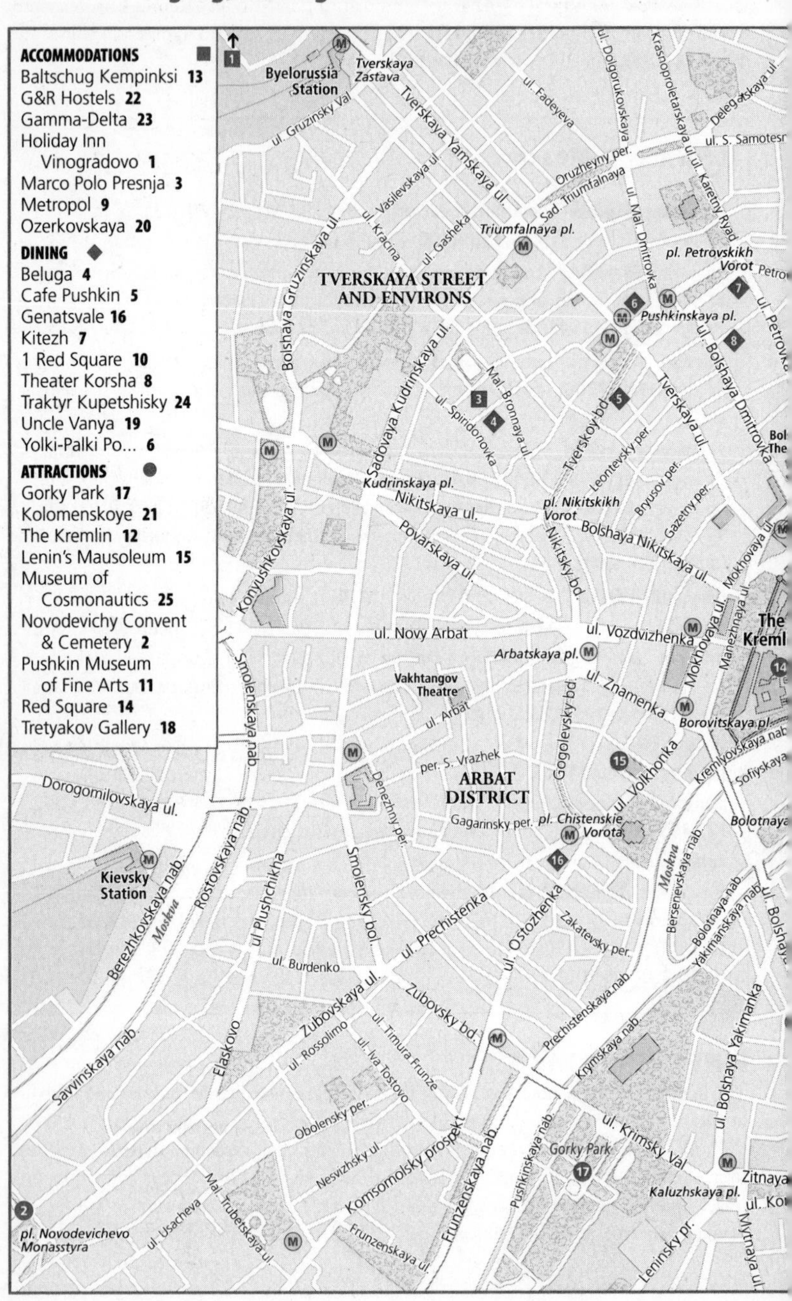
ACCOMMODATIONS
Baltschug Kempinksi 13
G&R Hostels 22
Gamma-Delta 23
Holiday Inn Vinogradovo 1
Marco Polo Presnja 3
Metropol 9
Ozerkovskaya 20
DINING
Beluga 4
Cafe Pushkin 5
Genatsvale 16
Kitezh 7
1 Red Square 10
Theater Korsha 8
Traktyr Kupetshisky 24
Uncle Vanya 19
Yolki-Palki Po... 6
ATTRACTIONS
Gorky Park 17
Kolomenskoye 21
The Kremlin 12
Lenin's Mausoleum 15
Museum of Cosmonautics 25
Novodevichy Convent & Cemetery 2
Pushkin Museum of Fine Arts 11
Red Square 14
Tretyakov Gallery 18
Byelorussia Station
Tverskaya Zastava
Tverskaya Yamskaya ul.
ul. Gruzinsky Val
ul. Fadeyeva
ul. Dolgorukovskaya
Krasnoproletarskaya ul.
Delegatskaya ul.
ul. S. Samotesn
Oruzheyny per.
Sad. Triumfalnaya
ul. Karetny Ryad
ul. Mal. Dmitrovka
Vasilevskaya ul.
ul. Kracina
ul. Gasheka
Triumfalnaya pl.
Bolshaya Gruzinskaya ul.
TVERSKAYA STREET AND ENVIRONS
pl. Petrovskikh Vorot
Pushkinskaya pl.
ul. Petrovka
ul. Bolshaya Dmitrovka
Sadovaya Kudrinskaya ul.
Mal. Bronnaya ul.
ul. Spiridonovka
Tverskoy bd.
Tverskaya ul.
Leontevsky per.
Bryusov per.
Gazetny per.
Kudrinskaya pl.
Nikitskaya ul.
pl. Nikitskikh Vorot
Bolshaya Nikitskaya ul.
Povarskaya ul.
Nikitsky bd.
Konyushkovskaya ul.
Mokhovaya ul.
ul. Novy Arbat
ul. Vozdvizhenka
Arbatskaya pl.
The Kreml
Manezhnaya ul.
Smolenskaya nab.
Vakhtangov Theatre
ul. Arbat
ul. Znamenka
Gogolevsky bd.
Borovitskaya pl.
per. S. Vrazhek
ARBAT DISTRICT
ul. Volkhonka
Kremlyovskaya nab.
Sofiyskaya
Dorogomilovskaya ul.
Denezhny per.
Gagarinsky per.
pl. Chistenskie Vorota
Bolotnaya
Kievsky Station
Berezhkovskaya nab.
Moskva
Rostovskaya nab.
ul. Plushchikha
Smolensky bul.
ul. Prechistenka
ul. Ostozhenka
Zakatevsky per.
Bersenevskaya nab.
Bolotnaya nab.
Yakimanskaya nab.
ul. Bolshaya
ul. Burdenko
Zubovskaya ul.
Zubovsky bd.
Prechistenskaya nab.
Savvinskaya nab.
Elaskovo
ul. Rossolimo
ul. Timura Frunze
ul. Iva Tostovo
Krymskaya nab.
Bolshaya Yakimanka
Obolensky per.
Komsomolsky prospekt
Frunzenskaya nab.
Pushkinskaya nab.
Gorky Park
ul. Krimsky Val
ul. Bolshaya Polyanka
Nesvizhsky ul.
Mal. Trubetskaya ul.
ul. Usacheva
Frunzenskaya ul.
Kaluzhskaya pl.
Zitnaya
Leninsky pr.
Mytnaya ul.
pl. Novodevichevo Monasstyra

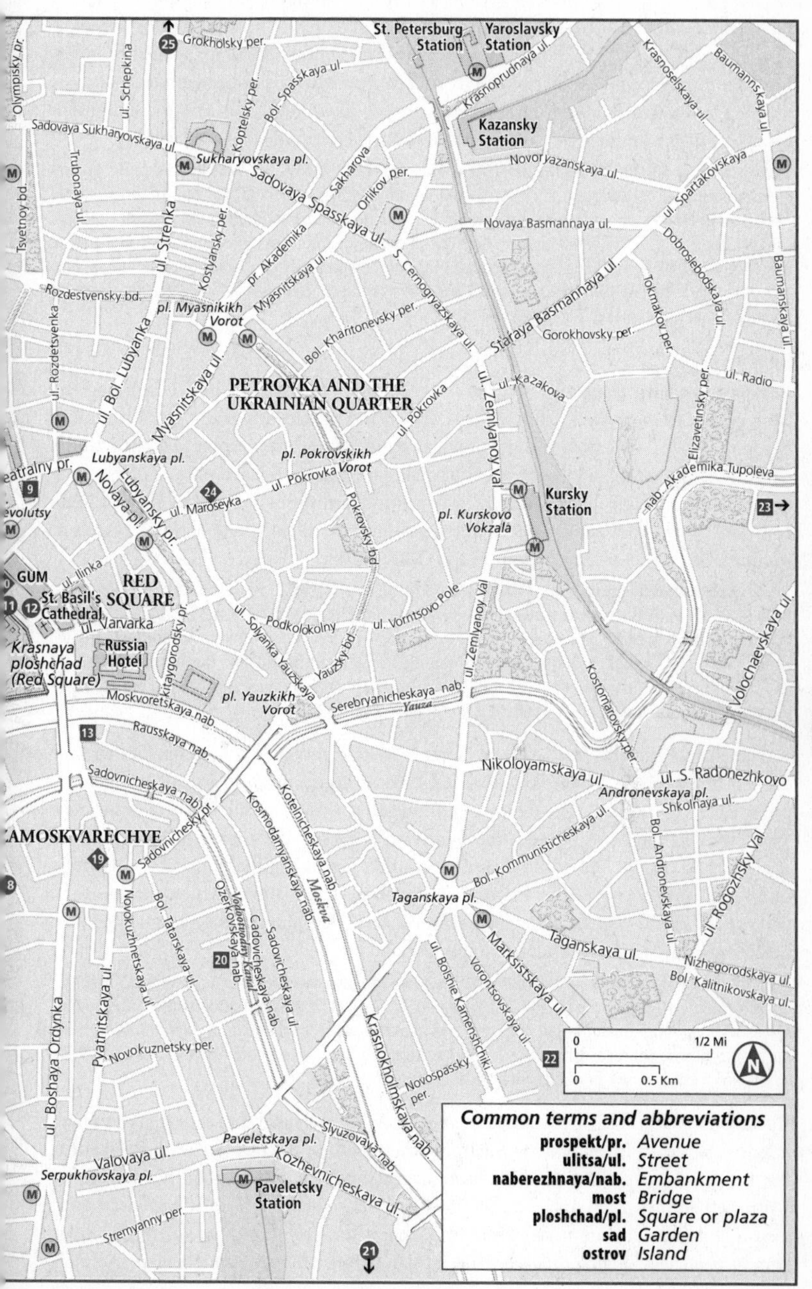

St. Petersburg Station
Yaroslavsky Station
Kazansky Station
Kursky Station
Paveletsky Station
PETROVKA AND THE UKRAINIAN QUARTER
RED SQUARE
ZAMOSKVARECHYE
GUM
St. Basil's Cathedral
Russia Hotel
Krasnaya ploshchad (Red Square)
Grokholsky per.
Bol. Spasskaya ul.
Krasnoprudnaya ul.
Krasnoselskaya ul.
Baumannskaya ul.
ul. Schepkina
Olympisky pr.
Sadovaya Sukharyovskaya ul.
Sukharyovskaya pl.
Sadovaya Spasskaya ul.
Koptelsky per.
Trubonaya ul.
Tsvetnoy bd.
Sakharova
Orlikov per.
Novoryazanskaya ul.
ul. Spartakovskaya
Novaya Basmannaya ul.
ul. Strenka
Kostyansky per.
pr. Akademika
Myasnitskaya ul.
S. Cernogryazskaya ul.
Dobroslobodskaya ul.
Baumanskaya ul.
Rozdestvensky bd.
pl. Myasnikikh Vorot
Bol. Kharitonevsky per.
Staraya Basmannaya ul.
Tokmakov per.
Gorokhovsky per.
ul. Radio
ul. Rozdetsvenka
ul. Bol. Lubyanka
Myasnitskaya ul.
ul. Kazakova
ul. Zemlyanoy val
Elizavetinsky per.
ul. Pokrovka
pl. Pokrovskikh Vorot
Lubyanskaya pl.
Teatralny pr.
Novaya pl.
Lubyansky pr.
ul. Maroseyka
ul. Pokrovka
nab. Akademika Tupoleva
Revolutsy
pl. Kurskovo Vokzala
Pokrovsky bd
ul. Ilinka
ul. Varvarka
Kitaygorodsky pr.
ul. Solyanka
Podkolokolny
ul. Vorntsovo Pole
ul. Zemlyanoy Val
Volochaevskaya ul.
Yauzky bd
Yauzkaya
pl. Yauzkikh Vorot
Serebryanicheskaya nab.
Yauza
Moskvoretskaya nab.
Kostomarovsky per.
Raushskaya nab.
Nikoloyamskaya ul.
ul. S. Radonezhkovo
Andronevskaya pl.
Shkolnaya ul.
Sadovnicheskaya nab.
Sadovnichesky pr.
Kotelnicheskaya nab.
Kosmodamyanskaya nab.
Bol. Kommunisticheskaya ul.
Bol. Andronevskaya ul.
ul. Rogozhsky Val
Moskva
Taganskaya pl.
Novokuznetskaya ul.
Bol. Tatarskaya ul.
Ozerkovskaya nab.
Vodootvodny Kanal
Cadovicheskaya nab.
Sadovicheskaya ul.
Marksistskaya ul.
Taganskaya ul.
Nizhegorodskaya ul.
Bol. Kalitnikovskaya ul.
ul. Bolshie Kamenshchiki
Vorontsovskaya ul.
Pyatnitskaya ul.
ul. Boshaya Ordynka
Novokuznetsky per.
Krasnokholmskaya nab.
Novospassky per.
Paveletskaya pl.
Slyuzovaya nab.
Valovaya ul.
Kozhevnicheskaya ul.
Serpukhovskaya pl.
Stremyanny per.
0 1/2 Mi
0 0.5 Km
N
Common terms and abbreviations
prospekt/pr. Avenue
ulitsa/ul. Street
naberezhnaya/nab. Embankment
most Bridge
ploshchad/pl. Square or plaza
sad Garden
ostrov Island

Very Expensive

Baltschug Kempinski ★★★ The Baltschug led the post-Soviet transformation of this district across the Moscow River from the Kremlin. Its pristine, buttercup-yellow facade immediately altered the neglected neighborhood of canals and abandoned churches. Just over the bridge is Red Square and its attendant activity; the bohemian bustle of Pyatnitskaya Street spreads out in the other direction, to the south. Don't miss the sumptuous brunch of prerevolutionary Russian delicacies and all the caviar you could want.

1 Ulitsa Balchug. ✆ **800/426-3135** or 495/230-6500. Fax 495/230-6502. www.kempinski-moscow.com. 232 units. $360 (£223) double; from $800 (£496) suite; $65 (£40) extra bed. AE, DC, MC, V. Metro: Teatralnaya, Kuznetsky Most, or Lubyanka. **Amenities:** 3 restaurants; 2 bars; indoor heated pool; health club; spa; Jacuzzi; 2 saunas; children's center; game room; concierge; tour desk; car-rental desk; limo; 24-hr. business center; Wi-Fi; shopping arcade; salon; 24-hr. room service; massage; babysitting; laundry service; same-day dry cleaning; nonsmoking rooms; executive rooms. *In room:* A/C, TV w/satellite, dataport, minibar, fridge, coffeemaker, hair dryer, iron, safe.

Expensive

Holiday Inn Vinogradovo ★ Kids This resort-type facility is unlike anything else Moscow has to offer. Well removed from the city, it's tucked in a forest 4km (2½ miles) beyond the bypass marking the city limits, not too far from the airport. The free shuttle takes awhile to get to and from town, but makes the place feel less remote. The plus side of such a distant locale is the availability of outdoor amenities unheard of at other Moscow hotels: horseback riding, as well as cross-country skiing in winter and watersports in summer. Guest rooms are generous in size. Kids eat free.

Dmitrovskoye Shosse, Estate 171. ✆ **877/477-4674** or 495/937-0670. www.ichotels.com. 154 units. $300 (£186) double, depending on when you reserve; from $380 (£235) suite. AE, DC, MC, V. 4km (2½ miles) north of Moscow Ring Rd. along Dmitrovskoye Shosse (visible from the hwy.). **Amenities:** 2 restaurants; 2 bars; indoor pool; health club; sauna; tour desk; transport desk; 24-hr. business center; salon; 24-hr. room service; massage; laundry room; same-day dry cleaning; nonsmoking rooms; executive rooms; bowling alley. *In room:* TV w/satellite, fridge, coffeemaker, iron.

Marco Polo Presnja ★★ A rare example of style, service, and affordability when it opened in 1993, the Marco Polo now faces greater competition in its category, and its prices have risen accordingly. Yet it remains one of Moscow's most coveted places to stay. The leafy neighborhood between the Boulevard Ring and the Garden Ring is ideal for strolling, and nearby Malaya Bronnaya Street offers several unusual shopping and dining finds you won't encounter on the city's main drags. The main attraction nearby is the park at Patriarchs' Ponds. Despite the hotel's relatively modest size, its guest rooms, bathrooms, closets, and corridors are spacious and airy.

4 Spiridonevsky Pereulok. ✆ **095/202-6061.** Fax 495/626-5402. www.presnja.ru. 72 units. $300 (£186) double; from $370 (£229) suite; $48 (£24) extra bed. AE, DC, MC, V. Metro: Pushkinskaya, Tverskaya, or Mayakovskaya. **Amenities:** 2 restaurants; bar and lounge; sauna; concierge; tour desk; transport desk; business center; room service; massage; laundry service; dry cleaning; executive rooms. *In room:* A/C, TV w/satellite and pay movies, minibar, fridge, hair dryer, iron.

Metropol ★★ The Art Nouveau mosaic by Mikhail Vrubel that tops the Metropol's facade sets it apart in era and in style from other hotels of its class. Some of its grandeur has faded in comparison to the newer luxury hotels in the neighborhood, but the Metropol, built in 1901 and last renovated in 1991, remains a historic and visual treasure. The rooms are compact for the price, but several offer antique writing tables or armchairs once belonging to aristocratic Russian families. The Metropol's western wall is still etched with stylistic letters reading: THE DICTATORSHIP OF THE PROLETARIAT IS READY TO FREE HUMANITY FROM THE YOKE OF CAPITAL.

1/4 Teatralny Proyezd. ✆ **499/501-7800** if called from abroad or 499/501-7800 if calling from Moscow. www.metropol-moscow.ru. 365 units. $365 (£226) double; from $750 (£465) suite. AE, DC, MC, V. Metro: Teatralnaya or Lubyanka. **Amenities:** 3 restaurants; nightclub and casino; health club; spa; Jacuzzi; sauna; concierge; tour desk; transport desk; limo; 24-hr. business center; shopping arcade; salon; 24-hr. room service; massage; laundry service; same-day dry cleaning; nonsmoking rooms; executive rooms. *In room:* A/C, TV w/satellite, dataport, minibar, fridge, coffeemaker, hair dryer, iron, safe.

Moderate

Gamma-Delta ★ Value This is the closest to a Western-standard facility in this price range. Lobby computer screens tastefully and helpfully display prices and services in Russian and English. Staff is accustomed to international travelers.

71 Izmailovskoye Shosse. ✆ **495/737-7070.** Fax 495/166-7486. www.izmailovo.ru. More than 1,000 units. $190 (£118) renovated double from $215 (£133); from $315 (£195) suite. AE, DC, MC, V. Metro: Izmailovsky Park. **Amenities:** 9 restaurants and bars; sauna; game room; concierge; tour desk; transport desk; business center; shopping arcade; salon; room service; laundry and ironing service. *In room:* TV w/ cable, fridge, hair dryer.

Ozerkovskaya ★★ Value A welcome addition to the hotel scene south of the Moscow River, the Ozerkovskaya occupies a new brick building set off from the road along one of the canals in the picturesque Zamoskvarechye. Eager staff and cozy yet spacious rooms make the Ozerkovskaya one of Moscow's best hotels in this category. Its location, deep in a residential neighborhood, is not exactly central, but it's certainly quiet. Tretyakov Gallery can be reached on foot; and the Paveletskaya metro station is about a 10-minute walk away. Rates include VAT and breakfast.

50 Ozerkovskaya Naberezhnaya, building 2. ✆ **495/777-1938.** ozerkovskaya@bk.ru. 25 units. $180 (£111) double; from $300 (£186) suite. AE, DC, MC, V. Metro: Paveletskaya. **Amenities:** Restaurant and bar; health club w/very small pool; sauna; billiard room; tour desk; transport desk; business center; salon; room service; laundry and ironing service; dry cleaning; executive rooms. *In room:* TV w/satellite, dataport, kitchen, minibar, fridge, hair dryer.

Inexpensive

G&R Hostels Though Moscow lacks hostels of the traditional sort, several independent entrepreneurs have taken over a floor or more of existing buildings and converted them into low-budget accommodations. G&R is one of the more pleasant and reliable in this category, and offers family-style units with private bathrooms and telephones, in addition to singles and doubles with shared bathrooms. The hostel can arrange for visas, a big plus in this price category. G&R is almost on top of a metro station (Ryazansky Prospekt), and the ride to the center takes about 15 minutes. Prices include VAT and breakfast, and discounts are available.

3/2 Zelenodolskaya St. ✆ **495/378-0001.** www.hostels.ru. 15 units. $30 (£19) single with shared bathroom; $48 (£30) double with shared bathroom; $70–$95 (£43–£59) family suite. MC, V. Metro: Ryazansky Prospekt. **Amenities:** Tour and transport desk; visa support; common kitchen; business center. *In room:* Some rooms w/cable TV, fridge.

WHERE TO DINE

In today's Moscow you can find food to satisfy all palates, in marked contrast to the decades of Soviet shortages. There are now restaurants to suit any pocketbook or craving—at any time of day or night. See also "Tips on Dining" on p. 577.

Very Expensive

1 Red Square (Krasnaya Ploshchad, 1) ★★★ RUSSIAN The name says it all. From the top floor of the National History Museum on the north side of Red Square, you can enjoy a meal as you gaze directly across the cobblestone expanse leading to St. Basil's Cathedral on the opposite end. The museum's neo-Gothic turrets and the location's historical significance imbue the restaurant staff and the Russian clientele with a sense of national importance. The menu is Russian and traditional, including a re-creation of the "tsar's menu" of a century ago.

1 Red Square (enter through Historical Museum). ✆ **495/692-1196.** http://redsquare.ru/english. Reservations recommended. Main courses $20 (£12) and up; business lunch $19 (£12). AE, MC, V. Daily noon–midnight. Metro: Ploshchad Revolutsii or Okhotny Ryad.

Theater Korsha ★★ RUSSIAN The haute couture attitudes, decor, and clientele of this restaurant fit perfectly with the luxuriousness of its specialty. The caviar is excellent and expensive, though not necessarily better than what you find in other top Russian restaurants. Caviar is served straight, in set quantities by the gram, and accompanied by a generous array of rich dark breads, pasta, and grilled vegetables.

3 Petrovsky Pereulok. ✆ **495/694-5038.** Reservations recommended. Main courses $20–$100 (£12–£62). AE, DC, MC, V. Daily noon–midnight. Metro: Pushkinskaya or Tverskaya.

Expensive

Cafe Pushkin ★★★ RUSSIAN Perhaps Moscow's most sophisticated 24-hour restaurant, the three-story Cafe Pushkin has the feel of an 18th-century mansion but dates from the late 1990s. Each of the floors has a different thrust, with a cherrywood bar and well-lit cafe on the first floor, a more formal dining room on the second, and a decadent and breezy summer cafe on the top. Standouts are *ukha,* a creamy, spiced fish soup; and grilled *sterlet* (sturgeon) with forest mushrooms.

26a Tverskoi Bulvar. ✆ **495/787-4085.** Reservations required for restaurant and summer terrace. Main courses $25–$60 (£16–£37). AE, DC, MC, V. 1st floor daily 24 hr., top floors daily noon–midnight. Metro: Pushkinskaya.

Kitezh ★★★ RUSSIAN Kitezh sees its purpose as upholding tradition and legend. If you have just one real Russian meal in Moscow, make it here. The restaurant is poised in a stone basement that re-creates a 17th-century farmhouse atmosphere, across from a 14th-century monastery on a quiet stretch of historic Petrovka Street, a great district for a post-meal stroll. Sauces are rich, divine, and heavy. This is one of the few Russian restaurants that do justice to beef stroganoff. Desserts include thick, Jell-O-like *kisel,* and light and buttery *bliny* with homemade jam.

23/10 Ulitsa Petrovka. ✆ **495/650-6685.** Reservations recommended. Main courses $12–$30 (£7.45–£19). AE, MC, V. Daily noon–midnight. Metro: Chekhovskaya.

Moderate

Genatsvale ★★ GEORGIAN This family-run restaurant—whose name means "comrade" in Georgian—is Moscow's best introduction to the colorful and flavorful cuisine of Georgia. The country-style dining hall is a welcome dose of earthiness on this street of chic restaurants. Try the finely ground lamb kabob, or the garlic-walnut paste rolled in thinly sliced eggplant.

12/1 Ostozhenka. ✆ **495/695-0401.** Main courses $10–$30 (£6.20–£19). MC, V. Daily noon–midnight. Metro: Kropotkinskaya.

Moments Banya Bliss

It's not on most tourist itineraries, but if you can squeeze it in, there's no better way to shed city grime and immerse yourself in Russian culture than to visit a banya. Something between a steam bath and a sauna, the banya has been an important cleansing and resting ritual for centuries. Traditional banyas are huts built alongside rural houses, where families take turns steaming themselves clean, then plunge into a tub of cool water or a nearby stream, or roll in the snow to cool off. In Moscow, banya culture ranges from elite spa-type facilities with expensive body masks and luxurious pedicures (for both sexes) to more proletarian facilities used by residents of communal apartments tired of waiting in line for the shower at home. Thought to cure many ills, the banya is a great rainy-day activity for tourists, too, if you pick one with a bit of history. In the women's halls, bathers treat the steam water with eucalyptus oil and coat their skin with honey, coffee grounds, or whatever other remedy they learned from grandma. In the men's halls, business deals are often made over copious beer and snacks. In both halls you're likely to see bathers beating each other (gently) with birch branches; the practice is believed to enhance the cleansing process.

Sandunovskiye Banyi, an ornate and cheerful 19th-century bathhouse, is a favorite with "new Russians" and Moscow-based expatriates. They have two levels of service for each gender. A 2-hour deluxe-level session costs $22 (£14); a 2-hour standard-level session costs $14 (£8.70). The differences between the deluxe and standard sessions are minimal; a deluxe session basically translates into more elegant furnishings and a larger steam room. Sheets, towels, and slippers can be rented for $1 to $4 (60p–£2.50), or you can bring your own. The deluxe level is offered Tuesday through Sunday from 8am to 10pm; the standard level is offered Wednesday through Monday from 8am to 10pm. You'll find the baths at 14 Neglinnaya St., buildings 3 to 7; the entrance is on Zvonarsky Pereulok (✆ **495/625-4631** or 495/628-4633; www.sanduny.ru).

Slyokhim parom, as the Russians say, or "Good steam to you."

Uncle Vanya ★★ RUSSIAN This cozy, artsy treasure left its original location in a theater basement to relocate to another basement in this even more cozy, artsy section of town. The restaurant takes its name from one of Anton Chekhov's plays. The menu of Russian favorites is accessible and safe, with highlights including cold sorrel soup *(zelyoniye shchi),* wild mushrooms, and buckwheat kasha.

16 Pyatnitskaya (entrance in courtyard). ✆ **495/232-1448.** www.dvrest.com. Main courses $5–$15 (£3.10–£9.30). MC, V. Daily 8:30am–midnight. Metro: Novokuznetskaya.

Inexpensive

Traktyr Kupetchisky ★ RUSSIAN To a Russian, the crayfish is a summertime staple as crucial to the national cuisine as caviar, and much more accessible. Bright red, just-boiled crayfish are the main draw at this spot, formerly known as Russian Crayfish, with variations such as boiled in beer, spiced, or doused in cream sauce.

 11/4 Maroseyka, building 1. ✆ **495/921-8545.** Main courses $10–$20 (£6.20–£12). No credit cards. Daily 11am–11pm. Metro: Kitai-Gorod.

Yolki-Palki Po . . . ★ (Value) CENTRAL ASIAN As soon as you shed your coat, you'll be greeted by a row of fresh ingredients that you heap into a bowl according to your mood and hand to the chef at the center of an enormous circular grill. The Mongolian barbecue–style concept is adapted with central Asian ingredients and Russian side dishes, and it has found huge success in Moscow.

Multiple locations, including 118 Prospekt Mira. ✆ **495/687-3005.** www.elki-palki.ru. Main courses $7 (£4.35). No credit cards. Daily 11am–5am. Metro: Alexeevskaya.

EXPLORING MOSCOW

Moscow is less a beautiful city than a collection of beautiful sights, many of them hidden beyond the expansive modern boulevards that Soviet governments bulldozed through town. The key to delighting in Moscow is to not let it overwhelm you. The things to see fall roughly into four categories: church-related, art-related, Soviet-related, and everything else. Try to get a taste of each, regardless of your interests.

Suggested Itineraries

If You Have 1 Day

Capturing Moscow in 1 day means hitting the **Kremlin** and **Red Square** early and branching out from there (see **"Walking Tour–Historic Moscow,"** below). In the evening, explore the artsy **Arbat** neighborhood.

If You Have 2 Days

Use your second day to immerse yourself in Russian art at the **Tretyakov Gallery** and wander the canals of **Zamoskvarechye.** Reserve the evening for **Pushkin Square** and lively **Tverskaya Street.**

If You Have 3 Days

On the third day in Moscow, spend the morning at **Novodevichy Convent and Cemetery,** a secluded spot that feels miles from the downtown rush. Then take a car or the metro to **Gorky Park.** After lunch, head to the **Pushkin Museum of Fine Arts,** and spend the evening on a bus tour that hits sights farther afield.

THE TOP ATTRACTIONS

Gorky Park ★ The most visited part of the park is near the entrance, where an amusement park, ponds, and street performers compete for attention. A space shuttle, designed for space flight but scrapped for lack of funding, is now parked along the river and open to visitors. Note the Lenin carving over the park's columned entrance.

Krymsky Val. Admission $1.75 (£1.10). Daily 9am–9pm. Metro: Oktyabrskaya or Park Kultury.

Kolomenskoye ★★★ (Kids) This park, museum, festival site, and religious-history tour is the jewel of Moscow's estate museums. Kolomenskoye gathers churches and historic buildings from the 15th to the 20th centuries in a huge green space perfect for picnicking, sledding, or lounging in the grass.

39 Prospekt Andropova. ✆ **499/612-5217.** Admission $1.75 (£1.10). Daily 8am–9pm; museum Tues–Sun 10am–5:30pm. Metro: Kolomenskaya.

The Kremlin This 28-hectare (70-acre) fortress emerged in the 12th century as a wooden encampment, and survived many an invader to become synonymous with modern totalitarianism in the 20th century. Physically it's still a citadel, surrounded by unscalable redbrick walls and tightly guarded gates, though the moat that protected its north and east sides was filled in nearly 200 years ago. Its oak walls were replaced with white stone ones in the 1360s, which were replaced again by 2.2km (1½ miles) of red-brick ramparts in the 1490s. Much of that brick remains standing.

Cathedral Square (Sobornaya Ploshchad) ★★★ forms a monument to Russian architecture of the 15th and 16th centuries, and its cathedrals deserve a thorough tour inside and out. The most prominent building on the square is the **Cathedral of the Assumption** ★★, a white limestone building with scalloped arches topped by almost chunky golden domes. Started in 1475 by Italian architect Aristotle Fiorovanti, this church is the most tourist-friendly of the cathedrals on the square, with detailed English labels on icons and architectural details.

Despite its name, the **Armory Museum** ★★ (✆ **495/921-4720**) holds much more than guns. The Russo-Byzantine building, dating from the 19th century, occupies the spot where royal treasures were housed since the 14th century and offers a sweeping introduction to Russian history. Exhibits include the Fabergé eggs exchanged by Russia's last royal couple, Tsar Nicholas II and Empress Alexandra.

Kremlin tickets available at Kutafya Tower in Alexander Gardens (✆ **495/203-0349**). www.kreml.ru. Admission to the Kremlin grounds and the Cathedral Sq. complex costs $12 (£7.45) for adults, $2 (£1.25) for students with ID and for children 7 and up. Admission to the Armory costs $14 (£8.70) for adults, $7 (£4.30) for students and for children 7 and up.

Lenin's Mausoleum (Mavzolei Lenina) ★★★ The embalmed body of the founder of the Soviet state is still on display in a mausoleum on Red Square. The stark Constructivist pyramid of red granite and gray and black labradorite was built in 1930, 6 years after Vladimir Lenin's death. Backpacks are forbidden; they must be left at the bag check by the Kremlin's Borovitsky. Visit after seeing the Kremlin, and then get your bags.

Red Square. No phone. Free admission. Tues, Thurs, and Sat–Sun 10am–1pm. Metro: Ploshchad Revolutsii, Teatralnaya, or Okhotny Ryad.

The Moscow Metro ★★ (Value) Most cities' public transit systems are useful eyesores. Moscow's is a masterpiece. Today it's the world's busiest subway system. Its oldest stations, dating from the 1930s and 1940s, are its grandest. Highlights include Ploshchad Revolutsii, with its bronze sculptures of Soviet swimmers and sailors holding up the marble columns; Kievskaya, with its mosaics portraying Ukrainian-Russian friendship; and Novoslobodskaya, with its Art Nouveau stained glass.

Museum of Cosmonautics (Muzei Kosmonavtiki) ★ (Kids) (Value) Housed beneath a giant aluminum monument of a rocket soaring into space, this museum is a tribute to the minds and might that put the Soviet Union head-to-head with the United States in the space race. It's far from the center of town (but right on top of a metro station).

Prospekt Mira 111. ✆ **495/683-7914.** Admission $1.50 (95p) adults, 75¢ (45p) children 8 and up. Audio guide in English $3.50 (£2.15). Tues–Sun 10am–6pm; closed last Fri of each month. Metro: VDNKh.

Novodevichy Convent & Cemetery (Novodevichy Monastyr i Kladbishche) ★★ If you visit only one holy site in Moscow, make it this one. The convent, founded in 1524, became over ensuing eras a carefully arranged complex of churches in a variety of architectural styles. Don't miss the **cemetery** behind the convent, which bears the unique gravestones of many Russian literary, musical, and scientific heroes.

Novodevichy Proyezd. ✆ **495/246-8526.** Admission to the grounds $7 (£4.30); a combined ticket including churches and exhibits $15 (£9.30). Cemetery admission $10 (£6.20). Cathedrals may be closed to tourists on Easter and feast days. Wed–Sun 10am–5pm. Metro: Sportivnaya.

Pushkin Museum of Fine Arts (Muzei Izobratitelnykh Isskustv imeni Pushkina) ★★ An impressive collection of French Impressionist works, ancient Greek sculptures, and Egyptian bronzes, as well as works by Rembrandt, Rubens, and the Italian Renaissance masters. Be sure to view the exhibition of controversial paintings stolen from European Jews by the Nazis and later seized by Soviet troops (Russians call them "rescued" artworks), including pieces by Renoir and van Gogh.

12 Volkhonka. ✆ **495/203-7998.** www.museum.ru/gmii. Admission $15 (£9.30) adults, $7.25 (£4.50) students and children 7 and up. Exhibits $3.50 (£2.20). Audio guides $10 (£6.20) available at the coat check downstairs. Tues–Sun 10am–7pm. Metro: Kropotkinskaya.

Red Square (Krasnaya Ploshchad) ★★★ One of the world's most recognizable public spaces, Red Square is as impressive in reality as it is on screen. The square was already famous by 1434, when it was dubbed "Trading Square." Its current name appeared in the 1660s, when the word *krasnaya* meant "beautiful" or "important" as well as "red." The name took on different connotations in the 20th century, when the red flag–bearing Communists staged massive parades and demonstrations on the aptly titled square.

Red Square (Krasnaya Ploshchad). No phone. Free admission. Metro: Ploshchad Revolutsii or Okhotny Ryad.

Tretyakov Gallery (Tretyakovskaya Galereya) ★★★ Newcomers to Russian art and connoisseurs alike leave awed by this collection of masterpieces. The gallery was Russia's first public art museum, and remains the premier repository of Russian art, starting with Orthodox icons dating from Russia's conversion in the 9th century, through to the naturalism of the 19th century, the Art Nouveau works of Mikhail Vrubel, and the 20th-century avant-garde works of Malevich and Kandinsky.

10 Lavrushinsky Pereulok. ✆ **495/230-7788.** www.tretyakovgallery.ru. Admission $11 (£6.80) adults, $7.50 (£4.65) students and children 8 and up. Audio guide $10 (£6.20). No credit cards, but there's an ATM. Small group tours in English $35 (£22) plus admission. Tues–Sun 10am–7:30pm. Metro: Tretyakovskaya or Novokuznetskaya.

WALKING TOUR HISTORIC MOSCOW ★★★

This walk covers several centuries of Moscow's history, and provides a sense of how the eras blend to make modern Moscow. It begins at Red Square, and continues through the neighborhood of **Kitai-Gorod,** with its showcase of Russian architecture from the 15th to 17th centuries. A good time to take this tour is a morning from Wednesday to Sunday, when crowds are thinner and exhibits open. Allow 2 to 3 hours.

❶ St. Basil's Cathedral

The oldest building on this tour, this 16th-century cathedral has come to symbolize Russia to the rest of the world, but it was almost torn down by Stalin as an anachronistic eyesore. Legend has it that a favorite architect rescued the cathedral by threatening to take his own life on its stairs.

When leaving the cathedral, turn right, away from the Kremlin, down Varvarka Street. Take the stairs on the right-hand side of the street down to the path that runs alongside a string of churches and mansions. This is one of the few sections of Moscow preserved as it was in centuries past. Continue to no. 4:

❷ English Courtyard (Angliisky Podvorye)

This wooden-roofed building is one of the oldest civilian structures in Moscow, a

1 St. Basil's Cathedral
2 English Courtyard
3 The Museum of the Romanov Boyars
4 St. George's Church
5 Cyril and Methodius Monument
6 Lubyanka
7 Church of the Archangel Gabriel & Church of St. Theodore Stratilites
8 Chistiye Prudy

16th-century merchant's center granted to English traders by Ivan the Terrible. The small exhibit inside is worth a visit for the building's interior and artifacts (labeled in English). It's open Tuesday through Sunday from 10am to 6pm (✆ **495/298-3952**).

Continue up the path, noting the yellow-and-white (and no longer functioning) Church of St. Maxim the Blessed. The next few buildings were once part of the Znamensky Monastery. No. 10 houses:

❸ The Museum of the Romanov Boyars

The Romanov Boyars (nobles) lived here before Mikhail Romanov was crowned tsar in 1613, launching the Romanov dynasty. The only original part of this building is the basement; the rest was added later to re-create conditions of 16th-century Moscow. The building was once part of a minicity that stretched to the Moscow River. The museum (✆ **495/298-3706**) is open Wednesday from 11am to 7pm, and Thursday to Sunday from 10am to 6pm (closed the first Mon of the month).

Head to the building next door, the last one along the row, just beneath the hotel driveway:

❹ St. George's Church

This church was built in two different eras, the 16th and 18th centuries, and its two parts remain different colors. It still holds regular services.

Head up the stairs to Varvarka proper, and continue down the hill. The street opens onto an intersection that can only be crossed by underground walkway. The sole remaining part of the 16th-century Varvarka gate tower is the white stone base, still visible in the underground passage. Once you're underground, continue straight along your trajectory from Varvarka. Take the first stairwell on your left aboveground. You should emerge in front of:

5 Cyril and Methodius Monument

Perched in the middle of Slavic Square, this monument portrays the two 9th-century monks credited with inventing the Cyrillic alphabet, used in Russia and many Slavic countries to this day. Up the hill behind the monument stretch the leafy slopes of Novaya Ploshchad (New Sq.), crisscrossed by shaded paths lined with benches.

Head to the plaza on the far side of Novaya Ploshchad, and look across it at a building that no Russian feels indifferent to:

6 Lubyanka

The Bolshevik secret police seized this granite-and-sandstone building from an insurance company in 1918, and its residents have spied on Russians ever since. Now it's the headquarters of the Federal Security Service, once led by President Putin.

Head back into the capitalist rush of modern Moscow by crossing over to Myasnitskaya Ulitsa, to the right of Lubyanka. Follow the street past a string of bookshops and cafes until you see Krivokolyonny Pereulok off to the right. Take this street (which translates as "Crooked Knee Lane") past the 18th- and 19th-century mansions now housing offices and apartments, until you reach two churches clustered together:

7 Church of the Archangel Gabriel & Church of St. Theodore Stratilites

The twisting gold dome of the Church of the Archangel Gabriel is the most noticeable of its nontraditional architectural features. Commissioned in 1705, the church is a clear example of the period when European classicism overrode Russian architecture, with grand buttresses and cornices not seen on most Orthodox churches.

Continue a few yards to the end of Krivokolyonny Pereulok. You'll emerge onto Chistoprudny Bulvar, a boulevard with a green space running down its center. Enter the park and head right, until you reach:

8 Chistiye Prudy

This area was referred to as "Dirty Ponds" in the days when it housed a meat market, whose refuse ran into the murky pools. The 19th-century city government cleaned it up and rechristened it "Clean Ponds," or Chistiye Prudy. Only one pond remains; it's a mecca for skaters and toddlers on sleds in winter, and for rental boats in summer.

SHOPPING

Just about any souvenir, bauble, or item of clothing you could want can be found just off Red Square, at the two city's major shopping centers: **GUM** and **Okhotny Ryad.** But Moscow's souvenir shopping mecca is the huge open-air bazaar open daily at **Izmailovsky Park** (near the metro station of the same name), in eastern Moscow, outside the Garden Ring. It has a huge selection of *matryoshka* nesting dolls, plus Russian space-program memorabilia, intricate and original jewelry, blue-hued Uzbek plates, lacquer boxes, and much more.

Kupina's (✆ **495/637-4940**) two stores on the Arbat offer Russian and European art and antiques, and **Alfa-Art** (✆ **495/230-0091**), an established gallery inside the New Tretyakov Modern Art Museum, holds auctions for its most valuable works as well as regular sales of its icons, paintings, and other items. For a great introduction to the Russian ceramic style known as Gzhel, with delicate blue designs painted on white porcelain and occasionally trimmed in gold, try **Gzhel** (✆ **495/491-7719;** www.gzhel.ru) on Ulitsa Svobody near Tushinskaya metro station. Hand-embroidered linens from the textile-producing towns along the Volga are a good buy, and can be found at **Vologodsky**

Len (✆ **495/232-9463;** www.linens.ru) in the Gostiny Dvor shopping center near Red Square.

The ornate **Eliseyevsky Gastronom** (✆ **495/650-0760**) on Tverskaya Street has an abundant collection of teas, sweets, and other Russian goods on display beneath its soaring ceilings, while **Aromatny Mir** (✆ **495/917-1160**) on Ulitsa Pokrovka near Kurskaya metro station features a broad selection of vodkas you won't find at home, as well as wines from the former Soviet republics of Georgia and Moldova, and rich Armenian brandies.

MOSCOW AFTER DARK

A large proportion of Moscow's tourists come primarily for its performing arts or, increasingly, its nightlife. Its reputation in both departments is well deserved. The most thorough English-language listings for theater, music, and movies are found in the Friday edition of *The Moscow Times* (www.themoscowtimes.com). Check *eXile* newspaper (www.exile.ru) for the latest hot clubs and bars.

Performing Arts

Bolshoi Theater Moscow's top dance venue remains the Bolshoi, the showcase for several generations of internationally adored ballet stars. Tchaikovsky's classics still form its backbone. Operas at the Bolshoi stick to the classics, such as *The Marriage of Figaro, The Barber of Seville,* and *Carmen.* Tickets must be purchased at least a week in advance. The Bolshoi is currently renovating its principal building, which will be closed to the public until November 2009. Until then, the second stage is hosting the main company and all the same top-tier performances. 1 Teatralnaya Sq. ✆ **495/250-7317.** www.bolshoi.ru/en. Metro: Teatralnaya.

Chaliapin House Museum You'll really feel transported to prerevolutionary Russia during a concert in this house, where opera singer Fyodor Chaliapin lived and performed for friends and family. A cluster of chairs around the piano ensures intimacy with the soloists and small ensembles who perform here a few nights a week. 25 Novinsky Bulvar (next to the U.S. Embassy). ✆ **495/605-6236.** Metro: Barrikadnaya.

Maly Theater The theater is called Maly ("small") only because it's across from the Bolshoi (which means "big" or "grand"), but the Maly's hall is full-size and its performances top quality. Most plays are in Russian, with an emphasis on classics from Chekhov, Ostrovsky, and Griboyedov. 1/6 Teatralnaya Sq. (across from the Bolshoi). ✆ **495/623-2621.** Metro: Teatralnaya.

Moiseyev Ballet Founded in 1937 by Bolshoi Theater choreographer Igor Moiseyev, this company sought to break free from the restraints of classical dance and has been putting on brilliant performances of their mixture of ballet and folk dance ever since. 31 Tverskaya St. ✆ **495/699-5372.** www.moiseyev.ru. Metro: Pushkinskaya.

Moscow Conservatory (Konservatoria) This is the most popular and most historic place to hear Russian and international classical music performed by the country's top orchestras and soloists. The conservatory, housed in an 18th-century mansion now fronted by a statue of Tchaikovsky, is still the premier training ground for Russian musicians. 13 Bolshaya Nikitskaya St. ✆ **496/629-9401.** Metro: Arbatskaya.

Dance Clubs & Bars

Conservatory This atrium bar on the top floor of the Ararat Park Hyatt Hotel is one of the few elegant and accessible places to watch Red Square at night. The ergonomic design and gorgeous customers are as eye-catching as the view from the wraparound windows. 4 Neglinnaya Ulitsa. ✆ **495/783-1234.** Metro: Teatralnaya or Kuznetsky Most.

Modest Charm of the Bourgeoisie (Skromnoye Oboyaniye Burzhuazi) This compact hall is the favored "preparty" spot of Moscow clubbers. It features lounge music in a mellow atmosphere to get you in the mood before the real party-hopping begins. It's open daily 24 hours. 24 Bolshaya Lubyanka. ✆ **495/623-0848.** Metro: Lubyanka.

Propaganda This spot features house, trance, and techno, and is popular with students, expats, straights, gays, artists, and young capitalists. Try to get a table upstairs for a little more space and a perfect people-watching angle. It's open daily from noon to 6am. 7 Bolshoi Zlatoustinsky Pereulok. ✆ **495/624-5732.** Cover Sat only, $3 (£1.85). Metro: Lubyanka or Kitai-Gorod.

Shtolnaya With beer taps at nearly every table, this is a fun but dangerous drinking hole. The taps are metered, but you always end up drinking more than you intended. 6 Zatsepsky Val. ✆ **495/953-4268.** Metro: Paveletskaya.

4 ST. PETERSBURG

St. Petersburg is Russia's principal port, and its geography and history make it immediately distinguishable from Moscow. St. Petersburg did not grow gradually from provincial backwater to major metropolis like its southern rival—this city was built up from the bogs, fast and furious, to be an imperial capital. Museums, palaces, and ballet and opera houses are where St. Petersburg's strengths lie.

VISITOR INFORMATION

The **St. Petersburg City Tourist Office** at 14 Sadovaya Ulitsa (✆ **812/310-2822**) does not have much more to offer than most hotels, but is worth a visit to find out about festivals or special events. An easy-to-read and detailed **map** is the bilingual "St. Petersburg Guide to the City." Look out for the twice-weekly *The St. Petersburg Times,* and *Afisha Petersburg,* which is the best weekly magazine for entertainment, dining, and shopping advice. See also "Visitor Information" in section 2 of this chapter.

The best tours of St. Petersburg are those done by **boat.** The smaller boats that cruise the canals give a closer view of the city's insides than the ferries that go up and down the Neva River. You can pick up a canal tour on Griboyedov Canal just north of Nevsky Prospekt, and on the Fontanka River just north of Nevsky Prospekt; prices run $3.50 to $7 (£2.15–£4.35) for a 1-hour tour.

GETTING THERE

BY PLANE International flights into St. Petersburg land at the renovated **Pulkovo-2 Airport** (✆ **812/704-3444;** www.pulkovoairport.ru), 10 miles south of the city limits or about a 30-minute ride to the center of town. You can arrange a taxi in advance by calling the **official airport cab company** at ✆ **812/312-0022.** Public bus no. 13 takes you to Moskovskaya metro station for a few rubles.

BY TRAIN Trains from Moscow arrive at **Moscow Station (Moskovsky Vokzal),** on Nevsky Prospekt and within walking distance of several hotels. From Helsinki, the trip ends at **Ladoga Station (Ladozhsky Vokzal)** on Zanevsky Prospekt. Other European trains arrive at **Vytebsky Station (Vytebsky Vokzal)** on Zagorodny Prospekt).

BY BUS A few tour companies offer bus tours to St. Petersburg from Scandinavia on top-class Finnish coaches. Buses arrive at **St. Petersburg Bus Station (Avtobusny Vokzal),** 36 Naberezhnaya Obvodonovo Kanala.

BY BOAT The port is 20 minutes south of the center. Most cruises include a bus trip to the center. Authorized taxis (regular taxis are not allowed into the port) cost around $35 (£22) each way. Return trips leave from Kazansky Cathedral on Nevsky Prospekt.

BY CAR Not including the long lines for Customs at the border, the 370km (230-mile) drive from Helsinki is about 6 hours. Once in St. Petersburg, head straight to your hotel and settle the parking question.

GETTING AROUND

BY PUBLIC TRANSPORTATION The **St. Petersburg metro** is a fast, cheap, and extraordinarily deep subway system that every visitor should try out at least once. Station entrances are marked with a blue letter M. The four-line system is easy to follow, with each line color-coded and transfers clearly marked. Trains run from 5:45am to 12:15am. Tokens cost 17 rubles (about 70¢/£45p) for one trip, or magnetic cards for 1, 2, 5, or 10 trips.

Two **tram** lines worth trying are the no. 14, which runs from the Mariinsky Theater up through the center of town and across the Neva; another is the no. 1, which runs through Vasilevsky Island, including a stop just outside the Vasileostrovskaya metro station. **Trolleybuses** run along Nevsky Prospekt and some other large avenues. Tickets for trams and trolleybuses cost 19 rubles (75¢/45p) and are available from the driver.

BY TAXI One reliable company to try is the official **Petersburg Taxi** (✆ **068**—that's right, just 3 digits; www.taxi068.spb.ru).

BY CAR Some rental companies to try are Hertz/Travel Rent (✆ **812/324-3242;** www.hertz.ru), Europcar (✆ **812/644-4418;** www.europcar.com), and Avis (✆ **812/327-5418;** www.avis-rentacar.ru). All have offices at Pulkovo airport and rent cars with or without drivers.

SUGGESTED ST. PETERSBURG ITINERARIES

If You Have 1 Day

Begin at **Palace Square** and the **Hermitage,** for an intense morning of history and art that provides context for the rest of the St. Petersburg experience. Next, take your pick from the sights on the **"walking tour"** later in this section, followed by a visit to the **Peter and Paul Fortress** and an evening stroll along **Nevsky Prospekt.**

If You Have 2 Days

Use your second day to take in the masterpieces of the **Russian Museum,** then visit the eye-catching **Church of the Savior on the Spilled Blood,** the sculpted **Summer Gardens,** and the prestigious banks of the **Fontanka River.** Shop in **Gostiny Dvor,** then use this evening for a visit to the renowned **Mariinsky Theater.**

If You Have 3 Days

A third day offers an ideal opportunity to whiz up the Baltic Coast to **Peterhof,** the palace Peter modeled partly on Versailles. The ride itself—on hydrofoil or ferry—is part of the adventure, offering a seafarer's view of the city and surrounding forest. Catch the ferry at the piers on Dvortsovaya Naberezhnaya in front of the Winter Palace.

Fast Facts St. Petersburg

American Express The main local office is at 23 Malaya Morskaya in the Beliye Nochi Business Center (✆ **812/326-4500**). It's open from 9am to 6pm and will cash traveler's checks. In the U.S., call ✆ 800/221-7282.

Currency Exchange Every St. Petersburg hotel, many restaurants, and all major streets have exchange booths *(obmen valyuty),* many open 24 hours. They have signs out front with the buy-and-sell rate for dollars and euros. For other currencies, try the booths in the underground walkway at Gostiny Dvor.

Doctor **American Medical Center St. Petersburg,** 78 Naberezhnaya Moiki (✆ **812/740-2090**) has Western-standard medical care and English-speaking staff.

Embassies The following addresses are for consulates based in St. Petersburg (embassies are in Moscow; see "Fast Facts: Moscow" in section 3): **United States:** 15 Furshtadskaya Ulitsa (✆ **812/331-2600); Britain:** 5 Ploshchad Proletarskoi Diktatury (✆ **812/320-3200**); **Canada:** 32 Malodetskoselsky Prospekt (✆ **812/325-8448**).

Emergencies For fire, dial ✆ **01;** police ✆ **02;** ambulance ✆ **03.**

Internet Access Most hotel business centers offer online access, though at steeper rates than the Internet cafes popping up around the center of town. Try **Quo Vadis,** at 24 Nevsky Prospekt, or **Café Max,** at 90/92 Nevsky Prospekt. Both are open 24 hours.

Postal Services The main city post office (Glavny Pochtamt) is at 9 Pochtamtskaya Ulitsa (✆ **812/312-8302**). Several international shipping companies serve Russia, such as FedEx (✆ **812/325-8825**) and DHL (✆ **812/326-6400**).

Telephone The city code for St. Petersburg is 812. For international calls from Russia, dial 8, wait for a tone, dial 10, then dial the country code. Access numbers in St. Petersburg are AT&T, 325-5042; MCI, 747-3322; BT Direct, dial 8 then wait for a tone, then dial 10-80-01-10-1044; Canada Direct, dial 8, then wait for a tone, then dial 10-800-110-1012.

WHERE TO STAY

Variation and innovation characterize St. Petersburg's hotel scene. The nicest and priciest hotels, and nearly all of the international chains, are clustered on upper Nevsky Prospekt. The huge Soviet-era hotel towers are farther from the center, and sometimes quite far from the metro. They offer better prices, but their quality is variable. The best price-to-quality ratio is found in the minihotels springing up around town. When choosing accommodations in St. Petersburg, bear in mind that it's a city of bridges that are drawn up in the wee hours to allow shipping traffic through. This means that if your late-night plans involve something on the other side of the Neva River from your hotel, you may be in for a long wait or a detour to get back.

Prices below are in U.S. dollars and British pounds and do *not* include breakfast or 18% VAT unless noted.

Very Expensive

Astoria ★★★ An example of Art Nouveau at its apex, the five-star Astoria offers 21st-century decadence in a prerevolutionary setting, overlooking St. Isaac's Cathedral with the Neva River in the background. The Astoria and adjacent Angleterre (see next listing) opened in 1912 on the site of a 19th-century English/Russian hotel venture. Unfortunately, the mirrored, Art Nouveau winter garden is open only for special events—peek inside and imagine the balls held here a century ago. The Astoria is an excellent stop for tea even if you're not staying overnight.

39 Ulitsa Bolshaya Morskaya. ✆ **812/494-5757.** 220 units. From $550 (£341) double; from $700 (£434) suite. Rates 10% higher May–July. AE, DC, MC, V. Metro: Nevsky Prospekt. **Amenities:** 2 restaurants; bar and lounge; pool; health club; spa; Jacuzzi; sauna; concierge; tour desk; car-rental desk; limo; 24-hr. business center; shopping arcade; salon; 24-hr. room service; laundry service; same-day dry cleaning; nonsmoking rooms; executive rooms; billiard room. *In room:* A/C, TV w/satellite, dataport, minibar, fridge, hair dryer, iron, safe.

Expensive

Angleterre ★★ Initially a wing of the Astoria, the four-star Angleterre shares a designer and a kitchen with its "sister hotel," though they're now under separate management. Today the Angleterre is a slightly less expensive, less well-preserved neighbor of the Astoria, but it is still a luxurious place to stay. The spacious guest rooms, many boasting wide windows, are decorated in warm woods that differ little from the Astoria's. The view of St. Isaac's makes a street-facing room worthwhile.

39 Bolshaya Morskaya Ulitsa. ✆ **812/494-5666.** Fax 812/494-5125. www.angleterrehotel.com. 193 units. $400 (£248) double (mid-May to mid-July $450 (£279); from $500 (£310) suite. AE, DC, MC, V. Metro: Nevsky Prospekt. **Amenities:** Restaurant w/live jazz pianist every evening; small indoor pool; health club; spa; sauna; concierge; tour desk; car-rental desk; limo; 24-hr. business center; salon; 24-hr. room service; laundry service; same-day dry cleaning; nonsmoking rooms; executive rooms. *In room:* A/C, TV w/pay movies and satellite, dataport, minibar, fridge, coffeemaker, hair dryer, iron, safe.

Grand Hotel Europe ★★★ This hotel has every right to call itself grand. Grandeur seeps from its ceiling friezes to its carpeting. Originally opened in 1875, it was completely rehauled for a 1991 reopening, and much of what seems prerevolutionary is recent re-creation, from the baroque facade to the Art Nouveau interiors. Its five floors surround a luscious winter garden and mezzanine cafe visible from inward-facing rooms. Even if you don't stay here, spend a lazy morning or rainy afternoon savoring tea from a silver samovar and listening to the harpist on the mezzanine. Guest rooms are elegant and modern.

1 Mikhailovskaya Ulitsa. ✆ **800/426-3135** or 812/329-6000. Fax 812/329-6001. www.grandhoteleurope.com. 300 units. From $310 (£192) double; from $790 (£490) suite. Rates 20% higher May–July. $40 (£25) extra bed. AE, DC, MC, V. Metro: Gostiny Dvor or Nevsky Prospekt. **Amenities:** 5 restaurants; 2 bars; health club; Jacuzzi; sauna; concierge; tour desk; car-rental desk; limos; 24-hr. business center; shopping arcade; salon; 24-hr. room service; massage; babysitting; laundry service; same-day dry cleaning; nonsmoking rooms; executive rooms. *In room:* A/C, TV w/satellite and pay movies, dataport, minibar, fridge, hair dryer, iron, safe.

Moderate

Marco Polo Litorin ★★ One of many appealing, accessible hotels opening on Vasilevsky Island, the Marco Polo Litorin stands out for its careful juxtaposition of modern art and 19th-century fireplaces. The hotel opened in 2003 and is still expanding. The staff pays individual attention to guests and to detail, which makes up for some of the standard hotel services it doesn't provide, such as laundry facilities. The bathrooms are large

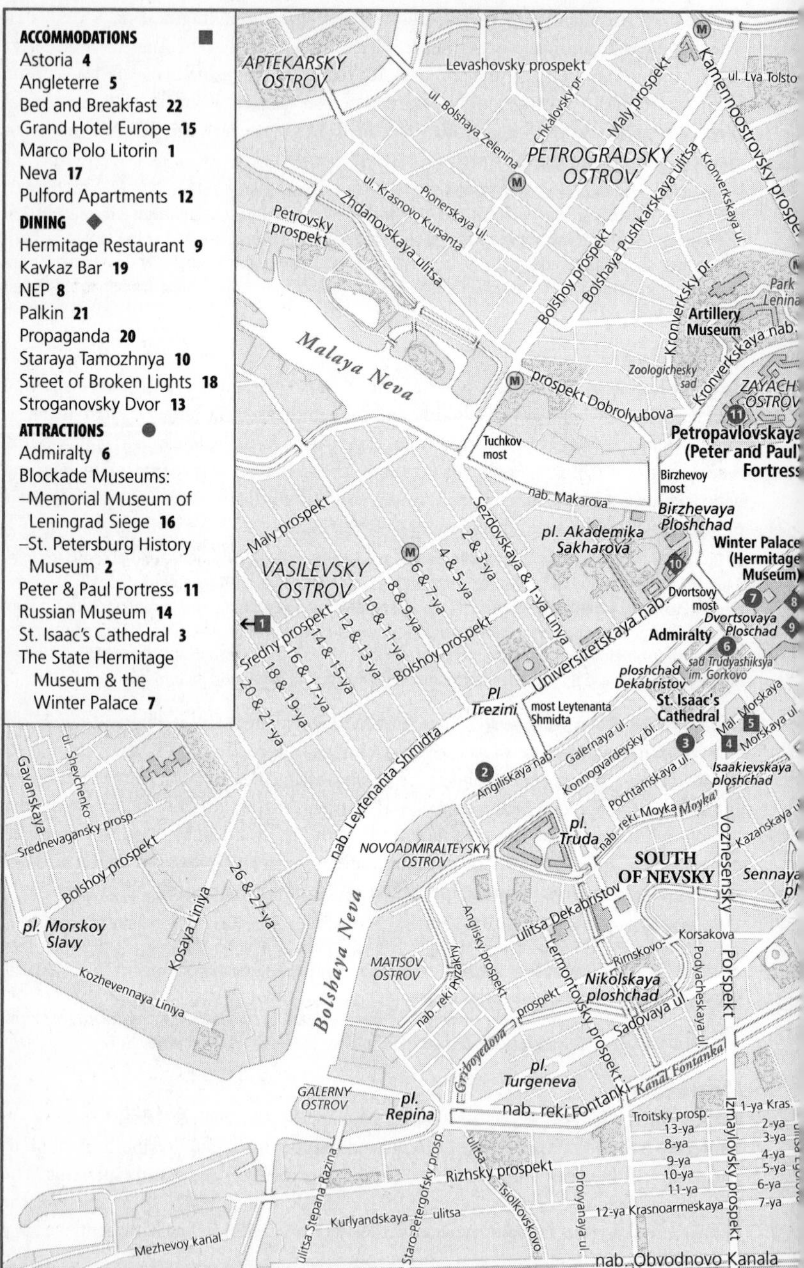
ACCOMMODATIONS
Astoria 4
Angleterre 5
Bed and Breakfast 22
Grand Hotel Europe 15
Marco Polo Litorin 1
Neva 17
Pulford Apartments 12
DINING
Hermitage Restaurant 9
Kavkaz Bar 19
NEP 8
Palkin 21
Propaganda 20
Staraya Tamozhnya 10
Street of Broken Lights 18
Stroganovsky Dvor 13
ATTRACTIONS
Admiralty 6
Blockade Museums:
–Memorial Museum of Leningrad Siege 16
–St. Petersburg History Museum 2
Peter & Paul Fortress 11
Russian Museum 14
St. Isaac's Cathedral 3
The State Hermitage Museum & the Winter Palace 7
APTEKARSKY OSTROV
Levashovsky prospekt
ul. Bolshaya Zelenina
Chkalovsky pr.
Maly prospekt
Kamennoostrovsky prospekt
ul. Lva Tolsto
PETROGRADSKY OSTROV
Bolshaya Pushkarskaya ulitsa
Kronverkskaya ul.
ul. Krasnovo Kursanta
Pionerskaya ul.
Zhdanovskaya ulitsa
Petrovsky prospekt
Bolshoy prospekt
Kronverksky pr.
Park Lenina
Artillery Museum
Kronverkskaya nab.
Malaya Neva
Zoologichesky sad
prospekt Dobrolyubova
ZAYACHY OSTROV
Tuchkov most
Petropavlovskaya (Peter and Paul) Fortress
Birzhevoy most
nab. Makarova
Birzhevaya Ploshchad
pl. Akademika Sakharova
Sezdovskaya & 1-ya Linya
2 & 3-ya
4 & 5-ya
6 & 7-ya
8 & 9-ya
10 & 11-ya
12 & 13-ya
14 & 15-ya
16 & 17-ya
18 & 19-ya
20 & 21-ya
Maly prospekt
VASILEVSKY OSTROV
Sredny prospekt
Bolshoy prospekt
Winter Palace (Hermitage Museum)
Dvortsovy most
Dvortsovaya Ploschad
Admiralty
sad Trudyashiksya im. Gorkovo
Universitetskaya nab.
ploshchad Dekabristov
St. Isaac's Cathedral
Mal. Morskaya
Morskaya ul.
Pl Trezini
most Leytenanta Shmidta
Galernaya ul.
Konnogvardeysky bl.
Angliskaya nab.
Pochtamskaya ul.
Isaakievskaya ploshchad
nab. Leytenanta Shmidta
Gavanskaya
ul. Shevchenko
Srednevagansky prosp.
Bolshoy prospekt
pl. Truda
nab. reki Moyka
Moyka
Kazanskaya ul.
NOVOADMIRALTEYSKY OSTROV
SOUTH OF NEVSKY
Voznesensky Porspekt
Sennaya pl.
26 & 27-ya
Kosaya Liniya
pl. Morskoy Slavy
Kozhevennaya Liniya
Bolshaya Neva
ulitsa Dekabristov
Angliisky prospekt
Lermontovsky prospekt
Korsakova
Rimskovo-Korsakova
MATISOV OSTROV
nab. reki Pryazhky
Nikolskaya ploshchad
Podyacheskaya ul.
Sadovaya ul.
Griboyedova
pl. Turgeneva
Kanal Fontanka
GALERNY OSTROV
pl. Repina
nab. reki Fontanki
Troitsky prosp.
13-ya
8-ya
9-ya
10-ya
11-ya
1-ya Kras.
2-ya
3-ya
4-ya
5-ya
6-ya
7-ya
Izmaylovsky prospekt
Rizhsky prospekt
ulitsa Tsiolkovskovo
Drovyanaya ul.
12-ya Krasnoarmeskaya
ulitsa Stepana Razina
Kurlyandskaya
Staro-Petergofsky prosp.
ulitsa
Mezhevoy kanal
nab. Obvodnovo Kanala

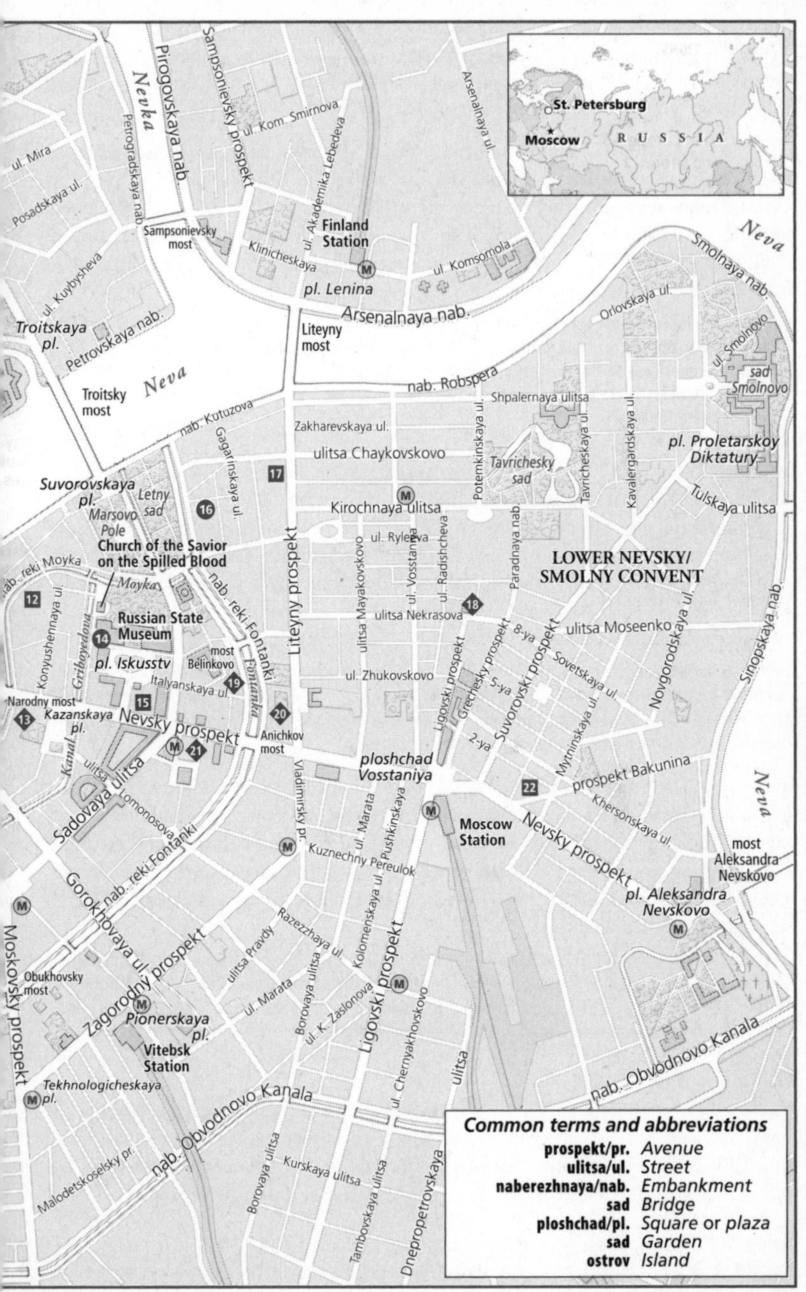
St. Petersburg
Moscow
RUSSIA
Neva
Nevka
Pirogovskaya nab.
Sampsonievsky prospekt
ul. Kom. Smirnova
ul. Akademika Lebedeva
Arsenalnaya ul.
Petrogradskaya nab.
ul. Mira
Posadskaya ul.
Sampsonievsky most
Klinicheskaya
Finland Station
ul. Komsomola
pl. Lenina
Arsenalnaya nab.
Liteyny most
ul. Kuybysheva
Troitskaya pl.
Petrovskaya nab.
Troitsky most
nab. Kutuzova
nab. Robspera
Shpalernaya ulitsa
Smolnaya nab.
Orlovskaya ul.
ul. Smolnovo
sad Smolnovo
Zakharevskaya ul.
Gagarinskaya ul.
ulitsa Chaykovskovo
Potemkinskaya ul.
Tavrichesky sad
Tavricheskaya ul.
Kavalergardskaya ul.
pl. Proletarskoy Diktatury
Suvorovskaya pl.
Letny sad
Marsovo Pole
Kirochnaya ulitsa
Tulskaya ulitsa
ul. Ryleeva
Church of the Savior on the Spilled Blood
nab. reki Moyka
Moyka
Liteyny prospekt
ulitsa Mayakovskovo
ul. Vosstaniya
ul. Radishcheva
Paradnaya nab
LOWER NEVSKY/ SMOLNY CONVENT
nab. reki Fontanki
Konyushennaya ul.
Griboyedova
Russian State Museum
ulitsa Nekrasova
ulitsa Moseenko
Novgorodskaya ul.
Sinopskaya nab.
pl. Iskusstv
most Belinkovo
Fontanka
ul. Zhukovskovo
Ligovski prospekt
Grechesky prospekt
8-ya
Suvorovski prospekt
Sovetskaya ul.
5-ya
2-ya
Mytninskaya ul.
Italyanskaya ul.
Narodny most
Kazanskaya pl.
Nevsky prospekt
Anichkov most
Kanal
ploshchad Vosstaniya
prospekt Bakunina
Khersonskaya ul.
Neva
Sadovaya ulitsa
ulitsa Lomonosova
Vladimirsky pr.
ul. Marata
Pushkinskaya
Moscow Station
Nevsky prospekt
most Aleksandra Nevskovo
Kuznechny Pereulok
nab. reki Fontanki
pl. Aleksandra Nevskovo
Gorokhovaya ul.
Razezzhaya ul.
Kolomenskaya ul.
Moskovsky prospekt
Zagorodny prospekt
ulitsa Pravdy
Borovaya ulitsa
Obukhovsky most
ul. Marata
ul. K. Zaslonova
Ligovski prospekt
ul. Chernyakhovskovo
Pionerskaya pl.
Vitebsk Station
ulitsa
nab. Obvodnovo Kanala
Tekhnologicheskaya pl.
nab. Obvodnovo Kanala
Malodetskoselsky pr.
Borovaya ulitsa
Kurskaya ulitsa
Tambovskaya ulitsa
Dnepropetrovskaya
12
13
14
15
16
17
18
19
20
21
22
Common terms and abbreviations
prospekt/pr. Avenue
ulitsa/ul. Street
naberezhnaya/nab. Embankment
sad Bridge
ploshchad/pl. Square or plaza
sad Garden
ostrov Island

and fully renovated. It's a long walk to the nearest metro, though compensation is the less frequented sights nearby, such as the cathedral on the embankment; the icebreaker *Krasin* docked nearby; and the Mining Institute, one of Russia's first universities.

12 Liniya 27 (Vasilevsky Island). ✆/fax **812/449-8877.** www.mpolo-spb.ru. 47 units. $125–$140 (£78–£87) double. AE, MC, V. Metro: Vasileostrovskaya. **Amenities:** Restaurant; sauna; tour desk; transport desk; business center; Wi-Fi; room service. *In room:* A/C, TV w/satellite, dataport, safe.

Pulford Apartments ★ This British-Russian company offers apartments all over town, but its prime spots are along the lanes between Palace Square and Nevsky Prospekt metro station. All apartments are renovated to Western standards, with fully equipped kitchens and bathrooms, and from one to several bedrooms. Maid service can be arranged as often as you like, as can any number of hotel-like services such as extra towels, theater tickets, cellphone rental, and visa help.

Main office: 6 Moika Embankment. ✆ **812/325-6277.** Fax 812/320-7561. www.pulford.com. From $130 (£81) double for 1-bedroom apt. AE, DC, MC, V. **Amenities:** Tour arrangements and personal guides; transport services; laundry service; dry cleaning; nonsmoking rooms; executive rooms. *In room:* A/C, TV w/satellite, dataport, kitchen, fridge, coffeemaker, hair dryer, iron, safe.

Inexpensive

Bed and Breakfast (Value) The only true bargain on Nevsky, this seven-room hostel was once a communal apartment in an imposing Stalin-era building. Rooms in the B&B range from a single with no window to a spacious triple with an expansive view. Bathrooms are shared but have shower and tub and are well maintained. A basic breakfast is offered—or can be made by you—in the common kitchen. A washing machine is available. The hostel's chief drawbacks are the dank and foreboding stairwell and the lack of an elevator to the third floor. Otherwise, this is an excellent, low-priced option.

74 Nevsky Prospekt. ✆ **812/315-1917** or 812/315-0495. www.bnbrussia.com. 7 units at Nevsky location, but other locations around town. $30 (£19) single; $40 (£25) double; $50 (£31) triple. No credit cards. Metro: Gostiny Dvor. **Amenities:** Tour and transport assistance; laundry service; common kitchen w/ fridge. *In room:* Coffeemaker, hair dryer, iron, safe on request.

Neva ★ The heavy wooden door opens onto a mirrored, marble staircase that dates back to the 1860s, when the hotel was built. The guest rooms have soaring ceilings and intricate molding, though beds are often creaky and windows lack modern insulation from street noise and drafts. The less expensive rooms have showers with no stalls; the suites all have modern bathrooms. The second-floor cafe serves breakfast in style. Several rooms have views of the Neva.

17 Ulitsa Chaikovskogo. ✆ **812/578-0-578.** Fax 812/273-2563. www.nevahotel.spb.ru. 133 units. From $100 (£62) double; from $150 (£93) suite. AE, MC, V. Metro: Chernyshevskaya or Gorkovskaya. **Amenities:** Restaurant and bar; sauna and very small pool; tour and transport desk; business center; salon; room service; laundry and ironing service. *In room:* TV w/cable, fridge.

WHERE TO DINE

St. Petersburg's current dining scene reflects its seaside and river-crossed geography, with fresh- and saltwater fish on every menu. Its eye-on-Europe heritage means that traditional Russian dishes are often upstaged by French-inspired terrines and roasts, or by pastas and pizza. St. Petersburg restaurants have a good quality-to-price ratio.

Very Expensive

Palkin ★★★ RUSSIAN If you want to splurge just once in St. Petersburg, do it here. The original Palkin opened in 1785 and became a mecca for aristocrats and intellectuals;

today's reincarnation opened in 2002 on the same spot. The interior today is at least as sumptuous as in the decadent days of Catherine the Great. Today, members of Russia's 21st-century elite make it a frequent stop, including friends of St. Petersburg native (and Russian president) Vladimir Putin. Chefs research menus of past centuries, including wedding feasts for grand princes, to create dishes like *sterlet* baked in white wine with a sauce of cèpes and crayfish.

47 Nevsky Prospekt. © **812/703-5371.** Reservations required. Jackets preferred for men. Main courses $40–$60 (£25–£37). AE, DC, MC, V. Daily 11am until last guest leaves. Metro: Nevsky Prospekt.

Expensive

Hermitage Restaurant ★★★ RUSSIAN/FRENCH The location right on Palace Square is what draws people here, but the inventive cuisine and atmosphere are what keep them coming back. Above a labyrinth of dining halls, the vaulted stone ceilings give the place the feel of a secret treasure cavern; works by local artists hang in the corridors. Each dining room is distinct in style, from the table sizes and shapes to the silverware and window coverings. The menu combines imperial-era favorites like pikeperch grilled with cèpe mushrooms from the surrounding forests, and more modern French-inspired favorites such as a delicately seasoned veal tartare.

8 Dvortsovaya Ploshchad (Palace Sq.). © **812/314-4772.** www.hermitage.restoran.ru. Reservations recommended. Main courses $14–$50 (£8.70–£31). AE, MC, V. Daily noon–midnight. Metro: Nevsky Prospekt.

Staraya Tamozhnya (Old Customs House) ★★ FRENCH/RUSSIAN This ornate, top-notch restaurant celebrates French culinary traditions the way Russian aristocracy of the 18th and 19th centuries did. A special truffle menu comes out in January, and the *pot-au-feu* with lobster pops up a few times a year. Keep an eye out for the pheasant with pine nuts and endive. The French cheeses and three-chocolate fondue are always divine. The wine cellar corner is cozy, and a light jazz ensemble plays most evenings.

1 Tamozhenny Pereulok. © **812/327-8980.** Reservations required for dinner. Main courses $21–$45 (£13–£28). AE, DC, MC, V. Daily noon–midnight. Metro: Vasileostrovskaya.

Moderate

Kavkaz Bar ★★ GEORGIAN For expats and visitors, this is St. Petersburg's most popular spot at which to sample cuisine from the former Soviet state of Georgia. Its Caucasus Mountain spices and fruits are not found in Russian cooking. Try the enormous *khinkali,* spiced meat dumplings you're supposed to eat with your hands; the tandoor-style chicken (chicken *tabaka*); or the eggplant slices slathered in walnut-garlic paste. If you want to try Georgian wine, stick with the dry reds.

18 Karavannaya Ulitsa. © **812/312-1665.** Main courses $6–$15 (£3.75–£9.30). AE, MC, V. Daily 11am–10pm. Metro: Mayakovskaya.

NEP ★ RUSSIAN Named after Lenin's New Economic Policy, an attempt at state-run capitalism in the 1920s that was crushed by Stalin's collectivization campaign, this restaurant is political only in name. Its prime location on the corner of Palace Square and the Moika River makes it rather touristy, but the fare is decent and filling and the prices not as high as they could be in this locale. Play it safe and order the ground-beef cutlets—or go all out and try the venison filet with bilberry and juniper, a modern rendition of traditional northern Russian fare. Sadly, the restaurant doesn't offer a view of its surroundings, since it's in the basement, but the ambience is convivial. The service can be warm or cold depending on the day and the waitstaff. Any mushroom dish is worth sampling; they are best in late summer and fall.

37 Naberejnaja Moiky. ✆ **812/571-75-91.** Main courses $15–$20 (£9.30–£12). No credit cards. Daily noon–1am. Metro: Nevsky Prospekt.

Inexpensive

Street of Broken Lights (Ulitsa Razbitykh Fonarei) ★ Kids RUSSIAN The main draw here is the extensive takeout menu, something unheard of elsewhere in town (other than at McDonald's). The decor and menu borrow from the Russian television series after which the restaurant is named, featuring cops and neighborhood dramas. The show and the restaurant are popular among families.

34 Ulitsa Radishcheva. ✆ **812/275-9935.** Main courses $8–$20 (£4.95–£12). AE, MC, V. Daily noon–midnight. Metro: Chernyshevskaya.

Stroganovsky Dvor (Stroganoff Courtyard) ★ RUSSIAN/EUROPEAN This cafe is cool, cheap, and convenient, and the atmosphere is so bizarre it's worth experiencing. The two-story restaurant is housed in a huge transparent tent plopped in the courtyard of an 18th-century aristocratic mansion. Customers can use special telephones placed at each table to call in orders—or to call occupants of other tables. Service is friendly and readily available.

17 Nevsky Prospekt (inside courtyard). ✆ **812/315-2315.** Sandwiches $3–$5 (£1.85–£3.10). No credit cards. Daily 24 hr. Metro: Nevsky Prospekt.

EXPLORING ST. PETERSBURG

St. Petersburg was a planned city from day one, and therefore makes sense to most visitors right away. The center of town is relatively compact, and English is increasingly used on street signs and billboards.

Admiralty (Admiralteistvo) ★★★ Overlooking Palace Square from a distance to the west is the Admiralty, once a fortified shipyard. It is now a naval academy that sadly is not open to the public. It's worth spending a few minutes admiring its 61m-high (200-ft.) spire, topped by a weathervane in the shape of a ship. Stand on the plaza beneath the spire and look toward the city: You're at the nexus of three major avenues—Nevsky Prospekt, Gorokhovaya Ulitsa, and Vosnesensky Prospekt. This is no accident, and is one example of the city's careful design. The building was one of the first in St. Petersburg, built to feed Peter the Great's dream of making Russia into a naval power.

Blockade Museums Two exhibits, both of them eye opening and tear jerking, trace the city's experience enduring 900 days of siege and isolation by Nazi forces from 1941 to 1944. The **Memorial Museum of the Leningrad Siege ★** is the more commonly visited, but no less impressive is **"Leningrad During the Great Patriotic War" ★★**, a permanent exhibit at the **St. Petersburg History Museum,** which is housed in a riverside mansion. The hall of children's photos and diaries is especially moving.

Memorial Museum of Leningrad Blockade: 9 Solyanoi Pereulok. ✆ **812/579-3021.** Admission $2.50 (£1.55) adults, $1 (60p) students and children 8 and over. Thurs–Tues 10am–5pm; closed last Thurs of each month. St. Petersburg History Museum: 44 Angliiskaya Naberezhnya. ✆ **812/117-7544.** Admission $3.50 (£2.15) adults, $2 (£1.25) students and children 8 and over. Thurs–Tues 11am–5pm. Metro: Nevsky Prospekt.

Peter and Paul Fortress (Petropavlovskaya Krepost) ★★★ Peter and Paul Fortress was one of Peter the Great's masterpieces. The citadel occupies small Hare's Island (Zaichy Ostrov) across from the Winter Palace, and contains a notable cathedral, the Museum of City History, a mint, an old printing house, a former political prison, and a long stretch of sandy beach packed with bathers in the summer. **Peter and Paul Cathedral ★★★**, named after the city's patron saints and erected in 1723, was St. Petersburg's first stone church. Two highlights are **walking along the fortress's southern walls** (tickets can be purchased at the stairs on either end) and watching (and hearing) the **daily cannon blast** at noon.

The fortress is on **Zaichy Ostrov (Hare's Island; ✆ 812/230-6431;** metro: Gorkovskaya). Entrance to the fortress grounds free. Admission to cathedral and other museums on the grounds $6.25 (£3.90) adults, $4 (£2.50) children. From 6–7pm, cathedral admission is free. Complex daily 10am–6pm. Museums and cathedral Thurs–Mon 11am–6pm.

Peterhof Palace and Park (Petrodvorets) ★★★ Unquestionably the number-one day trip from St. Petersburg, Peterhof lures visitors with its Versailles-inspired palace, overlooking a cascade of fountains and gardens opening onto the Baltic Sea.

Start with the **Great Palace,** built in 1715 by Jean Baptiste Leblond, and be prepared to squint at all the gold inside. Many visitors say the palace feels too magnificent to live in—and Peter felt the same, preferring **Monplaisir,** a small baroque bungalow close to the water's edge that was the first building in the Peterhof complex. In the lush park, the Monplaisir house, the small red-and-white Hermitage, and the **Marly Palace** (with a carved wood desk that Peter himself made) are well worth exploring, too. Before heading down into the park, spend a moment on the palace balcony to take in the view of the greenery and the **Grand Cascade** from above. Be sure to see **Samson Fountain,** with the biblical strongman tearing apart the jaws of a lion, symbolizing Peter's victory over Sweden in 1709.

Boat trips are the best way to get to Peterhof from mid-May to early October, not least because of the breathtaking view of the palace as you pull up to the Peterhof pier. **Russian Cruises** (**✆ 812/325-6120** or 812/914-0100; www.russian-cruises.ru) is well equipped and offers English-language commentary. From October to May the best way to go is by bus. Russian vendors hawk trips on direct buses from Nevsky Prospekt metro station.

2 Razvodnaya Ulitsa. **✆ 812/427-9527.** Admission to the palace $12 (£7.50) adults, $6 (£3.75) college students and children; admission to the park alone $7 (£4.35) adults, $3.50 (£2.15) students and children. Palace Tues–Sat 10:30am–5pm (closed last Tues of each month). Monplaisir and other buildings on the grounds have different hours.

St. Isaac's Cathedral (Isaakevsky Sobor) ★★★ St. Isaac's mighty, somber facade rose only in the mid–19th century but has become an indelible part of St. Petersburg's skyline since then. The church earned residents' respect during World War II, when it endured Nazi shelling and its grounds were planted with cabbage to help residents survive the 900-day Nazi blockade. Its interior is as awesome as its exterior, with columns made of single chunks of granite, malachite, and lazurite and floors of different-colored marble. If the viewing balcony around the dome is open, it's well worth a climb for the view of the city and of the cathedral from on high.

Isaakevskaya Ploshchad. **✆ 812/315-9732.** www.cathedral.ru. Admission $12 (£7.45) adults, $7 (£4.35) children. To climb colonnade, an additional $8 (£4.95) adults, $5 (£3.10) children. Thurs–Tues 11am–6pm; colonnade closes at 5pm. Metro: Nevsky Prospekt.

The State Hermitage Museum and the Winter Palace ★★★ The Winter Palace would be a museum itself even if it didn't hold the Hermitage Museum, one of the world's largest and most valuable collections of fine art. The permanent collection includes—among other treasures—more French artworks than any museum outside France. Halls no. 185 to 189 are worth a glance even if their labels, RUSSIAN CULTURE and

 STATE ROOMS, don't enthrall you. The Pavilion Hall, with mosaic tables and floors, marble fountains, engineering marvels, and a wraparound view, is a favorite for the whole family. The Impressionist and more recent works, including two rooms of early Picasso, are must-sees. Planning is key to any Hermitage visit, and an online tour can be a great preparation. Allow yourself a full morning or afternoon in the Hermitage itself—or a full day, if you can spare it. You won't regret it.

1 Palace Sq. Entrance to Hermitage main collection: through courtyard of Winter Palace, from Palace Sq. ✆ **812/710-9625** or 710-9079. www.hermitagemuseum.org. Admission to Hermitage Museum $18 (£11) adults, $3 (£1.85) students with ID, free for those 17 and under. English tours for up to 5 people by official museum guides $55 (£34). Admission to other buildings in the Hermitage collection $7.50 (£4.70) for each one, or a $26 (£16) ticket allows entrance to the main museum and 3 others of your choice over the course of 1 day. Main museum Tues–Sat 10:30am–6pm; Sun and Russian holidays 10:30am–5pm. Ticket office closes 1 hr. before museum closing. Metro: Nevsky Prospekt.

Summer Gardens (Letny Sad) ★★ This is the place to rest on a bench after a day of visiting museums, or to escape from the crush of city sidewalks—or to imagine how Peter the Great spent his summer afternoons. Peter brought in marble Renaissance-era statues from Italy to give the park a more European feel. He and his successors threw grand receptions here with dancing, drinking, and fireworks under the endless sun of the White Nights. Summer Palace is open to visitors, its rooms re-created as they would have been in Peter's time.

Entrance from Kutuzov Embankment (Naberezhnya Kutuzova) or Panteleimon Bridge (Panteleimonovsky Most). Park daily 10am–10pm. Free admission except during festivals. Summer Palace Wed–Sun 10:30am–5pm. Tickets $9 (£5.60). Metro: Gostiny Dvor or Gorkovskaya.

Russian Museum (Russky Muzei) ★★★ This museum should be on every visitor's itinerary, even those who know or care little about Russian art. It's as much an introduction to Russian history, attitudes, and vision as it is a display of artistic styles. Housing 32,000 artworks from the 12th to 20th centuries, the museum is best viewed with a tour guide or by using the English-language audio guide to ensure that you get the most out of its collection before you drop from exhaustion. The most popular rooms are in the Benois Wing, where works by avant-garde artists Malevich and Kandinsky attract international crowds. The Old Russian Wing deserves a good look, too, offering perspective on the evolution of Orthodox icon painting that helps you better appreciate any cathedrals you visit later. Note the Art Nouveau paintings and sketches of set designs for Diaghilev's Ballet Russe. Allow at least 2 hours.

4/2 Inzhenernaya Ulitsa. ✆ **812/595-4248** or 812/314-3448. www.rusmuseum.ru. Admission $15 (£9.30) adults, $8 (£4.95) students with ID, free for children 17 and under. English-language tour for up to 5 with official museum guide $65 (£40) plus entrance fee. Wed–Sun 10am–5pm; Mon and the day before holidays 10am–4pm. Metro: Gostiny Dvor or Nevsky Prospekt.

WALKING TOUR ST. PETERSBURG HIGHLIGHTS ★★★

This tour, starting at Palace Square, links key St. Petersburg sights with less important ones. The side streets and embankments are just as crucial to understanding the city as are the palaces, so look at everything, even between stops. Allow 2 hours.

❶ Palace Square

Stand at the Alexander Column in the center and turn around slowly, a full 360 degrees. Each building on the asymmetrical square emerged in a different era but they combine to create a flawless ensemble.

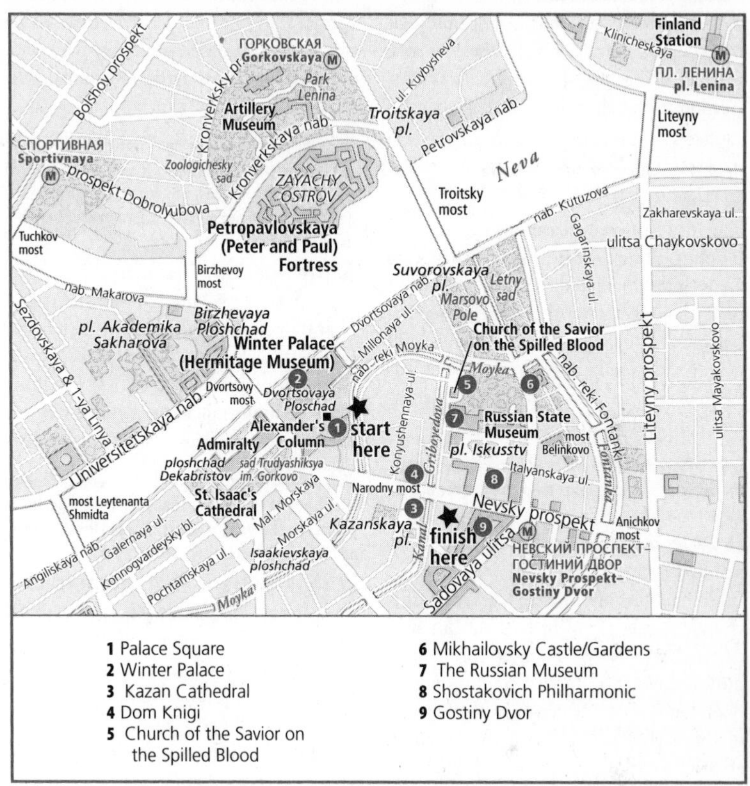

Nothing in this view, or this city, is accidental. Imagine the royal equipages pulling into the square, the tsarist army processions, the revolutionaries' resentment of all the square stood for—and the Communist-era appropriation of the square for holiday parades.

Walk north from the column to the courtyard of the:

2 Winter Palace

The palace's now tranquil courtyard bustled with court activity in Empress Elizabeth's and Catherine the Great's days, and with revolutionary activity 150 years later. You can pick up a museum plan while you're here, though a visit to the Hermitage deserves at least an afternoon or a full day to itself. As you leave the courtyard, take in the view of the curved General Staff building across the square.

Head left toward the Moika Canal, then turn right and follow it down to Nevsky Prospekt. Note the uniformity of the buildings along the canal, all in various shades of yellow, and the odd proportion of the wide bridges crossing the narrow waterway. Cross Nevsky and head left, until you reach the columned gray facade of:

3 Kazan Cathedral

Walking the length of the cathedral's concave colonnade gives you a stepped-back view of Nevsky on one side and a sense of the cathedral's scale on the other. Its modern, secular lines are almost reminiscent of the Capitol Building in Washington, built just 2 decades earlier. Compare this to other Orthodox churches you see around Russia. Even if you don't go in, note that the church's entrance is on the east side instead of facing the street, to satisfy Orthodox church canon.

Cross the avenue again and stop at the corner of Nevsky and Griboyedov Canal to admire:

❹ Dom Knigi

This Art Nouveau treasure is just another building along Nevsky, but worth noting are its glass dome and mystical mosaics. It once belonged to the Singer sewing machine company, whose name is still engraved on the facade. For decades it was Dom Knigi, or House of Books, Leningrad's main bookstore.

Cross Griboyedov Canal and head north along it, past the boatmen hawking canal tours, toward the dizzying domes of the:

❺ Church of the Savior on the Spilled Blood

Built 7 decades after Kazan Cathedral, this church sprang from an entirely different era and worldview. Though constructed during Russia's industrial and economic boom of the late 19th century, the Church of the Savior harkens back to the piled, etched, color-coated domes of medieval Russian churches. Inside, note the spot where Tsar Alexander II was assassinated by a revolutionary.

Walk around the cathedral along the outer edge of Mikhailovsky Gardens, stopping to study the undulating patterns of the cast-iron fences surrounding the gardens. Continue to follow the fence around to the entrance to the gardens.

❻ Mikhailovsky Castle & Gardens

The warm coral of the castle makes it look almost inviting despite its grim history. The paranoid Tsar Paul I had it built because the Winter Palace made him feel too exposed to threats from without and within his court. (Paul was right about the threats, but not about the security of his new home: He was assassinated by advisors soon after he moved in.) Mikhailovsky Castle is now the Engineering Museum.

Circle the palace and turn right onto Italianskaya Ulitsa, heading straight until you reach the Square of the Arts. Take a rest on a bench in this small rectangular plaza, then wander its circumference to study its components:

❼ The Russian Museum

This museum is housed in the triumphantly classical Mikhailovsky Palace (Dvorets). The optimism of the period when the palace was built (1819–25) is reflected in the mock war trophies that top its gates and victorious frieze.

Walk around the square past the Mussorgsky Theater (check out its repertoire of ballet and opera performances on the way), around the Grand Hotel Europe and across Mikhailovskaya Ulitsa to the:

❽ Shostakovich Philharmonic

Built in the 1830s, Russia's premier music hall has staged the country's leading works, from Tchaikovsky's concertos to Rachmaninoff's symphonies. It has hosted conductors including Sviatoslav Richter and, of course, Dmitri Shostakovich.

Continue down Mikhailovskaya Ulitsa to Nevsky Prospekt. Turn around and look at the Square of the Arts one more time from this perspective. Then turn left down Nevsky and continue to the underground walkway at the next intersection. Cross Nevsky through this passage, noting its lively commerce in pirated CDs, DVDs, and software. You'll emerge at:

❾ Gostiny Dvor

This 19th-century shopping mall has gone through several incarnations. Picture its early years, when it was a gathering place for the nobility looking for gifts to take to balls at the Winter Palace.

SHOPPING

Nevsky Prospekt is the city's commercial lifeline, and **Gostiny Dvor** shopping arcade concentrates all of Nevsky's riches in one two-story prerevolutionary mall. **Upper Nevsky** holds the posher shops, while **Lower Nevsky** (east of Moskovsky Train Station) is less pretentious. **Vernisazh,** an outdoor market across from the Church of the Savior on the Spilled Blood, is the city's most convenient and extensive gift bazaar.

For china and porcelain, try the **Lomonosov Porcelain Factory** (**✆ 812/560 8300**), opened in 1744 by Peter the Great's daughter, Empress Elizabeth I. Its craftspeople designed china for the royal family and nobility. After the revolution they produced plates with Constructivist Soviet art and propaganda slogans. Today it's been reprivatized, and sells both imperial and Soviet patterns.

Russian Icon (**✆ 812/314 7040**) on Bolshaya Konyushennaya (near Nevsky Prospekt) has an extensive array of icons on display. They're all recently made, meaning you'll have no problem taking them out of the country, but they follow the same rules icon painters have adhered to for centuries. The icons are more expensive than those at the monasteries, but the selection is larger.

Art Market This informal market in front of the Lutheran Church on Nevsky has been almost institutionalized in its many years parked here. A broad selection of paintings, watercolors, sketches, and photos is on display by the artists. The more original and less expensive pieces are usually displayed at the booths in the back. Prices are negotiable, and range broadly. Vendors speak English. 32–34 Nevsky Prospekt. Metro: Nevsky Prospekt.

Belazh This is an old standby on Nevsky, whose prices are higher because of its location but whose quality and selection of artworks and porcelain remain good. 57 Nevsky Prospekt. **✆ 812/310-6688.** Metro: Gostiny Dvor.

Panteleimonovsky Paintings, furniture, and tabletop collectibles may be found here, with an emphasis on Art Nouveau objects. 13/15 Ulitsa Pestelya. **✆ 812/579-7235.** Metro: Chernyshevskaya.

ST. PETERSBURG AFTER DARK

Most of St. Petersburg's liveliest and richest cultural events take place during the magical summer weeks when there is no "after dark," under the soft, elongated sunset of the White Nights. Of course, this city that considers itself Russia's cultural capital is alive with performances the rest of the year as well. The city's club and bar scene hasn't reached the superlative debauchery of Moscow's, but St. Petersburg's discos and casinos still offer plenty to shock and stimulate a Western visitor.

The Performing Arts

Jazz Philharmonic Hall Surprising at it may sound, St. Petersburg loves jazz, and this hall is its jazz shrine, where a large hall offers balconies and a nostalgic atmosphere. Performances are consistently excellent, with classically trained performers. Shows start at 7pm daily. Check out the Museum of Petersburg Jazz on the second floor. Zagorodnyi Prospekt 27. **✆ 812/764-8565.** Tickets $5–$10 (£3.10–£6.20).

Mariinsky Theater ★★★ Viewing anything in this theater makes you feel regal. The sea-green exterior encloses a five-tiered theater draped, embroidered, and gilded in blue and gold. Top-floor seats have a dimmer view of the performers but a close-up view of the ceiling frescoes that draw you right into their pillowy clouds and floating angels. The repertoire of the renowned and rigorous Mariinsky (formerly Kirov) Ballet features mostly classics such as *Sleeping Beauty* and *La Bayadere.* Tickets purchased at the box office are cheaper than those bought through your hotel, but availability is limited. 1 Teatralnaya Sq. **✆ 812/326-4141.** www.mariinsky.ru/en. Tickets $6–$18 (£3.70–£11) for 3rd balcony seats; $100–$150 (£62–£93) for orchestra. Metro: Sadovaya or Sennaya Ploshchad.

Peter and Paul Cathedral The cathedral inside the Peter and Paul Fortress is the main hall of the St. Petersburg Men's Choir, which carries on the tradition of its tsarist-era founders. A stunning setting for some stunning voices, with performances Monday and Friday nights. Peter and Paul Fortress (Hare's Island/Zaichy Ostrov). ✆ **812/767-0865.** Tickets run $15–$22 (£9.30–£14). Metro: Gorkovskaya.

Shostakovich Philharmonic Two halls, the Bolshoi (Grand) and Glinka (Small), stage symphonies, solo piano concerts, international festivals and competitions, and more, featuring music by Russian and international composers. The Grand Hall is home to the St. Petersburg Philharmonic but shares its stage with visiting performers. Both halls boast ornate and intricate interiors and superb acoustics, though they're in need of renovation. Mikhailovskaya St. ✆ **812/312-9871.** www.philharmonia.spb.ru. Tickets $20–$35 (£12–£22) in Bolshoi Hall; $5–$15 (£3.10–£9.30) in Glinka Hall. Metro: Gostiny Dvor.

Dance Clubs & Bars

Akvarel Several of the ship-restaurants along the north side of the Neva offer dance clubs at night, but this all-glass dockside restaurant/club is by far the sleekest way to party on the water. Door control gets fierce after 11pm; if you come for dinner and stay for the party you'll have no problem passing muster. 14a Prospekt Dobrolyubova. ✆ **812/320-8600.** www.aquarelspb.com. Metro: Sportivnaya.

City Bar This bar is run by an American and attracts a mixed Russian-expat crowd for its "Amerikansky Biznes Lunch" at midday and its lively bar at night. Beer, martinis, and a Sunday all-you-can-drink champagne brunch for just $12 (£7.45) are among its highlights. 20 Fourshatskaya Ulitsa. ✆ **812/448-5837.** Metro: Chernyshevskaya.

Jakata Consistently hip, and playing a mix of lounge, techno, and trance, this is the city's most authentic and least pretentious dance club. It's open daily 24 hours, but don't bother showing up before midnight. 5 Bakunina Ulitsa. ✆ **812/346-7462.** Metro: Ploshchad Vosstaniya.

Seven Seas This popular seafood restaurant has live music and private dining rooms. Live concerts take place on Saturdays. 26/2 Klinsky Prospekt. ✆ **812/495-3665.** Metro: Technologichesky Institut.

Slovakia

by Mark Baker

Slovakia's humble tourism motto, "A Part of Europe Worth Visiting," seems to sum up the country's rather modest ambitions when it comes to luring visitors. Just barely a teenager—Slovakia became an independent nation in 1993—the country still seems unsure of itself and what it has to offer. But the motto surely underestimates Slovakia's very winning charms. The mountains, starting in the hills of the Malá Fatra and running east to the Alpine peaks of the High Tatras, are some of the most starkly beautiful in Europe. And it's unlikely that any country in Europe, or anywhere else for that matter, has a castle with the pure drop-dead shock value of Spišský Hrad.

Slovakia's youthful capital, Bratislava, has shed some of its hulking Communist-era architecture and fixed up its charming Old Town. The result is a fun, lively, and energetic city that makes Vienna feel fusty and overly mannered and Prague feel forced and overly touristed by comparison. And the Slovaks' humility is part of the charm. The rudeness or arrogance you sometimes find in more popular destinations is absent here. Just let slip in conversation that you've come all the way from the United States, or Canada, or wherever, and the reaction you get will be nothing short of amazement. You'll feel like a treasured guest.

To be sure, you may have to put up with some relative hardships now and then. Standards for food and lodging, especially off the beaten track, are a slight step down from western Europe, and even perhaps lower than you might find in the Czech Republic or Hungary. But don't let that deter you. Relax, enjoy the largely unspoiled countryside, take a meal and a glass of wine in a traditional *koliba* restaurant, and let the natural warmth and hospitality of the people win you over.

1 GETTING TO KNOW SLOVAKIA

THE LAY OF THE LAND

Slovakia is a compact country, sandwiched between Austria and the Czech Republic to the west, Poland to the north, Ukraine to the east, and Hungary to the south. It borrows a little bit from each of its neighbors. Linguistically and culturally it's closest to the Czech Republic, with whom it shared a common state for more than 70 years. With the Poles, the Slovaks share a deep Catholicism, and here as in Poland, you'll see people lined up at the church door on Sunday morning. Hungary ruled over the Slovaks for 1,000 years until 1918 and the Hungarian influence is still evident, if difficult to pinpoint. The easiest-to-see example might be in the cooking. The Hungarians brought the peppers and paprika, and Slovak goulash has been the better for it ever since. The Austrian influence is also strong but hard to describe. Vienna, for Slovaks, remains the absolute pinnacle of class and manners, and every time a waiter nods or clicks his heels as he serves you your coffee or strudel he's echoing a notion of Viennese civility going back centuries.

THE REGIONS IN BRIEF

For a small country, Slovakia possesses a wealth of regional diversity, both cultural and geographic. The western third of the country includes the capital Bratislava and, except for a few hills running north of the city, is relatively flat. It takes in the Danube lowlands and much of the border region with Hungary. The mountainous central region, running from the Malá Fatra highlands east of Žilina to the country's highest peaks, the High Tatras, is considered quintessential Slovak territory. The far eastern third of the country defies easy description. While geographically it's mostly rolling hills, ethnically speaking it's diverse, including ancient communities of Poles, Hungarians, Ukrainians, and Germans. Here folkways and traditional wooden architecture dominate and religion is very important. A visit here is very much a trip back in time.

SUGGESTED ITINERARY: SLOVAKIA IN 1 WEEK

Slovakia is a relatively small country, with decent roads and a dense network of trains and buses. The following itinerary assumes you're arriving in Bratislava and have a week to see the country. It's laid out ideally for car travel, but can be adapted to train and bus schedules without too much trouble.

Days ❶–❷: Arrive in Bratislava

After resting at the hotel, head into the Old Town for a quick "get-acquainted" walk. The city's laid-back pace is a perfect way to adjust to time zone changes. On the second day, get a good breakfast and plan on doing more serious walking. Start in the Old Town and take in the castle and the former Jewish quarter. Treat yourself to a nice dinner tonight, since restaurant food outside of the capital (with a few exceptions) will be a significant step down.

Day ❸: Trenčín & Žilina

Head north and east along the Váh river, first to the enchanting castle town of Trenčín and then farther along to Žilina, the jumping-off spot for Malá Fatra National Park. If you're traveling by car, try spending the night at one of the places in or near the park; if you're traveling by train, Žilina makes for a more convenient overnight stop.

Days ❹–❺: The High Tatras

The High Tatras are about 3 hours or so by car east of Žilina (and about the same distance by train), so try to get an early start. Once you've found your way to one of the High Tatra resorts, use the Tatra Electric Railway to explore the other resort towns. Use the second full day for a long walk in the mountains, keeping in mind, of course, the usual precautions pertaining to mountain hikes.

Day ❻: Option 1, Dunajec raft trip; Option 2, Levoča & Košice

Depending on what you want to do and how much time you've got, at this stage you can decide to spend another day in the High Tatra region or push off farther east to Košice. If you opt for the first and you've got a sunny day, drive or take a tour bus to Červený Kláštor for an exhilarating raft ride down the Dunajec river. If you're ready to head east, follow the road to Košice (about 2 hr. east of Poprad by car). Be sure to stop in Levoča (which can be comfortably toured in a couple of hours) and at Spišský Hrad. Once in Košice, book a room at the Bristol (for a well-deserved splurge) and plan a meal at Le Colonial. You'll soon feel like the king of eastern Slovakia.

Day ❼: Return to Bratislava

From Košice the return trip to Bratislava will take the better part of a day (7–8 hr.), so start early. From Poprad and the High Tatras to Bratislava, it's about a 5- to 6-hour drive, depending on traffic. By train, it can take equally long or longer, depending on the type of train.

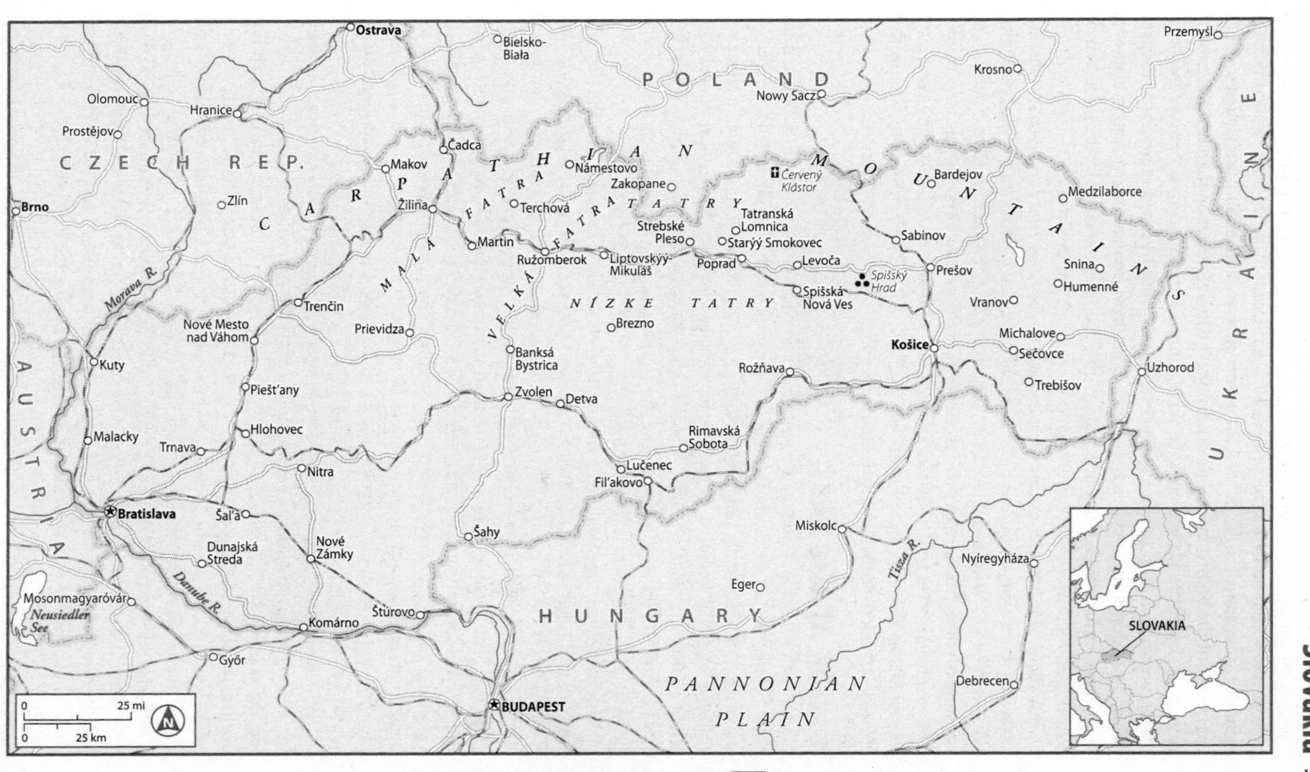
POLAND
CZECH REP.
AUSTRIA
HUNGARY
UKRAINE
CARPATHIAN MOUNTAINS
MALÁ FATRA
VEĽKÁ FATRA
TATRY
NÍZKE TATRY
PANNONIAN PLAIN
Ostrava
Bielsko-Biała
Przemyśl
Krosno
Nowy Sacz
Olomouc
Hranice
Prostějov
Brno
Zlín
Čadca
Makov
Žilina
Námestovo
Zakopane
Terchová
Martin
Ružomberok
Liptovský Mikuláš
Strebské Pleso
Tatranská Lomnica
Starý Smokovec
Poprad
Levoča
Červený Kláštor
Bardejov
Medzilaborce
Sabinov
Prešov
Spišský Hrad
Spišská Nová Ves
Snina
Humenné
Vranov
Michalove
Sečovce
Trebišov
Uzhorod
Košice
Brezno
Morava R.
Trenčín
Nové Mesto nad Váhom
Prievidza
Banská Bystrica
Kuty
Piešt'any
Zvolen
Detva
Rožňava
Rimavská Sobota
Malacky
Trnava
Hlohovec
Nitra
Lučenec
Fil'akovo
Bratislava
Šal'a
Šahy
Miskolc
Dunajská Streda
Nové Zámky
Nyíregyháza
Tisza R.
Danube R.
Mosonmagyaróvár
Neusiedler See
Eger
Štúrovo
Komárno
Győr
Debrecen
BUDAPEST
SLOVAKIA
0 25 mi
0 25 km
N

SLOVAKIA TODAY

Slovakia these days finds itself enjoying an economic and cultural heyday. Farsighted economic policies, including adopting a 19% flat-rate income tax and restructuring the public pension system, have allowed the government to reduce its budget deficit so much that the country qualified to adopt the European Union's common currency, the euro, as of January 1, 2009. This was no small achievement: Slovakia's euro adoption came years ahead of its main rivals, the Czech Republic and the country's former overlord Hungary. While switching to the euro caused some initial confusion and may even have allowed some shops to make a one-time price gouge, this was far outweighed by the pride Slovaks felt in meeting one of the E.U.'s toughest financial challenges.

But there were some concerns on the horizon. At press time, the global economic crisis was threatening to end—or at least significantly slow—the country's long-running economic boom. With fuel and energy costs rising, interest rates heading upward, and consumers cutting back, Slovakia's recent extraordinary economic growth rates of over 5% a year were in jeopardy. Visitors are not likely to notice the effects of any slowdown, but recent big drops in the value of both the U.S. dollar and British pound mean that Slovakia is no longer the budget destination it once was for many travelers.

A LOOK AT THE PAST

Slovakia is one Europe's youngest countries, dating only from January 1, 1993, and the amicable dissolution of Czechoslovakia into separate Czech and Slovak republics. While many on both sides at the time regretted the split, for Slovaks it represented a chance to realize a long-held ambition of forming an independent state. Slovak history goes back about 1,200 years, but for nearly the entire time—save for a few years during World War II when the Slovaks were permitted by the Germans to run a quasi-independent fascist puppet state—they were ruled by others.

The Hungarians first conquered the territory of modern Slovakia before the first millennium and ruled over the Slovaks for nearly 1,000 years, until the end of World War I. Slovakia was known on maps from the period simply as "Upper Hungary," and indeed Bratislava even served as the capital of Hungary during the Turkish occupation in the 16th and 17th centuries. The Hungarians suppressed Slovak culture and language, and the Slovaks were only one of a number of ethnic minorities—including enclaves of Poles, Germans, and Ukrainians—sharing the territory. The end of World War I saw the breakup of the Austro-Hungarian Empire, which gave the Slovaks a chance to split from Hungary and form an independent state together with the ethnically and linguistically similar Czechs.

The Slovaks profited greatly from the 70-year existence of Czechoslovakia, but there was also a bitter undercurrent of resentment against the authorities in Prague and a festering Slovak inferiority complex. It was only the collapse of Communism in 1989 that first opened the door to the possibility of a separate Slovak state. In 1992, with national politicians in Slovakia calling loudly for independence and Czech leaders fearful of the drag a poorer Slovakia would have on the national budget, the split was sealed and Czechoslovakia was finished. The "Velvet Divorce" was finalized on January 1, 1993. The years since independence have brought both ups and downs. Poor political leadership initially hurt the Slovaks in their bid to join the European Union and the NATO military alliance, but they eventually achieved both goals, joining the E.U. in 2004.

SLOVAK PEOPLE & CULTURE

With the country's expanse of unspoiled nature, Slovaks, generally speaking, tend to see themselves as a simple folk with a taste for fun, rich food, and strong drink. Folk music, while certainly an anachronism, can still be heard in some of the smaller towns and villages. Slovaks are known for being gregarious, generous, and loyal. On the negative side, they can be stubborn and nationalistic. Of course, these are generalizations. In reality there are as many "typical Slovaks" as there are people living there.

The vast majority of the population is ethnic Slovak, though a sizable minority of around half a million Hungarians lives in the south along the Hungarian frontier. There's also a large community of Gypsies, or Roma, spread out around the country, most living in squalor in the countryside or in decrepit public-housing projects in or near the large cities. The Roma represent a seemingly intractable problem for Slovakia. The Roma, with some justification, say they are routinely discriminated against and forced into substandard schools and living quarters. The Slovaks, for their part, say the Roma rigorously resist integration into mainstream life. There's truth on both sides, but no solution in sight.

SLOVAK CUISINE

As with culture, it's difficult to pinpoint Slovak cuisine with any certainty. If you had to generalize you'd be safe in saying it's similar to Czech and Austrian cooking, but spicier, more adventurous, and often better tasting. That means lots of meat dishes, with beef, pork, and chicken popping up on menus most often, but with a fiery taste that's often lacking in the countries to immediate west.

Many meals are built around the ubiquitous *halušky,* the Slovak equivalent of dumplings in the Czech lands. *Halušky* are little noodles made of potato meal, flour, and egg, which are then boiled and served as mains or sides. The national dish is *bryndzové halušky,* where the *halušky* share equal billing with a deliciously sharp, sour sheep's cheese and small chunks of bacon.

Mealtimes hold to the Continental standard. For breakfast *(raňajky),* Slovaks take a light meal that may only consist of a bread roll with tea or coffee, though hotels and pensions typically offer the standard table of cold cuts, cheeses, and cereals. Lunches are larger and usually served from noon until 2pm. Here you'll usually be offered two courses: a soup *(polievka)* and a main dish. Common soups include a deliciously sour cabbage *(kapustnica)* and vegetable *(zeleninová).* Mains are usually built around meat of some kind, with pork *(bravčové)* the most common, followed by beef *(hovadzie)* and chicken *(kurča).* You'll usually be expected to order a separate side dish. Potatoes *(zemiaky)* are the most common, usually served boiled or as fries, or something called "American potatoes," essentially large fries served with the potato skin intact (like steak fries). Dinners are more substantial, consisting of an appetizer, main course, and dessert *(dezert).* Desserts are normally built around pancakes of some sort, usually featuring chocolate and nuts, or fruit jam.

Vegetarians will find Slovak restaurants disappointing. Most restaurants offer salads, omelets, and fried cheese, but few if any meatless entrees. Menus typically include a section called "Meatless Dishes," but curiously these, too, generally contain a piece of ham or bacon.

LANGUAGE

Slovak is a western Slavic language, closely related to Czech. The two are mutually comprehensible. For centuries Hungarian was the official language in much of the territory of modern-day Slovakia, though command of Hungarian these days is limited mainly to ethnic Hungarians in the south of the country.

English speakers are likely to find the language something of a challenge. English is not widely known outside the larger cities, though nearly anyone can muster a few words in a pinch. This shouldn't deter you. Most museums and restaurants and anywhere else you're likely to go will have English information on hand. Almost every tourist information center and hotel will have a least one English speaker. If you know some German, that may help as well.

USEFUL WORDS & PHRASES

English	Slovak	Pronunciation
Hello/Good Day	**Dobrý deň**	*Doh*-bree den
Yes	**Ano/Hej!**	Ah-no/Hey!
No	**Ne**	*Neh*
Good morning	**Dobré ráno**	*Doh*-brey rah-no
Good evening	**Dobrý večer**	*Doh*-bree vech'-air
Goodbye	**Do videnia**	*Doh*-vee-*den*-ya
Good night	**Dobru noc**	Doh-*broo* nohts
Thank you	**D'akujem**	*Dyak*-oo-yem
Please/pardon	**Prosím**	*Proh*-seem
What's your name?	**Ako sa voláte?**	*Ah*-koh sa vol-*ah*-te?
My name is . . .	**Ja sa volám . . .**	*Yah* sa *vol*-ahm . . .
Nice to meet you	**Teší ma**	*Teh*-shee ma
Do you speak English?	**Hovoríte anglicky?**	*Hoh*-vor-ee-te *ahn*-gleets-key?
I don't understand	**Nerozumiem**	*Ne* roh-*zoom*-yem
How much is it?	**Kolko to stojí?**	*Kohl*-ko toh *stoy*-ee
Menu	**Jedálny lístok**	Yeh-*dahl*-nee *lee*-stoke
The bill, please	**Účet, prosím**	*Oo*-chet, *proh*-seem
Cheers!	**Na zdravie**	Nah *zdrah*-vye
Bon appétit!	**Dobru chut'**	Doh-*bru* hooty-a
Open	**Otvorené**	*Oh*-tvor-en-neh
Closed	**Zavreté**	*Zah*-vreh-teh

2 PLANNING YOUR TRIP TO SLOVAKIA

ENTRY REQUIREMENTS

There are no special requirements for entering Slovakia. Passport holders from the U.S., Canada, and Australia can enter the country without a visa and stay for 90 days. Passport holders from E.U. member countries, including the U.K., do not need a visa. Slovakia is a member of the E.U.'s internal Schengen zone, meaning you will not usually have to carry a passport if you are arriving directly from another Schengen country (Austria, Czech Republic, Hungary, and Poland)—though keep your passport with you just to be sure. This does not apply to the Ukrainian border.

A Note on Prices

While this book was being researched in the summer and fall of 2008, prices for goods and services, including restaurant meals, hotels and admissions, were still denominated in Slovak crowns. Prices here have been converted to euros at the prevailing rate of exchange (1€ = 30 Sk) but may differ slightly from the actual prices after euro adoption on January 1, 2009.

MONEY

Slovakia joined the E.U.'s euro zone on January 1, 2009, with the euro replacing the Slovak crown (Sk) as legal tender. The euro has bank notes of 500, 200, 100, 50, 20, 10, and 5 euros, and coins of 1 and 2 euros, as well as smaller denominations of 50, 20, 10, 5, 2, and 1-euro cent. At press time, 1 euro was equal to about $1.27 (but subject to considerable fluctuation).

While the euro is being phased in 2009, you may still see dual prices—euros and Slovak crowns—on some goods and services. Note that this is only to allow consumers to make price comparisons. Slovak crowns cannot be used to make purchases (so don't buy any on the black market). Banks will accept Slovak crowns for exchange until December 31, 2009. After that they are only good for the scrapbook.

Major credit cards are widely accepted at hotels, restaurants, and shops. Traveler's checks are less useful and must usually be cashed at banks. ATMs are ubiquitous in both big and small towns. They remain the best way to get cash on the spot.

WHEN TO GO

Slovakia has a continental climate with four distinct seasons. Summers are generally warm to very hot, and have reliably good weather. Winter is ski season in the resorts of the Malá Fatra, and the Low and High Tatras. Ski season starts in late December and runs through March. Spring and fall are generally ideal. The months of May, September, and October bring warm sunny days and crisp cool nights. By the end of October, hotels and many sights start shutting down for the winter.

Holidays

Offices, banks, museums, and many stores are closed on the following holidays, though some stores and restaurants remain open: January 1 (New Year's Day, Day of the Establishment of the Slovak Republic), January 6 (Epiphany), Good Friday, Easter Sunday and Monday (Mar/Apr), May 1 (Labor Day), May 8 (Victory over Fascism Day), July 5 (St. Cyril and Methodius Day), August 29 (Slovak National Uprising Day), September 1 (Constitution Day), September 15 (Day of Our Lady of Sorrows), November 1 (All Saints' Day), November 17 (Day of the Fight for Democracy), December 24 (Christmas Eve), and December 25 and 26 (Christmas).

GETTING THERE

BY PLANE Bratislava's regional airport *(letisko),* **M.R. Štefánik Airport** (© **02/3303-3353**; www.airportbratislava.sk) is 9km (5 miles) northeast of the city. **Czech Airlines/ CSA** (www.csa.cz) maintains regular air service to and from Prague. Budget carrier **Sky-Europe** (www.skyeurope.sk) flies to several European capitals, including London

Major Festivals in Slovakia

The major festivals in Slovakia usually celebrate either religious rites or the country's folk origins. Among the biggest religious celebrations is the annual **Maria pilgrimage** in Levoča the first **weekend in July**. Unless you're a pilgrim, or eager to see a pilgrimage in full force, try to avoid Levoča on that weekend; otherwise you'll find yourself elbow to elbow with 100,000 other people looking for hotel rooms and tables at restaurants. Nearly every village holds a folk festival of some sort or another during the summer months (too many to list here), but the granddaddy of them all is the **Východná festival** in **early July** in the town of Východná, not far from Liptovský Mikuláš. The **Pohoda Music Festival** (www.pohodafestival.sk) in **mid-July** in Trenčín is the highlight of the outdoor rock music season, drawing many of the best alternative and independent bands from around Europe and United States.

(Luton), Paris (Orly), Amsterdam, and Rome, and several smaller European cities. Other airlines that fly to Bratislava include the budget carrier Ryanair, Austrian Air, and Lufthansa. Vienna's **Schwechat** airport (✆ **431-7007-22233;** www.viennaairport.com), 67km (42 miles) west of Bratislava, offers more flights, and remains the only option for direct flights to and from North America. Bratislava is a 70-minute bus ride away (see details in the Bratislava section, below).

BY TRAIN Regular train service links Bratislava with Vienna (1 hr.), Prague (5 hr.), and Budapest (3 hr.). For exact times, check the **Slovak State Railway (ŽSR;** ✆ **02/18188;** www.slovakrail.sk) online timetable (be sure to use "Praha" to search for Prague, "Wien" to search for Vienna, and so on). Most international trains arrive at Bratislava's centrally located **Hlavná Stanica,** Predstanicne námestie 1 (✆ **02/18188**), about 20 minutes by tram or 10 minutes by taxi to the Old Town.

BY BUS The Slovak national bus carrier, **Slovak Lines** (✆ **0900/211-312;** www.slovaklines.sk), together with the Europe-wide consortium of bus operators, **Eurolines** (www.eurolines.com), maintains regular long-distance bus service from Bratislava to a number of European capitals and other cities, though this service is coming under increasing competition from budget airlines. Bratislava's main bus station is at Mlynské nivy 31 (✆ **02/12111;** www.cp.sk).

BY CAR Bratislava lies on a main central European motorway, linking Prague with Budapest. The drive to Bratislava from Prague (320km/198 miles) will take 3 to 4 hours, depending on traffic. From Budapest (250km/155 miles), expect to drive about 3 hours. The drive from Vienna (70km/43 miles) will take about 1 hour, but try to avoid travel on Fridays to miss frequent preweekend backups at the border crossing. Note that you will have to buy a special sticker to drive on Slovak highways. The sticker, available at border crossings and at major gas stations, costs around 5€ ($6.35) for 1 week, and 10€ ($13) for a month. If you rent a car in Slovakia, the rental should include a valid highway sticker.

BY BOAT It's possible to travel between Bratislava and Vienna by high-speed catamaran (about 75 min.). Check **Twin City Liner** (✆ **0903/610-716;** www.twincityliner.com). Boats depart from the main dock area on Rásuzovo náb, just behind the Devin

Hotel. Fares run from 16€ to 26€ ($23–$33) per person one-way. Regular ferry service is also available to Vienna and Budapest (about 4–5 hr.). Contact **LOD** (✆ **02/5293-2226;** www.lod.sk).

GETTING AROUND

BY CAR Car travel offers the most flexibility, and if your plans are to see some of the countryside away from the main cities, you should consider renting a car. To rent, you'll need a license that's valid in the country of origin (U.S. state licenses are acceptable), a major credit card, and a passport. Slovak driving rules follow Continental norms. A yellow diamond denotes a main road where you do not need to yield to incoming traffic at intersections. At unmarked intersections, yield to cars on the right. Cars on roundabouts have the right of way. Speed limits are 130kmph (81 mph) on four-lane highways, 90kmph (55 mph) on open roads, and 50kmph (30 mph) in villages and incorporated areas. Speed limits are rigorously enforced, and if caught you'll have to pay a spot fine of about 35€ ($44) or higher. The blood alcohol limit is zero. Slovakia has only a few stretches of four-lane, limited-access highway, so prepare yourself for some slow two-lane travel, where you're usually trapped behind a belching truck or a painfully slow bus. Remember to pass with care and only with a clear line of sight.

BY TRAIN Slovakia's aging but serviceable national rail line, **ŽSR** (✆ **02/18188;** www.slovakrail.sk), remains the best way to travel directly between most major cities, including Žilina, Trenčín, Poprad, and Košice.

BY BUS The national bus line, **Slovak Lines** (✆ **0900/211-312;** www.slovaklines.sk), operates a dense network of bus connections that, in theory, should be able to get you nearly anywhere in the country. Bus and train fares are similar and you should make your choice between the two based on convenience of departure times and connections. The Slovak Lines website has a convenient timetable for figuring out connections, but watch to use Slovak spellings for town and city names.

TIPS ON ACCOMMODATIONS

The number of newer, privately owned hotels is on the increase. If you arrive in town without a room, the best place to go is the local tourist information office. Many of these, including the helpful office in Bratislava, can advise on rooms and book according to your wishes. Failing that, look around for private rooms, usually identified by the word *ubytovanie* (accommodations) or *privat* on the outside. These are invariably bed-without-bathroom setups, usually in an unused part of the family home, but are almost always clean and cheap.

TIPS ON DINING

With disposable incomes on the rise, more people are eating out more often and the restaurant situation is improving dramatically. The transformation is easiest to see in Bratislava and Košice. That said, you may still find yourself in a small town with relatively few options aside from the ubiquitous pizzeria on the main square and a couple of unappetizing pubs, catering mostly to old guys crouched over beers. While you may occasionally find good food in an old pub, it's usually a safer—if less interesting—bet to go with the pizza. On the other hand, special folklore-type restaurants, sometimes with the word *koliba* in the name, are a real treat, usually serving traditional foods and grilled meats, occasionally with a live band or "gypsy" music to accompany the meal.

Fast Facts Slovakia

American Express There's no full-service American Express office in Bratislava, but some Amex services are offered through Agency Alex, Kuzmanyho 8 (✆ **02/5941-2200**).

Business Hours Stores and offices are generally open Monday to Friday 9am to 6pm. Banks are open Monday to Friday 9am to 4pm. Some larger stores have limited Saturday hours, usually 9am to noon. Museums and other tourist attractions are often closed on Mondays.

Doctors & Dentists Phone ✆ **155** in a medical emergency. In Bratislava, there's a doctor on 24-hr. call at the Ružinov clinic, Ružinovská 10 (✆ **02/4823-4113**). Private dental services are available at Drieňová 38 (✆ **02/4342–3433**).

Electricity Slovak outlets follow the Continental norm (220v, 50hz) with two round plugs. Most appliances that run on 110v will require a transformer.

Embassies **U.S.:** Hviezdoslavovo námestie 4 (✆ 02/5443-0861); **Canada:** Mostová 2 (✆ 02/5920-4031); **U.K.:** Panská 16 (✆ 02/5998-2000).

Emergencies In an emergency, dial the following numbers: police ✆ **158,** fire ✆ **150,** ambulance ✆ **155,** road assistance ✆ **154.**

Internet Access Internet cafes are located throughout Bratislava and in all larger cities. Rates vary but are around 1€ ($1.27) for 30 minutes online. Nearly all hotels will offer some form of Internet connection—either in-room dataports or wireless—and many will have at least one public computer for guests to use.

Luggage Storage & Lockers Railroad stations in large cities, including Bratislava's main station, have storage lockers or an attendant to watch luggage.

Mail The main post office is at námestie SNP 35, just outside the main gate to the Old Town. The post office is open Monday to Friday 7am to 8pm, Saturday 7am to 6pm, and Sunday 9am to 2pm. The rate for mailing a postcard or first-class letter to the U.S. or Canada is around 1€ ($1.27), and slightly less within Europe.

Safety Crime is generally low, but as everywhere use common sense.

Telephones & Fax Slovakia's country code is **421.** To dial Slovakia from abroad, dial the international access code (011 in the U.S.), plus 421 and then the local Slovak area code (minus the zero). The area code for Bratislava is 02. Other commonly used area codes are: Trenčín 032, Žilina 041, the High Tatras 052, and Košice 055. To call between cities within Slovakia, dial the area code (retaining the zero) plus the number. To call abroad from Slovakia, dial 00, and then the country code and area code to where you are calling. A call to the U.S. or Canada would begin 00-1 (plus the seven-digit number).

Time Zone Slovakia is in the Central European Time zone (CET), 1 hour ahead of GMT and 6 hours ahead of the eastern United States.

Tipping In restaurants, tip about 10% of the bill to reward good service. Round up taxi fares to the next even euro amount. Tip bellhops and tour guides a few euro coins, depending on the services rendered.

Toilets You will find decent public toilets in cities and towns throughout Slovakia. Expect to pay about .20€ (30¢) to use the facilities.

Water Tap water is generally potable and there are no specific health concerns. If in doubt, buy bottled water, which is cheap and widely available.

3 BRATISLAVA

Slovakia's youthful capital (www.bratislava.sk) has transformed itself from a relatively unappealing sprawl of postwar, Communist-era buildings into a relaxed and pleasant medium-size capital in the span of little more than a decade. The city's compact Old Town has been completely and stunningly renovated. Most of the area is restricted to car traffic, and in the evenings, it seems, the whole town converges on the center for a cup of coffee or a glass of wine. Plan on being thoroughly charmed, and you might even consider extending your stay.

Until relatively recent times Bratislava (known as Pressburg to the Germans, and Pozsony in Hungarian) was a sleepy port on the Danube River (Dunaj in Slovak). It was only in the post–World War II decades, under Czechoslovakia's then-Communist government, that the city exploded in population to the current around 500,000. The Communists were keen on building up the Slovak capital as a way of gaining Slovak support. You can see the results of this rapid buildup in the high-rise residences on the outskirts of town. The largest of these Communist-era housing projects, Petržalka, just across the SNP Bridge from the Old Town, holds something like 150,000 people.

Bratislava has played an important role in Hungarian history. During the Turkish occupation of Hungary, the Hungarians moved their capital here. No less than 11 Hungarian royals were crowned in Bratislava's St. Martin's cathedral on Dóm Sv. Martina down through the ages.

ARRIVING

By Plane

Bus no. 61 connects Bratislava airport with the main train station, Hlavná Stanica. The journey takes about 25 minutes. An **Airport Shuttle** service (© **02/4363-2305;** www.airportshuttle.sk) is available, with prices starting at 15€ ($19). If you are arriving in Vienna Schwechat airport, buses run frequently to Bratislava's main bus terminal. The ride takes 70 minutes and costs about 10€ ($13) each way. Several operators maintain regular limo and minibus service between Schwechat and Bratislava. The above **Airport Shuttle** service charges 50€ ($64) for up to four passengers.

By Train, Bus, Car, or Boat

See the general "Getting There" section on p. 613 for details about arriving in Bratislava by train, bus, car, or boat.

CITY LAYOUT

The area of most interest to visitors is the Old Town (Staré Mesto) and the adjacent Castle area, all situated north of the Danube. For restaurants, accommodations, and most of the attractions, you'll rarely stray from this area.

GETTING AROUND

ON FOOT The best way to see Bratislava and to get around in Old Town is to walk. Distances are not far, but you'll want to wear comfortable shoes because of the cobblestones.

BY TRAM Bratislava's tram system is comprehensive, though for traveling around the Old Town and the immediate area, you won't need it. Ticket prices vary by time. A 10-minute ticket, the cheapest, costs about.50€ (75¢). A 30-minute ticket costs.60€ (90¢). A ticket for large pieces of luggage costs.25€ (40¢). You can also buy day or multiday tickets for 1, 2, 3, and 7 days. Validate tickets on entering the tram and hold onto them until the end of the ride. The fine is steep for riding without a ticket. Trams generally run from 5am to 11pm. More information is available on the Bratislava Transport Company website: www.dpb.sk.

BY BUS Bratislava has an extensive network of buses and trolleys, and these are generally the only ways of reaching the more far-flung parts of the city. The ticketing is the same as for trams. Validate your ticket on entering the bus or trolley. Buses generally run from 5am to 11pm.

BY TAXI Taxis are relatively cheap and easy to find. Hail them on the street, at taxi stands, or call by phone. Watch that the driver switches on the meter, since dishonest drivers, relatively rarely now, may try to cheat you. Fares around town shouldn't be any higher than 5€ to 7€ ($6.35–$8.90). Two reputable agencies include **Fun Taxi** (✆ **02/16777**) and **ABC Taxi** (✆ **02/16100**).

BY BIKE The car-free Old Town is easily negotiated by bike, but there are few rental shops around. The rest of the city is less bike-friendly, with trolley buses, trams, and traffic to contend with.

VISITOR INFORMATION

The **Tourist Information Center** maintains four offices. The main office is located in the Old Town at Klobučnícka ul. 2 (✆ **02/16186;** www.bkis.sk), with branches at the airport, main train station, and passenger ferry port. The staff is efficient at supplying maps and suggestions of all kinds, as well as helping to arrange transportation and accommodations. The **Bratislava Tourist Service,** also in the Old Town at Ventúrska ul. 9 (✆ **02/5464-1271;** www.bratislava-info.sk), is a separate but equally helpful office, where you'll find plenty of maps and booklets as well as suggestions on what to see and where to sleep. The office runs daily walking tours (15€/$19 per person, in English and German). For a more fun tour, head to Hlavné námestie in the Old Town to catch the little red trolley through the Old Town. Tours last 30 to 45 minutes and are great for a quick orientation (✆ **0903-302-817;** www.tour4u.sk). **Bratislava Sightseeing Tours,** Pri Suchom mlyne 84 (✆ **0907-683-112;** www.bratislavasightseeing.com), offers off-the-beaten-track bicycle and bus tours, both within Bratislava and in the surrounding countryside, from May 1 through September.

WHERE TO STAY

You may experience sticker shock on arrival in Bratislava. The city attracts relatively few individual travelers and most of the properties are aimed at businessmen on expense accounts and the odd coach tour from Germany and Austria. If you do decide on one of the luxury hotels, bear in mind that it never hurts to bargain. Even the most expensive hotels have been known to slash rates on slow nights and weekends.

At the other end of the spectrum are private rooms. These vary greatly in comfort, cleanliness, and location. Some are real gems, situated in or near the Old Town and presided over by Slovak grannies who make sure everything is spotless. Others are less desirable, in public housing estates in far-flung residential neighborhoods. If you decide to go the private room route, insist on a room within comfortable walking or tram distance from the Old Town. The Tourist Information Center is a good source for private rooms; alternatively, check the **Bratislava Hotels** website (www.bratislavahotels.sk), which includes listings for hostels and pensions.

Very Expensive

Arcadia ★★★ Finds A lovely restoration of a 13th-century town house, with a gorgeous arcaded lobby and rooms that maintain many period elements—like fireplaces and wood-beamed ceilings—from the original structure. The rooms are furnished in 19th-century style, with bold reds and golds, as well de-rigueur-at-this-price-point modern elements like flatscreen TVs and DVD players. The cocktail and cigars bar off the lobby has the feel of gentlemen's club.

Františkánska 3. ✆ **02/5949-0540.** Fax 02/5949-0555. www.arcadia-hotel.sk. 34 units. 250€ ($318) double. AE, DC, MC, V. **Amenities:** Restaurant; spa; concierge; business center; salon; 24-hr. room service; dry cleaning; nonsmoking rooms. *In room:* A/C, TV, dataport, minibar, coffeemaker, hair dryer, iron, safe.

Marrol's ★ Beautiful boutique hotel with a Jazz Age theme, situated just outside the Old Town. The gorgeous lobby, with dark hardwoods and leather sofas, feels like out of the Great Gatsby, with a Billie Holiday soundtrack to enhance the mood. The rooms are retro sleek with soft greens and dark woods. The baths have 1930s-style black-and-white tiles. Ask to see room no. 102, with a private garden. You'll notice the bellhop is wearing white gloves.

Tobrucká 4. ✆ **02/5778-4600.** Fax 02/5778-4601. www.hotelmarrols.sk. 54 units. 250€ ($318) double. AE, DC, MC, V. **Amenities:** Restaurant; spa; concierge; business center; 24-hr. room service; dry cleaning; nonsmoking rooms. *In room:* A/C, TV, dataport, minibar, coffeemaker, hair dryer, iron, safe.

Radisson SAS Carlton Hotel ★★ Once the dowdy grande dame of Bratislava's prewar hotels, the Carlton has gotten a multimillion-dollar face-lift courtesy of the Radisson hotel chain and the result is easily Slovakia's finest big chain hotel. You'll find everything you would expect from a leading international hotel, packed into a lovely 19th-century neoclassical building along one of the city's nicest squares. The location is convenient for walking to the Old Town, the river, and the city's cultural facilities. Check the website for weekend specials.

Hviezdoslavovo nám. 3. ✆ **02/5939-0000.** Fax 02/5939-0010. www.bratislava.radissonsas.com. 170 units. 250€ ($318) standard double. AE, DC, MC, V. **Amenities:** Restaurant; spa; concierge; business center; shopping arcade; salon; 24-hr. room service; dry cleaning; nonsmoking rooms. *In room:* A/C, TV, dataport, minibar, coffeemaker, hair dryer, iron, safe.

Expensive

Devin ★ A quirky, local alternative to the Radisson SAS Carlton if you have a higher budget but want something a little different. The Devin dates from the 1950s and was once the hotel of choice for visiting Communist dignitaries. It's been thoroughly scoured and spruced up since then, but you'll still find a sort of old-school regalness to the well-proportioned rooms, as well as the lobby and reception area. The adjoining cafe is a classic midcentury period piece. The location, just away from the Old Town, along the

Danube, is excellent and especially convenient to the ferry docks. Parking and access to the hotel is easy, since the freeway runs nearby.

Riečna 4. ✆ **02/5998-5856.** Fax 02/5443-0682. www.hoteldevin.sk. 100 units. 155€ ($197) double. AE, DC, MC, V. **Amenities:** Restaurant; indoor pool; spa; concierge; business center; limited room service; dry cleaning; nonsmoking rooms. *In room:* A/C, TV, dataport, minibar, hair dryer, safe.

Hotel No. 16 ★★ Finds This dark-wood, cottagelike inn, tucked high above town in Bratislava's tiny villa quarter, is one part mountain chalet and one part boutique hotel. The rooms themselves are small but cozy, and ooze rustic charm. That's a ruse. They're wired with every modern convenience you're likely to need, including in-room Wi-Fi and plasma TV screens. Everything, from the furniture to the bathroom fixtures, feels sturdy and well crafted. The relatively remote location affords an illusion of seclusion, but the Old Town is still only a 10-minute walk away. If you arrive in town by plane, bus, or train, take a taxi and don't try to negotiate the twisting streets. Be sure to ask about discounts, since the hotel will cut rates on slow nights.

Partizánska 16. ✆ **02/5441-1672.** Fax 02/5441-1298. www.hotelno16.sk. 12 units. 130€ ($165) double. AE, DC, MC, V. **Amenities:** Restaurant; concierge; room service; dry cleaning; nonsmoking rooms. *In room:* A/C, TV, dataport, minibar, hair dryer, safe.

Perugia This medium-size Old Town hotel offers a decent mix of comfort and location, and for that reason it's often difficult to get a room (though it still feels overpriced). The emphasis is on contemporary style. A former baroque town house renovated in the 1990s by a well-known Slovak design team, the modern rooms have original art on the wall. In the summer, the welcoming terrace is often filled with friendly faced foreigners. The in-house restaurant serves very good Hungarian food.

Zelená 5 16. ✆ **02/5443-1818.** Fax 02/5443-1821. www.perugia.sk. 14 units. 180€ ($229) double. AE, DC, MC, V. **Amenities:** Restaurant; limited room service; nonsmoking rooms. *In room:* A/C, TV, minibar, hair dryer, safe.

Moderate

IBIS ★ Exactly what you'd expect from the European hotel chain that has pioneered the market for moderately priced hotels with central locations. Okay, so the lobby and hallways feel a little cramped, and the room is tiny and lacks, well, atmosphere. You're a stone's throw away from the Old Town and you have relative luxuries like in-room Internet and air-conditioning that would easily cost twice as much anywhere else. Note that only queen-size beds are available, no twins or triple rooms.

Zámocká 38. ✆ **02/5929-2000.** Fax 02/5929-2111. www.ibis-bratislava.sk. 100 units. 80€ ($102) double. AE, DC, MC, V. **Amenities:** Restaurant. *In room:* A/C, TV, dataport, minibar, hair dryer.

Penzión Gremium ★ The formerly funky Gremium has gone upscale in the past year, with a thorough renovation that left the rooms nicer and more comfortable but taken out some of the former hipster appeal. The coffee shop on the ground floor is now gone, replaced by an expensive restaurant. The chief draws here are the plain but comfortable rooms, the decent price, and the location, within easy walking distance of the Old Town.

Gorkého 11. ✆ **02/2070-4874.** Fax 02/2070-4874. 15 units. 85€ ($108) double. AE, DC, MC, V. **Amenities:** Restaurant.

Inexpensive

Old City ★ The only inexpensive hotel located within the Old Town has a few good things going for it. First is location, right in the heart of Bratislava's Old Town. The hotel

Bratislava Lodging, Dining & Attractions

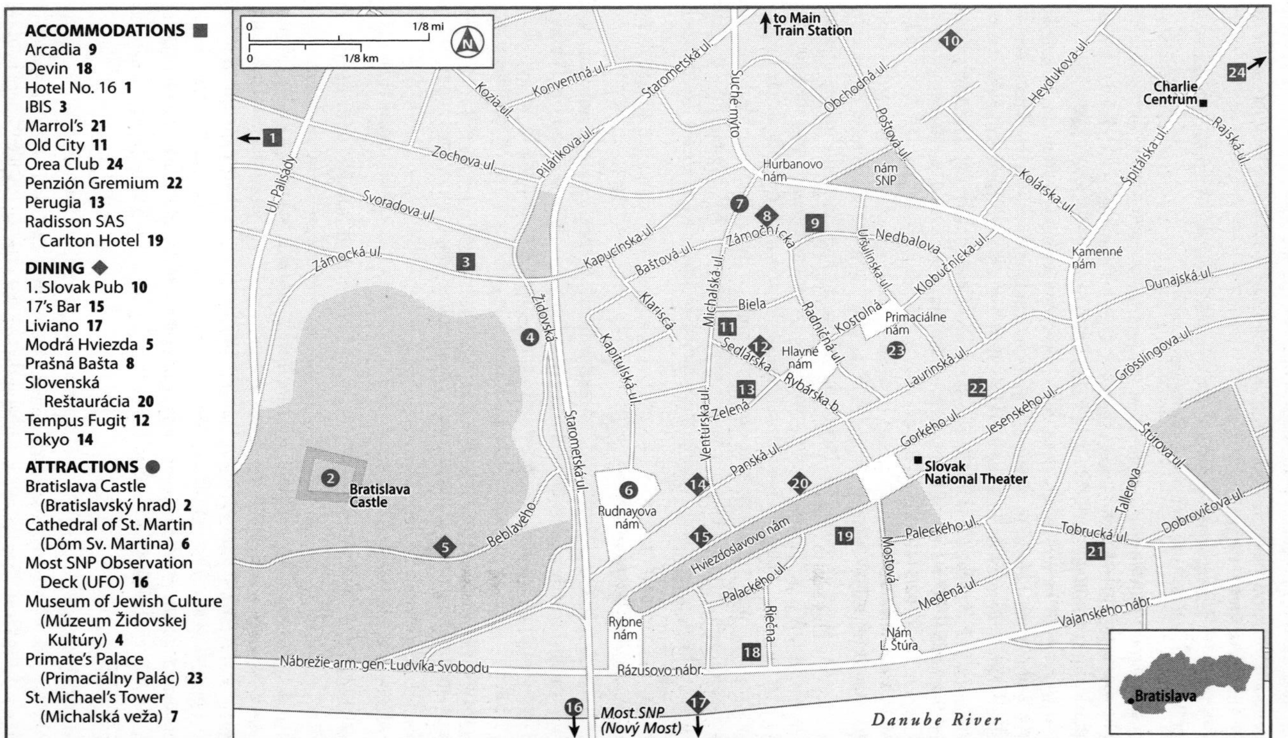

is also clean and nonsmoking throughout. On the downside, it's a four- or five-story walk up, and the rooms themselves are nondescript. Ask for one of the lower rooms in midsummer, since the rooms just below the roof can get hot. There's an Internet cafe on the ground floor to check e-mail.

Michalská 2. ✆ **02/5443-0258.** Fax 02/5464-8304. www.oldcityhotel.sk. 15 units. 60€ ($76) double. AE, DC, MC, V. **Amenities:** Restaurant. *In room:* TV, minibar, hair dryer.

Orea Club This former sport hotel on the grounds of the Slovak national tennis club is a good value alternative for budget shoppers. Orea is a midrange Czech hotel chain and that ensures good-quality bedding and cleanliness, even if the hotel itself resembles a dorm for tennis players (what it used to be). Ask for a room away from the parking lot. A big plus if you happen to play tennis; you can rent equipment on-site. The location is three tram stations away from the center, with the tram stop situated across the street.

Odbojárov 3. ✆ **02/2492-02111.** Fax 02/2446-35739. www.orea.cz. 30 units. 60€ ($76) double. AE, DC, MC, V. **Amenities:** Restaurant; spa; tennis courts; nonsmoking rooms. *In room:* TV, dataport, hair dryer.

WHERE TO DINE

Bratislava's restaurant scene has exploded in the past few years. The number of places has grown, the range of choices has increased, and, most importantly, the quality of what's on offer is much better. Most of the restaurants are clustered in or around the Old Town or near the castle. Bratislava is a relatively casual city and, aside from the fanciest restaurants in the high-end hotels, you can pretty much come as you are. Meal times are standard, with 7:30pm being the hardest-to-get reservation. Most restaurants serve late into the evening, especially during the summer, but don't let it go *too* late. Kitchens generally start closing down around 10pm or so.

Very Expensive

Liviano ★★★ CONTINENTAL Arguably Bratislava's best restaurant isn't in the Old Town at all, but rather across the river in the sprawling Communist-era suburb of Petržalka. Head chef Marcel Ihnačák trained with Britain's Jamie Oliver and has imported Oliver's philosophy of simple foods and fresh ingredients. Here, the emphasis is on local dishes with a Mediterranean flair like oven-roasted beef sirloin with pecorino cheese, served with beetroot, mashed potatoes, and arugula salad. The interior is simple and refined and provides a perfect foil for the food. Take a taxi here, since you're not likely to find it otherwise.

Kutlikova 9. ✆ **02/6828-6688.** Entrees 12€–18€ ($15–$23). AE, DC, MC, V. Daily 11:30am–11pm.

Tempus Fugit ★ CONTINENTAL Something about the simple, softly lit, modern decor pulls you in from one of the city's more chaotic side streets (an Irish bar is right across the street). The restaurant occupies three floors of a beautifully restored Renaissance building. The theme is less Slovak and more classic dishes with a French or Asian twist. Try the duck breast in a cherry sauce with a potato-cinnamon mash. Boasts one of the best wine collections in the Old Town.

Sedlárska 5. ✆ **02/5441-4357.** Reservations recommended. Entrees 13€–26€ ($17–$33). AE, DC, MC, V. Daily 11am–1am (last dinner orders 10:30pm).

Expensive

Modrá Hviezda ★ SLOVAK Come more for the traditional atmosphere than for the Slovak food, which is still very good. There's something about climbing the steps to the castle in the evening on the way here that makes Modrá Hviezda feel like a special outing. In warm weather, the terrace, with views over the Old Town and the futuristic SNP

Bridge (New Bridge), is *the* place to be. In colder weather, the rich interior feels more like a Gothic wine cellar. Sit back and let the waiters, some English speaking, guide you through the mains and wines.

Beblavého 14. ✆ **02/5443-2747.** Entrees 8€–13€ ($10–$17). AE, DC, MC, V. Mon–Sat 11am–11pm.

Slovenská Reštaurácia ★★ SLOVAK The ideal spot if you're looking for *bryndzové halušky* and other classic Slovak dishes in a highly traditional setting, complete with waiters in folk costumes, folk music—the whole nine yards. If this sounds too touristy, don't be put off. The food is excellent (this may be your only chance to try wild boar) and the clientele includes not only the inevitable tour buses, but also Slovak couples looking for good home cooking in their capital city.

Hviezdoslavovo nám. 20. ✆ **02/5443-4883.** Entrees 10€–13€ ($13–$17). AE, DC, MC, V. Daily 11am–11pm.

Moderate

Prašná Bašta ★★ Finds SLOVAK This well-concealed restaurant, just a couple steps away from the St. Michael's Tower, is an oasis for laid-back locals who know good food at good value when they get it. Sit outside on the back terrace in nice weather. There's usually a little combo band keeping things lively in the evenings. Start off with the spicy "Armenian" salad, and then move through the mains of mostly chicken and pork dishes, but more interesting and original than the usual Slovak menu. There's also a nice selection of vegetarian meals. Top it all off with a rich Hungarian chocolate cake called *somló.*

Zámočnicka 11. ✆ **02/5443-4957.** Reservations are recommended, especially for the terrace. Entrees 7€–10€ ($8.90–$13). AE, DC, MC, V. Mon–Sat 11am–11pm.

Tokyo ★ JAPANESE One of the few places in town that serves decent sushi. That might sound like a strange claim, but after a week or more in the wilds of eastern Slovakia, facing dinner after dinner of stuffed chicken breasts, you might welcome a lighter change of pace. The sushi is pricey by the piece, but a decent range of sushi-maki sets brings the price down to the affordable category. In addition to sushi, Tokyo serves decent Thai food, including staple noodle dishes and some spicy curries (though mild by Thai standards). The restaurant is light on atmosphere, so head here, like many Slovaks do, for a quick lunch instead.

Panská 27. ✆ **02/5443-4982.** Entrees 7€–10€ ($8.90–$13). V. Daily 11am–11pm.

Inexpensive

1. Slovak Pub ★ SLOVAK This mock-up of a traditional Slovak pub in the middle of bustling Bratislava manages to be both a raucous tavern and a visitor-friendly restaurant at the same time. The menu has dozens of variations of the national dish, *bryndzové halušky,* as well as *pirohy* (the Slovak variation of the Polish pierogi), goulash, and lots of grilled meats. Wash it all down with plenty of beer and be prepared to settle in for the evening. Fun.

Obchodná 62. ✆ **02/5292-6367.** Entrees 5€–7€ ($6.35–$8.90). AE, DC, MC, V. Daily 11am–1am.

17's Bar ★ PIZZA The place to go for pizza and beer in a casual student atmosphere. The pizza, served in typically thin-crusted, Slovak style, is some of the best in town. Try the Diavalo, with spicy Slovak sausage and red peppers. Sit on the terrace in summer or grab a wooden bench inside in winter. In keeping with the largely student clientele, the service and presentation are casual. Reservations not needed.

Hviezdoslavovo nám. 17. ✆ **02/5443-5135.** Entrees 3€–5€ ($3.80–$6.35). No credit cards. Mon–Sat 11am–11pm.

Bratislava is best suited to ambling. There are few "musts"; instead the **Old Town (Staré Mesto)** itself, with its inviting, laid-back mix of restaurants, cafes, and bars, is the primary attraction. The best place to start your exploration is at the main entrance to the Old Town, **St. Michael's Tower (Michalská veža).** From here, walk along the main pedestrian streets of Michalská and then Ventúrska, pausing to admire the detailing on the lovingly restored baroque and Renaissance housing stock. Alleyways fan out in all directions, and the best advice is simply to follow your nose. The core of the Old Town is small and can be covered in a couple of hours. The focal point of the Old Town is **Hlavné námestie,** the main square, lined on one side by the Old Town Hall and the other by a mix of restaurants and cafes. At some point, be sure to pay a visit to the city's cathedral, **St. Martin's (Dóm Sv. Martina),** situated just outside of the Old Town, following the signs. From here it's a short walk below the freeway to the **castle** side of the Old Town. The hike to the castle takes about 30 minutes. The views out over the Old Town are spectacular, but the castle itself is undergoing a long-term renovation and is something of a disappointment. From here, you can't miss the view of Bratislava's retro-futuristic bridge, the **Most SNP (New Bridge),** which links the Old Town to the sprawling housing project of Petržalka. On your return from the castle, walk through the **old Jewish quarter,** once situated in the area around Židovská.

Bratislava Castle (Bratislavský hrad) ★ This squat, square castle, high above the Old Town, is worth the climb to the top, if only for the fabulous view of the space-age bridge, the Most SNP (New Bridge), in the distance. The castle dates from the early 16th century. It burned to the ground at the start of the 19th century and stood as a ruin for almost 150 years before the Communist government started restoration work (still ongoing) in the 1950s. At press time the castle was closed for visitors for ongoing reconstruction and was not expected to open during 2009. You can still enjoy the view from the top—you'll just miss the castle museum's historical exhibitions which are a bit of a disappointment anyway.

Hrad. No phone. Tues–Sat 9am–5pm; Sun 1–5pm.

Cathedral of St. Martin (Dóm Sv. Martina) ★★ The city's most important church was neutered and neglected by the former Communist regime, who planned the main highway right past the church's front door. That was done intentionally as a way of snubbing religion in the name of modernity. Now the church is making a comeback, though it still feels a little lost and forlorn here. St. Martin's served as the main coronation cathedral for a procession of Hungarian kings and queens during the centuries of the Turkish occupation of Hungary.

Rudnayovo nám. No phone. Mon–Fri 10–11:30am and 2–4:30pm; Sat 10–11:30am; Sun 2–4:30pm.

Museum of Jewish Culture (Múzeum Židovskej Kultúry) ★ For centuries, Bratislava was one of the most important centers of Jewish scholarship in central Europe. The area below the castle—now covered over by the highway—eventually became the Jewish quarter, and was once home to as many as 20 schools and synagogues. The quarter survived largely intact until World War II, during which the puppet Slovak government—following the Nazi lead—deported the Jews (mainly to death camps in Poland). The Communist government after the war paved over the remains (in this case, by building a highway over them). The photographs and documents on display here tell the story.

Židovská 17. ✆ **02/5934-9142.** Admission 7€ ($8.90). Sun–Fri 11am–4:30pm.

Most SNP Observation Deck (UFO) ★ The very cool retro-futuristic SNP Bridge (now known officially as the "New Bridge") was built in the late 1960s and early '70s at the height of Communist excess. It was inspired by the optimistic futurism of the 1960s and looks like it sprang right out of an episode of *Star Trek* or *The Jetsons.* The circular observation deck atop the supporting tower rises some 90m (295 ft.) above the river below. The view from the top is great, but the shape of the deck, the winds buffeting the bridge, and the flowing river below all combine to cause a slight feeling of vertigo. The restaurant serves good, if expensive, food—and if you're eating at the restaurant, you can visit the observation deck for free.

Most SNP (New Bridge). ✆ **02/6252-0300.** Admission 7€ ($8.90) adult, 3.50€ ($4.45) children 15 and under; free if you are eating at the restaurant. Daily 10am–11pm.

Primate's Palace (Primaciálny Palác) ★★ A beautifully restored 18th-century palace that now serves as the seat of the mayor of Bratislava. It was here in 1805 that a victorious Napoleon Bonaparte and Holy Roman Emperor Francis I signed the Treaty of Pressburg following the Battle of Austerlitz (now Slavkov, near the Moravian city of Brno). You can tour the inside of the palace; the highlights include the **Chamber of Mirrors (Zrkadlová sieň),** as well as a valuable collection of tapestries.

Primaciálne nám. ✆ **02/5935-6111.** Admission 1.30€ ($1.65). Tues–Sun 10am–5pm.

St. Michael's Tower (Michalská veža) ★ A highly inviting entryway into the Old Town. The gate is actually part of the city's medieval fortification system, and you can still see the remains of the moat and bastion. The 50m (164-ft.) tower, topped with a statue of St. Michael himself, houses a small exhibition on weaponry; the top of the tower affords a postcard view over the Old Town.

Michalská. No phone. Admission 4€ ($5.10). Tues–Fri 10am–5pm; Sat–Sun 11am–6pm.

SHOPPING

Bratislava, as a modern European capital, has everything you might want or need. In terms of souvenirs, there are a couple of unique shops worth visiting. **Antikvariát Steiner,** Ventúrska ul. 9 (✆ **02/5443-3778**), is an antiquarian bookshop with a wonderful selection of old maps and prints, as well beautiful books (most in Slovak and German). If you're looking for more traditional folk art, including textiles, lace, and ceramics, try **Úľuv,** with locations at Obchodná ul. 64 and nám. SNP 12 (✆ **02/5273-1344;** www.uluv.sk). **Interpress,** Sedlárska 2 (no phone), carries a nice range of English-language newspapers and magazines.

BRATISLAVA AFTER DARK

As the nation's capital, Bratislava is the center of Slovak culture. The **Slovak National Theater (Slovenské národné divadlo)** maintains an active program of high-quality drama, opera, and ballet in season (Sept–June). The theater operates from two buildings: the "historic" building at Hviezdoslavovo nám. 1 (✆ **02/5443-1723;** www.snd.sk) and the "new" building at Pribinova 17 (✆ **02/5778-2534;** www.snd.sk). The **Reduta,** Palackého 2 (✆ **02/5920-8233**), home to the Slovak National Philharmonic, is an excellent venue for classical concerts. You can buy tickets at the box office, or ask at the tourist information office. To find out what's on, pick up a copy of *Kam do mesta (Where in the City),* the city's free monthly, available at tourist information offices and bars and restaurants. The English-language weekly *The Slovak Spectator* is also a good source for what's happening.

As for culture of the drinking and clubbing variety, there's no shortage of late-night bars, cafes, and music clubs. Most of the action is concentrated in and around the Old Town, and typically starts around 10 or 11pm and lasts until 1 or 2am.

Au Café Something a little different: an elegant open-air cafe on the opposite side of the Danube from the Old Town. It's the perfect spot to relax with a drink on a warm evening in summer, and also serves very good food. Take a taxi, since it's not easy to find for first-time visitors. Tyršovo nábrezie. ✆ **02/6252-0355.** www.au-cafe.sk.

Charlie Centrum An all-in-one alternative movie house, pub, and dance club. If you get bad weather, check out the excellent movie program here. The films are usually shown in their original language. Špitálska 4. ✆ **02/5273-1493.** www.charlieclub.sk.

Trafo ★ A popular dance club, with a rotating program of techno, disco, and "oldies." It's the club of the moment in the Old Town. Ventúrska 1. ✆ **02/2092-2744.** www.trafo.sk.

4 WESTERN SLOVAKIA & THE MALÁ FATRA

TRENČÍN

100km (62 miles) N of Bratislava

Trenčín (www.trencin.sk) is a welcoming town that has three things going for it: a picture-perfect, brooding castle; a small grouping of welcoming hotels and pensions at each price point; and a positive attitude. As recently as a few years ago, the town was in steep decline, with its major textile industries facing stiff competition from cheap Asian imports. That's changed as the town has begun to embrace the future and play up some of its cultural attributes. Trenčín is now host to arguably the best open-air alternative and independent music festival in the country, the Pohoda Festival (www.pohodafestival.sk), each July.

The city's history dates back to Roman times, when it served as a northern garrison town to protect the Roman Empire from Germanic tribes. On rocks below the castle, a fascinating Roman inscription dating from the year A.D. 179 and ordered by Emperor Marcus Aurelius, celebrates a Roman victory over the hordes (you can see it from the first floor of the Hotel Tatra). In the Middle Ages, the town grew in importance because of it position on the Váh River, astride one of the main trading routes linking the Baltic and Mediterranean seas. Trenčín achieved arguably its greatest place in history in the early 14th century as the seat of a renegade kingdom declared by Matúš Čák. Čák, who made the castle his residence, proclaimed himself the king of the Váh and the Tatra Mountains. His kingdom ended with his death 20 years later in 1321.

Essentials

GETTING THERE From Bratislava, the drive takes about 90 minutes in light traffic. Trenčín is also easily reached by train or bus from Bratislava or Žilina. Regular bus service links the city to Brno in the Czech Republic and points west. Trenčín's bus and train stations are next to each other and situated about a 10-minute walk through a park from the center of town.

VISITOR INFORMATION Trenčín's **Tourist Information Office,** Sládkovičova (✆ **032/16186;** daily Apr 15–Oct 15 Mon–Fri 8am–6pm, Sat–Sun 8am–4pm; Oct 16–Apr 14 Mon–Fri 10am–5pm, Sat 10am–noon), is just off the main square. The helpful staff can provide a local map and information on the sights, as well as good advice on hotels and restaurants. While the office doesn't book rooms, they keep a list of accommodations and can make a few helpful phone calls.

Where to Stay & Dine

Outside of mid-July during the annual Pohoda music festival, you shouldn't have any problem booking a room. Eating is a different story. There's not much aside from the (very decent) restaurants at the Tatra and pod Hradom hotels and a bunch of pizzerias and coffee bars along the main square.

Da Giuseppe ★ PIZZA The ubiquitous pizzeria on the main square in this case is actually not a bad choice for a simple and cheap meal. The menu includes all of the pizza combinations you'd expect, but the mozzarella with tomatoes and fresh basil stands out because they use real mozzarella. The service is slow.

Štúrovo nám. 5. No phone. Entrees 3€–4€ ($3.80–$5.10). No credit cards. Daily 11am–9pm.

Hotel pod Hradom ★★ The kind of family-run hotel every Slovak town needs. Clean, moderately priced, and comfortable, with a friendly staff eager to show off all that the hotel offers. The location is excellent on a quiet lane that runs below the castle and parallel to the main square. Choose the Hotel Tatra (below) if you're looking for a full-service hotel, but this will do if you're just looking for a clean bed. The restaurant here is excellent.

Matúšova 12. ✆ **032/748-1701.** Fax 032/748-1703. www.podhradom.sk. 12 units. 80€ ($102) double. AE, DC, MC, V. **Amenities:** Restaurant; spa. *In room:* TV, minibar, hair dryer.

Hotel Tatra ★★ Nicely refurbished turn-of-the-20th-century hotel retaining many Art Nouveau details. The rooms are a delight, evoking that idyllic time of the First Republic, the 20 years between the two world wars that both Slovaks and Czechs look back to with such fondness. The location, on the tip of the main square just below the castle, is perfect. Still, the hotel is probably overpriced for what it offers. The reception has been known to cut rates on slow nights. The restaurant is easily the best in town.

M.R. Štefánika 2. ✆ **032/650-6111.** Fax 032/650-6213. www.hotel-tatra.sk. 70 units. 120€ ($152) double. AE, DC, MC, V. **Amenities:** Restaurant; spa; concierge; salon; limited room service; massage. *In room:* A/C, TV, dataport, minibar, hair dryer.

Penzión pod Hradom ★ An excellent low-budget pick. The rooms are spotlessly clean and modern. The beds have crisp white sheets and nice big windows. Some open onto the castle above, while others open onto a quiet inner courtyard. The location couldn't be better: a 5-minute walk from the main square or a 15-minute hike to the castle.

Matúšova 23. ✆ **032/744-5028.** Fax 0032/744-2507. www.podhradom.sk. 5 units. 60€ ($76) double. AE, DC, MC, V. *In room:* TV, hair dryer.

Reštaurácia Tatra ★★ SLOVAK The house restaurant of the Hotel Tatra is one of the few upscale dining options in town. Don't expect nouvelle cuisine, but rather hearty Slovak dishes built around chicken and pork, but done very well. The wine list is extensive; ask one of the knowledgeable waiters for a recommendation.

M.R. Štefánika 2. ✆ **032/650-6111.** Entrees 8€–12€ ($10–$15). AE, DC, MC, V. Daily 11:30am–2:30pm and 6–10pm.

Exploring

Trenčín has a handsome and compact historic core, comprised of two central squares: a modern one, Štúrovo námestie, and a more traditional square, Mierové námestie, joined by the town's last remaining old town gate, the Dolná brána. Simply choose an entryway onto the square and walk.

To reach the castle, look for steps going up just before you reach the Hotel Tatra toward the end of Mierové námestie, or climb the stairs running off Farská ulica. It's a 15-minute climb to the top, with some beautiful views over the Old Town and Váh river valley.

Trenčín Castle ★★ Worth the climb for the marvelous views and a close-up look at the rambling structures that make up the castle complex. The restored interiors are only accessible via guided tour (though English tours are a rarity behind Slovak and German).

Hrad. No phone. Admission with 30-min. tour 2.70€ ($3.40), with 70-min. tour 4€ ($5.10). May–Oct daily 8am–6pm; Nov–Apr daily 9am–3:30pm.

After Dark

Trenčín nightlife is laid back and usually follows one of two patterns: The first is a comfortable meal at the restaurant at the Hotel Tatra followed by a stroll around the central square or maybe a climb to the castle to work off some of those calories. The second option is to have a couple more drinks at dinner and then line up at one of the clubs that line the main squares. The action starts around 10pm and goes until around 2 or 3am. It is not sophisticated in the slightest, but it can be fun if you're in the mood to dance.

ŽILINA

80km (50 miles) N of Trenčín; 180km (112 miles) N of Bratislava

Žilina (www.zilina.sk) is a brawny industrial town that's better known as the home of some of Slovakia's more conservative politicians than anything worthwhile for tourists. On the other hand, it's an important bus and train junction, as well as a major stopping-off point on the main east-west highway, so many visitors find themselves here for one reason or another. And if you have your own transportation, Žilina makes for a comfortable base to explore the Malá Fatra National Park. The town of Terchová, the center of the Malá Fatra region, is just a 25km (16-mile) drive down the highway.

Essentials

GETTING THERE Žilina lies on the main east-west highway and is a relatively easy drive from both Trenčín and Bratislava. Figure on an hour's drive from Trenčín and 2 to 3 hours, depending on traffic, from Bratislava. Žilina is also a major train and bus depot. There are frequent train connections to both Trenčín (70 min.) and Bratislava (2–3 hr.). The train is also the best bet for reaching Poprad and the High Tatras. The train station is a 10-minute walk from the main central square along Národná Street. If you're planning on heading to the Malá Fatra, the bus is the best bet. There are frequent bus connections to Terchová; figure on a ride of about 45 minutes. The bus station is east of the city center, about a 10-minute walk from the train station and from the center of the city.

GETTING AROUND The inner city is relatively compact and most of it has been restricted to automobile traffic, so walking is the only option.

VISITOR INFORMATION Žilina's tourist information office, Burianova medzierka 4 (✆ **041/562-0789;** www.selinan.sk), is situated in a private travel agency called **Selinan** on a small street just off of Mariánske námestie. They'll do their best to help you sort out the train and bus schedules, as well as recommend lodging and dining options. The office is open Monday to Friday 8:30am to 5pm.

Where to Stay & Dine

Žilina has several decent hotels, and you're not likely to have a problem finding a room. Another option, recommended if you have a car, is to continue on in the direction of Terchová for more rustic lodging in the hills. Most of Žilina's restaurants are clustered around the Mariánske námestie. in the older part of town. Though they all have different names and slightly different menus, they all serve the same nondescript food.

Dubná Skala ★ Žilina's nicest hotel opened in 2006. It's a contemporary boutique, with bold contemporary furnishings, hardwood floors, high-end room amenities like flatscreen TVs, and a wellness spa. The location is just a block from the central square. The restaurant is one of the best in town.

Hurbanova 345/8. ✆ **041/507-9100.** Fax 041/507-9101. 37 units. 140€ ($178) double. AE, DC, MC, V. **Amenities:** Restaurant; spa; concierge; business center; 24-hr. room service; dry cleaning; nonsmoking rooms. *In room:* A/C, TV, dataport, minibar, hair dryer, safe.

Grand A nicely refurbished, charming, older hotel just off of the Mariánske námestie. A thorough modernization in 2004 added the unexpected touch of Jacuzzis and air-conditioning (rare for these parts) in some of the "Lux" rooms. Given the shortage of good places to eat, the restaurant is fine for a meal. The rooms themselves are bright and airy. The helpful reception staff can help you with basic directions if you arrive on the weekend, when the tourist information office is closed.

Sládkovičova 1. ✆ **041/564-3265.** Fax 041/564-3266. www.hotelgrand.sk. 45 units. 100€ ($127) double. AE, DC, MC, V. **Amenities:** Restaurant; limited room service. *In room:* A/C in some, TV, dataport, minibar, hair dryer, Jacuzzi in some.

Trattoria Pepe ★★ PIZZA This is the warmest, cleanest, and most inviting place to eat in the center of Žilina. Unlike the restaurants that line Mariánske námestie, this small, family-run Italian restaurant honestly cares about the food and the service. The pizzas are at least two notches above average, with the cheese and other ingredients mostly fresh. The pastas are good. Eat in the garden terrace in nice weather.

J. Vuruma 5. ✆ **041/564-3555.** Entrees 4€–6€ ($5.10–$7.60). No credit cards. Daily 11am–9pm.

Accommodations & Dining Outside of Žilina

Bránica ★★ (Finds) This relatively new, upscale hotel is a destination in its own right, with beautifully groomed clay tennis courts, wine-tasting rooms, a full fitness center, and sauna. It's the kind of place you book for the weekend to take some time off after a hectic work schedule. The hotel is situated just along the main road between Žilina and Terchová, about 20km (12 miles) east of Žilina. It's possible to reach the hotel by bus (tell the driver where you're going and he'll drop you off at the far eastern edge of the village called Belá).

Belá. ✆ **041/569-3035.** Fax 041/569-3039. www.hotelbranica.sk. 24 units. 90€ ($114) double. AE, DC, MC, V. **Amenities:** Restaurant; indoor pool; tennis courts; health club and spa; bike and ski rental; concierge; limited room service; massage; nonsmoking rooms. *In room:* A/C, TV, dataport, minibar, hair dryer, safe.

Chata pod Malým Rozsutcom ★ SLOVAK This very modest traditional restaurant and pension situated about 30km (19 miles) east of Žilina, just east of Terchová, is one of the most authentic mountain cabins you'll see. The owners have set aside six tiny rooms with a bathroom on the second floor of their log-cabin home. The rooms can be chilly at night and hot during the day, but at the same time the experience is enjoyable

Malá Fatra National Park

Though they lack the natural drama of the High Tatras to the east, the Malá Fatra highlands feel more rustic and relaxed. The pristine park is one of the most popular in Slovakia for weekend mountain walks, bike rides, and, in winter, cross-country and downhill skiing. If you have a few days to spend, and are not rushing to those *other* mountains (the High Tatras), plan on spending a couple of days here. The administrative center of the region is Terchová, a long narrow village about 25km (16 miles) east of Žilina. Here you'll find the main tourist information office, Ulica sv. Cyrila a Metoda 96 (© **041/599-3100;** www.ztt.sk), as well as dozens of pensions and private rooms. The tourist office sells hiking maps and can help book rooms.

The European Union has provided funding for an extensive network of bike trails aimed at cyclists of all abilities. Throughout the region, you'll find chaotic, downhill "adrenaline" rides as well as more level trails for simply puttering around and enjoying the views. Pick up the pamphlet *On the Bicycle Across the Jánošík Region,* available at the tourist information office in Terchová. You can rent bikes at the Pension Malá Fatra in Terchová, Družstevná 176 (© **041/569-5413;** www.durko.sk).

because of the hospitality you're extended. Even if you're not staying here, stop in for a meal (daily 10am–10pm). It's hearty Slovak cooking in the best sense of the word.

Demkovska 7, Zázrivá. © **0908/785-092.** www.chpmr.sk. 6 units. 20€ ($25) double. AE, DC, MC, V. **Amenities:** Restaurant.

5 THE HIGH TATRAS & EASTERN SLOVAKIA

THE HIGH TATRAS/VYSOKÉ TATRY

150km (93 miles) E of Žilina; 350km (217 miles) NE of Bratislava

The High Tatras (www.tatry.sk) are Slovakia's biggest tourist draw, and a visit to the country is not complete without seeing these majestic mountains. It's not the hills' height that's so impressive—the tallest are only in the 2,600m (8,528-ft.) range. Rather it's the way that they vault, so dramatically and out of nowhere, from the flat grasslands around the town of Poprad to their lofty snowcapped peaks.

The High Tatras are commonly called the "world's smallest Alpine range." That's a reference to the relatively short length of the mountain chain, just 30km (about 20 miles) end to end. The Tatras are actually part of the much larger Carpathian range that begins its rise just outside of Bratislava and then draws a wide arc through northern Slovakia, southern Poland, and into Romania.

The High Tatra resorts enjoyed a brief golden age in the late 19th and early 20th centuries, when the wealthy classes from Hungary, Austria, Germany, and later Czechoslovakia came to ski or to ride out the hot summers in the mountains. Many of the most beautiful buildings, including the two "Grand" hotels in Starý Smokovec and Tatranská

Lomnica, were built at that time. The two world wars and the decades of Communism afterward put an end to all of that. These days, the High Tatras remain a popular tourist destination for Slovaks, Poles, and, increasingly, Russians, though it's hard to escape that bittersweet feeling of nostalgia for those good old days.

The Tatras have two main tourist seasons, summer hiking and winter skiing. Summer season starts in mid-June, when the trails to the peaks are opened up to the public, and runs through October. The hikes here are some of the best in central Europe, and if you enjoy walking, then pick up some maps and gear and plan on staying at least a few days. In terms of planning, it's possible to base yourself at one the main resorts and do a series of day hikes, or you can hike the complete range, bedding down each night in a series of simple mountain chalets situated at comfortable hiking intervals. For information on booking accommodations in mountain huts, contact the Tourist Information offices (see below).

It's also possible to hike across the peaks into Poland (and you no longer need a passport to do this), but note that the trails in the higher elevations and across the peaks are closed in winter from November 1 until June 15.

Ski season, depending on the weather, starts in mid-December and runs to mid-March. The best skiing is situated near Štrbské Pleso, but all three major resorts have lifts and ski-rental facilities.

Most of the best trail heads, hotels, and restaurants are clustered around the three main resort towns, which ring the peaks at an elevation of around 1,000m (3,280 ft.). All are easily reachable by car or electric railroad from the regional capital of Poprad.

At the far western edge is the resort of **Štrbské Pleso.** The word *pleso* means tarn and refers to the resort's large mountain lake. Štrbské Pleso, traditionally, was the most youth oriented of the resorts, and accommodations and restaurants were limited mostly to student-dorm-type facilities. As of this writing, however, the Kempinski Hotel Group was planning to open a massive five-star hotel along the edge of the lake in early 2009. This will certainly take Štrbské Pleso upmarket.

The resort of **Smokovce,** divided into "Starý" (old) Smokovec and "Nový" (new) Smokovec, lies in the middle and is about 18km (11 miles) east of Štrbské Pleso. Starý Smokovec has the largest station on the Tatra electric railroad and is a main junction for reaching the other resorts. This is the liveliest resort and has the best hotel and restaurant facilities. It's also close to the Hrebienok funicular, and makes a great base for hiking in the peaks.

The third of the bigger resorts is **Tatranská Lomnica,** about 6km (3¾ miles) to the east of Starý Smokovec. Tatranská Lomnica is quieter and boasts two of the area's best hotels. It's also close to the cable car to reach the peak of Lomnický Štít (2,634m/8,640 ft.). One disadvantage is that you'll have to travel a bit to get to the best hiking trails.

One note about the environment: A powerful windstorm struck the High Tatras in 2004, knocking down tens of thousands of trees in a matter of minutes. The damage was greatest in the area between Štrbské Pleso and Starý Smokovec. The authorities have done a good job clearing trees where they could and all of the trails are open, but you'll still notice extensive damage, especially in the lower ranges. Sadly, it will take a generation to fully restore the mountains to their former glory, but the beauty of the peaks and upper elevations remains intact.

Getting There

BY PLANE The High Tatras has a small airport, **Poprad-Tatry** field (**© 052/776-3875;** www.airport-poprad.sk), which offers limited passenger air service depending on the season. The airport is located about 5km (3 miles) outside of town and is reachable by car or taxi (but not public transportation). Currently the Bratislava-based budget carrier **SkyEurope** (www.skyeurope.sk) offers twice-daily flights from London's Luton airport. The Czech airline **CSA** (www.csa.cz) also offers regular flights to the Tatras from Prague, but these flights go to Košice airport, with a minibus transfer to Poprad (2 hr.).

BY TRAIN Poprad is a major rail junction and ŽSR state railroad train service is relatively frequent to and from Bratislava, Žilina, and Košice. From Bratislava, the journey on an express train takes about 5 hours; from Žilina, 2 hours, and from Košice, 2 hours. From Poprad station, the Tatra Electric Railroad runs directly to Starý Smokovec and Štrbské Pleso, about 30 minutes to Starý Smokovec and 1 hour to Štrbské Pleso. To reach Tatranská Lomnica, change trains in Starý Smokovec.

BY CAR Poprad lies on Slovakia's major east-west highway. The drive from Bratislava follows the Váh River north to Trenčín and Žilina, before turning east. Some of the drive is along four-lane highway and takes about 4 hours. From Košice, the drive is along mostly two-lane highway and takes about 2 hours.

BY BUS Bus service is frequent from Poprad to many regional cities and towns, including Bratislava, Košice, and Levoča. You can also use the bus station at Starý Smokovec, just on the edge of the resort in the direction of Tatranská Lomnica. The bus is often the best option for seeing the smaller towns in and around the Tatras. The tourist information offices can help you sort out the timetables and destinations.

Getting Around

BY TRAIN The Tatra Electric Railroad is cheap and efficient, and serves all of the major resorts. Trains run about every 45 minutes from Poprad to Starý Smokovec and on to Štrbské Pleso and several points in between. Travel to Tatranská Lomnica requires a change at Starý Smokovec. Ticket prices vary depending on the length of the journey. The price from Poprad to Štrbské Pleso is about 1.50€ ($1.90). Buy the tickets at ticket windows at stations and validate them in the trains.

BY CAR Excellent roads connect Poprad to all of the Tatra resorts. The travel time between Starý Smokovec and Štrbské Pleso (20km/12 miles) is 15 minutes.

BY BIKE You can easily rent a bike and move from resort to resort along the main road. The ride from Starý Smokovec to Štrbské Pleso is challenging, since there's an elevation change of about 300m (984 ft.) between the towns. Coming back it's all downhill.

ON FOOT Once you're at one of the resorts, walking is the only option for getting around. Walking between the resort towns is not a viable option since the distances are too far.

Visitor Information

The main **Tourist Information offices,** identified as **TIK,** in Starý Smokovec (✆ **052/442-3440**) and Tatranská Lomnica (✆ **052/446-8119;** www.tatryinfo.eu), can provide basic information and hiking maps, as well as book accommodations. The staff is also helpful in sorting out basic transportation questions. The **Mountain Rescue Service (Horská Záchranná Služba),** based in Starý Smokovec (✆ **052/442–2820;** emergencies ✆ 052/18300; www.hzs.sk), is the first place to turn in the event of an accident. The **Mountain Guide Agency (Spolok Horských vodcov)** in Starý Smokovec (✆ **052/442–2066;** www.tatraguide.sk) can provide guides to the summits, or for adventures like snowshoeing and rock climbing. A guide for a climb to the highest peak, Gerlach, will cost around 150€ ($191) for one person and about 175€ ($222) for two.

Where to Stay

The High Tatras have plenty of hotel rooms, and outside of the peak Christmas and New Year's season you'll have little problem finding a place to stay. The Tourist Information offices can help book hotel rooms and private accommodations. In addition to the hotels and pensions, many families offer private rooms. All hotels boost their rates by at least a third over Christmas and New Year's. The rates quoted below apply generally to the high skiing and hiking seasons.

Very Expensive

Grandhotel Praha Tatranská Lomnica ★★ If you're one of those people who love that faded elegance of the early 1900s, with billiard rooms, crystal-chandeliered cafes, and cocktail bars, look no further. The Grandhotel Praha was conceived for a time when the wealthier classes summered in the mountains to escape the heat of the cities. Alas, those times are gone, but the hotel still lives on in its former glory. The Praha went through some hard times under Communism but is now trying to reach out to a new clientele of young professionals and their families. The rooms have gotten a makeover and the bathrooms have been completely modernized. Still, enough exquisite period detailing remains to give aficionados of that *fin de siècle* fantasy something to sink their teeth into.

Tatranská Lomnica 8. ✆ **052/446-7941.** Fax 052/446-7945. www.grandhotelpraha.sk. 98 units. 130€ ($165) double. AE, DC, MC, V. Electric railroad station: Tatranská Lomnica. **Amenities:** Restaurant; indoor pool; health club and spa; bike and ski rental; concierge; limited room service; massage; nonsmoking rooms. *In room:* TV, dataport, minibar, hair dryer, safe.

Grand Hotel Starý Smokovec ★★ Like the Grandhotel Praha, the Grand Hotel Starý Smokovec is a beautifully faded anachronism trying hard to win over new customers. The hotel's immense "Alpine-Secession" facade (how else to describe it?), so au courant in 1906 when the hotel was built, smiles over the resort like a rich, benevolent auntie, lending a sense of grace and civility to the entire town. The large and comfortable rooms have been completely modernized. Ask for a room with a balcony for a commanding view of the valley. But the real draws here are the public areas, including the picture-perfect period-piece cafe, restaurant, dance room, and cocktail bar. The location is a big advantage, just a few steps up from the electric railroad station in Starý Smokovec and near to the funicular that will take you up to Hrebienok and some of the best hikes.

Starý Smokovec. ✆ **052/478-8000.** Fax 052/442-2157. www.grandhotel.sk. 83 units. 150€ ($191) double. AE, DC, MC, V. Electric railroad station: Starý Smokovec. **Amenities:** Restaurant; indoor pool; spa; bike and ski rental; limited room service; massage; nonsmoking rooms. *In room:* TV, dataport, minibar, hair dryer, safe.

Expensive

Hotel Tulipán/Best Western ★★ The only hotel in the area so far to be managed by a major Western hotel chain, and the Best Western polish shows through in staff training and in the modern, no-nonsense-but-comfortable rooms. The property is on the small side, occupying what looks like a big house just outside the center of Tatranská Lomnica, about 15 minutes walk from the electric railroad station. The on-site wellness center is small but spick-and-span. Unusual for Slovakia, all the rooms come with their own computers with Internet access and the hotel is nonsmoking throughout.

Tatranská Lomnica 63. ✆ **052/478-0611.** Fax 052/478-0614. www.hoteltulipan.sk. 15 units. 90€ ($114) double. AE, DC, MC, V. Electric railroad station: Tatranská Lomnica. **Amenities:** Restaurant; health club and spa; bike and ski rental; concierge; limited room service; massage; nonsmoking rooms. *In room:* Some A/C, TV, dataport (in-room computers), minibar, coffeemaker, hair dryer, safe.

Penzión Vila Park ★ This inviting, smaller hotel in the center of Tatranská Lomnica is particularly suited to walkers and climbers. The owner is a mountain guide, who can help you plan your assault on the peaks or gentler walks along the "Magistrale" hiking trail. Even the facilities seem aimed at purists. You won't find rowdy bars and smoky billiard rooms; instead it's simple, no-nonsense furnishings for those who are here to commune with nature. That said, the prices are relatively high for what's offered.

Tatranská Lomnica 37. ✆ **052/478-2310.** Fax 052/478-2308. www.vilapark.eu. 12 units. 75€ ($95) double. AE, DC, MC, V. Electric railroad station: Tatranská Lomnica. **Amenities:** Restaurant; bike rental. *In room:* TV.

Moderate

Hotel Smokovec ★ A cheaper alternative to the Grand Hotel, offering the same excellent location near the Starý Smokovec electric railroad station at about half the price. What you sacrifice is ambience. The simple, dormitory-style rooms were built for sleeping and not for lingering. That said, the standards for cleanliness and efficiency are high, and facilities like an indoor pool and wellness center offer good value for money. Ask for a room facing the mountains.

Starý Smokovec. ✆ **052/442-5191.** Fax 052/442-5194. www.hotelsmokovec.sk. 30 units. 70€ ($89) double. AE, DC, MC, V. Electric railroad station: Starý Smokovec. **Amenities:** Restaurant; indoor pool; health club and spa; bike and ski rental; limited room service; massage. *In room:* TV, minibar.

Villa Dr. Szontagh ★★ A lovely steepled mountain manor offering what you might expect of old-school hospitality: squeaky clean public areas, tasteful turn-of-the-20th-century period furnishings (the first-floor apartments are especially inviting), and a solicitous proprietor who is only too happy to guide you around the resorts. Villa Dr. Szontagh was one of the first traditional inns to open up in the immediate aftermath of the fall of Communism, and remains one of the best.

Nový Smokovec 39. ✆ **052/442-2061.** Fax 052/442-2061. www.szontagh.eu. 15 units. 60€ ($76) double. AE, DC, MC, V. Electric railroad station: Nový Smokovec. **Amenities:** Restaurant; spa; limited room service; massage. *In room:* TV, minibar, hair dryer.

Inexpensive

Hotel Tatry Clean if sterile dormitory-style rooms that are perfectly acceptable if the priority is saving money or if your initial choices are fully booked. The property itself is a charming, ramshackle sort of Alpine-style chalet, with an in-house Slovak restaurant serving pretty good food. It's popular among students and young families with children because of the prices. A small bunny slope with a tiny ski lift is just down the street.

Tatranská Lomnica 53. ✆ **052/478-2862.** Fax 052/478-2863. www.hoteltatry.eu. 14 units. 50€ ($64) double. No credit cards. Electric railroad station: Tatranská Lomnica. **Amenities:** Restaurant; spa. *In room:* TV.

Toliar ★ Basic dormitory-style accommodations in an older hotel/shopping arcade complex across the road from the Štrbské Pleso train station. The hotel attracts mostly students and younger couples who don't have the cash to splash out on plusher rooms. The location is convenient, and the rooms are plain but clean. There are a small sauna and wellness spa on the premises.

Štrbské Pleso 21. ✆ **052/478-1011.** Fax 052/449-2193. www.hoteltoliar.sk. 91 units. 50€ ($64) double. AE, DC, MC, V. Electric railroad station: Štrbské Pleso. **Amenities:** Restaurant; health club and spa; ski rental; massage. *In room:* TV.

Where to Dine

The quality of the food in the Tatras has lagged behind the quality of the lodging. To be sure, the restaurants have definitely improved, and all three main resort towns now have a clutch of three or four decent, privately run eateries. But, sadly, there are still no breakthrough restaurants on the scene. Most of the new places build on the traditional folk *koliba* theme and have broadly similar menus that are heavy on the grilled meats, schnitzels, and stuffed chicken breasts. For something different, consider taking a meal at the Grand Hotel in Starý Smokovec or the Grandhotel Praha in Tatranská Lomnica (see both above). The quality of the food will likely be higher than at the independent restaurants listed below and nothing can match that faded, old-world opulence. The beautiful crystal chandeliers, the perfect seven-pieces-of-cutlery place settings, and that oh-so-proper waiter will have you staring at the chicken breast on your plate with a renewed sense of civility. In keeping with the overall informality of the Tatra resorts, dress is casual. You might want to dress up for the two "grand" hotel restaurants, but clean, casual attire is all that's required.

Expensive

Koliba Starý Smokovec SLOVAK A newer version of the traditional *koliba* theme that tries and largely fails to capture the pleasant kitsch of the Zbojnícka Koliba (see below). Maybe it's the toned-down interior or the fact the waiters are not decked out in full Slovak peasant regalia. Still, the food is similarly good, with grilled chicken and trout featuring prominently on the menu. This is also a good place to sample local game, including venison steak and goulash. And the central location of this *koliba* in Starý Smokovec is much better than the Zbojnícka Koliba if you don't happen to be staying in Tatranská Lomnica.

Starý Smokovec (just behind the Starý Smokovec railroad station). ✆ **052/442-2204.** Entrees 7€–10€ ($8.90–$13). AE, DC, MC, V. Daily 4pm–midnight.

Zbojnícka Koliba ★★ SLOVAK A fixture on the High Tatras dining scene for several years now and certainly the best meal in town during Communist times. It hasn't changed much since then, and it's still pretty good. You'll find all of the classic *koliba* trimmings here: a picture-perfect cottage setting, a crackling, wood-burning fire in the middle of the room (sending sweet wood smoke out the chimney), spits of roast chicken over the open fire, wines served by the jug, and on some weekends an irrepressible Gypsy band, keen to play a folk song or two for a gratuity. It's kitschy for sure, but fun too.

Tatranská Lomnica (just next to the Grandhotel Praha), ✆ **052/446-7630.** Entrees 7€–10€ ($8.90–$13). AE, DC, MC, V. Daily 4–10pm.

Moderate

Reštaurácia Svišť ★ SLOVAK This relaxed, family-run pub restaurant is a welcome addition to Nový Smokovec, just a short walk west of Starý Smokovec. The clean, blonde-wood interior and the open fire at the center of the room keep things cozy, especially if it's cold or snowy outside (likely at least half the year). The roast pork, a house specialty, is served with sauerkraut and bread dumplings, with the added kick of black peppercorns.

Nový Smokovec 30 (a short walk from either the Starý Smokovec or Nový Smokovec railroad stations). ✆ **052/442-2454.** Entrees 6€ ($7.60). No credit cards. Daily 11am–9pm.

Reštaurácia Tatrasport Zampa ★★ SLOVAK The best food in Starý Smokovec is served at this unassuming set of picnic tables at the far eastern end of the resort near the road that leads to Tatranská Lomnica (across the road from the bus station). From the outside, it looks like a place cyclists might go to grab a cold drink before hitting the trails. But don't let appearances deceive. The house specialty, pork tenderloin served in a red wine–and-bacon reduction, is a cut well above the average cutlet. The menu features the standard mix of pork and chicken entrees, plus a "fresh vegetables" section for vegetarians (which means at least 1 night you won't have to eat fried cheese), all at prices that are well worth it. Tatrasport Zampa is one of the few places around to serve breakfast, which is something to keep in mind if you're staying in private accommodations where breakfast is not part of the deal.

Starý Smokovec 62. ✆ **052/442-5241.** Breakfast 3€ ($3.80). Entrees 5€–8€ ($6.35–$10). No credit cards. Daily 8am–10pm.

Inexpensive

Furkotka ★ SLOVAK You wouldn't expect to find such a clean and welcoming spot so close to Štrbské Pleso's shabby electric railroad station, but the family owners of this traditional Slovak restaurant maintain high standards. There are no standouts on the menu, but staples like fried pork cutlet and grilled chicken range from good to very good. The decent food at modest prices attracts a range of in-the-know day-trippers and local shop clerks on their lunch breaks. The large nonsmoking room in the back is great for families with kids.

Štrbské Pleso (right outside the electrical railroad station, across from the Hotel Toliar). ✆ **052/449-2167.** Entrees 5€ ($6.35). No credit cards. Daily 11am–10pm.

Exploring the High Tatras

Aside from simply hiking, biking, or skiing the hills, there's not much else in the way of must-sees or -dos. Here are some suggestions.

Cable Car to Lomnický Štít ★★ Kids One of the most popular activities in the High Tatras is to take the cable car to the top of the second-highest peak in the range, Lomnický Štít (2,634m/8,640 ft.). The *lanovka,* as the cable car is known, is located in Tatranská Lomnica, just to the left as you arrive on the road from Starý Smokovec. In addition to going to the peak, the cable car stops at two intermediate points, Skalnaté Pleso and Start. Skalnaté Pleso is a good departure point for mountain hikes, and Start offers a whole range of downhill adrenaline activities aimed at older kids and young adults, including riding downhill scooters and four-wheeled "Stanley riders." There's a restaurant at Skalnaté Pleso and a cafe, and even a small hotel at the top of Lomnický Štít. Get an early start as the lines at the ticket window can get very long. There's an information office next to the ticket window to help you sort out the various ticketing and price options. Be sure to bring a jacket or sweater along to the top. It's chilly up there, even in midsummer.

Tatranská Lomnica. ✆ **0903/112-200.** www.tldtatry.sk. Admission 13€ ($17; Tatranská Lomnica–Skalnaté Pleso and return); 20€ ($25; Skalnaté Pleso–Lominický Štít and return); 9.20€ ($12; lift plus 2 scooter rides). July–Aug daily 8:30–6:30pm; Sept–June daily 8:30am–4:30pm.

Funicular to Hrebienok ★★ Kids The funicular railway that begins just behind the Grandhotel Starý Smokovec and runs to Hrebienok station at 1,284m (4,212 ft.) is great fun for the whole family. You can use it to get an easy start on one of the great mountain hikes that lead off from here, or simply go up, walk around a bit, and come down. There's a small restaurant at the top where you can get a meal or a hot drink. For kids, in summer there's downhill tubing, and in winter, sledding.

Starý Smokovec. ✆ **0903/112-200.** www.tldtatry.sk. Admission 6.50€ ($8.25; round-trip), 5.50€ ($7; up only); 1€ ($1.25; 1 downhill tube ride). July–Aug daily 7:30am–7pm; Sept–June daily 8:30am–4:30pm.

Museum of the Tatra National Park (TANAP) ★ Kids A small, easily managed museum that details the founding of the Tatra National Park, with some nice displays of

A Good Walk

Although the High Tatras attract many serious hikers, there are trails for walkers of all abilities, and some of the most beautiful walks require only an intermediate level of skill and exertion. One of the best of these follows the beautiful, red-marked "Magistrale" trail for part of its length from just above Hrebienok to the mountain lodge at Sliezsky Dom (www.sliezskydom.sk) and back down to the electric railroad station at Tatranská Polianka (for a total walking time of 5–6 hr.).

Start the hike in Starý Smokovec, from where you can follow the green- or blue-marked trails for about an hour uphill to Hrebienok, an elevation difference of about 300m (984 ft.). If you want to save energy, take the funicular from behind the Grand Hotel up to Hrebienok. From Hrebienok pick up the red-marked Magistrale trail and follow the signposts in the direction of Sliezsky Dom. (Be careful, the signs here are tricky; you should be walking with the mountains to your right and the valley to your left.) The walk begins in the forest, and as you move uphill, the large trees gradually thin out and the dwarf pines start. After another hour of gradual climbing, you break through the tree line along ridges just below some of the lower peaks. Here, the views, both up and down, are nothing short of spectacular. After another hour or so, you'll round a bend and see the boxy Sliezsky Dom lodge in the distance. Stop in at Sliezsky Dom for a light hot meal. From here, you can follow the road down to Tatranská Polianka, or if you have the time and energy, take the green-marked trail. The walk from Sliezsky Dom down to the electric railroad station will take another 2 hours.

No matter how long or short a hike you're planning, there are a few rules to follow: Remember to get an early start to avoid getting stranded in an afternoon rain- or snowstorm; always wear sturdy shoes to avoid ankle turns on the descent; and always pack extra water, sunscreen, sunglasses, a water-resistant jacket, and a good map.

the tremendous variety of the flora and fauna native to the High Tatras. The exhibits include some stuffed bears, Tatra "grizzlies," several of whom are said to be still frolicking around the higher elevations.

Tatranská Lomnica. Admission 1€ ($1.25). Mon–Fri 8am–noon and 1–5pm; Sat–Sun 8am–3pm.

Shopping

Folk handicrafts, like lace or folk costumes, make for interesting, one-of-a-kind souvenirs. You'll see stands selling these items at all of the major resorts. Look especially in the parking lots, where the stands are set up to cater to visiting tourist buses. One of the nicest places to buy handmade folk items, including genuine folk costumes, textiles, and ceramics, is **Úľuv,** Tatranská Lomnica 36 (✆ **052/446-7322**). **Sport Risy,** Starý Smokovec 70 (✆ **052/478-2911**), is a good place to stock up anything you might need for a hike. They carry a full range of high-quality walking and hiking boots, fleeces, caps, and outerwear, and can give good advice on what you're likely to need.

Kids Rafting on the Dunajec ★★★

Just to the east of the High Tatras, the peaks end abruptly and the rolling highlands of eastern Slovakia start. This is the border region with Poland, and communities on both sides share a common folk culture and heritage going back hundreds of years. A short segment of the border is formed by the Dunajec River, a surprisingly narrow waterway that zigzags through some breathtakingly rocky crags, with Poland on the left and Slovakia on the right.

Daily from April to October, several tour operators run guided group floats down the river, starting from just outside the small town of Červený Kláštor, about 60km (37 miles) from the High Tatras. These trips are great fun and make for a special day out, particularly for the kids. The floats follow the river about 12km (7½ miles) to the town of Lesnica in the Pieniny National Park. The guides are dressed up in traditional Gorál (highland) folk costumes and can be quite entertaining (most speak only Slovak, but some can also manage a smattering of German and English). The entire trip takes about 90 minutes and costs about 14€ ($18) per person.

In Lesnica, you can get a drink or light meal at a little cottage restaurant before boarding a bus back to the rafting operator. If you have the time and energy, rent a bike and ride along a little path beside the river back to your car. It's easy to organize a trip from the High Tatras; simply inquire at your hotel or the tourist information office and they can book you on a coach tour. If you want to travel independently, one of the better organizers is **Rafting Pieniny** in Červený Kláštor (✆ **0907/477-412;** www.rafting-pieniny.sk).

After Dark

The Tatras, with an emphasis on athletic, healthy living, is alas no place to party. The bar at the Grand Hotel in Starý Smokovec occasionally books live entertainment in the evenings, so check with the front desk to see what's on. Otherwise, enjoy a slow meal, take a stroll around the town, and then fall asleep with a good book (that's why you came here in the first place).

LEVOČA

40km (25 miles) E of Poprad; 360km (223 miles) NE of Bratislava

Levoča (www.levoca.sk) is one of the best-preserved medieval towns in the country, boasting a charmingly tumbled-down square of Renaissance and baroque burghers' houses and a church with a 15m-high (50-ft.) wooden altarpiece that must be seen to be believed. Most of the sights can be taken in during an afternoon, but a cluster of nice hotels and a few good restaurants make Levoča an excellent place to plan an overnight stop. For centuries, Levoča was the leading town of a confederation of 24 towns and villages, known collectively as the Spiš, filling a large swath of central and eastern Slovakia. The Spiš towns came of age in the 14th and 15th centuries, following a series of devastating raids from the east that left the area devoid of population. To resettle the region, the Hungarian kings then in power invited German-speaking Saxons to form towns, and bestowed special trading rights on the towns to sweeten the deal. The Spiš soon became wealthy, and Levoča, which enjoyed the greatest number of these special trading privileges, emerged as the wealthiest of the lot.

Levoča reached its high point in the 16th and 17th centuries, and many of the most impressive buildings date from this time. The highlight of your visit will certainly be the town's beautiful cathedral, St. Jacob's, in the middle of the main square, and its exquisitely carved wooden altarpiece, the work of the local master Pavol of Levoča in the early 16th century.

Given the town's wealthy past, the state of modern Levoča comes as kind of a shock. In and around the beautifully crumbling facades of what were once the homes of the wealthiest merchants in the land, you'll see Roma children running around, mugging for the camera, and occasionally begging for a coin or two. Times are tough in the Spiš region these days, and brain drain has hit these towns especially hard.

The first weekend in July sleepy Levoča is turned upside down when tens of thousands of worshippers descend for the annual Marian pilgrimage. Most of the action takes places at the Marian church, the white building on a hill about a mile outside of town and easily visible from side streets running off the main square. If your visit happens to coincide with the pilgrimage, it probably goes without saying, don't even dream of finding a room.

Getting There

BY BUS The bus is the only way to get to Levoča using public transportation. The bus station is a short walk from the main square. The regional bus hub is in Spišska Nová Ves, about 10km (6¼ miles) away. Frequent buses ply the route daily from there to Levoča.

BY CAR Levoča is on the main road connecting Poprad to points east. The drive from Poprad takes under an hour. Košice is about an hour away to the east.

Visitor Information

The main tourist information office, **SUZ,** is situated on the main square, at Námestie Majstra Pavla 58 (✆ **053/451-3763;** www.levoca.sk). The office is a good first stop for brochures on the sites and can advise on hotel and restaurant options.

Where to Stay

Levoča is blessed with a few decent hotels, including arguably one of the best mom-and-pop hotels in the country. It's best to try to book in advance during the summer, and well in advance if you plan to be here in early July when the pilgrims hit town. In winter, you'll likely have the town to yourself.

Barbakan ★ The Barbakan is less overall appealing than the Satel (below), but welcoming and comfortable for an overnight stay. The hotel occupies three floors of a burgher's house, a block off the main square. The rooms, particularly the doubles at the back of the hotel, are well appointed, with hardwood floors, throw rugs, and roomy bathrooms with big new bathtubs. Whether you choose a double or a single, ask for a room away from the main road. The house restaurant is decent in a pinch, but the food is frankly better at the Satel and a couple of other restaurants around town.

Košická 15. ✆ **053/451-4310.** Fax 053/451-3609. www.barbakan.sk. 12 units. 43€ ($55) double. AE, DC, MC, V. **Amenities:** Restaurant; limited room service. *In room:* TV, dataport, minibar, hair dryer.

Penzión pri Košickej bráne A no-frills bed-and-bath pension, right next to the Barbakan and about 15m (50 ft.) or so from the main square. The building, which dates from the 16th century, is lovely, but the room furnishings are the standard-issue particleboard beds and desks. The four-bed apartment is spacious and represents real value if you're traveling in a larger group.

Košická 16. ✆ **053/469-9713.** Fax 052/452-2550. www.penzionkosicka.sk. 9 units. 30€ ($38) double. AE, DC, MC, V. **Amenities:** Restaurant.

Satel ★★ Finds This is Levoča's nicest hotel and one of the best small hotels of any Slovak town. The rooms are spotless, with inviting, modern furnishings and beautiful hardwood floors. Some of the rooms have the original Renaissance-era vaulting. Don't miss the gorgeous Renaissance-arcaded restaurant/cafe in the back. An on-site sauna and small wellness center add to the, frankly, unexpected charms of this family run inn. The location, right on the main square, is ideal, and the position away from the main highway means less noise at night.

Námestie Majstra Pavla 55. ✆ **053/451-2943.** Fax 053/451-4486. www.hotelsatel.com. 23 units. 80€ ($107) double. AE, DC, MC, V. **Amenities:** Restaurant; health club and spa; limited room service; massage; nonsmoking rooms. *In room:* TV, minibar, hair dryer, safe.

Where to Dine

The range of eating choices is smaller and less agreeable than the hotels, but fine for the length of time you're likely to be here.

Mama Mia Pizzeria ★ PIZZA This is better than most of the small-town Slovak pizzerias you're likely to run across. No surprises on the menu—you'll find the same combinations of cheese, ham, corn, sausage, bacon, and whatever else they can put on a pizza, but the crust is thinner and crispier than the norm. The main dining area is nonsmoking, and the two tables on the terrace command an inspiring view of the Marian church in the distance.

Veprova 4. ✆ **053/451-2020.** Entrees 3€–5€ ($3.80–$6.35). No credit cards. Daily 11am–10pm.

Slovenská Reštaurácia ★ SLOVAK The nicest spot in town for that traditional Slovak meal, either on the outdoor terrace in nice weather or in the warm, peasant-style dining rooms, complete with wagon wheels on the walls. The front room is nonsmoking. As you might expect, the emphasis here is on simple Slovak meals done well. The house specialty, a potato pancake stuffed with a spicy mix of pork and beef, is recommended.

Námestie Majstra Pavla 62. ✆ **0904/225-766.** Entrees 4€–8€ ($5.10–$10). No credit cards. Daily 11am–10pm.

Exploring Levoča

Levoča is essentially a one-horse town, and all of the main sights are perched along the town's oblong square, Námestie Majstra Pavla. The four freestanding buildings at the center form the most important complex of structures in town. Here you'll find the Roman Catholic Church, St. Jacob's (Chrám Sv. Jakuba), as well as the former town hall, the current town hall, and the main Protestant church. Start your exploration from St. Jacob's, with its fabulous wood-carved altar (the only absolute must-see) and move on from there. The Old Town Hall (Levočská Radnica) behind the church is recognizable from its handsome Renaissance arches dating from the 17th century. The original town hall, built in the 15th century, burned in a fire in 1550. In front of the Old Town Hall you'll see a large birdcagelike contraption. This is the so-called "cage of shame," once allegedly used to hold adulterous women. Across the street from the Old Town Hall is the Spiš Regional Museum. Take a stroll on both sides of the square to admire the old baroque and Renaissance housing stock in all states of repair and disrepair.

Spišský Hrad ★★★

Put this in the "Most Spectacular Castle You Are Ever Likely to See Built by a Civilization You've Never Heard Of" category. When the Spiš confederation of towns first got rolling in the 13th and 14th centuries, the towns lived in constant fear of devastating raids from the east. To ensure that would never happen again, the Spiš built this enormous castle, **Spišský Hrad** (✆ **053/454-1336;** www.spisskyhrad.sk), on the highest hilltop around. Nothing you've seen or read in the tourist brochures will prepare you for the shock of seeing this ghostly white ruin from a distance for the first time.

If you're driving from Levoča toward Košice, you'll catch a first glimpse around the village of Klčov, about 8km (5 miles) away. From that point, you won't be able to take your eyes off of it as the road winds you closer and closer. The view traveling in the opposite direction is even better. At night, it's given a garish blue-white lighting and seems visible from about half of eastern Slovakia.

The castle served the Spiš towns well until the mid–18th century, when it burned in a tragic fire. By that time, the threat of invasion from the east had passed and the castle was never rebuilt. Today the castle is a designated UNESCO World Heritage Site. You can climb up to the castle and walk the ruins by following a small road just beyond the village of Spišské Podhradie (traveling from Levoča toward Košice). Alternatively, you can take a bus or train to Spišské Podhradie and hike the 3.2km (2 miles) or so to the castle.

St. Jacob's Church (Chrám Sv. Jacuba) ★★★ The richness of the interior of this church is a testament to the town's former wealth and importance. Parts of the church date as far back as the 14th century. The high point is certainly the wooden altarpiece, carved over a period of 10 years by Master Pavol of Levoča in the 16th century. At more than 18m (59 ft.) in height, it's commonly described the world's largest of its kind. Look toward the bottom of the altar to see Master Pavol's carving of *The Last Supper.* You are not permitted to get too close to the altar, so buy a photograph of it (in the church) for a closer look. The faces of the disciples were apparently modeled on merchants living in Levoča at the time. Master Pavol's depiction is certainly humorous. St. John is shown sleeping in Christ's arms! Entry to the church is by guided tour only.

Námestie Majstra Pavla. ✆ **053/451-2347.** Admission 2€ ($2.55). June–Oct daily, tours on the half-hour 9am–4pm. Nov–May tours daily once an hour 8:30–11:30am and 1–4pm. Purchase tickets at the cash desk across from the church entrance.

After Dark

Aside from an after-dinner walk along the square and the side streets, there's not much to do in Levoča in the evening. The town shuts down almost completely by 10pm, and locals looking for action head for the relatively "big city" diversions in Spišská Nová Ves, about 10km (6¼ miles) away. Levoča maintains an active festival scene in the summer months. Ask at the tourist office if anything special is going on in and around town during your visit.

KOŠICE

100km (62 miles) E of Poprad; 400km (248 miles) E of Bratislava

Košice (www.kosice.sk), Slovakia's second-biggest city after Bratislava, has transformed itself from a smoggy, provincial backwater into one of the country's most attractive urban destinations within the short span of a decade. Much of the credit goes to the former Slovak president, and former Košice mayor, Rudolf Schuster, who vigorously promoted development of the city, including the extensive renovation of the main drag, Hlavná ulica. Hlavná is a stunner from end to end, a 30-minute corso that takes you past the country's biggest Gothic cathedral, its turn-of-the-20th-century State Theater, a lovely little park with a singing fountain, and, in warm weather, a never-ending row of outdoor terraces, packed with stylish coffee drinkers.

Košice has been an important market town on major east-west and north-south trade routes for centuries, and during the 16th and 17th centuries served as a bastion for the Hungarian nobility in their struggle against the Ottoman Turks occupying the Hungarian mainland. Just 20km (12 miles) from the frontier with modern Hungary, the city, in more recent years, has shuttled back and forth between Hungarian, Czechoslovak, and now Slovak sovereignty. The city still has a sizable Hungarian minority, and if you listen carefully you will hear Hungarian spoken on the streets.

Getting There

BY TRAIN Košice is a major rail junction and the ŽSR state railroad train service is relatively frequent to and from Bratislava and other large cities. From Bratislava, the journey on an express train takes about 7 hours. The train station is next to the bus station and is about a 10- to 15-minute walk from the center of the city.

BY CAR Košice lies at the eastern end of Slovakia's major east-west highway. The northern route from Bratislava follows the Váh river north to Trenčín and Žilina before turning east. Some of the drive is along four-lane highway and takes about 6 hours. From Poprad, the drive is along mostly two-lane highway and takes about 2 hours.

BY BUS Slovakia's national bus carrier maintains regular service from Košice to many regional cities and towns. The bus is often the best option, for seeing the smaller towns to the east. The tourist information offices can help you sort out the timetables and destinations. The bus station is about a 10-minute walk from the center of the city.

BY PLANE Košice Airport (✆ **055/683–2253;** www.airportkosice.sk) lies about 5km (3 miles) outside of town The budget carrier SkyEurope (www.skyeurope.sk) maintains regular flights to and from Bratislava and London's Luton airport. Regular air service is also available to and from Vienna and Prague.

Getting Around

ON FOOT Much of Košice's center, where most of the hotels, restaurants, and attractions are concentrated, is either closed to cars or allows only limited car traffic, so walking is the only option.

BY CAR It's best to leave the car in one of the city parking lots or at the hotel. Navigating the small streets of the inner city can be challenging and finding a parking spot on the side streets difficult.

BY BIKE Hlavná ulica has bike lanes running up and down its length, but it may be hard to find bike rentals. Inquire at the information center (below) or your hotel.

Visitor Information

The **Information Center for the City of Košice** is the main entry point for visitors. The office is conveniently located on Hlavná ulica 59 (✆ **055/625-8888;** www.kosice.sk). The helpful, multilingual staff can provide maps and guidance, as well as suggest hotels and pensions.

Where to Stay

If money is no object, you're in luck. Košice is blessed with two of the country's nicest expensive hotels—and choosing between the two is not easy. If you're watching your euros, there are plenty of other good choices around. The city information office can offer suggestions.

Very Expensive

Hotel Bristol ★★★ **Finds** Just what Košice needed: a hip designer hotel just a 5-minute walk from the city's main square and 2 blocks away from the best nightlife. You'll see the difference first in the sleek, clean modern lines of the lobby, with its hardwood floors and smart wicker chairs. The mix of style, comfort, and technology extends to the rooms, which are equipped with separate climate-control settings and dataports. Breakfast is the usual selection of meats, cold cuts, yogurts, and cereals, but the difference is that it's all fresh and the juice freshly squeezed.

Orlia 3. ✆ **055/729-0077.** Fax 055/729-0079. www.hotelbristol.sk. 20 units. 140€ ($178) double. AE, DC, MC, V. **Amenities:** Restaurant; indoor pool; health club and spa; limited room service; nonsmoking rooms. *In room:* A/C, TV, dataport; minibar, hair dryer, safe.

Zlatý Dukát ★★ **Finds** Fabulous reconstruction of a 13th-century town house, right on the main pedestrian thoroughfare Hlavná. Each of the rooms is done in a different contemporary look, but the designer had a keen eye for colors and textures, giving the hotel a feeling of style and energy. The public areas are used to show off the owner's collection of historic glassware, including some beautiful contemporary pieces and historical glass from the 1920s and '30s. The in-house restaurant gets high marks, and if it's any consolation, garage parking is included in the room rate.

Hlavná 16. ✆ **055/727-9333.** Fax 055/727-9344. www.hotelzlatydukat.sk. 34 units. 130€ ($165) double. AE, DC, MC, V. **Amenities:** Restaurant; limited room service; nonsmoking rooms. *In room:* A/C, TV, dataport; minibar, hair dryer, safe.

Expensive

Dalia ★★ This small, well-run hotel not far from the main square is a nice pick if the Zlatý Dukát and Bristol are booked. The rooms are spotless and quiet. The reception is friendly and the breakfast is good. There's a small Jacuzzi as an added bonus. The in-house restaurant has won local awards for quality.

Hlavná 101. ✆ **055/799-4321.** Fax 055/633-1717. www.hoteldalia.sk. 11 units. 110€ ($140) double. AE, DC, MC, V. **Amenities:** Restaurant; spa. *In room:* A/C (in some rooms), TV, dataport, minibar, hair dryer.

Moderate

Penzión Krmanova One of the best of a new breed of privately owned, in-town pensions. Despite the location, near a normally loud arterial roadway, the rooms are generally quiet because the house has thick walls. If noise is a concern, ask for a room overlooking the garden in the back. The modern, pastel furnishings won't win any design competitions, but the rooms are large and clean, and the beds and chairs still feel and smell new. The bathrooms have been completely renovated and some in the larger apartments have tubs. Aside from the rooms, the services are modest. Breakfast is not included in the price.

 Krmanova 14. ✆ **055/623-0565.** Fax 055/622-6483. www.krmanova.sk. 13 units. 90€ ($114) double. AE, DC, MC, V. **Amenities:** Nonsmoking rooms. *In room:* A/C (in some rooms), TV, fridge.

Inexpensive

Penzión Slovakia ★ Six cozy little rooms next to the Rosto steakhouse and across from the Bristol. The location, just up from Kováčska ulica., where the best clubs and cafes are located, is a major draw. You can't beat it for the price. The rooms, named after Slovak cities, are clean and roomy, with TVs, big beds, and armchairs. The bathrooms are on the tiny side, with showers. One drawback may be that the rooms, just below the roof, tend to get hot in midsummer. Ask for a room away from the street.

Orlia 6. ✆ **055/728-9820.** www.penzionslovakia.sk. 6 units. 50€ ($64) double. AE, DC, MC, V. **Amenities:** Restaurant. *In room:* TV, dataport.

Where to Dine

The restaurant scene in Košice is improving rapidly. As in Bratislava, the number of eateries is growing and the range of cooking is slowing starting to expand beyond the beef, pork, and chicken trilogy. Most of the best places to eat, and to go out for that matter, are not along the main Hlavná street, but just to the east of the main square, along Kováčska.

Very Expensive

Rosto STEAKHOUSE Local version of an American-style steakhouse, but less formal, featuring excellent aged beef imported from South America. This place gets crowded, especially at lunch. The grilling extends to chicken, pork, lamb, and whatever else can be cooked over an open flame. They also have a full range of Middle Eastern–style shawarma sandwiches, essentially shaved lamb, chicken, or pork served in a pita pocket.

Orlia 6. ✆ **055/728-9818.** Entrees 6€–14€ ($7.60–$18). AE, DC, MC, V. Daily 11am–10pm.

Expensive

Camelot ★★ SLOVAK The handsome decor mixes the best of the dark woods and high-backed chairs of traditional Slovak restaurants with a modern emphasis on clean lines and cleanliness. The Camelot theme extends to the menu, and the main courses are named for the Knights of the Round Table. Some combine the traditional Slovak emphasis on grilled meats with international, especially Asian, spices and sauces.

Kováčska 19. ✆ **055/685-4039.** Entrees 8€–10€ ($10–$13). AE, DC, MC, V. Daily 11am–midnight.

Le Colonial ★★★ CONTINENTAL This popular place, just off the southern end of Hlavná, never fails to impress. Maybe it's the inviting 19th-century "colonial-era" decor, the impeccable service, or the creative turns on traditional Slovak cooking that make it so special. Try the *escalope panee,* a chicken breast that's stuffed with sharp-sour sheep's cheese and lightly breaded and fried, served with little bunches of green beans wrapped in bacon. And that's just the start. Like lots of restaurants in Košice, to find it, you'll have to first walk through a rather uninviting little doorway off the main street. Your anxieties will be relieved once you walk into the warm and inviting interior. Good choice for a business meal or a romantic dinner for two.

Hlavná 8. ✆ **055/729-6126.** Entrees 8€–10€ ($10–$13). AE, DC, MC, V. Daily 11am–11pm.

Moderate

Villa Regia ★ SLOVAK A local favorite and reputed to be the best place in town for *bryndzové halušky* and other typical Slovak dishes. If you've come from the High Tatras or from one of the outlying areas, you'll recognize the dark woods and heavy tables and chairs as the hallmark of a traditional Slovak restaurant. At their best, and this is one of the best, these spaces run to the cozy and intimate, with the emphasis on food, drink, and close conversation. While the *halušky* come highly recommended, the full range of pork, beef, and chicken specialties is done well.

Dominikánske nám. 3. ✆ **055/625-6510.** Entrees 5€–10€ ($6.35–$13). AE, DC, MC, V. Tues–Sun 11am–10pm.

Exploring Košice

Almost all of the major tourist attractions are along or just off of the main square, Hlavná ulica. A sensible plan is simply to start at one end of the square and slowly walk to the other, admiring the baroque, Renaissance, and neoclassical facades that line the long street on both sides. The southern end of the square possesses the most important clutch of buildings, centered on the **Cathedral of St. Elizabeth (Dóm svátej Alžbety),** the biggest cathedral in Slovakia and the easternmost Gothic church of its kind in Europe. Next to the cathedral on the north side is the Renaissance-style **Urban's Tower (Urbanová veža).** On the other side is the **Chapel of St. Michael (Kaplnka svátého Michala),** with its valuable relief work on the portals. The chapel is older than the cathedral and dates from around the middle of the 13th century. Just here as well you'll see the entryway to a relatively recent archaeological find called the **Lower Gate (Dolná Braná).** It's certainly worth poking in to take a look at the fascinating medieval fortification systems that were built here some 700 to 800 years ago.

To the north of the cathedral, walking along Hlavná, you'll see a small park, complete with the locals' pride and joy: a "singing fountain." Just beyond the fountain is another local treasure connected to music, the handsome **State Theater (Štátné Divadlo).** The theater dates from the late 1800s and was built in the neoclassical, historical style that was so popular in Austro-Hungarian provincial capitals at the time. Farther along the square you'll see little gems here and there, hidden behind the day-to-day life of a bustling city. Be sure to take a look at the Art Nouveau facade at Hlavná 63, home to the Café Slavia and hotel of the same name.

Cathedral of St. Elizabeth (Dóm svátej Alžbety) ★★ The country's largest cathedral is a master work, both inside and outside. Admire the relief on the north side of the cathedral, and the immense carved wooden altarpiece, one of the biggest of its kind (but still short of the altar in Levoča). The nicest aspect of this cathedral is that it still plays a vital role in the lives of people living here.

Hlavná ulica. ✆ **055/622-1655.** Admission to the church free; 1€ ($1.30) to climb the tower. Daily 9am–6pm.

East Slovakia Museum (Vychodoslovenské múzeum) ★ Primarily of interest for the massive collection of gold coins, around 3,000 or so, that were originally minted in Kremnica from the 15th to the 17th century. The coins were hidden during raids on the city in the 17th century and were only discovered in 1935.

Hviezdoslavova 3. ✆ **055/622-0309.** www.vsmuzeum.sk. Admission 1.30€ ($1.65). Tues–Sat 9am–5pm; Sun 9am–1pm.

Lower Gate (Dolná Braná) ★ Košice residents remember with horror the mid-1990s, when pretty much the entire Hlavná ulica was torn apart during the city's general large-scale renovation. One of the more unusual finds at that time was this intricate system of medieval fortifications, town walls, bastions, and even sewage systems, now buried underground, going all the way back to the late Middle Ages.

Hlavná ul ✆ **055/622-8393.** Tues–Sun 10am–6pm.

The Warhol Family Museum of Modern Art ★

Although American artist Andy Warhol rarely admitted it, even saying once in an interview that he "came from nowhere," his family hailed from eastern Slovakia, emigrating in the early 20th century to Pittsburgh, Pennsylvania, where Warhol was born in 1928.

That in itself would not be remarkable were it not for a highly unusual museum in the town of Medzilaborce, in the far eastern region of Slovakia, that Warhol's family has established in the artist's memory. The **Warhol Family Museum of Modern Art** (✆ **057/748-0072;** www.region.sk/warhol) holds around two dozen of Warhol's original prints, including two of the famous Campbell's soup collection and a well-known portrait of former Soviet leader V.I. Lenin.

The museum alone is probably not worth a trip to this remote village on the Polish border, about 2 hours drive from Košice. Nevertheless, if your travels take you in this direction, perhaps on the way to southeastern Poland, a stop here is highly recommended—if only to see the stark contrast of Warhol's splashy prints and the relatively simple surroundings of his ancestral home.

Shopping

If you've been looking for a special wine store that carries the best Slovak wines, try **Cabinet,** Pri Miklušovej väznici 2 (✆ **055/622-5566;** www.vinotekacabinet.sk). The knowledgeable wine merchants there can guide you through the plonk to some very nice bottles.

After Dark

Košice, as the capital of the Eastern Slovak region, is a cultural center, and maintains an excellent program of music, theater, and the performing arts. Spring and fall tend to be the liveliest times of the year and an annual musical festival is held in May. For culture of the cocktails, clubbing, and carousing variety, the center of the action is Kováčska ulica, which runs parallel to the main square.

Cosmopolitan ★ Maybe a notch or two above the competition if you're looking for something a little quieter and more sophisticated. The cocktails here are probably the best in town, and you might even catch a special event, like a champagne tasting or something similar. Kováčska 9. ✆ **055/625-8419.**

Jazz Club Still going strong after several years as Košice's leading music club. Don't expect much jazz here, despite the name. Disco, techno, and pop are the genres of choice. Also includes an affiliated cocktail bar and decent pizza restaurant. This place can get very crowded on a weekend evening. Kováčska 39. ✆ **055/622-4237.** www.jazzclub-ke.sk.

Štátné Divadlo Košice ★★ The center of cultural life for Eastern Slovakia, with an active theater, ballet, and opera repertoire 9 months out of the year (the theater largely shuts down during summer). Tickets are available at the box office. Even if you don't see a performance, stop by to admire the handsome turn-of-the-20th-century building, one of the finest concert halls in central Europe. Hlavná 58. ✆ **055/622-1231.** www.sdke.sk.

Slovenia

by Keith Bain

It's been referred to as a pocket-size country, but Slovenia is perhaps more justly thought of as Europe's first "boutique destination." Crammed with jaw-dropping scenery and packing in more history than its marginal 20,273 sq. km (7,906 sq. miles) should allow, this tiny central European nation is studiously being developed as one of the finest tourism destinations on earth. You may have trouble pointing it out on a map, but with just over two million inhabitants, smart little Slovenia is already setting the tone for fashionable travel; in 2007, visitor numbers exceeded the country's population.

Only recently discovered by a select group of globe-trotters who've tuned into tales of its idyllic beauty, Slovenia is considerably more tranquil and sophisticated than any other destination cast under the "Eastern European" banner, with almost none of the hang-ups associated with its former Communist connections; 18 years after gently wresting itself from Yugoslavia, there's a fresh exuberance of spirit here suggesting a nation not only still enjoying its independence honeymoon, but simultaneously relishing a distinct cosmopolitanism that results from the myriad influences of its contact with diverse cultures.

Its good looks have drawn comparisons with Switzerland, a country that is twice its size, and while there are similarities, Slovenia's relative anonymity and lack of pretense mean that you can still enjoy yourself here for fewer euros. In fact, considering how much beauty is packed into such a compact space, it's got to be said that Slovenia offers tremendous value. Imbued with fantastic, scraggy mountains, turquoise rivers and silver lakes, vast subterranean caves, and just enough medieval castles to conjure up a fairy tale or two, Slovenia is one of those destinations you wish you could make your regular weekend getaway.

1 GETTING TO KNOW SLOVENIA

THE LAY OF THE LAND

Easy to miss on even the largest of maps, Slovenia is tucked into the armpit formed by Italy to the west, Austria to the north, Hungary to the east, and Croatia to the south. It's pretty much in the center of Europe, about the same distance from London as it is from Istanbul, and more or less midway between Moscow and Lisbon.

THE REGIONS IN BRIEF

Ljubljana is more or less in the center of the country. To the north, the **Julian Alps** on the Italian border form one natural perimeter of the **Triglav National Park,** synonymous with the triple-peak Triglav Mountains seen on the national flag. Triglav's proud peaks add to the splendor of the country's most cherished lakes, **Bled** and **Bohinj,** both defining features on the country's tourist trail. Tucked between Triglav and the Italian border is the fantastic **Soča River Valley,** a tour de force for travelers looking for river and mountain thrills. And stretched along the northern Austrian border is the Karavanke Mountain range, providing rewarding views as you drive anywhere north of the capital.

Slovenia's southwest is defined by its unique limestone formations that make up the unique region known as the **Karst,** a term that has been exported around the world to describe similar "Karstic" phenomena. Squeezed between Italy's Trieste and the border with Croatia is Slovenia's tiny slither of **Istrian coastline,** with fishing ports of distinctly Venetian influence. Finally, more mountains, wine lands, and remnants of a Roman and medieval past are found in the less traveled east.

SUGGESTED ITINERARY: SLOVENIA IN 8 DAYS

While you could rush around Slovenia and cover it quite extensively in just a few days, I recommend you take things easy and soak up this tiny country's myriad pleasures. Relax in and around its many pleasure spots and enjoy the possibility of adventures both hard and soft. Bear in mind that there are tolls on all highways; these are clearly marked and you can pay with a credit card.

Day ❶: Arrive & Head East

Pick up a prebooked rental from Ljubljana's international airport, and head east, to the salubrious town of Maribor, where you can stroll through gorgeous squares, lunch at excellent restaurants, explore a vast underground cellar, and enjoy a sundowner at the legendary waterfront area known as Lent. In summer, you may catch some of the excellent entertainment that forms part of the Lent Festival.

Day ❷: Ptuj, Then the Jeruzalem Wine Road or Otoček Castle

From Maribor, it's a short drive through gorgeous countryside to the ancient Roman city of Ptuj (pronounced pit-*ooey*), which you can explore in a few hours. Then head out to sample the fruits of the vine along the Jeruzalem Wine Road. Presuming you enjoy a liquid lunch, overnight at one of the wine farms, where you can also enjoy a traditional farm dinner. Alternatively, skip Jeruzalem and head south to the newly refurbished Otoček Castle where you can live out a royal fantasy, dining in its beautiful courtyard, sampling the famous local wine, Cviček, and then bedding down in the castle's luxurious quarters.

Day ❸: The Lakes

Strike out early back toward Ljubljana, but head instead to Bled, some 31 miles (50km) north; you should arrive well before lunch. Book a suite at Vila Bled; you can use the spa at sister hotel Grand Toplice, sunbathe on the private lido, or take one of the private boats and row yourself to Bled Island, where you can explore the lovely church. Take a relaxed stroll around the lake and drive or walk to the thousand-year-old castle perched above the water, before setting off to explore Lake Bohinj.

Days ❹–❺: Soča River Valley

If you're feeling adventurous, start your day by swimming out to the island and back. After breakfast set off north to the adventure resort of Kranjska Gora, which marks the starting point for the route over the Vršič Pass in the Julian Alps. You'll negotiate 50 hair-raising switchbacks in just 25km (16 miles) before reaching the other side—the Soča River Valley. You can indulge your spirit for adventure in Bovec (the best base for skiing on the slopes of the Kanin), but reserve accommodations near Kobarid—either at Casa Hiša Franko (which also offers the most exciting restaurant menu in

the country), or at nearby Nebesa, perhaps the most idyllic getaway in Europe. In Kobarid, visit the antiwar museum, and grab a map for the outdoor walking "museums" that you can undertake under your own steam, preferably in the early morning, before temperatures start to rise. Spend your second day white-water rafting and attending to other river- or mountain-bound adventures. At Hiša Franko, ask for a lunch basket and picnic on the banks of the nearby river.

Day 6: Piran

From the Soča Valley, it's a 2-hour drive toward the Istrian Coast, connecting with the main highway heading south. En route, stop at the Škocjan Caves, which are a scintillating 2-hour diversion. In Piran, take your time exploring the cobblestone streets and back alleys, cooling yourself in the refreshing waters of the Adriatic before settling in for an evening of seafood at Neptun. If you feel you're up for a party, head over to the nearby resort town of Portoroz where you'll find casinos, nightclubs, and merry-making crowds.

Days 7–8: Ljubljana

The highway leads directly from Piran to the capital; set out after an early-morning swim. Ljubljana has great charm and can be extensively explored on foot or bicycle. Head up to the castle for a good look at the layout of city, then explore Old Town, where you'll find plenty of stunning restaurants. In the afternoon, prioritize the art museums, but be sure to grab a seat at one of the lively cafe-bars lining the Ljubljanica River for sundowners. In summer, try to catch a festival performance at the **Križanke Summer Theater,** perhaps after an early dinner at AS. If you have the energy, prepare for a night of clubbing, or try to visit a selection of the city's best watering holes.

SLOVENIA TODAY

Having emerged from its 10-day war of independence practically unscathed, Slovenia is a country of tremendous stability and calm. A high-ranking E.U. official once referred to Slovenia as the "good pupil of the European Union," but in fact Slovenia could teach the rest of Europe (and much of the world, in fact) a lesson or two. A country that quietly gets on with the job of improving its position on the world stage, Slovenia consistently administers to all spheres of local life, thereby attracting foreign investment through both industry and—now that the crisis faced by its Balkan neighbors appears to have abated—also on the tourist front.

A LOOK AT THE PAST

Slovenes will tell you of a history fraught by outside rule; when independence was won in 1991, it was after a 1,000-year struggle.

Once the ancient home of southerly Illyrian tribes and Celts from the north, the Romans arrived here in A.D. 100, legendarily traversing the Julian Alps (named, in fact, for Julius Caesar) and creating the trade hubs of Emona (Ljubljana), Poetovia (Ptuj), and Celeia (Celje). Attila the Hun raged across Slovenia from the east, en route to Italy in the 5th century, causing the Roman settlers to regroup at the coast, where the port cities of Capris (Koper) and Piranum (Piran) were created.

Slavic tribes—the ancestors of contemporary Slovenes—arrived in the 6th century, bringing pagan superstitions and an agricultural lifestyle, and finally uniting to form the Principality of Karantania. But it wasn't long before the Slavs were forced to submit to the rule of the Frankish emperor, who converted them to Christianity. From the 14th century, Slovenia fell to the Habsburgs, who stimulated great resentment during most of their reign. War, Turkish invasion, and economic gloom were the ongoing themes in the 15th and 16th centuries. The coastal cities fell under voluntary protection of the Venetian Empire until the end of the 18th century, while the Ottomans repeatedly trampled through the region in attempts to take Vienna.

Germanic culture was encouraged among the elite, while the peasant classes occasionally rose up, determined to replant their Slavic roots. Slovene culture was touted by nationalist movements, and for the brief 4 years (1809–13) that Napoleon made Ljubljana the capital of his Illyrian provinces, the Slovenian language entered schools and government. In the mid-1800s, Slovenian nationalism reached its zenith; amid (largely unsuccessful) cries for nationhood and recognition of a unique identity, the call for Slavic unity could be heard pushing for the unification of all Serbs, Croats, and Slovenes. The second half of the 19th century was a period of industrialization, but this failed to prevent mass emigration by the country's poor.

In 1914, Archduke Franz Ferdinand was assassinated, sparking World War I between the Austro-Hungarian Empire and the Triple Entente (France, Britain, and Russia). Dragged into the fray, Slovenia was forced to fight to protect its homeland when Italy attacked.

When the Austro-Hungarian Empire collapsed in 1918, Slovenia was partially incorporated into the newly established Kingdom of Serbs, Croats, and Slovenes, which later became Yugoslavia ("Land of Southern Slavs") in 1929; coastal Slovenia was given to Italy.

In 1937 the half-Slovene, half-Croat Josip Broz Tito became party leader, and was the man at the helm when Hitler invaded Yugoslavia in 1941. After World War II, Tito headed up the Socialist Federal Republic of Yugoslavia, with Slovenia as one of six states. Tito played his cards right with both Eastern and Western powers, and—unlike other Eastern bloc countries—Yugoslavia enjoyed a fairly open relationship with the rest of the world.

To curb the tide of nationalism from Slovenes who resented their unbalanced contribution to the socialist economy, Tito gave cultural freedoms to minorities, and constituent states had some autonomy. In 1980, Tito's 35-year rule ended with his death in Ljubljana, opening the floodgates of political and economic disaster. Slovenia represented less than 10% of the Yugoslavian population but brought in over 25% of its export wealth, and with Tito's death Slovenes affirmed their desire to break free from their Balkan neighbors. In December 1990 over 90% of the population voted for independence which it declared in June 1991, sparking a short, bloody war with president Slobodan Milosevic. The small Slovene defense force resisted for 10 days before Milosevic was forced to withdraw his troops to focus on Bosnia and Croatia. Slovenia was formally recognized as an independent state in January 1992, joining the United Nations later that year, and the European Union in May 2004. Recently, Slovenia also became part of the Schengen zone, which means that border checks with neighboring Italy, Austria, and Hungary no longer exist.

SLOVENIAN PEOPLE & CULTURE

Slovenes, one of the smallest ethnic minorities on the Continent, are a proud, prosperous people, with a distinct cosmopolitanism that has evolved out of the assimilation of foreign and neighboring influences over the centuries. Seen as former-Yugoslavia's well-to-do sibling, Slovenia is a nation of vivacious, cultured, and gregarious people, and you'll find it easy to meet locals, many of whom speak several languages (typically Slovenian, English, German, and Italian). While city life is energetic and modern, you may also come across tiny bucolic communities where a traditional agricultural lifestyle is augmented with the odd beer festival or carnival, complete with a lineup of cheerful polka bands. For while they're considered a nation of hard workers, Slovenes love to kick back, relax, and party; with life this good, there's plenty to celebrate.

LANGUAGE

Most Slovenes you meet will understand English, so you won't have much call to try Slovenian, a complicated and difficult-to-learn South Slavonic language. Using Roman letters, written Slovenian includes three modifications of the letters s, c, and z, which receive a hacek top in order to slur them; thus, *š* sounds like "sh," *č*sounds like "ch," and *ž* sounds like "zh."

USEFUL TERMS & PHRASES

English	Slovene	Pronunciation
Hello	**Živijo**	jhi-*vi*-jah
Please/Can I help you?	**Prosim/Prosim?**	*pro*-sim

English	Slovene	Pronunciation
Goodbye	**Nasvidenje**	naz-vee-*dan*-ja
Good day/evening	**Dober dan/večer**	do-*ber* dun/*ve*-tcher
Good night	**Lahko noč**	la-*ko* noc
What's your name?	**Kako ti je ime?**	*kak*-o tee *ye*-may
Cheers!	**Na zdravje**	naz-*dra*-vee
Yes/No	**Ja/Ne**	ya/neh
Thank you (very much)	**Hvala (lepa)**	h-*vah*-la (lee-pa)
Excuse me	**Oprostite**	o-pros-*tit*-eh
Open/Closed	**Odprto/Zaprto**	od-*pr*-to/Zap-*pr*-to
Entrance/Exit	**Vhod/Izhod**	vod/*ee*-zod
Bon appétit	**Dober tek!**	dob-er tek

2 PLANNING YOUR TRIP TO SLOVENIA

VISITOR INFORMATION

The **Slovenian Tourist Board,** Dunajska cesta 156, 1000 Ljubljana, Slovenia (✆ **+386/1/589-1840;** fax +386/1/589-1841), is incredibly organized, pitching every aspect of the country on its excellent website (www.slovenia.info), from which you can download or order over a dozen different brochures.

ENTRY REQUIREMENTS & CUSTOMS REGULATIONS

Citizens of the U.S., Canada, the U.K., Australia, and New Zealand do not presently require visas for stays of up to 90 days. Check the Foreign Ministry website (www.mzz.gov.si) for any updates on visa and entry requirements. Visitors to Slovenia are exempt from Customs duty on items intended for personal use; additionally, you may import 200 cigarettes or 50 cigars, 2 liters of wine, and 1 liter of spirits, as well as 50 grams of perfume or .25 liters of toilet water. Visit www.carina.gov.si if you have any queries in this regard. There are no restrictions on cash brought into the country.

MONEY

Slovenia started using the euro in January 2007. Exchange facilities are widely available, as are ATMs and credit card facilities; you can swipe your card almost anywhere, including at gas stations.

WHEN TO GO

Slovenia is wonderful all year round, enjoying a mix of Alpine, continental, and Mediterranean climates. In winter, the Julian Alps are just one of many mountain ranges that are ideal for skiing and snowboarding. Be wary midsummer, however; in July, Slovenes take a break from everyday life and head for the coast (of Croatia, mostly). So while it's a great time to see the old towns in the east, the capital is rather quiet, and the coast crowded.

Major Festivals in Slovenia

The eastern town of Ptuj erupts with life on Shrove Sunday **(mid-Feb),** when 50,000 people assemble for the country's anticipated **Kurentovanje.** This winter carnival has revelers taking to the streets in spectacular Kurent masks and costumes—an outrageous pagan spring celebration that's become an awesome excuse for a raucous party. For 2 weeks in **late June,** Maribor hosts the **Lent Festival,** one of the most exciting cultural events in Slovenia, attracting great musical acts and supporters from all over Europe. In **mid-July,** Laško holds a weeklong beer festival, probably the best place to experience Slovenia's affection for drinking, polka bands, and live music. **Ljubljana Summer Festival** runs from **July through to the middle of September** and features performances of all kinds—film, theater, jazz, chamber music, opera, ballet, symphony concerts, theater, and puppetry. Ljubljana also hosts the **Druga Godba (The Other Music),** an alternative music festival scheduled around **late May;** while in **late June,** you can catch the **Ljubljana Jazz Festival,** the oldest jazz festival in Europe. In **mid-July,** the popular summer resort of Bled hosts **Blejski Dnevi (Bled Days),** a festival of music, craft markets, fireworks, and a candlelit lake.

On the **last Sunday in August,** Predjama Castle hosts **Erazem's Medieval Tournament,** complete with jousting knights on horseback and costumes from the Middle Ages. **The Cow's Ball (Kravji Bal)** happens at Lake Bohinj over the **second or third weekend in September;** the cows literally come home from the mountains and villagers set about their drink-fueled merrymaking. On **November 11 (St. Martin's Day),** look out for winemaking celebrations in the country's wine regions.

HOLIDAYS

Slovenian public holidays are New Year's Day (Jan 1), Prešeren Day (Feb 8); Day of Uprising Against Occupation (Apr 27), Easter Day and Easter Monday, Labor Day (May 1, 2), Statehood Day (June 25), Assumption (Aug 15), Reformation Day (Oct 31), Remembrance Day (Nov 1), Christmas Day (Dec 25), and Independence Day (Dec 26).

GETTING THERE

BY PLANE Slovenia's national carrier, **Adria Airways** (www.adria.si), has regularly scheduled flights over 20 European cities. Your best option for a reasonably seamless flight from North America or Australasia is **Air France** (www.airfrance.com), via Paris, which has flights from most major cities, and up to four daily flights to Ljubljana with its short-haul carrier, Régional. Flight time from Paris is about an hour. It's also worth checking out flights with **Austrian Airlines** (www.aua.com) and **Lufthansa** (www.lufthansa.com). British low-cost airline easyJet (www.easyjet.com) flies to Ljubljana from London's Stansted airport daily; the London-Ljubljana flight is 2 hours. **Czech Airlines** has flights from Prague, **Malev** flies from Budapest, and **Turkish Airlines** arrives from Istanbul. You could also consider flying to Venice or Trieste in Italy, and then getting a train or car for the short trip to Slovenia.

BY TRAIN Daily services connect Slovenia (usually by way of Ljubljana) with larger cities in neighboring countries. Venice (245km/152 miles), Vienna (385km/239 miles), Zagreb (135km/84 miles), and Budapest (491km/304 miles) are all an easy train ride away.

BY CAR You'll have little trouble driving into and around Slovenia. Be aware that border crossings with Croatia can get jam-packed in the summer; there is a great deal of vacation and business traffic passing in and out, and its entry points can get crowded.

GETTING AROUND

BY CAR Slovenia's size makes driving here very attractive; besides, you'll be able to get into many smaller villages unnoticed by those on trains and buses. Drive on the right-hand side and pick up a road map (from Tourist Information centers at the airport and in Ljubljana). On expressways, the speed limit is 130kmph (81 mph); on highways, 100kmph (62 mph); on secondary roads, 90kmph (56 mph); and in built-up areas, 50kmph (31 mph). Keep your headlights on at all times, wear your seat belt, and do not use your cellphone while driving. Carry your driver's license and insurance documentation at all times. Gas stations are ubiquitous; you can pay for gas using most credit cards.

Since June 2008, travel on Slovenian highways and expressways requires that all vehicles are in possession of a *vinjet* (vignette) sticker. Available at gas stations and valid for 6 months, they cost 35€ ($22) and mean that drivers no longer need to stop at toll booths (they've been decommissioned). If you rent a car, ask if the vehicle comes with the license; most do, but you will be fined between 300€ and 800€ ($186–$1,016) if you're caught driving on highways without one. Visit the website of the **Automobile Association of Slovenia** (www.amzs.si) for information about traffic and details of what to do in emergencies. This is also a good place to get the lowdown on Slovenia's complicated parking rules; you can also call their **Information Center** (✆ **01/530-5300**). For road emergencies, call ✆ **1987;** you'll get immediate roadside assistance and a towing service if necessary. You can also call their **breakdown assistance hotline** (✆ **01/530-5353**). For up-to-date **traffic information**, call ✆ **01/518-8518** or **080-2244.**

BY TRAIN Slovenia's train network is fairly extensive and reliable; it's also inexpensive. InterCity ("IC") trains are faster than *potniški,* or slow trains, which stop at every backwater village. English timetables are available at www.slo-zeleznice.si. Usually you'll be able to purchase tickets for domestic journeys at the station just before departure. Ticketing staff is incredibly helpful.

BY BUS Buses are slightly more expensive than trains, but the network is more extensive, allowing access to more remote destinations; they're also more frequent (except at weekends in some areas). Buses are operated by a number of local companies, and the larger towns have stations with computerized booking systems.

BY BIKE Slovenes love cycling and it's possible to rent bikes in most towns for countryside exploration. Cycling is also popular within cities and towns; in Ljubljana, where parking is problematic and distances are quite short, bikes are definitely the easiest and most economical way of getting around. While riding on highways is not permitted, you'll discover a vast network of bike trails that will take you through some of the most spectacular terrain in Europe.

TIPS ON ACCOMMODATIONS

Accommodations range from average to superb. There's a five-star classification system loosely reflecting the quality of hotels, but it certainly doesn't give a clear indication of price, which is dependent on demand. June through August is considered peak vacation season, when you should reserve accommodations well in advance, especially on the coast; the exception to this is the ski resorts that fill up between December and February.

To avoid high hotel costs, consider staying at a *penzion* or a small, family-run hotel; these might be referred to as *gostišče.* There are an increasing number of upper-end establishments, particularly in resort towns, spas, and in the capital. The country's hostels are among the very best in Europe.

TIPS ON DINING

Generally, you'll be choosing to eat in either a *restavracija* (restaurant) or a *gostilna,* which is more like a tavern with down-to-earth atmosphere. If there are accommodations attached to the tavern, they will probably be called a *gostišce,* making them a real "inn." *Okrepčevalnice* are snack bars where you can get in-between fillers or light meals. Meat (including horse) and fish feature heavily on the Slovene menu, and—depending on where you are—the cuisine shows some Austrian, Hungarian, or Italian influences; in Ljubljana there are a wide range of international dining establishments. ***Note:*** Like Italy, many upmarket restaurants in Slovenia add a "bread and cover" fee to your bill—in short, a 1€ to 3€ ($1.25–$3.80) cover charge that you must pay for the mere privilege of sitting at the table.

TOURS & TRAVEL AGENTS

Based in the U.K., **Just Slovenia** (✆ **44/1373/814230;** www.justslovenia.co.uk) arranges reliable all-inclusive personalized trips to Slovenia. Another British outfit is **Slovene Dream** (✆ **44/20/7737-3054;** www.slovenedream.com), which books tailor-made itineraries and accommodations at individually selected properties across the country. You will also discover links to various other agencies on the Slovenian Tourist Board website (www.slovenia.info).

Fast Facts Slovenia

Addresses Throughout this chapter, the following Slovene words may occur as part of an address: *ulica* (street), *cesta* (road), *trg* (square), *pot* (trail), and *steza* (path).

Airlines All the major airlines have offices either in Ljubljana or at the airport. **Adria Airways:** Kuzmičeva 7, Ljubljana; ✆ **01/369-1010,** airport ✆ **04/259-4339,** toll-free: ✆ **080-1300;** www.adria-airways.com. **Air France:** ✆ **01/244-3447** or 01/242-8403, airport ✆ **04/206-1674;** www.airfrance.com/si.

Area Code For Slovenia, dial ✆ **+386.**

Banks & Currency Exchange ATMs are your best bet for getting cash quickly, although credit cards are also accepted for cash advances at most banks.

Business Hours Shops should be open weekdays 8am to 7pm, and Saturday 8am to 1pm. On Sundays, some shops and services may open at 11am and do business until 5pm. Banks usually take a midday break between 12:30 and 2pm, and close at 5pm, and are open Saturday mornings until 11am or noon. Most attractions close on Mondays.

Car Rentals All major international car-rental agencies are represented; rates are competitive and vehicles are in excellent condition; always return the car with a full tank to avoid a 50% surcharge. **Avis: ✆ 01/583-8780;** www.avis.si. **Hertz: ✆ 01/239-6010;** www.hertz.si. **Europcar: ✆ 031-382-052;** www.europcar.si.

Drugstores *Lekarna* are found in all towns, and are open from early until 7 or 8pm. It shouldn't be too difficult to track down an all-night drugstore, or *dežurna lekarna.*

Electricity Local current is 220 volts. Outlets take plugs with two round prongs, typical to continental Europe. Plug and power adapters are necessary for appliances requiring 110 volts.

Embassies & Consulates All embassies and consulates are in Ljubljana. **U.S. Embassy:** Prešernova cesta 31; **✆ 01/200-5500;** fax 01/200-5555; www.us embassy.si. **U.K. Embassy:** Trg Republike 3/IV; **✆ 01/200-3910;** fax 01/425-0174; www.british-embassy.si. **Consulate of Canada:** Dunajska 22; **✆ 01/252-4444;** fax 01/430-3575. **Australian Consulate:** Dunajska 50; **✆ 01/425-4252;** fax 01/426-4721; austral.cons.sloven@siol.net. **Consulate of New Zealand:** Verovškova 57; **✆ 01/580-3055;** fax 01/568-3526; janja.bratos@lek.si.

Emergencies Dial **✆ 113** for police emergencies; fire service, **✆ 112;** ambulance, **✆ 112.** For nonaccident road emergencies, call AMZS at **✆ 1987.**

Internet Access Slovenia has good Internet service, although dedicated Internet cafes are few. Most hotels have in-room Internet connectivity.

Language See "Language" on p. 651.

Liquor Laws The legal age for drinking is 18.

Mail Post offices (look for signs that read POŠTA) are generally open weekdays 8am to 6pm, and Saturdays 8am to 1pm; mail service is efficient and reliable.

Maps Good maps are available at the airport, and tourist offices around the country will give you everything you might need to find your way around. Gas stations have also been supplied with a range of free maps produced by the Tourist Board.

Newspapers & Magazines You'll find heaps of useful tourist publications at the airport. ***The Slovenia Times*** is published in English every 2 weeks.

Police Dial **✆ 113.**

Restrooms Clean and user-friendly; you'll pay a very small fee to use public facilities at train and bus stations.

Safety & Crime One of Europe's safest countries, with a below-average crime rate.

Taxes & Service Charges VAT will generally be included in all quoted prices; at all hotels, there will be an extra "tourist tax" of around 1€ ($1.25) per night.

Telephones Use a phonecard, bought at post offices and newsstands, to use public pay phones, which are fairly ubiquitous; you can also call from a booth at the post office. Numbers in Slovenia have seven digits; this should be preceded by the two-digit area code if you're calling from a different region.

Time Zone Slovenia is 1 hour ahead of GMT.

Tipping Leave 10% to 15% for all good restaurant and bar service.

Water Slovenia's water is clean and delicious; in some areas, it's considered among the purest water in Europe.

Weather Information Dial **✆ 090-7130.**

3 LJUBLJANA

In many ways a fairy-tale city, replete with castle, the capital city has as its defining motif a dragon, which you will see on flags that flutter from bridges and buildings, in intriguing architectural embellishments throughout the city, and on marketing materials everywhere. The historic center is imbued with striking monuments and generous squares that suggest good urban planning. Graffiti artists mark these public spaces, often branding historic edifices with such unironic one-liners as "Ljubljana is a beautiful city." And it is. Graffiti aside, Ljubljana has a low-key buzz and an air of exuberance that extends to the artfulness of its buildings, its statuary, and its fountains.

According to legend, Argonauts may have laid the foundations of Ljubljana as they fled along the Ljubljanica River from the Black Sea to the Adriatic with the Golden Fleece 3,000 years ago; certainly the Romans established a city, Emona, here by the turn of the 1st century A.D. With Emona destroyed by the Huns, Slavic immigrants chose to build a city at the foot of what is now Ljubljana Castle Hill; it grew to become what was known 500 years later as Leibach and in 1144 as Luwigana. When the Habsburgs took over, this became their administrative center until they were expelled during World War I. In the mid–19th century the city's economic pull was enhanced when the railroad linking Vienna and Trieste was built through Ljubljana, and much of the city's prosperity came from its tobacco factory.

A university town, with cutting-edge ambitions, Ljubljana percolates with charm. It's long been a cultural center, home to one of Europe's oldest philharmonic societies, and now also to a swinging alternative youth and student culture, drawing international artists from all spheres. It's also the birthplace of celebrated architect, Joze Plečnik, who almost single-handedly reshaped the city, erecting many of its lovely buildings and developing its squares and bridges. Best of all, the city is small and compact, so you'll see plenty of it with little effort.

GETTING THERE

Although **Ljubljana Jože Pučnik Airport,** Brnik 130a (✆ **04/206-1000;** www.lju-airport.si), 23km (14 miles) from the city, isn't the busiest place in Europe, there are regular flights arriving from Paris, London, Prague, Zurich, Frankfurt, Budapest, Warsaw, and Munich, as well as an increasing number of other Europe cities. You can rent a car at the airport from **Avis** (✆ **01/583-8780;** www.avis.si) and return it when you fly home. Taxis into the city will cost 35€ to 45€ ($44–$57). Prearrange a **shuttle bus** through your hotel (it should cost 8€/$10 one-way) for a direct drop at your accommodations. Public buses also operate; these run from early until midnight; the bus trip (4.10€/$5.20) to the city lasts 45 minutes, and terminates at the city **bus station,** Avtobusna postaja, trg Osvobodilne fronte 4 (✆ **01/234-4600;** www.ap-ljubljana.si), which is also the main point of arrival and departure for other Slovene and European destinations. Ljubljana's **train station,** Železniška postaja, is next to the bus station, and has a currency exchange facility as well as tourist information office (✆ **01/433-9475**). The stations are a 10-minute walk from the center.

CITY LAYOUT

Most of the tourist action is within a small, compact area centered on Ljubljana's Old Town, which straddles a bend in the Ljubljaniker River. For more detail see "Exploring Ljubljana's Center," later in this chapter.

GETTING AROUND THE CITY

This is a city for walking, and you'll be irritated and frustrated if you try to explore it by car; finding parking—even on quiet days—is hellish. Hotels beyond walking distance of the center usually provide shuttle services, and taxis are very reliable.

BUSES Decent, comfortable public buses will get you wherever you need to go; the network is extensive and route maps clearly indicate when and where buses are going. Purchase bus tickets from newspaper kiosks and some shops (.80€/$1), or purchase a ticket on the bus using exact fare (1€/$1.25). A day-long bus pass costs 4€ ($5.10).

TAXIS Call ✆ **080-1190** to have a **Metro Taxi** cab pick you up; **Rumeni Taxi** (✆ **041-731-831**) is another option. Alternatively, you can hail a taxi on the street (more expensive than calling); you'll always find taxis at the station and smarter hotels.

OTHER To really get your bearings, consider a 90-minute **hot-air balloon ride** organized by the tourist information center. For a more down-to-earth sightseeing option, rent a **bicycle** (also from tourist information; see details below), or set out **on foot.** There are also **barge** trips up and down the Ljubljanica.

VISITOR INFORMATION

Ljubljana knows that tourism is where it's at, and there's a great deal of literature and assistance for visitors. Right in the heart of the Old Town, at one end of the Triple Bridge, is **Ljubljana Tourist Information Center** (✆ **01/306-1215;** www.ljubljana.si), an excellent source for sightseeing advice; it's also where you can buy the **Ljubljana Card** (13€/$16), a 72-hour discount passport that is most useful if you are able to use it for reductions on accommodations or car rentals, in which case you'll score major savings; otherwise, it'll mostly get you into museums and galleries for free, and give you unlimited bus travel. The **Slovenian Tourist Information Center,** Krekov trg 10 (✆ **01/306-4575/6;** daily 8am–9pm), provides assistance on the entire country. The train station hosts a **Tourist Office** (✆ **01/433-9475**), and there's an **Airport Center** (✆ **051-606-172**). Look out for information-packed ***Ljubljana in Your Pocket*** (www.inyourpocket.com), which carries capsule write-ups of just about every hotel, restaurant, club, bar, and attraction in town; it also carries contact details for just about anything you could imagine, and has maps.

CITY TOURS & GUIDED WALKS

You can join one of the city tours provided by **Ljubljana Tourist Information Center,** Adamič-Lundrovo nabrežje 2 (✆ **01/306-1215;** www.ljubljana.si); guides are knowledgeable and enthusiastic. If you prefer your independence (or don't want to tour with a group), you can hire a personal audio guide instead.

Fast Facts Ljubljana

American Express Kolodvorska 16; ✆ **01/430-7720;** Monday to Friday 8am to 5pm.

Area Code For Ljubljana, dial ✆ **01.**

Banks & Currency Exchange Exchange is available at banks and also at post offices. If you arrive by train, there's a facility at the station open until 10pm. ATMs are an easy way to draw euros throughout the day.

Drugstores Round-the-clock service at **Lekarna Ljubljana,** Prisojna 7 (✆ **01/230-6230**).

Hospital The city's main hospital is situated at Bohoričeva 4 (✆ **01/232-3060**). Near the center is **Health Center Metelkova,** Metelkova 9 (✆ **01/472-3700**).

Internet Access If for some reason there's no Internet at your hotel, head for the Slovenian Tourist Information Center on Krekov trg.

Police Dial ✆ **113.** Report any incidents at Trdinova 10 (✆ **01/432-0341**).

Postal Services **Glavna pošta** (main post office): Slovenska 32; ✆ **01/243-1960;** Mon–Fri 8am–7pm, Sat 8am–1pm.

WHERE TO STAY

Very Expensive

If you choose to research further you may come across the city's most expensive and, arguably, most glamorous hotel, **Lev** (www.hotel-lev.si), but note that it suffers from an alarming location on a busy central intersection and, frankly, is soulless.

Grand Hotel Union Comprising three centrally located hotels under one umbrella—Executive, Business, and Garni—Grand Union is aimed at business travelers, but pins its image to a sense of refinement (despite former Holiday Inn connections) apparent only in the elegant entranceway facade of the original (Executive) building. Built in 1905, it was then the most modern hotel in the Balkans, with a high-ceilinged sprawl of wide passages and shiny marble floors, behind that impressive Art Nouveau facade. Opt for the more expensive Executive part of the hotel only if you crave an inkling of historical ambience (it was good enough for Bill Clinton, apparently, although he no doubt had a suite); the Business wing may be in a less elegant 1970s building, but rooms are bigger and include great views of the castle and the city's rooftops from even-numbered units on the seventh, eighth, and ninth floors. All rooms in the Business section have balconies, whilst only half of the Executive units do. Although guest rooms are relatively spacious with manageable bathrooms (tub or shower) throughout, it's quite clear that the entire hotel is in need of a thorough face-lift (the last renovation was over a decade ago), and staff could do with a serious injection of character, too.

Miklošičeva cesta 3, 1000 Ljubljana. ✆ **01/308-1170.** Fax 01/308-1914. www.gh-union.si. 401 units. Executive 230€–276€ ($292–$351) double, 455€–546€ ($578–$693) suite; Business 223€–266€ ($283–$338) double, 372€–446€ ($472–$566) suite; Garni 181€–217€ ($230–$276) double, 286€–343€ ($363–$436) suite. Rates include breakfast and VAT. AE, DC, MC, V. **Amenities:** 3 restaurants; 3 bars; cafe; pool; fitness room; sauna; car rental; shops; hair salon; room service; massage; laundry; currency exchange. *In room:* A/C, TV, Internet, minibar, hair dryer, safe.

Hotel Ljubljana When it opened in 2004 (as the Domina Grand Media), this then-Italian-owned monolith was heralded as the world's most technologically advanced hotel, offering guest rooms packed with enough electronic gadgetry to make even the most hardened computer geek shriek with delight. Since being bought out by the Austria Trend group, however, many of those cool high-tech extras have disappeared and the new owners aren't yet sure how they plan to lure 21st-century travelers in the immediate future. Despite the hotel's poor location on a busy city intersection in a building that's more office block than anything else, once you're inside, things don't look quite so bad, particularly once you're away from the cold, lifeless marble lobby (escalators lead down to the casino and doors open on to a convention center). Guest rooms are spacious, carpeted, and design conscious, with patterned textiles and dark-wood furniture in a bland, formal style that gets its highest marks for spaciousness (closets and bathrooms are large, too), although you'll need a suite to really get a sense of luxury. Guests make use of a shuttle for the center, which is 3km (2 miles) away.

Dunajska 154, 1000 Ljubljana. ✆ **01/588-2500.** Fax 01/588-2599. www.austria-trend.at/lju. 214 units. 285€ ($362) double comfort; 335€ ($425) double executive; 410€–750€ ($521–$953) suite. Rates include breakfast. AE, DC, MC, V. **Amenities:** Restaurant; 2 bars; casino; business center; room service; wellness center; Thai massage; laundry. *In room:* A/C, TV, Wi-Fi, minibar, hair dryer.

Expensive

City Hotel ★ Kids A complete rebuild of a former eyesore has resulted in one of the city's most popular large hotels. A busy, cheerful lobby—where you'll find the bar, lounge areas, restaurant, and a fairly on-the-ball reception—is done out in eclectic, upbeat decor, with more colorful ambition than any recognizable style. Guest rooms are nonetheless rather pleasant—overtly minimalist with eye-catching primary colors and contemporary straight lines that make these accommodations more desirable than those at the nearby Grand Union (below), and that's despite the lack of amenities (not really a problem in a city where you'll be out exploring most of the time anyway). You'll also get a more comfortable rate (as little as 129€/$164 double during the busy summer months, although prices go up and down according to demand). Opt for either a quieter room facing the interior atrium, or—better still—one of six corner units that have small terraces from which you can see the castle and observe life on the streets below (no. 608 is the highest of these, with the best view, so book it now). You can also ask for either a carpeted or wood floor unit; all the rooms come with sufficient hanging and packing space, good bathrooms with both shower and tub. The hotel also offers "standard" rooms which are smaller and have fewer amenities, but since they're charged at more or less the same rate, are best avoided.

Dalmatinova 15, 1000 Ljubljana. ✆ **01/239-0000.** Fax 01/239-0001. www.cityhotel.si. 200 units. 129€–300€ ($164–$381) superior double; 400€ ($508) business suite; 500€ ($635) superior suite/apt. Rates include breakfast and VAT. AE, DC, MC, V. **Amenities:** Restaurant; bar; cybercafe; bike hire (free); tour and travel assistance; car rental; airport transfers; Wi-Fi; laundry. *In room:* A/C (most), TV, minibar, hair dryer, safe.

Hotel Mons ★★ Billed as Slovenia's first designer hotel and set at the edge of a thick green forest right at the outskirts of greater Ljubljana, Mons may be a little way out of the center (5km/3 miles away, in the suburb of Brdo), but is well positioned for quick highway access to the rest of the country, and there's a regular free shuttle into the city. Designed by Boris Podrecca, it's a bright glass-encased hotel, the chic modernism counterbalanced by its salubrious garden setting (which you're reminded of by views from practically every window). Guest rooms in pale tones and gleaming dark-wood floors continue the modernist theme; they're smart, comfortable, and easy on the eye—certainly the most attractive amongst the city's expensive hotels. The drawback here is that Mons is attached to a Congress Center, meaning that from time to time it fills up with delegates who, at meal times, throng to the self-service "market"-themed canteen-style restaurant, which is great if you're a conference attendee, but ultimately without charm. Rates are very reasonable, and when things are quiet, you might get a reduced rate, even without a reservation.

Pot za Brdom 55, 1000 Ljubljana. ✆ **01/470-2700.** Fax 01/470-2708. www.mons.si. 114 units. 140€–195€ ($179–$248) double; 260€–340€ ($330–$432) junior suite; 290€–385€ ($368–$489) suite; 25€ ($32) extra bed. Rates include breakfast and VAT. AE, MC, V. **Amenities:** 2 restaurants; bar; fitness room; sauna; bike

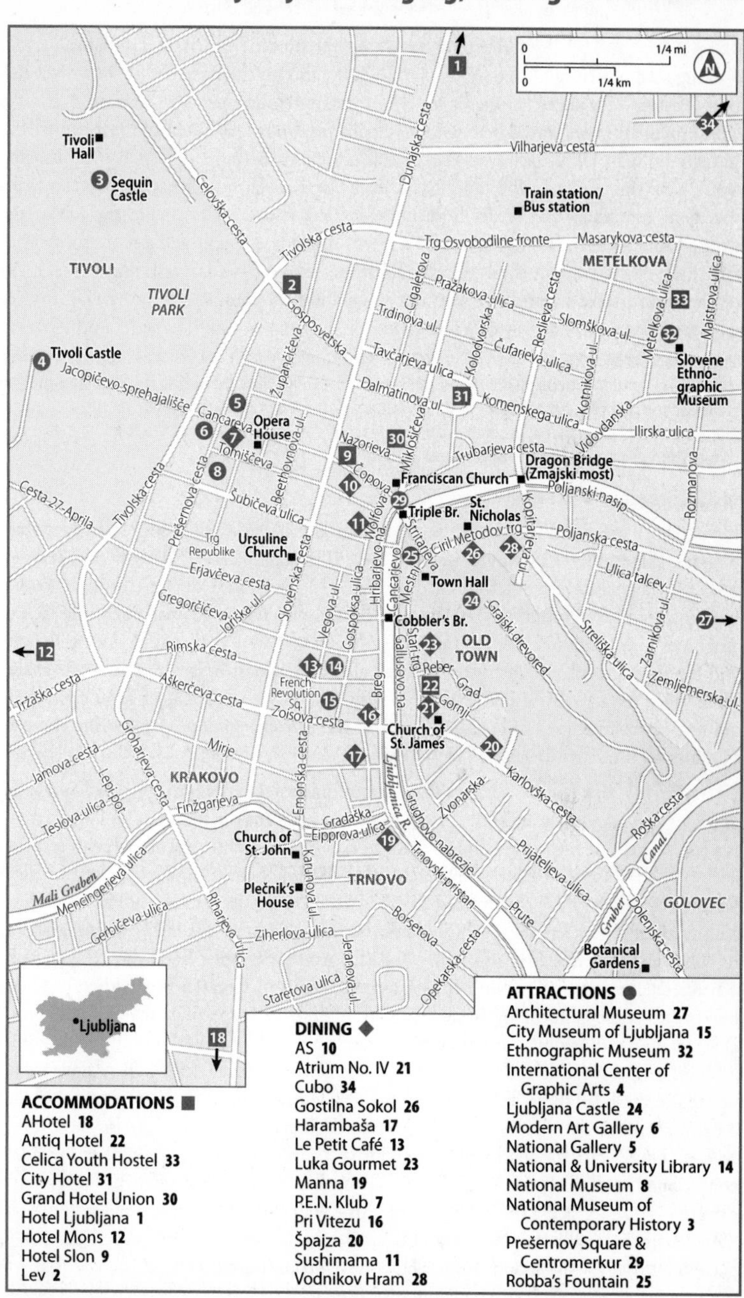
0 1/4 mi
0 1/4 km
N
Tivoli Hall
Sequin Castle
TIVOLI
TIVOLI PARK
Tivoli Castle
Jacopičevo sprehajališče
Celovška cesta
Tivolska cesta
Gosposvetska
Dunajska cesta
Vilharjeva cesta
Train station/ Bus station
Trg Osvobodilne fronte
Masarykova cesta
METELKOVA
Cigaletova
Pražakova ulica
Trdinova ul.
Tavčarjeva ulica
Dalmatinova ul.
Kolodvorska
Resljeva cesta
Slomškova ul.
Čufarjeva ulica
Kotnikova ul.
Metelkova ulica
Maistrova ulica
Slovene Ethno-graphic Museum
Komenskega ulica
Vidovdanska
Ilirska ulica
Trubarjeva cesta
Dragon Bridge (Zmajski most)
Franciscan Church
Poljanski nasip
Rozmanova
Župančičeva
Opera House
Cankarjeva
Tomšičeva
Beethovnova ul.
Nazorjeva
Čopova
Miklošičeva
Šubičeva ulica
Cesta 27 Aprila
Tivolska cesta
Prešernova cesta
Triple Br.
St. Nicholas
Ciril Metodov trg
Kopitarjeva ul.
Poljanska cesta
Ulica talcev
Trg Republike
Ursuline Church
Slovenska cesta
Wolfova
Hribarjevo
Cankarjevo
Mestni
Stritarjeva
Town Hall
Erjavčeva cesta
Gregorčičeva
Igriška ul.
Vegova ul.
Gosposka ulica
Cobbler's Br.
Grajski drevored
Streliška ulica
Zarnikova ul.
Rimska cesta
Stari trg
Gallusovo na.
OLD TOWN
Reber
Grad
Zemljemerska ul.
Tržaška cesta
Aškerčeva cesta
French Revolution Sq.
Breg
Zoisova cesta
Gornji
Church of St. James
Mirje
Groharjeva cesta
Jamova cesta
Lepi pot
KRAKOVO
Emonska cesta
Ljubljanica R.
Karlovška cesta
Teslova ulica
Finžgarjeva
Gradaška
Eipprova ulica
Grudnovo nabrezje
Zvonarska
Roška cesta
Canal
Church of St. John
Karunova ul.
Trnovski pristan
Prijateljeva ulica
Mali Graben
Mencingerjeva ulica
Plečnik's House
TRNOVO
Prule
Gruber
Dolenjska cesta
GOLOVEC
Gerbičeva ulica
Riharjeva ulica
Ziherlova ulica
Borsetova
Jeranova ul.
Opekarska cesta
Botanical Gardens
Staretova ulica
Ljubljana
ACCOMMODATIONS
AHotel 18
Antiq Hotel 22
Celica Youth Hostel 33
City Hotel 31
Grand Hotel Union 30
Hotel Ljubljana 1
Hotel Mons 12
Hotel Slon 9
Lev 2
DINING
AS 10
Atrium No. IV 21
Cubo 34
Gostilna Sokol 26
Harambaša 17
Le Petit Café 13
Luka Gourmet 23
Manna 19
P.E.N. Klub 7
Pri Vitezu 16
Špajza 20
Sushimama 11
Vodnikov Hram 28
ATTRACTIONS
Architectural Museum 27
City Museum of Ljubljana 15
Ethnographic Museum 32
International Center of Graphic Arts 4
Ljubljana Castle 24
Modern Art Gallery 6
National Gallery 5
National & University Library 14
National Museum 8
National Museum of Contemporary History 3
Prešernov Square & Centromerkur 29
Robba's Fountain 25

 rental; sightseeing; city shuttle; airport transfers; conference center; Internet; shop; room service; laundry; billiards; travel agency; jogging paths. *In room:* A/C, TV, Wi-Fi, minibar, hair dryer, safe.

Hotel Slon ★ One of the most conveniently situated hotels in Ljubljana, within walking distance from all the sights (although it's also on the busiest road in town), this Best Western "Premiere" property has a history stretching from 1552, when Archduke Maximilian allegedly stayed here with his elephant (*slon* means "elephant"); the hotel was actually built in 1937, however. Packed full of amenities (most of which you probably won't have time to use), the hotel often feels like a social hub, drawing regulars to its basement nightclub and smart little multi-leveled restaurant-bar. Like the lobby, the comfortable guest rooms have received a recent upgrade, giving them a more contemporary look, with easy-on-the-eye neutral shades, textured walls, and finer fabrics. All deluxe rooms have bathtubs; if you opt for a cheaper "comfort" room, you'll need to request either a tub or shower, if it matters.

Slovenska cesta 34, 1000 Ljubljana. ✆ **01/470-1131.** Fax 01/251-7164. www.hotelslon.com. 171 units. 190€ ($241) comfort double; 220€ ($279) deluxe double; 250€–360€ ($318–$457) suite. Rates include breakfast and all taxes. **Amenities:** 2 restaurants; breakfast room; cafe; delicatessen; nightclub; Jacuzzi; sauna; gift shop; Internet; room service; laundry. *In room:* A/C, TV, DVD (some), Wi-Fi, minibar, tea- and coffeemaking facility, hair dryer, safe, Jacuzzi (suites).

Moderate

If you don't mind being out of the center, an alternative with a slick, contemporary design is **AHotel ★**, Cesta dveh cesarjev 34D, 1000 Ljubljana (✆ **01/429-1892;** www.ahotel.si), a brand-new hotel (opened in 2008) located south of the city in Trnovo, a pleasant, upmarket suburb. There are just 26 ultraminimalist rooms, where the lack of amenities and in-room comforts reminds you that you should be out exploring the city and dipping into its vibrant riverside cafe culture. Breakfast is served, and while there's an outdoor terrace, and a lounge-bar done out in attractive wickerwork armchairs, there are few other amenities to distract you from the pressing matter of exploring the city. Doubles go for 125€ to 130€ ($159–$165).

Antiq Hotel ★★ (Finds) This still-new boutique hotel in the heart of Old Town—the entrance is marked by four potted "designer" trees adjacent the fountain on Gornji trg—is a sure winner as the most intimate place to stay in the capital. Decorated with assorted antiques, the interior is like an advertisement for Ljubljana's Sunday market; passages feature mirrors and original framed paintings, and there are interesting bits of original architectural detail. In the back, a small, tranquil, terraced garden is a fine place to unwind. Guest rooms are a mixed bag and charged accordingly: Book no. 1 if you want a spectacularly large room with ornate carpets, a carved wooden bed with sumptuous bedspreads and cushions, lovely closets, antique desk, and a seating area with sofa, armchair, and an old ottoman; even the bathroom is big and long, with his and hers basins, a bidet, and a separate toilet. Five beautiful new rooms have been added since Antiq opened in 2006; of these, no. 4 is by far the loveliest (and largest), with wood floors and a private indoor patio facing a walled, terraced garden (to which you also have direct access). There's also an apartment, done out in a more contemporary style with an air-conditioned loft bedroom and downstairs living area with its own kitchen; it even has a private rooftop terrace. On the other end of the scale are a number of small rooms with shared bathrooms for travelers on a budget. Breakfast (the only meal served here) happens in a bright, white indoor patio where the delicious buffet includes oranges that you can squeeze yourself for the ultimate fresh juice.

Gornji trg 3, 1000 Ljubljana. ✆ **01/421-3561.** Fax 01/421-3565. www.antiqhotel.si 16 units. 77€–89€ ($98–$113) double with shared bathroom; 144€–193€ ($183–$245) double; 204€–235€ ($259–$298) apt. Rates include breakfast and taxes. AE, MC, V. Children 3 and under stay free in parent's room. **Amenities:** Lounge; bar; room service; laundry. *In room:* A/C (some), TV, minibar, hair dryer, safe.

Inexpensive

Located in the Metelkova precinct, an area in the old part of town that is experiencing progressive urban renewal and a heady nightlife, **Hostel Celica** (✆ **01/230-9700;** www.hostelcelica.com; 16€–27€/$20–$34 per bed) offers a novel stay in what was once part of the barracks of the JNA (Yugoslav People's Army); the most celebrated rooms are converted prison cells (46€–54€/$58–$69 double), given a design makeover by a number of invited Slovene artists. You pay for the level of privacy that you enjoy: First-floor dorms have facilities shared by 40 people, while on the second floor there's one bathroom per dorm. Breakfasts are a touch better than the usual hostel fare, and linens and towels are provided free of charge. There's a self-service laundry, free Internet, and an on-site tourist agency that organizes trips through the city and throughout Slovenia.

WHERE TO DINE

Considering its size, Ljubljana has huge number of restaurants, most of them good. You'll find plenty of options along the Ljubljanica River, but these fill up quickly at dinnertime, so get there early. If you're looking for a place that tourists haven't discovered, try the **P.E.N. Klub** ★★, Tomisiceva 12 (✆ **01/251-4160**), in the headquarters of the Writers' Society. Near the parliament and behind the Opera House, this Bohemian-styled place is where local foodies, politicians, and intellectuals gather. You will however need to call ahead to check if it's open, and whether they can find a table for you.

Very Expensive

Considered by some to be the top eatery in Ljubljana, **Manna** ★★, Eipprova 1a (✆ **01/283-5294**), serves up expensive international fare with great flare and at expectedly upmarket prices. In some respects, the sparkling decor outshines the authenticity of the often over-elaborate cuisine which tends to favor exotic choices. Nevertheless, this was where First Lady Laura Bush was treated to lunch on her visit to the capital (and where you can—for 75€/$95—sample the menu created especially for her). Although problematically located some 3km (2 miles) from the center, if you have the time to trek out to **Cubo** ★★★, Šmartinska 55 (✆ **01/521-1515;** www.cubo-ljubljana.com), do so by whatever means. It's a smart, chic, decidedly contemporary place which savvy locals consider their favorite haunt—delighting in the Scandinavian-inspired decor as much as the superb, unpretentious, largely Italian menu (which changes regularly). The food is light, simple, and spectacular. Of particular merit are the desserts, which have already inspired this young establishment's first recipe book. Both Cubo and Manna are closed Sundays.

Expensive

AS ★★★ MEDITERRANEAN A casual terrace disguises a beautiful interior signaling this restaurant's excellent pedigree. Consistently producing top-notch food and attracting VIPs and celebs, this is the most centrally located of Ljubljana's growing selection of exclusive eateries. The menu (for which there isn't much need, thanks to on-the-ball waiters) changes according to the seasons, and is often based on whatever owner-chef Svetozar Raspopovic finds when he sometimes pops over to Trieste in neighboring Italy to pick up the day's inspirational ingredients. They might include those he'll use in his famous *pesce tartuffalo* (angler or monkfish filet with tartufi sauce)—although not on the menu, you should ask for it. A favorite starter is the shrimp, fresh from the Adriatic, marinated for 15 minutes and served raw and cold. Then order the excellent *tagliata,* made from two different cuts of individually flambéed beef medallions. If you're after fish, opt for the house-blended herb-and-spice-crusted sea bass, or tuna steak prepared on an open fire; there's also a divine clam and oyster pasta, and—amongst a number of many memorable risottos—one prepared with scampi and seasonal vegetables (like asparagus, zucchini, and chanterelles).

Čopova 5a, Knafljev prehod. ✆ **01/425-8822.** www.gostilnaas.si. Reservations essential. Main courses 18€–31€ ($23–$39). AE, DC, MC, V. Daily noon–midnight.

Pri Vitezu ★★★ INTERNATIONAL This riverside eatery is owned by Slovenia's very own "Naked Chef" contender, Luka Lesar, whose culinary flair has earned him high kudos amongst Slovenia's foodies. Specials are chalked up outside the beautiful multi-themed restaurant, and are usually based on whatever's freshest at the market (much of it straight from the Adriatic coast). Start with fragrant ginger soup or swordfish carpaccio, then order the unforgettable beef filet *a la Calabrese,* prepared with olives, dried tomatoes, capers, and cognac sauce. There's a selection of homemade cakes, but don't miss Luka's tiramisu. Incidentally, there's a toned down version of what's on offer here at **Luka Gourmet ★**, Stari trg 9 (✆ **01/4250118;** www.lunchcafe.net), where—due to its popularity—the trick to arrive early enough to get a table.

Breg 18–20. ✆ **01/426-6058.** Reservations essential. Main courses 14€–30€ ($18–$38). AE, DC, MC, V. Mon–Sat noon–11pm.

Moderate

If you're craving your weekly intake of raw fish, stop off at **Sushimama ★★**, Wolfova ulica 12 (✆ **01/426-9125**), a modern place in the heart of Ljubljana; it's one of the top sushi restaurants in central Europe, with a loyal local crowd. Go classic with *miso* soup, followed by *nigri* sushi and *kinako* with a pancake; the sashimi is fresh from the Adriatic. Another interesting option (as much for the lack of English menus as for the eclectic, fantastical decor), this time for Balkan dishes, is **Atrium No. IV ★★**, Gorni trg 4 (✆ **01/251-1069**), situated right next to Cerkev sv. Jakoba. Expect an energetic crowd scattered about the gorgeous little rooms decorated with framed pictures and painted in bright, dramatic colors. And don't forget to check out the outrageous ceiling decorations. Besides Sokol (below), another popular (and arguably less touristy) place to sample Slovene cuisine in the heart of Old Town, is **Vodnikov Hram,** Vodnikov trg 2 (✆ **01/234-5260;** www.vodnikov-hram.si), right near the funicular that takes you up to the castle.

Gostilna Sokol ★★ Value SLOVENE This superb upstairs *gostilna* is squarely aimed at tourists (why else would the servers be dressed in traditional costume?), yet it's managed to retain an authentic atmosphere. Wooden tables and stone floors, chunky wood paneling, wine barrels, hunting trophies, and an eclectic collection of paintings contribute to a real country-tavern vibe, underscored by the accompanying funky accordion music. Also, Sokol is a microbrewery where you can order beer made on-site. Dishes are prepared from the recipes of someone's grandmother and include such down-to-earth favorites as game goulash (served with bread dumplings), fried sausage with cabbage, and the very excellent medallions of deer with Mahaleb cherry sauce; hungrier diners need look no further than the venison plate, with deer steak, deer medallions, and wild boar, accompanied by various gravies. If you'd like to tempt fate, ask for the mushroom soup served in a bread bowl—it's literal, and you'd better take care just how much of the bowl you devour before the soup is done. Beyond the wide range of grilled steaks, there's also seafood, including a kilogram of grilled trout, and squid stuffed with cheese and ham. Hard as it may be, save room for a taste of Slovenia's traditional dessert, *Prekmurska gibanica,* a rich mix of cottage cheese, apples, poppy seeds, and walnuts.

Ciril Metodov trg 18. ✆ **01/439-6855.** www.gostilna-sokol.com. Reservations recommended. Main courses 6.50€–21€ ($8.25–$27). AE, DC, MC, V. Mon–Sat 7am–11pm; Sun and holidays 10am–11pm.

Špajza ★★★ SLOVENE/INTERNATIONAL When the restaurant was featured on Discovery Channel's documentary about Slovenia some years back, Špajza's reputation was sealed, and although its popularity with locals took a dip recently, this Old Town favorite is back on top. In summer you can dine in the outdoor courtyard, but at night you'll be drawn to the romantic, slightly informal indoor spaces, divided into different rooms. All the seafood is superfresh (it arrives daily from Croatia). Fish lovers could start with octopus salad or the mixed-fish plate, followed by the excellent John Dory, prepared with Mediterranean flair. But it is for its meat dishes that Spajza is known, with horsemeat the main specialty (when *špajza* appears on the menu, it means horse will be served); *špajzin file s tartufi* (horse filet with truffles) is a particular highlight, or so I'm told. For more reserved tastes, there's beef and veal, best topped with local mushrooms *(jurčki),* or—a personal favorite—medallions of venison with wild berries. Finish off with apricot and apple strudel, or homemade lemon cheesecake.

Gornji trg 28. ✆ **01/425-3094.** Reservations highly recommended. Main courses 14€–22€ ($18–$28). AE, DC, MC, V. Mon–Sat noon–11pm; Sun and holidays noon–10pm.

Inexpensive

There's a friendly atmosphere at **Harambaša,** Vrtna ulica 8, Krakovo (✆ **041-843-106**), which serves Bosnian pub fare in a space filled with antiques and junk—swords, coffeepots, and copper urns alongside postcards, newspapers, and Sarajevo sports team shirts. Food is simple: *Čevapi v lepinji* (spicy little sausages with bread), *sudukice* (Bosnian sausage), and *pola-pola,* another kind of sausage, best with *kajmak* cheese. A filling meal with beer and Turkish coffee (served with a cigarette) is under 6€ ($7.60).

Le Petit Café ★ Value FRENCH/CAFE This ultimate Sunday-afternoon cafe has a popular wooden terrace under a tree right on French Revolution Square; inside it's a little like an intimate Parisian cafe, with posters against exposed brick. It's a fine place for healthy breakfasts made with fresh ingredients, including homemade yogurt; in summer the drinkable lemon sorbet is a great quencher; in winter, sample the mulled wine. The menu is pretty casual, offering salads, pastas, and wholesome sandwiches (only the latter are available after 8pm). Good choices include beef carpaccio with truffles and Parmesan, served on rocket (arugula), gnocchi stuffed with rocket and ricotta cheese, and grilled filet of salmon with Trevisiano chicory and mozzarella. Daily specials are written on the blackboard.

Trg Francoske Revolucije 4. ✆ **01/251-2575.** Main courses 7.50€–16€ ($9.50–$20). No credit cards. Mon–Fri 7:30am–11pm; Sat–Sun and holidays 9am–11pm; may close later Fri–Sat.

EXPLORING LJUBLJANA

Exploring Ljubljana's Center

If you don't dally in the art galleries, you could see the whole of the city in a single day, starting at **Ljubljana's Castle** (reviewed below), which overlooks the entire city. The best buildings are in and around the finely preserved **Old Town,** a fine mixture of baroque,

Fun Facts City of Frogs & Dragons

Inhabitants of Ljubljana are sometimes referred to by a strange nickname: "frog people." While it seems a bizarre moniker to bestow upon a handsome tribe living in an equally attractive city, the name has its roots in Ljublana's ancient history when much of what is now the old part of the city was actually a swampland. The original inhabitants of this marsh lived on tiny islands, perhaps as natural protection against potential invaders, and this lifestyle earned them the unkind-sounding name "frog people." However, the city's marshy history also ties in with the ancient legend of the Argonauts and their leader, Jason, who supposedly slew a dragon here. Some researchers have theorized that "Jason" may very well have visited Ljubljana, and that the "dragon" was in fact a misinterpretation of the explosions resulting from various noxious gases given off by the decaying matter in the swamp.

Secessionist, and neoclassical buildings around a curve in the **River Ljubljanica,** and heavily beefed up by the city's designer laureate, Jože Plečnik. Life proceeds at a gentle, lively pace along and around the Lubljanica, defined by its cafe and bar culture, and the bridges linking the two banks.

A good place to find your bearings is **Prešernov Square ★★★**, centered on the statue of France Prešeren (1800–49), considered the "Father of the Nation," and the poet whose words are now the national anthem ("A Toast"). Take a seat under the eye-catching **statue** of Prešeren, and you could spend hours watching the constant ebb and flow of people. Also here is **Centromerkur,** marked by an Art Nouveau awning over the entrance; this is Ljubljana's oldest department store, in a gorgeous Secessionist building, Urbanc House, dating from 1903. This is roughly the heart of the Old Town, where young people meet to start their day (often on the steps of the looming **Franciscan Church**), or the night—often heading one way or another across **Triple Bridge (Tromostovje)** to get to their favorite riverside drinking spot. Across Triple Bridge you can take a left turn (at the Tourist Information Center) to reach the colonnaded covered promenade of the daily **crafts market;** alternatively, after crossing the bridge, continue on Stritarjeva, where you soon hit **Mestni trg,** marked by the beautifully remodeled **Robba's Fountain (Robbov Vodnjak),** originally completed in 1751 and celebrating the confluence of the three Carniolan rivers (the Ljubljanica, the Sava, and the Krka). The fountain is just in front of the **Town Hall (Magistrat),** which you can visit for free; exhibitions are occasionally held in the interior courtyard. Medieval Mestni trg is a defining part of Old Town, as is **Old Square (Stari trg)** at its southern, narrowing end. Together, Mestni, and Stari squares form a lively pedestrian cobblestone avenue lined with shops, restaurants, and cafes, and culminating with the massive early-17th-century **St. James' Church.**

As Mestni trg curves east, you'll notice the looming **Cathedral of St. Nicholas ★**, an important religious building in the baroque style, defined by its high dome and massive bell towers. Started in 1701, the cathedral was designed by Andrea Pozzo; its interiors are famous for frescoes by Quaglio, depicting miraculous moments in the life of St. Nicholas, the patron saint of all seafaring people. Worth a look are the bronze sculpted church doors, added for the 1996 visit of Pope John Paul II (whose image can be seen looking over the history of Slovene Christianity on the main doors).

Adjacent the cathedral is the **Market** ★, another of Plečnik's designs. Just north of the market, crossing the Ljubljanica out of Old Town, is **Dragon's Bridge (Zmajski Most)** ★★★; designed by Jurij Zaninovich and completed in 1901, four fabulously sculpted dragons adorn each corner of the bridge. Legend states that the dragons wag their tails in the unlikely event of an old virgin crossing the bridge. Just beyond the bridge, if you head east along **Trubarjeva cesta,** you'll encounter a distinctive student culture, with a succession of cheap cafes, adventure companies, and New Age shops such as the hemp-based cosmetics outfit, Extravaganja. Turn off Trubarjeva into **Vidovdanska cesta,** which soon gives way to interesting **Metelkova,** an area experiencing progressive urban renewal and a heady nightlife. Formerly the barracks of the JNA (Yugoslav People's Army), the buildings that comprise the Metelkova project have been reclaimed to serve as a center of alternative youth and student culture; this is steadily being transformed into Ljubljana's expanding museum quarter. The project has long been famous thanks to **Celica** ★, a prison-turned-hostel, known for its artistically renovated cells (p. 663); nonresidents can call ✆ **01/430-1890** to arrange a visit.

Near the Celica is Metelkova's highbrow **Slovene Ethnographic Museum** ★★, Metelkova 2 (✆ **01/300-8700;** www.etno-muzej.si), which sheds light on the relationship between humankind and the multitudinous objects that make up our world, be they part of survival, evolution, or everyday existence. You can join the pottery workshops that are held in the trendy-looking studio near the entrance. Or, better still, grab a drink at the cool cafe-bar (called **S.E.M.**) at the entrance.

Back in Old Town, on the western side of the river, **Congress Square (Kongresni trg)** is a fine urban park named in honor of the Congress of the Holy Alliance, for which it was laid out in 1821. Of note around the square are the **Ursuline Church** (1726), the **Kazina** (a 19th-c. establishment hangout), the *fin de siècle* **University** building, and the contemporaneous **Slovene Philharmonic Hall (Slovenska Filharmonija)** ★, which is the headquarters of the country's celebrated Philharmonic Orchestra, which traces its roots to the 1701 Academia Philharmonicorum, making it one of the world's oldest music societies.

Vegova ulica runs south from Kongresni trg, passing the **National and University Library** (reviewed below), and terminating at the 1929 **Illyrian Monument** (another of Plečnik's contributions), which marks **French Revolution Square (Trg Francoske revolucije).** Here, if you're interested to learn much more about the history of the city, you should take time out to visit the recently reopened **City Museum of Ljubljana** ★★, Gosposka 15 (✆ **01/241-2500;** www.mestnimuzej.si; Tues–Sun 10am–6pm). This is also where you'll find the **Križanke Summer Theater;** formerly the Monastery of the Holy Cross, it's now an outdoor theater venue used during the Ljubljana Summer Festival. The complex was redesigned by Plečnik in the 1950s.

Stretching past the open end of Kongresni trg is **Slovenska cesta,** the city's main road. Just north of the square is the "famous" **Nebotičnik "skyscraper."** Designed by Vladimir Subic, this is the "Rockefeller Center of the Balkans." Commissioned in the 1930s, it was then Europe's tallest residential building. Sadly, in recent years it became Ljubljana's favorite suicide spot, prompting the closure of the upper level to allow for the building of a protective fence around the top-floor perimeter.

West of Slovenska cesta is the gorgeous **Opera House** ★★, along Cankarjeva cesta; it was built in the neo-Renaissance style in 1892, and is worth seeing just for the loveliness of its facade, although it'll be undergoing renovation until around mid-2009. Farther west, on Prešernova cesta, are the two main art galleries (both reviewed below), and

Tivoli Park ★, where you can visit the **International Center of Graphic Arts** ★, Pod turnom 3 (✆ **01/241-3800;** www.mglc-lj.si), occupying mansionlike Tivoli Castle (it's a 10-min. walk from Old Town, or you can hop on a bus to Hala Tivoli). The Center hosts excellent temporary programs with diverse themes, from street art and film and theater costumes, to amazing record cover designs. Also in the park is Ljubljana's **National Museum of Contemporary History,** Celovška cesta 23 (✆ **01/300-9610;** www.muzej-nz.si), which makes for a possible diversion; exhibits highlight significant moments from 20th-century Slovenia.

Back near the Opera House the **National Museum,** Muzejska ulica 1 (✆ **01/241-4400;** www.narmuz-lj.si; Fri–Wed 10am–6pm, Thurs 10am–8pm), where the prize possessions include Slovenia's oldest discovered artwork (a 5th-century-B.C. Iron Age bronze urn known as the Vače Situla), the world's oldest wheel, and the earliest musical instrument. The museum occupies a neo-Renaissance palace built in 1883 to 1885; in the same building is the **Museum of Natural History.**

Just south of the museum building is **Trg Republike,** an unattractive square where concrete blocks hide **Cankarjev Dom,** a major space for cultural events and exhibitions. Also here is the **Parliament,** marked by an interesting sculpted relief around the entrance; the figures represent different aspects of social and industrial life.

Farther south of the center is the residential suburb of **Trnovo,** with a small, burgeoning cafe culture that attracts a mixed crowd; it's also where you'll find **Plečnik's House** ★, behind Trnovo Church at Karunova ulica 4 (✆ **01/540-0346;** www.aml.si; Tues–Thurs 10am–6pm and Sat 9am–3pm).

Top Attractions

Architectural Museum ★★ Somewhat off the beaten track, the city's Arhitekturni Muzej is likely to be a highlight for anyone interested in learning about the built environment—at least as far as it pertains to Ljubljana's urban planning god, Jože Plečnik. Housed in a 16th-century Renaissance castle, **Grad Fužine,** the "museum" is more accurately a tribute solely to Plečnik, centered on a condensed version of his "Paris Exhibition," which wowed visitors to the Pompidou 2 decades ago.

Fužine Castle, Pot na Fužine 2. ✆ **01/540-0346.** www.arhmuz.com. Admission 3€ ($3.80). Mon–Fri 9am–3pm; Sat 10am–6pm; Sun 10am–3pm.

Ljubljana Castle ★★ According to the legends, the dragon slain by St. George lived beneath the hill on which **Ljubljanski Grad** is situated, and around which the capital has grown. Start your exploration of the city up here, where you can climb up one of the watchtowers and admire the whole of Ljubljana, which turns out to be a little larger than it seems when you're caught up in the relaxed sybaritic ambience of Old Town. A new gondola-style funicular whisks you up to the castle in record time (departing from adjacent the puppet theater, not far from the market); at the top, there's a lovely terrace cafe and a good souvenir shop; the open courtyard plays host to many of the events during the Ljubljana Summer Festival. Disappointingly, the castle's **Virtual Museum,** which tells the city's story by means of a plodding stereoscopically projected 3-D documentary, is virtually unbearable; tickets to the **Outlook Tower** ★★ are combined with the virtual show, so people feel forced to endure it—you'd do well to steer clear of its patronizing tone and head directly for the views from the tower.

Ljubljanski Grad. ✆ **01/232-9994.** Funicular 3€ ($3.80) return. Castle entrance free. Funicular, Outlook Tower, and Virtual Museum 3.50€ ($4.45). Guided tours daily at 10am and 4pm June to mid-Sept; 4.50€ ($5.70). For private tours call ✆ **01/232-9994.** Castle Oct–Apr daily 10am–10pm; May–Sept daily 9am–11pm. Outlook Tower and Virtual Museum Oct–Apr daily 10am–6pm; May–Sept daily 9am–9pm. Virtual Museum screenings start every half-hour.

Modern Art Gallery ★★ Ljubljana's Moderna Galerija was designed by Plečnik disciple Edvard Ravnikar. It hosts a lively collection of Slovenian paintings, sculptures, and installation pieces from no earlier than 1950. Standout works include the excellent 1960s surrealist works of Štefan Planinc, and Jože Slak-Doka's graffiti-inspired mixed-media assemblages from the 1980s. There's some eyebrow-raising conceptual art definitely worth checking out, while the quality of temporary exhibitions that are regularly hosted here varies considerably. At press time, the gallery was closed for renovation, so call before you go, and there are plans to host part of the collection in Metelkova in the future.

Tomšičeva 14. ✆ **01/241-6800.** www.mg-lj.si. Admission around 4.50€ ($5.70) adults. Free admission Sat afternoon. Tues–Sat 10am–6pm; Sun 10am–1pm.

National Gallery ★★★ Housed in an interesting architectural juxtaposition of two 19th-century buildings linked by a modern structure in glass and steel, the Narodna Galerija holds the country's largest collection of Slovenian paintings, which are surprisingly good. Art enthusiasts will appreciate the thorough survey of the nation's early modern artists, including work by Mihael Stoj (1803–71), Biedermeier portraitist Joef Tominc (1790–1866), and the Slovene landscapes of Marko Pernhart (1824–71) and Pavel Künl (1817–71). Look out for the interesting works of "realist-Impressionist" Ferdo Vesel (1861–1946) and notable 19th-century painter Anton Ažbe (1862–1905). Also here are works by the first internationally reputable female Slovene artist, Ivana Kobilca (1861–1926), whose pale portraits are exquisitely ghostlike. Ivan Grohar's (1867–1911) modernist techniques include excellent use of color, and there are some striking canvases by Richard Jakopič (1896–1943). Galleries of older, classical works include 17th-century Hans Georg Geiger a Geigerfeld's *St. George Slaying the Dragon* featuring a rather sci-fi-looking beast.

Prešernova cesta 24. ✆ **01/241-5434.** www.ng-slo.si. Admission 7€ ($8.90) adults, 3.50€ ($4.45) seniors, students, and children. Free admission Sat afternoon. Guided tours Tues and Thurs 11am. Tues–Sat 10am–6pm; Sun 10am–1pm.

National and University Library ★★ Perhaps the most important of Pležnik's achievements, the nation's main library (Narodna in univerzitetna knijižnica) is remarkable for the unusual and fascinating design of its exterior walls; part brick, part concrete, and part stone, the redbrick walls are dotted with ancient Roman rocks that appear to be sliding toward the sky. Besides its intriguing design elements, the building is notable for the symbolism of the layout; apparently, the main stairway (as you enter) represents a journey into the light of knowledge. You may be tempted to take a book to the reading room, thanks to its rich furnishings and eye-catching chandeliers.

Rimska cesta. ✆ **01/200-1110.** www.nuk.uni-lj.si. Admission 2€ ($2.55). Guided tour 2.50€ ($3.20). Mon–Fri 8am–8pm, except July 10–Aug 19 when visiting hours are reduced.

SHOPPING

ANTIQUES Ljubljana's **antique flea market ★★★** unleashes its collectibles on the world every Sunday until 1pm. Strung along the edge of the Ljubljanica from the Triple Bridge as far south as it needs to go, it's a cornucopia of bright and faded memories, including some genuine treasures. It's also a great place to meet locals. Along Trubarjeva cesta, the one shop worth visiting is **Carniola Antiqua** ★★ (✆ **01/231-6397**), which carries Slovene art, antiques, assorted historic memorabilia and potentially classy retro gear displayed in a stylish manner that includes clever little museumlike window displays.

ART & IMAGES Exquisite photographs and photographic books are sold at **Galerija Fotografija,** Mestni trg 8 (✆ **01/251-1529;** www.galerijafotografija.si), which also hosts impressive exhibitions of international photographic work. Peruse and shop for paintings by Slovene artists at **Galerija Hest,** Židovska 8 (✆ **01/422-0000;** www.galerijahest-sp.si). **Art.si,** židovska 5 (✆ **01/421-0123;** e-mail art.si@lala.si), is the gallery of Andris Vitlinš, which sells bright contemporary paintings.

BOOKS Two of the finest bookstores in the country are **Azil,** Novi trg 2 ✆ **(01/470-6438;** http://azil.zrc-sazu.si), with an astonishing selection of books dealing with philosophy, art, film, and Slovenia; and **Knjigarna Behemot,** Židovska steva 3 (✆ **01/251-1392;** www.behemot.si). Architecture buffs should pick up the excellent *Architectural Guide to Ljubljana* by Andrej Hrausky and Janez Koželj; it features images and commentary on 107 buildings in the city. You'll find it at **Darila Rokus Gifts,** Gosposvetska Cesta 2 (✆ **01/234-9720;** www.darila.com), also good for other books on Slovenia and its culture.

GLASS & PORCELAIN Rogaška crystal is amongst the few brands for which Slovenia is internationally known, and there's finally an outlet in the capital. You'll find **Rogaška,** Mestni trg 22 (✆ **01/241-2701;** www.steklarna-rogaska.si), with its opulent glassware, opposite the Town Hall. Among the rash of touristy paraphernalia at **Darila Rokus** (see "Books," above), you'll find the distinctive "Janus" crystal wine–cum-coffee glass sets, which make lovely gifts. At **Galerija Marjan Lovsin,** Breg 8 (✆ **01/426-0402;** www.marjanlovsin.com), you can buy vases by Tanja Pak, who hails from a family of glassblowers, and is known for her distinctive "Drops" design. Slovenia's foremost **porcelain** artists, Katja Jurgen Bricman and Jure Bricman, are known for having had their unusual and unique porcelain jewelry modeled by Miss Slovenia in 2003. They have a gallery near Robba Fountain. **Porcelain Catbriyur,** Ciril-Metodov Trg 19 (✆ **041-499-528;** www.catbriyur.net), carries an exclusive range of porcelain cups, bowls, and jewelry.

HOMEWARE & FURNITURE To ogle Slovene style, visit **Nova,** Levstikov Trg 7 (✆ **01/426-0410;** www.nova-on.net), an inspirational furniture store and lovely nursery. You'll find gorgeous European-design homeware, ornaments, and simple furniture at **DOM Design,** Štefanova 6 (✆ **01/244-3460;** www.domdesign.si).

FASHION For the best in Slovenian designer wear, head to **Oktober,** Tobačna ulica 5 (✆ **01/425-4068**). Alternatively, **Pletilni Studio Draž,** Gornji Trg 9 (✆ **01/426-6041**), is a great little boutique promoting a number of emerging Slovene fashion designers. **Katarina Silk,** Gorni trg 5, next door to Antiq Hotel, deals in stylish silk garments.

FOODSTUFFS Showcasing produce from the Karst region, **Kraševka** ★★★, Ciril Metodov Trg 10 (✆ **01/232-1445;** www.krasevka.si), is a great place to stock up on organic cheeses, olives oil, stuffed olives, cured meats, honey, dried mushrooms, teas, herbs, and plum brandy.

SHOES & ACCESSORIES Accessorize with a fashionable handmade handbag by award-winning **Marjeta Grošelj,** Tavčarjeva ulica 4 (✆ **01/231-8984**). For eccentric shoes and boots with fancy buckles and interesting decorative motifs, you can't beat the idiosyncratic footwear made and sold at **Obulalnica Butanoga,** Levstikov Trg 8 (✆ **01/425-9888** or 041-334-701; www.butanoga.org), a little cobbler's boutique hidden down an alleyway off Levstikov trg; look for the hanging signboard across from St. James's Church.

WINE Pick up wine from Slovenia's top-rated Movia Estate (owned by Mirko and Ales Kristancic) at **Vinoteka Movia★★**, Mestni Trg 2 (✆ **01/425-5448**); the intimate wine cellar is not only a sales point, but an excellent place for tastings, accompanied by an informative pitch. For a wider range of vintages from all of Slovenia's wine-growing regions, visit **Dvor★**, Dvorni trg 2 (✆ **01/251-1257**).

LJUBLJANA AFTER DARK

Live Music, Theater & Opera

The performing arts are very much alive in the capital, and in summer there is likely to be street theater, especially in and around Old Town—keep eyes and ears pealed. For cutting-edge productions look out for shows conceived by **Draga Živadinov,** the native Ljubljaniker responsible for staging the world's first theatrical production in a weightless environment, somewhere far above Russia.

Theatergoers should make every effort to catch a show at the beautifully designed **Slovene National Opera and Ballet Theater★★★**, Župančičeva 1 (✆ **01/241-1700;** www.opera.si); performances by its 117-year-old resident company are critically acclaimed (**box office** ✆ **01/241-1764**). You can also ask about plans for the new, modern opera house, to be built in the next few years.

During the famous **Ljubljana Summer Festival ★★** (✆ **01/241-6000;** www.ljubljanafestival.si), performances of all kinds—film, theater, jazz, chamber music, opera, ballet, symphony concerts, theater, puppetry—are held in venues around the city. Main venues are Ljubljana Castle, and the **Križanke Summer Theater★★★**, Trg Francoske Revolucije 1. Križanke is also the venue for **Druga Godba ★★**, literally "the Other Music," an alternative music festival held in late May; and in late June, it hosts the **Ljubljana Jazz Festival★★**.

Classical music fans should attend a performance of the **Slovene Philharmonic★★★**, which enjoys a proud 307-year musical tradition; performances are held at the Philharmonic Hall, Kongresni trg (✆ **01/241-0800**). Look out for straight theater and musicals at the **Slovene National Theater,** Narodno Gledališče, Erjavčeva 1 (✆ **01/252-1511**), although the modern **Cankarjev Dom,** Trg Republike (✆ **241-7299;** www.cd-cc.si), is now the main venue for stage productions.

You can catch **live music** spilling out from the terrace of one of the popular cafe-bars at Triple Bridge, nightly in summer; a fun crowd gathers to take in the free entertainment. If you'd like to get a taste of Slovenia's **alternative music scene,** find out what's happening in the Metelkova cultural precinct; start your investigation at any of the Tourist Information offices, or simply wander along **Trubarjeva cesta** and pop your head into any of the trendy-looking stores, or you can opt to inquire at the **Celica Youth Hostel.**

Bars & Clubs

You could spend days just cruising for your favorite place to drink; virtually all of these establishments are cafe-bar hangouts equally good for coffee, beer, wine, and cocktails. Some also serve ice cream in summer (**Cacao ★★**, on the water's edge at Prešernov Square, is a favorite). Many places also carry light meals, so you can forgo restaurants entirely if you're in a party mood.

Drinking along the Ljubljanica is the most popular activity in town, and **Maček★**, Krojaška ulica 5 (✆ **01/425-3791**), inexplicably obsessed with pussycats, has long been *the* favored people-watching haunt. Still, there are some sexy alternatives, like **Fétiche Bar★★**, Stari trg 25 (✆ **040-700-370**), which scores high points for its dramatic interior decor and dark, broody design, complete with provocative poster-size images of models most of the clientele aspires to be. Electronic vibes set a relaxed mood at **Salon ★★**, Trubarjeva 23 (© 01/439-8760), a fun lounge bar with a distinctly shagadelic look—padded walls, plush sofas, gold drapes, and dazzling mirror-ball effect behind the small bar; you'll need to dress for success. Each summer, the garden of the Writer's Society (behind the opera house) hosts **Jazz Club Gajo ★★**, Beethovnova 8 (© **01/425-3206;** www.jazzclubgajo.com), where you can sit under the trees, or sip your drink in a hammock.

The only real club in the center is **Bachus ★★**, Kongresni trg 3 (© **01/241-8244;** www.bachus-center.com), and it draws a mixed crowd to its late nights of DJ-fueled fun, making this arguably Ljubljana's hippest discothèque.

4 THE JULIAN ALPS (JULIJSKE ALPE)

Vršič Pass in the Julian Alps ranks as the most exciting drive in Slovenia, its hairpin (and hair-raising) bends offering views of soaring peaks that define the northwestern corner of the country. Straddling Triglav National Park, and hemmed in by the Karavanke Mountains to the east and the Julian Alps range to the west, the lakes of Bled and Bohinj are two of Slovenia's most treasured resorts, both an easy getaway from Ljubljana and a great base for all kinds of outdoor adventures. Farther west, along the Italian border, and best reached via the aforementioned Vršič Pass, is the Soča River and the beautiful valley it has carved. Here, the tiny town of Kobarid retains memories of battles that raged along the border at a most critical time in the history of Europe. Besides sheltering some of the nation's finest restaurants and accommodations, Kobarid makes a fine base for exploring the valley by land or water. In winter, nearby Bovec fills up with skiers who prefer their adrenaline rush dusted with white powder.

THE LAKES

Bled: 50km (31 miles) NW of Ljubljana. Bohinj: 26km (16 miles) SW of Bled

Bled is a lake fit for a fairy tale—complete with dramatically situated cliff-top castle, an island church, and wraparound mountain scenery; the shock of its electric turquoise surface is emblazoned on tourism materials everywhere. Situated in a national park, Bohinj manages to resist the limelight, and hasn't seen so much overwrought development. A Swiss hydropath named Arnold Rikli (1823–1906) first developed health tourism at Bled after spending years "studying" the beneficial effects of its water, clean air, and sun. Today, it's one of the most fashionable destinations in Europe, drawing an upmarket crowd as well as loads of young trendsetters and outdoor enthusiasts from all over the world. It also draws hordes of day-trippers at the weekend, yet the crowds never seem to overwhelm the sheer loveliness of the resort, which offers plenty to do. Popular trips from Bled include the Babji Zob Caves and Vintnar Gorge. Also nearby is the exquisite town of **Radovljica.**

Essentials

Bled is reached by driving from Ljubljana along the expressway that goes to Jesenice; follow the signs from the Lesce turnoff. **Trains** from Ljubljana stop in the nearby town of Lesce, Železniška ulica 12 (© **04/294-4154/7**), where you'll need to catch one of the regular buses to Bled. **Buses** arrive at Avtobusna postaja Bled at Cesta svobode 4 (© **04/578-0420**). The **Tourist Information Office** is at Cesta Svobode 15 (© **04/574-1122;** www.bled.si), around the corner from the casino entrance.

The nearest train station for **Lake Bohinj** is at Bohinjska Bistrica, which isn't served by trains from the capital. **Buses** stop at Ribčev Laz, at the head of the lake, right near the office of the helpful **Bohinj Tourist Association (Turistično društvo Bohinj),** Ribčev Laz 48 (✆ **04/574-6010;** www.bohinj.si), open daily 8am to 8pm in summer. Buses also continue to Ukanc at the far side of the lake, although fitter types like to walk, and you can also opt for a boat ride across the water.

Where to Stay

Bled's infrastructure is fairly sophisticated, evident in its excessive lineup of large hotels, many of which cater to tour buses. Lake Bohinj has fewer options, and most of these are smaller pensions with homey accommodations at good rates; the tourist offices will be able to point you toward such bargains.

In Bled

Budget hunters who you don't mind bunking up and sharing bathroom facilities should consider spending the night at **Bledec Youth Hostel,** Grajska cesta 17 (✆ **04/574-5250;** www.mlino.si), one of Europe's best, with a terrace overlooking the lake. Still, it's a hostel; a big step up is quaint and lovely **Mayer Penzion,** Želeška 7 (✆ **04/576-5740;** www.mayer-sp.si), a family-run operation with comfortable en suite guest rooms (70€–75€/$89–$95 double) and a small cottage apartment (100€/$127 double) right near the lake; dining here is excellent.

If you want a touch of class, but can't face the chance of dour service at the Grand Toplice or wince at the prices at Vila Bled (both below), consider bedding down at **Hotel Lovec ★**, Ljubljanska 6 (✆ **04/576-8615;** www.kompas-lovec.eu), a part of the Best Western Premier chain with doubles for 133€ to 171€ ($169–$217). There are pricier deluxe units, too, but you should be more than comfortable in one of the standard rooms provided you book a lake-facing unit with a balcony.

Grand Hotel Toplice ★ Built in 1931, Bled's most opulent hotel is an ivy-covered stone building right at the water's edge. In summer, guests flock to the wooden deck that hovers over the water and affords immaculate views across the lake and up to the castle. Interiors are styled with antiques and Persian rugs, plenty of carved wood, and crystal chandeliers. You simply *must* reserve a lake-facing room (which all have balconies behind shuttered doors) to make the most of the most awesome setting in town. Indeed, the setting—and that staggering view (which also accompanies breakfast)—is what earns this fading grande dame a star. Sadly, service standards have fallen in recent years (and some of the public areas could do with an injection of vitality), but that doesn't detract from the sublime views. Although bedrooms aren't enormous, they're well proportioned, with parquet floors and air-cushioned mattresses, and decor signals an earlier era in luxury travel; suites are beautiful, with solid antiques. There's a full on-site spa, with naturally heated indoor pool fed by thermal waters and a drinking fountain with mineral water tapped straight from the earth.

Cesta svobode 12, 4260 Bled. ✆ **04/579-1000.** Fax 04/574-1841. www.hotel-toplice.si. 87 units. 156€–218€ ($198–$277) double; 250€–600€ ($318–$762) suite. Rates include breakfast and VAT. AE, DC, MC, V. **Amenities:** Restaurant; bar; terrace; lounge; outdoor pool; golfing privileges; spa w/thermal pool; sauna; spa treatments; room service; massage; laundry. *In room:* A/C, TV, Internet, minibar, hair dryer, safe.

Vila Bled ★★★ One of Slovenia's two Relais & Châteaux properties, this estatelike hotel is set in lovely gardens near the edge of the lake. Originally a royal villa, then rebuilt as a country retreat for Marshall Tito's favored guests in 1947, the hotel has since seen the likes of Prince Charles, William Hurt, and Jeff Bridges. Accommodations are divided between huge suites and fairly small doubles. Reserve a suite for a real sense of being on Tito's VIP list: Decked out with parquet floors, massive windows, and big Art Deco furniture, they have a distinctive Soviet atmosphere conjuring up memories of secret meetings in a smoke-filled haze. The 1950s styling includes idiosyncratic period pieces such as chunky telephones and gigantic ashtrays, and everything—from silverware to waste bins—has been monogrammed. The hotel has a private "lido" on the lake (basically a wooden deck for sunbathing), and boats are available so you can row yourself to Bled Island. Do visit the first-floor meeting room, where Tito had his private cinema; the walls feature Slavko Pengov's pro-Yugoslav frescoes dating back to 1947. Even if you don't spend the night, book a table at the **Vila Bled Restaurant** ★★★, offering the best food and service in town; dishes are better priced than you might imagine (mains range from 18€–28€/$23–$36). ***Note:*** At press time, there was news of changed ownership at Vila Bled, so there may be plans afoot that may impact services offered here.

Cesta svobode 18, 4260 Bled. ✆ **04/579-1500.** Fax 04/574-1320. www.vila-bled.com. 30 units. 208€–228€ ($264–$290) double; 228€–288€ ($290–$366) suite; 288€–318€ ($366–$404) superior suite; 688€ ($874) presidential suite. Rates include breakfast and VAT. AE, DC, MC, V. **Amenities:** 2 restaurants; bar; golfing; tennis court; spa baths; Jacuzzi; sauna; travel assistance; business facilities and meeting rooms; room service; massage; babysitting by arrangement; laundry; lakeside bathing area; rowboats; aromatherapy. *In room:* Fan, TV, minibar, hair dryer, safe.

Around Lake Bohinj

Vila Parc ★★ (Finds) Stylish and beautiful, Vila Park is a pitch-roofed chalet-style lodge with roughly cut lawns and a low wooden gate; behind its shuttered windows, there's a certain trendiness that's far removed from the rusticated pensions that dominate Ukanc, at the western end of Bohinj Lake. Opened in 2004, and still gleaming with the fresh appeal of a good idea, guest rooms and public spaces show contemporary style; they're done out in pale blue and mushroom shades, with crisp white linens that still feel brand new. Each room has a balcony and a lovely en suite shower. Downstairs, there's a gorgeous wood-floored restaurant and a lounge with hi-fi system, CD collection, and a selection of *National Geographic* magazines; in case you're here in winter, there's an inviting fireplace.

Ukanc 129, 4265 Bohinjsko Jezero. ✆ **04/572-3300** or 041-622-105. Fax 04/572-3312. www.vila-park.si. 12 units. 100€–120€ ($127–$152) double; 120€–140€ ($152–$178) double with half board. Rates include breakfast and taxes. AE, DC, MC, V. **Amenities:** Restaurant; bar; TV room and lounge; room service; laundry. *In room:* TV, Wi-Fi, safe.

Where to Dine

The best restaurant in Bled is at **Vila Bled** (see above). For something more down-home, **Glostina pri Planincu** ★, Grajska 8 (✆ **04/574-1613**) is so popular you'll have your menu whisked away before you've had a chance to make sense of the Slovenian listings. For a more relaxed atmosphere, head to nearby **Glostina Murka** ★, Riklijeva 9 (✆ **04/574-3340;** www.gostilna-murka.com). Operating since 1909, it offers authentic Slovene cuisine, including barley soup made with dried meat, and traditional pork sausages; veal steak is served with boletus mushrooms; the venison in a juniper berry sauce.

Purely for the lovely setting, it's worth stopping by for a light meal at **Vila Prešeren** ★, Veslaška promenade 14 (✆ **04/575-2510**), where you can spend hours savoring the moment over a glass of wine on the wooden deck right at the edge of Lake Bled. Their gateaux isn't half bad, either.

Gostišče Erlah ★ (Value) SLOVENE This relaxed little eatery near Lake Bohinj affords sumptuous mountain views from its covered garden terrace. Menus are on a wooden platter and there's a strong fish bias, with plenty of fresh trout. You can, however, get meatier items, like steak, turkey, or roast sausage (served with cabbage); there's also a mixed grill platter, and even burgers *(pleskavica)* for the kids. Particularly popular is the "Ukanc" plate for two, which comes with meat, turkey, and vegetables. Remember that Erlah is in the country, so service can be slow—not a problem considering how polite and gentle the staff is.

Ukanc 67, Bohinjsko jezero. ✆ **04/572-3309.** www.erlah.com. Main courses 6€–18€ ($7.60–$23). MC, V. Daily 7:30am–11pm in summer; weekends 9am–10pm in winter.

Exploring Bled and the Lakes

Allow time to dally around both of the lakes (both reviewed below), and definitely take to the waters if you're here in summer. Both lakes are starting points for rewarding hikes—either right around the lakes themselves or into the valleys and gorges nearby. It may be a serious splurge but consider reserving a scenic flight over the lakes; contact **Alpski Letalski Center** in Lesce (✆ **04/532-0100;** www.alc-lesce.si) to organize a panoramic flight over Bled, Bohinj, and Mount Triglav. Over and above the normal summer chaos, each July sees Bled host **Bled Days (Blejski Dnevi),** a festival that includes music concerts and ends with fireworks and the spectacular sight of thousands of lit candles floating on the lake. Earlier in the same month, there's a highly regarded festival of classical music (www.festivalbled.com). In August, Bled prepares for a lineup of world music entertainments as part of the **Okarina Etno Festival** ★★; concerts are inspirational and free.

Bled's pseudo-Gothic **St. Martin's Parish Church (Cerkov Svetega Martina)** ★ is situated below the castle, overlooking the lake. Consecrated in 1905, it is worth visiting for the intriguing interior frescoes by Slavko Pengov (the same artist responsible for the paintings in Tito's former cinema at Vila Bled); in particular look for the clever rendition of the Last Supper, in which Judas has been depicted as none other than Comrade Lenin!

Five kilometers (3 miles) northeast of Bled, the River Radovna has carved the mile-long **Vintgar Gorge** ★★, one of Slovenia's great natural attractions. Visitors can experience the spectacle of rushing rapids and gushing waterfalls, which include the 13m (43-ft.) Šum Waterfall, by traversing the bridges and walkways put in place since the end of the 19th century, when the gorge was first opened to the public. To get there, leave Bled via Prešerenova cesta, heading toward Podhom (there are plenty of signs), which marks the public entrance; there's a small admission fee. **Babji Zob Caves** ★★, named for the monstrous-looking "Hag's Tooth" rock formation above them, are some 4km (2½ miles) west of Bled, and require participation in a 3-hour guided tour.

Bled Castle (Blejski Grad) ★★ Backed by Mount Triglav and the Julian Alps, the real drama of Bled Castle is its striking position atop a sheer cliff, 138m (460 ft.) up. The castle traces its history back to 1004, and was once the center of an important self-sufficient state measuring 900 sq. km (351 sq. miles), and ruled by the bishops of Brixen. Today it's the most obvious of Bled's attractions, but perhaps a little jaded because of various restoration projects over the centuries. It houses a recently revamped museum that traces the history of the region over many millennia, and there's a chapel with lovely original frescoes. But the real reward for making the journey to the top (around 15 min. by foot via three different paths, or 5 min. by car, after which there's still a stiff climb up the final stretch): **Views** ★★★ from the castle ramparts are without equal. There's also a restaurant and ice-cream shop at the top, and if you want an unusual souvenir, you can bottle, cork, and label your own Slovenian vintage in the historic wine cellar.

Rečiška cesta 2, Bled. ✆ **04/572-9782.** www.blejski-grad.si. Admission 7€ ($8.90) adults, 3.50€ ($4.45) children. Daily 8am–8pm May–Oct; daily 8am–5pm Nov–Apr.

Lake Bled (Blejsko jezero) ★★★ Lake Bled is a jewel, pure and simple. Nestled between two great mountain ranges—the Karavanke and the Julian Alps, which tumble into Slovenia from Austria and Italy, respectively—there is something indescribably beautiful about the way in which the surface of the water changes through the day, wearing its striking turquoise facade when the sun is brightest, and maturing to a silver-blue as dusk descends. Swans swoop down over its surface, and gondolier-style oarsmen steer their *pletna* across the waters (transporting tourists for an outrageous fee), adding to the fairy-tale idea of the place; occasionally a fierce and noisy rowing regatta changes the energy entirely. To get a good idea of the size of the lake, and to appreciate it from every angle, walk the hour-long route around its perimeter. Adding to the drama of its setting is its darling islet forming a perfect centerpiece: You can row (or be rowed) to **Bled Island (Blejski Otok)** ★★★, but more adventurous types like to break the "official" rules and swim to it—an utterly invigorating exercise, this is highly recommended if you're a strong swimmer. On the island is the delightful **Church of the Assumption** ★★, dedicated to both Mary the Virgin and Mary Magdalene, and built on the site where the ancestors of modern Slovenes worshipped an ancient Slavic goddess. The pagan idol was broken down in the 11th century when Slovenes were Christianized. People from all over Slovenia come here to tie the knot on Saturdays, only to discover that the tradition of carrying the bride up the 99 stairs to the church is tough (many grooms, in fact, conduct test runs before the wedding day, in order to avert an embarrassing disaster). Inside the church, look out for the frescoed reference to Christ's circumcision, a seldom-seen reminder that Jesus was Jewish. ***Note:*** If you swim to the island, you won't be able to explore the church unless you ask someone to bring a change of clothing by boat.

Bled. ✆ **04/578-0500.** Admission to the Church of the Assumption 3€ ($3.80); daily 8am–sunset.

Lake Bohinj (Bohinjsko jezero) ★★★ Measuring over 4km (2½ miles) long, Bohinj is the largest permanent lake in Slovenia. Because it's inside Triglav National Park, it has been spared the rapacious development which has affected Bled, so there's no town on its shores; instead, there are small villages nearby and there's a road connecting its two ends, Ribčev laz and Ukanc, where you'll find a range of accommodations. Visible on the local flag, the **Church of St. John the Baptist** ★★, at the head of the lake, near Hotel Jezero, is Bohinj's best-known man-made attraction, mostly built in 1520 and renowned for its interior frescoes. For heart-stopping views of Bohinj and the Julian Alps, take the cable car up **Mount Vogel,** or head for the **Vodnikov razglednik viewpoint.** Bohinj's Tourist Association can suggest walks to bring you closer to the lake's many charms. From Ukanc, you can hike to **Savica Falls,** the best-known of Slovenia's 260 waterfalls, immortalized in France Prešeren's epic poem, *Baptism on the Savica,* published in 1836, and dedicated to his friend who drowned in the Sava a year before. The two-pronged waterfall measures 51m (167 ft.); the gushing water comes from Black Lake (Črno jezero) half a kilometer farther up. There's a small fee to be paid at the entrance to the path leading to a wooden pavilion that offers the best views of the falls.

Bohinjsko jezero. ✆ **04/574-6010.** www.bohinj.si/tdbohinj.

Tips Golfing at Bled

Slovenia's top golfing spot, **Bled Golf and Country Club** (www.golf.bled.si), is just 4km (2½ miles) from the lake, and includes thrilling views; the 18-hole King's Course was laid out by Donald Harradine, and is the country's oldest. Ask your hotel to book your tee time several days ahead of schedule.

Moments Vršič Pass: The Drive of Your Life

Slovenia's best drive traverses **Vršič Pass** ★★★, an awesome journey between Kranjska Gora, just north of Triglav National Park, over Mount Vršič, and down to the town of Trenta. The intense (and intensely beautiful) drive takes you through staggering views of soaring rocky peaks and lush, plunging valleys. It's the most spectacular way of traveling the otherwise short distance between Bled and the Soča Valley, but requires cautious driving to negotiate 50 numbered hairpin bends along the 25km (16-mile) roller-coaster route. At bend number eight, the **Russian Chapel (Ruska kapelica)** honors the 300-odd Russian prisoners of war who died in an avalanche while building the road; near bend 21 is the **cemetery** for the thousands more who died during construction, often starved or tortured to death. There are great viewing sites along the way; the highest point (at 1,611m/5,284 ft.) is **Vršič,** where there's a parking fee. Be aware that the road can be alarmingly narrow; some drivers speed in spite of this. Cows and sheep may stumble across the way; cyclists, too, are ubiquitous, but usually more alert.

Adventures in & Around the Lakes

Bled's **Lifetrek Adventures** ★ (✆ **04/578-0662;** www.lifetrek-slovenia.com) offers a variety of water- and mountain-based adventures to meet your level of experience. **3Glav Adventures** (✆ **041-683-184;** www.3glav-adventures.com) targets a younger crowd.

Skiing around Bohinj is arguably the best in the country from a scenic point of view. Cable cars whisk passengers from the western end of Lake Bohinj to **Ski Center Vogel,** from where there are chairlifts for skiers wishing to access some of the higher reaches of the Triglav Mountain range. In Bohinj, **Alpinsport** (✆ **04/572-3486;** www.alpinsport.si) is the place to hire an instructor and ski equipment.

For an adrenaline quick fix during the summer months when skiing is no longer possible, consider taking the plunge on Bled's new **summer tobogganing ride** (✆ **04/578-0534**), a 520m (1,706 ft.) high-speed descent on a fixed track that simulates the rush of winter tobogganing with Lake Bled spread out before you.

Besides offering scenic flights, **Alpski Letalski Center** (www.alc-lesce.si) runs gliding courses in two-seater and Alpine gliders, and Cessna flying courses for beginners. If you'd rather feel the wind beneath your feet, ask Alpski to arrange a tandem parachuting jump from 3,000m (9,840 ft.); you'll be enjoying the same perfect free-falling views enjoyed by jumpers during the world parachuting championships. **Pac Sports** (✆ **04/572-3461;** www.pac-sports.com) is the place to call if you feel like a spot of tandem paragliding instead: same breathtaking views but a lot less scary.

THE SOČA VALLEY: KOBARID & BOVEC

A haven for adventurers, the valley formed by the electric turquoise advance of the Soča—one of Europe's loveliest rivers—is scintillating. This part of the country is blessed with gorgeous mountain views, splendid towns, plenty of well-organized sports outfitters, and a people who are as charming as they are relaxed. It may be Slovenia's least developed region, with a dwindling population of just 19,000 (generally due to overeducation!), but it is likely to provide many of the defining moments of your visit to Slovenia. Kobarid is at the heart of the more exclusive and developed portion of the valley, offering its best accommodations, and two of the country's finest restaurants. Slightly north of Kobarid, Bovec is one of the prime adventure resorts in Slovenia; it's an excellent ski resort and ideal for access to the Soča River, which hosts a number of international rafting competitions. The valley is also great for biking, with extreme cycling races held around Bovec—and given the enchanting topography, a wonderful place to observe from the air, making paragliding particularly popular.

Getting There

From Bled and Bohinj, the most exciting way to get to Bovec or Kobarid is by driving over the Vršič Pass, via the Kranjska Gora winter resort; there is also a bus that traverses the pass at a very gentle speed.

Essentials

Kobarid's Tourist Information Office, Gregorčičeva 8 (✆ **05/380-0490;** www.lto-sotocje.si), is very helpful, and will make suggestions around which walks, bike rides, or other adventures are best suited to your schedule and ability. **Bovec Tourist Information Center,** Trg Golobarskih žrtev 8 (✆ **05/389-6444;** www.bovec.si), is largely geared toward providing information about sports activities, but will also help you find accommodations.

Where to Stay

Besides the recommended options below, budget hunters looking to sample local life can inquire at the tourist information offices about the opportunity to overnight in mountain cottages and stay in village homes. You won't find luxury, but you will take home an altogether different understanding of life in this tranquil valley; expect to pay between 20€ and 30€ ($25–$38) per person.

Dobra Vila Bovec ★★★ Value This handsome villa in Bovec offers a touch of class in a town that's generally geared more toward sporty types than those who prefer their adventures wrapped in elegance. It's easily the most gracious place in town, where, after a grueling day on the slopes, you can kick back in a wine cellar, or a library-style drawing room that's perfect for a glass of Slovene wine in front of the fireplace. In summer, there's a terrace and lawns with wonderful views upon which to laze. There's also a smart restaurant where fresh trout is always a sure thing. Guest rooms are big and bright with high ceilings and dark-wood floors; crisp white linens and beautiful bathrooms score high points. Should you be tempted to leave the villa's pleasing comforts, your hostess, Andreja, and her staff can help you book a variety of activities, from horseback riding to sky diving.

Mala vas 112, 5230 Bovec. ✆ **05/389-6400/3.** Fax 05/389-6404. www.dobra-vila-bovec.com. 10 units. 88€–135€ ($112–$171) double; 137€–168€ ($174–$213) triple; 173€–221€ ($220–$281) quad. Rates include half board and taxes. **Amenities:** Restaurant; wine cellar; sports and adventure activities; computer access; laundry; library; rooftop viewing area. *In room:* A/C, TV, DVD player, Internet, minibar, hair dryer.

Hiša Franko Casa ★★★ Value Just 3km ($1^3/_4$ miles) west of Kobarid, on the way to the Italian border, Hiša Franko is pure delight—the creative expression of husband-and-wife team Ana Roš and Valter Kramar. Gorgeous, simple, and dramatic, each guest room is designed to a particular color theme, and offers slick comfort. Choosing a favorite is difficult as each unit has a different shape and design, but all offer wooden floors, smart furniture, silk drapes, and plenty of space. Room nos. 9 and 10 share an amazing enclosed terrace with a chill-out lounge vibe, where you can relax on clever armchairs that light up. With the emphasis firmly on relaxation, there are no telephones, and you need to specify if you'd like to have a television or sound system in your room. A recommended outing is a picnic lunch at Nadiža River, which has Slovenia's cleanest and warmest water, naturally heated by white riverbed rocks.

Staro selo 1, 5222 Kobarid. ✆ **05/389-4120.** Fax 05/389-4129. www.hisafranko.com. 10 units. 110€–135€ ($140–$171) double. Rates include breakfast. 21€ ($27) extra bed. **Amenities:** Restaurant; bar; wine cellar; bike rental; room service; laundry; picnic arrangements; library and CD collection. *In room:* TV, hi-fi, minibar; hair dryer (all by request).

Hotel Hvala ★★ Value What started as a family restaurant in 1976 is quickly expanding into an upmarket hotel, already well known for its brilliant seafood (see Topli Val restaurant review, below) and now experimenting with luxurious suites and (in the near future) a very special spa for post-adventure pampering. A great three-floor hotel, this is the best place to stay in the center of Kobarid. The spotless accommodations have toothpaste-white walls and straightforward modern furniture; as the hotel is upgraded and expanded, however, contemporary designer luxuries are set to redefine the hotel's image. Guest rooms also have balconies and good-size bathrooms, most of which have tubs. While the main focus is on the extremely popular downstairs restaurant, your hosts will take excellent care of you, treating you like a guest in their home, and helping you get in touch with your adventurous side through one of the local activity companies.

Trg svobode 1, 5222 Kobarid. ✆ **05/389-9300.** Fax 05/388-5322. www.hotelhvala.si. 32 units. 104€–112€ ($132–$142) double; 138€–146€ ($175–$185) half board double; 160€–200€ ($203–$254) suite. 30% discount for children 11 and under. Rates include breakfast and VAT. **Amenities:** Restaurant; bar; sauna; bike rental; adventure-activity assistance; car rental; room service; laundry; fishing. *In room:* A/C (suite and 2 rooms), TV, hair dryer.

Nebesa ★★★ Finds Nebesa means "heaven," and it isn't much of an exaggeration, with each of the four private guesthouses, overlooking Kobarid and the Soča Valley, feeling as though it's on the edge of the world. Built in wood, with steeply pitched roofs, the little cottages are designed as a contemporary take on traditional mountain hay-houses. All things considered, they're perfect; the minimalist interiors (wooden floors and smart, simple contemporary furniture) draw attention to the large picture windows that frame those astonishing views you get from the lounge and the upstairs sleeping area. Each unit also has a porch, from which you can play god to the valley below. You also have your own kitchen with a fridge that's stocked for your basic needs. Guests have access to a communal dining area and kitchen, as well as a sauna and fitness room (with meditation and yoga areas). There's a sublime help-yourself cellar with on-tap house wine and prosciutto that you are welcome to shave yourself. From up here, you can see Italy and even feel a sea breeze from the gulf; the neighboring property is home to 30 deer, one of which is tame enough to come when called. What's more, your hosts epitomize Slovene hospitality and will introduce you to the truly debonair spirit of the nation.

Livek 39, 5222 Kobarid. ✆ **05/384-4620.** www.nebesa.si. 4 units. 239€ ($304) per guesthouse; 215€ ($273) per night 2-day stay. Rates are all-inclusive. **Amenities:** Dining room w/kitchen; wine cellar; wellness center w/pool, sauna, and yoga area; laundry. *In room:* Kitchen (fridge, stove, oven, kettle, toaster), hi-fi.

Where to Dine

Hiša Franko ★★★ EXPERIMENTAL You haven't dined in Slovenia until you've tried this hugely innovative restaurant just outside Kobarid. Making magic in the kitchen is Ana Roš, who gave up her career as a national skier when she fell in love, and then discovered a passion for food. Ana's imagination—fueled these days by French and Oriental influences—inspires a regularly changing menu, which might include such dishes as roe buck fillet with rhubarb chutney, and traditional estragon *štrukelj* (dumpling) or perhaps mini rabbit roulades filled with a pistachio, sage, and chocolate sauce. If it's available, try the suckling pig, sometimes served with rhubarb chutney and almond pâté; it's absolute bliss. As are the desserts, like fresh fig salad in sweet spices and red-wine jus with white chocolate foam and toasted almonds. Running the wine department is Ana's lovely husband, Valter Kramar, who trained extensively at Italy's Gradisca d'Isonzo, and knows his wines. He's been cultivating a stellar cellar for years, so this is one meal where you should splurge on a few of his five-star rated wines.

Casa Hişa Franko, Staro Selo 1. ✆ **05/389-4120.** www.hisafranko.com. Main courses 15€–22€ ($19–$28); side dishes 3€ ($3.80); degustation menus 40€–65€ ($51–$83). Cover charge 2.50€ ($3.20). AE, DC, MC, V. Wed–Sun noon–3pm and 7–10pm.

Topli Val ★★★ SEAFOOD This is one of the finest seafood restaurants in central Europe; no wonder regular diners come from across the border to join in the feasting that's best enjoyed on the small terrace on warm summer nights. Do yourself a favor: Ignore the menu and ask your debonair host, Aleš, to suggest what's hot. You'll be served wonderful creations dreamed up by Gorazd and his team. To start there may be a platter of perfect oysters, served with octopus carpaccio in a delicate zest with arugula and mushroom carpaccio, or giant scallops *(jakobove pokrovače)* prepared in olive oil and served with olives and rosa tomatoes. Then move on to whatever fish of the day is recommended; fresh from the Adriatic, it'll be grilled to perfection, and then lightly dusted with olive oil and pepper (from the largest pepper mill you'll ever set eyes on). If you want to sample everything, share the gourmet platter; it includes lobster, sea bass, scallops, mussels, and fish kabobs. Order a bottle of perfect, dry chardonnay from the Goriška Brda region, or one of the perfectly drinkable house wines bottled especially for Topli Val, to go with your meal. Finish with hot blueberries and ice cream, or the famous *Kobariški strukljі,* with ice cream and cinnamon.

In the Hotel Hvala, Trg svobode 1. ✆ **05/389-9300.** Main courses 7.50€–28€ ($9.50–$36). AE, DC, MC, V. Dec–Jan and Mar 15–Oct noon–3pm and 7–10pm.

Exploring Kobarid

Practically on the Italian border, Kobarid is known for the Battle of Kobarid (or Caporetto), which happened here on October 24, 1917, and is considered a key moment in World War I. Pick up a map from the **Tourist Information Office,** Trg Svobode 16 (✆ **05/380-0490;** www.lto-sotocje.si), and set out on the **Kobarid Historical Walk** ★★★, a 3- to 5-hour trail that takes you to some key war sites, and surveys some of the loveliest natural phenomena in the area, including the Kozjak Brook Waterfalls; at one point you'll cross the Soča River on a 52m (171-ft.) suspension bridge. A lovely way to spend the morning, the walk starts at the award-winning Kobarid Museum (reviewed below), considered one of the best of its kind in Europe.

Both Kobarid and Bovec are possible starting points for the **Walk of Peace** (www.potimiruvposocju.si), a newly designated commemorative trail which takes hikers to key positions—including outdoor museums and military cemeteries—along the Isonzo Front, a major conflict area during World War I. You needn't cover the entire route (which would take several days) to discover some intriguing historical sites and naturals vistas; pick up maps from either of the tourist offices.

If your time is more limited, but you'd like to fit in a **walk** through lush forest, there's a 2-hour trail that takes you past several pretty waterfalls, starting at the church of St.

Just; follow signs to Drežnica, and then head for the idyllic village of Koseč to find the church. The best **swimming** in the area is in the Nadiža River.

Kobariski Muzej ★★ Kobarid Museum is an antiwar museum designed to illustrate the senselessness of war. Several rooms, spread over three floors, are filled with war-related paraphernalia, photographs, and excerpts from journals and letters. On the first floor, the Black Room includes horrible photographs of survivors who were savaged by weapons of war. One man shown in profile has lost his nose and upper jaw—left with half his face, he is a dreadful irony juxtaposed with the display beneath of military medals and badges. Nearby, more grotesque photographs of mangled, skeletal war victim corpses are displayed over a number of defunct, "dead" weapons that may very well have been used in their slaughter. Much of the museum deals with the role played by Kobarid during World War I, and some of the displays (particularly those on the ground floor) don't make much sense. There is a 20-minute video, but you'll need to ask when the English version is to be screened.

Gregorčičeva 10. ✆ **05/389-0000.** www.kobariski-muzej.si. 4€ ($5.10) adults; 3€ ($3.80) students and children. Apr–Sept Mon–Fri 9am–6pm, Sat–Sun and public holidays 9am–7pm; Oct–Mar Mon–Fri 10am–5pm, Sat–Sun and public holidays 9am–6pm.

OUTDOOR ACTIVITIES IN THE SOČA VALLEY

Outdoor adventures are usually high on the list of priorities of visitors to this region; in winter there's great skiing, while in summer climbing, hiking, and river-based activities are among the best in the country. One of the top all-round outfits in the Soča Valley is Kobarid-based **X Point ★★★**, Stresova 1 (✆ **05/388-5308** or 041-692-290; www.xpoint.si), which offers rafting, kayaking, paragliding, canoeing, hydrospeeding, canyoning, trekking, and mountain-biking excursions; the company can also set you up with a good ski instructor. Ask owner Dejan Luzar about the company's multiactivity packages. If X Point can't oblige, try Kobarid newcomer **Positive Sport ★★★**, Markova ulica 2 (✆ **040-654-475;** www.positive-sport.com), also recommended. ***Note:*** Private use of the Soča for watersports activities requires a license costing 1.60€ ($2.05) per day.

CANYONING **X Point** has excursions (all equipment included) for different levels of experience; most outings last 2½ to 3 hours and cost around 48€ ($61).

HORSEBACK RIDING You can ride Lipizzaners in the Soča Valley through **Pristana Lepena** (www.pristava-lepena.com). Based in Trnovo ob Soči, between Bovec and Kobarid, **Alpin Action** (✆ **05/384-5504;** www.alpinaction.it) offers a variety of horse-riding packages.

MOUNTAIN BIKING Bovec's bike specialists are **Outdoor Freaks,** Klanc 9a (✆ **05/389-64/90** or 041-553-675; www.freakoutdoor.com); they can rent you a suitable mountain bike and put you onto a number of trails in the **Kanin mountain bike park** (www.mtbparkkanin.com), which opened in 2003. In Kobarid, contact Positive Sport (see above).

PARAGLIDING **Avantura** (✆ **041-718-317;** www.avantura.org) offers tandem paragliding in Bovec. **X Point** offers first-time courses as well as tandem jumps (99€/$126). Skiers should inquire about a combination package in which you paraglide from 1,800m (5,904 ft.) after being on the slopes.

RAFTING & KAYAKING **X Point** and **Positive Sport** (see both above) offer all-inclusive rafting excursions, with some four rapids (38€/$48 per person, including transfers); you'll spend some 90 minutes on the water. Positive Sport runs a kayak school. Also offered by X Point, **hydrospeeding** is a less taxing option, which involves wearing a wet suit and gripping a hand-held navigational board as the current sweeps you down the river.

SKIING & SNOWBOARDING High-altitude skiing in the Kanin Mountains is popular and rewarding. Cable cars take you into the mountain ski areas from **Ski center ATC Kanin,** Dvor 43 (✆ **05/389-6310;** 13€/$17), just beyond Bovec. The circular cabin cableway offers hourly departures from the ski center starting at 8am; the half-hour ascent takes you an altitude of 2,200m (7,216 ft.), from where there's skiing in winter (Dec 20 to early May) and fantastic hiking in summer. As of the 2008/2009 winter season, a new ski pass will be available allowing enthusiasts to sample the slopes on the Italian side of the border. To ask about the various ski passes, head for Bovec's **Information Office,** Trg golobarskih žrtev 47 (✆ **05/389-6003;** Mon–Fri 8am–noon and 1–4:30pm, Sat–Sun and holidays 8am–noon). Note that while out-of-bounds skiing is a possibility, it is dangerous, as navigation in the Kanin is difficult. Local adventure companies can design a bespoke skiing program for you, perhaps taking in three different sets of slopes—on Kanin, Kranjska Gora, and Vogel.

5 THE KARST & SLOVENIA'S TINY SLIVER OF COAST

An ancient word meaning "stone," Slovenia is where the word "Karst" was first coined, and refers to a rocky limestone plateau that links the Soča Valley to Slovenia's tiny piece of Istrian coast. Here you'll find spectacular cave systems, the best of which are the UNESCO-protected Škocjan caves; nearby is Lipica Stud Farm, where the glamorous Lipizzaner horses are sired.

Slovenia's Istrian coast stretches from the bottom edge of the Karst in the north to the Dragonja River in the south, which creates the border with Croatia; this 46km (29-mile) coastline has been a refuge for people since the 7th century, when the Roman Empire collapsed, and the first olive groves and vineyards were established by people fleeing marauders from the east. During the 13th century, these coastal principalities looked to Venice for protection, and so began 500 years of Venetian rule, a period that has imbued the port towns with a distinctive look and attitude that still today make this region a most pleasant sojourn, and possibly the ideal entry into Croatia.

POSTOJNA & ŠKOCJAN CAVES

Slovenia's Karst" landscape has hundreds of subterranean caves. Two of the most fascinating (and best-exploited) cave systems are Postojna and Škocjan, both filled with unbelievable limestone formations, and colored by different minerals, the result of thousands of years of rainwater seeping through the surface of the earth into the underground chambers. Over the eons, these drops of water have caused stalactites and stalagmites to mushroom throughout these vast otherworldly spaces where underground rivers, secret lakes, immense tunnels, and rock-hard formations that look like melted wax form the backdrop against which an unusual albino creature has evolved in almost complete isolation from life above the earth's surface.

Stellar Accommodations en Route to the Caves

Postojna can be visited as a half-day trip from Ljubljana, and Škocjan is near the coastal city of Piran. If you're traveling to either of the caves from anywhere in the Julian Alps, consider breaking up the journey with a night at **Kendov Dvorec** ★★★ (✆ **05/372-5100;** www.kendov-dvorec.com), a 14th-century manor situated roughly midway between Kobarid and Postojna. Accommodations are some of the most refined in the country, with just 11 luxurious guest rooms, furnished with smart antiques; doubles range from 150€ to 280€ ($191–$356).

Essentials

Postojna is situated roughly midway between Ljubljana and the Slovenian coast. Take the Ljubljana-Koper Highway, and follow the signs at Postojna. **Škocjan** is much nearer the coast, also easily reached using the highway. Trains from Ljubljana reach Postojna and Divača, near Škocjan. There is parking and information at the entrances to both sets of caves.

Exploring the Karst

Lipica Stud Farm & Riding Center (Overrated) Lipizzaners, bred here since 1580, are arguably the most intelligent horse breed; certainly their combination of strength and agility has turned them into excellent "dancers," able to perform a number of leaps and pirouettes in choreographed formations to the beat of music. Enthusiasts can visit the stables on a thoroughly dull guided tour, but unless you're hell-bent on traipsing through a series of stables (and sometimes seeing the poor beasts tethered in their stalls), or enjoy looking at collections of disused horse carriages, you really won't find much to hold your attention. If you want to see the famous horses and don't want to feel ripped off by the whole experience, your best bet is to arrive just in time to watch a **dressage performance** ★ (definitely call ahead to confirm these times, officially known as the "Presentation of the Classical riding school") or arrange to ride one of these magnificent thoroughbreds.

Lipica 5, Sežana. ✆ **05/739-1708.** www.lipica.org. Stable and stud farm tours 9€ ($11) adults, 4.50€ ($5.70) students and children. Guided tours Nov–Mar 11am, 1, 2, and 3pm Tues–Sun; Apr–June and Sept–Oct hourly 9am–5pm except at noon daily; July–Aug hourly 9am–6pm except at noon daily. Tour and dressage performance 16€ ($20) adults, 8€ ($10) students and children; Apr–Oct 3pm Tues, Fri, and Sun.

Postojnska Jama ★ Visited by more than 30 million people, the famous Postojna Cave has been an official tourist site since 1818; graffiti signatures prove it's been attracting visitors since the 13th century. The largest of the classic Karst cave systems, with a network of over 20km (12 miles) of chambers and galleries connected by passages and tunnels, this is, quite frankly, the Disneyland of caves, complete with a little tourist train, which each day propels thousands of noisy people through an artificial tunnel and into the heart of the cave system. Visitors then divide into groups on the basis of language (a terribly time-consuming process) before being led off on a tour of Postojna's most representative and exotic chambers; there are galleries with such telling names as Beautiful Cave, the Gothic Hall, and the Brilliant Passage. All in all though, it's a remarkable journey, with a second train trip that gets you even deeper into the system. Along the way, you'll also see the unusual "human fish," a salamander-type creature, or olm *(Proteus* *anguinus)*, that's blind and the color of Caucasian flesh, hence its fanciful nickname. Note that the caves are chilly (46°–50°F/8°–10°C), and walking surfaces slippery; bring something warm and wear nonslip shoes.

Jamska cesta 30, Postojna. ✆ **05/700-0103.** www.postojna-cave.si. Cave admission 19€ ($24) adults, 16€ ($20) students, 12€ ($15) children. Scheduled cave tours Nov–Mar 10am, noon, and 3pm; Apr and Oct 10am, noon, 2, and 4pm; May, June, and Sept hourly 9am–5pm; July–Aug hourly 9am–6pm.

Predjama Castle ★★ (Kids) A mere 10km (6¼ miles) from Postojna, the medieval Predjamski grad is dramatically situated on a 123m (403-ft.) cliff carved into the rock face. Legend has it that this was the hide-out of Slovenia's very own Robin Hood, named Erazem, who was more likely a rebellious thieving baron. Erazem incurred the intense hatred of the governor of Trieste, who laid siege to the castle, before cannonballing it and killing Erazem in 1484. Predjama remains a spectacular sight, perched defiantly against its rocky backdrop—very much the stuff that medieval fantasies are made of. Although the castle's curators have given the interiors a whitewashed museum feel, it's worth getting a ticket to explore inside, if only for the exhilarating views from its stone windows and balconies. Today, reliving the pomp and ceremony of the past is the annual Erazem's Medieval Tournament, with jousting scenes and costumes straight out of *A Knight's Tale;* the event happens in August.

Predjama. ✆ **05/751-6015.** www.postojna-cave.si. Admission 8€ ($10) adults, 7€ ($8.90) students, 5€ ($6.35) children. Guided tour available for a small fee. Nov–Mar daily 10am–4pm; Apr and Oct daily 10am–5pm; May–June and Sept daily 9am–6pm; July–Aug daily 9am–7pm.

Škocjan Caves ★★★ (Value) Far more alluring and peaceful than Postojna, cave exploration doesn't get much better than this. Skočjan is where the first Karstic discoveries were made, and the caves have been spared the onslaught of tourism thanks to the protection of UNESCO. So, no intrusive miniature trains or Disneyland adventure-park atmosphere; here there's a real sense of exploration. Moving through the 3km (1¾-mile) subterranean system (which includes rigorous stairways), you almost sense the voidlike drama of Silent Cave, and become increasingly aware of the subdued roar of the Murmuring Cave, coming from the underground Reka River. Besides spectacular stalactites, stalagmites, and rim limestone pools (resembling those in Pamukkale in Turkey), Škocjan includes what is believed to be the world's largest underground canyon, as well as awesome bridges and drop-away galleries where the vastness of the subterranean world (at one point you're told the parking lot is 140m/459 ft. above your head) undoes everything you think you know about the earth. (***Tip:*** While you wait for your tour to begin, don't miss the Belvedere Viewpoint, overlooking a magnificent gorge with a small waterfall.)

Škocjan 2, Divača. ✆ **05/708-2110.** www.park-skocjanske-jame.si. Admission 14€ ($18) adults, 10€ ($13) seniors and students, 6€ ($7.60) children, free for children 5 and under. Purchase tickets 30 min. before tour. June–Sept hourly guided tours daily 10am–5pm; Nov–Mar guided tours Mon–Sat 10am and 1pm, Sun and public holidays also at 3pm; Apr–May and Oct guided tours daily 10am, 1, and 3:30pm.

PIRAN & THE ISTRIAN COAST

Piran: 120km (74 miles) SW of Ljubljana

Piran is easily the loveliest place along Slovenia's tiny slither of Istrian Coast, drawing inevitable comparisons with Venice which—after 500 years of rule—it echoes in many ways; only here there are no canals—the entire city is built on dry land, rising to a low hill, along which defensive walls are built. Within walking distance of Piran is the modern seaside playground of **Portorož** ("Port of Roses"), with its strutting crowds and concrete resort hotels. Popular with pleasure seekers and always crowded during the peak summer months, it may be a worthwhile clubbing spot if you grow weary of Piran's more restrained nighttime tavern activity. North you'll find two more Italianate ports, Koper and Izola, neither of which is nearly as nice as Piran.

Essentials

While it's an easy drive along the highway from Ljubljana, getting into Piran itself can be a nuisance. If you're driving, you'll need to leave your car in the town's parking lot, just beyond the city limits, which is controlled by boom gates; from here there's a regular shuttle bus to transport you between the parking area and the town center. (You can enter Piran with your vehicle, but you're charged rather heavily for the time you spend on its few cramped roads, and you can forget about finding parking.)

Buses to Piran terminate at the **bus station** on Dantejeva ulica, located just outside the town proper; a short walk around Piran Port, along Cankarjevo nabrežje, takes you to Tartinijeva trg, at the town center. Trains from Ljubljana terminate in Koper, 10km (6¼ miles) northeast of Piran. Piran's helpful **Tourist Information Office** is in the City Hall building, Tartinijev trg 2 (© **05/673-4440**). The students who work there can help you with most anything, including trips to **Izola, Hrastovlje,** and **Sečovlje Salt-pans,** recommended if you have time.

Where to Stay

For the sake of convenience, historic Piran is where you should base yourself, but there are no luxurious options here. If you need your pampering there are numerous upmarket modern resorts with spa facilities that line the waterfront at nearby Portorož; of these, I'm expecting the brand-new **Kempinski Palace Portorož** (www.kempinski.com) to be the finest option on the block. It's a restored historic hotel dating back to 1910 grafted onto a modern construction, sporting multifarious architectural influences. The alternative is the **Grand Hotel Portorož** ★★ (www.hoteli-palace.si), which not only puts on a range of luxuries (including private beach access and some of the finest spa treatments in central Europe), but also frequently announces good-value deals, making its smart, bland rooms more affordable that you might expect. Back in Piran, serious budget hunters may be interested to hear of good-value **Val Hostel,** Gregorčičeva 38a (© **05/673-2555;** www.hostel-val.com), offering accommodations in two-, three-, and four-bed rooms for 22€ to 25€ ($28–$32) per person, breakfast included; facilities are shared, but clean.

Hotel Tartini ★ This classic hotel gets a star for its great position right on Tartini Square—which is why it's usually full in summer months. Other than this it's a fairly standard place with a slightly ramshackle feel; the atrium-style lobby was actually once a road, the hotel having been constructed from two separate houses that were on different sides of the street. The best thing about Tartini is the view of Piran's rooftops afforded by climbing to the gazebo above the second-floor terrace. Guest rooms are neat, clean, and dull, with furniture that's somewhere between *The Jetsons* and the 1980s; rooms with sea views are only a little more expensive and worth it for the chance to watch the subtle effects of light on the water. Tartini offers free parking for guests, although this is in the public lot outside the town.

Tartinijev trg 15, 6330 Piran. © **05/671-1000.** Fax 05/671-1665. www.hotel-tartini-piran.com. 45 units. 76€–120€ ($97–$152) double; 128€–192€ ($163–$244) suite. Rates include breakfast. **Amenities:** Restaurant; breakfast room; bar; cafe; terrace; meeting room; room service; laundry. *In room:* A/C, TV, Wi-Fi, minibar.

Max Hotel ★ Value In a pink four-story building at the high end of the town right near St. George's Church, this is Piran's most low-key accommodations option. More guesthouse than hotel, it's filled with thoughtful touches and is more intimate than anywhere else in town (you're handed a front-door key and reminded of the importance of an afternoon siesta). Some serious stairs lead up to six simply furnished but immaculate guest rooms. These too have pink walls, with small, original paintings and shuttered windows affording great views of the local cobblestone neighborhood (better the higher up you stay). There's a superstylish breakfast room downstairs with books and relaxing music; friendly proprietor Max goes out each morning to bring home fresh ingredients. Well located, away from the tourist bonhomie, Max is near Piran's nicest beach areas (including a little nudist spot) yet close to Tartini Square.

Ulica IX korpusa 26, 6330 Piran. ✆ **05/673-3436** or 041-692-928. www.maxpiran.com. 6 units. 60€–70€ ($76–$89) double. **Amenities:** Breakfast room; laundry. *In room:* TV, fan, hair dryer.

Where to Dine

Most of the restaurants that line Piran's waterfront are tourist traps; avoid them. One notable exception is **Ivo**★, where you'll find devoted fans queuing for a table in summer. If you want a break from Piran, head for the nearby town of Izola, and try harbor-side **Ribič**, where seafood is king.

Neptun ★★★ SEAFOOD Away from the crowds and away from the main drag, Neptun is in an intimate white space with exposed wood beams from which fishing nets are draped. Members of the Grilj family (who've worked the kitchen and tables since 1994) offer a warm, inviting atmosphere, and appease guests with polite reminders that everything is fresh and therefore requires some preparation time. No matter; you'll be provided with homemade bread, sardine filets, and homemade fish pâté while you wait. Ordering is easy: Ask for catch of the day, grilled and served with fried potatoes. Simple, straightforward, and utterly delicious. If you want something slightly richer, consider the "Neptun" fish filet, prepared with cream and pepper, but be sure to leave room for the unforgettable chocolate mousse.

Župančičeva 7. ✆ **05/673-4111.** Main courses 8€–24€ ($10–$30). MC, V. Daily noon–4pm and 6pm–midnight.

Exploring Piran

Occupying a horn-shaped promontory, Piran is a rambling rabbit warren of narrow cobblestone streets, back alleys, and squares. Small as it is, Piran is packed with detail, and there's lots to explore even if you do nothing more than wander around looking for emblematic references to Venice, like the famous winged lion of St. Mark you'll find on buildings all over the city; it's rather a privilege to get lost amongst the ancient brickwork. For a full-on view of the town, start at its inland perimeter wall up on **Mogoron Hill.** These **defensive walls** are believed to date from as far back as the 7th century, attaining their present form in the 16th century; today you can climb up the Gothic towers and look back at the town and Piran Bay. Down below, the town's center is marked by **Tartini Square (Tartinijev trg)** ★★, which celebrates the Piran-born violinist and composer Giuseppe Tartini (1692–1770), whose bronze effigy rises in the center of this marbled public space. At the southern edge of the square is **Hotel Tartini,** while the lovely 19th-century **City Hall,** the most impressive building here, is to the north. Southwest of the square is **Piran Port,** where a hundred or so boats and yachts are docked in the small harbor formed by a curve in the Piran promontory.

All around the square alleyways lead into a jumbled web of fascinating back streets; facing the square from the northeast is the red facade of the lovely old **Venetian House,** which marks one of the many narrow streets leading up to Piran's quaint tangle of churches, including the lovely **Minorite Convent** and its early-14th-century **Church of St. Francis of Assisi;** in summer, concerts are held in the convent courtyard. Along the northern wall is **St. George's Church,** rising above the sea-facing cliff walls. At St. George's, take a peek at the baroque interior and then climb the early-17th-century **campanile** (daily 10am–1pm and 4–9pm) for splendid panoramas. Then, continuing along Admaičeva ulica, you'll head back down to Piran's concrete **bathing area,** full of tourists in summer. Continuing west, you'll reach the tip of the Piran promontory, marked by the **Punta Lighthouse** and by **St. Clement's Church.** From the lighthouse, the promenade formed by Prešernovo nabrežje leads back toward the **Tartini Theater** at Piran Port, passing a slew of seafood restaurants in quaint Italianate houses on the one side, and the Adriatic's Gulf of Piran on the other; all along this concrete coast, bathers find a spot to sunbathe or dive into the warmish waters.

While there are plenty of places to stop for a drink, the most fun (and least expensive) has got to be the semidingy **Kantina Zižola** (www.piranjein.com; daily 9am until very late), in a corner of Tartini Square. There are tables outside, while the bar feels ever so slightly like a pirate's tavern (except for the upbeat music and handsome, bouncy staff) where you can search for a photo of Robert De Niro, who apparently stopped by here in 2004.

Shopping

Visit the studio of artist and artisan **Marko Jezernik** at **Studio Šterna,** Bolniška 8 (www.jezernik-sp.si), for some alternative reminders of your trip. Besides propagating Piran's alternative lifestyle—"essential," he says, "for the artist"—Marko sells satirical paintings, quirky T-shirts, and books of textual and visual impressions of life inspired by the perfect isolation of Piran; you can also pick up one of his idiosyncratic painted beehive panels. As a spirited nonconformist, Marko opens when he feels like it. On Tartini trg, in the Venetian House, visit the stylish outlet of the Sečovlje salt mine (see below), **Piranske Soline** (**© 05/673-3110;** www.soline.si), where you can purchase cosmetic salt, salted chocolate, and coarse sea salt, all beautifully packaged.

An Outing to the Sečovlje Salt Pans

One worthy excursion if you have the time and you want to escape the crowds that pack Piran in the summer is a trip to the nearby **Sečovlje Salina Nature Park ★★★** (**© 05/672-1330;** www.kpss.soline.si), right on the Croatian border. Here, natural salt is harvested from the sea using the same techniques practiced as far back as the 14th century. The protected wetland area, consisting of salt fields and mudflats, is also home to unique salt-loving plants (halophytes), specially adapted fish, and over 270 bird species. Call ahead to arrange for a ranger/guide to meet you; you'll get an introduction to the labor-intensive salt-farming methodology and a close-up look at some of the flora and fauna. You'll be stunned to learn just how much salt a single man can harvest in 1 day. Not only that, but the all-natural salt from these pans is perhaps the healthiest and best tasting you can find. The rare, unrefined "salt flower" harvested here is arguably the finest salt in the world; the on-site shop carries this as well as a range of salty healing products.

6 EXPLORING EASTERN SLOVENIA

Slovenes tell us that a few years back, **Celje,** the country's third-largest city, was the fastest growing in Europe. Whether or not this is true, it suggests just how much room for growth there is east of Ljubljana. Though Celje itself does not hold much to interest the first-time visitor, it's worth setting aside a few days in July to visit neighboring **Laško** ★, a gorgeous town that holds a weeklong celebration in honor of its main product: beer. Don't miss this lively festival if want to witness Slovenia's penchant for polka bands, street parades, and all-night merrymaking. Other than this, three destinations beckon in Slovenia's northeast: the salubrious riverside university town of **Maribor,** whose citizens seem entirely given over to idling in cafes and soaking up the atmosphere along its tiny waterfront; **Ptuj,** once a Roman stronghold; and, farther east, the vineyards along the peaceful **Jeruzalem Wine Route** (easily taken in as a day trip from either Ptuj or Maribor).

Not yet on the beaten tourist trail, but an important historic town in Slovenia's little-discovered southeast, is **Novo Mesto,** at the heart of some of the country's most pristine countryside and a good base for exploring a number of gorgeous villages or setting out to discover the region's unique wine vintage, Cviček. A visit here is also an opportunity to stay in a gorgeously restored 13th-century castle, in one of the most luxurious hotels in the country (see box below).

MARIBOR & PTUJ

There's a congenial air about **Maribor** (www.maribor-tourism.si), Slovenia's second-largest city. Straddling both banks of the River Drava, with its historic center to the north, Maribor evolved as a market town in the early 13th century. Today Maribor is a pleasant university town; its position at the foot of Pohorje Mountain, garlanded by winegrowing hills, gives it an idyllic aspect. The Drava itself has plenty of spots for swimming, fishing, and even sailing, while south of the center, Zgornje Radvanje is a base for mountain activities in the Maribor Pohorje ski resort.

It's worth climbing to the top of the **Cathedral Tower,** located in the historic center, to get a bird's-eye impression from the wraparound viewing platform, then exploring **Vinag Wine Cellar** ★★, Trg svobode 3, behind the renovated city castle (✆ **02/220-8111;** www.vinag.si); comprising 2km (1¼ miles) of subterranean caves that run right beneath the city, the cellar provides storage for up to 5½ million liters of wine. South of the castle is **Grajski trg,** a pedestrian cafe haunt, where flea marketers operate at weekends. Head south past more shops and bars to reach the city's main square, **Glavni trg,** fringed by lovely architecture and centered on Straub's majestic 18th-century **Plague Monument.** For many, the highlight of Maribor is a ramble along the waterfront promenade, centered on a small, salubrious area known as **Lent** ★★, the city's principal docking port before the arrival of the railway in 1862. Lent is defined by its pleasant bars and cafes, but the most famous attraction here is the **Stara Trta,** at 400 years supposedly the world's oldest living vine, and the June **Lent Festival** ★★★.

From Maribor, **Ptuj** ★★★ (pronounced pit-*ooey*) is a short drive along bucolic back roads. Called Poetovio by the Romans, Ptuj (www.ptuj-tourism.si) became a town in 977; with its hilltop castle and cobblestone streets, it feels every bit the medieval stone-walled fortress. Like Maribor, Ptuj straddles the banks of the River Drava; the Romans put greater Ptuj on the map when they grew the population to 40,000, transforming it into one of the largest provinces in the empire, an important trade point along the road linking the Mediterranean and Baltic seas. Today, the population has dropped to 20,000, but its Roman and medieval heritage continue to lend it considerable charm. Ptuj's Gothic-era **City Tower** marks **Slovenski trg,** at the heart of the old town. Near the foot of the tower is the **Orpheus Monument,** a 2nd-century Roman tombstone used as a medieval pillory to which wrongdoers were tied and ridiculed by the townsfolk. Behind the tower is the Gothic **St. George Parish Church.** Just beyond the church is the **market,** and nearby—on Mestni trg—the century-old **City Hall.** Beyond the square, along Kremplijeva ulica, is the **Minorite Monastery;** ring the buzzer marked ŽUPNIJSKA PISARNA, and a monk will arrive to take you on a tour. In summer classical concerts are occasionally held in the large open courtyard. Several routes lead up to the town's main attraction, 11th-century **Ptuj Castle** ★ (www.pok-muzej-ptuj.si), overlooking the city and affording panoramic views of the surrounding landscape; you can drive or walk up the steep cobbled pathways, or take the signposted steps from Prešernova ulica. Call ahead to book a guide (✆ **02/748-0360**).

Usually quiet, even empty, Ptuj comes to life each year on Shrove Sunday, when 50,000 people gather for the **Kurentovanje Festival** ★★★, when revelers take to the streets in their startling Kurent masks and fantastical traditional costumes in an outrageous pagan celebration that is traditionally an attempt to magically stave off winter, but is today an awesome excuse for a raucous party.

WHERE TO STAY & DINE

In the northeast, you'll probably want to bed down in either Maribor or Ptuj, preferably in the historic center, where there aren't a whole lot of options. Note that you can also stay along the Jeruzalem Wine Route.

IN MARIBOR **Hotel Piramida** (✆ **02/234-4400;** www.termemb.si; 120€–136€/$152–$173 double) is a bright, modern, professional business hotel just a few minutes' walk from Maribor's main drag. The room rate includes access to a recreational spa (pools, Turkish baths, saunas) just outside town. **Hotel Orel** (✆ **02/250-6700;** www.termemb.si; 110€/$140 double), entirely renovated in 2006, is a well-located, simple hotel in a historic building overlooking the main square.

Maribor has two excellent restaurants. Novi Svet pri Stolnici ★★★, Slomškov trg 5 (✆ **02/250-0486**), is a top choice for seafood from the Dalmatian coast; try the sole *(morski list)* with truffle sauce or share the Fish Feast *(ribja pojedina "Novi Svet"),* a seafood platter for two. **Toti Rotovž** ★★, Glavni trg 14 (✆ **02/228-7650;** www.mednarodne-kuhinje.com), has a massive subterranean cellar that dates from 1874. The international menu has a strong Slovene bias, highlighted by great choices like filet of red scorpionfish with truffles, roast veal, escalope of wild boar, and grilled squid. Finish with sour-cherry strudel, and be sure to order a bottle of local Vinag wine.

IN PTUJ Occupying a prime position on the town's oldest street, **Park Hotel Ptuj** ★, Prešernova 38 (✆ **02/749-3300;** www.parkhotel-ptuj.si; 108€–126€/$137–$160 double), is a welcome addition to Ptuj's accommodations scene; the neat guestrooms are furnished with antiques. Until the Park opened its doors, **Hotel Mitra,** Prešernova 6 (✆ **02/787-7455;** www.hotel-mitra.si; 61€–81€/$77–$103 double), occupying a historic building on the same street, was for many years the only place to stay in the center; at this writing the hotel was closed for extensive renovations, hopefully looking significantly improved, although this is likely to drive prices up. Reserve a room on the second floor; those higher up have ceiling windows preventing you from seeing out.

The nicest place to eat is **Gostilna Ribič** ★, Dravska ulica 9 (✆ **02/749-0635;** www.gostilna-ribic.si), where a seat on the riverside terrace is an ideal place to enjoy a bottle

Slovenia's Undiscovered Southeast

Less than an hour from Ljubljana, in Slovenia's little-known Dolenjska region, **Otočec Castle Hotel** ★★★, Grajska cesta 2, 8222 Otočec ob Krki (✆ **07/384-8900;** www.terme-krka.si), offers perhaps the finest overnight opportunity in the country, with 16 stylish, contemporary rooms and suites within the fabulously restored thick, solid walls of a distinctive castle built as early as 1252. Enjoying a romantic position on a pristine patch of green in the middle of the River Krka, it is the only island castle in Slovenia; I'm pleased to report that standards of comfort and service (which is friendly, intelligent, and personable) do justice to the aristocratic theme. While staying at the castle, you're able to use the facilities at the nearby Hotel Sport, including all kinds of spa treatments. But the piece de resistance is the excellent restaurant (in summer, the courtyard is magical) where you can sample the region's famous—and reputedly unique—light red wine, Cviček, accompanied by impeccable cuisine. Doubles cost 260€ ($330), including breakfast.

While Otočec may not be the most famous destination in the country, it's a perfect base from which to explore the nearby town of **Novo Mesto** (just 10 min. away), where one of Slovenia's best museums shelters a fascinating archaeological collection. Unraveled at the **Dolenjski Museum** is the country's ancient history, traced from the Stone Age through to the early medieval period. A particular obsession here are the "situla" (urnlike vases); an ancient people buried their dead in these urns, large numbers of which have been unearthed hereabouts. The Dolenjska region, of which Novo Mesto is the center, was especially well endowed with princely Situla gravesites, where the urns are especially decorated. Not far from Novo Mesto, you can visit a small, private open-air museum, **Musej na prostem Pleterje** (✆ **041-63-9191;** www.skansen.si), where you can take a peek inside a traditional wooden house; with prior arrangement, it's possible to sample wines made at the strict Carthusian monastery just across the road. You can then visit part of the monastery to buy more wines to take home; just don't subject yourself to the punishing audiovisual presentation about the monks. Alternatively, hire a bike from the museum and explore the surrounding hills and countryside.

Incidentally, more budget-conscious travelers will be thrilled to learn that Novo Mesto recently saw the opening of one of the finest hostels I've laid eyes on. **Hostel Situla** ★★★ (✆ **07/394-2000;** www.situla.si) has been fashioned from a historic building right on the town's main square and features designer dorms and private rooms with immaculate shared bathrooms. Mattresses are thick and firm, and even the linens have been specially designed to keep with the theme—the integration of archaeological heritage with modern design—that's suggested in eye-catching motifs throughout the building. There's a restaurant, bar, and wine cellar, and an on-the-ball staff with round-the-clock reception. Dorm beds go for 17€–19€ ($22–$24), whilst private singles are 22€ ($28) and doubles 44€ ($59). If there's a place that's likely to set a new standard for desirable budget digs, this is it.

of wine and some excellent freshwater fish. Particularly good is the trout *(postrv),* but you can fearlessly try the mixed seafood stew, served at the table.

Touring The Jeruzalem Wine Road ★★★

Drive 30km (19 miles) beyond Ptuj, to **Ljutomer,** where you can pick up a **Jeruzalem Wine Road** map from the tourist office (✆ **02/584-8333;** www.jeruzalem.si). Then head off for gorgeous vineyards and their accompanying cellars; 20km (12 miles) from Ljutomer is the hilltop village of Jeruzalem, so named by the crusaders. From here, set off for **Kog** for a memorable tasting at **Hlebec** ★★, Kog 108 (✆ **02/713-7060**). Owner-sommelier Milan Hlebec will pour noble vintages produced by his family—responsible for some 18,000 vines, including local favorite, *šipon.* You can enjoy a hearty lunch, and if you're not up for driving back, stay the night in the guesthouse, which has good en suites.

INDEX

See also Accommodations and Restaurant indexes, below.

General Index

Accommodations

Restaurants

A Guide for Every Type of Traveler

Frommer's Complete Guides

For those who value complete coverage, candid advice, and lots of choices in all price ranges.

Pauline Frommer's Guides

For those who want to experience a culture, meet locals, and save money along the way.

MTV Guides

For hip, youthful travelers who want a fresh perspective on today's hottest cities and destinations.

Day by Day Guides

For leisure or business travelers who want to organize their time to get the most out of a trip.

Frommer's With Kids Guides

For families traveling with children ages 2 to 14 seeking kid-friendly hotels, restaurants, and activities.

Unofficial Guides

For honeymooners, families, business travelers, and others who value no-nonsense, *Consumer Reports*–style advice.

For Dummies Travel Guides

For curious, independent travelers looking for a fun and easy way to plan a trip.

Visit Frommers.com

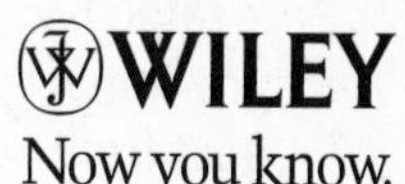

Frommer's® Complete Travel Guides

Alaska
Amalfi Coast
American Southwest
Amsterdam
Argentina
Arizona
Atlanta
Australia
Austria
Bahamas
Barcelona
Beijing
Belgium, Holland & Luxembourg
Belize
Bermuda
Boston
Brazil
British Columbia & the Canadian Rockies
Brussels & Bruges
Budapest & the Best of Hungary
Buenos Aires
Calgary
California
Canada
Cancún, Cozumel & the Yucatán
Cape Cod, Nantucket & Martha's Vineyard
Caribbean
Caribbean Ports of Call
Carolinas & Georgia
Chicago
Chile & Easter Island
China
Colorado
Costa Rica
Croatia
Cuba
Denmark
Denver, Boulder & Colorado Springs
Eastern Europe
Ecuador & the Galapagos Islands
Edinburgh & Glasgow
England
Europe
Europe by Rail
Florence, Tuscany & Umbria
Florida
France
Germany
Greece
Greek Islands
Guatemala
Hawaii
Hong Kong
Honolulu, Waikiki & Oahu
India
Ireland
Israel
Italy
Jamaica
Japan
Kauai
Las Vegas
London
Los Angeles
Los Cabos & Baja
Madrid
Maine Coast
Maryland & Delaware
Maui
Mexico
Montana & Wyoming
Montréal & Québec City
Morocco
Moscow & St. Petersburg
Munich & the Bavarian Alps
Nashville & Memphis
New England
Newfoundland & Labrador
New Mexico
New Orleans
New York City
New York State
New Zealand
Northern Italy
Norway
Nova Scotia, New Brunswick & Prince Edward Island
Oregon
Paris
Peru
Philadelphia & the Amish Country
Portugal
Prague & the Best of the Czech Republic
Provence & the Riviera
Puerto Rico
Rome
San Antonio & Austin
San Diego
San Francisco
Santa Fe, Taos & Albuquerque
Scandinavia
Scotland
Seattle
Seville, Granada & the Best of Andalusia
Shanghai
Sicily
Singapore & Malaysia
South Africa
South America
South Florida
South Korea
South Pacific
Southeast Asia
Spain
Sweden
Switzerland
Tahiti & French Polynesia
Texas
Thailand
Tokyo
Toronto
Turkey
USA
Utah
Vancouver & Victoria
Vermont, New Hampshire & Maine
Vienna & the Danube Valley
Vietnam
Virgin Islands
Virginia
Walt Disney World® & Orlando
Washington, D.C.
Washington State

Frommer's® Day by Day Guides

Amsterdam
Barcelona
Beijing
Boston
Cancun & the Yucatan
Chicago
Florence & Tuscany
Hong Kong
Honolulu & Oahu
London
Maui
Montréal
Napa & Sonoma
New York City
Paris
Provence & the Riviera
Rome
San Francisco
Venice
Washington D.C.

Pauline Frommer's Guides: See More. Spend Less.

Alaska
Hawaii
Italy
Las Vegas
London
New York City
Paris
Walt Disney World®
Washington D.C.

Frommer's® Portable Guides

Acapulco, Ixtapa & Zihuatanejo
Amsterdam
Aruba, Bonaire & Curacao
Australia's Great Barrier Reef
Bahamas
Big Island of Hawaii
Boston
California Wine Country
Cancún
Cayman Islands
Charleston
Chicago
Dominican Republic
Florence
Las Vegas
Las Vegas for Non-Gamblers
London
Maui
Nantucket & Martha's Vineyard
New Orleans
New York City
Paris
Portland
Puerto Rico
Puerto Vallarta, Manzanillo & Guadalajara
Rio de Janeiro
San Diego
San Francisco
Savannah
St. Martin, Sint Maarten, Anguila & St. Bart's
Turks & Caicos
Vancouver
Venice
Virgin Islands
Washington, D.C.
Whistler

Frommer's® Cruise Guides

Alaska Cruises & Ports of Call
Cruises & Ports of Call
European Cruises & Ports of Call

Frommer's® National Park Guides

Algonquin Provincial Park
Banff & Jasper
Grand Canyon
National Parks of the American West
Rocky Mountain
Yellowstone & Grand Teton
Yosemite and Sequoia & Kings Canyon
Zion & Bryce Canyon

Frommer's® With Kids Guides

Chicago
Hawaii
Las Vegas
London
National Parks
New York City
San Francisco
Toronto
Walt Disney World® & Orlando
Washington, D.C.

Frommer's® PhraseFinder Dictionary Guides

Chinese
French
German
Italian
Japanese
Spanish

Suzy Gershman's Born to Shop Guides

France
Hong Kong, Shanghai & Beijing
Italy
London
New York
Paris
San Francisco
Where to Buy the Best of Everything.

Frommer's® Best-Loved Driving Tours

Britain
California
France
Germany
Ireland
Italy
New England
Northern Italy
Scotland
Spain
Tuscany & Umbria

The Unofficial Guides®

Adventure Travel in Alaska
Beyond Disney
California with Kids
Central Italy
Chicago
Cruises
Disneyland®
England
Hawaii
Ireland
Las Vegas
London
Maui
Mexico's Best Beach Resorts
Mini Mickey
New Orleans
New York City
Paris
San Francisco
South Florida including Miami & the Keys
Walt Disney World®
Walt Disney World® for Grown-ups
Walt Disney World® with Kids
Washington, D.C.

Special-Interest Titles

Athens Past & Present
Best Places to Raise Your Family
Cities Ranked & Rated
500 Places to Take Your Kids Before They Grow Up
Frommer's Best Day Trips from London
Frommer's Best RV & Tent Campgrounds in the U.S.A.
Frommer's Exploring America by RV
Frommer's NYC Free & Dirt Cheap
Frommer's Road Atlas Europe
Frommer's Road Atlas Ireland
Retirement Places Rated